Special Praise for *Writing the Big Book*

"If you have read my husband's book, *Not-God: A History of Alcoholics Anonymous*, you may think as I did, that you have a good understanding of that history. And you would be wrong. *Writing the Big Book* zeroes in on the first five years in a way that no other history of A.A. has captured. And these years were critical. Like a good suspense novel, this book captures the day-to-day struggles these few intrepid men encountered over those years—in the heart of the Great Depression. How does a bunch of homeless alcoholics start a worldwide movement? Schaberg's book tells us how they did it, tiny step by tiny step."

Linda Farris Kurtz, author of *Recovery Groups*
Professor Emerita, Eastern Michigan University

"For many in recovery, Bill Wilson is a Moses freeing them from the bondage of addiction. As a result, a variety of myths have evolved around him, some encouraged by his own efforts to tell the story and to sell the spiritual program of Alcoholics Anonymous. Bill Schaberg does a great service to the Fellowship of Alcoholics Anonymous with his exhaustive examination of archival documents, separating myth from fact. The result is a clearer picture of the beginnings of A.A. and the development of the Big Book, along with a rich and compelling portrait of Bill W. Less myth produces a much better story. This volume is a must read for anyone interested in the history of A.A."

The Very Rev. Ward B. Ewing, D.D. Trustee and past Chair of the General
Service Board of Alcoholics Anonymous, Retired Dean and President of
The General Theological Seminary, New York, NY

"A stunning achievement. William Schaberg's eloquent storytelling rests upon a foundation of meticulous scholarship. Finally, we have a resource that draws upon decades of recent research to separate fact from myth regarding the origin of *Alcoholics Anonymous*. *Writing the Big Book* is the most important work on the history of A.A. since Ernie Kurtz's *Not-God*. It raises the bar for future studies on the history of addiction recovery mutual aid organizations."

William L. White, author of *Slaying the Dragon*

"Schaberg's study of *Alcoholics Anonymous* is a true gift to A.A. and its membership, past, present, and future. His monumental research and incredible thoroughness demonstrate that far from being "divinely inspired," the Big Book resulted from many perfectly flawed human beings working and living under difficulty and duress. The humanizing of the many figures in this story is invaluable. Schaberg gives a real sense of who each person was and what their crucial roles meant to A.A.'s fundamental piece of literature."

Kevin Hanlon, co-creator of the documentary *Bill W.*

"With tour-de-force exposition, *Writing the Big Book* details the chapter-by-chapter authoring of *Alcoholics Anonymous* and provides a revealing anthology of its primary contributors. Schaberg also debunks numerous long-standing beliefs of Big Book history. The revelations about Hank Parkhurst's role in particular cast a welcome and inclusive light on his critical importance, as he is shown to be a true unsung hero."

Arthur S., A.A. historian from Arlington, TX

"In-depth research and masterful presentation of previously unpublished facts about A.A.'s early history make for an explosive package. Schaberg humanizes the participants and clearly articulates how *Alcoholics Anonymous* emerged after a painful and arduous birth. It reveals the evolution of the Twelve Steps and the fundamental differences between Akron and New York meetings and cultures of sobriety in 1938. But far from dry historical record, *Writing the Big Book* is lively, fascinating, compelling, and insightful—more like a thriller than a documentary."

Jay Stinnett, independent scholar, A.A. historian from Sedona, AZ

"This is a book that A.A. historians will want to read and make footnotes to from now on . . . the product of incredibly detailed research in the archives at the central A.A. office in New York City and at Stepping Stones in Bedford Hills, New York, along with Lois Wilson's diary, and a host of other primary sources."

Glenn F. Chesnut, Author of fourteen books including *Father Ed Dowling: Bill Wilson's Sponsor,* Emeritus Professor of History, Indiana University South Bend

"*Writing the Big Book* surprises in how well it defines and demonstrates the actual condition of alcoholism, while so clearly rendering the portraits of its interesting cast of characters. I came away with a much better understanding of what some of my dearest friends and family struggle with as alcoholics, along with a deep appreciation for the work that went into the creation of A.A., and how profoundly the program has shaped our culture."

David Stickney, contributing editor of *The Nietzsche Canon*

WRITING THE BIG BOOK

WILLIAM H. SCHABERG

WRITING
the
BIG BOOK

THE CREATION OF A.A.

CENTRAL RECOVERY PRESS

LAS VEGAS

Central Recovery Press (CRP) is committed to publishing exceptional materials addressing addiction treatment, recovery, and behavioral healthcare topics.

For more information, visit www.centralrecoverypress.com.

Publisher: Central Recovery Press
3321 N. Buffalo Drive
Las Vegas, NV 89129

24 23 22 21 20   2 3 4 5

Library of Congress Cataloging-in-Publication Data
Names: Schaberg, William H., author.
Title: Writing "The big book": the creation of A. A. / by William H. Schaberg.
Other titles: Creation of Alcoholics Anonymous
Description: Las Vegas, NV : Central Recovery Press, [2019] | Includes
   bibliographical references.
Identifiers: LCCN 2019009154 (print) | LCCN 2019011861 (ebook) | ISBN
   9781949481297 (ebook) | ISBN 9781949481280 (hardcover : alk. paper)
Subjects: LCSH: W., Bill. Alcoholics Anonymous | Alcoholics Anonymous--History.
   | Alcoholics--Rehabilitation.
Classification: LCC HV5278 (ebook) | LCC HV5278 .S33 2019 (print) | DDC
   362.292/86--dc23
LC record available at https://lccn.loc.gov/2019009154

Photo of William Schaberg by Katie Settel Photography.
Front cover photo used with permission of Page 124 Productions, LLC.

Grateful acknowledgment is made to Alcoholics Anonymous World Services, Inc. (AAWS) to reprint brief excerpts from *Alcoholics Anonymous, fourth edition.* Permission to reprint does not mean that AAWS has reviewed or approved the contents of this publication, or that AAWS necessarily agrees with the views expressed herein.

All documents, images, and excerpts in this work that are from the Stepping Stones Foundation Archives are used with permission of Stepping Stones, the historic home of Bill and Lois Wilson, 62 Oak Road, Katonah, NY 10536, www.steppingstones.org, (914) 232-4822. No permission is granted whatsoever for any further use, distribution (online or otherwise), or reproduction.

Access to the Stepping Stones Foundation Archives and use of excerpts from its materials does not imply that the author's views or conclusions in this publication have been reviewed or are endorsed by Stepping Stones. The conclusions expressed herein, and the research on which they are based, are the sole responsibility of the author.

Cover design and interior by Sara Streifel, Think Creative Design.

To my Lady Sara
again, now, always

and

In loving memory of
King Dykeman
1934 – 2017
("continuously sober" 1956 – 2017)

"I'd just like to spin some yarns and they will be a series of yarns which cluster around the preparation of the good old book, *Alcoholics Anonymous*. Some people reading the book now, they say, well, that this is the A.A. Bible, and when I hear that, it always makes me shudder because the guys who put it together weren't a damn bit biblical. I think sometimes some of the drunks have an idea that these old timers went around with almost visible halos and long gowns and they were full of sweetness and light. Oh boy, how inspired they were, oh yes. But wait till I tell you . . ."

Bill Wilson
Speaking in Fort Worth, TX
June 12, 1954

"Well, this is switching back, but one of the things I feel vitally important is to get the story of how the book was actually written. We get so many distorted stories on the [West] Coast. People talk about the one hundred men that wrote the book. Actually, there weren't a hundred, as Bill will bear me out, but he said one hundred to make it sound good as though it really was going to work. The people talk as though there were one hundred men, that all went saintly and were taken straight up to heaven and God just guided Bill's hand—that Bill just sat there and let the words come through. Actually, it wasn't anything like that at all."

Dorothy Snyder
Interviewed by Bill Wilson
August 30, 1954

No . . . it wasn't anything like that at all . . .

TABLE OF CONTENTS

Acknowledgments

When I bought Jim Burwell's Multilith copy of the Big Book several years ago, I had no idea it would lead me—step by step—to the book you now hold in your hands. In the beginning, I was just trying to answer a simple question: "How many of these Multilith copies were printed?"

In 2007, that question introduced me to Amy Filiatreau, the A.A. archivist at the General Service Offices in New York City, who helped me secure permission to do research in their huge collection of documents. Fascinated with so much detailed and previously unreported information, my search expanded until it encompassed not just the Multilith copy (I never did discover how many of those were actually printed), but also the whole fascinating project of writing the book, *Alcoholics Anonymous*.

Amy left the GSO archives a few months after my search began, but her desk was filled by the amazing Michelle Mirza who has helped me in more ways than I can ever begin to count. She is the most professional, knowledgeable, and accommodating archivist I have encountered in my thirty years of scholarly research. Michelle and her equally accomplished staff (led by April Hegner), have been unfailing in their patience and proficiency while answering my ever-expanding list of questions and requests.

While the resources of the GSO archive are vast, the archival collection held at Stepping Stones (Bill and Lois Wilson's home in Katonah, NY) are equally impressive and important—especially for researchers interested in the early years of that couple's life and of A.A.'s history. I am grateful for the open access granted me to those records by Stepping Stones' executive director, Sally Corbett-Turco.

Supplementing those resources were the archives in Akron, OH (compiled by the dedicated and ever resourceful Gail L.), and the helpful people at the Rockefeller Archives in Sleepy Hollow, NY, and the Chester H. Kirk Collection on Alcoholism and Alcoholics Anonymous at Brown University's John Hay Library in Providence, RI.

In addition, A.A. is blessed with a host of amateur historians who do stellar work researching and writing about the history of the Fellowship. Arthur S. of Arlington,

TX and Jay S. of Sedona, AZ are two such scholarly men and both of them were early and tremendously helpful critical readers of this text. John K., a sophisticated student of A.A. history, also merits special thanks for his judicious suggestions and comments prior to publication.

Among professional historians, Ernest Kurtz was an early consultant on this project, but sadly he did not live to see it come to fruition. Ernie's continued advice and guidance as my work neared its end was sorely missed. On the other hand, the support and scholarship of the prolific author, Glenn Chesnut, has been an ongoing comfort and inspiration to me. But most worthy of special mention in that regard is my friend, Kevin Hanlon, co-producer and co-director of the recent documentary *Bill W.*, who has regularly acted as a sounding-board and critic, while being a constant source of additional information and insightful direction. Both of these gentlemen read an initial draft of this book and improved it greatly with their perceptive comments and critiques.

My friend David Stickney deserves particular thanks not only because he read and astutely critiqued the initial draft of this book, but also because this was the second time I have called upon David for his formidable editorial skills (he provided the same services for my first book, *The Nietzsche Canon*, prior to its publication almost twenty-five years ago).

And no one has been a more important advisor than Sid Farrar. He was an early champion of the nearly completed work, first introducing my book and me to the good folks at Central Recovery Press, and then taking on the job of editing the text into its final, publishable state.

I am also tremendously grateful for the energetic efforts of Central Recovery Press's managing editor, Valerie Killeen, its marketing manager, Patrick Hughes, and my CRP copy editor, Nancy Schenck. They have been amazingly enthusiastic about this project from the very start and have worked tirelessly and efficiently to bring it to press. Thank you all!

Finally, special thanks must go to the many sober members of Alcoholics Anonymous—several of whom read bits and pieces of this manuscript over the years and who informed and corrected my understanding of the Big Book and the program of Alcoholics Anonymous in private conversations and communications as this work progressed.

But *none* of this would have been possible without the constant support, encouragement, and collaboration of my wife, Sara Jaeger—friend, lover, amazing life-partner. She has been a helpful researcher, a wise counselor, a creative thinker, and an astute critic as she read and then repeatedly reread this text over the seven years it was being written. To her, I owe more than could ever be expressed in this all-too-short paragraph, so I will not try . . . except to say: "Thank you, my Love. Without you, it would not have happened at all!"

Author's Note

You will notice that on occasion, 'single quotation marks' are used for dialogue in this book. This has been done deliberately to distinguish them from those that appear with "full quotation marks."

"Full quotation marks" indicate that those are the *exact* words either spoken or written and that they can be found in that same formulation in the source cited.

Those with 'single quotation marks,' on the other hand, are not *verbatim* quotes.

For reasons of either brevity or clarity or, more likely, because the dialogue presented is a blending of two or more real "quotes," the words found within 'single quotation marks' have been lightly modified from what is recorded in the sources cited.

In taking these liberties, I have been scrupulously careful to preserve the original meaning or intent of what was said or written. It is simply a literary device to improve the flow of the writing and of the story.

If the exact words are required for these 'quotes,' you can find them by referring to the sources noted in the accompanying endnote citation.

CHAPTER ONE

Challenging the Creation Myths

~November 1934 to October 1937~

The book *Alcoholics Anonymous: The Story of How Many Thousands of Men and Women Have Recovered from Alcoholism* (commonly called "The Big Book" by A.A. members) is one of the most important and influential spiritual works published in the twentieth century. It describes a clear path that alcoholics—problem drinkers who are unable to quit drinking by willpower alone—can follow to achieve sobriety and then live a life free of alcohol. Since 1939, millions of men and women have taken the advice offered in this book, worked the program of recovery outlined in the Twelve Steps, and experienced the "spiritual awakening"[1] necessary to maintain their day-to-day sobriety. It is an amazing book for what it says, but even more so for the profoundly positive, life-changing impact it has had on millions of alcoholics and on the families and communities to which they returned with the newfound purpose of being "useful to others."[2]

As a product of the late 1930s, *Alcoholics Anonymous* is almost unique among important spiritual works because of the tremendous amount of contemporary evidence telling us how it was actually put together. For the historian, the most valuable sources are the wealth of 1930s documents preserved in several archives across the Northeast.* Taken together, these documents tell an almost day-by-day story of how A.A. survived and grew during its early "flying blind period"[3]—right up until April 10, 1939, the day on which the authors published the book that so carefully explained their program of recovery.

---

* Foremost among these are the Alcoholics Anonymous General Service Office Archive in New York City and the Stepping Stones Foundation Archive in Katonah, NY. Other valuable sources of primary documents and information about Alcoholics Anonymous are the Akron and Cleveland, Ohio A.A. archives, the Rockefeller Archives in Sleepy Hollow, NY, and the Chester H. Kirk Collection on Alcoholism and Alcoholics Anonymous at Brown University's John Hay Library in Providence, RI.

While these real-time documents provide the most unassailable evidence for what happened in Alcoholics Anonymous between late 1934 and early 1939, that history is further embellished by the later writings and statements of four early participants in the story: Bill Wilson (A.A.'s founder), Ebby Thacher (the man who first exposed Bill to the ideas that led to the creation of A.A.), Jim Burwell (an early atheistic member of A.A.), and Ruth Hock (A.A.'s first secretary). The word "embellished" is used here deliberately to emphasize the fact that each of these four major eyewitnesses has proven to be unreliable, to one degree or another, once their testimony is critically compared with the available archived materials.

This should not be surprising. At best, memory is a defective and self-deceptive faculty. Attention is not always paid and when it is, dates are regularly misremembered, while details are forgotten, left out, or compounded beyond recognition. Events are frequently too unimportant to be remembered accurately (if at all) and, sometimes, the unvarnished truth is just too painful or embarrassing to be told. And, perhaps most of all in relation to this present history, there is the human tendency to modify memories so that they more positively reflect later realities. We seem to naturally need to create a smooth story that neatly fits 'what happened' into 'where we are now.'

This frequent lack of accuracy is found not only among these four most prominent early narrators, but also in the later recollections of other early A.A. members. This is not meant to impugn *everything* that was said at some distance from the actual events, but knowing how defective and creative memory can be demands that we check and, if possible, correct those errors by comparing them with the more reliable, more believable evidence provided by contemporary documentation.

In short, any portrayal of the Big Book's history that relies solely on A.A.'s well-worn stories is doomed to tell an inaccurate tale. In contrast, the history presented here is, whenever possible (but alas, lacking sufficient sources, not always), based on a critical reading and judicious collation of contemporary evidence rather than later recollections. As such, the story that emerges frequently contradicts the memory-based recollections that have assumed such a dominant place in A.A.'s popularly accepted history. However uncomfortable this may be for some devoted A.A. readers, what follows here is definitely much closer to 'what really happened' (the historian's ever elusive goal) than to many of those later, more familiar stories.

Bill Wilson: A Consummate Storyteller

The primary revelation from this kind of critical research and investigation is that Bill Wilson, the man who contributed more 'factual' information than anyone else to the traditional story of A.A., was by far the worst offender when it came to accuracy regarding that early history. This may sound harsh to Wilson's many worshipful admirers in the Fellowship of Alcoholics Anonymous, but it is an undeniable fact—as will be shown repeatedly in the pages that follow. Wilson's divergence from the truth was so common and so pervasive that it can only be compared to a dark cloud looming over any attempt to write an accurate history of A.A's early years, obscuring and even falsifying what happened at several key points in the story.

Bill was a consummate storyteller and his stories were, almost always, liberal simplifications of the facts. Some of them, on closer examination, exhibit a casual and even blatant disregard for anything approaching historical accuracy. On one level, this is understandable. Facts are messy things and they beg to be tidied up so that people can make sense of the story being told without having to travel down too many distracting byways. A good story needs to be simple, straightforward, and dramatic.

Bill Wilson was a master at this.

But, there are times—important times—when he went far beyond anything that might be characterized as 'poetic license' or simply 'tidying up the story.' Bill's recounting of the facts is sometimes so wide of the mark that it can only be explained as willful, conscious mythmaking—the creation of a story specifically crafted to deliver a particularly clear image or an unmistakable lesson to the listener. All too often, Wilson's 'this-is-what-happened' accounts must be understood and treated as nothing less than parables, as fables he fashioned to instill some hope in the still-suffering alcoholic or to provide an instructive, uncluttered story about the celebrated origins of Alcoholics Anonymous. Historical truth with a capital "T" was not the point. For Bill, the point was that the story had to convey an important message about the program of recovery, and it needed to be dramatically delivered for maximum impact. In such cases, Wilson believed that this kind of falsification was more than justified (or, at least, inconsequential) just so long as it served his higher purpose.

This is hardly a new or radical observation about him. As the author of *Pass It On*＊ noted so candidly, Wilson was certainly "never reluctant to stretch a fact for the sake of emphasis" and he often spoke "in metaphor, rather than relating events as they actually happened." Moreover, Wilson "was never likely to pass up the opportunity to deliver a parable where he thought it could do some good" or "when he thought he could make a point or highlight a principle."[4] Bill Wilson wasn't just a great storyteller, he was, at times, a conscious and deliberate mythmaker.

Besides telling a meaningful story or altruistically mythologizing A.A.'s early history, Bill also bent the facts in substantive ways whenever the true story would have shone the spotlight too brightly in his own direction. He knew he needed to move himself off center stage and so, whenever possible, he altered the story and redirected the light elsewhere. As A.A. grew and his contribution became more widely known, Wilson became increasingly aware of the need to curb his natural tendencies toward grandiosity and to somehow temper the constant adulation that increasingly came his way as the founder of the movement, i.e., as "the man who saved *my* life!" Bill regularly sidestepped these ego traps by modifying the facts, changing the story in ways that deflected attention away from himself. As time went on, Wilson routinely gave liberal credit—in whole or in part—to other people for things that were actually his own accomplishments.

Finally, many aspects of the true stories just did not make for comfortable retelling once Alcoholics Anonymous became a successful national institution. This was the

---

＊   An "A.A. General Service Conference-approved" biography of Wilson and the early years of Alcoholics Anonymous.

case, for instance, concerning A.A.'s early partnership with the Oxford Group* and, especially, the tenacity with which the Akron members clung to the Group right up until the end of 1939 (and even beyond that). Another embarrassing story that raised serious problems for the Fellowship was the central role played by Hank Parkhurst— Bill Wilson's right-hand man from 1936 to 1939—because Parkhurst drank shortly after the book *Alcoholics Anonymous* was published. Whenever possible, mention of Hank and his contributions to the program were judiciously dropped from the stories told about those early years.

These four persistent tendencies toward creative reporting—uncluttered storytelling, willful mythmaking, deliberate self-deprecation, and the omission of uncomfortable facts—coupled with his notoriously bad memory for dates** mean that we should not blithely take anything Bill Wilson said at face value. To accept his stories and statements without the most rigorous kind of cross-examination would be the height of historical folly.

At the same time, this is not to say that *everything* he said was somehow less than truthful. Bill frequently relates facts and events that are completely uncontaminated by these more creative tendencies. But, given how often Wilson's version of events is contradicted by other sources, it is always wise to weigh his pronouncements against the testimony of others and, most important, to evaluate them in relation to the available contemporary records.

This caveat about Bill Wilson's reliability, however, in no way diminishes his towering stature in the history of twentieth century spirituality or in any way compromises the truly remarkable things he accomplished during his lifetime. Bill was a man of vision—a grand, universal, uplifting, deeply spiritual, life-saving vision—and the fact that he elected to tell uncluttered, instructive parables rather than historically accurate stories can hardly be held against him. Had he not done so, it is possible he would never have been successful in transforming his profound vision of widespread recovery into such a vibrant, spiritually enriching international reality—something that he most certainly did before his death in January 1971.

Ebby Thacher's Visit

A prime example of Wilson's creative mythmaking can be seen in his version of an encounter considered to be one of the pivotal moments in A.A. history: the hallowed story of Ebby Thacher's visit to his Brooklyn home in late November 1934. Bill sat on one side of the kitchen table drinking gin while his recently sober friend, Ebby, sat

---

* The Oxford Group was a twentieth century religious Fellowship (in the USA, largely Episcopalian) that tried to practice "First Century Christianity." More details about the Oxford Group will be supplied later.

** Ernest Kurtz, for instance, in his justly admired *Not-God: A History of Alcoholics Anonymous,* frequently wrestles with Wilson's inaccuracies as he tries to understand what actually happened and several of his endnotes make explicit references to "Wilson's atrocious memory for dates" and to his general lack of precision with the facts. See especially n. 18 and 24 on pp. 329 and 330 respectively.

opposite him. Bill told the story of this meeting repeatedly throughout his sober life,* but the most famous version of it appears in "Bill's Story," the first chapter he wrote for the book *Alcoholics Anonymous*:

> Near the end of that bleak November, I sat drinking in my kitchen. With a certain satisfaction I reflected there was enough gin concealed about the house to carry me through that night and the next day. My wife was at work. I wondered whether I dared hide a full bottle of gin near the head of our bed. I would need it before daylight.
>
> My musing was interrupted by the telephone. The cheery voice of an old school friend asked if he might come over. *He was sober*. It was years since I could remember his coming to New York in that condition. I was amazed. Rumor had it that he had been committed for alcoholic insanity. I wondered how he had escaped. Of course he would have dinner, and then I could drink openly with him. Unmindful of his welfare, I thought only of recapturing the spirit of other days. There was that time we had chartered an airplane to complete a jag! His coming was an oasis in this dreary desert of futility. The very thing—an oasis! Drinkers are like that.
>
> The door opened and he stood there, fresh-skinned and glowing. There was something about his eyes. He was inexplicably different. What had happened?
>
> I pushed a drink across the table. He refused it. Disappointed but curious, I wondered what had got into the fellow. He wasn't himself.
>
> "Come, what's all this about?" I queried.
>
> He looked straight at me. Simply, but smilingly, he said, "I've got religion."
>
> I was aghast. So that was it—last summer an alcoholic crackpot; now, I suspected, a little cracked about religion. He had that starry-eyed look. Yes, the old boy was on fire all right. But bless his heart, let him rant! Besides, my gin would last longer than his preaching.
>
> But he did no ranting. In a matter of fact way he told how two men had appeared in court, persuading the judge to suspend his commitment. They had told of a simple religious idea and a practical program of action. That was two months ago and the result was self-evident. It worked!
>
> He had come to pass his experience along to me if I cared to have it. I was shocked, but interested. Certainly I was interested. I had to be, for I was hopeless.[5]

---

* The story of Bill's early recovery was the only one any group ever wanted to hear when he was invited to speak. But, with each retelling, Wilson became increasingly bored with the endless repetition and he began to refer to it sarcastically as "the bedtime story." He would have been much happier just to skip over this bit of ancient history and move on to much more current and important topics in A.A. (See Hartigan, *Bill W.,* p. 136 and also *Unforgettable Bill W* and the *"bedtime story,"* http://www.barefootsworld.net/aabillwreadersdigest.html [retrieved April 24, 2013].)

Literally millions of alcoholics have read this story and been inspired by its message of hope and the possibility that they too might recover. It is one of the most famous encounters in the history of Alcoholics Anonymous, a seminal, founding moment of the Fellowship.

But Ebby Thacher, the man who supposedly sat on the other side of the kitchen table, told a completely different version of that story; one so far removed from Bill Wilson's account that it is hard to believe they were talking about the same event:

> So I called him up one night and I didn't get Bill, but I got Lois, his wife, and told her what had happened to me . . . Well, anyway, Lois said why don't you come over to dinner some night and then she mentioned a date and I said: "Fine."
>
> So, that night I went over, at half past five, I guess, in the evening, and I rang the bell at 182 Clinton Street, the only person home was an old colored man named Green* whom I had known for years, he had been with the family, Lois's family that is, and he said: "They're both out, both Mrs. Wilson and Mr. Wilson are out, but come on in."
>
> So, pretty soon Bill appeared and he'd been drinking but he wasn't too bad, and said "Hello" and this, that and the other thing and he's kind of taking me around. Then he made an excuse, he had to go out and get some ice cream, something else for supper and, of course, I knew what he was going after. I understand. I've done it so many times myself.
>
> So, then Lois came in. Now there was another girl invited; there was a girl invited because she lived upstairs—they'd made the place into an apartment. So we all sat down at dinner. And Bill's got it a little garbled in the book about it being across the kitchen table, but it don't make any difference, the idea is there. Now we got dinner and then we all moved upstairs—in those houses back there in the East most of the living rooms are on the second floor—so we moved up to the second floor and after a little hemming and hawing, Lois said: "Well, let's hear about yourself." So, I started in and I guess they got me wound up and I guess I talked until pretty near 1 o'clock in the morning.
>
> And I remember Bill said: "I'll walk to the subway with you." And I knew that he wasn't going to go for a drink, because he had a bottle in the house anyway. And on the way over he put his arms around my shoulder just before I went in the subway and said "I don't know what you've got, kid, but you've got something and I want to get it."
>
> Well, he didn't stop drinking right away, any more than I had stopped drinking back there that summer when the Oxford Group boys came to

---

* Mr. Green had been with Lois's family for years (he took care of the horse and carriage for Lois's father) and now lived in the cellar at 182 Clinton Street.

see me,[*] but the idea was in there and the idea happened to get in Bill's head.[6]

Ebby told his version of that evening in Brooklyn on several different occasions, always acknowledging that "the story you read in the Big Book is a little different." He once glibly explained those differences by noting that, after all, he happened to be sober that night, while Bill Wilson was drunk,[7] pointing out that there were "some details of that talk that Bill doesn't remember."[8]

Bill didn't answer the phone? Lois knew about Ebby's recovery before he arrived? Was the whole evening a set-up by Lois? No one, other than Mr. Green, was home when Ebby got there? No kitchen table? No private one alcoholic talking to another alcoholic conversation? They all had dinner together and then went upstairs into the living room? Lois and the girl who lived upstairs were there too? Bill, with his typical bravado, expressing an interest in Ebby's solution, but ever so casually and only in private while they were walking back to the subway in the early hours of the morning? It's not the same story at all. Not even close.

So, what really did happen that afternoon (or was it that evening?) in Brooklyn in late November of 1934? With two such contradictory reports, it would be helpful to have a contemporary account to verify one version or the other, but the closest thing we have to that is a round-robin letter that Lois Wilson wrote to three of her oldest friends on July 20, 1935—a full eight months after Ebby's visit. In that letter, Lois proudly announces that "Bill has stopped drinking thru the Oxford Group" and then explains that "last December Ebby Thatcher [sic] appeared sober for the first time in years and with a very strange story to tell about a religion called the Oxford Group which had cured him just as he was about to be committed to an insane asylum."[9] While this confirms the importance of Ebby's visit, Lois provides no details whatsoever other than to say it occurred in December, which actually contradicts Bill's claim that Ebby appeared "Near the end of that bleak November"—adding yet another layer of confusion to the story.[**]

With no other direct evidence to rely on, Ebby's version of the story is far more credible than Bill's for several reasons. First of all, he presents a coherent, linear narrative—beginning with Lois answering the phone and ending with his walk to the subway with Bill—and he supports that story with a wealth of specific, colorful details. If this is a story Ebby Thacher made up just to counter the more familiar version, it was an amazingly creative effort. Also, the fact that he told this story publicly when he knew he was being recorded, along with his open acknowledgment that it was significantly different from what Bill always said, surely carries significant weight when evaluating the integrity of his memories of that night. Thacher's story, after all, has the ring of messy truth to it while Wilson's presentation sounds like the polished parable that it is.

---

[*]   The story of how three Oxford Group men saved Ebby from a jail sentence in Vermont is another one of the legendary encounters in A.A.'s prehistory.

[**]   In her book, *Lois Remembers* (pp. 87-88), Lois's account of Ebby's visit closely follows Bill's version, but this is consistent with her loyal repackaging of her husband's version of his stories throughout her life and in that book.

None of this is meant to ignore the fact that Ebby Thacher had a hard time staying sober and that he was not always the most reliable witness. His later recollections of his time with the Oxford Group and his comments on early A.A. meetings and activities are occasionally 'back dated' so that they more closely reflect later developments within the program.* Still, the reasons for those lapses are evident and understandable—as noted earlier, memory frequently remembers what the present wants to hear—while the creation of a wildly fallacious story about that fateful meeting with Bill Wilson serves no useful purpose whatsoever.

Ebby Thacher's version is clearly more believable than Bill Wilson's and that, of course, begs the question: Why would Bill have strayed so far from the facts when he told his version of the story?

The short answer is that Wilson was taking one of his experiences and recasting it into a story with a message, a message that would in no way be complicated or confused by the messy details of what actually happened. The point of Bill's much simpler, more direct, and comprehensible story is to dramatically present one of the most basic, foundational beliefs of Alcoholics Anonymous, namely "that one alcoholic could affect another as no nonalcoholic could."[10] His story about Ebby's visit does this admirably: just the two of them are sitting at a kitchen table and their entire conversation is devoted to how his friend has successfully taken control of his drinking and has now come to pass his message of hope on to another suffering alcoholic. It was one drunk talking to another drunk, the only way that the message of recovery could have ever been delivered so effectively, so successfully. In fact, it was this very one-on-one conversation that became the first step of Bill's own journey on the road to recovery.

Wilson's version of the story is a parable, a mythic truth deeply embedded in his story of A.A.'s origins, emphasizing the fact that it all started with one alcoholic talking to another alcoholic, personally delivering the message of potential sobriety. Bill told the story this way because it made the point that he wanted to make. In such cases, the actual facts are distinctly secondary to properly packaging and selling the concepts. Wilson had no problem justifying the creation of this much simplified story because doing so served his higher purpose.

Even as he offered his alternate version, Ebby acknowledged that higher purpose, noting that the differences between his memory of that night and Bill's later recollections didn't really "make any difference" because "the idea is there" and "the principle of the thing is about the same."[11] And, indeed, as far as Bill Wilson was concerned, it was the idea and the principle of the thing that were far more important than any jumbled collection of actual facts.

Wilson's story had drama and impact, delivering an unmistakable message of hope. Thacher's did not.

---

* To supply just one example, Ebby said that "those early [Oxford Group] meetings we attended were basically the same as the A.A. meetings of today." (Fitzpatrick, *Dr. Bob & Bill W. Speak*, p. 24)

Bill's First Meeting with Dr. Bob

A few weeks after Ebby's visit, Bill found himself back in the hospital, laid low by his alcoholism for the last time. While there, he had a profound "white light" experience that transformed his life and he never drank again. Unemployed and virtually unemployable because of his drunken past, Wilson spent the next five months diligently trying to help other alcoholics stop drinking, but all his efforts to pass along the message and the method of his own recovery were a complete failure.

A business opportunity arose and he went to Akron, Ohio, to organize a proxy fight that, if successful, would have made him president of the National Rubber Machinery Company. But things did not go according to plan and the situation became tremendously stressful for him, so much so that one night he found himself severely tempted by alcohol. Fearing that he would drink unless he took some positive action to stay sober, he made several phone calls in search of a local drunk to help.

Those phone calls led directly to another key moment in A.A. history, when Bill Wilson met Dr. Bob Smith for the first time on May 12, 1935. The two men, one sober for exactly five months and the other still drinking, were introduced by Henrietta Seiberling, a leader in the local Oxford Group, who had been trying for months to help Bob get sober. That night, Bill and his new friend talked privately for several hours and afterward Bob Smith, who "had repeatedly tried spiritual means to resolve his alcoholic dilemma but had failed . . . began to pursue the spiritual remedy for his malady with a willingness he had never before been able to muster."[12] Bob stopped drinking that night and actually stayed sober for a few weeks before going back to the bottle again.[13]

In "Doctor Bob's Nightmare," his personal story that appears in *Alcoholics Anonymous*, Smith recounted the details of his last drunk:[14]

> This dry spell lasted for about three weeks; then I went to Atlantic City to attend several days' meeting of a national society of which I was a member. I drank all the scotch they had on the train and bought several quarts on my way to the hotel. This was on Sunday. I got tight that night, stayed sober Monday till after dinner and then proceeded to get tight again. I drank all I dared at the bar, and then went to my room to finish the job. Tuesday I started in the morning, getting well organized by noon. I did not want to disgrace myself so I then checked out. I bought some more liquor on the way to the depot. I had to wait some time for the train. I remember nothing from then on until I woke up at a friend's house, in a town near home. These good people notified my wife, who sent my newly made friend over to get me. He came and got me home and to bed, gave me a few drinks that night, and one bottle of beer the next morning.

> That was June 10, 1935, and that was my last drink.

On the authority of this story, June 10, 1935, has ever since been celebrated as the founding date of Alcoholics Anonymous, the first day on which two men—sharing a common solution and a commitment to sobriety—were both able to stay sober from that day forward.

But Bill Wilson wasn't the only early A.A. member who had a problem with dates. Bob Smith claimed he attended the American Medical Association (AMA) Convention in Atlantic City on this trip, but that meeting, it has subsequently been proved, started on June 10 and ended on June 14.[15] If Dr. Bob did in fact attend that Convention, then his first day of sobriety would have been the following Monday, June 17. Of course, it is also possible that Bob simply couldn't wait another week to go on this bender and lied about the date of the AMA Convention so that he could catch a train to Atlantic City one week early.

Is this incorrect date the result of a faulty memory or just the enshrinement of an alcoholic lie? We don't know. While this particular piece of misinformation is not particularly significant in the larger picture of A.A.'s history, it does highlight the fact that, during the 1930s, members were not paying careful attention to the details of their early sobriety and, on occasion, their stories were modified to cover up past indiscretions. Both of these failings will play a part—and need to be acknowledged and corrected whenever possible—in the story that follows.

A.A. Number Three and the "Flying Blind" Period

Back in Ohio, Dr. Bob Smith got sober for the last time and the two men frantically set to work trying to save alcoholics, believing that the best way to preserve their own sobriety was to try to help others who suffered from the same problem. According to Wilson, they began by visiting local hospitals looking for likely candidates and "their very first case, a desperate one, recovered immediately and became A.A. number three. He never had another drink."[16]

Once again, Wilson is mythmaking. This number three A.A. member was not the very first case they actually worked with after Smith got sober. In fact, there had been at least two rather dramatic failures before this first success: a Dr. McKay and Eddie Reilly (the man who famously threatened to kill Dr. Bob's wife, Anne, while chasing her around the house with a knife).[17]

Bill's claim that this new member was the very first case they worked on and that he recovered immediately and never had another drink is another parable, one that presents at least three of A.A.'s cherished ideals: the necessity of working with others, the fact that this newfound way of attaining sobriety could actually be passed on from one alcoholic to another and, perhaps most important, that their new method could result in permanent sobriety.

The point of Bill's story is that what had happened to him and then to Dr. Bob Smith wasn't just a fluke—it was something significant, revolutionary and, most important, repeatable. Offering a more historically accurate account would have been irrelevant to the message Bill was trying to deliver and would only have obscured the essential points he was trying to make.

Bill stayed in Akron for four months, working with Dr. Bob and a number of other drunks, but primarily carrying on his proxy fight—a battle he eventually lost. He returned to New York in late August 1935[18] without a job and little hope of finding one, leaving him ample time to continue his work with alcoholics. The following month, Bill had his first success in New York when Hank Parkhurst left Towns Hospital and stayed sober.* Over the next two years, several more local recoveries followed, but they were accompanied by a long list of failures.[19] Meanwhile, still sober back in Ohio, Dr. Bob was preaching the message of recovery to hospitalized drunks in Akron with significantly more success than Bill was having in New York City. The two men communicated with some regularity about their successes and failures via letters, telegrams, phone calls, and during Wilson's infrequent visits to Akron.[20] The Fellowship of recovered drunks was small, but their number was growing slowly and steadily.

Wilson later characterized the time from the beginning of his own sobriety (December 1934) to the publication of the book *Alcoholics Anonymous* (April 1939) as "the flying blind period,"[21] a time when the leadership and the members of the A.A. Fellowship were evolving their program of recovery using what can only be called a trial-and-error method. Wilson's point was that before the book was published there was no concrete formulation of their program of recovery, and, most especially, there were no clearly articulated Twelve Steps that drinkers could follow as a road map for getting and staying sober.

The Oxford Group

But to think the Fellowship was really just flying blind during this period presents an inaccurate picture of what was happening. While it is certainly true that this was a period of real uncertainty about what did and what did not work—one that involved ongoing experiments with their methods for staying sober—the groups in Akron and New York were in fact following a formula that they had adopted almost wholesale from the Oxford Group, an approach they soon began to modify and change in a number of different ways to suit their own particular needs.[22]

Contrary to popular belief, Bill Wilson was committed to the Oxford Group's approach to religion throughout the first two years of his sobriety. He attended their meetings (sometimes called "house parties"), witnessed about his personal experiences, participated in group "guidance" sessions, and generally followed the Oxford Group's recommendations on how to live a life based on the Four Absolutes (absolute honesty, absolute purity, absolute unselfishness, and absolute love) and the directions that he received directly from God during his "quiet time" sessions.[23]

Bob Smith and his Akron group were even more immersed in the local Oxford Group and they continued to be deeply committed to both its practices and its core

---

* Hank Parkhurst's story, "The Unbeliever," appeared on pages 194 to 205 of the first edition of *Alcoholics Anonymous*. His sobriety date of "September 1935" is given in the 'Questionnaire' on his alcoholism and recovery, which he filled out in late 1938 (GSO, Box 59, 1938, Folder B[1], Document 1938–201) and confirmed by a letter he wrote to Mrs. J. Frank Baird on September 2, 1938 (GSO, Box 59, 1938, Folder B[1], Document 1938–130).

beliefs (including an ongoing entanglement with many non-alcoholic Group members) for much longer than Bill Wilson.[24] In fact, Smith and the Akron alcoholics did not formally break with the Oxford Group until December 1939, a full two-and-a-half years after Wilson had officially severed his ties with the Group in New York City.

The Oxford Group, founded in 1921 by Frank Buchman, described itself as a First Century Christian Fellowship, i.e., a pre-dogmatic, pre-organizational religious group that endeavored to follow the most basic of Jesus's commandments: that they love one another.[25] They had no formal membership, no dues, no hierarchy, no churches, no paid leaders, and no new theological creed. It was instead a loose confederation of friends who identified themselves as having "surrendered their lives to God" in order "to lead a spiritual life under [His] Guidance" and to "carry their message so that others could do the same."[26]

This did not mean, however, that it had no prescribed beliefs or actions. The Oxford Group professed a moral code based on the Four Absolutes and recommended a daily morning period of quiet time in which all its members should seek to discover God's personal guidance for them; insights that would then govern their thoughts and actions throughout the coming day. (The validity of this guidance was to be tested or "checked" against the Four Absolutes, and also, on occasion, was to be reviewed by another member.)[27]

The Oxford Group was far more sophisticated and complex than this brief description allows, but it was, in fact, the soil in which Alcoholics Anonymous originally germinated.* A few of its practices and beliefs would be carried over directly into the new Fellowship of A.A. while many others would be significantly modified or completely abandoned as Wilson strove to extend the effectiveness and the reach of their new Fellowship and its developing program of recovery. The Oxford Group was vastly important and instrumental in launching Alcoholics Anonymous, but it was necessary that A.A. sever its ties with them if their new group was to ever gain the autonomy so essential for its future evolution and growth.

In October 1937, Bill Wilson, sober for just two years and ten months, left New York for Akron to actively begin the process of that complete separation. Having distanced his group of sober men in New York from the Oxford Group, he now had a vision for what they could become once they struck out boldly on their own and he had already formulated a plan detailing exactly how they should do that.

And one important part of that plan was that they should write a book.

---

* Readers interested in knowing more about what it meant to be a member of the Oxford Group at this time are advised to read *I Was a Pagan* by V. C. Kitchen (Harper & Brothers, New York, 1934), the story of one man's life and practices both before and after he surrendered his life to Jesus within the Oxford Group.

CHAPTER TWO

The Akron Vote

~October 13, 1937~

The first time anyone mentioned the idea of writing a book about the recently discovered method for getting and staying sober was in the fall of 1937. The suggestion came from Bill Wilson, who claimed that such a book was the only way to keep the message of recovery from changing with every new word-of-mouth transmission. More importantly, it would be the best way, he said, for them to spread the news of their great discovery farther and faster, thereby saving the lives of thousands of suffering alcoholics all across the country.

Bill frequently told the story of the time he made this proposal to a group of sober men in Akron, Ohio, and how they finally voted to approve his plan—by the slimmest of margins. Unfortunately, almost all the particulars in his story of that meeting are contradicted by contemporary documents.

The Akron Vote Story—Bill's Version

According to Bill, it was November 1937, two years and five months after Dr. Bob Smith's last drink, and he was visiting the Smiths in Akron. One night, the two men sat down and famously "counted noses," suddenly realizing that they now had a total of forty sober members in their Fellowship. Wilson says he got carried away with this proof of their success and immediately proposed that they launch three ambitious projects—a nationwide chain of alcoholic hospitals, paid missionaries to establish meetings all over the country, and a book that would explain their methods. Each of these, he thought, was necessary for them to expand their reach and save many more people than they were currently able to help. Smith questioned the wisdom of these ideas, although the idea of a book did have some appeal for him. He suggested that they call a general meeting of the Ohio members where the matter could be thoroughly discussed and submitted to a vote.

Over the years, Bill Wilson told several versions of the 'Akron Vote Story' and each time, he would include a few additional details about what happened that night. Taken together, these different accounts provide a rich and vibrant picture of those events as he wanted to present them. What follows here is not a direct quotation although it does include words, phrases, sentences, and paragraphs taken directly from Bill Wilson's writings and talks. Instead, it is a composite story (indicated here by the use of *italics*) cobbling together different details that he mentioned at one time or another in his various accounts of that fateful meeting in Akron.

In November of 1937, I had just lost my job, so I took a trip out West looking for work—visiting Detroit and Cleveland before stopping in Akron where I stayed with my friends, Dr. Bob and Anne Smith.[1] Late one afternoon in their living room, Bob and I sat around by the gas log—with Anne listening in—comparing notes on our recent successes and failures in sobering up alcoholics both in Akron and in New York.[2] As the stories multiplied, we began to realize that we had been even more successful than we had thought. Was this thing really working?[3]

'How many sober people do we actually have in our two groups—right now?" we wondered. Bob and I started counting noses and quickly realized that there was something like forty people who had maintained enough continuous sobriety to be considered real success stories.[4] And, just months or years before, each of these forty people had been hopeless, dying alcoholics! Sure, there had been a tremendous number of failures in getting to that number, but look at the number—FORTY. Clearly enough time had elapsed on enough desperate cases to prove that this was no longer just some questionable experiment; it was a proven and working method for getting drunks sober. We had found a cure for alcoholism![5]

The idea that we had discovered something new and truly effective began to sink in. The numbers, however small at this point, didn't lie. There could be no doubt that our little society for the salvation of drunks was really working and those forty former alcoholics provided concrete evidence to anyone who wanted proof that we had actually discovered a solution for the drink problem.[6] As the realization of what we had accomplished stole over us, we became ecstatic and immensely grateful to the power of God that had made it all possible. Bob, Anne and I literally wept for joy as we bowed our heads to give silent thanks for the gift that He had given us.[7]

But I am a salesman by nature[8] and much less grounded than my doctor friend, so I would sometimes go places that he just couldn't or wouldn't go—and this was one of those occasions. Given the realization that we had discovered something new, something that really worked, my enthusiasm and imagination quickly leapt into the realm of the fantastic.[9] Surely, I claimed, this was "the beginning of one

---

* Please note that the use of single quotation marks (') here—and elsewhere throughout this book—indicate that these are not the exact words spoken or written, but rather the substance of what was said or written—but using slightly different wording. Full quotation marks (")—one example of which begins lower on this page—are used to indicate the reporting of exact wording.

of the greatest medical, religious and social developments of all time . . . A million alcoholics in America; more millions all over the world! Why, we only [have] to sober up all these boys and girls (and sell them God) whereupon they would revolutionize society. A brand new world with ex-drunks running it. Just think of that, folks!"*[10]

After Dr. Bob had calmed me down a bit, I became more pragmatic and began to see the problems that we faced with a little more practicality.[11] I began by pointing out that, for the past three years, we had focused almost exclusively on the life and death question of personal recovery, working with just one drunk at a time. But if forty people could recover from the fatal ravages of alcoholism, why not four hundred, or four thousand—or even forty thousand?[12] Clearly there were that many suffering alcoholics in the country. In fact, there were far more than that! Why there were thousands and thousands of people right there in Ohio who were literally dying for lack of our help.[13] We had a solution, but so far our methods had been tremendously inefficient. Only forty alcoholics had been saved in the past three years. There had to be a better way!

'Can we really expect,' I argued, 'that every drunk in the country will travel to either Akron or New York to be schooled in our solution?[14] And, even if they could, how would they ever learn that they should do that, how would they find out about this revolutionary new solution since it was only transmitted by word of mouth?[15] And, even if they did somehow learn about it—by whatever method—and did come to Akron or New York, how could the sober folks there ever begin to cope with them all?'

The Grand Plan

The plan that I came up with that day as a better way of bringing our solution to the world—the plan that I then sold to Dr. Bob Smith—had three interlocking elements: paid missionaries, a chain of alcoholic hospitals and a book to explain our method of recovery.[16]

Missionaries were essential for spreading the message; there was just no other way to get the good news out there. Seasoned members from our two existing groups—I speculated that there were perhaps twenty of these—would have to temporarily give up their jobs (if they had jobs) and go out to establish groups and meetings in other cities around the country.[17] Clearly these people would have to continue supporting their families, so they needed to be paid for their work. But where would all that money come from?[18]

One source would be the profits generated by the alcoholic hospitals that we would set up around the country—starting with Akron and New York.[19] After all, Dr. Bob's practice had never really recovered and this would be a perfect way to utilize his talents while simultaneously helping thousands of alcoholics get sober. And we desperately needed our own hospitals because the regular hospitals really hated dealing with drunks; they were moving them out as fast as possible to take care of people they

---

*   This idea that they could "revolutionize society" was a central tenet and overarching goal of the Oxford Group.

felt had real problems.[20] Granted there would be substantial upfront investment costs to establish these hospitals, which would provide first class medical care and high-powered spirituality[21]—but once they were up and running on a profitable basis, they could easily generate enough money to pay for the missionaries.[22] Eventually, our society would have a whole chain of these hospitals, coast-to-coast, just like the new chains of drug stores and grocery stores that were currently springing up all around the country and making huge amounts of money for the people who invested in them.[23]

The profits from the sale of the book would also help defray the costs of supporting a national squad of missionaries. Just think about how many potential readers there would be for a book that offers a solution to alcoholism! And, you shouldn't just count the drunks; remember that this book will appeal to wives, relatives, friends, doctors, priests, ministers, psychologists and psychiatrists. Copies of this book will sell by the carloads and the profits from it should be more than enough to pay for those missionaries.[24]

And, beyond its fundraising possibilities, having a book would be critically important in its own right because the current word-of-mouth program was exactly that—something that was passed from man to man—and would certainly become distorted unless it was put on paper. Writing down the exact details of the method would ensure that it wouldn't get garbled and changed as it traveled around the country from one person to the next.[25]

Bob and I agreed that the word of mouth program we had been following so far could be boiled down to six essential propositions:

1. *We had admitted we were powerless over alcohol*
2. *Had gotten honest with ourselves*
3. *Gotten honest with other people about our defects*
4. *Made restitution to those we had harmed*
5. *Tried to carry the message to other alcoholics*
6. *Prayed to whatever God we thought there was[26]**

This was the essence of what we had been doing and without "a Book of Experience"[27] to explain it all in clear and concise language, it would surely get changed with each retelling.[28]

Worse yet, without having it all explained in black and white, we were laying ourselves open to any uninformed reporter's interpretation of what we were doing. That would surely lead to misunderstandings and to our method being held up to

---

* Note that these "six essential propositions" differ slightly from the expanded version of the early "six steps" quoted on page 160 of *Alcoholics Anonymous Comes of Age* and, even more so, from several other early versions of the so-called Six Steps that can be found in the literature and the archives. The questions surrounding the validity of these early six "steps" will be dealt with in Chapter Twenty-Three of this book.

ridicule as a racket by certain members of the press who would like nothing better than an opportunity to discredit us.[29*]

Finally, where would all this start-up money come from that would be needed for the hospitals, the missionaries, and the book? Clearly these projects would require tens of thousands, if not millions of dollars, so it would have to come from the rich. 'Think of all the money donated in the past to salvation projects that didn't work anywhere near as well as this new method we have for getting people sober,' I argued. 'Think of all the money that was poured into the failed Temperance and Prohibition movements over the years.'[30]

'What we have here is a proven project of human reclamation,' I stated with certainty. 'People will be more than willing to provide us with the cash when they see the amazing amount of human suffering that can be alleviated and the spiritual growth that will come about by using our methods.'[31]

Bob liked the idea of the book, but he had strong reservations about the missionaries and the hospitals.[32] *It all seemed so overwhelming and he worried that money and property would contaminate the beautiful Christian spirit that had been the foundation of our group from the very beginning. 'Wouldn't money, paid missionaries, and hospitals somehow ruin everything?' he wondered.*[33] *I did not share Bob's fears; I was confident that whatever problems might arise, they could all be overcome.*[34]

The Akron Squad Responds

Dr. Bob suggested we consult with the others, so he called for a special meeting of the Akron "Alcoholic Squad." 'Let's try these ideas out on them,' he said.[35]

The meeting was duly called and eighteen sober members arrived at T. Henry Williams's house, their regular weekly meeting place.[36] *By this time, I was wildly excited about the new approach. I could already see the movement spreading all over the world, if only we could get the approval for these three critical proposals from this group. Dr. Bob opened the meeting and then turned it over to me. I immediately went into my best salesman mode, enthusiastically pitching the ideas of paid missionaries, a chain of alcoholic hospitals, and a book of our experiences—pouring out a constant stream of arguments in favor of each proposal.*[37]

But, as the crowd grew progressively quieter, it was clear to me that the Ohio group didn't really approve of these ideas.[38] *I knew that, on a good day, they were a conservative and skeptical lot and these proposals were obviously far too revolutionary to be accepted without a heavy round of arguments.*[39]

---

[*]   This is not just paranoia on the part of early A.A. members. The liquor issue had been a burning social and political topic in America for decades—culminating in the disastrous Prohibition Era. Any alleged cures for drinking were popular topics for skeptical and even scornful investigative reporting throughout this time.

But it was worse than that. As soon as I finished my pitch, the group launched into a storm of outraged objections: 'We've got to keep this thing simple,'[40] they said. 'If you bring money into it, you'll be creating a professional class and the whole movement will be ruined.[41] Paid missionaries are a terrible idea. They would completely destroy our good will with new alcoholics and they wouldn't trust us anymore.[42] And, after all, Christ's apostles weren't paid missionaries—and that's the example we should be following here. They spread the word of God in a spirit of selflessness and that is exactly what we have been doing all along.[43] If you try to change that by paying people for that kind of service, it will absolutely ruin the whole thing!'[44]

Alcoholic hospitals fared no better. Several people complained that if we went into the hospital business, everyone would say that we were running a racket.[45] And they'd be right. Once you go into business, you have to deal with all of the problems that come up for every business, and we don't want any part of that. How, for instance, would we ever deal with the bankruptcy that inevitably happens to any business that has been around for too long a time? And, how could we continue to hold our heads up when offering our cure for alcoholism to a new man, if that recovery now comes with a price tag attached to it?[46]

The group also rejected the idea of a book. 'Jesus didn't have any pamphlets or books when He started out,' they argued.[47] 'All He had was a simple word of mouth method for carrying the message from person to person and from group to group. Why would we ever want to deviate from His example? Do you think the apostles traveled around with printed pieces of literature in their pockets?'[48]

'And, we absolutely do not need the publicity a book would bring down upon us. It would be a disaster! How could we ever handle all of the inquiries that this publicity would create? We'd be swamped with requests and we would have no way of dealing with them all.'[49]

These objections had a strong impact, but Bob and I rose to the challenge,[50] presenting counterarguments to the objections, although Bob was most vocal in his support of the idea of a book.[51]

I used all the arguments I had worked out the day before when talking with Dr. Bob, pointing out that we had a cure for alcoholism, but at the rate we were going it would be another ten years before it reached the outskirts of Akron.[52] 'If you keep it too simple,' I argued, 'we end up with nothing but anarchy and then everything gets really complicated. We've got to take some chances here if we are ever going to spread this thing to all of the dying people who need it.'[53]

And I wasn't above getting personal in my arguments when challenging the nay-sayers. I asked them: 'How can you people sleep at night when there are drunks in California who are dying right now because there is no way that they could ever hear about our solution?[54] And, are you really willing to allow the successful methods that we have so painfully developed over the past three years to become distorted and twisted into something completely different, just because we didn't make the effort to write them down and put them in a book?[55]

After a truly passionate discussion, which resolved little and left the meeting in what seemed to be an angry deadlock, it was grudgingly decided that a vote should be taken.[56] Over the strenuous objections of the minority, the Akron meeting finally voted to approve the proposals to employ paid missionaries, to establish a chain of alcoholic hospitals and to write a book. All three measures were carried by the slimmest of margins—two votes—with ten men voting in favor and eight casting their vehement 'No's.'[57]

I had gotten the approval I needed from Akron, but it was a very reluctant approval. I might have their grudging support for the three new initiatives, but they wouldn't exert any further energy to move this agenda forward. If I wanted missionaries, hospitals and a book—all of which would cost a tremendous amount of money—then I should just go back to New York and try to raise that money.[58] After all, that was where the money was and there certainly wasn't going to be any money coming out of Akron to support any of these projects.[59]

Such is the collective substance of Bill's several colorful accounts regarding the Akron Vote and A.A.'s momentous decision to write a book—the only one of these three ambitious proposals that ever became a reality. It is an appealing and lively story, capturing the elation of the moment, highlighting all of the problems that would surely come from rapid expansion, and painting a vibrant picture of the emotions that flared up on both sides of the issue. Equally vivid and clear are the positions taken by the two sides along with the anger and the tension generated by their heated arguments (and the uncertainty of who would eventually win). It is a wonderful story that deftly builds with suspense, culminating in the drama of Bill Wilson's victory in the final vote.

The problem is that many of the details reported in this story are simply not true and, even more important, Bill leaves out a host of important facts and critical factors that are essential for any understanding of what really happened that night in Akron. Fortunately for us, as the Fellowship grew, it generated (and preserved) more and more documents that can now be used to verify, modify, or contradict elements found in these frequently told tales of A.A.'s early history. In this case, the story that emerges from a careful collation of those primary materials is substantially different from the one that Bill Wilson told so many times over the years.

But before getting to a more historically accurate account of the Akron Vote meeting, any proper understanding of that gathering must begin with a recounting of what was going on in Bill Wilson's life during the year 1937, especially as it relates to his job, to the growth of the group in New York, and to his deteriorating relationship with the Oxford Group.

Bill and the Fellowship in Transition

Bill is frequently identified as a stockbroker,* but he never held a license to sell stock and today he would more accurately be described as a stock speculator or, more kindly, an entrepreneurial Wall Street analyst. In January 1937, he finally found a job with Quaw and Foley, a small New York firm that specialized in speculative business ventures. In the past, Bill had done occasional work for these two business friends—he described them as a "pair of good-hearted Wall Street Irishmen"[60]—but he now had a full-time job with his own desk and the use of a secretary whenever he was in town. But much of the time Bill wasn't actually in New York during 1937; instead he was traveling around the country visiting other cities, investigating promising business situations the firm hoped to turn to their own advantage. His destinations during the first seven months of the year included Boston (January and March), St. Louis (January and June), Detroit (January, February, May, and July), Cleveland (February, April, and May), Rochester (February), and Springfield (March).** On March 11, 1937, for instance, Lois writes that Bill was leaving for Boston to see "the chairman of Fisk Tire to be put on the board of directors."[61] Throughout the year there had been many such opportunities, but, in the end, no real successes.

All of this travel would have had a significant impact on Bill's participation in the regular recovery meetings that were typically held at his house in Brooklyn every Sunday night. In addition, the daily requirements of the new job surely limited the amount of time he could spend working with other alcoholics even when he was in town. But despite all these new responsibilities and his frequent absences, Wilson did manage to stay involved. He continued his active participation in a number of local Oxford Group activities while also maintaining his regular efforts to help his recovering friends in the small but growing Fellowship in New York City.

The group in New York was growing slowly, the number of sober members fluctuating as new people came in and tried to stay sober while others quit and returned to drinking. The estimated size of the New York group when Bill drove out to Akron in October 1937 was ten sober members; these included Wilson himself, Hank Parkhurst (First edition story: "The Unbeliever"), Fitz Mayo (First edition story: "Our Southern Friend"), Myron Williams (First edition story: "Hindsight"), Florence Rankin (First edition story: "A Feminine Victory"), Bill Ruddell (First edition story: "A Business Man's Recovery"), along with Silas Bent, Douglas Delanoy, Paul Kellogg, and Sterling Parker.*** The group may have been small, but they were all tremendously happy to be sober and they were doing their best to pass that gift of sobriety on to as many other people as possible.

---

*   Bill calls himself such in the 1955 "Foreword to the Second Edition" of the Big Book.

**   All dates are from Lois's Diary, 1937. There are gaps in this diary so it is possible that Bill Wilson did make additional business trips in 1937.

***   The exact composition of A.A.'s early membership is a subject of considerable controversy, and I am grateful to John B., a New Jersey A.A. historian who has done exhaustive research on the earliest members of Alcoholics Anonymous, for these names. Other possible New York candidates who may or may not have been counted as sober at this time would include Don MacLean and Wes Wynans. Most lists of early members typically include nine or ten other New Yorkers who are recorded as 'failures,' i.e., they did not stay sober for any appreciable length of time.

But more important than Wilson's new job or the slow growth rate of the New York group was the fact he had been gradually distancing himself from the Oxford Group in New York City, at first by holding "alcoholics-only" meetings at his house in Brooklyn and eventually by completely and permanently breaking all ties with the Oxford Group in April or May 1937. Wilson's participation in the Group and the events that led to his break with them will be dealt with in some detail in a later chapter. What is important here is Bill's mid-1937 realization that this newfound independence from the Oxford Group left them in the precarious position of having no underlying organization or structure for their new movement.

Although the members in New York had been growing progressively less dependent on the Oxford Group (while their Ohio counterparts remained deeply entrenched), they had, for more than two years, carried out their recovery activities under the loose and wide umbrella of the Group. This affiliation, however relaxed it may have grown over time, provided them with a basic framework for understanding who they were and how their own small group fit into the spiritual landscape of the community. Suddenly, finding themselves autonomous, Bill—who was undoubtedly supported and most likely pushed on this issue by Hank Parkhurst, his closest friend in the New York group—realized how essential it was for the new Fellowship to create their own identity, structure, and organization. Breaking their ties with the Oxford Group precipitated what might be called a management crisis within the recovery movement in New York, and it was clear that an ambitious plan and strong leadership would be needed to address and effectively resolve these issues. Something had to be done and it had to be done now!

Compounding this growing organizational vacuum was the fact that Bill Wilson was a man of vision; he knew they had been successful in getting a small but substantial number of people sober, and he was anxious to begin spreading the news of their new methods as far and as wide as possible. In the past, his group had been riding along comfortably on the broad coattails of the Oxford Group, using its connections to spread the word about their own success while ensuring some degree of respectability for those efforts by associating with this elite group of people. But, having irrevocably broken those ties, Wilson and his small band of recovered drinkers could no longer rely on the various local Oxford Groups to serve as their stepping stones, providing them with both the introductions and the credibility they would need to carry their message into new cities.* The time had come for them to take full control of their own movement and to reorganize themselves in a way that would facilitate a rapid and broad expansion of the Fellowship.

While there is no direct evidence that these plans to take control of their own destiny and to begin aggressively spreading the message of recovery nationwide were formulated before Bill traveled to Akron, there is convincing circumstantial evidence— especially the timing of Bill's actions once he got back home to New York City—

---

* Bill Wilson's many letters to Lois while he was in Akron for those critical four months of 1935, for instance, make constant references to the Oxford Group and to many of its specific members. Bill is clearly using these connections as a vehicle for the promotion of further introductions to other powerful and influential people in Akron—and he continued this behavior on behalf of his recovery movement after his return to New York.

indicating that this was the case. Similarly, all the evidence suggests that Bill had shared these plans with key members of the New York group before bringing them along to lend their support in Akron. Finally, it is hardly conceivable that Hank Parkhurst would not have had a strong and adamant voice in the formulation of these ambitious plans. Paid missionaries to spread the word across the country, the establishment of a chain of hospitals dedicated to the medical and spiritual treatment of alcoholics, and a book that would clearly describe their methods for getting sober was exactly the kind of grandiose thinking that Henry G. Parkhurst was most famous for.

But, in stark contrast to what was going on in the East, the Akron Fellowship still openly identified themselves as members of the "Alcoholic Squad" of the Oxford Group* and they were seamlessly integrated with many non-alcoholic members of the Group who attended their meetings every week. Bill's break with the Oxford Group and his plans to create a new organization and launch a nationwide campaign of expansion could only be seen by many of the Ohio members as an outright betrayal of everything they considered essential to their movement and a repudiation of the methods they thought of as critical to the preservation of their own sobriety.

Bill Plans the Akron Visit

In October 1937, Bill still had one week's vacation left from his job at Quaw and Foley[62] and he was using it for a road trip to Ohio where he planned to have some serious discussions with the Akron members about the future of their movement. It was time to bring the conversations that had been going on in New York City to the attention of the Ohio Fellowship and to gain their approval for these new plans so they could begin to move forward immediately.

In late September, Bill wrote Bob Smith about their proposed trip, saying he and Lois planned to arrive on Sunday, October 10 and that they were bringing two couples and another friend with them. On hearing the news, Dr. Bob was enthusiastic and he wrote back saying, "We can easily find room for as many as you want to bring for as long as you wish. Between Paul [Stanley], T. Henry [Williams] and ourselves we will have no trouble housing and feeding you and your gang."[63]

Paul Stanley** was no less excited about the upcoming visit, writing to Bill and Lois the Wednesday before they left:

> Dr. Smith just told me that we are to expect a visit from you over the week-end, and that two other couples, the Parkers and the Ruddells, are coming with you. Needless to say, we are looking forward to this visit with a great deal of anticipation and pleasure, as are all the folks with whom we spend so much time . . .
>
> We have made arrangements for a little dinner party at our house on Sunday. There may be a few of us who will be tied up in a little meeting

---

*   A name they commonly used to refer to their group. See, for instance, Amos, "History," p. 3.

**   Paul Stanley got sober in early July 1936 and his story, "Truth Freed Me!," appeared in the first edition of *Alcoholics Anonymous* on pages 336 to 339. T. Henry Williams was an ardent Oxford Group member who lent his house to the "Alcoholic Squad" on Wednesday nights for their weekly meetings (see, for instance, AA Main Events, 1937, Point 2 and *AACOA*, pp. 75–76 and 141).

Sunday evening for an hour or so. Then we are planning on having an evening session at T. Henry's house after that.

We hope we are not laying out a program that would seem to be too strenuous for you, but we feel certain that you will be amply repaid for the inconvenience that such a trip may cause by the pleasure that you will afford us by your coming . . .[64]

Paul's mischievous poke at Bill—hoping that the program he outlined would not "seem too strenuous" for him—likely refers to Wilson's frequent lounging postures (he preferred to sit or lie on the floor) and to his somewhat casual manners, two things that friends teased him about with regularity throughout his life. This kind of playful light-heartedness is an excellent example of the familial nature of the Fellowship at this time; Paul Stanley had already met Bill on at least one occasion in Akron[65] and, just two months earlier, he and his family had actually spent four days with the Wilsons in Brooklyn.[66]

But, contrary to Bill Wilson's frequent retelling of this story, he did not go to Ohio alone. He and Lois went and they were accompanied by two other couples, the Parkers and the Ruddells, along with their friend, Fitz Mayo.[67] Wilson, Mayo, and Ruddell represented three of the four driving forces within the New York Fellowship at that time, the fourth being Hank Parkhurst (who was not going to Akron). Fitz Mayo had quit drinking two months after Hank and quickly became a close friend of both Bill and Lois; he was, in addition, a committed and avid promoter of the new method of recovery. Bill Ruddell was at this time only seven months sober, but ten months later he would be elected as a trustee and the first Chairman of the Alcoholic Foundation. Sterling Parker, a much more recent addition to the group, had quit drinking just two months earlier.[*]

In October 1937, Wilson, Mayo, and Ruddell—along with Parkhurst—were the heart and soul of recovery in New York City, representing the solid core of sobriety that sustained the group. Bill wasn't going to Akron for these important discussions alone. He was bringing most of the firepower from his home group along with him to ensure at least some support for his ambitious proposals. The two separate—and, in many respects, very different—communities of ex-drunks were coming together for what might be called a 'family reunion.' Or perhaps it would be more accurate to say that the Fellowship that would later be called Alcoholics Anonymous was about to convene its first summit meeting.

It was time to chart a new direction for the fledgling movement.

---

[*] Fitz Mayo's story, "Our Southern Friend," has appeared, with edits, in all four editions of the book, and Bill Ruddell's story, "A Business Man's Recovery," appeared on pages 242 to 251 of the first edition. Both of these stories contain their individual sobriety dates. Sterling Parker is likely the gentleman born in Akron in 1900 who is known to have been a tire salesman in Ridgewood, NJ, in 1930. [I am extremely grateful to Jared L.—an A.A. historian from Pennsylvania who is a constant and incredibly generous source of reliable information on early A.A.—for these facts.] Sterling Parker wrote a letter to Bill Wilson on August 10, 1937 thanking him for a financial advance that Bill had given him the week before. This loan was made against Parker's future income working for Hank Parkhurst's business, Honor Dealers—presumably as a salesman (StSt, WGW 102.7, Correspondence–General–Friends/Associates [1937], WGW Box 25, Folder 29). In addition, Lois notes that Sterling Parker "sobered in 1937" (December 13, [1937] entry, Lois's List of Historical Dates, October 1937–May 1945: StSt LBW 203, Box 35, Folder 4).

However, on Friday, October 8, the day before the New York group planned to leave for Akron, something happened that had tremendous consequences for Bill personally and even more impact on the future history of Alcoholics Anonymous.[68] Bill Wilson lost his job.

Unemployed, Bill Begins His Real Job with A.A.

Bill later minimized his nine-month stretch of employment in 1937, saying that he took the job because he was in such desperate financial straits and that he had only "made a little bit of money" while working at Quaw and Foley.[69]* However true this might be, the job was substantive enough for him to receive a two-week vacation, which he tried to take in July with Lois and his old friend, Ebby Thacher.** Unfortunately, that trip ended a week early when Bill was called back to work unexpectedly with Lois noting ruefully in her diary that "Bill will get another week later for having cut this one short."[70]

Wilson claimed that the March stock market crash of 1937 was responsible for his layoff and that was surely the case; the losses of the previous March 10 are still rated as the second worst day in US financial history.[71] The economic fallout from that crash was serious, further depressing all aspects of the country's business for well over a year, and it clearly had a negative impact on Wilson's employers. Lois mentions that Quaw and Foley was forced to let Bill go "because they had nearly failed."[72]

This ended the last substantive job Bill Wilson would ever hold outside of Alcoholics Anonymous—a fact that would have a profound and continuing influence on all of his relationships with the community of recovered drunks for years to come. The immediate impact was that Bill found himself with more than enough time on his hands to aggressively pursue the fundraising and later the writing of the book.

Wilson was never happy with his ongoing lack of real employment and he would spend the rest of his life chasing the occasional job opportunities that came his way, while just as constantly trying to resign from the central leadership position that was always being forced back upon him by the Fellowship of Alcoholics Anonymous.*** In many ways, these two factors defined Bill Wilson's life from this point forward: he never again held a job outside of A.A. and he was never able to completely let go of the reins that controlled A.A.

The Akron Vote Story—What Really Happened

Job or no job, with or without a paid vacation, the New York contingent was driving to Akron for a big meeting with their Ohio counterparts. The time had clearly come

---

*   The Wilson tax return for 1937 claims an income of $2,825.00 from Bill's job and Lois's generally unprofitable interior decorating business. (StSt, Income Tax–Federal 1927–1961 [miscellaneous], LBW 210, Box 42, Folder 2).

**   This vacation was taken immediately after Ebby left Towns Hospital following his first sobriety 'slip' in May 1937 (see Lois's Diary, June 23, 1937).

***   Dipping into any of the folders containing Wilson's voluminous thirty-five years of correspondence that are carefully preserved at Stepping Stones will provide ample support for both of these observations. However, it must be noted that Bill Wilson's desire to hand over the leadership of A.A. to others was always tempered by a conflicting desire on his part to continue "running the show." He was a complicated and fascinating man.

to find a new and better way to spread the message of recovery, and that meant some important and difficult decisions had to be made regarding the future course for the Fellowship.

While Sterling Parker and his wife went on alone, Bill Ruddell and his wife, Kathleen, drove over to Brooklyn and picked up the Wilsons at noon on Saturday, October 9.[73] The party then traveled as far as Chambersburg, PA (half way between Philadelphia and Pittsburgh) where they stopped for the night. The next morning, they picked up Fitz Mayo outside Pittsburgh and then continued on into Ohio, arriving in Akron at 5:00 p.m. The New Yorkers received a hearty welcome and were entertained by the large crowd gathered at Paul Stanley's house for dinner. Following the festivities, Bill and Kathleen Ruddell went to stay at T. Henry Williams's house[74] while Bill and Lois left with Dr. Bob and his wife, Anne, and drove to their house[75] where the Wilsons spent the next five and a half days before returning to Brooklyn.[76]*

These colorful details about the Akron trip all come from Lois's diary. Unfortunately she made no diary entry for her first full day in Akron and we shall never know what, if anything else, she wrote in the next four pages because they have been torn out of the book. All of the diaries that Lois left are intact except for the one from 1937, which has seventy daily pages removed. Why she would have torn these pages out is a mystery and none are more mysterious (or more sorely missed) than these particular four pages. Without them we have no contemporary, first-hand information about what actually happened when the New York group was in Akron that week.**

Whatever Lois's motive, the only thing we know for certain is that the pages are missing and the information appears to be lost forever. It is possible she removed these pages because they contained some unflattering personal observations about Bill or about someone else who attended this meeting. Or, perhaps, Lois recorded something there she later found embarrassing, something she didn't want to leave to the prying eyes of the future. While either of these explanations might be true, the more likely reason Lois removed these pages is that the details recorded there would have substantially contradicted the story that was later told by her husband with such regularity. Above all else, Lois Wilson was a loyal wife.

Despite this lack of contemporary documents, we can surmise without too much fear of contradiction that the arguments put forward against Bill's proposals in the meeting, arguments that he does describe in such admirable detail, also contained a strong element of support for the Oxford Group that Bill does not mention. It was this tenacious loyalty to the Group that drove the Akron members' resistance, raising the stakes of their arguments to a much higher level than Bill's version of the story allows.

---

* In his tribute to Dr. Bob published in the Grapevine in January 1951, Bill states, a bit incorrectly, that he "spent a week visiting Dr. Bob" when they held this Akron Vote meeting.

** Lois definitely knew these pages were missing, and it is equally certain that she removed them herself. The transcripts that she submitted to the GSO Archive in late 1975 (GSO, Box 201, Folder A, Lois's Diaries—1937) already note these four pages as missing—along with the other sixty-six pages that have been torn out of this diary. (The date of Lois's donation of the typescripts was confirmed by the GSO Archivist, Michelle Mirza via a personal email in October 2011.) The seventy missing dates generally appear in small clumps of four or five pages each, and I have been unable to discern any pattern as to why these particular pages 'needed' to be removed.

As far as the Ohio group could see, these men from New York were not just suggesting an organizational revolution—they were proposing heresy.

If we did have Lois's missing diary entries, we might find answers to some of the questions that still plague our understanding of what actually happened during those days and nights in Akron. For instance, how active were the New Yorkers in the discussions and were they allowed to vote when it came to the final tally? And, if not, by whose ruling and what procedure were they excluded? In addition, if there was a total of forty sober members in October 1937 and ten of these were in New York, then why were there only eighteen Akron members attending this historically important meeting? Where were those other twelve recovered drunks? Or were there really only fourteen Akron members present at the meeting (after the four New Yorkers are subtracted from the given head count of eighteen) so that Bill Wilson only needed to convince five of those fourteen Ohio members to join the New Yorkers and Dr. Bob Smith to reach the needed majority of ten?

All interesting questions, but, unfortunately, unanswerable for lack of reliable contemporary evidence.*

There is, however, some near-contemporary evidence that there were, in fact, thirty-one sober members in Akron in October 1937. Four months later, in February 1938, Dr. Bob Smith hand-wrote a two-page list of all the people who were sober in Akron at that time. That list contains forty-three names along with each person's profession, number of dry months, drinking years, and age. If we subtract all of those who had four or less dry months, we are left with thirty-one sober "noses" that were likely counted in Akron at the time of the vote.[77]

Further confusing the issue, it is possible that these reputed forty sober men were not just a simple thirty-ten split between Akron and New York. Ten months after the Akron Vote meeting, in August 1938, Hank Parkhurst reported to the Alcoholic Foundation that there were ten members whom he claimed had "definitely recovered, but who are out of touch with the group."[78] If all or some of these out-of-touch members were a factor in reaching the number of forty when Bill and Bob counted noses then perhaps there were as few as twenty sober members in Akron at this time and not the thirty that is so commonly supposed.

Finally, it should also be noted that Bill Wilson was extremely flexible when it came to this revered number of forty. At one time or another, he said that when they counted noses that day in Akron, they had something that "looked like forty"[79] names or "I should guess, about forty members in all three cities [New York, Akron and

---

* Kathleen Ruddell's much later recorded interview opens with her brief account of this trip to Akron, but her memory for details (here and elsewhere) is very poor. She states, for instance, that "some other people" also made the trip [the Parkers], but she can't remember their names. She also says that they picked up "a young man" in Pittsburgh [Fitz Mayo], but she can't remember his name either. She claims that there "were sixty [or sixty-eight or sixty to eighty—the tape is not easily understood] at the big meeting, that we went out there for." Sadly, this eye-witness account of the "counting noses" meeting has no other details besides these excepting only the previously noted fact that the Ruddell's stayed at T. Henry Williams's house while they were in Akron. (Recorded interview with Kathleen Ruddell; GSO, recording archives). NOTE: Kathleen's claim that there were sixty (or sixty-eight or sixty to eighty?) attendees at this "big" meeting is certainly plausible if we factor in the New York visitors (and their wives) along with the Akron regulars (and their wives), and also include a healthy contingent of Oxford Group members who were not alcoholics. That large meeting would have been the 'regular' meeting—the one that they "went out there for"—and not the special meeting that Bob Smith called for alcoholics-only to consider Bill's proposals.

Cleveland]"[80]* or "a handful of, I don't know, thirty-five to forty maybe."[81] or "something like forty cases"[82] or "upwards of forty" and, finally, "two score."[83] It is a flexible number.

Bill and Lois left Akron at 4:30 in the afternoon of Saturday, October 16 and rode through the night with Sterling Parker and his wife, arriving in Newark, NJ, at 5:30 in the morning. They all ate breakfast at a local restaurant and then the Wilsons took the subway home to Brooklyn where they gratefully collapsed into their bed.[84]**

• • •

All of the facts noted above confirm that an important summit meeting was held in Akron in October 1937*** and that at least four New York members (three of whom were principal members of that group) attended the meeting, as did Lois Wilson and two other wives. These facts, along with the realities of Bill's business situation and his decisive break with the Oxford Group several months earlier present a significantly different story from the version that Bill Wilson told of what went on in Akron that week.

But however confusing the details might be for what actually happened in Akron in late 1937, a decisive vote was certainly taken and Bill Wilson was authorized to try to raise the money necessary for alcoholic hospitals, paid missionaries, and the writing of a book to explain how they had gotten sober. That vote was, however, a close, contentious, and grudging victory, and it is clear that Bill's bare majority was obtained only after he made some concessions. He agreed that he would not try to raise those lavish funds in Ohio nor would he be expecting any contributions to come from the Akron Fellowship. If he was really going to raise that kind of money, it would have to be done in New York City, the home of most of the nation's wealthy philanthropists. Finally, perhaps at least a few of these harshly contested votes were won based on the belief that this was all just another one of Bill Wilson's flamboyant pipe dreams. The

---

*   This is incorrect. There were no Cleveland members in October 1937.

**   The fact that Bill and Lois rode home with the Parkers raises the question of what had happened to the Ruddells who drove them out there. Did they leave earlier or did they perhaps travel further on before going back to New Jersey? Or did they leave at the same time but took Fitz Mayo along with them, leaving the Wilsons to make the less crowded ride back home with the Parkers?

***   Bill, in both an October 1945 *Grapevine* article entitled "The Book is Born" and in *AACOA* (p. 144), says that the meeting took place in the fall, but then on page 76 of *AACOA*, he specifies the month of November and the schematic "Landmarks of A.A. History" on page vii of that same book picks this up, listing November as the date of the meeting—which has subsequently been adopted in most narratives about the event.

This is clearly wrong and Kurtz (*Not-God,* p. 326, n. 57), for instance, speaks directly to the several problems involved in the dating of this meeting. Perhaps most important, he notes that if the November date was correct, then Bill is justly open to the accusations "of dishonesty and promotional over-zeal" that Kurtz notes others have made (*Not-God,* p. 329, n. 18) because he was already aggressively fundraising in New York in late October —an activity that this meeting supposedly authorized.

To resolve this problem, Kurtz suggests the possibility that late July 1937 is the correct date "according to information available from Lois Wilson's diaries," but I can find nothing in her diaries to substantiate a visit to Akron during that month—it only mentions that Bill was in Detroit in late July. Lois's entries for the year 1937 mention Bill visiting six different cities—but never Akron. In addition, there are no preserved letters to or from Lois and Bill in Akron during 1937—as there are for his 1935, 1938, and 1939 visits—which would make sense if Bill's only visit was this one in October when Lois accompanied him.

Given all of this, the month mentioned by Lois in her list of dates (*Lois Remembers,* p. 197) and substantiated by her diary entries for that month conclusively pinpoint the date of this meeting as happening somewhere between October 11 and 15—most likely at the regular Wednesday night meeting held on October 13.

likelihood of him being able to persuade the rich to contribute that much money to a bunch of drunks—even in New York City—seemed to be a remote possibility at best.

Now, all Bill had to do was get back to New York and prove them all wrong by actually raising the money needed to put his ambitious plans in motion.

CHAPTER THREE

Meeting Mr. Richardson

~*Late October to November 1937*~

Today, Alcoholics Anonymous has neither its own hospitals nor paid missionaries, and this creates the impression that these two ideas were just momentary delusions of grandeur, distractions from the real business of writing a book that would guide people along the road to sobriety. Nothing could be further from the truth.

Bill Wilson came home from Akron with exactly what he wanted: a mandate to raise the cash needed to launch his worldwide assault on alcoholism, and he threw himself wholeheartedly into that project. Obviously these ambitious plans would require thousands, perhaps even millions of dollars before anything could happen. So, for the next several months, securing those funds became the all-consuming priority in Bill's life, and it would continue to command a significant part of his daily activities for the next several years.

This total commitment to fundraising temporarily sidelined any plans to write a book, so much so that the thought of actually putting pen to paper would not resurface for another seven months. During those months, the core New York members, with a bit of assistance from Dr. Bob and one or two others in Akron, spent all of their time trying to raise the money needed to finance this expensive new vision of how they would deliver their message of recovery to the wider world.

The story of these fundraising efforts is interesting in itself, but it is also essential for any real appreciation of the history of the book that would finally be published in April 1939. Bill Wilson found that explaining the Fellowship's constantly evolving understanding of alcoholism and its solution to the non-alcoholics he approached for funds was a radical departure from the 'one drunk talking to another drunk' model he had been using for the previous three years. Suddenly, he needed to explain in precise detail the many things that problem drinkers instinctively grasped the first time they heard them. These potential donors weren't drunks and they couldn't make the intuitive leaps that Bill had come to expect when talking to fellow alcoholics; they certainly didn't respond to Wilson's usual pitch, as many drinkers so often did, by saying, "Oh yes, that's me too!"

So Bill was forced to create a whole new vocabulary for explaining what he knew about alcoholism, one that would make the problem and his new cure more readily understandable to a prospective non-alcoholic contributor.* In short, the trials Bill went through trying to raise money, the people he met, and the successes and failures he experienced, all influenced the ways in which he packaged his message so that it was more comprehensible to the audience he was addressing, and many of these adaptations became a permanent part of the way that Alcoholics Anonymous ultimately explained its program of recovery to the world.

It is hard to imagine what kind of book would have been written in October 1937 when the Fellowship was just twenty-eight months old. Certainly twenty-eight months is an impressive amount of experience with sobriety, but how much more perspective and expertise does an additional twelve months provide? As noted earlier, Wilson characterized this as the "flying-blind period," and with each additional month of sobriety, the Fellowship developed deeper insights into the nature of alcoholism and grew significantly in their understanding of the solution they were offering. "The Book of Experience,"[1] Wilson's wonderfully pragmatic early name for the proposed book that was eventually written in late 1938, was necessarily substantially different from the one that would have been written in late 1937, having benefited greatly from almost a full year's worth of additional work with alcoholics and alcoholism.

If for no other reason than this, Alcoholics Anonymous can be grateful for the distractions and delays caused by Bill's laser-like focus on his fundraising efforts in late 1937 and throughout 1938.

The New York Group is on Board

Driving through the night from Akron, Bill and Lois arrived back in Brooklyn early on Sunday morning and went right to bed, but at 11 a.m. they were suddenly awakened by one of their resident drunks who thought someone had broken into the house.[2]** Bill certainly needed all the sleep he could get on Sunday because he was planning a big week of fundraising and he wanted to get started as early as possible the next morning.

Despite his later claims that he convinced the New York group to support these new projects after he returned from Akron, Wilson had surely sold the smaller New

---

* "Cure" was the word that members of the Fellowship were actually using at that time: "Think of it, we have the cure for alcoholism. Even then we were still talking about cures" (AA Main Events, 1937, Point 12).

** At this time, the Wilson household included a revolving cast of characters who were trying to stay sober. Lois provides some wonderful details of this time from her own perspective in a front-page December 1944 *Grapevine* article entitled "Bill's Wife Remembers When He and She and the First A.A.'s Were Very Young."

York group on these three proposals well before he left for Ohio, and they were excited and anxious to get started now that he had secured Akron's approval for the plan.*

On one hand, it is easy to understand the enthusiasm of the New York members, which was in such stark contrast to the hostile reaction Bill had encountered in Akron. With nothing but a Sunday night meeting at Bill's house in Brooklyn to act as a foundation and support for their small group, they needed to fully acknowledge their recently declared independence from the Oxford Group and begin to create a structure and belief system that would serve as the cornerstones for the future growth of their fledgling society.

On the other hand, this ready support is a bit surprising because ten months earlier, the New Yorkers had unanimously vetoed Wilson's decision to take a job as a professional therapist at Towns Hospital, the preeminent drying-out spot in New York City.[3] It is likely that Bill's frustration at being denied that job the previous December—a job that would have provided some much needed income for the Wilson household—contributed to his formulation of these three ambitious schemes.** If the group had previously found working for someone else as a professional counselor unacceptable, they were now willing to support the wholesale professionalization of the Fellowship's methods with hospitals and missionaries—just so long as they, rather than someone else, would be in control of the entire operation.[4] Bill claims that after his Akron trip, the New York group was "in a state of extremely high excitement" about raising large sums of money,[5] so they had seemingly worked their way through whatever reservations they had entertained about professionalism ten months earlier. Or, perhaps it was the fact that the population of this small group had changed enough in the meantime that their "group conscience"*** on this sensitive topic had changed as well.

Bill also notes that Hank Parkhurst, his right-hand man in the New York group, immediately caught fire with the idea of raising money from the rich,[6] but it is much more likely that Hank had helped push Bill in that direction long before he left for Akron. Hank loved big ideas, and he certainly wanted to get "back into the big time."[7] If Bill Wilson ever needed any help in 'thinking big,' then Henry G. Parkhurst was exactly the right man to help him do that.

Hank Parkhurst

Parkhurst's business background provides ample evidence of his ability to 'play in the big leagues.' According to his resume, Hank received his early training at Burroughs

---

* Bill Wilson consistently claimed that he held a meeting in New York *after* the Akron meeting to get the approval of the New York members (see, for instance, AA Main Events, 1937, Point 12 and AACOA, p. 146), but there was really no time for him to have done this in the seven days available between his return from Ohio on October 17, when he started on a round of aggressive (but failed) fundraising efforts and his visit to his brother-in-law, Dr. Leonard Strong, on October 25.

** Stepping Stones has archived only four tax returns by the Wilsons prior to 1940, but even these four are helpful in understanding the ups and downs of Bill's and Lois's financial situation. Their 1927 return lists $9,287.60 in income. The following year, their income soared up to $21,645.41—a truly rich income in those days. By 1936, their annual income had fallen to $4,879.91 and in 1937, they filed a return showing income of just $2,825.00, presumably from Bill's job with Quaw and Foley and from Lois's generally unprofitable interior decorating business. Clearly, the Wilson household was in need of a job that could provide a steady income (StSt, Income Tax–Federal 1927–1961 [miscellaneous], LBW 210, Box 42, Folder 2).

*** This is an early A.A. concept that was later enshrined in the Second Tradition: "For our group purpose there is but one ultimate authority—a loving God as He may express Himself in our group conscience."

Adding Machine Company and then operated his own successful sales consulting firm before taking a job with Standard Oil of Indiana. He quickly climbed the corporate ladder there, rising from city manager, to divisional sales manager, to assistant general manager. He then left the company to form his own oil company, which he subsequently sold to Standard Oil, after which they rehired him. Hank's last job before meeting Bill Wilson was as the Assistant Wholesale Sales Manager for Standard Oil of New Jersey, a position he claimed put him in charge of 6,600 salesmen servicing 28,000 dealers.[8] Bill once mentioned that Hank was paid $40,000 a year for this job; a truly staggering amount of money in 1935, right in the middle of the Great Depression.[9]* This was the job Hank lost when he was fired for drinking in 1935.

The Honor Dealers Venture

In late November 1936, when Hank had been sober little more than a year, Bill arranged financing for a company named after him (HGP Inc.) that was about to launch a new business venture called Honor Dealers.[10] The start-up money came from Wilson and three of his Wall Street friends named Meschi, Jones, and Curry. Parkhurst owned a controlling 51 percent of the company, while the other four investors shared in the remaining 49 percent of the new business enterprise.[11]**

The venture, as Hank envisioned it, was to be a cooperative buying group for gasoline, oil, tires, and automotive parts, bringing together an ever-expanding network of independent service stations,[12] effectively bypassing the huge corporations that controlled the industry's supply lines (including the Standard Oil Company that had fired him the previous year).

Unfortunately, most of Honor Dealers' business records were lost in the company's frequent moves and eventual demise, but it was never a successful venture in any substantive way. But the scant surviving documents do provide clear evidence of Hank's chronic grandiosity and overconfidence regarding the prospects of this new business. In late March 1937, he was boldly predicting to Bill that he would be operating on "a break-even basis by the end of May."[13] Wilson accepted this glowing prediction at face value and sent Hank an additional investment check of a thousand dollars (actually, "Lois's check for One Grand") on April 1.[14]*** Six weeks later, Wilson was still a true believer, exclaiming to a business friend in Cleveland "we shall probably be in the clear within a month. Our success is virtually assured."[15] In the end, Bill's, optimism proved to be not just premature, but completely misplaced. Hank's flamboyant visions almost always exceeded the disappointing (and sometimes disastrous) results that inevitably followed.

---

*   On January 19, 1939, Silas Bent published an article entitled "There Is Hope" in the *Hackettstown Courier-Post* claiming that Parkhurst "had lost his $20,000 job on account of his drinking." Whether Bill's or Silas's number is correct, they both represented an enormous amount of annual income in 1935.

**   "Jones" was Charles M. Jones who contributed $2,500 to the venture (Bill Wilson to Chas. M. Jones, January 11, 1941, GSO, Box 200, Folder I, Bill: Business with Hank P. / 1937-1950). Curry was almost certainly William G. Currie (Hank called him Bill and uses this spelling for his last name in an April 11, 1937 letter to Bill Wilson (GSO, Box 200, Folder I, Bill: Business with Hank P. / 1937-1950). Currie later owned eight shares of stock in Works Publishing. The GSO and Stepping Stones archives have no further helpful citations for Meschi.

***   The exact source of this substantive check is unknown, but Bill's mention of it coming from Lois may be an indication that it was a Burnham family investment rather than a personal one.

Altogether too much has been made of Bill's relationship with Honor Dealers in the past. It has, for instance, been stated in several places online that Wilson was a paid salesman for the company, but there are no contemporary documents to substantiate this claim. In relation to his actually working at Honor Dealers, Ruth Hock stated categorically that the company's "profits were split between . . . Hank Parkhurst and my salary and the service station owners . . . Bill was too busy to go selling oil, windshield wipers, tires, and that sort of thing."[16] When Wilson was working during this period, he was deeply immersed in Wall Street-related activities rather than in attempts to sign up service stations for the Honor Dealers program, and whatever modest income the Wilsons enjoyed at this time came from those ventures rather than from any paycheck signed by Hank Parkhurst. It is well-known that Hank did employ several recently sober members from the New York group as Honor Dealers' salesmen (most notably Sterling Parker and, later, Jim Burwell[17]), but Bill Wilson was not one of them. The only contemporary evidence we have of his official involvement with Honor Dealers is his signature on a legal document dated December 5, 1938, identifying him as the company's "Secy. & Treas."[18]

There is also a widespread assumption (even more common among "historical" online postings) that Parkhurst and Wilson were, to a large degree, both active partners in running this firm. But, in his own writings, Bill provides no justification for this view and he was, in fact, always careful to explicitly note that the business, the office, and even the secretary, belonged to Hank Parkhurst.[19] More to the point, as this project was being launched, Hank wrote to Bill informing him that he and his three financial backers were to take a "strictly hands off" policy in relation to Honor Dealers. They were free to offer him financial backing, but that did not buy them the right to offer him any advice and that, going forward, they would have absolutely "no voice in [the running of] Honor Dealers."[20] It is hard to call this letter anything but rude as Hank bluntly asserts that he doesn't want "anyone to take any responsibility for approaching any manufacturers, [or] to have anything to do with these contacts, or figuring discounts . . . It is my job to head this. A backer either has confidence in that ability up to a certain amount of money or he does not."[21] Honor Dealers was, in short, a Hank Parkhurst project from start to finish.

Finally, it is also widely believed—based primarily on the impression created by statements later made by Honor Dealers' secretary, Ruth Hock—that Bill was a constant presence at the Newark, New Jersey offices throughout 1937 and 1938, but this is not supported by any contemporary evidence. On the contrary, Wilson was on the road pursuing business ventures throughout most of 1937 (as Lois's diary attests) and he had an office at Quaw and Foley while he was back in New York City. Bill did not become a regular visitor to the New Jersey office until mid-1938 when, for a few weeks, he used Ruth's typing skills to help him write the first two chapters of the Big Book and then some three months later when he began writing the book again in earnest. As Honor Dealers' business wound down and the Big Book project became more demanding, Bill spent more and more time in the Newark office using the secretarial services that were so readily available to him there.

Hank's overconfidence in his own business acumen would prove to be a fatal factor, but he had two real talents that characterized his Honor Dealers venture—the creative promotional pieces he put together for the business and the marketing ideas he constantly proposed to expand Honor Dealers. Hank was a real promoter. For instance, in his efforts to enroll new dealers in the cooperative, he created an elaborate presentation on the benefits of joining the co-op using a detailed Q&A format. (We shall see this same format used again later in Hank's proposed, but rejected, "Q&A Chapter" for the Big Book.)* Among his many marketing ideas, perhaps the most striking was a lottery he tried to organize in which all of the previous week's customers would compete to win substantial gift certificates redeemable for Honor Dealers goods and services.[22]

Confronted with a challenge, Hank Parkhurst was a man who naturally thought big (if consistently too big) and who then brought his substantial creative energy and powerful sales abilities to bear on his proposed solution to that challenge. But, despite all of Hank's grand visions, his legendary energy and his very best efforts, Honor Dealers was never really successful and it "slowly but surely declined" and then disappeared completely as the 1930s drew to a close.[23]**

Bill's Right-Hand Man

Hank Parkhurst is the forgotten man of early A.A. history, which is somewhat understandable given the fact that he had returned to drinking by September 1939 and never again regained permanent sobriety.*** However, other than Bill Wilson, there is no more central person in the history of the writing of the Big Book than Henry G. Parkhurst or more critical to the formulation of the program of recovery unveiled to the world when that book was published. Dr. Bob Smith did later supply a remote but helpful counterbalance to Bill's overly ambitious natural tendencies, but at this time it was Hank Parkhurst who was always at Bill's right hand, making ever more extravagant suggestions, offering encouragement for all of his bold plans, and pushing him to write the book while simultaneously arguing over exactly what should go into that book. More than anyone else, it was Henry G. Parkhurst who delivered the constant pressure that drove Bill Wilson to raise money, to write a book, and to formulate the Twelve Steps of recovery.

Hank got sober in September 1935 and, from that time until shortly after the publication of the Big Book, he and Bill talked regularly and were constantly in each other's company. In addition, their families were extremely close. Hank lived in New Jersey, first in Teaneck and then in Upper Montclair, with his wife, Kathleen, and their two young boys. The families were on such familiar terms that, as Lois notes, "in 1938 we spent at least half of our weekends with the Parkhursts in Jersey."[24] And, when

---

*   See Chapter Twenty-One: The Q&A Chapter for details on this rejected chapter.

**   In a January 11, 1941 letter to Charles M. Jones, one of the original investors in Honor Dealers, Bill Wilson advised him that the company was "legally dead at least for income tax purposes and since there is no hope it can be revived you will be quite correct in showing a total loss of your $2,500 investment in your income tax returns for 1940." (GSO, Box 200, Folder I, Bill: Business with Hank P. / 1937-1950)

*** See Chapter Thirty-One: Aftermath for more details on Hank's return to drinking.

the Wilsons were forced out of their home by foreclosure in April 1939—just two weeks after the Big Book was published—they immediately moved in with Hank and Kathleen Parkhurst.[25]

From 1936 to 1939, Hank acted as Bill's right-hand man in the New York Fellowship and Bill often referred to him as "my partner in the book enterprise"[26]—clearly acknowledging Hank's central and critical role in the writing, publication, and promotion of the Big Book. But, despite their closeness, the two men were also a bit wary of each other, an understandable reaction given their respective strong personalities. During several months in late 1938 and early 1939 as the book was being written, Bill and Hank regularly shared the office in Newark, New Jersey. It is hard to imagine the challenging dynamics of these two alpha males squeezed into one tiny office (along with one very attractive secretary) as Hank's business waned and Bill's writing of the Big Book progressed toward its successful completion.

The secretary, Ruth Hock, later characterized Hank as "a vibrant personality" and noted "that he was capable of strong likes and dislikes—that he seemed to be possessed of inexhaustible energy—and that he liked to make quick decisions."[27] While Bill is typically characterized as a salesman, everyone who knew the two men noted that Hank was a significant notch up from Bill in his energy level and his forcefulness. Bill himself acknowledged that Hank was a "super promoter" and "the greatest high pressure salesman I had ever known."[28] Jim Burwell, who also knew Hank well and actually lived with him in early 1939,[29] called him a "high-pressure human dynamo."[30] It was exactly these talents that Bill Wilson would repeatedly call upon to help him with all his early efforts to put A.A. on a sound financial footing and to get the book written and published.

Hank played an absolutely central role during the critical months between October 1937 and April 1939, making repeated and substantial contributions to the direction in which the Fellowship and the book were developing. Without Hank Parkhurst's ideas, enthusiasm, drive, and the vigorous push that he constantly gave to Bill Wilson, the history of A.A. in 1938, 1939, and the years beyond would have been significantly different. It is possible to imagine the creation and growth of Alcoholics Anonymous into the organization that we know today without the help of Dr. Bob Smith, but it is impossible to do so if the many substantive contributions made by Hank Parkhurst are eliminated from the picture.

Dreams of Easy Money Evaporate

Following the Akron meeting, Hank was excited about these new plans to expand their program and eager to bring some of his famous high-pressure energy to bear on the moneyed classes of New York City. Surely, these people would be willing to make significant contributions to support the Fellowship's revolutionary and proven method for saving drunks all over the country—if not all over the world.

Both men started by canvassing every wealthy person they had ever met and making cold calls on the many foundations headquartered in New York City.[31] After a hectic week of appointments and meetings, they were frankly astonished to discover their plans for saving alcoholics had aroused absolutely no interest among anyone they had contacted.* While some individuals showed a sympathetic interest in their pitch, the conversation always ended with a polite rejection: "Thanks, but no thanks." There just wasn't any cachet in saving alcoholics. On the contrary, potential donors seemed to feel there was something disreputable and unsavory about the whole proposal. Wealthy individuals couldn't see the value of aligning themselves with down-and-out drunks and they almost uniformly wondered out loud: Why would anyone bother trying to save a bunch of people who were responsible for creating their own misery? Wouldn't that money be better spent trying to cure tuberculosis or cancer, or find a better use if it was donated to the Red Cross? The foundations were even less willing to consider the proposals. Besides experiencing the same aversion to indigent alcoholics that the wealthy instinctively felt, they couldn't even decide how to characterize this proposed new venture—was it social, medical, or educational?[32]

Bill's and Hank's bright dreams of easy money quickly evaporated in the harsh light of reality; they couldn't find a single person or organization willing to make even a token donation. Their dismay is completely understandable. For decades, many of the rich in New York City had generously supported the Temperance Movement and then contributed heavily to the political forces promoting the passage of the constitutional amendment that authorized Prohibition. What was the problem here?

With hindsight, it seems that what Wilson and Parkhurst failed to realize was that the Temperance and Prohibition Movements were both "front-end" solutions to the alcohol problem. They were either trying to convince people not to drink in the first place or, failing that, to make drinking illegal so that nobody could buy alcohol and get drunk even if they wanted to. They had directed all of their energy into "preventing the creation of new drunkards, rather than the reclamation of those who were afflicted."[33] But what Hank and Bill were selling was a solution that claimed to solve the problem on the back end, by actively reforming and rescuing people whose lives had already been destroyed by drinking. They were appealing for money to reclaim real, hardcore, down-in-the-gutter alcoholics. This was certainly the messy end of the temperance business and categorically different from the more sophisticated approaches that had attracted such large sums of money in the past. Added to this was one final problem: this appeal was being made by two men who, by their own admission, had once been terrible drunks themselves. It all sounded just a bit too sketchy and more than a little improbable to everyone they approached.

Clearly, none of these people were interested in getting involved with *real* drunks.

---

* The use of 'a week' here is mandated by the fact that Bill returned from Akron on Sunday, October 17 and then visited his brother-in-law, Dr. Leonard Strong, in despair on Monday, October 25. This visit to Dr. Strong and its aftermath are the critical arguments for accepting a date prior to October 25 for the Akron meeting—as opposed to the November date that Wilson so frequently mentioned.

Bill's Brother-in-Law Saves the Day

Bill Wilson was in despair. Convinced that he possessed a cure for 'the drink problem' and that he knew the best way to deliver that solution to active alcoholics worldwide, he was amazed that he couldn't find anyone willing to spend money to help spread this new cure. Failure, especially when success seemed to be so close, was difficult to accept, and Bill grew more and more frustrated as he struggled to turn his dream into reality.[*]

This frustration brought on what he called "one of my imaginary ulcer attacks,"[34] symptoms that seemed to crop up with some regularity during this time. Just five weeks earlier, Lois had noted that Bill "started a home ulcer treatment."[35] A little over a year later, he would have his most famous imaginary ulcer attack on the day he claimed to have written the first draft of the Twelve Steps. The tensions caused by big problems seemed to express themselves in Bill Wilson's stomach and, at the moment, he had some very large and frustrating problems.

Bill felt that something other than a home remedy was called for to deal with this, so on Monday, October 25, he visited Dr. Leonard Strong, a successful osteopathic physician, who also happened to be his sister Dorothy's husband and one of his closest personal friends.[**] Bill later admitted this ulcer attack was really little more than a pretext to bend the always sympathetic ear of his brother-in-law. It is also likely that the visit was a calculated part of Bill's campaign to connect with more rich people—many of whom were Dr. Strong's patients and several of whom could be found among his circle of friends. It is unlikely that the ever-resourceful Wilson would have left a valuable opportunity such as his brother-in-law's wealthy acquaintances untapped, and his ulcer complaint provided the perfect opportunity for opening up that discussion with his friend.

Leonard Strong is a low-profile, but extremely important person in early A.A. history. He stood by Bill throughout the darkest hours of his active alcoholism to the extent that Wilson once described him as "my only remaining friend and the confidant of the worst of my drinking time."[36] Through it all, Strong continually provided compassionate support and encouragement for whatever might be helpful in overcoming Bill's alcohol problem and he had, on at least two occasions in 1933 and 1934, generously paid for Bill's expensive trips to Towns Hospital following his relapses.[37] Later, he would demonstrate his ongoing support by serving as one of the earliest non-alcoholic trustees on the Board of the Alcoholic Foundation, a position that he held from January 1939 until his retirement in October 1954.[38][***] But Dr. Leonard Strong's most important and singular contribution to the success of Alcoholics Anonymous occurred during this meeting with Bill Wilson on October 25, 1937.

---

[*]   While a week may seem like a short time frame for developing such a bitter case of despair, it must be remembered that Bill was a self-acknowledged alcoholic; a person typically addicted to 'instant gratification.'

[**]   Osteopathic medicine takes a significantly different, basically holistic, approach to the patient; treating all aspects of body, mind, and spirit. Osteopaths believe that rational treatments can only be based on the fact that the body is capable of self-regulation, self-healing, and health maintenance and that its structure and function are reciprocally interrelated. (Wikipedia article, *Osteopathic Medicine in the United States*, retrieved June 6, 2013)

[***] Bill incorrectly states in *AACOA* that Leonard Strong served on the Alcoholic Foundation "from its beginning in 1938 until his own retirement in 1955" (p. 14).

As Bill tells the story, he had blithely imposed himself on his brother-in-law, who somehow found the time to fit him into his busy schedule, and they sat down in Leonard's office for a talk. After briefly describing his symptoms, Bill abandoned that particular line of complaint and launched into a sullen and resentful diatribe. He bemoaned the "stinginess and the shortsightedness" of the rich who were not willing to contribute anything to "this great and glorious enterprise" that was already well on its way to success. "Think of it, Leonard, forty hopeless cases sober for two, even three years!" Strong was, of course, well aware of these facts and of Bill's attempts to raise money, but Wilson wouldn't let it go, complaining bitterly to his friend: "What's the matter with these people anyway?"[39]

Leonard listened patiently to this familiar tale of Bill's past successes and his current need for money and quickly realized this visit was less about his brother-in-law's physical condition than it was about fundraising. So, after Bill's tirade finally wound down, the doctor offered him something more than just a new prescription or another ulcer treatment; he took him across the hall to meet Dr. Wynn. This prominent doctor had recently retired as the New York City Health Commissioner and Strong was hoping that he might know someone in city government who could be helpful. But after listening to the two men for just a short while, Dr. Wynn told them that he wasn't interested in pursuing those political possibilities, but thought he could propose a much better solution. At first, he said that Bill should get in touch with the Rockefeller Foundation, but then almost immediately changed his mind and said that the man Wilson should really be talking to was John D. Rockefeller Jr. Bill was more than a little taken aback at this ambitious suggestion, so much so, that he actually blurted out skeptically: "Well, how about the Prince of Wales!"[40]

At this point in the conversation, Dr. Strong remembered that he once knew a girl in high school who had an uncle, the Reverend Willard S. Richardson, and that he had even taken a Bible Study class taught by Richardson at the time. 'I don't know if he is still alive or even if he would remember me,' he told Bill, 'but he used to be a friend of the Rockefeller family and he was, at one time, the head of the Laura Spelman Foundation before it became part of the Rockefeller Foundation. Why don't I call up Mr. Rockefeller's office and see if he is still there?" Bill, of course, thought this was a fabulous idea and he encouraged his brother-in-law to do so immediately.

Dr. Strong called and not only was Richardson still working for Rockefeller, he actually took the call and immediately expressed his delight at being reconnected with Dr. Strong. 'Why hello, Leonard,' he said cordially, 'where have you been all these years? I would certainly love to see you again.' Bill said that, unlike himself, his sister's husband was a man of few words and so he quickly came to the point. 'Mr. Richardson, I'm sitting here with my brother-in-law who seems to have come up with a new cure for

---

* This story of the long-forgotten girlfriend, who would date back over twenty years to 1916 or so, sounds a bit far-fetched and suspiciously convenient, but Dr. Strong himself confirmed this story in a recorded comment made at the April 1951 General Services Conference. (GSO, AA Conference 1951, Ref #0002, Tape 2 of 11, [B side], 02:47). The story of his attendance at the bible class comes from Leonard and Dorothy Strong's 1978 Interview with Niles Peebles (GSO, CD 619, Track 1, [22:10 – 24:20]).

alcoholism. He's had some real success with sobering up drunks and I was wondering if you might be interested in talking to him?'[41]

This might seem like a strange question to ask in the first phone conversation between two men who haven't spoken for a long time, but it didn't sound all that unusual to Willard Richardson. He had assisted John D. Rockefeller Jr. with his charity work for many years and, as just about everyone in the country knew, the Rockefellers were strict Baptist teetotalers who, for the past two generations, had liberally supported temperance reform and aggressively contributed to the political campaign for the passage of the Prohibition Amendment. They were renowned, if not notorious, for their opposition to alcohol and all of its effects.

The family deserved that reputation. In 1874, John D. Rockefeller Jr.'s mother had been a founding member of the Woman's Christian Temperance Union and, as she once told her son, she "might have joined them" praying and singing religious hymns in local taverns during that first year of the WCTU's existence except for the fact that she gave birth to him that same year.[42] She was, however, later known to join these "well-bred ladies" as "they surged into the saloons, falling on their knees and praying for the sodden sinners" they found there.[43] His father, John D. Sr., was just as ardently committed to the cause of temperance throughout his life. Among his many other contributions, he was the largest single financial supporter of the powerful Anti-Saloon League, and since its inception in 1893, had been pledging a generous 10 percent match for any funds that they might raise elsewhere.

The son, like his father before him, was known as the richest man in America and he had continued the family tradition of liberally funding the cause of temperance (although he had abandoned his support of Prohibition just a few years earlier when it proved to be such a disastrous and lawless failure). John D. Rockefeller Jr. was famous for his loathing of alcohol and had, for decades, been just as well known for voting with his checkbook for a wide variety of solutions aimed at eradicating the evil consequences of drink.[44]

If there was a huge pipeline of money that could be opened by someone presenting a successful solution to the drink problem, then the tap for that pipeline was surely located in the impressive new skyscraper just off Fifth Avenue in mid-town Manhattan. Strong was confident that his brother-in-law's cure for alcoholism would be a sure-fire topic of interest at Rockefeller Center—and he was right.

'Would I be interested in talking to him?' Richardson asked. 'Why certainly, Leonard! Please send him over to me.'[45]

Bill Meets with Willard Richardson

However casual this invitation may have sounded, Dr. Leonard Strong understood that an eminent, old-school gentleman like Willard Richardson—born one year after the Civil War and currently a distinguished minister who enjoyed a strong personal relationship with John D. Rockefeller Jr.—required a courteous and well-mannered approach. So the next day, following a custom all but forgotten in the modern world, he wrote a formal letter of introduction for his brother-in-law to present to Willard Richardson:

October 26, 1937

Mr. Willard S. Richardson
30 Rockefeller Plaza
New York City, N.Y.

Dear Mr. Richardson:

This will serve to introduce my brother-in-law, Mr. William Wilson, of whom I spoke in our telephone conversation yesterday.

His work with alcoholics appears very effective and I think merits your interest and possibly that of the Rockefeller Foundation.

Your courtesy in seeing him is greatly appreciated by me and I regret my inability to be present.

With kindest regards to yourself and family, I am

Sincerely,

Dr. Leonard V. Strong[46]*

Presumably that same day, Bill presented himself and his letter of introduction to Willard Richardson on the 56th floor of Rockefeller Center. At the time, this was the most famous business address in America, although it was modestly referred to as "Room 5600 at Rockefeller Center." But Room 5600 was in reality the very heart of the Rockefeller empire, an entire floor of elegant, wood-paneled offices from which John D. Jr. and his closest advisors ran the family's worldwide operations.

Bill must have felt a fair amount of excitement and trepidation as he approached this intimidating office; there was no bigger prize in American philanthropy than John D. Rockefeller Jr. And it wasn't just the huge wealth and power of the family and their Foundation that was impressive, it was also that they were already favorably inclined to support just about anything that might alleviate the devastation caused by alcohol. The Rockefellers! All that money! Exhilarating and frightening? Of course. But what better opportunity could a natural-born salesman hope for than the chance to pitch a fabulous and proven product to such a perfectly prequalified and very rich prospect?

He met Richardson in his office, and as Bill told the story several years later: "I sat down and told him about our exciting discovery, this terrific cure for alcoholics that had just hit the world, how it worked, and what we have done for them."[47] While this is a succinct account, it is more than a little abstract and hardly covers the wealth of personal details mentioned during their lengthy conversation. In Frank Amos's much more contemporary account of that meeting, he says that Bill told

---

*   This letter clearly contradicts some of Bill's later accounts of how he and his brother-in-law rushed right over to Rockefeller Center together at the conclusion of the original phone call.

"the story of how, after many vain attempts to discontinue the use of alcohol, he had achieved what he believed was a permanent cure, through what he termed a religious or spiritual process."[48] Bill almost certainly told Willard Richardson in some detail about his own years of despair and of the "white light" experience in Towns Hospital,* which preceded his dramatic recovery, and he undoubtedly mentioned the religious awakenings experienced by others who had since joined the Fellowship. An emphasis on the religious aspect of his recovery was surely the best way to sell their new solution to someone like Willard Richardson who had lived the past forty years of his life as an ordained Baptist minister—and that is most likely what Bill Wilson did.

Richardson was impressed with Bill's story. Amos says he found it "so sincere" and "so convincing"[49] that he asked Wilson's permission to share some of the details with a few of Mr. Rockefeller's other friends and promised to get back to him shortly. Bill, of course, readily agreed to all of this and, for his own part, said he was so elated by the success of the interview that in an instant his "ulcer attack disappeared."[50]

Richardson's Relationship with Rockefeller

Bill later reported, "after the interview, I learned that Mr. Richardson was closer to John D. Rockefeller Jr., than perhaps any person in the world. How could we miss!"[51] Willard Richardson was, in fact, extremely intimate with the junior Rockefeller and he had worked closely with him for many years. Lois aptly called Richardson his "spiritual advisor,"[52] and it may convey some idea of his importance to the Rockefeller family to note that when John D. Rockefeller, Sr. died the previous May (at the age of ninety-seven) it was the Reverend Willard Richardson who officiated over the private burial service at Cleveland's Lake View Cemetery.[53]

Willard Richardson met John D. Rockefeller Jr., in 1893 when they both taught Bible classes while attending Brown University in Providence, RI, and the two men became fast friends. The young Rockefeller was, of course, burdened with being the son of the richest man in America and he was quite awkward and uncomfortable when he first arrived at Brown. But Richardson was able to help his younger friend overcome these difficulties. As Rockefeller later noted: "He was a Senior when I was a Freshman and . . . Dick realized my lack of ease and poise and was sympathetic and understanding, a very lovable character, and the first man I ever brought home from college."[54] **

Although Richardson graduated from Brown (and went on to study at the Union Theological Seminary) at the end of Rockefeller's freshman year, the two continued their close friendship. Following the completion of his sophomore year, Rockefeller invited Richardson to join him on a summer-long bicycle tour through England.[55] Two years later, when they had both graduated from their respective schools, they rewarded themselves with another summer bicycle tour—this time pedaling their way from Holland through Germany and on into Switzerland.[56]

---

*   Bill's recounting of this experience in his Big Book version only says, "I felt lifted up, as though a great clean wind of a mountain top blew through and through" (*Alcoholics Anonymous*, 4th edition, p. 14), but elsewhere he refers to it explicitly and in much more detail as a "white light" experience (see for instance Wilson, *Bill W., My First 40 Years*, p. 145).

**   Willard Richardson was always called "Dick" by his close friends.

Following that bike tour, Willard Richardson was appointed one of the ministers at the Fifth Avenue Baptist Church in New York City, the church the Rockefeller family attended and supported during the first decades of the century. Then, in 1909, he left New York to assume the post of director of religious activities at the University of Minnesota. Even at this distance, Richardson and Rockefeller maintained their close friendship by mail, exchanging a host of letters in which they addressed each other as "Dear John" and "Dear Dick." In 1912, Willard Richardson returned to New York City and went to work directly for Rockefeller as a member of his personal staff. Six years later, when John D. Junior created the Laura Spelman Foundation (named for his mother), he appointed Richardson as one of the five original directors and he served as its principal executive during the first four years of the fund's operation. (In 1929, the Spelman Foundation was merged into the slightly older Rockefeller Foundation that had been set up by his father in 1913.)[57]

But even more important than this, especially for the kind of request that Bill Wilson would be making, Willard Richardson oversaw John D. Rockefeller Jr.'s private charitable contributions. These were made from John Junior's personal checkbook*— separate and distinct from the Foundation—and Richardson was put in charge of this fund when it was first set up in 1919, a position Rockefeller legally formalized in 1923.[58] Officially called the "Committee on Benevolence," this private fund had a number of honorary members, but the decision-making powers rested squarely with the smaller Advisory Committee and, from the start, Willard Richardson was Executive Director of that Advisory Committee. One report shows that from 1926 to 1930, the Advisory Committee approved and distributed over $2,750,000 of John D. Rockefeller Jr.'s personal money to various charities, projects, and people.[59] In 1934, Rockefeller legally dissolved the Committee on Benevolence, but he continued to rely on Richardson as his primary advisor for all of his personal donations.[60] In short, Willard Richardson was the one man that John D. Rockefeller Jr. turned to for guidance and counsel when deciding on how best to allocate his very generous private donations to charitable causes and to other projects that promised significant social and religious benefits.

Given all of this, Bill was absolutely correct in saying that "Mr. Richardson was closer to John D. Rockefeller Jr. than perhaps any person in the world." However, whether or not Wilson could "hit" or "miss" with his pitch to Richardson for some of those fabulous Rockefeller dollars was another matter entirely.

Laying the Groundwork for the Rockefeller Meeting

While Richardson went off to consult with some of Rockefeller's friends, Bill called Dr. Bob to tell him the news of the fabulous connection he had just made with the Rockefeller organization and to predict with confidence that they would soon have a significant amount of money in hand to begin these new projects. Bill's plan was to set up their first alcoholic hospital in Akron under Dr. Bob's supervision and he

---

*   John D. Rockefeller Jr. was called "Junior" by all of his close friends.

mentioned to Bob that it might be necessary for him to come to New York to help finalize whatever arrangements would be necessary to properly launch that project.

The Monday after that call, Bob wrote to Bill complaining that he had "been looking for a letter from you, but so far have been disappointed. Our business here *[i.e., Dr. Bob's medical practice]* has all gone to pieces so I hardly think that I should get East for a while." He wanted to know if Bill had received any news from the Rockefellers. "Let me know what the state of affairs is with these gentlemen who seem interested [and] if you have learned anything new lately." After recounting some details about two new drunks who had joined the group and telling an embarrassing story of how he had fallen asleep during dinner at a friend's house (because he had been working so late with an active drunk the night before), Bob came back to his anxiety about the current financial situation: "Let me know, Bill, if there are any recent developments because I feel that I should have to do something shortly to correct this situation here, if possible."[61] Clearly things were not going well in Akron and Bob needed to know if he could really count on the rosy financial picture Bill was so confidently predicting. Was there really going to be a hospital for alcoholics in his future? If so, it couldn't come at a better time for he was currently teetering on the brink of financial ruin.

Given the vehement hostility that several members in his group had earlier expressed about these plans, Bob Smith decided not to tell anyone in Akron about this conversation or about the imminent possibility that their new movement might soon receive substantial financial support from the Rockefeller Foundation to put Bill's ambitious three-pronged plan into action.*

But, Bill hadn't heard anything from Willard Richardson since their meeting, so he had no new information to offer. Finally, Dr. Strong received a letter describing what had been happening within the Rockefeller circle during the previous two weeks:

November 10, 1937

Dr. Leonard V. Strong
133 East 58th Street
New York City

Dear Dr. Leonard:

I have now had conferences with four men** whose judgment as to the interesting story of Mr. Wilson I think is good. I assure you that even my repeating of the story was impressive to them and they thought the matter very important. They were all inclined to agree with me that, if possible, any organization of this project and anything that tended to professionalize or institutionalize it would be a serious matter and quite undesirable. Some of them thought quite as highly of Mr. Wilson's experience as a religious one as they did of it as a liquor one.

---

* Subsequent events conclusively prove the truth of this statement.

** Since Richardson later introduced Wilson and his alcoholics to only three other gentlemen, it is possible that this fourth man was John D. Rockefeller Jr. himself.

I wonder if we could get together some time for a few minutes. While there is little more that I would have to add, I should like to meet Mr. Wilson and you. And if both of you, or Mr. Wilson himself, could lunch with me next week or in the fairly near future it would be a pleasure to me. You may let me know by letter or telephone as you would care to.

Very truly,

W. S. Richardson[62]

Richardson had taken Bill's agenda to the next level by talking to some of the most trusted members of Rockefeller's inner circle and they were impressed with the promise of this new cure for alcoholism. However, this fantastic news was immediately tempered with Richardson's explicit rejection of "any organization of this project" and of "anything that tended to professionalize or institutionalize it," which is exactly what Bill Wilson was planning to do with whatever money he might obtain from the Rockefellers.

That explicit rejection of professionalization is universally claimed to have occurred much later in this story, either during the December 13 dinner meeting with the Rockefeller group or, as stated more frequently, in John D. Rockefeller Jr.'s letter the following March. Obviously, that is not the case. The Rockefeller mantra that "money will surely spoil this thing" appears almost immediately—explicit, bold, and clear—in this first written communication from Richardson, just two short weeks after he made his initial contact with the Fellowship. Wilson was so consumed by his burning desire to save all the drunks in the world that he just couldn't see how a huge infusion of cash would radically change what had, up until then, been so successful as a small, person-to-person operation. But Richardson and his friends—men with far more experience and sophistication about the ways in which money can profoundly corrupt any enterprise—were instinctively aware that this was one project that would be more harmed than helped by generous outside donations.

This mixed message likely bothered Bill tremendously. Here were five rich and powerful men who were exactly the kind of people he needed to help him realize his dream. They believed his story about the discovery of a new cure for alcoholism, but they weren't willing to go along with his vision of how that recovery could be spread to the huge number of suffering alcoholics who so desperately needed it. Ever the salesman, Bill surely interpreted this to mean that although he hadn't yet closed the deal, he was at least halfway there; they accepted his new solution, they just weren't ready to sign off on his ideas about the best way to more effectively deliver that solution. Finally, the really good news was that he was going to get at least one more chance to present his case in person. He wasn't finished with his sales pitch yet . . . Willard Richardson wanted to have lunch.

Richardson did want to have lunch with Bill and his brother-in-law, but he explicitly claimed that "there is little more that I have to add." This certainly sounds like a diplomatic attempt to close the door on any more of Bill's arguments for professionalization. Most likely, Richardson's agenda for lunch was to propose the idea of an exploratory meeting between Bill's recovered alcoholics and the inner circle of Rockefeller's friends as a way to determine if there was any way his group might be helpful to the fledgling movement. Certainly, Richardson would need to explore this idea with Bill in person and get his consent before organizing such a meeting.

In two short letters, it was all arranged and at 1:00 p.m. on Tuesday, November 16, the three men sat down to a leisurely lunch.[63] However much Richardson may have hoped to forestall any further arguments, Bill would have none of it. He saw such a desperate need to expand their work that he just couldn't help himself. To his mind, it was imperative that a way be found to extend this new cure for alcoholism and it needed to be found as quickly as possible. Anything else would be unthinkable.[64]

According to Bill's later account:

> So I had lunch with the old gentleman and we went over this thing again and again and, boy, he's so warm and kindly and friendly. Right at the close of the lunch he said, "Well now Mr. Wilson or Bill, if I can call you that, wouldn't you like to have a luncheon meeting with some of my friends? . . . I believe they'd like to hear this story."[65]

Bill was a persistent salesman, especially when he believed passionately in his own point of view, so it is not hard to imagine him presenting his arguments "again and again"—no matter what Richardson had said in his letter. But, in the end, Willard Richardson held his ground, agreeing only to revisit the success of the movement and to discuss some possible involvement by the Rockefeller group at a meeting, which he would personally organize at some mutually agreeable time in the near future.

The Rockefeller Meeting Is Arranged

One possible date for this meeting, Monday, December 13, had obviously been suggested for the meeting since it is mentioned in a letter that Dr. Bob sent to Bill less than a week later:

11/22/37

Dear Bill !—

Glad to hear from you again and to learn that some interest is being evinced by the [Rockefeller] Foundation. I showed your letter to Paul [Stanley], T. Henry and Clarace [Williams] only. Paul says he thinks he can come to N.Y. on relatively short notice and so do I at least with a little financial assistance. The trip would have to be a little hasty, perhaps 2 days in N.Y. (12th + 13th) for I would feel that if I got that far East I should spend at least one day with [my] mother [in Vermont] so we would be gone away from here about a week. I should drive of course unless the roads are too bad. Probably could not come if we had to pay R. R. fares . . . Business is very slow now . . . Give my love to Lois please and keep me informed re[garding] developments.

As ever

Bob[66]

It is unfortunate that Bill's letter prompting this reply has not been saved; it would be interesting to know how he had characterized his lunch with Willard Richardson and to see exactly what his hopes and expectations were for this upcoming dinner meeting. But, whatever Bill had said, Bob certainly continued to be secretive about the whole affair, sharing his comments with only one sober member of the Akron group, Paul Stanley (T. Henry and Clarace Williams being non-alcoholic Oxford Group members). It is possible that Bob didn't want to raise false hopes, but it is much more likely—especially in light of later events—that he was judiciously trying to avoid the inevitable confrontations that would arise if the emotional arguments that still swirled around these projects had to be revisited.

For whatever reason, Bob Smith had decided it would be in his own best interest to keep this news very much to himself. The exact nature of his fears is unclear, but he was not willing to let any of the Akron members, other than Paul Stanley, know about the promising plans afoot for raising money in New York. As with almost all secrets, this decision to 'go dark' about what was happening in New York City necessarily engendered more and more duplicity on Dr. Bob's part as events unfolded.

The day after Bob wrote this letter, Willard Richardson sent Bill the details of the arrangements he was hoping to make for their meeting:

> Dear Mr. Wilson:
>
> After conference with one or two of our friends regarding the possible meeting with a few of the men who are serving with you in the important personal work about which you have told me, I learn that Mr. Scott, who seems to me to be the important one from our standpoint, will not be available until at least the second week in December. He suggests to me a meeting on the evening of Monday, December 13th. Would this be feasible from your standpoint? We might come together here at Rockefeller Center for a simple supper together and spend an hour or two afterwards in one of our offices in conference. Will you let me know whether this idea is satisfactory?
>
> Your suggestion of a Sunday afternoon meeting may be arranged later in the month or in the early part of January if that is more desirable to you. I find that our friends are a little loath to give up Sunday afternoon.
>
> Very truly,
>
> W. S. Richardson[67]*

---

*   Note that Wilson obviously had further correspondence or conversations with Richardson—at least about the Sunday meeting proposal—which has not been preserved.

Bill was, of course, delighted and more than happy to abandon his suggestion for a Sunday afternoon lunch. Now, he only needed to clarify exactly what Richardson's expectations might be for this dinner meeting:

Dear Mr. Richardson:

My friends and I gratefully accept your invitation to supper and to conference at Rockefeller Center on the evening of Monday December 13th.

So many of us have been so intensely interested and have this situation so much at heart that I have commenced to wonder how many should meet with you. The names of four out-of-town men, who ought surely to attend, occur at once. Then there are six or eight local men. Our feeling is that this meeting should be of an informative nature—that you and your colleagues be afforded the best possible chance to get the spirit, and the true cross-section of our activities. It is thought that a gathering of this size, while perhaps too large to discuss ways and means, would offer you the most accurate impression of the whole.

That is but a suggestion, to be amended as you gentlemen would have it. We shall gladly appear in any attendance you care to indicate.

May we therefore have a note from you, setting forth your pleasure as to numbers?

WGW:VB[68]*

Richardson replied two days later:

... I think it would be desirable for you to have the number of men present which you think will be really useful. We had not thought that more than ten altogether would be desirable, but inasmuch as the meeting is chiefly to give us information, it is best that you bring a sufficient number to do that in such a way as you deem best. We would meet, I think, as near six o'clock as possible and have the supper at once and then confer for as long as seems wise.[69]

Bill immediately contacted Bob to share this news, asking him to come to New York, and Bob responded on the last day of November:

Dear Bill !—

Great to hear from you and to learn of the Foundations continued interest. Talked to Paul [Stanley] a few minutes ago he says he will be very glad to

* At this time, the capitalized initials at the bottom of a letter indicate the writer (WGW = William G. Wilson) followed by those of the secretary/typist. There is no further evidence regarding exactly who "VB" was, although she was a typist at the firm of Quaw and Foley that employed Bill for nine months in 1937 and that he did freelance work for well into 1938. See, for instance, similar initials at the bottom of a letter from Bill to Hank Parkhurst on Quaw and Foley letterhead dated April 1, 1937 (GSO, Box 200 Folder I: Bill—Business with Hank P. / 1937–1950). Bill's use of "VB" as a typist was not a onetime occurrence since her initials appear at the bottom of four more letters that he wrote that are subsequently quoted here: December 6 and 17, 1937 and January 11, 1938 (all to Willard Richardson) and February 2, 1938 (to Frank Amos).

accept your kind invitation as do I also. So far as we know we can be there but unless you urge it I shall not bring anyone else besides Paul because I shall travel up into Vermont on my way back here, just a little short cut I thought up . . . We (Paul + I) expect we'll leave here early Saturday AM and get to *[unreadable word]* some time in the evening if we don't freeze to death in the Pa. mountains somewhere. Shall actually be glad to tuck my feet under your table and to see both you and Lois again . . . Let me know if there are any changes in the plans

Affctly

Bob[70]

Whatever reluctance Bob Smith may have felt about alcoholic hospitals and paid missionaries during Bill's October visit, he was now clearly in favor of those projects. His business had, as he noted in a recent letter, "all gone to pieces" and he was currently so strapped for cash that even the idea of paying for a train ticket to New York City was out of the question. Bill's success with the Rockefeller people held out the prospect of a useful and financially secure future for him. Given his current circumstances, that was an extremely tempting prospect.

The final arrangements were all but complete. A week before the meeting, Bill wrote to Richardson:

Replies are now in from out-of-town men concerned with our meeting of Monday, December 13th. Three of them will be present, with a fourth in doubt until later this week.*

It is the sense among us here, that fewer, rather than more than, ten may prove agreeable to you. It is thought eight or nine will attend, depending upon our friend yet uncertain.

We take it that the point of assembly will be your office—30 Rockefeller Plaza. Please do not hesitate to let us know of any change in arrangement that seems desirable or convenient to you. We join in appreciation of your kindness.[71]

Richardson was happy with all of these details, but concerned about the uncertain head count:

. . . you are right about the meeting place here at our office, 30 Rockefeller Plaza, at about six o'clock.

Whatever number of men seems most desirable from your standpoint will be all right. If you could let me know exactly this weekend or Monday morning, it will facilitate our eating arrangements.[72]

---

* The three out-of-town men were Bob Smith, Paul Stanley, and Fitz Mayo. Who the fourth "in doubt" member might have been is uncertain.

Everything was finally falling into place. In just seven weeks, Bill Wilson had gone from complete despair to his present state of elation over the private dinner that was now arranged for his own sober friends and a small group of John D. Rockefeller Jr.'s intimates. He and several other drunks were actually being invited into the inner sanctum of American capitalism and asked to make a presentation on their newfound method of recovery there. Given their success in getting people sober (and keeping them that way!), Bill was confident that he could persuade these men on the wisdom of his ambitious plans. All they had to do was agree to finance a chain of alcoholic hospitals, pay for a band of traveling missionaries, and support some writers as they produced a book. Small change for the Rockefellers.

Success was surely just around the corner.

CHAPTER FOUR

The Rockefeller Dinner

~December 1937~

Dr. Bob and Paul Stanley drove from Akron to Brooklyn, arriving late on Saturday, December 11. Bill had arranged a "set up meeting" for the night before the Rockefeller dinner, so all the recovered alcoholics gathered at his house Sunday evening to plan their strategy and rehearse their presentations for the next night. Hank Parkhurst and his wife, Kathleen, came in from New Jersey early on Sunday morning so that they could join everyone for breakfast. Ned Pointer, a recent addition to the New York group, was there and planned to spend the night.[1] Bill Ruddell, Joe Taylor, and Fitz Mayo rounded out the group of eight drunks who would be joining the Rockefeller group for dinner the following evening.[2]

We have met all these players before with the exception of Ned Pointer and Joe Taylor, both of whom would have been truly anonymous figures if it weren't for their starring roles during this first and most critical meeting with the four Rockefeller men.

Ned Pointer had quit drinking a short time before this meeting and he didn't stay sober very long. Bill notes that Ned "turned out to be a confidence man"[3] —in short, a con man. Lois gives some further details in a letter to Bill two months after the Rockefeller dinner: "The latest is that [on] Friday Ned Pointer and his wife absconded with a car, a new suit, and some of Hank's papers. Hank has notified the police . . . Ned called here Thursday and wanted to talk to you. Wes took the message. I hope Hank has exaggerated it all. Hank phoned today and asked Wes if he wanted to take over Ned's job."[4] It seems that Ned was another one of the recently sobered alcoholics who had been put on the Honor Dealers' payroll, but, like several others who were given this same opportunity, he quickly drank himself out of that position.

Joe Taylor had a more checkered career with sobriety. He first shows up in a letter Bill wrote to Lois in July 1936, but it's not clear whether or not he had quit drinking at that point.[5] During the next two months, both Ebby and Lois mention Joe in different letters and indicate that he is currently sober, with Lois providing some details: " . . . the drunks [here at home] seem to be all on a rampage and poor Joe is beside himself to know what to do with them all."[6] In the same February 1938 letter where Lois tells Bill about Ned Pointer stealing the car, she mentions that she just had supper with the Taylors. Ora Taylor, Joe's wife, had become one of Lois's good friends and she shows up with regularity in her diary, receiving nine specific entries in 1940. Lois was not the most faithful recorder of people's relapses, so it is not clear whether Joe was sober all of that time. Certainly, he was drinking on July 15, 1940, when Lois writes: "Had lunch with Ora. Joe still drunk. It's his vacation." (Perhaps Joe was abstinent only when he had to work?) But, what we do know is that Joe Taylor was sober enough in December 1937 to be invited to the Rockefeller dinner as one of the sterling examples of how well the new cure for alcoholism was actually working.

There are no detailed accounts of what happened at the Sunday night set-up meeting and that is truly unfortunate. How amazing it would be to eavesdrop as Bill and his friends made plans for convincing the Rockefellers that they should contribute millions of dollars for the recovery of alcoholics. What arguments did they all agree on and then rehearse so that they could convincingly establish their case that the old word-of-mouth method was just too slow and how critical it was to find a new approach that would allow them to save as many suffering alcoholics as possible—and as quickly as possible?

It is likely that Hank Parkhurst, certainly the most aggressive promoter in the room, expressed strong opinions about how the group should formulate their overall strategy, and he undoubtedly contributed several of the arguments eventually used in their presentations. If nothing else, it would be fascinating to know what kind of comments and kidding Hank had to endure that night. After all, just two years earlier, he had been fired by the Standard Oil Company, the very source of John D. Rockefeller's wealth. Was Hank's employment history considered an asset or a liability as they planned their strategy? Did they decide that his work history would be most useful to them as an example of the potential for human recovery or would it be better not to mention his former connection with the company at all? Also intriguing is the question of how Hank, a disgraced and disgruntled former employee, felt about being invited to sit down at a meeting held in John D. Rockefeller Jr.'s own board room. Did that please him or anger him? Or, did he, perhaps, see this as his latest and best opportunity to get back into the big time?

Sadly, the record provides no answers to any of these fascinating questions.

Who Was at the Meeting

The all-important dinner meeting was held at 30 Rockefeller Plaza at 6:00 P.M. on Monday, December 13, 1937.

Representing the New York and Akron alcoholics were Bill Wilson, Dr. Bob Smith, Hank Parkhurst, Fitz Mayo, Paul Stanley, Bill Ruddell, Joe Taylor, and Ned Pointer—a group of men who had been sober anywhere from three full years (it was two days after Bill's third anniversary) to just a few weeks.

In addition, the group felt an endorsement from the medical community would greatly bolster their credibility, so they invited two doctors familiar with their work to join them: Bill's brother-in-law, Leonard Strong and William D. Silkworth, the Chief of Staff at Towns Hospital, who was an enthusiastic supporter of Bill's new way of staying sober.

Towns Hospital was the most fashionable 'drying out' facility in New York City, the place where the city's well-to-do drunks went to get sober. It was Dr. Silkworth who famously told Lois in the summer of 1934 that Bill was a hopeless alcoholic and that "in order to keep [him] alive and prevent his going mad, [she] would eventually have to 'put him away.'"[7] During his final admission to Towns in December 1934, where Bill had his "white light" experience and feared for his sanity, Silkworth was the doctor who counseled him "whatever you've got now you'd better hold onto. It's so much better than what you had only a couple of hours ago."[8] Finally, it was this doctor's good judgment and his stern advice that convinced Bill Wilson to abandon his approach of trying to sell his profound religious experience to other drunks as the basis for their own recovery. "Stop preaching at them," Silkworth told him, "and give them the hard medical facts first. This may soften them up at depth so that they will be willing *to do anything* to get well. Then they may accept those [religious] ideas of yours and even a [God]."[9]* It was exactly this suggested approach that worked when Bill first talked with Dr. Bob in May 1935—thereby setting in motion the chain of events that had led them to this meeting with the Rockefellers.[10]

For his own group, Willard Richardson had invited three men to join him who were well known to John D. Rockefeller Jr.: Albert Scott, A. LeRoy Chipman, and Frank Amos.

In Richardson's opinion, Albert Scott was the most influential and important member of this select group, a fact he made clear by postponing the dinner meeting so that Scott could attend. When the group finally did gather, Albert Scott was the acknowledged leader for the evening, starting the presentations, moderating the speakers, and offering the first and most incisive reaction to what they had heard.

Albert Scott was president of an international engineering firm, Lockwood Greene, which helped build one of the skyscrapers at Rockefeller Center starting in 1938.[11] He was, however, well known to Rockefeller from a number of other areas of his life and John D. Rockefeller Jr. had an absolute trust in Scott's integrity and competence. In 1934, when Rockefeller was searching for someone to oversee the expenses for his massive, fourteen-building project at Rockefeller Center, he asked Albert Scott to do the final review on all the compiled project reports before they were presented to him.[12] In addition, Scott sat on the Board of Directors of the Rockefeller Center Corporation

---

* The actual quote in *AACOA* uses the words "spiritual" and "higher Power" rather than "religious" or "God" but the former are surely later substitutions by Wilson in an effort to make them conform to the terminology and beliefs that were current in A.A. in 1957 (the year that *AACOA* was published).

and served as its president throughout 1937.[13] The depth of Rockefeller's regard for him can be seen in a candid letter sent to a business associate in 1933, commending Scott to him as "a warm personal friend of mine whom I know intimately [and] for whom I have the highest regard both in his ability and his wisdom."[14]

Beyond his ability and wisdom, Albert Scott also impressed Rockefeller with his spiritual life. Rockefeller once described him as a man who "devoted much time and thought to the intensive study of social and religious movements."[15] In 1930, Rockefeller asked Scott to become the acting head of the Laymen's Foreign Mission Inquiry, which labored for two years before releasing its suggestions for sweeping changes to the scope of Christian missionary work in the Far East.[16] Locally, Scott was on the Board of Trustees of the wealthy and prestigious Riverside Church in New York City, serving as Chairman of that Board from 1932 until his retirement in 1945.[17] The creation of Riverside Church had been a personal project of John D. Rockefeller Jr., and the institution was largely built with the substantial contributions he had made in support of its interdenominational mission.[18]*

Even more important in relation to this particular meeting, Scott was one of Rockefeller's closest advisors on the question of alcohol. In early 1933, when the repeal of Prohibition was all but a certainty, he asked Scott to join another of his trusted advisors, Raymond Fosdick (who would soon become the head of the Rockefeller Foundation), in the creation of a report outlining and evaluating the effective ways the individual States could legislate and control alcohol, given the obvious and miserable failure of the national solution. A complete report of the Liquor Study Commission findings was published in late 1933 by Fosdick and Scott in a book entitled *Toward Liquor Control*—with a Foreword written by John D. Rockefeller Jr. himself.**

So, not only was Albert Scott one of Rockefeller's most trusted business associates, an intimate friend, and an important member of his religious community, he was also the one member of this group with the most direct experience dealing with the liquor problem and hence, Richardson's evaluation of his central importance at this meeting and the reason for the delay in scheduling their dinner.

A. LeRoy Chipman, like Willard Richardson, was a member of Rockefeller's personal staff and had his own office on the 56th floor of Rockefeller Center where he helped in the management of the huge real estate empire owned by the Rockefeller family.[19] His relationship with John D. Junior dated back to the turn of the century. They became close friends during the late 1910s and early 1920s when they took annual moose-hunting trips together in Canada.[20] The depth and durability of their relationship (in personal correspondence they consistently addressed each other as "Dear Chip" and "Dear Junior") is demonstrated by the fact that the friendship survived and flourished even after Rockefeller loaned Chipman the huge sum of $125,000 for his family business in 1921 and then had to write off $108,000 of that loan as a bad

* Rockefeller abandoned his Baptist upbringing in the 1920s and embraced a profoundly non-denominational approach to Christianity—even founding a church that would support and propagate those beliefs.

** See Levine, *Birth of American Alcohol Control*, which has important and interesting information on both Scott and Rockefeller and their attempts to promote post-Prohibition legislation to restrict the availability of alcohol without producing the lawlessness that had characterized Prohibition—and so appalled Rockefeller.

debt in 1924.[21] It is amazing to think that Rockefeller allowed this default to pass without acrimony or ongoing resentment, but very much to his credit and as a striking testimony to his deep feelings for Chipman, that is exactly what he did.*

Just as it was for Scott and Richardson, another critical element in their bond was Chipman's commitment to Rockefeller's religious community. "Chip" had a long history of teaching Bible classes at the Fifth Avenue Baptist Church during the first two decades of the century—where Rockefeller also taught classes—and, again like Scott, he later served on the Board of Trustees for Riverside Church.[22] In a telling assessment regarding his default on the loan, one of Rockefeller's financial friends noted " . . . if Chipman had given as much thought to his own business as he had to the affairs of the church, the outcome might have been more favorable."[23] Clearly Rockefeller valued his good friend's spiritual commitment much more than he did his business acumen.

Finally, it is worth noting that this friendship continued right up until their deaths. In 1950, when Chipman was applying for admittance to a local retirement home, Rockefeller provided a reference saying he had known him for over fifty years and that their relationship was "one of lifelong friendship." This was further supported by the fact that Rockefeller made arrangements to look after Chipman even after his own death, providing dramatic evidence of their strong spiritual connection and deep friendship.[24]

Richardson's final invitee was Frank Amos, a man who would play a prominent and colorful role in A.A.'s unfolding story over the next couple of years. Amos doesn't really fit the mold that defines the other three men because he was not an intimate friend of John D. Rockefeller Jr., and he has left no conspicuous evidence of any direct connection with the Rockefellers or their churches (although he was a graduate of Denison University in Ohio, a Baptist school that had been liberally supported by John D. Rockefeller, Sr. for many years).[25] In late 1937, Amos was vice president of the New York advertising firm, Maxon Inc., where he specialized in international companies and export advertising. While he worked with a large roster of prestigious clients, none of those mentioned in contemporary newspaper articles can be readily identified with any of Rockefeller's vast holdings or enterprises.[26]

There is also no evidence that Amos had any prior commitment to temperance or Prohibition. He did, however, have two brothers who were alcoholics and this very personal experience is the likely explanation for his abiding interest in Alcoholics Anonymous. Years later he claimed that both of his brothers "got straightened out, one of them long before A.A. was thought of, but by very similar means. It was a spiritual approach."[27] Amos certainly had a natural soft spot for the promise of recovery that Wilson was preaching and he seemed to be much more sympathetic to the actual drunks involved in this process than any of the other Rockefeller men. Frank Amos genuinely empathized with the desperation of active alcoholism and he came to believe deeply in Bill Wilson's mission and the possibility of reclaiming many, if not most,

---

* The amount of the default would be well over one million dollars in current dollars using even the most conservative conversion factor and as much as twenty million using others. (See http://eh.net/hmit/ for possible conversion rates and standards.)

of the world's alcoholics. As the year 1938 progressed, he became a true believer in Alcoholics Anonymous and its most enthusiastic non-alcoholic supporter.

Bill Wilson claims that Amos was "an advertising man who had worked on Mr. Rockefeller's Committee to see if he should discontinue his prohibition efforts,"[28] and this certainly sounds plausible. Rockefeller, famously unhappy with the lawlessness that had grown up around Prohibition, publicly advocated Repeal of the Prohibition Amendment in 1932 and it is entirely possible that an advertising man would have been included in any discussions of how best to manage this spectacular reversal of opinion. Amos was as likely a candidate as any other for that job.

Along those same lines, it is possible that Richardson included Frank Amos in this group because he felt that one solution to Wilson's dilemma of spreading the new method of recovery might well be found within the realms of publicity and advertising, rather than in hospitals and in paid missionaries. Certainly Amos's connections within the publishing industry later proved to be an extremely important factor in moving the book project forward and he was, among the Rockefeller contingent, always the most vocal and enthusiastic supporter of Bill's plan to write a book.

Finally, there is the silent presence of John D. Rockefeller Jr. hovering over this meeting. It is hard to imagine that Richardson would not have spoken to Rockefeller and received his blessing before proposing this dinner meeting to the other three men—all of whom were well aware of the position that John D. Junior currently held in relation to the alcohol problem. He had indeed abandoned Prohibition as a solution five years earlier, but Rockefeller had not given up his fight against the evils of drinking. In 1933, he had written eloquently and forcefully about his ongoing commitment to the battle against alcohol in the Foreword to Fosdick's and Scott's book, *Toward Liquor Control*:

> I was born a teetotaler and I have been a teetotaler on principle all of my life. Neither my father nor his father ever tasted a drop of intoxicating liquor. I could hope that the same might be true of my children and their children. It is my earnest conviction that total abstinence is the wisest, best, and safest position for both the individual and society. But the regrettable failure of the Eighteenth Amendment has demonstrated the fact that the majority of the people of this country are not yet ready for total abstinence, at least when it is attempted through legal coercion. The next best thing—many people think it a better thing—is temperance . . .
>
> As Senator Capper has aptly said: "We may repeal Prohibition, but we cannot repeal the Liquor Problem.". . . [therefore] to develop the habit of temperance in individuals, to take up again the slow march of education— this is the real and fundamental approach to the problem of alcohol.[29]

Knowing how abysmally ineffective this slow march of education had been in stemming the tide of drunkenness during the previous four years, this Foreword would have made exciting bedtime reading for Bill Wilson as he dreamed his dreams of expanding the work of recovery nationally. Rockefeller's passion and dedication could not be any clearer. Alcohol abuse was an issue that moved him deeply and his commitment to finding a solution was real and profound. All his close associates were well aware of this and they were equally committed to discover a new and effective way for dealing with this destructive problem.

It was Bill Wilson's fervent hope that this dinner at Rockefeller Center would convince them that he had indeed found just such a solution to "the Liquor Problem."

The Proposal Is Made and the Rockefeller Men Respond

Dinner for fourteen was served in the executive dining room at Rockefeller Center and enjoyed in the traditionally polite manner, without any mention of the business at hand. However, the real purpose of the evening began immediately after the meal when everyone reconvened around the large conference table in John D. Rockefeller Jr.'s private board room located next to his personal office.[30]

What could be more exciting than this! Bill was profoundly impressed with his surroundings and said: "I was told I was sitting in a chair just vacated by Mr. Rockefeller. This was really getting close. The big money was just around the corner."[31] If Bill Wilson, with his many years of exposure to the financial elite of New York City, was swept away by the place and the moment, it is hard to imagine the reactions of Dr. Bob and the others, to whom this must have seemed like something out of a completely different world. The eight recovered alcoholics were sitting at the very heart of the richest Foundation in the world and they were meeting with four men who had the power to recommend that large amounts of money be donated to their cause—if only they could make their arguments convincing enough.

It was an intense evening with the meeting lasting a full five hours.[32] If we presume the dinner took no more than two hours, this leaves a substantial three hours for Bill and the other recovered alcoholics to present their own stories and to make their appeal to Rockefeller's friends for funding.

Albert Scott chaired the meeting from the head of the table and at first there was some awkwardness about exactly where to begin. Whatever plans Bill and the others had made the previous night were momentarily forgotten in the face of these awe-inspiring surroundings. Finally, it was suggested that each man introduce himself and then tell the story of his own drinking and subsequent sobriety—and so they began. One by one, the alcoholics recounted the details of how they had gotten into trouble with liquor and described the depths to which they had sunk. Each then told how they had met Bill Wilson (or, in the case of Paul Stanley, Dr. Bob Smith) and outlined the process that led to their current full recovery. The stories profoundly affected the Rockefeller men, who listened intently as each man told his tale. Most especially, the four men were impressed by the fact that although "the basic principles of the 'cure'" described were certainly spiritual, the methods and the approach used were "not in accordance with any hard and fast dogma or rule of thumb procedure."[33] This was clearly a new and very pragmatic approach to getting and staying sober.

Having presented the candid details of their own lives, it was time for the alcoholics to turn the floor over to someone who could supply a professional and informed medical opinion regarding what they had just heard. Dr. Silkworth rose to the challenge, telling the Rockefeller men in no uncertain terms that:

> . . . he had treated a number of these ex-alcoholics present, some of them several times, and that not one of them, in his opinion, could have been permanently cured by any means known to medical science or to Psychiatry.

> He went on to state without reservation that while he could not tell what it was that these men had which had effected their "cure," yet he was convinced they were cured and that whatever it was, it had his complete endorsement.[34]

In his closing statement, Dr. Silkworth stated unequivocally that, based on his own extensive experience, he believed "alcoholism, medically, [was] an incurable disease," but that these men had certainly discovered a way to cure alcoholism and that their cure was beyond the realms of medical science.[35]

If the men's personal stories had not been enough, "these statements from an outstanding Psychiatrist* and a leading authority on the treatment of alcoholism," Amos reported, "made a profound impression upon the non-alcoholics present."[36]

Following Dr. Silkworth's testimony, Albert Scott, visibly moved, looked inquiringly around the table and asked: "So, gentlemen, what can we do to help you?"[37]

This was exactly the question that Bill Wilson had been waiting for all night and he immediately launched into his speech, describing the deadly slowness with which their group was growing and pleading for his plans to accelerate the spread of their recovery methods. What they needed, he said, were alcoholic hospitals whose profits would fund the equally necessary paid missionaries, while supporting the creation of a book to explain their methods. To accomplish all of this, he noted, would cost money. Actually, it was going to take quite a lot of money, although he never specified an amount. As he finished his presentation, Bill noted in closing that 'you must all realize that the need here is desperately urgent. We are fully aware that there are risks in the ambitious plans that I have just outlined, but the risk and the consequences of doing nothing at all would certainly be greater.'[38] Following his summation, Bill says that all the alcoholics, including Dr. Bob and both non-alcoholic doctors, chimed in with their agreement on each of these important points.[39]

The room grew quiet as everyone around the table considered what had just been said. Finally, Albert Scott broke the silence. 'Gentlemen, I am deeply moved by what I have heard. What you have described is nothing less than first-century Christianity in its most beautiful form! Up to this point, your work has been one of tremendous goodwill only, with one person carrying the message on to the next. But, won't money completely ruin that? Just think about what buildings and property, paid workers and managers would do to the immense power of your society as it is currently working.

---

*   Note that Amos incorrectly identified Silkworth here as a "Psychiatrist." He was, in fact, an MD, but not a psychiatrist.

I am truly afraid that the introduction of money and hospitals and paid field workers will dramatically change all of that. We should be very careful not to do anything that would create a professional or a propertied class within your society. Everyone here wants to do everything we can to help you—it is the reason we all came out tonight—but would it really be wise to spoil this great work of yours with money? I am very concerned that going down that road will do nothing but quickly destroy everything that you have already accomplished.'[40]

This line of argument was, of course, very familiar to Bill and his group. These were the Akron objections all over again, but repackaged from an upper-class, New York perspective.

Backed by his friends and supporters, Bill addressed the issue head-on and made what he considered to be his two most powerful arguments. 'Quite frankly, our movement will be ruined if we *don't* do these things,' he said. 'First of all, our message will become hopelessly garbled and distorted if we don't put it down in writing. A book is absolutely essential for our survival. Without a concrete statement of how this thing works, it will be constantly changing and misinterpreted by people everywhere. Worse than that, it will be held up for ridicule by reporters who would like nothing better than another juicy story that makes fun of the latest alcohol racket. And we will definitely need money to get that book written.' However, this wasn't his strongest argument and, just as he had done two months earlier in Akron, Bill drew a dramatic picture of what would happen—or more accurately, what would *not* happen—if these aggressive steps were not taken. 'Can you seriously say that you would be willing to let millions of alcoholics die while this new solution makes its way around the country with a painful and fatal slowness because the only way we can do that is by word of mouth? Where is the Christianity in that? We can save these people right now, but only if we get the money necessary to spread this new method of recovery and salvation as quickly as possible; and to do that we need our own alcoholic hospitals and our own paid missionaries. You have to realize that we are talking about life and death here! Right this minute, the money that you are so worried about is the only thing that stands between the people who are dying out there tonight and a life of productive sobriety tomorrow. We know how to save them, we only lack the money to do it.'[41]

Although Bill claims all of these arguments for himself, he could hardly have been the only alcoholic talking at this point in the meeting, especially with Hank Parkhurst sitting at that same table. Hank's prominence and his outspokenness with this group of men in the months to come are well documented and it is much more likely that these two promoters worked as a team, peppering the Rockefeller group with one argument after another in support of their position, with one man picking up from the other as each point was made. Heartfelt and passionate words, not to mention emotional appeals, were surely used that night, and it must have been a sight to behold as these two forceful salesmen made their case.

The Rockefeller men began to waver. There was just too much power in these men's stories and in their arguments to resist for long. Bill claimed that it was the logic of their presentation that impressed them and they began to yield under the force of that pressure.[42] However, their motives for conceding were likely far more emotional than rational. The alcoholic's appeal was not only insightful and incisive, its religious undertones were perfectly tailored for this particular audience. Whatever the exact cause, Bill says that the Rockefeller group finally "admitted that we did need money, at least *some* money," although they continued to argue throughout the meeting about the fact that "our movement ought never be professionalized."[43]

A More Limited Proposal: An Alcoholic Hospital in Akron

Acknowledging he had lost the argument for the big money, but won a substantive concession that something had to be done, Bill shifted gears and put forward a more limited proposal, one that had likely been discussed and rehearsed the night before. 'Whatever money you might be willing to contribute,' he suggested, 'should first be used to establish an alcoholic hospital in Akron that would be run by Dr. Bob.'[44]

This made perfect sense. Not only was Bob Smith in desperate financial straits (according to Bill he was "about to lose his house"[45]) and his proctology practice in disarray, he was also a trained physician who was well versed in this new method for quitting drinking. Even without a hospital, Bob had shown tremendous success in sobering up drunks. Just imagine the incredible good work that could be done if only he had the proper facilities! Wouldn't it be criminal to waste such a fabulous resource? Dr. Bob, working in his own alcoholic hospital, was surely the perfect way to test-drive their new vision for spreading this method of recovery nationally.[46]

Again, Bill didn't make these arguments alone; all of the presentations that night were very much a group effort. In the unedited version of his "Akron Report," written two and a half months later, Frank Amos provides some interesting details about this portion of the evening:

> At our meeting in Rockefeller Center, Wilson and [Paul] Stanley had suggested that perhaps a small hospital of from 30 to 50 beds could be established at Akron and Smith put in charge. Their idea was that this could be used primarily for handling cases from outside of Akron, which when cured and trained could go home and continue the work in their communities. They thought that without any publicity, except by word-of-mouth, patients could be secured from big corporations and other sources where ample funds to pay for hospitalization, would be available.[47]

It has frequently been alleged that Dr. Bob was reluctant to participate in this meeting and it has even been said that he completely rejected Bill's ideas about hospitals and missionaries, but this is later revisionist history, which promotes the more saintly, more spiritual image of Smith.* The letters Dr. Bob wrote to Bill preceding this meeting clearly contradict that view. In addition, Bob's secrecy about the real purpose for his

---

* For instance: "As Dr. Silkworth and some of the alcoholics were caught up in the enthusiasm many expressed pretty much the same opinion. Except, that is, for Doc and most of the Akron contingent present, who kept their reservations to themselves. They were reserving their right to question Bill's motives later." (Mitchell K., *How It Worked*, p. 93.) Everything mentioned in this quote is clearly contradicted by a number of primary documents relating to this meeting.

trip East is inexplicable if his only reason for coming to New York was to frustrate Bill's plan.

Instead, we have Paul Stanley, the trusted friend Bob brought with him from Ohio and the only Akron alcoholic who even knew about this meeting, taking the lead in an argument in favor of establishing an alcoholic hospital in Akron. Bob Smith was, in fact, a self-effacing man so it is not surprising that he did not make these arguments himself. But it is inconceivable that this very detailed proposal—right down to the number of beds—had not been discussed during the long drive from Akron and then further elaborated at the set-up meeting the night before. Dr. Bob was very much in favor of any plan that would provide him with a hospital, a living wage, and the opportunity to save alcoholics from the devastation caused by their drinking. How could he not be?

The agreed strategy seems to have been: 'If we can't get them to give their support for the whole program, then we should fall back and make a renewed appeal for their help in establishing an alcoholic hospital in Akron.' An incremental solution is better than no solution at all and this certainly looked like the most substantial, but still obtainable, concession they might be able to get from the Rockefeller group.

Amos's short summation presents a simple and detailed plan that had clearly been worked out well in advance of Bill's and Paul's presentation. It addressed, in a modest way, almost all of the issues previously raised. The plan covered not just the size of the hospital and the treatment involved, but also the way in which these newly cured patients could then be transformed into an advance guard that would leave the hospital and carry the message of recovery back to their hometowns. This would surely spread the word more quickly and more effectively, creating a geometric increase in exposure to their methods throughout Ohio.

Finally, it should be noted that this proposal's presumption that large corporations with ample funds to pay for hospitalization would be more than willing to finance these treatments is pure Hank Parkhurst and a theme he would return to with regularity throughout 1938 and early 1939. In Hank's vision, he need only make a few calls on the heads of big companies and they would immediately agree to single out the drunks in their organization and pay for their rehabilitation. Corporate leaders would be willing to do this because, according to Parkhurst, they were guaranteed a solid return on their investment when the newly recovered man came back to work as a much more productive employee. Hank was completely confident that this was an argument no sane businessman would be able to resist.

'Just give us one hospital with proper staffing,' the alcoholics said, 'and you will see this thing take off and begin to spread all over the state—saving thousands and thousands of lives.' This was a powerful argument, and the openness with which it was received by the Rockefeller men was encouraging. They made no promises, but they were certainly intrigued by this reduced and much more specific option for how they might help.

The biggest casualty of this presentation was, of course, the book. Having finally captured the attention of the Rockefeller contingent with their Akron hospital proposal, the alcoholics seem to have concluded that they would be pushing their luck to bring up the idea of funding for a book once again. One step at a time. It is likely that, if the hospital idea had not received such a positive response, they would have then made one more strategic retreat to an even more limited (and less expensive) proposal focused exclusively on the book. But, given the favorable reaction to the hospital idea, they were content to set the book proposal aside for the moment, knowing it could always be revived again sometime in the future.

Compelling Arguments Elicit a Promising Response

In his letter to Richardson three weeks earlier, Bill had noted that with such a big contingent of alcoholics present at this meeting, it would "perhaps [be] too large to discuss ways and means" although it "would offer you a most accurate impression of the whole."[48] Having already discussed the ways and means of their comprehensive proposal and then presented the singular hospital-in-Akron alternative that intrigued the Rockefeller men, it was now time to ensure everyone had an accurate impression of the whole. The alcoholic group felt a number of specific items still needed clarification to prevent any misunderstandings by their potential benefactors.

Frank Amos provides a summary of the particulars that Wilson, Parkhurst, Smith, Stanley, and the others wanted to communicate to the Rockefeller people that night:

> It [was] stressed by the leaders that . . . early publicity would be ruinous. It had been estimated that there are probably a million people in the United States who either are incurable alcoholics, or who are rapidly approaching that condition. It was obvious that too much publicity early in the development of the movement would result in the few present workers being swamped with requests from relatives and friends, and from alcoholics themselves, and as a consequence, the whole movement probably would bog down.
>
> It was pointed out also that a great many elements entered into the successful carrying on of this work. Alcoholics who were reasonably normal mentally in other ways, and who genuinely wanted to be cured of their alcoholism, were the type with whom they had achieved their greatest success. On the other hand, alcoholics who were mentally defective, or who were definitely psychopathic, had proven very difficult problems, and so far the percentage of 'cures' had been very low among these cases.
>
> Therefore, any steps taken were to be weighed very carefully, and it was believed progress should be slow and just as sure as possible.
>
> The members of this self styled Alcoholic Squad emphasized that they did not want this movement connected directly or indirectly with any religious organization or cult. They strongly stressed the fact that they had no connection whatever with any so-called orthodox religious

denomination, or with the Oxford [Group],* or with Christian Science or any other organized movement . . .

It was also emphasized that these ex-alcoholics were in no way, shape or form attempting to practice medicine. They were, when possible, cooperating with physicians and psychiatrists. Any practicing physician, who had been an alcoholic, could of course use his medical knowledge to advantage.[49]

No wonder it was a three-hour discussion. Clearly, there was still a lot of territory to be covered even after the alcoholic's presentations had been made, especially reinforcing the facts that the movement was currently not capable of dealing with a large number of new prospects, disavowing any possibility of success with mentally defective or psychopathic drinkers, and strenuously emphasizing that they were not affiliated with any religion nor did they consider themselves to be medically qualified on any level.**

As the evening drew to a close, the meeting adjourned on a high note with the Rockefeller group promising to process all this information individually and then meet as a group to discuss exactly how they might help. They would get back to Bill Wilson as soon as they reached a consensus on what should be done next.

Again, the greatest loss of the evening was that when the focus shifted from the larger national plans to the more specific Akron hospital proposal, the book project dropped completely out of sight—and would not come back into view again for another five months.

A Test Case for the "New Method"

But the evening wasn't over yet. As Bill Wilson headed for the door, Frank Amos caught up with him to talk about a friend who seemed to be a hopeless alcoholic. Almost everyone knows at least one drunk and this privileged group was no exception. If Bill's methods could sober up the hard cases they had heard about tonight, then surely it would work on a suffering alcoholic who was well known to both Frank Amos and Willard Richardson.

Imagine Bill's reaction to this. Despite the overall success of having forty sober members, his day-to-day failure rate with drunks was, by his own admission, "immense."[50] Now one of the key Rockefeller people, immediately following their presentation on a new method that claimed such tremendous success, was proposing he help sober up a friend of his. It amounted to nothing less than a test case and it must have felt very much like a potential trap to Bill Wilson. But Amos's suggestion certainly wasn't out of line; if Bill's solution was really so sure-fire, then why shouldn't

---

* Amos actually wrote "the Oxford *Movement*," which was something very different from the Oxford *Group*. The Oxford Movement was a nineteenth century English religious reform movement that attempted to reintroduce more Catholic practices back into the Church of England. It was famously led by John Henry Newman who eventually left the Church of England to become a Roman Catholic cardinal.

** Given Bob Smith's ongoing deep involvement with the Oxford Group in Akron (he would not break with the OG until December 1939, two full years after this meeting), it is likely that he was relatively quiet about this claim that they had "no connection whatever with any so-called orthodox religious denominations, or with the Oxford [Group] . . ."

it work for his friend too? That friend, Jack Darrow, had attended the same college as Amos, but at the moment, his life, according to Frank, was "in a desperate condition from every viewpoint."[51]

Bill managed to buy himself some time by talking about the current prevalence of alcoholism in America and saying that "almost every person, at all active in life, either had a relative or a friend in such a condition," which was surely an excellent reinforcement of everything he had been saying about the magnitude of the problem for the past several hours. But, after mentioning all the disclaimers he felt could reasonably be offered under such circumstances, Bill finally agreed to meet with Amos's friend and to "start work with him, providing [he] was willing."[52] Even this early in A.A. history, willingness was recognized as absolutely essential for any success in getting sober, so at least Bill had that much justification if he should fail to turn this new prospect around.

Before he met with Jack Darrow and just four days after their dinner meeting, Bill Wilson sent a formal thank you letter to Willard Richardson that gently kept the argument going while simultaneously showing the proper respect for the objections raised by Richardson and his colleagues:

> My friends and I wish again to acknowledge the kindness and interest shown us on Monday evening last.
>
> The problem is how best to get our message to the great numbers we are confident would literally take up their beds and walk, if they only knew. Being mostly business and professional folk, it is natural for us to think in terms of our respective techniques and you have helped us to sense the danger of over-emphasis or wrong use of them. We must, at all cost, put first things first.
>
> How then, to preserve sound spiritual construction, simplicity and spontaneity, at the same time making our experience as widely and quickly available as possible, is the conundrum.
>
> We who had the fortune to be with you, carried away an impression of good sense, friendliness and understanding, that is much appreciated and will be long remembered.[53]

No less gracious, Richardson replied the following Monday:

> December 20, 1937
>
> Mr. William G. Wilson
> 182 Clinton Street
> Brooklyn, New York
>
> Dear Mr. Wilson:
>
> I appreciate very much your letter of December 17th. Certainly it was a pleasure to meet the men you brought to us on Monday evening, and much more than a pleasure, a very valuable influence and help.

Just what to do to help you men serve others and not run into the difficulties of organization and professionalism is certainly a problem. I am sure we are thinking about it, and your four friends are getting together as early as possible this week.

May I express also my appreciation of your conferring with Mr. Darrow. He is a very dear friend of friends of mine, and I have known about him and his abilities and his weakness and sincerely hope and pray that you can be of help to him.

With regards and good wishes for this Christmas season.[54]

Even as Richardson was reassuring Bill of their ongoing commitment to help, he was also reminding him that he had a vested interest in seeing just how well Wilson's solution would work for this very dear friend of his friends.

A meeting between Bill Wilson and Jack Darrow was arranged within two weeks of the dinner, placing it just before Christmas. Although Amos provides no details, he notes that after this meeting, Darrow "accepted without reservation the principles of the 'cure' by a religious or spiritual approach"[55] and stayed continuously sober from that point on.

Bill Wilson must have been greatly relieved. He had passed the test!

Waiting for a Decision

For the alcoholics, life returned to something like normal, although a deep layer of expectation and concern hung over everything they did for the next several weeks. Waiting for such a potentially life-changing decision would make anyone more than a little anxious.

The day after the meeting, Bob Smith and Paul Stanley left Brooklyn and drove up to Vermont where they visited Dr. Bob's mother before traveling home to Ohio.[56] Back in Akron, they told no one of their meeting at Rockefeller Center, characterizing their trip East simply as a visit to see Bill Wilson and then Bob's mother.

Smith's continued secrecy about the Rockefellers is perplexing. It had been a very successful meeting and there was now the real possibility of him opening the first alcoholic hospital in Akron in the near future. However, given the close October vote and the ongoing distrust of Bill Wilson's motives by a large percentage of the Akron Fellowship, it is easy to imagine that this Rockefeller connection would not have been regarded as good news by many of the Ohio alcoholics. On the other hand, it was clearly long past time that this momentous information should have been shared with the local group.

But, beyond the likely opposition of several Akron members—all of whom nevertheless deeply revered Dr. Bob Smith and most of whom would follow him wherever he led—there was another and perhaps more important reason for Bob's silence both before and after his visit to New York City. That reason was Henrietta Seiberling. Bob was certainly not anxious to tell her about his plan to expand their religious work with alcoholics into the secular atmosphere of a hospital that he himself would be running.

Henrietta, who was not an alcoholic, had introduced Bill Wilson to Bob Smith and she took great personal credit for their success. Seiberling was an outspoken and forceful—some would say dictatorial—leader within the Akron Oxford Group, and she had strong opinions about the necessity of relying on a very specific brand of Christianity as the primary solution for the "drink problem," along with a deathly abhorrence of the evils that came with money. Henrietta later captured this succinctly when she said, " . . . one of the first things that the devil could have used [to destroy Alcoholics Anonymous] was having money, and having sanatoriums as the men were planning. Much to Bob's and Bill's and Anne [Smiths]'s surprise, I said, 'No, we will never take money.'"[57] Her use of the royal "we" here should give some idea of why Bob Smith was so reluctant to broadcast the fact that the Rockefellers might be making substantial contributions for the expansion of the alcoholic work in Akron. Henrietta Seiberling was not a woman to be tangled with lightly and it is more than likely that Bob was frightened of what might happen should he cross her so publicly.[58]

In New York, the group was pleased with the way the meeting had gone and they optimistically awaited the promised decision from the Rockefeller people. There was an early flurry of activity as Fitz left Brooklyn for Washington, DC and Bill and Ned Pointer traveled to New Jersey on some business that Lois does not specify. Otherwise, life went on more or less as it had been before the meeting.[59]

For his own part, after that intense evening at Rockefeller Center, Bill realized that his presentation skills could use some improvement. Wilson always believed in making a 'maximum effort' in everything he undertook, so later that month he and Lois took a Dale Carnegie course together on public speaking.[60] If this quest for money from rich individuals and organizations was going to require him to speak regularly before such distinguished groups, then anything he could do to improve his speaking skills would be worth the effort. Everything might, just possibly, depend upon it.

The year ended with a gala New Year's Eve party at the Wilson's house in Brooklyn. Lois's guest list shows almost thirty people attending this sober celebration, including most, if not all, of the New York group as well as a number of other friends and relatives.[61] Certainly, 1937 ended on an extremely high note and 1938 looked to be even more promising than that.

But, once the lively spirits of the New Year's Eve party faded, there was nothing left for them to do but wait patiently and anxiously for some positive words from Willard Richardson.

It turned out to be a longer wait than anyone expected.

CHAPTER FIVE

Dr. Bob's Hospital

~January to February 1938~

Willard Richardson promised Bill on Monday, December 20, that he and the others would meet later that week,[1] in other words, before the holiday; but Christmas came and went before the four men finally managed to get together. During the last week of December or the first week in January, they met to "come to some conclusions"[2] and "to try to determine what steps, if any, could be taken to help this movement."[3] Unfortunately, those conclusions needed some unspecified further approval (most likely from John D. Rockefeller Jr.) before Richardson thought they could proceed.

But Bill didn't know any of this for three agonizing weeks. What was happening? Finally, he learned from the newly sober Jack Darrow that Richardson had been sick, and using this information, he decided to reopen the lines of communication himself.

January 11, 1938

Mr. W. S. Richardson
Room 5600
30 Rockefeller Plaza
New York City

Dear Mr. Richardson:

We have all been concerned and sorry to learn from Jack Darrow that you have not been feeling well, and we very much hope that this will find you in better form.

It will be refreshing to you to know that Jack is making a splendid recovery and that all of us who have met him agree that he should have little or no difficulty in the future. He is very much in earnest, very willing and very aggressive in his attitude, all of which augers well. There has also been an opportunity to meet his wife, Mary, with whom everyone is much pleased.

And last, but not least, there is ground for believing that he may again resume his connection with Otis & Co. His present financial circumstances are quite embarrassing, but our experience is that this sort of trial is more salutary than otherwise.

Very truly yours,

WGW:VB[4]*

The letter was mailed to Rockefeller Center so it didn't reach Richardson immediately; it had to be forwarded to his home in Montclair, New Jersey, where he was recuperating. On the following Saturday, he sent Bill a reply:

119 Harrison Avenue
Montclair, N. J.

January 15, 1938

Dear Mr. Wilson:

Your good letter was brought to me here where I have unfortunately been sort of laid up for ten days. It has hurt me very much to feel that I could be of no help to you now. We had come to some conclusions and seemed only to need a final word to clear the way for a talk with you and one or two others perhaps.

I expect to get to the office Monday but the after-effects of bronchitis have been prolonged I judge, suiting the punishment to the desserts of the sinner.

Am happy to hear about Jack Darrow, have fully appreciated all you, by the grace of God, have done for him and have tried to express my deep and continued interest in all you men, in my times alone with the Master and the Father.

Amos and Chipman have tried to do something in my absence but I judge that they did not begin soon enough. Mr. Scott had to be away.

My high regard and my hope to see you soon.

Truly,

W. S. Richardson[5]

Wilson was delighted not only to be in direct contact with Richardson again, but also by the content and the tone of the letter. In the lower margin of the original copy,

---

* Note that, once again, the typist of this letter is "VB," the secretary from Quaw and Foley.

he wrote "Interesting & how! / Bill" and then undoubtedly passed the letter around to the New York members, showing that they were still in the game.

The four men had concluded that the establishment of an alcoholic hospital in Akron under the direction of Dr. Bob Smith sounded like a plausible idea, but it warranted further investigation before proceeding. In Frank Amos's account of his meeting with Richardson, Chipman, and Scott, he claims they spent considerable time discussing the details of Dr. Bob Smith's precarious financial situation and the proposal presented for funding an alcoholic hospital under his leadership in Akron. "In discussing these reports, [it was] decided to ask Mr. Amos to visit Akron and make a careful survey of the situation there. Mr. Amos's expenses were financed by the other three."[6] (In a later comment, Amos candidly noted "the plain fact was, I was broke," so the only way he could travel to Akron was if someone else paid his way.)[7]

Amos was going to Akron at the behest of the Rockefeller group to evaluate the possibility of making Dr. Bob's alcoholic hospital a reality, which, if that actually came to pass, would then launch a host of newly recovered drinkers out into the nearby states, clearly testifying to the success of this new method of recovery.

Bill and Dr. Bob: Their Relationship and Status as Co-Founders

Before following Frank Amos to Akron, this may be the proper place to pause and consider Bill Wilson and Dr. Bob Smith and the nature of their relationship at this time. Over the years, the image of these two men has become deeply encrusted with so many layers of adulation and myth that it is hard to recapture the reality of the moment and to see them as they were at this particular juncture in Alcoholics Anonymous history.

First of all, it is important to note that in early 1938 Dr. Bob Smith was not yet recognized by anyone as the co-founder of Alcoholics Anonymous. While this may be shocking to current members, the earliest discoverable instance of that term being applied to him is in the 1947 program for the Twelfth Anniversary celebration of A.A.'s founding held in Cleveland in mid-June of that year. In that write-up, it was noted that two years earlier, Cleveland had also hosted the Tenth Anniversary celebration where "Bill W. and Doc S., co-founders, [gave] their humble utterances of A.A. philosophy."[8] Tellingly, two years earlier, the June 1945 issue of the New-York-based *Grapevine* reported extensively on that Tenth Anniversary celebration, but there was no mention of anyone being a co-founder. Bob's elevation to that status seems to have begun in Ohio somewhere between 1945 and 1947, although it is worth noting that well into the 1950s, Midwesterners referred to Bill as the founder of A.A. and Bob as the co-founder.[9]

Bob Smith was certainly directly responsible for helping many Ohio people get sober at this time, but his individual contribution to the presentation of their program of recovery in the book *Alcoholics Anonymous* was relatively negligible. As Ernest Kurtz so bluntly stated: "Dr. Bob isn't really a co-founder of AA . . . a person with a much better claim to be a co-founder of AA would have been Hank Parkhurst.'" Indeed, Ebby and Hank both had better claims to the title of co-founder, but they both drank again and it made no sense—either from a marketing perspective or for the message it sends to other members—to christen either of these unrecovered alcoholics with the title of co-founder. But Dr. Bob Smith did not drink, making him the 'last man standing' among the important and effective early members and he was therefore the default winner of the title.

Actually, the fact that A.A. considers itself as having a co-founder is interesting in itself. Wilson could have easily claimed and held the title of sole founder, not only because he was the first person to get sober, but also because of his dedicated solo missionary work during the five months before he met Dr. Bob, his flexibility in relation to an evolving and pragmatic program of recovery, his creation of the Twelve Steps, his all-but-sole authorship of the Big Book, and his ongoing acknowledged position as the final arbiter of all things related to Alcoholics Anonymous from its inception right up until the late 1960s (among many other things).

But Wilson was well aware of his tendency toward grandiosity (to give just one example, at one point he favored the name "The B. W. Movement" rather than Alcoholics Anonymous[10]) and he took regular steps to counteract that particular character defect throughout his life. In addition, the more successful A.A. became, the more adulation he received from the people who felt he had saved their lives. As Kurtz noted: "Bill needed a co-founder so that he wouldn't be thought of as God"[11] and Wilson was extremely generous with his distribution of that title. Over the years, he bestowed co-founder status on such diverse people as William James, Dr. William Silkworth, the Reverend Sam Shoemaker, Anne Smith, and Sister Ignatia.** But the most important recipient of that self-effacing exercise was Dr. Bob Smith: the key player in Akron during A.A.'s formative years.

Because of their legendary co-founder status, Smith and Wilson have become iconic figures, with Bob typically being cloaked in the mantle of a humble, saintly doctor, and Bill more frequently cast in the role of the brilliant, but ego-driven salesman. While there are certainly elements of truth in both of these stereotypes, the two men's characters in early 1938 were far more complicated and nuanced than either of these two standard clichés would ever allow.

Despite his outgoing personal style, Bob Smith was a reticent man about his personal life, always holding his cards extremely close to the vest. Bill provided some wonderful testimony for this in a 1959 Akron talk in which he quoted Dr. Bob's

---

* Ernie's full statement—made in a formal, filmed interview with the author, Kevin Hanlon and Dan Carracino conducted on October 22, 2013—was: "Some people are going to shoot me for what I'm going to say right now, but Dr. Bob isn't really a co-founder of AA . . . Bill needed a co-founder so that he wouldn't be thought of as God. And he adopted Bob into this role. And I think Bob had the spirituality and the psychological smarts to realize this. And to go along with it. A person with a much better claim to be a co-founder of AA would have been Hank Parkhurst . . . [hearing that] people in Akron are probably rending their garments right now, so I hope the tailors in Akron will send me a commission . . ." (Full transcript, pp. 41–42). [The edited version of this interview entitled "A Reverence for History"—which does not include this particular quote—can be seen at https://vimeo.com/91456549—retrieved August 2, 2017].

** Several other people—from Henrietta Seiberling to Frank Amos to Clarence Snyder—claimed the title of co-founder for themselves.

comments on the night following his last drunk, which were made as a prelude to what later A.A.'s would call "doing a Fifth Step":

> Bob was a man of few words but what he said counted . . . He said, "I'm going to really go through with the kind of thing we've been talking about. I hit bottom all right. But that's only a starter. I'm a guy who would never make a full revelation about myself to any human being. I'm one of those damned Yankees who just bottle things up and hangs on and can't let go. So I'm going to get a housecleaning and you're going to listen."[12]

Given that frank confession, calling Bob Smith reticent might be a bit of an understatement. Sometimes, he could be positively secretive. At this point in the story, Bob Smith was playing a strangely silent game in relation to his friends in Akron and it is hard not to call this behavior anything but duplicitous. Whatever mitigating excuses Bob may have formulated in his own mind, he was not telling the Akron group about the truly significant (and critical to the future of their movement) things currently afoot in New York City. Acknowledging this is not to disparage Smith, but only to recognize he was not always the saint so consistently portrayed in A.A. literature and folklore. Despite his later distinguished reputation, Bob Smith was as human as the rest of us and this bit of deceptive secrecy is just one undeniable indication that there was far more complexity and depth to the man than can be found in the pious public image which he currently enjoys.

Two Very Different Men

The two men were very different on many levels and they were both aware of this. Bill once noted that "although we had many differences, we never had an angry word"[13] and Dr. Bob's son agreed, saying that "Dad often told me that, although he and Bill saw things from different angles, they never had an argument . . ."[14] However, it must be noted that both of these somewhat saccharine quotes were made years after the fact and fit all too neatly into the co-founder mythology that was already growing up around both of them by then.

The differences between the two men were real and substantial and it is a wonder there was no schism in early A.A. It is certainly true, for instance, that, in early 1938, Bob Smith had sobered up far more people in Akron than Bill Wilson had in New York. But there is absolutely no evidence Bob ever gloated over this fact or implied to Bill that his methods were so much more effective or that they should be adopted wholesale in New York City. Why he never did this, either directly or by implication, is a question worth asking.

Perhaps the best explanation is to remember that in early 1938, Smith—for all his importance within the Akron group—had not yet been proclaimed as a co-founder of the new movement nor did he then carry the gravitas that later came with that title. Back then, Dr. Bob was simply Bill Wilson's first and most successful sponsee. While the terms sponsor and sponsee—currently used in A.A. to designate a mentor and the new person being led through the Twelve Steps—had not yet been invented, the roles they describe were well established and fully operational within the program even at this time. Bob wasn't boasting about his greater success because to do so would be to show disrespect to the man who had literally saved his life two-and-a-half years earlier. Bob most likely had his own ideas on how things should work and he may have expressed some of those concerns to Bill in private conversations, but he consistently deferred to Wilson's decisions whenever they disagreed substantively on the evolving policies and procedures within A.A.

With so many acknowledged differences between them, it is unusual they did not have the kind of arguments one would normally expect under such circumstances. Still, it must be remembered these were not normal circumstances, but rather a situation where stubborn disagreement or even outright rebellion might well be the direct road back to drinking. (Witness Hank Parkhurst's slip from sobriety just eighteen months after this.) Given that reality, Bob Smith—despite his greater age and his impressive medical credentials—always accommodated Bill's desires and routinely yielded to his 'sponsor' as the final decision maker.

One of the fundamental and potentially contentious differences between them at this time was their approach and allegiance to religion. Bob Smith was far more devout and committed than Bill Wilson, characteristically claiming, as he did in 1945, that he "averaged at least an hour's reading each day for the past ten years on some religious subject . . . [always returning however] to the simple teachings in The Sermon on the Mount, the Book of James, and the 13th Chapter of Corinthians in the Bible for his fundamentals."[15] Dr. Bob was a believer and what he believed in were the fundamentals of the Christian religion.

Bill, on the other hand, read a wide variety of spiritual books, but the most important and influential of these was not the Bible. In fact, in a 1954 interview with T. Henry Williams, Bill claimed that when he first came to Akron in May 1935, he "hadn't looked in the Bible, up to that time, at all."[16] However true that may have been, what he had been reading with keen attention in 1935 was William James's *The Varieties of Religious Experience*, a 1902 work by America's leading philosopher-psychologist who emphasized the multiplicity of spiritual roads, all of which could be followed with equal success.[17] Although Bill's belief in God was profoundly deep and personal, he took a very eclectic approach to religion and would best be described as a seeker rather than a believer.

More important, Wilson—again following in the footsteps of William James—was a confirmed pragmatist, consistently shunning dogma and putting his faith in what worked. In its simplest form, Bill's credo was: "any good idea will work and any bad idea, when tried, will fail of its own weakness."[18] In both his personal life and in Alcoholics Anonymous, Wilson always preferred to investigate and embrace the solution that promised the best and most reliable results rather than committing himself to any particular rule or law. His emphasis on the practical versus Bob Smith's prescriptive approach would have accounted for many, if not most, of the difficulties these two men would have to navigate over the fifteen years of their relationship.

Finally, in early 1938 it would be easy to characterize Bill Wilson as the salesman who was constantly pushing his own ambitious plans to spread the message of recovery quickly across the country. This is, however, a very superficial description of the man (and his actions) and, as such, it is both inaccurate and unfair. While Bill was constantly coming up with fresh ideas for promoting their new solution for alcoholism, it was not so much his natural sales skills and his desire to win that pushed him at this time as it was his vision of universal recovery and a drive that can only be called messianic. Wilson knew he had the solution to a problem that afflicted thousands upon thousands of suffering alcoholics and he was desperate to show them the road to salvation. At this point, Bill felt like nothing so much as "the voice of one crying in the wilderness,"[19] and in his frustration, he responded by selling his vision just that much harder.

Wilson's reputation as a salesman—some of his detractors would go so far as to call him a snake-oil salesman—is as much his own fault as anything else. Where Bob was reticent, Bill was gregarious and constantly talking about himself, frequently including self-deprecating stories about his own grandiosity. While these stories were certainly true enough at times, misunderstandings about the point of these stories—Wilson was simply trying to keep his own ego in check—have created a legacy that unjustly tarnishes a man who was far more driven by a genuine desire to save others than he ever was to become rich and famous. Bill's efforts to raise money from the Rockefellers in the late 1930s certainly carried the promise of some future fame and fortune, but it was his sincere and heartfelt compassion for the alcoholic that truly engaged and drove him at this point of the story and throughout the remaining thirty-three years of his life.

Bill Wilson was his own worst enemy when it came to the charge that he was nothing more than a self-centered, self-serving salesman, bearing the full brunt of the disparaging remarks he so frequently made about himself both in meetings and in print. The current inflation of these publicly admitted character defects into the substance of his image creates a portrait that is grossly unfair to this compassionate, but driven man, maligning a heart that wanted nothing more desperately than to save as many lives as possible from the ravages of alcoholism—ravages that he himself knew and understood so well.*

Preparations for Frank Amos's Trip to Akron

In the two weeks following Richardson's letter, there was a flurry of activity as plans were made for Frank Amos's fact-finding trip to Akron. On Sunday, January 30, Amos and his wife visited the Wilsons in Brooklyn where the forthcoming trip and the proposed hospital were discussed in detail. Before leaving, Frank asked Bill for some advice on whom he should contact once he arrived in Akron.

Bill did some quick investigations and three days later, replied with a two-page, typed letter containing a wealth of concrete details about Dr. Bob's hectic activities in preparation for this visit.

---

* For a well-written and balanced (if poorly footnoted) portrait of Bill Wilson, see *My Search for Bill W.*, by Mel B. (Hazelden, 2000).

February 2, 1938

Mr. Frank Amos
c/o Maxon, Inc.,
570 Lexington Avenue
New York City

Dear Mr. Amos:

A friend writes me from Akron that the name of the Methodist minister is Dr. E. R. Brown, who is familiar with and, I understand, enthusiastic over Bob Smith's work. The alcoholics have frequently witnessed in his church. Mr. O. E. Meyerscough is the Baptist minister.

Concerning doctors you might consult, it is suggested that you call on Dr. Pinkerton, Dr. John Weber and Dr. Carl Steinke, all of the staff of the City Hospital, the first named being head of the general staff for the current year. Smith has practiced at this hospital for years. The institution has extended him the unusual courtesies with respect to treatment of his alcoholic cases. These men bear excellent reputations and can doubtless tell you all about Smith. The foregoing information was given me by Henrietta Seiberling, who has been a powerful influence in the alcoholic group, though she is not a part of it for that reason.

Another person whom I recommend highly to you is T. Henry Williams. He and his wife have maintained what amounts to a continuous "open house" for the alcoholics and their families, for the past two years. He is a non-drinker, deeply religious, has lots of horse sense and you can confide in him and depend upon him absolutely.

Smith's address is: 928 Second National Building, Akron. Phone: Hemlock 8523. Residence: Ardmore Avenue, Akron. Phone: University 2436.

Concerning possible sanitarium locations, Bob reports that the Fair Oaks Villa at Cuyahoga Falls, does not seem especially desirable. Although this is now being used as a sanitarium, he describes it as "old, wooden, cold and barny." He would evidently prefer a large house in the city of Akron which could be used for a sanitarium and perhaps, a general gathering place. He describes three places of this sort as having very large brick houses which could be used at once, without much outlay for changes.

Two of them are offered at $70,000 and have 8 to 12 acres of ground each. There is a third offered at $35,000. These places have 25 to 30 rooms, and could readily be expanded. I imagine that places of this sort are rather abundant as a lot of money has been made and lost in Akron in rubber. Although the asking prices seem high, I imagine that the present owners would be delighted to [enter into] a lease of a moderate period at any figure that would take care of the overhead. Smith is accumulating more data which he will have for you when you arrive.

I cannot tell you how much we appreciate your proposed trip. Smith has done a monumental job under great handicaps and we all earnestly hope that he will presently be enabled to accelerate and extend his great work.

Wishing you a successful journey and thanking you very much for the attendance last Sunday of Mrs. Amos and yourself, I am,

As ever,

WGW:VB[20]

Bob Smith was obviously anxious to do as much preliminary footwork as possible to maximize the effectiveness of Frank Amos's trip and had spent considerable time on this, first investigating an old sanitarium five miles north of Akron, and then looking at enough local real estate to narrow his choices down to three particular properties.

Also interesting is the fact that Bill is no longer talking about the small hospital proposed at the December dinner. He now refers to it as a sanitarium, possibly in an effort to avoid the image of the larger expenses that are so easily associated with the word "hospital." In addition, he notes this proposed sanitarium could also serve as a general gathering place for sober members of the Ohio group. Always a man with a keen business sense, Bill was underlining the fact that the Rockefellers could expect a dual return on any investment they might eventually make in one of these properties.

Amos Arrives in Akron

Frank Amos arrived in Akron on Friday night, February 11 and likely stayed with the Smiths, although his friends may have given him sufficient funds for a local hotel. He spent his first twenty-four hours in town with Bob and Anne Smith and the constant stream of alcoholic visitors who trekked through their home.[21]

This was an anonymous visit. As Amos notes, "only one other of the alcoholic group knew why I was there—that was Paul Stanley who was at the meeting we had in Rockefeller Center. I was introduced as a friend of 'Bill' Wilson's . . . and as a Christian layman deeply interested in their work."[22] Later, when being introduced to T. Henry Williams, Amos identified himself only as a man who was "speaking for four Christian laymen who were interested" in Dr. Bob's work with alcoholics.[23] There was no mention of the Rockefeller connection and no one suspected that Amos was there representing the richest man in America. This was clearly how Dr. Bob had decided to handle the situation and Amos had accepted his reasoning. As he explains in his report:

> I didn't ask the rank and file for solutions. I didn't regard it wise to even intimate that funds might be available for fear some short-sighted individual might feel that if one man was paid something, then others of them who give many hours to this work might also deserve remuneration.

This of course would ruin one of the finest features of this movement—the voluntary Christian service for sick humanity which they themselves need to keep them permanently "on the wagon."[24]

That is one way to explain the need for secrecy, but on closer examination, it raises more questions than it answers. Why, for instance, was it that the New York group had no problem with the idea of money coming to certain people so they could continue their work with alcoholics, while the supposedly much more Christian group in Akron needed to be kept in the dark about that possibility? Were the Akron members so contentious, so competitive, and so shortsighted that the very idea of available funds coming to one or more members (but not to all) was a situation that was just too volatile to risk talking about publicly? What was going on with this group that it was considered unwise to even intimate that funds might be available to some people for their work with alcoholics?

It is likely that the fear of dissatisfaction and dissention was based not so much on the potential personal jealousies that Amos mentions as it was on the belief that money would contaminate and derail the underlying foundations of sobriety, i.e., the "voluntary Christian service" as it was understood and practiced in Akron at that time. This belief that money was a corrosive, evil influence in and of itself is an idea clearly not shared in New York, where the members saw lavish financing as the solution to the challenges of expanding their reach rather than the beginning of the end of all their efforts.

Even more likely, the fear of talking about money in Akron was driven not so much by the fact that members of the group might object (although there were some who surely would), but that the non-alcoholic Oxford Group members, who regularly attended meetings and who were literally an integral part of the Alcoholic Group there, most certainly would. We have already seen Henrietta Seiberling's very emphatic and outspoken opinions on the evils of money and she was surely not alone in these beliefs. Bob had shared one of Bill's early letters about a possible Rockefeller connection with T. Henry Williams and his wife, Clarace, but they had obviously not been informed of any later developments since T. Henry didn't know that Amos was in Akron representing the Rockefeller interests.[25] Perhaps there had been some unpleasant repercussions from this earlier sharing with the Williamses, the kind of fallout that prompted Bob to go silent after that first bit of candor.

Certainly it was this ongoing and deep integration of the Ohio "Alcoholic Squad" into the Oxford Group—and vice versa—that led to an almost universal adoption of these sentiments against money in Akron and that necessitated Bob Smith's insistence on such absolute secrecy regarding Frank Amos's true mission.

Meetings with the Akron Fellowship

Amos spent most of Saturday meeting with several of the "fifty men, and, I believe, two women" who were now sober in Akron.[26] Over the course of this visit, he "met and talked with about half of these men with their wives and, in one or two cases, their mothers."[27] In support of his mission to investigate the possibility of funding a hospital for Dr. Bob, he was pleasantly surprised by the openness with which these former alcoholics discussed their Akron leader. "In private talks with many of them, without any prompting on my part, they emphasized how vital Smith was at this time to their work. Several told me they knew he was sacrificing his professional and remunerative work for this and that something must be done to help him handle both without spoiling either."[28]

Amos's claim of fifty-two sober members was close, but just a bit inflated. In the final report to John D. Rockefeller Jr., Amos included a two-page list made out in Dr. Bob's handwriting of the forty-one men and two women who were then currently sober in Ohio. (Each page has five columns with the name, profession, dry time in months, drinking years, and the age of each member in the group.)[29] Clearly Bob had been very successful in helping people get sober during the four months that had elapsed since they sat down and 'counted noses' the previous October.

On Saturday evening, after a full day in Akron, Paul Stanley and his wife, Hildreth, drove Frank eighty-five miles south to his hometown of Cambridge, Ohio.[30] On that drive, Stanley took the opportunity to present in detail his own opinion on why Dr. Bob should be given financial support:

> Most of us have our jobs and can make a good living. I am an insurance man and can go out aggressively for business. Smith as a reputable and ethical physician can't be an ambulance chaser or advertise himself. All he can do is to meet regularly with physicians, keep up his professional contacts, since from that source he, as a rectal surgeon, must get most of his surgical patients. At present his income is so low that he can't keep an office secretary and finds it difficult to meet his necessary home expenses. Either we must help him or he must give up most of this alcoholic work . . . [and] it would be criminal at this time, to lose Smith as [our] leader.[31]

Amos was traveling to Cambridge to visit relatives and to acquaint himself with the current status of the family business, a newspaper called the *Daily Jeffersonian*. He spent the better part of two days in Cambridge focused on his private affairs before returning to Akron late on Monday afternoon.[32]*

That evening, he dined with T. Henry Williams and his wife, Clarace, after which the couple opened their home to a special meeting of the Akron "Alcoholic Squad."[33] Amos noted that the Williamses "are devout and practical Christians [who] have become so impressed with the work of Smith and his associates that they turn over their home to them twice weekly for religious and social gatherings."[34]** According to Dr. Bob's own estimate "about 50–60 of the men and their wives gathered so he could see and talk to them."[35]

---

* Amos returned to Cambridge and the family business on January 1, 1940 as the paper's president and publisher, a job that he retired from in 1952 (Frank B. Amos to John D. Rockefeller Jr., March 25, 1940: RAC, Family, Group 2 OMR, Series P, Box 42, Folder 457; "Frank Amos, A Co-founder of Alcoholics Anonymous," Obituary, the *New York Times*, July 20, 1965).

** Presumably, these two occasions were the Sunday "religious" gathering and the Wednesday night "social gathering," i.e., what passed for an A.A. meeting in Akron at that time.

One of the worries about this Monday night gathering was that it might seem far too much like an Oxford Group meeting and mislead Amos about what was actually happening in Akron. This was not an unreasonable fear given the number of ardent, non-alcoholic members of the Oxford Group (not least of which was the indomitable Henrietta Seiberling) who attended that meeting. In addition, these gatherings were run using the model suggested by the Oxford Group for their own meetings. After Amos left, Bob wrote to Bill that "of course he heard some Oxford Group chatter but we tried to impress him with the fact that as far as the alcoholic set up was concerned we could not be identified with the [Oxford] Group and explained why such a set up was impossible. I think he understands things ok."[36]

Given what was going on in Akron at that time, Dr. Bob's confidence that Amos left with an understanding of these differences sounds more than a little optimistic. Even the Conference-approved A.A. history book, *Dr. Bob and the Good Oldtimers*, recaps this meeting and then wryly notes that, under the circumstances, Smith's hope that the Oxford Group connection would not be noticed was surely "more wishful than real."[37]

Amos's Later Observations on the Fellowship in Akron

In his two-and-a-half days in Akron, Amos did seem to get a clear understanding of what the alcoholic set-up was like in Akron. In his comprehensive historical report completed the following August, which includes details of this trip, Frank noted that:

> [At that time] the Akron alcoholics group was holding meetings weekly in the home of a friend. These meetings were attended by the alcoholics themselves, and members of their families. "Prospects" were invited whenever, in the opinion of the workers, they were of the type that could be helped.
>
> In many respects these meetings have taken on the form of the meetings described in the Gospels of the early Christians during the first century, but they have avoided some of the methods used by the Oxford Movement *[sic]* which, particularly with this class of people, had proved a handicap. Mr. Amos was invited to attend such a meeting, at which there were between fifty and sixty present.[38]*

In his report to John D. Rockefeller Jr. on the Akron visit, Amos provides a detailed, seven step outline of exactly how he understood the "alcoholic set up" in Akron to be working:

> They told me varying stories, many of them almost miraculous, but all remarkably alike in the technique used and the system followed. Briefly this system is:

---

* The comment here about "this class of people" refers to the fact that the Oxford Group focused on wealthy and well-to-do Christians for their membership and they were a bit reluctant to accept the down-and-out types who would more typically show up at meetings sponsored by their "Alcoholic Squad." It was likely this distinction between their own approach and that of the Oxford Group that Bob Smith emphasized to Frank Amos to differentiate themselves from the Oxford Group.

1. An alcoholic must realize that he is an alcoholic, incurable from a medical viewpoint and that he must never again drink anything with alcohol in it;

2. He must surrender himself absolutely to God realizing that in himself there is no hope;

3. Not only must he want to stop drinking permanently, but he must remove from his life other sins such as hatred, adultery and others which frequently accompany alcoholism. Unless he will do this, absolutely, Smith and his associates refuse to work with him.

4. He must have devotions every morning—a "quiet time" of prayer, and some reading from the Bible or other religious literature. Unless this is faithfully followed, there is grave danger of backsliding;

5. He must be willing to help other alcoholics get straightened out. This throws up a protective barrier and strengthens his own will-power and convictions;

6. It is important, but not vital, that he meet frequently with other reformed alcoholics and form both a social and religious comradeship;

7. Important, but not vital, that he attend some religious service at least weekly.

All the above is being carried out faithfully by the Akron group and not a day passes when there is not one or more new "victim" to work on with Smith as their leader by common consent.[39]

This description, which includes six "musts"—admission of incurability, total abstinence, absolute surrender to God, complete removal of sinful behaviors, morning prayer and meditation, and helping other alcoholics—along with two strong suggestions, may be startling to current A.A. members, but it is important to remember that this is still the "flying blind" period. There were, as yet, no Twelve Steps and no group called Alcoholics Anonymous. As Dr. Bob so eloquently attested eight years after this meeting: "Blindly groping for the truth, the early development of the activity in Akron was not easy. It was mostly by the trial and error method. We had no precedent whatsoever, gleaning a fact here and there as time went on. Eventually a generalized procedure was discovered with a reasonable hope of acceptance."[40]

Frank Amos's candid snapshot of what was happening in Akron in February of 1938 is a priceless record of how people in that time and place understood their quest for sobriety and the tools they were using to maintain it. It is unfortunate we have no similarly dispassionate eyewitness account of what was happening in New York at this same time for the sake of comparison.

Amos Learns More about Dr. Bob

The final day of Amos's visit, Tuesday, was set aside for interviews with several prominent people regarding Dr. Bob's character and reputation and also to look at the real estate possibilities Bob had selected for his consideration. In the course of the day, he did not meet with any of the ministers or doctors Bill Wilson had recommended; instead he arrived in Akron with "leads from his Rockefeller friends and out of his own acquaintance."[41] These included one of Ohio's foremost eye specialists along with another doctor, a general practitioner, who had been "cured by Smith and his friends," and a former judge who had served as Chairman of the Board of the Akron City Hospital for the past forty years. Amos listed Henrietta Seiberling and T. Henry Williams as the final two people he interviewed.

All of these gave Dr. Bob Smith the most glowing reports—now that he had stopped drinking. The opinions range from the former judge who "didn't claim to understand the method [of recovery] but whatever it was he said it worked and he was for it," to the formerly-alcoholic doctor who proclaimed that:

> Smith stood at the top of his profession . . . [and] was the keystone of the alcoholic reform movement there and that something must be done to help him so he could regain more of his remunerative practice and still give much of his time to this work. At present his work with alcoholics was taking an average of 10 hours a day. [He] thought Smith should head a small hospital for this purpose.[42]

Clearly the idea of an alcoholic hospital was looked on favorably by at least some of the Akron alcoholics. According to Dr. Bob's list of forty-three Ohio members,[43] this doctor was six months sober in February 1938, so he was likely present when the October vote was taken and, if so, he may well have cast one of the deciding "Yes" votes.

Besides conducting most of his interviews on Tuesday, Amos also had lunch and dinner with Dr. Bob and, in between, they visited two of the sites that Smith was recommending for his sanitarium. Amos commented that these "would cost probably $75,000 to $100,000 to purchase and equip," but he was careful not to give Bob Smith any hint of what his reaction might be to the idea of acquiring those properties.[44]

The day after Amos left Akron, Bob wrote to Bill with details about the "very delightful visit from Mr. Amos" noting that "he seemed very favorably impressed. If he were not, I certainly do not know what we could do to impress him . . . He is a very shrewd man and a very careful and thorough diagnostician. It was a great pleasure to meet such a Christian gentleman [and] it is too bad that there are not more of them."[45]

Despite all his talk of how "very favorably impressed" Frank had been, Dr. Bob sounded more than a little anxious and wondered whether Amos had talked to Bill about the Akron experience since his return to New York: "I shall be very glad to hear from you as to his impression of us."[46]

Bill Wilson described Amos as being "terrifically impressed" by his trip and then almost predictably added: "Our spirits soared!"[47]

Frank Amos's Akron Trip Report

Bill was certainly right about Frank Amos; by the time he arrived back in New York City, he was a true believer in this new way of getting and staying sober. Seeing such an impressive number of recovered alcoholics leading happy and productive lives was more than enough proof for a man who had suffered through some serious problem with drinkers in his own family.

Frank came home on Wednesday, February 16 and spent the next four days preparing a four-page report he entitled "Notes on Akron, Ohio Survey." He opened his Survey with a brief introduction explaining the origins of "the self-styled Alcoholic Group" in Akron, and then organized the rest of his findings under two major headings; the first detailing what he had learned about Dr. Bob Smith and the second with his observations about the Alcoholic Group itself.

Three Options for Financial Support

In an early version of his report, this final section also presented three possible ways that financial support could be offered to the Akron group.*

The first option offered was the suggestion made by Wilson and Stanley at the December dinner for a "small hospital of from 30 to 50 beds." After outlining the details of this proposal, Amos reported that "with this in mind I visited two sites which would cost probably from $75,000 to $100,000 to purchase and equip." Amos advised that "in my opinion we are not ready to recommend this," but he did hold out the possibility that "later some plan like this may be advisable."[48] In short, the proposed alcoholic hospital in Akron under Dr. Bob's direction was now just a remote future possibility.

It isn't known exactly why Amos lost so much of his earlier enthusiasm for the idea of funding an alcoholic hospital in Akron. Several passing comments within the document support the idea that 'money will ruin the Christian foundations of this movement,' but there is no detailed or explicit reason given why he abandoned the hospital proposal. Although she is not credited as such in his report, Henrietta Seiberling claimed to have the strongest influence on Amos's thinking in this regard. In a later interview, she stated unequivocally that it was "her impact on and guidance of Amos [that] was responsible for his favorable report" and, further, that "she and others [had] convinced Amos that money would indeed 'spoil this thing.'"[49]

A second option, which he tentatively approved, was a scaled-down version of the hospital proposal:

> A second plan I considered was to continue just as at present with the hospitalization at the City Hospital, thus not involving any added expense for that (it costs about $8.00 a day and requires from 5 to 8 days on an average). Then secure a smaller home with nice surroundings with accommodations for ten or twelve to use as a recuperating home for those who need it. A man (former alcoholic) and his wife could run this with a

---

* The complete text of the unedited report can be found in Appendix I on page 607 of this book.

maid and a cook. Probably one or two unmarried former alcoholics could reside there. Such a place probably could be purchased, furnished, and equipped for not over $25,000 to $30,000 and if done, should be with the firm understanding that it must be self-supporting except perhaps for whatever would be supplied Dr. Smith as outlined in the next paragraph.[50]

The final possibility, pertaining only to Dr. Bob, received considerably more attention because Amos was convinced it was the most viable option:

A third plan—which could be worked with or without the second plan—would be to arrange on a confidential basis, with only a small carefully selected committee knowing anything about it, for a monthly remuneration for Dr. Smith for a period of at least two years until the whole proposition could get well going and perhaps be absolutely self-supporting in every way.

Dr. Smith has a wife—a lovely, cultured lady who supports him to the limit in this work—and a son and daughter around the ages of 18 and 20. His modest home is mortgaged and he has not been able to keep it in proper repair.

He needs a competent secretary not only to receive his calls when not in the office (his office hours are from 2 to 4 P.M.), but one who is thoroughly sympathetic with this work and who could handle a lot of assignments and details with other reformed alcoholics, in routing them to see patients, passing on his instructions etc, etc. which Smith himself has to do now. Mrs. Smith has her hands full with the home and with her work with wives of alcoholics, also with an occasional woman alcoholic who turns up. Smith says that men can rarely work satisfactorily with women alcoholics. The sex problem makes it difficult. He, as a physician, can and has helped, but his wife and other wives must handle most of this, for which there is a growing need. Such a secretary would cost about $1,200.00 a year. Smith needs to keep a good car—he now drives an Oldsmobile of somewhat ancient vintage—to afford swift, safe, prompt transportation. He needs better office facilities not only for his regular paying patients, but to better handle these ex-alcoholics who come to him daily for inspiration and instruction. Altogether I think a sum of around $5,000.00 a year for at least two years should be made available to help make up for his loss of practice, to pay a secretary, and to meet expenses which he cannot possibly handle under present circumstances. I am sold on attempting this at once. The other suggestions can be worked out later, after more analysis and consultation.[51]

Strangely, even this very limited amount of financial support for Dr. Bob had to be arranged on a confidential basis, with only a few "carefully selected" people knowing anything about it. It can only be assumed that this condition of secrecy was necessitated by Dr. Bob's belief that any public knowledge of these payments would be damaging to both his reputation and his mission. Money was obviously an extremely sensitive topic within the Akron Fellowship.

Finally, Amos ended his Survey with a call to action regarding the other areas where recovery was also being pursued: "The situation right here in New York, also down in Maryland [where Fitz Mayo lived] deserve consideration. They can be taken up later but should not be overlooked."[52]

Amos Submits His Findings and a Decision Is Reached

On the Monday following his return to New York, Amos met with Richardson, Chipman, and Scott and presented his findings. More than anything else, he wanted to emphasize that, in his estimation, the work being done in Akron was little short of miraculous and that it deserved financial support if it was to be continued under Dr. Smith's leadership.[53]

Years later, Bill Wilson claimed that Frank Amos was so enthusiastic about what he had seen in Ohio that his original report recommended a Rockefeller contribution of $50,000 for the "recuperating house" described in the second part of his unedited Survey.[54] And Frank was hardly alone in his enthusiasm, which is clearly evident in the fact that just weeks after this meeting, Richardson, Scott, and Chipman would all lend their wholehearted support to the creation of the Alcoholic Foundation to raise substantial sums of money for the movement.

But, if all four men felt that the group needed and deserved significantly more funding, then why didn't they simply ask Rockefeller for the money? Why was their recommendation to John D. Junior only $5,000 rather than the $50,000 that Bill says Frank originally favored?

No matter what their individual opinions may have been, it seems clear that John D. Rockefeller Jr. was the reason the request was so steeply reduced. Based on their long relationship with him, Richardson, Chipman, and Scott all felt that a $50,000 donation would never be approved by the man who had the final say in this matter. Their discussion about Akron and how far they were willing to go with Rockefeller may have been contentious, but once a consensus was reached on a lesser number, Frank Amos was asked to edit his original version of the Survey. He did this in his bold, distinctive handwriting, omitting large sections of the text and adding the agreed upon particulars; he then turned the document over to Richardson for retyping.[55]

Two days later, Willard Richardson sent this revised Survey to John D. Rockefeller Jr. along with a carefully crafted letter in which he almost begs his employer to approve the modest request being made. Reading between the lines, Richardson's tone clearly acknowledges that this donation does not meet Rockefeller's usual standards and he all but pleads with him to make an exception in this case. This appeal is then reinforced with his explicit emphasis that it is not just Amos and himself who are so enthusiastic about this project, but that Chipman and Scott were also in favor of this donation, so much so that they would be happy to come by Rockefeller's office to present their reasons in person if he should think that necessary:

February 23, 1938

Dear Mr. Rockefeller:

You may recall my saying to you a few words about a group of men and women who have been saved from the worst forms of alcoholism by real religious experience. The impression as to the importance of their experience and activity of these people grows upon us. Through conferences and studies we have been trying to fully understand and to help these friends who are well scattered from Boston to New York to Baltimore, Cleveland and Akron, and who face a situation difficult to solve. The demands upon their time and strength by needy men and women are heavy. They cannot wisely organize or institutionalize the service. They can finance a certain amount of help for each other by a small revolving fund, which they are doing. But situations in two or three centres, especially Akron, present a problem and a real opportunity as we see it.

After careful consideration we asked Mr. Amos, who was to be in Ohio on business, to study the Akron situation thoroughly. He spent most of three days there and reported to us last Monday. His typewritten statement is attached but you probably will not need to read it. It bears out the truth of statements made to us. Briefly, Dr. Smith, an able man and the first convert in that section, is the leader of 40 or 50 men and women in that area. His leadership has lasted for nearly three years and is for another two years very desirable. But his hard experience with drink makes his rehabilitation as a specialist slow, and the demands made by the former and new alcoholics are heavy. Furthermore, he wants to help them medically and spiritually. He is connected with the Akron City Hospital and does important service there. But his office and home facilities are inadequate. His friends, as Mr. Amos's report indicates, think if he could be helped financially for one year, possibly two, he would be able by having a secretary, a suitable office, and some other aid, to get fully on his feet professionally and could develop some helpers in the group of good men there and in Cleveland who would take much of the burden of the liquor work. Mr. Amos estimates the cost to do this effectively at $5,000 for the two years.

We four men think this matter so important that we are bringing it to you as worthy of careful consideration. Mr. Scott, as you probably know, is to take a sort of forced vacation in Florida. He would be glad to give you his point of view and told me to assure you that he sincerely recommended your undertaking this interest. Mr. Chipman thinks as he does. Would you think best to allow us, under proper business arrangements, to provide the Akron situation with as much as is necessary up to $5,000 for one year, deferring consideration of a second year.

There is an abundance of material in the form of information we have received as to this entire body of men and women which we will be glad to give you. We are very much impressed with some of the leaders in Akron and in this city, as well as with the development of this service both from a drink and a religious point of view. However, we do not mean to be anything but wise in treatment of the undertaking considering the present conditions and possible growth of the work.

Very Truly,

W. S. Richardson
Mr. John D. Rockefeller, Jr.

O F F I C E[56]

Rockefeller Makes His Final Judgment
Richardson and Rockefeller most likely discussed this request more than once for it wasn't until three weeks later, on March 17, that Rockefeller rendered his final judgment*:

---

* There has been considerable confusion over exactly what happened at the meeting among the four Rockefeller men and also when Richardson talked with Rockefeller directly. Bill notes, for instance, that Richardson "was convinced of our point of view," and he reports "a long talk" in which Richardson tries, unsuccessfully, to convince Rockefeller that he should make a larger contribution (AA Main Events, 1938, Point 3). But the letter that Richardson sent to Rockefeller following the meeting of the four men does not support this scenario. If that "long talk" did take place, it was, perhaps, among the four members of the group but it also might have been with John D. Rockefeller Jr. himself but prior to the final drafting of this letter.

In *Not-God*, Ernest Kurtz is equally perplexed when trying to make sense out of the evidence surrounding these meetings and he offers an endnote with an intriguing, but unsubstantiated, explanation for all the confusion: "Rockefeller's practice, as I understand it, was to discuss orally and then have letters confirming consensus written." Kurtz notes that this is only "hearsay" evidence, but he leans on it nonetheless to explain his "refusal to decide here." (Kurtz, *Not-God*, p. 330, n. 23.)

If it is true that the documents we have in the archives were written *after the fact* to reflect the final agreement reached, then Wilson's recounting of Richardson's "long talk" with Rockefeller is plausible and even probable.

Interestingly, there are three minor and two substantive differences between the text of this letter saved in the Rockefeller archives (which is quoted here) and the one in the A.A. archives in New York City. Besides two typos and a slight difference in formatting of the A.A. copy, the Rockefeller version adds one short sentence that does not appear in the other copy. That sentence reads: "Furthermore, he [Dr. Bob] wants to help them medically and spiritually"—a statement explicitly acknowledging Dr. Bob's deep commitment to alcoholics on both of these important levels. But the major difference in the two versions has to do with exactly how much money the four Rockefeller friends are asking John D. Rockefeller Jr., to contribute, which is the very crux of the letter. The A.A. copy somewhat ambiguously requests "up to $5,000 for one year and possibly two?" (GSO, Box 59, 1938, Folder B, Documents 1938-7 & 1938-8) while the Rockefeller version effectively halves this request saying "up to $5,000 for one year, deferring consideration of a second year."

We would expect Richardson (and, even more certainly, his secretary) to be meticulous about the correctness of any letter that went out to John D. Rockefeller Jr., so the typos almost certainly identify the A.A. copy as the earlier version—one that was later corrected and into which a new, short sentence was added. But why change the $5,000 contribution from a possible two years to just one with a decision on the second year now being deferred and, almost certainly, forgotten?

Given the evidence of these two versions of the same letter, it likely that Kurtz' "hearsay" understanding about Rockefeller's practice of post-writing documents is correct and these two letters offer interesting testimony to this practice of creating after-the-fact letters to reflect the final resolution of earlier disagreements.

Dear Mr. Richardson:

I have read with care your memorandum of February 23rd and the accompanying data in regard to the work for drink addicts which you and a few friends have been interested in. What has been accomplished according to these records in regenerating human life is almost miraculous. I do not wonder at your interest in the work.

On the other hand, much as I would like to do what you gentlemen want me to do and agree to contribute $5,000 a year for two years to the support of the work, as you know it is contrary to our office policy to undertake the entire responsibility for any enterprise, or even a fifty per cent responsibility, unless we expect to carry it indefinitely or to its conclusion. This policy I am sure you agree has been proven, by our long experience, to be a wise one. I feel that it would be a mistake to deviate from it.

However, because of the interest of yourself and these other friends in the matter, I will provide a total of $5,000 for this enterprise. Because the service for which this sum is to be used is closely related to the Riverside Church, the friends who present the request to me being officers of the Church, I am making a contribution of $5,000 to Riverside Church as a non-quota item of the Benevolent Department, understanding that it will be dispensed for the object mentioned in response to your requisitions.

From my standpoint, it is understood that the money can be spent during one, two or three years as may seem to you wise, but that in any event you will not look to me for a further contribution for this object. If a somewhat different way of handling this proposed gift seems better, I shall be happy to adjust the terms as may seem best. This letter simply represents what I will do.

Very Sincerely,

John D. Rockefeller Jr.
Mr. W. S. Richardson

O F F I C E[57]

So much for Bill Wilson's dreams of getting huge sums of money out of John D. Rockefeller Jr. They were to get a one-time, but paid-out-over-time contribution of $5,000 specifically allocated to Dr. Bob Smith and "the Akron situation," but there would be nothing more. *Nothing more*. However stilted the language might be, what could be clearer than "in any event you will not look to me for a further contribution for this object"? Rockefeller's decision was not only unexpected, it was final. As Wilson noted, "this was terrifically discouraging news."[58]

Discouraging? It must have been crushing.

Incremental payments from the $5,000 would surely help Dr. Bob keep his head above water and allow him to continue his work with alcoholics in Akron* at least for a little while longer, but what about the people in New York? Despite Frank Amos's caution that "the situation right here in New York [and] also down in Maryland deserve consideration" and "should not be overlooked," that is exactly what happened; they were entirely disregarded by Rockefeller. The strategy of placing the emphasis on a hospital for Dr. Bob had completely sidelined the needs of the New York contingent, so much so that they were not even mentioned in the appeal that Willard Richardson made to Rockefeller.

If this was all the money they were ever going to get from Rockefeller, where could they turn next for the extensive funding needed to bring the message of salvation to the thousands upon thousands of alcoholics who were still suffering all over the country?

Their only choice was to go back to the beginning and to start over again.

One thing, however, was clear. The hope and the promise of Dr. Bob having his own alcoholic hospital in Akron—a hospital that would have served as a first big step in the expansion of their movement—was dead and it would never be seriously considered again.

---

* Bill Wilson incorrectly claims in *Alcoholics Anonymous Comes of Age* (p. 151) that "the small mortgage on Dr. Bob's place was paid off, and each of us began receiving thirty dollars a week," information that was subsequently picked up and repeated in *Pass It On* (p. 188). Neither of these claims are true. Jay D. Moore's exhaustive examination of Rockefeller's contributions points out that Smith was only paid in $200 monthly installments and states categorically: "There is no evidence that Dr. Bob's mortgage was paid off. A search of the Summit County Clerk's records show no lien cancellation for 855 Ardmore in 1938, 1939 or 1940." (*Alcoholics Anonymous and the Rockefeller Connection*, p. 140)

CHAPTER SIX

The Alcoholic Fund

~*March to April 1938*~

Bill learned about the contents of Willard Richardson's letter before it was even sent and he immediately went on the road, visiting Dr. Bob in Akron and then traveling to Maryland to confer with Fitz Mayo.[1] With him, he brought the sad news that Richardson would not be asking Rockefeller for a substantial contribution for a hospital (or even a sanitarium) and that the very best they could hope for was some modest financial support to keep Dr. Bob afloat. The grand strategy of initially raising as much as $50,000 from John D. Rockefeller Jr. —a strategy that looked like it was well on its way to success just one week earlier—had suffered a resounding defeat.

We have no records of the conversations Bill had with Bob and Fitz, but it is clear he was intent on salvaging whatever resources and opportunities he could from their recent association with the Rockefeller people. There must be some way they could capitalize on this connection and raise the money they so desperately needed. What should their next step be?

Whatever John D. Jr.'s opinion might be, his four friends realized that even if they would not be able to expand their efforts for saving alcoholics in the way they had originally hoped, the growing Fellowship would definitely need much more than this $5,000 contribution just to continue what they were already doing—especially on the East Coast, which would receive no benefit from Rockefeller's contribution. While the group might, in fact, be an outstanding example of first-century Christianity, they had to live in the real world and, as their work progressed in New York, food still had to be put on the table, mortgage payments must be made, and everyday expenses continued to pile up at an alarming rate.

According to Bill, neither Richardson nor Amos could "quite agree with Mr. Rockefeller"[2] and Wilson saw this as a perfect opening for further solicitation. Once back in New York he enlisted Hank's help and the two men began "working on" Amos and Richardson, visiting them several times a week.[3] They emphasized their ongoing expenses and their financial distress, noting that Hank's business, Honor Dealers, was in "terrific financial straits" and "on the point of collapse." Deprived of even this dwindling source of income, they painted a "horrendous picture" of how they would "have to give up [their] work on alcoholics if they didn't receive some sort of financial relief."[4]

Their persistence paid off and on Sunday, March 13—four days *before* John D. Rockefeller Jr. sent them his disappointing written response—both Amos and Richardson attended a "large meeting" of the New York group at Hank Parkhurst's house in Montclair, New Jersey, a location likely chosen to accommodate Willard Richardson, who lived in that same town. Like all of the meetings in those days, the gathering was a husband-and-wife affair with even Amos's wife, Mary, in attendance that night. This proved to be a landmark meeting for the future of Alcoholics Anonymous, for it was the one in which the idea of creating a foundation to raise money for the Fellowship was first proposed and seriously considered.[5]

The Foundation Idea

Establishing a foundation was most likely Wilson's or perhaps even Parkhurst's idea, but Bill later pleaded ignorance over "who actually made the proposal" and modestly suggested it was "probably" Richardson who first brought up the idea since he was "a foundation man himself."[6] Lois, however, remembers Gussie Kellogg (whose husband, Paul, had sobered up the previous July) as the person responsible for convincing Richardson a foundation would be the best solution for all of their financial problems.[7] Lois provides no further details on how or when this persuasive discussion might have taken place, but in her account it was not a conclusion Richardson arrived at without some outside influence.

Two days later, a smaller meeting—this one attended only by alcoholics—was held at Bill's house in Brooklyn, and here the group "talked foundation" far into the night.[8*] Despite the huge disappointment they felt over Rockefeller's pending refusal to make a large donation, they were all rejuvenated by this impressive new idea of creating their own foundation to solicit the rich on a tax free basis.[9] "Our new friends, Richardson, Amos [and] Chipman . . . had decided to back our idea for the formation of a Foundation," Bill said, noting they also agreed to lend them the use of their own names when they approached people or institutions for money. Wilson's spirits predictably soared: "This would mean indirect Rockefeller backing. How in the dickens could we fail under such circumstances!"[10]

Hope springs eternal . . . especially in Bill Wilson's heart.

---

* Lois notes that "Van, Hank and Kathleen, Joe and Paul and Fitz" were in attendance.

Lois Takes a Break from the Chaos at Home

While Bill was traveling around Ohio and Maryland trying to resolve their money problems, and then organizing meetings locally to formulate ambitious new plans for financing, Lois Wilson was at home dealing with the host of alcoholics who constantly camped out there.

"We had drunks all over the house," she said, "sometimes as many as five lived there at one time."[11] This would have been problematic enough if they had all been sober, but, more often than not, these fellows were out drinking and then rolling in at all hours of the night, frequently dead drunk. She reports one committed suicide in their absence (after having sold "about 700 dollars worth of our clothes and luggage"), while another "slid down the coal chute from the street to the cellar when we refused him the front door," and "two others took to fighting, and one chased the other all around the house with a carving knife."[12] The circus had come to town and it didn't look as if it would be leaving 182 Clinton Street any time soon.

Worst of all were the times when Bill was on the road, first during his 1937 job with Quaw and Foley, and then later in his efforts to coordinate the growing recovery movement. While Bill was away, Lois found herself home alone with the responsibility of caring for these resident alcoholics. This meant she was the only one available to nurse them through their drunks, babysit them when they were hung over, go out late at night looking for a sympathetic doctor, or even join them in the bar for a late night drink that might be needed to calm their nerves. In one famous incident, Lois says, "I was once suddenly taken sick, and when my sister arrived to nurse me, she found five men milling around in the living room, one of them muttering, 'One woman can look after five drunks but five drunks cannot look after one woman.'"[13]

This kind of domestic chaos had been the norm in the Wilson household for a few years and March 1938, while all this talk of starting a foundation was going on, was no exception. On March 9, Lois notes in her diary that "Tom Donahue came to live." The very next day, she says, "Russ drunk came home at 2 a.m." Two days later it got worse: "Wes, having had a drink, told me he liked me, etc. etc. etc." (Who knows what those three *et ceteras* encompass!) Finally, on March 17, the very day of Rockefeller's disappointing letter, Lois says she "told Russ about Wes."[14]

All this lunacy proved to be too much and Lois decamped the day after that discussion with Russ, going off by herself to stay with the Mayos, claiming she needed to go "to Maryland to rest."[15] Three days later, she wrote Bill a long letter thanking him for his love and "for seeing me through this hard time." Spring had already arrived at the Mayos' home in Cumberstone, MD, and she was sure the birds, the flowers, and the sunlight would revive her flagging spirits. But the instability that seems to just come naturally with alcoholic families was also rampant in Maryland where she had to deal with the dysfunctional Mayo clan and she wondered to Bill "if this is after all the best place for me to shake out of myself."[16] Despite all the local family tensions, Lois stayed in the Washington area for twelve days before returning to New York on March 30; taking the train into New York's Penn Station where Bill welcomed her back home again.[17]

Hank Parkhurst Proposes an Alcoholic Fund

Bill and Hank had certainly been busy during her absence. On Wednesday, March 16—the day immediately following the Brooklyn meeting where they had discussed their ideas for creating a foundation in such detail and the day before Rockefeller's decisive letter—Hank wrote to Frank Amos outlining his suggestions on how something he called "The Fund" might be established, organized, and administered. In Hank's proposal this would not be a legally incorporated foundation (which would be created later), but rather a simple method for collecting and distributing monies to support "this alcoholic work" right now.

Although the letter states over and over these are Hank's own ideas ("my thoughts," "my personal opinions," "I would suggest," "In my mind," "I believe," and "any suggestions contained herein are personal"),[18] the details in the letter had been recommended and approved by Bill Wilson from first to last. Across the top of one archived copy Hank has handwritten: "Copy to—Bill Wilson / Dear Bill: - This, along the lines of your suggestion."[19] If Bill had asked his number two man in New York to put forward some of his own ideas, it was likely a strategic ploy that would allow him to later modify or even disavow these proposals should they receive an unfavorable response from the Rockefeller people.

In his letter Parkhurst noted "the decisions that are made at this time" came "with grave responsibilities" because whatever model they adopted now might well be "followed later on a national basis." Hank's caution here underlines the fact that The Fund was originally conceived primarily as an arrangement for dealing with donations made in New York rather than as a proposed central headquarters for the growing movement. Dr. Bob Smith would have his contribution from Rockefeller to live on (the distribution of which would also be administered through this Fund), but the New Yorkers were still basically broke and they needed to begin raising money locally for their own support. Nevertheless, Hank's concern about "grave responsibilities" is certainly farsighted, for The Fund they soon established did, in fact, evolve over time into first the Alcoholic Foundation and then the General Service Office, which coordinates the service structure for the benefit of Alcoholics Anonymous today.

Hank characterized his proposed structure for The Fund as a "loose organization and administration," one that would oversee both the collection and the distribution of money for the recovery of alcoholics while diligently avoiding "professionalism" and continuing to promote "the unselfish, self giving" that had been the hallmark of all their efforts so far. Hank was not, at this time, advocating for a legally established foundation. His suggestion was simply that they organize a judicious and controlled short-term solution for accepting and allocating contributions; one that would preserve the current amateur nature of the enterprise while simultaneously creating a definite procedure for handling money that would be above reproach should hostile parties later make any investigations into their affairs.

Under Hank's scheme, contributions would be accepted only from "those who have received direct benefit" from their work, i.e., the individuals, and also the companies, who enjoyed the results of this newfound sobriety. These donations would eventually form the basis for an ongoing, self-supporting program that would carry the work of recovery far into the future. Of course there would be those who would want to contribute to The Fund on a "humanitarian basis," and their generosity would necessarily have to be accepted at first; but once sufficient contributions began to come in from individuals and companies who were direct beneficiaries, future humanitarian contributions would be refused and those already collected would be repaid as quickly as possible.

Hank proposed that an honest, "disinterested party, who is not an alcoholic" with some significant business background should be appointed to collect and administer The Fund. This Administrator would be instructed to keep the source of these donations secret—most especially from the recipients—revealing that information only to the appropriate auditor.

So much for the easy part.

More difficult would be how to distribute these funds in a fair and equitable manner; one which would not bestow "any stigma of receiving charity" on the recipients nor lead to the "professionalizing of their work," while at the same time forestalling all "jealousies and political possibilities." Hank suggested that:

> . . . three men initially be given access to the fund. These men to spend that part of their time that seems right toward co-ordinating this work. These men not to feel called upon to make reports or be pressed to show results. These men not to feel that they are drawing a salary, nor to feel that they had a permanent responsibility to carry forward the work on a full time basis.

Although not mentioned by name, the three men in question were obviously himself, Bill Wilson, and Fitz Mayo. Finally, regarding the delicate question of the actual distribution of money, Hank suggested "that these men, when in need of funds, call upon the administrator for them, being subject to his counsel."[20]

This is a summation of the main points of the letter since it wanders around a bit as Hank, in his typically rambling fashion, labors to make each point. (Although Bill Wilson is chastised at times for his poor writing skills, he was an accomplished prose stylist when compared to Hank Parkhurst.) But, however uneven the letter might be, it presented a persuasive enough case for The Fund to capture the attention and then the full support of both Frank Amos and Willard Richardson.

Ruth Hock Enters the Picture

For all of its central importance in the creation of the Alcoholic Fund,* Hank's letter is of interest on a completely different level because the initials "RH" appear at the very bottom, indicating that Hank's secretary, Ruth Hock, was the typist. Ruth had

---

* While the terms "Fund" and "Foundation" were used loosely and almost interchangeably during this time, Frank Amos later made a clear distinction between them, noting that the money from the Alcoholic Fund (founded in April 1938) had been moved to the Alcoholic Foundation (founded in August 1938) once that foundation was legally in place (see Frank B. Amos to W. S. Richardson, August 19 1938, GSO, Box 59, 1938, Folder B[1], Document 1938–114). In *AACOA*, Bill Wilson blends the two without any distinction and thus confuses the issue (see, for instance, p. 15 & 151).

certainly typed up reams of letters and invoices for Honor Dealers since being hired in January 1937, but this March 6, 1938, letter is the first concrete evidence of her having any direct secretarial involvement in the alcoholic side of Hank's activities.* It would, however, not be the last. In the months to come, Ruth would play an increasingly important role in the development and growth of A.A. and especially in the writing of the Big Book.

When she started work with Honor Dealers, Ruth Hock was a twenty-five-year-old married woman with a small son to care for. She was an accomplished typist who claimed she had never had any trouble finding work. "I was a very good secretary," she said years later, and if "I didn't like the various jobs I had at that time and, for one reason or another, I would simply tell them that I was quitting in two weeks and do so and I was always able to get a job. Of course, it was Depression times and you didn't work for much, but I actually came to [Honor Dealers] through an agency. Hank Parkhurst had contacted [them] for a secretary."[21]

Although Ruth was married at this time, her marriage was rapidly disintegrating and because of this she claimed she "needed to work desperately."[22] The fact that Honor Dealers offered her twenty-five dollars a week—three dollars more than she made at her last job—was an opportunity just too good to pass up.[23]

What she didn't realize when accepting this job was how genuinely caring and helpful her new employers would be. "Hank and Bill put me back together by giving me this opportunity and realizing my problems at the time," she later said, and she was so appreciative that "you couldn't have paid me to leave within a few months."[24] Both Hank and Bill quickly became warm friends, nicknaming her "The Duchess" or "Dutch" for short. (Ruth claimed this was brought on by both her German background and her take-charge attitude.)[25]

One instance of their generosity was an attempt to help both Ruth and Florence Rankin, a woman who was desperately trying to get sober at this time. They suggested it would solve both of their problems if Ruth hired Florence as her housekeeper and live-in babysitter and in September 1937, Florence Rankin wrote to Bill Wilson profusely thanking him for finding her the job with the Hocks. Under this arrangement, Florence moved in with Ruth, her husband, and their son, Gene, who was about to start kindergarten. They were not yet divorced, although Florence claimed in her letter that she hadn't "seen a great deal" of Mr. Hock in the three days she had already been there.[26] Ruth was delighted with the arrangement: "She came to live with us and she was a marvelous cook [and] she took wonderful care of my child, she was very good to him."[27]

---

* Ruth's recollections of her employment at Honor Dealers and of the early happenings in A.A. are frequently faulty in the extreme. For example, in a long 1955 letter to Bill Wilson, she claims to have been hired in January 1936—almost a year before the company was even formed. But she also makes no great claim to accuracy and, in fact, her letter to Bill begins with an explicit disavowal of having a good memory: "I do not guarantee the accuracy of any dates I may use [in this letter] . . . neither do I insist that my memory is absolutely accurate." (Ruth Hock to Bill Wilson, November 10, 1955; StSt, AA 326, Box 4, Folder 17)

I have accepted Ruth's claim that she was hired in January, but moved it forward one year to 1937. January seems to be a defensible choice since it is the month Ruth herself mentions and, in addition, it falls right between the actual start date of the business (late November 1936) and the date on the first of many letters preserved in the GSO Archive with Ruth's "RH" initials at the bottom (February 12, 1937: Box 200, Folder I, Bill: Business with Hank P. / 1935–1950).

Unfortunately, this social experiment ended abruptly three weeks later when Florence rather spectacularly started drinking again. According to Ruth: "Everything went fine until it was my birthday and Florence was going to cook me a dinner beyond all dinners with a birthday cake and all the rest of it. And when I got home, Florence was celebrating my birthday—but in a big way!"[28*]

This must have shocked Ruth, who claimed she was not "a bit familiar with alcoholism in any form."[29] Honor Dealers, however, provided her with a quick education on that side of life, as can be seen from her later description of her first day on the job (sent to Bill Wilson in a letter written eighteen years after the fact):

> I walked into the Honor Dealers office in Newark, NJ on Williams Street[**] one Monday morning—was interviewed by Hank—and started to work immediately that morning . . .

> By the end of that very first day I was a very confused female for, if I remember correctly, that first afternoon you had a visitor in your office and I think it was Paul Kellogg.[***] Anyway, the connecting door was left wide open and instead of business phrases what I heard was fragments of a discussion about drunken misery, a miserable wife, and what I thought was a very queer conclusion indeed—that being a drunk was a disease. I remember distinctly feeling that you were all rather hard hearted because at some points there was roaring laughter about various drunken incidents . . .

> The activity of Honor Dealers, as I remember it, was never of paramount importance—it seemed to me after I began to know most of you original men, that it was only a means to an end—that end being to help a bunch of nameless drunks. Having come from a thrifty German family I know that I thought if you two would spend as much energy and thought and enthusiasm on Honor Dealers as you did on drunks you might get somewhere . . .

> Anyway I soon stopped caring whether Honor Dealers was successful or not and became more and more interested in each new face that came along with the alcoholic problem and caring very much whether they made the grade or not . . .

> Well—the activities of Honor Dealers slowly but surely declined and there was more and more correspondence with drunks and more of them showing up in the office. In those days it was part of the procedure, if the

---

* Ruth's twenty-sixth birthday would have been celebrated on Tuesday, October 12, 1937.

** This is another example of Ruth's lack of accuracy in this letter and elsewhere: Honor Dealers didn't move to the William Street address until July 1938, so there is no way that she could have reported to that address on her first day of work for Hank Parkhurst. Such a flagrant mistake would also call into question the fact that the incident described actually took place on her "very first day" there.

*** Paul Kellogg is reputed to have gotten sober in July 1937. If Ruth's identification of Paul and the date are correct, then this may have been during one of his earlier attempts to get sober. Ruth does, however, qualify this identification with a rather specific "I think," so it may have been someone other than Paul who arrived that morning.

prospect was willing to go along, to kneel and pray together—all of you who happened to be there. To me, drunkenness and prayer were both very private activities and I sure did consider all of you a very revolutionary lot—but such likable and interesting revolutionaries![30]

Several years later, Ruth offered another glimpse of the kind of active drunks she had to deal with while working for Honor Dealers during those early days in New Jersey:

> . . . The first one I was really aware of was quite a nice looking gentlemen in a hat and a beautiful black overcoat, [who was] reeling, desperately reeling up the stairs . . . And, he wanted to see Bill Wilson and I insisted on knowing why and what his business was, and I thought that's what secretaries always did. And, he refused to give me any kind of name. He had to see Bill Wilson, and I said that Mr. Wilson was busy. It didn't get me anywhere anyway, but Bill finally heard us out there and came out and roared, "Hello, Bob! And "How are you today? Are we ever glad to see you!" and hauled him into the office.

> . . . They were in there a long time, laughing their heads off and I couldn't understand that. Here was this poor fellow, under the [influence], really in bad shape with liquor, and they were thinking it was funny, and he was telling them how he was afraid to go down the stairs alone because he might fall down, and that amused Bill.

> You know, the door was open . . . and the first thing I know, there was Hank and this man, Bob, and Bill [and they] were all kneeling around the desk and praying, and I desperately didn't know whether I was going to [stay or not] —I really didn't—it really worried me whether I ought to stay or not. I was 25 but I didn't think my father would approve at all! I really didn't.[31]*

Obviously, this was not going to be your typical run-of-the-mill secretarial job!

The Alcoholic Fund Is Established

The Monday after receiving Parkhurst's letter with his suggestions for the establishment and possible structure for The Fund, Frank Amos wrote back praising the proposal:

March 21st, 1938

Mr. Henry G. Parkhurst
No. 11 Hill St.
Newark, New Jersey

Dear Mr. Parkhurst:

---

* Typical of the problems that arise with many of Ruth's recollections, the former quote says that on her first day of work she encountered Paul Kellogg (who sounds sober in that account) while this quote relates that "the first one" to come to the office was a man named Bob (who was clearly drunk).

Your thoughts on the alcoholic work, expressed in your fine letter of March 16th, strike me as basically sound. I will show this letter to Mr. Richardson this afternoon and then should like to arrange for an early conference with you.

Thank you very much for writing it.

Sincerely,

Frank B. Amos[32]

Hank's letter was then duly passed on to Richardson, who was also favorably impressed, sending Amos a handwritten note a little over a week later on March 30:

Dear Frank:

I have read and reread this letter from Henry Parkhurst. It presents an interesting and I think valuable idea and method in a clear and complete manner. As I understand conditions this idea as well as that of possibly securing contributions or gifts on the plan suggested by Mr Wilson is to be further discussed and acted upon only on the decision of the leaders of the Group.

WSR[33]

Wilson's already formulated plan for securing contributions or gifts along with Hank's recently suggested organization of The Fund, were, according to Richardson, to be discussed in detail and decided upon by the leaders of the Group before moving forward. But at this point, Hank, Bill, and the other members of the New York group were certainly in agreement with all of these proposals, leaving only the leader of the Akron group to be consulted. It is interesting to note that later correspondence clearly indicates that if Bill did have any conversations with Dr. Bob about these matters, they were confined solely to the structure of this proposed mechanism for distributing the Rockefeller money (and any other monies they might collect), but did not include any talk about the larger issue of their plan to create a full-fledged foundation at some time in the near future. At this point, Bob's only 'need to know' was about how the Rockefeller money would be distributed to him, so that was the extent of Bill's discussion with him.

Dr. Bob Smith readily agreed to the establishment of the Alcoholic Fund and the distribution plan for the Rockefeller contribution. It is, in fact, hard to imagine he would have had significant reservations about any aspect of Bill Wilson's plans at this point or, for that matter, any objections to the future creation of a foundation. After all, he was in desperate financial straits and eager to start getting some of the money Rockefeller had donated for his support. On the other hand, it is equally difficult to imagine that Bob would then broadcast this news about the Alcoholic Fund or the monies he would soon be receiving from it to anyone within the Akron Fellowship. Taking money "for the work" was still a taboo subject in Ohio.

Once Bill had signaled his approval of Hank's proposal and Willard Richardson had given his blessing, Frank Amos accepted the position of the "disinterested party, who is not an alcoholic" to administer The Fund. He had already set up a special checking account to handle John D. Rockefeller Jr.'s contribution at a local branch of the Chase National Bank and this became the vehicle for handling all of The Fund's finances going forward. The first check drawn from that account was on March 18; it was for $500 and made out to Robert H. Smith M.D. of Akron, Ohio.[34]

Charles Towns of Towns Hospital Contributes to the Fund

Bill later said with regularity that they were unable to raise any money at this time beyond the single contribution from John D. Rockefeller Jr. for Dr. Bob Smith; otherwise, he said, "we didn't get one red cent, not one."[35] But, despite Wilson's repeated claims to the contrary, there was one person other than Rockefeller who was willing to contribute money to this fledgling movement and Bill had certainly factored him into his suggested plan for raising money through contributions and gifts.

That person was Charles B. Towns, the owner of Towns Hospital in New York City.* Not mentioning Towns in his later stories is another one of those understandable simplifications of the A.A. creation myth that Wilson told repeatedly throughout his life. The story of John D. Rockefeller Jr.'s contribution involved one of the most famous and richest men in the world and it was dramatic in the extreme. Mentioning that money was also contributed by Charles Towns would mean having to also explain in some detail who he was and why someone running a drying-out hospital was giving money to A.A. and, even more problematic, why A.A. was accepting money from him. In short, it made for an uncomfortable story, one that just begged for further elaboration and would likely be subject to criticism; so Charles Town's contributions to the movement were summarily deleted from Bill's version of the story.

Towns Hospital was a "very lucrative" establishment with a fashionable Central Park West address where it "catered to New York's social elite." The hospital had been founded in 1901 and, according to one reliable source, "was no more than a fancy, very expensive detoxification facility." It was expensive and patients were required to pre-pay for their treatment: "Towns would not admit anyone unless the fee was paid upon admission or a 'backer' guaranteed to pay the fee, which was $200 to $350 for a five-day stay."[36] **

Towns Hospital was the facility where Bill Wilson had gone to detox at least three times in 1933 and 1934 and where he had his "white light" experience during his final admission in mid-December 1934.*** Following that last visit, Towns generously

---

*   See Neidhardt's well-researched *King Charles of New York City* for an in-depth look at this fascinating man and his life.

**   Bill Wilson's brother-in-law, Dr. Leonard Strong, seems to have paid for all of his expensive stays at Towns Hospital although Bill implied that his mother may have covered the expense of his last admission (*Bill W., My First 40 Years*, p. 104). [Thanks to Arthur S. of Arlington, TX for bringing this last citation to my attention.]

***   There is some confusion over whether Bill was at Towns Hospital three times or four; a confusion caused, once again, by Wilson's bad memory and his casual attitude about details. While the late 1933 and December 1934 admissions are universally accepted, the question of whether Bill was in Towns once or twice mid-year in 1934 is questionable. In support of four visits, see for instance, *Pass It On*, which reports Bill in Towns Hospital "in the autumn of 1933" (p. 100), "a second time" [early summer? 1934] (p. 106), again "by midsummer of 1934," (p. 108) and finally in December 1934 (pp. 119–20). Most especially, see Kurtz (*Not-God*, p. 310, n. 26) for an informative and balanced treatment of the issue.

allowed Bill to wander the wards, preaching his own brand of recovery to any patient who might be willing to listen, despite the fact that he was personally skeptical about Bill's religious approach and originally uncomfortable with the enthusiastic cooperation extended to Wilson by his own Chief-of-Staff, Dr. William Silkworth.[37]

But by the time Bill was two years sober, Charles Towns had been won over by the impressive work he was doing. Seven years into the Great Depression Towns Hospital had still not bounced back to the level of prosperity it had enjoyed before the big financial collapse in October 1929. The days of the Roaring Twenties, "when wealthy actors and famous playboys had been willing to pour thousands of dollars a week into Towns's till for a little discreet drying out"[38] were long gone; but Charles thought he saw a way to increase his patient admissions along with his profits if he could just forge a working relationship with Bill Wilson.

In December 1936,* when Wilson was just two years sober, Charles sat Bill down and proposed he join the staff of the hospital as "a lay therapist," explaining the position would bring with it "an office, a decent drawing account, and a very healthy slice of the profits." Charles was confident that with Bill's help the hospital could be brought back to those lucrative 1920s profit levels and he produced several old financial statements to emphasize exactly how many "thousands of dollars a month" they could share between themselves if they were successful. Charles also made a strong argument that such an alliance would be "perfectly ethical;" after all, there was nothing wrong with becoming a lay therapist, was there? Why shouldn't Bill convert his newfound talent for getting people sober into a job that would produce a living wage for himself and for Lois? "Don't you see [that] you're getting the bad end of this deal?" Towns argued. "You are starving to death, and your wife is working at that [department] store. All around you, these drunks are getting well and making money, but you're giving this work [your] full time, and still you're broke. It isn't fair."[39]**

In late 1936, Wilson was deeply entrenched in the New York Oxford Group and the idea of his group financing their own chain of hospitals was still ten months in the future, so this offer seemed like the perfect way for Bill to successfully deliver the message of recovery to many more people. Surely, making an alliance with this respectable and well-run establishment would allow him to expand his reach while simultaneously helping to put Towns Hospital back on a solid financial basis.

It was a really fabulous offer!

Wilson later claimed he experienced "a few twinges of conscience" over this proposal, but it was an appealing prospect on a number of levels and he quickly convinced himself that Charles Towns was 100 percent correct about it being perfectly ethical. In fact, while riding the subway back home from that meeting, Bill decided he was

---

* There is considerable debate about the date of this offer from Towns, but December 1936 is surely the most likely. From January to October 1937, Bill was working for Quaw and Foley and would not have been tempted by this job. After October 1937, he was singularly focused on raising money for hospitals, paid missionaries, and the writing of a book—right up until the book's publication in April 1939.

** The dialogue quoted here is from Bill's much later *AACOA* retelling of the story (1957) so the reference in December 1936 to Lois's job at Loeser's Department Store, which she left in March 1936 (*Lois Remembers*, p. 104), is another example of Wilson's lack of accuracy about details. By December 1936, Lois was doing free-lance interior decorating jobs but, as she admits, she was so bad at properly billing for her services that she "brought little money into the household" (*Lois Remembers*, p. 105).

being divinely 'guided' (á la the Oxford Group) to accept this wonderful opportunity to become a professional lay therapist. After all, doesn't the Bible tell us the "laborer is worthy of his hire?"[40] Bill felt he *should* be paid for what he was doing.

This job offer is one of the more fateful turning points in A.A.'s history. Who knows what might have happened if Bill Wilson had actually become a lay therapist, working in the recovery field under the auspices of Towns Hospital? There is surely no predicting the "what ifs" of history, but it is highly unlikely A.A. would have ever developed in the way it did if the founder of the movement had sidelined himself at this early stage of its growth by becoming a paid professional who was focused on his own share of the profits being generated by a 'drying out' hospital in New York City.

When Towns made this offer there were perhaps five sober members (along with a smaller number of transients who were still having trouble with their drinking) attending the Sunday gatherings in Brooklyn.* At the next meeting, Bill enthusiastically described this wonderful new opportunity and was immediately met by a stony and disapproving silence from the group. According to his later recounting, "one of my friends"—almost certainly Hank Parkhurst who was never bashful about speaking his own mind and who certainly had the most influence in the group after Bill—finally broke the oppressive silence and said: "Don't you realize that you can never become a professional? . . . You tell us Charlie's proposal is ethical. Sure, it's ethical. But what we've got [here] won't run on ethics only; it has to be better. Sure, Charlie's idea is good, but it isn't good enough. This is a matter of life and death, Bill, and nothing but the very best will do."[41] The rest of the regular members quickly chimed in with their agreement. Severely chastised, Wilson immediately abandoned both his personal 'divine guidance' and his desire for gainful employment and acknowledged the greater wisdom of the group. He turned down the job at Towns Hospital.[42]**

Charles Towns was deeply disappointed, but he continued to have "a genuine personal interest" in the work Bill and the others were doing. As Wilson later told Amos, he was "a man who really likes to help people" and who was "prepared to help us in every possible way, whether he got any money in return or not."[43] In short, Towns was exactly the kind of man Bill could approach for help now that the New York group had been left with nothing but their own meager resources to fall back on.

Bill met with Charles and explained that while Rockefeller's contribution certainly sounded impressive, it had been specifically earmarked for Bob Smith and that he and the others would be forced to struggle along on their own. How could they possibly keep up all the work they were doing with alcoholics in New York, New Jersey, and Maryland without at least some sort of financial assistance? Bill then confided to Charles the details of the recently created Alcoholic Fund and their plans to incorporate as a legally recognized, fully functional, tax-exempt foundation at some

---

*   The meetings in New York were held on Sunday until they were moved to Tuesday nights on June 7, 1938 (Lois's diary, 1938).

**   In *Twelve Steps and Twelve Traditions* (first edition, pp. 140–42), Wilson—incorrectly placing the event in 1938 (as he incorrectly placed it in 1937 on p. 99 of AACOA)—characterized this meeting and its guidance as the foundational moment of A.A.'s Second Tradition: For our group purpose there is but one ultimate authority—a loving God as He may express Himself in our group conscience. Our leaders are but trusted servants; they do not govern.

time in the near future, emphasizing that both of these projects had the full backing of the Rockefeller people.

On April 1, 1938, Charles Towns responded to Bill's appeal by writing a $500 check to the Alcoholic Fund, noting on the check stub that the money was going to Frank Amos, the man who was now responsible for distributing all of the money collected by the Fund.[44] Much to Bill's relief and satisfaction, Charles specified the money was to be used exclusively to support the work being done by Bill Wilson, Hank Parkhurst, and Fitz Mayo.[45] Split between the three of them, this was not a tremendous amount of money, but they were delighted nonetheless.

Things were *finally* going in the right direction.

Fundraising Stalls and the Need for a Book Is Acknowledged

Having successfully structured and launched The Fund, Hank and Bill could now begin to solicit donations from the rich in earnest and they had wasted no time in doing exactly that. Bill, for instance, reports in one of his letters that he would be "calling on [the] General Motors man" on Monday, March 21 asking for financial support and stating confidently "there is nothing to worry about—not even money. It's all soon in the bag—I think."[46] Although their hope of raising one large sum of money directly from John D. Rockefeller Jr. had been dashed, they now had references and contact information for other potentially generous donors given to them by John D. Jr.'s friends. Securing funds from a variety of people would obviously take longer than if they had been able to get one large and decisive contribution from Rockefeller, but with the support and backing of his closest associates they were confident that the doors—and the checkbooks—of the wealthy would now be open to them. Unfortunately, this didn't prove to be the case.

Bill and Hank were also well aware they needed to establish a real foundation in order to secure the all-important tax-exempt status that would be so critical to their success, but the expense of setting up such a complex legal entity presented them with a formidable obstacle: how could they possibly pay for it? Until a proper solution to that problem could be found, they would just have to wait and meanwhile make whatever appeals they could for donations to the Alcoholic Fund based on the promise of future tax benefits.

But Bill Wilson was not good at waiting. Worse than that, he was haunted by the vision of alcoholics all over the country who were dying because they had no access to a solution he was convinced could save their lives. Six months earlier Bill had challenged the Akron members by asking them how they could possibly sleep at night when there were drinkers in California who wouldn't get the message of recovery until it reached them by word of mouth at some time in the distant future.[47] Now, half a year later, the movement had certainly grown locally in Akron and New York, but the drunks in Los Angeles and San Francisco were not one step closer to relief than they had been the previous October.

Bill's growing awareness that his more ambitious plans were completely dependent on large donations from the rich—and that the amount of time required to raise that much money was substantial—gradually began to shift his attention back to the third proposal he had made six months earlier: the writing of a book. A book, he realized, was certain to produce faster results and it was the perfect vehicle for clarifying their method and then delivering that message of recovery into every area of the country. In addition, when compared to hospitals and missionaries, a book would take far less time to complete and it would cost them significantly less money to produce.

Lack of money was their central problem according to Wilson. The reality was that after six months of hard work and high hopes, their fundraising efforts had been a dismal failure. Aside from a grudging, one-time donation of $5,000 from John D. Rockefeller Jr. and the $500 contribution from Charles Towns, not one other rich person or foundation had come forward to give them any money. These two contributions were enough to keep the leader's heads above water for a short time, but they did nothing to advance the larger plan of saving alcoholics all around the country.

Bill's goal and overall strategy remained the same—he wanted to spread the word as far and as fast as possible—but his experience during the past six months showed something more was needed. What could they be doing differently right now to reach more people, more quickly? Bill's, and almost certainly Hank's, answer to that question was a growing commitment to writing a book that would effectively present their method for getting sober to drinkers all across America.

The Book Idea Is Tested in Akron

With these thoughts in mind, Bill realized it was time for him to make another trip to Akron. If they were going to write this book then he would surely need the support and help of the people in Ohio to get that done. It was not the kind of job he was planning to take on all by himself.

He left New York for Akron on Wednesday, April 20.[48] Traveling with him was the newly sober Bert Taylor[49]* who would play a number of important roles in early A.A. history, not least of which would come in mid-1939 when he used his fashionable Fifth Avenue clothing business as collateral to secure a $1,000 loan so that copies of the still-unpaid-for book, *Alcoholics Anonymous*, could be liberated from the printer for sales and distribution.[50]** But, at this time, it seems Bill was hoping for more than just some personal companionship from Bert. Here was a man who had managed to get sober before losing everything he had and who might possibly be convinced to help with their fundraising efforts in a very direct way. And, if Bert's present financial condition wouldn't allow him to make a personal contribution, perhaps he could be convinced to approach one or more of his wealthy clients for donations to help finance the book they were planning.

---

* Herbert Taylor's sobriety date is frequently given as May 1938, but Bill mentions him as a new "prospect" as early as March 21, 1938 (Bill [Wilson] to Darling Susie [?], March 21, 1938: StSt, WGW 102.7, Box 25, Folder 24).

** Bert's business and then his apartment were also the sites of the first A.A. meetings held in Manhattan. In addition, Bert was, at one point, president of Works Publishing Company and he also served as an early trustee of the Alcoholic Foundation.

The two men left New York City together and Bill spent at least ten days away from home. Whether Bert was with him throughout this entire trip is unknown, although it is likely that they drove out to Ohio (and perhaps even back) in Bert's car.* In Akron, there were long conversations with Dr. Bob, and Bill participated in several private and group meetings with other members of the Akron "Alcoholic Squad" hoping to get some positive feedback on his plan for what should be done next.

The suspicion many Akron members felt toward Bill Wilson and their distrust of his motives had not dissipated much in the six months since that turbulent meeting the previous fall, and now here he was again with more of his grand ideas. Wally Gillam was one sober member who had attended the contentious October meeting, but seventeen years later he didn't remember the book being mentioned at that time.** His memory said that the argument in late 1937 was all about the money Bill wanted to raise for hospitals and missionaries. But, he later recalled, it was during these several meetings in April 1938—the ones held "after [Frank Amos] came out here"—that the proposed book was first brought up. "Two or three [meetings were held] at Williams's house" and two more "at the Lucas's a little later,"*** he claimed, and it was then the idea of writing a book was raised and discussed in such detail. Gillam's memories are surely selective, but they do underline the fact that the major issue being discussed during these April 1938 meetings was the writing of a book.[51]

Wally remembered Bill casually sitting on the floor as he made his proposal for a book at the Williams's house one night,**** but the Akron group was even more resistant to this New York idea than they had been in October. Several of the arguments raised earlier—for instance, those about Jesus and his apostles not needing any written or printed literature—were likely brought up and revisited in detail. But, what most troubled the people opposed to Bill's idea was the frightening consequences they would face if such a book were actually published. How could they possibly cope with all the requests for help that would then pour in on them? They would be overwhelmed! For all of Bill Wilson's grand plans, there was still no structure in place to deal with that sort of deluge, nor was there any likelihood one could be funded and created before a

---

*   As noted earlier, at this time, Bill was still doing occasional freelance work for his former employers, Quaw and Foley, and he (along with Bert?) may well have made a side trip to Anderson, Indiana to pursue a business venture for them on this same trip. See Wm. G. Wilson to Mr. Charles Parcelles [sic], July [*but really August*] 1, 1938 (GSO, Box 59, 1938, Folder B, Documents 1938–31 to 1938–34) mentioning that he had lately "been made a Director of the Pierce Governor Co." in Anderson, IN. (A contemporary ad for this company's products can be found in *Popular Mechanics* magazine, Volume 70, Number 3, September 1938, p. 127A.) Bill was still a Director of this company in 1940 as is attested to by several pieces of "To the Directors" correspondence that were sent to him by Pierce on January 24, 1940 (GSO, Box 200, Folder I, Bill: Business with Hank P., 1937-1950). Finally, it is interesting to speculate whether or not the Pierce mentioned in Lois's List of Historical Dates—Oct 1937–May 1945 ("Tom Pierce came into group in '38") had a familial relationship with this company and is perhaps the reason Bill got involved with the company in the first place. (Dec 13 [1937]; StSt, LBW 203, Box 35, Folder 4).

**   Wally's memory is almost surely at fault here since all other accounts and recollections universally confirm that the writing of a book was definitely a part of the package of proposals that Bill offered in October 1937.

***   Most likely the home of Tom and Maybelle Lucas. Tom's story, "My Wife and I" appeared in the first edition of *Alcoholics Anonymous*, pp. 287–95.

****   This is another classic example of Bill Wilson's casual demeanor when among friends. Some, like Henrietta Seiberling, took grave offense at this nonchalance. Henrietta, who was frequently vocal about her low opinion of Bill, once noted critically that he was "never standing when he could sit, and never sitting when he could lie down" (Ernest Kurtz in private correspondence with the author on September 16, 2011, quoting from his April 6, 1976 interview with Henrietta Seiberling. For a published reference to that interview, see Kurtz, *Not-God*, p. 315, n. 63).

book was published, *and* the Ohio people were generally not in favor of building such a structure in the first place.

'Wouldn't it be better,' they argued, 'if we just continued with the word-of-mouth program that has worked so well for us so far? If we keep doing what we are doing now, the message will get out to those people in California eventually. But, if you go ahead with your plan for a book, it will surely create an impossible situation for everyone and most likely destroy all of the good work we have done so far.'

Wilson was a consummate politician so the fact that he did not call for a vote during these April meetings is telling; he could only have been distressed by the resistance he felt on almost every side in Akron.[*] Unlike the meeting six months earlier, Bill was forced to leave Ohio without securing a mandate for the plan he considered so essential to the future success of their movement.[**]

Lois Holds Down the Fort

While Bill was away, the hectic pace never let up at the Wilson household in Brooklyn. A day or two after he left, Lois wrote him a warm letter ("I love you and I'm so lonely without you") recounting all of the comings and goings at Clinton Street, which included supper with Joe and Ora Taylor, some of Russ and Wes's latest escapades, the arrival of Fitz Mayo "an hour after you left," along with a pending visit from Florence Rankin who was "coming here to spend the night." In Bill's absence, there was some uncertainty over where the regular Sunday meeting should be held, but at the last minute it was decided—the decision seems to have been made by Lois and Kathleen Parkhurst—to keep it in Brooklyn rather than move it out to the Parkhurst home in New Jersey.[52]

Right after the meeting ended on Sunday night, Lois wrote Bill another warm and chatty letter ("I love you darling, and miss you terribly") that included one particular paragraph offering a rare glimpse of how early A.A. meetings were conducted in New York—this one held at the Wilson home in Brooklyn on April 24, 1938.

> There were 14 here today. I thought it was going to be terrible because all the old time men went off in little groups and left the two new guys with the women and Fitz was sick and terribly off the ball. But later everyone got together and Fitz made a grand and short witness. Wes was fine and Paul funny and tearful at the same time. Hank led.[53]

More details would be appreciated, but this is all Lois tells us and it is considerably more than we are offered anywhere else in contemporary documents about these early New York meetings. Few of her letters at the time mention meetings and most of her Sunday (and later Tuesday) diary entries for 1938 simply say "seminar"—her tongue-in-cheek way of referring to the weekly gathering of alcoholics.[54]

---

[*] Other than Bert Taylor, Bill had no other New York support at this April meeting . . . in contrast to the meeting held in the previous October.

[**] This reconstruction of the April meetings in Akron is based primarily on Wally's recollections (Oral History Transcriptions, Transcript Record of Wally [Gillam], Akron, Ohio, 12/12/54: GSO, Box 1 of 2, Box 1: 304680980) and Bill Wilson's long letter to Dr. Bob Smith in late June 1938 (Bill Wilson to Dr. Bob Smith, [June 22, 23 or 24], 1938: GSO, Box 59, 1938, Folder B, Documents 1938-25 to 1938-30).

Interesting here is her candid critique of the "old time men" for ignoring the two new men, leaving them with the women as they pursue their own conversations in smaller groups. (Was she reporting this to Bill with the implication that it would have been different if he had been there or was this just part of an ongoing conversation they were having between themselves about the proper conduct for participants at these weekly gatherings?) Although this is a minimal description, it does sound as if the speaker-discussion format that is still common in A.A. meetings today was already well established: Hank Parkhurst is the leader for the evening and Fitz Mayo is the featured speaker; his lead is then followed by comments made by other attendees, Lois noting Wes and Paul's participation in particular. (Also of interest is Lois's brief description of the regular inclusion of the wives at these meetings and the uncertainty over whether or not she is including them in the head count of fourteen.)

Besides making arrangements for this meeting, Lois had been busy with several other matters during the previous two days. She notes that since her last letter she had enjoyed "a cocktail supper and movie" with Ora Taylor on Saturday night and spent part of the weekend playing detective as she tried to determine who had made an expensive $3.65 call to Richmond, Virginia that showed up unexpectedly on their phone bill. She finally discovered that Tom, one of their current residents, was the culprit; he had called to find out "if an old girl [friend] of his had married." Lois also reminded Bill that she was leaving on Tuesday to visit her two sisters, Barb and Kitty—something she had been looking forward to "more than I have looked forward to anything for a year at least"—and wouldn't be back until Saturday. In her absence she had arranged for the activities at the house to be supervised first by Fitz Mayo and then by Jim Burwell.[55]

One thing clearly evident here is how much constant, frantic activity was going on among all of these New York alcoholics as they tried to stay sober together and to spread the message of recovery to others.

Things were definitely not boring in the Wilson household in 1938.

CHAPTER SEVEN

Bill's Stories

~Late May 1938~

Bill Wilson came home from Akron unsure of what to do next. He and Hank would continue trying to raise money for the new Alcoholic Fund from individuals, businesses, and other foundations, but what, if anything, should be done about this plan for a book? Most of the people in Akron were uncomfortable with the proposal and some of them were actively opposed to it. Maybe it *was* a bad idea.

It is not clear how openly and vigorously Bill had promoted the idea of writing a book in New York before he went to Akron, but it was definitely a central topic of discussion immediately after his return. Two months later* he wrote Dr. Bob a long letter explaining what had happened: "After getting home from Akron I had about concluded to let the book idea lie quiet while people thought it over." Certainly the real possibility of writing a book was something "you people had only just begun to consider" and the objections raised about the "dangers and difficulties of such a venture; particularly [the] fear of undesirable publicity" seems to have struck a cautionary note with Wilson.[1]

However, the Eastern members were typically unimpressed with Akron's objections. They wholeheartedly got behind the idea of writing their own book. "A lot of [the New York] people" thought the book was a great idea, and the most ardent champion turned out to be Frank Amos who was "quite afire" with the project, telling Bill that, in his opinion, "something ought to be started right away."[2] Since they were both much more in touch (and in greater sympathy) with their so-far unsuccessful fundraising efforts, it was clear to the New York members and the Rockefeller men that the amount of money needed for hospitals and missionaries was not likely to be forthcoming anytime

---

* The substance of this letter makes it clear that this is the first time Wilson had communicated with Smith since leaving Akron at the end of the previous April, almost two full months earlier.

soon and that the book proposal offered a far less expensive and much more acceptable vehicle for spreading the message of recovery quickly. With such limited resources, this was the place where they should be putting their time and energies.

Whatever part Bill may have played in these arguments (was he convinced or was he convincing?), he quickly adopted the position that a book was essential for them to move forward at this time. As he explained to Dr. Bob two months after the fact, he decided it was critical for them to make at least a tentative start on the book project:

> Considering the rate at which we grow, [Frank Amos], and others including myself, began to think that publicity would come anyhow. Why then not our own anonymous view of ourselves thus precluding the possibility that some one else garbled the situation before we had a chance to say anything. Thus we came to the conclusion that in a tentative way, a beginning should be made. In this fashion, having some definite proposals laid out and some printing done, we would have a concrete basis for discussion.[3]

And so, despite all the strong opposition he had so recently encountered in Akron, Bill Wilson began to write the Big Book in May 1938 and he did so without telling anyone in Ohio he had made that decision or that he had already begun to work on the project. Akron wouldn't be informed about any of these developments until Bill wrote to Bob in late June.

Parkhurst's Fundraising Plan for the Big Book

Besides Frank Amos, the New Yorker who was most excited about writing a book was Hank Parkhurst. This was definitely his kind of project, one that would utilize all of his formidable sales and promotional skills and allow him to make a substantial contribution to the growth of their new movement. Hank took a businessman's approach to most things—rarely missing an economic opportunity—and soon after Bill's return from Akron, he began to formulate a plan for how they might raise and then distribute the funds needed for the book project. Hank's persistence and creativity in relation to financing are just two of the great assets he would bring to the book project—without which the Big Book as we know it would never have been written and published.

Hank discussed these ideas in detail with Bill Wilson and Bert Taylor and then wrote one of his rambling letters addressed to both men in which he recapped his plan to make sure "we are thinking alike."[4]* The letter detailed how much money he thought would be needed to finance the writing and publication of a book and outlined how they might administer the collection and distribution of that money. Although this first version of Hank's plan to raise money for the Big Book was not successful, it does provide some interesting insights into how both he and Bill Wilson understood their situation at this time and how they planned to cope with it.

---

* Because this is such a poorly written letter, it *may* be misinterpreted here. Given that possibility, the letter is printed in full in Appendix II on page 613, inviting a different, more cogent reading by others should that be possible.

It is also worth noting that this May letter contains the germ of the idea which, five months later, would blossom into Hank's formation of The One Hundred Men Corporation. The fundamental difference between these two proposals was that this earlier version was premised on "donations" (really loans that would be repaid as quickly as possible from the book's profits) rather than on the sale of stock that would have cash value and also pay the shareholders ongoing dividends from the profits.

Hank begins his letter by reminding the two men of the plan to expand the current Alcoholic Fund into a fully-fledged foundation: "a non-profit foundation is being formed for the purpose of disseminating funds for the furtherance of work among alcoholics." It is his understanding "that donations are to be solicited to this fund for the purpose of financing the writing and publishing of a book for alcoholics." In Parkhurst's opinion, the "minimum amount" the foundation should raise for this publishing work is $15,000 and these donations should be solicited not as outright contributions, but with the understanding that they are loans to be repaid as soon as possible once the book was published and had begun to generate profits.

Working in tandem with this fundraising foundation, Hank proposed there would also be a "private marketing organization" (he also refers to it as a "publishing firm" in the letter) that would oversee the writing, marketing, and publication of the book. This independent concern would be responsible for paying all of the expenses needed to support these efforts both before and after the book was published. Note that, even at this early date, Hank Parkhurst was firmly committed to the idea that they should be publishing this book themselves.

Although Hank suggests $15,000 as the fundraising goal, he speculates that they will most likely need only $10,000 to bring the book to market. Should this prove to be true, once the book is published, "any remainder of the donations" would be "returned pro-rata to the subscribers," i.e., the remaining $5,000 would immediately be apportioned and returned to the individual donors.

Then, as the books began to sell, the first fifty cents of profit on each book would be returned through the Foundation to the lenders. Once the first 20,000 copies had been sold, the $10,000 balance in loans would have been paid back in full. In addition, he noted that after all these loans had been retired, the ongoing income of fifty cents per book would go directly to the new Foundation for their continuing work with alcoholic projects.

Although he began by claiming his reason for writing this letter was "to see if we are thinking alike," Hank's real purpose may have been fundraising. In the final line of the letter, he asks Bert (who was the principal addressee): "I understand that you are going to approach a certain individual for the sum of $500.00—who would put this $500.00 in for immediate promotional work?" This question seems less directed at Bert than at his prospective donor and the entire letter appears to have been crafted so that Bert could show it to one of his wealthy customers as evidence of the genuineness of his request for a $500 loan.[5]

It is more than likely that Bert did present this ambitious plan to his wealthy prospect, but it was ultimately unsuccessful. Later minutes of the Alcoholic Foundation show no such loan was ever made at this time.[6]

Unraveling the Plan

Without knowing more details from the prior conversations among these three men, it can be difficult to accurately summarize this letter. The first two paragraphs outlining Hank's plan are relatively straightforward, carefully explaining the details, noted above. But the third paragraph, one of Parkhurst's more tortured efforts, can be a challenge to unravel:

> Now we have the situation of the initial subscribers having been entirely paid off and the $10,000.00 would be entirely between the fund and the publishing firm. In this case all net profits of the publishing firm would go to the fund to the amount of $10,000.00—this in addition to the 50¢ per book, assured profit to the fund. To simplify all of the above, if the book is profitable the fund will receive 50¢ for every book that has been issued. The expense of writing and marketing would have been entirely paid out of the profits secured by the marketing company.

To bring some clarity to this cryptic paragraph, it must first be noted that something important has not been mentioned anywhere in this letter, namely that there will be more than a fifty cents profit on each book sold. Exactly how much that profit might be is never specified, but Hank clearly expects it to be substantial.[*] He does state categorically that "the marketing concern [has] assured the fund of 50¢ profit per book," but he never directly says how much more profit there will be from the sale of each book, only noting that these will become the "profits secured by the marketing company."

Given that additional information, one sentence here still needs clarification: "In this case all net profits of the publishing firm would go to the fund to the amount of $10,000.00—this in addition to the 50¢ per book, assured profit to the fund." It is the "this in addition to the 50¢ per book" that is confusing: Where does this extra $10,000 come from? The key phrase for understanding this is Hank's assurance "the fund will receive 50¢ for *every book that has been issued* [emphasis added]." Hank was promising the foundation that the "publishing firm" would not only pay the fund $10,000 to satisfy the donors (at the rate of fifty cents per book), it would also reimburse them an *additional* fifty cents per book (out of "all net profits of the publishing firm") until that $10,000 payout to the donors had been fully reimbursed. This would certainly delay the accumulation of profits by the "private marketing organization," but the foundation would then be able to claim they had actually received "50¢ for every book that had been issued"—over and above the necessary repayments to donors.

---

[*] Hank's instincts on the amount of money to be made on each book was confirmed months later when he and Bill visited an industry professional, Richard J. Walsh, the owner of the John Day Publishing Company, who predicted a net profit of $1.27 per book. (Printed promotional stock prospectus entitled "Alcoholics Anonymous," GSO, Box 59, 1939, Folder C, Documents 1939-144 to 157, p. 8).

To use Hank's own phrase, "to simplify all of the above," the "marketing concern" was committed to using the first part of the book profits to repay the $10,000 in loans and then to give the foundation their promised fifty cents *for each book sold*, all the while paying all the expenses associated with the writing, printing, publishing, and promotion of the project. After those expenses had been met, whatever "net profits" remained would be retained by the "publishing firm."

This leaves one other large and rather important element of the plan that was not being mentioned in any way. Under this scheme, Hank and Bill would not only be responsible for the activities and administration of the "marketing company," they would also be the owners of this "publishing firm" and, as such, they would stand to reap whatever financial benefits might come to the "private marketing organization." Hank does clearly note that this marketing-publishing firm would be "private" and, although the owners of the proposed company are never mentioned by name, they could only be Hank Parkhurst and Bill Wilson.*

Although this particular plan of Hank's never came to fruition, this is not the last time we'll see these two men putting themselves in line to be the primary recipients of whatever profits the book might generate. In October, Hank would roll out an almost identical scenario for The One Hundred Men Corporation, based on the sale of stock rather than loaned donations. But beyond that one difference, almost all of the other essential elements of that proposal had already been created, considered, and carefully formulated five months earlier.

Fundraising for the Book Falters; Charles Towns to the Rescue Again

Immediately after the Alcoholic Fund was established, Willard Richardson compiled a list with detailed information about a group of "wealthy men who might be solicited" and passed it on to Bill Wilson.[7] "Armed with [this] list of millionaires," Hank and Bill "gleefully set to work" trying to make appointments with people from this new pool of rich New Yorkers.[8] Once again, their spirits ran high. With this invaluable contact information and a referral from Richardson, it seemed impossible for them to fail in their efforts to secure donations to support the writing of their book.

Unfortunately, they quickly found they had to deal with the same exact objections they had encountered the previous October and November, only now these arguments were coming from a completely different set of prospects. This must have been frustrating in the extreme. Both Hank and Bill believed they had made some significant progress in the past six months, but here they were again, right back at the beginning. It was as if nothing at all had changed. According to Bill, the excuses they had to endure were fairly consistent, including a complete lack of understanding about alcoholism in general, uncomprehending questions about their methods of recovery, followed by demands for scientific proof to support their claims of success. Even more exasperating was the frequently raised question: 'Why should we try to save drunks,

---

* It would make no sense to suppose that the profits would be retained by some as yet unimagined extension of the recovery Fellowship; monies meant to benefit alcoholics could just as easily be directed to the proposed Alcoholic Foundation whose charter was to do exactly that (i.e., to support "the furtherance of work among alcoholics") rather than going to some other "organization."

anyway? Wouldn't this money be better spent preventing alcoholism in the first place rather than wasting it on these people who are already beyond any help?' It was as if there was a solid wall of misunderstanding, apathy, and second-guessing surrounding these rich New Yorkers and it was a wall these two men just couldn't seem to get over.

As Bill later confessed, "We were terribly disheartened."[9]

There was, however, one small success to celebrate that May. Bill Wilson had turned, once again, to his friend, Charles Towns, hoping he might convince him to make a loan along the lines of Hank's fundraising proposal to get the book project off the ground.* Charles was a successful businessman who had witnessed the ravages of alcoholism on a daily basis and he had a strong faith in this new method of getting sober; surely he would appreciate the huge potential human return on his small investment if it produced a book that would quickly and effectively spread the message of recovery to people all around the country.

The two men met in mid-May and Bill explained the current state of their affairs, including the desperate need to begin work on the book—a need, he pointed out, that was strongly supported by Frank Amos and the other Rockefeller friends. He also noted the fact that the $500 Charles had given them six weeks earlier had already been spent. Wilson must have made an extremely convincing case, for on May 18 Charles Towns contributed another $500 to the Alcoholic Fund, noting on his check stub that this payment was being sent to Frank Amos as an "Advance on [the] book."[10]

Given the fact that he was the only one besides Rockefeller to have given them any money up to this point, Bill's second appeal to Towns makes perfect sense. But why Charles was so responsive at this time is a bit more complicated because it raises the question of the relationship that was developing between his hospital and the new sobriety movement emerging in New York City. There is little doubt Charles Towns had great respect for Bill Wilson and he was, as Bill said, "a man who really likes to help people" and who was "prepared to help [A.A.] in every possible way, whether he got any money in return or not."[11] But it is also quite possible that some consideration for the welfare of his own business was on Charles's mind as he wrote that check.

Perhaps Towns had not yet given up on the idea of forging *some* sort of partnership with Bill Wilson, or possibly he was hoping to establish a working relationship with the growing A.A. movement, a connection that would likely deliver significantly more patients into his hospital beds. After all, what sort of impact could be expected at Towns Hospital if such a book were written and published, one that he must have assumed (correctly) would advise people to seek professional and medical assistance as a first step in their recovery from alcoholism?**

But, however complicated and intertwined Charles Towns's personal motives may have been, he did in fact put up the money that allowed Bill Wilson to start working on the creation of the Big Book in late May 1938.

---

* A.A. did later pay Towns back for all of his donations to both the Alcoholic Fund and the Alcoholic Foundation.

** The relationship between Towns Hospital and A.A. is certainly interesting and deserving of further study. Suffice it to note here that the *New York Times* report of the hospital's closing in early June 1965, mentions that while the regular charge for a stay there was "from $205 to $350 a week," A.A. members enjoyed a "special five-day rate of $125" ("'Drying Out' Hospital for Problem Drinkers Closes," *New York Times*, June 6, 1965).

And now, with that $500 "advance" on the book firmly in hand, it was time to start writing.

Bill Agrees to Start the Book and Makes a First Attempt

Bill wanted to begin immediately, but there were two important questions he needed to answer first: 'Exactly what should I write?' and 'How should I even start?' As he told Bob Smith a month later, he was convinced it was important to get their own point of view written and published in order to head off "the possibility that someone else garbled the situation before we had a chance to say anything."[12] That clearly explains his fears and one of the reasons why he thought it was so important to write a book, but it does nothing to define exactly what this "view of ourselves" would actually look like once it was put down on paper.[13] What *was* the 'ungarbled' version of their story, and how should it be organized so that drunks everywhere could read and understand it well enough to get sober?

An overview and an outline would certainly have been helpful, but at this point the creation of the first outline for the book was still five weeks away. The fact was that Bill didn't have a clue where he should start or how to go about writing this book.

Bill and Hank had several long discussions about this and Frank Amos was almost certainly consulted for his opinions on the matter. Charles's $500 contribution obviously wasn't enough to fund the writing of an entire book, but it would allow them to make a significant start. Ever the promoter, Hank was the likely source of the suggestion that they should begin by writing just a portion of the book. After all, if they could get two really good chapters written, they could surely use them as promotional pieces to raise the money needed to get the rest of it written. That was the place to start![14]

It is hard to appreciate the level of intimidation Bill must have felt as these discussions moved toward their inevitable conclusion. The people in Akron, including Dr. Bob, were not about to volunteer for this job and Hank Parkhurst was far from a good writer (whatever he might have thought of his own talents in that regard). From the very start it was clear that if anyone was going to be responsible for getting the book started it would have to be Bill Wilson. Intimidating? Indeed. Bill just knew he couldn't write a book—he'd never done anything like that in his entire life.

The two chapters that were soon written are evidence of the decision that had been made. The best way to start would be to produce a chapter presenting their understanding of alcoholism, one that included an outline of both the problem and their solution for recovery. This experience-based theory about the nature of alcoholism and how to recover from it would then be followed up by a true story, similar to the kind of 'witnessing' being done at their meetings. In this case it would be Bill Wilson's own story, providing concrete and convincing evidence of how their method actually worked and how it had produced a complete transformation in his life.

In the end, Bill Wilson agreed he would try to put together two chapters for a possible book with the understanding that, once written, these "definite proposals" would serve as a "starting point" and provide "a concrete basis for discussion" about how they could then go about creating the rest of the book.[15] Bill wasn't trying to write an entire book. He was just going to get the project properly started while at the same time producing something that could be used as promotional materials to raise the funds needed to take the book project to the next level.

Bill's First Failed Attempt

On Friday, May 20, two days after Charles Towns delivered his check as an advance on the book, Bill Wilson began to write.[16] He almost certainly started with his own story based on the presumption this would be the easier piece to write because it was based on his own experience. But even this straightforward bit of autobiography proved to be much more challenging than Bill had anticipated and he labored through two false starts before producing something he felt would be good enough for the proposed book.

The first of these failed attempts is preserved in a manuscript Bill handwrote on eight sheets of yellow legal paper.[17] The short, fourteen-paragraph story is entitled "The Strange Obsession" and Wilson opens it with a few dramatic lines, vividly sketching one of his last admissions to Towns Hospital:

> It was a hot night in the midsummer of 1934. I found myself at a noted address in Central Park West New York City. It was the Charles Towns Hospital for drying out alcoholics.
>
> Sobering and sweltering out a fearful hangover, I laid abed in an upstairs room. Downstairs the doctor looked across his desk at my wife Lois.
>
> She was saying, "Doctor, why can't Bill stop drinking? He always had great willpower. Yet here he is, facing ruin again, and still he can't stop. The more he struggles, the worse he gets. I am scared, heartbroken and confused. I know he is, too. He'd do anything—anything at all to stop. Tell me, Doctor, why can't he?"[18]

The rest of the manuscript is basically a monologue by the unnamed doctor, who is clearly Dr. William Silkworth, the Chief of Staff at Towns Hospital. The doctor is deeply moved by Bill's dilemma, but he doesn't know if he can "bring himself to tell Lois the truth" about her husband's condition. Finally relenting, he begins by explaining to "Mrs. W." that the most important thing she needs to know about alcoholics is that no matter how much they might want to control their drinking, they cannot and "their behavior becomes completely illogical and irrational—it really verges on insanity . . . Therefore the biggest fact about alcoholism is its obsessional nature. It is one of the most subtle yet most powerful compulsions known."[19]

After explaining this side of the problem in some detail, the doctor shifts his emphasis in the final paragraph by noting that, although this mental aspect is certainly critical, it is not "the whole story." He tells Lois "alcoholism is [also] a physical malady," one that is brought on by the alcoholic's "continued excess," creating a "serious physical reaction" that somehow makes them "allergic" to alcohol.[20] Then, just as the doctor is about to launch into a fuller explanation of this allergy, the manuscript ends abruptly, with the three final hand-written words appearing at the very top of the eighth page.

Why Wilson decided to terminate the story just as he was beginning to explain this second major characteristic of alcoholism is unknown. Perhaps it had already grown longer than he intended or, more likely, Bill thought better of putting so much emphasis on the doctor's explanation of alcoholism at the very beginning of his own story. Wouldn't that information be better saved for the chapter he would have to write next? After all, this was supposed to be his own personal story, a witness to the redemptive powers of their new method of recovery and not a detailed presentation of some new medical theory about addiction to alcohol.

Whatever his reasoning, Bill abandoned the story at this point and never returned to it.

Significant Points in the Rejected Draft

There are a number of interesting and important things worth noting in this short manuscript.

First of all, there is the dramatic and skillful way Bill handles his narrative. For a man whose only prior experience was writing the comparatively dry prose required for financial reports, this is a radical departure. The shift from the third-person to a first-person perspective requires a completely different set of writing skills, as anyone who has ever attempted to make that transition will readily confirm. But Bill does a credible job with this new style and his story immediately springs to life with a dramatic opening and is then quickly engaged by two genuine characters speaking in believable dialogue. This is really quite a remarkable achievement.

Admittedly there are problems. How could there not be with a first attempt such as this? Under the circumstances we can certainly forgive Bill for his "it was a dark and stormy night" opening along with the occasional awkward sentence and the obvious need for further editing. But this is just a first draft (and a discarded one at that), so any criticism of his writing style here would be unfair.

This unsuccessful attempt likely confirmed Bill's fears of how difficult it was going to be to write his own story and he abandoned the piece after just a few pages. Failure, however, did not distract him from the ambitious standard he had already set for himself. As his story amply demonstrates, Bill was reaching for a sense of immediacy and a gripping vitality that he hoped would have a powerful impact on any drinker who might read the story.

Second, it is also important to notice that even in this first attempt, Bill is already abiding by the principle of anonymity, referring to his wife only as "Mrs. W." Given the amount of shame then associated with alcoholism—a problem the public assumed to be caused solely by a lack of will power—it is easy to understand why anonymity was quickly adopted as a defensive measure by the early members of the Fellowship. Wilson's use of his last initial here stands as testimony that the principle of anonymity (later appreciated on a much broader level and eventually enshrined in two of A.A.'s

Twelve Traditions*) was already being respected as an important part of the program of recovery by late May 1938. Nor is this an isolated incident of anonymity. One month later, when Bill was writing to Dr. Bob informing him about the work already done on the book, he noted "nearly everyone [here] agrees that we should sign the volume, Alcoholics Anonymous."[21] (To be clear, this is not the suggested title of the book, but rather the way in which the authors would be identified on the title page.) In short, the foundational principle of anonymity was already being practiced to some degree in New York City by the middle of 1938.

A third item of interest here is the reference to "the Charles Towns Hospital" in the opening paragraph. This specific mention may have seemed appropriate given the fact that Towns was financing the writing project, but it undoubtedly caught Wilson's attention as a potential problem. The early Fellowship consistently recommended hospitalization for recovery, but this specific mention of one establishment by name must have sounded too much like an endorsement to Bill, one that someone looking to criticize their new method as 'a racket' might even try to characterize it as a paid endorsement. Later versions of "Bill's Story" would refer to his hospitalizations, but they would never again mention the name of the place where he was treated.

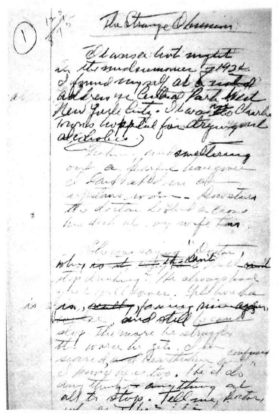

Finally, the short piece provides an excellent example of how Bill actually wrote at this time, the same method he would employ throughout the coming months as he created the remaining chapters for the Big Book.[22] Wilson would start by writing down a 'first pass' version of the text on yellow legal pads, continuously making changes as he went along. These sheets would then serve as the basis for any further edits as the text was taken to the next level of composition.

Although Bill's favorite method of writing on "yellow scratch pads"[23] was well known around the early Fellowship, none of the original pages used for the composition of the Big Book have survived. There is, however, a full-color copy of the first page of "The

Strange Obsession" posted on the internet[24] (see photo on previous page). This picture clearly shows how much editing was done during his first attempt to write in this new narrative style, providing striking evidence for the way Bill Wilson went about creating his texts during these middle months of 1938.

The photo also shows one other item of interest: the numbers "125 / 875" have been written in the upper left-hand corner of the sheet. Although the count is a bit off, this is clearly the number of words on the first page followed by the number to be found in the entire piece. (The published transcription of "The Strange Obsession" in *Bill W. My First 40 Years* counts 121 and 869 words respectively.) Bill obviously had some basic idea of how long he wanted his story to be and he was counting words to see how well he was doing. A month later, when he finally informed Dr. Bob of the progress being made with the book, Bill revealed that he had decided that each chapter "should run about five thousand words."[25] Wilson's practice of counting the words on each page will be seen again as the later chapters are finished and the Big Book begins to near completion.

Bill's Second Attempt: "The Original Story"

Bill's second attempt has been dubbed "The Original Story" and it was much longer than his targeted limit, running to almost 12,000 words. Despite this inordinate length, Bill had not even gotten sober yet by the time the manuscript ends. The typed story is thirty-six-pages long and it simply runs out mid-sentence at the bottom of the last page rather than reaching any conclusive ending.[26*] Clearly, organizing his materials and eliminating extraneous details were two of Bill's major problems as he began this project.

"The Original Story" starts when Bill was ten-years-old and tells how his parents' separation forced him to go live with his grandparents. There are some wonderful details here about his grandfather and grandmother Griffith along with a host of autobiographical information regarding his youth that might have been lost if he had never written this overly long version. Perhaps the most famous of these concerns a boomerang he made when he was a young man, a favorite Bill Wilson tale that he offered with regularity as an insight into his character and personality.

> I too was ambitious— very ambitious, but very undisciplined in spite of everyone's effort to correct that condition. I had a genius for evading, postponing or shirking those things which I did not like to do, but when thoroughly interested, everything I had was thrown into the pursuit of my objective. My will to succeed at special undertakings on which my heart were set was very great. There was a persistence, a patience, and a dogged obstinacy, that drove me on. My Grandfather used to love to argue with me with the object of convincing me of the impossibility of some venture or another in order to enjoy watching me 'tilt at the windmill' he had

---

* Given the abrupt ending, it is also possible that there were originally more pages to this story that have since been lost. It should also be noted that although the pagination runs seamlessly from page 22 to page 23, the numbered text on those pages jumps from line 658 to line 680 with some section of the story (typically about a half page of text) obviously missing here. For those who are interested, a full transcript of this story can easily be found online by searching for the first words in the text: "When I was about ten years old my father and mother" (using quotation marks as shown).

erected. One day he said to me—I have just been reading that no one in the world but an Australian can make and throw the boomerang. This spark struck tinder ~~and everything~~ and every activity was instantly laid aside until it could be demonstrated that he was mistaken. The woodbox was not filled, no school work was done, nor could I hardly be persuaded to eat or to go to bed. After a month or more of this thing a boomerang was constructed which I threw around the church steeple. On its return trip I went into transports of joy because it all but decapitated my Grandfather who stood near me.[27]*

Following this, Bill covers the rest of his life in some detail, including his marriage to Lois and his service in the First World War before going on to describe his activities during the Roaring Twenties and his increasingly destructive relationship with alcohol as the 1930s unfolded. But these biographical details are really only the prelude to what Bill considers to be the central reason for telling his story. As noted in the first version of the chapter, "There Is A Solution" (written almost simultaneously with these three versions of his own story), the ultimate purpose of the "personal narratives" appearing in their book would be to describe "the way in which [each writer] found or rediscovered the living God."[28]**

In this version, Bill's discovery of "the living God" is significantly different from what he always related in later accounts. When he finally reaches the "white light" moment of the story, Bill surprisingly talks as if it happened to him on the day his friend Ebby Thacher first came to visit him in Brooklyn:

> The man [who sat before me] was transformed; there was no denying he had been reborn. He was radiant of something which soothed my troubled spirit as tho the fresh clean wind of a mountain top [was] blowing thru and thru me. I saw and felt and in a great surge of joy I realized that the great presence which had made itself felt to me that war time day in Winchester Cathedral had again returned.[29]

Once again, this is a rejected draft and it is clear that this time sequence—that presents Bill as having his "white light" experience ("the fresh clean wind of a mountaintop blowing thru and thru me") while talking to Ebby that November afternoon in Brooklyn—is problematic. This is especially true because Bill Wilson continued to drink for weeks after Ebby left that day, a fact that all but obliterates his claim that this talk was "the great turning point of my life," the one where he stood "on the threshold of the fourth dimension of existence."[30]

In the final published version of his "Story," Bill would correct this problem by maintaining that during his talk with Ebby "that war-time day in old Winchester Cathedral came back again," but he would not mention the "great clean wind of a mountaintop [that] blew through and through" him until he was laying on his bed at Towns Hospital

---

* Quoted here without the distracting line numbers (which are explained later in this chapter).

** This sentence would be modified several times before being published in April of 1939 as: "Each individual, in the personal stories, describes in his own language, and from his own point of view the way he established his relationship with God."

during his final visit there as a patient—after which he never drank again.[31] Because he remained sober after that profound spiritual experience, the story has much more impact if it occurs in Towns rather than several weeks earlier. Placing his 'conversion experience' in the hospital offers strong experiential proof of Wilson's later claim about the sudden realization that "God is doing for us what we could not do for ourselves."[32]

But this is a relatively minor confusion and understandable given Wilson's constant revision and reordering of details to suit his own purposes. More interesting and important is Bill's first attempt to describe "the terms and conditions" his friend Ebby outlined for him if he wanted to stay sober. These were a set of "spiritual principles and rules of practice" that he characterized as "a practical workable twenty four hour a day design for living." These, he outlined in four expansive "steps:"

> One: Turn my face to God as I understand Him and say to Him with earnestness, complete honesty and abandon, that I henceforth place my life at His Disposal and Direction forever. [T]hat I do this in the presence of another person, who should be one in whom I have confidence and if I be a member of a religious organization, then with an appropriate member of that body.

> TWO: Having taken this first step, I should next prepare myself for Gods Company by taking a thorough and ruthless inventory of my moral defects and derelictions. This I should do without any reference to other people, and their real or fancied part in my shortcomings should be rigorously excluded. "Where have I failed" is the prime question . . . *[This is followed by an additional forty-one lines of explanation.]*

> Step number three required that I carefully go over my personal inventory and definitely arrive at the conclusion that I was now willing to rid myself of all these defects moreover I was to understand that this would not be accomplished by myself alone, therefore I was to humbly ask God that he take these handicaps away. To make sure that I had become really honest in this desire, I should sit down with whatever person I chose and reveal to him without any reservations whatever the result of my self appraisal. From this point out I was to stop living alone in every particular . . . *[This is followed by twenty-one additional lines of explanation.]*

> Step number four demanded that I frankly admit that my deviations from right thought and action had injured other people therefore I must set about undoing the damage to the best of my ability. It would be advisable to make a list of all the persons I had hurt or with whom I had bad relations. People I disliked and those who had injured me should have preferred attention, provided I had done them injury or still entertained any feeling of resentment towards them. Under no circumstances was I to consider their defects or wrong doing, then I was to approach these people telling them I had commenced a way of life which required that I

be on friendly and helpful terms with every body; that I recognized I had been at fault in this particular that I was sorry for what I had done or said and had come to set matters right insofar as I possibly could...

Bill's "step number four" is then followed by an additional ninety-five lines of explanation before the story ends abruptly in midsentence.[33]

The thirty-six-page typescript is physically peculiar in several ways and it bears absolutely no resemblance to anything known to have been typed by Ruth Hock. This suggests someone else helped Bill or that he once again turned to the services of "VB" (the secretary at his old firm, Quaw and Foley'), or perhaps he even typed the document himself. Inexplicably, each line of text begins with a number, running from 1 to 1180, making the story a bit difficult to read. Here is how the first six lines of the story actually appear in the original document:

1. When I was about ten years old my Father and mother

2. agreed to disagree and I went to live with my Grandfather,

3. and Grandmother. He was a retired farmer and lumberman. As I

4. see him in retrospect, he was a remarkable man After he

5. returned from the Civil War he settled in the small Vermont

6. town where I was later to grow up. His original capital con-

In addition to this strange practice of numbering each line, as shown above, the typist used an extremely deep indentation, forcing the text into little more than half of the available space on the page. It is overall a strange looking document with no explanation offered (or readily apparent) for its curious formatting."

The story itself has significantly less dialogue and much more narrative than Bill's first attempt and his writing skills are obviously challenged by this longer effort. As can be seen in the quoted sections, the text would need considerable editing to make it read smoothly. However, his discarded story does contain a few striking examples of Bill's improving writing skills as when—eight pages after relating the boomerang incident noted above—he talks about his later obsession with all things related to Wall Street and notes that "like the boomerang story, I could think of nothing else. Here I thought was the road to power. How little did I see that I was fashioning a weapon that would one day return and cut me to ribbons."[34] That is actually pretty good writing.

We have no idea how many drafts may have proceeded this typed version, but it is probable that this is a first one given the large number of obvious problems in the text.

---

* As noted earlier, several of Bill's letters from late 1937 and early 1938 (specifically, November 24 and December 6 and 17, 1937 along with January 11 and February 12, 1938) had been typed by "VB," a secretary working at Quaw and Foley. Two of Wilson's letters quoted earlier (January 11, 1938 to Willard Richardson and February 2, 1938 to Frank Amos) have the typist's initials of "VB" at the bottom. This is the same typist whose initials show up on an April 1, 1937 letter that Wilson wrote to Hank Parkhurst on Quaw and Foley stationery (GSO, Box 200 Folder I: Bill—Business with Hank P. / 1937-1950). These initials provide strong circumstantial evidence that Bill Wilson was still, on occasion, working out of the Quaw and Foley offices during the early months of 1938.

** Some legal documents are routinely typed with numbers preceding each line, but that numbering system typically runs for one page only, starting over with "1" on the next page. In this document, the numbers run consecutively, page-to-page, right up until the end.

Not only are there several crossed out words in the typescript (i.e., corrections made as the writing was being done—exactly like those we have already seen in the handwritten story, "The Strange Obsession"), but both the organization of the piece and the quality of the writing deteriorate noticeably as the story progresses. By the time Bill gets to the point where he is trying to explain the details of the recommended steps for staying sober, the narrative becomes something of a free-for-all with five pages of poorly organized information about Ebby's suggested program and Bill's own experience with it. There is little wonder why he abandoned the story at this point; it was obviously not turning out to be anything like the piece he had originally envisioned.

Comparing the "Four Steps" to the Twelve Steps

Still, a careful reading of the four steps quoted above reveals something interesting. Although Wilson wouldn't formally write the Twelve Steps for another six months, and they wouldn't be published until they had survived an additional four months of minor edits, the steps he outlines in this very early story explicitly contain eight of the final Twelve Steps and they do so in language strikingly similar to the version that would be published in April 1939:

Published Version of the Twelve Steps	"The Original Story"— Four Step Version
3. Made a decision to turn our will and our lives over to the care of God *as we understood Him.*	Turn my face to God as I understand Him and… place my life at His Disposal and Direction *[step one]*
4. Made a searching and fearless moral inventory of ourselves.	[Take] a thorough and ruthless inventory of my moral defects and derelictions *[step two]*
5. Admitted to God, to ourselves, and to another human being the exact nature of our wrongs.	I should sit down with whatever person I chose and reveal to him without any reservations whatever the result of my self appraisal . . . [and] to be really honest with myself and God *[step three]*
6. Were entirely ready to have God remove all these defects of character.	I was now willing to rid myself of all these defects moreover I was to understand that this would not be accomplished by myself alone, therefore . . . *[step three]*
7. Humbly asked Him to remove our shortcomings.	…I was to humbly ask God that he take these handicaps away *[step three]*
8. Made a list of all persons we had harmed, and became willing to make amends to them all.	Make a list of all the persons I had hurt or with whom I had bad relations. *[step four]*

Published Version of the Twelve Steps (continued)	"The Original Story"— Four Step Version (continued)
9. Made direct amends to such people wherever possible, except when to do so would injure them or others.	Approach these people telling them I . . . had come to set matters right insofar as I possibly could . . . [but] discretion should be used lest others should be hurt. *[step four]*
10. Continued to take personal inventory and when we were wrong promptly admitted it.	This principle of making amends was to continue in the future . . . *[step four]*

The Twelve Steps are the very essence and the main purpose of the book, *Alcoholics Anonymous,* so it is remarkable to find so many of them so clearly articulated (though not as well organized) in this first extended attempt by Bill Wilson to write down his own story. As noted earlier, the official formulation and numbering of the Twelve Steps was still six months in the future, but the comparison above shows Wilson was already well aware in late May 1938 that these eight actions had been central to his own recovery.

God as I Understand Him

Also worthy of significant attention here is Wilson's use of the phrase "God as I understand Him" in his first step. While the Twelve Steps are the core message of the Big Book, it is this open-ended flexibility in relation to a belief in God that has made those steps accessible to so many people and this is the first instance of that phrase surfacing in any of A.A.'s historical records.

Most every other feature of the steps can be traced back to earlier religious and spiritual traditions (or, as Ebby Thacher tells Bill in this version of the story: "they [are] spiritual principles and rules of practice . . . common to all of the worthwhile religions and philosophies of mankind"[35]); but it is the singular lack of dogmatism and the democratic freedom of choice that made the Twelve Steps of Alcoholics Anonymous so profoundly revolutionary. Such a pragmatic and very American approach, summarily dismissing thousands of years of doctrinal disputes, is a breathtaking innovation, transforming "the spiritual program of action"[36] suggested by Alcoholics Anonymous into a viable option for all but the most obstinate non-believers.

There is a tremendous amount of inaccurate A.A. mythology surrounding the inclusion of the phrase "God *as we understood Him*" in the Twelve Steps, most of which claims it was invented some six or seven months after making its first appearance here. Whatever conversations and arguments there may have been about the wording of the Third Step during the following December, January, and February (conversations and arguments that certainly *did* take place), it was already a part of Bill Wilson's religious vocabulary as early as late May 1938, appearing in a story reporting he had first heard that phrase a full three-and-a-half years earlier.

The exact origin of the phrase "God as I understand Him" is uncertain. Bill Wilson later claimed it was an essential part of the sobriety message his friend Ebby Thacher had brought to him in November and December 1934; but whether or not that exact phrase was actually used or if he was only presented with the general idea of flexibility regarding his religious beliefs is very much open to question.

For his part, Ebby was equally clear that this formulation had been given to him by members of the Oxford Group when they first approached him in July 1934 after his arrest for public drunkenness in Vermont. "They came right out with the statement," he said in a 1955 talk, "'Why don't you try turning your life over to God as you understand Him?' which was the principle, one of the principles, of the way the Oxford Group operated."[37*] Three years later in 1958 he expanded on this comment by saying that the Oxford Group people "were the ones who originated the phrase, believe in a God or a Higher Power as you understand Him."[38] Both of these reports put a severe strain on Ebby's credibility regarding this issue, for it sounds absolutely nothing like the Oxford Group and everything like the later Alcoholics Anonymous.

Ebby's claim that the Oxford Group espoused this sort of doctrinal openness flies in the face of everything we know about them. There are no other recorded instances of Oxford Group members using the phrase "God as I understand Him"—either as a way of introducing new members to their belief system or for any other reason. On the contrary, written reports of the Oxford Group activities and those found in Oxford Group literature uniformly present a narrow Christian version of their beliefs with a strong and decisive emphasis on Jesus Christ as the source of all goodness and salvation.[**] An openness of belief regarding this issue was *not* "one of the principles of the way the Oxford Group operated," nor would they have ever suggested the additional dilution of the concept of God into one of a "Higher Power."

Ebby was reading later A.A. history back into his own story and into that of the Oxford Group.

It is, of course, possible that one of the men recruiting Ebby had taken the liberty of presenting him with an open-ended concept of God in order to capture his agnostic attention; if so, it was an unusual and perhaps singular instance in Oxford Group history. Beyond that, it is always possible that, regardless of whatever might have actually been *said*, this was what Ebby *heard* and the recruiter let it stand since it produced the desired positive effect. This same questionability regarding 'what was said' and 'what was heard' would equally apply to what Ebby told Bill and what Bill took away from that talk.

---

[*] For details of Ebby's early encounters with the Oxford Group, see Mel B.'s *Ebby, The Man Who Sponsored Bill W.*, Chapter 6: "Cebra, Shep and Rowland."

[**] See *I Was a Pagan* by V. C. Kitchen (one of the most famous and widely read Oxford Group books, which was written in 1934, the same year that Ebby was first approached by OG members) for one excellent example of the all-pervasiveness of this fundamental focus and belief. Kitchen is uncompromising in his emphasis on Jesus Christ as savior and he makes absolutely no allowances for an easier, softer approach to the message that he is preaching: "[Members] have found that personal experience of Jesus Christ is the only thing that sets men's hearts on this . . . *limitless quest* of spiritual growth." (p. 125).

Whatever the original source of this innovative phrase, by late May 1938, "God as I understand Him" had entered Bill Wilson's lexicon of recovery and from there it would grow into a central tenet of Alcoholics Anonymous—where it would have a long and fruitful life.

Bill's Third and Final Attempt to Tell His Story

Bill's final attempt to write his own story produced a version that, in most places, closely resembles what is familiar to readers of the Big Book today, although several edits—some of them substantive—would be made to this first pass over the next ten months.* Wilson had finally gained enough control over the details of his own life to pare the story down to an acceptable 5,347 words while still hitting all of the points he thought were important to describe "the way in which he found or rediscovered the living God."[39]

However, the discipline that Bill needed to accomplish this was not something that came to him naturally; he had help. This third version of the story was produced at the offices of Honor Dealers in Newark, New Jersey, and it followed a pattern that would become well established a few months later as the writing of the Big Book was taken up again in earnest. According to Ruth Hock, Bill would typically arrive at Hank's office in the morning with a collection of yellow sheets on which he had sketched out roughly what he wanted to say.[40] He would then stand behind her and start talking as he improvised from his notes, telling her what to type. Ruth claimed this was the only way Bill ever worked with her because he really disliked dictating while she took shorthand notes. He wanted to see the results immediately. At first, Ruth was uncomfortable with this method, having never worked that way before, but she quickly "developed quite a speed to be able to keep up with this kind of dictation."[41] Years later, she reaffirmed that she and Bill always worked this way, even when writing letters, noting that the "whole manuscript [for the Big Book] was done with Bill standing behind me while I typed. He liked to speak awhile and then look it over, and he wanted it right then while his thoughts were working in the same vein."[42]

But Ruth wasn't the only other person in the office as this version of "Bill's Story" was being written. Hank Parkhurst was also present and he undoubtedly weighed in with his own thoughts and suggestions for edits as the work progressed. Years later, when Ruth was directly asked "Did Bill write the Big Book?," she claimed in no uncertain terms that he did, but she also acknowledged that Hank had "contributed a lot of ideas."[43] Hank Parkhurst was both opinionated and irrepressible, so it is hard to imagine how it could have been otherwise, given their close friendship and their even closer quarters during the entire writing process.

Whatever particular contributions may have been made by his two office mates, Bill finally managed to produce a version of his "Story" that covered all of the appropriate

---

* The full text of this early version of "Bill's Story" can be found in the second half of Appendix III starting on page 615.

bases in both his life and his recovery and he finished it without greatly exceeding the 5,000 word limit he had set for himself.

The first thing that is readily apparent from a careful reading of this story is how much of the writing actually came from "The Original Story" that preceded it. The new opening, for instance, contains several elements taken directly from that earlier version and then lightly edited:

Early June 1938 Version	Late May 1938 Version
At the age of ten I went to live with my grandfather and grandmother—their ancestors settled the section of Vermont in which I was to grow up. Grandfather was a retired farmer and lumberman; he nurtured me on a vigorous pioneering tradition.	When I was about ten years old my Father and mother agreed to disagree and I went to live with my Grandfather, and Grandmother. He was a retired farmer and lumberman. As I see him in retrospect, he was a remarkable man.

In addition to these many similarities there are several sections in the new version that were lifted wholesale and almost word-for-word out of the earlier one.

But the most important thing about this version is that Bill once again attempts to articulate the steps he took to recover from alcoholism, although this time he uses no numbers nor does he call them 'steps,' as he had in the earlier version. Here, the equivalent of the First Step appears when he tells of his meeting with Ebby, while an additional nine steps (#3, 4, 5, 6, 7, 8, 9, 11, and 12) are lumped together in his explanation of the actions Ebby suggested he take if he wanted to 'stay stopped' after he left the hospital.

Bill's "Steps" in Version Three Compared to the Published Twelve Steps

Once again, this can best be illustrated by comparing the published Twelve Steps with those found in this version of "Bill's Story:"

Published Version of the Twelve Steps	"Bill's Story" (Early June 1938)
1. We admitted we were powerless over alcohol—that our lives had become unmanageable.	Like myself he had admitted defeat. *(p. 20)*
3. Made a decision to turn our will and our lives over to the care of God *as we understood Him.*	I humbly offered myself to God, As I then understood Him, to do with me as He would. I placed myself unreservedly under His care and direction *(p. 21)*
4. Made a searching and fearless moral inventory of ourselves.	I ruthlessly faced my sins of omission and commission . . .made a list of people . . . towards whom I felt resentments. *(p. 21)*

Published Version of the Twelve Steps (continued)	"Bill's Story" (Early June 1938) (continued)
5. Admitted to God, to ourselves, and to another human being the exact nature of our wrongs.	I fully acquainted him with my problems and deficiencies. *(p. 21)*
6. Were entirely ready to have God remove all these defects of character.	became willing to have my new-found Friend take them away, root and branch. *(p. 21)*
7. Humbly asked Him to remove our shortcomings.	became willing to have my new-found Friend take them away, root and branch. *(p. 21)*
8. Made a list of all persons we had harmed, and became willing to make amends to them all.	We made a list of people I had hurt or towards whom I felt resentments. I expressed my entire willingness to approach those individuals, admitting my wrong. *(p. 21)*
9. Made direct amends to such people wherever possible, except when to do so would injure them or others.	I was to right all such matters to the utmost of my ability. *(p. 21)*
11. Sought through prayer and meditation to improve our conscious contact with God *as we understood Him,* praying only for knowledge of His will for us and the power to carry that out.	I was to test my thinking by the new God consciousness within . . . I was to sit quietly when in doubt, asking only for direction and strength to meet my problems as He would have me. Never was I to pray for myself, except as my request bore on my usefulness to others. *(p. 21)*
12. Having had a spiritual experience as the result of these steps, we tried to carry this message to alcoholics, and to practice these principles in all our affairs.	the moment I fully accepted them the effect was electric... I felt lifted up, as though a great clean wind of a mountain top blew through and through... I soon found that when all other measure failed, work with another alcoholic would save the day... my friend emphasized the absolute necessity of my demonstrating these principles in all my affairs. *(pp. 21–22)*

Although the phrasing of these "steps" are not always as dramatically similar to the published version as those that appear in "The Original Story," they clearly articulate the basic ideas or the actions to be found in each of those respective Steps. In addition, Bill had become much more concise when speaking about the program he followed to get sober. The earlier four step presentation had taken up almost six full pages, whereas eight of the nine Steps mentioned here are presented in less than a page and half.

It should also be noted that this "Story" contains three additional Steps (1, 11, and 12) that did not appear in the earlier version, (which ran from Steps 3 to 10). These three 'new' steps bring the total number mentioned by Bill Wilson in these two earliest attempts to write for the Big Book up to a total of eleven. The only Step missing here is the Second ("Came to believe that a Power greater than ourselves could restore us to sanity"), a Step that *would* appear in the final version of "Bill's Story" after it was added in just before the book went to press.

In short, it is remarkable how much of the final program of recovery that characterizes Alcoholics Anonymous is so clearly contained in these two versions of "Bill's Story," written in late May and early June 1938. While A.A.'s creation myth repeatedly boasts of how the Big Book is the product of a collective group effort, that claim completely ignores the fact that Bill Wilson single-handedly wrote down almost every key element contained in A.A.'s core teaching in his very first attempts to write material for the book, and he did so without serious consultation with any other members of the Fellowship. As more and more writing was done for the book, a detailed elaboration of these twelve points would gradually be developed, but the program that was finally presented to the world as the twelve suggested steps of recovery differs very little from what Bill Wilson had claimed was necessary for his own personal recovery from the start.

Bill Revises What Ebby Originally Told Him

Throughout both versions of his "Story," Bill gives full credit to his friend, Ebby Thacher, as the source of these suggestions on how to quit drinking and praises him lavishly for that singular contribution. Bill always portrays Ebby as the messenger of hope who was constantly prodding him to accept these "spiritual principles and rules of practice" and to apply them as a "practical workable twenty four hour a day design for living" if he wanted to stay sober.[44] Given Bill's gratitude and his profound sense of what he owed him, it is no wonder that, despite Ebby's continual slips back into drinking, Wilson identified him as his sponsor right up until Thacher's death in 1966.

But, given Bill's consistent habit of myth-making, it is important to note that this May 1938 report of what Ebby told him three-and-a-half years earlier is surely a significant modification of what would have been a much more religious conversation. Several essential elements in the program of recovery Ebby originally offered to Bill needed to be edited out because the New York Fellowship had abandoned them in the three-and-a-half years since those meetings. We have no way of knowing exactly what Ebby said to Bill in late 1934, but his presentations almost certainly mentioned the Oxford Group's Four Absolutes and included the need for Wilson to surrender his life to a Christian God. These and other Oxford Group ideas and practices would have been essential elements in whatever Ebby Thacher suggested to Bill Wilson in late 1934.*

Wilson's removal of these explicit and specific religious elements and his report that Thacher delivered a set of more generalized guidelines instead—closely resembling his own recovery experience—is certainly understandable given his purposes. But once again, the story presented here is more a reflection of the message Bill was trying to pass along than any kind of accurate presentation of historical facts.

---

* The problems with Bill's reporting of what Ebby told him that day will be discussed in more detail in the chapter on the writing of the Twelve Steps. In that same chapter, the predominance of Oxford Group teachings in early A.A. will be substantiated when we consider the first typed version of Fitz Mayo's story that explicitly refers to the Four Absolutes being presented to him as a critical element in the program of recovery in November 1935. (See pp. 450 – 451)

CHAPTER EIGHT

"There Is a Solution"

~Early June 1938~

The second chapter Bill needed to write was much more challenging. It was easy enough to defend whatever he might put down in his own "Story"; it was, after all, a straightforward retelling of his own experiences, an autobiographical account of what had happened to him personally. But writing a much more general chapter, one describing the reasons for their success in universal terms, was fraught with treacherous political problems because of the radically different ways Akron and New York understood and practiced the program of recovery in early June 1938.

The Akron Fellowship and the Oxford Group

It is hard to overstate the differences between the Akron approach to sobriety in mid-1938 and what was going on at that same time in New York. Ohio's brand of recovery was still exclusively based on the practices, principles, and beliefs of the Oxford Group, and the Akron alcoholics were seamlessly blended into that Group. There was no organization called Alcoholics Anonymous as yet, and as far as the newly recovered Ohio drunks were concerned, they were members of the Oxford Group and they owed their salvation to the fellowship and the belief system they had found within it.[1] That belief system was firmly based on the Christian New Testament and it advocated, among other things, surrender to God, daily prayer and "quiet time" to receive direct guidance from God, and a life of reformed behavior based on Absolute Honesty, Absolute Unselfishness, Absolute Love, and Absolute Purity.

While the typical Oxford Group focused their recruiting efforts almost exclusively on the wealthy and drew their membership primarily from within the Episcopalian community, key members in Akron had made unusual allowances in relation to this motley crew of recovered alcoholics. Despite the disapproval of some local members who suggested "the alcoholics [should] be screened so that only the most socially acceptable would be allowed in,"[2] both Henrietta Seiberling and T. Henry Williams had extended their strong support to the newly emerging "Alcoholic Squad" within their group, even if it meant ignoring the fact that many of these people had neither the social standing nor the economic resources usually considered prerequisites for membership in the Oxford Group.

The previous February, Dr. Bob had claimed that "the alcoholic set up [here in Akron] . . . could not be identified with the [Oxford] Group,"[3] but as already noted, even in "conference approved" literature that sentiment has been justly characterized as "more wishful than real."[4] While Dr. Bob may have not seen any formal affiliation between his work with alcoholics and the local Oxford Group, the members of the "Alcoholic Squad" certainly thought of themselves as Oxford Group members, a perfectly understandable conclusion since they were deeply committed to the principles promoted by the Oxford Group, and they were all attending a weekly meeting that was in every respect a typical Oxford Group gathering. The line Dr. Bob claimed to see separating his "Alcoholic Squad" from the Oxford Group was not self-evident to most of the recovering alcoholics in Akron at that time.

One dramatic example of Akron's adherence to Oxford Group practices was the requirement that each new member get down on his knees and publicly surrender his life to God before being allowed to attend the group's meeting. As Frank Amos had written the previous February, one of the six "musts" for recovery in Akron was that an alcoholic "must surrender himself absolutely to God, realizing that in himself there is no hope."[5]

In 1954, while preparing to write the book *Alcoholics Anonymous Comes of Age*, Bill Wilson interviewed most of the surviving early A.A. members in Akron and two of these transcripts provide conclusive testimony regarding this practice. The first comes from a man who sobered up in February 1937:

> <u>Bob:</u> . . . l was going to say the last thing I did there at the hospital before I left was to make a surrender, which I think was important.

> <u>Bill:</u> Like the Oxford Group—on your knees?

> <u>Bob:</u> Sharing completely—had to be done with another person. Pray and share out loud. The act of surrender.

> <u>Bill:</u> You know, in the first draft of the Twelve Steps, it said that people were to be on their knees, but the other drunks made me take it out.[*] That went back to this practice of surrender—you got on your knees and surrendered your life to the will of God. That was the process which you actually went through?

---

[*] Bill is referring here to the Seventh Step, which originally read: "Humbly, on our knees, asked Him to remove our shortcomings—holding nothing back."

Bob: Oh, yes. Of course, I've never forgotten that—it made a tremendous impression on me. I hear a lot, to this day, fellows talk about getting down on our knees to pray at night.

Bill: Oh yes, lots of people do it, to be sure, but this was a certain act of surrender?

Bob: Yes, this was very important at this time. There were no exceptions. You couldn't attend a meeting unless you had gone through that. You couldn't go to a meeting—you had to go through the program of surrender . . .[6]

Another comment made by a man who had his last drink two months after Bob in April 1937 confirms this:

Wally: . . . On the business of surrender which I think is probably the most important part of this whole thing, Dr. Smith took my surrender the morning of the day that I left the hospital. And, at that time, it was the only way you became a member—you became a member by a definite act of prayer and surrender, just as they did in the [Oxford] Group. I'm sorry it has fallen by the wayside . . .[7]

This necessity of making a public surrender before attending a meeting was an integral part of the Akron program throughout the late 1930s and well into the early 1940s. "If by accident you didn't make [your surrender] in the hospital," one early member recalled, then "you had to make it in the upper bedroom over at the Williamses' house"[8] just before the regular Wednesday night meeting began. "The men would all disappear upstairs," recalled Clarence Snyder's wife, Dorothy, describing a typical 1938 meeting. Then, "after about half an hour or so, down would come the new man, shaking, white, serious, and grim. And all the people who were already [sober] would come trooping down after him. They were pretty reluctant to talk about what had happened, but after a while, they would tell us that they had had a *real* surrender."[9]*

The meeting that followed these surrenders typically began with the group holding hands and reciting a prayer before they launched into a "quiet time during which [everyone] silently asked God for guidance."[10] In the beginning, these quiet times took up literally 50 percent of the meeting, but sitting in silence and "listening for guidance half the time . . . made the drunks very restless"[11] so the practice was gradually shortened. The leader for the evening would then open the meeting with a reading from Christian scriptures or some other religious writing, frequently relying on a popular Methodist periodical, *The Upper Room.*** Having set the tone with literature, the leader would then 'witness' for twenty to thirty minutes before inviting others, alcoholics and non-alcoholics alike, to do the same. Although "not too much was said

---

* Once the Ohio alcoholics made their formal break with the Oxford Group in late 1939, this practice of going upstairs and surrendering was transferred to Dr. Bob's house. Visitors are still shown that room at the top of the stairs in Dr. Bob's house and are often invited to get on their knees and say the Third Step prayer that is conveniently provided for them on a printed card.

** For an interesting discussion of the importance of this publication in early A.A. history, see *The Upper Room and Early A.A.* by Glenn C. (http://hindsfoot.org/uprm1.html - retrieved December 16, 2011).

about alcoholism or drinking in the testimonials" ("we were more interested in our everyday life than we were in reminiscing about drinking")." Dr. Bob was particularly adamant about full participation and he encouraged everyone to be brief in their comments so that each person would get a chance to speak. The meeting ended with the recitation of the Lord's Prayer.[12]

It was, in short, a very Christian affair, specifically based on the Oxford Group's religious model, and would hardly be recognized or acknowledged as an A.A. meeting by today's members. As Dorothy Snyder so wryly commented a few years later: "I often wonder how many of the people that come in now would agree with [the Oxford Group's] version of the Word of God or anything spiritual and really survive an experience like that—[it was] a regular old-fashioned prayer meeting."[13]

Bill Wilson and the Oxford Group

Bill Wilson had started out in early 1935 with a similarly strong connection to the New York Oxford Group, but his experiences were strikingly different from those of the people in Akron. While a vocal minority in Ohio actively embraced these new members, the New York chapter wanted little or nothing to do with the drunks Bill was regularly bringing into their meetings. It was a strained relationship from the very start, setting Wilson and the New York Oxford Group on a completely different trajectory from the one unfolding in Akron.

Having left Towns Hospital for the last time, Bill "constantly went to Oxford Group meetings" and he soon became a member of one of the smaller "teams" of men who regularly met and sat quietly as they listened for "the guidance of God for each one."[14] Curiously, Oxford Group guidance was rarely directed toward the person receiving it, but rather was intended for someone else within the group. Bill almost immediately began to have trouble with the guidance others were receiving for him. As Lois noted:

> The rest of the team would get guidance for him to work with such and such a person in order to "bring him to God." Bill usually had different guidance and felt no identity with the person they selected. He became a bit annoyed at being told what to do. He knew he could be far more useful working with alcoholics, with whom he could identify.[15]

The crux of the problem was clear. Bill Wilson wanted to spend all his time working with drunks and the Oxford Group members believed (and constantly received confirming guidance from God) that he should go out and get a job on Wall Street where he could mingle with the 'right' sort of people, people who would be much more appropriate candidates for membership in their Group. The practice of recruiting recovering alcoholics as new members, which was so generously tolerated in Akron, was at first actively discouraged in New York, and later soundly criticized and

---

* This in stark contrast to the more prominent focus on alcohol in the New York meetings of this time.

censured.* Given these evolving criticisms and restrictions, Bill's stubborn commitment to working with drunks generated a fair amount of friction as he began to pick and choose which guidance he would follow and which he would not. In spite of the specific instructions others so consistently received and passed along to him, Bill doggedly insisted his time and energy could best be spent trying to sober up and recruit people who were in trouble with alcohol.[16]

Or, as he so succinctly put it a few years later: "The Oxford Group wanted to save the world, and I only wanted to save the drunks."[17]

Because of this tension and the undercurrent of hostility, the alcoholic members in New York (whom Bill was recruiting not only from within the Group itself, but also from among the drunks at the Calvary Mission** and the patients in Towns Hospital) began to gather by themselves immediately after the regular Oxford Group sessions at Stewart's Cafeteria, a convenient and congenial spot just a few blocks from the regular Oxford Group meetings. But this eventually proved to be both too public and too unwieldy and, starting late in 1935, Bill moved these sessions to his house in Brooklyn where they began to hold regular "alcoholics only" meetings on Sunday nights.[18]

These early Brooklyn meetings began "using the Oxford Group principles"[19] and were remarkably similar to what was happening at T. Henry's house in Akron at that time, i.e., they started with some quiet time followed by Christian readings and then a talk by the leader (usually Bill) along with witnessing by other attendees, all of which was bookended by opening and closing prayers. But because they did not include any non-alcoholic members in their group—an integral part of the Akron format— the meetings in New York almost immediately began to evolve independently and to have a much more specific emphasis on alcohol than in Akron where drinking was rarely mentioned in their meetings. Given both of these changes, many of the practices specific to the Oxford Group began to fade away as it "became very clear" (as Wilson so delicately put it later) "that [the] drunks couldn't stand the Oxford Group pace."[20]

However, one Akron element that did linger for some time in New York was the belief that an alcoholic had to make an explicit surrender to God if he wanted to stay sober.*** The stories of both Hank Parkhurst and Fitz Mayo (who sobered up in September and November 1935, respectively) provide clear testimony that a complete surrender to God was considered an essential requirement for anyone trying to build a solid foundation for ongoing sobriety.

Hank's rather awkward and rambling stream-of-consciousness Big Book story (entitled "The Unbeliever") details the many agnostic arguments he formulated while lying in his Towns Hospital bed and then offered to Bill Wilson whenever he visited him there. But despite all his protestations of disbelief, Hank's story ends abruptly with a dramatic account of his surrender at the side of his bed: "Brrr, this floor is cold on my

---

* Wilson claims that this Oxford Group reluctance to work with drunks in New York was, among other things, driven by some frustrating and unfortunate experiences that Sam Shoemaker, the rector of Calvary Episcopal Church and the leader of the Oxford Group in the USA, had had with earlier attempts to save alcoholics (*AACOA*, pp. 64–65; *Bill W. My First 40 Years*, pp. 158–59).

** A rescue operation run by Calvary Episcopalian Church in New York City.

*** Whether or not, at this time, surrender was a requirement for attendance at New York meetings, as it was in Akron, is not known.

knees . . . why are the tears running like a river down my cheeks . . . God, have mercy on my soul!"[21]

Similarly, Fitz Mayo's present-tense Big Book story ("Our Southern Friend") recounts the details of his surrender to God at Towns Hospital:

> Suddenly I feel a wave of utter hopelessness sweep over me. I am in the bottom of hell. And there a tremendous hope is born. It might be true [that there is a God who could help me].
>
> I tumble out of bed onto my knees. I know not what to say. But slowly a great peace comes to me. I feel lifted up. I believe in God. I crawl back into bed and sleep like a child.[22]

This requirement for a complete, on-your-knees surrender continued to be an active part of the New York program for more than a year after these two men got sober, a fact that is illustrated in a letter Bill Ruddell sent to Bill Wilson several years after he wrote his own Big Book story, "A Business Man's Recovery." According to this more detailed version of his recovery, Ruddell says that as he was being discharged from Towns Hospital in February 1937, Dr. Silkworth referred him to Wilson, suggesting he was someone who might be able to help him stay sober. Desperate to stay stopped, Ruddell and his wife Kathleen almost immediately visited the Wilsons at their home in Brooklyn and, after some heartfelt discussion, Bill invited them both upstairs where, as Ruddell reminded him, "Kathleen and I knelt down in front of the fireplace in your upstairs parlor with both you and Lois and [I] made the surrender."[23]

But very shortly after this, during March and April 1937, Bill's relationship with the local Oxford Group began to deteriorate at an alarming rate. That spring, Wilson discovered the alcoholics at the Calvary Mission had been forbidden to attend the weekly meetings at his home in Brooklyn and had even been told they could not visit the Wilson house for dinner. Worse than this, he learned that word was spreading throughout the congregation saying the Wilsons were "not maximum," meaning they were not sufficiently committed to the Oxford Group program. This is perhaps the strongest criticism that could be leveled against a Group member without directly accusing them of sin. The end came when an associate pastor at Calvary Episcopal Church delivered a Sunday morning sermon directed against the "divergent work" of a "secret, ashamed sub-group" within the congregation; a clear and caustic indictment of Bill Wilson and the work he was doing with alcoholics.[24]*

---

* Both Bill's and Lois's published recollections of exactly when these negative responses from the Oxford Group and its members took place are either vague or contradictory. I have accepted Kurtz's version of the time sequence here because it agrees with Bill's "AA Main Events" recollections and also because it was based on two personal interviews with Lois Wilson. Regarding the timing of the break, it is worth noting that according to Lois's diary entries for 1937, she and Bill attended Oxford Group meetings on January 10, 21, 22, and 24, on February 7, 14, 21, and 28, and on March 11, 21, and 28, but after March 28, 1937, there is no further mention of any Oxford Group meetings in her diary. In addition, Bill notes in A.A. Main Events (1937, Point 1) that "it was probably in the early part of this year [1937] that we completely withdrew from the Oxford Groups in New York City."

The Decision to Leave the Oxford Group

The sermon was the final blow, crystallizing all of Bill's dissatisfactions with the Oxford Group. Deeply committed to his work with drunks and now finally admitting the "impossibility of carrying [on] the alcoholic work in the atmosphere of the Group,"[25] he decided it was time for a complete break. But Bill did not take this separation lightly, nor did he make the decision to quit the Oxford Group by himself. According to Ruddell:

> . . . the final parting came in the spring of 1937 because Kathleen and I started coming to meetings in your home in February of 1937, and we attended with you meetings on Sunday nights in Sam Shoemaker's church . . . As we remember it, the decision to disassociate from the Oxford Group was made at a meeting in your home, and at that time it was a very serious decision. You talked it over at one of the group meetings and the decision was made. This was, as we remember it, two or three months after [February of 1937.][26]*

A little over three years later Bill was pressed for an explanation regarding New York's break with the Oxford Group and he responded with a long and thoughtful letter, detailing at length eight reasons that made this separation necessary. Those reasons can be summarized as follows:

1. The "aggressive evangelism" of the Oxford Group

2. Their reliance on "excessive personal publicity or prominence"

3. The unacceptability of the word "absolute" before the virtues of honesty, purity, unselfishness, and love (four virtues that Bill rather testily claimed were "as much practiced [by A.A. members] . . . as by any other group of people")

4. The coercive nature of "guidance for others" and of the subsequent "checking" by those who had received that guidance to ensure that it was being followed

5. The practice of writing down guidance during 'quiet time' which, according to Bill "was too often made ridiculous by novices scribbling messages from God in notebooks"

---

* Jim Burwell in his wildly inaccurate late 1940s history, "The Evolution of Alcoholics Anonymous," said that the break from the Oxford Group occurred in September 1937. He repeated this claim a few years later in a letter to Bill Wilson dated January 17, 1957. Bill had sent out proof copies of *AACOA* to many people for comments and Jim's only quibble with the entire book was to note that "It does seem to me that I saw a copy of a letter from you and Hank to Sam Shoemaker, resigning from the Oxford Group and dated Sept. 1937... am I wrong?" (GSO, Box 29, Reel 13, 17.3 History Book, A. A. Comes of Age: Correspondence with Members Mentioned in Book, Document marked "p. 46"). Despite this observation, Bill did not change the dates in his book based on Jim's contention. As noted earlier, Burwell is the most unreliable witness we have for facts and dates in early A.A. history so I am reluctant to move the date of the break from the Oxford Group back by several months based on his testimony alone. In addition, no such letter has been found in the Shoemaker Archives. Still, it is possible that he is right on this one particular fact and that there was such a September letter. If that *is* the case, then although the group had made its decision in April or May 1937, they did not *formally* notify Shoemaker of that decision until a few months later. Whatever the exact date, it is clear that Wilson and the New York group had completely severed their relationships before Bill and the others went to Akron for the October, 1937 "counting noses" meeting and the subsequent vote taken there.

6. "We found" he observed with some irritation and judgment, "that the principles of tolerance and love had to be more emphasized in their actual practice than they were in the O.G., especially tolerance"

7. There could be no "religious requirement" for membership in A.A.

8. The kind of dogmatism demanded by the Oxford Group necessarily precluded Catholics from joining A.A.[27]

Given all of this, he noted:

> I am always glad to say privately that some of the Oxford Group presentation and emphasis upon the Christian message saved my life. Yet it is equally true that other attitudes of the O.G. nearly got me drunk again and we long since discovered that if we were to approach alcoholics successfully these would have to be abandoned. Recovery being a life or death matter for most alcoholics, it became a question of adopting that which would work and rejecting that which would not.[28]

This decision to leave the Oxford Group in New York was one of the most critical turning points in the history of Alcoholics Anonymous, marking a decisive step away from any preexisting organization or belief and a commitment to both an evolving operational structure and a set of principles that would increasingly be determined by pragmatic results rather than the dictates of any specific doctrines. Finally liberated from the structure, dogmas, and culture of the Oxford Group, the New York alcoholics were free to create a set of beliefs and practices based on their collective experiences, a process that soon evolved into something that looks very much like today's Fellowship of Alcoholics Anonymous.

A Pragmatic Approach to Religious Beliefs

The separation didn't mean Bill Wilson had abandoned everything he had learned during more than two years with the Oxford Group. They "had clearly shown us what to do," he admitted, but "just as importantly, we had also learned from them *what not to do* as far as alcoholics were concerned."[29] This meant that most of the specifically religious aspects associated with the Group along with their more authoritarian practices (such as team guidance and the Four Absolutes) were soon dropped in New York.[30]

But, if Bill and his group weren't going to follow the religious and evangelical route outlined by the Oxford Group, how then should they proceed?

The fact was Bill Wilson had been moving himself and his group away from a structured religious approach to sobriety well before the spring of 1937. Based on their collective experience, he had come to believe these men "had to be led, not pushed . . . [because many of them] just wanted to find sobriety, nothing else. They clung to their other defects, letting go only little by little. They simply did not want to get 'too good too soon.'"[31] In short, the Akron insistence that a new recruit "must remove from his life other sins such as hatred, adultery and others which frequently accompany alcoholism" and "unless he will do this absolutely, Smith and his associates refuse to work with him"[32] was not the model being followed in New York. The culture of the Fellowship on the East Coast was much more tolerant of what might be considered sinful behavior—just so long as the new recruit wasn't drinking.

In addition, most of Wilson's potential recruits were "awfully hard-headed guys"[33] who repeatedly had difficulties with many of the teachings of the Oxford Group. The program of recovery certainly required a strong religious foundation, but that foundation did not necessarily have to adhere to any specific set of beliefs or to the practices prescribed by any particular Church. Yes, you had to believe, but what you had to believe in was becoming more and more a matter of personal choice.

In that same 1940 letter where he talked about the reasons for leaving the Oxford Group, Bill was unusually candid about his own religious beliefs, confiding that:

> By degrees I find that I have become a rather orthodox Christian. But I do not find, at least within our group, that I can better serve God by demanding that anyone agree with me. If I can be used to help people find a consciousness of the Presence of God I hope I shall please Christ quite as much, if I still permit each individual to attach his own label to that experience. Of course this is no final conclusion on my part. I may be entirely wrong, but I fancy Christ Himself would prefer the hottentot* happily aware of God and usefully serving Him, than He would the most orthodox were he in a state of useless drunkenness. I think Christ would be interested in Christian results rather than Christian professions.[34]

It is, frankly, a radically pragmatic and amazingly democratic approach to the concept of religious beliefs; one that Bill Wilson carefully laid as a critical foundation stone in the creation of Alcoholics Anonymous.

A Broader Formulation of the Solution

The net result of Bill's break with the Oxford Group in New York was to accelerate his evolving understanding of alcoholism and to move him farther along the road toward a broader formulation of the solution, one that required not only a much more open religious component, but also one that emphasized the critical physical and psychological elements that needed to be addressed for a successful recovery.

As early as May 1935, Dr. Silkworth had criticized the fervor of Bill's religious approach. At that time, Wilson's failure to sober up a single person during the five months since he himself had quit drinking was driving him to the brink of despair and Silkworth was worried Bill himself might pick up a drink. "Stop preaching at them," he told the evangelical Wilson, "and give them the hard medical facts first. This may

---

* Referring to the Khoikhoi people who are native to South Africa. These days the term is considered derogatory.

soften them up at depth so that they will be willing *to do anything* to get well. Then they may accept those [religious] ideas of yours, and even a [God]."[35]*

The Medical Aspects

Silkworth's theories, his understanding of "the hard medical facts" about alcoholism, are most famously presented in "The Doctor's Opinion" (the opening chapter in the Big Book), which Bill Wilson once neatly summarized as *the obsession of the mind that compels us to drink* and *the allergy of the body* that condemns us to go mad or die."[36] Bill was very familiar with both aspects of this theory, not only from his own life experiences, but also from his observations of so many other drunks in the five months since he himself had achieved sobriety.

Bill took Silkworth's advice and had his first real success with the very next drunk he connected with: Dr. Bob Smith in Akron. During their first meeting in May 1935, Bill specifically told Bob about "Dr. Silkworth's description of alcoholism and its hopelessness," and armed with this knowledge, Bob "began to pursue the spiritual remedy for his malady with a willingness he had never before been able to muster."[37] Wilson continued with this strong emphasis when he returned to New York in late 1935, enthusiastically pointing out to new prospects "how hopeless they were medically" because "it was this technique that [had] apparently turned the corner with Bob."[38] As Bill began to see some success with his efforts in New York, his confidence in Silkworth's advice about emphasizing the medical hopelessness of the malady as the best place to start with a new prospect grew rapidly, and he embraced that approach as his own.

Unfortunately, it was exactly this strong emphasis on the medical aspects of alcoholism to which "the Oxford Groupers had very strong objections." They were insistent in their belief that there was a purely religious solution available for curing this problem; one that, if diligently followed, would certainly relieve the alcoholic of his compulsion to drink. Bill considered such a stance "truly a heartbreaker, for we felt we owed these [alcoholics] everything" that could help them, including an understanding of the important medical side of the problem.[39]

A Psychological Understanding

Besides religion and medicine, the final component in Wilson's evolving approach to recovery was a two-sided psychological understanding of the drinker's problems. The first half of that understanding was his identification of the "peculiar mental twist"[40] that he now believed to be at the very heart of the alcoholic's problem. Silkworth had explained how the phenomenon of craving invariably set in once an alcoholic took the first drink, but what baffled Bill Wilson was the complete failure of the alcoholic's ability to refuse that first drink—when he had no alcohol whatsoever in his body. Why was it that all the accumulated memories of past disasters (and of present promises)

---

* As noted before, the actual quote in *AACOA* uses the words "spiritual" and "higher Power" rather than "religious" or "God" but the former are surely later substitutions by Wilson in an effort to make them conform to the terminology and beliefs that were current in A.A. in 1957 (the year *AACOA* was published).

had absolutely no impact on his decision to *start* drinking? Wilson's own behavior—most notably at the beginning of his final drunken spree on Armistice Day 1934*—was inexplicable to him on any other terms than to admit that he was as sick in his mind as he was in his body.

The second psychological element didn't concern the source of the problem; it was related to the solution to the alcoholic's dilemma. Although Dr. Silkworth did not invent this idea, he can fairly be credited with clearly formulating an early explanation of the concept in his April 1937 paper entitled "Reclamation of the Alcoholic." That article outlines his own three-step medical procedures for the successful treatment of alcoholics and fully describes the last of these three steps, which he called "Moral Psychology."** This phrase has caused considerable confusion over the years because it appears twice in Silkworth's Big Book chapter "The Doctors Opinion" without any explanation of its exact meaning. But in this article, the doctor is clear that the primary function of moral psychology is to address the underlying egotism found in alcoholics "whose interests center entirely in themselves" and, when successfully applied, it liberates them to the point where they begin to "ask how they can help others."[41] The purpose of moral psychology then is to assist alcoholics in overcoming their perspective of extreme self-centeredness and encourage them to adopt an attitude of consideration and care for others. In Silkworth's opinion, this shift of perspective away from self and toward others was of paramount importance in keeping alcoholics from taking their next drink.

To illustrate this, Silkworth concluded the final section of this paper by presenting two case histories of successful reclamation through moral psychology (certainly Hank Parkhurst and Bill Wilson, although the details do not fit their stories exactly). In his description of the second patient (Wilson), Silkworth notes that:

> He gives part of his income to help others in his former condition, and he has gathered about him a group of over fifty men, all free from their former alcoholism through the application of this method of treatment and "moral psychology."

> To such patients we recommend "moral psychology," and in those of our patients who have joined or initiated such groups, the change has been spectacular.[42]

This belief that self-centeredness is the central problem for an alcoholic and that it can only be overcome by a life based on usefulness to others are two of the

---

* For Bill's detailed and dramatic account of his last slip on November 11, 1934, see *Bill W., My First 40 Years*, pp. 118–20.

** "We might define these three phases as follows: 1, Management of the acute crisis; 2, physical normalization and cell revitalization so that craving is eliminated, and 3, mental and normal stabilization, which naturally involves some 'normal psychology.'" (Silkworth, "Reclamation of the Alcoholic," p. 321) *NOTE*: the use of the word "normal" twice at the end of this sentence makes little sense here and even less in the face of what follows in this article. It is, in all likelihood, a typographical error and should read "moral" in both cases—as it does throughout the rest of the article.

most fundamental and often repeated premises to be found in the book, *Alcoholics Anonymous*.*

In brief, whenever Bill Wilson or other early A.A. members talked about psychology in relation to their program of recovery, they were referring to one or the other of these two concepts: either the insanity of taking the first drink (and the need for an effective spiritual defense against it) or the alcoholic ego (and of the need to cure that problem through a change of attitude and positive engagement with other people).

A Bigger Tent

Along with a broader approach to religion and the specific inclusion of both medical and psychological elements in his evolving understanding of recovery, Bill Wilson brought one more important personal factor into all of his work with alcoholics: he wholeheartedly believed everyone who had "an honest desire to stop drinking"** should be given the opportunity to get sober. Bill's compassion for the suffering alcoholic was genuine, deep, and profound; so deep, in fact, that he was reluctant to turn anyone away from his group in New York, no matter what their belief system might be. This dedication to an ever-expanding tolerance was one of the most influential and important ideas he took away from his negative experiences with the Oxford Group and his ongoing efforts to make the Fellowship more and more inclusive became one of the outstanding hallmarks of Bill Wilson's long leadership of Alcoholics Anonymous. Throughout his life, Bill continually worked to make A.A. into a bigger tent—and then one even bigger than that: a tent that increasingly embraced those who, for whatever reason, had previously been excluded from membership.

There are many stories attesting to Bill Wilson's efforts to open the doors of Alcoholics Anonymous a little bit wider every year. One typical example occurred at the A.A. Clubhouse in Manhattan just after the end of the Second World War. In those days, visitors entering the building were greeted by a member sitting at the front desk. One day in 1945, a relatively new member, Barry L., was working the desk when he was confronted by an unusual arrival—a black, ex-convict drunk and addict (there were no black members in New York at this time) who was hungry, broke, and homeless. The man also admitted to being a homosexual, an admission that came as no surprise to Barry since the fellow had long and flowing bleached-blonde hair that covered one half of his face while the other side revealed him to be an expert with makeup.

Barry was recently sober and he was not about to take responsibility for letting this man into the meeting, so he called several of the older members out of the back room to make the decision; but this only provoked a loud and wandering argument that clearly had no hope of resolution. Finally, in frustration, Barry got the man a cup of coffee and called Bill Wilson at his home in Bedford Hills, NY. He described the

---

* These two beliefs are so fundamental to the message of the book that a list of comprehensive references would necessarily be pages long. It is, for instance, a central message in Chapter Five ("Selfishness—self-centeredness. That, we think is the root of our troubles." p. 62) and there are at least seventy specific mentions of the need to be "useful," "helpful," "of service," or "altruistic" throughout the book.

** This phrase was explicitly used to describe "the only requirement for membership" in the "Foreword" to the first edition of *Alcoholics Anonymous* (p. viii).

prospective new member to Bill in detail and then said, 'We don't know what in the world to do with him. He needs all kinds of help.'

After a short silence, Bill asked Barry to run over the list of problems and objections one more time and Barry did so.

'Now,' said Bill, 'did you say he was a drunk?'

'Oh yes,' Barry replied. 'There's no question about that. He is definitely a drunk.'

After another brief silence, Bill made his decision and said, 'Well, I think that's the only question we have any right to ask.' Barry invited the man into the meeting.[43]

In Bill Wilson's A.A. *everyone* deserves a chance to get sober.

Perhaps even more important than Bill's broadmindedness in relation to the marginalized members of society was his growing acceptance of people whose beliefs about God were completely different from those of traditional Christianity and eventually, some that did not accept even the most basic Western concepts of divinity. One example of this enlarged religious tolerance appeared in print in 1957 when Bill related the story of the Twelve Steps being shown to a Buddhist leader for his approval. The monk read them over carefully and then commented, "Why, these are fine! Since we as Buddhists don't understand God just as you do, it might be slightly more acceptable if you inserted the word 'good' in your Steps instead of 'God.' Nevertheless, you say in these Steps that it is God *as you understand Him*. That clears up the point for us. Yes, A.A's Twelve Steps will certainly be accepted by the Buddhists around here." Bill admitted some members might find this to be a serious "watering down of A.A.'s message. But here we must remember," he continued "that A.A.'s Steps are suggestions only. A belief in them as they stand is not at all a requirement for membership among us."[44] It is the desire to stop drinking that qualifies someone to become a member of Alcoholics Anonymous; that and nothing else.

But in early June 1938, as Bill Wilson sat down to write this critical chapter for their proposed book, a chapter that was supposed to clearly outline the basics of their collective approach to sobriety, sophisticated problems involving gay black men and atheistic Buddhists were not even on the horizon yet.

In June 1938, the problem in New York City was Jimmy Burwell.

Challenges from Outspoken Atheists

Burwell came from Washington, DC, where he quit drinking on January 8, 1938. Two weeks later, he traveled up to New York to meet Bill Wilson and Hank Parkhurst. It turned out that Jim already knew Hank because eleven years earlier, Parkhurst had fired him from a very good job after he'd "totaled out three or four cars on him" while driving drunk.[45] No matter. Jim was really enjoying his newfound sobriety and this "swell pair of screwballs" (Wilson and Parkhurst) he had fallen in with. His only complaint was "all they talked of that first weekend was God" and then, along with the rest of the men at the regular Sunday night meeting, they always seemed to come back to praising the ways in which "God had touched [them] personally on the shoulder." As far as Jim could tell, it was all about God, and that was a serious problem because he was a man with a profound aversion to all things religious or theological. Jim Burwell was a confirmed and outspoken atheist.[46]

He was, in fact, the kind of man who would not have a chance of getting sober in Akron. It wasn't just his lack of belief that was a problem; many people (including Bill Wilson himself and his right-hand man Hank Parkhurst) had started out as agnostics or atheists. The problem was that Burwell was not the least bit shy about loudly proclaiming his disbelief and accompanying it with a liberal dose of sarcastic commentary about how stupid and unnecessary it was to expect someone to believe in God just because he wanted to quit drinking. What did God have to do with it? There wasn't a glimmer of hope that Burwell would ever make a personal surrender to God (either in public or private) and in Akron, as already noted, a new member was not admitted into the group until he had fulfilled that basic requirement.

In New York, however, Wilson's desire to be inclusive and his reluctance to turn away anyone who wanted to stop drinking had already overridden many of these old beliefs and he insisted Burwell be given a chance; Bill was confident that sooner or later Jimmy would come around to a belief in God or, if not, then he would surely drink.* Hank endorsed this liberal approach and even went so far as to hire Burwell (who had an excellent record as a salesman just so long as he wasn't drinking) to go on the road selling automobile polish for Honor Dealers.** Going one step further, Hank even agreed to put Jimmy up in his house in Montclair, NJ, whenever he wasn't out on the road traveling.

But for months, Burwell neither changed his mind about God nor did he drink; he just became an increasingly more vocal and annoying 'problem child' within the group. By his own description he was a shock to the Sunday night meetings at Bill's house in Brooklyn: "I was a menace to serenity those first few months, for I took every opportunity to lambaste that 'spiritual angle' as we called it, or anything else that had any tinge of theology." His constant outspoken condemnation of the God idea upset the New York members so much that, according to Jim, they "held many prayer meetings hoping to find a way to give me the heave-ho, but at the same time stay tolerant and spiritual." The group was, however, never able to resolve that perplexing problem so by default Jim was allowed to stay.

---

* This belief that exposure to the program of recovery as embodied in the Twelve Steps would eventually lead a person to either believe in a personal God or a drink was one of Bill Wilson's lifelong beliefs. In his May 1944 address at the annual meeting of the Medical Society of the State of New York Section on Neurology and Psychiatry he said: "the new man . . . sometimes eliminates 'the spiritual angle' from the Twelve Suggested Steps to recovery and wholly relies upon honesty, tolerance, and 'working with others.' But it is curious and interesting to note that faith always comes to those who try this simple approach *with an open mind*— and in the meantime stay sober." In the same vein, see the lines that follow his 1957 comments regarding the Buddhist story that are noted above (from *AACOA*, p. 81).

** This was most likely for a product made by a company called Stain-Ox that was located in Roselle, NJ. In his Big Book story, Jim incorrectly states that "Bill and Hank had just taken over a small automobile polish company," but there is no evidence that Hank had anything other than a distribution deal with this company; Bill called it simply a "promising interest" in Stain-Ox in a January 7, 1939, document (One Hundred Men Inc., GSO, Box 59, 1939, Folder C, Document 1939-26 to 1939-32, p. 6). Supporting this contention of a distribution deal is the fact that Stain-Ox was one of the original investors in Works Publishing (eight shares for $200); something that would not have happened if Hank had been required to put up the money for those shares. He was broke. (See the list of shareholders in Works Publication dated May 15, 1940; GSO, Box 61, Folder D, 1940—Works Publishing Company, p. 76.) *NOTE:* This is a typical example of the wildly inaccurate statements that Burwell so commonly makes in relation to factual details. Because of this, I have been extremely hesitant to accept many of his claims at face value and have relied on secondary source substantiation whenever possible. This is not to say that everything Jim said was inaccurate, but the percentage of his statements that are contradicted by contemporary documents is certainly high.

Bill Wilson wrote his own description of what it was like during those first five months of 1938 when Jim Burwell showed up at the meeting every week, ranting about the God problem:

> Like a four-ton bomb, the new member exploded among [our] small group of [drunks]. As we were then very young, no one had ever seen anybody like Jimmy. Jimmy knew just what he was after; he wanted to stop drinking.
>
> There was no doubt about it. Enthusiastic—sincere—aggressive—he was all of these. But Jimmy was a man of fixed ideas; very fixed, as we soon discovered.
>
> Rising to his feet at a meeting, Jimmy stridently declared, "[Damn] this God business! It's the bunk. I don't need it to make [this] program work. And neither does anybody else. It's a lot of superstition. We ought to stand on our own feet, get honest and work with other alkies. That's program enough. Let's skip the God stuff."
>
> And so the trouble started.
>
> . . . Was it not our experience that we must live by spiritual principles or drink and so die? Of course, it was. The spiritual "angle" was the heart of the program. Some of us had been unbelievers, but we had come open-minded to [the group] and had acquired faith. But here came a man shouting that the very grace by which we were living was ridiculous.
>
> We tried every conceivable means of [bringing] Jimmy around—gentle remonstrance, angry argument, condescending pity, the advice [that he was destroying our] newcomer's chances by his awful heresy, exclusion from our councils and finally the threat of expulsion from [our group]. None of these devices worked. As well [try to] soften cold steel in a candle flame.[47]

Burwell was proving to be an enormous challenge to Wilson's desire for an open door policy, but whatever the difficulties and however uncomfortable it might have been at times, Bill persevered in his tolerance and his commitment to the principle that the only requirement for membership was an honest desire to stop drinking. And on that score, Jimmy absolutely qualified.

But Burwell's presence wasn't the only problem. His candid and unrepentant disbelief while he continued to stay sober encouraged Hank Parkhurst to become increasingly more open about his own feelings that the group was placing far too much emphasis on the religious angle and that they would have more success with new prospects (and drive fewer people away) if they would just confine themselves to the psychological aspect of recovery. In Hank's opinion, the most effective way to gain a newcomer's attention was to talk to him about how powerless he was over the first drink (the "peculiar mental twist" that took him back to drinking) and about his need to become more selfless and caring for others (moral psychology).

Hank has frequently been portrayed as an agnostic or even an atheist—mostly based on his reported insistence on leaving God out of the Big Book. As Wilson later noted, Parkhurst "had been very agnostic" and it was because of this that "he thought a psychological book should be written."[48] But Parkhurst's outspoken objections to Wilson's constant emphasis on religion was not because he had no faith in a Higher Power. Hank *was* a believer, but his faith was much more along Deist lines than anything else.* Given this different understanding of God, he credited his own sobriety more to the psychological changes he had made than he did to the powerful hand of the providential God to which Bill always gave credit.

More than that, he felt that such an explicit religious emphasis would prove to be a marketing disaster. He knew his own history and how resistant he had been to "the God idea" while he was drinking and he feared Bill Wilson's constant mention of God and religion would alienate the majority of active alcoholics from the very start and thereby deny them any possible chance of recovery.

Jim Burwell's volatile presence in the group provided Hank with the perfect foil for making his increasingly strident arguments about the need to de-emphasize the religious and present their program in a book that used much more general, psychological terms that would not immediately drive away readers. While admitting the religious component was important for any long-term sobriety, Hank felt just as strongly that recovery would be accessible to more people if it was presented to them from the psychological viewpoint first, with the religious elements being slowly introduced at some time later in the process.

Given all of these circumstances, Wilson's challenge was beyond formidable; it seemed impossible. How could he possibly write something that would accommodate the very different and liberal opinions being adopted by his group in New York City, while simultaneously satisfying the much more rigid Oxford Group model practiced by the larger contingent of sober men out in Akron?

Among his many talents, Bill Wilson was an accomplished politician, and he could be absolutely brilliant when dealing with the squabbling factions clamoring for his attention and approval throughout his many years as the unofficial leader of Alcoholics Anonymous. But in this case, it was just not possible to satisfy these two divergent and conflicting approaches simultaneously so, in the end, Bill chose to steer a middle course by focusing primarily on his own experiences in New York, while making every effort to present those experiences in a way he hoped Dr. Bob and the other Ohio members would find acceptable.

---

* Merton M.'s unfinished and unpublished manuscript, *Black Sheep*, focuses primarily on Hank Parkhurst and he repeatedly (and credibly) makes the point that "Hank was neither an atheist nor an agnostic" after he got sober (see, for instance, *Black Sheep*, p. 48). Support for that understanding of Parkhurst's religious convictions will be presented later in the story here.

Bill Writes the New Chapter

Finally putting pen to paper, Wilson began by boldly titling this new chapter "There Is A Solution," and then plunged immediately into the religion versus psychology controversy then raging in New York by citing the professional opinion of one of the world's leading psychiatrists. Bill presented this head-on confrontation as a story about "a man we know" who "had searched the whole world for a solution to his alcohol problem" before finally traveling to Europe where he consulted with "a noted doctor and psychologist having world eminence in his specialty." This was the famous A.A. story of Rowland Hazard and Dr. Carl Jung, a tale familiar to the New York members and one that had certainly been passed on to the drunks in Akron.[*] Despite the extensive treatment Rowland received from Jung, he had slipped back into drinking and the doctor, in frustration, declared him incurable, saying that, in his judgment, he "was utterly hopeless, could never regain his position in society, and would have to place himself permanently in an institution or hire a bodyguard if he expected to live long."[**]

Bill followed this dramatic opening with a short teaser paragraph noting that despite this alarming and fatal prognosis "our friend lives and is a free man. He does not have to have a bodyguard, nor is he confined." After a professional diagnosis like that, how could this possibly be true?

Rather than presenting the conclusion of Rowland Hazard's story here (it appears later, near the end of the chapter), Bill pauses for dramatic effect, claiming "We, of ALCOHOLICS ANONYMOUS, now know at least one hundred men" who "have been the victims of a common calamity and have collectively experienced almost every known variety of human misadventure and misery." But it is these same men who have discovered "a common solution" to their problem with alcohol and "a way out with which we can absolutely agree." These last six words were surely overly optimistic, but then Wilson was creating something intended as a sales piece to promote donations as much as it was meant to be a how-to presentation on recovery and a positive stance of unanimity was critical to both of those goals.

Nor is this "common solution" or the "way out" immediately described. Once again, Bill sidesteps the issue he has just introduced and spends the next two pages establishing the credentials for these "one hundred men" who "as a group . . . have had four years of intensive and unique experience on which to draw" and who "during this

---

[*] The often told A.A. version of this story has frequently eluded attempts at corroboration. For an in-depth investigation and some interesting conclusions about the disputed facts of this story, see "Stellar Fire: Carl Jung, a New England Family and the Risks of Anecdote" by Cora Finch (available at http://hindsfoot.org/jungstel.pdf - retrieved March 4, 2012). For one interesting theory on how this story came to Bill Wilson through Cebra Graves who supposedly heard it directly from Rowland Hazard, see Jared Lobdell, "Progress Report: The Messengers to Ebby: Cebra G." in Vol. III, no. 7 of *CASQ, Culture Alcohol & Society Quarterly*, p.12.

[**] Unless otherwise noted, the quotes here from "There Is A Solution" are taken from the earliest version of the chapter I have been able to locate, a reduced copy of a typed original in the Stepping Stones archive that has the title "Alcoholics, Anonymous." at the top of the page in pencil (StSt, AA 501.1, Alcoholics Anonymous—Early Draft of Chapter "There Is A Solution," Box 13, Folder 24). Stepping Stones preserves a later, edited version of this chapter (in the same folder), while GSO has archived an even later, edited version (GSO, Box 59, 1938, Folder B, Documents 1938—53 to 63). Note that all of these were typed on 8½" x 14" (legal) paper. The first two are twelve pages in length and the GSO copy is eleven pages long. See Appendix III starting on page 615 for a full transcript of the text used here.

time . . . have most intimately touched some two hundred cases of acute alcoholism."* This has typically been done, he says, by having one "ex-alcoholic who has found this solution, and who is properly armed with certain medical and psychiatric information" carry the message of their common solution directly to another suffering alcoholic. Wilson then goes on for almost two pages about the absolute necessity of expanding this work with the publication of a book that will suggest "a definite program of action and attitude to everyone concerned in a drinking situation." Such a book, he notes, will necessarily involve "a great deal of discussion . . . of matters medical, psychiatric, social and religious;" subjects which are, by their very nature, "highly controversial." But he quickly reminds his readers that, as these discussions progress, "we are most anxious not to appear in a role of those who would preach or reform, as we deem such attitudes ill befit the kind of people we have been and to some extent still are."

Having spent almost five pages on these preliminaries, Wilson finally arrives at the heart of the matter and offers three critical questions that he claims will frame the general outline of the book, questions he feels would have by now occurred to anyone with enough interest in his subject to have "read this far:"

1. Why it is that all of us became so desperately ill from drinking?

2. How and why have we all recovered from an utterly hopeless condition of mind and body?

3. What do I have to do to get over it?

"The main purpose of this book," he states confidently, "is to exhaustively, definitely and specifically answer those questions and to let you know what you can do about it."

In the next two pages Wilson briefly describes a "moderate" drinker and then a "control" drinker before launching into a long and detailed description of "the true alcoholic;" a picture that he admits is not comprehensive but that he hopes will "suffice for the moment to roughly identify him in the mind of the reader." This is the man we are talking about and here is what his problems look like in graphic detail. How did he ever come to such a place and what is it about his drinking that has made him "so desperately ill"?

The Problem: Insanity

Perhaps the most striking example of genius in all of Bill Wilson's writings occurs in the next two and half pages of this manuscript as he pinpoints the central problem of the true alcoholic and identifies it with the moment of insanity just before the problem-drinker—with no alcohol whatsoever in his body—picks up the first drink:

---

* This "four years" of group experience (not to mention the "one hundred men") is completely inaccurate given the date of the writing. In June 1938, Bill was sober just three-and-a-half years and Dr. Bob (the second oldest person in sobriety after Ebby's slip in April 1937) had only three years of sobriety. The same claims are made in both of the other two early archived version of this chapter. Contemporary mention of the "one hundred men" claim can also be found in a letter Bill wrote in August 1938 (Wm. G. Wilson to Mr. Charles Parcelles [sic], July [but really August] 1, 1938 (GSO, Box 59, 1938, Folder B, Documents 1938-31 to 1938-34) and appears again, along with the "four years" assertion in an undated "To Whom It May Concern" letter that Wilson wrote, most likely in mid-July 1938 (GSO, Box 59, 1938, Folder B, Document 1938-49). Perhaps this is just simple exaggeration (a defect that Wilson was consistently prone to) or these inflated numbers may have been used in anticipation of what the situation would be on the book's projected publication date.

The almost certain consequences that follow taking a glass of beer do not crowd into the mind and deter us. If these thoughts do occur, they are vague or hazy and become readily supplanted with the old threadbare idea that this time we shall handle ourselves like other people. There is a complete failure of the kind of defense that would keep one from putting his hand on a hot stove . . .

[Now,] all of these observations would be quite academic and pointless if our friend never took the first drink, thereby setting in motion the terrible cycle that everyone has seen so many times . . . If hundreds of experiences have shown him that one drink means another debacle with all its attendant suffering and humiliation, how is it that he takes that one drink? What has become of the common sense and will power that he frequently displays with respect to other matters?

These are inspired and penetrating questions and they lead Wilson to the inevitable conclusion that "the real problem of the alcoholic centers in his mind rather than in his body." Usually the alcoholic "has no more idea why he took that first drink than you have," and there is no possible explanation for this complete lapse of "common sense and will power" other than to admit that he suffers from some form of temporary insanity.

This is a startling diagnosis: the alcoholic's *real* problem isn't his drinking, it is his *thinking*; more specifically, his thinking during the brief moments just before he picks up the first drink.

At a certain point in the drinking of every alcoholic, he passes into a state where the most powerful desire to stop drinking is of absolutely no avail . . . The fact is, that all of us for reasons which are yet obscure, have entirely lost the power of choice with respect to alcoholic drinks. Our so-called will power with respect to that area of thinking and action becomes virtually non-existent. We are unable at certain times, no matter how well we understand ourselves, to bring into our consciousness with sufficient force, the memory of the suffering and humiliation of even a week or a month ago.

This is a unique insight into the very heart of the mystery of alcoholism and an ingenious reformulation of the drunkard's most basic problem; it is already and exactly *there*, fully blown, *before* he ever drinks. This belief is firmly based on Bill Wilson's own experiences during the years when he was so desperately trying to stop drinking. His final, month-long drunk began on November 11, 1934, a day on which he traveled out to Staten Island to play some golf and, along the way, struck up a conversation with another passenger on the bus. The bus broke down and, while they waited for its replacement, Bill told the story of his drinking life to his new friend and explained he was sober now and could never again drink alcohol in any form. An hour later, the two men sat together at a bar finishing their lunches when:

we were almost ready to leave when my mind turned back again to Armistice Day in France, all the ecstasy of those hours. I remembered how we'd all gone to town. I no longer heard what my friend was saying. Suddenly, the bartender, a big, florid Irishman, came abreast of us, beaming. In each hand he held a drink. "Have one on the house, boys," he cried, 'It's Armistice Day." Without an instant's hesitation I picked up the liquor and drank it. My friend looked at me aghast. "My God, is it possible that you could take a drink after what you just told me? You must be crazy." And my only reply could be this, "Yes, I am."[49]

This is a clear-cut and very personal example of the insanity that precedes the first drink, and it proved to Wilson that, in some perverse and inexplicable way, his primary problem was mental rather than physical. The man who woke up on that Armistice Day morning had recently completed an extensive round of professional treatment and he was supremely confident that his newly acquired self-knowledge would protect him from drinking. But after this incident it was obvious that self-knowledge—along with every other avoidance technique he had ever tried—would always fail him in the moments just before he started to drink again. At some unpredictable time in the future, whatever mental defense he might have developed would be forgotten and disappear in the instant before the first drink was raised to his lips. Then the crazy cycle of drunkenness would begin again for "once [the alcoholic] takes any alcohol whatever into his system, something happens both in the bodily and the mental sense, which makes it virtually impossible for him to stop." Disaster was inevitable. Whatever confidence a drunk might have in his ability to resist that first drink, it would eventually and inevitably prove to be a delusion. Even if a "true alcoholic" does manage to stop drinking for some period of time, there was no way he can ever stay stopped.

The Solution: A "Deep and Effective Religious Experience"

Given this penetrating and frightening analysis of the problem, was there no hope? In fact, he claimed, "there is a solution, and how glorious was the knowledge of it to us."

The solution, Bill explained, requires that certain actions be taken, including extensive "self searching" along with "the leveling of our pride [and] the confession of our sins of omission and commission." He also notes that, at first, "almost none of us liked" the idea of doing any of these things, but once "we had come to believe in the hopelessness and futility of life as we had been living it" and had seen this process "really worked in others," then "there was nothing left for us to do but accept the proposals placed before us."

And now, beyond these suggested actions, there is one other element absolutely essential to sobriety that Wilson could no longer avoid. While the alcoholic's *problem* can be understood in medical and psychological terms, the *solution* is most certainly religious in nature. The "GREAT FACT is just this and no less; that all of us have had deep and effective religious experiences which have in every case revolutionized our whole attitude toward life, toward our fellows and toward God's great universe."

Furthermore, "the central fact of our lives today is the absolute certainty that the Creator of you and me has entered into our hearts and lives in a way which is to us new and beautiful and has there commenced to accomplish those things which by no stretch of the imagination were we humanly capable of."

Self-searching, a reduction of pride, and the confession of our sins are all necessary actions, but they are only effective when carried out in the context of a new and "revolutionized" attitude that comes from having a "deep and effective religious experience." Both the actions *and* the experience are necessary if there is to be any hope of truly quitting drinking and of being able to begin a new life of wholesome and continued sobriety.

From his long experience with drunks Bill knew exactly what kind of reaction to expect once his alcoholic readers were confronted with this revelation:

> Is it possible that this announcement has given you a severe jolt, followed by thoughts something like these—"Oh, so that's what it is, I'm so disappointed, I had begun to think these fellows knew what they were talking about." But let us assure you that you should be cheered up . . . for we think that no one should miss THE GREAT REALITY which we have been lucky enough to find . . .

Wilson is almost pleading here: please don't go away in despair; please do not close your eyes to this wonderfully effective solution. Where you are now, we have already been and while we were there, we tried every imaginable—and ultimately unsuccessful—way to stop drinking. But now, we have finally found something that works and it has worked for all of us. If you can believe just that much, then hopefully you will be able to agree with us that:

> There is no tenable middle of the road solution. You are in a position where life is becoming impossible, and if you have passed into the region from which there is no return through human aid, you have just two alternatives. One is to go on to the bitter end, blotting out the consciousness of your intolerable situation as best you can. Or, you can surely find what we have found, if you honestly want to and are willing to pay the price.

Bill immediately tempers the need for a "deep and effective religious experience" by emphasizing he is not talking about some sort of instant conversion. No one expects, he told his readers, that you are "going to get rightly related to your Creator in a minute. None of us found God in six easy lessons, but He can be found by all who are willing to put the task ahead of all else."

Carl Jung and William James
Having so far offered a solution based on the experiences of one hundred sober men, Bill now returns to the story of Rowland Hazard and Dr. Jung and shares that great psychologist's professional opinion about the *only* possible cure for alcoholic drinking;

an opinion that aligns perfectly with the religious solution Bill has just insisted is so essential to any recovery:

> On the bare chance that our alcoholic readers still think they can do without God, let us complete for you the conversation which our friend was having with the celebrated European man of medicine. As you will recall, the doctor said—"I never have seen one single case in which alcohol mindedness was established in the sense you have it that ever recovered." Naturally, our friend felt at that moment as though the gates of hell had closed on him with a sickening clang. He then said to the doctor, "Is there no exception?" The doctor answered, "Yes, there is. The sole exceptions in cases such as yours have been occurring now and then since early times. Sporadically, here and there, once in a while, alcoholics have had what are called vital religious experiences. I am not a religious man, to me these occurrences are a phenomena. They appear to be in the nature of huge emotional displacements and rearrangements. Ideas, emotions and attitudes which were once the guiding forces of the lives of these men, are suddenly cast to one side and a completely new set of conceptions and motives commence to dominate them . . ."

Rowland was, at first, greatly pleased by this news since, as he told Jung, he was already "a very good church member." But the doctor quickly dashed this cavalier optimism by noting that "his faith and his religious convictions were very good so far as they went, but that in his case they did not spell the vital religious experience so absolutely imperative to displace his insanity with respect to matters alcoholic." Jung made it perfectly clear he was not talking about a typical run-of-the-mill religious belief in God demonstrated by regular attendance at church. Such a faith would have absolutely no effect on Rowland's ability to stop drinking nor could it ever be "successful with an alcoholic of your state of mind." Jung insisted it was "imperative" for Rowland to experience something much more "deep and effective" than just a commonplace belief in God and noted that, unless Rowland found such a "vital religious experience," he would never be able to stay sober.

Directing his attention back toward the reader, Bill writes that:

> You and I would say that the patient was on a very hot spot, [and] that is probably what he did say and feel. So have we, when it began to look to us as though we must have a vital religious experience or perish. Our friend did finally have such an experience and we in our turn have sought the same happy end, with all the ardor of drowning men clutching at straws. But what seemed at first to be a flimsy reed has proved to be a loving and powerful hand of God. A new life has been given us, or if you please, a design for living that really works.

Having addressed the religion versus psychology controversy by citing the opinion of a world-famous European psychiatrist who believed the only solution was a "vital religious experience," Wilson now begins the final three paragraphs of the chapter by once more combining psychology with religion; but, this time, approaching it from a completely different perspective.

Rather than introducing yet another authority to confirm the necessity of a God-centered solution, Bill takes that point to be proven and moves on to his next important insight by citing William James (at the time the most famous and revered of all American psychologists) to substantiate the fact that there was absolutely no need for this God-centered solution to be tied to any particular set of beliefs or prescribed practices. Wilson refers the reader to James's important and influential 1902 book, *The Varieties of Religious Experience*, presenting it as conclusive psychological proof that there are "a multitude of ways in which men have found God." He then goes further and claims that this open approach to theology is the very one adopted and endorsed by each of these one hundred men:

> As a group, or as individuals, we have no desire to convince anyone that the true God can only be discovered in some particular way. Anyone who has talked with all of us would soon be disabused of the idea. If what we have learned, and felt, and seen, means anything at all, it indicates that all of us, whatever our race, creed or color, are children of a living Creator with whom we may form a new relationship upon very simple and understandable terms, the moment any of us become willing enough and honest enough to do so. Therefore, we waste no time in the kind of religious disputation which has so frequently torn people apart.

These men, who have individually discovered that flimsy reed, which later proved to be the "loving and powerful hand of God," have all come to their beliefs by different paths, and there is no particular set of dogmas or religious practices they subscribe to or that they will demand of you. Nor do they care what church you belong to or even if you go to church (although most of them do). "We feel that should be entirely one's own affair." Attendance at church is an individual decision to be made "in the light of [each man's] past association, his newly found religious experience, his convictions and preferences, and above all, his future usefulness."

Bill then ends the chapter with a final paragraph noting that "the next few chapters" will have "the personal narratives of several of us" describing "the way in which [each writer] found the living God." "We hope," he says, "that no one will be disturbed that these stories contain so much self revelation" or think they exceed the bounds of good taste. They are necessarily candid so "that the reader may get a fair cross section and a clear cut idea of what has really happened, and why we think it happened." But most important, these stories are written in the hopes that the alcoholic reader will readily identify with them and having made that identification, will "be persuaded to say, 'Yes, I am one of them; I must have this thing.'"

Bill's Religious Perspective

What would likely be surprising—and, in some cases, even shocking—to many current A.A. members in this early version of the chapter is the repeated insistence that the solution for alcoholism is specifically "religious" in nature, a word that drags a fair amount of baggage into the discussion. Perhaps none of these would be more surprising than Dr. Jung's observation that the only hope for recovery from drinking is be found in a "vital religious experience"; a dramatically different prescription from the frequently quoted "vital spiritual experience," which appears in the Big Book today.

Bill is aware of this problem and he is constantly reminding the reader that when he says "religious," he intends that word to be understood in the most flexible and open-ended way possible. He almost pleads with the reader to keep an open mind on this question of religion, pointedly claiming that the word is meant to encompass "nearly every conceivable . . . shade of belief" and, "we have no desire to convince anyone that the true God can only be discovered in some particular way." The religious solution is explicitly understood to be as accommodating as possible, allowing people to approach and resolve whatever issues they might have with God in absolutely any way they find acceptable. Bill's final appeal to William James's book, *The Varieties of Religious Experience*, is meant to emphatically underline the fact he is talking about a religious solution that comes with no formal dogma and with no prescribed religious practices.

Later edits to this chapter would significantly tone down the impact and the implied message of the word "religious" by repeatedly replacing it with the much gentler "spiritual"; a word that undoubtedly comes with some baggage of its own, but nowhere near as much as the more specific "religious." To most ears, that word almost necessarily implies "church" and "dogma," while "spiritual" might be understood to apply to a meaningful life that is lived independent of any formal religious organization.

But just how open was Bill in this early version of "There Is A Solution" to "nearly every conceivable . . . shade of belief"? It does not require a careful reading of the text to realize that Wilson is very much a man of his own time, culture, and upbringing and when he uses the word "religious"—despite all of his protests to the contrary—he was identifying with a specific concept of God to the exclusion of all others. Whatever later liberalizations may have been introduced by the substitution of spiritual for religious or by Bill's consistent efforts over the years to open the doors of A.A. ever wider, the open concept claimed for religion here does not embrace a whole host of the "varieties" so candidly acknowledged in William James's book, a study that includes investigations into the religious beliefs of Pagans, Hindus, Buddhists, and Sufis (among others).

As his language consistently shows, when Wilson uses the word "religious" here, he is talking about the belief in a personal, providential God, very much along the lines of the God of Abraham, who is to be the ultimate source of salvation for alcoholics. When it comes to recovery, he is not talking, for instance, about the indifferent Creator God of the Deists or about any of the other more liberal concepts of "God as you understand Him." Bill Wilson's God is "the Creator of you and me," the "living Creator" and "the living God." He is a God with "a loving and powerful hand"; one who is capable of "entering into our hearts and lives" where He can "accomplish those things which by no stretch of the imagination were we humanly capable of." This is a God who wholeheartedly offers each of us the opportunity to form a very personal and direct relationship with Him and on whom we can absolutely rely for help to overcome the insanity that precedes the first drink.

Like almost everything else in the chapter, this conception of God came from Bill Wilson's own personal experience, it is the foundation of a belief system he adopted when he first got sober and it is the one he maintained for the rest of his life. Since Bill's own God was a providential God—one you could pray to with the full expectation of receiving an answer to your prayers—that is the God he explicitly described as the "glorious" solution to the problem of uncontrolled drinking in this first version of "There Is A Solution."

Further Distancing from the Oxford Group

While it is interesting to note that what Bill writes is little more than a generalized version of his own personal experience, it is what he does *not* say here that is even more striking. He makes no specific or implied mention of the Oxford Group and he carefully avoids using any of their traditional terminology (Absolutes, quiet time, checking, etc.). Beyond this, Bill also rejects the Group's particular Christian practices as being unnecessary for their solution and in their place, he wholeheartedly endorses William James's infinitely broader definition of what qualifies as a valid religious experience.

Where then does that leave the very successful Akron prescription for getting sober; an approach that, in almost all of its important particulars, has been either completely ignored or significantly watered down in this chapter?

A little over a year earlier Frank Amos had noted in his report that there were six different 'musts' in the sobriety solution he found in Akron. In this chapter, four of these are certainly touched on, although their presentation has been considerably softened (the word "must" in this sense is not used in Bill's first version of "There Is A Solution"):

> An alcoholic <u>must</u> realize that he is an alcoholic, incurable from a medical viewpoint and that he <u>must</u> never again drink anything with alcohol in it

> He <u>must</u> surrender himself absolutely to God realizing that in himself there is no hope

> He <u>must</u> be willing to help other alcoholics get straightened out . . . [50]

But the other two "musts" are not mentioned or even implied in this first attempt at what was supposed to be a comprehensive outline of how the so-called "one hundred men" (the majority of whom were in Akron) had managed to stay sober. Completely missing are:

> Not only must he want to stop drinking permanently, but he <u>must</u> remove from his life other sins such as hatred, adultery and others which frequently accompany alcoholism . . .

> He <u>must</u> have devotions every morning—a "quiet time" of prayer, and some reading from the Bible or other religious literature. Unless this is faithfully followed, there is grave danger of backsliding; . . . [51]

Bill has come out strongly for his own vision of alcoholics who are saved by the intervention of a providential God, but while doing so he has softened or abandoned a large amount of what was considered to be the very core of recovery and sobriety in Akron. Would Dr. Bob and the other Akron members be able to follow him down this new path?

Exactly how Bill thought these slights might be received in Akron is unclear, but his blatant omissions and rejections would certainly offend the non-alcoholic Oxford Group members who were so deeply intertwined with Akron sobriety, not to mention how they might upset those sober members of the Ohio "Alcoholic Squad" who thought of themselves primarily as Oxford Groupers and who credited the Group (and its way of life) with saving their lives.[*] But, however deeply committed these sober members might be to the Oxford Group, Wilson was clearly articulating a position that flew directly in the face of that partnership and decisively distanced him from everything he felt was wrong with the Oxford Group, including all of the unnecessary baggage and entanglements such an alliance entailed.

Wilson's significantly moderated presentation of the first four "musts," and his complete elimination of the other two, speaks volumes about his vision for the future of their growing Fellowship. It is not just that he makes no mention whatsoever of the Oxford Group here; instead, the chapter emphatically describes a group that will not tolerate the "religious disputation which has so frequently torn people apart" and further states "that it is no concern of ours as a group what religious bodies we shall identify with as individuals." In fact, "not all of us have [even] joined religious bodies." Essentially, he says, we are a group of men who wholeheartedly embrace the "varieties of religious experience" approach and we are committed to honoring *whatever* religious beliefs our members feel will take them "a step toward new growth and [a greater] availability for God's purpose."

Given the timing of this writing and what was then going on in Akron, this first version of "There Is A Solution," can hardly be read as anything other than Bill Wilson's Declaration of Independence from the Oxford Group and, for that matter, from every other religious organization imaginable.

---

[*]   This was certainly the case when the book was finally published. "If the alcoholics in Akron had their problems with the Big Book, members of the Oxford Group had even more. There was the impression that it was commercial, for one thing. Another reason they were disappointed was that there was no mention of the Oxford Group in the book. Furthermore, the Twelve Steps had replaced the four absolutes, which were not mentioned, either." (*Dr. Bob and the Good Oldtimers*, pp. 154–55.)

A New Path to Sobriety

At this point, it is important to take a few steps back in order to fully appreciate the startling vision and leadership Bill Wilson displays in this first version of "There Is A Solution."

By defining the solution as primarily religious—while pointedly insisting it must not be affiliated with any particular dogma or church—Wilson has resolutely staked out the basic grounds upon which the future Fellowship of Alcoholics Anonymous would be built. His solution is progressive, pragmatic, democratic, and expansive. It is a vision conceived in an open-ended and inclusive spirit going far beyond anything imagined in the restrictive religious outlook adopted by Dr. Bob Smith or to be found in the psychology-first perspective advocated by Hank Parkhurst. Bill has categorically rejected the pitfalls of an Oxford Group connection while simultaneously refusing to reduce their proposed solution to mere psychology. His vision, even at this early date, is already broad, brilliant, and uncompromising. Wilson has seen what would be needed to capture and hold the attention of the thousands (and later the millions) of people he is trying to reach with his "Solution" and he has gone there with confidence.

As he first started to write, Bill might well have set for himself the goal of creating an extremely broad explanation of their solution, one wide enough to encompass both the Oxford Group sobriety of Akron and the more liberal psychology-based model favored by the vocal minority of Parkhurst and Burwell in New York. It would have been the safest and the most political thing for him to do under the circumstances. But the simultaneous accommodation of both perspectives was impossible and Bill was not about to compromise his own vision by capitulating to one or the other of these views exclusively. Instead, he rejected the pointed, single focus of both camps and drafted a far-sighted vision of recovery radically different from the extremely limited views then being advocated by his two main compatriots.

"There Is A Solution" is pure Bill Wilson; a clear and forthright presentation of a new path to sobriety, one that is firmly rooted in his own experience and that would, a few months later, begin to blossom and grow into the Big Book of Alcoholics Anonymous.

Given the chance, Dr. Bob Smith might have written a chapter very different from this; one with an explicit Christian message and a far more dogmatic approach to the requirements for sobriety. Knowing this, Wilson was justifiably nervous about the reception this chapter would receive in Ohio. It might be difficult to predict how Dr. Bob would react to this particular presentation of their solution, but Bill had been stung all too frequently and much too recently by the angry resistance of many Akron members to doubt there would be severe opposition once they had the opportunity to read what he had written. It was a situation that called for delicate handling.

But however uncertain or confrontational the Ohio reaction might prove to be, it was a problem that lay in the future. Hank Parkhurst, on the other hand, was sitting in the same office while Bill dictated "There Is A Solution," and he was not about to give up his own vision of sobriety without an argument.

CHAPTER NINE

Hank's Ideas

~Early June 1938~

Hank Parkhurst was not happy. He had his own very definite ideas about what should be going into this chapter describing their common solution—"a way out with which we can absolutely agree"[1]—and those ideas ran in a completely different direction from the one Bill Wilson was taking. At this time, Hank did believe in a "universal power,"[2] but his idea of a "Power greater than himself" was significantly different from the providential God Bill insisted was so necessary for recovery. Several months later Hank would categorically state his theological beliefs by saying, "I understand God as a great undefinable, unexplainable Power which will help me if I keep in tune with it."[3] Keeping in tune with a Power is significantly different from praying to and expecting to receive help from a personal God. Parkhurst's faith rested much more firmly on the belief that the best way to approach an active alcoholic was to talk about the insanity of the first drink and then emphasize the positive effects of moral psychology, initially avoiding any overt mention of the religious part of the solution.

Sharing a small office, Hank couldn't help but overhear as Bill dictated the new chapter to Ruth, and he was convinced that making a "vital religious experience" and a complete reliance on God central to the solution was a terrible mistake. Such an upfront insistence on religion and theology, he thought, would drive people away from their new method of recovery and severely cripple the book's appeal and sales. Wasn't this book supposed to attract problem drinkers rather than drive them away?

Hank Writes Down His Own Ideas

Parkhurst was a man of strong opinions with a talent for forceful persuasion, so even as Bill was creating the first draft of "There Is A Solution," he was jotting down his own thoughts about what should and should not be put into the book; ideas that were radically different from those Wilson was just then incorporating into the chapter he was writing.

Hank sketched out his own loosely organized thoughts about the contents of the book and how to promote it on eleven handwritten sheets (two of which were written on both sides). These pages, which Bill labeled in his own hand as "Hank's ideas," reveal a seemingly unbridgeable chasm between their very different understandings of the proper road to sobriety. This disagreement was nothing new, but as Bill wrote these chapters in late May and early June 1938, it suddenly became an unavoidable point of contention. Hank's strident push for his own vision of recovery created a decisive fork-in-the-road for their relationship, one that would gradually and inexorably widen over the next fifteen months as these and other differences continued to crop up and intensify. All the arguments these two men had been able to successfully sidestep or sweep under the carpet during the previous two-and-a-half years of their friendship were about to become unavoidable; they could no longer be ignored.

The sharp contrast between them also offers insight into the dynamics of the very real conflicts alive in the New York City group at this time, as well as the depths of the local problems Bill had to confront and try to resolve (especially in relation to his own right-hand man) as he began to write this critical chapter. Whose vision and explanation of recovery was going to prevail and be presented to the world at large? Would it be Bill Wilson's God-centered sobriety, so firmly based on a personal religious experience, or the much more secular approach favored by Hank, built on four practical steps and a solid foundation of moral psychology?

The notes labeled "Hank's ideas" were never meant to be, as some have claimed, an outline for the new book. The first page is the only one that presents anything even vaguely resembling this, but if Parkhurst had intended these notes to be a general plan for the book, then he would surely have provided far more details about the "List of Chapters" he mentions there.

Fourteen Points

Rather than an outline, what Hank jotted down in his own random fashion were some general ideas and observations to facilitate a conversation with Bill about his personal opinions

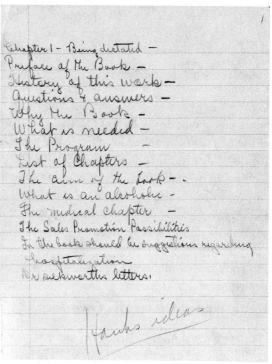

Courtesy of Stepping Stones Foundation Archives

regarding the book in general and about the chapter then being written in particular. His grandiose plans for promoting the book were intermixed with these ideas, but more than anything else, Hank was looking to change Bill's mind about the contents of the book. Central to that discussion are the fourteen points noted on his first page, elements that Hank thought should definitely be included in any book attempting to describe their program of recovery.

The fourteen points were:

- Chapter 1—Being dictated—
- Preface of the Book—
- History of this work—
- Questions + answers—
- Why the Book—
- What is needed—
- The Program—
- List of Chapters—
- The aim of the book—
- What is an alcoholic—
- The medical chapter—
- The Sales Promotion Possibilities
- In the book should be suggestions regarding hospitalization
- Dr Silkworths letters.[4]

Eight of these receive no further elaboration in the following ten pages, so they should at least be noted here again individually as being critical to Hank's vision for the book:

- Preface of the Book—
- What is needed—
- The Program—
- List of Chapters—
- The aim of the book—
- The medical chapter—
- In the book should be suggestions regarding hospitalization
- Dr Silkworths letters.

By far, the most significant of these eight is Hank's introduction of the all-inclusive phrase "The Program" to describe what actions they were taking to stay sober. It seems to be the first appearance of this ubiquitous A.A. phrase in any of the archived documents, and it is possible that Hank Parkhurst invented it as he was jotting down these notes. Obviously someone had to use that phrase for the first time and its appearance here is the first recorded instance we have of that happening.* Also of interest here are Hank's last three points, all of which focus on the important medical aspects of the problem and include his call for the use of letters (note the plural) from Dr. Silkworth. The famous letter of recommendation from Silkworth (that would later appear so prominently in the beginning of "The Doctor's Opinion") would not be written for several more weeks, but it is likely the doctor had already been approached on this and agreed to supply them with letters of recommendation. Silkworth was an enthusiastic supporter of their work and he could surely be counted on to do whatever was needed to help them further their cause.

Following this first page, again in no particular order, are ten additional sheets—each with a number and title—providing more details about the six remaining points mentioned on the first page:

2   Why the Book.

3   Questions + Answers—

4   Sales Promotion Possibilities
    (back side) Publicity / Newspapers

5   Suggestion for Chapter 1—

6   Mail Order

7   Title Page

8   Observations –
    (back side) ["Observations" continued]

9   [no title, but "Observations" continued]

10 Alcoholism

11 [no page number or title, but a numbered list of 25 professions
    to be included in the story section [5]

Hank's writing, as already noted, can be confusing even when he was striving for clarity, but these notes were never meant to rise to that level, which makes any summary of them even more challenging. The additional ten pages do, however, present a relatively well-organized picture of his position once they have been sorted out and grouped under two general headings:

(1) What Hank thought should and shouldn't be put into the book, and

(2) his explanation of the planned marketing campaign for the book.

What *Should* Be in the Book

Under the first heading Parkhurst makes three relatively minor suggestions for what should be in the book along with a fourth that is fairly significant (and certainly close

---

* Bill Wilson mentions "a practical program of action" on page 19 of his "Story" and notes on page 4 of the first version of "There Is A Solution" that the book they were planning to write was one "which ought to suggest a definite program of action and attitude for everyone concerned in a drinking situation," but neither of these uses of the word "program" carry anything like the weight and the significance that Hank captures with such clarity and brevity in his catchphrase "The Program."

to his heart). But then in his long fifth "observation," Parkhurst becomes much more critical, launching into an open attack on the approach being taken by Bill Wilson in "There Is A Solution," and then explaining his own ideas about the proper way to present their program of recovery to the public.

The first suggestion for the book blends two of Hank's original fourteen points ("Chapter 1—Being dictated" and "History of this Work") into a single recommendation. He notes the chapter currently being dictated to Ruth Hock should include:

> A History of the work—Possibly this could be carried on the first two pages of the book.
>
> This history should establish proof of success of the work and carry hope to everyone that reads that much.
>
> The opening to the book should arouse the emotion of hope.[6]

Bill's own opening for this chapter—his presentation of the first part of Rowland Hazard's story—certainly holds out a dramatic promise of hope for anyone afflicted with alcoholism ("But our friend lives and is a free man. He does not have to have a bodyguard, nor is he confined."), but it does not start out with the history of the work that Hank suggests. Although Bill does provide something of an overview of the work in the most general terms in the early pages of "There Is A Solution," he does so without presenting any kind of comprehensive or linear history, which is clearly what Hank is suggesting here. Beyond Rowland's hopeful story (which he had in all likelihood already written as the beginning of the chapter) Bill ignores this particular piece of advice.

Hank's second recommendation provides an abbreviated outline and an incomplete answer to the question raised in his tenth point from page 1: "What is an alcoholic?"

> Alcoholism
>
> May be best be [sic] defined to the average person by pointing out its leading symptoms and indicating how these reactions differ from the affects of alohol [sic] on normal persons
>
> 1. Total inability to control drinking once drinking is started.
>
> 2. Anti social behavior of these people when intoxicated
>
>   A. marked insanity
>
>   1. little relation [to] that persons normal behavior. or [to an] ordinary exuberant drinker or drunk
>
> [NOTE: written down the left hand side of this page—in block letters rather than script]:
>
> [Al]coholism a total [i]nability to control drinking when once started[7]

If there is one page here showing the very sketchy nature of these notes, this is surely it. Hank struggles even more (and quits much sooner) than Bill does in trying to create a simple and straightforward definition of the alcoholic. Wilson certainly labored mightily to define the alcoholic in "There Is A Solution," but he, like Hank, was never able to compress the tremendous complexity of alcoholism into a single, brief, but acceptable explanation. Instead, Bill wrote at great length about and around the subject in the new chapter before he finally stopped trying on page 7, claiming "the description [of the alcoholic offered so far] should suffice for the moment to roughly identify him in the mind of the reader." Evidence of Bill's surrender here is the word "roughly." What he had written was the best he could do, but he was aware that this description was still extremely vague and imprecise. Both men were learning first hand the difficulty of capturing the essence of the alcoholic in a concise, but comprehensive description.

Hank's third suggestion for the book is an interesting list of twenty-five different career types that should be represented among the many recovery stories they were planning to include in the book. Such a wide variety would dramatically demonstrate how the problem of alcoholism (and the solution) cuts across both social and economic lines:

1.	Broker ✓	13.	Judge ✓
2.	Surgeon	14.	Insurance ✓
3.	Politician	15.	Teacher
4.	Executive ✓	16.	Upholsterer
5.	Sales Manager. ✓	17.	Gardener
6.	Author. ✓	18.	Salesman
7.	Radio man. ✓	19.	Book Agent
8.	Laborer. ✓	20.	Fast car driver
9.	Accountant. ✓	21.	Farmer
10.	Proprietor very large retail business ✓	22.	Laboratory technician
11.	Housewife ✓	23.	Banker
12.	Mechanic ✓	24.	Athlete
		25.	Oil man[8]

It's not too difficult to guess that the first two stories would be written by Bill Wilson and Dr. Bob Smith. Number three is Bill Dotson (AA #3, a politically connected lawyer) who had been a city councilman and, according to the Big Book, entered a political campaign immediately after he got sober.[9] The fourth is surely Hank Parkhurst himself. A further alignment of the sober members at this time and their jobs would probably result in a comprehensive list of exactly who was expected to represent each of these professions. While the reason for the check marks is not specified, it seems that these indicate New York members Hank (or Bill) had already convinced, or expected to convince, to write their stories for the book. Those professions without check marks would be supplied by the Ohio alcoholics.*

Parkhurst's fourth proposal was that one of the book's chapters should be written in a Q&A format. We have already noted his fondness for this type of sales pitch at Honor Dealers, so it is not surprising to see him advocating the same approach here. Hank even supplies a few potential questions to give some idea of exactly what he has in mind:

Questions + Answers—

1. The question is often asked—where does the money come from for this work?

2. How do I know this will work with me?

    Why is this method better than any other religious method? (It is not—this is only a step toward a religious experience which should be carried forward in Christian fellowship no matter what your church)

3. Will I fail if I cannot keep my conduct up to these highest standards?

4. What happens when an alcoholics [sic] has a sexual relapse?

5. There is so much talk about a religious experience—what is it?[10]

This is an interesting and revealing set of questions. The first one about money is obvious and could be expected in relation to any organization offering a new solution for alcoholism. The second and fifth questions both relate to religion and pointedly end with the unanswered "what is it?" question about the religious experience, while the parenthetical remark in the second question fails to shed any clarifying light on a possible response to that question. It is a vexing question and Hank had no answer in mind; instead, he was reminding Bill Wilson that any talk about religious methods and experiences would necessarily have to be followed by an explanation of exactly what was meant by that. But perhaps most intriguing, and of the highest personal interest to Henry G. Parkhurst, are the third and fourth questions, both of which relate to moral failings, especially sexual misconduct. This was a real and ongoing problem for Hank— as later events will reveal—so it is no wonder he felt this was an issue worthy of being directly addressed in the book.

The idea of including a Q&A chapter was something Parkhurst would cling to tenaciously for the next six or seven months and he even went so far as to actually write a rather long and detailed version of this proposed chapter, a chapter Bill Wilson eventually rejected.**

---

*   It is interesting to note the fact that Hank is well enough informed about the "brethren" in Ohio that he could produce a list like this showing all of their professions.

**   Hank's rejected Q&A chapter will be discussed in detail in Chapter Twenty-One.

What Should *Not* Be in the Book

Finally, Hank's most sustained piece of writing in these notes (spanning both sides of page 8 and continuing onto page 9) presents his ideas about what Bill should *not* be putting into the book and what he would like to see substituted in its place. He offers these blunt and contentious remarks as his own "observations:"

Observations—

One of the easiest and most talked of things among us is a religious experience.* I believe that this is incomprehensible to most people. Simple + meaning[ful] words to us—but meaningless to most of the people that we are trying to get this over to.—In my mind religious experience— religion—etc.—should not be brought in. We are actually irreligious—but we are trying to be helpful—we have learned to be quiet—to be more truthful—to be more honest—to try to be more unselfish—to make the other fellows troubles—our troubles—and by following four steps we most of us have a religious experience. The fellowship—the unselfishness— appeals to us.

I wonder if we are off the track.

A very good merchandizing procedure is to find out why people do not buy our products—it is good reasoning to find out WHY—I am fearfully afraid that we are emphasizing religious experience when actually that is something that follows as a result of 1-2-3-4. In my mind the question is not particularly the strength of the [religious] experience as much as the improvement over what we were. I would ask a man to compare himself as follows after say a month –

#1—As compared to 2 months ago do you have more of a feeling that there is a power greater than you

#2—Have you cleaned out more completely with a human being than ever before?

#3—Have you less bad things behind you than ever before

#4—Have you been more honest with yourself + your fellow man— Have you been more thoughtful of people with whom you are associated—Has your life been cleaner both by thought + action— Have you looked at others less critically and yourself more critically this past 30 days. You will never be perfect but the question is have you been more perfect?[11]

---

* Long before Bill Wilson added the clarifying appendix on "Spiritual Experience" [1941], Hank Parkhurst had already identified this as a subject that was harder to talk about in a meaningful way than it was to come up with a definition of "the alcoholic."

Before looking more closely at these comments, it should be noted that perhaps the most important sentence here is the middle line in which Hank acknowledges: "I wonder if we are off the track"—a sentence in which he has individually underlined the words "I" and "wonder." Hank doesn't claim they *are* off track or even think or suspect they *might be* off the track. He says he is just wondering about that possibility. This is an obvious nod of respect toward Wilson and a tacit acknowledgment of his central authority within the group, but it is the only hint of concession Hank makes to Bill's vision throughout these three pages of his "Observations." Otherwise, he is direct and very much to the point, exposing the profound differences between his own understanding of what constitutes a proper and accessible program of recovery and the one Bill was then putting down on paper. Hank is not just suggesting Bill's belief in a religious and God-centered foundation should be toned down or modified; he is advocating Bill's explanation be abandoned and something totally different put in its place.*

As usual, the tone of Hank's message is quite clear, but on closer inspection the precise meaning becomes surprisingly elusive and any attempt to paraphrase it must cross a minefield of possible misunderstandings. What, for instance, does Hank mean when he says in the first sentence that "a religious experience" is one of the "easiest . . . things among us"? Easiest to get? Easiest how? Easiest what? Or easiest in what way? It is not possible to consider this fourth word without being caught in the "incomprehensible" and "meaningless" elements of Hank's own statement rather than concentrating on the position he is about to attack. Perhaps Hank meant to say that talking about religious experiences comes easily to us, but he doesn't *actually* say this; so however plausible that interpretation may be, it ultimately remains speculative.

Despite this annoying lack of precision, the first paragraph is remarkably straightforward in its attack on Bill Wilson's religious solution; Parkhurst describes it as something that will be "incomprehensible" and "meaningless" to most people and predicts that such a presentation will completely fail to deliver the message of recovery to the people who need it most. In Hank's opinion neither religion in general nor religious experience in particular (whatever that is) should be mentioned in this book; religion as such has nothing to do with what they are actually doing to help people get sober. Although we can talk about "a power greater than you," there is nothing at all religious about our method, and Hank thought it was best described as "irreligious."

Hank thinks the focus needs to be put back where it properly belongs—on a desire to be more helpful, more quiet, more truthful, more honest, and especially more unselfish. These are the truly productive virtues of their method, the positive results of adopting a program of moral psychology, and they can only be worked out in this

---

* It is surprising to note that Hank's "Observations" make no mention whatsoever of Bill's brilliant analysis of the problem—being powerless over the first drink—that is such a central topic of "There Is A Solution." Bill's understanding that "plain insanity" was the very crux of the problem necessarily led him to a theological solution since his own experience had repeatedly proven how ineffective psychology and self-knowledge were in the face of these "strange mental blank spots" that inevitably led the alcoholic back to drinking.

world—in the very meaningful and comprehensible world of fellowship with other people.

Parkhurst is thoroughly convinced that all this talk about religion and religious experience would just not be helpful to anyone trying to get sober. On the contrary, it would actually drive people away. If the program is to be successfully spread then it must start by emphasizing those elements that appeal to people, like fellowship and unselfishness. These are the benefits that can most successfully be 'sold' to alcoholics. But if the program of recovery is packaged as a fundamentally religious solution, then it will be impossible to find many 'buyers' out there who will be interested in what the book is offering.

If the program is not to be presented as a religious method or a religious experience, how then should it be packaged so that it would most likely appeal to drunks, convincing them to "buy our product"? Hank is certain the proper way to accomplish this is to emphasize the four steps for recovery; steps he claims are the real reasons why so many of their group have been able to recover. Once taken, these steps have resulted in "*most* of us [having] a religious experience," (emphasis added) but even some who have not had a religious experience have been able to recover. According to Hank, the book needs to be talking primarily about these four steps and not focusing exclusively on the expected positive results of those steps, i.e., the eventual religious experience.

This is an important perspective, but unfortunately Hank doesn't say exactly what those four steps are, making it difficult to evaluate his suggestion properly. A casual reader might be tempted to think the four numbered items at the bottom of his "Observations" are the steps Parkhurst is recommending, but they are simply a yardstick for measuring the positive results of not drinking once the drunk has been sober for a month or so; they are not the four steps one must take to get sober in the first place.

So, what are the "1-2-3-4" steps that Hank is talking about here?

Hank's Four Steps

It could be argued that the four items noted in that same sentence with the four steps are what Hank had in mind, i.e., learning to be (1) more helpful, (2) more honest, (3) more unselfish, and (4) more caring for others. But these are hardly the makings of a new and revolutionary program for getting sober and it is hard to imagine Hank would seriously suggest Bill offer these four pious platitudes in place of his own much more vigorous religious program.

Given the early growth of the Fellowship out of the Oxford Group, it has been suggested that Hank's four steps are a direct reference to the four practical spiritual activities the Group recommended to people who wanted to be "spiritually reborn, and to live in the state in which [the Four Absolutes] are the guides to our life in God." Those four spiritual activities were:

1. The Sharing of our sins and temptations with another Christian life given to God, and to use Sharing as Witness to help others, still unchanged, to recognize and acknowledge their sins.

2. Surrender of our life, past, present, and future, into God's keeping and direction.

3. Restitution to all whom we have wronged directly or indirectly.

4. Listening to, accepting, relying on God's Guidance and carrying it out in everything we do or say, great or small.[12]

The striking similarity between these points and some of the later Twelve Steps is hardly surprising given A.A.'s early attachment to the Oxford Group, but it is unlikely Hank Parkhurst would be suggesting that Bill Wilson fall back on the principles and practices of the Oxford Group as a way to avoid introducing a strong element of religion into the presentation of their new solution for alcoholism. Not only would this be an open admission of allegiance to the Oxford Group, but—even if they were somehow repackaged for presentation—there would still be far too much God in these activities for them to be considered as serious candidates for Hank's four steps.

The most likely explanation is that Hank was referring to the four numbered steps Bill had talked about at such length in the earliest full version of his "Story"—the one written just prior to Hank's composition of these notes.* It certainly would have been politic for Parkhurst, as he argued for such a radically different approach to the book, to frame those suggestions in terms Bill had so recently acknowledged as central to his own experiences while getting sober. In his "Original Story," Wilson had detailed the four steps and claimed they were the cause of his sobriety and the foundation of a "practical workable twenty four hour a day design for living."[13] This earliest articulation of the steps covered five pages and was, as already noted, something of a free-for-all of poorly organized information. But, however cluttered his first presentation of these four steps may have been, it is possible to eliminate many of the side comments and over-explanations packed into those five pages, revealing the following central ideas as the essence of Bill's earliest four steps:

---

* For the purposes of clarity and narrative flow, I have presumed that Bill Wilson wrote all three versions of his "Story" before he began to write "There Is A Solution" (see Chapters Seven and Eight). It is, of course, always possible that Bill wrote the "Original Story" and then started on "There Is A Solution" before returning to his own personal narrative and doing the major revisions that resulted in "Bill's Story." The fact that Hank advocates for Bill's "four steps" here in his notes, suggests that this kind of reordering of the time line for when Bill actually wrote the two long versions of his "Story" is certainly defensible and might even be used to explain Bill's elimination of any numbered "steps" from his later version.

1. Place your life in the hands of God as you understand him—forever.

2. Make a thorough and ruthless inventory of all moral defects and immoral actions.

3. Be willing to get rid of all these defects and immoral actions and realize that you can't do this alone.

4. Make amends for all past transgressions.[14]

This is a program Hank Parkhurst could support without argument and it is highly likely these are the steps he was advocating as the primary focus for the book about their new solution. They definitely would qualify as being irreligious just so long as the explanation of "God as you understand him" is broad enough to allow for the inclusion of an impersonal and vague "universal power,"[15] "a great indefinable, unexplainable Power"[16] and therefore not so overtly religious. In addition, these four fit well with the other requirements Hank mentions in his notes: they qualify as actions that can be taken in the "1-2-3-4" fashion and, once completed, could be expected to result in a religious experience, an experience which would then "be carried forward in Christian fellowship"[17] (quietly, honestly, and with unselfish caring for others). They would also be likely to produce after just one or two month's time some very positive answers to the four critical questions Hank suggests be put to any newly sober man who had followed these steps.

If in fact these are the four steps Hank had in mind—and there are no other likely candidates to be found in the records*—then perhaps his argument with Bill Wilson's vision wasn't quite as contrary as his rather abrasive tone makes it sound. Parkhurst believed that once people had successfully completed these four steps they would, in most cases, acquire some sort of religious experience; but this religious experience was understood as the *result*, rather than the *cause* of, their sobriety.

This might be glossed over as little more than a cart-before-the-horse argument, but the differences between the programs advocated by these two men are actually much more substantive than that. Hank just does not believe the religious experience has anything to do with *getting* sober; it is something positive that will likely happen after—but only after—some length of sobriety had been achieved. It is certainly a wonderful thing once it happens, but it is neither the religious experience itself nor "the strength of the experience" that really makes the difference. What matters are the changes brought about by working the four steps and it is these four actions that make it possible for a person to successfully stop drinking.

Each man was obviously locked into a defense of his own experiences while getting sober, insisting that what had happened to him personally should now serve as the universal model for others. Bill had a "white light" experience in Towns Hospital and then got sober, so he was emphasizing the primacy of an encounter with God followed by a list of actions to be taken to enhance and preserve that sobriety. But Hank, along with almost all of the other New York members, had never had

---

* See, however, pages 444 – 45 and 455 for two other remote possibilities for this list of four steps.

such a unique and profound religious experience. Their sobriety was the product of the four steps they had been told to incorporate into their lives and their continued abstinence was dependent upon them first completing and then continuing to work on those four steps. Hank's "Observations" basically chastise Bill for sticking too closely to his own experience and presenting it as their collective wisdom while completely ignoring the very different paths taken by the majority of the members in New York City.

These differences fueled a running argument and the two men would continue to disagree on these basic issues with increasing intensity over the next several months—right up until the day the book went to press. But in June of 1938, Bill rejected both Hank's criticisms and his suggestions and the two chapters were circulated as he had written them with only minor revisions over the next several weeks. However, three months later, when the writing of the Big Book began again in earnest, the effects of this ongoing disagreement can clearly be seen in the constant adjustments Bill made to new chapters as he wrote them; chapters that included at least some accommodations for Hank's understanding of the proper path to recovery.

Parkhurst may have lost this first battle, but he would continue to fight for his own approach and, in the course of those skirmishes, he would win a few significant victories for the inclusion of at least some elements of his point of view into the final text of *Alcoholics Anonymous*.

Promoting the Book

The second general group of "Hank's ideas" all relate to his plans for promoting the book and this was one area where Bill Wilson was more than willing to let him have his own way, candidly admitting Parkhurst "was used to such business."[18] For the moment Bill had taken ownership of the book project and he was not about to give up control over the content, but he willingly deferred to Hank when it came to marketing. Wilson was genuinely impressed with Parkhurst's previous expertise in this area and he counted on Hank's talents when it came to the promotional side of business, an area where he had almost no real experience himself. For the next year, Henry G. Parkhurst would be the source of several ambitious ideas for marketing their new book and Bill Wilson would lend his enthusiastic support to each of these grand schemes in the hope that the book would quickly generate some substantial profits while carrying their message of recovery to people all over the country.

Hank's estimate of how many people might be buyers of their book was impressive and he began his outline of the marketing plan by describing the huge niche market he saw already waiting for just such a volume—over one million alcoholics in the United States alone—and by noting this large and desperately needy audience would surely make it possible for the book project to become self-supporting very quickly.

Why the Book

It has been estimated by the Rockefeller Foundation that there are over a million incurable from medical or psychiatrical [sic] standpoints, alcoholics in the United States.

These men realize their vital need and are desparately [sic] seeking the answer. The book should be so written that it will prove the answer to these people.

The work has become so broad that full time assistance and direction is needed. This costs money (which has been offered by foundational funds) however the alcoholics believe it should come from within their own experience.[19]

Hank then expanded this already huge market by adding several other groups and professions that could be counted on to buy a book offering a real solution for alcoholism, groups that should therefore be included in any accurate accounting of the potential market for the book:

Sales Promotion Possibilities
The Market—

1. Over million alcoholics (Rockefeller Foundation)

2. At least [a] million non alcoholics that have definite alcoholic relatives

3. Every employer of 100 or more people

4. Those that take an academic interest

5. Two hundred and ten thousand ministers

6. One hundred sixty nine thousand physicians

7. The total would be well over three million prospects[20]

This "well over three million prospects" is pure Hank Parkhurst—a typically exaggerated estimate by a man whose enthusiasm almost always outdistanced the realities of the situation. Hank consistently looked at any new and potentially lucrative business project through rose-colored glasses and then vigorously sold that colorful picture to anyone who would listen. And Parkhurst was not just convinced by his own arguments, he was also extremely convincing. Over the next several months both he and Bill Wilson took up the mantra that, given this huge potential market, there was no way they could fail, claiming, "this book would sell by [the] carloads."[21] Those "carloads" they kept mentioning, it should be noted, were *railroad* carloads.

Hank's plan for getting the word out to this large, eager audience was to publish four separate news bulletins in the month before the book's release and then to mail out a prepared article about the work to every newspaper in the country immediately prior to the book's publication. He was confident that this sort of media saturation would allow them to effectively tap into an enormous pent-up demand, creating huge sales for the book just as it was being offered for sale.

Publicity

Newspapers

When book is nearly ready to leave the presses a short matt (?) article should be sent to the 12,285 newspapers in the U.S.

This article would briefly cover the work as it has gone to date. Case histories would be covered. —It possibly would be a brief case history of the work and announcement of the book.

At least four news bulletins should be published at weekly intervals, ahead of the book.[22]

Exactly who would be handling the logistics of this massive mailing and how it would be paid for is left to the reader's imagination or, perhaps both Bill and Hank presumed the foundation would have raised enough money by that time to easily cover the mailing costs (at three cents a stamp, the mailing of 50,000 pieces would cost $1,500) along with the printing and all of the labor involved in such an ambitious undertaking.

Then, in anticipation of the huge response expected from all of this newspaper publicity, Hank advised that a system be organized and put in place well before the first mail order requests started to pour in:

Mail Order

A form letter of acknowledgment must be worked out.

This will acknowledge the receipt of the enquiry and will inform that the writer can secure the book by mailing a check for two dollars or through their local bookseller who can secure from

Alcoholics Anonymous, Inc

Post Box xxxx

The profits of the book are administered by a foundation for promotion of cure and understanding of alcoholism.[23]

Most fascinating about Parkhurst's mail order plan is the foregone conclusion that they would be directly selling the book themselves, rather than turning the project (and the copyright) over to an established publishing house for release and distribution. Hank had done the math. If they were going to sell more than a million copies of this book then it would be foolish to share those profits with a middleman who had no vested interest in curing alcoholism. Instead, Hank was planning to keep all that money and turn some of it over to a foundation "for [the] promotion of [the] cure and understanding of alcoholism" with the balance of the profits being retained by the "publishing company." Of all Hank Parkhurst's many contributions to the creation of the book *Alcoholics Anonymous*, his ongoing insistence that they must maintain ownership of their own text was the most astute and perhaps the most important.

Also worthy of note, both here and in several other places throughout Hank's pages of ideas, is the mention of a foundation. The idea of creating their own foundation had not been abandoned since the detailed discussions of the previous March, but now, with the possibility of these huge profits from a best-selling book, the need for a foundation became even more important. The existence of a tax-exempt foundation that reinvested the book's profits into further recovery work would be critical for establishing their credibility with donors and for emphatically distancing themselves from the alcohol-related rackets that proliferated during these post-Prohibition times. It would be another two months before this new sense of urgency about establishing a real foundation would come to fruition, but it seems that the writing of these two chapters and the possibility of actually publishing a book supplied the additional push Bill and Hank (along with Frank Amos and Willard Richardson) needed to begin moving that project forward in a much more substantive way.

One final note of interest here is his original estimate that the books would sell for $2.00 each (cash, no checks!). This was a fairly reasonable, even inexpensive, price for a hardcover book at this time, but, by the following February, Hank would inflate that price to a hefty $3.50 a copy. A big price for a Big Book.

Hank Names the Book, the Group, and the Foundation

In a category all by themselves, and of singular importance, are the sixth and seventh pages of "Hank's ideas," which contain the first use of the words "Alcoholics Anonymous" to indicate the name of the group, the title of the book, and the name of the foundation that would be publishing that book. This phrase seems to have materialized almost spontaneously within the New York Fellowship around this time, for, as Bill Wilson later commented, it was just a short step for them to go from calling themselves "a bunch of nameless drunks" to saying they were members of "Alcoholics Anonymous."[24]

The story has been widely circulated—evidently based on Jim Burwell's erroneous comment in his "Evolution of Alcoholics Anonymous" —that a man named Joe Worden was the inventor of this phrase, but Joe wasn't even a member of the group at this time; he joined A.A. several months later in December 1938. In 1955, when Bill Wilson was asked who came up with the title *Alcoholics Anonymous*, he replied "who first suggested the title, I don't know. But I do remember that Joe Worden, the derelict and broken-down ex-partner on the New Yorker* did plug that title heavily, though I don't think for a minute that he invented it."[25] Joe was around for the much later arguments about the book's possible title, but, given the evidence in these notes,

---

* This, too, is erroneous. Worden had worked for *Metropolitan Magazine* in New York City, but was never a partner at the *New Yorker* magazine, (See for instance: http://health.groups.yahoo.com/group/AAHistoryLovers/message/8085 - retrieved August 5, 2012.)

it seems likely Hank Parkhurst was the person to first suggest the name *Alcoholics Anonymous* for the book.

As Hank was proposing this phrase as the name of the group, the title of the book, and the name of their new publishing company / foundation, Bill also used it in the first draft of "There Is A Solution," as the group's name ("We, of ALCOHOLICS ANONYMOUS, now know at least one hundred men . . ."[26]) and very shortly after that, he wrote to Dr. Bob that "Alcoholics Anonymous" was the name "nearly everyone agrees" should be used to identify the authors of the book and that it might even make a fine name for the foundation they were hoping to establish.[27]

Since Hank's notes were sketched while Bill was still dictating "There Is A Solution," it is impossible to know whether he was borrowing from Bill or if Bill had inserted that phrase into the new chapter after reading Hank's notes. Whatever the case, within a few days, "Alcoholics Anonymous" had emerged as a universal description for the group in New York, being liberally applied to just about everything associated with the work including the name of group, the title of the book, the authors of the book, and the name of the foundation that would be publishing the book. Both men were evidently pleased with this new coinage.*

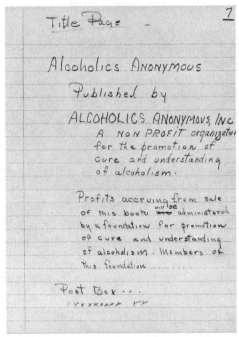

Courtesy of Stepping Stones Foundation Archives

The exact text of Hank's title page suggestions were as follows:

Title Page

Alcoholics Anonymous

Published by

ALCOHOLICS ANONYMOUS, Inc

A NON PROFIT organization
for the promotion of
cure and understanding
of alcoholism.

---

* It has been impossible to pinpoint the exact dates when Hank wrote his notes or when Bill worked on "There Is A Solution" although they both likely happened during the first week of June. Lois mentions—without any further substantiation—June 15, 1938 as the date that "the name 'Alcoholics Anonymous' was used for the first time." (*Lois Remembers*, p. 197). The first use definitely didn't occur any later than June 15, but despite what Lois says, it was two (or perhaps even three) weeks earlier than that date that the phrase "Alcoholics Anonymous" first appeared and began to gain some common currency.

Profits accruing from sale
of this book will be administered
by a foundation for promotion
of cure and understanding
of alcoholism. Members of
this foundation . . .

Post Box . . .

xxxxxxxxx xxx[28]

Jim Burwell's Final Drunk

At this time, an important confirmation of Bill Wilson's insistence on a particularly religious solution came from an unexpected quarter. Just as he was putting the finishing touches on this new chapter with its explanation of his theory about "the insidious insanity of that first drink" and the futility of any recovered alcoholic thinking he "can do without God," the most rebellious member of the New York group supplied some striking evidence that, at first, seemed to confirm both of Bill's key points.

Jim Burwell went out and got rip-roaring drunk.

On June 11, five months sober and still derisively ranting about the "God stuff" whenever he got a chance, Jimmy was on the road in Boston, where he had just completed a successful week selling automobile polish to the owners of local gas stations. It was midday Saturday and two of Jim's prospective customers invited him to lunch, completely unaware that they were about to present him with the perfect opportunity for displaying the "peculiar mental twist"[29] that allows an alcoholic to return to drinking, no matter how unjustified or ridiculous his reasoning might seem to everyone else.

According to Jim's own account, the three men went into a restaurant and

> . . . ordered sandwiches, and one man said, "Three beers." I let mine sit. After a bit, the other man said, "Three beers." I let that sit too. Then it was my turn—I ordered, "Three beers," but this time it was different; I had a cash investment of thirty cents, and, on a ten-dollar-a-week salary, that's a big thing. So I drank all three beers, one after the other, and said, "I'll be seeing you boys," and went around the corner for a bottle. I never saw either of them again.[30*]

Amazingly, there was no thought of refusing that first beer and, with that opportunity missed, it must have been a real pleasure (and a torture?) for Jim to sit there toying with the thought of those three frosty glasses on the table and realizing that one of them was *his*. Nor did it ever occur to him he could simply push those two untouched beers over to his clients rather than order the third round. But, having done that, Jim's perverse alcoholic mind told him that thirty cents was, after all, thirty cents,

---

* Jim's story. "The Vicious Cycle," was first published in 1955 in the second edition of *Alcoholics Anonymous* and has since appeared in both the third and the fourth editions.

so there was just *no other choice* but for him to drink his three beers as fast as possible and, that done and already way too far down the road to quit now, he immediately moved on to something stronger.

Jim sold off his remaining automobile polish samples for ready cash and, for the next few days, stumbled around New England in a drunken state, spending his nights in cheap hotels while he peppered his boss, Hank Parkhurst, with telegrams demanding money. Reading between the lines, Hank knew exactly what that meant, so he never responded to any of these pleas. When Jim finally did managed to reach him by phone, Hank Parkhurst fired him.[31]

Completely abandoned, Burwell spent a wretched night in a second-rate hotel in Providence where he "nearly died from the worst seizure he had ever had"[32] and woke up the next morning wallowing in his loneliness and burdened with a feeling of despair profoundly intensified by the realization that he had just cut himself off from the only people in the world who had any real understanding of him and his problem.[33] Still drinking, but resolved to go back and make a fresh start with the group in New York, Jim made his way to New Jersey where, late on a Wednesday night, he quietly snuck back into Hank Parkhurst's house and put himself to bed.[34]

The next day, June 16, 1938, became Burwell's new sobriety date and he never drank again. When he died on September 8, 1974, Jim was the oldest surviving sober member of the group of drunks who had been around while the Big Book was being written.

The Group as Higher Power

During the first raucous months of his sobriety, Jimmy had presented a real challenge to members of the New York group; they had absolutely no idea how to deal with this strident atheist who repeatedly rejected the most basic tenet of their approach to sobriety. Burwell always claimed that in the early part of 1938, during his first stint of sobriety, some members of the New York group had literally gathered together and prayed that he would drink. Such a fate, they thought, was inevitable and the sooner it happened, the better; once Jim drank they would have positive proof that an alcoholic couldn't stay sober unless he wholeheartedly embraced their version of a religious, God-centered solution.

Now those prayers had been answered, but the much-desired slip didn't turn out to be the simple, comfortable solution everyone had hoped it would be.

Three days after Jimmy drank, the regular weekly meeting at Wilson's home in Brooklyn was held on a Tuesday night for the second time (they had previously always met on Sundays).* Hank, who had received several telegrams from Burwell by then, would certainly have announced the news of Jim's relapse to everyone who hadn't already heard about it. At this time, any return to drinking was a "terrific catastrophe"[35] for every member of the group, undermining whatever confidence they might have

---

* Lois's diary, 1938 notes this shift clearly on June 7. Previously, these gatherings, (which she referred to as "seminars" in her 1938 diary entries) had been held on Sunday nights, but, for whatever reason, the decision was made to move the meeting to Tuesdays. The regular weekly gatherings of the East Coast contingent would continue to be held on Tuesday nights in Brooklyn until ten months later when the Wilsons lost their home in a foreclosure proceeding.

about the sustainability of their own sobriety. Back then, "we'd go anywhere [to sober someone up]," Bill Wilson said, "no matter how unpromising"[36] and, whenever someone did drink in those early days, everyone else "would come running, because we were still very afraid of ourselves and no one knew who might be next. So there was a great concern about the brother who got drunk."[37]

"But in Jimmy's case," Bill noted, "there was no concern at all."[38] No one even stirred to help him. "Leave him alone!" they said, "Let him try it by himself for once; maybe he'll learn a lesson!"[39] What today's A.A. members call "tough love" was already being practiced by the New York Fellowship and nobody felt this more deeply than Jim Burwell who lamented, "now even my own kind had turned against me."[40]

When Jim finally did make it back to New York and into the meeting, he told them he had experienced his own kind of spiritual awakening, one where he "saw for the first time that those who . . . at least honestly tried to find a Power greater than themselves"[41] were definitely onto something:

> When the others saw my altered attitude, they took me back in, but for me they *had* to make it tough; if they hadn't, I don't think I ever would have stuck it out. Once again, there was the challenge of a tough job, but this time I was determined to follow through. For a long time the only Higher Power I could concede was the power of the group, but this was far more than I had ever recognized before, and it was at least a beginning. It was also an ending, for never since June 16, 1938, have I had to walk alone.[42]

Jim Burwell's reliance on the group as his higher power, rather than the God described by Bill Wilson in "There Is A Solution" or even something as vague as Hank Parkhurst's "universal power," marks a major turning point in the ongoing evolution of Alcoholics Anonymous; one that would have significant repercussions over the next several months as more chapters of the Big Book were being written, and which would, in the end, have a profound and lasting impact on the future development of A.A.

The radical idea that GOD (Group of Drunks) could be "God as I understand him" had just been born.*

---

* In telling Burwell's story, I have included two plausible quotes from *Twelve Steps and Twelve Traditions* where Bill Wilson tells Jim's story using the pseudonym "Ed" (see 1st edition, pp. 147–49). It must be noted that Bill takes significant liberties with the facts of "Ed's" story in the *12&12* in order to make a larger point. Glenn F. Chesnut, in his excellent "Jim Burwell: early AA's first famous atheist," rightly takes Wilson to task for "gravely altering and distorting Jimmy Burwell's real story" by recasting it into "the genre of the traditional Protestant frontier revivalist conversion story." The sentiments and statements attributed to "Ed" in that reading do not in any way correspond to Burwell's own version found in the Big Book, nor are they supported by any of Jim's many recorded talks nor does it jibe at all with an article that he wrote for the May *Grapevine* on his anniversary in 1968 entitled "Sober for Thirty Years." In that article, Burwell is clear that his own belief in a higher power had, over the years, evolved first from a reliance on "the A.A. Fellowship," then into a belief that "God and Good were synonymous" [shades of those Buddhists mentioned on *AACOA*, p. 81] and, finally, to "meditating and trying to tune in on my better self for guidance and answers." This is hardly a "conversion" story in the sense that Wilson understood and retold it.

CHAPTER TEN

The Outline

~Late June 1938~

With two chapters of the proposed book finally in hand, it was time to find out if this writing experiment would prove to be an effective tool for raising money. Ruth typed up the latest versions of "There Is A Solution" and "Bill's Story" and Hank put them together into "a neatly gotten up brochure."[1] Different from their positions in today's Big Book, "Bill's Story" was placed second in the package, in partial fulfillment of the promise made at the end of "There Is A Solution" that "the next few chapters are the personal narratives of several of us."[2] Hank's promotional brochure was accompanied by a letter of introduction, which included the request for an appointment to discuss in more detail the great success they were having in their work with alcoholics.[*]

Two Chapters Are Mailed to the First Prospect

On Friday, June 17, this tidy presentation was mailed off to their first prospect, Jeremiah D. Maguire, the president of the Federation Bank & Trust Company in New York City. The initial contact information likely came from Willard Richardson, who knew Maguire not only as a prominent New York banker, but also as member of the Advisory Committee for Chase National Bank (popularly known as "the Rockefeller bank").[3]

Maguire was genuinely impressed by the materials Bill sent him and, despite his busy schedule, he responded the following Tuesday.

---

[*]   Unfortunately, there are no copies of this cover letter to prospective donors preserved in either the GSO or the Stepping Stones archives.

June 21, 1938.

Mr. William G. Wilson,
Henry G. Parkhurst, Inc.,
11 Hill Street,
Newark, N. J.

Dear Mr. Wilson:

I acknowledge your letter of the 17th, transmitting a very interesting brochure which I have not read intently, but such extracts as I have had [the] opportunity to read prove the document a very interesting one and I shall take the first opportunity to read it more at length. On my return from the Bankers Convention, which will be some time during the coming week, I will try to work out an appointment with you.

Meanwhile with kind regards, I am

Yours faithfully,

Jeremiah D. Maguire

President
FEDERATION BANK AND TRUST COMPANY[4]

Success! Hank Parkhurst had been right; a small sampling from the proposed book was an outstanding way to get the attention of rich New Yorkers who had an interest in the alcohol problem. Maguire's letter probably arrived in Newark on Wednesday, June 22, and Bill's undated response was likely sent out two days later on Friday, the 24.

172 *[sic]* Clinton Street,
Brooklyn, New York.
Phone Main 4-3220.

Jeremiah T. *[sic]* Maguire
Federation Bank & Trust Co.
New York City, N. Y.

Dear Mr. Maguire:

Your letter came in the other day and its thoughtful consideration is appreciated.

Since forwarding you the first two chapters of our book we have prepared an outline of the remainder which I think you will be interested to look over.

I have just dictated a letter to Dr. Robert Smith of Akron Ohio. You will recall him as the man out there who has helped between sixty and seventy others to recover; his own case being an outstanding example. It occurs to me that a copy of this letter which I am enclosing may give you a clearer idea of what is going on and how we are progressing.

This letter is being written from my home in Brooklyn so that you now have this address as well as that of our Jersey office. Hoping that I shall see you.

Bill[5]

There are several things worth noting in this letter. First of all, the rather informal signature line attests to the fact that Bill was not a man who was easily intimidated by the rich and famous. Six weeks later he would close another letter to Maguire with the much more formal "Wm. G. Wilson,"[6] but at this point, the confidence inspired by the banker's warm and enthusiastic response had encouraged him to adopt a decidedly familiar tone. Also of interest is Bill's mention of Dr. Bob Smith as someone Maguire would recall as the person who was doing such outstanding work with alcoholics in Akron. The only source of that information would have been the earlier letter sent to Maguire, providing at least one small glimpse into the contents of the cover letter that accompanied the brochure. Finally, Bill mentions his letter is being written from his home in Brooklyn, which raises the question of who might have done the typing for him.* A copy of the letter he had just dictated to Dr. Bob was also being included, but it is unclear whether that letter had been dictated in Brooklyn (and, if so, then to whom?) or if it was one of several copies produced earlier in the day (or the day before?) at the office in New Jersey. Adding to this uncertainty is the fact that neither the Maguire letter nor the one to Dr. Bob Smith have a date on them, something which is unexpected from Ruth Hock with her otherwise consistent professionalism (although the street address error was one she would make again in other letters that do carry her signature as typist at the bottom).

But beyond these intriguing elements, the truly important piece of information contained in this second letter to Maguire is Bill's revelation that during the past week they had prepared an outline for the remainder of the book. This outline provides an early glimpse into exactly how Hank and Bill envisioned the whole book project would come together and what it would contain once finished. The outline is actually the "List of Chapters" Hank had so recently suggested as a key requirement for moving the promotion of the book forward. After discussing his ideas with Bill, and this time with Wilson's active encouragement and input, Hank had created a comprehensive outline for the book, one that showed precisely how the two recently completed chapters would fit into the projected whole.**

---

* Lois Wilson is not a candidate for the typist at this time because she was away from home visiting her sister, Barbara, from June 22 to June 25. (Lois's diary, 1938)

** The language and style used in this outline are unlike anything else Wilson ever wrote, but it does nicely match other prose efforts we have from Parkhurst—leaving no doubt in my mind that Hank was the author of this piece.

Tom Thacher's Suggested Intro to the Book Proposal

But Hank Parkhurst wasn't the only one working on promotion materials for the new book during that third week in June. Tom Thacher, one of Ebby's older brothers, had been to dinner at the Wilson's house on Thursday, June 16, where he participated in a long discussion about the book project. Following that conversation Tom put together a neatly typed sheet with his own suggestions for how the book could most effectively be presented to prospective donors. This document was neither an outline of the book nor a cover letter, but rather a short piece of writing Tom thought might serve as an effective introduction to the two chapters that followed.

Thacher had been invited to dinner because his youngest brother, Ebby, had just returned to New York, expressing a serious desire to quit drinking again and Bill Wilson, in his efforts to muster whatever support he could for the friend who had helped him get sober, had suggested Tom join them for dinner to lend some fraternal encouragement.

Ebby Thacher had originally sobered up and "given his surrender" on November 1, 1934, and then, a few weeks later, carried his message of recovery to Bill Wilson.[7] But, in April 1937, he fell off the wagon and, two months later, found himself in Towns Hospital trying to get off the booze one more time. At first, Ebby's efforts were successful; but one month later, when he left the protective arms of the New York fellowship and returned to his job in Albany, he almost immediately started drinking again, this time heavily and continuously, and he went on doing so for most of the next year.[8] By mid-June 1938, alcohol had once more brought him to his knees and he was desperate to stop. Whenever his drinking overwhelmed him, Ebby turned to the one man he knew he could always count on for help, arriving at the Wilson household on June 14—just in time to make an appearance at the Tuesday night meeting.[9] Given the contrast between Ebby's sudden reappearance announcing his desire to get sober again and Hank's report that Jim Burwell was out drinking again, it must have made for a very inspiring meeting that night in Brooklyn.

Unlike Burwell, Ebby Thacher had not only enthusiastically embraced the religious solution, he was also the man who had first brought that solution to Bill Wilson. Given this uniquely central position within the Fellowship's story, and fueled by Bill's ever vigilant concern, Ebby received generous support from the New York members, including an invitation from one of its most sober members to spend the entire summer on his farm in Maryland. As Ebby tells it:

> In 1938, I came down and spent some time with Bill and during my visit, Fitzhugh Mayo from Maryland came also to visit Bill and he suggested that I return to Cumberstone, Maryland, where he lived, and spend some time with him, and we could have a good time together working around the place, where Fitz had done most of his drinking. So I went down and met his wife, daughters, and son. He and Bill were moving about the country a great deal, the idea of the book was beginning to bud, and I was left with the family there . . . I had a lovely summer.[10]

Before Ebby left for Maryland, Lois prepared him a special home-cooked meal and his brother Tom was invited to join them.[11] Thomas Thacher, twelve years older than Ebby, had attended Princeton University, had been the vice president and general manager of the family business before its collapse in 1922, and was currently an investment broker with an office located in Manhattan.[12] Tom was well known to the Wilsons; he and his wife had even attended Bill and Lois's New Year's Eve party the previous December.[13]

Lois's dinner was held on the night before Bill mailed off their first solicitation package to Maguire and, from Tom's enthusiastic response, it seems clear that the main topic of conversation that evening was the best way to sell the idea of the proposed book to prospective donors. Tom felt a general one-page introduction was needed to immediately capture the reader's attention and draw him into the two chapters that followed in the brochure. A day or two after the dinner he sent Bill a typed one-page letter containing his "hurried suggestion along the lines we talked" of the best way to properly introduce the two new chapters.

Tom begins his proposal with a short handwritten disclaimer across the top of the page, noting that "the suggested title and signatures are merely thoughts that occurred and like the rest of the outline below may not fit the picture at all." Underneath this, the typed introduction is organized under five section headings, each followed by a short body of text, (which makes liberal use of capital letters) creating succinct and persuasive points about the importance and the worthiness of the book project.*

The first section is entitled simply "ALCOHOLISM," and Tom's lead sentence quotes the observation made by Dr. Jung that opens "There Is A Solution": "I have never seen one single case, in which alcohol-mindedness was established in the sense you have it, THAT EVER RECOVERED." Tom follows this with the claim that this astute evaluation applies not to just one individual, but to "several hundred thousands of our fellow citizens" and "will soon be applicable to a half million more."**

In the "INCURABLE" section, which comes next, he notes that three years earlier an unnamed alcoholic had "found a haven of self control" and then discovered an approach that allowed him to pass this on to others, thereby creating "a circle of self control and right living" for one hundred men "of every FAITH and CREED" who "have been returned to Society as useful members."

The third header, "ANONYMOUS," describes these men as driven by a simple Christian spirit and devoted to just one "common purpose—TO HELP THEIR FELLOW MAN." Each of them is deeply committed to helping their fallen brethren attain a life of sober usefulness, and they do this by following a "definite procedure" that had been developed by trial and error and which has produced "truly remarkable results."

The next-to-last section proclaims "each man is writing a brief outline of his life" and that these will be published in a book entitled "ONE HUNDRED MEN by VICTORS ANONYMOUS." That volume will also present concrete information

---

*   See Appendix IV on page 637 for the complete text of Thomas Thacher's introduction.

**   Given Tom's accurate quote from "There Is A Solution," it is reasonable to presume that Bill had given him a copy of the brochure that Hank had put together.

about the disease of alcoholism and emphasize the benefits of psychoanalysis and medical treatment for treating the illness.

Tom entitled his fifth and final section "PROGRAM" and it is the longest of them all. Here he emphasizes the dire need for a volume of this kind, claiming, "nothing like this has ever been done before." Such a book, he says, is surely needed and would almost certainly be a best seller, but it will require outside financial assistance if it is ever to be completed and brought to market. Regarding that large projected sale, he notes all profits would be "turned over to a FOUNDATION . . . that will be dedicated to the perpetuation of SELF CONTROL and the RIGHT METHOD OF LIVING."

The entire piece is then signed at the bottom by "VICTORS ANONYMOUS."[14]

Tom Thacher's Unique Take on the Book

Tom Thacher's one-page introduction is remarkably well written for something that was put together so quickly. It is packed with a large amount of well-organized, concise information, making cogent arguments using pithy sentences and effective language. But whether or not it is a completely accurate reflection of the discussion at dinner that night is another matter entirely. Tom admits what he has written "may not fit the picture at all" and that sounds like an astute assessment—especially if one focuses on the two prominent references to self-control as the key to recovery. (It is hard to imagine Bill Wilson invoking self-control as a primary pathway to sobriety.) Nor does Thacher mention religion in any explicit way other than to note that these one hundred men operate with a simple Christian spirit and represent every faith and creed. Instead he emphasizes the disease concept of alcoholism and touts the benefits of psychoanalysis and medical treatment as critical to the solution. It is unlikely these were the exact points Bill was trying to impress upon Tom that Thursday night, but it is always problematic to sort out 'what was said' from 'what was heard' whenever uncertainties such as this arise.*

Beyond these possible misunderstandings and misrepresentations, one item of great interest is Tom's confident statement that the book would contain one hundred different life stories, each of which would tell "the HOW and from WHENCE the spirit of righteous living was reborn in" each man. Such a book would presumably have just one chapter of exposition ("There Is A Solution") followed by a large collection of real-life stories that would collectively elucidate the benefits of psychoanalysis and medical treatment—but little or nothing else. Whatever Tom's understanding may have been, it is unlikely this was Bill Wilson's conception in mid-June 1938 of how the book would be organized. In all likelihood, he had already embraced the more expansive vision Hank Parkhurst was just then in the process of outlining for the book.

Also worth noting is Tom's reluctance to use the word "Alcoholics" as part of the book's title or as the name of the group. Clearly Bill had suggested this terminology since the letter originally used that phrase in four different places in bold capital letters. But Tom obviously found the term distasteful and he very deliberately went back over

---

* If only Lois's diary indicated that Hank Parkhurst had also attended this dinner then these misunderstandings and the heavy emphasis on psychology and medicine would make more sense. Perhaps Hank *was* there and she just failed to mention his presence.

the letter, erasing the four instances of the word "ALCOHOLICS" as best he could and substituting "VICTORS" in their place using black ink. (A handwritten sidebar apologizes to Bill for these last minute edits asking him to "Excuse the stereographic work please.") The word "victor" certainly has a distinctly positive ring to it, conveying an optimism lacking in the darker and more pejorative "alcoholic." But, "VICTORS ANONYMOUS" conveys absolutely no information about the victory being won, while "ALCOHOLICS ANONYMOUS" leaves no doubt about the problem that needs to be conquered.

Tom's final contribution was important. He notes that "the suggested title and signature are merely thoughts that occurred" to him and concedes these may not fit what Wilson has in mind. Identifying the authors as "Victors Anonymous" certainly didn't fit as far as Bill and Hank were concerned, but Tom's suggestion to title the book "One Hundred Men" was a huge success, immediately capturing both of their attentions. This title was quickly and enthusiastically adopted and would have a prominent and interesting history over the next several months as the book project moved toward completion. Hank was particularly smitten with the phrase, and he later used "One Hundred Men" not only as the working title for the book, but also as the name of the corporation that he formed to finance and promote it.[15]

Since there are no surviving copies of either Bill Wilson's cover letter or the promotional brochure itself, it is impossible to say whether Hank and Bill ever adopted Tom's suggestion of including a single-page introduction with the chapters they were sending out, but changes were constantly being made to the text of those two chapters so it is possible that this might have been done. A liberally edited version of Tom's introduction would probably have made a valuable addition to their brochure, serving as an effective tool for quickly grabbing the reader's attention and enticing them to look further into the document.

Parkhurst's Outline Establishes the Book's Contents

In the third week of June, Hank Parkhurst created a comprehensive outline for the proposed book, one far more ambitious than Tom Thacher's straightforward idea of compiling and publishing one hundred real-life stories on recovery. (What else would one expect from Henry G. Parkhurst but a more ambitious plan?) Hank's outline significantly scaled back the number of personal stories and then added ten additional expositional chapters on a wide variety of topics related to the problem of alcoholism and its solution.*

According to Parkhurst, the book would open with the two chapters already written: "There Is A Solution" ("Introduces Alcoholics Anonymous. There follows a description of ourselves, the alcoholic problem and our solution. The chapter is general and casts [a] shadow of that to follow.") and "Bill's Story" ("Narrative One. An alcoholics [sic] life experience—How he found the answer."). These two would then be followed by thirteen chapters of personal stories; Chapters 3–10 presenting one story each ("the

---

* See Appendix V on page 641 for the complete text of Hank's outline.

narrator of the first story introduces others, will tell what they were like and what they have found") while Chapters 11–15 would include four shorter stories each ("these will contain groups of stories written by alcoholic men and women") for a total of twenty-nine personal stories of recovery. This is just one less than the actual number of stories published in the first printing of the Big Book ten months later; the difference being caused by the last-minute addition of a story called "Lone Endeavor." It is also interesting to notice that Hank thought it would be necessary to add some appropriate editorial comments at the end of each of these stories, "emphasizing and analyzing" any significant points of interest they might have raised.[16] Hank was planning to exercise some editorial control over the stories submitted—most likely anticipating that, if nothing else, the Akron stories would require some oversight.

Note also, that Hank once again uses the phrase "Alcoholics Anonymous" as the name of the group (and perhaps even as the name of the book; he is typically unclear).

Following the personal stories, the next ten chapters Hank describes are remarkably prophetic in predicting the topics that would actually be covered in the Big Book. Since none of those chapters have titles—they were simply numbered 16 through 25— perhaps the clearest way to illustrate the accuracy of his vision is to list the titles of the chapters that currently appear in the first 164 pages of the book, *Alcoholics Anonymous*, followed by the corresponding quotes from Hank's outline, in which he describes the suggested contents for each of the proposed chapters:

> *The Doctor's Opinion*: "Testimony of a well known physician who has specialized a lifetime with alcoholics. At his hospital he has seen many of us recover whom he has pronounced incurable. It will also cover the problem in lay language from the medical and psychiatric point of view." *[Hank's Chapter # 17]*

> 1 & 2. *There Is a Solution* and *Bill's Story*: *[already written]*

> 3. *More About Alcoholism*: "Devoted to the vagaries of the alcoholic mind, bearing especially on mental and emotional states. Having observed each other under new conditions, we think our experiences will be of immense benefit to alcoholic readers. It will give the medical profession the intimate view of these mens *[sic]* minds they so much desire." *[Hank's Chapter #18]*

> 4. *We Agnostics*: "Most of us were honest in being agnostic. This chapter is so directed." *[Hank's #16]*

> 5 & 6. *How It Works* and *Into Action*: "Having secured the confidence of the alcoholic reader we tell him just what he can do about it. Detailed instructions for working out his situation with his priest, pastor, reader *[?]*, wife or best friend will be given. Our experience shows that a man can do this if he follows directions. Great numbers can be touched by the book in this fashion." *[Hank's Chapter #19]*

7. *Working with Others*: "We observed that once an alcoholic has a spiritual experience he must throw himself into work for others. It is preferable that he work with other alcoholics for he can do things which no one else can do. This chapter will detail just how to help others and build up a new group of friends. This chapter will give a blind address, to which an alcoholic who has recovered, and is helping others, may write. When the correspondence indicates real results, we shall contact and draw them into fellowship." *[Hank's Chapter #20]*

8 & 9. *To Wives* and *The Family Afterward*: "Dealing with wives, relative and friends, showing them how they may help." *[Hank's Chapter #21]*

10. *To Employers*: "Herein employers will be given the new view of alcoholism as it affects their interests. Many specific suggestions will be made, as to how in the best interest of all, the employer may handle the myriad situations which are so baffling to him at present." *[Hank's Chapter #22]*

11. *A Vision for You*: "This chapter will disclose our life as a group, our work as a group, our present situations, and our attitude toward the outside world of life and business. We shall show how our simple common denominator works in the every day world." *[Hank's Chapter #24]*

This is a remarkable achievement. In this earliest outline, Parkhurst has accurately accounted for each of the chapters that would eventually be published in the book and he has almost perfectly designated the correct number of stories that would appear in the first printing. It is hard to understand Bill Wilson's later dismissive comments that they had been "unable to come up with any genuine outline for the publication" and that all he had to work with while writing the book was Hank's "hastily drawn-up list of possible chapter headings."[17] No genuine outline? The order of appearance here is a bit off, but Hank has rather accurately articulated the contents of each of the published chapters (not just supplied possible chapter headings—which, in fact were *not* supplied) and his outline must have been more than a little helpful when the writing of the book began in earnest in late September. The outline provides a suggestive template for each new chapter as it was being written and, perhaps most significant, there are no chapters in the Big Book that are *not* suggested in Hank Parkhurst's outline.

Two Chapters That Weren't Included
There were, however, two chapters in Hank's outline that never made their way into the book. The first of these was to be "devoted to the potential alcoholic," which Parkhurst thought necessary so that "the potential alcoholic and others may definitely recognize the symptoms before great consequences develop" *[Hank's Chapter #25]*. The inclusion of the phrase "and others" is interesting since it presumes people who might know a potential alcoholic would, first of all, have been reading this book and then understood it well enough to warn him about his incipient problem, thereby referring

him to the book to gain some insight into how he might avoid the pitfalls of his budding alcoholism. And while the spirit of helpfulness would be a clear motivator for delivering such a warning, it is equally clear that the big problem with writing such an enlightening chapter would be the necessity of providing a definitive answer to Hank's earlier question: "What is an alcoholic?" Such a definition would be the only way to differentiate the poor out-of-control drinker from his potential alcoholic brother, and we have already seen what an impossible challenge it had been for both Bill and Hank to produce a simple and straightforward answer to that question.

Although this proposed chapter was never written, both the idea of and the phrase "potential alcoholic" do make a number of appearances in the Big Book: in "Bill's Story" ("I studied economics and business as well as law. Potential alcoholic that I was, I nearly failed my law course . . ."); in "More About Alcoholism" ("Potential female alcoholics often turn into the real . . ." "[We] see large numbers of potential alcoholics among young people everywhere . . .," "Though you may be able to stop for a considerable period, you may yet be a potential alcoholic . . . ," "But the actual or potential alcoholic, with hardly any exception, *will be absolutely unable to stop drinking on the basis of self-knowledge* . . ."); and in "To the Employer" ("That company may harbor many actual or potential alcoholics . . ."). In addition to these specific references, the possibility of someone being just a potential alcoholic informs much of the discussion on the nature of alcoholism in the Big Book, from the "moderate drinkers . . . hard drinkers . . . real alcoholics" distinctions described in "There Is A Solution", to the four categories of problem drinkers so extensively outlined in the chapter "To Wives."[18] Although it did not receive its own chapter, the concept of someone being a potential alcoholic did receive a fair amount of treatment and notice throughout the book.

Hank's remaining suggested chapter was never written, nor does the topic he intended to cover in it receive much direct mention in the Big Book. It was to be devoted to an insightful analysis of what had *not* worked for them in their efforts to get people sober and it was meant to serve as a guide for newly recovered alcoholics and those who were involved in the all-important job of working with people who were still drinking.

Chapter Twenty Three.

We shall emphasize that we have no cure all. The sufferer must be willing to recover and cannot be too much handicapped by other great mental and nervous abnormalities. Our failures with many such types will be analyzed at length. We have learned more from our failures than our successes. This should be a valuable chapter for new men and women, that they may recognize their handicaps and may readily perceive the difficulties of those they seek to help.

In June 1938, this was seen as an essential chapter for the book and Hank had convinced Bill it would make an important contribution to the cause of recovery. When Wilson wrote to Dr. Bob Smith immediately after this outline was completed, he referred to it favorably as "the chapter on failures,"[19] and, shortly after that in another letter, he all but quotes Hank's pragmatic criteria for this chapter by saying "I feel that I have always learned more from the failures than from the successes."[20]

A chapter called "On Failures" (or perhaps "Our Failures"?) would have made for compelling reading, especially since there had been so many of them. Identifying which cases should be included would have presented a challenge, not only in the sorting out of the individual causes of failure, but also in relation to the preservation of those former members' anonymity. Bill later gave some idea of how this chapter might have read when he commented to Dr. Bob Smith that "the story of a fellow like Ernie* would be omitted from this series [of success stories], but could be included in the shorter narrative or perhaps, considering his wonderful comeback with powerful effect in the chapter on failures."[21]

In addition, Hank felt it was important to underline the fact that a successful candidate for sobriety could not be too "handicapped by other great mental and nervous abnormalities." There was a fair amount of talk at this time in both New York and Akron about how impossible it was to help people who were burdened with serious emotional problems above and beyond their alcoholism. Both the leadership and the other members of A.A. were constantly trying to distance themselves from the walking wounded they encountered with such regularity in the shelters and missions of the inner cities. This disclaimer about the inability of unstable people to get sober would be slowly tempered over the next several months and finally modified to the point that the first paragraph of the fifth chapter in the Big Book, "How It Works," would end by noting "there are those, too, who suffer from grave emotional and mental disorders, but many of them do recover if they have the capacity to be honest." Emotional and mental issues would admittedly create an additional layer of complications for active alcoholics, but this does not categorically preclude them from getting sober. Only those who are "constitutionally incapable of being honest with themselves"[22] would be left to suffer that unfortunate fate.

Bill's Letter Announcing the Book to Dr. Bob

Almost five weeks after he had started writing in earnest, and one week after going public by mailing out two chapters to a potential donor, Bill Wilson finally sent a long letter to Dr. Bob Smith announcing he had not only launched the book project, but that it was already well underway.** This is an important letter, not only for a proper understanding of the evolution of the Big Book, but also for the insights it provides into the relationship between these two men at this time. Most notable is the fact that Bill had not been in touch with Bob Smith since his last visit to Akron almost eight weeks earlier—an amazingly long time to have absolutely no contact between these

---

*   Ernie Galbraith was an early Akron A.A. member who got sober, slipped after a year and then, seven months later, regained his sobriety. His story, "The Seven Month Slip," appeared in the first edition of the Big Book on pages 282–86.

**   This letter carries no date, but it is clearly the one referred to in Bill's second letter to the banker, Maguire, in which he mentions that he had "just dictated a letter to Dr. Robert Smith of Akron Ohio." Given the probable date of June 24 for the Maguire letter and the fact that Dr. Bob's letter had just been dictated, this letter to Bob can confidently be dated as going out on either June 22 or 23 or perhaps even as late as Friday, June 24. The definitive element in this dating is that the second letter to Maguire and this letter to Dr. Bob Smith about the book both contained a copy of the outline that Hank Parkhurst had created the previous week.

two groups, especially with such an important project just getting started. It only serves to underline the fact that, up to this point, the book was a New York project only, and understandably so; the two chapters Bill sent to Bob along with his letter were proof in black and white that the brand of sobriety being practiced in New York City was far different from what was happening in Akron. Bill was fully aware of how stark these differences must appear and the letter reflects his best efforts to sell what he had already written (and circulated) to Dr. Bob and to the other Ohio members of the group newly named, Alcoholics Anonymous.

Bill begins a bit sheepishly by explaining why he has launched this project in spite of the strident opposition the Akron group had expressed to him just two months earlier.

> Dear Bob:
>
> I have been most remiss but there have been reasons. After getting home from Akron I had about concluded to let the book idea lie quiet while people thought it over. I found however that a lot of people including Frank Amos had got quite afire. Frank thought something ought to be started right away. I told him that you people had only just begun to consider the matter and pointed out at length the dangers and difficulties of such a venture; particularly our fear of undesirable publicity. Considering the rate at which we grow, he, and others including myself, began to think that publicity would come anyhow. Why then not our own anonymous view of ourselves thus precluding the possibility that someone else garbled the situation before we had a chance to say anything. Thus we came to the conclusion that in a tentative way, a beginning should be made. In this fashion, having some definite proposals laid out and some printing done, we would have a concrete basis for discussion.[23]

Bill was willing to admit his own part in the decision to launch this book project; but even while doing so, he artfully sidesteps much of the responsibility by placing it squarely in the lap of John D. Rockefeller Jr.'s associate, Frank Amos. The clear implication is that Amos's opinion carried more than enough weight to override the Ohio objections and effectively decide the issue. Bill not only agreed with Frank, he also argued that their recent phenomenal growth had made it absolutely essential that they write down their own anonymous view of themselves and of their program for recovery. Only by making such a preemptive strike could they prevent some outsider from writing about them first; someone who would surely get the message all wrong and end up painting an unfavorable picture of them. Surrendering to Amos's pressure and believing it was essential that they get into print sooner rather than later, Bill had made a tentative attempt at the book, one which could now serve as the basis of an ongoing discussion about how the rest of the book should be put together.

What is not said here—at least not directly—is that the New York group, in a stunning disregard for collective decision-making, had unilaterally vetoed all of

Akron's objections and begun to write the book on their own and without any further consultation with the Ohio members.

The letter continues with details on the progress they had already made with the project:

> As a starting point, I have, with the help of the folks here, dictated and mimeographed two chapters of the proposed book one in the nature of an introduction and the second my own story. These I enclose to you together with a rough outline of the contents of other chapters.
>
> I imagine you could use this material as a sort of trial balloon and a starting point for discussion of what you folks out there believe the book ought to contain.

Wilson was confident (or at least he was trying to sound as confident as possible) that the reality of these two finished chapters along with an outline of the entire book would change the negative opinions he had encountered in Akron several weeks earlier and allow the Ohio group to begin a positive discussion of the merits of the individual chapters, rather than continuing to protest the fact that a book was being written in the first place.

> Although I have made the beginning, I feel that the completed book should represent the work of many people; particularly the individual stories which I think should be as little edited as possible. They will naturally be the heart of the book and must represent the feelings, experiences, and personalities of those who write them.

Bill's disavowal of primary authorship here is based on the proposed centrality of the personal stories which, according to the outline, were to be prominently positioned in the front of the book and were projected to take up more than 60 percent of the entire text. Who would be responsible for writing the remaining ten chapters called for in Hank's outline is a question he never addresses.

Regarding those personal stories, Bill now tried to further assuage some of Akron's expected hostility by offering the writing of one these stories to Dr. Bob's wife, Anne Smith:

> As you will note, the chapter outline calls for nine stories of a chapter each about the same length as my own. My feeling is that Anne should do the one portraying the wife of an alcoholic. We have here [in New York] a very striking story in the person of Florence Rankin who is an alcoholic and also the wife of an alcoholic. She has been alright for about nine months and has a very unusual and powerful witness. It may be that like Anne she should have a chapter to herself.

This is Bill Wilson at his political best. He is well aware of the opposition to this project in Akron and he is sensitive to the resentments his proposal will generate. What better way to defuse that animosity than by making an offer to the beloved "mother" of Ohio A.A., asking her to write one of the most prominent stories in the proposed book, the one telling the story of recovery from the perspective of an alcoholic's wife? Wilson seems confident this would provide a significant Akron counterbalance to what could only be perceived as a predominately East Coast enterprise. The inclusion of Anne Smith's personal story would amply demonstrate this wasn't just a New York project and Bill even sweetens his offer further by promising that Anne need not fear being the only woman writing her story for the book; Florence Rankin would also have her own story in the back.

If Anne Smith had accepted this generous offer, it might have gone a long way toward facilitating the acceptance of the book project in Akron, but she immediately and unequivocally declined the honor. The short, two-page story, entitled "An Alcoholic's Wife," did appear in the first edition of the Big Book and was eventually written by Marie Bray, the non-alcoholic wife of another Akron A.A. member.*

Regarding those nine full personal stories, Bill explained that:

> Then we might, beginning with myself, take several of us in consecutive order omitting any who have fallen from grace. The story of a fellow like Ernie would be omitted from this series, but could be included in the shorter narrative or perhaps, considering his wonderful comeback with powerful effect in the chapter on failures.

Bill's concept of how the stories would be arranged is identical to the list of twenty-five professions Hank Parkhurst had created earlier in the month for the story section.[24] They would start with Bill, who had the most time sober, and then present "in consecutive order" the stories of the others who had gotten (and stayed) sober. This would obviously mean that Bob's own story would appear second in the series:

> It is thought each of these nine chapters should run about five thousand words. Then we might have five chapters each consisting of five witnesses of about one thousand words each selected mostly I should think, consecutively except for some especially striking case and the witnesses of a couple of beginners.

The nine long stories by those with the most sobriety would be followed by twenty-five shorter stories that would also be presented in chronological order—although a couple of stories by beginners might be inserted in this section for dramatic effect. Note that Bill has increased the number of stories in these multiple-story chapters to five short stories each; one more than Hank's outline suggestion of four stories in each of these chapters. Also of interest here is Bill's mention that the suggested length for all the chapters in the book should be 5,000 words; a target he most likely arrived at while

---

* There is a popular A.A. legend that Bill originally offered the writing of the chapter "To Wives" to Anne Smith. But as the text of this letter makes clear, Wilson is offering her one of the choice, longer stories that would eventually appear in the back of the book, not one of the expositional chapters that would later appear in the front. In this apocryphal story of conflict, Lois is pictured as being outraged when Bill—having previously made this offer to Anne—refuses to let her write "To Wives." Lois was, in fact, extremely angry at Bill's refusal to let her write that chapter, but only because she felt she was the most qualified person to do so. Nowhere, in any of Bill's or Lois's writings or recorded talks is there any mention of Bill offering "To Wives" to Anne Smith or of that previous offer being the cause for Lois's anger. See Hartigan, *Bill W.*, p. 114, *Lois Remembers*, p. 114 and *Pass It On*, p. 200 for three versions of this story—none of which make any mention of Anne Smith or of Bill's alleged offer to her.

struggling to write those first two chapters which, at this early stage, numbered roughly 5,800 and 5,350 words respectively.

Bill then graciously moves away from this proposed conception of the book and invites Dr. Bob and the other Ohio members to liberally edit what he has done and even to freely invent something completely different if they think that might be best.

> The foregoing are suggestions only. We can never tell where the next best idea may come from and who will make a still better suggestion. So please take the picture I have sketched and do not hesitate to add, subtract and multiply it in any way which occurs to you all. I am not suffering at the moment from any pride of authorship so let everyone do their best and if they like their worst.

Despite this generous request for criticism, Bill just couldn't restrain his natural talent for being the director and he immediately goes on to offer Bob concrete suggestions on how to present the two chapters and the outline and then gives an exhaustively detailed account of what should go into each of the individual stories, stories he was expecting the Ohio members to start writing in the very near future.

> It might be a good idea if you showed this stuff around generally and then asked people to write their own stories in their own language and at all the length they want; covering those experiences from childhood up which illustrate the salient points of their character. Probably emphasis should be placed on those qualities and actions which caused them to come into collision with their fellows and those things which lay beneath the tendency to excessive drinking. The queer state of mind and emotion preceding the first drink, the first medical attention required, the various institutions visited; these ought to be brought in. There ought to be a description of the man's feelings as he met our crowd, his first sense of God being with him, his feeling of hopelessness and now his sense of victory, his application of principles to his everyday life including domestic, business and relations with other alcoholics; the release he gets from working with others, the victories God has given him, the problems which still face him and his progress with them; these are other possible points. When this is done we can sit down with the authors one at a time and fit their story into the pattern of the book. Everyone should write with feeling not laying it on too thick however and above all let's not try to be literary it will be much better to be guided.

This final word "guided" refers, of course, to the guidance one receives from God during quiet time, the practice Frank Amos had cited in his report as being so critical in the Akron program of continued sobriety—a practice they believed had to be faithfully followed every morning to prevent the "grave danger of backsliding."[25] The Oxford Group's suggested method for quiet time required people to sit with "a pencil and note-book so that [they might] record every God-given thought and idea that comes

to [them] during our time alone with Him, that no detail, however small, may be lost
. . ."[26] This is the model Bill was advising the Ohio members to use when writing their
own stories, relying primarily on God's inspiration rather than attempting to produce a
polished literary work.

Bill concluded this section of his letter by telling Dr. Bob he wanted him to assume
responsibility for promoting this project in Akron.

> I can't say how soon I shall get to Akron for we are in the throes of raising
> more money to carry on with. But if you could get the ball rolling along
> these lines it will be great. This will greatly facilitate tying up the packages
> quickly and neatly later on.

Bill would not be coming back to Ohio any time in the near future, nor did he plan
to do anything further to sell this project to the Akron members. That was Bob's job
now and he would also be held responsible for getting the Ohio members to actually
begin writing their personal stories.

Having covered all the important details regarding the book, and passed
responsibility for the Ohio portion of this project on to Dr. Bob, Bill proceeded to the
topic that had consumed almost all his time and energy since he had finished writing
the two chapters:

> Now about money matters. In the first place I am sure we could use quite
> a bit to carry on the general work for the next year. Situations are bound
> to arise which will need some underpinning. Moreover it is going to take
> time and money to get this book out and put it into circulation.

The "general work" mentioned is what Bill and Hank were doing every day,
working with both new and old drunks, along with the time and money they were
spending on promotion as they solicited donations from the rich to support these
efforts. Since, at this time, neither of these men had any real outside source of income,
it is understandable that Wilson felt they would require quite a bit of money if they
were going to maintain the office in Newark and continue to pay all of the other
normal living expenses necessary to keep food on the table and a roof over their heads.
This need for financial assistance was self-evident to the people in New York, but
Bill understood that his reasoning had to be laid out explicitly to counter the Akron
abhorrence of money and their belief that it would only act as a contaminant to the
work being done.

Where this money would come from was still something of a mystery, although
Wilson and Parkhurst were confident the book was a viable product and they were
equally certain that, if it was promoted and sold properly, it would eventually generate
more than enough profit for them to carry on. In addition, they were not the only two
people in New York who were feeling so confident about this venture:

> In this latter connection we are told by Silas Bent that if we can produce a
> book as useful and as moving as the first two chapters suggest it may have
> a very large sale. You will remember Silas as an alcoholic we worked with

out here. He is a star reporter and writer and was at one time editor of the New York Times Sunday magazine. He thoroughly knows all the ropes we shall need and offers his services as an editor or as a writer, if we so desire.* He thinks that prior to the publication of the book articles based upon it should be published in the Readers Digest, Saturday Evening Post, etc. Or perhaps some of the chapters of the book itself. This would ensure a very large sale of the volume if it is any good. We think we can get some of the life insurance companies to recommend in their advertising that people read the book.

Nervous about the Ohio response to these two chapters, Bill is happy to report that a local professional has pronounced them useful and moving and notes he is confident they will prove to be effective marketing tools for the book. *Readers Digest* and *The Saturday Evening Post* were the two most widely read magazines at the time and, in this age before television, they were (along with radio) the primary vehicles for communicating with the American public. Bill's mention of them here is surely ambitious, but as later events would prove, his hopes for using these two magazines to help expand the A.A. movement were not completely unfounded. The possibility of publishing an article about the book in *Readers Digest* would consume a considerable amount of Bill's and Hank's energy over the coming months, but it was the eventual publication of the Jack Alexander article on Alcoholics Anonymous in the March 1, 1941, issue of *The Saturday Evening Post* that would produce exactly the kind of explosive results that Bill predicts here.

Wilson's concluding idea that life insurance companies would become active partners in the promotion of the book may seem a bit strange today, but this was one of Hank's most cherished convictions at the time. Parkhurst was thoroughly convinced that life insurance companies, whom he claimed constantly paid out large settlements for drinking-related deaths, would quickly realize the benefits they could reap by reducing the number of active alcoholics among their insured customers. There is a plausible logic at work here, but the life insurance companies never fully appreciated Hank's argument and his prediction that they would happily spend money to advertise this new cure turned out to be another one of his many unrealistic expectations for the book.**

---

*   Wilson' facts are, again, not quite accurate although Silas Bent *was* an accomplished writer. According to Wikipedia, Silas Bent (1882–1945) was an "American journalist, author, and lecturer, [who] began newspaper work in 1900 in Louisville, Kentucky, on the *Louisville Herald*. After three years he moved to St. Louis and joined the staff of the *St. Louis Post-Dispatch* as reporter and assistant editor. He was appointed assistant professor of theory and practice of journalism at the University of Missouri School of Journalism when the school was opened in 1908, but resigned that position in February 1909 to return to the *Post-Dispatch*. Later, he did publicity work in Chicago and then spent thirteen years in New York City. As a freelance writer he contributed articles to the *New York Times*, *Harper's*, and *The Atlantic* among others. Bent's most famous work is *Ballyhoo* (1927), a critical survey of newspaper practices; he also wrote *Strange Bedfellows* (1929), a book on contemporary political leaders; a biography of Justice Oliver Wendell Holmes, Jr., and *Buchanan of the Press* (Vanguard Press, 1932), a novel about a reporter's career set in St. Louis." (http://en.wikipedia.org/wiki/Silas_Bent - retrieved March 3, 2013) Also worthy of mention here is the story told by Lois in her book about Silas getting seriously drunk and ill in Connecticut and Bill rushing out there, calling a taxi and taking him to Towns Hospital in New York. (See *Lois Remembers*, p. 102)

**   See Finan *Drunks: An American History*, p. 251 for an interesting discussion of what happened when, in 1964, the insurance companies finally did begin to acknowledge that Hank Parkhurst might have been right on this point.

Despite the fact that Bill had openly invited criticism, there was something very finished about these two chapters and the outline mailed to Akron; it was a neat and tidy package, presenting a formidable challenge to any would-be critic. What Bill had sent could easily accommodate an occasional suggestion or correction, but the self-contained completeness of it all discouraged wholesale rejection unless that person was willing to undertake a complete rewrite of both the outline and the individual chapters. Wilson had already put in the hard work needed to get this far in the project and there was really no one in Akron with the time, energy, commitment, talent, or willingness to make the effort necessary to create a completely different version of the book.

Perhaps realizing this, Bill offered Bob a very open-ended question near the end of this letter, generously inviting his opinions on a matter that had not yet been decided at all—the title of the book:

> By the way, you might all be thinking up a good title. Nearly everyone agrees that we should sign the volume, Alcoholics Anonymous. Titles such as 'Haven, One Hundred Men, Comes the Dawn, etc.' have been suggested.

While there was general agreement that the authors should remain anonymous, Hank's suggestion for titling the book *Alcoholics Anonymous* had obviously not yet gained much traction. And why should it? There were so many other much more colorful titles to be imagined. Here Bill mentions just three, but the list of possible titles would grow significantly over the next seven months as "naming the book" became something of a popular parlor game among the New York members.

Bill then asked Bob another open-ended question and supplied some context for that question:

> What would you think about the formation of a charitable corporation to be called, let us say 'Alcoholics Anonymous'? Money coming in from the book could be handled through it as well as any funds arising from contributions by corporations [who] benefited by our work.

> We should always remember that perhaps some day our activities will be scrutinized by hostile microscopes with the idea of proving we are a racket. If we now form a corporation whose control is exercised by a board composed largely of disinterested and non-alcoholic people, we shall have closed the door to such criticism. The trustees of this corporation could administer any other enterprises we might want to engage in; such for instance, as sanitariums.

As it was in "Hank's Ideas," the idea of forming their own foundation was now clearly in the forefront of Bill's mind and so, for the first time, he tells Bob Smith of their plan to create a foundation, sharing not only his justifications for that plan, but also outlining the way in which the foundation would be structured and what kind of responsibilities and duties it would have—including the oversight of any sanitariums they might establish. This same formula would be brought up again a few weeks later when Bill convinced Dr. Bob to become one of the trustees of the foundation (which was finally set up in early August).

In the final paragraph, Bill supplies Bob with some specific details about their work with potential donors, explaining the current status of their efforts and their hopes.

> It is expected that we can obtain from friends of Frank Amos suitable "To whom it may concern" letters introducing us to people of means. The plan is to approach such people saying that we need funds to carry on our general work and to publish this book. They will be shown chapters of the book and will be told that we intend to become self supporting within one year, but that we shall need financial assistance in the meantime. So we are hard at work in the money department out here and I have no doubt that we shall raise what we need. When this is accomplished some of us will probably come out for a visit at which time we can develop matters further.

Bill is being a bit duplicitous here in failing to note that the fundraising plans were already well launched, Maguire having had this kind of promotional package in hand for a week when this letter was written. Still, it is worth noting that one feature included in the initial presentation letter emphasized their commitment to being fully self-supporting within a year. Wilson's confidence in this matter—however misplaced—is almost charming to see.

Finally, things are firmly on track and significant progress is being made on what needs to be done to spread their solution across the country!

Bill closes with a warm salutation for everyone in Ohio and a postscript containing something of a mixed-message:

> Meanwhile, salutations to the alcoholic brethren and God be with you all!
>
> Much yours,
>
> [signed] Bill
>
> p.s. I believe Frank Amos concurs. Let us know what you think.
> *[handwritten above the typed strikeout]*
>
> ~~p.s. I am mailing Frank Amos a copy of this letter and I think he concurs for the most part in its contents. Please let us know what~~[27]*

Once again, there is mention that a duplicate copy of this letter has been made and it is being used to apprise other people of the current state of their efforts. This seemingly generous final solicitation that Bob "let us know what you think" comes packaged with the implicit reminder that these are not just Bill's ideas; they also have the endorsement of Rockefeller's man, Frank Amos. There is a certain symmetry to this postscript, one which hardly creates an open invitation for any kind of serious criticisms; the letter opened with an emphasis on Frank Amos's enthusiastic approval

---

* Although this important letter has been dealt with as separate pieces, the text here is complete and in order when taken all together.

of the book project and ends with his much more sweeping approval of most of the items discussed in this letter. If Bob had any objections to what was being done in New York City then he would not just be disagreeing with Bill (and Hank), he would also be rejecting the concurrence of one of John D. Rockefeller Jr.'s intimates.

Frank Amos's Letter to Albert Scott

The Rockefeller men were, in fact, in full support of all these efforts. Amos, the member of the group who was most involved with A.A.'s day-to-day activities in New York City at this time, had already received a copy of the two chapters and the outline and he was delighted to see that the book project had finally been launched. He was also impressed with the writing Bill had done so far and felt it provided convincing evidence for the credibility of the growing Fellowship and for their solution to alcoholism. On the same day Wilson was writing his second letter to Maguire, Amos sent a letter to the leader of the December 13, 1937 Rockefeller meeting, Albert Scott—who had just returned from an extended medical leave in Florida—giving him a summary of the progress "the self-styled Alcoholics squad" had made during Scott's four-month absence and included copies of the outline and the first two chapters of the book.

> June 24th, 1938
>
> Mr. Albert L. Scott
> Lockwood Greene Engineers Inc.
> 30 Rockefeller Plaza
> New York City
>
> Dear Mr. Scott:
>
> Since your return I have wanted an opportunity to tell you in detail the developments in the activities of the self-styled Alcoholics squad, both here and at Akron. The work has been going on splendidly and every day evidences are piling up which strengthen my conviction that these fellows not only are on the level but have developed a Christian technique which if earnestly followed out is, and can be, effective in a majority of cases of this character.
>
> There are two things that these men are particularly anxious about. One is that along carefully worked-out logical lines their influence can gradually be spread to other parts of the country. The second is that they can gradually become self-supporting, so far as this particular work is concerned.
>
> I have been in constant consultation with the leaders here and just recently paid a brief visit to Akron, spending my entire time with Dr. and Mrs. Smith and Paul Stanley. Smith and Stanley were two of the group who we met in our original meeting.

After securing a great deal of expert advice from various quarters, including two writers of national reputation, they have decided to bring out a book. They hope that the revenue from the sale of this book will be of material financial assistance. Their desire is to have this a cross section of experiences from a large number of the group, selecting only those who have been in this work long enough to convince the leaders that they are permanently cured and therefore good practical examples.

The idea is for the book not to bear the name of any author but to be by "Alcoholics Anonymous." They figure that it may take a year to complete it and they have offers to have it carefully edited by two writers of national reputation, one of whom is Floyd Parsons*, providing this proves desirable.

It is hoped that endorsements of the book and of this work can be incorporated in it over the names of at least one outstanding physician of national reputation and at least one person who is likewise well known, thus adding great strength and authenticity of [sic] what the book contains.

I am sending you a rough draft of the first dictation. The first page is not to be part of the book but is outlining the purpose of it. The rest is a rough beginning on Chapter I and on the first story of an ex-alcoholic. If you can spare the time and strength, I wish you would read this, if possible, within the next few days and let me know what you think of it. In fact, if you can spare the time, I should like to come over and discuss the matter with you for a half hour or so.

I am more than ever impressed with the sincerity and the practical ability of these gentlemen and believe it is well worth our while to back it up in every possible manner.

Mrs. Amos joins me in warmest regards to Mrs. Scott and yourself.

Sincerely yours,

Frank B. Amos[28]

It is hard to miss how Amos's enthusiasm for the work of the "self-styled Alcoholic squad" has grown since Scott left for Florida in late February.[29] In Frank's opinion, these men appear to have found a cure for alcoholism and their efforts are therefore "well worth . . . every possible manner" of support from Mr. Rockefeller's friends—

---

* Silas Bent, mentioned in Bill's letter to Bob Smith was the first of these "writers of national reputation" and his accomplishments have been described in a previous footnote. Floyd Parsons was, according to *The Palm Beach Post* (in a February 4, 1931, story entitled "Floyd Parsons Talks at Rotary Gathering"), a "noted writer and reportorial investigator of Saturday Evening Post fame" —although I can find no instances of him writing any stories for the *Post* after 1931. There is no evidence that either Bent or Parsons ever edited the text of the Big Book. But Parsons would make one further appearance in the Prospectus that Hank Parkhurst prepared in late October of 1938, for the One Hundred Men Corporation in which he noted that "Among other sales promotional possibilities that must be followed up is the offer of Floyd Parsons to write an article based upon the book for the Saturday Evening Post. Mr. Parsons is very well acquainted with the editor and believes an article would be acceptable." (GSO, Box 59, 1939, Folder C, Unnumbered copy of "Memo on 100 Men Corp.," p. 8) This, of course, never happened. *The Saturday Evening Post* article on Alcoholics Anonymous was written by Jack Alexander and did not appear until March 1, 1941.

especially now that they have adopted a strategy of becoming self-supporting rather than depending on the large outside contributions they had previously sought and which Scott had been so sure would ultimately be the ruin of all their work.

Albert Scott's reaction to this was positive and he wrote a strong letter of recommendation for Bill Wilson to use as an introduction to the list of millionaires they had already been given. Scott's letter and several other testimonials were then added to the brochure that Hank prepared as the primary device for getting appointments with potential donors.[30] Going forward, Amos would frequently consult with Bill Wilson and Hank Parkhurst and they, in turn, would come to rely on him as the primary conduit for passing along information about their progress to the other members of the Rockefeller circle.*

A Slip Averted

It had been a busy couple of weeks and the stress of it all had taken a toll on the Wilson household. Lois actually missed the finalization of the outline and the late-June letters to Maguire, Smith, and Amos because she left Brooklyn on Wednesday, June 22, to visit her sister, Barbara. Returning home three days later, she and Bill went over to New Jersey to spend Saturday night with the Parkhursts and then stayed on for Sunday dinner.[31]

There is no way of knowing exactly what happened between Bill and Lois during the forty-eight hours following her return, but the next day there was a huge blow up at the house in Brooklyn—which was not an altogether unusual occurrence in the Wilson's marriage.** Lois dramatically describes their argument saying, "I got mad at Bill and he dashed out to take a drink, but went to Parkhursts instead."[32] Her diary provides a bit of additional color, noting that after she "got mad at Bill," he "went over to Jersey for lunch" and that the fight had been so bad that he "came close to taking a drink."[33]

At this point, the idea of Bill Wilson running out to a bar and getting drunk after three-and-a-half years of continuous sobriety is a profoundly disturbing thought and it is hard to imagine how Alcoholics Anonymous would have ever survived such a crushing blow. But however thirsty Bill may have been that morning, he exhibited just enough spiritual sanity to act on his second, rather than his first, thought and he turned to his friend, Hank Parkhurst, for help rather than picking up the first drink.

---

* Wilson says that "meetings of the Alcoholic Foundation were held I think every week at that time . . ." i.e., "during June, July and August" of 1938 (AA Main Events, 1938, Points 13 & 14), but the foundation wasn't formally created until August 11 and there are no records of any meeting of the Alcoholic Fund during that time period. There is, however, considerable evidence of regular, on-going meetings between Bill Wilson and Hank Parkhurst with Frank Amos at his office during this three-month period. (See for instance, AA Main Events, 1938, Point 6.)

** In her book, Lois Wilson admits to having a temper and relates several instances where she lost it (see, for instance, *Lois Remembers*, pp. 17, 70, 127-28 along with the two citations that follow here). The most famous of these was the "shoe incident" of 1936 or early 1937: "One Sunday Bill casually said to me, 'We'll have to hurry or we'll be late for the Oxford Group meeting.' I had a shoe in my hand, and before I knew what was happening, I had thrown it at him and said, 'Damn your old meetings!'" (*Lois Remembers*, p. 98). In addition, in the next-to-last paragraph in her book she revisits the topic of her temper and the fights she had with her husband: "I regret that I occasionally lost my temper with Bill. I said earlier that I had it under better control most of the time, and so I did. But in spite of Bill's amiability, at times he tried my patience with his inattention to details, which I had to rectify. The pressure would build up until finally I exploded. Bill hated these episodes and would do almost anything to avoid them, and I tried hard to control myself." (*Lois Remembers*, p. 169)

Once again, "one drunk talking to another drunk" proved to be the critical element in preserving sobriety.

It would be interesting to know the specifics of their conversation that afternoon in Montclair, NJ. Was Bill, for instance, taking advice from Hank on how to stay sober; or did Hank just commiserate with him on his marital troubles? Perhaps even more so, it would be fascinating to know whether Bill Wilson publicly acknowledged how close he had come to drinking when he moderated the regular Tuesday meeting the next night. How their founder, the most sober member of the group, had successfully navigated his way through such a strong temptation would have surely made for an interesting topic of discussion at that meeting.*

But Bill didn't drink. When he woke up on the morning of Tuesday, June 28 he was still a man who could, with a clear conscience, go forth and preach the message of recovery he believed in so fervently. He must have been greatly relieved and pleased to be sober that day, for he had passed a tremendously challenging test. He also must have been proud of the remarkable amount of progress made in the previous five weeks. Two proposed chapters of the book had been written and were already being circulated among their supporters and potential donors. There was even a detailed outline of what the entire book would look like once it was finished. In addition, the Ohio group had been formally notified that he had begun the book project and copies of the first two chapters and an outline had been sent to Dr. Bob's group for their consideration. Finally, members in both New York and Ohio had been explicitly asked to start writing their own personal stories of recovery for inclusion in the book. The volume that would describe their new method of recovery and spread that news across the country was decidedly and decisively under way.

But the publication of the book, they speculated, was still a year away. What needed to be done right now was to execute the plan to raise money that Bill had described in his letter to Dr. Bob.

Bill Wilson had never been more committed to a course of action than he was to these fundraising efforts. And with this professional-looking promotional package for their writing project in hand, he was again confident that, this time, he would be able to convince wealthy donors to make large contributions that would carry them through the projected twelve months of writing, and he was equally positive he would be able to make those donations start coming their way very soon.

Imagine his despair if he could have known then that there would be no contributions whatsoever in the near future and that it would be another three months before he would find his way back to writing more chapters for this all-important new book.

---

* Although Jim Burwell is not the most reliable of witnesses, his comments on how these early Brooklyn meetings operated appear to be accurate: ". . . we held a Tuesday night meeting at Bill's house. There were seven or eight men sitting around in a circle and Bill Wilson sat in the corner with a little three-legged stool, one of these antique sewing stools. And he would do all the talking and we would do all the listening and answering the questions because he had all the book sense." *(Markings, Your Archive Exchange,* Volume 30, Number 3, Fall 2001, p. 2: http://www.aa.org/en_pdfs/f-151-markings_fall-2011.pdf —retrieved March 16, 2013). Bill Wilson candidly confirmed this general picture in a 1955 talk to the Manhattan Group by noting that "at Clinton Street [in Brooklyn], I did most of the talking." (http://www.silkworth.net/aahistory/print/manhattan_group_1955_2.html —retrieved March 16, 2013).

CHAPTER ELEVEN

Chasing Testimonials

~July 1938~

Before actually approaching any more new prospects for money, Bill decided he should first solicit some favorable medical opinions about the work they were doing and about the two chapters already written. These testimonials could then be used to create a solid professional foundation for the appeals he would be making to prospects on the list of millionaires given him by Willard Richardson[1]. On July 1, he and Fitz Mayo left Brooklyn, taking the train down to Maryland for what would be the first leg of an eleven-day road trip in search of strong endorsements from some of the nation's most important doctors and psychiatrists.[2]

Fitz Mayo

John Henry Fitzhugh Mayo (at this time more than two-and-a-half years sober) was the second most important man—after Hank Parkhurst—helping Bill Wilson with the work on the East Coast, and his name is frequently mentioned in Frank Amos's correspondence and notes during this time. Despite the fact that Fitz lived in Cumberstone, Maryland—fifteen miles south of Annapolis and 30 miles due east of Washington, DC—he had become one of Bill's closest and most trusted friends. Off by himself in Maryland, Fitz today would be called a "loner" (someone staying sober without the help a nearby A.A. group), but he tempered his isolation by frequently traveling 230 miles north to stay with Bill and Lois in Brooklyn. For their own part, the Wilsons returned the favor by visiting Fitz and his family at Cumberstone with such regularly that Lois could say (with just a bit of exaggeration) that she and Bill had "practically commuted to his home" in Maryland.[3]*

As Bill Wilson's other early stalwart in A.A., Fitz Mayo could hardly have been more different from Henry G. Parkhurst; the two men were, in fact, almost polar opposites. Hank was a loud, confident, high-energy man of action and Fitz was "a charming, aesthetic, impractical, lovable dreamer."[4] While Fitz was subject to spells of lethargy and depressive bouts of self-pity, Hank's emotional life revolved around his boisterous enthusiasm and seething resentments. The two men also stood at opposite ends of the critical debate over religion in A.A. Hank was something of a Deist, while Fitz had returned to the Episcopalian faith of his minister father and he had done so with a deep and abiding commitment. His faith in God was unshakable and his conviction that God was responsible for the gift of his sobriety unquestioned.

Mayo's dreamy, impractical nature is evident in the checkered business life he led before getting sober at the age of thirty-eight. His first job was in the accounting department of a large company where he was responsible for collecting receivables. Having lost that job, he moved on to try his hand as a traveling salesman. He then became a real estate salesman and after that, a teacher at a boy's school in Norfolk, Virginia. Failing at that, he finally decided to become a farmer, working a plot of land at Cumberstone, which was near his original hometown in Maryland.

Fitz's married life was fraught with similar ups and downs. Married in 1921, he and his wife Elizabeth had three children over the next ten years, but their relationship was hardly a smooth one—an understandable situation given his increasingly morose drunken habits. But even after he quit drinking in late 1935, Fitz candidly admitted that members of the family continued to annoy him and marital discord seemed to be more the rule than the exception in the Mayo household. While sober, he once abandoned his "wife at home sick" to board a train after being "unkind to her in leaving." In his Big Book story, "Our Southern Friend," Fitz relates an incident similar to this, confessing in his first person, present-tense narrative: "Things are not going so well at home. I am learning that I cannot have my own way as I used to. I blame my wife and children. Anger possesses me, anger such as I have never felt before. I will not stand for it. I pack my bags and leave", and goes to stay with understanding friends.[5]

In all likelihood those understanding friends were the Wilsons, who found themselves deeply enmeshed in the Mayo's marital problems on more than a few occasions over the years. In February of 1938—four months before this July road trip—Lois had written to Bill, who was then visiting at Cumberstone: "Why don't you bring Fitz back with you and come home soon. The more I think about it, the more it seems to me that Fitz ought not to live at home yet, that he isn't yet ready to tackle the family, that they are all happier when he is away and he himself a different man."[6] Three weeks later, Lois was herself on an extended trip to Cumberstone and she wrote Bill that she had just told Elizabeth "how fine Fitz was [doing] and in spite of wanting him better it probably hurt her to think he is fine as soon as he gets away from home."[7] Despite

---

* There are ample entries in Lois's diary and numerous references to Maryland travel in the letters between Lois and Bill to lend some credence to this statement.

his two-and-a-half years of sobriety, Fitz Mayo had not yet acquired enough emotional stability or resiliency to successfully navigate the turmoil of his own family life.

Nor was Fitz successful in getting people sober using the methods he had learned in New York. Back in Maryland, he desperately missed the Brooklyn fellowship and did his best to recreate that same type of community on a local level. But it wasn't working for him and it wasn't working for others. "A man calls me on the phone," he recounts in his Big Book story. "Will I take a young fellow who has been drinking for two weeks to live with me? Soon I have others who are alcoholics and some who have other problems. I begin to play God. I feel that I can fix them all. I do not fix anyone . . ."[8] Abandoning his attempts to sober up people at home (one can only imagine how much this must have aggravated his already unstable family situation), by March 1937 Fitz was trying to run a mission in the nearby town of Shadyside. This project was neither successful nor very long-lived; Lois even placed the word "mission" in scare quotes when she mentions visiting there in her diary.[9] And, all this work with alcoholics in Maryland wasn't the only thing going poorly for Fitz. Leaving his family to fend for themselves, he frequently decamped to nearby Washington, DC, where he stayed with his sister, Agnes, who worked there. Although these efforts did finally produce some slim positive results, they were meager indeed. In late 1937, Fitz got a friend named Jackie Williams sober and Jackie, in turn, sobered up Jim Burwell; but then Jackie drank again (and eventually died drunk), while Jim left for New York where he carried out all of his subsequent 1938 escapades.* For all his hard work, Fitz had almost no luck in actually getting people sober. Perhaps the problem was his consistently strong emphasis on God when delivering his appeals, but whatever the cause, as Bill Wilson later admitted, "near-failure dogged his efforts for years."[10]

Grievously compounding all of these issues, the work brought in no money whatsoever and the Mayos were in desperate need of significant financial support; their large household and Elizabeth's ongoing medical problems demanded at least a moderate flow of regular income for them just to keep their heads above water.**

Bill and Fitz Set Out

Taking the train from New York City, Bill and Fitz first stopped in Maryland and then traveled farther south to Suffolk, Virginia, a city immediately west of Norfolk, where they spent the night with Dr. Charles Hedges and his wife, Margaret. Hedges was one of the ten New York success stories Hank Parkhurst would describe in his presentation to the Board of the Alcoholic Fund one month later as "definitely recovered, but who are out of touch with the group."[11]

---

* There is some wonderful irony in this sequence of events. Fitz and Jim had grown up together and knew each other well. As the controversy over what should and should not be put into the book, Fitz would find himself at one end of the spectrum advocating for a specifically religious program while Jim was positioned at the other end demanding a strictly psychological approach. Today, they are buried just a few feet from each other in the Christ Episcopal Church cemetery in Owensville, MD (Wikipedia, Jim Burwell Named Article, retrieved June 28, 2013).

** There are numerous references to Elizabeth's poor health and frequent visits to doctors and hospitals in Lois's diary and letters.

Hedges had been the director of the prestigious Johns Hopkins Hospital in Baltimore during the late 1920s and early 1930s before becoming superintendent for New York City's Roosevelt Hospital early in 1934. Two years later, his drinking had spun so far out of control that he was "kicked off the staff" of the hospital. He finally quit drinking in January or February 1937 with the help of Wilson and Parkhurst, and once sober almost immediately petitioned Bill Wilson for assistance with his brother-in-law, Paul Kellogg who also desperately needed to stop drinking (something Paul did in July 1937, but with later mixed results).[12]

Dr. Hedges Is on Board

Bill says when they met again in Virginia—where Hedges now worked for the local public health service—he couldn't help but notice "that Charles's skepticism had gone;" implying the doctor had been something of a agnostic when he first came through the Fellowship. Much to Bill's amusement, he discovered that not only was Hedges no longer a skeptic, he was now a fervent and active believer in the religious solution that had been offered to him in New York in early 1937. Wilson notes wryly, "there were [even] traces of his being over 'grouped'"—implying that Charles Hedges was now deeply involved with the local Oxford Group.[13]

Bill and Fitz gave Charles a full report about the general state of affairs in both New York and Akron and then explained their plans for the book project, proudly showing him the two chapters already written and the outline for how the rest of the book would be organized. Hedges "got up a lot of steam right away" and, in his enthusiasm, immediately volunteered to help his two friends with introductions to some former colleagues at Johns Hopkins, the most respected medical school and teaching hospital in the country.[14]

This was almost more than Bill and Fitz could have hoped for. Johns Hopkins was established in 1889 and it quickly became the founding institution of modern American medicine; its importance in transforming the antiquated practices then used in the United States (and the world) can hardly be overstated. During its first forty years of existence, Johns Hopkins had revolutionized the art, the science, and the teaching of medicine, constantly inventing new medical procedures and life-saving operations while training a host of well-educated doctors to carry that knowledge out into every area of the country. In July 1938 there was no more important or prestigious medical establishment in the country, so any testimonials Bill and Fitz might garner from members of its staff would be the most valuable and impressive professional endorsements they could possibly get.[15]

Two Johns Hopkins Psychiatrists Weigh In

Charles Hedges claimed he was still in touch with several leading people on the psychiatric staff and he insisted on driving Bill and Fitz over there to meet them. The three men drove 230 miles up to Baltimore and Hedges arranged an interview with Dr. Leslie Hohman and Dr. Esther Richards, two doctors that, Hedges claimed, were "considered tops in Psychiatry."[16] At the time, both doctors were active on the staff at

Johns Hopkins Hospital and served as Associates in Psychiatry when teaching at the University.*

By now, Bill was well practiced at this presentation and he launched into his explanation of who they were and what they were doing. He then "gave them . . . the two chapters of the book to read, asking that they point out where we were wrong in any of our statements about the hopelessness of alcoholism and the mental conditions surrounding it." Wilson claims that, based on what he had just heard, Dr. Hohman responded with a statement that pleased him immensely:

> . . . Hohman tossed the ball right back with the flat pronouncement that in his judgment, we were one hundred percent correct in our attitudes and belief about the true alcoholic. Pointing to Fitz and me he said, "I will go even further than you people have and make the flat statement that alcoholics of your type are 100% incurable on any basis save religion. Although I am not a religionist, I have great respect for its powers in these cases. If I can possibly avoid it, I never take such a case as yours. They are too heart-breaking."[17]

What could be clearer or more supportive than this for Wilson's thesis about "the hopelessness of alcoholism and the mental conditions surrounding it"? As far as Bill was concerned, he had just received the ultimate seal of approval from the most respected psychiatrist in the country and, bundling this with Dr. Jung's earlier diagnosis of Rowland Hazard, he claimed that "we now have the authority of the best man in Europe and of Johns Hopkins on the question of incurability." Let any alcoholic who thinks he can successfully moderate his own drinking take note of this lethal diagnosis: All of his efforts are doomed to failure and his only hope of a cure is to "commence to seek God with ardor and at once."[18]

Another issue which came up during this interview was the firm conviction expressed by both Hohman and Richards that A.A. would need to clearly define and avoid those unfortunates who could not be helped by their religious cure for alcoholism. As noted earlier, this was not a new topic of discussion within the Fellowship; there had already been a fair amount of exclusionary talk about people with problems other than alcohol, people who were therefore impervious to their solution. In the outline for the book written a few weeks earlier, Hank had noted that the alcoholic sufferer "cannot be too much handicapped by other great mental and nervous abnormalities. Our failures with many such types" prove that this cure will not work for everyone.[19] Dr. Richards was particularly adamant on this point, claiming those who have suffered "organic deteriorations" from their drinking along with those who were "constitutional"

---

* Dr. Leslie B. Hohman (1891–1960) received his MD from Johns Hopkins University in 1917 and then served as a first lieutenant in the US Army during WWI. He finished his psychiatric training and residency at Johns Hopkins after the war and attended graduate school in Vienna in 1924. He served as an Instructor in Psychiatry at Johns Hopkins from 1920–1922, as an Associate in Psychiatry from 1922–1943 and ended his career at Johns Hopkins as an Assistant Professor from 1943 to 1946. He was subsequently a professor of psychiatry at Duke University from 1946 to 1960.

Dr. Esther Richards (1885–1956) received her MD from Johns Hopkins University in 1915 and then served as an Assistant Instructor there from 1917 to 1918. For the new term in 1918, she was promoted to full Instructor and then again promoted in 1920 to Associate in Psychiatry. Richards spent her entire career at Johns Hopkins where she developed a specialty in child psychology.

psychopaths must be carefully avoided as potential candidates for membership in Alcoholics Anonymous.

Providing perhaps more medical details than even Bill Wilson was looking for, she told him,

> . . . it [is] very necessary that you have some competent psychiatric check on the type of alcoholics you can be expected to be of value to. The signs of organic brain disease deterioration are something that a layman cannot detect, and many doctors are in the same boat. These signs are found in a careful examination of the brain and cord, and they represent damage which is in the nature of defect rather than disturbance in functioning. These organic deteriorations and the constitutional psychopath are two types which you can not have any success with, and I think even the most enthusiastic in your midst would not be disheartened by such failures.[20]

Wilson, along with most other early members of Alcoholics Anonymous, was extremely sensitive to the percentage rate of their success and Bill was constantly guilty of inflating those numbers.[21] In Akron, the standards were far more stringent than New York (excluding anyone who didn't first make a public surrender), but, at this time, both groups were doing their best to exclude those who suffered from "grave emotional and mental disorders."[22]

Following the initial interview, Bill thanked Charles Hedges profusely for being so "instrumental in setting afoot big things at Johns Hopkins" and then he and Fitz returned to the farm at Cumberstone. Giving Dr. Hohman time to read over the chapters, the two men returned to Johns Hopkins a few days later—this time with Ebby Thacher in tow—for a follow-up interview.[23] Hohman was even more positive and enthusiastic about their work and "much impressed" with everything he had read. Bill commented that he again confirmed his belief in "the proposition that drunks of our type have to get out from under on a spiritual basis." There was just no other option. The doctor then gave them "a lot of valuable advice about our manuscripts and our procedure" and noted that "from the standpoint of a psychologist he could find no fault whatever with our procedure, our theories about ourselves, and our mental state." Hohman was in complete agreement with everything he had read in "There Is A Solution" and "Bill's Story." Wilson noted that his only "criticism was devoted . . . to showing us how we could better express our ideas and avoid controversy."[24*]

Bill confessed he felt "huge delight" as he listened to Dr. Hohman's sweeping validation of his theories about alcoholism and the doctor's agreement that their program of recovery was the only one that had any hope of success. This was exactly the kind of professional endorsement Wilson had hoped to gain on this trip; one that he was confident would prove to be an effective selling tool once he got back to New York and again had to face that host of rich, but skeptical, potential donors.

---

* It is likely that, once he was back in New York, Bill made several substantive changes to "There Is A Solution" based on Hohman's suggestions, thereby accounting for at least some of the severely reduced text found in the Multilith printing.

A Loan from Agnes Mayo

But none of these wonderful testimonials put any immediate cash in the bank and the balance there was running precariously low. Frank Amos had been making regular payments to Dr. Bob Smith from Rockefeller's contribution to the "Alcoholic Fund" ($500 in March, $450 in April, $500 in May and $200 in June) and he had also been giving cash to Wilson and Mayo from the monies sent to him by Charles Towns ($200 to each of them on both May 9 and May 27 and a final $200 to Bill on July 5).[25]* Curiously, Amos makes no mention of sending any money to Hank Parkhurst, presumably because he was still generating at least a small amount of income with his Honor Dealers operation.

While this left a comfortable balance in the Rockefeller account specifically earmarked for Dr. Bob Smith and his work in Akron, it exhausted the $1,000 Towns had contributed to the Alcoholic Fund for Wilson and his friends. Once again, they were flat broke. Given their desperate financial situation, on Monday, July 11, Bill made one last stop in Washington, DC, before catching the train back to New York City, visiting Fitz's younger sister, Agnes. Unlike her brother, Agnes Mayo had a thriving career and an excellent job. She was Secretary of the Corcoran School of Art in Washington[26] and the kind of person who had always been careful with her money. Bill was hoping to convince Agnes to dip into her savings and offer them some "substantial assistance . . . in bridging the gap of the next few months" by making him a short-term loan of $1,000, promising to pay it back in less than three months. Since the average salary in the U.S. at this time was less than $2,000 a year,[27] this was a significant amount to be loaning Bill; but to his great relief, Agnes agreed to his request and he left Washington, DC's Union Station with a check for the full amount in his pocket.

It was the perfect ending to a long and very successful road trip; Wilson was coming home with strong positive endorsements from two of the country's most respected psychiatrists and he had even secured enough cash for them to continue their full-time fund raising efforts for at least a couple of months. It must have made for a very exhilarating train ride back to Penn Station in New York City.

Bill returned to Brooklyn that night, Monday, July 11,[28] and the following Thursday he wrote Agnes a letter detailing the specific arrangements for the loan and his promise to pay it back in full by October 1:

> My dear Agnes:
>
> I cannot tell you how grateful we all are for your substantial assistance. It will be most helpful in bridging the gap of the next few months.
>
> After consulting with Mr. Frank B. Amos, custodian of our fund, it will simplify matters if I assume personally the obligation to repay you $1000, which you have loaned me as of July 11th, 1938.

The understanding is that I may have the use of this money until October 1st at 6% interest. On or before that date I fully expect to be able to repay you out of funds which I am collecting on behalf of the alcoholic work. In the event that all or part of this sum cannot be paid by October 1st, I would like to continue the loan on the same basis until January 1st, 1939, by which time we shall certainly have received ample funds.

I am today depositing this check with our custodian, Mr. Amos. It is understood, however, that the other funds which already have been contributed to this purpose and which have been specified definitely for certain phases of the work are not now—nor will be—available for repayment of this loan to you. In other words, it is my personal obligation, in which my associates join me wholeheartedly, to raise additional funds out of which we will make this repayment. Though I would like to make the other funds, previously contributed, surety for you, I find that under the terms by which they were donated these funds cannot be used for repayment of any borrowed money. As we agreed, your personal security lies in our ability to raise this money, of which I have no doubt whatsoever.

I am sending this letter in triplicate and wish you would return two copies on which you have stated your approval of the arrangement as outlined above. One of these I shall turn over to Mr. Amos. I have just endorsed your check and deposited it with him as trustee.

Affectionately yours,

Bill Wilson

William G. Wilson

WGW:lm[29]

There are a number of interesting things worth noting in this letter. First of all, Bill's assumption that it will simplify matters if he takes personal responsibility for the loan implies he had earlier assured Agnes that the funds already deposited in the Alcoholic Fund would stand as security for her loan. Frank Amos had obviously disabused Bill of this understanding, pointing out that the only possible surety for Agnes's loan would be his personal promise to raise sufficient funds before the loan came due on October 1. Wilson was once again supremely confident in his own abilities as a successful fundraiser; this time specifically during the next eleven weeks.

In addition, despite the fact that this was now a personal loan, Bill makes it clear that his guarantee is just a necessary formality regarding the mechanics of repayment. This was not really a personal loan and the check was not going to be deposited into the Wilson's bank account. Instead, it was being handed over to Frank Amos with Agnes's check endorsed over to him as the trustee of that fund. Bill was being absolutely scrupulous in relation to the handling of this money, hoping to avoid any possibility of some later investigator unearthing the story and alleging he had been using his work with alcoholics to line his own pockets.

Also of interest is Bill's promise to pay 6 percent interest on this loan. A typical annual interest rate on bank deposits in 1938 was 3.5 percent, so this was an excellent short-term investment for Agnes Mayo. Whether Agnes was a tough negotiator or Bill was just sweetening the deal to make it more attractive is unknown. Curiously, for someone with such business acumen, Bill Wilson does not specify "per annum" as the term in this letter. However it is unlikely Wilson was promising to pay a 6 percent interest rate on a loan with a term of less than three months. Much more likely, the "per annum" is implied here based on the conversation he had with Agnes Mayo in Washington D.C. the previous Monday.

A minor, but final item of interest are the initials "WGW:lm" following the signature line. The home address listed at the top of the page identifies this letter as coming from 182 Clinton Street in Brooklyn, but there is no further information about who this new typist might be. At this time, none of the members of the New York group had the initials "lm" nor did any of their last names begin with "m" (other than Fitz Mayo, who did not type this letter to his sister). Although Bill had previously identified some of his letters as being typed in Brooklyn, this is the first one to provide any clue as to who the mysterious home-typist might be, but that clue is so insubstantial that we are left with little more than a nameless assistant who was helping Wilson with his at-home secretarial work. It does, however, provide conclusive evidence that, at this time, Wilson did have resources other than Ruth Hock to help him with his occasional typing needs.

Agnes accepted both Bill's explanation and his conditions for the loan, signing her name next to the "Approved" line at the bottom of the letter and sending two of these countersigned copies back to Wilson.[30]

A Flurry of Letters

The next day, Bill abandoned his mystery typist in Brooklyn and traveled to Newark where he dictated at least eight letters to Ruth Hock. Several of these provide most of the details we have about Bill's road trip with Fitz Mayo, but when taken together, they provide something more important: a wonderfully revealing snapshot of one day in the life of Bill Wilson as he was living it on Friday, July 15, 1938.

Bill's first letter was a straightforward thank you to Dr. Leslie Hohman at Johns Hopkins, telling him how much he appreciated meeting him and expressing his gratitude for the "very real interest" the doctor had shown in their program of recovery. Wilson reminded Hohman of his offer to continue reviewing and critiquing their book "as we get further on with our writing," and expressed his hope that theirs would not just be "a one-sided arrangement," but that "it will turn out that we can be of real use to you in some fashion or other" in the future.[31] Bill was not about to let this prestigious connection with Johns Hopkins slip away from him and he fully intended to continue fostering as close a relationship as possible with Dr. Hohman.

A Thank You to Dr. Hedges

His next letter went to Dr. Charles Hedges, sincerely thanking him for the introduction he had engineered with the two famous psychiatrists at Johns Hopkins and reiterating how pleased he was with the results of their trip to Baltimore. Wilson also informed him that he had not yet followed up on another contact Charles had provided, a Professor Hammond in New York City.* Bill is curious to know if Hedges had written to Hammond yet and asked if he "should bring up Owen Young's name" when talking with Hammond. "It strikes me that he might be an exceptionally good approach to Mr. Young but I do not want to do anything which would disturb your relationship with [Hammond], or which would seem unreasonable to him, so if you would rather have Mr. Young not mentioned, I wish you would let me know.[32] Charles Hedges had obviously dropped Hammond's and Young's names together in the same conversation and now Bill was wondering if he could use this Hammond connection to get a personal introduction to Owen Young.

Mention of Owen Young's name here attests to Wilson's grand vision for approaching the most prominent millionaires in New York City for contributions. Having successfully secured at least some money from the richest man in America, it seemed perfectly logical to Bill that he should continue his fundraising efforts by making direct appeals to other men who sat very near the pinnacle of the country's economic pyramid. Owen D. Young was exactly that kind of man: he had created the Radio Corporation of America (RCA) in 1919, helped found the National Broadcasting Company (NBC) in the mid-1920s, and had been sitting on the Board of Trustees for the Rockefeller Foundation since 1928. In 1932 Young was even considered a strong 'dark horse' candidate for the Democratic presidential nomination—an honor that went to Franklin D. Roosevelt instead.[33] Young was a titan of industry, but Wilson was confident he could enlist him in their cause once he was given the chance to make an appeal based on the two chapters from his book, these new testimonials he had just received, and the fact that they had already sobered up a remarkable number of men.

Bill assured Charles Hedges that if there were any objection to him asking Hammond for an introduction to Owen Young, it would not be a problem. "We have other approaches to him," he noted confidently.[34] Obviously Wilson was aware of Young's position as a trustee of the Rockefeller Foundation and he was equally confident Willard Richardson would be able to facilitate an introduction for him, should that prove necessary.

Keeping the New York Group in the Loop

In an effort to keep the Rockefeller group well-informed about all of his activities and as closely involved in their progress as possible, Bill's next three letters were sent to Albert Scott, Willard Richardson, and Frank Amos. The first of these went to Scott,

---

* There are no further details provided about Professor Hammond, here or elsewhere, but he is most likely Dr. Graeme Hammond, an American neurologist and sportsman who advocated for physical exercise as a treatment for nervous disorders. Hammond was professor of nervous and mental diseases at the NYU School of Medicine throughout his entire professional career and was, in addition, an Olympic fencer (a very elitist sport at that time) who was, according to the Unites States Fencing Hall of Fame, "generally regarded as the father of American fencing." (Named Wikipedia article, retrieved March 28, 2013).

thanking him for the fine letter of recommendation he had sent them, assuring him it would be "used discreetly and with regard to good taste." Scott's letter had been mailed on July 1, so Bill also made the necessary apologies for his delayed response, explaining he had been out of town recently. Bill then profusely thanked Scott and his associates for the "monies you have placed at our disposal, the lengths to which you have gone to look after our needs, and the spirit in which these things have been done."[35] Wilson could hardly have been more generous in his praise of Scott and the other members of the Rockefeller circle; they were, after all, the solid foundation upon which he was hoping to build a broad network of other wealthy supporters and donors.

Scott's brief letter of introduction (multiple copies were supplied) vouched for his faith in the new movement, making it a valuable piece of paper in New York City in 1938; one that would surely open a number of important doors, allowing Bill, Fitz, and Hank to make their appeals directly to some of New York City's most elite citizens.

Lockwood Greene Engineers Inc. / 30 Rockefeller Plaza / New York
[printed letterhead]

July 1, 1938

To Whom It May Concern:

This will introduce William G. Wilson, J. Fitzhugh Mayo, and Henry G. Parkhurst.

These men are part of a fellowship of one hundred ex-alcoholics who have recovered on a basis which in most aspects is new. Most of them had been pronounced medically incurable.

I have followed their work with much interest and know personally that these men have sound medical endorsement. I gladly vouch for what they may say to you.

Truly yours,

Albert L. Scott

President[36]

It should be pointed out that this claim of success for "one hundred ex-alcoholics" by July 1, 1938 is an inflated number—more good marketing than an accurate reflection of the true number of sober A.A. members at that point. It is also worth noting that "one hundred" is the number constantly and consistently bandied about—without any increase whatsoever—for the next nine months, right up until the day the book was published in early April. To accept the accuracy of this number on July 1, 1938 is to believe either no further recoveries were made during the following nine months (unlikely) or that Bill Wilson consistently disregarded all of the additional members gained between July to April (equally unlikely). One hundred is much more believable as the number of the successful recoveries by the time the book was published (although even this has been challenged), but at this point of the story, "one hundred ex-alcoholics" was more smart marketing than any kind of accurate reflection of reality.

Bill had Ruth type up two extra copies of his letter to Albert Scott and sent these along with his letter to Willard Richardson, asking that the extra copy be passed on to A. LeRoy Chipman. Wilson also repeated his invitation to the three Rockefeller men, one he had obviously made several times before:

> ...let me say again that we should like to have yourself, Mr. Chipman and Mr. Scott come to any or all of our [Tuesday night] gatherings without waiting to be asked. Certainly in the case of you gentlemen, we shall gladly waive the heavy drinking that has qualified us for Alcoholics Anonymous. By common consent, you gentlemen are in the fold. We think you are one of us, and there are no honorary members.[37]

The casual use of "Alcoholics Anonymous" here provides concrete evidence that this new name had decisively entered the vocabulary of the New York Fellowship in the six short weeks since its first appearance in "Hank's Ideas" and "There Is A Solution."

Bill then had Ruth type up yet another copy of his letter to Albert Scott and he sent this one to Frank Amos. There was no need to extend a Tuesday-night invitation to Amos; he was already close enough to Wilson and Parkhurst to have accepted their offer to visit the weekly meeting on more than one occasion (usually bringing his wife with him).[38] Frank was much more involved in the day-to-day operations of the Fellowship at this point—receiving regular office visits from both men—so Bill's letter focused on a recent and very exciting development in their plans to spread the program beyond the confines of just Akron and New York.

> Dear Frank:
>
> I am enclosing a copy of our letter of thanks to Mr. Scott.
>
> Just received an enthusiastic letter from our Springfield protegee [sic] which is also enclosed with a copy of my reply. These two letters will give you a clear idea of how this thing takes root and how it is likely to spread. It is just a question of getting live wires of this description into action throughout the country, and then being able to follow them up and help them out.
>
> I feel that the book will uncover hundreds of men of Mr. Furlong's description.
>
> Much yours,
>
> *Bill*
>
> WGW:RH[39]

Ray Furlong: Spreading the Word beyond Akron and New York

The Springfield protégée was Ray Furlong,* and the great news in his letter was that he was back in Springfield, Massachusetts, staying sober and doing his very best to spread the work among the other alcoholics there. Despite his lack of immediate success, Ray was the perfect example of what Bill Wilson had been advocating for months: One man would get sober and then go back to his home town, carrying the message about their program of recovery to others and offering his own sobriety as proof of its effectiveness. If this could work with a man who had been exposed to the Fellowship directly, there was no reason to think it wouldn't also work for someone who was introduced to their program by simply reading the book.

Furlong had spent a week at Towns Hospital in early 1938, but he started experimenting with "a little controlled drinking" shortly after he arrived back home. Predictably this spun out of control in fairly short order. After a particularly spectacular drunk on Tuesday, June 6, his wife packed him up the next morning and drove him 150 miles to New York City where she redelivered him to Towns Hospital. Calming her fears of yet another relapse, Dr. Silkworth assured her that this time, he felt "he really had something . . . that would work" for Ray.

Three days later, Silkworth's promised solution arrived in the person of two members of the New York Fellowship—one came during the day and another visited him later that night—who told Furlong they had been exactly like him not so long ago, but now they were free of their obsession for drink. The next day was Sunday and Ray was visited by a third recovered alcoholic who carried a spiritual message, one that Furlong later described as "a simple, day to day, plan of faith." The bedridden man was not just convinced, he surrendered completely, making a "final agreement . . . to let God be first in my life"** after which, he claimed, "the whole outlook and horizon brightened up in a manner which I am unable to describe except to say that it was 'glorious.'"[40]

This turnaround was so convincing that the following day Ray's new friend insisted he leave Towns Hospital and come stay at his home in New Jersey, which Furlong did. The next night, Tuesday, June 14, Ray was taken to the meeting in Brooklyn where he would have heard about Jim Burwell's on-going slip and also been introduced to Ebby Thacher who was just returning from his own recent bout with alcohol. At that meeting, Ray said he found a group of men who were just like himself, but "telling of a liberty of living unmatched by anything I had ever seen." He felt like he was home at last.[41]

Shortly after this Ray returned to Springfield, rejoined his wife in their stationery store business, and began to set his life in order. Essential to that recovery was the need

---

* The letter is from R. A. (Roland Arthur) Furlong of Springfield MA who has been mistakenly identified as Ralph Furlong (another contemporary Massachusetts resident). I have called him "Ray" here based on Jim Burwell's use of that name in his handwritten list of "Those Dry + Active Since AA Book 4/1/39" and in his identification of the author of the first edition Big Book story, "Another Prodigal [Son]" (Burwell's copy of the Multilith Printing is currently in the author's collection). Such a name would be likely for a man who so frequently went by his initials: R. A. Adding an additional layer of complexity to this confusion over R. A.'s identity is the fact that Roland also went by the nickname "Bob" (supposedly his father preferred that name for him) and, because of this, he has been incorrectly listed in some A.A. documents as "Robert." See Dodd, *The Authors*, p. 37 and Jared L.'s excellent research on the topic posted to AAHistoryLovers, Message #9280: http://health.groups.yahoo.com/group/AAHistoryLovers/message/9280 (retrieved, June 29, 2013).

** An interesting mid-1938 instance of "getting a surrender to God" before the new man has left the hospital—still a common practice in Akron, but much less frequently noted in New York by this time.

to work with others, but all of his initial attempts failed and, with the typically alcoholic expectation of being wildly successful in his first three or four weeks, he wrote to Bill Wilson in some despair, wondering what he was doing wrong, asking for advice and suggesting perhaps he needed to come back to Brooklyn for a short refresher course. Bill's response (a copy of which was sent to Amos along with Ray's original letter) was both enthusiastic and candid:

Mr. R. A. Furlong,
Empire Stationers,
305 Bridge St.,
Springfield, Mass.

Dear R.A.:

You bet your life you and your wife can come. Plan to stay the night with us.

We have the meetings on Tuesday evenings during the summer. They are usually held at my house, but not always so you had better give us a few days notice so we can let you know if there is any change of plan or possible omission of the meeting.

I cannot tell you how delighted I am about what you say about yourself, your wife, and those men you are working with. We know that you are on the right track, and it was the impression of everyone who talked with you down here that you would be sure to make good, particularly if you took an interest in seeing that others enjoy the chance you have. Christ as an idea is fine, but Christ in action is a power which has no limitation.

We have had a slew of experience working with these drunks. It is sometimes a heart-breaking business and we have learned not to be disturbed when our desires in the matter were not fulfilled. These men, as a class, remind us of a forest through which a great fire has swept. All of the trees are charred on the outside and there appears to be no worthwhile timber left, but a good part of the trees were once strong and the wood was straight grained. We have discovered in our work that if these are not too badly charred, they make great timber; even better for their seasoning in the fire. But those trees which are bent and knotted and useless before the fire are likely to remain that way whatever we do.

It is true that anything is possible through Christ, but I think we assume a great deal, considering our own incapacity to demonstrate His principles, if we think everybody we touch is going to get well. We have had a lot of conceit knocked out of us in that direction. However, the way to learn is to keep on working. I had some hard schooling myself, for the first eight or ten cases I dealt with never got anywhere, and there have been lots more since. I feel that I have always learned more from the failures than from the successes. And don't take yourself or these men and their problems too seriously. I believe that God wants us to be naturally and joyously happy, to be otherwise is to limit our effectiveness in this skeptical old world.

Yours,

Bill

WGW:RH[42]

One thing that stands out starkly in this letter is Wilson's explicit mention of Jesus Christ as God, something he rarely did in print. Bill is almost certainly responding here to the use of Christ's name in Ray's letter, but it is also obvious Wilson is very comfortable with this kind of religiously specific talk. That is hardly surprising since all of the believing members of Alcoholics Anonymous in New York at this time were Christian, and any talk among themselves about religion or spirituality would necessarily have been framed in those terms. One further reason for Bill's comfort level with talk of Christ as God was the fact that, at this time, readings from the New Testament were still a regular part of the meeting format for A.A., even in Brooklyn. Given all of those circumstances, who else would you talk about when you talked about God?

Also of interest here is Bill's metaphor of the forest devastated by a great fire. This sounds very much like a figure of speech he had developed and perfected for use in his presentation to potential donors and one that he uses again in later letters. The fire is a rich metaphor, one that can cut both ways. As Wilson emphasizes, despite outward appearances, some of these charred timbers are not only salvageable, but actually better for having been seasoned in the fire. On the other hand, harkening back to Dr. Richards's point that there are some damaged people who just can't be saved, he notes there are those who are "bent and knotted and useless *before the fire*" [italics added] and they "are likely to remain that way whatever we do." Alcoholics Anonymous members were completely dedicated to working with drunks who could be saved, but they had no interest in squandering their time and energy on those who were hopeless—for whatever reason.

Reverend Ward: A Link to Wealthy New York Donors

The seventh letter Bill wrote that day went to the Reverend C.E.B. Ward, an activist Presbyterian minister with deep contacts among rich donors in New York City.* Willard Richardson had encouraged Bill to meet with Ward but, despite phone calls and letters, the two men had managed to miss each other throughout late June and the first half of July.[43] Bill was anxious to talk to Ward and was hoping he could convince

---

* Clement E. B. Ward and his wife, Blanche, co-founded Marvel House in 1914 and the League for The American Home in 1929. Both of these charities were based in New York City (with Marvel House maintaining a participating country home in Mountain View, New Jersey). The charter of Marvel House was "to establish in the great cities of America, Christian homes of vocational guidance for struggling youths. Each home group consists of ten to fifteen under the supervision of a Christian man and wife or mother-hearted woman . . . Supported by voluntary contributions and board at cost." (*The New York Charities Directory*, Charity Organization Society, New York, 1918, pp. 180-181)

him to come to Brooklyn to attend one of their Tuesday night meetings so that he could see with his own eyes the miracles being worked there:

My dear Mr. Ward:

"The best laid plans 'o mice and men gang aft agley.'"* What with being unable to reach you on the phone, and having been out of town for some time, we have not gotten together as Mr. Richardson suggested we might.

Each Tuesday evening, at my house, 182 Clinton Street, Brooklyn, we have an informal meeting of ex-alcoholics and their families to which newcomers may come for assistance. These meetings are so informal they may startle you a bit, but they do meet our needs. We would like you to come to the next one, if you so desire, so that we may become better acquainted.

My Brooklyn telephone number is Main 4-3220 and you take either the Eastside or Westside subway from New York, getting off at Borough Hall, where you will be within three or four blocks of my house. People commence to drop in around six o'clock, and we have a buffet supper. Everyone stays as long as they like, which is sometimes for the night. So for next Tuesday evening please feel that you are one of us, and on that afternoon will you phone my house and let whoever answers know that you will be there?

If you cannot make it this Tuesday, please feel free to come later, though you might phone in advance as sometimes the meetings are omitted or held at another place.

Very much yours,

Wm. G. Wilson

WGW:rh[44]

Both this letter and the one to Ray Furlong mention that people occasionally stayed overnight after the meeting, so "The Wilson Hotel" was obviously still open for business on Clinton Street. Bill also tells Ward a buffet supper was always served, making it sound as if Lois was buying and preparing enough food for the entire group each week, but this was really more of a pot-luck affair with food contributions coming from the wives who also attended these meetings.

Keeping Dr. Bob Informed

Having addressed all of A.A.'s helpers and potential supporters on the East Coast, Bill's final letter of the day went to Bob Smith, providing him with a recap of his

---

* A slight misquote from Robert Burns' 1785 poem: "To a Mouse, on Turning Her Up in Her Nest with a Plough." The exact line, in the Scottish idiom, reads "The best-laid schemes o' mice an' men / Gang aft agley," which is usually translated into standard English as "The best-laid schemes of mice and men / Often go astray."

trip "down south barnstorming through Maryland, Virginia and Washington, etc." and proudly reporting on their success with the two famous psychiatrists at Johns Hopkins. Bill assured Dr. Bob these endorsements would make a significant difference in their effort to raise money. "The old juggernaut [of fundraising] bounces along," he told Smith, "still in low gear, but shifting soon, I think, to second."

For Bill Wilson, shifting into second gear meant he would now be so caught up in fundraising that he had no idea when he would be able to visit Akron again, certainly not any time in the near future. Explaining this delay, he notes that "Mr. Scott has just given me letters of introduction and we plan to put the bite on such people as Owen D. Young, Mr. Stettinius, Sloan and such like without delay." Bill's sights could not be set any higher. In addition to the already mentioned Owen D. Young of RCA and NBC fame, Bill now plans to solicit Edward Stettinius, Chairman of the Board of U.S. Steel (and later Secretary of State under F.D.R. and Harry Truman), and also Alfred P. Sloan, the President and C.E.O. of General Motors.[45] Bill Wilson was clearly not intimidated by the prospect of making his pitch to these titans of industry who were among the richest and most powerful men in the country.

Bill signed off this exuberant and chatty letter to Bob without asking for either his opinion or his consent on any of these weighty matters. It was either a foregone conclusion or perhaps Bill just didn't feel he needed it. He simply closes the letter by sending "best wishes to dear Annie and yourself, and all of the whirling dervishes— Amen."[46] That final salutation sounds lighthearted enough, but it is unclear whether his "whirling dervishes" comment was Bill's jesting way of referring to the Akon brethren or if it was a private joke between the two men about the Akron group members—both sober and non-alcoholic—who were still so outraged by Wilson's efforts to raise large sums of money to further his plans for the expansion of A.A..

Whatever Bill meant by that remark, given all of his own frenzied activity on this particular Friday, July 15, 1938, anyone looking for a "whirling dervish" could start right there in Newark, New Jersey. There was surely no need to travel all the way to Akron to find one.

An Office Downgrade

But dictating letters wasn't the only commotion going on at the Honor Dealers office—Bill and A.A.'s temporary headquarters—that week. The business had just gone through an upheaval, having moved with all of their furniture from the ninth floor at 11 Hill Street (where they had been located for at least a year and a half) into smaller and more economical space around the corner and one block north at 17 William Street. That kind of packing and unpacking is both time-consuming and disruptive, so it is not surprising Bill waited until Friday the 15th before heading over to Newark for Ruth's help in typing these letters.*

Strangely, Bill didn't seem to have any idea Hank was planning to move Honor Dealers to a new location on July 1st. In his June 24 reply to the Maguire letter, he had

---

* There is an old business maxim: "Two moves equals one fire," which may be appropriate here.

noted "this letter is being written from my home in Brooklyn so that you now have this address as well as that of our Jersey office."[47] But, the only address Maguire had been given for the New Jersey office was 11 Hill Street and it is hard to believe Bill Wilson would have made this kind of mistake with such an important potential donor. It is, of course, possible Bill was so completely disconnected from the day-to-day operations at Honor Dealers that he had no idea the lease was about to run out and that a move was imminent. But it is also possible that Hank had gotten himself into some serious trouble with the Hill Street landlord and was forced into this hurried move at the last minute.

In any case, the lease for Hill Street was terminated at the end of June and Honor Dealers began operating out of their new William Street location on July 1, 1938. By July 15 when Ruth typed these letters, she was neatly crossing out the "Eleven Hill Street" line on the preprinted "Henry G. Parkhurst" stationery and typing in the "17 William Street" address directly underneath it.*

The new offices, a small two-room suite numbered 601, were on the sixth floor of the building and Hank's business would stay there throughout the time Bill wrote the remaining chapters of the Big Book. Ten months later, Henry G. Parkhurst Inc. was forced to move again, this time when the sheriff appeared at his door in May 1939 with an eviction notice for non-payment of rent. Even in the face of this disaster, the ever-resourceful Hank managed to negotiate a deal so that he and Ruth could move into a much smaller office on the other side of the same floor of the building (#604).[48] It was, Bill claimed, "a tiny room barely big enough to contain Henry's large desk, his overstuffed chair, a couple of file cabinets, and Ruth and her typewriter. For callers there was standing room only."[49] Such was the rapidly declining fortune of Honor Dealers.

Doctor Richards Approves of the Book

During the week following this flurry of communication, Bill received a letter from Dr. Esther Richards that validated all his enthusiasm for the visit to Johns Hopkins. Dr. Hohman had read the two chapters of the book almost immediately and had been lavish in his praise when Bill, Fitz, and Ebby visited him a few days later. Although Richards attended this second meeting, she had not yet read the two chapters and didn't do so until Sunday, July 14. But, once done, she was equally impressed with the prospectus package they had left her. The very next day, she wrote Bill a letter expressing her enthusiastic support for the work he was doing, providing him with a testimonial letter full of specific, concrete professional praise for all of his recovery efforts:

---

* Interestingly, only five of these eight letters—those going to Hohman, Scott, Richardson, Amos, and Ward—were typed using this preprinted "Henry G. Parkhurst" letterhead and were obviously meant to be seen as coming from the professional offices of Alcoholics Anonymous. The other three letters to A.A. members—Hedges, Furlong, and Smith—were considered personal and therefore had the Brooklyn address listed at the top of the page as their point of origin.

Baltimore, Maryland

July 18, 1938

Mr. William G. Wilson,
182 Clinton Street,
Brooklyn, New York

Dear Mr. Wilson:

Yesterday for the first time I had a chance to look over the prospectus of Alcoholics Anonymous. I can give it no higher compliment than to say that I read through the first two chapters without stopping, so gripping was the presentation of the material. If all the chapters are like these two you will have a book that will hold its readers spellbound. These two chapters are the embodiment of what makes any book great. They have something to say and what they have to say is presented in clear, concise, graphic words. It carries the reader on and on with pictures that tell their story of real life facts. There is no attempt at highbrow theories veneered with scientific and psychological wordiness. What you say carried the conviction of truth. I know that you have a great thing in this message and if you keep it on the same plane the book will go over hot. I think you should get an A No. 1 physician who has a wide knowledge of the alcoholic's medical and social problem to write an introduction.

I am keeping the manuscript for a bit but will return it presently. I should indeed like to have the manuscript of the succeeding chapters when they are ready. Needless to say if there is anything I can do to be of help in the presentation of this book or in the furtherance of your work I would consider it a privilege to be called upon.

With kind regards, I am

Very sincerely yours,

Esther L. Richards

Esther L. Richards, M. D.[50]

If Wilson had any doubts about his ability to write a book, this letter must have allayed at least some of those fears and convinced him that he did, in fact, have the necessary talents to be an effective prose writer. What could be more positive than Richards's opinion that the chapters were gripping, that they hold the reader spellbound, and her conviction that the book would "go over hot" once it was completed? It's hard to imagine any letter being more favorable than this—even if Bill had written it himself.

Wilson had copies of Dr. Richards's letter made and this glowing testimonial was included in all future mailings that went out to prospective donors.

The next Friday, Bill was once again in New Jersey, this time dictating a long reply to Richards. Given her open-ended invitation to be helpful "in preparation of this book, or in the furtherance of your work," Wilson was happy to explain to her in great detail exactly where they were in the development of their program and what their immediate needs were.

Bill Makes His Case for Finding Donors

He opened the letter with a half-page of pleasantries, thanking Richards for her "spontaneous and enthusiastic reaction" and then offered her this perspective on the origins of their program of recovery:

> ... As you see, we have been finding our way along in a way which we had feared was rather haphazard and amateurish, though some of us felt as long as three years ago, that out of old and well known elements we might compound a synthesis which would possess new and rather startling powers in this field ...

This explanation of the origins of the A.A. program is wonderful in its candid admission of the debt they owe to "old and well known elements" while simultaneously claiming that the synthesis they have forged from those elements was something new and startling in its effectiveness.

Having dispensed with the formalities, Bill began his presentation of their current dilemma:

> Our work thus far has been on a part time, voluntary basis ... [but] we have now come to a new phase of the work, and there is one aspect of it which we are approaching very gingerly and reluctantly. That is the question of how we can carry on from this point without several individuals spending the greater part of their time at it. The publication of this book, the acceleration of our personal work, the building up of sufficient individuals who will be trained to cope with the influx of new patients who are bound to appear as soon as the book is published—how to handle this situation has been a puzzle. Those of us who ought to be spending for the next year or two a great deal of time in the work, are confronted by the necessity of either being subsidized to do so, or else letting up on the alcoholic activity and paying more attention to business. Most of us feel that this thing has to go on if we have to live in tents.

> A beginning has been made by some friends of Mr. Rockefeller and a very modest subsidy has been placed at the disposal of one of our most effective men,* who has a group of about seventy cases in Akron, Ohio. This man is a surgeon who has been obliged to neglect his practice in order to keep up the work. The underwriting takes care of his bare necessities for a year, with the thought that he will secure some additional surgical work.

---

* Another explicit mention of the fact that Rockefeller's contribution was meant specifically for Dr. Bob Smith and not for any other members of the Fellowship—however needy they might be.

Though we are most anxious that this thing be not professionalized, or that no one have a vested interest in a job, it begins to look as though several more people will have to be similarly provided for to carry our experiment on for another year, and to get out our book . . .

Wilson's key emphasis here is on the very temporary nature of their need for a subsidy to support several more people so they can carry on the work. But, he claims, this need for financial help should go away rather quickly once the book is published, allowing them to become self-supporting.

We feel that the book will provide some revenue, and that at a later date we can easily fill any number of sanitariums with these people, if it became apparent to the public that any of them were really getting well. So we are positive that the time will eventually come when we will be self-supporting. By temperament we are a pretty independent lot and do not like being subsidized by charitable sources, nor would we care to be taken care of by any of the large foundations or churches. Our power for good depends to quite an extent on absolute independence of religious sects or institutions. We are seeking to make our experience available on a universal and worldwide basis; hence we would prefer not to become too heavily committed in any way, to any person or denomination . . .

This is a revealing paragraph with its vision of "any number of sanitariums" under their control and his unequivocally stated position of "absolute independence of religious sects and institutions." The integrity of both of these important features was to be ensured by a foundation—here creatively called "Fellowship Anonymous"—that they are in the process of setting up. This foundation will administer the funds they collect in such a fashion that their work will be above reproach or criticism by skeptics:

We are setting up a sort of foundation of our own, which will be called, let us say, Fellowship Anonymous. This will be administered by non-alcoholics who are responsible and disinterested. All of our money transactions will be handled through this corporation. This is the best thing we could think of to forestall any criticism that as individuals we are trying to capitalize our knowledge of what to do for alcoholics . . .

Wilson then follows with the interesting conviction that the most likely source of donations to this foundation will be the great, but "soul-less," corporations of America:

Our idea in raising funds is to go to the large corporations. These companies are riddled with alcoholics, both actual and potential. We can offer them our services, and I have no doubt we can return a lot of talented men to their jobs. Therefore, a corporation, however soul-less, has a direct financial interest in such a result. One of my best friends* used to make forty thousand a year with the Standard Oil Company, and they had to let him go because of drinking. It cost them a lot of money to train him for

---

* Hank Parkhurst.

such a responsible position, and a lot more to train a man to fill his place. Why then should not such a company contribute to our fund? They will spend millions to find a new kind of solder for a tin can, so we think they will help along our experiment for much the same reason . . .

The notion that a corporation willing to spend "millions to find a new kind of solder for a tin can" should also be willing to spend a few thousand dollars to preserve their investment in talented personnel is an argument Bill used in more than one letter and, it seems safe to assume, was also a part of the presentations he made to wealthy industrialists whenever he was given the chance to do so in person.

At this time, Johns Hopkins was the richest and best funded hospital in the country; so Wilson closed his letter with the veiled suggestion that perhaps Dr. Esther Richards might have some knowledge of one or more of these wealthy donors: "I hope I have not been taking liberties in writing you at this length, but we want your real opinion touching these matters. Perhaps you can make some helpful suggestions or criticisms."[51]

Two-and-a-half weeks later when Esther Richards finally responded to Bill, she gracefully sidestepped the entire issue of money and the question of who might be a potential donor, focusing instead on her contention that there are a large number of mentally challenged people who would not be suitable candidates for Wilson's brand of recovery. Her tacit response made it clear that Bill should not expect to receive any help locating or courting donors from that particular source.[52]

A High Profile Connection: Dr. Richard Cabot

Either later that same day, or sometime over the weekend, Bill Wilson visited Towns Hospital where he met with both Charles Towns and Dr. William Silkworth. He wanted to strategize with them about how he could most effectively approach potential donors and, in the course of these discussions, he asked both men for their written recommendations concerning the work they were doing. In addition, he requested their help in soliciting the support of other medical authorities, hopefully famous doctors whose names would be instantly recognizable to the wealthy patrons of New York City.

On Monday, Towns wrote to Bill:

July 25, 1938

My dear Wilson:

After our talk I thought this matter over, and as I had promised to write something to you regarding the work, and I thought this was an unusual opportunity for me to state all of the findings to Dr. Cabot, and in this way, kill two birds with one stone.

Very truly yours,

Charles B. Towns [53]

Although the Towns letter to Dr. Cabot has not been preserved, his letter was positive enough that Bill included a copy of it in the future solicitation packages he sent out to prospects.[54]

Dr. Richard Clark Cabot was famous not only for his prestigious lineage ("So this is good old Boston / The home of the bean and the cod / Where the Lowells talk only to Cabots / And the Cabots talk only to God'"), but also for his tireless advocacy of the downtrodden and the poor. He believed that economic, social, family, and psychological conditions underpinned many of the problems that patients brought to the Outpatient Department he ran at Massachusetts General Hospital. In 1905, Cabot invented the position of "social worker" to assist him at the hospital, and even went so far as to pay her salary when the hospital refused to do so. When Cabot finally left Mass General in 1919 (to take up the chair of Harvard's Department of Social Ethics), the hospital finally agreed to pay the wages of the thirteen social workers he had personally employed for the past several years. Dr. Cabot was also a medical innovator in the field of hematology and the author of more than a dozen books relating to medical, social and ethical topics.[55]

Shortly after Charles Towns's letter was mailed, Bill followed up by sending Cabot a copy of the two chapters of the proposed book along with his own personal appeal, repeating many of the details (and even some of the same phrases) he had used in his letter to Dr. Richards:

> July 1938
>
> Dr. Richard C. Cabot,
> 101 Brattle St.,
> Cambridge, Mass.
>
> Dear Dr. Cabot:
>
> Mr. Charles B. Towns tells me he has written you concerning some work which has been going on among alcoholics here in New York and in Akron, Ohio. At his request I am enclosing the two opening chapters of an anonymous volume which we shall publish sometime during the next twelve months. This material will give you the general idea of the nature and temper of our work.
>
> As you will see, we have taken certain old and well known elements and have related them in such a way as to produce a synthesis which has some new and novel results and characteristics. You will observe the central idea is that an alcoholic, who has had a spiritual experience upon the simple basis which is outlined, and who is armed with certain information about the physical and mental aspects of his own malady, can apparently do for another sufferer those things rarely, if ever, accomplished by a nonalcoholic.

---

*   Doggerel poem "Boston Toast" by Harvard alumnus John Collins Bossidy (http://en.wikipedia.org/wiki/Boston_Brahmin—retrieved April 15, 2013).

The great promise of the thing, of course, is that each man in his turn, must see that still others recover, or perhaps perish himself. This provides impetus and a growth possibility which greatly excites the imagination of those of us who are close to the situation.

We have never developed any accurate statistical information, but I should say that we have dealt with about 200 cases in all, about half of whom seem to have recovered. Doctors tell us that, almost without exception, we have been problem drinkers of a class commonly regarded as next to hopeless.

We want to place these facts in your possession for whatever use they may be to you, and it may be that you would like to investigate, or become in some fashion or other a part of our effort.

As you see, we are about to publish a book, and in addition it has become necessary for a number of individuals to spend much time at the work. We think that within a year the work, through channels unnecessary to discuss here, will become self-supporting. In the meantime, we frankly need some assistance.

It seems right that you should know these facts, so I hope you will not regard this letter as a solicitation for a contribution. However, your personal interest, advice, and approval will be much prized by all of us.

Sincerely yours,

Wm. G. Wilson

WGW:rh[56]

There is no known response from Cabot and it is unlikely he even bothered to write back (a fairly predictable reaction given his notoriety, his current retirement and the fact that he was in failing health and died just nine months later).

The Silkworth Letter

While Charles Towns's testimonial letter generated no lasting results, Bill's request that Dr. Silkworth write about the success of their work did produce something of genuine importance. As his endorsement, Silkworth sent Bill the following letter of introduction; a letter which would later become—in slightly modified form—an integral part of "The Doctor's Opinion," the opening chapter of the Big Book:

July 27, 1938

TO WHOM IT MAY CONCERN:

I have specialized in the treatment of alcoholism for many years.

About four years ago I attended a patient by the name of William G. Wilson. Though he had been a competent business man of good earning capacity he was an alcoholic of a type I had come to regard as hopeless.

In the course of his third treatment he acquired certain ideas concerning a possible means of recovery. As part of his rehabilitation he commenced to present his conceptions to other alcoholics impressing upon them that they must do likewise with still others. This has become the basis of a rapidly growing fellowship of these men and their families. This man and over one hundred others appear to have recovered.

I personally know thirty of these cases who were of types upon which other methods had failed completely.

These facts appear to be of extreme medical importance. Because of the extraordinary possibilities of rapid growth inherent in this group these events may mark a new epoch in the annals of alcoholism. These men may well have a solution for thousands of these situations.

You may rely absolutely on anything they say about themselves.

Very truly yours,

W. D. Silkworth MD

W. D. Silkworth, M. D.[57]

The doctor had obviously accepted Wilson's contention that there were more than one hundred current success stories in A.A. and he bolstered this claim by saying he personally knew thirty of these cases in New York (leaving a balance of the often noted seventy member in Akron).

Before being published in the Big Book, the specific reference to a patient "by the name of William G. Wilson" was removed and the single word "who" was substituted. There were some other, minor, cosmetic changes made to the text, but the substance of the letter was left untouched.

Bill's Cover Letter for the Book Proposal

Having collected all of these glowing references, the final element Bill needed was a cover letter to introduce these endorsements and the two chapters of their proposed book to prominent businessmen. The form letter he created contained a brief and excellent presentation of his case and ended with a classic salesman's closer—his request for an appointment to discuss the matter further.

182 Clinton St.,
Brooklyn, N. Y.

During the past four years approximately one hundred men have recovered from acute alcoholism. We have been told by authorities at The Johns Hopkins Hospital that persons of this class are largely incurable by medical means. As you are no doubt aware, alcoholism ranks with cancer and tuberculosis as a problem. Economically and socially it is more destructive than either.

The United States is said to contain one million people who are actual or potential alcoholics. This refers to those who are really sick, and not to those who merely drink too much. Until recently, there has been no answer for any substantial part of those who suffer from this common malady.

As a citizen and a business man, we think that you will be interested to know that this group of one hundred men have apparently found the answer to a most baffling human problem

Enough has been done to suggest that wholesale recoveries may be possible. Medical men who understand our procedure express this opinion, as the attached letters suggest. One of these is an introduction from Mr. Albert L. Scott, who is President of Lockwood Green Engineers, Inc., and also Chairman of the Board of Trustees of Riverside Church. He has taken a nationally prominent part in studies of the alcoholic problem.

Dr. W. D. Silkworth of Towns Hospital, New York City, and Dr. Esther L. Richards of the Psychiatric Department of The Johns Hopkins Hospital, further vouch for what is taking place.

Our fellowship is about to publish an anonymous book describing our experiences and methods. This book ought to drive the entering wedge for an expansion of our activities. As you will see from the attached manuscript, we are not 'reformers' in the usual sense of the word. We merely wish to be helpful to those who suffer from alcoholism. Our services have been entirely voluntary and free.

As one of the fellowship. I am approaching you with two things in mind. Our work has now reached the stage where we frankly need the assistance of a number of men prominent in American life. The second point is that we wish to make our knowledge and methods more useful to the American home and business.

Should you wish to see me, when may I call upon you?

Sincerely yours,

Wm. G. Wilson

WGW:RH[58]

Bill had spent the entire month of July soliciting testimonials praising the work A.A. was doing in the hope these professional endorsements would prove to be the perfect introduction for him and his organization as they approached some of the richest men in the country for donations. Who could possibly resist their request for contributions in the light of these overwhelmingly positive statements?

That was the theory. Now, it was time to find out if that theory would actually work in practice.

CHAPTER TWELVE

The Alcoholic Foundation

~August 1938~

Bill had developed a passionate new focus for his fundraising efforts. Having successfully convinced John D. Rockefeller Jr., the richest man in the country, to contribute to their cause, he saw no reason why his next target shouldn't be Henry Ford, the second richest man. The revolutionary automaker's distaste for alcohol was even more notorious than that of the Rockefeller family, who were generally described as being "drys." Henry Ford was a "superdry."[1] He was so adamant in his opposition to drinking that early in his career he formed a fifty-man "Social Department" within the Ford Motor Company to intrusively investigate the moral conduct of all his employees. This group was instructed to fire any man who was caught drinking (or even if he was found to have liquor in his home).[2] Ford had been such a fervent supporter of Prohibition that when the possibility of repeal loomed in 1931, he threatened, "if booze ever comes back to the United States, I am through with manufacturing... I wouldn't be interested in putting automobiles into the hands of a generation soggy with drink."[3] Economic self-interest quickly overrode that ominous threat when repeal went into effect in December 1933, but Ford's conviction that alcohol was one of the greatest evils afflicting Western civilization was a foundational belief throughout his life.

Bill Tries to Reach Henry Ford through Charles Parcells

Here was someone who would surely be more than willing to offer significant financial help to their new movement—if only Bill could find the proper way to approach him. Wilson's brother-in-law had been the key to meeting Willard Richardson and then accessing Rockefeller, but how could Bill go about securing a similarly impressive introduction to Henry Ford? After some careful thought, Wilson decided Charles

Parcells, one of his Detroit business acquaintances, might be just the man to help. He wrote Parcells a four-page letter on August 1, 1938, presenting a detailed summary of the current state of affairs within Alcoholics Anonymous while simultaneously asking for his advice on the best way to approach Ford.*

Parcells was a successful businessman, the principal in a Detroit brokerage firm that bore his name and, during the years 1946 and 1947, he would serve as President of the Detroit Stock Exchange.[4] Bill hadn't seen Charles for almost a year (he mentions in passing "the unpleasantness of last fall" which likely refers to him losing his job at Quaw and Foley the previous October), but he confidently announces he has since "come right side up" and has even been "made a Director of the Pierce Governor Co.," a company that "shows a lot of promise." So much promise, Bill says, he "would like to talk at length with you about it when next I get out there."**

But news of a wonderful new stock opportunity was not the purpose of the letter. Wilson notes that the last time they met, Parcells had been so interested in his work with alcoholics "that I feel you would like to know what has happened, moreover I think that you can possibly be of a great deal of help to us in Detroit." Bill then spends a full page telling him about their growing success (100 recoveries—seventy in Akron and thirty in New York—out of 200 attempts), of their plans to write a book, and about the fabulous endorsements they have just secured from a psychiatrist at Johns Hopkins along with several other prominent professionals. Bill suggests Parcells could get an excellent picture of the current state of the work by just reading the two chapters and the outline he has enclosed in the mailing, carefully pointing out that "although our material has to have a great deal of emotional pep, you will notice that the religious angle is presented in a very broad and sane manner," and that "we have acquired a great deal of medical and psychiatric information about ourselves" that is also included in these chapters as an important part of the overall picture.

Specifically distancing himself from the Oxford Group (which he was much more deeply involved with when the two men had last spoken of these matters), Bill pointedly notes that "some of the religious thoughts have come from the so-called Oxford Group, although the Group got these mostly from the Lord's Prayer and the Sermon on the Mount," and that his own group has subsequently drawn on "many other sources, selecting those ideas and attitudes which experience has shown are most useful." Moreover, they have realized it is "quite important, even imperative, that we do not align ourselves with any particular institution or denomination." He then underlines this point by saying, "as it now stands, our religious presentation is so broad, that a Catholic, a Jew and an Agnostic, or even a Hottentot***, can go for it," and they were "most anxious to keep it that way."

---

* The date on the document preserved in the GSO archives (Wm. G. Wilson to Mr. Charles Parcelles [sic], July 1, 1938: GSO, Box 59, 1938, Folder B, Documents 1938–31 to 1938–34) is actually July 1, 1938 but the letter mentions several events that did not take place until later that month (for instance, Wilson's encounters with the Johns Hopkins psychiatrists and Silkworth's letter of recommendation), so the typed date is clearly wrong. Since Wilson does mention Dr. Silkworth's letter (which was dated July 27) and does *not* mention the Alcoholic Foundation (whose documents are dated August 5), the letter can be confidently identified as being written sometime between these two dates. The mistaken date is easiest to explain by presuming that Ruth Hock absentmindedly typed the former month, July rather than the new one, August.

** See the footnote on page 103 for our previous discussion of the Pierce Governor Co.

*** Referring to the Khoikhoi people who are native to South Africa. These days the term is considered derogatory.

This is a revealing statement for Bill to be making in early August of 1938, one clearly showing how far he had come in his understanding of the religious component of sobriety since he had last spoken with Charles Parcells in mid-1937.

Finally, Bill comes to the point, noting, "as much as I dislike to introduce the money element into this picture, I don't see how it can be avoided." After explaining why money is needed at this time, he immediately gets specific and says they would be able to "use at least twenty-five thousand dollars to excellent advantage over the next twelve months, to carry on the general work and to get the book out." Then, just as quickly, Bill allays any fears Parcells might have that he was about to ask *him* for a donation by saying they have already formulated a plan for raising the money and what he really wants from Charles are his comments and suggestions on this plan. If he could just write back to Bill with his honest opinion on these matters, that would "be plenty of contribution as far as you are concerned."

Bill Wilson has already described this proposed plan to others, but here it is laid out in greater detail. They are going to begin by approaching large corporations as a source of funding for their group. It is self-evident and logical that these corporations would have a vested interested in reclaiming their fallen executives and the expense of doing so is almost nothing when compared to what they now typically spend to discover some new industrial product or process. "For a corporation, or its officers personally to foster this sort of effort would not only be humanitarian; it should be good for business. We are, therefore, about to approach the heads of big business in this country with the idea that we can be helpful to them, and that they can be helpful to us, if they so desire."

After two-and-a-half pages of prelude, Bill finally gets to the real purpose for the letter by stating categorically that "Henry Ford is on our list" of potential donors, telling Parcells this is exactly where Wilson hopes he can be "a great deal of help to us in Detroit."

He then refers Parcells to the attached letters of recommendation—one from Albert Scott ("a friend of Mr. John D. Rockefeller")* and two from prominent doctors. Bill states confidently he has "no doubt these letters are strong enough so that we could see anyone in this country without further introduction"—except perhaps, Henry Ford. "I do think, however, that in Mr. Ford's case, a word of recommendation from somebody in Detroit would be helpful. Perhaps you are the man, if you want to be, or, you may know somebody who would be willing to do so."

Immediately reinforcing this built-in excuse for not getting involved, Bill tells Charles he is not "going to feel badly if you conclude that you had rather not be concerned with this thing" and mentions two other avenues for approaching Ford he has already considered. The first of these was still an open option: "It may be that we should see Mr. Ford's publicity man, Mr. Cameron, first, about these things; I frankly don't know, and would like to have you tell me what you really think [about that]." The second option was one Bill had already dismissed: "Dr. Sladen came to my mind, but I rejected the idea as he is definitely associated with the Oxford Group and

---

* This is one of the rare uses of Rockefeller's name in public correspondence at this time. Notice too that there is absolutely no mention, here or elsewhere, about the money Rockefeller had given them. That contribution had obviously come with the stipulation that it remain strictly anonymous.

he might therefore carry the idea to Mr. Ford that this is an Oxford Group matter, which it definitely is not." Dr. Frank J. Sladen had been Physician-in-Chief at Detroit General Hospital since 1914 when Henry Ford took over financial responsibility for the hospital and embarked on his plan to make it a rival to Johns Hopkins in both power and prestige.[5]

In his conclusion, Wilson tells Parcells that, whatever the case, he would appreciate it if he could "please look over the [enclosed] material . . . and let me know . . . what you think ought to be done about it in Detroit?"[6]*

We have no record of Charles Parcells's response, but over the next several months Bill Wilson, in his typically tenacious fashion, would relentlessly continue his efforts to make direct contact with Henry Ford through whatever avenues he could find. Besides a later unsuccessful attempt by Charles Towns to provide an introduction to Ford,[7] Bill and the recently sober Archie Trowbridge visited with Dr. Sladen and Dr. Dwight C. Ensign—an intern specializing in addiction—at Detroit General Hospital in early March 1939.[8] That visit seems to have made a favorable impression upon both of these important doctors, but it did nothing to get Bill any closer to the great man himself.**

But none of these efforts ever produced the all-important face-to-face meeting with the great automobile maker or the result that Bill Wilson so desperately wanted: a ringing endorsement from Henry Ford along with a generous contribution as a concrete expression of his commitment to their new method for staying sober.

Bill Seeks Dr. Bob's Support

Henry Ford wasn't the only person Bill Wilson was aggressively pursuing during those early days of August. The other major target was Dr. Bob Smith whose support he needed to ensure that the Akron group didn't wander off on some completely divergent path of its own. At this critical juncture Wilson realized just how crucial it was that everyone be moving in the same general direction and he was committed to doing everything in his power to make sure that happened; it was the only way to prevent the movement from coming apart at the seams and flying off into several different rival factions.

---

* Wilson, a life-long Republican, closes this letter with one of the rare political comments to be found in his early (sober) letters, telling Parcells that "The Great American Swindle seems to have most decidedly moved from Wall Street to Washington, but I still think we are all coming out right side up in the sweet bye and bye."

** Although Bill dismissed Dr. Sladen in his letter to Parcells as an approach to Henry Ford, he obviously established contact with Sladen several months later. There is a first edition copy of the Big Book (in the author's collection) with an inscription dated April 20, 1939—just ten days after the book was published—from Dr. Sladen to Dr. Dwight C. Ensign noting: "Recall: / Bill Wilson p. 10 / Archie Trowbridge p. 332." These two doctors had obviously met with Bill and Archie prior to that date. Dr. Ensign worked with addicts at Detroit General (see his online article from 1931, "Metabolic Studies During Morphine Withdrawal from a Human Addict", which he co-authored with Sladen) and Trowbridge was the man who brought A.A. to Detroit from Akron. His story "The Fearful One" appeared in the first edition of the Big Book and in every edition since as "The Man Who Mastered Fear." His sobriety date is variously given as September 1938 (a number of online sources), November 1938 (Jim Burwell's handwritten list in his Multilith Copy—now in the author's collection) and December 1938 (Dodd, *The Authors*, pp. 105-107).

Fundraising for a Foundation

Dr. Bob was still hopeful that an alcoholic hospital could be opened in Akron under his leadership, but that would only happen if money could be found to fund it; so although he was still locally silent on the matter of money, Bob was firmly committed to Bill's fundraising efforts. In a long letter to him in late June, Bill had asked:

> What would you think about the formation of a charitable corporation to be called, let us say 'Alcoholics Anonymous'? Money coming in from the book could be handled through it as well as any funds arising from contributions by corporations [who] benefited by our work.

> We should always remember that perhaps some day our activities will be scrutinized by hostile microscopes with the idea of proving we are a racket. If we now form a corporation whose control is exercised by a board composed largely of disinterested and non-alcoholic people, we shall have closed the door to such criticism. The trustees of this corporation could administer any other enterprises we might want to engage in; such for instance, as sanitariums.[9]

Wilson's inclusion of the final word "sanitariums" here is hardly subtle, but it underlines the very real possibility that they would be establishing an alcoholics-only recovery facility in Akron just as soon as the money became available. And when that happy day did come, all the wonderful work Dr. Bob Smith was presently doing with alcoholics could then be performed in a first-rate facility with adequate medical and spiritual resources along with—best of all—a regular paycheck for the director.

Three weeks later, in Bill's July 15 letter to Bob, he makes no mention of the possibility of setting up a foundation, although he did tell him about their plan "to put the bite" on several very rich and prominent men over the next few weeks. These fundraising activities, he said, made it impossible to predict when he might be coming to Akron again.[10] But, even without a visit to Ohio, the two men did manage to have a detailed discussion during the next two weeks (via either telephone or unsaved correspondence) about the creation of a foundation, discussions that resulted in Dr. Bob Smith agreeing to serve as one of the trustees of the new Alcoholic Foundation. This must have pleased Bill immensely. Not only did his acceptance of this public position more firmly cement Smith's commitment to the ambitious New York plans, it also allowed them to add his name to their masthead, immediately bringing a much needed tone of professionalism and respectability to the foundation.

Getting the Akron Squad's Stories for the Book

But establishing a foundation wasn't the only thing they discussed during those late July talks. Wilson was anxious to get the Ohio members committed to his vision for A.A. and he thought the best way to do that was to get them actively involved in the book project. He wanted Smith to be much more aggressive and insist that the Akron "Alcoholic Squad" start writing their own stories for the proposed book.

Bill had already sent him a copy of Hank's list of the professions (and the obvious corresponding members—the majority of whom were in Akron) that he wanted to include in the stories section. So how were those stories progressing and how soon could he expect to see some finished copies of those stories coming in from Ohio?

Whatever the substance of their earlier discussions, Bob had some questions about exactly what Bill was looking for and he wrote back asking for clarification. Smith's letter has been lost, but Wilson's reply on August 7, supplies some candid advice on how the Ohio members should go about writing their personal stories.

> Dear Bob:
>
> Thanks for your good letter.
>
> About the stories, I should say that everyone should write at whatever length they want to; the more, the better. Then the thousand word manuscripts can be edited down to the right size. The idea is that a chance word or phrase or experience may be the most telling point of the story, which would be missed entirely if people were trying to restrict themselves to a given number of words.
>
> Enclosed herewith are three letters vouching for us, and I am enclosing enough copies so that they can be attached to the four manuscripts you have.
>
> We are now laying the pipes to Owen D. Young, Henry Ford, and Thomas Lamont.* What is going to happen, of course, remains yet to be seen.
>
> Very much yours,[11]

It is interesting to note Bob's question was not in relation to the longer 5,000 word stories written by the most sober men—Wilson had already provided copious details on these in an earlier letter and he had also supplied his own story as a model for how these might be written—but about the shorter versions he was hoping to get from more recent members. Bill justifies his suggestion that everyone "should write at whatever length they want" by casually noting these free-form stories would be edited down for proper length once the book gets closer to its final assembly. Unspoken, but clearly implied here, is that those final editing decisions would be made by the people in New York.

But the most unexpected revelation in this letter is Bill's enclosure of copies of three letters vouching for their group that should be "attached to the four manuscripts you have." The previous October the Ohio members had been emphatic that there would be no fundraising done in Akron. If Bill wanted to raise money for his overly ambitious and moneyed schemes, they said, then he could just go back to New York and look for donors there. The "Alcoholic Squad" in Ohio would have nothing to do with it. But remarkably, at this point in August 1938, Bill obviously expects Dr. Bob Smith to

---

* Thomas W. Lamont was the head of J. P. Morgan, the most important single financial institution in New York City, if not the country.

take these four manuscripts and use them locally to solicit donations for the Alcoholic Foundation; there is just no other plausible explanation for why he would send Bob these recommendation letters. Admittedly New York was then the richest city in the country, but Akron had more than its fair share of millionaires. Most prominent among these was Harvey Firestone who was not only a committed member of the Oxford Group, but also a man with a strong and vested interest in promoting sobriety.* Bill may have convinced Dr. Bob that Firestone would be an excellent prospective donor for their group or perhaps—since he was surely aware of the famously close friendship between Harvey Firestone and Henry Ford—he was hoping that by making a good impression on Firestone, their group might thereby gain a favorable and powerful introduction to Ford.

Setting up the Foundation

All the months of talk and speculation about setting up a tax-exempt foundation finally came to fruition on Friday, August 5 when the necessary paperwork was finally ready to be signed. One major reason for the delay was the significant legal costs of setting up such a foundation, money the leaders of A.A. clearly did not have as they struggled to make ends meet on a day-to-day basis. The problem was solved when Frank Amos enlisted the services of a young lawyer named John Wood who agreed to draw up the necessary paperwork *pro bono.*** This was quite a coup for Amos since Wood was a rising star in Root, Clark, Buckner, and Ballantine, one of the most important and prestigious law firms in New York City, and his services would have been prohibitively expensive otherwise.*** John Wood was also, according to Amos, motivated by his "knowledge of this movement and [his] sympathy for it," and was so committed that he not only drew up the necessary documents, but even agreed to serve as one of the first five trustees of the new Alcoholic Foundation.[12]

Having taken on the assignment, Wood's job was almost immediately complicated by what Bill Wilson later called "a legal riddle."[13] The foundation was to be set up in such a way that the decision-making powers would always rest with a majority of non-alcoholics rather than with the alcoholic trustees. Wood spent considerable time trying to create a pair of definitions that would legally differentiate between those who had

---

* Harvey Firestone's alcoholic son, Bud, had been sobered up by Sam Shoemaker in 1931; a radical transformation that prompted the Firestones to head "a civic committee, which invited a team from the Oxford Group to hold meetings in the city over a ten-day period" in January of 1933 thereby creating a strong and ongoing presence for the Group in Akron. (Newton, *Uncommon Friends*, p. 88). See also *Dr. Bob and the Good Oldtimers*, p. 55.

** In *AACOA* (p. 153), Wilson gives Frank Amos sole credit for securing Wood's services, but it was in all likelihood the Rockefeller connection that was the deciding factor here. Doing a favor for Richardson, Scott, Chipman (and Amos) was clearly in the best interest of an ambitious young man who belonged to such a well-connected firm.

*** John E. F. Wood joined this law firm in 1929 and later advanced to become a named partner (*American Bar Association Journal*, Volume 58, June, 1972, p. 581). At this time, Root, Clark, Buckner, and Ballantine was one of the largest and most powerful law firms in the country. Founded in 1906 by Elihu Root, Jr. and Grenville Clark, the firm went through many personnel changes over the years, but perhaps none more important than the 1917 addition of Elihu Root Sr. (former Secretary of War, Secretary of State, Senator from New York and winner of the Nobel Peace Prize) to its roster of prestigious lawyers. The firm numbered among its clients such notables as Andrew Carnegie, Marshall Fields and AT&T and was an influential player in Washington politics. They had, for instance, under Grenville Clark's leadership, been critically instrumental in defeating President Franklin D. Roosevelt's attempts to "pack" the Supreme Court in 1937. (See http://www.fundinguniverse.com/company-histories/Dewey-Ballantine-LLP-Company-History.html, retrieved June 25, 2011.)

never had a problem with alcohol and those who were sober ex-drinkers, but he never found a way to resolve that thorny dilemma. While this was an incredibly frustrating challenge for the young lawyer, it only amused members of the regular Tuesday night meeting in Brooklyn, one of whom reportedly quipped: "Well, that's a cinch—a nonalcoholic is a guy who *can* drink and an alcoholic is a guy who *can't* drink."[14]

Unfortunately John Wood needed something more legally specific than this to resolve his problem. If neither Bill Wilson nor Hank Parkhurst—two men with years of experience with alcoholics and alcoholism—could not come up with a short, but conclusive definition for the alcoholic, then how could they possibly expect this young non-alcoholic lawyer to resolve the issue for them in just a few short weeks? In fact, Wood never did discover a solution to his problem, but like any good lawyer, he did find a way to work around it. According to Wilson, he "finally gave up [his] attempt to describe an alcoholic in legal terms" and suggested they could sidestep the whole problem by just writing up and signing a simple trust agreement rather than applying for a formalized charter for the foundation.[15*]

And that is exactly what Wood did. He created a thirteen-page "Trust Indenture" which placed control of the Alcoholic Foundation in the hands of five trustees. These trustees were to be

> divided into two classes, to be known respectively as Class A and Class B. Trustees in Class A are intended to be persons who are not and have not been alcoholics; Trustees in Class B are intended to be persons who have been alcoholics. The purpose of the division of the Trustees into such classes is to provide for representation of alcoholics among the Trustees and at the same time to insure that the majority of the Trustees at all times will be persons who are not and have not been alcoholics.[16]

Having successfully dodged the problematic issue of defining exactly who was and who wasn't an alcoholic with this simple statement of fact, Wood then went on to note that "if any Class B Trustee is found to have consumed any alcoholic beverage after his election to the office it shall be the mandatory duty of the other Trustees to remove him at once." Well, at least that was clear enough!

The duties of the trustees would include ensuring that the money collected by the Alcoholic Foundation was put to the proper purposes and here it becomes clear that the ambitious plans Wilson had formulated for his group the previous October—a string of hospitals, paid missionaries, and a book—were still very much a part of his ongoing plans (with a few new items added along the way just for good measure):

> The Purposes
>
> The purposes of the Foundation to which the fund is to be applied by the Trustees are:

---

* A cursory online search for the legal differences between a "charter" and a "trust indenture" under US or New York State law in 1938 did not produce any meaningful results for someone (the author) untrained in the law.

1. The relief and rehabilitation of persons suffering from or threatened with alcoholism and its attendant problems by conducting or participating in or giving financial or other assistance to any of the following activities:

a. Personal work of a religious (but non-sectarian) nature among alcoholics.

b. The maintenance of places of rest and recuperation for alcoholics.

c. Providing financial assistance in the form of loans or gifts to alcoholics.

d. Research in the field of alcoholism and related problems.

e. The publication and distribution of books, pamphlets and other literature on the subject of alcoholism or designed to assist alcoholics in overcoming their difficulties;

2. The making of gifts of money or property to other charitable or religious organizations having the same or similar purposes, no part of the net earnings of which inure to the benefit of any private stockholder or individual and no substantial part of the activities of which is carrying on propaganda or otherwise attempting to influence legislation; and

3. Any and all activities which in the judgment of the Trustees will assist in the restoration of alcoholics to normal life.[17]

As Bill said years later, they thought the Alcoholic Foundation "ought to be chartered to do just about anything within the field of alcoholism except lobby for Prohibition,"[18] and that's exactly what John Wood empowered the foundation to do.

After defining the election and terms of the trustees, articulating what powers they did and did not have in relation to money, and describing the administrative offices of the foundation and their individual responsibilities, the Indenture went on to create an Advisory Board that would "consult and advise with the Trustees with regard to carrying out the purposes of the Foundation.* The functions of the advisory board, however, shall be merely those of consultation and advice and the Trustees shall retain the full powers and responsibilities of their office."

The first three Class A Trustees were John Wood, Frank Amos, and Willard Richardson. The two Class B Trustees were Bill Ruddell (the man who had accompanied Bill Wilson to Akron the previous October) and Dr. Bob Smith. Both

---

*   While the Trust Indenture calls this group the "Advisory Board," the name was almost immediately changed in all future references to the "Advisory Committee"—a change that is respected here in later mentions.

Bill Wilson and Hank Parkhurst were elected to the Advisory Board along with Albert Scott and A. LeRoy Chipman.[*]

It is interesting to note the strong similarities and also some significant differences between the structure of the new Alcoholic Foundation and the way John D. Rockefeller Jr. had set up his own "Committee on Benevolence" so many years earlier. Rockefeller's Benevolence Committee had a number of honorary members on its Board of Directors (as are Wood and Smith here), but the real decision-making powers rested squarely with his Advisory Committee whose powerful Executive Director was Willard Richardson (which is not the case here). The Alcoholic Foundation made no official distinction among the four members of the Advisory Board and no single member was designated as its Executive Director.

Still, even in this reduced capacity, the Advisory Board would function as the center of action within the Alcoholic Foundation. Under this model, Dr. Bob's presence as one of the trustee is a position that fully acknowledges his commitment to the project of raising and spending money, while simultaneously recognizing that the 450 miles separating him from New York City would prevent him from being any kind of force in the day-to-day decision making process. Wilson and Parkhurst would be the primary channels for the information presented to the trustees and they would therefore be in the position of having the most influence over any decisions the trustees might make.

The Initial Meetings of the Foundation

The paperwork was dated and delivered on Friday, August 5, but it wasn't until the following Thursday, August 11, that the first meeting of the Alcoholic Foundation was actually held.[**] The delay was necessary because Dr. Bob Smith would not be coming to New York City for the meeting so the documents had to be mailed to him for his signature and official notarization. Each of the other four trustees had their copies signed and notarized on August 5, but Smith's signed copies of the Indenture Trust

---

[*]   Bill Wilson's recollections in *AACOA* regarding the formation of the Alcoholic Foundation are, as usual, not completely accurate. He claims that it was set up in May of 1938 (rather than August) and that his brother-in-law, Dr. Leonard Strong, was one of the first trustees (with no mention of Wood). [See *AACOA*, p. 152.] Both of these claims are contradicted by the contemporary documents. Note that Dr. Strong did become a trustee of the foundation but not until January 18, 1939 (Minutes of Trustees Meeting of the Alcoholic Foundation, January 18, 1939: GSO, Minutes: Alcoholic Foundation / 1938-1944 / Duplicates, Folder: 1939).

[**]   There has been tremendous confusion over the exact date of the first meeting of the Alcoholic Foundation caused by the misdating of a single document. The handwritten notes for this meeting preserved in the GSO archive carry the date April 11, 1938 at the top of the first page. That handwritten date was then carried over into the typed version of the "Minutes of the first meeting of The Alcoholic Foundation" done by Ruth Hock. The date is indisputably wrong. The first meeting of the Alcoholic Foundation took place on AUGUST 11, 1938, and this date is verified by all of the other preserved documents surrounding this event along with those of the second meeting that was held a week later on August 18, 1938. For instance, the minutes of the first meeting directly reference a proxy letter received from Dr. Bob Smith that Frank Amos had requested from him on August 8 and that comes with the date of August 11 on the top line. In addition, the minutes of the second meeting specifically note that the first meeting had been held on August 11 and Frank Amos confirms that date in several other documents. These discrepancies are so obvious that when Nell Wing (the first A.A. Archivist) filed the first Frank Amos letter mentioned above, she added a handwritten note at the bottom of the page, (which she signed and dated 1976) as follows: "(see April 11, 1938 = first-meeting minutes. These minutes, penciled draft as well as typewritten, seem to refer to events taking place at the Aug. 11 meeting. Perhaps 'April' was a slip of the pencil and got transferred to the typed notes.)" Indeed. To defend this single instance of the word "April" in these documents, it is necessary to question the veracity of at least a half-dozen other documents from August 1938. On the other hand, conceding that the handwritten word "April" should be corrected to "August" makes all of these contradictions instantly disappear. (Documents quoted in this footnote are, respectively: GSO Box 59, 1938, Folder B, Documents 1938-19 & 1938-18a; Folder B [1], Documents 1938-107/8, 1938-114 & 1938-115[a].)

(which was notarized on the 10th)[19] along with his hand-written proxy letter authorizing Willard Richardson to vote in his stead, did not arrive in New York until August 11. (In fact, Dr. Bob Smith was unable to attend any of the official trustee meetings during this critical 1938 period.)

The First Meeting

With everything in hand, Amos, Richardson, and Ruddell (John Wood was absent) met in Room 5600 at Rockefeller Center. Dr. Bob's proxy—"I hereby appoint Mr. W. S. Richardson to represent me at the meeting of the trustees of The Alcoholic Foundation & to vote for me as he sees fit. I instruct him, however, to vote for Mr. Frank B. Amos for Treasurer of said Foundation."[20]—was duly read and accepted and within just a few minutes Bill Ruddell was elected as permanent Chairman of the Alcoholic Foundation and Frank Amos became its temporary Secretary and the permanent Treasurer.[21]

The two remaining Rockefeller men, Chipman and Scott, were then elected to the Foundation's Advisory Board (thereby cementing the commitment of all four of Rockefeller's friends to this new Foundation) along with Bill Wilson and Hank Parkhurst. Two of these new members, Chipman and Parkhurst, were present at the meeting; Albert Scott and Bill Wilson were not.[22]

Having taken care of the administrative formalities, Hank Parkhurst was then called upon "to recount the work to date . . . in the Eastern section" and he delivered a report noting that:

41 alcoholics have recovered and are currently "on the ball"

6 alcoholics are in the questionable class

12 alcoholics upon whom a great deal of time has been spent, but who are so difficult that the cases are classified as practically hopeless

10 alcoholics who have definitely recovered, but who are out of touch with the group

At present, they have over 25 prospects[23]

Since the Ohio contingent was, at this time, commonly referred to as being in a "western city and its environs,"[24] these figures represent the current status of recovery in New York, New Jersey, and Washington. If there had really been just ten sober members the previous October and if Hank's August numbers are accurate, there would have been a solid fourfold increase (or fivefold if we are meant to include those "out of touch" members with the 41 who have "recovered") in the number of sober members in the East since Bill and Dr. Bob had "counted noses" in Akron.

While Hank had suggested to Amos in mid-March that neither he, nor Bill, nor Fitz should be "called upon to make reports or be pressed to show results,"[25] this kind of growth in just ten months was certainly the kind of report Parkhurst was anxious to make. Such impressive numbers lent solid credibility to the desperate need for money so they could continue this obviously effective work of saving alcoholics. Regarding those needed contributions, Hank concluded his presentation by providing some details on "Mr. Wilson's and his own activities toward raising funds for the Foundation."[26] Although the minutes are not explicit, beside the contribution from Rockefeller in March, Hank likely reported on the monies they had already received from Charles Towns and the $1,000 Bill had managed to borrow from Agnes Mayo. Beyond that, we can safely assume Hank then painted a glowing picture of their current plans for approaching some of the richest men in the country including Owen Young, Thomas Lamont, Alfred Sloan, Edward Stettinius, and Henry Ford.

In his new role as treasurer, Amos then "went into budget and office matters for the information of the Trustees," producing the necessary paperwork to be signed by three of them so that an "unincorporated association account" could be opened at a local bank for the future management of the Foundation's money.

And so on that high note and with great hopes for the future, the first formal meeting of the Alcoholic Foundation (which would later evolve into the General Service Office of Alcoholics Anonymous) was unanimously adjourned.

Why Bill Wilson did not attend this important meeting is something of a mystery and completely unexpected at such a critical juncture for the group. The reason for his absence is neither noted in the minutes nor mentioned in Lois's diary or in any other contemporary document. The meeting *was* called at the last minute—on the same day Bob Smith's signed copies of the Trust Indenture and his proxy letter arrived—so perhaps Bill had a prior commitment to meet with some rich or well-connected New Yorker on that day, one he just couldn't afford to cancel. But whatever the explanation, Bill's absence definitely provided Hank Parkhurst with an opportunity to take center stage and proudly recount for the trustees all of their current successes in the East.

The Second Meeting

It is also interesting to note that neither Wilson nor Parkhurst attended the second meeting of the Alcoholic Foundation, which was held just seven days later on Thursday, August 18. We know Bill had left for Maryland the previous Saturday[27] (chasing the possibility of opening a sanitarium for alcoholics in Washington, DC), but the reason for Hank's absence and his exact whereabouts on that day are uncertain. This second meeting was attended by Richardson, Amos, and Ruddell, along with A. LeRoy Chipman who was sitting in as a representative for the Advisory Committee.

Other than reading and accepting the minutes from the previous meeting and the Treasurer's report with the particulars of the new bank account he would be opening the next day, the entire agenda was devoted to the transfer of John D. Rockefeller Jr.'s contribution from the Alcoholic Fund to the new Alcoholic Foundation. For some reason this involved "considerable discussion" before the three men unanimously agreed to transfer the $2,150 still remaining from "an anonymous donor for the alcoholic work being done in Akron, Ohio" into the Foundation's new account. It is more than likely this prolonged discussion centered on the fact that the money could only be transferred with "the stipulation that it be used exclusively for the work at Akron," making it explicit that the money could *not* to be spent for any of the other purposes stated in the organization's charter. Having approved the transfer with that restriction, the trustees then authorized Frank Amos to send Dr. Bob Smith a check for $200 on the first of each month, starting in September and continuing until the following April.[28]

The next day Frank Amos was still busy with foundation work. He wrote Willard Richardson informing him he had just returned from the bank where he closed the joint account they had maintained for the Alcoholic Fund and transferred the remaining balance into a new account established for "the Alcoholic Foundation which came into existence on August 11, 1938." Frank also wanted to bring his report of receipts and disbursements up to date and he did so by noting there had been no new contributions since the last accounting and that he had written just one check for $200, which was mailed to Dr. Bob Smith on August 1.[29]

Amos Writes a History of the Foundation

After spending some considerable time with Frank Amos in Akron the previous February, Bob Smith had characterized him as "a very shrewd man and a very careful and thorough diagnostician,"[30] and it was exactly these qualities which prompted Amos to spend the rest of that Friday afternoon dictating and proofing an eight-page document he entitled: "History of the Alcoholics movement up to the formation of the Alcoholic Foundation on Aug. 11, 1938.'" Amos was profoundly aware that he was involved in the creation of something revolutionary and, conscious of his position at the epicenter of this major historical event, he felt it was important to record the details of how the movement had begun and been set in motion so that they would be properly preserved for posterity.**

Frank's "History" tells a detailed story about the December 1937 meeting at Rockefeller Center and the conference held among the four Rockefeller men immediately afterward before going on to describe his trip to Akron and then recounting the concerns over money, which led to the creation of the Alcoholic Foundation. Amos supplies a wealth of information in this document that appears nowhere else in the contemporary record, making it a valuable piece of writing for any comprehensive history of Alcoholics Anonymous, and we must be grateful to Frank for his foresight and his commitment to getting all of these wonderful details down on paper.

The following Monday, in the interest of historical accuracy, he took the additional step of asking both Hank and Bill to review and correct this document before it was finally typed.

---

* See Appendix VI on page 645 for the complete text of Frank Amos's "History . . ." A careful reading of that "History" will show that many of the unique details presented earlier in this book can be traced directly to this "History."

** Frank Amos's obituary published in the *New York Times* on July 20, 1981 reflected Amos's own view of his centrality to the creation of Alcoholics Anonymous. The article was headlined "Frank Amos, A Co-Founder of Alcoholics Anonymous" and noted that he was "one of the five original members of Alcoholics Anonymous . . . Mr. Amos . . . was a nondrinker who along with four other men founded A.A. in 1937. Mr. Amos helped select the name and for years was a nonalcoholic trustee for the organization's general service unit." Despite some half-truths here, it is worth noting that throughout 1938 Frank Amos was, after Bill Wilson and Hank Parkhurst, arguably the next most important moving force shaping Alcoholics Anonymous into the organization that it is today.

570 Lexington Ave.
New York City

August 22, 1938

Mr. Henry G. Parkhurst
17 William Street
Newark, N. J.

Dear Hank:

It is my intention that the attached memorandum which Miss Dore wrote for me be placed in the permanent record of the Alcoholic Foundation so that in future years anyone reading the minutes will know the history of the movement from the time that we four became interested in it.

I would appreciate it if you would read it over very carefully. If you find anything wrong or if you have any suggestions of any kind for improving it, please let me know. I think Bill Wilson should also read it before it is finally typed.

I have two or three intimate friends who are already fairly familiar with this work to whom I want to give a copy of this along with your prospectus of the book. As soon as you and Bill have passed on it, it can be copied and I should like to have about six copies including the original.

Sincerely yours,

Frank B. Amos

Despite the additional review by these two direct participants there are still some misstatements in this account (in particular, with dating), but these are minor.* Frank Amos's "History" did an outstanding job of presenting the backstory of Alcoholics Anonymous, which was largely missing from the outline, and the two chapters included in the prospectus of the book. The document would therefore provide an excellent introduction to the work for his friends who, on the basis of their friendship alone, would likely have read all of these additional eight pages. Beyond these few friends mentioned in his letter to Hank, it is unknown whether Bill and Hank ever included any of their extra copies of the Amos "History" in the promotional packages sent out to prospective donors after the middle of August. Frank Amos certainly felt it made a valuable addition to any appeal they might make to potential donors and he obviously intended them to use it as such.

From another perspective, it should also be noted that Amos's efforts amounted to nothing less than the "history of the work" that Hank had insisted should be included in the first chapter of the book.[31] It is even possible—especially considering Amos's

---

* Amos, for instance, claims that Bill Wilson first met with Willard Richardson "during *December* of 1937" and stating that his own trip to Akron was made "about *the 1ˢᵗ of February.*"

request for Parkhurst's input—that Hank had encouraged Frank to write up this detailed account. But whatever the exact impetus for creating this valuable document, it is to both men's everlasting credit that it was written, reviewed, and then preserved for the historical record.

Judge Casey and the Prospect of a DC Sanitarium

While the disappointingly small contribution from Rockefeller had ended any hope of Dr. Bob running an alcoholic hospital in Akron, Bill received a letter in early August that quickly developed into the possibility that they might be able to open their own sanitarium for drunks in Washington, DC, in the very near future. This was such a solid and tempting opportunity that Bill Wilson lost most of the next month as he tried to turn his dream of founding this first (of what he hoped to be many) A.A. sanitarium into a reality.

The exciting news came in a letter from Victor Heiser, the president of the National Association of Manufacturers, who told Bill, "I thought perhaps it might be of interest to you to know that Judge Walter J. Casey of the Police Court of the District of Columbia has expressed interest in the Towns treatment for alcoholism and drug addiction. It would probably be advisable for you to get in touch with him."[32]* *Perhaps* this might be of interest? Wilson was, of course, very interested and elated by the news. This was exactly what he hoped would start to happen with increasing regularity; as people became more familiar with their work, they would begin to talk about the amazing success rate of Alcoholics Anonymous and this would lead to a growing number of personal recommendations just like this one. Bill's vision of how they could network to reach more and more potential donors was finally beginning to work.

Wilson had been introduced to Heiser by "one of Mr. Rockefeller's associates"[33] (likely Willard Richardson) and they had met sometime earlier (probably during the third week of July), but Bill had been disappointed by that meeting. "It seemed at the time as though he had little interest," he told Fitz when writing him with news of this judge in Washington, "but apparently he took fire to some extent," passing their promotional package along to other interested parties and eventually catching the attention of Judge Walter Casey.[34]

Bill wrote back to Heiser a few days later, thanking him for the referral and noting that:

> It so happens that one of our most active men lives near Washington, and I have asked him to call upon Judge Casey.

---

* Again, it is impossible to know exactly what Bill said about the "Towns treatment" at their meeting or to know how Heiser heard that part of his story. If Bill was most actively pursuing money for a chain of hospitals, then talking about Towns Hospital and their success rate as a prototype along with his own experience there would likely have played a prominent part in his presentation.

I think you will be interested in the enclosed letter, which I did not have with me the other day, from the Chief Physician of Towns Hospital.[*]

Please let me know of any case of alcoholism where you think our group might be helpful, and please also forgive my tardiness in acknowledging the very pleasant interview I had with you.[35]

Finally they had a solid lead (and a possible job) for Fitz Mayo—one that was right in his own backyard. On Monday, August 8, Bill wrote Fitz, enclosing a copy of Heiser's letter, and gently suggesting, "perhaps you will want to call on Judge Casey,"[36] Fitz didn't need much in the way of encouragement and he managed to get an appointment with the judge that very week.

According to Bill, Judge Walter J. Casey was "a most public spirited man" and "very influential in the District of Columbia."[37] In addition, he had a fair degree of notoriety as a no-nonsense judge, not only in Washington, but also nationally. Just two years earlier, he had famously jailed a sitting US Congressman who had publicly declared Casey could "go to hell" after the judge issued a warrant for his arrest. A year later, the judge gained even more national attention when his picture appeared in a *Life* magazine article describing how he had sentenced a woman to a year in jail for child beating.[38] (Years later, Judge Casey also showed up in the May 1947 issue of the A.A. *Grapevine*, which quoted extensively from a paper he had written entitled: "A Judge's View of Alcoholism.")

Given his job of presiding over the local Police Court, it is not surprising that the judge had "dealt extensively with drunks in his court, and [had] wondered for years what could be done about it."[39] Bill Wilson was confident he had the definitive answer to the judge's question of what could be done about it and that Casey's influence would provide them with the opportunity to establish the first official A.A. sanitarium in Washington, which "could easily be the starting point for other model set ups of the same kind."[40]

In the beginning, everything looked extremely positive. During Fitz's first meeting with Casey the judge "took fire right away and wanted to know what we proposed."[41] That was all Fitz Mayo needed to hear; he immediately telephoned Brooklyn, and Bill Wilson caught the next train south for Washington, DC, where he stayed for the next ten days.[42] During that week and a half he and Fitz made several calls on the judge during which they "suggested that enough funds ought to be raised by private subscription to rent a house in Washington this winter and open a farm on the outskirts next spring."[43] Their plan was to accept "selected cases only" in order to build up "a strong team down in that District."[44] Once presented with this proposal, Casey grew even more enthusiastic and claimed "there would be little difficulty in raising the money among his friends for such an experiment" with the ultimate plan being that "if, after a year trial, the experiment proved successful . . . there would be no trouble in

---

[*]   The fact that Bill did not have a copy of Silkworth's letter with him during their meeting—even while speaking so glowingly of the "Towns treatment" —suggests that Wilson had met with Heiser sometime after his return from Maryland on July 11, but before Dr. Silkworth letter was written on July 27.

getting the District to make a larger contribution for a still larger effort."[45] Finally they were really getting somewhere!

Casey was as good as his word, discussing their proposal with "some of his friends, who include the Chief Commissioner of the District of Columbia, the President of the Washington Board of Trade, the Head of the Elks, and some other prominent business people." After listening to the judge's presentation and reading over the two chapters of the book, several of these gentlemen suggested a meeting be organized where they could speak directly with the recovered alcoholics and then make a coordinated plan for their next step forward.[46]

While Bill claims the suggestion for this meeting came from Washington, the proposal so closely mirrors the successful meeting with the Rockefeller team the previous December that Wilson (or his glowing account of that dinner) was likely the original source of this idea. But, whoever formulated the plan, the organization of the meeting quickly floundered and Bill's hopes of repeating the Rockefeller Center success turned into a long drawn out affair that eventually spilled over into late September and then dragged on until November.

Bill and Fitz came back to Brooklyn on August 23, arriving just in time to attend the Tuesday night meeting.[47] Both men had several appointments with prospective donors that week in the City where, once again they encountered uncomprehending resistance and even pleas of poverty from other foundations. Fitz received one particularly heartfelt response from a Mr. Bullis, the Executive Director of The National Committee of Mental Hygiene, claiming they were currently running an annual deficit of $20,000 and actively discouraging Mayo from contacting any of their regular donors. They needed the money themselves.[48]

The following Monday, August 29, Fitz was still in Brooklyn and the judge had not yet been able to establish a date that worked for everyone he wanted to attend this meeting. Fitz sent him a letter of encouragement, holding out the prospect that Dr. Bob might even be able to join them for the discussion in Washington:

> Dear Judge Casey:
>
> When you have determined on the date for the meeting which you proposed, will you please notify Mr. W. G. Wilson at 182 Clinton St., Brooklyn, N.Y., as much in advance as possible?
>
> We may be able to get a doctor who has been free from liquor for three years, and who is head of a large group of ex-alcoholics in Akron, Ohio, to come on. This man has had quite a lot of experience both from the spiritual and medical standpoint, with many cases.
>
> I imagine there will be about six of us present.
>
> Cordially yours,
>
> (F. Mayo)
>
> JFM:Rh

P.S.

I expect to be at my home next Saturday, Sept. 3rd in the event you can get your group together next week.

On that same day Bill wrote a letter to Dr. Bob telling him all the details of this recent development in Washington, (which he knew would be "of exceptional interest") and describing the "definite proposal for that area, which would include some sort of a Community house in Washington this winter, and next spring a farm on the outskirts." Finally, he informed Bob that it looked as if a meeting would be held "shortly after Labor Day, say about the 7th or 8th of September" and that

> we think we ought to appear in Washington in some strength. It is probable that Fitz, Don McClain [sic], Hank Parkhurst, yourself, and myself should be there if possible. We think you will be especially needed because you can tell the gentlemen first hand about the kind of experience you have had out there, because this is the sort of thing we will seek to develop in Washington and Baltimore.*

> Though the exact date of the meeting is not set, I am wondering if you can arrange to come to it in case it seems necessary at the time, and in the event we can provide you with the wherewithal . . . It isn't absolutely necessary that you come to the meeting, but it would certainly be helpful we think.[49]

Dr. Bob Visits New York

The August 29th date on the letter quoted above is problematic (and probably wrong) because the very next day Bob Smith arrived in Brooklyn and it is hard to understand why Bill would have bothered to write in such detail and ask so many questions if he knew he would actually be speaking to Bob the following day.** Dr. Bob, his wife Anne, and their son Bob arrived at the Wilson house on Tuesday, August 30, and stayed for three days.[50] In all likelihood, they were on their way to Vermont to visit Bob's mother over the Labor Day weekend and—as he had done the previous December—made this

---

* Bill was confident that any progress made in Washington, DC, could be effortlessly spread to Baltimore, telling Bob in this same letter: "Through contacts we have made at Johns Hopkins and elsewhere in Baltimore, it is probable that we can also get some Baltimore people interested in this project."

** It is always possible that the Smiths dropped in without any significant advance notice, but if this is not the case then two other solutions suggest themselves for the perplexing date on this letter. The first is that Ruth Hock had, once again, typed the wrong date on the letter. She was not, after all, a "letter perfect" typist, having gotten Dr. Bob's middle initial wrong here—a mistake she made on two other letters to Smith in 1938 (July 15 and August 7)—and having typed Bill Wilson's address incorrectly as "172" rather than 182 Clinton Street on three letters that same year (June 24 and two on August 8¹), not to mention the misspelling of Dr. Heiser's name on the August 8 letter to him. The second possible explanation might be found in the inscrutable final line of this letter, which reads: "Signed in Mr. Wilson's absence." This is the only GSO archive letter from 1937 to mid-1939 that has this peculiar statement and, since Ruth claimed that Bill always insisted on dictating directly to her typing, it is more than a bit problematic. Had Wilson dictated the letter some day earlier and she just now retyped it and signed it in his absence? Whatever the explanation, it seems unlikely that Bill would be so unaware of Bob's imminent arrival and that he would be sending this letter to Akron the day before he knew he would see him in Brooklyn. If that is the case then the correct date for this letter is most likely sometime in the previous week—before Bob's arrival but after Bill's return from Washington, DC, on August 23.

side trip to New York; this time to catch up with Bill and to spend some time with the other members of the Eastern group.

The two men had not seen each other since Wilson's last trip to Ohio the previous April and he had written only four letters to Bob during those intervening four months.* It would be helpful to have copies of any letters Bob may have written during this time; we know there was at least one, which Wilson references by saying, "thanks for your good letter,"[51] but it did not survive. Still, there is no indication of any glaring gap in their correspondence during those four months other than the necessary discussion about Bob Smith's election as a trustee of the Alcoholic Foundation, (which, as already noted, might have been negotiated with a phone call). Such a minimal amount of communication over these critical four months severely challenges the popular A.A. myth regarding the close contact and constant interaction between these two men during this period.

The Smiths arrived just in time for Bob to participate in the regular Tuesday night meeting,[52] but unfortunately we have no record of what he thought about the very different style and substance of that meeting. By late August 1938 the format in Brooklyn had been evolving for well over a year and was now significantly different from the Oxford Group meetings being held at T. Henry William's house every Wednesday night in Akron. The New York meetings were not only far less religious in tone, they also placed a much greater emphasis on alcohol—both the participant's past history with drinking and the importance of not picking up the first drink—which was not happening in the Ohio meetings.** It would be fascinating to know just how approving and even comfortable Bob Smith felt when he came face-to-face with such glaring differences, but he has left us with no record of his reactions.

In addition, we have no information about what opinions (if any) Bob Smith may have expressed about the recently launched book project and especially about the two chapters Bill had mailed him two months earlier. Did he approve or disapprove of the overall plan, should they make changes to the outline, and what did he really think about those two chapters? Did he offer any criticisms or suggestions at all? In addition, what kind of progress had been made (or not made) in Akron on the stories needed for the book? And, if he hadn't already sent it to Bill, did Bob perhaps show up in Brooklyn with a draft of his own story for the book? If nothing else, Bill Wilson was surely curious to know if the book project had gathered any recent support among those Ohio members who had been so vocal in their condemnation of the idea just four months earlier. Did Bob have anything to say about any of these issues?

---

* These were: the long, late June (22, 23, or 24) letter telling Bob that he had gone ahead and written the first two chapters of the book; a July 15 letter with details about the Virginia/Baltimore trip; an August 7 letter with Bill's expectations for the stories being written in Akron (and his hopes that Bob would do some fundraising there), and this oddly dated August 29 letter, which is quoted above with all its details about what had been happening in Washington, D C.

** On the lack of focus on alcohol in Akron: "Wally G . . . noted that not too much was said about alcoholism or drinking in the testimonials. 'That was conversation the alcoholics had among themselves. T. Henry was apt to have a number of Oxford Group guests who were visiting. Their witnessing would have nothing to do with alcohol. You would be surprised how little talk there was of drinking experience even among ourselves,' Wally said. 'That was usually kept for the interview with new prospects in the hospital. We were more interested in our everyday life than we were in reminiscing about drinking.'" (*Dr. Bob and the Good Oldtimers*, pp. 140-141)

There were also those still very contentious issues surrounding money and hospitals. It would be invaluable to know the substance of any conversations they might have had about their ongoing fundraising efforts and the role of the newly created Alcoholic Foundation, along with the strong possibility they might imminently be opening the first A.A. sanitarium in Washington, DC. And finally, there was the very real possibility that they would soon be receiving some prominent national publicity since that August 30 meeting was also attended by an observer from the *Readers Digest* who had been invited to sit in by Hank Parkhurst in the hopes that the *Digest* would write a favorable article about the success of their movement.[53]

This was, after all, the only time during the year 1938 that Bill Wilson, Hank Parkhurst, Fitz Mayo, and Bob Smith—the four most important and active members of early Alcoholics Anonymous—ever had a chance to sit down together and have a meaningful discussion about the future of their movement.* Bob's and Fitz's presence in New York allowed for nothing less than a summit meeting of A.A., and yet we know absolutely nothing about what they talked about, what opinions might have been offered, or what plans may have been formulated regarding these pressing issues.

Despite the likelihood that interesting and even important things were discussed during Dr. Bob's three-day trip in New York, the only answer we have regarding this host of intriguing questions comes in a letter Bill wrote to Bob the week after he left Brooklyn: "It was certainly great to have you folks with us."[54] That is all the contemporary information we have about what happened during those three days. Perhaps the insistence that these important issues *must* have been addressed during those three days is just our wish that they *had* been discussed and the details preserved so that we could have a better understanding of the personalities and the dynamics of Alcoholics Anonymous's early history.

Instead, it may have been that the only thing happening during this visit was that Bill and Bob, along with Hank and Fitz, sat around in grateful wonderment over how radically different their lives were now that they had found a way to stop drinking and how happy they were just to be sober. While it would not be completely surprising for alcoholics to focus so exclusively on themselves for three days, it remains unlikely that none of these important topics were discussed during this singular visit. What is surprising is that nothing of importance or value seems to have come out of those talks with Dr. Bob Smith. A few weeks earlier Bill Wilson had noted "the old juggernaut bounces along,"[55] and it apparently continued to bounce along in exactly the same direction and in exactly the same way as it had already been going—without any meaningful input for change from Dr. Robert H. Smith.

The DC Sanitarium Experiment Fails

Unfortunately, the early September dates Bill had first mentioned to Bob for the meeting in Washington did not work out and on September 8, he wrote again asking Bob to reserve the following week as a possible date for the meeting: "Fitz has seen

---

* The only previous meeting of these four men had been held the night before the Rockefeller dinner the previous December.

Judge Casey again in Washington and it looks as though the Washington meeting would take place Thursday or Friday of next week, which will be the 15th or 16th. I am not positive of the exact date, but will let you know the minute we find out."[56]

On that same day Bill wrote a letter to Don MacLean, a sober Police Court judge who lived just north of Albany* (and who was almost certainly one of the ten members Hank had reported at the first Foundation meeting as being recovered, but out of touch with the group), asking him if he would join them for this important meeting in Washington. "Like yourself, [Judge Casey] has dealt extensively with drunks in his court and has wondered for years what could be done about it . . . Our observation of the Judge tells us that you and he are bound to click, so we all very much hope that you can be there on Sept. 15th or 16th. Bob Smith is coming in from Akron, and Hank, Bill Ruddell and myself will go from New York. Perhaps we can arrange to drive from here down together. I think Fitz has enough room to put us up, so there should be little expense."[57]

Bill was all business as he did everything in his power to prepare the grounds for this critical meeting, mailing Fitz a copy of Frank Amos's "History" and suggesting "perhaps Judge Casey ought to read [it] before the meeting", and then asking Mayo if there was any "prospect of getting the Baltimore [i.e., the John's Hopkins] contingent for the Washington meeting." Everything that could be done was being done to make this as successful as—if not more successful than—their first meeting with the Rockefeller team eight months earlier.

Then, although Bill Wilson was reluctant to admit it, the whole enterprise began to slowly unravel. Near the end of September Bill finally wrote Dr. Bob a letter confessing: "[I] shouldn't have kept you in suspense about the Washington situation. It turns out that Judge Casey is in the hospital after an operation: the matter stands just where it did before, but it looks as though he would be unable to do anything about it for three or four weeks. Will let you know when."[58] Elsewhere, Bill says Casey "was supposed to be out [of the hospital] and reconsider this thing shortly after October 1st"[59] but he later amended that date, noting that the Judge was still ill and without his leadership it was unlikely that the group of Washington businessmen would be able to "consider the matter before October 15th."[60] Even in early November Bill was still "most hopeful that Judge Casey and the Washington businessmen . . . will presently come forward with a proposal" on the sanitarium, claiming he had "the strongest kind of feeling [that] this is going to happen."[61]

It never did.

Whatever might have been going on with Judge Casey (and with his friends), part of the problem seems to have been Fitz Mayo who, for some unknown reason, developed a strong aversion to the entire project. In the third week of September Fitz wrote Bill a letter detailing his many financial woes, offering several possible solutions, but while

---

* For details on the life of Donald MacLean, see his obituary in the January 29, 1958 issue of *The Times Record* of Troy, NY, page 13. [Special thanks to Jared L. of Pennsylvania for tracking down this man with the name that could be spelled so many different ways!] Wilson's letters consistently misspell his name ("McClain") and elsewhere he refers to MacLean as a banker (for instance in AA Main Events, 1936, Point 8: "We had isolated out of towners like Fitz Mayo and Don MacLean, a banker who lived at Cohoes, New York."). This is not entirely untrue since, besides his primary professions as lawyer and judge, MacLean also served as a trustee of the Cohoes Savings Bank.

doing so he "expressed his reluctance to again approach the Judge."[62] Wilson doesn't elaborate on why Mayo was so reluctant to pursue this seemingly golden opportunity, but a few weeks later he did report his reaction to Fitz's wife, Elizabeth, saying:

> this annoyed me a little bit for it looks to me like the Judge is the sole prospect at the moment for a regular income, to say nothing of the general desirability of getting someplace with the work in Washington. The situation over there seemed so obviously the best bet from every standpoint that I wrote Fitz a pretty stiff letter designed to dynamite him into action . . . On rereading it I can see how I have possibly discouraged him from looking elsewhere, though to nothing like the degree that he seems to have conveyed to you. It was the most intelligent letter I know how to make to keep him steered down the middle of the road in the direction of immediate bread and butter. If you think best I shall write him correcting any impression that he should hold back on looking for anything that will produce results.[63]*

Fitz, with Wilson's approval, finally decided to begin "doing some alcoholic work in Washington immediately, even if it be only on a shoestring." Bill thought this was a worthwhile plan because he felt "it will spur Judge Casey and his friend to do something all the sooner" and it would also "build a fire under the Foundation Trustees, if I can indicate that Fitz is actually at work in Washington."[64] Neither of these things happened. No money was ever raised in Washington, DC, and the possibility of opening the first A.A. sanitarium there became less and less of a topic of discussion among the Eastern leadership as the year drew to a close and the plan finally fell out of sight completely as renewed work on the book began to demand more and more of everyone's time and attention.

Bill Wilson was deeply attached to his dream of establishing a chain of A.A. hospitals and it would take more than just this abject failure in Washington to kill it. Despite the fact that he had wasted the better part of a month on the project, Bill would continue to believe that a chain of sanitariums, sponsored and staffed by A.A. members, would eventually prove to be their best hope for carrying the message of recovery out into the greater world. It was a dream he would cling to for several more years before abandoning it completely.**

---

* Neither Fitz's letter to Bill nor Bill's response have been saved. We only know of both letters from this letter that Bill wrote to Elizabeth.

** The Knickerbocker Hospital project of the 1940s is just one example of Bill's ongoing attempts to have an A.A. hospital.

CHAPTER THIRTEEN

This Week Magazine

~*September to October 1938*~

It had been three full months since Bill Wilson had written any new material for the book. It wasn't that absolutely no progress had been made on the project, but it was minimal at best. Bill rather lamely admitted to Dr. Bob on August 29 that "a little more has been done on the book, but not much,"[1] and he similarly told Don MacLean on September 8 that "some more progress has been made on the book,"[2] but he offered no further details. Perhaps this was because whatever recent progress there may have been was in relation to their efforts to confirm the acceptability of what Bill had written so far and to establish that, once finished, the book would prove to be as marketable as they hoped it would be.

Sometime in mid-June Wilson and Parkhurst solicited a professional opinion on the first two chapters during a visit with Floyd Parsons (the former *Saturday Evening Post* writer), who pronounced the book to be a worthy effort and agreed to help with the editing once it was finished.[3] Best of all, Hank and Bill left with the writer's commitment to do an article once the book was published, along with his confident assurance that he would be able to get that story placed in *The Saturday Evening Post*.[4] On August 3 Wilson wrote Parsons a belated thank-you note, asking him to "forgive my tardiness in acknowledging the pleasure which Mr. Parkhurst and I had in your company the other day," and sending him copies of Dr. Silkworth's and Dr. Richard's letters "for your further information." This was really little more than a courtesy letter, clearly intended to reassure Parsons that the book was still a viable project and reiterating how much Bill appreciated his offer of assistance in promoting it.[5]

---

*   It is interesting to note that enough copies of the first two chapters had been typed for one to make its way to Cohoes, NY.

Ongoing Edits to the Two Chapters

The only other progress Wilson might possibly claim was the ongoing cosmetic edits to the two chapters. While the overall format of "There Is A Solution" and "Bill's Story" remained fundamentally the same over these three months, Bill continued to make small revisions to the text every time Ruth had to retype them. The changes were mostly confined to small additions or deletions as he tried to sharpen the impact of his sentences and to clarify the message he was trying to deliver. Commenting on this particular part of the process, Hock later noted ". . . there were thousands of small changes and rewrites—constantly cutting or adding or editing."[6] Ruth also claimed that she retyped these chapters "at least 50 times."[7]*

For example here are three early versions of just one paragraph from "There Is A Solution" showing the progressive edits which were made with each retyping. *(Deletions from the previous version are noted by ~~strikeouts~~ and additions appear in **bold italics**):*

Stepping Stones Version 1, *[June, 1938]:*

If by chance you are, or have begun to suspect that you are, an alcoholic, we think there is no tenable middle of the road solution. You are in a position where life is becoming impossible, and if you have passed into the region from which there is no return through human aid, you have just two alternatives. One is to go on to the bitter end, blotting out the consciousness of your intolerable situation as best you can. Or, you can surely find what we have found, if you honestly want to, and are willing to pay the price. After years of living on a basis which now seems to us wholly false, you are not going to get rightly related to your Creator in a minute. None of us has found God in six easy lessons, but He can be found by all who are willing to put the task ahead of all else.[8]

Stepping Stones Version 2, *[June-September?, 1938]:*

If by chance you are, or have begun to suspect that you are, an alcoholic, we think ~~there is no tenable~~ *you have no* middle of the road solution. You are in a position where life is becoming impossible, and if you have passed into the region from which there is no return through human aid, you have just two alternatives. One is to go ~~on~~ to the bitter end, blotting out the consciousness of your intolerable situation as best you can. Or, you can surely find what we have found, if you honestly want to, and are willing to pay the price. After years of living on a basis which now seems ~~to us~~ wholly false, ~~you are not going to get~~ *we did not become* rightly related to ~~your~~ Creator in a minute. None of us ~~has~~ *have* found God in ~~six~~ easy lessons, but He can be found by all who are willing to put the task ahead of all else. *That goes for you too!*[9]

---

* If this is not an outright exaggeration, the constant retypes could be explained by the fact that they did not have these chapters offset printed in quantity, but rather typed up multiple carbon copies whenever Hank or Bill had depleted the store of previous copies they were constantly sending out in their efforts to raise money.

GSO Version, *[June–September?, 1938]*:

If by chance you are, or have begun to suspect that you are, an alcoholic, we think you have no middle-of-the-road solution. You are in a position where life is becoming impossible, and if you have passed into the region from which there is no return through human aid, you have ~~but~~ *just* two alternatives. One is to go *on* to the bitter end, blotting out the consciousness of your intolerable situation as best you can. Or you can surely find what we have found, if you honestly want to, and are willing to ~~pay the price~~ *make the effort*. After years of living on a basis which now seems wholly false, we did not become rightly related to our Creator in a minute. None of us have found God in easy lessons, but He can be found by all who are willing to put the task ahead of all else. ~~That goes for you too!~~[10]

Throughout these three versions, the number of words remained fairly constant (156, 155, and 146 respectively), but the impact of the language was changed subtly—for instance with the dropping of the too clichéd "six" from the "easy lessons" comment and the addition (and subsequent deletion) of the pointed accusation, "That goes for you too!"

From Bill Wilson's perspective it was important that he continue to sharpen the text as much as possible, but at this time, there was no pressing need for him to begin writing any new chapters. These two served their primary purpose as promotional pieces in June, July, and August, and Bill continued to use them throughout the rest of 1938 as his opening wedge for securing appointments with some of the most important and prestigious men in New York and Washington.

Fundraising Efforts Continue

As usual, Bill set his sights high. In early September he prevailed upon his old employer, Clayton Quaw, to join him and Hank Parkhurst for a preliminary meeting with Fredrick Yeager, the private secretary to Thomas W. Lamont, the senior partner at J. P. Morgan & Co.[11]* Yeager was enthusiastic about their proposal and he was confident Lamont would responded positively, but after this auspicious beginning the head of J. P. Morgan disappointed them all, telling his secretary to write Wilson how "he regrets that he is unable to offer any assistance" because "the enterprise is entirely outside of his bailiwick." Returning the package of documents to Wilson, Yeager consoled him with his "personal regrets that the negotiations proved unsuccessful" and suggested Bill might have better luck if he approached "the personnel executive of large organizations where such matters come under their personal supervision."[12] This was little more than a polite brush off—with just a bit of sympathy thrown in to soften the blow.

---

*   It is not unlikely that Clayton Quaw was the reason they were able to actually get this appointment.

It is difficult to understand why Wilson and Parkhurst were so consistently unsuccessful with the rich men they approached in New York City during the summer and fall of 1938. Bill was upset by these repeated failures, complaining that

> it is inconceivable to us, when we observe the amounts of money raised for other purposes, that we cannot quite readily secure adequate funds to carry forward a work of the probable importance of this one . . . Obviously we had not yet discovered how to go about it . . . We simply have not reached the right people in the right way.[13]

Wilson's frustration is understandable, but just how likely is it that all of these men would have been so completely deaf to the worthiness of the cause they were promoting?

Perhaps the problem wasn't that Hank and Bill hadn't found the right people or the right way. Perhaps it was the successes they were so proud of—the early contribution from John D. Rockefeller Jr. and their current alliance with his closest associates—that were the very source of their undoing. The community of the rich is small and incestuous and it is not inconceivable that one response to learning of Rockefeller's support for A.A. would be to wonder why John D. hadn't come up with a larger donation himself if he was so convinced about the worthiness of this cause. After all, Wilson and Parkhurst weren't looking for *that* much money—only something like $30,000—an amount that was little more than pocket change to Rockefeller. Had word of the fact that Rockefeller thought money would spoil the project already become so well known among the New York elite that it provided them with a readymade excuse for saying "No" without any fear of troubling their conscience? In the face of the universal and summary rejection of all their appeals, this may well have been the case.

Even more ambitious than his hopes at J. P. Morgan were Bill's plans for two meetings he encouraged Fitz to set up in Washington, DC. Before the Judge Casey project completely unraveled, Wilson encouraged Mayo to make contact with Stanley Woodward and Colonel Edwin Watson—two important members of the White House staff—and convince them they should attend the meeting then being organized by the Judge.[14] This was shooting very high indeed! Colonel Watson was President Roosevelt's personal military aide, and Woodward was the White House Chief of Protocol, two men who were not just in daily contact with the President of the United States, but also well known to be among his closest personal friends.[15*] Could Bill Wilson have had any greater hopes for the proposed Washington D.C. meeting than to have it attended by two men who shared the confidential ear of Franklin Delano Roosevelt?

But all of this came to naught. Despite these grandiose plans and all of their efforts, by late September Wilson was forced to admit he was "rather ashamed to say that outside of Mr. Towns' generous contributions, we have not secured a red cent."[16] The game plan they had been following for the past several months was obviously not working, nor was there any real hope that it would start working in time to relieve

---

* Given Bill Wilson's famously low opinion of Franklin Roosevelt, we can only take this as a measure of the lengths that he was ready to go in his efforts to make A.A. successful.

the growing desperation of their current financial situation. A completely different approach was clearly needed.

Not surprisingly, Henry G. Parkhurst had a plan.

Hank Approaches Silas Bent about a *This Week* Magazine Article

Predictably Hank's new plan had to do with promotion and fundraising. His scheme hinged on the wide circulation of a story praising their work and his certainty that such publicity would generate tens of thousands of inquiries from the public. But it was the second half of his proposal that proved to be the most important. He claimed that once this well-placed article had put them in touch with a huge and receptive audience, they would then respond to all inquiries by offering several chapters from the soon-to-be-finished book for just $1 ("the price of a pint of cheap whiskey"), thereby raising enough money to finance the writing of the rest of the book.[17]

Floyd Parsons had promised them national exposure in *The Saturday Evening Post* once the book was published, but what they desperately needed right now was enough cash to support themselves while they wrote, edited, and published the book. Bill, Hank, and Fitz were flat broke and quickly slipping deeper into debt as they struggled to cover their regular household expenses.[18] Something had to be done immediately and Hank's plan for capitalizing on this proposed wide-ranging publicity sounded like the best way to raise money quickly, maximizing the resources they already had on hand.

One of their members, Silas Bent, had a working relationship with *This Week* magazine, a syndicated Sunday supplement distributed locally by *The New York Herald Tribune*. This magazine had a weekly nationwide circulation of over five million copies[*] and Hank was sure an article in *This Week* was the perfect vehicle for producing the publicity they so desperately needed. How could they fail to raise some money once they had received such penetrating national exposure?

Bill Wilson had met Silas Bent in Towns Hospital in November 1935 and helped him become the third sober member of their group in New York City. But less than a year later, Silas had a spectacular slip, drinking himself into a stupor that lasted for several weeks before his wife placed a desperate phone call to Wilson. Bill took the next train from Grand Central to Old Greenwich, Connecticut, and found his friend practically unconscious and in a seriously deteriorated state. In a panic, Wilson called a cab and dashed the drunken and dangerously ill man down to Towns Hospital where Dr. Silkworth pronounced Bent to be on death's door, holding out little hope for his survival. Silas, however, quickly proved the doctor's dire prediction wrong by making an amazingly quick and full recovery.[**]

---

[*] In the prospectus for the One Hundred Men Corporation prepared more than a month later, Hank Parkhurst claimed a weekly circulation of five and a quarter million copies for *This Week* (Printed promotional stock prospectus entitled "Alcoholics Anonymous," GSO, Box 59, Folder C [1], Documents 1939 – 144 to 157, p. 6). Bill Wilson said circulation was seven million in his letter to Frank Amos, September 26, 1938 (GSO, Box 59, Folder B[1], Document 1938-145 to 1938-151, p 5).

[**] Lois tells this story with rare gusto in *Lois Remembers* (p. 102). It is unlikely that Silas Bent was one of the more stable members of the group and the day he achieved permanent sobriety (if at all) is not known. It is telling that his story was not included in the Big Book, strongly suggesting that despite his prodigious writing skills, his length of sobriety was not to be trusted.

The next time Silas shows up in the records is the long letter Bill wrote to Dr. Bob Smith in late June 1938 reporting on Bent's glowing opinion of the two chapters just written and his high hopes for the proposed book. Wilson reinforced Bent's credibility as a critic by reminding Bob that Silas was "a star reporter and writer" who "was at one time editor of the New York Times Sunday magazine."[19]

Whatever his past writing accomplishments (and they were, in fact, considerable),* Bent was at this time regularly supplying copy for the "Page 2" feature in *This Week* magazine.[20] Hank approached Silas and suggested he make a more substantial contribution by writing a full-length article about their success in getting people sober. Hank also mentioned that whatever Silas might write, he should include a paragraph that would "guardedly disclose [their] need for funds." Once this article was read by "several hundred thousand families where the alcoholic problem exists," A.A. would surely receive a huge number of requests for information and help, providing Bill and Hank with an opportunity to sell copies of the already-written chapters to many of the people who wrote for help and thereby raise the money needed for their ongoing support.[21]

Hank had no doubt that if Silas wrote and submitted such an article, it would be published; and he was not too far wrong. By mid-September Bent had finished the piece and submitted it to Gerald Mygatt, the Managing Editor of *This Week* magazine. Mygatt responded enthusiastically on September 19 saying that "personally, I think it's most interesting" and he promised Bent a prompt answer once the publisher and the owner of the magazine found the time to read it.[22] On the same day that Mygatt was writing this first response to him, Hank, Bill, and Lois drove out to Old Greenwich for a talk with Silas about the *Tribune* article.[23] If they were about to receive such massive favorable national exposure, then they needed to formulate a plan for handling the deluge of requests for help which would surely be generated by this publicity. It would be interesting to know more about these conversations (unfortunately, no record has survived), but given the typical over-the-top optimism of the participants in that discussion, we can only presume the plans they made that day were both ambitious and elaborate.

The need for such planning, however, was called into question the very next day when Mygatt raised the first of several complications. He wrote to Silas telling him the publisher had now read the article "with interest," but they both felt that something important was missing. Would it be possible, he asked, "to incorporate in the article a description of how the cure works?"

> What it boils down to is that you tell us and the reader that this new cure exists—and then don't tell us anything about it.
>
> Could this be written in the first person by some man who has actually gone through the process? Such an article would be extremely valuable to us and extremely interesting to any reader with an alcoholic problem anywhere on the horizon. As it stands, Mr. Field [the publisher] and I

---

* For some details previously given on Silas Bent's career, see the footnote found on page 193.

agree the piece fails to hammer its real interest home—and the real interest lies perforce in the process rather than in the fact that "there is hope." I will hold the piece here awaiting your reply.[24]*

This was very bad news indeed. While they already had such a first person account in "Bill's Story," they didn't want to publish that in the magazine. Instead, that was exactly what they were hoping to sell to the interested parties who read the magazine article. In addition, Bill had not yet written any general description of how the cure works, a labor that would prove to be the greatest single challenge of his life and perhaps his most important accomplishment. But at this point Wilson was still almost three months away from his first serious attempt to produce a comprehensive explanation of how the cure actually worked.

Silas passed along copies of this correspondence to Bill and suggested they had reached an impasse that only he could resolve. "I believe the best thing for you to do is to see Gerald Mygatt, but you must make an appointment to the minute; you can't just drop in on the guy. Even so, he may keep you waiting."[25] In short, all of the problems of revising the article to the publisher's satisfaction had now been dropped directly into Bill Wilson's lap.

The Third Foundation Meeting: The Lack of Money

But Bill had more pressing problems to deal with first. At 3:00 p.m. on Friday, September 23, just two days after Silas's report of the problems with the *This Week* article, Wilson made a dramatic presentation of their desperate need for money at the third meeting of the Alcoholic Foundation at Rockefeller Center. In attendance were Willard Richardson, Frank Amos, A. LeRoy Chipman, and Hank Parkhurst; absent were John Wood, Bill Ruddell (who sent a proxy to Frank Amos), and Dr. Bob Smith (who had written a short letter on September 3 outlining a request he wished to make of the other trustees).[26]** The meeting was completely focused on money and, more particularly, on their lack of money. Amos gave a treasurer's report noting there was still a balance of $2,000 from the Rockefeller contribution along with a $500 check received from Charles Towns and an anonymous donation of $50.*** Frank also reported the Towns donation of $500 had already been distributed to Wilson, Parkhurst, and Mayo ($150, $150 and $200 respectively) as the donor had requested. Finally, he reported the regular monthly payment of $200 had been sent to Dr. Bob Smith earlier that month.

---

* The following January, an article written by Silas Bent entitled "There Is Hope" was published in the Hackettstown Courier-Post. Given Mygatt's use of that phrase in quotes in his letter to Bill, it is possible that the Hackettstown piece was just a recycled version of what Silas had written for "This Week" magazine.

** Note that there are two sets of minutes for this meeting; the second of which (GSO, Minutes: Alcoholic Foundation / 1938-1944 / Duplicates) contradicts the first set in a few places and, based on those differences, appears to be the earlier version. Both documents were used in the presentation of the meeting that is given here.

*** In an alternate set of minutes for this meeting, it is noted that $650 of the Rockefeller money (not $2,000) was currently in the Foundation's account. While this is likely more accurate than the $2,000 mentioned in the official minutes, neither number seems to be 100 percent accurate in relation to Rockefeller's total contribution and the payments already made to Dr. Bob Smith. These minutes also note that the anonymous $50 contribution "was secured by Mr. Amos from Mrs. Charles S. Burke" (GSO, Minutes: Alcoholic Foundation / 1938-1944 / Duplicates).

Following this report, the first piece of new business was how to respond to Dr. Bob Smith's letter requesting the trustees take $400 from the money that would be paid to him in March and April 1939 and give it "at once to Mr. William G. Wilson and his associates." Since Rockefeller had donated these funds for Smith's exclusive use, this prompted a frank discussion which

> disclosed that Messrs. W. G. Wilson and H. G. Parkhurst—indispensable leaders in this movement for the redemption of alcoholics—had used up all their private funds and much borrowed money in the carrying on of this work and that either some funds must be supplied them or they would have to seek private employment at once of a nature which would take them away most of the time from this work in which they are exceptionally capable leaders. The Trustees . . . [decided] that for some time to come it would be vital to keep particularly Messrs. Wilson and Parkhurst in the New York Metropolitan area, entirely on this work providing it were at all possible to secure funds which would barely meet their actual expenses. No other funds being available at this time, the Trustees reluctantly accepted Dr. Smith's request and authorized the treasurer to pay this $400.00 over to Messrs. Wilson and Mayo.*

This decision was followed by the trustees reviewing the entire financial situation "at great length" and finally resolving that they would organize an "informal meeting of [the] Trustees with others interested . . . in an effort to raise funds to carry on this work." Although the minutes do not say so, it is clear from comments Bill Wilson made shortly after this meeting that Richardson (most likely prompted by Amos) was considering the possibility of re-approaching John D. Rockefeller Jr. for more money—this despite his employer's firm declaration the previous March that "you will not look to me for a further contribution for this object."[27] That pronouncement was so uncompromising that Richardson thought such a request could only be made with the active support of Albert Scott and it was agreed that he should be consulted on these matters as soon as possible because the immediate financial situation was so urgent. In preparation for that meeting, Amos asked Wilson to write out a fully detailed statement of their current financial distress, a document which could serve as a starting point for the planned discussion with Albert Scott the following Wednesday.

The Proposed *This Week* Article is Discussed
The final financial item to be discussed at the meeting was the proposed *This Week* magazine article and this raised something of a moral dilemma for Bill. On the one hand, he was nervous about not mentioning their plan for national publicity to the trustees before making that commitment, but he was equally worried the Rockefeller

---

* In the alternate (and almost certainly earlier) set of minutes for this meeting, it is noted that rather than approving this reallocation of $400 to Wilson and Parkhurst, that "no action was taken" (GSO, Minutes: Alcoholic Foundation / 1938-1944 / Duplicates). This contradiction might be explained by accepting that "no action taken" was the actual decision made by the trustees that afternoon, but that the transfer was approved once Willard Richardson had a chance to sound out John D. Rockefeller, Jr. on the matter and the minutes were subsequently modified to reflect that decision. *NOTE:* On page 338 of his well-researched book *Alcoholics Anonymous and the Rockefeller Connection*, Jay D. Moore, confirms that the foundation made a payment of $200 each to Hank and Bill on September 29, 1938—so the motion *was* approved.

men might veto the project and force them to cancel it outright once they learned the details of the proposal. Despite these fears, Wilson launched into

> a brief discussion of proposed publicity in the New York Herald Tribune Magazine called "This Week." It was suggested by Messrs. Parkhurst and Wilson that if such a step were taken promptly, new sources of contribution might be disclosed and that perhaps chapters of the book now under preparation could be sold to those seeking help. This would, they said, make a spiritual beginning in many homes and possibly permit Mr. Parkhurst and the office at Newark, N. J. to be retained.

> All agreed that this course had its disadvantages; that it might not produce much revenue; that it might flood us with inquiries which could not be looked after; that it might put us in a wrong light with the general public; that it might create the impression we were more interested in money than in spiritual matters.

Having noted in the course of this discussion that more chapters of the book were "now under preparation," Bill expanded on this by giving

> a report on the progress of the book which he has been writing, the purpose of which will be to give workers and alcoholics alike a powerful written help in pointing them toward spiritual redemption from alcoholism through reading of exactly how some one hundred former alcoholics had been redeemed. There was much discussion as to methods of publishing this book and promoting its sale, but nothing definite was decided.

In the end, the group simply ran out of time and, in addition to a lack of consensus about the best way to go about publishing and promoting their book, "no decision was made with respect to the Herald Tribune matter and its possible good or bad consequences."[28]

Although Wilson left this meeting with no clear solution to their dire financial situation, there was at least the hopeful possibility that Albert Scott could be persuaded to open a dialogue with John D. Rockefeller Jr. about making another (and perhaps even more substantial?) contribution to their group.

Bill's Letter Paints a Dire Financial Picture

Responding to Frank Amos's suggestion for a summary document he could present to Albert Scott, Bill wrote one the longest and most impassioned letters of his life in which he detailed "the position with reference to our alcoholic work, of Fitz Mayo, Hank Parkhurst and myself." The opening line, striking a tragically biblical note, was classic Bill Wilson: "So far as I can see, we three have 'sold all our sheep and goats.'"[29]*
He followed this dramatic opening with two paragraphs detailing Fitz Mayo's grave

---

* This mention of "sheep and goats" is an Old Testament reference to the flocks of animals kept by the pastoral Israelites of that time. In a pastoral economy, once you had sold all your sheep and goats, you had nothing whatsoever left to live on. For the complete text of this important and informative letter, see Appendix VII on page 651.

situation, noting that he "has gradually liquidated his livestock, equipment and farm. His house only is left . . . he is also in debt to his sister . . . [and] he has no income of his own at all." Unless Mayo could get some immediate relief, Wilson said, "he may be lost to us so far as much alcoholic work is concerned [and] when our book comes out we shall surely need man power of his kind." Knowing Amos wanted him to be specific about their needs, Bill noted that Fitz could "scrape by for a while on $200.00 a month, but will need more eventually."

Hank Parkhurst was in even worse shape than Mayo, a situation Wilson described in some detail over the next several paragraphs. Hank's business was failing and he "has no income and is running into debt at an alarming rate. He is at least two thousand dollars in the hole now." But more important, Hank's services "were going to be badly needed in the alcoholic work, which would obviously expand so much on publication of our book." In fact, no one was better or more "effective with businessmen of his own type" than Henry G. Parkhurst. In addition, Hank was needed for the critical role of looking "after the publicity and distribution of the volume... There is no one in our crowd who has been sober long enough, has the business capacity and energy, and would be available, save Hank." His services, Wilson declared categorically, "will be invaluable" in bringing the book to press and then promoting it.

Added to Hank's personal expenses were the costs of maintaining the office and his secretary in New Jersey which, Bill notes, are "now useful to me because I am dictating the book there and looking after an ever increasing correspondence." It would, of course, be possible to close it down immediately and thereby save some money, but they would desperately need an office to deal with "the labor entailed by the huge volume of inquiries and pleas for assistance which will surely descend upon us when the book is out." Quite frankly, if that happened and they had no office to serve as a base of operations, "the situation would be chaotic." In addition, if "the equipment and furnishings we now possess" were sold off and had to be re-purchased in just a few short months, it would "cost two thousand dollars to duplicate" them. On the other hand, Bill estimated it would cost only "about $600.00 per month to carry Hank, the office and a secretary" during the brief time before the book's publication, which would then begin to generate the income needed to sustain themselves.

Wilson's own situation was hardly any better. His "Wall Street income [had] stopped" the previous fall and although he has "since been made Director of a promising company,"* the fees paid by this Midwest firm were only "nominal."* To make things worse, he was in debt.

> During the past year, so that I could keep on and have a free hand with this work, I have gone fifteen hundred dollars into debt. I have given my personal notes for twelve hundred dollars. This money was shared with Hank and Fitz. Contributions amounting to fifteen hundred dollars were secured from Mr. Charles B. Towns. This money was likewise divided among the three of us and has all been spent.

---

*   The company Bill refers to is The Pierce Governor Company,

Having brought up the subject of Charles Towns, Wilson next went into a long discussion recounting his past relationship with the New York City Hospital and its owner, telling the trustees how Towns had offered him a job and the subsequent decision to reject that offer* along with any other kind of formal affiliation with the locally-famous drying out spot.

> We did not go along with Mr. Towns at that time because we felt there was a better way. We did not want any man's chance of finding his God and getting over his alcoholism prejudiced by accusations, however ill-founded, that we were too commercial. On this point we have been bending over backward ever since and I am very glad we have. But our financial backs have been broken with the bending!

Moving Ahead on a Less Than Ideal Basis

Having effectively eliminated Charles Towns and his hospital as a potential source of income, Bill states—in a not-too-subtle reference to John D. Rockefeller Jr.—that the ideal solution would be "to have access to adequate funds given by understanding people, quietly and without expectation of personal publicity or reward." Although he realizes this is the "ideal set up" and "perhaps we cannot have that," nevertheless:

> we could well use thirty thousand dollars during the coming year to place the knowledge of our solution in every home and to follow up this initial step. It will be unfortunate if we bring out a book which is sure to create a huge demand for help, at least by correspondence, and then be totally unprepared to take care of the situation. Though the book alone will undoubtedly do much good, it will fall short of this objective if publication finds us without men or money to carry it through. It is imperative we be ready. This is no time to bog down. The next six months are critical. The general work ought to be pushed and a foundation built that will withstand the pressure which is inevitably coming . . .

> As there are no funds yet in sight to carry the work upon the ideal basis we would like, we are plainly faced with the question as to whether we should go ahead on something less than an ideal basis. Or shall we stick to our vision of the ideal yet accomplish little or nothing for lack of money.

> For example, we could let the status of the work revert to where it was a year ago. Those of us now active could go back to business. In that event we might continue to grow at such a rate that perhaps several hundred more men would be reached over the next few years. But what shall we say of the many thousand who might pass out of the picture just because we failed to let them know? May they not be obliged to suffer because we are

---

* Even at such a close remove Wilson could get his time line wrong. Here he claims that the job offer from Towns almost certainly received in December 1936—had come "about a year ago, before we met you gentlemen," i.e., in September 1937.

now too timid, too conservative, or too fearful of what people may say?...
Assuming that the Trustees, by private contribution, think it unlikely we
can take care of the situation, should we not consider other means?

The New York Herald Tribune, for example, seems willing to carry an
article descriptive of our work, which would guardedly disclose our need
for funds. I refer to their Sunday Magazine called "This Week." This
section of the Tribune is widely syndicated. It has a weekly circulation
of seven millions. Perhaps it would bring our work to the attention of
several hundred thousand families where the alcoholic problem exists.
The managing editor of "This Week" thinks that twenty thousand of
them would get in touch with us. We could offer these families, say five
of the vital chapters of our book in photo-lithographic form. We could
frankly let them know about our finances and the necessity for money to
publish the book and take care of this aftermath. We could ask them one
dollar for these chapters . . .

. . . Admittedly, this is not the best possible approach, but would it not be
better than to drift? Frankly, I don't know. We would much like the advice
of the Trustees on this point.

Bill next revisited the possibility of making some kind of commercial arrangement
with Towns Hospital ("Again, I am not sure. What do the Trustees think?") and then
offered yet another option, one in which he would "concentrate entirely on the book,
letting Fitz and Hank, and the office from out of active participation," but even this
would cost a significant amount of money: ". . . these expenses, allowing myself two
hundred and fifty dollars a month to cover everything, will amount to fifteen hundred
dollars for six months."

To sum up then; It seems doubtful whether the status quo of all three
of us can be maintained during the month of October for less than one
thousand dollars. That would be six hundred to Hank and the office, two
hundred to Fitz and two hundred to me. Perhaps Fitz can get through
October without any more money, though he could certainly use it. In any
event he will be flat on November first, unless the Washington business
men pick up the load.

Six Pointed Questions for the Trustees

Having spent the better part of six pages arriving at this inescapable and unpleasant
conclusion, Wilson then organized all of these details into six comprehensive questions,
which he challenged the trustees to answer.

With the foregoing in mind, does it not seem proper that the Trustees
consider and perhaps come to some conclusion at their next meeting on
the following questions:

1. Assuming that contributions can be obtained, should the Foundation attempt to maintain the three of us in active work for, let us say, six months?

2. Should the Trustees decide that status quo should be maintained, how are we going to do that for the month of October?

3. Do the Trustees think there is a real likelihood that we can maintain the status quo ($1,000.00 a month) for six months on the basis of private contributions only?

4. In the event the Trustees think it improbable we can maintain the status quo for six months by private contribution, what is their pleasure with respect to the proposal we augment our income through the Herald Tribune publicity, the sale of book chapters, and perhaps a closer working arrangement with Mr. Towns?

5. If the Trustees think it impossible or undesirable to maintain the status quo by any of the foregoing methods, what do they think of the proposal that I continue alone on the book?

6. If it is decided I continue on the book, what is their advice as to how I should be financed? Should I immediately commit myself to Mr. Towns or not?

These were not rhetorical questions. Bill was genuinely looking for answers and insisting his Rockefeller friends not only acknowledge the reality of their dire situation (and their own complete failure to raise any money during the past several months), but also make a serious effort to formulate a working solution for these pressing problems. Bill did, however, manage to temper this insistence a bit in his closing statement.

> Though I have expressed some personal views, I would like to make it clear I shall not be at all disturbed if they are vetoed. Hank and Fitz and I are sensible that our thinking, at this time of financial embarrassment, may be warped. We would like the Trustees to help us guard against this possibility. We must, at all costs, avoid being driven into arrangements we might later regret.

> Though we are grateful we have you gentlemen to go to, we do not want to cast too much responsibility on the shoulders of our ever-willing Trustees.

> Let us say once more how much we appreciate the time and devotion which you Frank, Mr. Richardson, Mr. Chipman, Mr. Scott, and Mr. Wood have given this undertaking. Please do not take our problems too seriously.

> After all, God has a way of working things out if we are willing to be used as He would like.

Sincerely yours,

William G. Wilson[30]

Challenging the Rockefeller Trustees

The previous December, Bill Wilson had forged what seemed to be an amazingly fortunate alliance with four of John D. Rockefeller Jr.'s closest associates in the hope that, with their help, he would be able to open the wallets of wealthy New Yorkers and garner substantial contributions for their cause. Nine months later, Richardson, Amos, Chipman, and Scott had been responsible for facilitating just one donation—$5,000 from John D. himself—with absolutely no money coming from any of their other many contacts and recommendations. Wilson's frustration with this complete failure—and the dwindling prospect that this plan would produce any positive results in the near future)—was fast eroding what little remained of his original confidence that the Rockefeller group would be their passport to financial security.

With his six pointed questions, Bill Wilson had thrown down the gauntlet, giving the Rockefeller men one last chance to propose a solution for their disastrous situation. Despite the conciliatory closing paragraphs, Wilson knew if these men could not come up with a realistic and viable way for them to support themselves throughout the next six months, then other means—perhaps even arrangements they might later regret—would have to be entertained. Whatever might happen, Bill Wilson had no intention of walking away from his plan to rapidly expand the reach of their program of recovery, even if such a decision required him to take several giant steps away from the Rockefeller connections that had originally held out so much hope and promise.

On September 27, the day after he wrote this long letter, Bill explained to Silas Bent the extent and import of his current dilemma with the trustees and the reason he had not yet contacted *This Week* magazine.

> . . . As you know, The Alcoholic Foundation has five trustees, three of whom are closely related to the source from which we have already derived some funds, and from which it looks as though we presently might get some more. I favor the Herald Tribune publicity at this time because it would bring in a great number of inquiries for help. To the people who wrote in we could send five vital chapters of our book—the backbone of it. We might charge one dollar for these chapters and thus make enough profit on them to help us over the tight spot we are now in . . . A considerable advance demand for the book might be created. Actual contributions, or sources thereof, might come to light.
>
> I am urging these points upon the trustees. It seemed to me that they should be consulted and their approval secured, before we go to bat, for money or no money, we want to do this thing in the best possible way. One of the trustees, Mr. Frank Amos, approved the Herald Tribune

project, but, as luck would have it, we cannot get down to cases with the other two until next week.

So I have not gone to the Tribune, for if, by an off chance, the trustees felt this publicity unwise at the moment, we might feel quite uncomfortable.

Though I suppose I occupy, in an unofficial way, a position of considerable authority in this work, I do not think it wise for me in a case like this to take action first and tell the trustees afterwards. I am sure you will agree.[31]

Wilson was hoping the Rockefeller trustees would endorse his plan to publish the story and he was also, at this point, still reluctant to go against their wishes or advice. He did not want to place himself in the uncomfortable position of acting before receiving their approval, but this stance would change dramatically with their subsequent failure to come up with a reliable means of ongoing support for them. Bill's "sheep and goats" letter was, in fact, the last time he would throw himself and his growing movement at the feet of these four men in such an abject way. Their failure to raise money for him and his team left him no choice but to turn away from these rich friends and become more receptive to the promotional and profit-making schemes Hank Parkhurst was constantly suggesting. The time was fast approaching when, in desperation, Bill would begin to exercise his "position of considerable authority in this work" and start taking actions that were contrary to the advice being offered by the Rockefeller men.

The Question of Dues Is Raised

Bill had told Silas Bent that John D. Rockefeller Jr. might be considering another contribution and "it looks as though we presently might get some more" money from him. That same day, Bill also wrote to Bob Smith, telling him the renowned preacher, Dr. Harry Emerson Fosdick* was back in town and that A. LeRoy Chipman planned to enlist his support for their cause and then, once his "enthusiasm is aroused, I think the boys intend to use that as a means of putting some heat on the Big Chief."[32] But more than Fosdick, Wilson's highest hopes were pinned on Albert Scott whom Frank Amos had agreed to approach and arrange a meeting so that the money issue would be discussed in detail. Bill was confident Scott would be able to broker a deal that included another Rockefeller contribution and thereby resolve the laundry list of intractable financial problems he had presented to the Foundation.

Although Bill referred to it as "a Trustee meeting,"[33] the meeting with Albert Scott held on Wednesday, September 28 was not a formal gathering of the Alcoholic

---

* Harry Emerson Fosdick (1878-1969) was "one of the most prominent liberal ministers of the early 20th century" and the original pastor at Rockefeller's Riverside Church. He was deeply involved with many facets of Rockefeller's religious affairs while his brother, Raymond, was at this time the president of the Rockefeller Foundation. Also of note, Harry Emerson Fosdick later wrote a favorable review of the book, *Alcoholics Anonymous* when it first came out. (Wikipedia, Harry Emerson Fosdick, Named Article—retrieved October 26, 2013)

Foundation and no official minutes were kept of what happened there.* Scott sat down with Frank Amos and, most likely, A. LeRoy Chipman (and possibly even Willard Richardson), but there were no alcoholics invited. Bill's expansive letter, with its six pointed questions, was the only presence they had at the meeting. That letter did, however, provide the primary focus for the discussion as Albert Scott was sounded out on whether or not he thought it might be a good idea to approach John D. Rockefeller Jr. for another contribution.

He did not.

Instead, Scott took a completely different and unexpected approach, insisting that the members of Alcoholics Anonymous show good faith by taking primary responsibility for the financing of their own organization before he would be willing to make any suggestion to Rockefeller (or to anyone else) about further donations to their cause. He wanted Wilson and Parkhurst to approach their members and ask "each ex-alcoholic . . . to contribute something, however little, to the Alcoholic Foundation regularly, preferably weekly." Scott considered this demonstration of self-support absolutely "vital as a preliminary" to securing any "larger subscriptions from outside sources."[34] This was not the first (nor the last) time that a proposal of enforced regular dues for A.A. membership would be made, but Scott's intransigence at this time made it one of the more fateful presentations of that idea in the history of Alcoholics Anonymous. Wilson and Parkhurst felt it left them with no other option than to begin significantly distancing themselves from their Rockefeller colleagues.

Bill and Hank Reject the Dues Idea

The day after the meeting, Frank Amos invited Bill and Hank to his office and told them of Scott's fixed position on the question of financing. In a letter he wrote to Albert Scott the following Tuesday, Amos said that, on hearing this news, Wilson and Parkhurst "endeavored to canvas the situation from every angle," but could not, in the end, find any way they could agree to his proposal. From their perspective and experience, it was wrong on far too many levels.

> . . . they feared the results of such a plan at this time and stressed the following pertinent points.

> 1. Every ex-alcoholic, to be sure of remaining permanently sober, must keep active, working with others for their emancipation. Otherwise they definitely face a recurrence of the disease with death or the insane asylum their destination. Therefore, regular "dues" are not necessary to keep them active or interested.

---

* The next official meeting of the Alcoholic Foundation did not occur until four months later on January 18, 1939 (GSO, Box Title: Minutes: Alcoholic Foundation / 1938-1944 / Duplicates). Those minutes do not include a reading of the minutes from the previous meeting so it is impossible to state categorically that no meetings had taken place in the intervening four months, but there are no other minutes preserved in the GSO archive from that time. In addition, the headstrong and willful pursuit by Wilson and Parkhurst of their own plans to write and publish the Big Book—contrary to the advice of the Rockefeller trustees—would certainly go a long way toward explaining the lack of any such formal meetings during that time.

2. Every ex-alcoholic with any funds whatever is being called on constantly to contribute to the desperate needs of others who are destitute. Their wives and families, seeing personally this need, do not object seriously to these individual gifts.

3. The moment this work is put on what they would consider a dues paying basis, the wives would want to know the purpose of these "dues." When it became known—as it soon would—that this money was to provide for two or three leaders, it would cause serious trouble in many families. Family dissension is frequently a factor in causing an ex-drunk to drop the "ex."

   We must all remember that this situation is different from the average church, service club or non-profit organization. In most cases the wives and families have suffered cruelly for years through the husband's depravity. Now that they are redeemed, it is only natural that these wives expect their husbands to concentrate their meager resources on providing food, clothing, education, etc. They will respond to desperate individual cases before their own eyes— and are doing it liberally—but they rebel against systematic dues to a central organization.

4. Even where they accepted the regular contribution idea and "came through," they then would feel that all requests for relief should be referred to the Alcoholic Foundation. As we are not the U.S. Government with taxing power and ability to issue "I.O.U's," we could not, and should not for some time to come, undertake to finance the general rehabilitation costs. The individual help—man to man—is vital and should be continued indefinitely.

5. Last February, Parkhurst put the proposition of monthly contributions up to a large number of the New York alcoholics who accepted the plan in principle. Several of the wives, however, raised a kick and the plan was abandoned for the time being. Upon being consulted, Dr. Smith advised emphatically that such a plan attempted at present with the Akron crowd, would be demoralizing.

These are strong and persuasive counter-arguments and Frank Amos agreed with them wholeheartedly. "For nine months," he told Scott, "I have kept in almost daily touch with this work. It is my conviction that we should not yet attempt this organized giving. When larger numbers of the ex-alcoholics become rehabilitated economically, such a plan should be evolved." But definitely not now.

Amos's Alternate Plan
Despite this unanimous disagreement, Albert Scott's reputation and his close personal relationship with Rockefeller required nothing less than a respectful response. "After

you read this memorandum," Frank Amos allowed, "if you are still convinced" such a move is "vital," then "both gentlemen agree to have me go before their crowd" to present this proposal. Clearly, Wilson and Parkhurst were intent on distancing themselves as far as possible from this suggestion, placing the full responsibility for the scheme (and whatever fallout might occur from it) directly onto Frank Amos and his three Rockefeller friends.

In the hope that Scott would not require him to do something that he and these two men completely disagreed with, Amos offered his own alternate plan for responding to Bill Wilson's six questions.

At this period I recommend:

(a) That the four of us—you, Richardson, Chipman and myself—endeavor at once to raise $10,000.00;

(b) That we ascertain what advance we can get from a publisher on the book. This might be sufficient for Wilson's bare expenses while writing it;

(c) That Parkhurst continue until November 1st to try and secure contributions;

(d) That Parkhurst handle, with Miss Hock, the secretary, such office detail as is necessary until November 1st.

(e) If by November first, all of our efforts have failed to secure sufficient funds to maintain Parkhurst, secretary and office until April first, that we abandon, for the present, the suggestion to take over the Newark office and leave Parkhurst free to re-enter business on a full time basis.

(f) That we maintain the principle that the work among alcoholics must be voluntary, but that we endeavor for as long a period as necessary to provide funds so that

Wilson can pursue his work as an author of "One Hundred Men" and

Parkhurst can handle the business end of our operations.

Amos closed his letter to Scott by noting he was "crowded with rush work" and trying to clear his desk before leaving on Friday morning for a three-week vacation. He would therefore not be available for a private conversation to give full information on anything that might have been left out of the memo. Instead, he provided Scott with Bill's contact information and suggested "you ask Wilson to come to your office as soon as convenient for you. He can make clear any points and give you the correct picture."[35]

Whether or not Albert Scott ever called Bill for that appointment is unknown, but his insistence that A.A. become self-supporting by instituting a policy of enforced weekly dues was not implemented. It is also not clear to what degree Scott and the others ever embraced Amos's suggestion that they commit themselves to quickly raising $10,000 to support the three men until the following April. Whatever efforts they may have made, no such sum was ever raised. On the other hand, Frank's all-important suggestion "that we ascertain what advance we can get from a publisher on the book" would, in just a few days, lead Bill Wilson and Hank Parkhurst—in defiance of the advice they were receiving from the Rockefeller contingent—to embark upon an ambitious plan to publish the book, *One Hundred Men*, on their own.

• • •

To avoid any confusion, it is important to emphasize that the name of the proposed book at this point was not *Alcoholics Anonymous*, but rather *One Hundred Men*. That title was first suggested by Ebby Thacher's brother, Tom, when he wrote his proposed Introduction entitled "Victors Anonymous" the previous June.[36] At that time, both Wilson and Parkhurst had enthusiastically adopted the name and it was the one they had bandied about with regularity whenever they spoke about the proposed book during the following months. From this point in early October of 1938 up until mid-February of 1939, the title *One Hundred Men* would become much more prominent in all their correspondence and other preserved documents, being constantly mentioned as the name of the proposed book and also as the name of the corporation Hank Parkhurst would soon organize in an effort to raise money for the book project. The decision that led to the selection of *Alcoholics Anonymous* as the title of the Big Book was still several months away.

This Week Article Rejected

Like the ill-fated Washington project, the possibility of publishing an article in *This Week* magazine limped along for another two months before it was decisively rejected by the publisher on November 25.[37] Silas Bent had advised Bill on September 21 that he should call on the magazine's Managing Editor, Gerald Mygatt, but that appointment was delayed by the excitement of the late September trustee meetings, Wilson's ongoing writing for the book, and Parkhurst's aggressive efforts to raise money. Almost two months later, Bill finally wrote to the editor, reminding him of his earlier request for changes to Silas Bent's article and of Silas's promise that he and Hank Parkhurst would be calling to offer their assistance in making those changes. Bill apologized for the immoderate delay, but offered no other explanation than to say that there were "several reasons we could not see you then." More important, he wanted to correct Mygatt's impression that this piece was no longer relevant because "an article about our work" had recently been published in a competing publication, *The American Weekly*. Wilson assured Mygatt "that the article [in that magazine] had no relation to our activities whatever. So I assume that you are still interested." Bill then ended by playing what he must have considered to be a powerful trump card.

> Mr. W. S. Richardson, secretary to Mr. John D. Rockefeller, Jr. knows about us. He has given us much of his time and effort. It turns out he is a friend of Mrs. Meloney [the owner of *This Week* magazine], and has been good enough to let her know that you may rely upon what we say.

Mr. Parkhurst and I would like very much to call as soon as you are at liberty.[38]

A flurry of correspondence went back and forth between Wilson, Amos, Mygatt, Richardson, and Meloney for two weeks before the owner finally replied with finality "the piece is not for us."[39] This must have been tremendously disappointing for Wilson and Parkhurst. Bill had done everything he could to get *This Week* to run the article—including sending Willard Richardson a sample of some language he thought should be used in the letter to Mrs. Meloney, (which Richardson ignored, writing his own text instead).[40] All to no avail.

This appears to be another one of the fortunate failures that so dominate the early history of Alcoholics Anonymous. If an article had been printed in *This Week* magazine—which had a national circulation of at least five million copies—in September or November 1938, it may well have proved more disastrous than beneficial to the fledgling movement. The article might have produced an overwhelming response and thousands of requests for help—requests they were simply not capable of dealing with at a time when they had less than one hundred members, just two weekly meetings, no book explaining their method for staying sober, and no infrastructure in place for organizing and responding to those desperate requests.

When Jack Alexander's famous article on A.A. appeared in *The Saturday Evening Post*—which had a national circulation of three million copies—on March 1, 1941, it produced a tidal wave of attention and requests for help. But by that time the movement had two thousand members[41] and a book of instructions on how to stay sober, along with meetings that were springing up all over the country and a New York office that, however understaffed, had been functional for more than two years.

The rejection of Silas Bent's article by *This Week* magazine was a very large blessing in disguise for Alcoholics Anonymous.

CHAPTER FOURTEEN

"More about Alcoholism" and "We Agnostics"

~September 1938~

Despite the challenges of dealing with the ongoing excitement created by the trustee's meeting, composing the long "sheep and goats" letter, and Albert Scott's disappointing call for regular dues at A.A. meetings, Bill Wilson was able to finally begin to write new material for the Big Book. Although the proposed *This Week* article was never published, Hank's ambitious plans for it depended on two interconnected events: Silas Bent would write the article and, just as critically, Bill Wilson would start writing for the book again—a task he had successfully avoided for the past three months by repeatedly claiming he was *not* an author.

Hank Keeps the Book Moving Forward

But Parkhurst was adamant. They needed additional chapters to justify the $1 price for what he would be sending out to people asking for help and Bill was the only person qualified to do the writing. Once Hank had convinced Silas to take on the article—something that happened during the first or second week of September—he immediately began to pressure Bill to write more chapters so they would have sufficient material ready when the piece was published. Hank thought if they had five chapters to send out, people would feel they were getting fair value for their investment of one dollar.

Once again, Hank was playing a critical and central role in moving the book project forward. Without his insistence that Bill start writing again in September 1938, the Fellowship may never have had a book at all or, if one was eventually written, it would have been published long after April 1939 and released with a text (and perhaps even a program) significantly different from what exists today. Bill candidly acknowledged on several occasions that Hank was his "partner in the book enterprise",[1] and when Ruth Hock was asked about Parkhurst's input, she readily admitted he "contributed a lot of ideas"[2] and suggestions while the book was being written.

Ever the salesman, Hank's greatest accomplishment was this constant promotion of the Big Book. While Parkhurst didn't actually write the book (other than the chapter, "To Employers" and his own story, "The Unbeliever"), his voice was always the loudest one raised in support of the project, at first convincing Bill to write "There Is A Solution" and his own story as promotional pieces (despite all of the objections being raised in Akron), and then creating his prophetic outline of what the book would contain when it was finished. Three months later, in the face of their ongoing failure to raise any money from the rich, Hank suggested that their next best fundraising strategy would be to finish several more chapters of the book so they would have something substantial to sell to *This Week*'s readers. When that project eventually fell through, Hank raised his sights once more and decided that if they could just get the book written and published, it would surely generate an ongoing income stream for their growing movement and thereby put Alcoholics Anonymous on a solid financial footing.

Throughout the entire process Hank Parkhurst was deeply involved with anything and everything relating to the book project, but his most important contribution was surely this ongoing, increasing, and at times strident insistence that a book had to be written and published. If Hank's focus seems to be more on the book's potential profits than on how many drunks might be saved, that is no reason for any of today's A.A. members to feel anything other than the most profound gratitude for Henry G. Parkhurst. He was the singular, monumentally persuasive force driving first the writing, and then the publication of the Big Book.

So while Hank's scheme for raising money with an article in *This Week* ultimately failed, his aborted plan was the direct cause of another decisive turning points in the history of Alcoholics Anonymous: Bill Wilson finally assumed full responsibility for writing the rest of the book and began to do just that.

Bill Writes the Next Two Chapters

Bill claims he "probably got down to serious writing about September 15, 1938"[3] and this is one of those instances where his memory for dates seems to be reasonably accurate; it certainly fits with all the other known facts in the story. Bill took the next two chapters proposed in Hank's outline (after discounting the twenty-eight personal stories and what later became "The Doctor's Opinion") and began by writing one chapter "devoted to the vagaries of the alcoholic mind, bearing especially on mental and emotional states" and another "directed" toward "most of us [who] were honest in being agnostic."[4] When finished and fully polished, these two chapters would appear in the Big Book under the titles "More About Alcoholism" and "We Agnostics."

At the time, it wasn't just Hank's outline driving the order of the content for these next two chapters. Bill was actually returning to the two central points he had made in "There Is A Solution" and devoting an entire chapter to each of them in an effort to drive home his foundational beliefs that, (a) the central problem for the alcoholic is that he has absolutely no effective mental defense against the first drink, and (b) the only proven solution to this problem was a total reliance on God. If the compulsive drinker wanted to have a real chance at continued sobriety, then he must first admit he was personally powerless over the problem, and then surrender himself to God as the only source of hope for his recovery.

Once the Twelve Steps were written in early December, these two chapters would be seen as a full exposition of the first two steps. Bill made this clear in Chapter 5 ("How It Works"), where he first articulates all of the steps and then declares the first two have already been fully covered in the book, so the reader is "now at step three"[5] —which he then goes on to talk about in detail.

Unfortunately, aside from the two earliest chapters ("There Is A Solution" and "Bill's Story"), we have no other rough drafts of the chapters found in the front half of the Big Book. Early versions of those chapters were either discarded with each rewriting, or they were lost when the office moved from Newark to New York City. Ruth Hock noted in an April 12, 1940 letter to Hank that when they moved to New York, "we took all the furniture there was at 17 Williams and left only some cartons of paper, etc."[6] Might those cartons of paper have contained the discarded rough drafts? The earliest versions we have of the other nine expositional chapters are found in the Multilith edition—the prepublication version of *Alcoholics Anonymous* that was offset printed in mid-February of 1939 and privately circulated for criticism. That text had already been reviewed by some members of the Fellowship, and it had been subjected to considerable editing by Bill Wilson and two professional editors.*

It is important to note that the earliest drafts of the first two chapters pre-date the writing of the Twelve Steps, while the other nine chapters can only be found in a form that incorporates whatever edits may have been made to them after the Steps were created in early December 1938. This is a major disappointment since it is clear from Bill's letters that these two newest chapters were originally circulated in a very rough form and it would be illuminating to see how they read in that early stage of their development.

On September 27, less than two weeks after he started to write again, Wilson sent them off to Dr. Bob Smith commenting:

> Two more chapters of the book ["More About Alcoholism" and "We Agnostics"] are close to completion. I am enclosing the original dictation on two of them so you can get a rough idea. You will understand that what I am sending you is just the rough, uncorrected outline. Will let you have the polished product when ready.[7]

---

* Details about the Multilith Copy and the two editors, Janet Blair and Tom Uzzell, are given in Chapters Twenty-Seven and Twenty-Eight.

Of course significant revisions were made to both of these two original dictations: first in the revised versions sent to Dr. Bob Smith on November 3,[8] and then on an ongoing basis as they got closer to the Multilith printing of the book. Just as the 5,810 word first draft of "There Is A Solution" was cut by more than 2,000 words before being printed in the Multilith edition, it is possible that both of these chapters started out as much longer compositions, and were then rewritten, edited, and cut down in size before they arrived at the text we find in that first available version. On the other hand, it is likely that the discovery of a first draft of either of these new chapters would not reveal anything substantively different from what we find in them today. Just as the central ideas of "There Is A Solution" remained intact and were, in fact, clarified by the ongoing editing process, these two chapters would almost surely follow the basic outline of what is found in them today. (The only significant difference being the substitution of the word "spiritual" for "religious" throughout—a change already made, for instance, while editing Dr. Jung's important observation in "There Is A Solution" and in several other places in the two earliest chapters.)[*]

The Real Alcoholic Is Powerless

As already noted, Bill Wilson was intent on making a clear-cut case in these chapters for the two beliefs he considered essential to their program of recovery. The first of these was the inability of the true alcoholic—no matter how great his resolve or his degree of self-knowledge—to avoid picking up the first drink.

In "There Is A Solution" Bill had written:

> At a certain point in the drinking of every alcoholic, he passes into a state where the most powerful desire to stop drinking is of absolutely no avail . . . The fact is, that all of us for reasons which are yet obscure, have entirely lost the power of choice with respect to alcoholic drinks. Our so called will power with respect to that area of thinking and action becomes virtually non-existent. We are unable at certain times, no matter how well we understand ourselves, to bring into our consciousness with sufficient force, the memory of the suffering and humiliation of even a week or a month ago.[9]

But rather than presenting yet another more detailed explanation of this absolute lack of power, Bill took the more dramatic story-telling approach in "More About Alcoholism," presenting three real-life stories and one striking analogy in the hopes that one of these four might grab the alcoholic reader's attention in a way that a simple statement of fact never could. Before introducing those stories, Bill wanted to emphatically state that being powerless over the first drink was not just a temporary condition or a passing disability: It was a permanent condition if you were a real alcoholic.

---

[*] While the Multilith Copy version of "More About Alcoholism" uses the word "spiritual" six times, "religious" only appears once and in that case appears in the doctor's comment in the next to last paragraph of the chapter where he claims that "Though not a religious person, I have profound respect for the spiritual approach . . . "

Most of us have been unwilling to admit we were real alcoholics. No person likes to think he is bodily and mentally different from his fellows. Therefore, it is not surprising that our drinking careers have been characterized by countless vain attempts to prove we could drink like other people. The idea that somehow, someday he will control and enjoy his liquor drinking is the great obsession of every abnormal drinker. The persistence of this illusion is astonishing. Many pursue it into the gates of insanity or death.

We learned that we had to fully concede to our innermost selves that we were alcoholics. This is the first step in recovery. The delusion that we are like other people, or presently may be, had to be smashed.

We alcoholics are men and women who had lost the ability to control our drinking. We know that no real alcoholic ever recovered this control. All of us felt at times that we were regaining control, but such intervals— usually brief—were inevitably followed by still less control, which led in time to pitiful and incomprehensible demoralization. We are convinced to a man that alcoholics of our type are in the grip of a progressive illness. Over any considerable period we get worse, never better.

We are like men who have lost their legs; they never grow new ones. Neither does there appear to be any kind of treatment which will make alcoholics of our kind like other men.[10]

Bill followed this strong opening with a long list of the ways members of the Fellowship had tried "to prove themselves exceptions to the rule," employing "every form of self-deception and experimentation" in an effort to claim they did have some power over the first drink. But sooner or later, all of these strategies ended in abject failure and the alcoholic inevitably returned to drinking.

As testimony to the absolute permanence of this condition Bill's opening story presents the case of a man of thirty, who realizing he had a problem with alcohol, decided to quit drinking until he had made his fortune. He did so and finally retired after a successful and happy business career characterized by twenty-five years of bone-dry sobriety. The man then "fell victim to a belief which practically every alcoholic has—that his long period of sobriety and self-discipline had qualified him to drink as other men." This presumption proved fatal, for although he was a healthy man at retirement, he went to pieces quickly and was dead within four years.* This story provides a powerful lesson and reaffirms the truth that "we have seen . . . demonstrated

---

*   Identifying the unnamed alcoholics who appear in the Big Book has become something of a cottage industry among students of A.A. history and this case is no exception. While no specific candidate has ever been offered who neatly fits the specifics of this story, it has been suggested with some regularity that Bill Wilson "borrowed" the story from a book called, *The Common Sense of Drinking* by Richard Peabody (Little, Brown, and Company, Boston, 1931). There is, in fact, a somewhat similar story on pages 123–24 of that book, but it seems to be about a different individual altogether. There is no mention of the man's age in *Common Sense* and it took that gentleman only "five years" to "make the million" rather than the twenty-five years mentioned here, and he died five to six years after resuming drinking versus the four mentioned in Bill's version. Rather than considering Wilson's story as a creative elaboration on Peabody, it is more likely that these are actual details about someone Bill knew from personal experience or whom he had heard about from the personnel at Towns Hospital.

again and again: 'Once an alcoholic, always an alcoholic.'"* In short, "if you are planning to stop drinking, there must be no reservation of any kind, nor any lurking notion that someday you will be immune to alcohol."

Bill then spends the next several paragraphs wrestling with a distinction between the "potential" and the "real" alcoholic in the hope that this will help the reader evaluate and clarify his own condition. The potential alcoholic seems to be someone who can stop for a prolonged period of time, but can't stop once he has started drinking, while the real alcoholic finds it absolutely impossible to avoid the first drink for any appreciable length of time even after he has stopped. Such a man has lost the power to choose whether he will drink or not and it is exactly here that we find "the baffling feature of alcoholism as we know it—this utter inability to leave it alone no matter how great the necessity or the wish." The real alcoholic just can't avoid alcohol for any significant length of time; he always comes back to drinking in fairly short order.

The Insanity of the First Drink

The man in the story made a conscious decision to resume drinking—it had been his plan to do so for twenty-five years—and the result was fatal. But what about the fellow who has every intention of never touching another drop of alcohol in his life and still picks up the first drink? According to Wilson this is the very heart of the compulsive drinker's problem and he spends the rest of this chapter graphically exploring the mental processes that precede the first drink. "What sort of thinking dominates an alcoholic who repeats time after time the desperate experiment of the first drink? Friends, who have reasoned with him after a spree that has brought him to the point of divorce or bankruptcy, are mystified when he walks directly into a saloon. Why does he? Of what is he thinking?" And, most important, what are "some of the mental states that precede a relapse into drinking, for obviously this is the crux of the problem"?

For his first illustration, Bill offers the story of Jim, a sober car salesman who one day stops at a roadside place to get a sandwich for lunch. He had no intention of drinking and had eaten there many times during the months he had been on the wagon. Shifting into the first person, Bill allows Jim to tell the story in his own words:

> ". . . I sat down at a table and ordered a sandwich and a glass of milk. Still no thought of drinking. I ordered another sandwich and decided to have another glass of milk.
>
> "Suddenly the thought crossed my mind that if I were to put an ounce of whiskey in my milk, it couldn't hurt me on a full stomach. I ordered a whiskey and poured it into the milk. I vaguely sensed I was not being any too smart, but felt reassured, as I was taking the whiskey on a full stomach. The experiment went so well that I ordered another whiskey and poured it into more milk. That didn't seem to bother me so I tried another."

---

* Once again, Wilson has been accused of lifting this phrase from Peabody's *Common Sense of Drinking* and here there is a bit more plausibility to the charge. On page 82 of his book, Peabody claims, in italics, that "*once a drunkard always a drunkard—or a teetotaler!*" The word 'alcoholic' was supposedly just coming into common usage in the mid-to-late-1930s. Wilson's other famous 'lift' from Peabody appears in the first draft of "How It Works" which says "Half measures will avail you nothing." Peabody had written in *Common Sense*: "Halfway measures are of no avail" (p. 99).

Thus started one more journey to the asylum for Jim. Here was the threat of commitment, the loss of family and position, to say nothing of that intense mental and physical suffering which drinking always caused him. He had much knowledge about himself as an alcoholic. Yet all reasons for not drinking were easily pushed aside in favor of the foolish idea he could take whiskey if only he mixed it with milk!

Whatever the precise medical definition of the word may be, we call this plain insanity. How can such a lack of proportion, of the ability to think straight, be called anything else?

Bill's use of underlining here is meant to drive home "the peculiar mental twist" that allows someone to make such a ludicrous decision. What would you call this other than plain insanity? Real alcoholics consistently exhibit a "curious mental phenomenon" that readily entertains whatever "insanely trivial excuse for taking the first drink" might come up and then permits that "insane idea" to win out. "Our behavior," Bill says, is nothing less than "absurd and incomprehensible with respect to the first drink."

In an attempt to further emphasize the absurdity of this kind of thinking, Wilson offers the ludicrous analogy of a passionate (but frequently injured) jaywalker, claiming that his behavior is no more preposterous than it was for Jim to pour that first shot of whiskey into his milk.

In the beginning, the jaywalker "gets a thrill out of skipping in front of fast-moving vehicles" and does so with impunity for years; but then his luck deserts him and he "is slightly injured several times in succession. You would expect him, if he were normal, to cut it out." But he doesn't. Worse and worse injuries occur and still he can't seem to quit. "Finally, he can no longer work, his wife gets a divorce, he is held up to ridicule. He tries every known means to get the jaywalking idea out of his head. He shuts himself up in an asylum, hoping to mend his ways. But the day he comes out he races in front of a fire engine, which breaks his back."

"Such a man," Wilson pointedly asks, "would be crazy, wouldn't he?"

This analogy, he admits, may sound "too ridiculous" to the reader—*but is it really?* If the alcoholic were to substitute his failed attempts to quit drinking with the jaywalker's problems, "the illustration would fit us exactly. However intelligent we may have been in other respects, where alcohol has been involved we have been strangely insane. It's strong language—but isn't it true?"

Although it had not yet been written, the point being made here is that the alcoholic is basically insane in regard to the first drink and in desperate need of the sanity promised in the Second Step: "Came to believe that a Power greater than ourselves could restore us to sanity." The insanity that step was designed to relieve is to be found exactly here—in the split second when, while still absolutely sober, the "peculiar mental twist" comes into play and convinces the alcoholic that it is perfectly reasonable for him to take that first drink.

As a graphic example of this strange mental deficiency, Bill now presents his final story, this one about Fred,[*] the successful businessman who, much to his surprise, finds himself hospitalized with "a bad case of the jitters" as a result of his drinking. A bit depressed about this embarrassing situation, he resolves to quit drinking completely, never thinking he might not be able to do so. Fred would just "not believe himself an alcoholic, much less accept a spiritual remedy for his problem." He was completely confident he could resolve his current dilemma all by himself.

Fred left the hospital and was successful with his no-drinking plan for some time and quite "frankly did not believe it would be possible for [him] to drink again." But he did drink again; and the circumstances forced him to accept A.A.'s hypothesis that there is a "subtle insanity which precedes the first drink"—a moment of irrationality that overrides every level of self-confidence, self-knowledge, and willpower. Here was a man who was "absolutely convinced he had to stop drinking, who had no excuse for drinking, who exhibited splendid judgment and determination in all his other concerns, yet was flat on his back nevertheless."

According to Fred's own account, he was on a business trip to Washington; it was "the end of a perfect day" and there was "not a cloud on the horizon." He was on his way to dinner when "as I crossed the threshold of the dining room, the thought came to mind it would be nice to have a couple of cocktails with dinner. That was all. Nothing more." Fred ordered a drink and then later another and yet another, resulting in a drunken spree lasting several days. How did this happen?

"As soon as I regained my ability to think, I went carefully over that evening in Washington. Not only had I been off guard, I had made no fight whatever against that first drink. This time I had not thought of the consequences at all. I had commenced to drink as carelessly as though the cocktails were ginger ale." How to explain this chain of events other than to say that best intentions, self-awareness and the firmest resolve were all discarded in a moment that could only be described as one of those "strange mental blank spots" that plague the real alcoholic and takes him directly back to drinking in spite of all his promises—whether made to himself or to others.

Surrendering to the truth of his powerlessness over alcohol, Fred agreed to accept the spiritual answer and the program of action offered by A.A. and, like so many others who faithfully followed that program, he became sober and was able to stay that way.

Wilson concludes the chapter with a ringing endorsement of A.A.'s conclusions regarding the first drink which is offered by a staff member of a world-renown hospital,[**] followed by a short paragraph hammering home the two most important points in this chapter (and serving as an introduction to the next): "Once more: the alcoholic at certain times has no effective mental defense against the first drink. Except

---

[*]   Fred is generally presumed to be Harry Brick who got sober in June 1938 (see, for instance, Dodd, *The Authors*, pp. 13–14). Brick's story, "A Different Slant," appears on pp. 252 – 53 of the first edition of *Alcoholics Anonymous*.

[**]   Although this sounds very much like something Dr. Silkworth might have said, this quote has been attributed to Dr. Percy Poliak of Bellevue Hospital in New York City by several students of A.A. history (see, for instance, AAHistoryLovers message 10,238: https://groups.yahoo.com/neo/groups/AAHistoryLovers/conversations/messages/10238). Dr. Poliak (sometimes erroneously called "Pollick") was identified in *AACOA* (p. 88) as "a psychiatrist who had been impressed with A.A. as he had seen it at work in Bellevue Hospital in New York."

in a few rare cases, neither he nor any other human being can provide such a defense. His defense must come from a higher Power."

The time had now come for a much fuller discussion on the delicate subject of belief in God.

A Power Greater Than Ourselves

The essence of the next chapter Bill wrote is neatly captured in the later wording of the Second Step: "Came to believe that a Power greater than ourselves could restore us to sanity;" this is the only way the alcoholic can overcome the insanity of the first drink. But rather than just bluntly stating the fact that one hundred men had come to believe and thereby been able to stop drinking, Wilson needed to present some persuasive arguments to convince an active alcoholic that he could and should join them in their beliefs about the power of God.

Bill had told Bob Smith he didn't much care for the first draft of "We Agnostics," claiming he thought it was "too preachy" and he felt that it was "rather disconnected." Given his almost impossible task, this is completely understandable; how could he even begin to make an effective argument for the necessary belief in God *without* sounding like a Sunday school preacher? No wonder he suggested to Bob that perhaps it "might better be done . . . in the form of a dialogue between one of our former agnostics and a tough minded bird lying in a hospital bed."[11] Presenting arguments for the existence of God as part of a bedside conversation would have sounded much less like a church sermon and might have proved more appealing to non-believers, but as far as we know, Bill never went down that more literary road.

Whatever he wrote, Wilson knew he needed to do everything in his power to avoid the reaction expected from an alcoholic who had just been told that God was a necessary part in this solution: "Oh, so that's what it is, I'm so disappointed, I had begun to think [you] fellows knew what [you] were talking about."[12] Above all else, Bill wanted the reader to keep an open mind and to engage in an exploration of what he called "the God idea." His worst fear was that the agnostic or atheist would reach this point in the book and then just slam it shut, effectively closing off any further discussion.

Wilson tried to make this inclusive point clear from the very beginning by choosing a collegial title of "We Agnostics" for this chapter. He could have just as easily called it "The Agnostic" or "You Agnostics" or even something like "The Agnostic's Dilemma"—all of which would have immediately set up a confrontational scenario. Instead, Bill quickly makes two specific references to the "We" of his title by noting that originally about half of the Fellowship had been strangers to any sort of spiritual experience and, more specifically, that "something like fifty of us thought we were atheists or agnostics" when first introduced to the Fellowship.[13] But even these committed non-believers soon realized the choice they faced was to either "be doomed to an alcoholic hell or be 'saved.'" These two harsh options, Wilson admits, are not always easy to face, but however much agnostic members may have tried to avoid the

God issue, "after a while we had to face the fact that we must find a spiritual basis of life—or else"—the "or else" being a return to drinking and a life that could only be characterized as an alcoholic hell.

Having hopefully established some rapport with the non-believing reader, Bill now referred back to the drinker's lack of power regarding the first drink, summing up the essence of his position—and the critical challenge presently facing the atheist or agnostic in eight short sentences:

> Lack of power, that was our dilemma. We had to find a power by which we could live, and it had to be A Power Greater Than Ourselves. Obviously. But where and how were we to find this Power?

> Well, that's exactly what this book is about. Its main object is to enable you to find a Power greater than yourself, which will solve your problem. That means we have written a book which we believe to be spiritual as well as moral. And it means, of course, that we are going to talk about God.

God as We Understand Him

When writing this chapter Bill was trying to be as open-ended as possible in his talk about the essential "spiritual experience" and the need for a "spiritual basis of life", and he emphasized that liberal approach throughout by using phrases like "A Power Greater Than Ourselves" and "your own conception of God" and even "God, as you understand Him." But many contemporary A.A. readers completely miss the point Wilson was trying to make in "We Agnostics" because they read the chapter from a twenty-first-century perspective, one which incorporates the tremendous liberalization the phrase "God as we understand Him" has gone through during A.A.'s subsequent history and development. This later and much greater flexibility regarding "God as we understand Him" allows some alcoholics to understand God as a "Group Of Drunks," or "Good Orderly Direction," or the "Gift Of Desperation," or even the "Great Out Doors." While this widely expanded approach has been a boon to the growing membership of Alcoholics Anonymous, it goes far beyond anything Bill Wilson ever intended when he wrote "We Agnostics" in September of 1938.

Today's more liberal contemporary understandings of "God as we understand Him" are put forward under the misconception that this level of freedom of choice was exactly what Bill Wilson meant when he used those open-ended phrases in "We Agnostics." It wasn't. Instead, Bill had two fundamental and very restrictive presumptions that informed all of his writing in this chapter, presumptions that twenty-first-century A.A. readers so easily fail to notice because of their own current expectations of the text.

Spiritual Means Belief in a Personal God

The first of these is Wilson's belief in the complementary equations that "spiritual = God" and "God = spiritual." Bill makes it clear in the first six paragraphs of this chapter that there is absolutely no avenue for accessing the spiritual other than through a belief in God. This strict equivalency rejects out-of-hand every other avenue for having a spiritual experience along with any alternate path for discovering a spiritual basis for life. While such an exclusive position is far from today's more liberal attitudes in A.A., it is completely consistent with Bill Wilson's upbringing, with the beliefs and values of the earliest members of the Fellowship, and is perfectly aligned with 1930s American culture (which was far more religious than it is today). More open conceptions of "God" and "spiritual" that were adopted later must therefore be firmly set aside in order to reach a proper understanding of what Wilson was actually saying when he first wrote this chapter.

Bill's second fundamental presumption lies buried within his claim that readers can believe in any conception of God they might like. What is understood in that claim, but never explicitly stated, is that this new belief must be in any *providential* God you want to believe in—a God to whom you can pray, with whom you can make conscious contact, and on whom you can absolutely rely for the help needed to avoid the first drink. Bill offers an open-ended invitation for alcoholics to believe in "a Supreme Being" or "an All Powerful, Guiding, Creative Intelligence" (along with a number of other Impressively Capitalized Titles), but never, for instance, does he offer as an object of belief the God of the Deists—who believe He created the universe and then removed Himself from the realm of human affairs—or any of the other less involved, less accessible conceptions of divinity that have been suggested over the millennia by religious teachers, mystics, and philosophers.

If you want to get sober, you must align yourself with a *personal* God with whom you can have a *personal* relationship. There is no other option.* Again, Bill was not being duplicitous here; this fundamental assumption was not only what had saved his own life,** it was the foundational, common currency of belief throughout the Fellowship at that time as well as for religious people across the country. Wilson didn't feel he needed to be explicit about this point when talking about "the God idea"; it was simply a given in the context of that time and place and, in addition, completely obvious from the amount of direct help the alcoholic would need from this Supreme Being.

If you want to stop drinking, you must find a spiritual basis of life, and that spiritual basis can only be found by believing in a Supreme Being with whom you can establish a personal relationship.

---

* This was stated much more explicitly in a Chicago pamphlet written in 1940 or 1941 (the words "spiritual experience" still appear in their version of the Twelfth Step): "All that is required is a recognition of a Supreme Being which would help us were He sincerely petitioned." (available online at http://silkworth.net/aahistory/impressions.html - retrieved September 28, 2015).

** See, for instance, the mid-1938 version of "Bill's Story:" "In a power greater than myself I had always believed. I had often pondered these things. I was not an atheist . . . I had little doubt that a mighty purpose and rhythm underlay all. How could there be so much of precise and immutable law, and no intelligence? I simply had to believe in a Spirit of the Universe, which knew neither time nor limitation. But that was as far as I had gone. With preachers, and the world's religions, I parted right there. When they talked of a God personal to me, which was love, superhuman strength and direction, I became irritated, and my mind snapped shut against such theory . . . But my friend sat before me, and he made the point blank declaration that God had done for him what he could not do for himself . . . In effect he had been raised from the dead; suddenly taken from the scrap-heap to a level of life better than the best he had ever known . . . That floored me. It began to look as though religious people were right, after all. Here was something at work in a human heart which had done the impossible. My ideas about miracles were drastically revised right then . . ." (GSO, Box 59, 1938, Folder B, First Two Chapters of the Proposed Book; Trust Indenture, Documents 1938-53 to 1938-75, p. 20).

On Being Willing to Believe

Noting that while most active alcoholics think the God idea is best ignored or rejected out-of-hand for a variety of reasons, Bill then launched into an eight-paragraph 'soft sell' of that idea by stating and restating the cornerstone in his argument, namely that very little is required to start your journey on this road to belief. There is absolutely no requirement to accept anyone else's conception of God; your own conception "however inadequate, [is] sufficient to make the approach." "The Realm of the Spirit is broad, roomy, all inclusive; never exclusive or forbidding. It is open, we believe, to all men" and all we are asking is that you "lay aside prejudice and express even a willingness to believe in a Power greater than" yourself. He all but begs the reader not to "let any prejudice you may have against spiritual terms deter you from honestly asking yourself what they mean to you." Instead:

> You need ask yourself but one short question. "Do I now believe, or am I even willing to believe, that there is a Power greater than myself?" As soon as a man can say that he does believe, or is willing to believe, we emphatically assure him that he is on his way. It has been repeatedly proven among us that upon this simple cornerstone a wonderfully effective spiritual structure can be built.

The double mention here of being "willing to believe" is striking and likely evidence that Wilson had read William James's book, *The Will to Believe,* and then embraced its central point. On the book's first page, James characterized his first chapter as a "an essay in justification *of* faith, a defense of our right to adopt a believing attitude in religious matters, in spite of the fact that our merely logical intellect may not have been coerced."[14] The right to simply adopt a belief (rather than having to prove it logically) was a foundational principle of William James's philosophy and it is the central argument Bill Wilson presents to his skeptical readers in "We Agnostics."

Once again stressing the fellowship of unbelievers, Bill notes that despite a lifetime of "obstinacy, sensitiveness, and unreasoning prejudice," many A.A. members have found that when "faced with alcoholic destruction, we soon became . . . open minded on spiritual matters . . . In this respect, alcohol was a great persuader" allowing us to finally admit there just might be a Power greater than ourselves, one who could make it possible for us to lead an entirely new, alcohol-free life.

Belief in God Is an Idea That Works!

Wilson now arrives at the most challenging part of the chapter—his arguments for a belief in God. Here was a task that had stymied great minds for millennia, but Bill makes it clear he is not intimidated by that fact: "The reader may still ask why he should believe in a Power greater than himself. We think there are good reasons. Let us look at some of them." He then launched into a series of arguments—actually more pragmatic demonstrations than logical arguments—that, despite being somewhat disjointed, exhibit a solid understanding of his audience and how he might best gain their confidence and agreement.

Wilson begins by appealing to the scientifically minded, noting the ease with which people accept current scientific theories (such as electricity), so long as they are "firmly grounded in fact." But how do we get to that point of ready acceptance? We get there, he says, by beginning "with a reasonable assumption as a starting point," explaining that "nowadays, [everybody] believes in scores of assumptions for which there is good evidence, but no perfect visual proof." To demonstrate this concept, Bill invites the reader to consider "the prosaic steel girder", which according to science is really just "a mass of electrons whirling around each other at incredible speed." Things are obviously not always what they seem on the surface and "outward appearances are not inward reality at all." Clearly, there are many things we believe in, but for which we have no real visual proof.

So just as there are these precise laws of science that "hold true throughout the material world"—in spite of what our senses may tell us—could there not also be a spiritual element, "an All Powerful, Guiding, Creative Intelligence," underlying and supporting this material world? Bill contends that, actually, when you think about it, to believe anything less would be to join forces with those who claim "that life originated out of nothing, means nothing, and proceeds nowhere." He asks, isn't it the height of intellectual arrogance to believe that our senses and our human minds are "the last word, the alpha and the omega, the beginning and end of all"?

Dramatically shifting gears, Bill now makes a series of practical arguments that prove him to be an apt student of William James's pragmatism—the claim that the truth of any proposition is to be found in the results it produces. While the skeptic spends his time "cynically dissecting spiritual beliefs and practices," he completely ignores the fact that "people of faith have a logical idea of what life is all about" and are living lives that demonstrate "a degree of stability, happiness and usefulness which we should have sought ourselves." The truth is that we agnostics "never gave the spiritual side of life a fair hearing."

Quoting the 1928 presidential candidate Alfred E. Smith, Bill invites the reader to "look at the record"[15] and to carefully note that "one hundred men and women . . . have come to believe in a Power greater than themselves" and thereby had "a revolutionary change in their way of living and thinking." He then turns this impressive record into a direct challenge: "When one hundred people, much like you, are able to say that consciousness of the Presence of God is today the most important fact of their lives, they present a powerful reason why you too should have faith."

Beyond this, the larger record that Wilson wants the reader to examine includes historical figures who have succeeded in the face of "superstition, tradition, and all sorts of fixed ideas;" people like Columbus, Galileo and, his favorite example, the Wright brothers. Why, in just thirty years, he says, "the conquest of the air is almost an old story" and today many people consider the prospect of exploring "the moon by means of a rocket" inevitable.* Isn't it clear, he says, from all of these examples that "the spirit of modern scientific inquiry, research and invention" relies upon "the ease with which we discard old ideas for new, by the complete readiness with which we throw away the theory or gadget which does not work for something new which does." Bill is making the point that it is exactly this kind of open-mindedness that has been the key and indispensable ingredient for the progress made in science over the past few centuries.

For alcoholics, he says, belief in God is exactly like that: It is an idea that works, while our old ideas did not. He asks: Doesn't it make sense that we apply the same ease with which we change our mind in scientific matters to our stubborn doubts about the existence and the power of God? "We agnostics and atheists were sticking to the idea that self-sufficiency would solve our problems [but] when others showed us that 'God-sufficiency' worked for them, we began to feel like those who had insisted the Wrights would never fly."

"Logic," Bill says, "is great stuff. We liked it" and therefore "we are at pains to tell [you] why we think our present faith is reasonable, why we think it more sane and logical to believe than not to believe, why we say our former thinking was soft and mushy when we threw up our hands in doubt", saying we just couldn't decide one way or the other about the existence of God. But soft and mushy thinking was no longer an option for us. We had become "alcoholics, crushed by the self-imposed crisis we could not postpone or evade" and find that now we have no choice but to "fearlessly face the proposition that either God is everything or else He is nothing. God either is, or He isn't."

A Choice Must Be Made

At this crucial point, Bill throws down the gauntlet and dramatically demands of the reader: "What is your choice to be?"

Having stated categorically that the present faith in God by one hundred recovered alcoholics was "reasonable . . . sane and logical," Wilson now does his best to justify that claim. "Arrived at this point, we were squarely confronted with the question of faith" and we could no longer "duck the issue." But for all his earlier bravado about looking at the good reasons for belief, Bill abandons his direct prose style here and begins the argument for faith by painting a flowery image of "the Bridge of Reason" leading to "the desired shore of faith" where "friendly hands are stretched out" welcoming those with "flagging spirits" to "the promise of the New Land." Despite this glowing scene, he admits that, having come this far, many agnostics find that they just cannot abandon their absolute faith in "the God of Reason" and take the final "step ashore" to the "New Land" of faith in God.

Wilson then takes this dilemma and turns it on its head, asking those who are reluctant to take this final step if their clinging to "the God of Reason" isn't also "a certain kind of faith? For did we not believe in our own reasoning? Did we not have confidence in our ability to think? What was that but a sort of faith?" He then

---

* It is worth noting that despite the obvious boldness of this statement, Wilson was historically closer to the 1969 moon landing (just thirty-one years in the future) than he was to the Wright brother's first flight at Kitty Hawk (which had occurred thirty-five years earlier in 1903).

catalogues a number of other kinds of faith to be found in everyone's life; not only faith in Reason but also faith in "people, sentiments, money and ourselves" along with a sense of worship in relation to Nature and our feelings for loved ones. "It is impossible," he claims, "to say we had no capacity for faith, or love, or worship. In one form or another we have been living by faith and little else."

> Hence, we saw that reason isn't everything. Neither is reason, as most of us used it, entirely dependable, though it emanate from our best minds. What about people who proved that man could never fly?

> Yet we had been seeing another kind of flight, a spiritual liberation from this world, people who rose above their problems. They said God made these things possible, and we only smiled. We had seen spiritual release, but liked to tell ourselves it wasn't true.

> Actually we were fooling ourselves, for deep down in every man, woman, and child, is the fundamental idea of God. It may be obscured by calamity, by pomp, by worship of other things, but in some form or other it is there.

In recapping this long, argumentative section, Bill notes that despite all his best efforts to convince the agnostic, "we can only clear the ground a bit for you." But, he says, if you are open-minded and pay careful attention to "our testimony" on this issue, it may allow you to "sweep away prejudice," enable you "to think honestly" and encourage you "to search diligently within yourself . . . With this attitude you cannot fail. The consciousness that you do believe is sure to come to you."

But Bill wasn't done yet. Not completely trusting in all he had written so far, he presents his final argument for belief, the story of Fitz Mayo (identified here only as someone who will appear later in the book): a man whose "story is so interesting that some if it should be told now." Despite a deeply religious upbringing, Fitz had rejected God and fallen into an alcoholic way of life filled with nothing but "trouble and frustration." Finding himself in a drying-out hospital, he was "approached by an alcoholic who had known a spiritual experience," but this encounter only enraged him:

> Our friend's gorge rose as he bitterly cried out: "If there is a God, He certainly hasn't done anything for me." But later, alone in his room, he asked himself this question: "Is it possible that all the religious people I have known are wrong?" While pondering the answer, he felt as though he lived in hell. Then, like a thunderbolt, a great thought came. It crowded out all else:

> "WHO ARE YOU TO SAY THERE IS NO GOD?"

> This man recounts that he tumbled out of bed to his knees. In a few seconds he was overwhelmed by a conviction of the Presence of God . . . He had stepped from bridge to shore. For the first time, he lived in conscious companionship with his Creator.

On that night, three years ago, this man's "alcoholic problem was taken away" and it has never returned:

> God had restored his sanity.

> Even so has God restored us all to our right minds. To this man, the Revelation was sudden. Some of us grow into it more slowly. But He has come to all who have honestly sought Him.

> Draw near to Him and He will disclose Himself to you![16]

According to Wilson, this is the only hope you have if you want to successfully avoid that treacherous first drink.

Bill as the Sole Author

Many modern readers have been critical of the writing in this chapter, so a few words about its composition may be helpful.

Wilson's authorship of the Big Book has been challenged—most famously by himself—but it is clear from everything he writes during this time that, at this point, he was *the* writer. There is no mention whatsoever in contemporary records of the much touted collaborative editing process (which did, to some degree, occur later). In fact, all the 1938 evidence supports Bill Wilson as being the sole author of these chapters. His writing was, however, being criticized and critiqued by Hank Parkhurst and Ruth Hock, the two people who were constantly present as he dictated the book at their Honor Dealers office in Newark. In what proved to be a less than fruitful attempt to help with the book, both Ruth and Hank took a semester's worth of short story writing classes at New York University at this time[17]* and, in those classes, they learned just enough that "they were constantly trying to advise" Bill on how he might improve his prose style. This interference did not sit particularly well with Wilson, who noted bluntly that, in this regard, he "didn't go for Hank's advice very much."[18]

Given this acknowledgment of Parkhurst's unsolicited advice, it is probable that it was Hank's suggestion that the chapter "We Agnostics" might be improved if Bill would just recast the whole thing "in the form of a dialogue between one of our former agnostics and a tough minded bird lying in a hospital bed."[19] This interesting suggestion sounds much more like the ambitious (and recently schooled) Hank Parkhurst than anything Bill Wilson would have come up with on his own. Hank was certainly interested in the creative side of the writing project as can plainly be seen in the flamboyant stream-of-consciousness style he adopted when writing his own story, "The Unbeliever," for the Big Book:

> I know that history Doc . . . how the spiral tightens . . . a drink . . .
> unconscious . . . awake . . . drink . . . unconscious . . . poured into
> the hospital . . . suffer the agonies of hell . . . the shakes . . . thoughts

---

* It is also possible that these short story classes were at the famous School of Journalism at Columbia where Tom Uzzell—who later edited the Big Book—was known to have taught. A.A. lore claims that Uzzell taught at NYU when, in fact, he was only known to have been on the faculty of Columbia University. Ruth's assertion here could be a similar error.

running wild . . . brain unleashed . . . engine without a governor. But hell Doc, I don't want to drink! I've got one of the stubbornest will powers known in business. I stick at things. I get them done. I've stuck on the wagon for months. And not been bothered by it . . . and then suddenly, incomprehensibly, an empty glass in my hand and another spiral started. How did the Doc explain that one? He couldn't.[20*]

Once again we have these two powerfully opinionated men disagreeing on what should and shouldn't be put in the book. But, as Wilson said at this time (in a slightly different context), he occupied "a position of considerable authority in this work"[21] and since he "didn't go for Hank's advice very much,"[22] he just continued to compose the book in the way he thought best.

The New Chapters Go to Dr. Bob

In addition to Hank Parkhurst, there was Dr. Bob's opinion to be considered, and Bill sent these two new chapters off to him on September 27 with the following comments:

> The chapter, "More About Alcoholism," seems to meet with general approval. See if you can think of some other points which should have been covered in it. The chapter, "We Agnostics," I do not like so much. It is still "too preachy" and rather disconnected. It might better be done on an entirely different basis. In the form of a dialogue between one of our former agnostics and a tough minded bird lying in a hospital bed. What do you think? Perhaps it would be well not to show everybody these chapters, except where you think people can contribute some new ideas which can be incorporated in the final write.[23]

Besides Bill's candid comments on his uncertainty about the writing process, this letter makes it clear that the collaborative team writing later claimed to have taken place throughout the entire creation process for the Big Book was not yet operational. He does mention that "More About Alcoholism" had met with general approval in New York, but as later testimony will show, he meant that everyone simply agreed with it without offering any serious comments or criticism.

Nor did the Akron people make any substantive critiques or contributions to these chapters. As we shall see in much more detail in Chapter Sixteen, "the chapters of the book were sent to [Dr. Bob Smith] for debate and inspection out there [but] he never passed them around very much, merely writing me saying he thought they were all right."[24]

Whatever faults and problems may be found in "More About Alcoholism" and "We Agnostics" today, they were the work of William G. Wilson and no one else. It was from start to finish his own creation.

---

* Ruth Hock later noted that Hank's story was written in this style because of what he had learned at the "short story courses" they took at this time (Ruth Hock's 1978 Interview with Niles Peebles, GSO, CD 876, Track 1, 18:15 to 18:45).

CHAPTER FIFTEEN

The One Hundred Men Corporation

~October 1938~

Albert Scott's insistence that A.A. must become self-supporting through mandatory weekly contributions before any other solicitations of the rich—especially of Mr. John D. Rockefeller Jr.—called for a strong response. The very next day, Thursday, September 29, Bill and Hank met with Frank Amos to formulate an alternate plan of action. The three men carefully crafted, reviewed, and then edited their response before it was mailed off to Scott on Tuesday, October 4. Amos concluded this letter with six recommendations he wholeheartedly approved, the first three and most important of which were: (1) that the four Rockefeller men "endeavor at once to raise $10,000;" (2) that "we ascertain what advance we can get from a publisher on the book [that] might be sufficient for Wilson's bare expenses while writing it;" and (3) that "Parkhurst continue until November 1 to try and secure contributions."[1]

Regarding the first recommendation, the Rockefeller contingent did make at least some fundraising efforts during this time, but once again they proved to be completely unsuccessful and raised no new monies to support the work.* Wilson was discouraged by these failures, at one point complaining to Amos:

> I talked to Chipman over a week ago [and] he said they would do the best they could but he had no need to see me. Neither have we heard from Mr. Scott about the prospect he had in mind . . . [it is] sad that our personal

---

* The only preserved records of any effort in this direction are a denial letter sent to Frank Amos by the Institute of Public Administration (Luther Gulick to Frank B. Amos, October 7, 1938; GSO, Box 59, Folder D.2, Document 13) and Willard Richardson's solicitation of Mrs. E. L. Ballard on November 3 (GSO, Box 59, Folder B[1], Document 1938-175) and the subsequent submission of an application for assistance to the Davella Mills Foundation (a group with which Mrs. Ballard was associated). However, according to the director of the Foundation, that request "was brought to the attention of our Trustees without seeming to arouse any interest on their part" (Stanley Hutchinson to Willard S. Richardson, December 28, 1938, GSO, Box 59, Folder B[1], Document 1938-192).

losses do not concern the Trustees but we think they should [concern them] because our financial wellbeing has a direct bearing on the work and Hank's presence in the picture has a very large bearing on the success of the book and its aftermath.[2]

At this point, Bill had at least temporarily abandoned his earlier hopes that the Rockefeller connection would prove to be the gateway to large contributions and the Alcoholic Foundation would be "a great receptacle for the rich to deposit their money in."[3] He was finally beginning to concede to himself that this was just not going to happen—at least not at any time in the near future—and he actively began to consider any other option which might bring some ready cash into their empty check books.

It is important to note that in Amos's third proposal Hank Parkhurst was considered to be the point man for approaching the rich and securing contributions. As Wilson had noted just a few days earlier, Hank was "now doing a great deal of [their] efforts to raise money"[4] and this was a position he had held at least since the previous July when Bill went south to collect testimonials for the new movement. In their honest pursuit of this suggestion, both Wilson and Parkhurst continued working their own list of promising new contacts, with Hank making direct appeals while Bill wrote solicitation letters.[5] But, once again, their best efforts produced nothing. There was no money coming in from any new outside sources and now, more than ever, they seemed to be completely on their own.

Finding a Publisher for the Book

This left only Amos's second substantive recommendation as a possible source of ready cash, namely that they abandon the idea of publishing the book themselves[6] and investigate the possibility of finding a publisher who would give them an advance on the proposed work. Fortunately, Frank had a friend named Eugene Exman who was the Religious Editor at Harper and Brothers, the prestigious New York publishing house, and he enthusiastically suggested to Bill that "perhaps he would be interested in your new book. Why don't you go down there and show him the few chapters you have done? I'll fix it up for you."[7] Frank quickly set up an appointment for Bill and Hank and the two men "got there in a hurry,"[8] meeting with Exman in his office either on Friday, September 30 or sometime during the first few days of October.[*] Bill brought copies of "There Is A Solution" and his own story along with them to this important meeting.

---

[*] Over the years, Bill Wilson claimed a wide variety of contradictory dates (for instance: July, August, September, late summer & early fall) for this meeting with Exman: "at the Trustee's meeting, July 1938, Frank Amos suggested . . ." (Bill Wilson to Jack Alexander, December 13, 1949: GSO, Box 29, Folder 17.1, AA History: Miscellaneous Materials, p. 2), "One day, probably in August 1938, Frank Amos said . . ." ("How the Book Alcoholics Anonymous Came About," in *The Book That Started It All*, p. 210), "at a meeting around September 1st, 1938 . . ." (AA Main Events, 1938, Point 15), "it then being late summer of 1938 . . ." (Bill Wilson speaking in Atlanta, GA, July 14, 1951, GSO, CD, BW115) and "at one of those meetings in the early fall of 1938 . . ." (*AACOA*, p. 153)—to note just five different dates. Lois was much more specific, but no more accurate, claiming that Bill met with Exman on Tuesday, September 6, 1938 (Lois's Important Dates 1937-1945, StSt 203, Box 35, Folder 4). None of these dates are correct. Given the amount of financial details Bill presented in his "sheep and goats' letter of September 26, most especially with all of the information on their best source of potential money—the article to be published in *This Week* magazine—it is inconceivable that he would not have mentioned the fact that Eugene Exman of Harper had offered him a $1,500 advance on the book if that had already occurred. Therefore, that meeting must necessarily have followed the September 26 letter and also

The Proposal to Harper Is Accepted

Bill was nervous about showing these two chapters to a professional publisher and, painfully aware that he had never written anything like this before, he approached this meeting with considerable "trepidation."[9] But his fears proved to be groundless. After the two men provided Exman with a bit of background on who they were and recounted some of their successes over the past three years, the two chapters were dutifully handed over. To Wilson's surprise and extreme relief, Gene Exman thoughtfully scanned[10] them and then showed immediate interest[11] in what he was reading. "Why Mr. Wilson," he said, this is "rather interesting. Could you do a whole book like this?" Bill claims he was shaking when asked that question, but he "lied valiantly and said, 'Of course, of course.'"[12] Exman next wondered how long it would take for him to finish such a book and Bill—erring on the side of caution—suggested it might be nine or ten months before he would be able to deliver a finished manuscript.[13] Exman was delighted with this and suggested they come back again later after he had a chance to present the idea of publishing their book to Cass Canfield, the president of Harper and Brothers.[14]

On their next visit, Eugene Exman announced he had excellent news: Harper was definitely interested in publishing their book and they would be happy to offer a $1,500 advance against future royalties of 10 percent on all sales.[15] Exman explained this advance "would be deducted from your account when the book is finished in 1939"[16] and they would need to sell 5,000 copies of the book before the advance would be paid back in full.[17] (Note this means that Harper was projecting a $3 list price for the book.) This was a generous offer for a first-time author, one which Exman, having heard of their current financial difficulties from his friend Amos, hoped "would help things along"[18] and make it possible for Wilson to devote himself exclusively to finishing the book.

Hearing this, Wilson's immediate reaction was "pretty exciting."[19] "It made me feel like I was an author or something,"[20] he said, and, typical of Bill, he found himself "in the clouds."[21] After all, it was exhilarating "to know that a firm like Harper wanted the book and that an editor of Gene's caliber believed it was going to be good."[22] The two men immediately set off for Frank Amos's office to tell him about the offer and Bill was delighted "to see Frank's face light up as he heard the news,"[23] this in spite of the fact that Wilson had already begun to have serious doubts about the wisdom of accepting Harper's offer.

Hank Convinces Bill to Self-Publish

Wilson's elation had actually begun to fade shortly after they left the meeting with Eugene Exman as Hank Parkhurst immediately began to revisit all of his objections to having someone else publish their book. He had been curious to learn Harper's evaluation of the book's potential, but as far back as May, Hank had been insisting they

---

came after they had met with Frank Amos on September 29 to plan their response to Albert Scott during which the first mention was made of a possible publisher's advance on the proposed book. It is likely that Amos made the appointment for Wilson and Parkhurst shortly after this meeting, but scheduled it for some time before he left on his three-week vacation on Friday, October 7. This would place their first appointment with Exman either on Friday, September 30 or during the first few business days of the following week.

should maintain control of their most important written asset and he had not changed his mind on this critical point since then. Harper and Brothers' offer only reinforced and confirmed his belief that they should publish the book themselves; in fact, he was "vigorously opposed"[24] to giving up control and turning their manuscript over to a professional publishing house.* As usual, Hank had a laundry list of arguments he felt justified his position and he presented them in the most forceful way possible.

What, he said, if this book "should prove to be the main textbook of A.A., why would we want our main means of propagation in the hands of someone else? Shouldn't we control this thing?"[25] And besides, he contended that if a fine publisher like Harper thinks they can easily sell 5,000 copies of this book, he and Bill shouldn't have to settle for a paltry royalty of thirty cents on each copy when much more profit could be made on every single book by doing the printing and publishing themselves. In addition, this $1,500 may be enough to keep the author solvent for the next six months, but it provides nothing for the rest of them, not to mention the expenses involved in maintaining the office. To support their entire operation for six months, he noted, would require four times what Harper is offering.[26] Finally, and most important, he pointed out that the royalty check would be completely spent by the time the book came out and there would be no further money from the publisher until substantially more than 5,000 copies had been sold. So, how would they pay for the people and the facilities needed to respond to the "thousands of cries for help from alcoholics and their families" that would surely pour in once the book was published and began to receive favorable publicity?[27]

Individually these were persuasive arguments, but taken together they were unassailable, a fact Bill Wilson found both impressive and depressing. At this point he was forced to admit they had to publish this book themselves, but at the same time, he had no idea how they could go about doing that and was equally sure the Rockefeller trustees would not be in favor of turning down this windfall of $1,500. As one might expect, Hank Parkhurst saw no particular problem with either of these two difficulties.

A Break with the Trustees

When they told Amos and Richardson about the offered $1,500 advance, Bill says the two men "smiled happily as they heard the details . . . it was the first ray of hope [they] had seen in months" and they were "unanimous in their opinion that the Harper deal was the answer" to their problems and the best way to resolve their current critical lack of money.[28] Bill had been afraid of this response and, although he was not anxious to go against the advice of these two stalwart supporters ("to flatly disagree with these wonderful friends," he said "was the toughest possible assignment"[29]), he felt he had no other choice but to do exactly that.

Reluctantly, Bill and Hank shared with these two men their grave reservations about the long-term consequences of accepting Harper's offer and carefully recounted each of their objections with all the persuasive force and conviction they could muster. This

---

* Had Harper acquired the book, it is interesting to speculate on how many printings and editions would have been published before they insisted on major revisions to the text—either to promote increased sales or to update the book so that it more accurately reflected the changes in American culture and in Alcoholics Anonymous itself.

was an argument they desperately wanted to win, but as they feared, neither Amos nor Richardson were particularly impressed with their reasoning and they overrode them by constantly coming back to their primary objection:[30] "Why, this will never work," they said. It just "can't be done. Authors never publish books and get away with it . . . you are on the wrong track."[31] Wilson claims he and Parkhurst then "politely, but pointedly, reminded them there was no money in the Foundation" and, given that fact, they saw no reason why they should simply "hand this newcoming book" over to Harper rather than holding on to the ownership and control themselves.[32] These could not have been particularly pleasant meetings and when everyone had finally had their say, they "ended on a dismal note. We were a hung jury [and] no conclusion or verdict was reached."[33]*

Wilson was convinced they should refuse the Harper offer, but he wasn't above second-guessing himself when faced with such a momentous decision and he finally decided to get an expert opinion from the only man he knew with extensive experience in this area—Harper editor Eugene Exman.

> Still much disturbed about the whole business, I went back to Gene Exman and frankly explained to him what was about to happen. To my utter amazement, he agreed, quite contrary to his own interest, that a society like ours ought to control and publish its own literature. Moreover, he felt that very possibly we could do this with success.[34]

This bit of unexpected advice from Exman "did not register at all when it was transmitted to the Trustees,"[35] and Wilson must have found his inability to change their minds extremely frustrating. Despite the fact that this agreement with their plan came from a reliable and authoritative source, the "Trustees stood pat"[36] and refused to agree with Bill's and Hank's decision to self-publish the book. Wilson and Parkhurst had recently disagreed with Albert Scott over his insistence that they collect mandatory dues at each A.A. meeting, and now they found themselves on the other side of the fence in this all-important argument with Amos and Richardson. It was an unexpected and disconcerting reversal for everyone.

A little more than two weeks earlier, Bill had written, "though we are grateful that we have you gentlemen to go to, we do not want to cast too much responsibility on the shoulders of our ever-willing Trustees."[37] As he later noted, the primary impact of Eugene Exman's advice had been to "give Henry and me the kind of encouragement we so much needed"[38] and the two men now felt they had no choice but to assume the burden of those responsibilities themselves, signaling an even greater estrangement from the Rockefeller contingent. This was an outcome no one would have predicted on September 26 when Bill had so carefully crafted his dramatic 'sheep and goats' letter detailing the severity of their current financial situation and pointedly challenging the trustees to come up with a workable solution. Their growing alienation from

---

* While telling this and other stories about the last three months of 1938, Bill Wilson consistently claimed that these (and similar) exchanges occurred during formal meetings of the Alcoholic Foundation. There are, however, no records or minutes of any meeting being held between the third meeting on September 23 and the fourth, which was held four months later on January 18, 1939. Given that there were really only two non-alcoholic trustees (the lawyer, John Wood, never attended a meeting after the formalization of the paperwork), Bill's and Hank's meetings with these two men were on a one-on-one basis rather than occurring within the format of a formal trustee meeting.

Rockefeller's friends was surely the last thing Wilson would have predicted as an outcome when he threw down the gauntlet in that letter, intending more than anything else to move Albert Scott in the direction of approaching John D. Rockefeller Jr. for yet another substantial contribution.

Instead, they now found themselves completely rejecting these men's considered advice and, in fact, setting off on a course that was in direct opposition to their mentors' wishes.

Another Loan from Charles Towns

If the Rockefeller trustees and advisors were unalterably opposed to the self-publication of the book and could not be counted on to raise any immediate cash to support the writing then there was just one other person to whom Bill could reliably turn for help. Charles B. Towns had given him a $500 check in mid-May specifically in support of the book project and he had made another, more general $500 contribution in late August that had been judiciously divided and distributed to Wilson, Parkhurst, and Mayo as they needed it.[39]

The May check had made it possible for Bill to write the first two chapters of the book, and now Charles Towns seemed to be the only person willing to step up and provide the money that would be so essential if Wilson was to devote his time to writing the rest of the book. But Bill was worried that taking any more money from Towns might be misconstrued as an overt endorsement of his New York hospital and he had spent almost two full pages of his 'sheep and goats' letter detailing the history of his relationship with Towns and evaluating the positive and negative aspects of taking any further monies from him. But, after all of these plusses and minuses had been carefully noted and evaluated, it still came down to the inescapable fact that, as Bill candidly told the trustees, "the only certainty of funds is Mr. Towns [and] I think he is willing to finance the completion of the book, if no other way can be found."[40]

In the two weeks since Bill had written that letter, no other way had been found and, in fact, several formerly high hopes had been completely dashed. This left Charles Towns as their only viable option.

Towns Agrees to Finance the Rest of the Book

Towns was certainly willing to finance the completion of the book and indeed he later claimed he had "voluntarily proposed" to loan Wilson enough money to finish it. In Charles's own recollections of that conversation, recounted in a later letter to Bill, he said, "I voluntarily proposed that you hire a stenographer, which you considered could be done for $25 per week and [you said that] all you wanted was an advance of $50 per week for yourself and I told you to go ahead."[41]* Once they had made the decision to reject the Harper advance, Bill had no other choice but to accept Charles Towns's generous offer.

Having reached that decision, they came to an agreement in the second week of October and Charles wrote Bill his first check on October 14, 1938 and continued making regular payments over the next several months, generally sending him a check on the eleventh of each month.[42] Bill confirmed the details of this October arrangement the following January in a letter to Frank Amos, plainly telling him that "Mr. Towns has subsidized me at the rate of $200.00 per month, plus $100.00 more per month for [Ruth Hock] who has worked with me" and that it was this arrangement which had allowed him to finish writing the book.[43]

Deciding to accept this money from Towns—which Wilson always acknowledged as a loan and that was dutifully repaid in full over the next few years[44]—was the only way Bill could survive once he rejected the trustee's advice regarding the Harper advance. At this critical juncture, Wilson was well aware that taking money from the man who owned Towns Hospital might be misconstrued by suspicious people and expose them to the accusation of participating in a racket to make money from other people's suffering, but Bill felt this was a risk they would just have to take. There really was no other choice.

Making this deal all the more attractive and even more difficult to refuse was the fact that Charles Towns's allowance of $300 a month for five months was identical to the $1,500 Bill would have received from Harper. The loan could be repaid from the book profits once it was published, while the publisher's advance amounted to an outright purchase. Rejecting the Harper advance and agreeing to take Towns's money was the obvious, logical path to take, achieving all of their major goals by financing the ongoing writing while simultaneously retaining ownership and control of the book and, in addition, allowing them to use the profits from the book immediately after it was published to finance the work rather than waiting for more than 5,000 copies to be sold before they would see any further royalties from the publisher.

According to Towns, his arrangement with Wilson included the fact that they had "discussed the subject of the manuscript before it was written and agreed upon a policy"[45] regarding how the writing and review process would be accomplished and Bill was no less regular in his compliance with this part of the agreement than Charles was in sending the monthly check. Just days after receiving the first payment, Wilson sent a copy of a new chapter off to Towns for his review, noting briefly, "Here's the latest. Still going strong, many thanks to you."[46]

Exactly which chapter this might have been is uncertain. Certainly Towns had already seen the frequently revised versions of "There Is A Solution" and "Bill's Story",

---

* It is important to note that this letter, detailing Charles Towns's own recollections of financing of the book in 1938–39, was written in 1945 and sent to Bill because he was so incensed that John D. Rockefeller Jr. had received credit in a recently published article for extending that help when, as Towns noted, "he had nothing whatsoever to do" with it. Charlie expected that Bill would be "very much surprised at the writer's lack of the actual history of the beginning of the Alcoholics Anonymous group" although Towns's claims in this same letter that he was the person who had originally proposed the idea of a book to Bill and that he insisted Bill was the only person who could write it are more than a little off the mark in terms of the actual history of the beginning of the Alcoholics Anonymous group that we have seen so far.

so it was likely a reworked and more polished version of "More About Alcoholism" or perhaps even "We Agnostics" (which had only been available in "the original dictation" of a "rough, uncorrected outline" when Bill had sent them to Dr. Bob three weeks earlier).[47]

Charles was delighted with what he read, responding on October 19:

> Dear Bill:
>
> Received your letter this morning and I think this chapter is wonderful. I cannot help but marvel at the way you are able to analyze and present this phase of your work, and I am satisfied that with the other material this book will contain, the semi-religious nature—it is going to immediately create an interest among the ministers of the world. The way in which you have presented this is entirely your own, and it could not be more clearly presented.

Obviously Charles was not going to be a very critical or intrusive reviewer when it came to Bill's writings, but the next paragraph shows that Towns was not bashful about offering some creative marketing suggestions for the book.

> I believe in time, as far as the Rockefeller Institute is concerned, John D. will find that it is up to him to present a copy to every religious institution in the world, and many public libraries. In other words, I think that he could distribute about five hundred thousand copies; also, I believe when Fosdick reads this material he will be the man to interest Mr. Rockefeller.
>
> I am more than pleased with what you have done.
>
> Very truly yours,
>
> Charles B. Towns[48]

Whatever the origin of this ambitious idea of Rockefeller distributing a half million copies of the book (had Charles been talking to Hank Parkhurst?), it was not the last time this suggestion would be made, although the project never caught the imagination of the great philanthropist and therefore never came to fruition.

Charles B. Towns was not a rich man—certainly not on the order of John D. Rockefeller Jr. and his friends—but his confidence in Bill Wilson and his program of recovery far exceeded the combined faith of all of those men and he demonstrated that faith by writing these all-important monthly checks. When talking about the essential help he gave at this decisive point in the story, Charles Towns claimed he had "never sought any credit nor publicity in this matter and I don't care for any,"[49] but it is a sad fact that this man—one of the great unsung heroes in the story of the writing of the Big Book—continues to receive so little credit for his critical role in making it possible for the book to be written.

Parkhurst's Plan: Sell Stock in a Separate Publishing Company

The biggest problem with the Towns's arrangement to support Bill Wilson (and Ruth Hock) for the next several months was that Hank Parkhurst still had no income to pay his mortgage, support himself, his wife and children, and cover the monthly expenses of maintaining the office in Newark. Some other source of money was clearly needed and, with the prospect of a published book on the near horizon, Hank just "champed at the bit" to take the group in a completely different direction than the one they had pursued for the past year.[50]

The weekend after Bill received his first check from Towns, the two men found themselves in Hank's back yard in Montclair, NJ, where Parkhurst marshaled his considerable promotional skills to sell Bill on the idea that it was time for them to ignore the advice offered by the non-alcoholic trustees and advisors and declare their independence from the ineffective Alcoholic Foundation. According to Hank, what they needed to do was to form their own publishing company—even if that meant they "would have to forget about the Foundation"[51]— and then sell stock in that company to raise the cash they so desperately needed.[52] Wilson called Parkhurst a "terrific power-driver" and a "hard-hitting salesman" and his later recounting of Hank's arguments and his style that afternoon in New Jersey as he "sold his bill of goods" seems to capture accurately the force of the dynamic presentation Parkhurst made to him that day.[53]

> Look here, Bill, why do we bother any more with those Trustees and that Foundation? Those folks have not raised a cent and they are not going to. Why don't we put this proposed book on a business basis and form a stock company? Let's sell shares to our own folks right here in New York. If we give them a real argument, I'll guarantee they will get up the dough.[54]

Wilson later claimed that as "an ex-Wall Streeter" he "had already toyed with this notion . . . but Henry had much bigger ideas and he breathed confidence" to such a degree that Bill was soon swept away by this tempting and adventurous new business scheme.[55] The exact nature of Hank's bigger ideas became clearer as he explained his proposal for how the stock plan would work. Parkhurst suggested that they issue six hundred shares of stock, retaining two hundred shares each for themselves (as author and business manager) while selling the remaining two hundred shares for $25 each, thereby raising the $5,000 needed to support both him and his office-based promotional activities for the next several months.[56]

While Bill was attracted to the idea of selling stock as a way to support Hank for the next several months (not to mention the fact that he would be receiving $5,000 worth of stock for his work as author), he was more than a little concerned about how the trustees would react to this radical new approach to fundraising. In fact he was convinced they "would never agree to [this] scheme" and he worried that "to flatly disagree" with these men might seriously "hurt their feelings;" something he desperately wanted to avoid lest it should jeopardize access to future charitable donations. "But Henry's skin was thicker than mine," Bill noted. "He was implacable; he said that it simply had to be done, and I finally agreed."[57]

A Break with the Rockefeller Group

Ever the salesman and as a concession to Bill's growing anxiety over the trustees, Hank proposed they offer the foundation a financial incentive in the hope that this might make it easier for the non-alcoholic trustees to accept his plan for a stock offering. Parkhurst suggested the new publishing company pay the Alcoholic Foundation a "full royalty of 35¢" on every book sold—this being a nickel more than the thirty cents offered by Harper, and thereby increasing the Foundation's potential profits from each sale by almost 17 percent. As a businessman, this was an argument that made perfect sense to Hank Parkhurst and he presumed it would have an equally powerful impact on the reluctant trustees.

Once they had worked out the details of the new plan, Bill and Hank "were so overcome by this idea that [they] burned up the telephone to [Willard Richardson in] New York and even to Ohio where Frank Amos" was still enjoying his three-week vacation.[58] Having presented the basic outline of the new company and the stock plan, the question was simple enough: "Would you therefore be in favor that [we] make an effort to secure stock subscriptions for a corporation to take over the book on the terms [we] have just described?"[59] Bill had "anticipated that the reaction would be bad, and it certainly was."[60] Neither Richardson nor Amos approved of the idea and they both "counseled caution" before they took any further steps to implement this rash new venture.[61] But Bill Wilson "knew we would have to go through with the deal despite all the objections"—it was the only way they could keep their heads above water while getting the book written—although he found this prospect "depressing."[62] Making such a dramatic break with his Rockefeller friends was the last thing he wanted to do. But it had to be done.

The One Hundred Men Corporation Is Formed

"The very next day," Wilson and Parkhurst "went to a stationery store and bought a pad of stock certificates."[63] Back in the Newark office, Hank had Ruth Hock type "One Hundred Men Corporation, par value $25.00" at the top of each blank share and then confidently signed his name across the bottom as "Henry G. Parkhurst, President."[64]* Wilson later claimed that on seeing this, he "protested" over "these irregularities," but "Henry said there was no time to waste; why be concerned with small details?"[65] If this did happen, it is unlikely it was much of an argument because the entire One Hundred Men Corporation was a Hank Parkhurst project from start to finish and the money

---

* Bill Wilson repeatedly and consistently told this story of the stationery store and just as regularly reported that the name "Works Publishing, Inc." was typed across the top of these blank certificates. This is, in fact, incorrect; an error made either by a faulty memory or simply for the sake of a smoother story. The original name for the publication company was "One Hundred Men" and this was the name used in all of the many references made to the new company in documents created between mid-October 1938 and mid-February 1939. The name "Works Publishing" makes its first appearance in the record on February 14, 1939 in the minutes of a meeting of the trustees of Alcoholic Foundation (GSO, Box 59, 1939, Folder C, Document 1939-44a) and its newness is attested to by a letter from Bill Ruddell—most recently the Chairman of the Alcoholic Foundation and now a member of its Advisory Committee (see the minutes of that February 14, 1939 for this change in position) and the owner of five shares of stock—to Hank Parkhurst less than two weeks later on February 27th asking "What's this "Works Publishing Co'?" (GSO, Box 59, 1939, Folder C, Document 1939-158). Ruth Hock wrote a reply to this letter the next day and in the postscript she noted that "We, that is the One Hundred Men Corp, are Works Publishing Co. H.G. will write you about it." (GSO, Box 59, 1939, Folder C, Document 1939-159). If there was such an explanatory letter, it has not been preserved.

they were trying to raise was going to be used to support him, not Wilson. Who else but Hank should be President of this new publishing company?

And so, the new company to raise money for the book project and to ensure that they "control this thing"[66] had been created with the help of a few blank stock certificates and the bold stroke of a pen. Now they just had to figure out how to package the company in such a way so that people would spend some of their hard-earned cash to buy those rather dicey looking, home-made shares of stock.*

Selling Stock for Profit vs. One Drunk Helping Another

Before moving on to Hank's sales promotion campaign, there are a number of important things that need to be noted about this stock offering.

To begin with, it was perfectly reasonable for Hank Parkhurst to suggest in October that they raise money by selling something of potential value. The previous May in his letter to Bert Taylor and Bill Wilson, Hank had proposed that "donations" to the Alcoholic Foundation would be solicited to finance the writing and publishing of a book for alcoholics.[67] But, in the intervening five months, despite the fact that these donations were actually loans to be repaid out of the book's profits, they had not been able to convince a single person other than Charles Towns to contribute to this important project. Towns had written a $500 check in May and another in August,[68] but, other than these two contributions secured by Bill Wilson, Hank Parkhurst's plan had been an abysmal failure.

Given that disappointment, it was almost predictable that Hank's next step would be to offer an economic incentive to those willing to finance this phase of the book's publication. If generosity of spirit and the desire to support a worthy cause could not motivate people to open their checkbooks, then perhaps it was time to fall back on the always-reliable profit motive to get the funds he needed. An infusion of cash was absolutely essential if they were ever going to get the book published and if the only remaining way to raise those funds was to appeal to people's selfish economic interests then so be it. It might not be the ideal solution, but it seemed to be the only option left at that point. Without some source of significant financing, all their hopes of publishing a book would collapse like the proverbial house of cards.

This shift from donations to the sale of stock was both radical and fateful. Parkhurst was now enlisting support for the book project (and indirectly for himself) by promising buyers they would make money from their investment, injecting the always-

---

* It is worth noting that this is not the first time Hank Parkhurst formed a corporation by simply issuing stock certificates. In late November 1935, when he was just two months sober, Hank created "Sharing, Inc." by this same means. The company was reputedly a Delaware corporation and "authorized to issue 3,000 shares of stock;" the certificates were signed by Hank as President and Bill as Treasurer. Bill Wilson's stock certificate ("Number 4") was for 150 shares and dated November 29, 1935 (GSO, Box 200, Folder J). *NOTE 1*: Sharing Inc. was "a fund raising venture for Honor Dealers" (Moore, *Alcoholics Anonymous and the Rockefeller Connection*, p. 111). Lois also makes this claim but mistakenly says the company was formed "in the fall of 1936" (*Lois Remembers*, p. 101)—rather than in the fall of 1935 (as stated on the actual stock certificate). *NOTE 2*: The only other real-time documentation mentioning Sharing Inc. are two personal letters from Bill to Lois (dated April 1936 and July 16, 1936). Each of these has "Sharing Inc.,11 West 42ⁿᵈ St., New York City" hand-typed and centered across the top as if it were letterhead (GSO, Box 200, Folder K). *NOTE 3*: Although the July 16 letter noted above says that "the boys at Q&F seem pretty well pleased with my work," the Quaw & Foley offices were located at 30 Broad Street at this time (GSO, Box 200, Folder I) and not on 42ⁿᵈ Street—so Bill was not running Sharing, Inc. out of the Quaw & Foley offices.

contentious financial element—the fear that 'money is going to ruin this thing'—into the very heart of all their efforts. With his stock scheme, Hank abandoned the virtuous 'let's do this because it's the right thing to do' approach and adopted instead an unmistakably mercenary appeal for people to 'join us in this book project because you will make a lot of money!'

Other than the potentially harmful effects this decidedly materialistic approach might have on the New York membership, the great downside of Hank's stock plan was that with this one fateful decision, he had realized all of Akron's worst fears about New York's obsession with money. People buying stock in this publishing company were no longer making donations to generously support an emerging Fellowship that promised sobriety to the suffering alcoholic. Instead, they were writing checks because they had been promised a substantial return on their investment. The altruistic, "one drunk talking to another drunk" movement had suddenly been turned into a racket, an organization seriously tainted by the explicit promise that people could make some easy money off of it.

Fortunately, Dr. Bob avoided—at least for the moment—the explosion that would have resulted had the Akron members heard about Hank's stock plans. He was so dubious about the whole scheme (although he did "consent" to it), that, after listening to Bill's explanation of the plan, he suggested that "it would be unwise at this stage to lay the matter before the Akron membership."[69] Bob judiciously concluded there was already more than enough hostility in Ohio toward Bill Wilson and the New York way of doing things without it being further inflamed by this news of Parkhurst's money-making scheme for the book. Smith concluded that the best way to handle this potentially volatile situation was to simply not mention Hank's stock offer to the Akron membership at all. Once again—just as he had done with his secret trip to meet the Rockefeller group in December and his lack of candor about Frank Amos's connections with John D. Rockefeller Jr. during his Akron visit the previous February—Bob decided it would be best to just leave the Ohio group in the dark about this sensitive and sensational information.

Joint Ownership of the Proposed Enterprise

But the possibility that this profit-making scheme might corrupt the New York Fellowship paled in comparison to the fact that, besides selling 200 shares of stock, Hank was making the very generous gift of an additional 200 shares each to himself and Bill Wilson. As noted in an early version of the prospectus for The One Hundred Men Corporation: "Two hundred shares will be issued to the author, and two hundred shares will be received by another member of our group, an experienced publicity man, who will undertake the business conduct of the enterprise and handle the sale of the volume."[70]

What might be seen to be an overly generous gift of stock in the new company was, from Hank's perspective, simply appropriate compensation for all the work he and Bill were doing to create the book and then launch it as a successful business venture. At this stage, this $5,000 asset was nothing more than a paper profit, one that would be completely worthless unless they produced and successfully marketed the book. But if they did manage to publish a best seller, then the profits from those sales would generate significant dividends for all of the stockholders, including Hank Parkhurst and Bill Wilson.[71]

In the Prospectus he would soon create, Hank predicted that the sale of 15,000 copies would generate a profit of $10 per share (after the initial investment of $25 had been returned) along with the more aggressive prediction that selling 100,000 copies would result in a dividend of $150 per share. Parkhurst even went so far as to speculate that, "Although it seems ridiculous, one estimate has been made of half a million volumes within two years time. Should this come, over nine hundred dollars per share would be returned."[72] These are clearly not insignificant numbers, especially for two men owning 200 shares of company stock: a dividend of $10 would pay them $2,000 each, one of $150 would return $30,000 and, in the unlikely event that Hank's "ridiculous" prediction of half a million copies in two years actually did come true, they would have each received $180,000 in dividends during that time.

Numbers like these lend at least some credence to the resentful comments made by Hank Parkhurst's son many years later, including the one "that his father and Bill both expected to make a million dollars from the project."[73] However close that allegation may be to the truth, Hank Parkhurst's formation of the One Hundred Men Corporation and his outright gift of 200 shares to both himself and Bill Wilson obviously put these men in line to make quite a lot of money from the book should it prove to be successful.

But even more disturbing than this is the fact of who now actually owned the new company. Bill later candidly acknowledged that "the New York alcoholics and their friends could buy one-third of these shares for cash. The other two-thirds would be distributed between Henry and me for our work."[74] What this casual statement fails to make clear is the plain fact that if Wilson and Parkhurst held 400 shares between them and the remaining stockholders controlled a total of only 200 shares, then the publishing company (*and the book*) would belong to Bill Wilson and Hank Parkhurst rather than to Alcoholics Anonymous. Suddenly, the question Hank asked Bill while he was trying to convince him to adopt this stock proposal—"Shouldn't we control this thing?"[75]—takes on a completely different meaning from the one so commonly understood today.

This startling fact of their joint ownership of the company and the book has been all but lost in the mythology that has grown up around the early years of The One Hundred Men Corporation (which later became Works Publishing Co.). Bill rather blithely states in *Alcoholics Anonymous Comes of Age* that their intention was that "our society would organize its own publishing company" because "a society like ours ought to control and publish its own literature."[76] But, at this point in the story, it wasn't the society organizing the publishing company and it wasn't the society who would control the book it published. That control would lie with Hank Parkhurst and Bill Wilson and with no one else.

On some level, this is understandable and perhaps even forgivable. To begin with, the two men were completely broke and, as they had told the trustees the previous September, if they could not secure some sort of ongoing financial support, they would have to stop working with alcoholics and apply for regular jobs just to put food on the table and pay the mortgage. In October 1938, commandeering the income from a successful book looked to be the only plausible way for them to get a steady income stream—both in the short and long term—for themselves and for the work that needed to be done. In addition, the two active non-alcoholic trustees of the Foundation, Frank Amos and Willard Richardson, were both unalterably opposed to this scheme to self-publish a book and they would surely have blocked any funds from leaving the Foundation's coffers in support of a project they considered to be completely unworkable.

A Disastrous Misstep

But, whatever justifications might be offered and however unavoidable it may have seemed at the time, this stock offer was the single most serious misstep made by Bill Wilson during the so-called "flying blind" period of A.A.'s history. Yes, the responsibility for both the idea and the promotion rests primarily with Hank Parkhurst, making it easy enough to argue that it was his mistake and not Bill Wilson's. But characterizing Parkhurst as "the serpent in the garden" of this selfless new recovery movement is just too convenient, completely ignoring the fact that Bill undeniably accepted the apple Hank offered him and took a bite.

Less than two years later, everyone had realized that this stock scheme—despite its success in sustaining Hank Parkhurst and his promotional efforts from November through April—was a complete disaster. In May 1940, Bill and Hank signed their 400 shares over to the Alcoholic Foundation and, with a 1942 loan from John D. Rockefeller Jr. negotiated by A. LeRoy Chipman, the foundation bought back all of the $25 shares at face value, and thereby assumed ownership of both the publishing company and the book.[*]

Advice from a Successful Publisher

The first thing needed if they were going to sell this stock was some hard facts about what would be involved in this amateur publishing venture, facts demonstrating that the new company would be established on a solid business basis, allowing them to present a "real argument" when pitching the stock to local A.A. members.[77] Fortunately, someone within their immediate circle had a personal friendship with Richard J. Walsh, the owner of the John Day Publishing Company, and actually knew him well enough to secure Hank and Bill an appointment.[78] This introduction was no small matter.

---

[*]   In an April 3, 1945 letter, Bill claims that when he and Hank voluntarily gave up their stock in 1940, it was "earning about $5 a share" making its "cash value per share . . . about $25"—meaning they had made donations worth $5,000 each. In that same 1945 letter, Wilson says that "today" his 200 shares would "conservatively" be worth $37,500. (William G. Wilson to Leonard V. Harrison, GSO, Box 65, Folder C [1 of 2], Document 52), Some details on the colorful and contentious story of how the stock was retired can be found in *AACOA*, pp. 189–190, *Pass It On*, pp. 235–36 and Hartigan, pp. 119–20, but a full scholarly treatment based on primary document research is clearly called for.

Walsh's company was the publisher of, among other books, *The Good Earth*, one of the great blockbuster novels of the 1930s. (The book had been the #1 best seller in both 1931 and 1932, it won the Pulitzer Prize in 1932, and was the work most responsible for the author, Pearl Buck, receiving the Nobel Prize for Literature in 1938.[79])

Richard Walsh gave Wilson and Parkhurst a considerable amount of his time and attention, providing them with reliable and valuable information on the "printing, credit and sales" of a self-published work along with his own confident prediction of "an unusual sale for the volume." Perhaps most important was his assurance that, given their circumstances and their desire to maintain control of the proposed book, "he could not see where this venture would gain through using an established publisher."[80] This was exactly what Bill and Hank had been hoping to hear—yet another professional opinion confirming the validity of their plan to publish the book themselves.

According to Walsh, the printing of the book should not cost any more than thirty-four cents a copy. This, taken with the royalty of thirty-five cents to the Alcoholic Foundation and an allowance of five cents for packaging and drayage would result in a maximum cost of just seventy-four cents per book. If the book had a retail price of $3.00 a copy, it would produce a gross profit of eighty-eight cents on each book sold through a bookstore (after deducting the traditional "jobber's discount" of $1.38) and a $2.07 gross profit on every copy sold by direct mail (after allowing nineteen cents each for wrapping, addressing, and postage). Walsh presumed that as a result of the publicity Hank was then so busily planning, they would be able to sell at least one book via direct mail order for every two books sold in stores, resulting in an average gross profit of $1.27 per book.[81]

This was wonderful news to the fledgling publishers. If Hank needed any further convincing about the feasibility of his vision for the One Hundred Men Corporation, these numbers decisively confirmed all of his most optimistic hopes. This was going to be a *very* profitable business venture and once he projected those profit numbers onto the fantastic number of books he envisioned selling, it made the investment of a mere $25 for one share in the One Hundred Men Corporation look like a tremendous bargain.

How could the folks in New York not "get up the dough" when presented with such a sure-fire proposition as this?[82]

The New York Members Aren't Buying

Bill was excited by what they had learned from Richard Walsh, but these projections made Parkhurst wildly enthusiastic and he immediately began aggressively selling the New York members, pushing them to jump on this fabulous opportunity while they still had the chance. Bill reported that Hank "descended like a whirlwind on the New York alcoholics" and "buttonholed them one by one, persuading, browbeating, hypnotizing." He said that Parkhurst knew all the "stratagems of the super-salesman" and he used every one of them in his effort to separate people from the $25 (or more) needed to make this investment. Meanwhile, Bill claims he "was no second-rater at this sort of thing" himself and he "followed right along," backing up all of Hank's arguments and prodding people to take out their checkbooks. According to the two promoters, this was a once-in-a-lifetime, ground-floor offering that people would be just crazy to miss.[83]

Nobody was buying.

Over and above the fact that most of the newly recovered men had absolutely no disposable income, they were also very skeptical of the basic argument Hank and Bill were trying to sell. Wilson said the typical alcoholic's response was often accompanied by a "stony look" and the disdainful observation that "you fellows certainly have some nerve! You mean to say you're asking us to buy stock in a book that you haven't even written yet?"[84] It sounded like a hare-brained, pie-in-the-sky scheme rather than a solid business proposition to these people.

Despite Hank's "violent promotion,"[85] they found it impossible to sell even one share of stock. "Obviously [they] needed still stronger arguments"[86] if this ambitious new fundraising effort was ever going to get off the ground:

> Henry was not discouraged. He still had ideas. "Bill," he said, "you and I know this book is going to sell. And Harper thinks it will sell. But these New York drunks just do not believe it. Some take it as a joke, and the rest talk high and holy about mixing a spiritual enterprise with money and promotion. But if they really did think that the book would sell, they would buy the stock all right, and fast.[87]

Parkhurst was convinced that the promise of national publicity was the best way for them to start getting some traction with their sales efforts. If they could just get a commitment from one of the big national magazines to print an article promoting the book just as it was about to be published, they would surely be guaranteed a huge sale in the first few months that *One Hundred Men* was out.

Good Housekeeping *Is Approached*

The first magazine approached was *Good Housekeeping* where they met with the editor, William Bigelow.[88] The appointment had been set up by an established author named Wainwright Evans who had published two books in the late 1920s, and who had almost twenty years of freelance writing experience to his credit. His connection with the growing A.A. movement is unclear, but it may well have been the result of the many articles he had published on the occult and the paranormal, a topic that held an abiding interest for Bill Wilson throughout his life.[89*] Evans was clearly well enough known to Bigelow that he was able to secure a meeting after he sent the editor a letter regarding the work being done with alcoholics and requesting an appointment.[90]

Wainwright Evans accompanied Bill and Hank to the meeting and Bigelow was so impressed with their presentation that he asked Evans "to submit an outline of the

---

* While Wilson's attraction to and involvement with spiritualism is not touched on directly in this work, it was, in fact, a prominent and pervasive element in his basic beliefs system as can be attested to by such items as the "Spook Book" held in the Stepping Stones Archive (StSt, WGW 101.7, Box 7, Folder 4) which records the results of séances and Ouija board pronouncements made during the early 1940s (almost all of which proved to be incorrect).

completed article which he believed would be used by the magazine just prior to the issuance of the book."[91] This was what the three men were hoping to hear and Hank Parkhurst must have been overjoyed to see his plan for getting them some substantial and reputable national publicity unfolding so flawlessly on their very first attempt. An article like this in *Good Housekeeping* magazine would generate literally thousands of requests for the book!

Evans quickly finished his detailed outline and submitted it to Bigelow, but it turned out that the management at *Good Housekeeping* had some of the same issues and questions raised by *This Week* magazine the previous month. "Though by no means unfavorably disposed"[92] toward the proposed article, the editor subsequently told Evans, there were several serious concerns that would need to be addressed before his magazine would be willing to print this article.[93] It must be remembered that this was the heyday of the famous Good Housekeeping Seal of Approval—one of the earliest and most successful consumer protection efforts in history—and the magazine was not about to publicize any new solution for alcoholism until Wilson and Parkhurst had provided them with answers to several difficult questions.

Bigelow pointed out the problematic fact that they were anonymous, which was all well and good in itself, but raised the question of what he should do with the flood of inquiries they would undoubtedly receive after publishing this article and he wanted details on how these inquiries were going to be used once Wilson and Parkhurst received them. The editor also suspiciously questioned whether the fantastic results were really what they claimed them to be, which was a difficult proposition to prove to a skeptic's satisfaction. "Furthermore," the editor asked, "is there going to be any continuity to the work?" and exactly "what is going to be done for, or said to, the distressed people who write asking for an answer?"[94]

Relating this battery of still unanswered questions to Frank Amos almost three months later, Bill Wilson noted that, "of course, we can't answer all these questions yet, because we do not know what our finances will be or what the trustees think should be done."[95] Bigelow's questions and his demand for answers was a stark reality check on how unprepared A.A. was at that time to field any kind of effective response if they were faced with an onslaught of appeals for information and help—which was the problem Wilson had been complaining about so bitterly since the publication of their own book became a real possibility. They were, after all, nothing more than a small handful of men (and one secretary), possessing no infrastructure for handling such requests and having no visible means of support either for themselves or for their fledgling organization.

Like the proposed piece in *This Week* magazine, the possibility of publishing Wainwright Evan's article in *Good Housekeeping* limped along for several more weeks without any real resolution until, despite Parkhurst's and Wilson's reluctance to give up hope, it was finally abandoned as yet another failed attempt to convince the national media to publicize their fabulous new cure for alcoholism.

The Readers Digest *Meeting*

A few days after their visit to *Good Housekeeping*, Wilson and Parkhurst had a much more successful trip to Pleasantville, NY, where they met with Kenneth Paine, the Managing Editor of *Readers Digest*.[96] This was perhaps their most ambitious attempt at national publicity, given the *Digest*'s monthly circulation of twelve million copies[97] and with individual magazines being passed around among several readers and many being bought for the sole purpose of being prominently displayed in the waiting rooms of professional offices across the country. It was a magazine read by more Americans every month than any other publication.

Exactly how they managed to secure this appointment with a well-placed and powerful man such as Paine is uncertain.[*] As noted earlier, a reporter from the *Digest*, had attended a regular Tuesday night meeting in Brooklyn on August 30th, presumably in pursuit of a potential story. This appears to have been another one of Hank Parkhurst's attempts to get national publicity for A.A. and, two day later, he followed up the reporter's visit with a letter to Dewitt Wallace, the founder and owner of *Readers Digest*:

> Sept. 1, 1938
>
> Mr. Dewitt Wallace,
> c/o Readers Digest
> Pleasantville, N. Y.
>
> Dear Sir:
>
> The writer is one of a group of ex-alcoholics who held a meeting last Tuesday evening, Aug. 30th, which your Mr. McCarthy attended.
>
> Mr. McCarthy informed us that he was making a staff report on this meeting.
>
> If you are interested in the significance of the work several of us would be glad to drop in to see you at Pleasantville in order to give you a more personal glimpse.
>
> Thanking you for your interest as expressed by Mr. McCarthy, we are,
>
> Yours very truly,
>
> HGP:RH[98]

---

[*] It is possible that Dr. William Silkworth provided the necessary introduction to *Readers Digest* although this is far from certain. Wilson had noted in a September 8, 1938 letter to Fitz Mayo (GSO, Box 59, Folder B[1], Document 1938-137) that he had "discovered that Dr. Silkworth lives in a house owned by Mr. Wallace, the proprietor of the *Readers Digest*. Dr. Silkworth is planning to call on Mr. Wallace as quickly as he can make an appointment." However, it does not seem that any such appointment occurred in late 1938 since Wilson later wrote to Frank Amos (January 4, 1939; GSO Box 59, 1939, Folder C, Document 1939-7 to 1939-10) that "Dr. Silkworth, of Towns Hospital, rents a house of Mr. Wallace, owner of The Readers Digest. The doctor feels that he is favorably known to Mr. Wilcox, Business Manager of that publication. We have just given the doctor a manuscript of the book, which he expects to present, through Mr. Wilcox, to Mr. Wallace, urging upon him the desirability of this article and vouching for what he has seen in his hospital." These are certainly interesting possibilities, but, unfortunately, not real proofs.

While there is no preserved response to this, it seems someone within the A.A. circle had some sort of personal relationship or contact within *Readers Digest* and, six weeks later, had been able to facilitate the scheduling of this critical meeting for Wilson and Parkhurst.

The two men made the hour-long drive up to Pleasantville, NY and arrived at Kenneth Paine's office in a state of high excitement. Paine was interested in what they had to tell him and he listened attentively as Bill and then Hank "drew a glowing picture of [their] fellowship,"[99] describing for him "this wonderful budding society"[100] along with its recent development and growth.[101] They also did not fail to mention ("in a discreet way,"[102]) the high interest of Mr. Rockefeller and some of his friends,[103] and Bill made at least passing reference to the fact that he had recently spoken with Harry Emerson Fosdick and received his blessing for the work they were doing.[104] Wilson then presented Paine with the two sample chapters from the book, which he said was "then in the process of being written" and gave him sufficient time to read them over.[105]

The editor was duly impressed, commenting that he found these two chapters to be more than good; they were positively "inspired."[106] With such a favorable response, Wilson (or, more likely, Parkhurst) went for the close by asking if an article describing a group such as theirs would not "be a matter of tremendous interest to the Readers Digest?"[107] Kenneth Paine's reply was "most enthusiastic"[108] and he admitted that, yes, "this is just exactly the kind of thing the *Readers Digest* would like. We'd love to do a piece about your promising young society. One alcoholic talking to another. All very dramatic. Yes, we'll put a feature writer on it"[109] and he then spoke about how he intended to give the article considerable space[110] in that issue of the magazine.

Having gotten this far and beginning to feel a bit more confident, Hank pressed on to make sure they had an explicit understanding about what he considered to be the most critical element regarding this proposed article. "But, Mr, Paine," he asked, "will you mention the new book in this piece?" The editor replied definitively that "Yes, we will mention the book."[111] The two men were elated, but the editor's intention to start work on the story immediately posed something of a problem for them. While an article published in the *Digest* would be a huge coup, it would do them little good if it came out too far in advance of the publication of the book. Asking for a favor at this point may have seemed presumptuous, but they really had no choice; so Hank politely asked Paine if the piece could be timed so that it would appear just as their book was being published,[112] explaining that once they had their "methods set out on paper," they would be much better prepared to respond to the "thousands of inquiries" that an article in the *Digest* would generate.[113] Kenneth Paine instantly understood their dilemma and asked how long it would take to do the book. Wilson suggested it should be ready for publication sometime in the spring of 1939 and the editor was more than happy to work with that deadline.[114] "When your book is ready next spring," he said, "let me know and I think we can put a feature writer to work. This should be a great story."[115]

Their meeting lasted an hour[116] and concluded with Paine assuring them that they had "a deal",[117] along with his promise that he would "take [the story] up with the editorial board" as soon as possible and "when the time is right . . . we'll put a special feature writer on this thing and we'll tell [everyone] about your society."[118] Wilson and Parkhurst could not have been happier. They had just successfully negotiated the placement of a story about Alcoholics Anonymous in a national magazine with a paid monthly circulation of twelve million copies, an article that would surely bring them more publicity than even Hank had ever imagined in his wildest dreams.

The two men "reached for [their] hats and sped back to New York." Now, they "had some real ammunition" and enough solid arguments to assure even the most skeptical buyer that they would "someday get their money back."[119] Both men were confident that the promise of a story in *Readers Digest* (especially one that would be timed to appear just as the book was published), finally "gave [them] the argument" they needed "to pry the money loose from the drunks."[120] Surely, with the help of *Readers Digest*, they would be able to sell some of those $25 shares of stock!

Hank's Prospectus

With this firm commitment from *Readers Digest*, Hank Parkhurst immediately went into promotional overdrive, "sitting up nights working on a prospectus" explaining the sure-fire profitability of the proposed book business.[121] After some considerable editing, he had Ruth Hock type up multiple copies for him and Bill to use while promoting the $25 shares in The One Hundred Men Corporation.

This original typed version of this prospectus was eight pages long (a few weeks later there would be a slightly revised twelve-page version which was typeset)[122] and it opened with a "Brief Resume of the Work of ALCOHOLICS ANONYMOUS."[123] Hank was wasting no time in taking this opportunity to finally present the historical background for A.A. that he considered so important to selling their solution and that, back in early June, he had suggested to Bill as the ideal opening for the book arguing that:

> A History of the work—Possibly this could be carried on the first two pages of the book.
>
> > This history should establish proof of success of the work and carry hope to everyone that reads that much.
>
> The opening to the book should arouse the emotion of hope.[124]

In the brief resume of the work in the prospectus, Hank actually used Bill's full name ("William G. Wilson") and gives him sole credit for "certain ideas" that "came to him which form the basis of the events which have since transpired." But Parkhurst is not about to squander this chance to promote his own, much less religious, understanding of their solution and he quickly goes on to note how "doctors and psychiatrists have agreed that the only way out for the true alcoholic is through a so-called spiritual experience and it matters little what form this experience takes." Furthermore, he says, this "spiritual feature must be simple and understandable" if it is to be "acceptable to the ordinary men of the world" and its presentation must be packaged with "accurate and reliable medical information" if the "new prospect" is to be "readily persuaded that he was hopeless." But William G. Wilson's most brilliant contribution, he claims, went far beyond just simplifying this spiritual feature and recognizing the importance of accurate medical information; all of these elements have been well-known to professionals for years but they had been employed with comparatively little success when it came to sobering up alcoholics. According to Hank, Bill's major insight came when he "conceived the idea" that this failure to help the suffering drinker "was because the matter was so often presented to an alcoholic by a non-alcoholic" and this universally lopsided approach did not provide the "sufficient basis for mutual confidence" so critical for success. Wilson "realized that one alcoholic could gain the confidence of another to an extent that no other person in the world could" and that, once this "idea took hold of [his] imagination," it led him to a vision of "one alcoholic helping another [and] that one helping still another" as the only truly effective way to spread the message of recovery and of bringing sobriety to an increasingly large number of drunks. According to Hank's retelling of their story, A.A.'s singular success was more the result of fellowship between alcoholics than any other single factor.

Hank then briefly recounted Bill's trip to Akron and related how it resulted in three Ohio men recovering before he returned home to New York. In the three years since then, "about two-hundred cases of hopeless alcoholism have been dealt with" and "about fifty percent of these have recovered" with the net result that "the original Akron three have expanded themselves into more than seventy" and "scattered about New York and in the seaboard states there are about forty" men who have completely recovered from their previously insoluble problem with drink.

Having outlined the basic backstory of A.A., Hank then launched into a section he entitled "The Present Program." He began by stating categorically that "it has been felt vitally necessary to spread the work widely and get it on a sound basis rapidly," noting that the first step in this process "has been the establishment of a trust known as The Alcoholic Foundation." After briefly describing the structure and responsibilities of the foundation, Hank then moved on to the real topic under consideration, the need for the "education and instruction" of an "estimated million alcoholics in this country" in "the nature of the disease and its cure" and the decision therefore to publish a book "based upon the past four years experience" so that their "definite program of attitude and action" could be offered to everyone affected by the malady. In conclusion, he noted "the publishing of this book, to be known as One Hundred Men is the subject of the attached material."

With all this groundwork carefully in place, Hank then presented details of "The Proposal," namely their plan to form "The One Hundred Men Corporation" whose purpose would be to publish the "One Hundred Men" book. Shares of "non-assessable" stock, issued by a Delaware corporation, would be offered in this new company for $25 each and the proceeds of the sale would be used "to promote publicity, sales and to publish the book." Painfully aware of just how little disposable income there was among the recovering drunks in New York, Hank created a convenient time-payment program claiming that if you could not afford the full price of $25 a share, then the company would be willing to accept "five dollars for each share subscribed at the time of subscription" along with the promise that an additional $5 per share would be paid "each thirty days for four months after subscription." If Hank couldn't "pry the money loose from the drunks"[125] in one lump sum, then he would be more than happy to take it out in five monthly installments of $5 each.

With these concrete details of past performance and the specifics of his proposal now on the table, Hank then proceeded to list the "Facts" which he considered pertinent when "considering the possible success of the volume—One Hundred Men," breaking these "Facts" down under three different general headers: "Publicity," "Established Publisher's Opinion," and "The Possible Market."

The first of these, "Publicity," was the most extensive and to Parkhurst's mind, the most persuasive of all the "Facts." He listed here seven numbered items, although the first and last of these were not actually publicity items but rather about the testimonials provided by doctors regarding "the foundational soundness of the work" and the fact that "established publishers" were confident that "this volume seems assured of the most unusual publicity preceding publication of any book they had known." But sandwiched between these two were three short but impressive paragraphs recounting their very positive meetings with *This Week*, *Readers Digest* and *Good Housekeeping* along with two reports of the sensational responses to recently published articles—one in *The Saturday Evening Post* ("The Unhappy Drinker," January 15, 1938) and the other, "a very obscure article" by Dr. Silkworth which had appeared in "a small New York Medical journal."[126] Reading Hank's enthusiastic retelling of their meetings with all three of these magazines, one could easily assume that favorable articles about Alcoholics Anonymous and their new book would be appearing in all three simultaneous with the release of the book. This was, of course, simply not true. While Bill and Hank left *Readers Digest* with the understanding of a firm commitment, both *This Week* and *Good Housekeeping* had expressed grave reservations about the articles and requested further clarification—which was never provided.

Next, in "Established Publisher's Opinion," Parkhurst revealed Harper's offer of a $1,500 advance (something the publishers would never do, he said, unless they thought it was a "sure fire book") and the fact that Richard Walsh of John Day Publishing had met with them and had, among other things, "predicted an unusual sale for the volume." These two impressive and well-informed testimonials regarding the marketability of the book from such respected publishing houses should allay any fears regarding the projected sales to be expected once the book was published.

Hank then launched into his third general category of "Facts"—"The Possible Market"—and it was here that he abandoned the world of recent past history and began to make some wild predictions of the potential sales for the book. In "Hank's Ideas," his handwritten speculations composed at the beginning of June, he had claimed there were 210,000 clergymen and 169,000 physicians who would surely be interested in buying this book.[127] Now, less than four months later, these numbers had more than doubled, with Parkhurst assuring the prospective stock purchaser that this book "should appeal to the five hundred thousand Clergymen in this country [and also to] the three hundred and fifty thousand physicians." In addition to these previously considered professions, Hank Parkhurst now added "the twenty odd thousand established Psychiatrists" and noted confidently that "the problem is one of pressing concern to large corporations" and asserted, "we know also that special reprints should be interesting to insurance companies." While he had speculated the previous June that "the total would be well over three million prospects,"[128] in the face of these newly expanded and much more impressive numbers, Hank was at a loss to even guess at the potential market, leaving the final number of books they might sell up the reader's imagination by asking rhetorically "who can estimate the possible sale?"

The "Corporate Set-up"

With this tantalizing question floating in mid-air, Hank now began the fourth major section of the prospectus that he called "Corporate Set-up." The first half of this presented the "budget that runs to April 1st" and outlined the declining scale of profits that would be "apportioned among the shareholders" (80¢ on each of the first 1,000 books, 70¢ each for the next 1,000 books and 60¢ on the following 2,000) or "until the subscriptions have been returned."

The budget—which noted that $1,500 had already "been extended as a loan to insure the writing of the volume"—listed the following nine categories along with their costs:

BUDGET TO APRIL 1st, 1939.

Author	$1,000.00
Directional & Sales Promotional work	1,800.00
Office rent	480.00
Steno.	650.00
Office Expense (estimated)	240.00
Incidental expense	500.00
Printing plates	700.00
1000 volumes	350.00
Art work	250.00
	$ 5,970.00

To forestall sticker shock or any too careful questioning of these numbers, Parkhurst immediately followed this budget with a page-long, detailed accounting of the projected costs for printing, publishing, and distributing the book. These were the previously mentioned numbers supplied by Richard Walsh of John Day Publishing Company; numbers that promised "an average gross profit of $1.26" for every volume sold.

Finally, Hank had arrived at the punch line of his entire presentation, the section of the prospectus he called simply "Profits." Coupling the huge projected market he had so confidently outlined with Richard Walsh's assurance of the substantial amount of profit to be realized on each book, Parkhurst just could not restrain himself as he detailed the fabulous returns anticipated from this sure-fire investment:

> By June first, the [$25] subscription would have been returned. Then, if the following sales are reached the profit per share would be:

15,000 volumes first year—	
per share return after money back	$10.00
25,000	30.00
50,000	75.00
100,000	150.00

> Although it seems ridiculous, one estimate has been made of half a million volumes within two years time. Should this come, over nine hundred dollars per share would be returned.

Having made a fairly well-organized and, for Hank, relatively articulate presentation of all these arguments, the final section, called "Operation of the One Hundred Men Corporation," seems to be an afterthought and it reads like something that had just been stuck on the end of this prospectus, a catch-all list of facts and figures that he hadn't been able to blend into the previous text. But in reality, what Parkhurst was primarily trying to address in this section was an objection that would plague Alcoholics Anonymous for many years to come and had, even at this early stage of their development, already grown into a burning question: Why did A.A. need an office and a staff to carry on the work of organizing a program that was basically transmitted by word-of-mouth, by one drunk talking to another? At this time, the primary focus of the question was the shareholder's concern that much of those enticing profits would simply disappear into the overhead costs of maintaining Hank and his office. This question of an official A.A. office was of particular interest to Hank Parkhurst since he was the one running that office and he was totally dependent on it for his livelihood. If the A.A. office went away, then so did his only current source of income. In justification of maintaining it, Parkhurst asserted that "during the time of the writing of the book, and while sales promotional and directional duties were going on, the necessity of an office is apparent" and he mentioned several tasks (working with Floyd Parsons on a possible *Saturday Evening Post* article, following up with a host of NYC-based national church offices, canvassing the National Library Board, and securing articles in the American Medical Society's publications) to support that assertion. In addition, he said, once the book was published, "if sales are going at a very rapid rate, there would be no question as to the necessity of the office" although he conceded that if this most likely of all scenarios did not materialize, then the office would seem to be unnecessary and could be closed.[129]

The Prospectus Is Completed and Shares Are Sold

Over the next couple of weeks, Hank continued to work on the prospectus, adding a decorative title page (reading simply "Alcoholics Anonymous") and writing two more pages of text before he had the document typeset and professionally printed. The major addition was a full-page "Foreword" containing "certain information" that should be known to the reader before considering the "attached proposal." This included a fairly detailed explanation of the allergy theory of alcoholism which, according to Hank, "informed doctors and psychiatrists" now consider to be "just as much a disease as cancer," along with an emphasis on the "indisputable fact that during 1937, thirty-five percent of the life insurance turn downs were due to alcoholism." Taken together, these particulars demonstrate that "there exists today an alcoholic problem which takes its place in seriousness with cancer and syphilis." In contrast to this distressing situation, "over the past four years over one-hundred true alcoholics have recovered, who from the standpoint of medicine and psychiatry, were considered hopeless." Noting "these men have dubbed themselves Alcoholics Anonymous," Parkhurst explained that the name was "adopted because of the nature of the work, because of the desire to keep away from notoriety, and because the work is strictly non-sectarian." The second new page, which appeared at the very end, was a fill-in-the-blanks subscription form to be completed by the stock purchaser and mailed along with a check (made payable to the Alcoholic Foundation or to Henry G. Parkhurst) to either Hank at 17 William Street in Newark or to William J. Ruddell in Hackettstown.[130]

With the marshaling of all these impressive facts and arguments, Hank went back to the local alcoholics and finally began to sell some shares of stock to them, to their friends and to a miscellaneous collection of non-alcoholic supporters. As a lot, the New York members "were pretty poor"[131] and many who couldn't afford the $25 needed to purchase a single share of stock, adopted the five-monthly-payments plan Hank had devised for exactly these circumstances. These buyers agreed to make their first monthly payment on November 15—solidly placing Hank's greatest sales success in the two or three weeks immediately prior to that date—and committed to make an additional $5 payment on the fifteenth of each following month until March 1939. In addition to financially challenged A.A. members, some of their friends also opted for this time-payment program (including several people who bought more than just one share of stock).[132]

Bill Wilson later claimed that "practically all of [the New York members] subscribed" to this initial stock offering,[133] but the official May 15, 1940, list of subscribers does not support this.[134] Despite Hank's best efforts, there was still considerable resistance in New York to his speculative venture. Of the forty-three people (and one company, Stain-Ox) who did buy shares of stock, only ten were current A.A. members—all of whom were from the New York group (including Jack Darrow, a New York member who moved to Cleveland, shortly after the Big Book was published).[135*]

Because they were never even told about stock or the Prospectus, no one in Ohio ever bought a share of stock.

A total of forty-four recovered alcoholics, friends, relatives and business relations purchased one-hundred-seventy-nine shares of stock over the next six or seven months, producing an adequate, but uneven income stream for Hank that eventually totaled $4,475[136] and thereby moved his dream of making The One Hundred Man Corporation a successful publishing enterprise one step closer to reality.

---

* When Darrow moved to Cleveland, he immediately began attending meetings at Abby Golrick's house that started in May 1939 (Bill Wilson's 1954 Interview with Jack Darrow, Oral History Files, GSO, New York). Besides Darrow, the other nine members of the New York group to buy stock were: Norman Hunt, Bill Ruddell, Bert Taylor, George Williams, Fred Breithut, Harold Sears, Robert Furlong, Grenville Curtis, and Wallace von Arx. *NOTE*: Bill Wilson rather frequently mentioned that there were forty-nine stockholders, but that number includes five people who held shares that had been "issued for services rendered" rather than purchased for cash. These five were Ruth Hock, Ray Campbell, Charles Leahy, Harry Brick and Wallace von Arx (who was counted twice—once as a purchaser and here again as a receiver of stock for services rendered (Ibid.).

CHAPTER SIXTEEN

Meanwhile, Out in Akron . . .

~*October to December 1938*~

In October 1937, when Bill Wilson first suggested the idea of writing a book, the Akron group voted to support his proposal, but only by the slimmest of margins. At that time, close to half of the Ohio members were intensely opposed to the idea and argued vigorously against it. Six months later Wilson was back in Akron once again pushing the idea of writing and publishing their own book, but in the meantime the balance had shifted away from him, and the Akron members were even more hostile than they had been during his previous visit.* The atmosphere during those April meetings was so negatively charged that Bill didn't even call for a vote on the issue, knowing he would lose if he tried to get their formal consent.

By the beginning of November 1938 several chapters of the proposed book had been sent to Akron for Dr. Bob's approval as Bill became more and more insistent that Ohio members with substantial sobriety write out their personal stories of drinking and recovery and send them to New York for inclusion in the book. But the group's approval of Wilson and their acceptance of his vision for the Fellowship had deteriorated even further during these additional six months, so much so that a large majority of the Akron members, who were now being pressed to participate in a project they strongly opposed, were in open revolt against what they saw as Bill Wilson's money-grubbing approach to sobriety.[1]

---

* Another possible way of understanding this shift might be that when Bill revisited Akron in April 1938, he was unaccompanied by several members of the New York contingent who had been there with him the previous October and that, without their support, the majority was now solidly against him and his plans.

Akron and New York Are Far Apart

At this point, the Ohio group had not yet been told Hank Parkhurst was selling stock in The One Hundred Men Corporation—something they would not learn until Bill's visit to Akron in March 1939. Of the 179 shares Parkhurst finally managed to sell—not one was bought by an Akron member, including Dr. Bob Smith—nor did anyone in the newly sobered Cleveland group (that still regularly drove down to Akron to attend the Wednesday night meeting at T. Henry Williams's house) ever buy any stock.[2] Bill said that the Ohio people "subscribed no money whatsoever"[3] to the book project and they were keeping themselves as far removed as possible from Bill Wilson and his ambitious plans for spreading their newfound solution across the country. From their perspective, all of these grandiose New York projects were little more than misguided and egotistical schemes, each of which was fatally contaminated by the unavoidable need for money.

By this time, the New Yorkers had proudly adopted the name "Alcoholics Anonymous" along with the completely separate identity this new name implied. But the Akron people, Bill ruefully noted, were "still thinking they were Oxford Groupers" and as such, they were "dubious of the doings in New York"[4] and almost uniformly opposed the idea of publishing the book. They considered it a "dangerous undertaking" for a variety of reasons.[5] With this deeply suspicious attitude toward all things originating on the East Coast, the Ohio contingent remained steadfastly and piously aloof from the book project and unresponsive to all of Bill Wilson's pleas for support.

Bill later claimed Dr. Bob "consented" to the formation of the One Hundred Men Corporation and the sale of its stock to raise money, but he almost immediately contradicts this rather limited concession (consent hardly implies enthusiastic agreement) by simultaneously reporting that as he gave his consent, Smith advised that they should first "try this [stock] idea out on the Board of Trustees" and stated they "surely could not ignore" the Board and their opinion on such an important matter.[6] But that is exactly what Wilson and Parkhurst had done—completely ignored the trustees and their advice after lengthy consultations—so Bob's alleged consent amounts to little more than a token acceptance of Hank Parkhurst's plans for the One Hundred Men Corporation. Tellingly, Bob Smith himself never bought a share of stock; this despite the fact that just two months earlier he had lobbied the trustees to distribute $400 of his Rockefeller money to Wilson and his associates to alleviate their desperate financial situation.[7] Not spending a minimum of $25 to support this all-important New York initiative is certainly a strange and significant omission on Dr. Bob Smith's part.

Further, when Wilson approached Smith with the task of asking Akron members to invest in the new corporation, Bill says Dr. Bob was dubious about the whole project, claiming he thought it would be unwise to mention it to his Ohio members. "Some promotion might be justifiable in New York" he noted, "but few Akronites would be able to see it."[8] Bob's claim that the purchase of stock might be perfectly appropriate for New York, but would be unacceptable in Akron, starkly underlines the very real differences between these two groups and highlights the deep-seated Ohio mistrust of all things New York. At this point, other than their common pursuit of sobriety along generally spiritual lines, the methods and the perspectives of the two groups could hardly have been more different. Ohio was still explicitly religious and deeply committed to Oxford Group principles and practices while, by this time, New York had been following an increasingly secular (but still decidedly spiritual) path of recovery for well over a year.

Getting Stories from the Akron Group

While Bob Smith successfully dodged any responsibility for promoting the stock offer in Akron, he had made a firm commitment to Bill Wilson that the Akron members with substantial sobriety would supply him with their personal written testimonials for the book.[9] The *Personal Stories* section was supposed to make up at least half of the book, and with the majority of those recoveries living in Ohio, it was essential that they be written and sent to Bill as soon as possible so they could be added to the growing manuscript. By way of setting a good example, Bob Smith wrote his own story;[10] however most of the Ohio members were simply not willing to take the time or make the effort to commit their recovery stories to paper.

Bob did have enough influence with some of the Ohio members to convince them to write their own accounts, but even among those few who were willing to go along with him on this project, there was the usual problem of "trying to get [them] to do things on a deadline," and this only resulted in more and more "nagging [by Dr. Bob] to get the stories written."[11] Dr. Bob's son, Smitty, and his adopted daughter, Sue, both twenty-years-old in late 1938, recalled members of Alcoholics Anonymous coming to their house at night to write their stories under Bob Smith's supervision. "The guys would come over and sit at the old dining room table," Smitty said, "with a yellow tablet and a Big Chief pencil. They weren't literary people [and] this wasn't easy for them."[12] But the stories did begin to get written.

It is almost certain that this small handful of personally written stories were among the first sent off to Bill in late October 1938.[13] But most of the Akron members just could not be moved; they had no intention of participating in the book project. "There was quite a bit of argument about [the stories] as I recall," Sue Smith Windows said,[14] and Dorothy Snyder confirms this, claiming that the fall of 1938 was a "time of real serious contention" in Ohio. "There was so much controversy over the book," she said, and such direct opposition to the entire project by a significant number of people, that there was a real fear that "the whole Akron group was going to break up over" the argument.[15]

Dr. Bob Finds a Writer to Produce More Stories

According to Dorothy, Dr. Bob was "in great grief" over this major disagreement and completely at a loss over what more he could possibly do to move the stories project forward. Then Smith got a lucky break that he quickly turned to his own advantage.

He "found a bum down on Akron skid row who had been a newspaper man and quite a famous one in his time—Jim Scott."[16] Jim's drinking career had taken him all over the world, and in his travels and travails, he had created a wildly varied resume. In addition to his work with newspapers, Jim had been an English bookie and a rare book dealer interspersed with jobs as a factory worker, sailor, hobo, soldier, publicity man, editor, advertising manager, and WPA administrator.* But it was Jim's writing talents that Bob Smith needed right now, and he felt if he could "only straighten Jim up, he would really be able to help" him get the personal stories written; stories that, by now, Bill Wilson was constantly nagging him about.[17]

Jim did manage to stay sober (it was not his first attempt to quit drinking in Akron A.A.), in no small part because he was taken in for several weeks by Tom Lucas and his wife; certainly an act of Christian charity, but also an insurance policy against Scott drinking again and thereby ruining any chance of his helping Dr. Bob find a way out of the current dilemma.[18] Despite all of Dr. Bob's encouragement and "talk about the boys getting their stories boiled down—just a couple of pages, very brief,"[19] so far nothing much had actually been "boiled down." Jim Scott looked like just the man to step in, take charge, and finally start getting some stories written about the Ohio members' experiences.

Over the next few months, if your name was on Bob Smith's list of targeted writers and you had not yet submitted your story, he would, as one Akron veteran put it, send Jim Scott over to sit down and "listen to you recite your story", after which Jim would go back home and "write it up for you."[20] If the Akron drunks weren't willing to take the time to compose their own stories, then the version produced by a well-informed professional writer would just have to do. Dr. Bob was at first unsure whether or not this ghostwriting arrangement would be acceptable to Bill, but when he told him about the plan, Wilson approved of it. He was in favor of whatever it would take to get the stories actually written and mailed off to him in New York.[21]

Jim Scott was "always careful to leave the flavor, the character of the person"[22] in the stories he was writing. At times this must have been a real challenge, because even this "easier, softer way" of getting things down on paper was not without its share of serious problems. Some people were still so categorically opposed to the whole project that, according to one early Akron member, the ghostwriting often involved Jim Scott having to "drag it out of these poor fellows" before he could get enough material to create a coherent narrative. As one particular example of an unenthusiastic participant, this old-timer specifically mentioned "poor old Joe Doppler," whose story "The European Drinker" appears in the first three editions of the Big Book. Doppler must have been a particularly reluctant and difficult case to have triggered such a clear and compelling memory during an interview given sixteen years after the fact.[23]

Fourteen different Ohio stories were submitted to New York in time to be included in the pre-publication, trial-run Multilith edition of mid-February 1939,** while

---

* See Jim Scott's original Big Book story entitled "Traveler, Editor, Scholar" (Alcoholics Anonymous, 1ˢᵗ edition, pp. 254–64). Scott's story was later edited and appeared in both the 2ⁿᵈ and the 3ʳᵈ editions on pp. 251–60 under the title "The News Hawk."

** "Multilith" is a trade name for an offset printing process and press that became something of a generic brand name for short-run printing in its day. There will be significantly more information on this trial-run Multilith printing later in this book.

another four arrived later, but still in time to be included in the *Personal Stories* section of the Big Book when it was published in April.* Dr. Bob's daughter Sue was back in school at this time and claimed she "typed some of [these stories] up myself at the business college,"[24]** noting she did so because she needed the practice for her school work.[25] Jim Scott wrote a majority of those first fourteen stories and Lois Wilson, for one, was grateful for Jim's writing skills, later complimenting him and noting that, because of his efforts, the Akron stories "were better written than those from New York."[26]

An Akron Member Pulls His Story and Fuels Dissension

One of these Ohio stories had a particularly contentious history, creating a flashpoint for all the Akron mistrust of Bill Wilson and his book project. Del Tryon, "a little gambler in Akron . . . was going to write his story,"[27] and he did actually produce a four-page account of his drinking and recovery—most likely with Jim Scott's help—entitled "Ace Full—Seven—Eleven." But, before it could be published, Del told Dr. Bob he didn't want the story used and withdrew it from consideration.[28] According to Dorothy Snyder, Tryon pulled his story because "he thought that this [book project] was all a fraud," and the most likely explanation of exactly what Tryon meant by fraud was that he had some deep-seated suspicions regarding "Bill's personal aspirations from the sale of the book"[29]; i.e. he was convinced any money made would go directly into Bill Wilson's pocket.

It was this dramatic withdrawal and Tryon's outspoken accusations against Wilson—allegations readily believed by so many in Akron—which fueled the bitter arguments that left some members fearing that the Akron group might break up over the controversy.[30] This was not just a minor complaint made by one member of Akron A.A.; it was a widespread and acrimonious argument threatening the very existence of the group. Dr. Bob's son, Smitty, confirmed this years later, noting "there were big egos and big fights over the writing of the Big Book. There was a lot of suspicion. There was even a rumor around Akron," he said, "that Dr. Bob and Bill had known each other well before they met at Henrietta's [and] that this was a con job they were putting on people."[31]

In this overheated atmosphere, the mistrustful Del Tryon insisted that if Bill Wilson was going to be making money off of this book, then he should receive some royalties from those sales or, at the very least, he should be paid for the use of his story.[32]

After Del withdrew his story, Dr. Bob prodded him to reconsider and eventually convinced him to resubmit it.[33] Tryon's story did appear in the mid-February pre-publication Multilith printing of the text, but once more he decided that the book project was nothing but a scam to line the pockets of the people in New York City. Sometime in late February or March 1939, he withdrew his story again, and it did not appear in the *Personal Stories* section when the Big Book was published in April. It is

---

* Note that only seventeen (not eighteen) Ohio stories appeared in the Big Book because one story was withdrawn before the publication of the book.

** These were most likely the handwritten stories done at the Smith house under Dr. Bob's supervision, but may also have included stories with hand edits made to Jim Scott's original typed versions.

sad to see the huge green "X" pencil lines cancelling each of these four pages in the Master Copy of the Multilith printing, but even sadder to read the note Bill Wilson has handwritten across the top of the first page identifying this as "Del Tryon's story" and commenting that the writer "thought the book was a racket and so withdrew this."[34]

Del Tyron evidently became something of a *cause célèbre* in Akron, and the allegations he used to support his on-again, off-again submission provide concrete and important evidence of the highly charged and deeply suspicious fears that ran through Ohio A.A. whenever Bill Wilson's name was mentioned. The man's abandonment of the Oxford Group and his insistence on the need for money to successfully spread the message of recovery were anathema to most Akron members, and they made it clear that they wanted absolutely nothing to do with him or with any of his grand schemes, including writing their personal stories for his proposed book.

A.A. #3 Refuses to Submit His Story

There was at least one other important casualty in this fiercely negative debate: the personal story of Bill Dotson, the first person Bob Smith and Bill Wilson had successfully sobered up in Akron, did not get written at this time. The man universally recognized as A.A. #3 refused to submit his story, so his first-person account of Bill's and Bob's early and successful visit to his hospital bed did not appear in either the Multilith printing or in the first edition of the Big Book. Dotson was held in particularly high regard by the local A.A. members and he had secured a prominent spot on the list of potential Big Book story writers Hank Parkhurst had put together in June. There, Dotson was the third writer mentioned, listed simply as the "Politician," appearing immediately after the "Broker" [Wilson] and the "Surgeon" [Smith].[35] (Parkhurst's identification of the lawyer Dotson as a politician was based on the fact that he had been an Akron city councilman and ran in a political campaign immediately after he got sober.[36])

There is no contemporary explanation for why Bill Dotson did not write his own story nor is there any explicit contemporary confirmation of the fact that he actually refused to write one. But it is impossible to think that Bill Wilson didn't expect him to write a personal account of his recovery for the Big Book and almost as hard to imagine Bob Smith never asked him to do so. Still, A.A. #3 never submitted a story for publication and its absence was a glaring rebuke to both Bill Wilson and to the whole book project.

In 1952, Dotson was asked why his story had not appeared in the first edition of the Big Book and he replied rather lamely "that he hadn't been much interested in the project or perhaps thought it unnecessary."[37] This cavalier comment makes no sense at face value. In late 1938, such a blatant lack of interest or an evaluation of the project as unnecessary was nothing less than a complete rejection of Wilson's plans to publish a book.

The most plausible explanation for this refusal was revealed years later when Dr. Bob's son wrote his memoirs and noted that one point of serious contention in 1938 was that "a lot of the guys thought they ought to get paid for" writing their stories and "Bill D. was one of them."[38] On one level, this is understandable. If you were convinced the book was a racket whose only purpose was to make money for a few New Yorkers, asking for a share of the profits would have been a contentious but not entirely unreasonable position to take. If that was Dotson's position in 1938 (and all the available evidence supports this), then it is understandable why he would want to avoid owning such a negative position in 1952 when the success of the book was obvious to all and instead, claim he just wasn't much interested and "perhaps thought it unnecessary."

Whatever his reasoning had been in 1938, fourteen years later Bill Dotson had obviously changed his mind; he noted in that same later interview that "Bill Wilson had [recently] come out to Akron to record his story" and that the version Wilson would be writing based on that meeting "would be in the next edition of the book."[39] By this time, when the revised second edition was already being planned, Bill Dotson had come to the belated conclusion that perhaps the book project hadn't been just an unnecessary racket after all and he had finally decided to allow Bill Wilson to include a version of his story in the book.**

The Founder of A.A. in Chicago Is Also a Holdout

Not quite as critically central as Dotson's story, but also a significant omission from the first edition of the Big Book, is Earl Treat's important account of his drinking and recovery. This is strange because Earl had been sober for more than a year when the call for stories went out, and his work in spreading the message of recovery to his native Chicago would have been an important and inspirational story to feature in the book. Earl was somewhat removed from the Ohio scene during this time, having returned to Illinois shortly after he got sober, but throughout 1938 he regularly visited Akron every three weeks or so as insurance against drinking again[40] and to get his "spirits recharged and to work with other alcoholics."[41]

Earl's attempts to start a local A.A. group in Chicago were unsuccessful until sometime during the summer of 1938 when a business acquaintance asked him for help with a drunken employee who, much to Earl's surprise after so many other rejections, was actually interested in trying this new approach to sobriety. Finally given the chance, Earl "did not feel adequate to pass the program on to him alone" and therefore suggested the new man "take a trip to Akron for a couple of weeks, which he did." Having completed the course there, the new man returned to Chicago and together they established the first A.A. group in Chicago.[42]

This real-life story of how the message could spread to another major city is so important that it is difficult to imagine why it did not appear in the first edition of the

---

* Ernest Kurtz appears to suggest in *Not-God* (see p. 74) that Dotson's story was judiciously withheld from the book because it was felt that his "credentials" (social position, education, and early religious training) were so high that they would create a false impression of what was required to get sober. Then, in an endnote (#45, p. 333), he also offers the reported explanation that Dotson's story was not submitted because "he was too humble." These are hardly convincing arguments given the equally high "credentials" of several other members whose stories did appear in the book and the fact that Dotson's story has since been included in the 2nd, 3rd, and 4th editions of *Alcoholics Anonymous*.

** The version that Bill Wilson wrote for Dotson is entitled "Alcoholics Anonymous Number Three" and it appears on pages 182–192 of the 2nd, 3rd, and 4th editions of the Big Book.

Big Book. One likely reason is that during his frequent trips to Akron, Earl Treat had imbibed more than enough of the controversy raging there to agree with Del Tryon that the book was a racket, and so refused to submit his own story. Earl never offered an explanation for why his story was not in the first edition of the book, but the most plausible assumption is that his objections were the same as Tryon's and Dotson's, i.e., if money was going to be made from the publication of this book then he deserved to be paid for his contribution to it.

One thing is sure: The atmosphere in Akron in late 1938 was toxic whenever the topic of writing stories for the proposed book was mentioned.

Bill Sends New Chapters to Dr. Bob

On Thursday, November 3—just seven weeks after he had started to write again—Bill Wilson sent Dr. Bob a letter that included two revised chapters and three new chapters along with some pointed criticisms of his own writing style.

> Dear Bob:
>
> I am enclosing you five chapters two of which you have already seen in the rough. All these can be improved a lot, and I agree that the chapter of the Agnostics should be longer, and perhaps somewhat different in character. I am turning this stuff out as fast as I can, being only once corrected dictation. You can't call it serious writing. After I get all through with these general chapters on the present basis, I will edit them as carefully as I can, bearing in mind the criticisms and suggestions from anyone who wants to make them.
>
> So you might be showing this stuff around, asking people what they really think. I find it is pretty hard to get people to voice their real opinions, as they are too much afraid of hurting the author's feelings. So I wish you would make a special effort to get people to speak their minds.
>
> In my opinion the stuff I have done is not always clear, is sometimes too long winded, and may not always be the best possible presentation. So I wish you would tell people to speak up or forever hold their peace. I hope to get out there about December first for a week or two so we can cover these matters better.
>
> Everybody who has seen the personal stories from Akron thinks they are great.
>
> Many regards to all, and much love to my Annie.
>
> Yours,
>
> WGW:RH[43]

Early Akron Stories Are Acknowledged

Unfortunately, there is no further information—here or elsewhere—about exactly which personal stories had been sent off to Bill in New York during October. Since the ones Jim Scott would create were still a few weeks away, in all likelihood these were taken from the small handful of Ohio stories written by the individuals themselves. Bill Wilson later noted that Jim Scott "must have ghostwritten about twelve or thirteen stories"[44] and if that estimate is correct, this leaves room for only five or six of the eighteen stories from Ohio that could have been written by the Akron members themselves. Of these, we know that Dr. Bob wrote his own story ("The Doctor's Nightmare")[45] and that William Van Horn submitted his own personal account ("A Ward of the Probate Court").[46] Besides these two confirmed authors, it is likely that Paul Stanley, Dr. Bob's confidante and his travel companion to the December dinner at Rockefeller Center, would have written his own story. Beyond his close and confidential relationship with Bob Smith, the brevity of Paul's story—"Truth Freed Me!"—was just 862 words long (and one of only three Akron stories to be less than 1,000 words),* also strongly suggests that he was the author of his own story.

One other candidate Dr. Bob may have convinced to write his own story as early as October would be Ernie Galbraith. He was the fellow Bill Wilson had specifically mentioned to Bob Smith in his late June letter regarding the proposed book: "The story of a fellow like Ernie . . . could be included in the shorter narrative or perhaps, considering his wonderful comeback with powerful effect in the chapter on failures."[47] Ernie was a frequent visitor at the Smith household and at this time, quite popular with both Bob and Anne,[48] so it is highly possible that, at Bob's insistence, he was one of those few Akron members who did agree to write his own story. Ernie's tale, as Bill had suggested, emphasized his early failure in A.A. and was predictably enough entitled "The Seven Month Slip." Adding to the circumstantial evidence for this possible early date of composition is the length of Ernie's story; like Paul Stanley's, it was substantially shorter (just 1,260 words) than most of the stories authored by Jim Scott (most of which ran from 2,000 to 3,000 words each).

The New Chapters

But more important than which of the personal stories had already been sent in to New York is the perplexing question of which chapters of the book were included with this November 3 letter.

The two chapters Smith had already seen in the rough were "More About Alcoholism" and "We Agnostics." They had been sent to Akron five weeks earlier, along with Wilson's note that they were "the original dictation" and were coming to him in "just the rough uncorrected outline," with Bill's promise that he would send along "the polished product when ready."[49] Here were the more polished versions. After receiving those two first drafts, Dr. Bob had told Bill he thought the chapter to the agnostic should be longer and suggested it might be better if it were "different in character"

---

* The other two under-1,000-words stories from Ohio were "A Close Shave" (588 words) and "An Alcoholic's Wife" (518 words).

from the version Bill had sent him. Wilson acknowledges both of those suggestions in his letter, but he also owns that he hasn't bothered to do any kind of major rewrite to achieve the different character that Bob had recommended, nor is he confident that he has lengthened it enough to meet Smith's expectations.

Bill was asking for suggestions and promising to edit the manuscript with those suggestions in mind, but at this point he wasn't making any significant changes in response to the few criticisms he had already received. At least for the moment, he was noting incoming suggestions as he continued to "turn this stuff out as fast as I can" with the promise that they would be edited later "after I get through with these general chapters on the present basis" (i.e., "the present basis" being in the form, style, and language that came to him most naturally).

Although the titles of the three new chapters are never specified, there is a very short list of possible candidates, so it is not difficult to make an educated guess as to which these might have been. Bill had not yet written the Twelve Steps (which would not happen until sometime during the first week of December), so by way of elimination, these three new chapters would not have included either "How It Works" or "Into Action," both of which provide concrete details for working the Twelve Steps and could not have been written prior to the creation of the Steps themselves.

That leaves only five other published chapters from which to choose. It seems natural to presume that "To Wives" and "The Family Afterward," a nicely matched pair, would have been written in tandem with each other and they were almost certainly two of the new chapters sent out to Ohio with Bill's letter. It is possible that the third new chapter was "To Employers," but this is extremely unlikely since it is the only general chapter in the book not written by Bill Wilson but by Hank Parkhurst, so it would hardly qualify as one of the chapters Bill was claiming to be turning "out as fast as I can." And finally, because "A Vision For You" contains evidence strongly suggesting that it was the last chapter to be written, we are left with only "Working With Others" as the most likely candidate for the third new chapter sent to Bob Smith in early November. Certainly working with others was such an integral and essential part of the program that it would not have required the writing of the Twelve Steps to have been thought worthy of having its own chapter; it was, in fact, one of the most basic components of the program of recovery and the one element that was considered absolutely necessary for people hoping to stay sober.[*]

Repeated Attempts for Feedback from Akron

This was the third time Bill had sent chapters of the book to Dr. Bob asking for his comments and opinion. But it is interesting to note the differences in Wilson's three requests for feedback and also the varied instructions he sent about who else in Akron should be shown these proposed chapters and why.

---

[*] "I soon found that when all other measures failed, work with another alcoholic would save the day." (*Alcoholics Anonymous*, 4th edition, "Bills Story," p. 15). "Practical experience shows that nothing will so much insure immunity from drinking as intensive work with other alcoholics. It works when other activities fail." (Ibid., "Working With Others," p. 89).

In late June, when he sent Smith the recently finished versions of "There Is A Solution" and "Bill's Story" (along with Hank Parkhurst's detailed 'Outline' for the book), Bill included a five-page letter suggesting that Bob "could use this material as a sort of trial balloon and a starting point for discussion of what you folks out there believe the book ought to contain." Note that Wilson, ever the politician, has deftly sidestepped the fact that just two months earlier, over half the Ohio members had been vigorously opposed to the writing of any book at all. In a tacit acknowledgement of this fact, Bill does explain his rationale for going ahead with this project despite the objections so recently raised in Akron. He also spends a fair amount of time giving reasons why "it is going to take time and money to get this book out and put into circulation" (another Ohio hot button) before finally asking Bob Smith what he thinks might be a good title for the proposed book.

But all that was just packing material for the central and overriding purpose of this long June letter, which was to "get the ball rolling" on what Wilson clearly considers to be Akron's most important contribution to the book: the writing of the personal stories. Bill spends more than two full pages giving detailed instructions for those who should be writing their stories, how long each one should be, and precise directions for what he would like to see covered in each of these stories. Then, with these guidelines so carefully and explicitly in place, he tells Bob Smith "it might be a good idea if you showed this stuff around generally and then asked people to write their own stories." Having passed along this laundry list of particulars telling the Ohio members how he expected them to participate in the project and presuming that these potential authors would have read his own story, Wilson wraps up his instructions to Bob Smith by giving him a solid nudge about his own responsibilities in relation to this project, saying, "if you could get the ball rolling along these lines it would be great . . . [and] greatly facilitate tying up the packages quickly and neatly later on."

Bill's blithe assumption that the stories would be written doesn't leave any room for Bob Smith to argue, although at one point in the letter, Wilson does rather generously allow some openness to feedback.

> The foregoing are suggestions only. We can never tell where the next best idea may come from and who will make a still better suggestion. So please take the picture I have sketched and do not hesitate to add, subtract and multiply it in any way which occurs to you all. I am not suffering at the moment from any pride of authorship so let every one do their best and if they like their worst.[50]

While this is an honest and open invitation for all the Akron members to review what had been written in these two chapters and to make suggestions for changes, this last phrase acknowledges that Dr. Bob might have some trouble selling this program to his local members. And as noted earlier, taken all together these two polished chapters and the detailed outline must have presented a formidable package, a *fait accompli* that would require a large amount of work by anyone wanting to make significant changes to Wilson's proposals. To many in the Ohio Fellowship, this must have looked like a ship that, despite all of their strenuous objections, had already sailed and was now set on an irreversible course. Since their negative opinions about the writing of a book had been so flagrantly disregarded, their only remaining option was to simply boycott the entire project.

Bob, even more aware than Bill of the dissention surrounding this volatile topic, shared these new materials with very few people in Akron.

Three months later, in late September, Bill sent Bob the rough drafts of "More About Alcoholism" and "We Agnostics," again asking for his personal opinion. But since these chapters had nothing to do with the personal stories Wilson was trying to get out of Ohio, he was even more circumspect about who should be shown this new material and cautioned Smith that "perhaps it would be well not to show everybody these chapters, except where you think people can contribute some new ideas which can be incorporated in the final write."[51] Clearly Bill was worried that many, if not most, of the Akron members would be more interested in opposing the project outright than they would be in making anything resembling constructive criticisms to the proposed text, and he was asking Bob to confine the circulation of these writings to those who seemed at least favorable to the project and might be willing to make a positive contribution.

At the same time that Bill is suggesting Bob significantly limit the number of people who would be shown these two chapters, he also requests that those few readers confine their comments and criticisms to "new ideas which can be incorporated in the final write," i.e., he is not soliciting major changes to the text, but rather asking for edits and contributions that might be fit neatly into what he has already written.

Input Is Limited
Five weeks after that, on November 3, the two newly revised and three completely new chapters arrived in Ohio, heralding the fact that this book was no longer just a speculative project; it was something that *was* going to be written and published. This reality demanded that the Akron people begin making some sort of critical contributions to the book or at least sign off on what Bill had written so far. In an effort to make that happen, Bill tells Bob (in two previously quoted paragraphs, but worthy of being repeated in this context):

> So you might be showing this stuff around, asking people what they really think. I find it is pretty hard to get people to voice their real opinions, as they are too much afraid of hurting the author's feelings. So I wish you would make a special effort to get people to speak their minds.

> In my opinion the stuff I have done is not always clear, is sometimes too long winded, and may not always be the best possible presentation. So I wish you would tell people to speak up or forever hold their peace. I hope to get out there about December first for a week or two so we can cover these matters better.[52]

Bill is beginning to sound just a little bit desperate here. He hasn't received any substantive feedback from Ohio in response to his last two letters, and without some sort of response, he fears the book project will be seriously compromised. In his previous letter, he had suggested "it would not be well to show everybody these chapters," but he has now begun to realize that unless the Akron people make a contribution to the book or at least sign off on the text before it is published, it will never be 'their' book. This book *would* be going to press sometime in the near future, so now was the time for "people to speak up or forever hold their peace," or they would have no say in how the announcement of their Fellowship's new program of recovery would be packaged and presented to the American people.

In another letter written on the same day that he mailed these five chapters to Dr. Bob, Bill tells a Cleveland member named Bill Jones that he has just sent "Doc Smith some more chapters" and notes that he wants "people to say what they really think" about them. "After all," he tells Jones, "we are trying to write the best possible book; one which reflects the view of the group, rather than the individual. So if you have any ideas after you read the stuff over, speak up. You know the old maxim: 'Spare the rod and spoil the child.'"[53]*

Wilson presumed Jones would be given the chance to review this material, but it is not certain if he was even on the list of those who were being shown those new chapters as they arrived. In 1954, when Bill asked Bob Evans, an Akron member who got sober in February 1937, for his impressions of the time when the book was being put together, Bob replied that, of course he remembered when "you started coming through with these rough drafts" but notes, "we didn't show them to too many people," although he proudly admits that he "was one of the chosen few" who did get a chance to see them. When Wilson pressed him for more details, Evans said:

> Of course, we were very serious about the thing. We were quite awed by the realization that it was beginning to take form. There wasn't much we could do to add or subtract from the information that you put down . . . I can remember going over the draft with Doc in his home there and down at Hildreth and Paul Stanley's and Tom Lucas's. Those were the main fellows looking at the draft.[54]**

---

*   Given what is known about the actual writing process for the book up to this point, Bill's use of the word "we" here is more editorial than collaborative. While he was trying to write something that captured "the view of the group" regarding their method for getting and staying sobriety, he was relying almost exclusively on his own personal experiences in formulating his presentation of that method.

**   Dorothy Snyder claimed in her 1954 interview that "Bill would write the chapters and send them to Akron. We would read them in the Akron meeting and he wanted any comments and corrections on them so then they would be read there and then sent back to Bill." This direct contradiction of Bob Evans' testimony bothered the authors of *Dr. Bob and the Good Oldtimers* so much that they tried to resolves this discrepancy by likening it to an accident that was seen from different angles by different witnesses (see pp. 152–53). Elsewhere, Dorothy notes that she and Clarence were often houseguests of the Smiths in those days and she specifically mentions the late night session at Dr. Bob's house where they reviewed Chapter 5, "How It Works," the day that it arrived. It is likely that these meetings with select readers at Dr. Bob's and other's houses (as Bob Evans remembers them) are the same Akron meetings that Dorothy Snyder is referring to in her interview. It is all but impossible to imagine Bob Smith (or anyone else, for that matter) reading these rough drafts aloud at the Wednesday night meetings held at T. Henry Williams's house—which included many non-alcoholic Oxford Group members and lacked explicit mention of the alcohol problem—and then asking for comments and criticisms. (GSO filing cabinet drawer marked "Oral Histories," Folder marked: Murphy, Dorothy Snyder / Akron OH / August 30, 1954)

Doctor Bob Smith was showing these chapters only to those who were in favor of the book being written and he was conducting those review sessions in the privacy of these members' homes. Those who were categorically opposed to the project were being left out of the review loop. And of those who did get a chance to read the chapters, none of them ever offered any significant changes or made any substantive constructive criticisms of what they were reading.

As Bill Wilson so neatly summed up the so-called Akron review process: "the chapters of the book were sent to [Dr. Bob Smith] for debate and inspection out there [but] he never passed them around very much, merely writing me saying he thought they were all right."[55]

No Direction from Dr. Bob

This lack of any widespread or critical review was evident in the comments Dr. Bob offered in his response just four or five days after receiving these five chapters, telling Bill he was basically happy with everything that had been written so far. Wilson was expecting much more feedback than this and he was disappointed that the largest contingent of the A.A. Fellowship was completely uninterested in generating any serious criticism for these five important chapters of the book. Bill had made it clear he felt his writings needed significant revision or at least some help with polishing, and this obvious lack of engagement by everyone in Akron must have been quite frustrating for him. A little direction, at least from Bob himself, would have been appreciated, but his tentative nod of acceptance was clearly the most Bill could expect to get from Ohio. Despite his repeated request for checking and criticism of the proposed chapters, Akron offered him "nothing but the warmest support."[56]

Writing back almost immediately, Wilson's brief, two-sentence opening paragraph conveys not only his disappointment, but also the depth of his resignation regarding this notable lack of enthusiasm and input from anyone in Ohio:

> Nov. 9, 1938
>
> Dr. R. H. Smith,
> Akron, Ohio.
>
> Dear Bob:
>
> Glad to hear you liked the chapters I sent you. I wish you would be more critical of them, for I think they can be improved a lot. I have but two more of the general chapters to write, and then I shall come out.[57]

And that is all we ever hear in the contemporary documents about the weighty criticisms and critiques allegedly sent from Ohio in relation to the Big Book. "Glad to hear you liked the chapters . . . I wish you would be more critical." Bob Smith now had in his possession at least six of the ten general chapters, and neither he nor anyone else in Ohio was offering any meaningful help in shaping the text that would determine the future of their movement.

Hank Parkhurst's Questionnaire

Bill didn't belabor his disappointment; he was just going to have to accept the fact that Akron wasn't going to engage with the book project. But there was another issue he was hoping Dr. Bob might be able to help him with, and that now took up the balance of this letter. Hank Parkhurst had devised a questionnaire he wanted every A.A. member to fill out so that New York would have some kind of hard data to present in reply to the inevitable questions they anticipated coming their way from skeptics, especially from those within the medical community.* While Bob claimed he was fine with what Bill was writing for the book, he was decidedly not happy about this proposed questionnaire and he didn't think any of the other Ohio members would be either.

Having wistfully acknowledged Bob's lack of criticism for the five chapters in the first paragraph of his letter, Bill spent the remainder of his letter arguing for the validity and importance of the questionnaire in the most diplomatic language he could muster:

> I share your feelings about the questionnaire, hating very much to do anything which smacks of institutionalism, or a liver pill testimonial.
>
> Yet, I think it good sense we have such information on hand. We are making some claims in this book which, medically speaking, are rather staggering. They are certain to be questioned. To have an easy means of authentication may come in handy.
>
> As you know we are approaching The Readers Digest, Good Housekeeping, Saturday Evening Post, etc. We are also going to want some eminent doctor and or business man to write a foreword for this book. He may have neither the time nor inclination to investigate our claims exhaustively. Nevertheless he will want to be sure of what he is getting into. So it would seem wise to have this kind of information in the filing cabinet. Of course we shall never use the information publicly, but it may be very important as a private exhibit to responsible people.
>
> If however you feel very strongly that we should not make this request of the fellows, please feel free to say so. Our success is not going to stand or fall on a flock of testimonials, but they may help a lot in the immediate future.
>
> My very best to all the folks.
>
> Yours
>
> WGW:RH[58]

---

* There is no direct evidence that Hank Parkhurst was the author of this Questionnaire, but it is hard to believe that Bill Wilson would have had either the time or the inclination to create this document. In addition, Hank's business background and his exclusive responsibilities for publicity and promotion in relation to the book, make him the most likely candidate for creating both the document and the arguments to support it. Given all of that, I feel confident in ascribing the creation of this Questionnaire to Hank Parkhurst.

The Questionnaire was an 8½" x 14" sheet with twenty-seven questions covering important aspects of each respondent's drinking career and recovery. As Bill said, this would be important information to have on hand for any professionals who might be thinking of aligning themselves with their burgeoning movement.

There are ten completed copies of this Questionnaire in the GSO archive in New York City. The one below contains the questions found in all copies along with the typed response offered by Hank Parkhurst when he filled out his form in December 1938:

QUESTIONNAIRE

Name Henry G. Parkhurst

Address 344 North Fulton, Montclair, N. J.

Age 32 *[sic . . . Hank was 43 when he filled this form out]*

Occupational History (Try to give from beginning) Advertising salesman, warehouse Railroad Construction, Express Co, Railroad Freight handling, concrete block manual labor, specialty sales, printing press sales, detail sales, dental manufacturing, oil salesman, oil executive, oil wholesale, gas appliance manufacturer, button manufacturer.

Educational History Grade, High School, college.

At what age did serious drinking start? 21

At what age did uncontrolled drinking start? 36

Years of uncontrolled drinking 2

When drinking, how long did sprees last? Two days to two weeks, last one in *[sic]* three months.

What was average period between sprees in last two years of drinking? Three or four months.

Date of original change September 1935

Number of slips and periods between slips None

How long since last slip? 3 years, 3 months

Try to give some comparison between former drinking habits and those since the change. No comparison. Have done no drinking.

How strong was religious background as a child? Medium

What was religious history after leaving influence of childhood home? Agnostic

Number of hospitalizations. 12

Effect of hospitalizations? After first one, seven months on wagon. Little effect afterwards.

Number of times physician in attendance? Once.

Effect of physicians attendance? None. (Hospitalization)

Number of different psychiatrist consulted. 1

Effect of psychiatrical treatments? None

Number of jobs lost through drinking? Two

Now employed? ?*

Marital results of drinking? (Divorce, separation?) Separation

Is family reunited? Yes

During drinking were any religious approaches made and what were the results and attitudes? No[59]

While ten New York A.A. members dutifully filled out their questionnaires,** no one in Akron, including Dr. Bob Smith, ever did so. However much value such data might have brought to the publicity and publication efforts for the book, this was one more New York project that Dr. Bob decided the Akron folks just didn't need to know about.

As far as we know, these questionnaires were never put to any practical purpose. The ten completed forms were filed away in a drawer for future reference and never used.

---

* What an interesting answer on this question by Hank in December 1938! Was he employed or not? The question mark here directly addresses the fact that Honor Dealers was all but dead, and he was unsure of his current position within the growing A.A. movement.

** Besides Hank Parkhurst, questionnaires were completed by Jim Burwell, Horace Chrystal, William Emerson, Norman Hunt, Florence Rankin, Harold Sears, G. C. Sherwood, J. L. Williams and Bill Wilson (GSO, Box 59, 1938, Folder B[1], Documents 1938-197 to 1938-206).

CHAPTER SEVENTEEN

"Working with Others"

~October to November 1938~

October 1938 was a busy month for Bill Wilson. During the first week he lost the support of the Rockefeller trustees when he rejected the advance from Harper and Brothers and then became immersed in all of Parkhurst's publicity ventures (not least of which required the two of them to visit the managing editors of both *Good Housekeeping* and *Readers Digest*), plus all of Hank's frantic efforts to launch the stock offering for The Hundred Men Corporation. Yet somewhere in the midst of all that furious activity Bill found time to do major revisions on the two "rough, uncorrected outlines"[1] he had sent to Bob Smith at the end of September, and then produce first drafts of three completely new chapters—all five of which, as already noted, were mailed off to Dr. Bob for his review on November 3.

Bill's Working Relationship with Ruth Hock

Throughout October Bill had been "commuting every day from 182 Clinton Street [in Brooklyn] to Newark",[2] where he gave Hank whatever help was needed and then spent the rest of his day working on the book. By this time Honor Dealers "had gone broke" and there was "nothing left but a very large desk and a few plush chairs for the customers—now empty."[3] However, the "big thing that was left was Ruth Hock, who began to take [Wilson's] dictation on the chapters for the book under preparation."[4] As noted earlier, Bill didn't like Ruth taking shorthand notes as he talked; instead, he preferred to stand behind her, speaking at a measured pace, while she typed directly from his dictation. She would then hand him the typescript to read over before starting on a second version that incorporated his further thoughts and corrections. "He liked to speak awhile and then look it over," Ruth once commented, "and he wanted it right then while his thoughts were working in the same vein."[5]

Reminiscing about these times in a 1955 letter, Hock reminded Wilson how he would:

> ... arrive at the office with those yellow scratch pad sheets I came to know so well. All you generally had on those yellow sheets were a few notes to guide you on a whole chapter! My understanding was that those notes were the result of long thought on your part after hours of discussion pro and con with everyone who might be interested ... As I look at it today the basic idea of each chapter of the book and the twelve steps is still essentially today what you scribbled on the original yellow sheets. Of course there were thousands of small changes and rewrites—constant cutting or adding or editing ... [6]

Ruth later added a bit more color to this picture by noting that Bill was a chain-smoker who "would pace back and forth expounding his ideas" and "at various intervals he would include his philosophizing off the subject using lengthy, flowery metaphors that would later [have to] be edited out."[7] These off-the-subject rambles sound perfectly reasonable if the only thing Wilson brought into the office were just a few notes to guide him on the writing of a whole chapter, as opposed to a more detailed outline of what he wanted to say. Lengthy extemporizing and flowery metaphors were very much in Bill Wilson's style and it would have been hard for him to resist those two tendencies while working under such loosely organized conditions.

Still, it is a captivating scene to imagine: Bill Wilson, standing behind Ruth Hock, completely immersed in the creative process, suggesting numerous small changes and rewrites and making constant additions, deletions, and edits to the text. It was an unorthodox way to go about writing a book and, as he admitted to Bob Smith, these first drafts were far from well-organized or polished prose: "I am turning this stuff out as fast as I can, being only once corrected dictation," he said, and concluded "you can't call it serious writing."[8] But the writing was getting progressively more "serious" with each retyping; something Ruth claimed—perhaps with a bit of exaggeration—she had to do "at least 50 times" before the book was finally published.[9]

However many times Ruth may have retyped the chapters, none of these interim copies were saved, so we have no record of the more polished October versions of "More About Alcoholism" or "We Agnostics," nor were any of the "once corrected dictations" for these three new chapters ever filed for future reference. This is unfortunate. While we have some idea of what was added and, more important, deleted from "There Is A Solution" and "Bill's Story," there are no comparatively early drafts of any of these other chapters allowing for similar comparison and analysis.

As already noted, besides the two May-June chapters, the earliest available version of all the other chapters are found in the Multilith Copy printed in mid-February 1939 and, while the Multilith text is in many instances notably different from what was finally published a little less than two months later, the changes made there were almost exclusively confined to specific word choices rather than to any significant additions or deletions.* Access to any of these earlier, ever-changing drafts might have shown substantial ongoing cuts and rewrites, but at this point it is impossible to imagine what those changes might have been. Still, the Multilith text is different enough from the published version to provide us with some important insights into Bill Wilson's evolving ideas about what should go into the book and how it should be presented.

One Alcoholic Working with Another

Although Hank had supplied a succinct description of the book in his mid-June outline,** Bill needed no prompting to know that the first of his three new chapters, "Working With Others," deserved a prominent and separate place within the work. In 1938, carrying the message of recovery to the suffering alcoholic was the central responsibility of every man who wanted to preserve his own sobriety and, by this time, the Fellowship had amassed almost four years of experience—both positive and negative—from their many attempts at sobering up other problem drinkers.

Dr. Bob's access to local hospitals regularly put him in touch with many alcoholics in need of help, while Bill's close relationship with Towns Hospital supplied a steady stream of prospects for the New York members. Beyond that, word of their success was driving potential members toward the Fellowship with growing frequency in both communities. Those years of solid experience made Bill's writing of "Working With Others" a much easier task than the more challenging chapter to the agnostic, or even the two he had already finished on alcoholism. Here, at least, was a much less controversial topic, one on which there was some general agreement between Akron and New York regarding what did and did not work when approaching a new prospect.

If nothing else, over the past three years they had reached an accord on two foundational principles for Alcoholics Anonymous: first, that the message of recovery was best delivered by one alcoholic speaking directly to another alcoholic, and second, that reaching out to help another person was the single most effective way to ensure your own continued sobriety. Both of these tenets were based on Bill Wilson's own experiences as he struggled to stay sober, but they had been confirmed by the experiences of almost every other early member of A.A. since then.

The Meeting with Dr. Bob Laid the Foundation

Bill's unqualified faith in these two principles was dramatically established in May 1935 when he travelled to Ohio with a team of investors attempting to take over National Rubber Machinery, a small Akron tool company. It was Bill's first substantial job since leaving Towns Hospital the previous December and he was desperate to succeed, especially since he had been promised the presidency of the company should they win

---

* Excepting only the long addition made to "Bill's Story," which incorporated the Second Step into his account of his own recovery. This important change will be dealt with at the appropriate point in the story.

** "We observed that once an alcoholic has a spiritual experience he must throw himself into work for others. It is preferable that he work with other alcoholics for he can do things which no one else can do. This chapter will detail just how to help others and build up a new group of friends." (Outline: Chapter Twenty, StSt, AA 501.1, Box 13, Folder 16; Publications Alcoholics Anonymous [1939 – (sic)] – Outline of chapters.)

control.[10] However, not long after his arrival in Ohio, it became clear that they were unlikely to secure enough proxy votes to win the fight. Wilson's partners in the venture went back to New York, leaving him behind to do his best, but with little real hope for success. Bill was stranded in Akron with just a few dollars in his pocket.[11]*

It was depressing enough that Wilson had spent the previous five months diligently trying to get a number of different men sober without scoring even one success. Now the shining prospect of winning this proxy fight (along with the promise of a big job) looked as if it too would end in failure. Bill was bitterly disappointed, so much so that he suddenly realized just how dangerously close he was to picking up a drink. His "white light" experience at Towns Hospital was five months behind him and he feared the impact of that event had grown so weak it might no longer be enough to keep him sober.

> Alone now in the hotel I paced up and down the lobby. There was a bar at one end, a church directory at the other. I would look into the bar where, it being Saturday afternoon, the local boys and girls were beginning to get an edge on. Then I would wander out and look absently at the church directory listing the services to be held next day. Into the bar I finally wandered, with a vague idea that I'd buy a bottle of Ginger Ale. Maybe I could scrape up an interesting acquaintance. Suddenly I got scared to death. I realized this was the beginning of the usual rationalization which led me to the first drink . . . Still walking back and forth between bar and church directory my panic increased. The pull of the bar became terrific, I was really tempted this time. But still I could think straight. What should I do? Then I suddenly realized how much helping other alcoholics had helped me—even though none had got well themselves. I'd have to find an alcoholic in Akron, and find him quick.[12]

This is arguably the most seminal moment in A.A. history. Wilson's growing awareness that he might actually pick up a drink was followed by a startling new insight: "I realized as never before how working with other alcoholics [over the previous five months] had played such a great part in sustaining my original experience" and "I thought to myself . . . 'I *must* find another alcoholic and help him so that I can remain free.'"[13]**

---

*   Besides the subsequent events recorded here, it is interesting to speculate on the very different future (if any) of Alcoholics Anonymous if Wilson had been successful and moved to Akron in mid-1935, something he was planning to do. As he told Lois: "The life is so different here and so interesting, it would make a brand new girl of you in six months—and I am pretty sure we are headed toward Akron." (Bill Wilson to Lois Wilson, May, 1935, StSt, WGW 102.4, Box 27, Folder 76).

**   These three quotes, along with several other retellings by Bill (and also by Lois, see *Lois Remembers*, p. 95), repeatedly make the point that this was the first time Wilson noticed the direct connection between his own continued sobriety and his efforts to get others sober.

There is an often-repeated A.A. urban legend that Lois Wilson was the first to notice this fact, but the source of that story has proven to be surprisingly elusive. Supposedly, just before he left for Akron, Bill was depressed and complaining about his lack of success in getting even one person sober during the previous five months. At that point, Lois allegedly disagreed with him saying something along the lines of: "Well that's not true, Bill. If nothing else, *YOU* stayed sober!" It would be wonderful to use this tale to support A.A.'s belief that the best way to stay sober is to carry the message of recovery to another alcoholic, but without a single shred of discoverable evidence in its favor (other than the fact that it sounds like something that certainly *ought* to be true) its appearance here must be limited to a footnote.

This was an historically important insight. While the thirsty Bill Wilson paced in the lobby of the Mayflower Hotel, it was not just his own sobriety, but perhaps the whole future of A.A. which hung in the balance. Fortunately, in his desperation, this self-described "rum hound from New York"[14] decided his salvation lay in reaching out to another alcoholic and he picked up the phone and made several calls which eventually led him to the all-important meeting with Dr. Bob Smith.* These actions not only preserved Wilson's own tenuous sobriety, they also resulting in Smith eventually getting sober.[15]

Because of this incident (and so many more like it which followed), Wilson believed that carrying the message to another alcoholic was the most fool-proof way for the newly sober man to avoid picking up the first drink. In addition, this activity was acknowledged as a profoundly spiritual one in and of itself. The chapter "Working With Others" (as it appears in the Multilith printing) opens with a strikingly strong statement establishing the privileged position that one alcoholic talking to another held in the early Fellowship: "Practical experience shows that nothing will so much insure your own immunity from drinking as intensive work with other alcoholics. It works when other spiritual activities fail."[16]** Working with others was explicitly considered to be the single most practical spiritual exercise to ensure continued sobriety. And, in case that important point had been forgotten by the reader as he made his way through the many details presented in this chapter, Bill firmly restated it just six paragraphs from the end: "If you are spiritually shaky," he wrote "you had better work with another alcoholic;" it was the very best way to preserve your own sobriety.

Beyond the spiritual benefits of working with others, it must be remembered that throughout 1938 there were only two Alcoholics Anonymous meetings in the world—one in Brooklyn on Tuesday nights and the other held in Akron every Wednesday—and at this time the primary activity pursued by A.A. members was not going to meetings, it was trying to help another alcoholic get started on the path to sobriety. The practice of reaching out to others wasn't just one more element in the quest for sobriety, it was literally the most important thing early members did on a day-to-day basis in their efforts to stay sober.

While most of the initial work with new men in Akron was being done during their hospital stay,[17] the experience Bill describes in this chapter is more closely modeled on the methods used in New York, where the new man was typically approached either

---

The anecdote is, quite frankly, such a great story that if it were true, surely either Bill or Lois would have recounted it at some time, most likely with considerable relish (just as they both candidly told the shoe throwing incident). But there is absolutely no evidence that either of them ever told this story in a recorded talk or in any of their writings. Instead, they both ascribed Wilson's first realization of this fact to the day he was in such distress in Akron in May 1935—as noted above.

* Another cottage industry among students of A.A. history are the many attempts to reconcile the different details offered at different times about this famous phone call: how many people were called before Bill made the all-important connection with the Reverend Tunks that led him to Henrietta Seiberling? Were the calls made from the phone booth (costing perhaps up to 50¢ for 10 calls) or where they made from his room? Did the Oxford Group people already know of Bill's presence in Akron and were they already planning for him to help Dr. Bob Smith? Whatever the exact details, the connection was made and Bill Wilson was introduced to Dr. Bob in their famous carriage house meeting shortly after this.

** The word "spiritual" was deleted from that final sentence when the book was published two months later and the Hazelden facsimile clearly shows that this was Hank Parkhurst's doing. He has drawn dark black lines through the word 'spiritual' and used an arrow to indicate his reason, which is written at the top of the page: "Page 27, Paragraph 3, #12—specifically says a "spiritual experience." This refers to the original form of the Twelfth Step as printed in the same book that, at least in Hank's opinion, made its reference here redundant.

before he became a patient or immediately after he had left the hospital.[*] In addition, it is important to note that the candidates approached in 1938 in both Ohio and New York were almost exclusively middle-class business men. In a contemporary letter, Bill confirms the desirability of this kind of candidate, noting that "the type of alcoholic who recovers most readily is the man who has begun to get some place in business and then is cut down by this hellish sickness."[18] This was the kind of prospect most frequently approached with the new program of recovery and the chapter Bill wrote detailing the best way to carry this message clearly reflected that fact.

The Salesman Makes His Case

One of the most prominent features of Bill's writing style in the Big Book is his constant selling of the A. A. program. On page after page Wilson's experience as a professional salesman[**] consistently colors the ways he presents his information, building an argument to successfully sell his conclusions to the reader, and then close the deal. (Perhaps the most striking example is the one found in the chapter "We Agnostics," which occurs after five pages of discussion on the necessity of adopting a belief in God: "When we became alcoholics, crushed by a self-imposed crisis we could not postpone or evade, we had to fearlessly face the proposition that either God is everything or else He is nothing. God either is or He isn't. What was our choice to be?"[19]) Over the years, some readers have been put off by this pervasive salesmanship, but selling is very much a part of Bill Wilson's style when it comes to the program of recovery, and his writing constantly veers in that direction as he drives home his points and tries to win each of the arguments he has set up.

"Working With Others" presents the most sustained example of this approach as Bill opens the chapter with several pages of advice that sound like nothing so much as a "Sales 101" training course. After extolling the benefits of carrying the message to others, he cautions against approaching the newcomer like "an evangelist or reformer," saying that kind of approach is likely to just "arouse . . . prejudice," and he reminds the man making the pitch that "to be helpful should be your only aim." He warns to not ever present yourself as a Temperance preacher or a Prohibitionist, that those approaches have never worked with alcoholics in the past and they will surely alienate your prospect.

The first step Bill suggests for winning over a new convert is to 'know your prospect,' one of the cardinal rules of salesmanship, or as he so bluntly puts it, "find out all you can about him." He suggests that the man carrying the message should first talk to

---

[*]   See, for instance, Bill Ruddell's letter to Bill Wilson from January 26, 1957 (mentioned here on p. 147) detailing how in February 1937, Dr. Silkworth had given him Wilson's name and phone number as he was leaving Towns Hospital and recommended that he contact Bill if he really wanted to stay sober.

[**]   Bill's primary job functions as a Wall Street entrepreneur were to (1) identify a stock that was a good candidate for growth, (2) form a small group of investors to buy significant shares of that stock, (3) sell other investors on the wonderful potential for this stock, thereby increasing the price through greater demand and "buzz" in the Financial District, and then (4) selling the stock at a profit. Wilson was, in fact, a sophisticated and astute analyst of undervalued stocks and he was an equally expert salesman when it came to convincing other investors to follow his lead and to buy into the new target company. (For just one instance of this see the details Bill provides on the Akron proxy fight in his audio biography [Bill Wilson—Autobiographical Recording]—Writings 1954—Recollections of his early life—recorded with Ed Bierstadt at Hotel Bedford Sept. 1954: StSt, WGW 103, Box 31, Folder 15]).

the prospect's wife to "get an idea of his behavior, his problems, his background, the seriousness of his condition, and his religious leanings." Armed with this information, Bill says, the investigator should then be able to "put yourself in his place" and so get some idea of "how you would like him to approach you if the tables were turned." In other words, arrive with an approach that has already been carefully tailored to this particular man.

The next traditional sales step would be to 'qualify your prospect,' so Bill advises that "it is wise to wait till he goes on a binge" and then "wait for the end of the spree, or at least a lucid interval" when the family can ask him "if he wants to quit for good and if he would go to any extreme to do so." If the man replies positively, then the family should mention that they know someone who has solved his own problems with drink and who tries to help others as "a part of his own recovery." In short, Wilson suggests starting with a willing (and hopefully hurting) prospect who has already admitted he is open to suggestions for change.

However, if the prospect rejects any help because he is still in denial about his problem, or if he thinks he can solve his drink problems on his own, then a bit of subversive advertising is suggested; a ploy that might be thought of as 'effectively using your promotional materials.' In these cases, Bill advises leaving a copy of the book, *Alcoholics Anonymous*, lying around the house where he can see it in the hopes it will attract his attention during his next interval between drunks. If his disastrous drinking career hasn't already brought him to his knees, then perhaps reading about this powerful and proven new solution will capture his attention and arouse some hope in him.

As a fairly strict rule-of-thumb Wilson warns against approaching the prospect through his family and suggests the best way to make a proper impression on the new man is to secure a professional referral from a doctor or an institution. Bill strongly recommends medical help for those trying to get sober, noting that "if your man needs hospitalization, he should have it." Then, once he is a patient, "let the doctor tell him he has something new in the way of a solution" and "when your man is better, let the doctor suggest a visit from you." (Note how Wilson casually presumes that A.A. members already have a working relationship with a particular institution and at least one of the doctors who works there—as he and his group had with Dr. Silkworth at Towns Hospital.) Wilson was aware that by the time the typical drunk requires a hospital visit, he would likely be paying little or no attention to his family's incessant complaints, but that a professional opinion might break through the many layers of denial continually employed to justify his ongoing drinking career.

Gaining a New Prospect's Confidence

Wilson then launches into several pages of step-by-step advice for how to approach and hopefully sell the new man on sobriety during a first visit. This particular section— which includes fourteen substantial paragraphs that make up a full one-third of "Working With Others"—is actually the heart of the chapter. This first meeting is of paramount importance because failure here means no further contact with the man, while success guarantees at least the possibility of a second meeting.

Speaking directly to the recovered member who will be visiting the stricken drunk, Bill suggests that he first gain the drinker's confidence by engaging "in general conversation" with him, and then after a while, turning "the talk to some phase of drinking." Bill contends that by being candid about your own drinking career, about your "habits, symptoms and experiences," you should be able to convince him that "you know all about the drinking game." Once he accepts you as someone who has had significant personal problems with drinking, "commence to describe yourself as an alcoholic. Tell him how baffled you were . . . [and] give him an account of the struggles you made to stop." Having carefully prepared this groundwork, Wilson advises that now is the perfect time to explain to him about "the mental twist which leads to the first drink," for this is truly the heart of the problem. "If he is an alcoholic, he will understand you at once."

If you have gotten that far with your new man, Bill suggests you "continue to speak of alcoholism as a sickness, a fatal malady" and dwell on the "hopeless feature" of the disorder caused by "the queer mental condition surrounding that first drink [which] prevents normal functioning of the will power." Explain to your prospect "that many are doomed" because they "never realize their predicament" or ever come to understand just how insidious and deadly alcoholism really is.

As you are concluding this 'gaining the client's confidence' section by reciting "your personal experience," Wilson warns you must be careful "not to brand [the new man] an alcoholic. Let him draw his own conclusions. If he sticks to the idea that he can still control his drinking, tell him that possibly he can—if he is not too alcoholic. But insist that if he is severely afflicted, there is little chance he can recover by himself."

By concentrating on the details of the problem and the revolutionary diagnosis of alcoholism as a fatal illness (most clearly exhibited by the "mental twist" which inevitably precedes the first drink), Wilson is cleverly trying to entice the listener into becoming an active participant in the conversation. "Even though your protege may not have entirely admitted his condition, he has become very curious to know how you got well. Let him ask you that question, if he will." That is surely the ideal outcome—capturing the prospect's attention so completely that he begins to ask you for more information—but if he does not fall for that traditional sales ploy, then it is time to "proceed with the rest of your story."

Spiritual Principles in Everyday Language

This necessitates introducing the idea of God, and Bill suggests dealing with this often-problematic issue head-on, no matter what a man's beliefs or lack of belief might be. "Stress the spiritual feature freely," he boldly advises. "If the man be agnostic or atheist, make it emphatic that he does not have to agree with your conception of God. He can choose any conception he likes, provided it makes sense to him. The main thing is that he be willing to believe in a Power greater than himself and that he live by spiritual principles." In dealing with non-believers, Wilson highly recommends using "everyday language to describe spiritual principles" for "there is no use arousing any prejudices" he may already have. And at all costs, avoid introducing any "theological terms and conceptions . . . no matter what you own convictions" might be. These would almost certainly be 'deal-breakers.'

Even if your prospect already belongs to a religious denomination, you must still be careful in how you handle this topic of God, for he may know far more about the subject than you do. "Let him see that you are not there to instruct him in religion. Admit that he probably knows more about it than you do, but call to his attention the fact that however deep his faith and knowledge, there must be something wrong, or he would not drink." Why is it that his own very fine religious convictions have failed him in relation to alcohol, while "the general [spiritual] principles common to most denominations" which you have been using to stay sober are working so well for you? Perhaps it is because you have engaged in a number of actions demanded by those common principles. Obviously, "faith alone is insufficient. To be vital faith must be accompanied by self sacrifice and unselfish constructive action." Or, as Bill would later write in the "Into Action" chapter, the program of recovery is in essence a "spiritual program of action."[20]

A Program of Action, Not a Crusade

Having emphatically dealt with the necessary reliance on God (or, at the very least, on "a Power greater than himself"), it was now time to start talking about the "program of action." Bill suggests being very specific here. Tell the new man "how you made a self-appraisal, how you straightened out your past, and why you are now endeavoring to be helpful to him . . . show how important it is that he place the welfare of other people ahead of his own." Be prepared, for there may be a negative reaction to this. Having been given some idea of exactly what will be asked of him if he means to stay sober, "your candidate may give reasons why he need not follow all of your program." Do not be discouraged and "do not contradict such views. Tell him you once felt as he does, but you doubt if you would have made much progress had you not taken action." If nothing else, "maybe you have disturbed him about the question of alcoholism. That is all to the good. The more hopeless he feels, the better. He is [then] more likely to follow your suggestions."

Returning once again to a theme that informs this whole chapter, Bill emphasizes that "you will be most successful with alcoholics if you do not exhibit any passion for crusade or reform. Never talk down to an alcoholic from any moral or spiritual hilltop, simply lay out your kit of spiritual tools for his inspection. Show him how they worked with you." While the words "crusade and reform" have now lost most of their historical impact, a 1938 reader would have clearly understood them as referring to the Temperance and Prohibition movements that had so dominated the cultural and then the political life of the country for the previous seventy years. It must be remembered that Prohibition had ended just five years before this and anyone reading these words would have grown up under the shadow of those militant and increasingly effective political campaigns to banish alcohol. Similarly, the "moral and spiritual hilltop" mentioned here stands in for all of the preachers and ministers who railed so loudly against alcohol (or at least excessive drinking) in support of those two movements. According to Bill Wilson, these are two paths that members of Alcoholics Anonymous should never try to walk down. That would be fatal to your argument. Those approaches just do not work. Instead, the best way and most proven way to present your position is to tell your story in terms of what has worked for you.

But even a well-conducted first interview does not always produce the desired results. Perhaps "he is not interested in your solution," but rather "expects you to act only as a banker for his financial difficulties or a nurse for his sprees." If so, just "drop him until he changes his mind." And, "if your prospect does not respond at once" do not be discouraged. "Search out another alcoholic and try again. You are sure to find someone desperate enough to accept with eagerness what you offer. It's a waste of time and poor strategy to keep chasing a man who cannot or will not work with you."

The Pitfalls of Money and Family

But, if you are successful, and your man "says he is prepared to go through with . . . The Program of Recovery," then there are still several common pitfalls to be avoided, especially those surrounding money and family. Wilson notes that the man who is "broke and homeless" may need some help getting a job and "a little financial assistance" at times and perhaps even a place to stay "for a few days." Bill cautions that taking someone into your home calls for "discretion" to ensure "he is not trying to impose upon you for money, connections, or shelter" and you also need to be sure "he will be welcomed by your family." But serious problems can still arise when working so closely with a newly sober man, and Wilson graphically relates some of these, all of which are based on his own personal experiences.

> It may mean the loss of many nights' sleep, great interference with your pleasures, interruptions to your business. It may mean sharing your money and your home, counseling frantic wives and relatives, innumerable trips to police courts, sanitariums, hospitals, jails and asylums. Your telephone may jangle at any time of the day or night. Your wife will sometimes say she is neglected. A drunk may smash the furniture in your home, or burn a mattress. You may have to fight with him if he is violent. Sometimes you will have to call a doctor and administer sedatives under his direction. Another time you may have to send for the police or an ambulance.

But, even if some of these are what must be done to achieve continuous sobriety, it is still an outstanding bargain.

Bill cautions, however, that you must be vigilant and careful around all of these issues because "the minute we put our work on a social service plane, the alcoholic commences to rely upon our assistance rather than upon God . . . [and] we simply do not stop drinking alcohol so long as we place dependence upon other people ahead of dependence on God."

Along with financial problems, domestic issues almost always plague the newly sober man; they are the price he typically pays for his years of neglecting the family while drinking. Arguments and faultfinding are common (and understandable) as the family tries to come back together again, but they "are to be avoided like leprosy." Instead, the newly sober man must "concentrate on his own spiritual demonstration" and, with any luck, his family will recognize the changes in him and perhaps even "want to join [him] in a better way of life." But if not, "let no alcoholic say he cannot recover unless he has his family back." If he begins to go down that road of complaint, "remind your prospect that his recovery is not dependent upon people. It is dependent upon his relationship with God." Whatever family disagreements there may be, "take care not to participate in their quarrels." "If you have been successful in solving your own domestic problems," the most you might want to do is to share some personal stories about how that was accomplished. Real life stories are "worth any amount of preaching or criticism" and they are surely the best way for you to be most helpful in these situations.

A New Relationship with Alcohol

Then, in the final eleven paragraphs of the chapter, Bill Wilson suddenly shifts gears, taking his focus off the new man and the proper way of delivering the message of sobriety and begins to tell the A.A. member who is carrying this message all of the wonderful things he is now free to do because he himself has had a spiritual awakening. These comments—delivered in a fairly stern and directive tone—are somewhat unexpected and may seem misplaced here, but they give Wilson the opportunity to make several interesting and important observations about alcohol and alcoholism, remarks he obviously feels are essential to any thorough discussion of how to effectively work with others.

Bill starts these comments in a direct and challenging fashion:

> Assuming we are spiritually fit, we can do all sorts of things alcoholics are not supposed to do. People have said we must not go where liquor is served; we must not have it in our homes; we must shun friends who drink; we must avoid moving pictures which show drinking scenes; we mustn't go into bars; our friends must hide their bottles if we go to their houses; we mustn't think or be reminded about alcohol at all. Experience proves this is nonsense.

To Bill, it should be clear this is nonsense, and alcoholics will know it is nonsense because their experience tells them those things are simply not true because, "we meet these conditions every day" without drinking. Experience has proven that "any scheme of combating alcoholism which proposes to shield the sick man from temptation is doomed to failure." The solution is not to be found in isolation. An alcoholic must comfortably coexist with alcohol whenever and wherever it appears and if a man cannot do this, then it is clear he "still has an alcoholic mind" and that there is "something the matter with his spiritual status."

So our rule is not to avoid a place where there is drinking, <u>if we have a legitimate reason for being there</u> . . .

You will note that we made an important qualification. Therefore, ask yourself on each occasion, "Have I any legitimate social, business, or personal reason for going to this place? Am I going to be helpful to anyone there? Could I be more useful or helpful by being somewhere else?" If you answer these questions satisfactorily, you need have no apprehension. You may go or stay away, whatever seems best. But be sure you are on solid spiritual ground before you start and that your motive in going is thoroughly good . . .

In addition, when he does find himself in a drinking situation, there is no need for the alcoholic to sit there suffering "with a long face . . . sighing about the good old days." Instead, Wilson advises, "if it is a happy occasion, try to increase the pleasure of those" around you and "let your friends know they are not to change their habits on your account."

Your job now is to be at the place where you may be of maximum helpfulness to others, so never hesitate to go where there is drinking, if you can be helpful. You should not hesitate to visit the most sordid spot on earth on such a mission. Keep on the firing line of life with these motives, and God will keep you unharmed.

Once again he emphasizes that "we are careful never to show intolerance or hatred of drinking as an institution . . . Every new alcoholic looks for this spirit among us and is immensely relieved when he finds we are not witch-burners." Instead, because of this new and more open attitude toward alcohol, Wilson hopes that someday "Alcoholics Anonymous will help the public to a better realization of the gravity of the alcohol problem. We shall be of little use if our attitude is one of bitterness or hostility. Drinkers will not stand for it."

Some passages in this final section of "Working With Others" have often baffled and perplexed modern members of Alcoholics Anonymous because, on the face of it, Bill's advice contradicts more recently held beliefs in A.A. about the necessity of avoiding drinking situations whenever possible. Most troubling to some is Wilson's casual faith that a truly sober man should have no problem whatsoever going into bars or any other place where alcohol is a prominent part of the landscape. Later experience has suggested that, however well protected a man might be by his new spiritual condition, it is far wiser not to tempt fate by plunging into drinking situations except under specific and compelling circumstances.

But an awareness of what Bill was actually talking about as he brought this chapter to a close—never explicitly mentioned, but again, easily recognized by anyone who read it in 1938—can be helpful in understanding the real purpose of this dramatic closing. Wilson's final eleven paragraphs in "Working With Others" are, more than anything else, an attempt to positively describe in the strongest possible terms the differences he sees between the beliefs and practices of Alcoholics Anonymous when compared to those so widely promulgated by the Temperance and Prohibition movements over the previous several decades.

Bill calls these much-touted Temperance and Prohibition beliefs about the necessity for isolation, and even the complete abolition of alcohol, "nonsense." Who says a recovered alcoholic can't safely be around alcohol and that the only solution is to separate himself from a drinking society? That is what the evangelists, the reformers, and the witch-burners have always said, but Bill reassures the alcoholic that it just isn't so. And it's true that the avoidance, isolation, and abolition ploys prescribed for so many decades as a cure for alcoholism had never worked. Ex-problem-drinkers can neither ask society to ban alcohol nor can they be expected to live their lives in isolation from it. Instead, Wilson proposes that the solution must come from within each man and it must be based on his solid relationship with God. The old formulas and the old solutions have never worked and they never will, but this completely new understanding of the drink problem along with the new solution for curing it most certainly does.

Bill would have the alcoholic finally admit that the fault lies neither in alcohol itself nor in the bottles holding the booze, nor even in the people who sell it, but rather deep within himself. Any further fight against the presence of alcohol in our lives or in the lives of the people around us is doomed to failure and must be acknowledged as such if there is to be any progress whatsoever toward a reliable and sustained recovery. Driving home this point—that the solution rests solely with the individual and the work he must do to effectively challenge and overcome his own disease—Wilson ends this chapter with a brief but potent final paragraph that he underlines for special emphasis.

> <u>After all, our troubles were of our own making.</u> <u>Bottles were only a symbol.</u>
> <u>Besides we have stopped fighting anybody and anything.</u> <u>We have to!</u>

He is stating in plain language that blaming outside forces is the road to failure, but if you look to yourself and rely on God's help, you will surely be invincible in all your future relations with alcohol and alcoholics.

CHAPTER EIGHTEEN

"To Wives"

~October to November 1938~

Perhaps no chapter in the Big Book is more dated and more reflective of its own time than "To Wives." The prejudices and preconceptions regarding women that were so much a part of the cultural landscape in 1938 are glaringly on display in almost every paragraph here. At this time, Bill Wilson and his cohorts in the Fellowship—predominantly middle class American men—generally understood the word "alcoholic" as an almost exclusively male noun, with women relegated to the role of subservient helpmate in every area of a couple's life.

On one level, this should surprise no one. Women had been actively fighting for recognition and respect for more than a century in America, but had won the right to vote only *eighteen years* before this chapter was written. The long American arc of women's liberation stretching back to Frances Wright in the early 1800s and extending through Susan B. Anthony and other early fighters for women's equality throughout that century had made some progress, but only some. Still to come for the feminist movement was the emergence of "Rosie the Riveter" during the Second World War and the gradual acceptance of women working outside the home in the 1950s. This would be followed by the tumultuous rebellion that broke out in the 1960s in response to the callously dismissive treatment women had endured during the previous twenty years of financial prosperity and growth.

But beyond the pervasive 1938 cultural deprecation of women, there were two additional factors operative in early A.A. history that produced an almost total identification of the word 'alcoholic' with the married man rather than a married woman.

Prejudices Against Women Alcoholics

The first of these was the hostile prejudice against women alcoholics at the time. While a man could be an alcoholic and still preserve some semblance of respectability or, at least be granted that status once he became sober, the woman alcoholic was uniformly characterized as a disreputable fallen creature who was unlikely to ever regain her former reputation. This was based on the belief that while drinking, she had surely compromised her virtue to such a degree that she could never again be the kind of woman who would be received in proper society. It was a flagrant double-standard, creating the firm conviction that almost all of the females who came into A.A. (wives of highly successful men were at times exempted[1]) automatically deserved to be categorized as promiscuous, disgraced, and generally unredeemable women.[2]

The Akron group's experience with "absolutely the first woman [they] ever dealt with"[3] only reaffirmed this prejudice. Lil arrived on the scene in late 1935, but rather than securing her place as the first woman to get sober in Alcoholics Anonymous, Lil's notoriety rests on a torrid evening she spent with Victor, another early member, as they consummated their affair on the examination table in Dr. Bob's office (while Bob was off playing cards for the evening). Things got even more out of hand later that same night when Victor announced it was time for him to go home and the intoxicated Lil insisted on continuing the party. She started running around the office, rummaging through Bob's cabinets, stealing pills and stuffing them in her mouth. Victor had to call another member for help before they could subdue Lil and get her safely tucked away in Dr. Bob's basement where she temporarily sobered up.[4] Lil's uninhibited episode proved to be a bad omen for the future of women in the still unnamed Ohio recovery movement.

Not surprisingly the biggest barriers to the acceptance of women in early A.A. were the wives of the men who attended meetings. "Every woman who came in alone was like a warning signal to all the wives. They were scared to death of them."[5] In late 1939 the first woman to come into Cleveland A.A. was reportedly "so bad" that the wives "wouldn't allow her in their homes."[6] The position taken by the wives was that "no lady would do a thing like that,"[7] the emphasis being firmly placed on their understanding of the word "lady" and the unspoken licentiousness of "that." "Nice women," they believed, just didn't drink to excess and those who did were therefore not nice.[8] This unforgiving attitude persisted well into the 1940s when, for instance, a member reported overhearing one woman alcoholic advising another: "Be darn careful how you handle yourself around these wives. They think you're the babe their husband went out with."[9]*

But women weren't the only problem; the men could be just as bad and often acted in ways that did nothing to alleviate their wives' fears. In mid-1939 a woman

---

* This low opinion of women in A.A. was, unfortunately, not confined to the 1940s nor were the wives of members the only ones who professed it. Female A.A. members could be equally harsh on their sisters in recovery. There was a front-page article published in the October 1946 issue of The A.A. *Grapevine* entitled "Women in A.A. Face Special Problems" written by Grace O. of Manhattan that is literally shocking to twenty-first century sensibilities. The author's indictment of women in this long article will reward any reader seeking a better understanding of the significant prejudices and barriers blocking a woman's path to sobriety in A.A. during the mid-1940s (and beyond).

named Sylvia Kaufman arrived in Ohio from Chicago. She was thirty-three-years-old, beautiful, and rich, a "glamorous divorcee with $700 a month alimony," and she was in need of some help with her drinking problem. When Dr. Bob introduced her to the group the men were "only too willing to talk to her after they saw her." Sylvia, it turned out, was so pleased with Bob Smith and his friends that she decided to take up residence in Akron and "this caused great consternation, since her presence threatened to disrupt the whole group." The wives were not about to leave their men alone in a room with this beautiful temptress. Finally, someone shrewdly suggested to Sylvia that "it would mean a great deal more if she could go back and help in Chicago" rather than stay in Akron and this idea immediately appealed to her. Sylvia was summarily escorted to the train station by several members and she left for the Windy City, much to the relief of Dr. Bob and all of the A.A. wives in Ohio.[10]*

But perhaps the most important and influential opinion on the issue of women in early Akron A.A. was that of Dr. Bob Smith himself; he was notorious for his distrust of women alcoholics, believing they had no place in A.A. meetings and wondering if they were even capable of getting sober. When he was first told Sylvia was on her way to Akron, he "threw up his hands and said, 'We have never had a woman and will not work on a woman.'"[11] But, by that time, Sylvia was already on her way. "He just didn't know how to handle them," his son remarked.[12] Confronted with yet another new female prospect, Bob just shook his head and said: "I think I'd better work with the men, because the women . . . I'm not sure. I don't know." In his awkward uncertainty, Bob Smith turned new women over to his wife, Anne, and to any of the other wives who could be convinced to shoulder the burden of explaining the program of recovery to their fallen sisters.[13] As Frank Amos so candidly commented in his February 1938 report: "Smith says that men can rarely work satisfactorily with women alcoholics. The sex problem makes it difficult. He, as a physician, can and has helped, but his wife and other wives must handle most of this, for which there is a growing need."[14]

Of course the real problem here was the threat of extramarital sex. Bill Wilson "recalled 'explosions' which took place around the 'out-of-bounds romance' and the arrival of alcoholic women at meetings. 'Whole groups got into uproars, and a number of people got drunk,' he said. 'We trembled for A.A.'s reputation and for its survival.'"[15] In Akron, Bob Smith, accepting the denigrating prejudices of his day, acknowledged the fact that "most of the women came in with the label 'nymphomaniac,'"[16] an attitude that presumed there would just naturally be the lurking danger of sex whenever men and women mixed at A.A. meetings. This fearful mindset regarding women members was neatly captured in the pithy and pejorative Akron saying, "Under every skirt, there is a slip" (a "slip" being a return to drinking). The prevailing attitude was: *Beware of these women; they are dangerous to your sobriety!*

---

* Sylvia Kaufman drank on the way back to Chicago, but did finally quit a few months later. Once sober, she joined forces with Earl Treat and they became the two most important and active founding members of A.A. in Chicago. Her story, "The Keys to the Kingdom" (which makes no mention of these early difficulties in Ohio), appears in the second, third, and fourth editions of *Alcoholics Anonymous* (starting on pages 304, 304 & 268 respectively). Fourteen years after writing her story, Sylvia wrote a post-script in a January 1969 article in the AA *Grapevine* entitled "Don't Take Our Word For It." According to member list index cards kept by the Chicago group, Sylvia's date of sobriety was September 13, 1939, which likely makes her the first woman to achieve permanent long-term sobriety in Alcoholics Anonymous. She died on October 31, 1974.

To put it bluntly, men who regularly drank to excess were alcoholics, but women who did so were sluts.*

The New York Group Accepts Florence Rankin

We have no direct contemporary information on the treatment of women in the early New York meetings, but the ready acceptance of Florence Rankin, despite all of her repeated slips, does provide evidence for Bill Wilson's more inclusive approach to membership in the group. It is unlikely her inclusion came without its share of problems, but Florence was extended at least the same sort of tolerant acceptance given, however grudgingly, to the militant atheist, Jim Burwell. Both the woman and the atheist were in one way or another seriously out of step with the rest of the group, but they were admitted to their meetings nonetheless.

As was typical in Akron, it was the wife, Lois Wilson, who made the first A.A. contact with Florence, having been brought to her hospital bed by Rankin's ex-husband Larry (one of Bill's old drinking companions from his Wall Street days).[17] When Florence was released, Lois took her home and introduced her to Bill who seems to have had no problem working directly with this new member. After a few days, Florence was sent out of town to live with another recently recovered alcoholic and his wife, presumably because the Wilson household in Brooklyn was overrun with single males who were trying to stay sober and didn't need the distraction of this woman's presence.[18]

Regarding the difference in the level of acceptance in New York and Akron, it is instructive to note that the only story by an Ohio woman appearing in the first edition of the Big Book ("An Alcoholic's Wife") was less than two full pages and was written by Marie Bray, the wife of an alcoholic. In New York, Florence, noting that she was "the only 'lady' alcoholic in our particular section," wrote a full-length story (more than eight pages long) entitled "A Feminine Victory" recounting the details of her drinking career and her long succession of slips before going on to celebrate the turnaround that resulted in her first full year of sobriety. Finally, Bill Wilson's inclusion of Florence's story in the book was a clear invitation to women everywhere, announcing they would be welcome in Alcoholics Anonymous if they truly wanted to solve their drinking problem.*

The second factor having a profound effect on the writing of "To Wives" was the fact that—despite the deliberate fiction that it was the work of the non-alcoholic "wives of Alcoholics Anonymous"—the chapter was entirely written by Bill Wilson, an alcoholic man.

---

* As the endnotes attest, most of the foregoing information on the experience of women in early A.A. comes from just a few pages of *Dr. Bob and the Good Oldtimers*, highlighting one of the most glaring gaps in our current understanding of the early years of Alcoholics Anonymous. It is criminal that there is still no serious and insightful study—based on thorough research using primary documents—to tell the story of women's fight for acceptance in A.A. from 1935 to 1945. This is a truly important story and one can only hope that someday soon an able historian will take it on as a doctoral dissertation or a full-blown book-writing project. It is desperately needed.

Bill Denies Lois's Request to Write the Chapter

There are numerous citations on the internet and elsewhere in print[19] claiming the Akron Archive contains evidence that Marie Bray, the wife of the Akron A.A. member Walter Bray, wrote a preliminary draft of "To Wives," or at least lent a hand in the writing of that chapter. However a recent thorough search of the Akron Archives produced no such evidence, nor was the existence of any such evidence known to the long-time archivist who was responsible for creating that collection. It can only be presumed that this bit of bad information grew out of someone's misunderstanding of the fact that Marie Bray did actually write a chapter entitled "An Alcoholic's Wife" for the story section of the book. (This was the same story chapter Bill had offered to Anne Smith the previous June, but she had declined to write.)[20]*

Lois was probably aware Bill had offered Anne Smith the opportunity to write one of the full length stories for the back of the book and that Anne had refused him. But Lois was not as modest or retiring as Anne Smith. In the almost four years that Bill had been sober, she "had begun to realize how distorted the relationships in families of alcoholics could often be, how important it was for families to understand about alcoholism and to rearrange their thinking."[21] Given all of that, Lois thought writing this chapter was "something she was much better qualified to do"[22] than her husband, so what could be more logical than to assume that Bill would offer her the opportunity to put all of this hard-won knowledge to good use by writing "To Wives" for his book?

But that was an offer Wilson was not willing to make.

According to Lois, when she "shyly suggested" to Bill that she should write this chapter (and perhaps also "The Family Afterward"), he answered with a firm "No," telling her "he thought the book, except for the stories, should all be written in the same style."[23] This is an interesting excuse (and one we shall see Wilson use again later), but it is more than a little self-serving, reflecting Bill's growing sense of ownership and control of the book project as each of the newly finished chapters began to pile up.

However, Bill's reasons for not wanting Lois to write the chapter were, in all likelihood, a bit more complex than this simple-sounding desire for uniformity in style or even his own control issues. For one thing, as he wrote more of the book, Wilson came to appreciate just how difficult it was to write accurately and clearly about the alcoholic condition, and "To Wives" would surely have to address several of these sensitive and complicated questions—not least of which was "What is an alcoholic?" Given that reality, Bill was unwilling to delegate this challenging task to a non-alcoholic, fearing they would almost certainly get the tone wrong or, at least, offer some unacceptable explanation of alcoholism or some wrong advice on how to handle certain delicate situations involving the newly recovered man.

In fact, Bill would once more wrestle with trying to produce an accurate definition of the alcoholic in this chapter, but it was most likely this last point—the way to properly deal with a newly recovered man—that was decisive in his refusal to turn this project over to Lois. As Francis Hartigan noted in his 2001 book, *Bill W.*:

* See the footnote on p. 190 of this book for the previous discussion of the fact that Bill Wilson never asked Anne Smith to write "To Wives."

In all things, Bill Wilson was, first and foremost, an advocate for the still suffering alcoholic. It is hard to appreciate today the tentativeness of the early sobriety of the typically middle-aged, late-stage, alcoholics he was familiar with. As heartless as it might seem from the wife's point of view to ask her to continue to treat her husband as a fragile child, if it could buy him precious time to achieve some degree of emotional stability before her long bottled up resentments boiled over, it was something that Bill would do.[24]

And that is just what he did in this chapter, constantly stressing the major concessions the wife must make to support the new man's still tenuous sobriety, while simultaneously absolving the drinking husband from substantive responsibilities for his actions. One could hardly count on the long-suffering wife to see the issue from this more permissive and forgiving perspective. Still, Lois felt she was more qualified than anyone else to write this chapter and she might well have been; but if she had done so, "it is quite likely that the content would have been different."[25] An understatement, indeed.

Finally, there is the worrisome problem of the marital discord that might arise if Bill was forced to severely edit something Lois had written so that it conformed to the perspective he wanted to see presented in this chapter. Avoidance is a common tactic in many marriages and this likely figured in Wilson's decision to sidestep such a potentially explosive minefield by simply writing the chapter himself. Saying "No" is a single argument. Ongoing edits and corrections might have resulted in more disagreements than Bill Wilson was willing to contemplate or tolerate.

Lois was furious at being treated so dismissively. "I was mad," she said, adding that "I wasn't so much mad as hurt. I still don't know why Bill wrote it. I've never really gotten into it—why he insisted upon writing it."[26] Years later, when she was questioned on this again, it was still a sensitive topic, one that continued to rankle; "I don't think I have ever gotten over it," she said. "It *still* makes me mad just to think about it."[27*]

Given all of the above cultural biases and the short but stormy history of women in early A.A., along with the fact that "To Wives" was written by a man masquerading as a woman, it is hardly surprising to find that this chapter contains the most patriarchal writing to be found in the Big Book.

Bill Speaks for the Wives

Bill opens the chapter with an acknowledgment that "thus far our book has spoken of men," but he notes "what we have said applies quite as much to women," that "our activities in behalf of women who drink are on the increase," and that "there is every evidence that women regain their health as readily as men if they follow our suggestions."[28] So, clearly women are welcome in Alcoholics Anonymous and the

---

* I would suggest that the sentiments in this paragraph ("I still don't know why Bill wrote it" and "I don't think I have ever gotten over it") provide some interesting insights into the Wilson's marriage in relation to the levels of communication that prevailed there and to the resentments that obviously remained unresolved for decades.

principles of the program are just as valid for them as they are for any of their male counterparts.

Having given this scant, but important bit of recognition to female drinkers, Wilson notes that the ravages of alcoholism affect many family members, but especially impact the wife. There is, however, reason for hope because "among us are wives . . . whose problem has been solved." Bill then concludes his three introductory paragraphs with a deliberately deceptive promise: "We shall let the wives of Alcoholics Anonymous address the wives of men who drink too much. What they say will apply to nearly everyone bound by ties of blood or affection to an alcoholic."

And so with a double-space and four short dashed lines to indicate a change of speaker, Bill Wilson begins his impersonation of the wives of Alcoholics Anonymous, women who in one uniform voice will deliver the message he considers so important for the wife of a drinking man to hear and heed.

Borrowing from the powerful and proven one-drunk-talking-to-another-drunk model, this section opens by saying "As wives of Alcoholics Anonymous, we want you to sense that we understand you as perhaps few can . . . [and] we want to leave you with the feeling that no situation is too difficult and no unhappiness too great to be overcome." This hopeful promise is followed by an attempt to generate some immediate sister-feeling by offering a few likely shared experiences:

> We have traveled a rocky road; there is no mistake about that. We have
> had long rendezvous with hurt pride, frustration, self-pity, misunderstand,
> *[sic]* and fear. These are not pleasant companions. We have been driven
> to maudlin sympathy, to bitter resentment. We have veered from extreme
> to extreme, ever hoping that one day our loved ones would be themselves
> once more.

Shifting from these common problems to some shared but failed solutions, the wives now present a sympathetic catalogue of the ways they have unsuccessfully tried to deal with their drunken husbands (so similar to Wilson's laundry list of methods tried by alcoholics who want to quit drinking[29]):

> We have been unselfish and self-sacrificing. We have told innumerable
> lies to protect our pride and our husbands' reputations. We have prayed,
> we have begged, we have been patient. We have struck out viciously. We
> have run away. We have been hysterical. We have been terror stricken.
> We have sought sympathy. We have had retaliatory love affairs with other
> men.

Acknowledging the complete failure of these tactics, "the wives" now present six paragraphs elaborating the many troubles often caused by drunken husbands ("our homes have been battle-grounds," "we seldom had friends in our homes," "there was never financial security," "sometimes there were other women," "the bill collectors, the sheriffs," "they struck the children") followed by two paragraphs relating more possible solutions to these seemingly insoluble problems ("perhaps . . . we got a divorce" or "finally sought employment ourselves" or "we began to ask medical advice").

Laying the groundwork for the coming A.A. solution, "the wives of Alcoholics Anonymous" freely admit that "under these conditions we naturally made some mistakes," and then present several paragraphs detailing the confusion and bafflement they felt when confronted with the mystery of their husband's illness. They agree this mystery must be acknowledged, but if you honestly want him to recover, "don't condemn your alcoholic husband no matter what he says or does. He is just another very sick, unreasonable person. Treat him, when you can, as though he had pneumonia. When he angers you, remember that he is very ill."

This admonition for understanding, forgiveness, and acceptance sets the tone for much of what follows; the basic message to the wife will be that she must do everything in her power to help her husband get sober, no matter how unfair or unreasonable that may seem to her at the time. This is not going to be a presentation of how the wife can best take care of herself, but rather a set of instructions on what must be done if she really wants her husband to quit drinking forever. Here Bill's presentation once again follows the outline Hank had created the previous June, where he suggested a chapter "dealing with wives, relative and friends, showing them how they may help."[30] This chapter is not going to be about how they may survive, it's about how they may *help*.

However there is one situation that overrides this general rule of forgiveness and tolerance that "the wives" want to note before concluding this section. "There is an important exception to the foregoing," they write. "We realize some men are thoroughly bad-intentioned, that no amount of patience will make any difference." The wife is told that if her husband is like this, "don't let him get away with it" and take whatever measures are required to save yourself and your children from further misery—if necessary even by leaving him.

Dealing with the Four Types of Alcoholics

In contrast to the three different types of alcoholics Bill had already offered in "There Is A Solution" (the moderate drinker, the hard drinker and the real alcoholic[31]), "the wives" now confidently claim that "the problem with which you struggle usually falls within one of four categories" and they provide a detailed outline for each of these four types.

> <u>One</u>: Your husband may be only a heavy drinker. His drinking may be constant or it may be heavy only on certain occasions . . . Sometimes he is a source of embarrassment to you and his friends. He is positive he can handle his liquor, that it does him no harm . . .

> <u>Two</u>: Your husband is showing lack of control, He is unable to stay on the water wagon, even when he wants to . . . He is remorseful after serious drinking bouts and tells you he wants to stop. But when he gets over the spree, he begins to think once more how he can drink moderately next

time . . . He has begun to try, with or without your cooperation, various means of moderating or staying dry . . .

Three: This husband has gone much further than husband number two . . . and the weary round of sanitariums and hospitals has begun. He admits he cannot drink like other people, but does not see why. He clings to the notion that he will yet find a way to do so. He may have come to the point where he desperately wants to stop but cannot . . .

Four: . . . He has been placed in one institution after another. He is violent, or definitely insane when drunk. Sometimes he drinks on the way home from the hospital. Perhaps he has had delirium tremens. Doctors shake their heads and advise you to have him committed. Maybe you have already been obliged to put him away . . .

The critical difference between these four types is the degree to which the drinker is willing to quit. The first is still "positive he can handle his liquor," the second, driven by increasing problems, continues to "tell you he wants to stop," the third "desperately wants to stop but cannot," while the fourth has given up all hope of ever quitting, he's the one who "drinks on the way home from the hospital."

With this neat outline in place, the next sixteen paragraphs advise the drinker's wife on what she can expect—depending on which of these four categories her husband falls into—and what actions she should take to be helpful to him. In each case, the actions suggested for setting the drunken husband on the road to recovery rely almost exclusively on readings from the book, *Alcoholics Anonymous*. "The wives" are confident that the book will prove to have all the information necessary for transforming an active drinker into a sober member of A.A.

Half of these paragraphs concentrate on "husband number one" because "oddly enough" he is often the most difficult to deal with. Confronted with this kind of drunk, "the first principle of success is that you should never be angry" and "the next rule is that you should never tell him what to do about his drinking." Unless these two rules are strictly followed, your husband will likely consider you as nothing but "a nag or a killjoy," and then he will use that characterization as an excuse for more drinking during which time he "may seek someone to console him—not always another man."

With this devastating threat hanging over her head, the wife is encouraged to initiate a "frank and friendly talk about his liquor problem" with her husband, but "be sure you are not critical during such a discussion. Attempt instead, to put yourself in his place. Let him see that you want to be helpful rather than critical" and "when a discussion does arise, you might suggest he read this book, or at least the chapter on alcoholism." This is followed by the rather strange suggestion that it might be helpful at this point to take the focus off the husband and put it on some of his drinking friends. Once the "number one" husband has gained some understanding of alcoholism (from his wife and from reading the book), then he might be willing—because "drinkers like to help other drinkers"—to take an interest in some of his alcoholic acquaintances and even "be willing to talk to one of them, perhaps over a highball" about his drinking problem. (Exactly how this bizarre recommendation might move the husband closer to sobriety is never clarified.)

If the conversational gambit fails, "drop the subject for a time" and wait for him to bring the book up again—something he will usually do. In the meantime, while waiting for him to revive the topic himself, "you might try to" redirect your efforts and "help the wife of another serious drinker."

When dealing with the second type of alcoholic husband, "the same principles which apply to husband number one should be practiced." In addition, it is suggested that after his next binge, you "ask him if he would really like to get over drinking for good. Do not ask that he do it for you or anyone else. Just would he <u>like</u> to?" If he replies positively, "the wives" recommend an even stronger focus on the book, with the ever-helpful wife carefully pointing out some of the most salient insights for her husband's consideration. If this does not produce the desired results, they recommend just leaving him alone for a while. "The seed has been planted in his mind" and now "he knows that over a hundred men, much like himself, have recovered . . . Sooner or later, you are likely to find him reading the book once more."

"If you have a number three husband, you may be in luck. Being certain he wants to stop, you can go to him with this volume as joyfully as though you had struck oil." But, if your husband does not respond favorably, then "cheerfully see him though more sprees. Talk about his condition or this book only when he raises the issue. In some cases it may be better to let the family doctor present the book. The doctor can urge action without arousing hostility."

Men in the fourth category may seem "quite hopeless, but that is not so. Many of Alcoholics Anonymous were like that" and, although everyone had given up on them and "defeat seemed certain . . . often such men have spectacular and powerful recoveries." If the reader's husband is one of these and if he is currently committed somewhere, then she is told to show him "this book," and then consult with his doctor about the possibility of him giving this program an honest try. If her husband "can convince you and your doctor that he means business, you should give him a chance to try our method, unless the doctor thinks his mental condition abnormal or dangerous." In a strong note of positive reassurance, "the wives" then relate the story of four men confined to a state institution who were recently given just this kind of chance to "try our method," and only one of them has returned to the hospital. "The others had no relapse at all. The power of God goes deep!"

If the husband is not currently confined, but should be because he is "too dangerous" to himself and to others, "we think the kind thing is to lock [him] up." The "women" follow this sad admission with a paragraph on the harsh realities of such commitments, the product of some real life experiences with such situations.

> As a rule, an institution is a dismal place, and sometimes it is not conducive to recovery. It is a pity that chronic alcoholics must often mingle with the insane. Some day we hope our group will be instrumental in changing this condition. Many of our husbands spent weary years in institutions. Though more reluctant than most people to place our men there, we

sometimes suggest that it be done. Of course, a good doctor should always be consulted.

The Benefits for Wives

Now "the wives" dramatically shift the focus from the husband to the wife herself, extolling the benefits she can gain by following the suggestions found in the book. With this new understanding of her husband and the nature of his illness, she is now better equipped to deal with neighbors and friends ("explain to such people that he is a sick person"), with his children ("the same principle applies . . . use your energies to promote a better understanding all around"), and with his employer ("let your husband explain. Your desire to protect him should not cause you to lie to people"). Should this last tactic result in the husband losing his job, the wife should "regard it in a different light. Maybe it will prove a blessing! . . . Time after time, this apparent calamity has been a boon to us, for it opened up a path which led to the discovery of God."

This final line serves as an opening for "the wives" to expand upon the further benefits that a careful reading of the book can provide—even if her husband doesn't quit drinking. After all, the general idea that a "much better life" can be had if only it is "lived upon a spiritual plane" applies just as much to the wife as it does to the husband.

> If God can solve the age-old riddle of alcoholism, He can solve your problems too. We wives found that like everyone else, we were afflicted with pride, self-pity, vanity, and all the things which go to make up the self-centered person; and we were not above selfishness or dishonesty. As our husbands began to apply spiritual principles in their lives, we began to see the desirability of doing so too.

"The wives" point out that the major stumbling block for many of us who found ourselves in this situation was that, at first we "did not believe that we needed this help. We thought, on the whole, we were pretty good women . . . But it was a silly idea that we were too good to need God. Now we try to put spiritual principles to work in every department of our lives. When we do that, we find it solves our problems too."

If both you and your husband do put these principles into practice, they advise, you are "going to be very happy," but that does not mean all of your problems will disappear overnight. On the contrary, you are entering a phase where "growth has just begun" and where "there will be ups and downs. Many of the old problems will still be with you," but "a better way of life will emerge when they are overcome." However, throughout this period of adjustment,

> You must not expect too much [of your husband]. His ways of thinking and doing are the habits of years. Patience, tolerance, understanding, and love are your watchwords. Show him these things in yourself and they will be reflected back to you from him. Live and let live is the rule. If you both show a willingness to remedy your own defects, there will be little need to criticize each other.

Lessons Learned the Hard Way

Moving toward their conclusion, "the wives" now mention two things that frequently cause conflict in the home after a man has quit drinking. First of all, there is the likely "resentment that love and loyalty could not cure our husbands of alcoholism" and second, "you may become jealous of the attention he bestows on other people, especially alcoholics." Regarding the first, "when resentful thoughts come, pause and count your blessings. After all, your family is reunited, alcohol is no longer a problem." In relation to the second complaint, remember "he must work with other people to maintain his own sobriety" and "it is a real mistake if you dampen his enthusiasm for alcoholic work." But, "if you cooperate, rather than complain, you will find that his excess enthusiasm will tone down."

One final thing that would surely bother the long-suffering wife is if her husband came home drunk some night. If he owns his mistake in picking up the first drink and is aware that "he must redouble his spiritual activities if he expects to survive . . . you need not remind him of his spiritual deficiency—he will know of it. Cheer him up and ask him how you can be still more helpful."

Approaching the end of the chapter, "the wives" have just a few important, final points they would like to emphasize for the benefit of the woman who struggles with an alcoholic husband.

> Even your hatred must go. The slightest sign of fear or intolerance will lessen your husband's chance of recovery. In a weak moment he may take your dislike of his high-stepping friends as one of those insanely trivial excuses to drink.

> Never, never try to arrange his life, so as to shield him from temptation. The slightest disposition on your part to guide his appointments or his affairs so he will not be tempted will be noticed. Make him feel absolutely free to come and go as he likes. This is important. If he gets drunk, don't blame yourself. God has either removed your husband's liquor problem, or He has not. If not, it had better be found out right away. Then you and your husband can get right down to fundamentals. If a repetition is to be prevented, place the problem, along with everything else, in God's hands.

Acknowledging that much of the foregoing may have sounded rather strident, "the wives of Alcoholics Anonymous" try to soften these blows by closing on a conciliatory note.

> We realize we have been giving you much direction and advice. We may have seemed "preachy." If that is so, we are sorry, for we ourselves, don't care for people who preach. But what we have related is based upon experience, some of it painful. We had to learn these things the hard way. That is why we are anxious that you understand, that you avoid these unnecessary difficulties.

And "the wives" close by saying to the other wives out there who may soon be with them: "Good luck and God bless you!"

Wives' Culpability

"To Wives" is a mixed and jumbled bag filled with "much direction and advice," but the overall message to the wife is clear: Although both God and your husband share some responsibility in the matter, the heaviest burden of responsibility for whether or not your husband will ever quit drinking rests squarely on you—the wife of the alcoholic. After carefully reading this chapter, one might reasonably conclude that the unhelpful wife is the cause of most slips and Wilson's response to this has been fairly summarized as a collection of demands requiring the wife to "continue to treat her husband as a fragile child"[32] if she wants him to stay sober. In addition, as the wife struggles to make the best of this bad situation and to follow the "direction and advice" offered in this chapter, the drinking husband is largely exempted from any of the consequences caused by his drinking escapades.

Speaking for the wives, Bill suggests there are many ways for a wife to be "helpful" under these circumstances, all of which include a heavy emphasis on the virtues of "patience, tolerance, understanding, and love" and take the slogan "live and let live" as a rule. But he says that there are many more ways in which a wife's wrong actions can cause her husband to drink and these must be avoided at all costs. He admonishes: Don't try to reform your husband. Don't complain about your husband. Don't condemn your husband. Don't be critical of your husband. Don't be resentful of your husband. Don't question your husband. Don't argue with your husband. Don't be angry with your husband. Don't embarrass your husband. Don't lecture your husband. And, finally, "never, never" tell your husband what to do. He contends that failure in any one of these areas will likely give him "one of those insanely trivial excuses to drink"—and then it will be your fault when he goes out drinking again.

This overall perspective of the wife's proper place in a marriage and the heavy responsibility she supposedly bears for her mate's drinking is certainly the most striking feature of the chapter. That such an outlook on marriage was so confidently offered by the writer (and so readily approved by his male cohorts in Alcoholics Anonymous) tells us more about Bill Wilson and the state of marital relationships in middle-class America in the late 1930s, than it does about the best ways for a wife to be helpful in keeping her husband sober. It also provides a stark insight into just how desperately Bill wanted the new man to stay sober, even to the point of casually and comfortably foisting this huge burden of guilt off onto the wife should her husband ever go back to drinking.

Fortunately, the Al-Anon Family Groups were officially organized thirteen years after this chapter was written, providing a much needed counterbalance. Founded as an independent group for partners, relatives, and friends of alcoholics, it promotes a much more reasonable approach to marital relations than the one presented here. While suggesting numerous ways to be helpful when dealing with a troubled partner, friend, or relative, Al-Anon's emphasis is more firmly placed on the benefits that a Twelve Step program can offer to the suffering non-alcoholic, even while he or she continues trying to help the alcoholic in their life.

Beyond Wilson's gross overstatement of the wife's culpability in her husband's drinking, there are two other notable features in "To Wives" worthy of mention.

Further Defining the Alcoholic

The first of these is Bill's attempt, once again, to provide a definitive description of the alcoholic. His earliest try, in "There Is A Solution," offered three types of drinkers. The moderate drinker is briefly described there as having "little trouble giving up liquor entirely . . . [he] can take it or leave it." The hard drinker gets a longer paragraph, noting that he suffers more from his drinking than the moderate drinker, but with the proper negative motivation, such a man "can also stop or moderate, although he may find it difficult and troublesome." However, the real alcoholic—who is presented in a detailed, page-long paragraph—has lost "all control of his liquor consumption," "he is always more or less insanely drunk" and gradually deteriorates until he "begins to appear at hospitals and sanitariums." Bill admits this portrayal "is by no means a comprehensive picture of the true alcoholic . . . but this description should identify him roughly."[33]

In "To Wives," Wilson revisits this thorny problem of formulating an accurate definition of the alcoholic and attempts to supply a more comprehensive picture in four long paragraphs, each of which details a different category of men who suffer from too much drinking. While the earlier distinctions centered on whether or not the three types *could* give up drinking, these four new categories reformulate the question, asking whether the problem drinker really *wants* to quit and, if so, just how badly does he wants to do that?

In the intervening months, Bill seems to have concluded that intention rather than actual behavior might be the best way to make fruitful distinctions between the different types of drinkers. Men in the first category here have no intention of stopping, those in the second definitely want to want to stop, the third group includes drinkers who desperately want to stop but cannot, and the fourth is made up of men who, no matter how willing they might be, have despaired of ever quitting and are now hopelessly confined to an institution.

This shift is subtle, but it resonated with Wilson and he continued to find it useful in explaining his understanding of the best path to sobriety from this point forward. For instance, in March 1941 when he published the appendix entitled "Spiritual Experience" in the second printing of the Big Book, the element of *"willingness"* was identified as one of the three *"essential"* and *"indispensable"* factors necessary for recovery.[*]

But, for all of Bill's effort, these new categories are still far from a comprehensive definition of the alcoholic and they clearly lack any of the scientific criteria that the medical and psychiatric professions demand as a valid diagnostic tool. Later A.A.s,

---

[*]   *Alcoholics Anonymous* (4th edition) on pp. 567–68. The other two elements are *honesty* and *open mindedness*.

recognizing this ongoing lack of a precise, accurate definition for alcoholism, have been heard to neatly side-step the issue by noting that 'alcoholism is a disease that can only be *successfully* diagnosed by the patient.' It is an interesting and helpful reformulation of the problem.

The Book as the Solution

Another notable feature in this chapter is the complete reliance on the book *Alcoholics Anonymous* as the only lifeline offered to these wives and husbands struggling with the drink problem. The faith "the wives of Alcoholics Anonymous" have in the power of the book is almost boundless and it is this, and this alone, that they offer as a beacon of hope to the hard-pressed women they are addressing.*

The exclusive emphasis on the book may seem odd at first, but this one-solution-fits-all approach is understandable when seen in the context in which the chapter was written. It must be remembered that in October 1938, there were no A.A. hospitals, no A.A. missionaries, no other A.A. literature, no treatment facilities of any kind preaching 'the program of recovery,' no other local sober men, and most important, just *two* A.A. meetings being held weekly in the entire country. The only thing a woman reading this book had to rely on was the book itself. There were simply no other support mechanisms in place at this time. The book was either going to carry the message of recovery to her suffering husband, all by it itself, or it would not.

It was the *only* available option at this time for saving the still-suffering alcoholic.

---

* To help husband number one, "you might suggest he read this book, or at least the chapter on alcoholism." Husband number two is to be offered a more vigorous introduction to the book: "Show him your copy of this book and tell him what you have found out about alcoholism. Show him that the writers of the book understand as only alcoholics can. Tell him some of the interesting stories you have read . . . ask him to look at the chapter on alcoholism." For husband number three (he who wants to quit but cannot), it is suggested that you "go to him with this volume as joyfully as though you had struck oil. He may not share your enthusiasm, but he is practically sure to read the book." If not, perhaps his doctor could convince him to do so. Finally, for the institutionalized husband, wives are advised to "see that your husband gets this book" and that you "give him a chance to try our method," but only if you and his doctor are convinced "he means business."

CHAPTER NINETEEN

"The Family Afterward" and the Authorship Question

~October to November 1938~

For the next chapter in the Big Book, "The Family Afterward," Bill Wilson shifted gears and assumed a new persona, speaking in the voice of the "families of Alcoholics Anonymous."[1] Under this thin guise, he goes beyond talking about just the wife's role in her husband's recovery and describes at length the changing dynamics in a family confronted with "father's" sudden adoption of the sober life, mentioning specific problems they will likely face and offering some solutions based on A.A.'s collective experience up to that time.

Given that Bill authored both of these chapters, it is almost comical to see him open "The Family Afterward" by backpedaling and undercutting the overprotective suggestions "the wives of Alcoholics Anonymous" had offered in the previous chapter:

> Our women folk have suggested certain attitudes a wife may take with the husband who is recovering. Perhaps they created the impression that he is to be wrapped in cotton wool and placed on a pedestal. Successful readjustment means the opposite. All members of the family must meet upon the common ground of tolerance, understanding, and love.

So, finally we are going to learn something about the newly sober husband's responsibilities—along with those of the other family members.

Wilson warns that everyone in this newly reconfigured family unit—the alcoholic, his wife, his children, and even his 'in-laws'—will have their own idea about how the new arrangement should work. But if anyone demands that the others concede to their particular vision, it will only result in discord and unhappiness. Instead, each family member must give up the desire to have his or her wishes respected and abandon all attempts "to arrange the family show to his liking." Rather than each member contentiously trying to manage these new changes, it is now a question of what each person can give to the family rather than what they can take under the new setup.

The Obstacles Ahead

With this perilous warning of the pitfalls that lay before each family member, including the newly sober father, Wilson makes a promising proposal: "Suppose we tell you some of the obstacles a family will meet; suppose we suggest how they may be avoided—even converted to good use for others." All family members, he cautions, will "remember when father was romantic, thoughtful and successful," and now that he is sober, "family confidence in dad is riding high." Everyone thinks, "the good old days will soon be back." But Wilson states in graphic terms that nothing could be farther from the truth! "The head of the house has spent years in pulling down the structures of business, romance, friendship, health—these things are now ruined or damaged. It will take time to clear away" all that wreckage and perhaps even years to complete the construction of what needs to be built in its place.

Confronting the Past

So, what is the biggest obstacle the family will face on this new road of sobriety?
   It is the past:

> Now and then the family will be plagued by spectres from the past, for the drinking career of almost every alcoholic has been marked by escapades, funny, humiliating, shameful, or tragic. The first impulse will be to bury these skeletons in a dark closet and padlock the door. The family may be obsessed with the idea that future happiness can be based only upon forgetfulness of the past. Such a view is quite self-centered and in direct conflict with the new way of life.

Quoting Henry Ford, who famously extolled experience as "the thing of supreme value in life," Bill notes that this maxim "is true only if one is willing to turn the past to good account." But with proper and judicious use, "the alcoholic's past thus becomes the principal asset of the family, and frequently it is the only one!" As such, it must be honestly acknowledged and then used wisely.

Such an attitude not only allows the alcoholic to grow in "willingness to face and rectify errors and convert them into assets," it is also helpful to other families who are struggling under similar circumstances:

> We think each family which has been relieved owes something to those which have not, and when the occasion requires, each member of it who has found God, should be only too willing to bring former mistakes, no matter how grievous, out of their hiding places . . . [for] in God's hands,

the dark past is the greatest possession you have—the key to life and happiness for others.

But before exploring the ways in which the sharing of intimate information between the families of Alcoholics Anonymous actually operates, Bill offers a word of caution about confessing past sexual indiscretions. There are limits to what should and should not be revealed. Sometimes, he says, "in the first flush of spiritual experience," partners will confess to extra-marital affairs and then forgive each other, only to have the aggrieved party later "unearth the old affair and angrily cast its ashes about." These kinds of growing pains can hurt a great deal and they have driven more than one alcoholic back to the bottle. Given that potentially disastrous result, "our rule is that unless some good and useful purpose is to be served, past occurrences are not discussed." Some parts of the past are just better left buried.

However, among members of the Fellowship, we "have few secrets. Everyone knows about everyone else." Wilson acknowledges that in ordinary life such intimacy would likely "produce untold grief," because it would invariably lead to "scandalous gossip, laughter at the expense of other people, and a tendency to take advantage of intimate information." But, among ourselves, he confidently states, these are rare occurrences. We "do talk about each other a great deal," he says, but this talk is tempered by an attitude of love and tolerance. We are also careful to keep whatever confidences someone might share with us to ourselves unless we are sure he would approve. This is critical, because if we do not, the criticism or ridicule that may result "has been known to raise the very devil. We alcoholics are sensitive people [and] it takes some of us a long time to outgrow that serious handicap."

Economic Problems

Having spent the first third of the chapter on these preliminaries, Wilson devotes the middle third to explaining the two basic ways in which a recently sober man typically reacts to his new life: "At the beginning of recovery a man will, as a rule, take one of two directions. He may either plunge into a frantic attempt to get on his feet in business, or he may be so enthralled by his new life that he talks or thinks of little else." Bill warns that whichever of these two paths he might choose, certain family problems will arise. Here, the members of Alcoholics Anonymous think they can be helpful because they have hard-won experience with both of these roads so commonly taken by recently sober men.

If a new man elects the first course and "rushes headlong at his economic problems," Wilson suggests it will likely prove to be a mixed blessing. At first, the family members will be delighted because they feel their financial troubles are about to be solved, but they quickly become less pleased "as they find themselves neglected" by the now tired and preoccupied father. Dad pays little attention to the children, he is inattentive to his wife, and frequently acts out irritably. When the wife and children, expecting a much happier home life, react critically to these unpleasant changes, resentments grow between family members. Nobody is getting what they wanted or what they think they deserve from dad's new life of sobriety.

"This sort of thing must be stopped," Bill states emphatically. "Both father and the family are wrong, though each side may have some justification. It is of little use to argue and only makes the impasse worse." To the wife and children he recommends patience.

> The family must realize that dad, though marvelously improved, is still a sick man. They should thank God he is sober and able to be of this world once more. Let them praise his progress. Let them remember that his drinking wrought all kinds of damage that may take long to repair. If they sense these things, they will not take so seriously his periods of crankiness, depression, or apathy, which will disappear when there is tolerance, love, and spiritual understanding.

But the husband too must make some significant concessions and changes.

> The head of the house ought to remember that he is mainly to blame for what befell his home. He can scarcely square the account in his lifetime. But he must see the danger of over-concentration on financial success. Although financial recovery is on the way for many of us, we found we could not place money first. For us, material well-being always followed spiritual progress; it never preceded.

> Since the home has suffered more than anything else, it is well that a man exert himself there. He is not likely to get far in any direction if he fails to show unselfishness and love under his own roof.

With the proper amount of attentive consideration and mutual concern, "each member of a resentful family begins to see his shortcomings and admits them to the others," thereby laying the "basis for helpful discussion . . . little by little, mother and children will see they ask too much, and father will see he gives too little. Giving, rather than getting, will become the guiding principle."

Spiritual Intoxication
But what if the husband chooses the second path, completely embracing his recent spiritual experience and "overnight . . . becomes a religious enthusiast." This can be even more disruptive for the family than the man obsessed with financial recovery. Bill describes how this can play out in an alcoholic's freshly minted sobriety.

> He is unable to focus on anything else . . . There is talk about spiritual matters morning, noon and night. He may demand that the family find God for themselves in a hurry, or exhibit amazing indifference to them and say he is above worldly considerations. He tells mother, who has been religious all her life, that she doesn't know what it's all about, and that she had better get his brand of spirituality while there is yet time.

The family will probably react to this by looking "at their strange new dad with apprehension, then with irritation" and they may even become "jealous of a God who has stolen dad's affections." They become critical and, in their neglected state, begin to wonder if dad really is "so spiritual after all . . . why all this concern for everyone in the world but his family?" They may even begin to "suspect that father is a bit balmy!"

Under these circumstances, Wilson pleads for the family's understanding, pointing out that many members of A.A. have gone through just this same sort of elation and indulged in "spiritual intoxication." Given time, such a man will come to his senses and realize he has been suffering from a distortion of values and that "his spiritual growth is lopsided." The wife and children must be patient. With the help of a "sympathetic family, these vagaries of dad's spiritual infancy will quickly disappear."

If, however, the family relentlessly condemns and criticizes him, "this fallacy will take a still greater hold on father" and he will retreat farther into himself, believing he has now "become a superior person, with God on his side." Despite his neglect and irresponsibility toward the family, the proper response is to accept these "alarming and disagreeable" manifestations of his new spiritual life and "let him go as far as he likes in helping other alcoholics." In the long run, working with others "will do more to insure his sobriety than anything else." The man who takes the spiritual path is building a much firmer foundation for his sobriety than the man who "is placing business or professional success ahead of spiritual development. He will be less likely to drink again, and anything is preferable to that."

Wilson assures the family that an early overemphasis on the spiritual life is common among newly sober men, but just as common is the eventual recognition of the childishness of this "world of spiritual make-believe." Once that happens, this "dream world [is] replaced by a great sense of purpose, accompanied by a growing consciousness of the power of God in our lives" and of His desire for us to keep our feet firmly planted on the ground where "our work must be done." In short, "we have found nothing incompatible between a powerful spiritual experience, and a life of sane and happy usefulness." Just be patient.

Bill's final advice to the wife facing this kind of challenge is to forgo any opposition to her husband's new spiritual life and simply join him. It may prove to be the best defense. "Nothing will help the man who is off on a spiritual tangent so much as the wife who adopts the self-same program, making a better practical use of it."

Eight More Changes to Face
In the final third of "The Family Afterward," Bill spends the first twelve paragraphs addressing eight "other profound changes" that the family may face once father has gotten sober:

- Struggles over who now wears "the family trousers" ("liquor incapacitated father for so many years that mother became head of the house")

- Dad's new outside interests and his resulting absences ("mother and children may demand that he stay home")

- The need to balance alcoholic and non-alcoholic friends ("the couple ought to frankly face the fact that each will have to yield here and there, if the family is going to play an effective part in the new life")

- The possibility of becoming church members ("a helpful suggestion only . . . there is nothing obligatory about it . . . each individual must consult his own conscience")

- The insistence on laughter and enjoying life ("we aren't a glum lot . . . we are sure that God wants us to be happy, joyous, and released")

- Recovery of bodily health ("we are convinced that a spiritual mode of living is a most powerful health restorative . . . but this does not mean that we discourage human health measures")

- The possibility of sexual impotence ("some of us had this experience, only to enjoy, in a few months, a finer intimacy than ever . . . we do not know of any case where this difficulty lasted long")

- And finally, the need for dad to reclaim his children's love and respect ("in time they will see that he is a new man and . . . when this happens they can be invited to join in morning meditation")

Additional helpful advice, based on A.A. members' past experiences, is offered for each of these problems.

In summation, Bill notes that however the family may respond to the obstacles they meet, the alcoholic must continue to live his own life on a spiritual basis. "The others must be convinced by his changed life beyond a shadow of a doubt. He must lead the way. Seeing is believing to most families who have lived with a drinker."

Sobriety is Primary

This might have served as an effective ending for the chapter, but Bill Wilson is unable to let this stirring conclusion stand on its own. Instead, he ends with a real-life story that seems strikingly out of place here and sounds contrary to much of what has just been said, reverting to the tone and tenor of "To Wives" and once again emphasizing just how much responsibility the wife bears for her husband's sobriety:

Here is a case in point: One of our friends is a heavy smoker and coffee drinker. There was no doubt he over-indulged. Seeing this, and meaning to be helpful, his wife commenced to admonish him about it. He admitted he was overdoing these things, but frankly said that he was not ready to stop. His wife is one of those persons who really feel there is something rather sinful about these commodities, so she nagged, and her intolerance finally threw him into a fit of anger. He got drunk.

Of course our friend was wrong—dead wrong. He had to painfully admit that and mend his spiritual fences. Though he is now a most effective member of Alcoholics Anonymous, he still smokes cigarettes and drinks coffee, but neither his wife nor anyone else stands in judgment. She sees she was wrong to make a burning issue out of such a matter when his more serious ailments were being rapidly cured.

First things first! We have two little mottoes which are apropos. Here they are: "LIVE AND LET LIVE" and "EASY DOES IT."[2]

Bill is admonishing that, if the wife had only realized that her husband's sobriety was of primary importance ("First things first!") and therefore allowed him to continue indulging in his "sinful" behaviors ("LIVE AND LET LIVE"), he would never have gotten drunk again. Love and tolerance must be the wife's code ("EASY DOES IT!") or she will pay the terrible price of finding her husband once more back in the bottle.

The Myth of Collective Authorship

With six of the ten "general chapters"[3] now available in rough format, it might be time to pause and consider one of the most pervasive myths in Alcoholics Anonymous, namely that the writing of the Big Book was a completely collaborative affair—the collective work of the first one hundred men who got sober. But that was certainly not true at this point in the story. By the time he had completed the first draft of "The Family Afterward," Bill Wilson had singlehandedly written more than half of what would eventually make up the front portion of the book, and he had done so with little or no substantive input from members of the Fellowship—other than Hank Parkhurst.

Recapping what we have already seen from contemporary records, Akron's response, right up until the middle of November, was simply to say they liked the six chapters already sent to them. Given this disappointing lack of response, Bill complained to Dr. Bob that he wished he "would be more critical of them, for I think they can be improved a lot,"[4] and he elsewhere noted that, despite the fact each of these chapters was sent to Ohio "for debate and inspection," Dr. Bob "never passed them around very much, merely writing me saying he thought they were all right."[5] In 1957 Bill tried to soften this indictment a bit by writing that "copies were sent to Dr. Bob for checking and criticism in Akron, where we had nothing but the warmest support"[6]—a judgment that uses faint praise to veil the fact that Akron may have sent back lots of warm support, but no checking or criticism.

Things in New York were a bit different, but not different enough to generate any kind of serious criticism for what Bill had written so far. "I find it is pretty hard," he told Bob in early November, "to get people to voice their real opinions, as they are too much afraid of hurting the author's feelings."[7] Whatever reasons there might be for this New York reticence, the result was that Wilson was writing in a virtual vacuum with little substantive feedback from the group about what he had written.

Given this overwhelming evidence for Wilson's sole authorship of the book up to this point, along with his explicit complaints about the lack input from others, it is perfectly reasonable to wonder where this popular and persistent creation story of an elaborate collaborative writing process for the text of the Big Book came from.

No one was more complicit in promoting this collective-writing myth than Bill Wilson himself who, after the book was published, increasingly minimized his own responsibility for the text and began to actively circulate the fiction that the book had been written by "We of Alcoholics Anonymous." One reason for this duplicity was the need to bolster the illusion that the book was a report of the collective experience of "one hundred men and women who have recovered from a seemingly hopeless state"[8] rather than being just a condensed version of Wilson's personal experiences and observations during the first four years of his sobriety which, for the most part, is what it was. The power of the communal experience, rather than that of any one individual, was increasingly recognized as one of the most important parts of the message promoted by Alcoholics Anonymous, and it was therefore vitally important that the story of the book's origins be presented as a participatory group effort rather than the work of just one man.

In addition to this larger purpose, Bill had an important personal reason for making light of his authorship of the Big Book. As the new method of recovery spread across the country, Wilson grew increasingly uncomfortable with the mantle of sanctity that was constantly being foisted off onto him by these new groups and members. Knowing how much this kind of hero worship played directly into his desire to be 'the number one man,' Bill realized he needed to put a number of serious checks on his ego, and one of the ways he did this was to regularly downplay his central importance in the writing of the book.

The Role of the New York Group

When talking about the time the Big Book was written, Bill consistently minimized his own part by offering some variation on the fact that "every paragraph of that book as originally dictated was torn in shreds and put back again"[9] by the members of the New York group. "We fought, bled, and died our way through one chapter after another,"[10] he claimed. Emphasizing the early origins of this process, Wilson later wrote about how "the hassling over the four [sic] chapters already finished had really been terrific. I was exhausted. On many a day I felt like throwing the book out the window."[11]*

Jim Burwell, the only other attendee to leave a record of these chapter-by-chapter review meetings, always told a similar story, reporting for instance that Bill "would take one copy of [each new chapter] to the Tuesday night meeting and [he] would read it

---

* Bill mistakenly implies here that "How It Works" was written immediately after the four chapters that precede it in the published version of the book.

over and we would chop it apart and give our suggestions," after which Wilson would "make notes in the margin" with the changes he would need to make.[12*]

How then can this frequently presented picture of extensive substantive editing of the six earliest chapters be squared with Bill's complaint to Dr. Bob in early November that he found it "pretty hard to get people [in New York] to voice their real opinions" because "they are too much afraid of hurting the author's feelings"?[13]

It can't.

The stories Bill and Jim told after the fact were the ones that created the mythology of how the Big Book was written, but those stories are overwhelmingly contradicted by contemporary records. While there was some group criticism later on, it was just not happening at this stage of the writing process, no matter what Wilson and Burwell later said about the matter.

Bill's difficulty in getting people to voice their real opinions about these six chapters was certainly real and it had several sources. One cause of the New York member's restraint was the fact that Wilson was such a dominant force in the weekly Brooklyn meetings where, as he once candidly admitted, "I did most of the talking."[14] He was, after all, the founder of the movement, the leader of the group and the man who was fundamentally responsible for each of these men's sobriety. Who else was qualified to speak about alcoholism with such conclusive and uncontested authority?

Bill's honest admission of his control over these meetings is consistent with Jim Burwell's recollection of how a typical A.A. meeting operated in New York during 1938.[**] "There were seven or eight men sitting around in a circle," he said, "and Bill Wilson [sat] in the center . . . he would do all the talking and we would do all the listening and answering the questions because he had all the book sense."[15] Elsewhere Jim elaborated on this picture by noting "it was a round table discussion with Bill in the center, and everybody was shooting at him and getting what information he had . . . gotten from his books. We thought he was really a walking encyclopedia on alcohol. There were only four or five books and Bill had read them all."[16]

This hardly sounds like an open-forum meeting with multiple opportunities to offer significant criticism of what the founder had just written on the nature of alcoholism and the problems facing a newly sober man.

Another problem with the scenario painted by both Wilson and Burwell is the sheer difficulty of having Bill read each new chapter out loud—from the only available copy—and then expecting each member to make substantive and helpful critiques (paragraph by paragraph!) after he was finished. It is worthwhile to pause and think about exactly how this might have worked. Did the members make notes about what they thought could or should be changed as Bill read? Or did they rely on their memories to recall those things that needed improvement, bringing them up

---

* In this same talk, Jim also erroneously claimed that "Akron did the same thing" (i.e., made notes for corrections in the margins of the copies that Bill sent to them) and then mailed these back to New York where the original and these two sets of suggested changes "were brought together by Bill." Based on contrary evidence, from both contemporary sources and several of Bill Wilson's later accounts, Burwell's report of detailed, annotated critiques of each chapter coming back from Ohio is just another piece of blatantly bad information that must be added to his already long list of gross inaccuracies.

** We can accept Burwell's report on these meetings with some measure of credibility because it serves as "second source" confirmation for Wilson's own admission that he "did most of the talking" in New York meetings.

individually once he was finished reading? Or did they just interrupt Wilson as he went along, stopping him whenever they heard something objectionable or that they thought needed to be changed? It is, quite frankly, hard to imagine any of these scenarios being the least bit plausible (or fruitful) given the known dynamics of the Brooklyn meetings.

And, finally, how much did they *really* care? Were they so concerned about what Bill Wilson had written that they were willing to openly challenge him on any of these seemingly incidental issues?

Everything he had written in the six chapters up to "The Family Afterward" could be characterized as either a detailed diagnosis of the disease of alcoholism or a summary of the problems the alcoholic would face in getting and staying sober. These were, as Bill noted, general chapters, covering a wide variety of topics and it is unlikely that members of the Tuesday night group would find any of this so questionable that they would challenge the man who was not only their leader, but also the man they readily acknowledged as having the most knowledge of the disease. The first six chapters probably generated little more criticism in New York than they did out in Ohio. Bill's comprehensive explanation of the alcoholic's *problem* just wasn't controversial enough to generate critical attacks from these New York members.

Whatever group criticism he did receive—which Wilson claimed he had been looking for all along—did not begin in earnest until December when he rolled out two new chapters ("How It Works" and "Into Action") with the Twelve Steps, his numbered *solution* to the alcoholic's problem. Bill's concise articulation of what must be done to get and stay sober was something the New York members were willing to argue about. Whatever truth there may be in the supposed "real mauling"[17] given to every paragraph by the New York contingent, it would have to wait for the appearance of these chapters containing the Twelve Steps along with Wilson's detailed instructions on how to go about applying them to your life.

But even here, as shall be detailed later, the group was not the main source of this criticism, nor did most of it come during the Tuesday night meetings. Hank Parkhurst, along with (to a lesser degree) Fitz Mayo, were the primary critics, and their objections or suggestions for changes occurred in private discussions with Bill, some surely in Brooklyn, but most in the Newark offices of Honor Dealers. Other than this, there is no credible evidence for any such significant participatory group criticism of what Wilson had so far written for the book.

Input Three Months before Printing

However there is one plausible scenario for some significant group input that may have been at work before mid-November and was part of the review process during the final three months before the Multilith copy was printed in mid-February 1939.

Bill Wilson's statement about the difficulty of getting people in New York to offer their real opinion does not necessarily mean there were absolutely no suggestions for changes during those final months as the book moved toward completion. Given Bill's specific claim that there were no strong criticisms that might "hurt the author's feelings" being voiced at this time, we can be fairly confident no one was standing up at these Tuesday night meetings saying things like "Bill, that's just wrong" or "But you can't say that!" or even the less personal "So, what is *that* supposed to mean?"

But this does not preclude the possibility that people would listen attentively as Bill Wilson read each new chapter and then offer thoughtful suggestions for additional material that might be added to what they had just heard. Given Bill's stature and recognized primacy within the Brooklyn group, this scenario presents a much more believable picture of how the editing process may have actually operated in New York City in late 1938. Rather than a free-for-all in which every paragraph was violently "pulled apart and suggestions added by all those present,"[18] readings most likely concluded with one or more member making an observation along the lines of: "Hey, Bill, how come you didn't say anything about X, Y, or Z in there?" or "You know what else might fit well into this chapter?" This "easier, softer way" of reviewing the chapters and respectfully offering suggestions for additional text would have avoided hurting the author's feelings while still allowing members to make reasonable contributions to the rapidly growing text.

Because we have neither the "once corrected dictations"[19] mailed to Akron in September and November, nor any of the interim versions between then and the following February, it is impossible to say exactly when the New York group might have started offering these kind of recommendations and requests for additional material. In early November when Wilson bemoaned the lack of significant input, he may have been specifically referring to criticism of what he had already written rather than these sort of suggested additions. But as noted above, if this less critical add-on process was not operative before mid-November, it did come into play sometime soon after that.

The notion that the New York input was more about adding material than criticizing what had already written is supported by a careful reading of the texts in these earlier chapters. For instance, there are a number of places in the three chapters just considered where paragraphs or sections seem to have been tacked on or feathered into the chapters Bill was reading to the group on Tuesday nights. These suspected add-ons stand out as abrupt and unexpected changes in direction—at times almost non sequiturs—or because they sound more like a misplaced afterthought rather than a logical extension of what comes immediately before it.

Consider, for example, the final eleven paragraphs in "Working With Others," which shifts the chapter's perspective from detailed instructions on how to properly deliver the message of recovery to a new man and suddenly begins to extol the benefits that come to the sober man who is now spiritually fit, elaborating on the fact that he can "do all sorts of things alcoholics are not supposed to do." As noted earlier, the purpose of this section is to differentiate the sober A.A. member from all of the noisy Temperance and Prohibition preachers that have preceded him and to detail the many strengths and opportunities available to him now that he has God on his side, keeping him safe from the first drink, even in a variety of previously dangerous situations.

While it may have been Wilson's original plan to have a section such as this close the chapter, the subject matter shifts so dramatically from the presentation to the presenter—all but abandoning the topic of working with others—that it sounds distinctly like something added later. The shift here may be because Bill couldn't think of a more effective close for "Working With Others," but it is just as likely that it appears here because someone suggested this type of information should be included somewhere in this chapter, so Wilson just added it on at the end.

The same premise might explain the inclusion of those two strident paragraphs that appear so abruptly just before the conciliatory conclusion of "To Wives." The "Even your hatred must go . . ." paragraph just doesn't flow logically from the talk of spirituality that immediately precedes it, and this is followed by the even more abrasive admonition to "Never, never try to arrange his life . . ." Both of these paragraphs show a significantly shift in tone and seem distinctly out of place in relation to what the wife has just been told, making it probable they were written after the fact and then dropped in here to satisfy the suggestion that the closing needed to be much more forceful, dramatic, and explicit if it is was ever going to make a real impression on the wife.

Similarly, "The Family Afterward" ends with the unfortunate "case in point" story of the man who drinks after being nagged by his wife about his "sinful" over-indulgence in cigarettes and coffee. How this story relates to what immediately precedes it— the well-organized and detailed explanation of eight profound changes that can be anticipated when a man first gets sober—is something of a mystery. More likely, it was Wilson's response to some New York member insisting that this instructive story be included.

Each of these examples displays a sudden change of direction, disrupting the logic and the flow of what came before it. Readers confronted with this kind of jumbled presentation in the Big Book frequently conclude that Bill Wilson just wasn't a very good writer, but perhaps the fault lies less in a lack of writing skills on the part of the book's primary author and more on the much-touted collaborative creation process of the Big Book.

Hank Parkhurst's Contributions

Hank Parkhurst was, however, another story completely. Unlike the other New York members, Hank did not have to wait until Tuesday night for a first look at what Bill Wilson was writing. He was sitting right there in the small Honor Dealers' Newark office, listening, criticizing, and offering his opinions as Bill and Ruth created first drafts of each new chapter.

Ruth tells us Bill would arrive in the office with "yellow scratch pad sheets . . . [with] a few notes to guide [him] on a whole chapter" and that "these notes were the result of long thought on [his] part after hours of discussion pro and con with everyone who might be interested."[20] Ruth's choice of words here about Bill consulting with "everyone who might be interested" is worth noting because it provides at least some evidence that not everyone *was* interested in talking about the book or at least not in relation to these six early chapters.

Having arrived in Newark with these few notes in hand, it is hard to believe Bill would (or even could) have avoided a discussion with Hank about them before he began dictating to Ruth. Who besides Wilson himself was more interested in what was going into each new chapter of the book than Parkhurst? Hank was genuinely passionate about the content of the Big Book and deeply committed to creating something that would effectively present their message of recovery to the world, and do so in such a way that the book would become an instant best seller. His own financial future and the all-important ability of Alcoholics Anonymous to become self-supporting through large sales of the book absolutely depended on it.

Parkhurst was the person closest to Wilson as he composed these critical first dictations, a fact Bill later freely acknowledged, calling Hank his "partner . . . in the book enterprise,"[21] a partnership that was not limited to their mutual involvement in the business side of the project. Parkhurst's continual presence during the actual writing of the book in Newark provided him with more chances to influence Wilson than anyone else in the Fellowship and he seized that opportunity by arguing with Bill for his particular point of view on recovery. As we have seen, Hank was never bashful about offering his own thoughts. On the all-important topic of what should go into the book, he wasted no time in emphatically advocating for his own perspective, first by submitting his contrary "Ideas" to Bill in early June, and then by creating his prophetic outline for the book a couple of weeks later. A lively dialogue between the two men surely continued over the next three months, but when Bill finally returned to writing for the book in mid-September, Hank was given the golden opportunity of speaking his mind with specific regularity.

Beyond Bill's own testimony, the fact that Hank made substantial contributions to the book is confirmed by Ruth Hock, the only other person who was an eyewitness to this process. When specifically asked about Parkhurst's input, she readily admitted he was present throughout the Newark writing period and claimed that he "contributed a lot of ideas" to the book, and then added emphatically, "he really did."[22]

However, Bill was not very receptive to most of Hank's comments and suggestions. Beyond the running arguments over content, style was also an issue. As noted earlier, Hank had recently taken a writing school course after which he was constantly advising Bill on how to improve his prose style. These suggestions did not sit particularly well with Wilson, who later noted rather bluntly that in this regard he "didn't go for Hank's advice very much."[23]

Hank Loses the God Argument

But much more confrontational were Parkhurst's contrary opinions about what should and should not be going into the book. He had strong convictions that Wilson had been unable to change over the past several months. For example, Hank was still opposed to the strong religious slant Bill was giving to their solution and he continued to advocate for his June position that "religion—etc.—should not be brought" into the picture when describing their method of getting sober.[24] Wilson claims that during this early period, Parkhurst even went so far as to demand "the word 'God' [be] deleted from the book entirely."[25] It is hard to imagine a position any further from what Bill was then writing for the Big Book.

But Hank decisively lost that argument—and he clearly did so early on—as can be seen from even a cursory reading of the first six chapters so far written. A quick search of those chapters—as printed on just thirty-nine pages of the Multilith copy— finds sixty-nine instances of the word "God" and that does not take into account any of the references to the divine "He" or "Him," nor to any of the other names for the providential Deity that appear so frequently in these pages. Given the ubiquity of the word "God" and similarly regular references to the Supreme Being, it is hard to imagine that Bill made any effort at all to tone down the number of explicit references to God in response to Hank's criticisms. On this issue, he completely dismissed Hank's arguments for a purely "irreligious"[26] approach and remained faithful to his original plan of presenting a basically religious solution to the problem of alcoholism. As with Parkhurst's critical comments about his writing style, Bill obviously didn't go for Hank's advice very much when it came to his suggestions for a basically non-religious approach.

God Plus Moral Psychology

In opposition to Bill's strong emphasis on God, Hank had lobbied for a purely psychological explanation of their solution, one that was firmly based on the moral psychology of ego reduction and a life of increased usefulness to others:

> We are actually irreligious—but we are trying to be helpful—we have learned to be quiet—to be more truthful—to be more honest—to try to be more unselfish—to make the other fellows troubles—our troubles— and by following four steps we most of us have a religious experience. The fellowship—the unselfishness—appeals to us.[27]

Bill actually agreed with most of this, recognizing Dr. Silkworth's ideas on moral psychology as a critical element in any meaningful and sustained recovery, but he didn't feel it was sufficient by itself for keeping someone sober. Wilson's model for gaining and maintaining sobriety was a much more balanced approach, incorporating spiritual, psychological, and physical parts, but with the greatest emphasis being placed firmly on the spiritual. Still, his agreement with the real need for ego reduction and a life redirected toward usefulness to others made it easy for Bill to include any number of references to the importance of moral psychology in what he wrote—noting, in just one dramatic example, that the recovered man's main job was to "be of maximum helpfulness to others."[28] Beyond frequent references throughout these six chapters to the need to get outside of oneself and to become a useful participant in society, one chapter, "Working With Others," was devoted almost exclusively to usefulness and little else.

Under these circumstances, it is impossible to say how much of the moral psychology and the regular emphasis on usefulness to others found in Bill Wilson's writings should be credited to Hank Parkhurst. But, with Bill's lavish inclusion of

Hank's beloved psychological and altruistic elements in the text, it would hardly be fair to say that Parkhurst lost all his arguments with Wilson about the content and the tone of the Big Book. Bill was willing to emphasize the psychological aspect Hank considered so singularly important, agreeing that it was indispensable for recovery, but he just wasn't willing to abandon his belief in the central importance of religion or to remove the constant mentions of God as a critical and essential element of that solution. In the end, Bill clung to these spiritual elements, but he did blend them with the psychological solution that can be found so generously sprinkled throughout each of the chapters he wrote.

With this fundamental disagreement raging between them these ongoing arguments could not have been easy for either man to navigate—the Honor Dealers' office in Newark became the battleground where the biggest fights over the Big Book were actually waged. More than in meetings, this was certainly the place where Bill Wilson and Hank Parkhurst "fought, bled, and died [their] way through one chapter after another"[29] and perhaps even where "every paragraph of that book as originally dictated was torn in shreds and put back again"[30]

Hank was that sort of combative guy and he was hardly likely to restrain himself for fear of hurting the author's feelings. Within the confines of their small office, the outright rejection of both his stylistic suggestions and his exclusively non-religious solution must have caused more than a little anguish. Under these circumstances, it is not hard to imagine why Bill later claimed that "On many a day I felt like throwing the book out the window."[31] And, perhaps, Henry G. Parkhurst along with it.

But Hank was nothing if not tenacious. Despite the fact that Bill consistently ignored so many of his ideas, Parkhurst would continue to fight for the inclusion of his own perspective and presentation—wherever they might fit in—right up until the final hours before the book actually went to press.

Addressing Marital Infidelity

Besides the three suspicious tacked-on endings already mentioned, there are several other places where paragraphs appear to have been incorporated into what was already written for the Big Book. One further example, found in "The Family Afterward," should be mentioned in this regard for its multifaceted importance.

In that chapter, Bill says that sober members and their wives who have wrestled with marital problems "should be only too willing to bring forward mistakes, no matter how grievous, out of their hiding places" and to share them with the new member and his wife. These revelations—along with the story of their successful resolution—are essential for showing newcomers how they too can gain victory over such terrible family problems. However difficult and counterintuitive it may sound, Wilson encourages sober members to speak openly and candidly with others about these delicate family matters because "in God's hands, the dark past is the greatest possession you have—the key to life and happiness for others. With it you can avert death and misery for them."

Skipping the next paragraph for the moment, Bill opens the following paragraph by noting that A.A.'s have few secrets and that "Everyone knows all about everyone else ...," an observation that flows smoothly and logically from "the dark past is the greatest possession you have" comment just noted. It continues the thought and fits perfectly into the point Bill is trying to make about the need for group members to be open and candid with each other, up to and including the sharing their darkest secrets. Complete openness and honesty about past family difficulties is, he says, one of the important and critical ways we can be truly useful and helpful to each other.

However, sandwiched between these two paragraphs, there is another that takes a sudden and unexpected turn into the question of marital infidelity.

> It is possible to dig up past misdeeds so they become a blight, a veritable plague. For example, we know of situations in which the alcoholic or his wife have had love affairs. In the first flush of spiritual experience they forgave each other and drew closer together. The miracle of reconciliation was at hand. Then, under one provocation or another, the aggrieved one would unearth the old affair and angrily cast its ashes about. A few of us have had these growing pains and they hurt a great deal. Husbands and wives have sometimes been obliged to separate for a time until new perspective, new victory over hurt pride, could be re-won. In most cases, the alcoholic survived this ordeal without relapse, but not always. So our rule is that unless some good and useful purpose is to be served, past occurrences are not discussed.

This small, self-contained side trip is directly contrary to the prior advice of being candid about "the dark past." It abruptly interrupts the argument being made about the necessity of talking openly about difficult family problems within the group and introduces an entirely different scenario—the question of how to talk (or not talk) with your spouse about past marital infidelities. This is certainly important information, but it is distracting to Bill's point about one couple helping another and it really does not fit in here (although it might be as good as any other place to drop this delicate subject into the chapter).

The question of how to deal with the admission of past infidelities (or the revelation of details should those infidelities already be known) is certainly a common problem for many newly sober men and it is mentioned several times in the Big Book—this being perhaps the most direct and explicit.[32] As a caution to the new man, it makes sense that this point should be made somewhere in this discussion, but its appearance here is more of a distracting aside than an element in Bill's main point. It is almost as if someone had said: "Listen, Bill, if you are going to talk about couples making revelations about 'the dark past,' then you had better make sure people understand you are not talking about *that* part of the dark past!"—and Wilson complied.

If that explanation is as plausible as it seems, then the next question would be who or what might have prompted this insertion. The suggestion may well have come from someone at the Tuesday night meeting making a comment similar to the one noted above, but there are a number of other possible candidates.

Bill's Sexual Past a Factor?

For instance, Bill Wilson himself may have decided, after the fact, that just such a paragraph was needed here. Certainly he was no stranger to the problem. The question of his own possible infidelities while drinking was one he had addressed, however circumspectly, in each of his three versions of "Bill's Story."

> Though I managed to avoid serious scrapes and partly out of ~~loyalty,~~ extreme drunkenness, I had not become involved with the fair sex, there were many unhappy scenes in my apartment. *[Original Story version]*[33]

> There were many unhappy scenes in our apartment . . . There had been no great infidelity. Loyalty to my wife, and sometimes extreme drunkenness, kept me out of those scrapes. *[May-June 1938 version]*[34]

> There were many unhappy scenes in our sumptuous apartment. There had been no real infidelity, for loyalty to my wife, helped at times by extreme drunkenness, kept me out of those scrapes. *[Multilith edition version]*[35]

There is an interesting progression here, from extreme drunkenness being "partly" the reason for not becoming involved with other women, to indulging in "no great infidelity" out of loyalty to Lois and "sometimes extreme drunkenness," to "no real infidelity" because of "loyalty" and "at times . . . extreme drunkenness." Whatever indiscretions Wilson may have committed while drinking, he was clearly not about to admit them in print nor is it likely he ever made any admission of guilt beyond this when talking to his wife, Lois.

Still, the careful reader has to wonder just how far a potential relationship would have to go before "extreme drunkenness" (i.e. either passing out or impotence) becomes the saving factor, preventing the betrayal of one's marriage vows. It is equally interesting to speculate on exactly what kind of behavior short of intercourse (or even including intercourse) might still allow the claim to "no *great* infidelity" or "no *real* infidelity" in the mind of a 1938 American male. One must wonder, too, about Lois's reaction when she first read each of these different versions.

But whatever stories Bill had been telling Lois about his relationships with other women during his drunken years, she was clearly not buying it, for in each of these stories there is only one phrase that repeats in each of these versions, namely the "many unhappy scenes" that were played out between Bill and Lois at home—whenever he finally did get home.

In short, if Bill Wilson had been unfaithful during his drinking days, he was obviously following his own advice about nondisclosure for he clearly never owned or disclosed that behavior to his wife.*

Ruth and Hank Have a Vested Interest in the Topic

Another possible candidate is Ruth Hock who had taken a semester-long short story writing course at NYU along with Hank Parkhurst around this time.[36] Having done so, she may have naturally felt qualified to offer comments and suggestions to Bill Wilson as he wrote. (Actually, it would be hard to imagine her not doing this to some degree throughout the free-form writing process in which she played such a prominent role.)

The question of whether or not to discuss past indiscretions was certainly something that Ruth had heard more than a little office talk about over the years. In fact, forty years later, she was still able to recount one harrowing Oxford Group story she had overheard about the real pitfalls inherent in these delicate situations.

> One of [the Oxford Group's] basic tenets was that, if you had ever harmed anybody, anyone at all in any way . . . you were . . . to go to that person, confess everything . . . [and] apologize. Do your best to make up for whatever had happened.

> The only trouble Bill found with that was that—and this happened, actually, twice in the New York area—where men had done this. In one case, the man . . . explained to his wife that he'd been unfaithful with this lovely girl [who] lived right across the street, but it would never happen again, and he was sorry and so on. Well, the first thing that happened, of course, over came the husband [of the lovely girl]. Then this [story] began to go from whisper to whisper, from one to another, and you don't keep that kind of thing secret—the minute you spread it that way—and, anyway, there was a great deal of trouble about it.

---

* This brings up a question that is outside the scope of this study but certainly relevant to these comments, namely the persistent A.A. rumor that, in his later years, Bill Wilson was a serial adulterer (or, as Susan Cheever would have it in her book, *My Name is Bill,* a "sex addict.") Despite the frequency with which this story has been retold by A.A. people who are critical of Bill, the claim has never been verified.

A.A.'s preeminent professional historian, Ernie Kurtz, was intrigued by the persistence of these rumors and he spent considerable time and effort during the last few years of his life trying to determine the truth or falsity of these allegations. Drawing on his close ties with other students of A.A. history and speaking directly with both Cheever and Francis Hartigan (two writers who had made accusations along these lines), Kurtz determined that in every instance he could find and trace back, the source for the stories of Bill's serial infidelities relied on the testimony of just one man, Tom Powers. Powers had been a close friend of Wilson's during the 1940s and 1950s, but, in the mid-50s, they had a tumultuous falling-out and it was then that he began spreading stories about Bill's repeated, illicit sexual conduct. Kurtz was significantly skeptical about these accusations because, as he noted in a recorded interview made on October 22, 2013, Powers "had offered this as an item of his knowledge but there was no evidence beyond that" for Wilson's misbehavior. Kurtz believed that if Bill had been as indiscriminate and flagrant in his behavior as Powers alleged, then there would certainly be other sources willing and able to provide supporting evidence. (This interview, *Ernest Kurtz: A Reverence for History,* can be streamed from the homepage of Page 124 Production at http://www.page124.com/. The quote here is from the section entitled "The Gold Standard: Two Independent Sources," which begins at 14:53). This lack of a "second source" does not, of course, disprove these rumors, but it should give one significant pause before wholeheartedly believing them. That was certainly Ernest Kurtz' conclusion. *NOTE* that none of this is meant to deny the fact that Bill Wilson did have a long-term, extramarital affair with Helen Wynn in the closing decades of his life. See the sensitive, but candid treatment of this topic in the documentary film, *Bill W.,* released by Page 124 Productions in 2012.

And that's when they began to realize that maybe that wasn't the best thing in the world [to be so candid] if it hurt the other person.[37]

While an awareness of these Oxford Group failings could have prompted a suggestion from Ruth about including this cautionary paragraph in "The Family Afterward," there might have been another, more personal reason for her wanting this plea for secrecy about extra-marital affairs to be included in the book.

Hank Parkhurst was known to have considerable troubles with marital infidelities throughout his life. While details about his past (and future) dalliances are frequently anecdotal, Hank's marriage to Kathleen was deteriorating severely at this time, so much so that they would separate several months after this and she would successfully file for divorce on September 23, 1939.[38] As Lois wrote, "for some time Hank's marriage had not been going well. He had many arguments with Kathleen, and they were planning to get a divorce."[39] Lois was actually part of that divorce filing—an unexpected thing given her husband's close relationship with Hank. But Lois did submit an affidavit at Kathleen's urging in which she noted, among other things, that Hank had been separated from his wife for ten weeks in early 1939 and had been living with the Wilsons at 182 Clinton Street during that time.[40*]

As Hank's attention wandered from Kathleen, he began to focus more and more on his own secretary, the very attractive Ruth Hock. In support of Lois's story about Hank moving in with them for ten weeks in early 1939, Ruth later claimed that Parkhurst "had broken up with his wife just prior to the Cornwall Press trip [i.e., the final week of March 1939] and soon thereafter began making overtures to [me]."[41] This date for the start of their affair is most likely self-serving because Hank had almost certainly been pursuing Ruth for several months at that point. Lois, for instance, mentions that his marriage "had not been going well . . . for some time,"[42] implying the affair had begun well before the Cornwall trip took place. In addition, Hank being thrown out of his own house in early January would strongly suggest that the affair started some time prior to that.

In this regard, it is important to note that Parkhurst's overtures were not unwelcome at first. Ruth was very open to them. "I thought highly of Hank,"[43] at that time, she said, and we "were *very* interested in each other."[44] While the exact date their affair started is unknown, Ruth said that throughout this time Hank "was just an unhappy man and, as Bill used to say: 'When you're unhappy, be careful because you're getting into trouble' and Hank was" doing just that—with Ruth Hock's encouragement.[45] Hank wanted her to become his wife,[46] she said, and she candidly admitted, "I had at one time seriously considered marrying him."[47] But, once he started drinking again, "marriage [became] an impossible thing for us" and the entire affair was over and done with by the fall of 1939.[48] Since Hank had pursued his divorce from Kathleen with every intention of marrying Ruth, this reversal of her affections caused some serious

---

* Merton M., who unearthed these details while writing his *Black Sheep* manuscript, admits that there is contradictory information presented in these primary documents, most especially the fact that Lois's dates don't correspond to Kathleen's sworn statement that they were separated from May 9, 1939. This last date is also compromised by other contemporary documents strongly implying that the Parkhursts did not completely separate until sometime in June at the earliest. Of course, all of these allegations could be—and most likely are—true. The end of a marriage is rarely a neat and tidy affair.

problems for both of them, and also for Bill Wilson who found himself caught squarely in the middle of this illicit affair.[49]

Under these circumstances, both Hank Parkhurst and Ruth Hock would have had a vested interest in making this addition to the text—one which explicitly absolved the adulterous partner from the need to candidly confess these transgressions to his wife—and either or both of them may well have lobbied for the insertion of this new paragraph into "The Family Afterward."

But whoever may have been responsible for the addition of this particular paragraph, it will have to serve here as just one—but far from the only—example of the type of ongoing edits being done to the text of the Big Book before it was finalized for the Multilith printing in mid-February 1939.

CHAPTER TWENTY

Hank Parkhurst: Managing Editor and "To Employers"

~November 1938~

Hank Parkhurst may well have been the busiest man in A.A. during the final months of 1938. In addition to being increasingly distracted with Ruth Hock, he was trying to sell shares in The One Hundred Men Corporation while continuing to lay the foundations for a national promotional campaign to coincide with the book's release. Adding to all this frantic activity, Hank was also about to write two chapters for the Big Book as well has having taken on the job of finding and hiring an editor to review the manuscript once it was completed.

In early November, with most of Bill's time devoted to writing, Hank assumed the role of managing editor. Both men were aware of their status as amateurs and knew it was essential to find someone with some real writing and publishing experience to edit the manuscript before it went to press. Parkhurst, still unhappy with much of what had been written, may well have thought someone with an impressive enough set of credentials might be able to critique the substance of Bill's writing and steer the book more in the psychological direction that he had in mind. But whether or not this was actually part of Hank's agenda, both men agreed the book needed to be reviewed by a professional and Parkhurst took charge of that phase of the project.

Potential Editors Eliminated

Several potential candidates for editor had presented themselves during the past few months. Back in mid-June Hank and Bill had met with Floyd Parsons, a nationally known writer for the *Saturday Evening Post*, who agreed to help them edit the work once it was more nearly finished.[1] But Parson's offer to edit the book was, for some unknown reason, never mentioned again (perhaps Floyd's services were just too expensive). Four months later, Parkhurst's only reference to Parsons was in relation to his promise to write an article for the *Saturday Evening Post* that would coincide with the book's release.[2] Neither of these possibilities ever came to fruition.

Within the Fellowship, Silas Bent had many years' experience as a professional writer and editor and he too had offered to edit the book before it was published.[3] Unfortunately, Silas was having trouble just staying sober and, as we have seen, despite his acclaimed reputation as an author, he did not write (and perhaps wasn't even asked to write) his own story for the book. As the work moved swiftly toward completion, Silas Bent was obviously no longer a viable candidate for the job of editor.

More recently, one of Bill's friends had given a copy of the first two chapters to a man named Arthur Scott and he marked them up extensively as he read them. In mid-October, he wrote to Wilson, telling him that "as an editor of 15 years experience, I just could not help editing the m.s. as I went along, and I hope you will pardon this. In any case what I have done will make the m.s. more acceptable to a printer, though I fear some of the typing will be apt to puzzle him a bit. I have also marked a few queries which need attention." Scott went on to qualify himself as a former alcoholic who had recovered through a deep and abiding belief in the power of God, telling Bill he wanted "to offer you whatever my editorial knowledge and ability may be worth to you in this noble and Christlike work."[4] While Arthur's generous offer of his services was perfectly in line with A.A.'s limited resources, it appears that his editorial suggestions were not and we never hear of him again. If Arthur Scott's letter and his suggested edits were ever brought to Hank's attention, he dismissed him as a potential candidate, deciding to find a much more qualified (and far less religious) editor for the book.

None of these people fit the profile Hank was looking for in an editor. He felt the book needed and deserved the best critical review and he was committed to finding the most experienced and professional editor possible. To his mind, a proper editing job—one that improved whatever amateurish mistakes they might have made while writing—was the critical step needed for the book to become a best seller. And as usual, Parkhurst had set his sights very high. He wasn't just looking for a best seller, he actually had serious hopes their book would become a Book of the Month Club selection, something that would guarantee them immediate nationwide exposure and a truly huge initial sale.[5*]

Two Editors Chosen

With these criteria in mind, Hank began his search for a professional to review, critique, and correct their book. But rather than hiring just one editor, Parkhurst rather quickly decided on two: Thomas H. Uzzell would review the overall format of the book,[6] while Janet M. Blair would more minutely edit the text. Uzzell may have suggested this

---

* In the beginning of 1939, The Book of the Month Club had 360,000 subscribed members who, each month, would elect to receive or not receive the Club's monthly selection (http://www.fundinguniverse.com/company-histories/book-of-the-month-club-inc-history/ - retrieved August 7, 2015).

creative approach. Dividing the editorial responsibilities between himself, a prominent (and expensive) literary critic, and Blair, a qualified but less prestigious (and therefore less costly) text editor, would effectively reduce the overall expense of the editorial work and keep the costs within A.A.'s limited budget.

Lois later claimed that Uzzell was someone "whom Hank knew,"[7] but she offers no further details on what their relationship might have been. By far the simplest explanation of how Parkhurst knew Uzzell would be that he was a teacher at the NYU writing school where, around this time, Parkhurst and Hock were taking a semester's worth of classes on how to write short stories.[8] While the plausibility of this scenario is supported only by circumstantial evidence and inference, it is certainly the least complicated explanation for how Hank may have met Tom Uzzell and it might also help explain how he was introduced to Janet Blair. As we shall see shortly, it is possible Uzzell knew Janet Blair through a mutual acquaintance, so it is not unlikely that Tom was the person who recommended her to Parkhurst. Even more speculative, but still within the realm of possibility, would be that Blair was one of the teachers at Uzzell's own writing school when he recommended her to Parkhurst.[*] In a telling comment, Ruth Hock once noted that the Big Book was "edited by a New York editor and his office staff."[9] If this is true, then Janet Blair was that staff member.

There are certainly other ways to explain how Parkhurst might have met and hired Uzzell and Blair as complementary editors, but the New York University scenario is the most appealing for its simplicity and for the way it fits so neatly with the known facts, few though they may be.

Tom Uzzell to Help Shape the Book

However they met, the first person Hank chose to help shape the book was Thomas H. Uzzell, a fifty-four-year-old author and established critic with an impressive list of literary accomplishments. In an early January letter to Bill Wilson, Hank enumerated his credentials:

> Mr. Thomas H. Uzzell, former editor Collier's Magazine, writer of several books, contributor to Collier's, Saturday Evening Post, etc. As you know, hardly a year goes past when one of Mr. Uzzell's writers do not appear on the best sellers list. Incidentally, this might be interesting to you. Such books as The Good Earth, If I Had Four Apples, The Outward Room, three Book-of-the-month Club books, and best sellers for months after publishing, were submitted to him for criticism and final designing.
>
> In the publishing and literary world, I know there is no one so well established and looked up to as Mr. Uzzell.[10][**]

---

[*]   Uzzell's writing school was very successful during the 1930s and he was known to employ people as his "assistant" and to act as a "teaching agent." (See, for instance, his employment of Eleanor [Berdon] Pearl in these jobs during 1937 and 1938 as noted in the Smith Alumni Quarterly, November 1937, p. 110 and November 1938, p. 108; retrieved online August 7, 2015). Janet Blair may well have been one of these teaching agents.

[**]   Hank's telltale "as you know" implies that this letter was written not so much to bring all of these wonderful details about Tom Uzzell to Bill's attention as it was to write a letter that could be passed on to impress others—as it was subsequently circulated to members of the Rockefeller group to convince them of the rightness of their decision to publish the Big Book themselves.

Tom Uzzell regularly placed advertisements in writing magazines offering "professional training"[11] to new writers along with his services as a freelance "literary critic" for those with finished manuscripts. If he and Hank did not meet through the NYU writing school, then Parkhurst may have located him by responding to one of these many ads. In one, Uzzell detailed his experiences as an editor, published author, and writing teacher and then, under a bold headline entitled "Selling Talk," he encouraged unpublished authors to contact him for advice "because I know my business—analyzing, collaborating, selling—because my reports are absolutely honest, prompt, [and] sympathetic, thousands of unarrived writers have come to me for help. Why not you?"[12]* His resume was certainly impressive, and this was exactly the kind of 'closer' sales question that would have caught Hank's attention if he had read that particular ad.

It is also possible Tom Uzzell came to Parkhurst's attention through a more personal recommendation. In his description of Uzzell's accomplishments noted above, Hank mentions that he had been involved in the "criticism and final design" of *The Good Earth*. This suggests Parkhurst may have first heard about Tom Uzzell from Richard Walsh, the head of John Day Publishing Company, publisher of *The Good Earth*, during their long meeting the previous month. Among all the other topics covered in that informative session with this candid and extremely helpful industry insider, one of Hank's questions may have been "So, who might be a good person to edit our book?" and "Tom Uzzell" could have been Richard Walsh's answer.

But however Parkhurst made the connection with him, Uzzell's professional credentials were remarkable, attesting to his long and successful career as both writer and editor. From the 1910s to the 1930s, he was a regular contributor to an impressive list of magazines including the *Saturday Evening Post, Scribner's, Mumsey's,* the *Writer's Digest, Woman's Home Companion,* the *Saturday Review,* the *American Scholar,* the *North American Review,* and *Collier's* (where he served as Fiction Editor for two years).[13] In addition, his books at this time included *Narrative Technique* (1923) and *Writing as a Career* (1938). The first of these, a textbook on writing, was so popular that it went through several editions over the next three decades.

As might be expected of a man with such noteworthy experience and high reputation, Tom Uzzell's services were not inexpensive. In the magazine ad for his services as Literary Critic, under the rather direct and challenging header entitled "What the Truth Costs," Uzzell tells his potential customers his "fee for a single manuscript is $5 for 5,000 words or less and a dollar a thousand above that."[14] This makes it easy to calculate how much his services would cost if Hank Parkhurst hired him for the job. Since the front half of the book in the Multilith printing was just under 50,000 words and the story section slightly less than that, Uzzell's estimated bill for the most basic literary review of the book would have been roughly $100.

Finally, it is worth mentioning that in his role as teacher and literary critic, Tom Uzzell was a great debunker of the "holy mystery" of writing and the "genius" of writers.

---

* I am grateful to Arthur S., the A.A. historian from Arlington, Texas, for providing me with a copy of this advertisement. Similar ads placed by Uzzell can be found online in the 1920 issues of the *Writer* magazine and in the 1922 issues of the *Editor* magazine.

He once claimed, "if there is such a thing as literary gift . . . meaning any endowment that comes without working at it, I have never been able to find it after years of working with both literary successes and failures." In support of this, he asserted his firm belief that "the people that succeed at authorship . . . seem to have something to say, with energy and egotism to say it, and need the money. These qualifications come pretty close to being those needed for success in any profession or business."[15] It would be hard to imagine a better description of the situation Wilson and Parkhurst found themselves in; they clearly had something important to say, there was no lack of energy or egotism in what they said, and they were very much in need of money.

Tom Uzzell's credentials as a professional editor met all of Hank's criteria and his supremely confident tone (he once referred to himself in an ad as "the foremost American teacher of creative writing"[16]) would have also spoken directly to Parkhurst's own perspective on the world. On so many different levels, Thomas H. Uzzell was his perfect candidate for this job.

Janet Blair as Text Editor

But before he actually met with Uzzell, Hank had lunch with his second candidate, the woman he hoped would become editor for the text of the manuscript.[17] This was the sixty-one-year-old Janet Blair, who had served as secretary to several famous authors throughout her long career in New York City, and who later ran a secretarial school based in her home town of Peekskill, New York, forty-five miles due north of New York City on the Hudson River.[18] But, during late 1938, Janet was clearly open to assuming a variety of freelance jobs to help support her family.

Over the previous two decades in New York, Janet had worked as secretary for a number of academics and authors with occasional breaks in her employment as demanded by ongoing family issues.* For instance, throughout 1916 and into early 1917, Blair was secretary to the author Ida Tarbell, but then left her employ for several months to have a baby. Returning to the job in early 1918, she managed Tarbell's busy schedule and her correspondence for the next three years. Ten years later, she was once again working for Tarbell and continued to do so for approximately two more years. Beyond that, the two women remained distant friends, exchanging birthday wishes and Christmas cards and occasionally scheduling lunch dates when they both happened to be in New York City at the same time.[19]

It is more than a little ironic that Hank Parkhurst would even consider Janet Blair for this job given her long personal history and close relationship with Ida Tarbell. From the mid-1920s onward, Tarbell wrote primarily as a Lincoln scholar with many books and magazine articles about the sixteenth president to her credit. But throughout the first half of her career, she was the most famous of the "muckrakers"—the name given to early twentieth century magazine writers who specialized in sensational exposés

---

* Besides her sister's health issue (which required her presence in Nova Scotia on one or more occasions), Blair's husband was laid off from his railroad job (at least twice) and also had some serious medical issues that demanded her undivided attention. Similarly, her daughter had some recurrent health problems during the late 1920s. (See Janet Blair to Ida Tarbell, November 9, 1921, February 23, 1928, and August 22, 1935; accessible in pdf format from Allegheny College at http://sites.allegheny.edu/tarbell/—retrieved July 27, 2015).

of the disreputable, destructive, and even criminal business practices so common to American capitalism at that time. As such, Tarbell almost single-handedly invented the profession of "investigative journalist" and she had done so most prominently in her brilliant, merciless, and scathing exposé of the Standard Oil Company. This she published in a series of nineteen articles serialized over two years in *McClure's Magazine* starting in 1902 and then put into book form as *The History of the Standard Oil Company* in 1904.[20]

Ida Tarbell was not just famous, she was positively notorious as the woman who had publicly humiliated and exposed John D. Rockefeller, Sr., characterizing him as a mean-spirited, miserly, money-grubbing man who was perhaps the cruelest, most vicious, and the most untrustworthy titan of industry the country had ever produced.* As noted in one brief biography of her:

> Tarbell capped the series [in McClure's] with a two-part character study that revealed her fixation with the man she had been studying for the better part of five years. Focusing on Rockefeller's weary appearance, she called him "the oldest man in the world—a living mummy," and accused him of being "money-mad" and "a hypocrite." "Our national life is on every side distinctly poorer, uglier, meaner, for the kind of influence he exercises," she concluded. Rockefeller was deeply hurt by this last attack from "that poisonous woman," as he called her, but he refused to engage in any public rebuttal of her allegations. "Not a word," he told his advisors. "Not a word about that misguided woman." [21]**

It is possible Parkhurst was unaware of Blair's connection with Tarbell, but that seems improbable since it was almost certainly the most prominent and important item on her resume. And if Hank did know about this connection, it is a wonder he didn't worry about the consequences once the Rockefeller people discovered he had hired an editor who was so closely associated with the family's single greatest enemy. If Parkhurst was at all bothered by this potential problem, he dismissed it—for whatever reason—as being irrelevant to his decision to hire Mrs. Janet Blair on her own merits.***

The other famous person Blair had worked for during this time was the academic Walter B. Pitkin,[22] who in 1932 authored the immensely popular, *Life Begins at 40*. Pitkin's book was a publishing phenomenon, becoming the number one non-fiction best seller in 1933 and staying on that list in the number two position throughout 1934.[23] Walter Pitkin had taught philosophy and psychology during his first five years at Columbia University, but then spent the next thirty years from 1912 to 1943 as one of the most famous teachers in their renowned School of Journalism.[24]

---

*   See Chernow's outstanding biography of John D. Rockefeller, Sr., where Chapter 22: Avenging Angel (pp. 425–65) is devoted to Tarbell. There he notes that this series was "one of the most influential pieces of journalism in American business history" and the one in which "Ida Tarbell turned America's most private man into its most public and hated figure." (*Titan*, p. 438)

**   Tarbell's well-documented revelations about the predatory practices of Standard Oil finally led to its breakup (into 34 different companies) in 1911 when the Supreme Court ruled it to be in violation of the Sherman Antitrust Act (Wikipedia, Standard Oil, Named Article retrieved August 6, 2015).

***   Since this was during the three-month period when Wilson and Parkhurst had distanced themselves significantly from the Rockefeller contingent—a connection that would not be firmly reestablished until January of 1939—it may also have been that Hank Parkhurst felt he didn't need to worry about what they would think about his decision.

More than a little intriguing is the fact that Tom Uzzell had worked for Walter Pitkin for two years in the early 1920s as his "associate and manager,"[25] a position that required Tom to frequently "substitute for him in Columbia School of Journalism fiction classes."[26]* The first ads Uzzell ran for his mail order writing course in 1922 actually claimed he was teaching "a new method . . . [that] has been devised by Professor Walter B. Pitkin, the leading university teacher in the field."[27]** While this connection may have been just coincidental, it is possible Blair and Uzzell knew of each other through their mutual relationships with Walter Pitkin and if so, this might be another avenue whereby Tom Uzzell knew and recommended Janet Blair to Hank Parkhurst.

However Hank was introduced to Janet Blair, they met for lunch—most likely on Friday, November 4—and he was so impressed that he offered her the job. In a long letter written on Monday, November 7, Parkhurst promised to send her a check later that same week as a retainer confirming their arrangement. He also told her he had discussed her "criticism fee with Mr. Wilson and we both agree that you are eminently fair and thank you for your real generosity." This suggests that Hank had negotiated a reduction in Blair's regular fee based either on A.A.'s limited budget or on the worthiness of their life-saving program (or both).

In that same letter, Parkhurst went into some detail about the current state of the writing project and his estimation of when it would be finished:

> According to schedule, Mr. Wilson will be through with the first write of the book by December 5th. As you know, there is a considerable portion of our group in Akron. Before starting to rewrite, Mr. Wilson wants to go over the contents of the book carefully with the people out there.
>
> In setting up our calendar we have allowed ample time and there is a good possibility that we may be two weeks ahead of schedule. However, December 19th is the day we have set when we expect Mr. Wilson to have a complete first write of the book, with full suggestions from the Akron group.

Subsequent events would prove this schedule to be unrealistic: the manuscript was nowhere near complete on December 5 (it is even uncertain whether the Twelve Steps had been written by that time, let alone the two chapters based on them) nor did Bill ever get out to Ohio for consultation with the Akron contingent in December. That didn't happen until March 1[28]—a full month after he had turned the manuscript over to Janet Blair for editing in early February.

Hank followed this with a rather offhanded comment that revealed a number of things about his recent activities: "As you know," he wrote, "I am going to have a talk with Mr. Uzzell in regard to the format of the book and this will be covered within the

---

* This advertisement and several others attest to Uzzell's years at Columbia University, rather than the often quoted, but likely incorrect statement that he was on the faculty at New York University. (See, for instance, this misattribution in *Pass It On*, p. 204.) It is, of course, always possible that he did teach some classes at NYU in addition to his well-known duties at Columbia.

** The year before Uzzell began advertising his mail order course, Walter Pitkin had published full page ads for his own mail order course under the bold headline: "You Can Learn Story Writing - $5." The ad actually quoted Tom Uzzell on how valuable Pitkin's method had been in teaching him how to write saleable stories. (*The Independent*, April 16, 1921, p. 418.)

next two weeks." Parkhurst had clearly already decided to hire Tom Uzzell prior to this lunch and he told Blair about Uzzell's involvement during that meeting, explaining their different areas of responsibility within the project. His plan to hire two editors charged with different tasks was obviously already in place before Parkhurst met with Blair.

Having confirmed her employment, outlined the probable work schedule and reaffirmed the dual responsibilities for editing the book, Hank then asked about the best way to proceed going forward.

> Now what is the soundest procedure for us to follow? Should we wait until the first write is completed and until Mr. Wilson has finished his Akron check-up and then rewritten and sharpened up the entire book, which we figure will be done by January 1st, before submitting it to you? Or should we begin to send chapters along to you now? As you agreed at lunch the other day, it would not be well for the author to have these suggestions until he is through with his first write. On the other hand, it might save time for you and it might get the book more thoroughly in your mind if we begin to send along first writes to you. What are your suggestions?

It is interesting to note that Parkhurst says Blair had told him at lunch that "it would not be well for the author to have these suggestions until he is through with his first writes," but he still wonders whether or not they "should . . . begin to send such chapters along to you now?" and then asks for her thoughts on the matter. Perhaps you had to be at that lunch meeting to fully understand this paragraph, but it very much sounds as if Hank is asking Janet to reconsider a firm opinion that she had already offered him on the subject.

Finally, Parkhurst asks if it would be helpful for Blair to actually meet and talk with Bill Wilson before she begins this project.

> What do you think of bringing Mr. Wilson up to see you [at your office in Peekskill] or meeting him sometime in New York? He has an absorbing story to tell you which would probably consume three or four hours. Would this affect your criticism or would you prefer to wait and hear about it all later? I ask this from the standpoint of the book, as I know you are intensely interested from a personal standpoint and want to meet him.

Blair's reply has not been preserved so there is no way of knowing what her response might have been to all of these questions, but much of that reply would have been based on Hank's proposed schedule which began to slip almost immediately. Whether Janet Blair and Bill Wilson ever met is unknown. The letter makes clear, however, that Hank was planning to meet with Tom Uzzell within two weeks and in all likelihood that meeting took place as scheduled. But all of these other deadlines would be pushed back significantly over the next several weeks and it would be three months before Janet Blair ever received a copy of the manuscript for editing.

But what is most important in this letter is the clear evidence that Parkhurst had taken complete control of the editing process and had already engaged two people to do their respective jobs in relation to the manuscript. Hank would continue to act as managing editor of the book right up until the day it was published.

Hank Finally Sells Some Stock

Besides assembling his team to edit the book, Parkhurst spent the first two weeks of November diligently trying to sell shares of stock in the One Hundred Men Corporation. Using typed copies of the sales prospectus he had created, Hank talked to as many people as he could, hoping to convince them to invest in this outstanding new opportunity. But, even with the glowing promises made in his initial sales offering, closing these deals proved to be more difficult than he had expected.

During his first burst of energetic selling, Hank did convince one company and seven different people to purchase twenty-six shares of $25 stock outright. The biggest investor, Stain-Ox Corporation (the company that made the auto polish marketed by Honor Dealers) bought eight shares. Another eighteen shares went to business friends and associates (including William Currie, one of the original investors in Honor Dealers and Clayton Quaw, Bill Wilson's former employer) and one lone member of A.A. (Norman Hunt bought a single share).[29]* This generated a much needed $650 in ready cash to help with Parkhurst's ongoing expenses, but as Bill Wilson had noted in his 'sheep and goats' letter in late September, Hank was already in debt to the tune of $2,000 and he needed at least $600 a month just to maintain his own household and the office in Newark.[30] While $650 was certainly a positive and much appreciated infusion of cash, it was too little and too late to get Hank even close to caught up on his bills.

An additional seven buyers could only afford to buy a total of thirty-four shares once Hank had offered them his "$5 a month for 5 months" payment plan. Three of these investors were members of the New York Fellowship and the other four were either their friends or relatives. George Williams (who reportedly got sober the previous June) bought twelve shares on time, while Bill Ruddell and Herb Taylor committed to purchase five shares each over the next five months. The remaining stock was bought by Herb Taylor's mother (five shares) and one of his business associates (four shares) and two of Bill Ruddell's friends (who purchased one and two shares respectively).[31]**

The first payments for all of these bought-on-time investments were due on November 15 and could be counted on to generate $170 in cash every month for Hank from November through March—if payments were actually made on time. If the $650 already received for outright purchases was budgeted over the next five months (i.e., $130 a month) and added to this time payment income, Parkhurst would have a

---

* The subscribers listed on this comprehensive document, prepared on May 15, 1940, are arranged in the chronological order in which they made their purchases. This is conclusively confirmed when the list is correlated with the many letters that Ruth Hock wrote in early 1939, either reporting on the outright sale of shares or asking for more timely monthly payments.

** The connections between Taylor and Ruddell and these other buyers is confirmed in several of Ruth Hock's letters of early 1939.

monthly income of $300, just half of the amount he needed to stay solvent, but better than nothing.

At this point, a careful analysis of the 1940 Stock Subscriber list shows something surprising: these sixty shares (bought by fourteen different people and one company) were all purchased before November 15, 1938 and Hank did not sell *any* more shares of stock between that date and the first week of January, 1939.[32]* Clearly, his efforts to sell more stock in The One Hundred Men Corporation were completely suspended during the last six weeks of the year as his energies were redirected to his own writings for the book, the organization of the editorial review team, the arguments that would surface and dominate the Fellowship throughout December once the Twelve Steps were written and the final assembly of a review manuscript for Tom Uzzell.

Bill Lets Hank Write "To Employers"

However little acceptance Hank may have so far received for his ideas about the proper contents of the Big Book, he was now given the opportunity to do some writing of his own for the book and he was hoping he would be able to show Bill Wilson some concrete examples of how he thought that job should have been done all along.

When it came to business matters, Wilson consistently deferred to Parkhurst's greater expertise, freely acknowledging his much more extensive experience within the corporate world. Bill had never held a job managing a large number of people nor did he ever regularly report to a more senior person within a corporate structure. Hank, on the other hand, had spent most of his professional life immersed in just such a large and hierarchical business environment; it was the place where his sales and leadership skills had been developed and perfected over the years. In his last job with Standard Oil of New Jersey, Parkhurst had been an Assistant Wholesale Manager, being paid the handsome salary of $40,000 a year.[33] In this important and lucrative position, he was responsible for the performance of 6,600 salesmen servicing 28,000 dealers,[34] whose sales he then had to justify to his own manager.

Who then was more qualified than Parkhurst to write a chapter entitled "To Employers"? Not only was Hank's business experience far superior to anyone else then sober in A.A., he had also proven to be one of the most successful members in delivering the message of recovery to businessmen who drank too much. In late September Bill wrote to Frank Amos reporting that Parkhurst was then busy with fund raising and publicity efforts, but also "doing a great deal . . . in the general work, where he is most effective with business men of his own type. In Montclair where he lives, three men of this description came to his attention only yesterday through his family physician."[35] In every respect, Hank was the group's most experienced and competent member when dealing with business and with businessmen.

---

* In his January 4, 1939 letter to Frank Amos, Bill Wilson claims that "ninety three shares have been subscribed for in cash" by that date. Exactly where this number came from is uncertain, but it is conclusively contradicted by the detailed May 15, 1940 Subscribers List. One possible explanation might be that Bill had asked Hank for a number and Parkhurst had—not untypically—replied with one that was based more on promises and expectations than actual sales. (Wm. G. Wilson to Frank B. Amos, January 4, 1939; GSO, Box 59, 1939, Document 1939-7 to 1939-10.)

In addition, Bill must have been relieved to admit that there was at least one chapter of the book where he could defer to Hank. Here was perhaps the best way to ease some of the constant pressure coming from Parkhurst about what was being written—let him do some of his own writing for the book! Hank was anxious to make a significant contribution and "To Employers" was the logical place for Bill to give him free rein to do just that.

Finally, this was to be Hank's chapter because of his passionate commitment to the pet theory that large corporations would be more receptive to their new solution than anyone else. Parkhurst fervently believed that whatever time and money a company spent to get a talented employee sober, that investment would be generously returned to them as soon as the recovered man was back on the job. Bill did an excellent job of describing Hank's logic on this topic in an August 1938 letter.

> We have found that the type of alcoholic who recovers most readily is the man who has begun to get some place in business and then is cut down by this hellish sickness. It is logical, therefore, for us to approach the large corporation in this country as a source of the proposed prospect for our group . . . They spend thousands in training a man, and then are obliged to toss him onto a scrap heap. Sometime he is very hard to replace. Our experience tells us that just before or just after they have tossed him onto a scrap heap, we could set maybe as high as 50% of those fellows back in the ring with a punch such as they never had before. Hence, for a corporation, or its officers personally to foster this sort of effort would not only be humanitarian; it should be good for business.[36]

The key point here—and in the chapter Hank would write—is that, in addition to any altruistic considerations, it just made good business sense to invest in a man's recovery. Rather than firing this once valuable employee as an incorrigible drunk and an irredeemable liability, wouldn't it make better sense for the company to help him turn his life around and once again become a valuable asset to the corporation?

Hank's early-June outline for the book had captured the essence of this and provided a framework for what would be covered in his chapter: "Herein employers will be given the new view of alcoholism as it affects their interests. Many specific suggestions will be made, as to how in the best interest of all, the employer may handle the myriad situations which are so baffling to him at present." [Hank's Chapter #22][37]

That outline suggestion would provide the basic content of the chapter.

But that still left Bill with one glaring problem—Hank's atrocious writing style. Given the rather staid and conservative target audience for this chapter, Parkhurst would not be experimenting with any of the more flamboyant techniques he had so recently learned in school, such as the stream-of-consciousness presentation he had already used when writing his own story for the book. But then Hank's normal prose style could be quite as torturous as even this more extravagant attempt at creative writing.

Bill was aware of this and he resolved the problem by claiming the right to edit Hank's chapter as he saw fit, noting (as he had once told Lois) that "he thought the book, except for the stories, should all be written in the same style."[38] It was difficult to argue with this insistence on the need for uniformity; certainly readers should not be forced to make adjustments to different writing styles as each new chapter unfolded. Ruth Hock provides striking testimony to Bill's reservation about Hank's writing in something she wrote to Wilson in late 1955. They had been exchanging letters about A.A.'s early history and in one of them she told Bill she had just remembered "the fact that Hank wrote the first draft of the chapter 'To Employers,' but that you corrected it and, in a sense, rewrote it in your own words."[39]

Whatever Hank might write, Bill was committed to making sure it blended in seamlessly with all of the other chapters. This presents the reader of "To Employers" as printed in the Multilith Copy with a challenging problem: how to tell which parts should be ascribed to Hank Parkhurst's original draft versus those that could be credited to Bill Wilson's later rewrite?

Original Outline Abandoned

Using the same technique he had employed for "To Wives," Bill opens "To Employers" with an introductory statement, presenting the author of the chapter to the reader.

> One of our friends, whose gripping story you have read, has spent much of his life in the world of big business. He has hired and fired hundreds of men. He knows the alcoholic as the employer sees him. His present views ought to prove exceptionally useful to business men everywhere.

> But let him tell you:[40]

Curious here is the fact that Bill informs the reader he has already read the personal story of the man writing "To Employers." In other words, whenever Wilson wrote this introduction, he was still under the impression that they would be following the sequence and organizational format called for in Parkhurst's original outline for the book—i.e., with the personal stories preceding all but one of the general chapters. Unfortunately, there is no further evidence to indicate when this particular sentence may have been written. It can only be said that by late December or early January (when the typescript of the book was submitted to the editor, Tom Uzzell), this format had been abandoned, with all of the personal stories (including Wilson's) now appearing after the general chapters. Surprisingly this bit of misinformation about having already read Hank's story—actually nothing more than a typo at this point—managed to survive ongoing edits and made its way into the Multilith copy, being corrected only at the last minute just before the printing of the book.

It would be interesting (and perhaps even important) to know exactly when and how this decision to abandon Hank's original format for the book was made, but unfortunately there is no mention of that decision in any of the contemporary documents nor in any of the later writings or comments by the participants.

Writing the Chapter

Following a double space to indicate a new writer, Hank Parkhurst opens the chapter by immediately establishing his business credentials: "I was at one time assistant manager of a corporation department employing sixty-six hundred men." He then immediately proceeds to tell the dramatic stories of three men he fired for drinking, each of whom committed suicide: one jumped from a hotel window, another put a shotgun in his mouth and pulled the trigger, the third hung himself in the family woodshed. This fate, Hank says, may well have been his own if it were not "for the intervention of an understanding person" who gave him a new perspective on alcoholism and thereby saved his life.

Without even pausing to mourn this tragic loss of human life and the profound effects it must have had on these three men's families (this was obviously not going to be a chapter that pandered to the emotions), Parkhurst immediately leaps into a bold outline of his basic argument: "My downfall cost the business community unknown thousands of dollars, for it takes real money to train a man for an executive position. This kind of waste goes on unabated. Our business fabric is shot through with it and nothing will stop it but better understanding all around."

Hank goes on to say how difficult it can be for the employer to develop a correct understanding of the alcoholic. He notes that, despite the fact that "nearly every modern employer feels a moral responsibility for the well-being of his help" and would like to do the best he can for all of his employees, misunderstandings about the true nature of the problem all too often get in the way when it comes to dealing with men who are plagued by drink. Rather than just explaining this difficulty, Hank dramatically demonstrates it with the real-life story of one of his friends, a bank executive who had struggled to deal with an alcoholic co-worker. Hearing about his friend's situation, Parkhurst spent "two hours talking [with him] about alcoholism, the malady. I described the symptoms and supported my statements with plenty of evidence." All to no avail. His business friend was sure the man was done drinking because he had recently "taken a cure, looks fine, and to clinch the matter, the board of directors told him this was his last chance."

Parkhurst scoffed at this naïve optimism, claiming that unless the man was brought into "contact with some of our alcoholic crowd" or, at least, given a chance to hear his story, he would soon be headed for "a bigger bust than ever." But this advice was rejected out of hand and Hank realized that, despite his best efforts during this two-hour conversation, "my banking acquaintance had missed the point entirely." The result, he said, was exactly as he had predicted: "Presently the man did slip and, of course, was fired." The upside of this story only came after A.A. members contacted the man following his dismissal and "he accepted our principles and procedure." Because of his willingness to change, he now found himself "on the high road to recovery."

But the man had been fired rather than being offered this simple new solution. Hank was not just frustrated, he was indignant. How could his friend, an accomplished and intelligent businessman, be so blind to his arguments and personal testimony about the subtlety and power of this disease? "To me, this incident illustrates a lack of understanding and knowledge on the part of employers—lack of understanding as to what really ails the alcoholic, and lack of knowledge as to what part employers might profitably take in salvaging their sick employees."

Addressing the first point—how an employer can ever come to understand "what really ails" the alcoholic—Parkhurst insists it must begin with the employer disregarding absolutely everything he knows about drinking. "Whether you are a hard drinker, a moderate drinker, or a teetotaler . . . to you, liquor is no real problem. You cannot see why it should be to anyone else, save for the spineless or the stupid." But Hank stresses that this kind of attitude is useless when dealing with an alcoholic. The employer must constantly fight against his "ingrained annoyance that [the alcoholic] could be so weak, stupid and irresponsible." To do so is a grave and often-fatal misunderstanding of the problem. Instead, Hanks says, you must remember, "that your employee is very ill" and "seldom as weak and irresponsible as he appears" to you.

The second point—understanding what employers can do to help their drinking employees—is more complicated. Having readily acknowledged his ignorance of alcoholism, the employer must then decide whether or not the drunken employee is worth saving. On this issue, Hank thinks there can be little question: "Take a look at the alcoholic in your organization. Is he not usually brilliant, fast thinking, imaginative and likeable? When sober, does he not work hard and have a knack for getting things done?" The implication is that, of course, it makes sense to rehabilitate and save such a valuable asset. Once this decision is made, "whether the reason be humanitarian, or business, or both, then you will wish to know what to do."

As a first step in that process, Hank contends that the employer must be willing to reconsider his existing misapprehensions, to the point where he can concede that this "employee is ill," but still valuable to the company and, as such, worth forgiving "what he has done in the past." He asks the employer to consider whether or not he can "shelve the resentment you may hold because of his past absurdities? Can you fully appreciate that the man has been a victim of crooked thinking, directly caused by the action of alcohol on his brain?" This last observation is followed by some extremely dubious medical testimony (even for 1938) about how drinking can increase the "pressure of the spinal fluid" thereby creating "a fevered brain" which is the cause of the alcoholic's irrational actions. Whatever nonsensical "scrapes" an employer may discover in an alcoholic's past behavior (and there may be some "pretty messy ones"), he must accept these as the result of alcohol's abnormal impact on his brain. The drinking employee needs understanding and forgiveness, not censure.

Hank then warns the employer about the man who really does not want to stop, but who is more than willing to take advantage of "your attempt to understand and help." If you find yourself with such an employee, he says, "you may as well discharge him, and the sooner the better." But these, he says, tend to be the exceptions. "There are many men who want to stop right now, and with them you can go far. If you make a start, you should be prepared to go the limit, not in the sense that any great expense or trouble is to be expected, but rather in the matter of your own attitude, your understanding treatment of the case." Once again, the employer's need for proper understanding is pointed out as the critical element.

Hank now begins to lay out step by step directions (similar to those found in "Working With Others") for how to approach a drinking employee. First, qualify your prospect; does he really want to stop drinking and will he "go to any extreme to do so?" Parkhurst gives detailed instructions here on difficult questions that must be asked of the alcoholic employee and he offers explicit warnings about the tactics and strategies that are often used by lying or insincere drinkers when challenged in this way.

Once the employer is convinced the man is sincere, he should tell him that "a certain amount of physical treatment is desirable, even imperative." If he accepts this definite course of action, offer "to advance the cost of treatment if necessary, but make it plain that any expense will later be deducted from his pay. Make him fully responsible; it is much better for him." Finally, if he accepts the proposal, point out to him that

> physical treatment is but a small part of the picture. Though you are providing him with the best possible medical attention, he should understand that he must undergo a change of heart. To get over drinking will require a transformation of thought and attitude. He must place recovery above everything, even home and business, for without recovery he will lose both.

Hank follows this bit of ambitious advice (it is, quite frankly, hard to imagine an employer credibly informing an employee that he must "undergo a change of heart" and "a transformation of thought and attitude" based on nothing more than a reading of this book) with his worries that the employer's own belief system may be the greatest stumbling block to the drunken employee ever hearing about this new solution. He explicitly cautions the employer against any prejudices he might have against A.A.'s spiritual approach and the professed need for a drinking employee to acquire a spiritual experience to successfully stop drinking. "After all," Hank says as he again addresses the employer directly, "you are looking for results rather than methods" and "you will surely agree that it may be better to withhold any criticism you may have of our method until you see whether it works." In short, don't let your own beliefs prejudice you (or your employee) against the essential spiritual elements in A.A.'s "Program of Recovery."

Continuing with his advice for "what part employers might profitably take in salvaging their sick employees," Hank suggests that once the newly sober man returns to work, the boss "call him in and ask what happened," questioning him about his recovery and what he thinks he must to do in order to preserve it. This invitation to an open conversation may result in the man admitting to shocking things, such as the padding of his expense account or his earlier plan to steal the company's best clients and take them with him to another job. Revelations such as these are fairly normal, Parkhurst says, once a man has "accepted our solution which, as you know, demands rigorous honesty." However distressing these confessions may be, Hank advises the employer to "charge this off as you would a bad account and start afresh with him."

He also warns that problems with the man's home situation and with office politics once he is back on the job should also be expected and dealt with as quickly and fairly as possible. Parkhurst contends that both of these call for candor and understanding on the part of the employer for "the greatest enemies of the alcoholic are resentment, jealousy, envy, frustration, and fear." The employer should avoid situations that generate these kind of feelings at all costs and anything he can do to reduce tensions will result in the newly sober employee professing "undying loyalty" to the manager and to his company.

Finally, Hank points out that the former alcoholics may now become a workaholic. If so, "don't let him work sixteen hours a day just because he wants to. Encourage him to play once in a while. Make it possible for him to do so." And, if he wants to work with other alcoholics in need of his help, even during business hours, "don't begrudge him a reasonable amount of time. This work is necessary to maintain his sobriety."

Hank follows this with three catchall paragraphs regarding what to expect from the man who has been sober for just a few months. First, he says, you may want to include him in conversations with other problem drinkers in your organization. He may be very helpful to you in these situations, even when dealing with more senior men. Second, it is critical that you completely trust this employee and not, for instance, become suspicious if he should call in sick one day. Nor should you worry about protecting him from any drinking situations that may normally arise in the course of his job. Finally, if he does have a slip, Parkhurst says you must do your best to evaluate his sincerity about staying sober. "If you are sure he doesn't mean business, there is no doubt you should discharge him. If, on the contrary, you are sure he is doing his utmost, you may wish to give him another chance."

Hank then spends three paragraphs expounding his theories about how the work of recovery should be fruitfully pursued within a large corporation. He proposes that junior executives, who are often put in compromising positions because of their coworker's drinking, be given the book to read. Once this has provided them with a sufficient understanding of alcoholism, they should then feel free to go to their drinking friends within the company and say something like this:

> Look here, Ed. Do you want to stop drinking or not? You put me on the spot every time you get drunk. It isn't fair to me or the firm. I have been learning something about alcoholism. If you are an alcoholic, you are a mighty sick man. You act like one. The firm wants to help you get over it, if you are interested. There is a way out, and I hope you have sense enough to try it. If you do, your past will be forgotten and the fact that you went away for treatment will not be mentioned. But if you cannot, or will not stop drinking, I think you ought to resign.

The possibility that this scenario might actually work to the company's benefit (or to the junior executive's) seems remote at best and it is hard to believe Parkhurst was ever seriously committed to it. But, somehow, the idea of distributing the book and then encouraging conversations similar to this made perfect sense to him and he confidently advocated that large companies adopt it as a way to ferret out and then reclaim the alcoholics within their organization.

"It boils right down to this," Hank says. "No man should be fired just because he is alcoholic. If he wants to stop, he should be afforded a real chance. If he cannot, or does not want to stop, he should usually be discharged. The exceptions are few."

In case the point has been somehow missed, Parkhurst once again highlights the financial benefits of addressing this problem. "We don't expect you to become a missionary," he tells the employer. "Being a business man is enough these days. But we can sensibly urge that you stop this waste and give your worth-while man a chance." Doing so is just a good business decision.

His final caution is against being one of those men who prefers to deny the problem rather than dealing with it and he offers the story of a vice president of a large industrial concern who claimed confidently that "we don't have any alcohol problem." Hank scoffs at this and categorically states this executive "might be shocked if he knew how much alcoholism cost his organization a year." Hank advises the employer that, if he is one of those who is ignorant or in denial about the extent of the alcohol problem within the company, "you might well take another look down the line. You may make some interesting discoveries."

Since the reader is a business man, Parkhurst presumes he would appreciate "a summary of this chapter," so he offers the following ten concise steps:

One: Acquaint yourself with the nature of alcoholism.

Two: Be prepared to discount and forget your man's past.

Three: Confidentially offer him medical treatment and cooperation, provided you think he wants to stop.

Four: Have the alcohol thoroughly removed from his system and give him a suitable chance to recover physically.

Five: Have the doctor in attendance present him with this book, but don't cram it down his throat.

Six: Have a frank talk with him when he gets back from his treatment, assuring him of your full support, encouraging him to say anything he wishes about himself, and making it clear the past will not be held against him.

Seven: Ask him to place recovery from alcoholism ahead of all else.

Eight: Don't let him overwork.

Nine: Protect him, when justified, from malicious gossip.

Ten: If, after you have shot the works, he will not stop, then let him go.

As a final testimony to the effectiveness of this approach, Hank closes, as he opened, with a bit of his own experience:

Today, I own a little company. There are two alcoholic employees, who produce as much as five normal salesmen. But why not? They have a better way of life, and they have been saved from a living death. I have enjoyed every moment spent in getting them straightened out. You, Mr. Employer, may have the same experience!

God Is Omitted from the Text

There are a few notable things in this chapter that distinguish it from those Wilson had already written. Most prominent is the complete omission of the word "God" from the text, a concrete example of the rule Hank had been urging on Bill for the past several months. In that same vein, the word "spiritual" appears only twice in this version of the chapter. Interestingly, both were deleted before the Big Book went to press, which may well imply they had been added by Wilson and then later removed by Parkhurst, returning the text to the purity he advocated with such consistency.

More than that, it would have been easy to justify these two deletions since they occur in these sentences that place unusual and distinctly unscientific responsibilities upon the physician attending the alcoholic: "The doctor should approve a spiritual approach. And besides, he ought to tell the patient the truth about his condition, whatever that happens to be. The doctor should encourage him to acquire a spiritual experience." This sounds suspiciously like something Wilson might have added in the belief that the group's experience with Dr. Silkworth, who enthusiastically supported the religious approach offered by A.A., would prove to be the model for medical men across the country. That belief was optimistic in the extreme and not even true among doctors who actually took the time to read the book, so the deletion of these lines proved to be an excellent editorial decision.

But beyond the expectation that doctors everywhere would rally to support A.A.'s newfound spiritual solution, it seems like a strange and unlikely way to handle this situation. Why completely spare the employer the responsibility of recommending A.A's explicitly religious solution while placing that task squarely on the doctor's shoulders? Why wouldn't the employer be the most likely person to recommend a spiritual approach to his employee, emphasizing the need to "acquire a spiritual experience" if he wants to stay permanently sober? Why leave it to the doctor?

Outside of these two later-deleted references, Hank is consistently, even willfully vague and ambiguous about spiritual issues, completely sidestepping the religious elements so prominently found in all the other chapters. Throughout, he barely makes passing mention of the spiritual aspects of "the Program of Recovery" and then only in the most offhanded way, usually giving it a psychological spin. Parkhurst's most direct reference comes when, as already noted, he advises the employer to tell his drinking employee "he should understand that he must undergo a change of heart" and that "to get over drinking will require a transformation of thought." In keeping with his overall intentions, this suggests something much more like a psychological change than the religious transformation called for in the rest of the book.

When at one point Hank does make explicit mention of the program's "principles and procedure," he presumes these need no further explanation because the employer has just read the book where all of that is explained in detail. Beyond this, the only specific application of the program Parkhurst does mention is the need for the newly sober man to be rigorously honest which, he says, is demanded of all who have accepted "our solution."

Read the Book—but Don't Mention It to the Employee

Hank simply assumes the employer has not only read the book, but completely understood and digested its spiritual content and then—in spite of any possible reservations he might have—decided to try this new approach with one of his more troublesome employees. This is a lot to presume given Parkhurst's recent experience with his friend the bank officer who, after two hours of intense one-on-one conversation, still failed to understand the nature of alcoholism and the necessity of pursuing a spiritual solution.

Even more strangely, the employer was also advised to make no mention whatsoever of the book to the alcoholic. This is in striking contrast to the advice Bill offered in "To Wives," where he repeatedly encouraged the wife to bring the book to her husband's attention, even suggesting she read significant passages to him in an effort to engage his interest in the possibility of recovery. Hank, on the other hand, warns against even mentioning the book's existence. When first cross-examining the employee about his willingness to quit drinking, Parkhurst explicitly tells the employer, "Not a word about this book." Not a word! Similarly, the junior executive is advised that "he need not, and often should not show [the book] to the alcoholic prospect." The only person to be told about the book is the doctor. "I suggest you draw our book to the attention of the doctor who is to attend your patient during treatment." The doctor is then given the task of introducing the book to the alcoholic patient ("Five: Have the doctor in attendance present him with this book, but don't cram it down his throat") and of making sure it is "read the moment the patient is able—while he is acutely depressed, if possible."

Exactly why the book would prove to be such an effective tool in the wife's hands (and the doctor's), but not in those of the employer (or the junior executive) is never explained. Perhaps Parkhurst felt that asking him to advocate for the book was just too far outside the realm of good business practices, where a request to do so would put him in the possibly uncomfortable position of having to endorse a book—and a particular solution—that contained such specifically religious elements.

• • •

Despite whatever changes Bill Wilson may have made to this chapter, it still exhibits—especially as it was printed in the Multilith copy—Hank Parkhurst's tendency to write in a wandering fashion, straying off topic with regularity and occasionally leaving out important connecting thoughts. This makes any logical, schematic outline of the chapter difficult, something that can only be done by ignoring the more distracting digressions (for instance, the spinal fluid theory*) while simultaneously filling in the logical gaps, which regularly appear in the chapter.

Given this overall lack of organization, it is natural to wonder about the remarkable ten-point summary offered at the end. This list clearly, comprehensively, and concisely describes the message that can be difficult to decipher from any casual reading of "To Employers." Was this something Bill added to the text? It certainly seems to have been put in by someone who thought it was necessary to bring a bit more clarity to this rambling chapter. Whatever its origin, it was deemed redundant and unnecessary—most likely by Hank Parkhurst himself—and this excellent numbered summary was deleted in the weeks just before the book went to press. This is unfortunate. If clear communication with the employer was the goal of this chapter, then the removal of that list was a decidedly poor editorial decision.

However disjointed and disorganized "To Employers" may have been when it was first written, it shines like a positive beacon of clarity when compared to the next chapter Hank Parkhurst produced in the hope that Bill Wilson would include it in the book.

---

* Hank's idea of heightened spinal fluid pressure causing a "fevered brain" probably came from Dr. Silkworth who in his 1937 article "Reclamation of the Alcoholic" noted that when treating a new alcoholic patient it was necessary to "relieve the pressure in the brain and spinal cord." (Silkworth, "Reclamation of the Alcoholic," April 21, 1937 in Medical Record, A National Review of Medicine and Surgery, The Medical Journal and Record Publishing Company, Inc., New York, Volume 145, pp. 321–24.)

CHAPTER TWENTY-ONE

"The Q&A Chapter"

~November 1938~

"To Employers" wasn't the only chapter Hank Parkhurst wrote for the book. He also suggested they include a "Question and Answer Section" and he went so far as to produce a fifteen-page sample to show how that chapter might actually look.[1*] Despite the fact that Bill Wilson rejected this proposal, it is well worth exploring in some detail for two reasons. Not only does it provide a candid and insightful glimpse into Hank Parkhurst, the man and his personality, it also contains a detailed snapshot of how Alcoholics Anonymous was working in New York City in late 1938—at least from one man's perspective.

The Honor Dealers Q&A as a Model

Hank had used this Q&A format several years earlier in a promotion piece sent out by Honor Dealers, believing it was an effective way to promote products and services to customers—especially to reluctant customers. Parkhurst was trying to convince gas station owners to join his collective buying group, and his theory seems to have been that a mailed list of questions and answers allowed the potential client to wade through all of the usual objections before receiving an actual sales call. Hank believed this strategy got him just that many steps nearer to closing the sale when he stopped by to make his in-person sales pitch.

---

* The title on this document notes that it "has been proposed for the book." This is helpful in dating the document in late 1938 rather than relying on the early 1939 numbering arbitrarily given to it by the GSO Archive. A draft of the complete book went to Tom Uzzell in late December so this writing surely precedes that event. Also, Hank's Q&A chapter makes no mention whatsoever of the Twelve Steps or of their explicitly spiritual elements so it was almost certainly written before Bill Wilson had formulated those steps in early December. These two correlations with later events place the date of composition for Hank's effort sometime in November (or possibly even late October) 1938.

Certainly one of the most attractive features of this kind of presentation is the illusion of intimacy and trust created by packaging the message as a one-on-one conversation. For instance, the Honor Dealers piece reads as if one businessman were having a casual but completely candid conversation with another. In fact, the talk in this dialogue—of which only a few paragraphs have survived—is so honest that it begins (mid-answer unfortunately) with a full accounting of just how poorly the organization has been doing financially during its first year.

> Men, cars and daily expenses has been slightly over $14,500.00—Telephone $613.00—Stationery and printing $1,051.00—Postage $390.00—Furniture and Fixtures $1,530.00—Incidental expenses $752.00—Rent $1,500.00—Making a total expenditure of $20,336.00—Against this expense has been a gross income of $2,062.85.[*]

70—How can such a loss go on?
We went into this with the full knowledge that it was expensive and that it would be well into the second year before real income began to come in. Today the income is increasing.

71—How will the financial loss be recovered?
We have constantly gone on the theory that every man is fair. If you help him to make money he is willing to pay you for that service. We know that this will eventually be profitable and believe dealers will be glad to see us take a fair share of the profits.

71-A—Is the development of the organization going too slowly?
Naturally it would be pleasing to see it go faster, but actually there is no harm in this slow development. If it went faster, dealers would profit to a greater extent, however we must remember that dealers share the power to wait. On products not handled by the organization no change in Honor Dealers buying procedure has taken place. This power to wait is one of your strongest points. We do not have to take on any products immediately, because we are not keeping any dealers from being supplied with sales necessities.

72—Will Honor Dealers last?
No one can guarantee that anything will be permanent. However, Honor Dealers are over a year old and have five nationally advertised buying connections. A dealer cannot lose by being an Honor Dealer.

---

[*] These financial numbers may well be important to A.A. historians investigating the period shortly after the Big Book was published when Wilson and Parkhurst got into a heated argument over the cost of the furniture Bill had moved to the new office in New York City, here noted as costing $1,530 during the first year.

73—What does a dealer have to sign?
Nothing except the lease on the sign. Every man's word must be as good as his bond and therefore a contract is not needed. The signed lease is for the protection of the dealers.[2]

Once again Parkhurst's prose leaves much to be desired, but the general ideas are clear enough, and might be even clearer if we had access to the sixty-nine questions preceding these. But it was this same kind of format that Hank had in mind for the book.

Why Do A Q&A Chapter?

Although his early June outline for the book did not include a Q&A chapter, just prior to creating this outline Parkhurst had suggested several important questions he felt should be answered in the book if it was to be effective in any way. In his roughly sketched "Ideas," Hank proposed to Bill that the following topics should be included and addressed directly:

Questions + Answers—

1. The question is often asked—where does the money come from for this work?

2. How do I know this will work with me?

   Why is this method better than any other religious method? (It is not—this is only a step toward a religious experience which should be carried forward in Christian fellowship no matter what your church)

3. Will I fail if I cannot keep my conduct up to these highest standards?

4. What happens when an alcoholics [sic] has a sexual relapse?

5. There is so much talk about a religious experience—what is it?[3]

Questions about money (#1) and the issues of moral conduct (#3) and, more specifically, sexual misconduct (#4) along with a number of other questions Parkhurst thought would be important to the prospective member are well covered in his proposed chapter. But, true to his ongoing aversion to any detailed talk of religion and how spirituality might actually work within the program of recovery (#2 and #5), those issues are given short shrift and are dealt with in only a cursory fashion.

Two Arguments for the Chapter
There are at least two likely arguments Hank might have put forward for including a Q&A chapter such as this in the book.

First, it would be a good way to anticipate and respond to the objections that would just naturally occur to the reluctant alcoholic as he read through the Big Book. By deliberately anticipating these objections and then addressing them in a straightforward manner, it might be possible to overcome the reader's resistance before he became too entrenched in his own negative responses. Hopefully, anything that forestalled such a rejection would provide the reader with a greater opportunity to honestly consider their proposed solution and perhaps even to accept it.

Second, a Q&A chapter would serve as an in-print substitute for the all-important "one alcoholic talking to another alcoholic" conversation that was so universally acknowledged as the proven way to secure new members for A.A. Before the book, these one-on-one dialogues were the only way the message of recovery had been carried; they were the solid and indispensable foundation upon which every successful member's sobriety had so far been built. Since face-to-face conversations were so fundamental to attracting new members, why wouldn't they want to provide the distant reader who had nothing but the book to rely on with the most faithful representation of that kind of personal encounter they could possibly create?

A Q&A chapter in the book would accomplish both of these worthwhile goals simultaneously.

The Questions and Answers Fail to Deliver

Sadly, despite Hank's best intentions, the ninety-four questions and answers he proposed for this chapter failed to deliver on either of these two promises.

For one thing, the questions did not address most of the important concerns any newcomer would need clarified to properly understand what was being asked of him. There can be little doubt that Parkhurst's questions had been raised by potential members at one time or another, but they were far from the ones needed to convince a new man of the truths presented in the rest of the book or to emphasize the actions needed for him to get sober. The vast majority of the questions exhibit an almost casual disregard for the substance of the program of recovery, concentrating instead on a wide variety of lesser issues that arise only after a man has been sober for some period of time.

For instance, the chapter opens with two questions that focus on what other people might think of a man who refused to take a drink.

> **What is your answer when asked to have a drink?** *[1]*
> On the first invitation I refuse. If there is insistence I explain I cannot handle it and a drink would eventually lead to a bender. If the party is interested, I explain I am one of the unfortunate people whom alcohol seems to poison much in the way certain pollens poison hay fever sufferers.

> **What are people's reaction when you explain you are an alcoholic?** *[2]*
> I have never seen it fail to arouse sympathetic interest and respect for meeting the question honestly.[4]

---

* Note that these *[bracketed italicized numbers]* after each question do not appear in the original document. They are inserted here as a handy reference for their location within the Q&A Chapter and to provide some sense of how questions have been reordered here for clarity and some semblance of a better organization. The complete text of the Q&A Chapter is reproduced in Appendix VIII on page 661.

This is hardly the dramatic and gripping opening one would expect for an honest and searching dialogue between two men discussing what is basically a life-and-death situation. Unfortunately, most of the questions that follow are similar to these in their focus on the mundane, primarily talking about what happens when a man stops drinking rather than providing any information on what must be done in order to get sober in the first place.

Subjectivity, Confusion, and Inconsistency Mar the Text

In addition to its many lackluster questions, Hank's chapter also failed to deliver because almost all of his responses are so intensely personal, clearly expressing just one man's experience and opinions rather than answering in a more general way as a spokesman for the program. The next four questions provide an excellent example of this decidedly individual focus.

How long since you had a drink? *[3]*
Three and a half years.

Don't you ever desire a drink? *[4]*
Of course. Seldom a day passes when I do not wish I could drink.

Do all alcoholics who have used this method wish they could drink? *[5]*
No. The desire to drink seems to be taken away instantaneously in some cases. Others lose it after a period of months.

What is there about liquor or the use of it you still desire? *[6]*
I miss the glow of well-being which comes from two or three drinks; the instant removal of tiredness or worries.

These are undoubtedly honest answers on Hank's part, but they do little to encourage a man who might be looking for a way to stop drinking. Who would elect to go three and a half years without a drink, all the while craving one on a daily basis? Is this really the most appealing way to open the chapter if your intention is to capture the attention and interest of the drinking reader? Hardly. The reader has just been informed, in the space of the first six questions, that once he quits drinking he will be constantly confronted with awkward situations (where he will be the conspicuous teetotaler who must explain himself to the drinkers present), all the while being plagued by a daily desire to drink.

The next fourteen pages are similar to this, with many secondary questions being asked and followed by Hank's individual responses. Throughout, Parkhurst dominates the discussion with at least thirty explicitly personal answers and another twenty or so that present his own experiences and opinions in a more general way. It is very close to an 'it's all about Hank' performance, offering telling insights into Parkhurst's life and personality for any future biographer.[*]

And all of this comes with an abundance of the confusing and inconclusive statements that typically litter Hank's writings. For instance, in the questions above, Parkhurst tells the new man that the desire to drink leaves some A.A. members "instantaneously" while others lose it "after a period of months," but that for him "seldom a day passes" when he does not crave a drink. An inquisitive newcomer would almost certainly want to ask: "Well, if most members lose their desire to drink so quickly, why do *you* still crave a drink on a daily basis after three-and-a half years of sobriety?" That is certainly an important question (and one that begs for a Parkhurst answer), but the issue is simply sidestepped and never addressed again.

Such confusions and lost threads run rampant throughout the chapter. In terms of organization and clarity, it is Hank Parkhurst at his all-time worst. Categorizing or talking about these questions in any rational fashion is challenging because they follow no logical pattern, jumping from one topic to the next (and then often coming back to an earlier one again) without any semblance of order or logic. However, if the most personal questions and responses—which do provide some substantial bits of information about the author—are sorted out, those that remain can be grouped under a few different headings.

Slips Get a Lengthy and Mixed Treatment

The general topic that gets more attention than any other is about those who return to drinking. If nothing else, when taken together, the sixteen questions on this topic provide some interesting information about both Hank Parkhurst's own sobriety and the New York A.A. program in late 1938. The first two questions in this group appear on the second page, providing a set-up for those that follow.

> **Did any of your friends, who are members of Alcoholics Anonymous, drink again?** *[10]*
> Yes. Many of them have had what we call slips.

> **What do you think causes slips?** *[11]*
> There are so many things, it is hard to define. Generally, I believe the man has been missing some of the more important points such as passing this on to another alcoholic, not putting first things first, dishonesty with self or others, not joining in the fellowship, getting angry at people or conditions, boredom, etc.

The nine questions that immediately follow this deal with each of these failings in turn, emphasizing their individual importance to the man who wants to stay

---

[*] The lack of a proper, well-researched biography of Henry G. Parkhurst is one of the most glaring gaps in current A.A. scholarship. Hank played an absolutely central and critical role in A.A.'s early history and such a book would surely make an important contribution to our understanding of the early years of this recovery movement. Again, one can only hope that someday soon an able historian will take on this project as a doctoral dissertation or as a full-blown book-writing project.

sober. Two are particularly interesting in relation to Parkhurst's own attitudes and his understanding of A.A.'s beliefs.

What do you mean by putting "first things first"? *[15]*
If a man is suffering from an incurable disease, I claim the first and most important for him is to do everything possible to recover from that disease. If a man is suffering from alcoholism, I believe the most important thing to him should be his recovery from his malady. In other words, first things first. Recovery should come before a job and everything else, for if the man does not recover, he will have no job or anything else anyway. An alcoholic is generally inclined to forget that he has spent many years getting into his present condition and is impatient for all difficulties to clear up immediately.

"First things first" seems to have been Hank Parkhurst's favorite A.A. slogan, appearing seven times in this chapter. This fuller explanation of his understanding of its central importance to sobriety is worth noting carefully because he considered it to be so critical to the process of recovery. Later, in response to another question, he made a further elaboration by saying "To keep first things first . . . of course, that means for me to keep a proper relation with the Power that enabled me to recover." *[41]*

Answering another question on slips, Hank is a bit judgmental at first, but then goes on to speak rather eloquently about the democratic underpinnings of Alcoholics Anonymous.

Why does boredom cause slips? *[20]*
To be brutally frank, I believe the man who gets plastered because he has become bored is generally a snob. He thinks he is a little better than the people whom he contacts and so he gets bored. While I do not claim that everyone in the fellowship must like every other person, I do believe that if a person sincerely searches for admirable qualities in other people, he will be able to find them. If a man really tries to help another person or persons, I believe life becomes so interesting he has no time to be bored.

Having canvassed the details for each of these pitfalls, he then wanders off for ten questions (relating to his own experiences, the reason A.A. focuses only on drunks, and his marital and financial history) before returning to the topic of slips once again on page 5.

Have you ever nearly slipped? *[31]*
Yes. Several times.

How did you escape? *[32]*
The first time I phoned one of the other alcoholics and told him I was afraid I was going to take a drink. He asked if I would wait until he got out to the house, and I agreed. When he arrived we talked over the desire

and the things which were bothering me and strangely, the desire left me. Another time, I called one of the gang and he suggested reading the Bible and praying before I took the first drink. I never took that drink. The third time, I made careful plans and then simply told one of the bunch I was going to. Instead of getting all excited, he simply said, "So what. Go ahead and have a couple for me." I took a nap and when I woke up I could laugh at it, the desire was gone. Another time when in the biggest crisis of my life,* which previously would undoubtedly have caused me to drink, I got to work helping others before the desire even had a chance to start to bother me.

Still later, on page 9, Hank presents his final three questions on slips.

When a man calls to tell you he is on the verge of a slip, what do you do for him? *[53]*
That is hard to define. So much depends on the man himself. One thing I always do is to say a silent prayer and ask him to get all his gripes off his chest. However, I usually tell him it may be right for him to go on a bender because I feel it may be necessary to prove certain things. I cannot get excited because anyone is going to get drunk. As I look at it, that will not presage the coming of the end of the world. I find that when a man is talking to someone who understands and actually does not care whether he is going to get drunk, he is apt to get his thinking on the right track and will not go on the bender.

When a man goes ahead anyway and then calls you up to tell you he has slipped, what do you tell him? *[54]*
I tell him not to bother me. I'm not in the business of pinning up anybody's diapers. When he gets through and sincerely wants to quit drinking, give me a ring and I'll see if I can be helpful.

When a man has had a slip should he attempt to hide it? *[55]*
We have found that to be one of our greatest dangers. The man is so ashamed of it, he generally has been so proud of his record that the temptation is great to pass it off. This, of course, is going right back to the old ways and is dangerous. If a man slips, my attitude is . . . So what? that isn't important, what is important is whether he is going to slip again. I clearly remember what a man once told me. He said, "An alcoholic who thinks no one knows about his drinking is like an ostrich with his behind in the air and his head in the sand."

---

* How unfortunate that Hank mentions this "biggest crisis of my life" since getting sober, but provides absolutely no further details!

These sixteen questions present a vibrant and fascinating picture of Hank Parkhurst in action in early A.A., reflecting not only his own understanding of sobriety and slips, but also the practices that were accepted in New York at this time. Certainly the cavalier "Go ahead and have a couple for me" and the belief that it may be acceptable and even necessary for a man to go on a bender so that he can "prove certain things" to himself about his drinking are far from the reactions and beliefs typically found among most of today's A.A. members.

A Personal (and Confusing) Take on God

Hank's initial list of the possible causes for slips—in his response to question *[11]* noted above—is important not only for what it says, but also for what it doesn't say. While there are some passing references, the most conspicuous missing element is the almost complete absence of God and the spiritual element. Hank's diagnosis of why the new man returned to drinking is based on a laundry list of worldly things: his failure to work with others, his bad attitude, dishonesty, isolation, anger or boredom. But he makes no mention whatsoever of the explanation repeatedly offered throughout the rest of the Big Book, namely that the slipper had not done the work required for "the necessary vital spiritual experience" that would ensure his sobriety; that he had, on some level and in some important way, "failed to enlarge his spiritual life."[5]

This is not to say that Parkhurst makes no mention of God or spirituality in this chapter, but when he does, it is often presented in a rather jarring and almost confrontational manner. At one point—improbably sandwiched between two completely unrelated questions—Hank asks:

> **Isn't this nothing more or less than old fashioned revivalism?** *[43]*
> I am forced to say, So What? It works! There is nothing that could place me in a more untenable position or make me do more ridiculous things than I did when in the grip of uncontrolled drinking.

This blithe concession, with absolutely no objection or qualification, that the program's solution could be accurately described as "revivalism" —the most incendiary kind of preaching and religious conversion imaginable—along with a response claiming that recovery may require the new member to adopt a ridiculous and even untenable position is almost shocking. It flies in the face of everything else written for the book up to this point and all but jumps off the page as a mocking challenge to Bill Wilson's entire formulation of the recommended road to sobriety.

Although this is a stand-alone question without prelude or follow up, scattered throughout Hank's personal responses there are small bits of information about his own understanding of God and the role He played in his sobriety. These include three

---

* This is an interesting choice of words since, at this time, the term 'revivalist' most commonly brought to mind Billy Sunday, the popular early twentieth-century preacher who gained national prominence with his month-long revival campaigns in cities all over the country and later through his radio broadcasts. Sunday was a 'hell fire and brimstone' sermonizer who called for the conversion of his listeners and their surrender to Jesus Christ. (See Wikipedia, Bill Sunday, Named Article—retrieved August 22, 2015).

significant mentions of God which, taken together, paint an interesting picture of Parkhurst's own experiences with the spiritual and the divine.

> I understand God as a great, indefinable, unexplainable Power which will help me if I keep in tune with it. *[64]*

> I believe some power outside of me has straightened my thinking in regard to the inevitable results of one drink. *[7]*

> To keep first things first . . . of course, that means for me to keep a proper relation with the Power that enabled me to recover. *[41]*

The first of these provides a much clearer description of Parkhurst's basic beliefs than the simple universal power Bill Wilson says he had come to believe in by this time.[6] Hank's response of "a great, indefinable, unexplainable Power" comes after the question, "What is your vision of, or what do you understand, by God?" Before answering that question, Parkhurst noted that his understanding of God "is unexplainable. When I begin to worry about that, I generally realize I am getting into a field where far greater minds than mine have argued and failed for years." While this sounds vaguely agnostic, Hanks' beliefs were much more substantive than that. He did not agree with those who saw this unresolvable controversy as an excuse to deny or be indecisive about the fact that at "a great, indefinable, unexplained Power" (note the capital "P") actually does exist.

Parkhurst was a believer, but the God he believed in was not the personal, providential God that Wilson referred to so consistently throughout the Big Book. This can be seen in Hank's careful choice of words when he talks of an impersonal "Power *which* will help me if I keep in tune with *it*" rather than the more personal and providential "Power *who* will help me if I keep in tune with *Him*" that Bill would have written here. Parkhurst's beliefs diverged radically from Wilson's petitionable Supreme Being. For Hank, God was a large and powerful but impersonal force, something that was forever incomprehensible, unknowable, and mysterious.

This begs the question of exactly what kind of relationship (if any) Hank Parkhurst believed was available to him with this God who had enabled him to recover by straightening out his thinking about the dangers of the first drink. Exactly how God went about performing this miracle of recovery is not mentioned anywhere, but Hank certainly does not credit it to the agency of a personal, providential God. Also worth noting is that the solution presented here is purely psychological rather than spiritual in nature, and strikingly similar to the "change of heart" and the "transformation of thought" Hank had mentioned in his chapter "To Employers" as being essential for the man who wants "to get over drinking."[7]

However this transformation actually did come about, Hank claims sobriety is something he will be able to maintain just so long as he keeps a proper relation with God, something he does by continuing to stay in tune with the Power that brought about his change of heart. Once again, this presents the familiar Parkhurst problem of trying to decide exactly what he means. What is the proper relationship and what does it mean to be in tune with God? More important, but unanswered, is what does one have to *do* to stay in tune and to maintain this proper relationship? Hank does credit the God of his own understanding with initially straightening out his thinking about the first drink—however that may have happened—but it would appear that the maintenance of this life-saving attitude falls squarely on his own shoulders from that point forward.

Some understanding of how this might possibly work for Parkhurst is provided by several questions he answered about his own religious practices in this proposed chapter.

Do you go to church? *[49]*
Not regularly, but more than before. Probably I will become a regular church goer, but just at the moment (I may be fooling myself, but) I believe I am doing some church work every day. What I am trying to express is that every man should work that problem out for himself.

Do you have any religious services? *[91]*
If you mean in the sense of organized religion, no. I believe our meetings are more or less the get-together of a fellowship.

Do you study the Bible? *[60]*
If you mean regularly, no. On the other hand, I have read the Bible a great deal more, and with more understanding the past three years, than all my life before. However, many of the fellowship are constant students of the Bible. A man's religious study, I believe, is entirely his own affair.

Is the Bible confusing to you? *[61]*
Yes, many times. Probably though because I am iconoclastic and do not study it enough.

How often do you pray? *[62]*
Many times a day.

What is your prayer? *[63]*
Thy Will Be Done . . . AND MEAN IT.

Somewhat confusing here is Parkhurst's self-identification as an iconoclast ("a person who attacks cherished beliefs . . . as being based on error or superstition"[8]) while simultaneously claiming he prays many times each day. Whatever Hank's antagonism may have been toward the Bible, it did not affect his ability to pray the simple prayer "Thy Will Be Done" with daily frequency. This implies that while his conception of God was not to be found in either the Old or the New Testament, it was a Power which was clearly in charge of the universe and whose "Will" could only be ignored or disrespected at one's peril. Such a God would require Hank to regularly turn his own will over to "Thy Will" and to accept things as they are with the faith that all will work out for the best in the end. This all sounds more Stoic or Daoist than Christian.

While these suggestions regarding Hank's spiritual beliefs *can* be supported from the textual evidence found in the Question and Answers Section, they must always be tempered by the understanding that Hank was never the clearest of writers, so misunderstandings and misinterpretations are always a real possibility.

Marital Infidelity Is Explored

As one more example of this kind of confused writing, consider the much more worldly and personal topic of marital infidelity that gets a brief, but revealing Hank Parkhurst answer.

> **I understand that most alcoholics get into sexual messes. Is that true?** *[33]*
> Yes.

> **What is your attitude about possible future sexual troubles?** *[34]*
> If you are speaking of unfaithfulness, I feel the same way about that as I do about liquor. I am taking no stand on this question. I can only say I hope I will not get mixed up in any such difficulties. On the other hand, I have seen married men nearly thrown into an alcoholic slip by a sexual mix-up and the soundest advice I have heard given was, "you are terribly upset because you have been trying to live in the perfection of Jesus Christ and now that you find you are not as perfect as He was, are you going to add more troubles, such as drinking will bring? Or are you going to pick yourself up and be better in the future? Not better as the world sees it, but better as your vision of yourself sees it?"

The "I am taking no stand on this question" is certainly a curious response to an inquiry about unfaithfulness, especially with the additional comment that "I feel the same way about that as I do about liquor." Hank's point seems to be that when it comes to alcohol, some people can drink safely and others cannot, and the difference can only be successfully identified by the man himself. In the same way it seems, adultery is troublesome for some men, but not for others and those who cannot tolerate being unfaithful must make that decision for themselves. According to his response, Parkhurst seems to be saying that adultery is not *always* a problem, just so long as the man who is being unfaithful can do so without unfortunate consequences.

It is uncertain exactly what practical advice, if any, is being offered here to the man who is currently cheating on his wife. Should he stop seeing the other woman completely? Instead, Hank's "soundest advice" is that he may just need to lower his expectations regarding his moral behavior and stop trying to be so perfectly Christ-like.* The final admonition to "be better" not "as the world sees it, but better as your vision of yourself sees it" only compounds the confusion. What could those two final sentences possibly mean in relation to being unfaithful to one's marriage vows? This

---

* This may well have been a not-so-subtle slap at the Oxford Group's insistence on "Absolute Purity."

entire response is pure Hank Parkhurst, sounding fairly coherent when read quickly and inattentively, but lacking in any kind of clarity once it has been read more slowly and carefully.

The A.A. Fellowship Gets Its Due

After slips, the general topic that receives the most attention is A.A. itself, with fifteen questions and answers devoted to it. These begin with a pair of queries on why Alcoholics Anonymous maintains such a singular focus.

If this works so well with alcoholics why would it not work with others who are in trouble? *[25]*
Undoubtedly it would. We see many of our families use the same approach to reach a happier way of existence.

If it could be successfully applied in other ways, why do you limit your work to alcoholics and those close to alcoholics? *[26]*
There are several reasons. Because of the things I have done, I am particularly able to interest alcoholics. Second, I am not a part, or trying to be a part of any religious movement. Third, one of the strongest things to me is the fellowship which has been built among men who have a common problem. Fourth, and most important to me, is the fact that working with alcoholics gives focus to my work and does not spread or diffuse it.

One page later, Hank returns to the topic of fellowship ("one of the strongest things to me"), stating the importance of their weekly meetings and providing details about how those meetings were run in late 1938.

How important in your mind is the fellowship? *[35]*
I think it is one of the most important elements. It allows newcomers to look us over, it allows the members of the fellowship to discuss their problems with others who have had similar problems. Many men get away from the weekly meetings, haven't time for one reason or another, and in most cases, I notice they have an eventual slip.

What are these weekly meetings? *[36]*
I am only familiar with them in three localities. At one of these, members who are interested decide who is to lead the meeting after the group gathers. He leads the group in the Lord's Prayer and then asks different ones to tell their stories. The meeting is closed with the Lord's Prayer. In the other two localities, the meeting is generally just a social get-together where the gang sits around and talks, sometimes in a large circle, sometimes in small groups. Occasionally this evolves into a meeting where some members tell their stories.

Why do you tell your story? *[37]*

I know my own story and when I am asked to tell it, it is generally because someone thinks it will be helpful to some of the newcomers. Actually all we have is the ability and willingness for each to tell their own story. The attitude is more or less, "Here is what I was . . . Here is what I did . . . Here is what happened . . . And here I am." By this telling of stories, newcomers may more or less identify themselves or things they have done with those things we did. As long as we stick to our own story, we are never in danger of preaching.

Parkhurst's first description of a meeting is obviously the Akron format. Whether he knew these details from personal experience (there is no record that Hank ever visited Dr. Bob in Ohio) or got his information from Bill is uncertain. The other two meetings mentioned are the New York version of the weekly gathering. Hank was claiming his own house in Montclair, NJ as the second site for East Coast gatherings since several meetings had been held there by this time. (Meetings were not held in Cleveland until after the book was published.) The contrast between these two formats—one rather formal and religious and the other much looser with no mention made of prayer—is just one more acknowledgement of the significant differences between A.A. in Ohio and New York at this time.

Defining an Alcoholic and His Likelihood of Success in A.A.

Then, in five questions (from two different pages), Hank attempts to formulate his own yardstick for who is and who isn't an alcoholic.

Do you ever tell a man he is an alcoholic? *[89]*

No. That is strictly a matter for him to decide. We tell him what we did and why we are sure we are alcoholics. He must decide for himself whether he is an alcoholic.

Do you identify different kinds of drinking? *[90]*

The casual drinker who takes an occasional drink. The social drinker who drinks when socially inclined. The heavy drinker who drinks a great deal. And the alcoholic.

What do you believe identifies an alcoholic? *[68]*

I believe an alcoholic, broadly speaking, is a man who cannot control his drinking. He cannot stop drinking when he knows that more will harm him. Nor can he stop drinking when he actually wants to.

Do you suggest this indiscriminately to men you believe to be alcoholics? *[66]*

No. Generally I talk to the man, and if he expresses interest, I tell him my story.

How do you present this to a man? *[67]*
First I tell him my story up to the time I discovered I was an alcoholic. By telling him my story, my drinking exploits, the tales of the shakes, how I hid bottles, etc. Then I generally steer the talk to the subject of alcoholism. If the man decides that he is an alcoholic, (that is a thing I cannot decide for him) I tell him how I got well and the cases of others who got well. I then put him in touch with other members of our fellowship. If the man wants it, he can get it.

In question 68, Parkhurst once again attempts to formulate a definition for the alcoholic, a challenge he and Bill had been wrestling with for well over a year. While Hank does qualify this description by claiming that he is speaking broadly, what he has written is a straightforward and practical description that would likely resonate with anyone who was in trouble with alcohol. Interestingly, this is not too far from one of Bill Wilson's attempts to do the same thing a bit earlier. In the opening paragraph of "We Agnostics," Bill had written: "If, when you honestly want to, you find you cannot quit entirely, or if, when drinking, you have little control over the amount you take, you are probably alcoholic."[9] Wilson, too, realized the inadequacy of this definition and qualified it with the word "probably." But whatever the words might be, the final decision—as Hank definitely notes—always rests with the drinking man himself. Only he can fruitfully decide whether he is or isn't an alcoholic.

Hank also included some questions about the likelihood of success in A.A..

What do you think of a newcomer's chance of recovery through this method? *[65]*
I believe that to be unpredictable although I have yet to see a failure where a man sincerely wanted to get well and where he would follow strictly the experience of the rest of the men who have recovered.

You speak at length of slips, it would appear that slips are common. Is that so? *[19]*
I would estimate that fifty percent who have accepted our method, have had no slips, and that everyone who has been sincere in their desire to recover has been so much better there is no comparison, even though they have slipped.

The answer to the first question here is a nicely phrased variation on what Bill Wilson would later write as the opening sentence in Chapter Five, "How It Works:" "Rarely have we seen a person fail who has thoroughly followed our directions."[10]* There was obviously a deeply held belief within the Fellowship that "if you just do what we have done, you will be successful in your sobriety." In the final accounting, it was a completely pragmatic program arguing that it "has worked for us and there is no reason it shouldn't work for you too, if only you give it an honest try."

---

* The word "directions" was later changed to "path" in the first edition of *Alcoholics Anonymous*.

Finally, there are three minor catch-all questions on A.A..

Do you or your friends in Alcoholics Anonymous hate liquor? *[75]*
Personally I serve liquor in my home to people who can control the use. Some of the group however have a hatred for what liquor has done to them.

Don't you think and talk of alcoholism too much? *[76]*
Maybe you're right. Anyway you are talking like a lot of our wives.

On the other hand, I have recovered and the thing is should I talk about it a great deal, or should I not talk about it at all, and do a lot of drinking?

Is there anything to join? *[88]*
Of course not. There is no membership list, or anything to sign.

Most interesting here is that Hank kept liquor in his house and served it to guests. This is one of those ongoing controversies in Alcoholics Anonymous, so it is worth noting that this pioneer member had decided the presence of booze in his house was not a problem. In fact, he was simply following the guidance given in Bill Wilson's early draft for "Working With Others:" "Many of us keep liquor in our homes . . . Some of us still serve it to our friends, in moderation, provided they are not people who abuse drinking."[11] However, some of today's A.A. members might point out that Hank Parkhurst was drunk a year after writing this and then wonder if the ready presence of alcohol in his house might have been one of the factors which allowed him to so easily pick up the first drink. It *is* a fascinating question.

Doctors and Psychiatrists, the Foundation, and a Curious Ending

Another important topic, Hank's opinion regarding doctors and psychiatrists, is addressed with four direct questions. In the first, Hank claims that "doctors and medical treatment for the alcoholic . . . most definitely have their place in any program of recovery," *[45]* but he does not mention or recommend any particular form of treatment. When it comes to psychoanalysis and psychiatric treatments, Parkhurst claims "anything which enables a person to better understand themselves and their thought processes, is well worth while" and notes approvingly that "after analysis I understood myself better and could identify more of my thoughts." But, he then negatively qualifies the overall value of this by saying analysis "still left me with nothing to tie to but myself. And I had always failed myself before." *[38]* The presumption from that answer would have to be that working with other alcoholics and becoming a part of the Fellowship (or, perhaps, that "unexplainable Power") had provided Hank with the "tie" he needed to keep his thinking straight about the dangers of the first drink.

Finally, speaking for once as a spokesman of the program, Hank offers eight questions *[80-87]* about A.A.'s lack of formal organization and in his responses, provides details about the workings of the Alcoholic Foundation. These questions and answers carefully repeat information that has frequently been given elsewhere: about the need for money to carry on the work, the fact that contributions come "from people who have benefited," and how the non-alcoholic trustees are in the majority and thus control of the finances, etc. It is the perfect set of answers to Hank's June question of "where does the money come from for this work?"[12]—effectively dispelling any suspicions the new man might have about this being just another money-making racket.

The proposed chapter then sputters to an inconclusive and even embarrassing end with two final non-sequitur questions, the last of which is almost incomprehensible (although it is thankfully, for Parkhurst's sake, credited to another member):

> **What do you mean by the beer experiment?** *[93]*
> Many times a fellow gets the idea if he had always stayed on beer, he would not have had his trouble. Or he has the idea that beer will not harm him. They generally try to drink nothing but beer and end up on liquor. Or they get as bad on beer as on anything else. Having learned their lesson, they generally say they tried the beer experiment.

> **To what do you attribute your not drinking now?** (Another member answers) *[94]*
> When leaving institutions I had no one to talk to about my problems. I was afraid to phone people for fear they would recall something I had done. I feel, however, that I have made up for it by doing time in the laughing academy. Because of my fear, I would phone someone I had met in the institution. Loneliness, I guess you would call it, and the other bird from the cuckoo hatch would feel the same way. Since meeting this crowd, there has been no barrier of what I have done because they understood and generally can match my experience with something as bad or worse.

Two New York Members Respond

Hank actually circulated this document among the New York members in what could only be seen as an effort to drum up support for his proposed chapter. In response, we know he received at least two reactions: one of which was decidedly positive and the other negative.

Horace Maher

Horace, who had sobered up the previous September,[13*] took the chapter seriously enough to send Hank and Bill his hand-written suggestions for additions and changes, saying that, in his judgment, he thought the proposed chapter was "a fine idea."[14] Horace's enthusiasm is almost predictable if we look at the story he wrote for the Big

---

* Horace's story, "On His Way," appeared in the first edition of *Alcoholics Anonymous*, pp. 375-377.

Book in which he sounds very much like one of Hank Parkhurst's A.A. protégés. Maher concludes his short, three-page story in *Alcoholics Anonymous* with this paragraph:

> The simple words "Thy Will Be Done" and the simple ideas of honesty and of helping others are taking on a new meaning for me. I should not be surprised to find myself coming to the astounding conclusion that God, whoever or whatever He may be, is eminently more capable of running this universe than I am. At last I believe I am on my way.[15]*

The "I should not be surprised to find myself" is Horace's way of saying he had not yet fully accepted the astounding conclusion that God was capable of running the universe without his help. That, combined with his emphasis on the simple—both in the words of the prayer "Thy Will Be Done" and in the "ideas of honesty and of helping others"—outlines a program which sounds very like what Hank had been advocating throughout his Q&A chapter. In many ways, it is a paragraph that Parkhurst might well have written about himself.

As already noted, Horace opens his comments by stating "the Q & Answer section is a fine idea." Given the number of criticisms cited above, the fact that Horace thinks the proposed chapter, as written, would make such a fine addition to the book comes as something of a shock. Maher seems to have completely missed all of the wandering confusion and the bad writing—not to mention some of the questionable advice on how to get and stay sober. Confirming his high opinion, Horace suggests that only eleven of the ninety-four questions need minor adjustments (and one more question needs to be added) to make the chapter ready for publication. Whatever Maher's critical abilities may have been, he was obviously sympathetic to Parkhurst when it came to the format, style, content, and logic of this proposed chapter.**

Because of the informal way in which Horace wrote up his suggestions,*** it is not always easy to associate each of them with a specific question in the Q&A chapter, but it is possible to identify the proper correspondence for most of them. Those that can be correlated present a few interesting observations on A.A. from the perspective of a recent member.

One of Horace's challenges suggests that Hank's answer to question *[19]*—where he asserts "I would estimate that fifty percent who have accepted our method have had no slips"—is a gross underestimation. Specifically, Maher states he think "50% <u>who have accepted</u> method is much too low." Unfortunately, Horace doesn't go so far as to suggest what number he thinks might be more appropriate in response to that ever-important question.

---

*   Horace's story did not appear in the Multilith printing so he would have written it sometime between mid-February and late March 1939.

**   It is worth noting that Horace Maher's written suggestions for additions and changes to Hank's proposed chapter are the *only* written example we have from the archival records of a member critiquing materials proposed for the Big Book. As such, it might be seen as one concrete example of the kind of responses Bill Wilson might have received from the membership when he asked for suggested changes to his own chapters.

***   Horace was working with a typed nine-page version of the chapter rather than the fifteen-page retyping that is preserved in the GSO archives. He had numbered these pages himself and when making his comments included the page and question number on that page to show what he was suggesting should be changed. Most of these can be matched by internal evidence, but a few of them are so indeterminate ("P-6-Q-2—Would suggest elimination of second sentence in Answer") that they cannot be conclusively identified.

Regarding questions *[38]* and *[39]*, Maher thinks the "point should be more emphasized that psycho-analysis and psychiatrical results rest with the person—we go beyond that." Again, what a greater emphasis on the ways that "we go beyond that" might actually work and look like in print gets no further elaboration in Horace's suggestion.

To the question "Outside of the Bible what book has been most helpful to you?" *[48]*, Hank had cryptically and incompletely responded by identifying only the author, "Thomas Mason's . . . ," leaving us with an incomprehensible answer which provides just enough information to mystify, but not enough to be helpful.* Horace suggests that A.A.'s own forthcoming book, "'Exit' (?) by Alcoholics Anonymous," might be the best answer for Hank to give here. (The parenthetical question mark he put after the title highlights the fact that it was still undecided exactly what the book would be called.)

The one suggestion that would have been most enlightening had Parkhurst acted on it was Maher's request that he respond more fully to the question "What are these weekly meetings?" *[36]*. Horace thought Hank's answer should "be elaborated a little." Indeed, any additional information Parkhurst might have supplied on how the New York meetings worked in late 1938 would have added immensely to the scant descriptions we currently find in the contemporary records, providing important insights into the workings of early A.A.

Horace's last suggested change was to supply his own response to the incomprehensible answer that closed the chapter. Maher suggested his own reply to "To what do you attribute your not drinking now?" would be:

> I attribute it to the <u>lifting</u> from my shoulders of the constant weight of the alcoholic problem from which I had not <u>been free</u> day and night for almost twenty years. To the knowledge that of myself I could never do this and to the firm belief that as long as I continue to the best of my ability, the thought process and the way of life that has been shown me, I shall have that help from God.

Once again, it seems that Horace is almost channeling Hank here. Actually, his "as long as I continue to the best of my ability" line is a clearer explanation of what Parkhurst was trying to say when writing about staying in tune with God and having a proper relationship with that Power. According to Horace, you simply continue to do the footwork called for by this "way of life" while maintaining the essential new "thought process" regarding the first drink and your sobriety will be assured.

Finally, Maher suggested one question to be added to the chapter:

> **Q—To what words can all your answers be boiled down when you are questioned by doubting or antagonistic people?**
> Ans—To these—"So what—it works."

---

* A diligent search of the Internet by the author produced no likely candidate for a book by a Thomas Mason that Hank might have turned to for help. But, on reading an early version of this manuscript, the eminent A.A. historian, Glenn Chesnut, suggested that perhaps this was a book called *The Methodist Magazine*, which was written by Thomas Mason and published in 1818 (https://www.forgottenbooks.com/en/books/TheMethodistMagazine_10792660 - retrieved May 7, 2018).

This is a repetition of Hank's response to the question about "revivalism" *[43]*, but here it is presented as a universal answer, one that should be used to silence all doubters. "So what—it works," was likely a common slogan in Alcoholics Anonymous at this time. It was based on the belief that the best way to avoid complicated and never-ending discussions with dissenters and unbelievers would be to rely on the pragmatic argument that truth can best be discovered in the results—and we most certainly have the results that you want. So, try it!

Bill Wilson

Wilson's response to Hank Parkhurst's suggested chapter was completely different from Horace Maher's, something we know conclusively from the fact that neither the proposed "Question and Answer Section," nor anything remotely like it, ever appeared in either the Multilith Copy or in the book itself. Over and above the disorganization and the confused writing, there can be little wonder why Bill reacted that way.

For one thing, the Q&A chapter presents just one man's account of sobriety, something that directly contradicts Wilson's consistent presentation of the book as the collective viewpoint of the Fellowship. While Bill did primarily write from his own experiences, he regularly packaged them to sound as if they reflected the consensus of the whole group. Hank's proposed chapter flagrantly violated this inclusive principle, shifting the voice of authority from a group consciousness to that of just one man.

Even more important from Bill's perspective and his stated purpose of the book, the chapter completely failed to address the question of "precisely how we have recovered," (a phrase that was printed entirely in capital letters in the "Foreword" to the first edition[16]) and focused instead on the problems and complications which typically arise once a man gets sober. Wilson just didn't think the book was the place to discuss how to handle the delicate social situation of explaining why you weren't having a cocktail tonight; he was completely focused on telling a man what he had to do to stop drinking and then stay stopped.

Even if it had been well organized and well written (which it most certainly was not), the proposed Q&A chapter just didn't fit anywhere into the Big Book. Its radically different voice and style—not to mention the often peculiar subject matter—was just too far afield from everything else Bill had already written for it to ever be seriously considered for inclusion.

It would be fascinating to know the conversations these two men had regarding this proposed chapter—how Bill went about telling Hank it was not going to be included in the book and how Hank reacted to that news. But Wilson had a much larger issue facing him in late November 1938. He was beginning to realize he needed to write something significantly more explicit about their program of recovery and, in all likelihood, reading Hank's suggested chapter for the book gave him a clear idea of the direction he did *not* want to go with his explanation of how the program of recovery actually worked.

Sometimes, negative cues are the best way to see the direction that we really *do* want to pursue.

CHAPTER TWENTY-TWO

"A Vision for You"

~November 1938~

November had been a busy month for Bill Wilson. Besides dealing with Hank's two writing projects—and whatever fallout, personal or otherwise, that may have accompanied those efforts—he continued to polish the seven chapters already written and started work on "A Vision For You," the chapter which would appear at the end of the first half of the book.

In addition to all the distraction caused by this ongoing editing and writing, a truly disappointing event—one that would have a significant impact on Wilson personally and on his subsequent writing of the Twelve Steps—occurred in the first week of November. Ebby Thacher was back in town and he wasn't doing well. Ebby had spent a successful and sober summer on Fitz Mayo's farm in Maryland "looking after Fitz's kids."[1] While there, most of his time and attention had been focused on the Mayo's youngest daughter who was seven years old and stricken with diabetes. Thacher reported his primary job that summer was to take her swimming and watch over her and he concluded with some satisfaction that he "had a lovely summer" with the Mayos.[2]

Ebby Thacher's Struggle to Stay Sober

Fitz and Ebby arrived back in Brooklyn on Tuesday, November 1st and attended the regular meeting there that night.[3] But, just a few days later, Ebby Thacher was dead drunk again, or as he candidly admitted in his later reminiscence, "I, of course, reached for the bottle again and was soon in trouble."[4] Trouble indeed. Not only did Ebby get rip-roaring drunk, he also took two other residents of the Wilson's 'sober house,' Brooke Blackford and George Heyman, along with him on this drinking spree.[5] Bill was furious, and when he found Ebby and Brooke both drunk again the next day, he threw them out of the house before they could embarrass themselves or anyone else at the meeting that night.[6]

Back on the street and with nowhere to go, Thacher was told about "a place in New Jersey called the Keswick Colony of Mercy for drunkards'" and he went there shortly after Armistice Day (November 11). Ebby spent the winter with that group, immersing himself in their very Christian approach to sobriety, which of course was nothing new to him given his earlier involvement with the Oxford Group.[7]

But religion wasn't working for Ebby Thacher anymore; he just couldn't stay sober. Even when Jack, his politically influential older brother, got him one of the choice jobs available at the New York World's Fair held during the summers of 1939 and 1940.[8][**]

> I did not sober up. I managed to drink and hold [that job] sufficiently well, and with so many people there, and crowds, I wasn't noticed much. I got away with it all summer until the fair closed in the fall, and I started up with some old cronies in Brooklyn, drinking it up pretty hard. Then in the spring [of 1940], I went to see my boss . . . and convinced her that I was again on the straight and narrow and would she give me back my job? I held that and fell off again that summer and in the fall. I again went to this place in New Jersey and spent the winter there.[9]

Throughout at least parts of this period Lois reports that Ebby was sober and even attending meetings,[10] but if his own report is accurate, he could only have created that impression by showing up on Lois's doorstep on one of his "'good" days. By his own account, he was nowhere close to sober for any length of time from early November 1938 until he secured a government job in Philadelphia as an associate inspector of naval materials shortly after the attack on Pearl Harbor in December 1941 (a job that allowed him to keep his distance from alcohol for most of the following year).[11]

Bill Wilson could never quite figure out what was missing from Ebby's program and it was a question that genuinely troubled and perplexed him. Years later he noted that Thacher was "sicker than I realized" and speculated that what "caused his backsliding later on" was most likely the fact that he "took little interest in other alcoholics."[12] According to Bill, Ebby just never adopted the "when all other measures fail, work with another alcoholic" model of recovery or acted on the group's belief that "nothing will so much insure immunity from drinking as intensive work with other alcoholics. It works when other activities fail."[13] Ebby Thacher clearly preferred the "lone wolf" model, even if it meant that he continued to drink.

Lois basically agreed with Bill's assessment, but her opinions on the subject of Ebby's constant relapses went even further.

> After those first two years in the Oxford Group, why did Ebby get drunk?
> It was he who gave Bill the philosophy that kept him sober. Why didn't it

---

[*]   Amazingly, this group is still around today. See their website (http://www.americaskeswick.org/support/help-now/colony-of-mercy) for more information.

[**]   Both of those years, the New York World Fair opened at the end of April and closed at the end of October (Wikipedia, Named Article, retrieved September 23, 2015).

keep Ebby sober? He was sincere, I'm sure. Perhaps it was the difference in the degree of wanting sobriety. Bill wanted it with his whole soul. Ebby may have wanted it simply to keep out of trouble. Or maybe he *couldn't* want it with his whole soul, because he was too ill. Beyond that crucial visit with Bill, Ebby seemed to do very little about helping others. He never appeared really a member of AA. After his first slip many harmful thoughts seemed to take possession of him and he appeared jealous of Bill and critical, even when sober, of both the Oxford Group and AA.[14]

Whatever the cause, Ebby's ongoing inability to stop drinking and stay sober would haunt Bill throughout the month of November and play a significant role in his thinking as he moved closer to the day he would finally write down the Twelve Steps in early December.

Towns Seeks Henry Ford's Endorsement

Wilson had been sending each new chapter of the book (and perhaps even some of the more significantly altered rewrites) to Charles Towns as visible proof that his monthly support check was being put to good use. Charles was "greatly pleased" with everything he read and consistently encouraged Bill to continue writing, enthusiastically urging him to finish the project as quickly as possible. At this time, no non-alcoholic was a bigger cheerleader or more supportive of the plan to complete this book and bring it to press than Charles B. Towns.[15]

But as the manuscript grew, Bill began to worry more and more about the "problem of securing the right person . . . to authenticate [the] book." Wilson thought it was of paramount importance that someone famous—someone with instant name recognition—be persuaded to write a Preface or Foreword to their book, one that would vouch for their work and lend credibility to the chapters that followed. This, he said, was so critical that until they secured "such an endorsement . . . obviously, publication of the book [would] have to wait."[16]

Besides the clear value of such a name endorsing their solution for alcoholism, Bill had two other reasons for his refusal to publish until he could include such a prominent public testimonial. First, he was convinced that a glowing endorsement by a really famous man would generate enormous publicity and thus guarantee them a large initial sale of the book. In addition, with such a high-profile endorsement in place, Wilson was confident they could easily raise the $2,500 needed to print the book along with whatever funds would be required immediately after publication to maintain their operation until the book royalties began to cover expenses.[17]

Bill's dream candidate for this prominent person to write such a Preface had long been and continued to be the celebrated carmaker, Henry Ford. A more famous name—with a legendary hatred for alcohol and an established commitment to temperance—could hardly be imagined. Bill discussed the problem with Charles Towns and enlisted his support in his attempts to make contact with Ford. Trading on their past relationship—however brief and tenuous it may have been in 1914 or 1915—Charles wrote a letter of introduction for Bill on his personal letterhead addressed to Henry Ford:

> November 16, 1938:
>
> Mr. Henry Ford,
> Detroit, Mich.
>
> Dear Mr. Ford:
>
> This will introduce to you Mr. William G. Wilson.
>
> Mr. Wilson has had remarkable success during the last four years in the rehabilitation of the alcoholic drinker. His work has a semi-religious background, and he has summed it up in a manuscript which is now ready for the press, except for the Foreword. In considering the matter of someone who would give this publication the prestige it should have, I could find no one I thought would be so eligible to do this, as yourself.
>
> You doubtless can recall the conditions under which we met some years ago, before the opening of the Ford Hospital.* In view of my special work and your interest in trying to reclaim the alcoholic unfortunate, I was invited to Detroit as your guest, and as a result, two physicians associated with your Sociological Department, brought to my hospital in New York a dozen patients addicted to drugs and alcohol, and the results were satisfactory to all concerned.
>
> I would appreciate any consideration you may give this request.
>
> Very sincerely yours,
>
> Charles B. Towns
>
> CBT:[18]

Towns' mention of the fact that the manuscript as "now ready for the press, except for the Foreword" is a bit problematic since this was certainly not true on November 16, 1938. However, Charles's claim can be understood in three possible ways. First of all, saying the book was ready for the press would make the need for a foreword just that much more pressing and thereby, hopefully, elicit a swifter response from Ford. Claiming 'we are only waiting on you before we can bring this great news of recovery to suffering alcoholics everywhere' sounds very much like a ploy to catch Henry Ford's attention and to get his consent as quickly as possible. Second, by this date Charles Towns may have already seen a draft of "A Vision For You," which Bill would have informed him was to be the last chapter in the front half of the book. From that perspective, and unaware that Wilson still had two very critical chapters to

---

* Ford Hospital began operations on October 1, 1915. (Henry Ford Hospital, Wikipedia, Named Article—retrieved October 10, 2015).

write (something Bill Wilson was most likely not aware of himself in mid-November), Towns' misconception that the book was complete would be perfectly understandable. Finally, it is possible—although least likely—that Charles wrote this letter with the understanding that Bill would not use it until the book had actually reached that point of completion.

Like the letter Leonard Strong had written to introduce Bill to Willard Richardson more than a year earlier, Towns' letter was meant to be first mailed and then handed over as a formal introduction during the first meeting with the addressee. Unfortunately, the actual use of such a letter was predicated on getting an appointment with the great man, and this was something neither Towns nor Wilson ever managed to do. Seven weeks later, in his January 4 letter to Frank Amos, Bill was still looking for someone to facilitate this all-important connection with Henry Ford and he earnestly noted that "the discussion of . . . the manner of approach" to people such as Ford and other prominent men "should, perhaps, be one of the main considerations of the next Foundation meeting."[19] If the Rockefeller people couldn't open that particular door for them, then who could?

However there is no record that Bill Wilson ever met with Henry Ford and therefore he never had the opportunity to present Charles Towns's letter or to get a polite face-to-face refusal of his request. Whatever attempts Bill made to reach the legendary automaker were successfully blocked by one of the many functionaries who typically surround and buffer the super-rich from ever having to deal with such solicitations directly.*

A Vision for How to Get and Stay Sober

Wilson knew that sooner or later he would have to face the challenge of creating a chapter that outlined in the clearest possible terms the actions needed to get and then stay sober. It was, he later commented, a problem that "had secretly worried the life out of" him for months before he finally got around to writing it.[20] But, so long as there was even one other chapter still to be written, Bill would elect to work on that rather than face the intimidating task of trying to put down on paper the exact details of their program of recovery.

Once again he may have been guided by Hank's mid-June outline enumerating the elements that should be found in their book, and perhaps even referred back to the handwritten "Ideas" Parkhurst had offered him shortly before creating his outline. But whether Bill formally did this or not, it is certain that Hank was still constantly arguing with him on a number of fronts, hoping to win approval for his own perspective on a wide variety of issues. In his "Ideas," Hank had suggested they include—even begin with—a history of the work in order to "establish proof of success of the work and carry hope to everyone" who read it.[21] Although Bill had not opened the book that way,

---

* Lois actually does mention a meeting between Bill and Henry Ford (*Lois Remembers*, p. 121), but she gives no date for this encounter. If such a meeting did occur, it happened much later in the story and certainly not before the book was published. See also the March 11, 1926 entry in her *Diary of Two Motorcycle Hobos* for a recounting of the time Bill Wilson did *not* want to meet Ford.

he was now about to close it with just such an account. In a similar vein, Hank's outline had proposed they include a chapter that "will disclose our life as a group, our work as a group, our present situations . . ." *[Hank's Chapter #24]*[22] and these points would also be fully addressed in this new chapter.

Bill incorporated both of Hank's suggestions into "A Vision For You" by presenting a detailed history of their beginnings as a group and then strongly suggesting that this should serve as the model for any reader trying to build his own community of local sober men. The chapter was nothing less than an earnest presentation of the extremely high hopes both Wilson and Parkhurst had for the book and their confidence that it would not only carry the message of recovery to isolated individuals, but also provide a concrete and practical plan that would spark the formation of Alcoholics Anonymous groups all across the country.

The Alcoholic's Isolation

Bill opens this final chapter by clearly stating one of the alcoholic's most distressing problems, the terrible isolation endured by both active and recovered alcoholics, offering a particularly graphic description of that painfully secluded state. Wilson paints this depressing picture in just four paragraphs* using some of the most ostentatious and elaborate writing found in the Big Book. Bill was certainly known to produce his fair share of purple prose over the years, but the writing here is so ornate and extravagant that it is enough to make one wonder if he didn't start this chapter by modifying and correcting a document originally written by Hank Parkhurst and that some of Hank's verbal excesses had simply slipped through the cracks during the editing process. The following quote (from the second paragraph of the chapter) more than adequately demonstrates these flowery excesses:

> As we became subjects of King Alcohol, shivering denizens of his mad realm, the chilling vapor that is loneliness settled down. It thickened, ever becoming blacker. Some of us sought out sordid places, hoping to find understanding companionship and approval. Momentarily we did— then would come oblivion and the awful awakening to face the hideous Four Horsemen—Terror, Bewilderment, Frustration, Despair. Unhappy drinkers who read this page will understand![23]

This florid account of the drinker's isolation is followed by an almost equally grim prediction of the loneliness the ex-alcoholic will face once he quits drinking. Although sober, he will now "be unable to imagine life either with alcohol or without it. Then he will know loneliness such as few do. He will be at the jumping-off place. He will wish for the end." In despair, such a man will desperately ask: "Am I to be consigned to a life where I shall be stupid, boring and glum, like some righteous people I see? I know I must get along without liquor, but how can I? Have you a sufficient substitute?"

---

* This refers to the first four paragraphs found in the Multilith edition and also in the 1st, 2nd and 3rd editions of *Alcoholics Anonymous*. For some unknown reason, the 4th edition printing of this chapter splits the first paragraph in two (after the end of the first sentence) so that, in that edition of the text, these comments would apply to the first five paragraphs.

The Fellowship as the Solution

Having so luridly illustrated the problem, Wilson is only slight less effusive in his presentation of the wonderful solution he claims to be so close at hand.

> Yes, there is a substitute, and it is vastly more than that. It is a Fellowship in Alcoholics Anonymous. There you will find release from care, boredom, and worry. Your imagination will be fired. Life will mean something at last. The most satisfactory years of your existence lie ahead. Thus we find The Fellowship, and so will you.

In a nutshell, this is the promised "Vision" that Bill is offering the new man—a meaningful life lived within a growing community of sober men, free from boredom, care, and worry; a life that will prove to be not just exciting, but truly richer and more satisfying than anything the reformed drunk has ever experienced before.

But however tempting all of these benefits might sound to the newly sober man, he would understandably still be confused about how such wonderful things could actually happen to him, not to mention being intimidated by the many challenges that such a radical change in his life would present. His expected responses are likely to be: "How is that to come about?" and "Where am I to find these people?" To this, Wilson confidently replies:

> You are going to meet these new friends in your own community. Near you alcoholics are dying helplessly like people in a sinking ship . . . Among them you will make lifelong friends. You will be bound to them with new and wonderful ties, for you will escape disaster together and you will commence shoulder to shoulder your common journey . . .

> . . . The practical answer is that since these things have happened among us, they can happen again. Should you wish them above all else, and should you be willing to make use of our experience, we are sure they will come.

Referring the reader back to the explicit directions provided in "Working With Others" on how to approach and aid others, Bill notes that implementing these suggestions will surely result in several local families adopting the A.A. solution. Once that happens, the leader of this growing sober community would want to know more of how to proceed from that point and Wilson proposes that the best way to answer that question would "be to describe the growth of the Fellowship among us." Rather than delivering a list of step-by-step directions on what to do next, Bill tells a long and detailed story (thirty-four of the fifty-six paragraphs in this chapter) about how the Fellowship was first established and then grew in Akron, Ohio.

The Fellowship's Beginnings and Success in Akron

Typical of many A.A. stories, Bill devotes three-quarters of his narrative to the backstory of how A.A. first began in Ohio (this being the "Working With Others" part of the account) before he gets to the stated purpose of this long section, the information the new man will want to know about how to proceed once others in his own area have achieved sobriety.

Bill opens by telling of his business trip to Akron in late April of 1935 and how the failure of that venture brought him dangerously close to a drink. Faced with the "the old, insidious insanity—that first drink," he realized his only hope for staying sober was to reach out to another alcoholic. This provides the background for his initial meeting with Dr. Bob Smith, followed by the ups-and-downs of Smith's first attempts to stay sober. Once they had successfully negotiated those problems, the two men realized "they must keep spiritually active" if there was to be any hope for them to remain drink-free, so they set off to find a "first class alcoholic prospect" to work with. This led to their encounter with Bill Dotson ("the man in the bed") at a local hospital and his acceptance of their program of recovery (which is detailed in a long section that includes a fair amount of dialogue among the three men). The first phase of this foundational story then concludes with Wilson noting that after several failures to find others, a fourth man turned up who also agreed to follow their suggestions and successfully stopped drinking.

Bill had now reached the point in the story where, after spending three months in Akron, he finally returns to New York City, leaving three men behind in Ohio who had to cope with the problem of how to preserve both their individual and collective sobriety. He wrote that these men

> had found something brand new in life. Though they knew they must help other alcoholics if they would remain sober, that motive became secondary. It was transcended by the happiness they found in giving themselves for others. They shared their homes, their slender resources, and gladly devoted their spare hours to fellow-sufferers. They were willing, by day or night, to place a new man in the hospital and visit him afterward. They grew in numbers.

The next six paragraphs continues the Akron saga by describing the fact that over the next year and a half, seven more men were successfully recruited and this small group maintained their sobriety by structuring their days in such a way that they saw

> much of each other [and] scarce an evening passed that someone's home did not shelter a little gathering of men and women, happy in their release, and constantly thinking how they might present their discovery to some newcomer. In addition to these casual get-togethers, it became customary to set aside one night a week for a meeting to be attended by anyone or everyone interested in a spiritual way of life. Aside from fellowship and sociability, the prime object was to provide a time and place where new people might bring their problems.

Bill then goes to some lengths describing "the stimulating and electric atmosphere of the place" where they meet each week and the loving and understanding companionship that permeates these gatherings. There, the newly sober man is reconnected with the men who visited him in the hospital and "in an upper room of this house, [having heard] the story of some man whose experience closely tallied with his own . . . he capitulated entirely." There, he realizes he has found a "haven at last," one where he discovers a "very practical approach to his problems, the absence of intolerance of any kind, [along with] the informality, the genuine democracy, [and] the uncanny understanding" that uniformly characterizes this new program of recovery. Over the past three years, Bill proudly states, this group has grown significantly and now boasts "sixty or eighty" members who attended the weekly meetings.

Concluding this long Ohio saga, Wilson lyrically expands his vision for the newly sober man, describing the many benefits that await him if only he works to replicate this "gay" Akron scene in his own home town.

> But life among Alcoholics Anonymous is more than attending meetings and visiting hospitals. Cleaning up old scrapes, helping to settle family differences, explaining the disinherited son to his irate parents, lending money and securing jobs for each other, when justified—these are everyday occurrences. No one is too discredited, nor has sunk too low to be welcomed cordially—if he means business. Social distinctions, petty rivalries and jealousies—these are laughed out of countenance. Being wrecked in the same vessel, being restored and united under one God, with hearts and minds attuned to the welfare of others, the things which matter so much to some people no longer signify much to them. How could they?

A Model for How A.A. Can Work

This detailed presentation of the founding of A.A. in Ohio—comprising almost sixty percent of the chapter—serves a number of purposes simultaneously. For one thing, Bill has finally satisfied Hank's ongoing insistence that the book include "a History of the work," although he had done so in a way that fit within his own understanding of the proper layout for the book. In addition, the Akron story was a perfect way for Wilson to offer the new man a model for how groups could be organized and share their collective sobriety once they have begun to grow beyond just a few men. But perhaps most of all, this long section explicitly recognizes Dr. Bob Smith's tremendous success in Ohio—giving generous credit where credit was due—and thereby, hopefully, calming some of the negative reactions that were still coming out of Akron whenever the book project was mentioned.

Almost bending over backwards, Bill diligently strives to present a frank and honest account of the way the Akron program of recovery (so different from that in New York) actually worked. Although he is careful to never mention the Oxford Group by name—a fact that might have annoyed some Ohio members since "the Akron people, still [thought] they were Oxford Groupers"[24]—Wilson does give credit to certain unnamed "outsiders [who] became interested" in their Fellowship and notes that one couple even went so far as to offer their home to the group for their weekly

Wednesday night meeting.* Bill also clearly emphasizes the fact that this gathering was open to anyone interested in a spiritual way of life, underlining the fact that recovering alcoholics were not the only people who attended these weekly meetings. In addition, several Oxford Group practices, such as the description of the new man's surrender "in an upper room of this house" and the explicit admission that these members were all "united under one God," were also freely acknowledged.

While the claim that the Akron group was united under one God was certainly true at this time (the Ohio program of recovery was still explicitly and exclusively Christian), it would not have been possible to say the same thing of the more pluralistic approach then being taken in New York. As noted earlier, several members of that group (most especially Jim Burwell and Hank Parkhurst) were actively advocating and practicing a much more flexible approach to divinity than would ever be tolerated in Akron.**

Despite these differences, by candidly and explicitly presenting all of these Akron elements in his retelling of the group's founding, Bill Wilson had effectively moved the Ohio model to center stage and held it up as the template for ongoing collective success in Alcoholics Anonymous. He had, for all intent and purposes, given the Akron people their own chapter in the book.

A Universal Solution

After these thirty-four substantial paragraphs devoted to Ohio, Wilson casually downplays the subsequent events in New York, devoting just two paragraphs to the fact that "under only slightly different conditions, the same thing is taking place in several eastern cities." Even here, Bill devotes most of these two paragraphs to the work being done by an understanding and helpful doctor in a "well-known hospital for the treatment of alcoholic and drug addiction," before adding that "in this eastern city there are informal meetings such as we have described to you, where you may see thirty or forty" people in attendance. So much for any elaboration on the different brand of A.A. then being practiced in New York City.

Having told the reader how the Fellowship was established, grew, and spread in these two areas, Wilson returns to his promotion of the expansive vision promised by the chapter's title. "Some day," he says, "we hope that every alcoholic who journeys will find a Fellowship of Alcoholics Anonymous at his destination," and he notes that currently several sober members, who are salesmen, were going about introducing the A.A. message into other communities. But, even without this kind of direct support, he

---

* Those two Oxford Group members were T. Henry and Clarace Williams whose home at 676 Palisades Drive in Akron served as the site of Akron's Wednesday night meetings from sometime in mid- to late-1935 until December of 1939. It has been alleged that this weekly Oxford Group meeting—which included members of the "Alcoholic Squad" during the time period noted above—began in April of 1935 (just prior to Bill Wilson's arrival in Akron and for the expressed purpose of allowing Dr. Bob Smith the opportunity to admit his drinking problem in relative privacy) and continued at that same address until sometime in 1954. (See, for instance, http://www.barefootsworld.net/aathe_chain.html and http://silkworth.net/aahistory_names/namesw.html - retrieved October 17, 2015.)

** Although this "united under one God" statement may sound dogmatic and prohibitively exclusive to many of today's A.A. members (a large portion of whom have adopted a much more liberal, non-providential approach to the concept of God), the line does still appear in the text of the Big Book; see p. 161 of the most recent edition.

advises, "though you be but one man with this book in hand . . . we believe and hope it contains all you will need to begin."

He goes on to encourage the reader to not be discouraged, to not let himself be overwhelmed.

> We know what you are thinking. You are saying to yourself: "I'm jittery and alone. I couldn't do that." But you can. You forget that you have just now tapped a source of power so much greater than yourself. To duplicate, with such backing, what we have accomplished is only a matter of willingness, patience and labor.

Once again Bill reinforces his point by telling a story, this one about a member of the Fellowship who recently ("only a few days ago at this writing") had moved to a new town where, after "but a few weeks," he discovered that it "probably contained more alcoholics per square mile than any city in the country." The man contacted a prominent local psychiatrist who had "certain responsibilities for the mental health of the community." This doctor freely admitted his inability to provide any meaningful help to active alcoholics and he agreed to the man's suggestion that the A.A. program should be tested "among his patients and certain other alcoholics from a clinic which he attends." This doctor's acceptance resulted in an introduction to "the chief psychiatrist of a large public hospital" who also agreed to try this new method with "still others from the stream of misery which flows through that institution.'"

> So our fellow worker will soon have friends galore. Some of them may sink and perhaps never get up, but if our experience is a criterion, more than half of those approached will become Fellows of Alcoholics Anonymous. When a few men in this city have found themselves, and have discovered the joy of helping others to face life again, there will be no stopping until everyone in that town has had his opportunity to recover—if he can and will.

This belief in the universal applicability and accessibility of their new method of getting sober is typical of Bill Wilson's enthusiasm about recovery. He was certain it would be successfully adopted wherever and whenever it was given an honest opportunity to succeed.

---

* The identity of this "former alcoholic" who had recently moved and "was living alone in a large community" is unknown. Several online sources suggest that it was Hank Parkhurst in Montclair, NJ, but Hank and Kathleen moved there in June 1937, which is attested to by Lois's diary entry for June 5, 1937: "To Montclair to see Parkhursts and their new home." Another candidate frequently mentioned is Jim Burwell and the facts presented here closely match his experiences on first moving to Philadelphia—but that did not happen until February 1940. Finally, Archie Trowbridge's experiences when he returned to Detroit from Akron also fit this description almost perfectly, but Archie didn't make his trip back to Detroit until the first week of March 1939—at least two weeks after this story appeared in the Multilith printing of the book. (See Archie's 1948 Christmas talk, available online, which specifies "In March . . ." and provides details about how Bill Wilson, who left for Akron on March 1 [Lois's diary entry for that date], accompanied him on that trip. This correlation confirms that they were in Detroit together on March 6 and 7, 1939.) Perhaps, if nothing else, Burwell's and Trowbridge's strikingly similar experiences show that this model—move to a new town, contact local medical man, get a favorable response, and begin to work with alcoholics there—was fairly common and had happened to some as yet unidentified other member in some other city—either in November 1938 (when this chapter was first written), or sometime before mid-February 1939 (when the Multilith copy was printed with the ongoing edits). Perhaps the best candidate for this "former alcoholic" is Bill Ruddell who moved to Hackettstown, NJ sometime in late 1938 and was actively trying to work with others in that new locale. If that is true, perhaps this is a clue to how the initial contact was made with the famous Dr. Howard whose identity will be discussed in some detail later.

The "Road of Happy Destiny"

In his stirring conclusion—considered important enough to be regularly read aloud at some A.A. meetings today—Bill Wilson concludes the front half of the book on a high note. He begins by emphasizing their thoroughly pragmatic approach to recovery and then proclaims the benefits that are freely available to the new man, if only he abandons himself to God "as you understand God'" and then carefully follows the pathway to recovery that has been methodically laid out for him.

> Our book is meant to be suggestive only. We realize we know only a little. God will constantly disclose more to you and to us. Ask him in your morning meditation what you can do each day for the man who is still sick. The answers will come, if your own house is in order. But obviously you cannot transmit something you haven't got. See to it that your relationship with Him is right, and great events will come to pass for you and countless others. This is the Great Fact for us.
>
> Abandon yourself to God as you understand God. Admit your faults to him and your fellows. Clear away the wreckage of your past. Give freely of what you find, and join us. We shall be with you, in the Fellowship of The Spirit, and you will surely meet some of us as you trudge** the Road of Happy Destiny.
>
> May God bless you and keep you—until then.[25]

Towns Approaches the AMA

Charles Towns was particularly pleased with this new chapter, so much so that he immediately included it in one of his many efforts to publicize and promote the Fellowship. Bill later praised Charles, noting he was consistently "raising heaven and earth to get publicity for us"[26] and in November, Towns's attempt to get publicity for them took the form of a long letter to the American Medical Association "setting forth his observations on [the] work" and requesting their support for this new method of curing alcoholism. Along with that letter, Charles sent the AMA a copy of "A Vision For You," thinking it would provide some concrete evidence of the spectacular results this new method was currently having out in the real world.[27]***

---

* Note this reversion to a more open and liberal understanding of God that effectively contradicts the "one God" concept just proclaimed so definitely in the Akron story. It should be noted though that this glaring inconsistency (separated by just ten paragraphs) may well have been caused by a later (December? January? early February?) addition of this phrase "as you understand God" into the steps and elsewhere in the text.

** "Trudge" is perhaps the single most troublesome word in the entire Big Book, frequently questioned by members who have found the dictionary definition ("to walk slowly and heavily because you are tired or working very hard") contrary to the very sense of the sentence, and also unacceptable because it runs counter to their own experiences in recovery. It is true that the "Road of Happy Destiny" hardly seems to be a place where one would "trudge" in this dictionary sense, but it was the word that Wilson chose and used from the very beginning and, based on the evidence found in the annotated Multilith Copy, it doesn't appear that anyone who read the manuscript ever questioned it. (See Hazelden's *The Book That Started It All*, p. 108.)

*** Charlie Towns's initial letter to the American Medical Association, the AMA's response and Towns's answer to this have not been saved. However, Bill Wilson did relate all of the details given here in his January 4, 1939 letter to Frank Amos—just a few weeks after they had occurred.

Towns's letter was convincing enough to generate "great interest" at the AMA, but like *This Week* magazine and *Good Housekeeping*, his proposal raised issues that troubled the reader. An official of the Association responded promptly enough to Charles, but he included several questions that he felt needed to be answered before a proper response could be formulated. A few weeks later, when Bill Wilson recounted the story of this exchange to Frank Amos, he noted that the AMA had wanted to know "what sort of organization we were, who the officers were, what we used for money and where Mr. Towns figured in?"[28]

Towns had no ready answers for these questions and, feeling more than a little challenged, he asked Bill to help him draft a reply. Wilson later explained that they had responded to the American Medical Association by saying

> that there was no organization in the conventional sense of the word; that for the past four years the work has been financed by the alcoholics themselves; that recently the Alcoholic Foundation had been formed to administer matters of money, etc; that the majority of trustees of that Foundation were disinterested and well known in New York City, that a few modest donations had been made to The Foundation; that the work would never be on a fee or professional basis; that outsiders could not deal with this group in financial matters touching the work without approval of the trustees; and finally, that Mr. Towns had advanced certain monies to promote publication of the book, but that Alcoholics Anonymous had not obligated themselves to him in any way (except for return of his money); that Mr. Towns hoped and expected his business would increase on account of our group, because men in it had taken his treatment and liked it, and would probably recommend that others do likewise if the occasion warranted. Mr. Towns stated explicitly that that was his only relationship with us; and that he saw no reason why it should ever be any different. He also added that the Towns treatment was in use in Akron, with his consent, but at no profit to himself.[29]

This last bit of information about the Towns treatment being used in Akron is interesting but a bit perplexing. At the time, the most commonly used treatment to allay the cravings for alcohol in Ohio was a forced regimen of sauerkraut, tomatoes, and Karo corn syrup—which was most definitely not "the Towns treatment." As Ernie Galbraith, the first man successfully recruited into A.A. after Bill Dotson, remembered:

> There were lots of recommendations made, diets of tomatoes, sauerkraut, corn syrup, which we found out were all experimental, but at the same time, in those days Bill and Doc were anxious to try anything that any M.D. could suggest that might be able to take away any craving for a whiskey. I can remember that tomato deal and that corn syrup that they used to lap up over there in the kitchen by the case—I can see it now—Doc with tomatoes and a big can of Karo, a big spoon—you got to the

place where it almost gagged you, taking it straight. Doc did back down on the sauerkraut. He kept up the tomatoes and corn syrup for years.[30]*

Despite Wilson's and Towns' carefully crafted answers, the AMA did not respond to this request until the following October when, six months after its publication, they reviewed the book, *Alcoholics Anonymous*, in the *Journal of the American Medical Association*. That review was short and negative in the extreme. After characterizing the group as "an organization which would save other addicts by a kind of religious conversion," it dismissively concluded that

> the book contains instructions as to how to intrigue the alcoholic addict into the acceptance of divine guidance in place of alcohol in terms strongly reminiscent of Dale Carnegie and the adherents of the Buchman ("Oxford") movement. The one valid thing in the book is the recognition of the seriousness of addiction to alcohol. Other than this, the book has no scientific merit or interest.[31]

So much for the 1938 hopes that the American Medical Association would support A.A.'s program of recovery.

Wishing Bill a Happy Birthday

November ended on a high, but somewhat unusual, note. Bill Wilson turned 43 years old on the 26th of the month and early that day he received a phone call from Dr. Bob Smith wishing him a "Happy Birthday."[32] But Bob said nothing to prepare him for the flurry of at least eleven celebratory telegrams that arrived at Clinton Street later that day. One, from New York, was sent by an otherwise unknown person, Mary Lewis, who wished "MAY YOUR BEAUTIFUL EFFORTS TOWARD HUMANITY SEE MANY MORE HAPPY BIRTHDAYS YOUR BOOK WILL PROVE TO THE WORLD YOUR SACRIFICES AND GOODNESS." Another local telegram, originating in Brooklyn, was signed from "ALL OF US" and read "HAPPY BIRTHDAY BILL. WE FEEL THIS AN APPROPRIATE TIME TO LET YOU KNOW HOW THANKFUL & GRATEFUL WE ARE THAT GOD CHOSE YOU TO HELP US OVER THE ROUGH SPOTS."[33]

The other nine telegrams all came from Akron, sent by Bill Dotson, Archie Trowbridge, Paul Stanley, Ernie Galbraith, Tom Lucas, T. Henry Williams, Dick Stanley, Wally Gillam, and Walter Bray (frequently including their wives as co-signers). Most of these messages confined themselves to standard, short greetings and wishes that Bill's day would be happy, but a few were a bit more expansive. Bill Dotson included "THE WISH THAT EVERY OTHER DAY OF THE YEAR WILL BE HAPPY, TOO" and Paul Stanley's hope for Wilson was that he might have "MANY MORE OF SUCH YEARS OF USEFULNESS." Paul's brother Dick

---

* In his 1958 Founder's Day talk in Akron (available from GFTapes.com) Bill Wilson claimed that using tomatoes, Karo syrup, and sauerkraut were his own suggestion— based on his contemporary understanding of the "scientific" physical needs of the recovering alcoholic. He describes the scene at Dr. Bob's house where both of them open cans of tomatoes and jars of sauerkraut and eat them cold. Bill said that Bob quickly gave up the sauerkraut; he just couldn't get it down every morning.

offered "CONGRATULATIONS ON THE ANNIVERSARY OF THE BIRTH OF SUCH AN ALL-ROUND GOOD FELLOW AND LOYAL FRIEND," and the William's didn't forget to include "LOVE TO LOIS" in their message.[34]

The telegram from the New York group (signed: "All of us") said they felt it was "an appropriate time" for such a demonstration of love and support, but other than this unhelpful clue, it is hard to know exactly what might have prompted this effusive outpouring. It is also noteworthy that this is the only year in which this seems to have happened; there are no birthday telegrams in the GSO archives from the previous years or for the years immediately following this. They only appeared in 1938.

But whatever the impetus, it was clearly an orchestrated effort. Interestingly, the New Yorkers felt they were well covered by one collective telegram, while the people in Ohio sent individual greetings. It could be imagined that perhaps Dr. Bob Smith had initiated and encouraged the Akron members to do this in an attempt to show some much-needed appreciation and support for Bill Wilson, acknowledging his central role in the founding of Alcoholics Anonymous (and also, tangentially, for the book?). But, however likely it might be to imagine the scenario of Dr. Bob Smith using his influence to rally support for Bill's big project, it must remain just that—speculation.

CHAPTER TWENTY-THREE

Writing the Twelve Steps

~December 1938~

Ebby was still drinking and it didn't look as if he was going to stop anytime soon. This was both frustrating and painful for Bill because there seemed to be nothing more he could do for the man who had first brought him the gift of sobriety. Thacher was definitely on a run and even his current residence in a New Jersey evangelical Christian community wasn't helping him to control his drinking. If Ebby's intimate knowledge of the effectiveness of the spiritual solution and his experiences during a couple of significant periods of sobriety couldn't keep him sober, then what possibly could? Bill found the whole situation baffling.

At the same time, Hank Parkhurst was relentlessly pushing him to write a much more secular version of their solution and had offered his own completely non-religious chapter, "To Employers," along with the proposed "Q&A Chapter" as two concrete examples of how their program of recovery could be packaged and presented to the world. But even in the face of Hank's constant barrage of suggestions, Bill steadfastly refused to take the book in the direction his friend insisted was so necessary if they were going to turn it into a runaway best-seller and thereby get people sober all across the country. Despite these persistent arguments, Bill continued to write about a method of recovery that relied primarily on a Supreme Being and the spiritual solution so essential for any successful attempt to quit drinking.

A Challenge of Heroic Proportions

In addition to all this personal turmoil, Bill had a much larger problem. He had finally reached the point where he had to put down on paper a set of clear instructions on how to get sober—something so "airtight" that the rationalizing alcoholic wouldn't be able to "wiggle out" of it no matter how hard he tried.[1] Doing so in a way that hopefully addressed Ebby's difficulties, while simultaneously incorporating at least some aspects of Hank's more secular approach, seemed to be an impossible task. Further complicating the matter, any set of instructions would have to acknowledge and accommodate the much more orthodox religious program practiced by Dr. Bob Smith and the sober men in Akron.

How to satisfy all of these profoundly contradictory constituencies was a challenge of heroic proportions.

By the first week of December,[2]* Wilson could not hold off any longer. He had to write something that described in precise detail "how [the] program of recovery from alcoholism really worked." Eight expositional chapters had already been drafted and edited providing more than "enough background and window-dressing" for the book.[3]** Finally, he was going to have to put down in black and white and in simple declarative sentences "a definite statement of concrete principles,"[4] telling the new man exactly what he had to do to get sober and then stay that way. It was the seemingly insoluble problem that he had been dodging for far too long, one that he later admitted "had secretly worried the life out of me" for some time.[5] Finally, it was time to stop procrastinating and to start writing.

At this most critical and important juncture in the story—for nothing is more central to the book *Alcoholics Anonymous* than the program of recovery outlined in the Twelve Steps—there are, unfortunately, no primary documents mentioning the actual writing of the steps. It is an unexpected gap in the otherwise rich archival records that provide a robust and vivid picture of early A.A. history from late 1937 right up until this point in late 1938. But now, at arguably the single most significant moment in the entire story, any historical account must rely solely on the stories Bill Wilson told much later about how he wrote the Twelve Steps. There is not one document preserved from December 1938 (or from the months immediately after that) to either confirm or contradict his version of what happened. It is simply not mentioned. Compounding the problem, and raising serious suspicion about Bill's absolute accuracy here, is the fact that the first recorded instance of him telling the well-known story of how he wrote the Twelve Steps appears in a letter he wrote to Jack Alexander on December 13, 1949,[6] a full eleven years after the event. How so much time could have elapsed without this important story being told sooner is a mystery.

This is truly problematic. As has been noted here repeatedly, Bill Wilson was no great respecter of the actual facts when it came to A.A. history. When he wrote or talked, his purpose was not to deliver a precisely accurate accounting of what had

---

* Despite three references (see endnote) verifying this timeline, it is likely that all three depend on a single AA Main Events source. Given the extremely tight compression of events necessary to accommodate a composition date as early as December 1, it is *possible* that Bill Wilson first wrote the Twelve Steps in mid- to late-November rather than early December.

** Whenever he told this story of writing the Twelve Steps, Bill repeatedly claimed that the chapters were written in the order in which they appeared in the book. He makes this claim most clearly in *AACOA*: "Up to that time I had done my own story and had drafted three more chapters with the titles 'There Is A Solution,' 'More About Alcoholism,' and 'We Agnostics.' It was now realized that we had enough background and window-dressing material, and that at this point we would have to tell how our program for recovery from alcoholism really worked. The backbone of the book would have to be fitted in right here." (p. 159) This makes for a good story, but, as the forgoing chapters make abundantly clear, the truth was far more complicated than this simplified explanation.

actually happened. And, whenever inconvenient or messy details were encountered, Bill would modify them (sometimes significantly) and then streamline the whole story for the dramatic impact he felt was necessary to underline the specific moral or inspirational message he was trying to deliver to his audience.

The previous chapters have supplied more than enough evidence that historians who rely on Bill's talks or writings for reliable historical information do so at their own peril. But in relation to this particular event—the day he first formulated and wrote down the Twelve Steps of Alcoholics Anonymous—we have no supporting contemporary documents whatsoever to rely on for confirmation or contradiction. There is only Bill's later version of the story, a story he told a number of times throughout the 1950s and 1960s.

What follows here is *not* a direct quote from Bill Wilson, although it does include many words, phrases, sentences and even whole paragraphs taken directly from his later talks and writings. Instead, it is a composite story (indicated by the use of *italics*) cobbling together different details he mentioned at one time or another during his various recountings of the day he first wrote down the steps.

The Day Bill Wilson Wrote Down the Steps

The stock in our new company wasn't selling anywhere near as well as we had hoped and some of the New Yorkers were really unhappy about the fact that we were even trying to raise money in this way. A couple of A.A. members came over to my house in Brooklyn and we got into a big argument about the whole arrangement. The discussion got so heated that at one point we were actually yelling and screaming at each other.[7] It was upsetting for everyone, but it hit me particularly hard. Why couldn't these guys see how essential this money was for us to finish and publish our book and realize this stock offering was the only way for us to get that done?

But worries about what these money arguments might be doing to our group (and being still mad as hell at those two guys for refusing to buy any stock[8]) wasn't the only problem I had on my mind that day. We had reached the troubling point where I knew something had to be done about the rest of the book[9] and it was a problem that had secretly worried the life out of me for some time.[10] Clearly, the distant reader would need a broader and deeper articulation of the program of recovery than we had already presented in the book, and whatever was written would have to be as clear and comprehensive as possible.[11] Knowing the alcoholic's ability to rationalize, I realized something airtight would have to be written.[12] What was needed was a set of specific directions, a definite statement of concrete principles that these drunks just couldn't wiggle out of no matter how hard they tried.[13]

These problems brought on another one of my imaginary ulcer attacks[14]—my typical reaction to stress in those days[15]—and then, to make matters worse, I fell into one of my depressive snits.[16] The combination of these two argumentative guys and the impossible challenges I was facing with the book had put me in a really bad frame of mind.[17] I was feeling dejected[18] and discouraged[19], but most of all, I was suffering from a terrible case of self pity.[20] I finally went upstairs to the second floor bedroom and laid down on the bed in an attempt to soothe my ulcer. But once there, I was completely overwhelmed with just one thought: "Poor me! Poor Bill Wilson!"[21]

However uninspired[22] I may have felt, I was still nagged by the thought that I had to come up with a broader and deeper concept of the program, one that was much more explicit[23] than the six word-of-mouth steps which had gradually evolved since Ebby first visited me in the fall of 1934.[24] Having arrived at what is now Chapter Five, we realized that a specific program of recovery had to be laid down if we were going to make any further progress with the book.[25] Slowly my mind came into some kind of focus,[26] and as I lay on the bed, I ran over in my head the word-of-mouth program that was currently in use and then jotted them down.[27] Although the six steps of that program were subject to considerable variation, they were approximately as follows:[28]

1. *We admitted that we were licked, that we were powerless over alcohol.*

2. *We made a moral inventory of our defects or sins.*

3. *We confessed or shared our shortcomings with another person in confidence.*

4. *We made restitution to all those we had harmed by our drinking.*

5. *We tried to help other alcoholics, with no thought of reward in money or prestige.*

6. *We prayed to whatever God we thought there was for power to practice these precepts.[29]*

Obviously this was just too loose; there were far too many loopholes here that an argumentative alcoholic[30] could exploit to wiggle out of doing what he had to do to get sober. What we needed was an absolutely explicit program[31] for these people to follow. I also worried that if I simply wrote down those six steps, they would be too big for the reader to digest all at once. I decided that what I needed to do was to break them down into smaller pieces,[32] making them not only more explicit, but also much easier to understand and less subject to misinterpretation.

Although I was still far from anything that could be described as a spiritual mood,[33] I was well aware this was something that absolutely had to be done. I relaxed and asked for guidance[34] and then picked up a pencil and the cheap yellow tablet[35] lying beside me on the bedside table. With that tablet of paper propped on my knee[36], I finally began to write, splitting up our word-of-mouth program into smaller pieces.[37] My purpose was to draft more than six steps, [but] how many more I did not know . . . With a speed that was astonishing, considering my jangled emotions, I completed the first draft [in] perhaps half an hour. The words kept right on coming. When

I reached a stopping point, I numbered the new steps [and saw] they added up to twelve. Somehow this number seemed significant. Without any special rhyme or reason I connected them with the twelve apostles.[38]

I had started with the idea that we needed to broaden and deepen the basic concepts of the program by making them more explicit, but that was the only idea I had when I began to write.[39] The most amazing thing about this experience was that I didn't seem to be thinking at all as I wrote.[40] The words just flowed out of me and I've come to believe that these Steps must have been inspired—because I wasn't in the least bit inspired myself while I was writing them.[41] I have no idea why I wrote the Steps down in that particular order or why they were worded as they are.[42]

I paused to read over what I had written[43] and one thing I noticed right away was that I had certainly enlarged the scope of the six steps considerably.[44] One of the reasons for this was that I had significantly changed the order of their presentation. Most especially, in our six step program, we had held off mentioning God until we got to the very end and that was the only mention we made of Him. (We were afraid any earlier mention might scare off some of the drunks before they even got in the door![45]) But, for reasons unknown to me, my new formulation not only mentioned God several times throughout, but I had moved Him right up to the very beginning of the Steps.[46] Whatever, I didn't pay much attention to that at the time. I actually thought it all sounded pretty good.[47]

The Sole Author

The fact that there is no contemporary evidence to support any of the details in Bill's account of writing the Twelve Steps is troubling and troublesome because a careful examination of Bill's story reveals some serious difficulties with his version of what happened that day.

Before exploring those problems, there is one fact that is beyond any doubt: Bill Wilson was the sole author of the Twelve Steps of Alcoholics Anonymous. His singular responsibility for writing the Steps has never been seriously challenged, although on occasion A.A. urban legends have credited Dr. Bob Smith or the Reverend Sam Shoemaker as either the author or the co-author of them. However, since both men publicly and categorically denied having had anything to do with the writing of the Steps,[*] Bill's authorship remains clear and unchallenged.

Beyond this one undeniable fact, Bill's ready willingness to play fast and loose with the past naturally begs the question of why he might have told the story of the creation of the Twelve Steps in this particular way. While many of those details might well be true—several parts of his story are certainly plausible—there is a very real possibility

---

[*] In one of his last major talks (Detroit, December 1948), Dr. Bob Smith stated categorically: "I didn't write the Twelve Steps. I had nothing to do with the writing of them." (see http://silkworth.net/aahistory/drbob1948.html - retrieved November 7, 2015). Similarly, Sam Shoemaker, speaking on June 17, 1962 in Charlotte, NC, said: "To set the record straight, that there has gotten going in AA, a kind of rumor that I had a lot to do with the 12 steps. I didn't have any more to do with those 12 steps other than that book [??] had. Those Twelve Steps, I believe came to Bill by himself, I think he told me they came to him in about 40 minutes and I think it's one of the great instances of direct inspiration that I know in human history . . ." (Wikipedia, Sam Shoemaker, Named Article—retrieved November 7, 2015).

that the first writing of the steps wasn't actually the sudden, inspired event he so frequently reported. Instead, it is possible their creation was a much more judicious and deliberate affair, a process of formulation—whether conscious or unconscious—over several weeks of reviewing and contemplating his own experiences while getting sober.[*]

Another Version of How the Steps Were Written

However, there is a very different story about how Bill wrote the Twelve Steps, one he told almost two full years before he rolled out this story of being inspired to break down an existing Six Step program. That earlier version appears in a letter Paul Kirby Hennessy wrote to Bill Wilson on October 19, 1948 recounting in some detail Bill's earliest version of the story of the day he first wrote the steps.[48]

Ten months earlier, on January 31 of that year, Paul had accompanied Bill and Lois on a train ride from New York City to Washington, DC. They were to attend an A.A. Regional Banquet there the following night and Hennessy was scheduled to speak about the late Fitz Mayo. According to Paul, the "conversation [on the train] naturally veered toward [Fitz] and then to the 'Twelve Steps.'" Once that topic had been raised, Hennessy says that Wilson "described to Eileen Barrett[**] and myself the evolution of the 'Twelve Steps.'" Paul reminds Bill that when he finished, "I said that this was the first time I had ever heard the story and that I believe it was of sufficient importance to commit to writing. I am still of that opinion."

In his October letter, Paul asks Bill to review the enclosed document, saying that if it "needs amplification or clarification, please let me know" so that changes can be made. If, however, Wilson finds it to be correct, Hennessey asks him to indicate so by initialing one of the two enclosed copies and then sending it back to him.

In the same envelope was a memo dated October 12, 1948 entitled "BILL'S STORY OF THE EVOLUTION OF THE 'TWELVE STEPS." In his third person narration of Wilson's conversation on the train, Hennessy states:

> Bill said that Fitz himself had no actual part in the writing of the "Twelve Steps" but that his spiritual perception and influence were a definite factor in their formulation.

> Bill went on to explain how the pioneers in A.A. fought, thought—and prayed—their way through to recovery. In his effort to rehabilitate himself the alcoholic was obliged:

> 1. To admit he was powerless over alcohol.

> 2. To make an inventory of his own character.

---

[*] Here I must disagree with Ernest Kurtz who found Bill Wilson's *AACOA* version of how the steps were created "scrupulously accurate" (Kurtz, *Not-God*, p. 331, n. 31). Ernie's praise for Bill's honesty about this seems overly generous and more than a little confusing since, in his very next endnote, he says that the "exact formulation of these six 'steps' was contrived by Wilson only as he set out to record the history in *AACA*" (Kurtz, *Not-God*, p. 331, n. 32). I would suggest that Wilson "contrived" more than just the Six Steps in his story of the writing the Twelve Steps.

[**] In his letter, Hennessy never clarifies exactly who Eileen Barrett was. She may have been a legal associate but his comment quoted below that he "dictated" his version of this conversation to her would imply she was a legal secretary rather than an associate.

3. To put trust in God.

4. To work with other alcoholics.*

> As it stood, this program needed clarification. Bill sat down and began to figure out the various phases of his own recovery. Setting them down on paper, he found there were twelve separate and distinct steps.[49]

Hennessy, a Rhodes Scholar and a practicing lawyer, notes for clarity's sake (and rather legalistically) in his final paragraph that "As soon as we reached Washington on that trip last January, I dictated my version of Bill's story to Eileen Barrett who agreed with my version as outlined. This memorandum has been compiled from the original draft, which is now before me, and also from a subsequent conversation with Bill." Paul's mention of a subsequent conversation strongly implies that Wilson had since confirmed this version of the story—why else would Hennessy even bother sending him this memo for his written approval?

This is a significantly different story from the one that later became so famous.

Bill's Recovery Experience as Basis for the Steps

Besides the presentation of an interesting *Four* Step program, Wilson's claim that he "began to figure out the various phases of his own recovery" (rather than breaking down some earlier version of the steps) and then used those phases of his own recovery to formulate the Twelve Steps is a startling admission. According to this earliest available version of the story, the Twelve Steps weren't the result of a sudden inspirational expansion of the fellowship's collective experience (Six Steps which had "gradually evolved"[50] since Ebby's 1934 visit), but rather a judicious reformulation of the most important elements Bill could identify in the different actions he himself had taken on the road to sobriety.

The creation of the Twelve Steps based on Wilson's own experience is, in fact, a much more likely scenario than the later claim of an inspired elaboration of the supposed Six Steps. When Bill wrote the first two drafts of his own "Story" the previous May, the first explicitly contained eight of the later Steps and the second mentioned ten of them. As already noted here, combining these two lists from May provides us with eleven of the Twelve Steps.** It is not beyond the realm of possibilities that when he began to formulate his "definite statement of concrete principles"[51] Wilson had taken some time to reread his own story to refresh his memory on what he had already written about the steps he himself had taken to get sober.

Frankly, it is a significant stretch to imagine how the Twelve Steps could have ever been the result of his decision to break those Six Steps down "into smaller pieces."[52] The Six Steps quoted in the italicized section above contain only two full and four partial Steps, while the Four Steps Bill mentioned to Paul Hennessy contains just two full and two partial Steps. Even taken together, these lack almost all of the actions

---

* Is it possible that these were the "four steps" that Hank Parkhurst had mentioned in his June 1938 "Ideas"?

** See pp. 121–22 and 125–26 of this book for further details.

suggested in the fully realized Twelve Steps. To break those Six Steps up into smaller pieces and transform them into the Twelve Steps would have required a tremendous amount of creativity, including the addition of several new ideas and a number of specific, previously unmentioned actions that would have to be taken.

On the other hand, to see the newly packaged steps as a direct reflection of Bill's own recovery experiences presents no such problems. On this December evening, six months after first writing his own "Story," Bill was simply recycling the material found there and repackaging it into a more organized and neatly numbered format.

Deflecting the Spotlight

Questioning Wilson's veracity on this particular story naturally begs another question. Why would he even bother to change his 1948 account of judiciously reviewing and transcribing his own experiences into the Six Step story he later told? Why not just continue with the story Paul Hennessy heard on the train? The most plausible explanation is that this change was another one of Wilson's many attempts to direct attention away from himself and to dim the spotlight constantly shone on him for his central role in the creation of Alcoholics Anonymous.

This is not only plausible; it is highly likely. During the years of A.A.'s early success and growth, Wilson had a significant problem keeping his own ego in check. Something that, years later, he would candidly admit.

> From the start the [proposed] title [for the book] "The Way Out" was popular. If we gave the book this name, then I could add my signature, "By Bill W."! After all why shouldn't an author sign his book? I began to forget that this was everybody's book and that I had been mostly the umpire of the discussion that had created it. In one dark moment I even considered calling the book "The B. W. Movement." I whispered these ideas to a few friends and promptly got slapped down. Then I saw the temptation for what it was, a shameless piece of egotism.[53]*

This paragraph is just one illustration of the ego problems Bill struggled with—could there be a better illustration of his grandiosity than "The B. W. Movement"?—and also evidence of his later efforts to downplay his central role as the founder of A.A. As his notoriety and reputation grew within Alcoholics Anonymous (and beyond), Wilson used all of his storytelling skills in a campaign of self-effacement, a concerted and calculated effort to minimize his singular responsibility for the creation of A.A. This effort to lower his profile went far beyond just polishing the facts to make a more dramatic and easily comprehensible story. Bill Wilson was an active mythmaker, constantly creating stories that spread the credit for his own actions to as many other people as possible.

---

* The thought of Bill 'whispering' either of these ideas "to a few friends" should bring a smile. What a genuinely human moment! And which friends? The thought of him flying this particular trial balloon past Hank Parkhurst certainly does *not* seem very likely.

The text quoted above is a perfect example. Over the last twenty years of his life Wilson consistently asserted that he wasn't *really* the author of the Big Book. It was "everybody's book," a distillation of the collective experiences of the first one hundred men, a book they had written and presented to the world. He would frequently declare that his only role was as the "umpire of the discussion that had created it"[54]—a claim he repeated whenever he was given the chance. This is so far from the truth as to be almost laughable, but it is a perfect example of the purposeful reformulation of A.A. history, of creative storytelling, that Bill regularly used to protect himself from his own ego. Mythmaking proved to be his best defense against the 'you are the man who saved my life' adulation that followed him everywhere throughout the rest of his life.

Regarding the story of how he became the umpire of the text, Wilson said that during the arguments following his presentation of the Twelve Steps, he despaired "of satisfying everyone [and] I finally asked that I might be the final judge of what the book said. Seeing that we would get nowhere without such a point of decision, most of the group agreed. We began to carry on again."[55*] Perhaps the closest Bill ever came to telling the truth about his 'I was just the umpire' myth came in a 1960 speech where he noted that "I was awful leery of the rows [over the book] but that situation looked better because I had been appointed the umpire. That if I would listen carefully, that I finally could take a decision about it."[56] There is some hidden irony in this comment about his appointment as the person authorized to take a decision on the book for it clearly implies that the A.A. members in New York (or was it just Hank and Fitz making these demands?) did not think Bill *was* listening carefully enough to their suggestions—or why would they have negotiated such a condition for granting him the power to decide what should and should not go into the book?

Perhaps the most obvious example of Bill recasting events to draw the spotlight away from himself, a reformulation that goes far beyond good storytelling and crosses over into intentional mythmaking, is the ever-expanding proliferation of "co-founders" of Alcoholics Anonymous over the years. This is the most prominent of Bill Wilson's attempts to take the focus off his sole responsibility for starting A.A., keeping it alive and nurturing it whereby he all but single-handedly wrote the Big Book and became the sole author of the Twelve Steps, its core teaching. Over the years, the number of co-founders grew and grew as Bill liberally spread the credit for the creation of A.A. in every available direction, attempting to lower his own justifiable claim to be A.A.'s undisputed founder.[**]

In this same myth-making way, Bill's revision of the 1948 story of writing the Twelve Steps based on his own experiences into one where the Steps were the result of breaking up the Six Step word-of-mouth program—something which happened almost automatically and "must have been inspired"[57]—serves exactly the same purpose. Wilson could not deny he was solely responsible for creating the steps, but

* "Most of the group"? That is certainly an interesting loose thread that Bill just leaves hanging in this version of the story.

** This ever-expanding list of A.A. "co-founders" has already been noted here on pp. 69–70. For just one example of Wilson's active part in this mythmaking, when Jack Alexander requested historical details for a 1950 follow up article on A.A. ("The Drunkard's Best Friend" in *The Saturday Evening Post*, April 1, 1950), Bill concluded his five-page response by saying: "I suppose founders have news value. But please, Jack, go easy on Smith and me. I'd also appreciate it if his part in the story could be as prominent as mine. Thanks." (December 13, 1949; GSO, Box 29, Folder 17.1, AA History: Miscellaneous Materials, p. 2).

this new inspired story redirected the credit for their invention away from him as much as possible by saying he was simply "breaking down" the collective wisdom of the group at that time and that while doing so, he had to "think little at all"[58] for "the words kept right on coming."[59] This often repeated story later prompted Sam Shoemaker to characterize the writing of the Twelve Steps as "one of the great instances of direct inspiration that I know in human history."[60]

Sam's evaluation was one that suited Bill Wilson's purposes exactly.

The Six Step Program Myth

One particular element in Bill's story—the details of the Six Step program supposedly being followed before the Twelve Steps were created—has generated considerable attention from A.A. members over the years. Most of that interest, however, has been driven by the misconception that there actually was a definite universally agreed upon and rigorously followed program of recovery in place before Wilson invented the Twelve Steps. This mistaken belief was directly and decisively addressed in a recent online comment by the respected religious scholar and A.A. historian Glenn Chesnut.

> There is no evidence that there was any formal set of "Six Steps" being listed and followed by people in AA prior to Bill Wilson's writing of the Twelve Steps in early December of 1938. People who like things neat and tidy, with lists to memorize, tend to get carried away with this idea of six steps, and start imagining early AA meetings with a window shade mounted on the walls, displaying the list of "The Six Steps" . . . and everybody sitting around memorizing and analyzing "the Six Steps."[61]*

Wilson is surely to blame for this misunderstanding because he mentions this Six Step program in such a concrete, definite way and with such regularity in his later writings and talks. But it is important to note that, while his lists create the impression of this being a specific, detailed program for recovery, even in his most widely quoted presentation of the alleged Six Steps, Bill does qualify what he is about to say by noting this is just one version of what was a "pretty consistent procedure," that this procedure was nonetheless "subject to considerable variation," and they are only "approximately as follows."[62] Note well that "considerable variation" and the "approximately."

Tellingly, there is no mention of the Six Step word-of-mouth program in any of Wilson's writings or talks until May 1949—ten-and-a-half years after he supposedly used them as the foundation for his creation of the steps.** That month, speaking before a convention of the American Psychiatric Association in Montreal, Bill categorically stated there had been an early Six Step program, but he did not present them as

---

*   Chesnut's mention of window shades refers to the two pull-down displays (one for the Twelve Steps and the other for the Twelve Traditions) that are commonly seen in A.A. meeting rooms. More than one wit has cynically commented along the lines that "A.A. is the only major spiritual movement in history that proudly displays their entire teachings on two window shades."

**   Bill did refer to what might be considered a Five Step program while addressing the New York Medical Society in May of 1944, but these five were his *reduction* of the Twelve Steps ("Boiled down, these Steps mean, simply:") not the original, shorter program out of which they were supposedly extrapolated. See *Three Talks to Medical Societies by Bill W., Co-Founder of AA*, Alcoholics Anonymous pamphlet, p. 29. Also published as "Basic Concept of Alcoholics Anonymous" in the *New York State Journal of Medicine*, Volume 44, August 1944.

something that had evolved, or that they had been subject to considerable variation over time as he later claimed in *Alcoholics Anonymous Comes of Age*.[63] Rather, in his first presentation of the Six Step formula, Wilson said they were exactly what Ebby Thacher had communicated to him during their first encounter in late November 1934.[*]

> While disagreeing with many tenets of the Oxford Group, my former schoolmate did, however, ascribe his new sobriety to certain ideas that this alcoholic and other Oxford people had given him. The particular practices my friend had selected for himself were simple:
>
> 1. He admitted he was powerless to solve his own problem.
>
> 2. He got honest with himself as never before; made an examination of conscience.
>
> 3. He made a rigorous confession of his personal defects.
>
> 4. He surveyed his distorted relations with people, visiting them to make restitution.
>
> 5. He resolved to devote himself to helping others in need, without the usual demand for personal prestige or material gain.
>
> 6. By meditation he sought God's direction for his life and help to practice these principles at all times.[64]

Although a few words here are slightly different, this list corresponds closely to the more famous presentation in *Alcoholics Anonymous Comes of Age*[65] (quoted verbatim in the italicized story above)—excepting only for the substitution of "meditation" for "prayer" in the Sixth Step. However, it is important to note once again, in this, its initial appearance, Wilson claims that this was the essence of the program of recovery from the very start rather than—as he repeatedly said later—something that gradually evolved over time.[66]

The point here isn't to minutely examine every variation of the Six Step program Bill Wilson ever offered—there are several and he was clearly not paying much attention to the changes he was constantly making[**]—but rather to demonstrate and emphasize the fact that his mention of a Six Step program first saw the light of day more than a

---

[*] Contradicting the claim that Ebby created the Six Step program, Wilson admitted in a 1960 talk that "Before the Twelve Steps were written, these ideas were circulated in some six word-of-mouth steps. I don't remember that anybody in particular formulated these." (Wilson's talk at the National Clergy Conference on Alcoholism, 1960: http://www.silkworth.net/religion_clergy/01052.html - retrieved November 6, 2015.)

[**] Those interested in making such comparisons can begin by checking Bill Wilson speaking in Atlanta, Georgia, July 14, 1951, (recording acquired from Dicobe Media Inc., Bellevue NE, 68005); "A Fragment of History: Origin of the Twelve Steps" (*Grapevine*, July 1953; reprinted in *Language of the Heart*, p. 200); Bill Wilson speaking to the Manhattan Group, New York City, December, 1955 (http://recoveryspeakers.com/bill-w-1955-manhattan-group-about-the-early-days/ - retrieved December 2, 2015); Bill Wilson speaking before the New York City Medical Society on Alcoholism, April 28, 1958 (pamphlet: *Three Talks to Medical Societies by Bill W., Co-Founder of AA*, Alcoholics Anonymous Work Services, Inc., p.12—available online at A.A.'s website); the copy of Bill's April, 1953 handwritten version of the "Original AA Steps" (http://hindsfoot.org/steps6.html); and AA Main Events, 1937, Point 9—to cite just six instances where Wilson explicitly outlined the Six Step word-of-mouth program. Note that any comparison of these and other versions should not fail to also acknowledge the Four Step program that Bill offered Paul Hennessey in 1948 in the letter quoted above. Finally, one other Six Step program of note is found in Earl Treat's story which was first written and published in 1955—eighteen years after he was supposedly introduced to them by Dr. Bob Smith. It appears in the second, third, and fourth editions of the Big Book under the title "He Sold Himself Short" (pages 292, 292 & 263 respectively).

full decade after the Twelve Steps were written and that these lists of Six Steps were never presented in any kind of consistent or definitive way. As Ernest Kurtz noted, this formulation of the word-of-mouth program was something Bill Wilson later "contrived"[67] for his own purposes as a literary device—a storytelling convenience—and it has been recognized as such by all serious A.A. historians.

Despite Wilson's 1949 claim that these Six Steps harken back to the very beginning of his own sobriety, they do not. In later revisions of this story, Bill acknowledged that the program of recovery had changed considerably since Ebby first visited him in 1934. It had certainly evolved to the point where there was *some* sort of routine approach helping people stay sober in December 1938, but there is no mention of anything in the early records even remotely resembling Bill's reputed Six Step program. In Wilson's defense it could be claimed that the historian's maxim, "absence of evidence is not proof of absence," might apply here, but there actually is a tremendous amount of contemporary documentation showing exactly what people were doing to get sober before Bill wrote the Twelve Steps—and none of it suggests anything like his alleged Six Step program.

Members' Stories Reveal a Procedure for Recovery

These solid contemporary sources—a first draft of Fitz Mayo's story, Frank Amos's 1938 report, and the thirty personal stories written for the Big Book in late 1938 and early 1939—provide detailed accounts of the "pretty consistent procedure"[68] being followed by A.A. members in both Ohio and New York before the steps were written. While this evidence does support a fairly consistent set of procedures for stopping drinking, they bear little resemblance to the semi-formal Six Step program Wilson later described.

Fitz Mayo's Story

Fitz Mayo's initial draft of his Big Book story (titled "Me and John" *[i.e. Barleycorn]*) was written in mid-1938 and it provides a brief glimpse at the 'steps' and the program of recovery being practiced in New York City when he got sober in late 1935. This initial draft (which is much shorter than the later version entitled "Our Southern Friend"") clearly highlights the dramatic evolution in the New York City program between late 1935 and late 1938. It also amply illustrates the kind of changes involved in the editing of at least some of the New Yorkers' personal stories as the book got closer to publication.[69]

In both the first and the published version of his story, Fitz finds himself a patient at Towns Hospital where he is approached by a man** who tells him that however hopeless he may feel, "there are men on the streets of New York today who were worse than you, and they don't drink anymore." In the earliest draft, when Mayo wondered how this could be possible,

---

* See *Alcoholics Anonymous* (1ˢᵗ edition), pp. 226–41 and (with ongoing edits) in all subsequent editions of the Big Book.

** Students of A.A. history have speculated that the man at Towns Hospital who was familiar with A.A. work at this early stage, just months after Bill had returned from Akron, was likely Silas Bent.

... the man asked would you be willing to try to live on a new basis—to try to live up to ideals, by trying to be absolutely honest, absolutely pure, absolutely unselfish, and absolutely loving in all your relationships with your fellow man, to get rid of this drink problem?

"Of course I would" I declared without much thought—"I'd do anything."

"Then all of your troubles are over" said the man, and he left the room.[70]

In this first draft, Fitz describes a program of recovery—such as it is in this extremely abbreviated form—that is pure Oxford Group. Salvation from alcohol can be had by adopting the Four Absolutes as the guiding principles of your life and then acting accordingly.

This is not surprising given Bill's strong connection with the Oxford Group in late 1935—a connection that lasted right up until mid-1937. Lois Wilson, in one of her rare departures from the stories her husband always told, acknowledges this when she claims that Bill had to write the Twelve Steps because "the six Oxford Group principles that the Fellowship had been using were not definite enough."[71] Whatever steps there might have been in A.A. prior to mid-1937 could only be described as Oxford Group steps, and it was these that formed the basis for whatever evolved after the New York group declared their independence in mid-1937.

But by the time Mayo's story was printed in the Multilith edition just a few months later, the text of this central paragraph had been changed considerably.

Then he asks me if I believed in a power greater than myself, whether I call that power God, Allah, Confucius, Prime Cause, Divine Mind, or any other name. I told him that I believe in electricity and other forces of nature, but as for a God, if there is one, He has never done anything for me. Then he asks me if I am willing to right all the wrongs I have ever done to anyone, no matter how wrong I thought they were. Am I willing to be honest with myself about myself and tell someone about myself, and am I willing to think of other people instead of myself and of their needs; to get rid of the drink problem?[72]

The original version of this encounter—which is surely how that conversation actually went—was rewritten to conform to the changes in the New York program over the intervening three years. Rather than being pressed to accept the Four Absolutes (something Ebby almost certainly recommended during his famous late-November visit to Bill rather than the Six Steps Wilson later claimed), Fitz was now reporting that he was asked if he had *any* kind of belief in God and if he would be willing to take an honest personal inventory, share it with another human being, make amends for past wrongs, and overall become a less self-centered, more loving and caring person—all of which had now been brought into line with at least five of the newly minted Twelve Steps.

Frank Amos's Story

Frank Amos prepared another contemporary report describing the program of recovery after his visit to Ohio in February 1938. In "Notes on Akron," he identifies seven actions required of a new man adopting the Ohio system for staying sober:

1. An alcoholic must realize that he is an alcoholic, incurable from a medical viewpoint and that he must never again drink anything with alcohol in it;

2. He must surrender himself absolutely to God realizing that in himself there is no hope;

3. Not only must he want to stop drinking permanently, but he must remove from his life other sins such as hatred, adultery and others which frequently accompany alcoholism. Unless he will do this, absolutely, Smith and his associates refuse to work with him.

4. He must have devotions every morning—a "quiet time" of prayer, and some reading from the Bible or other religious literature. Unless this is faithfully followed, there is grave danger of backsliding;

5. He must be willing to help other alcoholics get straightened out. This throws up a barrier and strengthens his own will-power and convictions;

6. It is important, but not vital, that he meet frequently with other reformed alcoholics and form both a social and religious comradeship;

7. Important, but not vital, that he attend some religious service at least weekly.[73]

There is certainly a rough correspondence here between some elements in this system and the later Six and Twelve Step programs of recovery: an admission of defeat, surrender to God, the need for prayer and meditation, and the requirement of working with others. But even these similar-sounding Ohio steps (#1, 2, 4, and 5 above), are delivered in phrases much more strident and directive than anything found in either of Bill's later formulations. In addition, there are several elements here (items #3, 5, and 6 above) that are not found in either the Six or the Twelve Step versions: the absolute requirement to cease sinful acts, the need for regular meetings with other alcoholics, along with a strong suggestion for weekly church attendance. Should another reminder be needed, Amos's report underlines the diverging nature of the Akron and New York programs—significant differences that are reported to be the very essence of the Ohio system just nine months before Bill Wilson sat down and wrote the Twelve Steps.

Members' Stories 1938–1939

The final source of contemporary evidence for the early program of recovery comes from the thirty stories written for the Big Book in late 1938 and 1939. If there actually had been, as Bill claimed, a pretty consistent procedure of Six Steps before December 1938, it would be reasonable to expect those steps to be mentioned—either in whole or in part—in the stories written by sober members during the two months before and the three months immediately after that December. But this is not the case. While making amends and working with others are referred to a few times in those stories, the only Steps that consistently show up throughout these stories are the admission of defeat and the necessity of surrendering your life and your drinking problem to God. In fact, if someone were to just read the stories in the back of the first edition of the Big Book, they would readily and logically conclude that it was the decision to surrender to God which was solely responsible for saving all of these men (and one woman) from their former lives of self-destructive drinking.[*]

But this central and necessary surrender to God doesn't even make an appearance in Bill's reputed Six Steps.

Given Amos's reported Akron requirement that a man "must surrender himself absolutely to God realizing that in himself there is no hope," it comes as no surprise that the Ohio stories are the most explicit on this point. Of the eighteen personal stories they contributed to the book, fully sixteen of them candidly acknowledge a belief in and dependence on God as either the sole or the primary explanation of how they got sober.[**] The sixteen short excerpts below make that point abundantly clear, providing repeated evidence that the admission of powerlessness and a surrender to God—of both your drinking problem and your life—are the two most important elements required of a man who really wants to stop drinking.

> If you think you are an atheist, an agnostic, a skeptic, or have any other form of intellectual pride which keeps you from accepting what is in this book, I feel sorry for you . . . Your Heavenly Father will never let you down! [The Doctor's Nightmare, p. 193]

> "You've been trying man's ways and they always fail," he told me. "You can't win unless you try God's way." . . . That day I gave my will to God and asked to be directed. [The European Drinker, pp. 214 & 215]

> No conviction was necessary to establish my status as a miserable failure at managing my own life. I began to read the Bible daily and to go over a simple devotional exercise as a way to begin each day. Gradually I began to understand. [Traveler, Editor, Scholar, pp. 263-264]

---

[*]   Wilson was later forced to acknowledge this, so much so that the second printing of the first edition (March 1941) included a new Appendix (pp. 399–400) that was later titled, "Spiritual Experience." There he noted that, "Though it was not our intention to create such an impression, many alcoholics have nevertheless concluded that in order to recover they must acquire an immediate and overwhelming 'God-consciousness' followed at once by a vast change in feeling and outlook." This new Appendix then went on, as best it could, to undo that impression.

[**]   This count includes Del Tryon's story, "Ace Full—Seven—Eleven," which was printed in the Multilith edition, but withdrawn before the publication of the Big Book. The two Akron stories that do not specifically mention God's role in their sobriety are "Riding the Rods" [pp. 303–316] by Charlie Simonson and "Fired Again" [pp. 325–31] by Wally Gillam. The first of these emphasizes Fellowship as the critical factor in his recovery and the second only notes that the alcoholics who visited him in the hospital "imparted to me the necessary knowledge and mental tools which have resulted in my complete sobriety."

All my life, he said, I had been doing things of my own human will as opposed to God's will and that the only certain way for me to stop drinking was to submit my will to God and let Him handle my difficulties. *[The Back-Slider, pp. 270-271]*

Spiritually . . . I have found a Friend who never lets me down and is ever eager to help. I can actually take my problems to Him and He does give me comfort, peace, and radiant happiness . . . For all of these blessings, I thank Him. *[Home Brewmeister, p. 281]*

I only know that as long as I seek God's help to the best of my ability, just so long will liquor never bother me. *[The Seven Month Slip, p. 286]*

. . . they were living proof that the sincere attempt to follow the cardinal teachings of Jesus Christ was keeping them sober . . . I acknowledged my fault to God and asked His help to keep to the course I had to follow. *[My Wife and I, p. 295]*

I learned the secret. They had a religious experience. I was willing, and renewed my acquaintance with God and acknowledged Him as a reality. I found it easy. I came to life and have been free now for two years. I hope never to take another drink. *[A Ward of the Probate Court, p. 301]*

But if friends and fellowship were to disappear tomorrow I don't think I would be dismayed. Back of all that there is the knowledge that I have a Divine Father—that as long as I try to walk as He has laid down for me to do throughout my life, nothing of ill can befall me, that if I wish I can be sober for the rest of my life. *[Ace Full—Seven—Eleven, Multilith Printing, Personal Stories, p. 65]*

They made it very plain that I had to seek God, that I had to state my case to Him and ask for help . . . Every morning I read a part of the Bible and ask God to carry me through the day safely . . . I've been sober for two years, kept that way by submitting my natural will to the Higher Power and this is all there is to it. *[The Salesman, pp. 322-323]*

And it was so simple. The sum and substance of it seemed to be that if I would turn to God, it was very probable that He could do a better job with my life than I had. *[The Fearful One, p. 334]*

Are you right with the Father who knows your needs before you ask? If so . . . your help comes from an ever present and all powerful Father. *[Truth Freed Me!, p. 338]*

I feel that the combined effort of these three Christian gentlemen made it possible for me to have a vital spiritual experience. *[A Close Shave, p. 349]*

Why not avail myself of this all wise, ever-present help?

This I did. I ask for, accept, and acknowledge this help, and know that so long as I do, I shall never take a drink and what is more important, though impossible without the first, all other phases of my life have been helped.

There is, it seems to me, four steps to be taken by one who is a victim of alcoholism.

First: Have a real desire to quit.

Second: Admit you can't. (This is hardest.)

Third: Ask for His ever present help.

Fourth: Accept and acknowledge this help. *[The Car Smasher, p. 367]*

Since giving my husband's problem to God I have found peace and happiness . . . My husband and I now talk over our problems and trust in a Divine Power. We have now started to live. When we live with God we want for nothing. *[An Alcoholic's Wife, p. 379]*

A religious awakening was conveyed to me through some unseen force . . . I have found a new life and I know as long as I do the few things that God requires of me to do, I never will take another drink. *[The Rolling Stone, p. 390]*

The New Yorkers, despite their vaunted reputation for greater skepticism, were only slightly less demonstrative in their stories about the centrality of God's role in their remarkable recoveries. In addition to Bill's own story, ten of the other twelve East Coast stories make this claim explicitly.*

He raised my hopes so high, it looked as though he had something. I don't know, I guess I was so sold that I expected him to spring some kind of a pill and I asked him desperately what it was. And he said "God." And I laughed. *[six pages later]* Brrr, this floor is cold on my knees . . . why are the tears running down my cheeks . . . God have mercy on my soul. *[The Unbeliever, pp. 199 & 205]*

. . . are you willing to give up? Are you willing to say: "Here it is God, all mixed up. I don't know how to un-mix it, I'll leave it to you." *[A Feminine Victory, p. 221]*

"The thing I do is to say 'God here I am and here are all my troubles. I've made a mess of things and can't do anything about it. You take me, and all my troubles, and do anything you want with me.' *[Our Southern Friend, p. 237]*

---

* The two New York stories that did not reference God in any way were "A Different Slant" [pp. 252–53] by Harry Brick and "Hindsight" [pp. 370–74] by Myron Williams. The first of these does not even fill two pages and, at less than 400 words, is the shortest story in the first edition of the book. Myron's story only says, "What I heard was hard to believe but I wanted to believe it. What's more I wanted to try it and see if it wouldn't work for me. It worked and is still working."

. . . it had never occurred to me that He, in His Infinite Wisdom knew much better than I what I should have, and be, and do, and that if I simply turned the decision over to Him, I would be led along the right path. *[A Business Man's Recovery, p. 249]*

From that day I gave and still give and always will, time everyday to read the word of God and let Him do all the caring. Who am I to try to run myself or anyone else? *[Smile with Me, at Me, p. 347]*

A belief in the basic spirituality of life has grown and with it belief in a supreme and guiding power for good . . . The first step I took when I admitted to myself for the first time that all my previous thinking might be wrong. The second step came when I first consciously wished to believe. *[Educated Agnostic, p. 355]*

Then the next day a fine fellow came, and in a halting but effective way, told how he had placed himself in God's hand and keeping. Almost before I knew it, I was asking God to clean me up. *[Another Prodigal Story, p. 361]*

I should not be surprised to find myself coming to the astounding conclusion that God, whoever or whatever He may be, is eminently more capable of running this universe than I am. At last I believe I am on my way. *[On His Way, p. 377]*

These men were thinking straight . . . had given themselves, *their minds*, over to a higher power for *direction* . . . The day I made my first efforts in this direction an entire new world opened up for me. Drinking as a vicious habit was washed completely out of my consciousness. *[An Artist's Concept, p. 385]*

I knew that the only way to combat this curse was to ask the help of that greater Power, God . . . God is my only chance. *[Lone Endeavor, p. 395]*

A Loose and Simple Path to Sobriety

This constant and uniform refrain of asking for God's help as the primary solution to the alcohol problem and the lack of any other common, specific steps to be taken to achieve sobriety is overwhelming contemporary evidence that there was no agreed upon and accepted Six Step program before December 1938. Instead, all these reports show members following a very loose and simple path to sobriety, one that might be most easily summarized in three basic steps:

---

* This story of the California man, Pat Cooper, who got sober after reading a copy of the Multilith printing, was actually written by Ruth Hock based on correspondence sent to the Alcoholic Foundation by the newly-sober Cooper and his mother. The New Yorkers were so excited someone had stopped drinking just by reading their book that they famously took up a collection for a bus ticket so that Cooper could come East. But when the bus arrived in New York, Pat didn't get off and he was finally found curled up under the back seat, sleeping off a hangover. His story was withdrawn when the second printing of the book was published in March 1941 (Burwell, "Speech at Hope Manor," p. 17;. Dodd, *The Authors*, p. 51).

1. Admit you're licked

2. Surrender your life to God

3. Act accordingly (i.e. pray, meditate, help others)*

Given this overwhelming evidence regarding the essence of the program of recovery as it was being practiced up until late 1938, Bill Wilson could not have been more correct when he said "a definite statement of concrete principles"[74] absolutely had to be formulated and included in the book, something that the rationalizing alcoholic just couldn't "wiggle out" of it no matter how hard he tried.[75] This was *way* too loose and subject to far too many interpretations to ever be effective. It could hardly even be called a "program of action."

By this time the point should be abundantly clear. Other than the references scattered throughout "Bill's Story," the reputed Six Steps receive no significant mention in any of the other thirty stories written for the Big Book. This universal silence is surely an "absence of evidence," but it is so uniform and so overwhelming that Bill's claim of a more sophisticated Six Step word of mouth program is revealed to be a fiction—one he created to avoid acknowledging that the Twelve Steps were based almost exclusively on his own experience.

An Inspired Event

Despite all these controversies and quibbles, there is no denying that Bill Wilson created something important, unique, and profound in early December 1938. His Twelve Steps have not only helped millions of people stop drinking since that time, they have also served as the foundational principles for scores of other life-saving recovery programs worldwide. Whatever the circumstances and whatever the source, Bill Wilson's Twelve Steps are revolutionary in their simplicity, their clarity and their effectiveness. Given the confusing and contradictory conditions under which he labored, it was an accomplishment so amazing that many people have agreed with Wilson's later observation that the creation of the Twelve Steps was a truly inspired event. Others claim Bill's formulation of this intensely spiritual set of suggestions as a program of recovery was nothing short of miraculous. And, indeed, for a man who was still several days short of celebrating his fourth year of sobriety, it *was* nothing less than a miracle.

The "Original" Twelve Steps

Bill's first draft of the Steps has been lost, so any attempt to reconstruct how they might have read in their original unedited form involves a fair amount of speculation. Still, if we presume that Wilson's first version was, as he said, "a set of specific directions,

---

*   Jim Burwell confirmed this simple Three Step program in his 1947 talk at Hope Manor: "First of all, you had to place your power in God completely, right now and not tomorrow morning. That was No. 1 . . . So the first step was believing in God. The second step was admitting that you had trouble with alcohol. The third step was catharsis. It was very broad." (Burwell, "Speech at Hope Manor," p. 13) The Webster's definition of catharsis is "a purification or purgation of emotions that brings about spiritual renewal or release from tension."

a definite statement of concrete principles that these drunks just couldn't wiggle out of,"[76] then it is logical to presume they would have been couched in some very directive language, the same kind of language found throughout the Multilith printing of the book produced just two-and-a-half months later. Assuming that change in voice and tone, it is possible to start with the Twelve Steps as they appear in the Multilith printing and reverse engineer them by deleting the few changes Bill said were later made to his first draft. Such a change in voice coupled with the delete-and-restore procedure produces a version of the 'original' Twelve Steps that would likely reads something very close to this:

1. Admit you are powerless over alcohol — that your life has become unmanageable.

2. Come to believe that God could restore you to sanity.

3. Surrender your will and your life over to the care and direction of God.*

4. Make a searching and fearless moral inventory of yourself.

5. Admit to God, to yourself, and to another human being the exact nature of your wrongs.

6. Be entirely willing for God to remove all your defects of character.

7. Humbly, on your knees, ask God to remove your shortcomings — holding nothing back.

8. Make a list of all persons you have harmed, and become willing to make complete amends to them all.

9. Make direct amends to such people wherever possible, except when to do so would injure them or others.

10. Continue to take personal inventory and when you are wrong promptly admit it.

11. Seek through prayer and meditation to improve your contact with God, praying only for knowledge of His will for you and the power to carry that out.

12. Having had a spiritual experience as the result of this course of action, try to carry this message to others, especially alcoholics, and to practice these principles in all your affairs.

With this new radical outline in hand, Bill now had to sell it to the rest of the A.A. members—not just to those in New York who were so deeply divided over the religion vs. psychology controversy, but also to the profoundly religious members of the Oxford Group's "Alcoholic Squad" out in Ohio.

---

*   Ernest Kurtz speculates that this step originally said: "Made a decision to *surrender* our will and our lives . . . " (*Not-God*, p. 331, n. 34) and it might have been as simply phrased as "Surrendered our will and our lives to the care and direction of God."

CHAPTER TWENTY-FOUR

Editing Bill's Steps

~December 1938~

According to Bill, he didn't have long to wait before he encountered the first negative reaction to his brilliant new formulation of their program of recovery. Just minutes after the Twelve Steps were written, he said he walked downstairs and discovered some strong resistance already waiting for him in the kitchen.

> At this moment a couple of late callers arrived. One of them was my boon companion of those days, Howard A. With him was a newcomer, dry barely three months. I was greatly pleased with what I had written, and I read them the new version of the program, now the "Twelve Steps." Howard and his friend reacted violently. "Why twelve steps?" they demanded. And then, "You've got too much God in these steps; you will scare people away." And, "What do you mean by getting those drunks down 'on their knees' when they ask to have all their shortcomings removed?" And, "Who wants all their short-comings removed, anyhow?" As he saw my uneasiness, Howard added, "Well, some of this stuff does sound pretty good after all. But, Bill, you've got to tone it down. It's too stiff. The average alcoholic just won't buy it the way it stands."[1]

The Arguments Over Religion vs. Psychology

The exact identity of this "Howard A." has proven to be a real mystery,* casting some doubt on Bill's recollection of the entire exchange; but whatever the truth might be

---

* The only known sober A.A. named Howard before 1939 was Dr. Howard Searl, an Akron member who stopped drinking in January 1937. (See Frank Amos's detailed mention of him in the February 1938, "Notes on Akron / Ohio Survey," p. 1.) *Pass It On*

about this particular encounter, Wilson's presentation of the Twelve Steps did touch off a wave of arguments in New York. His succinct formulation of "the steps we took, which are suggested as your Program of Recovery"[2] quickly brought to a head all the resentments that had been quietly festering just below the surface between those New York members who wanted the book to be a powerfully religious document and those who thought it should be a psychological book.[3] Bill had complained to Dr. Bob just one month earlier that he was finding it "pretty hard to get people to voice their real opinions, as they are too much afraid of hurting the author's feelings,"[4] but all that changed in December. The Twelve Steps were the catalyst that dragged all of those long simmering disagreements over religion, spirituality, and belief out into the open where they could no longer be ignored.

A.A. mythology claims that these loud and contentious arguments dominated the Tuesday night meetings in Brooklyn throughout the month of December, but that was not the case. The disagreements that did arise at those meetings were of the more genteel sort already mentioned here as members made relatively minor suggestions for changes they thought Bill should make to what he was writing for the book. Striking testimony to the relative civility of these discussions comes from Tom Birrell, who was a newcomer when he attended the New York weekly gatherings in late-November and December 1938. In a talk recorded years later, Tom supplied some lively and colorful details about what happened at those important meetings.

> . . . after the meatballs and spaghetti or whatever we had, this same tall, lanky guy [Bill Wilson] came out of the dining room with a legal pad and he sprawled out on the floor with his back to the folding doors and he started to read what he had written on this legal pad—and that was one of the chapters of the Big Book. And, of course, it made little or no sense to me at the time, maybe I was too fogged up or didn't get the full significance of this thing, but, at any rate, I listened while these folks wrangled: "change a comma here," "a question mark here." One said "You don't put that in, put this in" and finally the meeting was ended.[5]*

---

has a footnote on p. 206 claiming that this Howard A. was really Horace C. and that Bill used a pseudonym here because of a dispute between them and he "did not wish to offend [Horace C.] by using his name." While this would be true of the "Howard" mentioned on pp. 186 and 192 of *AACOA* (the facts there perfectly correspond to Horace Chrystal's A.A. Board activities during those times), the mention on p. 161 does not match up at all with what we know of the man. Most especially, Horace wasn't even sober on the day the Steps were written. He didn't stop drinking until December 16, 1938, at least two weeks after Bill wrote them. (See Horace Chrystal's Questionnaire, GSO, Box 59, 1938, Folder B[1], Document 1938-198 that has this as the date of his sobriety and also the second unnumbered document in GSO, Box 59, 1939, Folder C which lists his sobriety date as December 1938.). This leaves no obvious candidate for who this late night visitor, "Howard A.," might have actually been although he does sound suspiciously like Hank Parkhurst who had certainly been Bill's "boon companion of those days."

* Birrell says he attended "four, five, or six" meetings in a row before drinking again on December 23, 1938, which would put his earliest attendance at a meeting in Brooklyn on the fifteenth of November (or possibly the twenty-second or the twenty-ninth of that month if the "four, five" count are more accurate). Tom only drank again for four weeks before getting permanently sober on January 16, 1939, after which he went on to play several prominent and important roles in A.A.'s early years. Note that this talk, while occasionally leaning on *AACOA* for some incorrect details, provides a wealth of very specific and colorful information about A.A.'s early years that could only be supplied by a man who was actually there at the time.

This picture of Bill sprawled out on the floor* as he reads aloud from a hand-written yellow legal pad is the most captivating and compelling image we have of the group participation in the editing of the Big Book. Birrell's story of those December nights puts the listener right in the room with Wilson and the other A.A. members as they try to fine-tune their message for getting people sober all across the country.

Since eight of the ten expositional chapters had already been written by this time, Bill could only have been reading from his rough drafts of "How It Works" and "Into Action," the two chapters which explain in detail what was involved in actually working the Twelve Steps. Listening to this, the Clinton Street members "wrangled" over commas, question marks, and made some suggestions for revisions to the text. It is an appealing picture, but hardly the legendary fights— "we fought, bled and died our way through one chapter after another"[6]—so often depicted in later recountings.**

There definitely *were* big fights, first over the Twelve Steps, and then about the way Bill was explaining them in the two final chapters he was creating for the book. But those loud and contentious arguments took place at the Honor Dealers office over in Newark, not at the meetings in Brooklyn. As Ruth Hock later noted, the major changes made to the Steps and the book were "fought out in the office when you and Hank and Fitz and I were present."[7]*** Rather than arguing publicly at the weekly meeting, Bill, Hank, and Fitz had wisely decided to have it out in private at the Honor Dealers office, where they could be as combative and confrontational as they liked without fear of splitting the New York group into openly warring factions. Jim Burwell consistently claimed it was "the trio" of Bill Wilson, Hank Parkhurst, and Fitz Mayo who ran A.A. during these early days,**** and Ruth's testimony about these arguments in Newark certainly lends some credibility to that observation.

Fitz Loses the Argument for a Religious Approach

It was there that Fitz, who "made constant journeys to New York in order to reinforce the conservative position,"[8] pled his case for a specifically Christian book. The foundations of Fitz's own recovery were deeply religious (specifically Episcopalian) and he insisted that their program of recovery had to be explained using Biblical terminology and presented as a "doctrinal" and explicitly Christian solution to alcoholism. This approach

---

* Yet another eyewitness report of Wilson's casual demeanor when among friends bears additional testimony to Henrietta Seiberling's previously noted critical observation that Bill was "never standing when he could sit, and never sitting when he could lie down" (Ernest Kurtz in private correspondence with the author on September 16, 2011, quoting from his April 6, 1976 interview with Henrietta Seiberling. For a published reference to that interview, see Kurtz, *Not-God*, p. 315, n. 63).

** Bill Wilson was the primary source for these stories as noted above and in many other comments such as his claim that "when [the Twelve Steps] were presented to the meeting a few days later at Clinton Street, all hell broke loose. This was heresy, we'd done fine on six, why twelve?" (AA Main Events, 1938, Point 22). Jim Burwell's many talks also contributed much to this misinformation. For instance, speaking in San Diego on June 15, 1957, he said that "Bill would read [the chapters] to us. We'd all take shots at it. 'Well, this thing ought to be changed, that ought to be changed.' So every word in that wordage of the book there was culled, double culled, by alcoholic 'lawyers,' every loophole [investigated and closed]." (29:08 to 29:23; https://www.youtube.com/watch?v=ZzZYvaLy52o—retrieved December 19, 2015).

*** Bill supported Ruth's contention that these arguments took place in Newark, noting that "Present were Fitz, Henry, our grand Secretary Ruth and myself. We were still arguing over the Twelve Steps . . ." (Hunter et al., *Women Pioneers*, p. 81.)

**** Burwell makes five specific mentions of "the trio" being the decision-making body in early A.A. in his "The Evolution of Alcoholics Anonymous" —claiming that together they decided to quit the Oxford Group, write a book, and then publish it themselves. However, questionable some of those claims may be (Fitz is otherwise never specifically mentioned in relation to the book decisions), these Newark discussions do provide at least some supporting evidence for Jim's claim.

found some support among a few other New York members (Bill specifically mentions Paul Kellogg who "was even more emphatic [than Fitz] about this"[9]) and it was surely what most of the "Alcoholic Squad" in Akron would have expected to find in any book explaining how they got sober.

But however vehemently Fitz may have argued for his position, Bill Wilson had already made all the concessions he was going to make in the direction of a purely Christian solution for alcoholism. Such a specifically religious approach was almost universally recognized by A.A. members as the very thing that had thwarted the missions in all their past efforts to save drunks. At least on this point, Wilson was in complete agreement with the largest contingent in the New York group, who had no problem at all with the use of the term God throughout the book, but who were "dead set" against any "theological propositions" or religious doctrines being mentioned.[10] While, at this time, the suggested road to recovery included a regular habit of reading the New Testament,[11] Bill clearly recognized that such a specifically Christian emphasis would sabotage any hope they might have of successfully reaching out to agnostics and atheists, not to mention the problems it would cause for both Catholics and Jews.

Exactly what Bill might have said to placate Fitz Mayo on these issues is not known, but then no one ever described Fitz as a great debater or as a man who was comfortable fighting for his own perspective. Instead, Mayo was regularly characterized as "one of the most lovable people that A.A. will ever know"[12] and as "a charming, aesthetic, impractical, lovable dreamer."[13] In fact, his personality was the exact opposite of Hank Parkhurst's, so it seems a bit unfair to learn that Bill more or less threw Fitz to the wolves by letting Hank act as his proxy in this fight. While his two primary colleagues battled, Wilson sat back and watched as Parkhurst and Mayo engaged in "a hot argument . . . about the religious content of the coming volume."[14] It was a fight Fitz had no hope of winning.

Hank Loses the Argument to Completely Remove God from the Steps

On the other hand, Bill's arguments with the much more confrontational Henry Parkhurst were so loud and antagonistic that they could not escape later comment: "A terrific argument ensued between Hank and me,"[15] Wilson said, and it seemed to last forever—the "heated discussion went on for days and nights."[16] Hank had absolutely no intention of conceding he might be wrong about what he wanted. Once Fitz's pleas for a Christian book had been successfully demolished, Parkhurst began to attack Wilson for his constant, explicit references to God in both the Steps and throughout the book. He was convinced this would not only drive people away from their solution, but even worse, destroy any hope of the book being a best seller. Despite the fact that so much was already written, Hank still had not given up hope that they would publish a psychological book, one that "would lure the alcoholic in" and that "once in, the prospect could take God or leave Him alone as he wished." Bill found this to be a shocking proposal and refused to even consider it.[17]

Wilson justified his inclusion of these frequent references to God by citing his personal experience: "I'd had this very sudden experience and was on the pious side,

[so] I'd larded these Steps very heavily with the word 'God,'"[18]* Doing so made perfect sense to Bill (and was in keeping with his penchant for relying primarily on his own experience), but Hank would have none of it and they raged against each other in a fierce running battle—Wilson called it a "perfectly ferocious argument"[19]—in which neither man was willing to concede an inch of ground to the other.

Finally, after a "hellish fight,"[20] Hank realized there was no hope of convincing Bill all of these references to God should be removed from the Steps and he adopted a fallback position: 'Could we, at least,' he argued, 'get rid of this demand that people get down on their knees in the Seventh Step and then tone down the rest of this religious language by using some more general, less theologically specific synonyms for the word "God"?' Parkhurst proposed using "Higher Power" and "a Power greater than ourselves" as general, open-ended substitutes and suggested that the first appearance of the word "God" be followed by the more expansive and explicitly flexible phrase "as we understood Him."[21]

Besides arguing that they needed to provide some way for agnostic and atheist alcoholics to find an entry point into the steps, Hank's strongest contention for these changes would have been the fact that Bill had already used the phrases "power greater than myself" and "God, as I then understood Him" in his own "Story."[22] If these beliefs and perspectives had been so essential to Wilson's own recovery, why shouldn't they be offering that same level of openness to all the new people who were trying so desperately to get sober?

Bill did not want to change anything in the steps, and even in the face of Hank's constant and aggressive onslaught, he absolutely "refused to budge on this."[23] Weren't they, after all, perfect just the way he had first written them? In late June, Bill had told Dr. Bob Smith he was "not suffering . . . from any pride of authorship,"[24] but that was definitely not the case six months later. Wilson was firmly entrenched in defending the Steps exactly as he had created them and he "heavily resisted these objections"[25] on every front. Bill was not about to change a single word. (So much for the 'I was just an umpire' claim that he later made with such regularity.)

Besides, having successfully resisted the changes Fitz Mayo wanted to make, how could he possibly capitulate to Hank Parkhurst and include these more liberal phrases?

Bill Finally Concedes Some Changes

But Hank just would not give up, and after days of arguing and badgering, Bill Wilson finally began to weaken. He later admitted rather sheepishly that "it took a bit of persuasion," but Parkhurst's relentless insistence that they had to soften some of the God talk was wearing him down and he finally conceded "very grudgingly" to make at least some of the suggested changes.[26] Bill doggedly refused to take out the need for people to get down on their knees in the Seventh Step (that particular requirement would not be deleted until three months later when, after several more weeks of acrimonious fighting, he finally and "very reluctantly . . . took that phrase out"[27]). But

---

* This is another, though less explicit, admission by Wilson that the Twelve Steps were mainly based on his own experience rather than the collective experience of the group.

he did agree to use the phrase "a Power greater than ourselves" rather than "God" in the Second Step, and to add "as we understood Him" after the word "God" in the Third Step (but not to the Eleventh Step where it would not appear until four months later).

That was absolutely as far as Wilson was willing to go.

He had fought tenaciously and valiantly, but Bill was not particularly gracious in defeat. It clearly pained him to make these concessions, but he "finally went along,"[28] all the while defending his view that the original Steps were perfect. It would take some time before Wilson realized and acknowledged how critical these phrases were to their success and finally conceded that Hank Parkhurst had been right—especially about his insistence on adding "as we understood Him" to the Third Step. But Bill was always stubbornly proud of the fact that these modifications were the "only change[s] in the Twelve Steps as written"[29] and that "there were no other changes in the original draft."[30] They were, he claimed, *almost* perfect just as he had first written them.

However, when Bill did finally realize how important these changes were, he enthusiastically embraced them, calling them a "terrific ten-strike,"[31]* noting that "as we understood Him" was "perhaps the most important expression to be found in our whole AA vocabulary."[32] That and the phrase "Higher Power," he said, "have proved lifesavers for many an alcoholic. They have enabled thousands of us to make a beginning where none could have been made had we left the Steps just as I originally wrote them."[33] Most especially, he acknowledged that adding the phrase "as we understood Him" to the Third Step had made "a hoop big enough so that the whole world of alcoholics can walk through it."[34] It was a change that "enabled people of fine religious training and those of none at all to associate freely and to work together. It made one's religion the business of the A.A. member himself and not that of his society."[35] A ten-strike indeed.

The Origin of "God as We Understood Him" in Question

Wilson hardly exaggerates when he notes that "God as we understood Him" is perhaps the most important expression to be found in A.A.'s lexicon. That short phrase has made membership in A.A. possible for millions of people who otherwise would have never been able to cross over its threshold into sobriety.

So who was responsible for the addition of this critically important phrase?

Jim Burwell always claimed credit for adding "as we understood Him" to the Steps. His earliest recorded statement on this came in a talk he gave in March of 1947:

> . . . Then we took the God. This is about the only thing I have given to this thing. I said, "Bill, I am agnostic." We had quite a tussle. I had been staying sober. So had Hank. After a time we decide to put in there "as you see it," which in my estimation is right because you are not putting pressure on them. It was the only way I could do it.[36]

A year or so later Jim heavily revised that speech into his "Evolution of Alcoholics Anonymous," which noted simply that "after days of wrangling between Bill, Hank,

---

* The phrase refers to a perfectly thrown bowling ball, which knocks down all ten pins at one time.

Fitz and myself . . . another thing changed in this last rewriting [and that] was qualifying the word God with the phrase 'as we understand Him.' (This was one of my few contributions to the book.)" Then in 1955, when his story "The Vicious Cycle" made its first appearance in the second edition of the Big Book, he made the same claim about making this "contribution to their literary efforts."[37]

It is interesting and important to note that in none of these instances does Jim ever claim he invented the phrase "as we understood Him." Burwell just says he was the one who insisted it be added to the Third Step so that atheists and agnostics would have some flexibility in interpreting and then working the suggested program of recovery.

As already noted here, when Bill Wilson wrote the first two versions of his own story the previous May, that phrase had appeared in each of them. In the first, he claimed Ebby had told him to "turn my face to God as I understand Him" as the first step in his recovery[38] and in the second, while describing the early steps he took, Wilson said "I humbly offered myself to God as I then understood Him."[39] Since this second version of "Bill's Story" had been widely circulated during the previous six months, Burwell could hardly say he had invented this "most important expression to be found" in the A.A. vocabulary. But he did unequivocally claim that inserting that phrase into the Third Step was his own contribution to the Steps.

While Jim's claim has never been publicly challenged, there is some interesting private correspondence between Ruth Hock and Bill Wilson in 1955 calling Burwell's claim into serious question. Before she wrote her often-quoted letter of November 10, 1955, Ruth and Bill had already exchanged three letters in which he asked her to help clarify some historical details for him. One of the questions he asked was about Jim's alleged responsibility for suggesting they put "as we understood Him" into the steps. According to his own recollections, Wilson said:

> Finally, we had a big hassle in the Newark office between, as I remember, Hank, Fitz, you and me. Fitz was for more God and more theology— Hank was for little or none at all. The result of this argument was the phrase, "God as we understand Him" which was, of course, a ten-strike. Whether or not Jimmy Burwell was present, I can't remember. In a historical piece he wrote about this period, he claimed he had great influence on the Twelve Steps. I certainly think he had some because of his agnosticism, but whether it was direct or not, I can't remember.[40]

Two weeks later, Ruth's reply supported Bill's memory of those events.

> . . . the few things you mentioned basically agree with things as I remember them, but I'll be darned if I can remember that Jim Burwell ever took any active part in any of the writing of the book or the 12 steps or the name of the book. Certainly, he was never in on any of the office conferences that I remember although he undoubtedly had an effect through the endless discussion that went on at meetings and homes as did everyone who came to meetings at that time . . . [41]

Jim claimed that he, Bill, Hank, and Fitz had wrangled for days over these issues—almost certainly in the Newark office—but Ruth contradicted this emphatically in her letter. Bill was pleased to learn Ruth's recollections matched his own.

> I was most happy for your testimony about Jim Burwell's part in the early days. In my own mind, I've gone overboard to give him credit. The story he wrote up about the early days was printed,* you may know, and it has considerable circulation out on the [West] Coast where he now is. In a way, I suppose all our recollections are suspect . . .[42]

In short, 'I don't remember it the way Jim does (and I am pleased to hear that your memories are the same as mine), but I can hardly call him out on this issue since he has made these claims so publicly.' Bill, ever the politician (and well aware of Burwell's singular status as one of the very few early members still alive and sober in 1955), felt compelled to support Jim in his claim—or at least, not to contradict him—no matter what his own memory of the facts might be. For instance, five years later we find him making one of his typical statements about this, giving Jim credit by telling an audience that "this expression [was] coined, I think, by one of our former atheist members."[43] The "I think" was Wilson's not so subtle way of noting the questionability of that claim as once again he directed attention away from himself.

The key question Bill had asked Ruth was whether or not Jim had any direct input into this decision and neither of them could remember him being present or participating in the Newark arguments where that famous compromise was made. But both of them did allow that Burwell likely had some significant *indirect* impact on the steps, with Bill noting, "I certainly think he had some [influence] because of his agnosticism," and Ruth conceding he "undoubtedly had an effect through the endless discussions that went on at meetings and homes." While Jim clearly believed his own version of the story, the truth likely falls much closer to what Bill and Ruth remembered.

However, this is not to say that Jim Burwell did not have some substantial indirect responsibility for the inclusion of "as we understood Him" in the Steps—but only to question some details in his own version of the story. It is highly probable, for instance, that Jim's participation in this decision occurred not only in the regular Tuesday night meetings (where such things were discussed in a relatively calm fashion)—and perhaps even one-on-one with Bill Wilson before or afterwards—but also in the more insistent discussions held at the Parkhurst house in Montclair where Burwell was staying at the time.[44] Living there gave Jim many opportunities to badger Hank about the need to tone down "the God stuff" and to constantly reinforce Parkhurst's own belief that less religious language should be used in the Steps. Hank would have been using Jim's intransience on this issue as a foil to support his own arguments with Bill over the need to make at least some concessions in the steps to accommodate those drinkers who were theologically challenged. Bill later admitted as much by noting that Hank "argued, he begged he threatened. He quoted Jimmy to back him up."[45]

---

* Bill is referring here to Jim's "The Evolution of Alcoholics Anonymous, a history of A.A."

While all the available evidence supports the fact that Hank Parkhurst was the one making the forceful arguments for the inclusion of "as we understood Him' into the steps, he was driven to such stridency by the constant harassment of the long-term guest at his home back in Montclair, Jim Burwell.

Akron's Late Review of the Steps in Chapter Five

There is a final question of interest that needs to be addressed: What influence and impact did Akron have on the formulation of these Twelve Steps?

Over the years, Bill Wilson made starkly contradictory statements about Ohio's participation in reviewing and critiquing the Twelve Steps. In one talk he said, "out in Akron they kind of went along with it,"[46] while in another he noted "out in Akron, the drunks ripped them Twelve Steps all in small pieces."[47] In his usual inaccurate fashion, Bill was likely referring to different timeframes, or perhaps to different people's reactions. Whatever the case might be, on the face of it these two comments are impossible to reconcile without much more contemporary information.

In his 1957 book, *Alcoholics Anonymous Comes of Age*, Bill claimed that both Paul and Dick Stanley saw the Twelve Steps early on and they both "liked the new steps very much." But the Stanley brothers could not have seen the Steps until sometime after the middle of December 1938. Like everyone else in Ohio, they had to wait for Bill to finish writing Chapters Five and Six ("How It Works" and "Into Action") before they would be given the opportunity to review the new Steps. By that time, the number and most of the wording in them were almost a foregone conclusion.

Indisputable evidence for this late arrival of the Steps in Ohio comes from Bill Wilson's December 13 letter to Dr. Bob Smith in which he addresses several issues, but which makes it clear they have not spoken or otherwise communicated since they had last talked on Bill's birthday, November 26.

> Dear Bob:
>
> You have probably already heard from Frank [Amos]. The matter required Mr. Richardson's signature and it was his secretary who messed up the play by throwing your little document into her wastebasket. Frank tells me he has sent you another.
>
> But it was so wonderful to have your phone call followed by all those telegrams. Not a one had come in at the time I heard your voice over the wire, but they piled in soon after in quantity. I wish I had the addresses of all those who sent them so I could acknowledge every one. But I certainly do want to thank you and all the rest of the folks so much and I hope you will be sure that every single one knows how I appreciated those wires. It's the kind of thing that makes you think life is worthwhile.
>
> God bless you all for thinking of me.

On the book, we are going hell bent for election. It is practically complete, and I will send you the rest of the chapters within two or three days.

Next step is to make, after one editing, photolithic* copies of the whole works. There will be plenty of copies for everyone and then there will be no excuse for people not saying what they think. Or, as the wedding ceremony says, "Forever hold thy peace."

The money situation is not too bad, but it could be an awful lot better. Nothing to worry about right at this minute.

Don't think I shall be able to get out there for two or three weeks. Send in what stories you have.

Thanks once more for the birthday greetings. They put up a lot of heart in me.

Yours,

Bill[48]

Bob and the rest of the Akron members were going to see the two final chapters of the book as soon as they were completed, but since they wouldn't be ready for mailing for another "two or three days," the earliest they could have arrived in Ohio was December 17 or 18. Once there, they would be shown to the people Bob had decided were most favorable to the book project, as opposed to those who condemned it out of hand. Among that select group were the Stanleys, who Bill said "continued to report their approval" once "the remainder of the book text [was] developed, based on the Twelve Steps."[49]

Whenever those chapters did arrive in Ohio, they caused a stir among the folks who read them. Clarence Snyder's wife, Dorothy, recalled: "I'll never forget the time the fifth chapter came out . . . *Our* fifth chapter. I was staying all night with the Smiths, and Anne and I sat up, and we read the thing until four in the morning. And we thought, 'Now, this is it. This is really going to bring people in.'"[50] Unfortunately Dorothy fails to mention exactly where Clarence and Dr. Bob might have been that night or what they thought of the new chapter and of the Twelve Steps.

But Akron's real chance to review this new material wouldn't come until after "the whole works" had been professionally edited and Multilith copies of the book had been printed up for general distribution to all the A.A. members. Once that happened, the Ohio members who were still firmly attached to the Oxford Group were not pleased. They were "disappointed" that "there was no mention of the Oxford Group in the book" and that "the Twelve Steps had replaced the four absolutes, which were not mentioned either."[51] It was certainly not an unexpected response, and is one that lingers in Akron right up until the present day.

---

*   The printing process used for making the Multilith trial edition of the book is sometimes called "photolithic" (as here) and also "mimeograph" in other contemporary correspondence.

The Evangelical Approach of the Original Twelfth Step

While further changes would be made to the Twelve Steps as they neared their final publication date on April 10, 1939 (and even beyond that point), one striking feature of Bill Wilson's original version received little comment at the time and in later writings about the Steps. As "the trio" focused their fight on Bill's insistence that people kneel down to ask for the removal of their shortcomings, and on the advisability of using less religious substitutes for the word "God," no objections seem to have been raised about the universal evangelical approach that was explicitly advocated in Wilson's final Step.

As Bill first wrote it, the Twelfth Step said: "Having had a spiritual experience as the result of this course of action, we tried to carry this message to others, especially alcoholics, and to practice these principles in all our affairs." The idea that this "spiritual experience" (i.e., the direct result of working the steps) could then be spread not only to alcoholics, but also to all "others," was a lingering remnant of the Oxford Group's overarching goal of expanding until they had revolutionized American society—and eventually the rest of the world.

While the need to practice these principles in all their affairs was something under the direct control of each individual, the plan to also carry this message of spiritual awakening to non-alcoholics is ambitious in the extreme. It harkens back strongly to the sentiments Bill once described as overwhelming them during the "counting noses" meeting in Akron in October 1937.

> Once this spectacular notion [of rapid growth] gripped us, our thinking underwent a sudden change. Our alcoholic imaginations certainly had a field day. By temperament most of us are salesmen, promoters. So we began talking very big. Mere boxcar numbers wouldn't do. We went astronomical. Undoubtedly, we said, this was the beginning of one of the greatest medical, religious and social developments of all time. We would show the medical profession and the sky pilots where they got off! A million alcoholics in America; more millions all over the world! Why, we only had to sober up all these boys and girls (and sell them God) whereupon they would revolutionize society. A brand new world with ex-drunks running it. Just think of that, folks![52]

Wilson was a man of vision, and as he looked into the future he saw the possibility of Alcoholics Anonymous not only impacting drunks all across the country, but also a majority of the population that had no problem whatsoever with their drinking.

This was pure late-1930s Bill Wilson. Fortunately, the phrase "to others, especially alcoholics" was changed to include only alcoholics before the Steps saw the full light of day in the published version of the book.

CHAPTER TWENTY-FIVE

"How It Works" and "Into Action"

~December 1938~

Once Bill had solidified his position as the "umpire"—which in reality meant that, despite protests from both sides of the spiritual aisle in the New York group, he kept the Twelve Steps almost exactly as he had written them—he began to use the Steps as a ready-made outline for what would become the two central chapters of the book: "How It Works" and "Into Action." These were written, edited, and polished throughout December and then, near the end of the month, added to the manuscript, completing the first draft of the book.

"How It Works": Steps One through Four

The opening two and a half pages of "How It Works"—which contain the essence of the Alcoholics Anonymous program—are read at the beginning of most A.A. meetings worldwide. In fact, members hear them so often that their full meaning and significance can easily be lost in the endless repetition. This is unfortunate because, however stilted the language may occasionally sound to twenty-first-century ears, what Bill Wilson crafted in their final edited form was an attention-grabbing introduction to the steps, followed by a powerful summation of their essential and critical importance for gaining and maintaining sobriety.

However, the earliest available version of "How It Works"—the one found in the Multilith printing of mid-February 1939—is significantly different from what gets read at A.A. meetings today. In that earlier opening, the language is far more directive and the overall tone might even be described as officious. Here, Bill's constant use of the pronoun "you" (rather than the later "we") is so pervasive that the introduction sounds more like a strident sermon than a friendly announcement of a new solution for alcoholism. Wilson's writing is so preachy and autocratic that it all but begs for the later edits which significantly softened this harsh and insistent tone.

In the Multilith printing of the book, Bill begins the chapter with a clarion call to action, trying to impress the alcoholic with how important it is for him to be totally committed to the actions called for in the Steps that will follow. He promises the drinker that if he is dedicated, and conscientiously follows them, he will almost surely succeed for, "Rarely have we seen a person fail who has thoroughly followed our directions."[1]*

The Three Ingredients for Success

Having opened with this dramatic promise, Bill immediately goes on to warn the reader about the single greatest obstacle facing anyone who is trying to get sober. While there are a host of barriers he could have mentioned here—pitfalls that regularly sabotage the best efforts of many still-suffering alcoholics (family relations, financial problems, job issues, unemployment, lack of willingness, peer pressures, agnosticism, and atheism)—Wilson chose instead to focus on just one essential requirement for sobriety: honesty. Bill tells the suffering alcoholic that success is all but assured, but only if the effort is based on a foundation of complete honesty. Any attempt made without rigorous honesty, especially without resolute self-honesty, will almost certainly sabotage the reader's chances for a successful recovery.

> Those who do not recover are people who cannot or will not completely give themselves to this simple program, usually men and women who are constitutionally incapable of being honest with themselves. There are such unfortunates. They are not at fault; they seem to have been born that way. They are naturally incapable of grasping and developing a way of life which demands rigorous honesty. Their chances are less than average. There are those, too, who suffer from grave emotional and mental disorders, but many of them do recover if they have the capacity to be honest.

Even people with severe mental problems—those people Dr. Esther Richards had warned Bill he would never be successful with[2]—are given a fair chance at getting sober, but only if they can be rigorously honest with themselves and about themselves. Wilson forcefully warns the reader that, without this critical ingredient, his "chances are less than average."

Bill then goes on to mention another necessary ingredient for success, pleading for courage and perseverance, telling the reader he must be willing to go to any length in relation to the suggestions he is about to make and begging him "to be fearless and thorough from the very start."

---

* There is a persistent A.A. legend that Bill Wilson once said that if he had to change just one word in the Big Book, he would change this "Rarely" to "Never." But Wilson, ever averse to absolutes, denied this, stating categorically that he "had never considered this change." (*A Summary: Ask-It Basket*, General Service Conference of Alcoholics Anonymous, 1951–1978, p. 46).

Finally, in addition to honesty and courageous follow-through, there is one last essential element the drinker will need if he is to get sober: he must completely surrender himself to God.

> Remember that you are dealing with alcohol—cunning, baffling, powerful! Without help it is too much for you. But there is One who has all power—That One is God. You must find Him now!

> Half measures will avail you nothing. You stand at the turning point. Throw yourself under His protection and care with complete abandon.

The Steps are the Solution

Having outlined the three requirements necessary for success, Bill at last presents the details of the solution promised in the first chapter of the book and while doing so, he transitions from the very directive "you" statements that have so far dominated the opening of this chapter to the more tempered and accessible "we" language found throughout the Twelve Steps.

> Now we think you can take it! Here are the steps we took, which are suggested as your Program of Recovery:

> 1. Admitted we were powerless over alcohol—that our lives had become unmanageable.

> 2. Came to believe that a Power greater than ourselves could restore us to sanity.

> 3. Made a decision to turn our will and our lives over to the care and direction of God as we understood Him.

> 4. Made a searching and fearless moral inventory of ourselves.

> 5. Admitted to God, to ourselves, and to another human being the exact nature of our wrongs.

> 6. Were entirely willing that God remove all these defects of character.

> 7. Humbly, on our knees, asked Him to remove our shortcomings—holding nothing back.

> 8. Made a list of all persons we had harmed, and became willing to make complete amends to them all.

> 9. Made direct amends to such people wherever possible, except when to do so would injure them or others.

> 10. Continued to take personal inventory and when we were wrong promptly admitted it.

11. Sought through prayer and meditation to improve our contact with God, praying only for knowledge of His will for us and the power to carry that out.

12. Having had a spiritual experience as the result of this course of action, we tried to carry this message to others, especially alcoholics, and to practice these principles in all our affairs.

On first reading, such a list would appear overwhelming to anyone trying to get sober. The reader was almost certainly hoping for an easier, softer set of directions and Wilson immediately acknowledges this.

> You may exclaim, "What an order! I can't go through with it." Do not be discouraged. No one among us has been able to maintain anything like perfect adherence to these principles. We are not saints. The point is, that we are willing to grow along spiritual lines. The principles we have set down are guides to progress. We claim spiritual progress rather than spiritual perfection.

Always the pragmatist focused on action and its practical results, Bill immediately follows this first presentation of the program of recovery by underlining the fact that the Twelve Steps are meant to be guides for an ongoing process of spiritual progress rather than a way of arriving at a place of unattainable perfection.

Wilson then moves on to point out that the first four chapters of the book have already presented detailed information on the First and the Second Steps that he neatly summarizes as three salient points:

> Our description of the alcoholic [in "There Is A Solution" & "More About Alcoholism"], the chapter to the agnostic ["We Agnostics"], and our personal adventures before and after ["Bill's Story"], have been designed to sell you three pertinent ideas:
>
> (a) That you are alcoholic and cannot manage your own life.
>
> (b) That probably no human power can relieve your alcoholism.
>
> (c) That God can and will.

However, if this presentation of facts has not persuaded you of your own powerlessness over alcohol and of the need to appeal to God for a solution— "if you are not convinced on these vital issues"—then you have completely missed the point of what has been written so far and, if that is the case, "you ought to re-read the book to this point or else throw it away!"

Very directive—and 'tough love' indeed!

God Is the Director

However, if you are convinced of these three pertinent ideas (i.e., if you have already accepted Steps One and Two) then "you are now at step three." With these words, Bill begins his detailed examination of the rest of the program of recovery, starting with an explanation of Step Three. "Just what did we mean," he says, when we told you to turn your life and your will over to the care and direction of God and "just what did we do" to accomplish this ourselves?

The first thing the reader needs to realize, he says, is that "any life run on self-will can hardly be a success" and that the very heart of the alcoholic's problems can be found in his selfish willfulness. To illustrate the point, Wilson offers a colorful analogy, painting a detailed picture of the "actor who wants to run the whole show." This is the man who thinks he is (or at least thinks he should be) the director. He is someone who certainly believes he is in control. He is forever trying to arrange things with the firm conviction that, if he could only successfully do so, he would surely make his life (and that of everyone around him) just "wonderful."

But Wilson claims this is so wrong-headed that it is almost laughable. The actor who insists on being the director necessarily struggles against all the other would-be directors in his life, causing a host of problems that radiate out and affect everyone around him. In one of the most challenging statements to be found in the book, Bill notes that the aspiring director's basic problem is that he is "a victim of the delusion that he can wrest satisfaction and happiness out of this world if only he manages well." But this idea that managing well will lead to happiness is really just a crippling delusion, one that masks the reality of the alcoholic's deep and pervasive egotism.

> Selfishness - self-centeredness! That, we think, is the root of our troubles. Driven by a hundred forms of fear, self-delusion, self-seeking, and self-pity, we step on the toes of our fellows and they retaliate. Sometimes they hurt us, seemingly, without provocation, but we invariably find that at some time in the past we have made decisions based on self, which later placed us in a position to be hurt.

> So our troubles, we think, are basically of our own making. They arise out of ourselves, and the alcoholic is almost the most extreme example that could be found of self-will run riot, though he usually doesn't think so. Above everything, we alcoholics must be rid of this selfishness. We must, or it kills us!

With the problem so clearly defined, Bill moves on to the solution, telling the alcoholic that he must turn his life and his will over to the care of God—He who is the true Director.

> First of all, quit playing God yourself. It doesn't work. Next, decide that hereafter in this drama of life, God is going to be your Director. He is the Principal; you are to be His agent. He is the Father, and you are His child. Get that simple relationship straight. Most good ideas are simple and this concept is to be the keystone of the new and triumphant arch through which you will pass to freedom.

Bill promises the reader if "you sincerely take such a position, all sorts of remarkable things follow" and, after enumerating several of these positive consequences, he claims that any man who turns his will and his life over to the care of God will soon be able to face life successfully. "As you become conscious of His presence, you begin to lose your fear of today, tomorrow, or the hereafter. You will have been reborn."

But what do you actually have to *do* to turn your life over to the care and direction of God? Wilson answers that question by offering some very concrete instructions.

> Get down upon your knees and say to your Maker, <u>as you understand Him</u>: "God, I offer myself to Thee—to build with me and to do with me as Thou wilt. Relieve me of the bondage of self, that I may better do Thy will. Take away my difficulties, that victory over them may bear witness to those I would help of Thy Power, Thy Love, and Thy Way of life. May I do Thy will always!"

Bill immediately emphasizes the open, non-denominational freedom the reader has regarding this prayer, explicitly noting that the wording is "quite optional so long as you express the idea" of your complete surrender to God and then say the prayer without reservation. Make up any prayer you like, he says, just so long as it reflects the essential idea of your sincere and complete surrender to God, similar to what is expressed in our suggested prayer.

A Personal Inventory

From here, Wilson points out that this decision (and its heartfelt expression in prayer) is only a beginning. Having successfully completed the Third Step, it is now time to "launch out on a course of vigorous action" that starts with the housecleaning called for in the Fourth Step. A personal inventory—similar to the commercial inventory any successful business must regularly perform—needs to be taken. Though the decision to turn your life over to God

> is a vital and crucial step, it can have little effect unless at once followed by a strenuous effort to face, and to be rid of, the things in yourself which have been blocking you. Your liquor is but a symptom. Let's now get down to basic causes and conditions . . . <u>This is step four</u> . . . We take stock honestly. First, we search out the flaws in our make-up which have caused our failure. Being convinced that self, manifested in various ways, is what has defeated us, we consider its common manifestations.

From this point on, the rest of Chapter Five is devoted to a detailed description of how to write the three inventories needed to successfully complete this step. Each of these three separate personal accountings—of resentments, fears, and sexual behaviors—is intended to produce an increasingly clearer picture of the ways in which selfishness and self-centeredness have manifested themselves in the alcoholic's day-to-day life and caused so many of his problems.

Resentments

The first list focuses on resentment because according to Wilson, it is "the 'number one' offender," the thing that destroys more alcoholics than anything else. The reason, he claims, is simple. Resentments are the primary cause of "all forms of spiritual disease," which is the alcoholic's core problem— drinking has left him spiritually damaged. "We have been not only mentally and physically ill, we have been spiritually sick," and this is where the recovery process must start—with spiritual recovery. "When the spiritual malady is overcome, we straighten out mentally and physically."

Resentments are infinitely grave, he writes. They are like poison that cuts us "off from the sunlight of the Spirit." To live fruitful, happy lives we must be free of anger, and the only hope of doing that is through "the maintenance and growth of a spiritual experience." The first step to becoming free of anger is to make a list of our resentments, putting them all down on paper.

Bill then provides a simple three-column example of how to do this. The name of the person resented goes in the first column, the cause of the resentment appears alongside it in the second column, and the reason for the resentment is written in the third. The first column of this "grudge list" should include not only people, but also "institutions or principles with whom you are angry." In the third column, the reasons for the anger should be described by one of seven things affected by the cause: the alcoholic's self-esteem, pride, security, pocketbook, ambition, and personal or sex relations.

To be effective, the list must be thorough, honest and "as definite as this example:"

I'm resentful at:	The Cause	Affects my:
Mr. Brown	His attention to my wife.	Sex relations Self-esteem (fear)
	Told my wife of my mistress.	Sex relations Self-esteem (fear)
	Brown may get my job at the office.	Security Self-esteem (fear)

Wilson goes on to provide three more first-column examples ("Mrs. Jones," "My employer" and "My wife") along with the causes and affects opposite each of these in the next two columns.

Once finished, the writer's first response to this comprehensive list would almost certainly be to conclude that this world and its people are often quite wrong. But Bill says that stopping there would doom us to a life of futility and unhappiness, because harboring such feelings results in "the usual outcome . . . that people continue to wrong you and you stay sore" and "the more you fight and try to have your way, the worse matters get." Such a scenario leads back to just one thing—the insanity of alcohol: we drink again.

But, seen from a completely different perspective, you will realize that clinging to a belief in "the wrongdoing of others, fancied or real, has [the] power to actually kill you" and the awareness grows that "these resentments must be mastered, but how?"

Wilson offers two possible solutions.

The first suggests a different way of reacting to difficult situations. "Never argue. Never retaliate," he counsels. Instead, the newly sober man should acknowledge, "that the people who wrong you are spiritually sick," and then "ask God to help you show them the same tolerance, pity, and patience that you would cheerfully grant a friend who has cancer." Once again fulfilling his earlier promise to explain exactly what to do, Bill offers the following prayer as the most appropriate response: "This is a sick man. How can I be helpful to him? God save me from being angry. Thy will be done." Once requested, Wilson is confident that divine guidance will "show you how to take a kindly and tolerant view of each and every one" of these "sick people."

The second solution is more introspective and in some ways more challenging. Wilson suggests that resentments can be relieved by taking the focus off the offender and looking at your own contribution to the situation. It is essential to examine and then own the part you played in each of these hurts. To do this, he advises the alcoholic to

> Take up your list again. Putting out of your mind the wrongs others have done, resolutely look for your own mistakes. Where have you been selfish, dishonest, self-seeking and frightened? Though a situation may not be entirely your fault, disregard the other person involved entirely. See where you have been to blame. This is your inventory, not the other man's. When you see your fault write it down on the list. See it before you in black and white. Admit your wrongs honestly and be willing to set these matters straight.

Bill's explicit instructions here require that a fourth column be added to the inventory, one detailing whatever personal mistakes, fault, or blame may have contributed to this resentment. More than just constantly acknowledging the sickness of others, this admission of some personal responsibility for what happened is a way of gaining *permanent* relief from the spiritual malady that afflicts those who are plagued by deep and pervasive resentments.

Fears

Moving on to the next inventory, Wilson asks the reader to notice that the word fear is bracketed alongside the difficulties with Mr. Brown and also alongside each of the other three people presented in his example. Fear, he says, touches all aspects of our lives. It is "an evil and corroding thread [in] the fabric of our existence." It causes us more trouble and misfortune than we can ever realize until we take a hard look at the ways in which it is controlling our lives. The first step toward eliminating these fears is to take another inventory.

Review your fears thoroughly. Put them on paper, even though you have no resentment in connection with them. Ask yourself why you have them. Isn't it because self-reliance has failed you? Self-reliance was good as far as it went, but it didn't go far enough. Some of us once had great self-confidence, but it didn't fully solve the fear problem, or any other. When it made us cocky, it was worse.

Writing such a list clarifies the magnitude and pervasiveness of fear which, almost unnoticed, drives our behavior. But how to be free of this insidious tyranny? Bill notes that the members of Alcoholics Anonymous believe it is possible to vanquish fear. They are convinced there is a better way that has allowed them to overcome the terrible impact fear has had in their lives and to arrive at a place where they can "match calamity with serenity." They have learned that the key to success in this area is to put their trust in the infinite God rather than their finite self. Once again, the reader is encouraged to pray: "Ask Him to remove your fear and direct your attention to what He would have you be. At once, you will commence to outgrow fear."

Fearful himself that this constant mention of God and prayer might be alienating the reader—such a reliance being commonly regarded as a sign of dependent weakness rather than autonomous strength—Wilson makes an impassioned plea for a new understanding on this issue.

You must never apologize to anyone for depending upon your Creator. You can laugh at those who think spirituality the way of weakness, Paradoxically, it is the way of strength. The verdict of the ages is that faith means courage. All men of faith have courage. They trust their God. Never apologize for God. Instead let Him demonstrate, through you, what He can do.

He tells us that a searching and fearless inventory will uncover the unacknowledged fears that drive so much of your behavior, but the solution is immediately at hand: God will temper (and even relieve) this ubiquitous scourge of fear from your life, if only you will ask Him.

Sexual Behavior

"Now about sex." Without pausing for breath, Wilson opens the next paragraph with this one short sentence, which is guaranteed to grab the reader's attention. Suggesting that the reader "can probably stand an overhauling" in this area, he notes that it has so far been necessary for everyone who joined the Fellowship. But before addressing this troublesome topic, Bill prefaces his remarks with a paragraph distancing himself from the quagmire of conflicting opinions surrounding this delicate subject. Labeling both the Puritan and the modern psychological approaches as extremes—"one school would allow man no flavor for his fare and the other would have us all on a straight pepper diet"—he states unequivocally that Alcoholics Anonymous wants to stay out of this controversy. We are not here, he says, to promulgate one correct theory about your sexual behavior. In fact, "we do not want to be the arbiter of anyone's sex conduct. We all have sex problems. We'd hardly be human if we didn't." The only important question is: "What can we do about them?"

Once again the proper approach begins with an inventory. He instructs readers to review their own sexual conduct over the years and while doing so, honestly admit the ways in which they were at fault in these situations. "Where have you been selfish, dishonest, or inconsiderate? Whom did you hurt? Did you unjustifiably arouse jealousy, suspicion or bitterness?" Perhaps most important, "what should you have done instead?"

"Get all of this down on paper and look at it," Bill advises, and then "subject each relation to this test—is it selfish or not?" Once an honest, self-critical evaluation of past sexual behaviors has been created, it will readily inform the new perspective needed to "shape a sane and sound ideal for your future sex life." Again, prayer is the recommended way to approach this process: "Ask God to mould [sic] your ideals and help you to live up to them."

"Whatever your ideal may be, you must be willing to grow toward it," and if that requires making "amends where you have done harm," then you must be willing to do just that. If complications and questions arise, once again turn to God in meditation and ask, "what you should do about each specific matter. The right answer will come, if you want it." While it may be tempting and even desirable to consult with others about these problems, Bill cautions that "Some people are as fanatical about sex as others are loose. Avoid hysterical thinking or advice." When all else fails, remember, "God alone can judge your sex situation."

But what if, after all this hard work—reviewing your past and creating a new sexual ideal for your life—you still slip back into old sexual behaviors and patterns?

> Does this mean you are going to get drunk? Some people will tell you so. If they do, it will be only a half-truth. It depends on you and your motive. If you are sorry for what you have done, and have the honest desire to let God take you to better things, you will be forgiven and will have learned your lesson. If you are not sorry, and your conduct continues to harm others, you are quite sure to drink. We are not theorizing. These are facts out of our experience.

Finally, if sex continues to be troublesome, the best course is to fall back on this advice: "when all other measures fail, work with another alcoholic." Rather than succumbing to sexual temptations, "throw yourself the harder into helping others. Think of their needs and work for them. This will take you out of yourself. It will quiet the imperious urge, when to yield would mean heartache."

Having eliminated all these old excuses for drinking, it makes no sense for the alcoholic to continue sabotaging his life and happiness with foolish and destructive sexual behavior. Instead, Bill admonishes him to get right with God and begin to actually live the sane and sound sexual ideal he has formulated for himself. An alcoholic must do this or he is likely to drink again.

• • •

In the concluding two paragraphs of Chapter Five, Wilson provides a recap of the Fourth Step actions, noting that "if you have been thorough about your personal inventory, you have written down a lot by this time," and he then lists several practical benefits that should result from these efforts. The last of these—"you have listed the people you have hurt by your conduct, and you are willing to straighten out the past if you can"—is a strong foreshadowing of the Eighth Step, which will be addressed in the next chapter.

Finally, Bill reminds the reader of the foundational truth that underlies all of these efforts—namely that "God did for us what we could not do for ourselves"—and hopes that by now the reader is convinced of the truth of that statement. He then briefly reviews the work just done and concludes by congratulating the reader on having made a good beginning by becoming more honest with himself about himself. Wilson then closes the chapter with a question meant to draw the reader directly into the next one: Having come this far, he asks, "Are you willing to go on?"

"Into Action": Steps Five Through Eleven

With the first four steps now fully explained, Chapter Six, "Into Action," provides explicit instructions for working each of the next seven steps. In the Multilith printing, the Fifth Step is dealt with in just under two pages, and then Steps Six and Seven are covered in one paragraph each. Most of the next four pages are taken up with the many challenges of Step Nine (Step Eight getting only the briefest of mentions) followed by roughly one page each explaining Steps Ten and Eleven. Throughout, the emphasis is consistently placed on the actions that must be taken to successfully *do* each of these steps.

Admitting Wrongs to Another Person
Opening this chapter with a discussion of Step Five, Bill notes that the contents of the "searching and fearless moral inventory" taken in Step Four are already known to God and, of course, to the person who wrote the inventory. But such a solitary self-appraisal, i.e., merely admitting these things to yourself, is insufficient and, in the group's experience, positively dangerous.[3] The natural reluctance of intimately discussing yourself with another person simply must be resolved for "if you skip this vital step, you may not overcome drinking." Bill cautions that newcomers who have avoided this humbling experience almost invariably get drunk again. "They only thought they had lost their egoism and fear; they only thought they had humbled themselves. But they had not learned enough of humility, fearlessness and honesty, in the sense we find it necessary, until they told someone else all their life story."

Emphasizing the constant fear and tension which comes from hiding the resentments, fears and nightmare memories of the past, Bill leaves the reader no "wiggle room" whatsoever, stating categorically that "you must be entirely honest with somebody if you expect to live long and happily in this world." He admits that finding a trustworthy person with whom you can share the whole truth may be challenging, but he is confident everyone should know (or be able to find) a minister, priest, doctor, psychologist or "a close-mouthed, understanding friend" with whom they can take this intimate and confidential step.

Once that person has been selected, the directions for Step Five are concise and concrete. With the written inventory in hand, the alcoholic should waste no time in setting up an appointment for a long talk with the person he has chosen. At the beginning of their talk, the alcoholic is instructed to explain two very specific things to his confidant by candidly telling him "what you are about to do and why you have to do it." Having thus established the life-and-death importance of this exchange, the new man is told to "pocket [his] pride and go to it! Illumine every twist of character, every dark cranny of the past . . . withholding nothing."

Bill promises the reader once this all-inclusive confession has been completed, he will experience some miraculous results.

> . . . you will be delighted. You can look the world in the eye. You can be alone at perfect peace and ease. Your fears will fall from you. You will begin to feel the nearness of your Creator. You may have had certain spiritual beliefs, but now you will begin to have a spiritual experience. The feeling that the drink problem has disappeared will come strongly. You will know you are on the Broad Highway, walking hand in hand with the Spirit of the Universe.

Then, immediately following this revealing and rewarding conversation, the Fifth Step requires one final action to be taken in private.

> Return home and find a place where you can be quiet for an hour. Carefully review what you have done. Thank God from the bottom of your heart that you know Him better. Take this book down from your shelf and turn to the page which contains the twelve steps. Carefully read the first five proposals and ask if you have omitted anything, for you are building an arch through which you will walk a free man at last. Is your part of the work solid so far? Are the stones properly in place? Have you skimped on the cement you have put into the foundation? Have you tried to make mortar without sand?

These Fifth Step instructions are followed by two short paragraphs briefly explaining how to go about taking the next two Steps in the program of recovery.

Removing Character Defects

Wilson claims that if the alcoholic can answer these questions about the thoroughness of the work done in Step Five to his satisfaction, then it is time to look at Step Six. This is simple enough. Honestly ask yourself, he says, if you are "now perfectly willing to let God remove" all of these objectionable qualities from you and from your life.

However, if you discover that you "yet cling to something you will not let go," then once again prayer is the answer: you must ask God to help you be willing. Whatever it takes to become entirely willing to have these defects of character removed must be done before moving on to Step Seven.

Once there is willingness to have all of your shortcomings removed, the following Step can be completed by getting down on your knees and humbly saying a prayer which sounds "something like this: 'My Creator, I am now willing that you should have all of me, good and bad. I pray that you now remove from me every single defect of character, which stands in the way of my usefulness to you and my fellows. Grant me strength, as I go out from here, to do your bidding. Amen.'"

If you become willing—"holding back nothing"—and humbly pray to God that He remove all of your character defects, then you have successfully completed Steps Six and Seven.

Listing the People Harmed

With these two solitary Steps successfully completed, it is time to step back into the real world—the world of other people—and move on to Steps Eight and Nine. Both of these call for actions that must be taken fearlessly. If the alcoholic is hesitant or resistant here, he will soon learn the harsh truth of the Biblical warning, "Faith without works is dead,'"and he will likely drink again.

Surprisingly, the instructions for the Eighth Step are almost as brief as those given for Six and Seven. The action required does not even include creating a new list of the people you have hurt: "You have a list of all persons you have harmed and to whom you are willing to make complete amends. You made it when you took inventory." This harkens back to two statements Bill made at the end of the previous chapter while discussing the Fourth Step: "You have listed the people you have hurt by your conduct, and you are willing to straighten out the past if you can" and "You must be willing to make amends where you have done harm, provided that you will not bring about still more harm in so doing."

So, although the Eighth Step list has already been written, Bill believed that the alcoholic may not yet have the required willingness to make complete amends to them all. If that willingness is lacking, then Bill says he must pray to God until it comes. And whatever his reluctance, he has to remember, "you agreed at the beginning <u>you would go to any lengths for victory over alcohol</u>"—and that now requires him to make direct and personal amends to all of the people he harmed during his drinking career.

Making Amends

Wilson begins the long section on making Ninth Step amends with a strong warning about what you should not do as you try to make amends.

---

* This quote, from the Epistle of St. James in the New Testament (James 2:26), was reputed to be Anne Smith's favorite expression regarding spiritual growth and recovery (*AACOA*, p. 7). The quote was also extremely popular in early Ohio A.A., "so much so that 'The James Club' was favored by some as a name for the Fellowship"—rather than Alcoholics Anonymous. (*Dr. Bob and the Good Oldtimers*, p. 71)

> To some people you need not, and probably should not emphasize the spiritual features on your first approach . . . [for] it is seldom wise to approach an individual, who still smarts from your injustice to him, and announce that you have given your life to God . . . He is going to be more interested in your demonstration of good will than in your talk of spiritual discoveries.

Keeping this firmly in mind, Bill recommends a dramatic way to begin this process. "Take the bit in your teeth," he says, and approach a man you have hated for "he is an ideal subject upon which to practice your new principles." Whatever might have occurred between the two of you in the past, set aside any thought of your own injuries and "simply tell him that you realize you will never get over drinking until you have done your utmost to straighten out the past . . . to sweep off your side of the street."

Wilson admits such a conversation may certainly be difficult, but once done, the results are often unexpected. And he counsels that, even if the encounter does not go well—if, for instance, the man should throw you out of his office—to not be discouraged. "You have made your demonstration, done your part. It's water over the dam." While you *are* trying to put your own life in order by making these amends, "this is not an end in itself. Your real purpose is to fit yourself to be of maximum service to God and the people about you" and you will have begun to successfully move toward that goal once you have done your part with this step.

Raising a typical problem faced in recovery, Bill notes that most alcoholics owe money, and he states categorically that dodging creditors is no longer an option. They must be confronted honestly. Explain the cause of your past problems, he advises, and then negotiate "the best deal you can . . . You must lose your fear of creditors no matter how far you have to go, for you are liable to drink if you are afraid to face them."

In an effort to emphasize just how serious and thorough the new man must be in cleaning up the wreckage of his past, the next five paragraphs address how to make amends when to do so might result in criminal prosecution and even incarceration. "Perhaps you have committed a criminal offense which might land you in jail if known to the authorities. You may be short in your accounts and can't make good. You have already admitted this in confidence to another person, but you are sure you would be imprisoned or lose your job if it were known." What should you do under circumstances such as this?

> Although these reparations take innumerable forms, there are some general principles which we find guiding. Remind yourself that you have decided to go to any lengths to find a spiritual experience. Ask that you be given the strength and direction to do the right thing, no matter what the personal consequence to you. You may lose your position or reputation, or face jail, but you are willing. You have to be. You must not shrink at anything.

Wilson immediately tempers this uncompromising tone by strongly suggesting that, under such dire circumstances, the new man should first consult with others and then "use every means to avoid [the] wide-spread damage" that might result from these efforts to make amends. Bill does this by telling the story of a member who was facing jail time because he failed to pay his first wife's alimony. People in A.A. suggested that, before turning himself in to the judge, he should write to his ex-wife, apologizing for his past behavior and promising to act differently in the future (while including a good-faith check with the letter). Bill reported that this attempted reconciliation was successful and "the whole situation has long since been adjusted" to everyone's satisfaction.

But such an easy success may not always be the case. "If, after seeking advice, consulting others involved, and asking God to guide you, there appears no other just and honorable solution than the most drastic one, you must take your medicine. Trust that the eventual outcome will be right."

Sometimes, even though the offense might not be a prosecutable crime, radical measures may still be called for. To illustrate this, Wilson relates the story of a member of the Fellowship who had denied ever receiving money from "a bitterly-hated business rival" and then used that incident to destroy the man's reputation. What could possibly be done to set right this old affair without dire consequences to himself, to his partner and to his family? Finally deciding that something must be done or "he would soon start drinking again, and all would be lost anyhow," he stood up in church one Sunday and publicly confessed his wrongdoing. However difficult and embarrassing this may have been at the time "his action met widespread approval, and today he is one of the most trusted citizens of his town."*

Having given several examples of how to make amends outside the home, Bill spends the next four paragraphs wrestling with the question of how to address the serious domestic problems that may have resulted from the reader's past relations "with women in a fashion you wouldn't care to have advertised." Do you tell your wife the particulars of these affairs or not? Wilson replies with a judicious "Not always, we think," and then goes on to explain several scenarios of what might happen should you have to admit your fault to her. Here, Bill offers perhaps the most insensitive and self-serving line to be found in the entire Big Book, blithely claiming, "if you can forget, so can she." Building on this, he suggests with equal nonchalance that, when it comes to past infidelities, the best thing would be for each party to "decide that the way of good sense and loving kindness is to let bygones be bygones."

But even if you have somehow managed to avoid any of these adulterous situations, Bill claims "there is still plenty you should do at home," and he offers the following colorful analogy to illustrate that point:

> The alcoholic is like a tornado roaring his way through the lives of others. Hearts are broken. Sweet relationships are dead. Affections have been uprooted. Selfish and inconsiderate habits have kept the home in turmoil. We feel a man is unthinking when he says that sobriety is enough. He is

---

* The conclusion of this story notes that "This all happened three years ago" placing it in December 1935. Given the extremely limited number of people in the Fellowship at that time, the "friend" who would have stood up and made this speech was most likely Hank Parkhurst although it may also have been one of the very early members in Akron.

like the farmer who came up out of his cyclone cellar to find his home ruined. To his wife, he remarked, "Don't see anything the matter here, Ma. Ain't it grand the wind stopped blowin'?"

Rather than adopting such a thoughtless and inconsiderate attitude, Bill says that instead, the alcoholic must realize "there is a long period of reconstruction ahead" and his job is to take the lead in this reconstruction. He must "clean house with the family, asking each morning in meditation that your Creator show you the way of patience, tolerance, kindness, and love." It is here, within the family, more than anywhere else, that the new man must remember that "the spiritual life is not a theory. You have to live it."

The Promises

In conclusion, although there will be many challenges while making these Ninth Step amends, Bill offers what have since become popularly known in A.A. as "The Promises"*:

> If you are painstaking about this phase of your development, you will be amazed before you are half through. You are going to know a new freedom and happiness. You will not regret the past nor wish to shut the door on it. You will comprehend the word serenity and know peace. No matter how far down the scale you have gone, you will see how your experience can benefit others. That feeling of uselessness and self-pity will disappear. You will lose interest in selfish things and gain interest in your fellows. Self-seeking will slip away. Your whole attitude and outlook upon life will change. Fear of people and of economic insecurity will leave you. You will intuitively know how to handle situations which used to baffle you. You will suddenly realize that God is doing for you what you could not do for yourself.

> You say these are extravagant promises. They are not. They are being fulfilled among us—sometimes quickly, sometimes slowly. They will materialize in you if you work for them.

A Daily Reprieve

"This thought," Bill says, "brings us to step ten, which suggests you continue to take personal inventory and continue to set any new mistakes right as you go along." He notes that this does not just happen overnight, but should continue throughout a lifetime. Constant vigilance is critical for "it is easy to let up on the spiritual program of action and rest on your laurels. You are headed for trouble if you do, for alcohol is a subtle foe. We are not cured of alcoholism. What we really have is a daily reprieve." In

---

* These are, of course, not the only "promises" to be found in the Big Book. A careful reading will show that most steps are followed by 'promised' changes and benefits.

this daily examination, Wilson recommends the alcoholic "continue to watch yourself for selfishness, dishonesty, resentment, and fear. When these crop up, ask God at once to remove them. Discuss them with someone immediately. Make amends quickly if you have harmed anyone."

Tucked in between these admonitions is a long paragraph proclaiming an important benefit for those who have finally reached the Tenth Step. Wilson promises that by this time sanity will have returned and "you will seldom be interested in liquor." This new attitude toward alcohol allows the ex-alcoholic to "feel as though you had been placed in a position of neutrality. You feel safe and protected. You have not even sworn off. Instead, the problem has been removed. It does not exist for you." Bill contends that this glorious release is something that has just been given to you. It "has happened automatically" once you have successfully completed the first ten Steps.

Bill then closes these four paragraphs on the Tenth Step by mentioning one other important gift that comes to those who have faithfully followed the prescribed directions up to this point: "Much has already been said about receiving strength, inspiration, and direction from Him who has all knowledge and power. If you have carefully followed directions, you have begun to sense the flow of His Spirit into you. To some extent you have become God-conscious. You have begun to develop this vital sixth sense." In short, you will find that you are now living your life on a completely different spiritual plane.

But despite having reached this impressive new level of God-consciousness, still "you must go further and that means more action"—namely, the actions required by the Eleventh Step.

Prayer and Meditation

"Step eleven suggests prayer and meditation. Don't be shy on this matter of prayer. Better men than we are using it constantly. It works, if you have the proper attitude and work at it." Wilson notes that it would be easy to be vague about this matter of prayer and meditation, but instead he says that he would like to offer "some definite and valuable suggestions."

Here, Bill faced a serious challenge. It would be easy enough to make suggestions about prayer using generic language that would please most everyone within the Fellowship. But the Oxford Group had a very specific way of doing meditation which they called "quiet time," the purpose of which was to receive "guidance" directly from God. This method was still being faithfully practiced by Dr. Bob Smith and by most of the other Ohio members of the Fellowship. If Wilson were to talk about meditation by explicitly explaining the particulars of "quiet time" (and the desired guided result), the knowledgeable reader might well have identified this as an Oxford Group teaching, and this was an association Bill Wilson was determined to avoid. But if he were to leave out any direct references to quiet time, he was just as likely to offend many of the Akron and Cleveland people who were so devoted to that practice. It was the one Ohio practice that Frank Amos had noted members "must have . . . every morning—a 'quiet time' of prayer, and some reading from the Bible or other religious literature. Unless this is faithfully followed, there is grave danger of backsliding."[4]

Bill managed to walk this thin line by interspersing several Oxford Group beliefs and practices throughout these "definite and valuable suggestions" on meditation, but he did so in such a way that they would not readily be identified as having come from the Oxford Group.

Wilson's suggestions for a daily morning meditation practice were substantive. "When you awake tomorrow morning," he said, you should begin by making a thorough review of the previous day's activities. Ask yourself several searching questions about your behavior and intentions ("Were you resentful, selfish, dishonest, or afraid? Do you owe an apology? . . ." etc.) during the past twenty-four hours. Once this honest self-appraisal was complete, "ask God's forgiveness for any wrong. Ask to be shown what to do."

Having thoroughly dealt with yesterday, the reader is to move on to consider the twenty-four hours ahead. But before finalizing his plans for the day, he must be sure to "ask God to guide your thinking" and for His help in avoiding self-pity, dishonest and self-seeking motives. Once this is done, "your thought life will be placed on a much higher plane." If you have some particular problem facing you today, "ask God for inspiration, an intuitive thought or a decision. Relax and take it easy. Don't struggle. Ask God's help. You will be surprised how the right answers come after you have practiced a few days."

Having carefully and critically reviewed yesterday and asked for God's help to properly navigate your way throughout today, he says, "conclude the period of meditation with a prayer that you be shown all through the day what your next step is to be." With that commitment firmly in place, Bill promises the newly sober man that he will be able to go through your day with confidence. Should you become agitated or doubtful, he says, simply, "be still and ask for the right thought or action. It will come."

Once again, Wilson specifically underlines the fact that there are absolutely no religious dogmas implied in any of these suggestions.

> If you belong to a religious denomination which requires a definite morning devotion, be sure to attend to that also. If you are not a member of a religious body, you might select and memorize a few set prayers which emphasize the principles we have been discussing. There are many helpful books also. If you do not know of any, ask your priest, minister, or rabbi, for suggestions. Be quick to see where religious people are right. Make use of what they offer.

But Bill reminds the reader that whatever you do, you have to *do* it. "It works—it really does," but you won't know that until you have actually given some sort of formal meditation practice a try.

"Working with Others": Step Twelve

Bill concludes the chapter by returning to one of his constant refrains throughout the discussion of the Steps. "But that is not all," he says. "There is action and more action. 'Faith without works is dead.' What works? We shall treat them in the next chapter which is entirely devoted to step twelve."

In fulfillment of this promise, Wilson then took the already-written chapter, "Working With Others," and positioned it directly after "Into Action." He did this despite the fact that what he had written earlier focused almost exclusively on the middle part of the Twelfth Step ("we tried to carry this message to others, especially alcoholics") while completely ignoring the opening and closing requirements of the step ("having had a spiritual experience as the result of this course of action" and "to practice these principles in all our affairs").

Wilson likely felt the chapters immediately following "Working With Others" ("To Wives," "The Family Afterward" and "To Employers") sufficiently covered the need to practice these principles in all of the alcoholic's affairs. However, the first part of the step—about having a spiritual experience as a result of all this work—was nowhere specifically addressed in the book. Perhaps this was in tacit acknowledgement of Hank Parkhurst's earlier observation: "One of the easiest and most talked of things among us is a religious experience. I believe that this is incomprehensible to most people. Simple + meaning[ful] words to us—but meaningless to most of the people that we are trying to get this over to."[5] It wasn't until the second printing of the Big Book in the March 1941 that Wilson added "Appendix II" (later entitled: "Spiritual Experience") in his first concerted attempt to explain that critical part of Step Twelve.

• • •

All of the chapters for the front half of the book were now written. Bill smoothed out whatever rough edges he could see as Ruth typed up the final review copy that Hank would submit to his friend, Tom Uzzell, for critical comments. It is hard to imagine the exhilarating sense of accomplishment these three must have felt when they finally got to hold that completed manuscript copy in their hands for the first time.

They had actually done it. They had written a book!

The Book Goes to the Editor and Is Approved by the Board

~January 1939~

As 1938 came to a close, the New York group celebrated with another New Year's Eve party, this one held at Hank Parkhurst's house in New Jersey. One of the charming things about these early 'ringing in the New Year' parties was that "instead of cheering" at midnight, everyone held hands and said The Lord's Prayer.[1] At the previous year's party, much of the excitement had been driven by the expectation that they would soon receive a huge donation from John D. Rockefeller Jr.—a hope decisively crushed less than three months later. Now, as the calendar turned over to 1939, the future once again looked bright, but this time those prospects were much more firmly under their own control; Bill had finally completed the first pass of what they expected to be a bestselling book and a manuscript copy was being prepared for submission to a professional critic. All of the hard work they had put into this project during the previous three and a half months would soon begin to pay substantial dividends, greatly expanding the reach of the Fellowship and guaranteeing the group's financial security well into the future.

Bill had invited Frank Amos to join them that night, but for some unspecified reason, he and his wife could not attend. Instead, Frank sent a letter expressing his regrets.

December 31st 1938

Dear Bill:

Words are an inadequate vehicle of expressing depth of appreciation.

You and your "gang"—may their tribe increase—have been an inspiration to Mary and me far beyond our ability to measure.

On the occasion of your New Year's Eve party we send you—all of you—our greetings and love. May every one of you be instrumental during 1939 of bringing at least one sufferer to spiritual redemption. By January 1940, we can talk of <u>two hundred men</u>.

Affectionately,

Frank and Mary Amos[2]

Getting the Rockefeller Men's Support

The fact that Frank Amos thought a doubling of their membership during the next year was an ambitious goal implies just how complete the break had been between the leaders of the New York Fellowship and the Rockefeller men during the previous three months. Frank seems to have had no idea that a first draft of the book had been finished and was now moving quickly toward publication. If he, a professional advertising man, had been aware of the book's imminent release, he would have surely known that they could expect much more than a doubling of their numbers in the very near future.

Albert Scott's negative response to Bill's desperate "sheep and goats" letter in early October—his firm "No" to any additional outside funding, his insistence they start charging membership fees, and his advice that they take Harper Brothers' $1,500 advance and let them publish the book—had certainly backed Wilson and Parkhurst into a small corner where they could either accept those completely impractical directions, or defy the Rockefeller contingent and adopt a course of action these men considered to be pure folly. Hank and Bill chose the latter, but they also decided to spare the trustees any real knowledge of their decision and of the actions they were taking to implement it. As Bill continued to write the book and Hank began to sell stock, they had little or no further contact with Amos, Richardson, Chipman, or Scott—driven either by the fear of their harsh disapproval, or because they wanted to avoid an argument that might completely alienate these important friends whose help they would surely need in the future.

But the time for silence and secrecy was over. A rough draft of the book was done (partially financed with money borrowed from Charles Towns) and stock in the new company had been issued and sold. The Rockefeller men might not be happy about any of this, but by now there was no going back. Wilson and Parkhurst were resolutely committed to their current course of action. Still, several serious problems remained (which, as we'll see, are all connected to making contacts with the rich and famous) that could best be handled by the four Rockefeller men.

Soon after the New Year's Eve party, Bill finally told Frank about the important changes that had occurred since early October. Given that everything they had done was in direct opposition to the trustee's former advice, it is difficult to imagine Amos's first reaction. But Wilson and Parkhurst were not to be dissuaded, and Amos realized that if the foundation was going to remain a viable part of the Fellowship's mission, it was time to get behind these new plans. Challenging them at this point would be futile.

The first thing Amos did was to consult with Willard Richardson, who suggested that these developments must be brought to the attention of the Board of the Alcoholic Foundation and given careful consideration. He recommended "that another evening dinner and meeting should be held soon so that all these matters can be thoroughly discussed and, if possible, a constructive, forward program determined upon."[3] What Richardson was suggesting was not a regular Board meeting, but rather a large dinner party/meeting similar to the one held more than a year earlier when the alcoholics had first met the Rockefeller men. To begin organizing that meeting, Amos sent out a letter to the trustees and members of the Advisory Committee along with a few others (Fitz Mayo was included in this distribution), briefly explaining the current state of affairs and telling them "we shall try to arrange a dinner and evening meeting within the next ten days or two weeks at which your presence is desired."[4]

The notices went out on Friday, January 6 and they included copies of two additional important letters Frank had received from Bill and Hank. Amos suggested that each recipient "carefully read the attached and, in advance, formulate your ideas, so far as possible, on what should be done," noting that at the meeting they would be asking "Messrs. Wilson and Parkhurst to supplement the attached letters with more intimate accounts of what has been accomplished among alcoholics during the past year and what they believe is needed to carry on this work."[5]

Bill's Letter Makes the Case

Frank noted that the enclosed four-page letter from Bill Wilson, dated Wednesday, January 4, was written "at my request," in which he asked Bill to outline "certain accomplishments and problems all deserving prompt and constructive consideration."[6] Amos's suggestion that Wilson write a comprehensive letter is similar to the one he made in September, but the tone and tenor of Bill's January letter is completely different from his last long letter. Rather than abjectly pleading for help, Wilson projected a new-found confidence and sense of control, almost casually telling the trustees "quite a bit has happened in the alcoholic department since the last meeting of the Foundation," (which had been held on September 23) and saying he will now "endeavor to bring you up to date and set forth the problems which most concern us at the moment."[7] The shift from humble supplicant to assured presenter of facts is striking. In addition, Bill made no requests for approval of the actions they had taken in this letter. Instead, he presented a detailed account of their accomplishments and followed this with a list of four current problems that need to be resolved, clearly indicating what the Rockefeller men could do to be helpful should they choose to do so.

The first page and half of Bill's letter recaps the writing of the book, provides detailed information on the money borrowed from Charles Towns, and notes that stock in the One Hundred Men Corporation has been issued and sold. All of this, he says, was done with just one purpose in mind: to write and bring to press a book explaining their method of recovery. That book, he confidently reports, "should be in the hands of our printer about March 1." With the manuscript now complete and publication just weeks away, "our position is much improved" because donors and any potential writer of the "Foreword" along with "publications in which we seek articles, can now see precisely with what they deal . . . and can now judge intelligently whether our proposals are entitled to their favorable consideration."

Despite these significant accomplishments, there are, he notes, several "problems coming before the trustees at this time [which] may be resolved into four main categories. Here they are:

1. Securing of proper publicity in such periodicals as Readers Digest, Saturday Post, Good Housekeeping, etc.

2. To persuade suitable persons of prominence to read our book, investigate our situation, and vouch for our work in a preface to the volume.

3. To secure funds in an amount which we estimate at $2500.00, to pay printing costs, to maintain an office and staff able to handle the large number of inquiries and problems which the book will undoubtedly provoke.

4. To consider in detail, and to lay down guiding principles and policies which we ought to bear in mind after the appearance of the book."

The remaining two and half pages of the letter are taken up with his report of "how we stand right now on each one of these points." This amounts to a recounting of his and Hank's most recent activities along with direct or implied suggestions for what the trustees might do if they wish to be helpful going forward.

Beginning with the problem of securing publicity, Bill tells about their meetings with *Readers Digest* and *Good Housekeeping* and notes their success with these two prestigious publications along with the nagging questions they faced during each of those encounters: "Are these results what Messrs. Parkhurst and Wilson claim them to be? Furthermore, is there going to be any continuity to the work? What is going to be done for, or said to, the distressed people who write asking for an answer?" Bill noted that similar problems arose when Charles Towns contacted the American Medical Association "setting forth his observations on our work and enclosing the last chapter of our book." The AMA "wanted to know what sort of an organization we were, who the officers were, what we used for money, and where Mr. Towns figured in." Wilson ruefully observes that "of course, we can't answer all these questions yet, because we do not know what our finances will be or what the trustees think should be done." In short, the ongoing problem of uncertain financing was having a negative impact on every aspect of their efforts, including their ability to get free publicity from two of the most popular magazines in the country and compromising the possibility of an endorsement by the AMA.

Concluding the "proper publicity" section of the letter, Bill notes that

Hank Parkhurst has mapped out an extensive program which can be used to promote the sale of the book. He has also laid out office procedures, and a system for handling inquiries. So, subject to the advice of the trustees, we are prepared to go ahead with the publication of the book and are organized to take care of the mail which will come in. Provided, of course, we have the means to do it, and it seems the desirable thing to do.

Bill's deferential implication that there might be some question of proceeding with the publication of the book and that the decision to do so would be subject to the advice of the trustees is more a matter of polite politics than actual fact. There was no possibility—other than insurmountable financial difficulties—they were *not* going to publish this book. Bill is clearly proud that, other than the troubling questions raised by *Readers Digest, Good Housekeeping* and the AMA (which could all be easily resolved with money), he and Hank had effectively made contact with two of the largest magazines in the country and received assurance that they would be interested in running articles about their new book once it was published.

What the trustees do need to pay the most attention to, he says, is the second issue (one of "immediate and paramount importance"), which is the problem of finding the right person to endorse the book and its methods. Wilson considers this as critical, because once a famous and reputable man has done so "we ought to get anything we need in the way of publicity, and we can much more readily raise the $2500.00 which will be needed to print the book and to maintain the status quo until the book royalties and contributions to The Alcoholic Foundation take up the slack." All of these doors would open easily, he claims, if only the right person could be persuaded "to read our book, investigate our situation, and vouch for our work in a preface to the volume." Bill mentions some possible candidates for this job ("Mr. Ford, Dr. Carel [sic], the Mayo brothers, Dr. Fosdick"), but notes that little has been done in this direction and so the "discussion of such names and the manner of approach should, perhaps, be one of the main considerations of the next Foundation meeting." Bill's implication here is that, given their familiarity with many rich, powerful, and prominent men, the Rockefeller people should take on the responsibility for getting this job done.

Moving on to the important problem of money—calling it "the sinews of war"[8] —Bill notes that, "to get the book printed, to continue our office, etc. will require $2500.00." This, he points out, is "equivalent to the sale of one hundred shares of stock in the book corporation" and he is confident cash buyers can be readily found for those one hundred shares once the preceding two problems, publicity and authentication, have been successfully addressed.

Skipping over any details about how the sale of these one hundred shares might actually be made, Wilson then presents an ingenious plan which would "resolve all our financial difficulties at one fell swoop."

> Touching money, another alternative presents itself. Suppose we could find, for example, a public spirited person or persons, who would agree to buy at, let us say, half price, five or ten thousand books. These books might

be distributed by the buyer to ministers, doctors, or hospitals, of which there are six to seven thousand in the Unites States. Or again, they might be placed in libraries; or perhaps better still, in hotel rooms along with the Gideon Bible. This last might be the best bet for all, for almost every man of us has passed hours of terror and depression in those lonely cubicles. Under these conditions, the book would hit the man at the most receptive moment, and it would be introduced accidentally, instead of by another person. The approach in those places would be perfect.

Granted a firm order from people of unquestioned credit, we could easily persuade a printer to undertake the work without any money in advance, and to raise funds on the sale of stock with such an order in hand, would be nothing.

So possibly some thought should be given to a list of people who might be approached on this basis. An order of this kind would resolve all our difficulties at one fell swoop. It would put the whole venture in the clear and enable us to pay off Mr. Towns and the cash subscribers for stock. Further royalties and profits from the book could then be immediately applied to the work without having to make these deductions.

No one was fooled by Bill's "suppose we could find, for example, a public spirited person . . .": The proposal was aimed directly at John D. Rockefeller Jr. The suggestion that Rockefeller might be convinced to buy and then freely distribute copies of the book had been put forward by Charles Towns the previous October when he speculated that the great man should be persuaded to buy "five hundred thousand copies" and then give them away.[9] Bill seems fairly confident Rockefeller might actually agree to this plan, although for the purposes of the present proposal, he judiciously reduced the suggested initial order from Charles's half-million copies to a much more reasonable five or ten thousand.*

Finally arriving at the fourth and final problem, Bill solicits the trustee's advice on the "many matters of policy" that should be resolved before the book is published and he does so by asking seven specific questions:

- Will the Alcoholic Foundation maintain an office?

- Shall its address and the names of the trustees be disclosed?

- In our literature shall we make any public appeal either expressed or implied for funds?

- How shall the details of The Foundation work be administered?

- In the book itself, shall we invite people to write to The Alcoholic Foundation, or the publishing company?

---

* Despite the overwhelming logic of this ambitious solution to their money problems, neither Rockefeller nor any other philanthropist ever seriously entertained this proposal.

- Shall the activities of The Foundation and the publishing company be consolidated or kept separate?

- How can we be helpful to Mr. Towns within strictly ethical limits? For he has certainly played fair with us.

Frank Amos's cover letter had requested that everyone carefully read Bill's letter and then formulate their ideas on what should be done. In support of this, Wilson concludes his letter with a single sentence paragraph containing a neat summation of everything which had gone before along with a polite request: "Publicity, authentication, money and policy; upon these things we would very much like the help and advice of the Trustees."

The Book Goes to the Editor

Bill Wilson had written the Twelve Steps and then Chapters Five and Six in four weeks (or less) and, by the end of the year, a full version of the book was complete. With this first draft in hand, Hank Parkhurst was anxious to get a copy to the editor, Tom Uzzell, as soon as possible. Ruth may have even finished typing the final review copy before the New Year's Eve party on Saturday night, but whenever she finished, Parkhurst mailed the manuscript to Uzzell, most likely on the first Monday or Tuesday of the year. (Mail delivery, it must be remembered, was extremely efficient in 1939. For instance, at that time New York City had as many as six daily deliveries to business addresses and a minimum of three residential deliveries every day but Sunday.[10]) Uzzell almost certainly had the manuscript in his hands by Tuesday, January 3 and, after reading it, wrote Hank an enthusiastic letter with his favorable first impressions. Tom's letter has not been preserved, but shortly after he received it, Hank wrote to Bill liberally quoting various portions of Uzzell's extremely positive response, telling him "If I were you, I would be intensely proud of this opinion."[11]

Hank's letter to Bill was the second enclosure in the packet Frank Amos sent off to the trustees. It was included because it provided not only a favorable professional opinion of Bill Wilson's writing, but more important, the editor's conviction that the book was sure to be a commercial success. Hank opened his letter by recapping Thomas H. Uzzell's impressive credentials and then went on to let Uzzell speak for himself:*

> He says: "I spent last evening with the manuscript. I knew, of course, what the document was, but on reading additional chapters and surveying the job as a whole, I found myself deeply moved, at times full of amazement, almost incredulity, and during most of the reading I was extremely sympathetic. My feeling at the moment is that you should certainly hold on to the production and distribution of this volume, if you can, for she ought to go far, wide and handsome, and net those concerned a neat

---

* It is highly likely that Hank's letter to Bill was really put together for the sole purpose of impressing the trustees and potential investors. Bill almost certainly knew who Tom Uzzell was—Hank had met with him already about this project in early November—and what his credentials were. Additionally, it is hard to imagine that, upon receipt of Uzzell's letter, Hank wouldn't have immediately called Bill Wilson on the phone and read it to him or just handed it to him since he was living with the Wilsons at this point after Kathleen threw him out of the Montclair house.

profit. You have here an extremely urgent problem, you have a successful defiance of medicine, you have a religious story, you have a deeply human story, and, lastly, you have a whole flock of happy endings—my God! I don't know what else you could want for a good book. I believe in it most emphatically."

He further says, "The whole book needs the final shaping of a professional hand." And then goes on at considerable length into mechanical details with which I will not bother you.

But it is interesting that he ends his letter as follows: "I understand better now the enthusiasm you revealed in your talks with me about this work. I thought you were exaggerating somewhat, but now I have joined the choir invisible."[12]

Could there be any doubt after such a glowing review and the promise that the book would surely sell well and turn a fair profit that the trustees could do anything other than find some way to raise the $2,500 so desperately needed to bring this wonderful book to press?

More Stock Can Now Be Sold

Once the book was in the hands of the editor, Bill Wilson was, at least temporarily, relieved of his writing duties, and able to turn his attention more fully toward selling stock in Works Publishing. Hank's letter to him—with all those glowing quotes from Uzzell and his prediction of the book's all but certain success—served as a convincing promotion piece for these sales pitches and Bill likely brought it with him to show potential investors whenever possible. Making copies of this letter, sending out solicitations, and typing up acknowledgements for the receipt of stock payments kept Ruth Hock busy throughout the first two weeks of January, so much so that on January 11 she apologized to Bill Ruddell for a late response by explaining she had "been running around in circles"[13] lately and was just now getting around to crafting a response to his letter.

That same day, Ruth typed up letters acknowledging the receipt of a check for the full payment of five shares of stock from Bill's former boss, Clayton Quaw, and another to John Parker in Boston for one share. Both of these, along with an acknowledgement sent out six days later for full payment of eight shares of stock sold to F. E. Miller, were clearly the result of Bill Wilson's January sales efforts.[14]

The Trustees Meet

On Wednesday, January 18, twelve days after Frank Amos had mailed out his invitation packets, the trustees of the Alcoholic Foundation finally met. It was their first meeting in almost four months and, although Frank had originally promised them a dinner followed by an evening meeting, it turned out to be a much simpler affair held in Willard Richardson's office at 3 o'clock in the afternoon.

Perhaps the biggest news was that Dr. Bob Smith was in town and attending his first meeting of the Alcoholic Foundation. As a trustee, Bob had previously only cast his vote by mailed-in proxies, but for this meeting he traveled to New York City to be an active participant in the decision-making process. Smith's physical presence was likely driven by the fact that the foundation was about to approve the direction Wilson and Parkhurst had taken since their last meeting and his support was considered critical for the acceptance of these significant changes. Bob's presence was also needed to form a working quorum of three trustees since neither Bill Ruddell, the Chairman of the Board, nor the attorney, John Wood, were able to attend.

Two New Trustees Are Added and a Membership Count Is Made

The meeting opened with a reading and acceptance of the minutes from their last meeting on September 23 and then moved on to the first order of business, a "discussion which resulted in the unanimous opinion that the Board of Trustees should be increased in number." Following that discussion, Willard Richardson made a motion that the Board "be increased in number from five (5) to seven (7), adding one each in Class A and Class B."[15] Dr. Bob immediately seconded this and the resolution passed unanimously. Richardson then nominated Bill's brother-in-law, Dr. Leonard V. Strong, to be the new Class A (non-alcoholic) trustee and Bob Smith again seconded. Dr. Bob then nominated Harry Brick as the new Class B (alcoholic) trustee—a motion that Richardson seconded. Both men were then elected unanimously.[16]*

These two choices produced mixed results. Leonard Strong would serve as a trustee until his retirement in October 1954, but Harry Brick's term proved to be much shorter than anyone expected. Harry had gotten sober the previous June and he was a successful businessman.[17] While his personal account, "A Different Slant," is the shortest story to appear in the first edition of the Big Book,[18] his drunken sprees and ultimate recovery are covered in much more detail at the end of the chapter "More About Alcoholism" where he appears as "Fred, a partner in a well known accounting firm."[19] Unfortunately, Harry Brick drank the following December, triggering his automatic removal from the Board.

Following the election of these new board members, an update was given on the overall progress of the Fellowships in both Ohio and New York:

> Details of the work being done among alcoholics in and around Akron were given in most interesting and inspiring fashion by Trustee Smith, who is the unofficial head of that fellowship. It is estimated that there are now around 75 redeemed alcoholics in the Akron section and new ones are being contacted and worked on continually.

---

* There is a persistent story (online and in several books) that Harry Brick was elected to replace the drunken Bill Ruddell. This is completely untrue. Ruddell was sober and extremely active in selling shares of their stock at this time. He continued as Chairman of the Board of Trustees until February 14, 1939 when his resignation from that position was accepted and he was elected to the Foundation's Advisory Committee instead (Minutes of the Board Meeting, GSO, Box 59, 1939, Folder C, Document 1939-44a).

William G. Wilson, one of the leaders of the fellowship in the New York metropolitan district, reported on the work among alcoholics in that district and estimated that there were at least 60 reformed alcoholics in that district with a large number of new ones being contacted continually.[20]

These reports are interesting because the numbers are more credible than the estimates found in other contemporary documents. This census count was presented for the record in an official foundation meeting, one in which both of the leaders were present and listening to each other. They attest to the fact that the former 70/30 split in membership between Akron and New York had moved toward a more equal distribution—with Akron claiming 56 percent of the membership and New York 44 percent.

Also worth noting is that Dr. Bob is identified here as the unofficial head in Akron, while Bill Wilson only gets credit for being "one of the leaders" in New York—wording which alludes to Hank Parkhurst's central role in the Eastern group at that time.

Bill Presents the Book and It Is Approved

Following those recaps, Wilson gave a long report on the purpose and progress of the book—tentatively named "100 Men"—describing the steps they had been forced to take because "friends and workers in this fellowship had failed to raise sufficient funds by contributions to cover the necessary expenses involved in the writing of this book and handling of all details incident thereto." Interestingly, the word "stock" is never mentioned in the minutes. Instead it says "it had been decided to form an organization for the preparation and printing of this book, and contributions had been accepted for this purpose." Distancing themselves as much as possible from this venture, the trustees also note that "the Alcoholic Foundation does not have any legal connection whatsoever with the organization or operation of this to-be-formed publishing company," although the Foundation has agreed to accept "a contribution of $0.35 per volume sold if and when the book is published and put on sale."[21]

The other issues raised in Bill Wilson's four-page letter were then addressed.

> The trustees of the Alcoholic Foundation, as individuals, were asked to render advice and such other possible assistance in connection with the preparation and publishing of this book. The sentiment to render all such possible assistance was unanimous, but the Alcoholic Foundation, not having any funds available, could not at this time contribute toward this project.[22]

This unanimous desire of the trustees to render assistance as individuals meant that the non-alcoholic trustees had reversed their earlier opposition to the self-publication of the book and agreed to throw their support behind the fledgling One Hundred Men Corporation. They did this in the most tangible way possible—by voting with their checkbooks. A few days after the meeting, Willard Richardson and A. LeRoy

Chipman both bought two shares of stock for $50 and shortly after that Dr. Leonard Strong mailed in a $125 check for five shares.[23]*

Bill's and Hank's gamble to strike out on their own in defiance of the advice offered by the Rockefeller men had paid off. Richardson and Chipman may not have been entirely happy about the course they were taking, but at this point, they had no other choice. They could either completely distance themselves from the One Hundred Men Corporation or give it their blessing, which they emphatically decided to do with their stock purchase.

While Dr. Bob Smith was an active presence at the Board meeting, there is no evidence he was similarly active in reviewing the just completed manuscript of the book. Wilson had repeatedly complained about his lack of criticism and input for the book and now here he was—a captive audience in New York. With the first pass at the book not only complete, but already in the hands of a critic, Bill would surely have wanted to know Bob's candid opinion of what he had written and perhaps even asked for help with some corrections. But, while Wilson does later talk about the changes Tom Uzzell made to the manuscript, he makes no mention of any suggestions being offered by Dr. Bob Smith at this time or, for that matter, at any other time.

The Board meeting was held on a Wednesday afternoon, but there is no record of when Dr. Bob arrived in New York, or of when he returned to Ohio. If his travel plans permitted, he would have most likely come into town the previous day so he could prepare for the meeting and attend the regular Tuesday night meeting in Brooklyn, but even this is not mentioned in the archived records.** Other than his votes at the trustee's meeting, Bob seems to have come and gone in New York without leaving any other significant traces.

The First Article about A.A. Is Published

On January 19, the day after the Board meeting, the very first public notice of Alcoholics Anonymous appeared in a New Jersey newspaper, *The Hackettstown Courier-Post*.*** The article was entitled "There Is Hope," and the opening paragraph identified the author as Silas Bent****, noting he was a "former Sunday Editor of the New York Times and author of many well known books."[24] While this sounds like a Hank Parkhurst project,

---

* Strangely Frank Amos, the venture's greatest promoter among the Rockefeller men (but also the least affluent), did not buy any stock. Nor did Albert Scott, a titular member of the Advisory Committee, who does not seem to have been consulted on any level at this point of the conversation.

** The only contemporary note from this time is one of Lois's infrequent and spare early 1939 diary entries, this one from January 19, the day after the Board meeting, where she tantalizingly, but unhelpfully, writes: "Fiasco." A fight with Bill? Some problem with Dr. Bob? A fight between Bob and Bill (or Hank in some combination thereof)? A complication with one of the regular tenants of the Wilson household? Some issue with her all-but-defunct interior design business? There is, unfortunately, no way to know.

*** The most commonly available copy of this article (online and at the GSO archive) is a scan of a torn copy with words truncated and missing down the right-hand side and several words missing at the bottom. However, the archive at Stepping Stones does contain a full copy of the piece with all the words intact. (StSt, AA 501.1, Box 13, Folder 15).

**** Exactly why Silas Bent was writing a publicity piece for Alcoholics Anonymous at this time, but not his personal story for the Big Book, remains a mystery. Given his credentials and talents, he would have presumably been the first person Bill Wilson would ask to write his story. The most likely supposition is that Silas continually slipped in the program and was therefore not considered a good example of sustained recovery—but this explanation is pure speculation with nothing more than circumstantial evidence to support it.

it was almost certainly Bill Ruddell who was responsible for the placement of this article in his hometown paper.*

Without naming names, Silas tells the story of Hank Parkhurst who, "when I met him, three years ago . . . had lost his $20,000 a year job on account of drink," but who had been totally abstinent since then. Bent said he was offering that man's story here because it offers hope of redemption to a million alcoholics in this country, and then he immediately goes on to provide the first public description of Alcoholics Anonymous.

> The man is one of a remarkable fellowship, a sort of secret order, dedicated to reclaiming those who are fatally given to the cup. There are more than 100 of them scattered through the United States. The group is noteworthy, to begin with, in that no man or woman who comes under the wing is asked to sign a pledge or to sign anything else on the dotted line. Nobody is asked to pay. Admission to the order means no initiation fee, no annual dues, nor regalia and no ritual. It is anonymous because if its members were known they would be overwhelmed with more pleas for their volunteer help than they could handle. Therefore new recruits are found by word of mouth, by grapevine in the underworld of those who have reached the end of the tether.

> Those fellows are not reformers. There is nothing holier-than-thou about them. They are former drunkards, the sort of guys any tippler might like to meet at a bar today, if they were still at it. The tie that binds them is the tie of an escape from common disaster; the radiance which shines in their faces is the eagerness to help others escape.[25]

Silas goes on to describe how open and democratic this new organization is and then tells the story (once again without names) of Rowland Hazard's visit to Dr. Carl Jung and his subsequent almost miraculous release from his alcoholic compulsions. Bent ends this short piece with glowing praise for these men who "have found the solution to one of the world's oldest problems," but offers no way for the reader to contact this secret order, which remains completely anonymous.

Bill Ruddell sent off multiple copies of the article to Hank Parkhurst and Ruth Hock wrote back thanking him for sending them, noting that they "hadn't received the papers as yet but will probably come in tomorrow."

Although there was no contact information in Silas Bent's article, it was the first announcement to the world that there was a new path to recovery for the country's suffering alcoholics. A cure for the drink problem had been discovered and it was currently working for "more than 100 of them scattered through the United States"!

---

* Ruddell lived at 108 Harvey Street in Hackettstown at this time (see Secretary [Ruth Hock] to Wm. J. Ruddell, January 5, 1939: GSO, Box 59, 1939, Folder C, Document 1939-4), which was over forty miles from Hank's house in Montclair, NJ. Ruddell was also then working at the American Saw Mill Machinery Company in Hackettstown (Secretary [Ruth Hock] to Wm. J. Ruddell, January 25, 1939, GSO, Box 59, 1939, Folder C, Document 1939-41).

CHAPTER TWENTY-SEVEN

Editing the Manuscript

~January to March 1939~

Hank Parkhurst had spoken with Tom Uzzell sometime just before Thanksgiving and they agreed that, once the manuscript was completed, he would review the format of the book and then turn it over to Janet Blair for further editing.[1] When Uzzell finally received the manuscript in early January, his first reaction was extremely positive, but he also made the critical comment that "the whole book needs a final shaping by a professional hand"—an obvious pitch for his own services. Hank reported this to Bill noting that Uzzell went "on at considerable length into [the] mechanical details" of this shaping, but unfortunately he was no more specific than that in his letter, telling Wilson "I will not bother you" with those details now.[2] That was an unfortunate omission; we would love to know some of those details today.

Conflicting Accounts of Tom Uzzell's Contributions

In the past, there has been significant confusion over the extent of the changes Tom Uzzell made to the text of the Big Book. We have direct testimony on this issue from Bill Wilson, Ruth Hock, and Jim Burwell—three people who were present or close to that process at the time—but their versions of the story substantially contradict each other and are further tainted by their general unreliability when it comes to anything like historical accuracy in relation to details.

In his 1947 speech at Hope Manor—one that was full of historical inaccuracies—and its subsequent revision as "The Evolution of Alcoholics Anonymous," Jim Burwell says when Uzzell edited the book "practically nothing was done to the personal stories of the individual members and there was less than [a] 20% deletion from the original manuscript."[3] Such a 20 percent cut, he notes, "was very, very low," adding that, in his understanding, an editorial deletion of "thirty-five percent is [considered] good for a well known author."[4]

Ruth Hock's most detailed statement on this matter came in a 1955 letter to Bill Wilson where she notes that "it had been agreed, for one thing, that the book, as written, was too long but nobody could agree on where and how to cut it." So it was given to Uzzell who "cut the book by at least a third as I remember it and in my opinion did a wonderful job on sharpening up the context without losing anything at all of what you were trying to say . . . and the way you said it."[5] Twenty-nine years later, she was quoted as saying the editor had cut the book in "half—from 800 pages to 400 pages"—a reduction of a full 50 percent.[6] But this quote is almost certainly based on two telephone interviews with Ruth conducted by the A.A. historian Bill Pittman in July 1982 and January 1983. In his 1986 book, *The Way It Began*, he reported that Ruth claimed the percentage was even higher than this saying "Tom Uzzell had to edit out 800 pages to reach" the 400 pages contained in the first edition of the Big Book. This means that according to Ruth's later recollection, the original text was cut down by a full two-thirds—from 1,200 pages to 400.[7]

These huge and widely divergent estimates are further compromised by the fact that Ruth talks about the deletions in relation to the 400-page first edition printing of the book, while what the editors would have been dealing with was an original typed manuscript of the text before it was edited for the Multilith printing. Since the Mulitlith copy amounted to only 156 typed pages, it is clear that Tom Uzzell never saw anything like 800 (let alone 1,200) pages of original material.

Wilson himself remembered the editor had only "sharpened up the English but [he] didn't change much of anything excepting to take my story out of the story section where it had been the number one story and insisted on using it to open the book. What is now Chapter 2 ["There Is A Solution"], I had intended to be Chapter 1."[8] Bill gives no clue whatsoever about how much of that sharpening up may have come from deleted text (rather than just cosmetic word changes), nor does he anywhere indicate the overall amount of text Uzzell might have deleted. Given Wilson's well-documented resistance to making any significant changes to what he had already written—despite his occasional disavowal, Bill's pride of authorship was immense—this reluctance to be more specific about the extent of the editor's cuts is understandable.

Compounding the problem of these strikingly contradictory accounts—ranging from he 'didn't change much of anything' to 'he slashed the text by two-thirds'—is the fact that all three principals completely ignore Janet Blair's significant involvement in the editing process, making no mention whatsoever of her substantial presence in the project or of her contribution to the changes made both before and after the Multilith printing. All three give the credit for whatever editorial changes may have been made exclusively to Tom Uzzell, an attribution clearly contradicted by Blair's several letters to and from Parkhurst and Wilson during the first three weeks of February 1939.

What we do know is that when Tom Uzzell received the manuscript, Bill Wilson's story was prominently positioned in the back along with the rest of the individual stories, and that he was responsible for moving it to the front, insisting it should be the opening chapter in the book. However much Wilson may have welcomed this advice (it is hard to forget his temptation to call this new group "The B. W. Movement"[9]), it was certainly not something he could have comfortably suggested himself. Moving his story to the front violates the unity and equality created by having all of the stories together in the back; but Bill's first-person account of his successful recovery is a dramatic and effective way to open the book, grabbing the drinker's attention with a credible real-life story and giving him an excellent reason to continue reading in search of the information needed to bring about his own miraculous recovery from alcoholism.

Deletions to Bill's Story

As already noted, the only chapters for which we have early drafts—i.e., versions circulated before they appeared in the Multilith printing—are "There Is A Solution" and "Bill's Story." By comparing these earlier versions to the text of the Multilith Copy we can clearly see the extent of the changes made, although we cannot be certain that all of these edits were the work of the two editors. There is always the possibility that at least some of them were made by Bill Wilson before he turned the manuscript over to Tom Uzzell in early January.

The First Seven Paragraphs Are Cut

The first striking difference between what Wilson wrote nine months earlier and "Bill's Story" as it appears in the Multilith printing is the wholesale deletion of the first seven paragraphs, which contain a wealth of information about his early life.

> At the age of ten I went to live with my grandfather and grandmother—their ancestors settled the section of Vermont in which I was to grow up. Grandfather was a retired farmer and lumberman; he nurtured me on a vigorous pioneering tradition. I see, now, that my grandfather was the kind of man who helped make America.

> Little did anyone guess I was to be of the war generation, which would squander the savings, the pioneering traditions and the incredible stamina of your grandfather and mine. Ambitious but undisciplined—that was I. There was a genius for postponing, evading and shirking; but a certain dogged obstinacy and persistence drove me to succeed at special undertakings upon which my heart was set.

> Especially did I revel in attacking the difficult or the impossible. Grandfather said, for instance, that no one but an Australian could make and throw the boomerang. No school work done, no wood box filled and little sleep was there, until a boomerang had circled the church steeple, returning to almost decapitate him. Having accomplished this, my interest ceased.

So it was with my ambition to be a ball player; for I was finally elected captain of the team at the little Seminary I attended after leaving country school. Someone told me I could never sing, so I took up voice until I had appeared in a recital, then, as with the boomerang, my interest ended abruptly. I had commenced to fuss with the violin. This became such an obsession that athletics, school work, and all else went by the board much to everyone's consternation. I carried fiddling so far I failed to graduate. It was most embarrassing, for I was president of the Senior Class. So collapsed a certain legend of infallibility I had built around myself. Repairing this failure, I attempted to enter a leading technical school. Because of fierce enthusiasms I had displayed for matters chemical and electrical, It [sic] was assumed I was destined to become an engineer. At Boston, I failed the entrance examinations dismally. My people were heartbroken and my self sufficiency got another severe deflation.

Finally I commenced electrical engineering at an excellent military college, where it was fervently hoped I would get disciplined. No such thing happened. As usual I had good grades when interested but often failed when not. There was an illuminating instance concerning my calculus teacher. Not one formula would I learn, until all of the theory underlying the subject was made clear. At the library, I pored over the researches of Leibniz and Newton, whose genius had made calculul [sic] possible. Loving controversy, I argued much with my instructor, who quite properly gave me a zero, for I had solved only the first problem of the course. At this juncture, and quite conveniently for me, the United States decided to go to war.

We students bolted, almost to a man, for the First Officers Training Camp at Plattsburgh. I was commissioned second Lieutenant of artillery, electing that branch rather than aviation or infantry. For when I lay in my bunk at night, I had to confess I did not want to be killed. This suspicion of cowardice bothered me, for it couldn't be reconciled with the truly exalted patriotism which took possession when I hadn't time to think. Later, under fire abroad, I was relieved to learn I was like most men; scared enough, but willing to see it through. I was assigned to a post on the New England coast. The place is famous for its Yankee trading and whaling traditions.

Two far reaching events took place here. I married; had my first drink and liked it. My wife was city bred. She represented a way of life for which I secretly longed. To be her kind meant fine houses, servants, gay dinners, cultivated conversation and a much envied sophistication. I often felt a woeful lack of poise and polish. These inferiorities were later to drive me cityward in quest of success, as I suppose they have many a country boy.[10]

These paragraphs were originally followed by the line, "War fever ran high in the New England town . . ." and this now became the gripping opening sentence, having significantly more dramatic impact than the lackluster "At the age of ten I went to live with my grandfather and grandmother . . ." The rest of that new opening paragraph tells of Bill's discovery of alcohol as a young Army officer and how in his loneliness, he turned more and more to drink for relief.

Bill's Wartime Experiences Shortened

The next few paragraphs dealing with Bill's wartime experiences were also severely edited, but the results there were less fortunate. Uzzell's deletions may have resolved one particular problem, but they immediately caused another. After Tom's edits, all that remained of the original text was:

> We landed in England. I visited Winchester Cathedral. Much moved, I wandered outside. My attention was caught by a doggerel on an old tombstone:
>
> > "Here lies a Hampshire Grenadier
> > Who caught his death
> > Drinking cold small beer
> > A good soldier is ne'er forgot
> > Whether he dieth by musket
> > > Or by pot."
>
> Ominous warning—which I failed to heed.[11]

Bill's simple statement here that he was "much moved" at Winchester Cathedral has puzzled many readers of the Big Book over the years, especially since later in that chapter he makes two more specific references to his spiritual experience there. The first simply notes that when Ebby originally visited him with the message of recovery "That war-time day in old Winchester Cathedral came back again"—which tells us nothing about what it was that came back and why. The second mention is a bit more expansive, but still provides only a partial glimpse of what happened to him that day in England:

> The real significance of my experience in the Cathedral burst upon me. For a brief moment, I had needed and wanted God. There had been a humble willingness to have Him with me—and He came. But soon the sense of His presence had been blotted out by worldly clamors, mostly those within myself. And so it had been ever since. How blind I had been.[12]

Both of these later references to Winchester were originally written with the presumption that the reader was already familiar with the specifics of the profound experience he had there before sailing for France in 1918. But Uzzell had taken out all the overtly religious details from that first account, likely fearing that such an immediate introduction of God into the story would dissuade many readers from going any farther in the book.

The earlier version of the text provided concrete details for why Bill was so moved that day in England:

> We were in England. I stood in Winchester Cathedral with head bowed, in the presence of something I had never felt before. Where now was the God of the preachers? Across the Channel thousands were perishing that day. Why did He not come? Suddenly in that moment of darkness—He was there! I felt an enveloping comforting Presence. Tears stood in my eyes. I had glimpsed the great reality.
>
> Much moved, I wandered through the Cathedral yard. My attention was caught by a doggerel on an old tombstone.

> > "Here lies a Hampshire Grenadier
> > Who caught his death
> > Drinking cold small beer
> > A good soldier is ne'er forgot
> > Whether he dieth by musket
> >   or by pot."

> My mood changed. A squadron of fighters roared overhead. I cried to myself, "Here's to Adventure." The feeling of being in the great presence disappeared.[13]

Uzzell's deletion of all these specifics about Bill's "white light" experience at Winchester did, in fact, spare the reader an encounter with the issue of God on the very first page of Chapter 1; but since those details were never reintroduced later in the story, anyone reading this chapter would necessarily be perplexed by the two much less specific references to the incident that were left in the text.

Beyond these two major upfront deletions, "Bill's Story" received fairly minor editing by the editors. The early version of his story had 5,347 words while the Multilith printing used just 4,339—an overall reduction of 1,008 words, or 19 percent of the text. But 742 of those words were cut almost wholesale from the very beginning of the story, leaving just 266 words cut from the rest—an editorial deletion of less than 6 percent.

Edits to "There Is A Solution"

We know some of the changes made to "There Is A Solution" were edits made by Bill Wilson before he turned the manuscript over to Tom Uzzell in January. While the outline and format of that chapter remained the same over the months following its composition, Bill continually made small revisions to the text every time Ruth Hock retyped it. In the three earliest preserved drafts of this chapter, most of those changes are confined to the removal of words or the alterations of phrases as Wilson worked to increase the impact of his sentences and to clarify the message he was trying to deliver.

For example, here are three different versions of just one paragraph from "There Is A Solution" (a short description of Rowland Hazard's first meeting with Dr. Carl Jung) showing the progressive edits Bill made with each retyping of the text (deletions from the previous version are noted by ~~strikeouts~~ and additions by ***bold italics***). This is followed by the editors' version of that same paragraph as it appeared in the Multilith printing.

Stepping Stones Version 1 *[June 1938]*:

He had for many years before his encounter with this noted doctor, floundered desperately from one sanitarium to another. He had consulted several of the best known American psychologists and on their recommendation, he had gone to Europe and confined himself for a year in an institution there, at the same time, being under the care of this celebrated physician.[14]

Stepping Stones Version 2 *[June–September? 1938]*:

He had for many years before his encounter with this noted doctor, floundered ~~desperately~~ from one sanitarium to another. He had consulted several of the best known American psychologists and on their recommendation, he had gone to Europe and confined himself for a year in an institution there. ***A***t the same time, ~~being~~ ***he was*** under the care of this celebrated physician.[15]

GSO Version *[June–September? 1938]*:

~~He had~~ ***F***or many years before his encounter with this noted doctor, ***he had*** floundered from one sanitarium to another. He had consulted several of the best known American psychologists. ~~and~~ ***O***n their recommendations~~,~~ he had gone to Europe and confined himself for a year in an institution. ***T***here~~. At the same time,~~ he was under the care of this celebrated physician.[16]

Multilith Copy Version *[February 1939]*:

For ~~many~~ years ~~before his encounter with this noted doctor,~~ he had floundered from one sanitarium to another. He had consulted ~~several of~~ the best known American ~~psychologists~~ ***psychiatrists***. ~~On their recommendations,~~ ***Then*** he had gone to Europe, ~~and confined himself for a year in an institution. There he was under~~ ***placing himself in*** the care of ~~this~~ ***a*** celebrated physician ***who prescribed for him***.[17]

Uzzell and/or Blair were obviously much more aggressive in their edits than Bill had been with his fine-tuning attempts. Bill was tweaking the text; the editors were doing some serious rewriting.

One more example should suffice to illustrate the kind of progressive changes Bill Wilson made to "There Is A Solution" compared to what happened after it was in the hands of professional editors.

<u>Stepping Stones Version 1</u> *[June 1938]*:

If by chance you are, or have begun to suspect that you are, an alcoholic, we think there is no tenable middle of the road solution. You are in a position where life is becoming impossible, and if you have passed into the region from which there is no return through human aid, you have just two alternatives. One is to go on to the bitter end, blotting out the consciousness of your intolerable situation as best you can. Or, you can surely find what we have found, if you honestly want to, and are willing to pay the price. After years of living on a basis which now seems to us wholly false, you are not going to get rightly related to your Creator in a minute. None of us has found God in six easy lessons, but He can be found by all who are willing to put the task ahead of all else.[18]

<u>Stepping Stones Version 2</u> *[June-September? 1938]*:

If by chance you are, or have begun to suspect that you are, an alcoholic, we think ~~there is no tenable~~ *you have no* middle of the road solution. You are in a position where life is becoming impossible, and if you have passed into the region from which there is no return through human aid, you have just two alternatives. One is to go ~~on~~ to the bitter end, blotting out the consciousness of your intolerable situation as best you can. Or, you can surely find what we have found, if you honestly want to, and are willing to pay the price. After years of living on a basis which now seems ~~to us~~ wholly false, ~~you are not going to get~~ *we did not become* rightly related to your Creator in a minute. None of us ~~has~~ **have** found God in ~~six~~ easy lessons, but He can be found by all who are willing to put the task ahead of all else. *That goes for you too!*[19]

<u>GSO Version</u> *[June-September? 1938]*:

If by chance you are, or have begun to suspect that you are, an alcoholic, we think you have no middle-of-the-road solution. You are in a position where life is becoming impossible, and if you have passed into the region from which there is no return through human aid, you have ~~but~~ *just* two alternatives. One is to go *on* to the bitter end, blotting out the consciousness of your intolerable situation as best you can. Or you can surely find what we have found, if you honestly want to, and are willing ~~to pay the price~~ *make the effort*. After years of living on a basis which now seems wholly false, we did not become rightly related to our Creator in a minute. None of us have found God in easy lessons, but He can be found by all who are willing to put the task ahead of all else. ~~That goes for you too!~~[20]

Throughout Bill's ongoing edits, the number of words remained fairly constant (156, 155, and 146 respectively), but by the time the paragraph appears in the Multilith printing, it has been drastically reduced to just ninety words:

Multilith Printing Version *[February 1939]*:

If ~~by chance~~ you are, ~~or have begun to suspect that you are, an~~ *seriously* alcoholic, we ~~think~~ *believe* you have no middle-of-the-road solution. You are in a position where life is becoming impossible, and if you have passed into the region from which there is no return through human aid, you have ~~just~~ *but* two alternatives. ~~O~~: one is to go on to the bitter end, blotting out the consciousness of your intolerable situation as best you can; and the other, to find what we have found~~;~~. *This you can do* if you honestly want to, and are willing make the effort. ~~After years of living on a basis which now seems wholly false, we did not become rightly related to our Creator in a minute. None of us have found God in easy lessons, but He can be found by all who are willing to put the task ahead of all else.~~[21]

Both of these examples clearly demonstrate the talents of a professional editor. Extraneous verbiage and distracting thoughts have been removed, leaving a much more direct and effective story line. Bill's first attempt at the chapter certainly needed this kind of skillful editing throughout—an understandable need given that this was a first effort by an inexperienced author tackling a complicated subject.

Also worth noting is that these improvements to the text removed nothing essential from the earlier version, nor was anything of significant importance deleted. Here, as elsewhere, sentences have been modified for clarity or removed wholesale as being irrelevant to the point Bill is trying to make. Judging from these examples, it is clear the editors did in fact do "a wonderful job on sharpening up the context without losing anything at all" of what Bill Wilson was trying to say.[22]

While most changes were along the lines illustrated above, at times entire paragraphs or sections were deleted for clarity or lack of relevance. One example is the following deleted paragraph that had originally appeared just before the three-questions section of the "There Is A Solution."

For example, it is surprising to most of us that we have not developed a downright hatred for John Barleycorn and all his works, that we have not become intolerant and impatient with those who like to drink, for many sincerely believe that they should not be deprived of an age old privilege and pleasure just because a lot of people are softened and made sick by it. We are sure we have a way of life which, if adopted generally, would render excessive drinking a stupid and impossible practice. Most of us strongly feel that real tolerance of other people's shortcomings and viewpoints, and a decent respect for the opinions of mankind, are qualities which greatly enhance our usefulness to others, for in the last analysis our very lives as ex-alcoholics depend upon the constant thought of others, and how we may help meet their needs.

This run-on paragraph can only be described as an embarrassment of riches. It presents a number of randomly connected thoughts that, at best, need to be repackaged into several different paragraphs. As it stands, it is an excellent example of the 'everything but the kitchen sink' type of writing Bill occasionally adopted in his earliest attempts. At some point, Wilson (or, much more likely, one of the two editors) realized just how jumbled this paragraph was and how irrelevant it was to the argument being made at that point in the story and it was simply deleted rather than modified.

All these examples conclusively demonstrate that, despite Bill's ongoing minor changes, the text was still desperately in need of the much more substantial edits made by Tom Uzzell once he received the manuscript, or by Janet Blair after Tom had shaped it.

Radical Cuts Were Made

Bill's longest version of "There Is A Solution" contains an impressive 5,810 words, while the shortest is roughly 5,400 words, and these numbers are reasonably close to his projected target of 5,000 words per chapter. But the Multilith printing contains only 3,616 words, a dramatic 37 percent reduction of the shortest surviving original text. While some of these edits may have been made by Bill Wilson before turning the manuscript over to Tom Uzzell, his ongoing changes were most likely minimal and similar to the ones shown above. As Ruth noted, the book was just too long and nobody could agree on how to cut it.[23] If nobody—especially Bill Wilson—could agree on the necessary edits, then those more radical cuts could only have been the work of an outside editor.

If we combine the number of words in the original versions of these two stories (11,157) and compare that to a similar count from the Multilith versions (7,955), it shows the two editors had cut almost 29 percent from the originals. This same percentage might hold true for the rest of the chapters, but it would also be reasonable to presume that Bill's writing became progressively better once he got serious about finishing the book in mid-September, so much so that the editors' deletions might have been less than those made to his two earliest efforts. While it is plausible to argue that Bill's prose would have necessarily improved as the book progressed, it is more difficult to assess the effect of the ongoing suggestions and insertions that might have been made by the members of the New York Fellowship. While these may have improved the other nine expositional chapters—leaving them in much less need of drastic cutting when the manuscript was finally delivered into the editor's hands—it is just as likely that the suggestions Wilson had to cobble into his own text were among the probable suspects for later deletion or serious modification.

Without the pre-Multilith versions of the nine later chapters there is no way of determining exactly how much the editors cut from the finished manuscript they were given. But the examples above strongly suggest Jim Burwell may have been on the low side when he claimed there was somewhat less than a 20 percent deletion of text,[24] and Ruth Hock may have been a bit high with her original estimate that the editors cut the book by at least a third.[25] The percentage deleted probably fell somewhere in between these two. However, given these numbers, Bill Wilson's claim that, other than repositioning his story in the book, the editor made only cosmetic changes is woefully inaccurate.[26] The editors did more than just sharpen up the English and they did so by making both substantive deletions and significant corrections to the text.

Janet Blair's Contributions

Other than moving "Bill's Story" up to the front of the book, and his possible contributions to the edits described above, we do not know what specific changes Tom Uzzell made to the manuscript; but we do know a bit more about the edits Janet Blair made. When she finally received the manuscript, it had already been reformatted according to Uzzell's suggestions and this created some immediate problems for her. When just two chapters of the book were available, "There Is A Solution" had always come before "Bill's Story." But now, with Tom's reordering, she found the opening of the new Chapter 2 confusing. On Monday, February 6, after her first weekend's work on the book, she wrote Hank Parkhurst expressing her concerns and offering a solution.

> Dear Mr. Parkhurst:
>
> I am enclosing Chapters 1 and 2. It is all so amazingly interesting, and I feel the urgency of getting it out so keenly that I am tempted to rush ahead; but, remembering what you said, I have gone over these two chapters each three times.
>
> I could never say, I find, that "This is the best I can do." Who could? But, within reasonable limits, it is.
>
> Mr. Parkhurst, may I say a word about the continuity? It bothers me a little. Chapter 1, is Bill's story. Right? Bill's story includes a description of the terrible dilemma in which he was when his friend came to him; it includes what the doctor thought; it includes a brief account of the fellowship. It tells the solution.
>
> When I started Chapter 2, I thought from the first line I was beginning the story of another man, as the first page is just that. On page 2, you leave him, and go on to tell of the fellowship and alcoholics in general. On page 8 you return to the man, and for about a page tell us more about him; the rest of the chapter is general.
>
> In Chapter 2, you never mention Bill or his friend, although the "solution," as you call Chapter 2 is given in Chapter 1.
>
> I'm not suggesting a change. Maybe I am the one who is befogged; but I am supposed to represent the reader, and I felt I should tell you this. At this moment, it seems to me it would have been smoother, to start Chapter 2 on page 2, "We, of ALCOHOLICS ANONYMOUS, know one hundred men who were once just as hopeless as Bill," and so on.

Then somewhere in the chapter, say at the bottom of page 8, put in page 1, about the man who consults the European doctor; tell all about him that you have in this chapter told in two different places; then finish the chapter as you have it.

In other words, Bill's story, as told in detail in Chapter 1, is more impressive than the shorter account of the man, and a better lead off for the remark with which page 2 starts.

I'd be awfully glad to have a line as to your reaction to my markings.

Sincerely,

Janet Blair

2 more chapters will be mailed Tuesday[27]

This letter is informative on several levels. First of all, it clearly illustrates the value of engaging a professional editor, someone with a fresh set of eyes and the ability to suggest creative solutions for previously unseen problems. Janet Blair's observation that "There Is A Solution" would read much better if the two parts of Rowland Hazard's story about visiting Dr. Carl Jung were consolidated in the back of the chapter certainly made the opening much less confusing. Once noticed, this was so obvious that her suggestion was readily taken and the story appeared that way in the Multilith printing. Unfortunately, whatever other changes she may have suggested are not mentioned and her edited copy has not been preserved.

Also worth noting is that while this letter with edits for Chapters 1 and 2 was sent off to Hank Parkhurst on Monday, she was working so fast that she planned to have the next two chapters done and in the mail to him by the end of the next day. One can only imagine what sort of pressure Hank Parkhurst was putting on her to get this job done as quickly as possible so that they could move the book project forward without any unnecessary delay.

But perhaps most perceptive is Janet Blair's questioning why Chapter 2 was called "There Is A Solution" when the solution has already been "given in Chapter 1." She had not yet read any of the following chapters, but she realized the completeness of the solution already outlined in "Bill's Story." Given that full presentation of the solution, the title of Chapter 2 confused her. This is a very astute observation on her part, one that confirms our earlier contention that the full solution—i.e., the equivalent of the Twelve Steps—had already been supplied in "Bill's Story."

Finally, there is her reluctance to push this particular point ("I'm not suggesting a change"), which shows a bit of hesitation on her part as she tries to feel out just how far she can go with her changes, a hesitation she reemphasized in the final sentence of the letter where she candidly asks for Hank's reaction to her edits. From past experience Blair surely knew some authors could be more obstinate than others when it came to making editorial changes; so with these, her first suggested edits, she was judiciously testing the waters to see if this one big change and her other suggestions were going to be accepted gracefully or not.

She need not have feared. Bill Wilson was surprisingly amenable to almost all of her suggestions. The following Wednesday, when he would have had at most four edited chapters in hand, he graciously accepted the work she had done so far:

Feb. 8, 1939

Mrs. Janet M. Blair,
904 South St.,
Peekskill, N. Y.

Dear Mrs. Blair:

I am very grateful that you have the perception to understand what it is I want to say and the ability to say it so well. You have certainly cleared up our manuscript.

I also want to thank you for your interest and painstaking effort.

In effect, I have agreed with all you have done. Upon one or two minor matters I have taken the bit in my own teeth, but you may set that down to Vermont perversity and be assured that I heartily agree with you in your corrections after all.

Very much yours,

Wm. G. Wilson

WGW:RH[28]

Bill is not exactly clear here over whether he really "agreed with *all* you have done" (emphasis added) or whether he is still holding out on "one or two minor matters," but it is certainly a generous response from a man who had previously been decidedly obstinate whenever people tried to change anything he had written.

More suggested changes were to come. By the time she got to "Working With Others," Janet Blair was confidently (but very politely) suggesting that the lead paragraph had to be deleted for clarity's sake. She had obviously already made substantial comments trying to fix the first two paragraphs of the chapter, but decided at the last minute this would just not do.

Read this first

Memo. To Authors: Please note that this is written after I wrote the penciled and typed comments on the first and second paragraphs of Chapter seven.

The more I think about it, please Sirs, the more it seems to me that this first paragraph doesn't belong here at all. Every time I read the page, I feel a gap between the paragraphs, I finally analyzed it this way:

What does this chapter deal with anyway? Working with other alcoholics, as a vital part of the cure. Right? If that is right, what are these people (religious, but alcoholic) doing in the picture? Presumably they illustrate the fact that faith without works is dead—that is "works" in general, not, of course, the work of helping other alcoholics, what are we talking about, since they themselves cannot very well do that until they are cured.

When I tell you that one time I read the page I thought these religious people were the ones "you" were supposed to carry the message to, you will sense the confusion.[29]

Unfortunately we have no copy of the text before she worked on it, so there is no way of knowing exactly what was deleted here; but there is no paragraph in the Multilith printing that matches this description. Blair's questionable first paragraph was just deleted.

The final letter Janet Blair wrote to Bill Wilson went out on Monday, February 20 and things were not as amicable as they had been two weeks earlier. After mentioning some "enclosed lines" (unfortunately not saved) that she thought might be of interest, Janet noted that, while the job was not yet finished, her bill for services rendered was now past due: "I'd be grateful for half the $35 by the end of this week. I understand, of course, that the job is not finished, as I have some 20,000 odd words to go over yet. I wish I could afford to do the work for nothing, but I just can't. And I need the money!"[30]

Blair does not specify whether the remaining 20,000 words were in the front section of the book (which would include "To Wives," "The Family Afterward," "To Employers," and "A Vision For You") or if they comprised the final ten (of twenty) stories in the back. However, at the pace she was working—Blair had edited four chapters containing almost 16,000 words in the four days between February 3 and February 7—she was almost certainly talking about the ten stories that still needed to be edited when she wrote this letter just two weeks later.

But the most interesting thing about this is that while Janet Blair was complaining about her lack of payment and the amount of work still remaining on February 20, Wilson and Parkhurst had already sent the manuscript off to the printer a few days earlier. Finished Multilith copies of the book were available either late that same day or the next morning when, on February 21, Frank Amos explicitly tells Willard Richardson the "photo-lith copies of the book are now completed and I am sending one copy with this [letter]." Amos also confirms that Janet Blair had not yet finished her work on the story section, telling Richardson "the main part of the book has been carefully edited, but the individual stories, occupying the last half of the book, still must undergo considerable editing."[31] Hank and Bill were so broke they couldn't stay current with Blair and still afford to pay the offset printer, so they simply sent the manuscript out with the final ten stories unedited. Janet's work on those stories (and on ten more which had not yet been sent to New York) would have to be done without the prompt payment she was so anxious to get from Wilson and Parkhurst.

The Editors Are Paid—Two Contrasting Experiences

The Works Publishing financial report from June 1940 states that the "Book critics" (note the plural) were paid $375 for their work, but there is no indication of how much of this was paid to Tom Uzzell and what went to Janet Blair.[32] Jim Burwell claims Uzzell was paid $300 to edit the book,[33] but he makes no mention of Blair or how much she might have been compensated. As noted earlier, Tom's 1933 advertisement claimed he charged $1 for each 1,000 words for his services as "Literary Critic,"[34] which would have mandated a fee of $100 for this manuscript of just under 100,000 words. Uzzell's billing could hardly have tripled in just five years, nor would such a radical escalation have justified Wilson's claim to Amos that "because of his interest in our work, [Uzzell's] charge will be modest."[35] It is always possible that Burwell got the details wrong (it certainly wouldn't be the first time that happened) or, improbably, that the manuscript was originally three times longer before the Multilith Copy was printed. But if Burwell's $300 number is correct for Uzzell's pay, then perhaps the editor took a more aggressive role than just literary critic while working on this book and then charged Wilson and Parkhurst whatever was appropriate for those additional editorial services.

Whatever Tom's bill might have been, there is no evidence that he later hounded Bill or Hank for payment. Presuming he was paid promptly, a fair share of that may have come from a $200 loan that Honor Dealers—signed for by Parkhurst as President and Wilson as Secretary & Treasurer—had secured just a few weeks earlier from the Madison Finance Company in Newark. Hank had to put up his 1937 Ford convertible coupe as collateral and Honor Dealers promised to pay the money back in monthly installments of $18 each (excepting only the final payment of $15) over the next year.[36]

Janet Blair was not so lucky. If Burwell's number of $300 is correct, then Blair would have received just $75 for all the work she did on the manuscript. The previous November, Parkhurst had told her "your criticism fee [has been discussed] with Mr. Wilson and we both agree that you are eminently fair and thank you for your real generosity," promising to send out a retainer check later that week.[37] Clearly, Janet had also offered Hank some sort of modest fee structure; an understandable move given the economic climate at the time and the fact that she was nowhere nearly as famous as Tom Uzzell; and finally that, in 1939, a woman in business was always paid significantly less money than a man, no matter what the job.

How much, if anything, she had been paid before her February 20 letter (asking for at least half of the $35 owed on a past due bill) is unknown, but given the fact that more than this was owed to her later, it is certain that she continued to work on the still unedited portions of the manuscript even after the Multilith Copy was printed. On April 21, eleven days after *Alcoholics Anonymous* was published, Hank wrote her a sheepish letter regarding the long outstanding invoice.

> Dear Mrs. Blair:
>
> I know that excuses, etc do not pay bills. However, I do want you to know that we are all so ashamed of the way your bill is lagging behind.

Incidentally, we had set up, as a surprise to you, the idea of bringing you a check for $50.00 for the excellent work you did on the book. Note that I said bring you a check, not send. There were so many things that happened, that we wanted to sit down and tell you all about them. The financial situation has been such that every day we have expected money, and the lack of receipt has become actually ridiculous to us.

One of the members of Alcoholics Anonymous will tell his story on "We The People" program, Tuesday evening, April 25th, 9 P.M. Columbia Broadcasting System. If you have time to listen, we would like you to hear it. Let us know what you think of it.

We are mailing you a completed volume of the book under separate cover.

Yours very sincerely,

Henry Parkhurst

HGP:RH[38]

The book Hank sent her had the following dedication boldly inscribed across the top half of the front flyleaf in his distinctive hand:

To Janet Blair:

Whose work
and editing of this
book was so
eminently helpful.

Henry G Parkhurst[39]

While the inscribed copy did arrive, Janet Blair's $50 check did not. Despite Hank's assurance of its imminent hand delivery, Works Publishing just couldn't manage it. More than three months later, Ruth Hock was delegated to write a letter of abject apology that she sent along with Blair's final payment.

Dear Mrs. Blair:

I know that the positive sound of the following sentence will be music to your ears in comparison with the negative note of our previous letters.

I am enclosing [a] check in the amount of $50.00.

Mr. Wilson has asked me to remind him the first time he gets to the office that he wants to write you a letter of appreciation.

Meanwhile, I write for Mr. Parkhurst and myself to thank you for the invaluable work you did on the manuscript and for your patience and consideration during this delay in payment.

The book is making the progress of the turtle in his famous race and the results will be as successful. The Rev. Harry Emerson Fosdick has written a powerful review of the book which we hope will appear very soon in the Sunday Book Section of [the] Herald Tribune. Also Morris Markey, the writer for quite a few popular magazines and papers, has written an article on the work and on the book for Liberty, to appear some time in August. Publicity such as this will, of course, give the turtle powerful momentum.

Though I haven't the pleasure of knowing you, I certainly hope to. I am forwarding your "Short Story Writing" by Pitkin under separate cover.

Sincerely,

R. Hock
Secretary[40]

The final paragraph raises an interesting point: Janet had obviously loaned Hank a copy of her former employer Walter Pitkin's famous book on how to write effective short stories to help him as he edited the personal stories. That book may also have been read by Ruth Hock before she ghost-wrote the "Lone Endeavor," the last story to appear in the first printing of the Big Book.

Hank Parkhurst Edits the Stories

While Janet Blair had not yet worked on all of the stories in the back of the book, Hank Parkhurst most certainly had. As Bill later noted, "it was thought that each New Yorker with a real record of sobriety" should try to write his own story, but since none of them had any writing experience, the stories they produced were very much in need of an editorial hand. "Since New York had no one comparable to Akron's newsman Jim [Scott]," Hank Parkhurst took on the job of smoothing out these "amateur attempts," bringing them into line with what he thought should appear in the book. Bill said Hank's aggressive editing generated "plenty of trouble" among the first-time authors who were resentful he was significantly changing what they had worked so hard to produce. The "cries of the anguished" over these edits did eventually subside, but only after considerable arguments over what was seen as Parkhurst's high handedness in reworking their stories.[41]*

But Hank wasn't just making changes to the New York stories; he was also editing those that came in from Akron. The extent of the changes Parkhurst made to the twenty stories—from both New York and Ohio—that appeared in the Multilith printing are unknown because we have no earlier versions to compare them with. But the final ten stories that did eventually appear in the book weren't submitted until *after* the Multilith Copy went to press and the Stepping Stones archive contains handwritten originals for five of these. Three were from Akron ("An Alcoholics Wife" by Marie Bray, "The Car Smasher" by Dick Stanley, and "The Rolling Stone" by Lloyd Tate) and

---

* While Wilson claims here that both he and Hank edited the New York stories, the only changes seen in the preserved versions of those edited stories are all in Hank Parkhurst's handwriting.

two were written by New Yorkers ("Hindsight" by Myron Williams and "On His Way" by Horace Maher). They are all in different handwritings and therefore represent the authors' original submission of their stories for the book (confirming the fact that Jim Scott did not ghost-write them nor did Sue Smith type them up for submission).

In these archived copies, the liberal changes made by Hank Parkhurst can be clearly seen in his own hand, and by comparing these to what appeared in the book just a few weeks later, it is also possible to track the changes made after Hank had finished his initial edits. Although there is only circumstantial evidence to support this, those additional changes were probably made by Janet Blair.

Hank's edits could be surprisingly aggressive. He frequently crossed out entire pages or eliminated whole paragraphs (sometimes several in a row), regularly deleted sentences, and routinely made word changes to what had been submitted. The final edits—made after Hank's first round of changes, but before the stories appeared in the book—were usually less audacious and more generally cosmetic, but they show that Janet Blair (if this was, indeed, her handiwork) was also not shy about making substantive deletions to the text when she felt it was necessary to improve the flow of the story.

The extent and type of changes made by Parkhurst and Blair can be illustrated by examining "An Alcoholic's Wife." That story is just nine paragraphs long, one of the shortest to appear in the book. Written by Marie Bray, it presents her perspective on the problems of dealing with her husband, Walter, and his alcohol problem.

The text of her story presented below is annotated in three ways. The ~~double lined cross-outs~~ were made directly to Marie Bray's handwritten copy by Hank Parkhurst. The ~~single line deletions~~ were made sometime after that, but before the book was printed. (These, as noted above, were most likely by Janet Blair.) The words that appear in ***bold italics*** were then added, either to replace the deletions, or to smooth out rough spots in the text.

An Alcoholic's Wife

I have the misfortune, or I should say the good fortune of being an alcoholic's wife. I say misfortune because of the worry and grief that goes with drinking, and good fortune ~~to find~~ ***because we found*** a new way of living.

My husband did not drink, to my knowledge, for several years after we were married. Then we started on an occasional Saturday night party. As I drank nothing except an occasional highball I soon became what was called a "wet blanket." The parties became more frequent and more often I was left at home.

I would sit up and wait for him ~~to come home and~~. As each car passed the house I would return to walking the floor and crying and feeling so sorry for myself, thinking, "~~There I was~~ ***Here I am*** left at home to take care of the baby and him out having a good time."

When he did return sometimes on Sunday and sometimes a week later, it usually called for a scene. If he was still drunk I would put him to bed and cry some more. If he was sober it would mean I would say all the things I had been thinking and cry some more. He usually got drunk again.

I finally went to work as the bills worried me. I thought if I worked and got the bills paid he would quit drinking. He had no money in the bank but would write checks as he knew I would pay them for the boy's sake and in the hopes that each time would be the last.

I thought I should have a lot of credit ~~for that,~~ as I was paying his bills, taking care of the house and baby, besides my work, making as much money as he was, doing without things I wanted so he could have a good time.

I always went to church and thought I was living a Christian life. After my husband came in contact with ~~the group that made him surrender~~ *Alcoholics Anonymous* I thought our troubles were over as *I was sure* all our trouble was his drinking.

I soon found out that there was a lot wrong with me. I was selfish with my money, time, and thoughts. ~~I was selfish about my money because it is God's money and I wanted to use it not as God wanted me to.~~ I was selfish about my time ~~as~~ *because* I was always tired and had no time left for my family's pleasure or to do God's work. All I did was go to Sunday School and Church on Sunday with the boy and thought that was all God wanted me to do. I would be irritable and lose my temper and say all manner of things which usually called for another drunk and me pitying myself all over again.

Since ~~my sacrifice trying to live this quality of life~~ *giving my husband's problem to God* I have found a peace and happiness. I know that when I try to take care of the problems of my husband I am a stumbling block as my husband has to take his problems to God the same as I do.

My husband and I now talk over our problems and ~~ask God what to do with them~~ **trust in a Divine Power**. We have now started to live. When we live with God we want for nothing.[42]

The double-lined deletions in the third and the last four paragraphs were made by Hank Parkhurst and the substituted words immediately after them are also in his hand. The single line cross outs and the other added words are presumed to be Janet Blair's more restrained editorial contribution to this story. Note that while Janet's edits are largely cosmetic, Hank's are much more substantive. Parkhurst removed Marie's specific mention of "the group" (knowledgeable people might well identify this as the Oxford Group) and he substituted "Alcoholics Anonymous." He also completely deleted a sentence that made specific mention of "God's money" (which also mentioned how

He wanted it to be used) and then removed the redundant use of the word "God" in the final paragraph, substituting the more open concept of "Divine Power" in its place, curiously changing the words so that it now calls for "trust in" God rather than "asking God what to do." Did that just sound too much like Oxford Group guidance?

In all, Marie Bray's original text comprised 552 words, but by the time it finally appeared in print, the joint editors had pared the story down to 518—a reduction of just 6.2 percent.

Dick Stanley's story, "The Car Smasher" was not treated so gently. His original, handwritten submission was 2,695 words long, but by the time Parkhurst and Blair were done with it, there were only 1,502 words left—they had deleted more than 44 percent of Dick's original text. That story is too long to reproduce here in full,[*] so a few paragraphs will have to suffice to give some idea of the edits Parkhurst and Blair made. (NOTE: the notations used above for edits—~~double line~~ [for Parkhurst], ~~single lined~~ [for Blair], and ***bold italic*** [for additions]—are also used here):

The Car Smasher

During the first week of March, 1937, through the grace of God, I ended 20 years of a life made practically useless ~~by my not being able to do~~ ***because I could not do*** two things.

First, ~~being~~ ***I was*** unable to not take a drink.

Second, ~~being~~ ***I was*** unable to take a drink without getting drunk.

Perhaps a third as important as ~~these~~ ***the other*** two should be added; my being unwilling to admit either of the first two.

~~As a~~ ***With the*** result I kept trying to drink without getting drunk, and kept making a nightmare of my life, causing suffering and hardship to all those relatives and friends who tried so hard to help me and whom, when I was sober, I took the greatest pleasure in pleasing.

~~As a boy, I had taken a pledge in a religious church not to drink until I was 21. This pledge, I kept.~~

The first time I drank anything strong, or in greater quantity than a glass of beer, I got disgustingly drunk ~~whereas the other fellows had a drink and went on into dinner. I stayed in the bar and as each group came in, I had a drink with them and when the groups failed to arrive fast enough, I went on myself with the result I~~ ***and*** missed the dinner ***which had been*** arranged ~~by a church~~ for me ~~because I was shortly to be married~~ ***in honor of my coming marriage.***

I had to be taken home and remained in bed the following day; ~~far~~ more sick than I thought a human could be and live. ~~But~~ ***Yet***, until two years ago ***I*** periodically ~~having been doing~~ ***did*** the same thing.

---

[*]   The complete, fully annotated text of "The Car Smasher" can be found in Appendix IX on p. 677.

Making money was always pretty easy when I was sober and worked. ~~When I was nineteen, through the help of a friend, I acquired a piece of land, cut it into lots, sold it and within a year had made a profit larger than most successful men made their first ten business years. I bring this up only to show one more reason why I should have no drink[?].~~

All right when sober—absolutely helpless with a drink aboard. But I seemed to have had the idea that making money or a living was something to take or let alone.[43]

Most noticeable here are Hank's deletions of Dick taking "a pledge in a religious church" and Blair's elimination of details about his spree before the dinner party, including the fact that it was arranged by a church. It appears that any unnecessary references to formal religion were being deleted whenever possible. Similarly, the overly detailed description of Dick's early business career was deemed far too distracting to the point the story should be making—and it was ruthlessly edited out.

This practice of eliminating early life details, especially business details, is seen in almost all of Hank's edits. In "The Rolling Stone," the third original Akron story preserved in the archive, Hank completely eliminated the first two and half pages as unimportant, but left the remaining ten and half pages largely untouched. While he did make a few word changes to the remaining text, he had obviously decided Lloyd Tate's style of writing had a flavor that he didn't want to lose, so he wrote boldly across the top of the first page: "Miss H / No grammatical changes please."[44] One can only presume this meant that Ruth Hock was also an active participant in the editing process, at least to the extent that she felt free to make grammatical changes as she typed up the revisions which had been made to each story.

Hank was equally ruthless with the New York stories. Myron Williams submitted a fifteen-page handwritten manuscript for a story he called "Hindsight," but Hank crossed out the first seven and half pages, eliminating a wealth of details about Myron's early life. Following these deletions, Hank wrote the word "Start" in the middle of page 8, with a small arrow in the left margin pointing to the word "FIRED" which he printed out in bold capital letters. Although Parkhurst did reject half of the pages in Williams's story, it should be noted that, because of the way it was handwritten, his deletions amounted to only 38 percent of the original text.[45]

Hank's edits certainly gave the story a much more powerful opening, but the tale Myron told in those first seven and a half pages was eloquent in its description of how fear had dominated and completely run his life before he quit drinking. The word "fear" actually appeared four times in the deleted text, two of which Myron wrote out in bold capital letters.[46] Parkhurst's edits did make for a more concise and dramatic story, but it resulted in a substantive loss of a moving and emotional backstory and eliminated any hope of understanding what this particular man considered to be the primary driving force behind his alcoholism.[*]

---

[*] There are two Parkhurst notes handwritten at the bottom of the last page of this story. The first simply says "See me about this," which is likely directed toward Ruth Hock. The second is more interesting, saying: "Editor's Note—this man died from malnutrition one week after writing this story." But this line was inexplicably later crossed out in light red pencil.

Parkhurst took a similarly drastic editorial pen to the shorter story submitted by his friend, Horace (Popsy) Maher. The original handwritten submission was just eight pages long, but after Hank made some initial edits to the first page, he decided that the writing (or the story line) was just so hopeless that he simply crossed out the entire page and then also lined out the long second paragraph on page two. Maher had not put a title on his story, so Parkhurst made that decision for him and boldly wrote across the text of the completely crossed out first page: "<u>Title</u> On His Way." Hank's cuts to this story were not as drastic as those made to Myron's "Hindsight," but Popsy's manuscript was cut by roughly 15 percent.

Fitz Mayo's Story Expands

For some inexplicable reason, while everyone else's story, including Bill Wilson's, was being cut and edited, Fitz Mayo's personal story grew by well over 250 percent. His earliest attempt called "Me and John" [i.e., John Barleycorn] was a tidy 1,588 words long.[47] But, by the time Mayo's story appeared in the Multilith printing, it had been renamed "Our Southern Friend" and had grown to be an impressive 4,272 words.

"Me and John" was written very early in the process, a supposition that is suggested and supported by the fact that Fitz's first attempt is typed in the same strange format used for the long (almost 12,000 word) earliest version of "Bill's Story." Both of these documents are typed on 8½" x 14" legal paper and have exactly the same unusual arrangement—the text is deeply indented a full 2" and each line is individually and consecutively numbered. These two stories are the only examples of this unusual format found among any of A.A.'s archived documents, strongly suggesting that Fitz wrote "Me and John" during one of his frequent trips to Brooklyn, this one in late May 1938 while Bill was making his first attempts at his own "Story." The two accounts were probably typed by the same person and at the same time. It is even possible, albeit much more speculative, that Fitz Mayo was the typist for these two stories and that this very different format was his own creation.

Why Fitz was encouraged to write a longer story is a mystery. The most critical elements in his tale—his stay in Towns Hospital, his famous quote about "Who are you to say there is no God?" and the fact that he fell on his knees to pray—all appear in the earlier version, although not quite so concisely and dramatically as what finally appeared in the book. Surprisingly, other than some reorganization in this last part of his story, the major change was that Fitz added page after page of exactly those things Hank was so diligently deleting from all of the other stories: copious details about his early life, his family, and his business career. By the time Mayo was finished with his rewrite, those three elements completely dominated the expanded story.

Fitz's longer story also shows him using a distinctive new writing style: the entire account is cast in a first person, present-tense voice that he had not used in the earlier version. "Our Southern Friend" uses this attention-grabbing, present-tense format throughout, with Fitz opening many paragraphs with lines such as "I am in church," or "I am in another fellow's room in college," or "I am examined for the draft." This new style can seem a bit obvious and contrived as the story goes on, but it does give the reader a feeling of stark immediacy as he reads through the many phases of Fitz Mayo's life.

Whether this change in style was prompted (perhaps guided?) by Hank Parkhurst, who seemed bent on making each story as distinctive and lively as possible, or was the result of Fitz Mayo reading the Walter Pitkin book, *Short Story Writing*, that was floating around the Honor Dealers office, is unknown; but the difference between his two stories is dramatic in the extreme. Fitz was clearly reaching for exactly the kind of effect Bill Wilson had warned Bob Smith against the previous June when he instructed him to caution the Ohio writers "above all let's not try to be literary."[48] Fitz Mayo was definitely shooting for a literary effect when he rewrote this story.

But even Fitz's expanded story wasn't safe from the editor's pen; there were changes made to the original typed copy preserved at Stepping Stones and to the story as it appeared in the Mulitlith Copy. These changes were typical of what was done to other stories, although not so extensively. Sometime shortly before it was first printed, someone (most likely Janet Blair) cut the first three paragraphs and moved them to the very end of the story and also deleted three fairly long sections from the first few pages consisting of 12, 23, and 17 lines of type respectively.

While there is no documented evidence to explain why Mayo's story grew while all the others were shortened, one suggestion might be that Hank encouraged Fitz to write more about himself as some sort of consolation prize for losing the argument about putting more emphasis on God in the Big Book. It is also possible that Bill, driven by this same reasoning, may have suggested Fitz expand his story; or perhaps he did so because he felt the shorter version did not give Fitz the recognition he so richly deserved. After all, Wilson's own story was more than 4,300 words long and Hank's was almost 3,800. Someone may have felt that publishing the first version would be perceived as a slight to Fitz who had been a central figure in the New York Fellowship from the very beginning. If so, allowing him to expand his story (to almost the same length as Bill's), may have been suggested as an effective way to give appropriate credit to the second man to get sober after Bill Wilson returned to New York in late 1935.

Whatever the explanation, there is no contemporary evidence (or even hints) for why Fitz Mayo was encouraged or allowed to expand his story. It is an interesting anomaly and a mystery.

The Multilith Printing

~February 1939~

In the first week of November, Bill had written Dr. Bob telling him the Ohio members needed to "speak up or forever hold their peace" regarding the proposed chapters he had been regularly sending to Akron. He also said he hoped "to get out there about December first for a week or two so we can cover these matters better."[1] But the creation of the Twelve Steps and the writing of Chapters Five and Six had taken up the month of December and then January was spent editing the book, reactivating his connection with the Rockefellers, making plans for the book's release, and trying to keep everyone's head above water financially. By mid-February, it was time for everyone in the Fellowship to be given a chance to see exactly what was going to be printed in the book and to have their say regarding any final edits or additions they might want to make.

A Pre-Publication Version Is Planned

Dr. Bob Smith had been in town for the January 18 trustee's meeting. Perhaps it was during this visit that they decided to print an inexpensive pre-publication copy of the text and distribute it to all the members for their consideration. Whenever that decision was made, a month after Smith's visit Wilson and Parkhurst assembled all of the necessary elements to create a pre-publication version of the book that could be reviewed by all the sober men (and one woman) in Alcoholics Anonymous.

However, there were other reasons beyond seeking the approval of all the recovered alcoholics for a trial version of the book at this time. Someone—Wilson later claimed "I do not remember who"—sounded an additional note of caution about rushing to publish this text. "How do we know for sure," they said, "that this book will be widely acceptable to everybody? Maybe it still contains medical errors or material that might offend our friends in religion."[2] So, it wasn't just the drunks who were going to get a chance to review the book's contents before it went to press. Doctors, psychiatrists, judges, priests, and ministers would also be asked to comment and suggest whatever changes they thought might be necessary or appropriate.

Jim Burwell noted two more plausible reasons for printing up pre-publication copies of the book. He said, "These we would use as a promotion for more stock selling and at the same time to get the possible endorsement of well-known people." Along with every copy they mailed out to "possible prospective stockholders, we [also] sent out a prospectus for our corporation" in the hope that it might catch their interest as a potentially profitable investment. Neither of these plans ever came to fruition. No new candidates stepped forward to write a stirring Foreword endorsing Alcoholics Anonymous and, Jim confirmed that, despite all their hopes, "we did not get one new stockholder."[3]

Whether for review by the Fellowship, medicine or religion, or as an appeal for endorsements or to promote investments, Bill and Hank were printing up Multilith copies of the book and sending them out to "everyone we could think of who might be concerned with the problem of alcoholism."[4]

The Board Meets Again

On February 14, the leadership of the Alcoholic Foundation assembled in Willard Richardson's office for their second meeting of the year. Three Rockefeller men—Richardson, Amos, and Chipman—attended along with the newest non-alcoholic trustee, Dr. Leonard Strong. The alcoholic trustees Bill Ruddell and Harry Brick were also present, but Dr. Bob Smith was not. According to the minutes, Bill Wilson was represented by a letter he wrote "regarding the progress of the book which he is writing," but neither Hank Parkhurst nor Albert Scott attended this meeting.

The first order of business was that Bill Ruddell resigned his position as a trustee of the Foundation. The reasons were unspecified in the minutes, but were probably related to the pressures of his job in Hackettstown, coupled with the presence of a new baby at home.* Ruddell's request to be relieved of his duties was "reluctantly accepted," but he was immediately elected as a member of the Advisory Committee, while trustee Harry Brick was elected Chairman pro-tem in Ruddell's place.[5]**

Frank Amos then presented an informal report on the monies received and distributed since this "informal organization started in December 1937." The trustees further "agreed that a formal report would be made at the next meeting and at the same time an effort would be made to determine upon a definite budget for a definite period of operation for the foundation—then endeavor to raise funds to meet that budget."[6]

---

* In a February 21, 1939, letter to Bill Ruddell, Ruth Hock asks: "How is Mrs. Ruddell and Henry Griffen Parkhurst Ruddell Jr. coming along?" Was Ruth being facetious with this comment? (Jr.?) And, if she was actually reporting fact, it is interesting that the baby was named after Hank and not Bill.

** It has been alleged with some regularity that Bill Ruddell was removed as a trustee because he drank, but that could not have been the case. If it had been true, there would have been no "reluctance" about accepting his resignation nor would he have immediately been elected to serve on the Foundation's Advisory Committee.

As always, money was the most important issue at hand and the trustee's postponement of any substantive discussion of this critical problem until the next meeting is exactly what had driven Wilson and Parkhurst to begin selling stock in an effort to raise the money they so desperately needed *right now*. The minutes of the meeting make mention of their efforts, acknowledging the existence of the "newly formed publishing company," noting its name is Works Publishing Company and that it had offices at 17 William Street, Newark, New Jersey.

The minutes go on to explicitly underline the fact that there was no relationship between the new company and the Foundation, stating that "it was again emphasized that the Foundation has no legal connection with the Works Publishing Company, is not responsible for its acts, and does not exercise any supervision over it." But while the trustees were adamant about making a distinct separation between these two entities, they also noted that "the sympathetic cooperation of individual members of the Trustees Board of the Foundation is, of course, well understood."[7]

The Rockefeller men had formally capitulated and agreed that A.A. should self-publish their book.

The One Hundred Men Corporation Becomes Works Publishing

This is the first time the name Works Publishing appears in any of the contemporary documents. All previous mentions of this "newly formed publishing company" had referred to it as "The One Hundred Men Corporation," but that was no longer the case. In fact, the name was so new that even someone as deeply involved in the organization as Bill Ruddell was surprised and confused by the change, writing to Hank Parkhurst on February 27 for some clarification and asking pointedly: "What's this 'Works Publishing Co'?"[8] Ruth Hock responded the next day, noting in a postscript: "We, that is the One Hundred Men Corp., are Works Publishing Co." and she assured Bill that Hank would "write you about it."[9]

Works Publishing Co. was clearly a Parkhurst/Wilson enterprise being run without prior consultation with any other members of the Fellowship—up to and including an alcoholic trustee.

Bill Wilson later claimed that the name, Works Publishing was chosen in October when he and Hank went into a stationery store and bought a pad of blank stock certificates. But as we have seen, the name of the company at that time was The One Hundred Men Corporation. When the idea of changing the name did come up in early 1939, Wilson says he and Parkhurst had at first disagreed, but "after some debate," Hank suggested the name Works Publishing Co., claiming "that this book would be the first of many great works we would do"[10]—and Bill concurred.

Without even acknowledging Bill's version of this story, the author of *Pass It On* states that, "how the title [Works Publishing] was chosen is a matter of some dispute; some said it was named for the Akronites' (particularly Anne Smith's) favorite quotation from James, 'Faith without works is dead'; others said it was named for a favorite slogan of the membership, 'It works!'"[11] However charming these stories may be, they both sound like the result of a group discussion and decision, something that never happened. Besides Bill Wilson's candid account of this being a decision he and Hank Parkhurst made by themselves, Bill Ruddell's ignorance regarding the new name speaks rather dramatically and conclusively against the possibility that anyone else in the Fellowship was ever asked for their opinion on this topic.

Bill was clear that the company's new name was Hank's idea and the explanation offered for his grand choice ("this book would be the first of many great works") sounds far more like Henry G. Parkhurst than any thought of him choosing a meaningful Biblical reference to please the people in Akron or the possibility he was referencing a popular A.A. slogan. Hank's reason for choosing this name reflected his heartfelt belief that Works Publishing was destined to grow into a great and ongoing venture.

The Book Gets Its Title

But there was another far more pressing naming problem to be decided, one that had been the subject of lively discussions within the Eastern group for several months: "What was the title of this new book going to be?" Shortly after Bill finished writing the first two chapters, the New Yorkers began arguing over what title would best describe the contents of the book while simultaneously capturing the attention of potential buyers. In his late June letter to Dr. Bob Smith, Bill Wilson had suggested offhandedly, "by the way, you might all be thinking up a good title," and noted that in New York "titles such as 'Haven, One Hundred Men, Comes the Dawn, etc.' have [already] been suggested."[12]

Over the next few months several more titles were proposed, including "'The Empty Glass,' 'The Dry Way,' 'The Dry Life,' 'Dry Frontiers,' and 'The Way Out.'"[13*] In January, Horace Maher suggested to Hank that "Exit" might be a good title for their book.[14] Everyone was in the game. Bill later recounted that "voting on what the title of the new book should be became one of the major occupations" in meetings. "The more we tried," he said, "the more difficult it all seemed. Some wanted a novel-like title. Others wanted it titled like a textbook. Perhaps a couple hundred were suggested."[15]

Finally, after all these suggestions and arguments, the choices came down to two major contenders: *Alcoholics Anonymous* and *The Way Out*. As previously noted, Hank Parkhurst had first proposed the title *Alcoholics Anonymous* when he submitted his "Ideas" to Bill Wilson in early June,[16] but that suggestion had fallen by the wayside over the next few months as *One Hundred Men* became popular. Then, for whatever reason—be it the presence of one sober woman in the group (whose story was to appear in the back of the book), or a growing realization that a significant number of women would be joining the Fellowship in the foreseeable future—*One Hundred Men* began to fade as the possible name for the publishing company and for the book.

That shift gave *Alcoholics Anonymous* a second chance. Although the name had never really gone away, it now reentered the contest with some strong support from both Bill Wilson and Hank Parkhurst. In the group's arguments, Bill later remembered they

---

* These are certainly interesting and plausible titles noted in *Pass It On*, but once again, this book supplies no supporting references for where that information might have come from.

had at least one strong ally in this fight. This, he said, was Joe Worden, "the derelict and broken-down ex-partner on the New Yorker, [who] did plug that title heavily,"[17]* making a solid impression on the group with his arguments. Joe "saw great merit in the title of Alcoholics Anonymous" and he argued effectively for it, although as Bill remembered, "in the early discussion, he and I were the only proponents of it."[18] (This last comment casually ignores Hank Parkhurst's vigorous support for the name *Alcoholics Anonymous*—as contemporary evidence clearly shows.) The group, finally given a solid opportunity to make a collective contribution, was obviously putting a fair amount of time and energy into choosing the title for the new book.

Perhaps most important from Hank's and Bill's point of view was that Tom Uzzell was adamant that they should call their book *Alcoholics Anonymous*, insisting it was the perfect title. Tom's passionate support for this title was something Ruth Hock vividly recalled years later:

> I remember that during an appointment with Tom Uzzell, we discussed the various name possibilities and he immediately—very firmly and very enthusiastically—stated that "Alcoholics Anonymous" was a dead ringer both from the sales point of view because it was "catchy" and because it really did describe the group to perfection. The more this name was studied from this point of view the more everybody agreed and so it was decided.[19]

This last bit is another example of hindsight rewriting history. At the time, everyone did not agree on that name. As Bill later noted, "the debate on the title went on heavily during the fall and spring months," and finally the group adopted *The Way Out* as the title of the new book "by a narrow margin"—with *Alcoholics Anonymous* coming in second as the "the runner-up in popularity."[20] This did not please Wilson, who had long favored the losing title. "I didn't like this at all," he said. "I thought the title was altogether too trite. *Alcoholics Anonymous* said what we were, besides it had an air of mystery which was enjoyable."[21]

As noted, Hank Parkhurst was also strongly in favor of the name *Alcoholics Anonymous* and he was equally unhappy with the outcome of this vote. Disappointed with the results of the group conscience, Hank devised an end run around that decision. On February 9, he "wired Fitz Mayo in Maryland asking him to go to the Library of Congress in Washington and find out how many books were called *The Way Out* and how many were called *Alcoholics Anonymous*."[22]** When Fitz's response came back two days later,[23] it was exactly what Hank had been looking for:

1939 Feb 11 AM 12 19

WA 13 50 NL=CA WASHINGTON DC 10
HENRY G PARK HURST
182 CLINTON ST BROOKLYN NY=

---

* See p. 172 of this book for an earlier, fuller discussion of Joe Worden.
** In both of the cited references, Bill Wilson incorrectly takes credit for asking Fitz to undertake this investigation.

NO TITLE CAN BE REGISTERED IN COPYRIGHT OFFICE TO SECURE MONOPOLY OF ITS USE STOP LIBRARY OF CONGRESS HAS 25 BOOKS THE WAY OUT 12 THE WAY NINE THIS WAY OUT NONE ALCOHOLICS ANONYMOUS NONE COMES DAWN MY PET STOP OUR TRIP TO BROOKLYN DEFINITELY OFF- BUSINESS BRISKER AM WRITING. =

FITZ.[24]

Given that there were already twenty-five books entitled *The Way Out*—and despite Mayo's ongoing preference for *Comes the Dawn*—Wilson and Parkhurst simply declared *Alcoholics Anonymous* was going to be the title of the book. Or as Bill later said, "we left the title 'Alcoholics Anonymous' in the copy that went to the printer"[25]—a candid admission that they had already typed up the master copy with that title on the presumption the Fellowship would go along with whatever they wanted.

The fact that Fitz's telegram was addressed to Hank contradicts several facts in the story Bill repeatedly told over the years about this incident. Parkhurst formulated this strategy for overturning the group's decision and he contacted Mayo to set that plan in motion. How else to explain the fact that Fitz addressed his reply to Hank rather than to Bill? While this small change in the story is intriguing and relatively unimportant, it does provide one more striking example of how Henry G. Parkhurst's central role in the publication of the Big Book was so consistently written out of the story once he returned to drinking.

Nor was this the only creative liberty Wilson took with the story. He always—very colorfully, but incorrectly—said that Fitz had reported there were twelve books called *The Way Out* registered with the Library of Congress, rather than the twenty-five clearly noted in his telegram. He claimed that this allowed him to successfully argue with the group that it would be flying in the face of superstition for them to publish a thirteenth book with that title.[26] Whether Bill fabricated that number when he reported the results of Fitz's search to the New York members in February 1939 or added it in later to spice up his version of the story is unknown, but one or the other must be true given the text of the actual telegram.

Once again, Bill Wilson just could not resist telling a better story—even when doing so meant ignoring the clear facts of the situation.

Hank's Separation and His Decisive Ten Weeks with Bill

There is one important thing to be noted in the telegram Fitz sent to Hank, namely that he addressed it to Parkhurst, but directed it to Bill Wilson's home address in Brooklyn. This is the only other contemporary evidence we have to support Lois Wilson's statement (in her September 22, 1939 affidavit regarding the Parkhursts' divorce) that Hank was separated from his wife, Kathleen, for ten weeks in early 1939 and, during that time, he lived with them at 182 Clinton Street in Brooklyn.[27] Obviously something serious had occurred in the Parkhurst household, either at the New Year's Eve party, or some time shortly after that. Hank was not welcome at home and so became one of the several transient A.A. members in residence with the Wilsons in Brooklyn.

Supporting the fact that Hank lived in Brooklyn for most of the first three months of 1939, Ruth Hock later noted that Parkhurst "had broken up with his wife just prior to the Cornwall Press trip"[28]—a trip that occurred in late March. Final confirmation that Hank's ten-week stay in Brooklyn must have occurred during the first three months of the year comes from the fact that the bank repossessed the Wilson's house in Brooklyn on April 26, 1939, leaving them homeless. On that day, with nowhere else to turn, Bill and Lois "went to [the] Parkhursts,"[29] who had obviously reconciled—however temporarily—by that date.[30]

It is certainly tempting to imagine what happened during the two-and-a-half months Bill and Hank lived in such close and constant proximity—at the exact time when the elements of the book were being pulled together, edited, and finalized for publication. It would be wonderful to have some record of the conversations and arguments they had around the kitchen table in Brooklyn, but such personal one-on-one debates and decisions rarely find their way into contemporary historical records. While we can safely presume that these two primary movers in the writing and publication of the Big Book consulted with each other daily during this time, we have no way of knowing any of the details of those conversations.

Hank's ten-week residence in Brooklyn and his day-to-day interactions with Bill Wilson again underline the prominent role he played in the shaping and finalization of the Big Book's text. But we hear nothing of this in the later tales of this critically decisive period. Once again, Hank's significant participation and his immense contribution to the book's creation have been dropped from the story due to the inconvenient and embarrassing fact that he was drinking again before the year was out.

Dr. Silkworth Writes "The Doctor's Opinion"

In the minutes of the February 14 trustee's meeting, Frank Amos noted that Bill had reported via letter on the progress of the book "he is writing." Unfortunately, that letter has not been preserved, but he almost certainly provided some details of the joint editing job being done by Uzzell and Blair (and perhaps even Hank's work on the stories), along with the fact that they were just days away from having a pre-publication Multilith copy of the text available for review and a final critique. Wilson's letter also likely made mention of the fact that, although they had not yet found a prominent person to write a Preface endorsing their program of recovery, the book now included a chapter titled "The Doctor's Opinion," written by Dr. William Silkworth, which strongly supported the work they were doing.

"The Doctor's Opinion" contains two short statements written by Bill Wilson, the first introducing a letter from Silkworth, and the second serving as a preface to the doctor's longer statement enthusiastically endorsing the solution advocated in the book. Exactly how these two men went about cobbling these different elements together is unclear; nor is it known how (or if) they edited each other's work. We also do not know whether Silkworth's chapter was part of the manuscript submitted to Uzzell in early January, or if it was completed sometime later that month or even in early February—although Wilson's letter to Frank Amos on January 4 could be read as confirming that the chapter had not been written at that time.

The idea of publishing a strong endorsement of their program from Dr. Silkworth goes all the way back to "Hank's Ideas" written in the first week of June. At the bottom of the first page of his notes, Parkhurst explicitly states that "Dr. Silkworth's letters" should be included in the book.[31] Frank Amos confirmed the ready acceptance of this idea a few weeks later in a letter to Albert Scott: "It is hoped that endorsements of the book and of this work can be incorporated in it over the names of at least one outstanding physician of national reputation and at least one person who is likewise well known, thus adding great strength and authenticity of what the book contains."[32] If any further encouragement were needed, after reading the first two chapters of the book, Dr. Esther Richards of Johns Hopkins wrote Bill strongly advising that, "I think you should get an A No. 1 physician who has a wide knowledge of the alcoholic's medical and social problem to write an introduction" for the book.[33]

Just days after receiving this letter from Richards, Bill asked Dr. Silkworth to write a "To Whom It May Concern" letter of recommendation that he could use in his fundraising efforts, which the doctor happily supplied on July 27.[34] It was this letter (found here on page 225), which in slightly modified form, served as the first part of Silkworth's contribution to "The Doctor's Opinion." Bill introduced this letter with the chapter's opening paragraph.

> We of Alcoholics Anonymous believe that the reader will be interested in the medical estimate of the plan of recovery described in this book. Convincing testimony must surely come from medical men who have had experience with the sufferings of our members and have witnessed our return to health. A well known doctor, chief physician at a nationally prominent hospital specializing in alcoholic and drug addiction, gave Alcoholics Anonymous this letter:[35]

Silkworth Remains Anonymous

There were a few cosmetic changes made to Silkworth's original letter, but there were also three more substantial edits worthy of note. In his July letter, the doctor specifically identified the patient he attended four years earlier as "William G. Wilson," but in the Multilith version Bill's name has been edited out and replaced with an anonymous "who." There is also a much more positive spin put on the sentence "because of the extraordinary possibilities of rapid growth inherent in this group these events *may* mark a new epoch in the annals of alcoholism." That sentence now reads much more emphatically "because of the extraordinary possibilities of rapid growth inherent in this group *they mark* a new epoch in the annals of alcoholism." Finally, Silkworth's original statement that "These men may well have a *solution* for thousands of these situations" has inexplicably been changed to "These men may well have a *remedy* for thousands of these situations." (Perhaps "remedy" was thought to sound more medical than "solution.")

But the most unexpected change is that the doctor has chosen to remain as anonymous here as Bill Wilson. The original letter had been typed on Towns Hospital letterhead and signed "Very truly yours, / W. D. Silkworth M.D.," but in "The Doctor's Opinion" this has been changed to "Very truly yours, / (Signed) - - - - - M.D." This seems to defeat the very purpose of the letter: to present the testimony of a physician of national reputation who would readily be identified as an expert. Deleting the doctor's name and relying only on his own contention that he has "specialized in the treatment of alcoholism for many years" significantly diminish the letter's impact.

Without a name, how are we to know if this isn't just some quack doctor running one of the many rackets that prey on unfortunate alcoholics seeking relief? While that is one possible (and unfortunate) way to interpret the doctor's anonymity, his decision to leave his name off the endorsement letter was most likely driven by the other side of the argument. Opening the book with a statement from the chief physician at Towns Hospital in New York City might well have left A.A. open to the charge that it was endorsing Towns Hospital in an effort to bolster its business. It may have been decided the best way to straddle that delicate issue would be to simply claim the author was "a well known doctor, chief physician at a nationally prominent hospital specializing in alcoholic and drug addiction" (as Bill did in his introduction to the letter) without specifically identifying the name of that hospital. Less likely, but always possible for lack of any contrary evidence, is that Silkworth, who had published several articles in medical journals regarding his theories about alcoholism and his extensive experiences with alcoholic patients, was reluctant to so publicly link his name and reputation to this new, but still largely untested, method for recovery.[*]

The Rest of the Chapter

Bill follows Silkworth's letter with three paragraphs of his own which served as a preface to the doctor's longer endorsement of Alcoholics Anonymous that take up the rest of the chapter:

> The physician who, at our request, gave us this letter, has been kind enough to enlarge upon his views in another statement, which follows. In this statement he confirms what anyone who has suffered alcoholic torture must believe—that the body of the alcoholic is quite as abnormal as his mind. It does not satisfy us to be told that we cannot control our drinking just because we were maladjusted to life, that we were in full flight from reality, or were outright mental defectives. These things were true to some extent, in fact, to a considerable extent with some of us. But

---

[*]   Note that while Silkworth's name did not appear in any of the sixteen printings of the first edition of the book (1939–1954), his full name was included in the first printing of the second edition (1955) and has appeared in every printing since then. The change was presumably due to the fact that, in the interim, A.A. had proven to be so successful nationally that fears of this being construed as an advertisement for Towns Hospital were no longer likely. Other explanations might rest on the fact that Dr. Silkworth had died three years earlier and also that, by this time, Towns Hospital was in decline (it closed its doors in 1965) and therefore would have been an unlikely candidate for promotion by A.A.

we are sure that our bodies were sickened as well. In our belief, any picture of the alcoholic, which leaves out this physical factor is incomplete.

The doctor's theory that we have a kind of allergy to alcohol interests us. As laymen, our opinion as to its soundness may, of course, mean little. But as ex-alcoholics, we can say that his explanation makes good sense. It explains many things for which we cannot otherwise account.

Though we work out our solution on the spiritual plane, we favor hospitalization for the alcoholic who is very jittery or befogged. More often than not, it is imperative that a man's brain be cleared before he is approached, as he has then a better chance of understanding and accepting what we have to offer.

The longer statement from Dr. Silkworth that follows this contains some of the most frequently quoted passages found in the Big Book.

Silkworth's Theories of Alcoholism and Endorsement of A.A.

The doctor begins by admitting how powerless the medical profession has been in the past in its attempts to cure this problem: "We doctors have realized for a long time that some form of moral psychology was of urgent importance to alcoholics, but its application presented difficulties beyond our conception." Silkworth's understanding of "moral psychology" has already been discussed here in some detail,* but in this passage he sums up that understanding by noting that the men of Alcoholics Anonymous advocate for "the Power which pulls chronic alcoholics back from the gates of death" and that they are singularly unselfish, pursue no personal gain, and exhibit a community spirit that "is indeed inspiring to one who has labored long and wearily in the alcoholic field."

Silkworth then makes a concise presentation of his own theories about alcoholism and its intractability: "We believe, and so suggested a few years ago, that the action of alcohol on these chronic alcoholics is a manifestation of an allergy; that the phenomenon of craving is limited to this class and never occurs in the average temperate drinker."** The obvious solution is that "these allergic types can never safely use alcohol in any form at all . . ." But how to accomplish this? It is, he says, astonishingly difficult to break this habit once it has taken hold of a man, even though it continually brings his life to ruin. "Frothy emotional appeal seldom suffices. The message which can interest and hold these alcoholic people must have depth and weight. In nearly all cases, their ideals must be grounded in a power greater than themselves, if they are to re-create their lives." And, it is exactly that method of overcoming this problem that is "covered in such masterly detail in these pages."

If cynics find such an endorsement "somewhat sentimental," Silkworth invites them to "stand with us a while on the firing line, see the tragedies, the despairing wives,

---

* See pp. 139–40 for a previous discussion of "moral psychology."

** For Silkworth's published theory on the alcoholic allergy see "Alcoholism as a Manifestation of Allergy," *Medical Record, A National Review of Medicine and Surgery,* The Medical Journal and Record Publishing Company, Inc., New York, Volume 145, January to June, 1937, pp. 249–51.

the little children" and then witness "the solving of these problems" before dismissing this new "community movement" which "has contributed more to the rehabilitation of these men" than anything else he has ever seen.

The doctor follows this glowing testimonial with perhaps the most powerful and perceptive paragraph in the chapter:

> Men and women drink essentially because they like the effect produced by alcohol. The sensation is so elusive that, while they admit it is injurious, they cannot after a time differentiate the true from the false. To them, their alcoholic life seems the only normal one. They are restless, irritable and discontented, unless they can again experience the sense of ease and comfort which comes at once by taking a few drinks—drinks which they see others taking with impunity. After they have succumbed to the desire again, as so many do, and the phenomenon of craving develops, they pass through the well-known stages of a spree, emerging remorseful, with a firm resolution not to drink again. This is repeated over and over, and unless this person can experience an entire psychic change there is very little hope of his recovery.

Is there then no hope? "Faced with this problem, if a doctor is honest with himself, he must sometimes feel his own inadequacy . . . One feels that something more than human power is needed to produce the essential psychic change" most especially because "many types do not respond to the ordinary psychological approach."

Silkworth then makes his own attempt to classify the different types of alcoholics, admitting that such a task is "most difficult" and in the end can be reduced to one common symptom: alcoholics are people who "cannot start drinking without developing the phenomenon of craving." This is a condition that "has never been, by any treatment with which we are familiar, permanently eradicated. The only relief we have to suggest is entire abstinence." Such a categorical statement, he says, "immediately precipitates . . . a seething cauldron of debate. Much has been written pro and con, but among physicians, the general opinion seems to be that most chronic alcoholics are doomed."

Silkworth refuses to jump into this debate, pointedly asking instead: "What is the solution?" He then, very pragmatically suggests "Perhaps I can best answer this by relating an experience of two years ago."

The doctor then offers two real-life stories from his own practice, beginning with a patient he had first encountered three years earlier (who is not named, but who is obviously Hank Parkhurst). After describing the patient's pitiful condition on admission, Silkworth notes that before leaving the hospital he "accepted the plan outlined in this book" as a solution to his problem. One year later, that same man returned to Towns Hospital and he was so changed— "from a trembling, despairing, nervous wreck, had emerged a man brimming over with self-reliance and contentment"—that even after a lengthy conversation, the doctor says he "was not able to bring myself to feel that I had known him before. To me he was a stranger . . ."

The second story is of another patient (again, not named but obviously Fitz Mayo) whose "alcoholic problem was so complex, and his depression so great, that we felt his only hope would be through what we then called 'moral psychology,' and we doubted if even that would have any effect. However, he did become 'sold' on the ideas in this book. He has not had a drink for more than three years."

Leaving aside the "seething cauldron" of scientific debate, Dr. Silkworth finds this kind of pragmatic proof conclusive and he therefore advises "every alcoholic to read this book through, and though perhaps he came to scoff, he may remain to pray."

The Source of the Chapter and Its Position in the Book

It has been claimed that the bulk of this second long statement came from a journal article on alcoholism that Dr. Silkworth published in July 1939. This is only partially true. "The Doctor's Opinion" contains twenty-eight paragraphs and of these, nine can be found in his "Psychological Rehabilitation of Alcoholics" published in the *Medical Record* five months after the Multilith printing was released. That article was clearly written sometime after mid-April, because it specifically notes that the whole story of Bill Wilson's recovery and the group's program of recovery "is admirably told in a book written by them entitled 'Alcoholics Anonymous.'"[36] Silkworth had lifted several parts of "The Doctor's Opinion"—most notably the historical stories of Bill, Hank and Fitz— and neatly fit them into this much more scientific article addressed to the professional community. In short, Silkworth's Big Book contribution was a piece of original writing rather than something excised from a previously written professional article.

Also worth noting about Silkworth's appearance in the Multilith printing is the numbering of the pages. "The Doctor's Opinion" goes from "Page 1." to "Page 4." This is followed by "Bill's Story," which begins on a new "Page 1." and then runs consecutively until the end of "A Vision For You" on "Page 76." (After this, the pagination for the back half of the book begins again with "Personal Stories 1.")

This separate numbering of "The Doctor's Opinion" strongly suggests that the chapter wasn't submitted until the very last minute, most likely shortly before the already-finished typing of the book was to be handed over to the pre-publication printer. Supporting this theory is the fact that when the book was published in early April, Dr. Silkworth's chapter was incorporated into the full text of the book, appearing on pages 1–9 with "Bill's Story" beginning on page 10.

On the other hand, when the second edition of Alcoholics Anonymous came out in 1955, "The Doctor's Opinion" was once again relegated to a prefatory position in the book, now (and forever after) being numbered in Roman numerals while "Bill's Story" now commanded the page "1" position. Whatever the reasons may have been for this back-and-forth positioning of "The Doctor's Opinion," they have never been explained to anyone's satisfaction.

The Foreword

Another last-minute addition to the text of the Multilith copy was the "Foreword," which opens with the optimistic claim that "We, of Alcoholics Anonymous, are more than one hundred men and women who have recovered from a seemingly hopeless state of mind and body. To show other alcoholics PRECISELY HOW THEY CAN RECOVER is the main purpose of this book."

The rest of the "Foreword" goes on to articulate several key principles, some of which would, over the next ten years, find their way into the Twelve Traditions of A.A.:

- "It is important that we remain anonymous . . ."

- "We would like it clearly understood that our alcoholic work is an avocation only . . ."

- "When writing or speaking publicly about alcoholism, we urge each of our Fellowship to omit his personal name, designating himself instead as 'a member of Alcoholics Anonymous' . . ."

- "Very earnestly we ask the press also, to observe this request, for otherwise we shall be greatly handicapped."

- "We are not an organization in the conventional sense of the word."

- "There are no fees or dues whatsoever."

- "The only requirement for membership is an honest desire to stop drinking."

- "We are not allied with any particular faith, sect or denomination, nor do we oppose anyone. We simply wish to be helpful to those who are afflicted."*

The early appearance of these principles provides substantial evidence for the consistency of purpose maintained by Bill Wilson and Alcoholics Anonymous from this, the group's earliest publication, right up until the Twelve Traditions were formally adopted eleven years later in 1950.

Pricing the Book

Then, at the very bottom of this "Foreword," one final important fact about the book is slipped in parenthetically, noting that: "(This multilith volume will be sent upon receipt of $3.50, and the printed book will be mailed, at no additional cost, as soon as published.)"

How much to charge for the book had been a hot topic within the Fellowship for months. Bill later recalled that:

---

* I am grateful to the ever-perceptive A.A. historian, Arthur S., of Arlington, TX, for bringing these similarities to my attention.

we fixed the retail price of the book at $3.50 [and] this figure was the result of long and heated arguments. Some members had insisted on a $1.00 book,* others wanted a $2.50 printing. They had turned deaf ears to Henry's plea that we *must* make something on the deal or else we could never operate a headquarters office, much less payoff the shareholders.[37]

Hank was rightly insisting that the book had to make money if the organization was to have any chance of survival. The book would be their only secure source of income in the foreseeable future and the paradox was that the more copies they sold, the more their expenses would grow for maintaining a central office to respond to the increased inquiries and lending much needed support to the growing membership.**

Parkhurst had originally proposed a retail price of $3.00 for the book and this was the amount he consistently used when calculating the potential profit on each copy in his One Hundred Men Corporation prospectus.[38] It was also the price the publisher, John Walsh, had considered perfectly appropriate for a book such as this, especially because Hank and Bill had pitched it to him as a textbook, a term they consistently used when referring to the book.[39]

In early 1939, novels typically sold for less money than this—John Steinbeck's *The Grapes of Wrath*, published just four days after *Alcoholics Anonymous*, was longer (464 versus 400 pages) and sold for $2.75—but textbooks were always priced higher. Between the time of their meeting with John Walsh and the writing of the "Foreword," Wilson says that he and Hank had "looked up in the New York Times book review and we priced textbooks in there; and we found that the cheapest textbook that you could get (this was to be no novel, of course), the cheapest one was three bucks, the most expensive one listed there was around five bucks."[40] Given that evidence, paying $3.50 for their very valuable, even life-saving textbook on sobriety was clearly a bargain. With his typical tenacity, Parkhurst met all comers on this issue and he "finally won through,"[41] defeating all the arguments offered in support of a cheap price for the book.

As a consolation to the vanquished, Wilson claimed they "directed Mr. Blackwell [the printer of book] to do the job on the thickest paper in his shop" and, because of this, "the original volume proved to be so bulky that it became known as the 'Big Book.'" In addition to placating the losers, he said, they also did this "to convince the alcoholic purchaser that he was indeed getting his money's worth."[42]

Typing Up the Text

With all of these necessary elements finally in place, a clean, typed copy of the final text had to be prepared for the offset printer. While Hank had given Ruth marked up copies of the personal stories to be retyped,[43] further handwritten edits were constantly

---

* Clarence Snyder always insisted that a $1 copy of the book should be made available to newcomers and he alleged that Bill Wilson had promised him this would happen just as soon as the plates and the printing costs were recovered. It was one of the central issues in Clarence's ongoing list of resentments about Bill Wilson. (see Recorded interview with Clarence Snyder, GSO, CD 614; Tape 2: A.A. Niles Peebles Research—Clarence Snyder (1978); [16:00 – 16:40].

** Jay Moore, in his well-researched *Alcoholics Anonymous and the Rockefeller Connection*, notes that even this source of income would prove inadequate, at best allowing the group to break even some time in 1952. The shortfall from the book income—even with a $3.50 price tag—was soon apparent and the need for group contributions became unavoidable. (Moore, pp. 203, 226–31).

being made to the text—by Parkhurst and Janet Blair and perhaps even Bill—which meant the entire manuscript had to be neatly retyped with all those last-minute changes. As the number of pages grew to 164, this essential task became more and more formidable, far exceeding the amount of time Ruth Hock had as she juggled all her other office duties. Even more so than usual, Ruth was constantly busy in early 1939, answering the phone, greeting visitors, typing multiple copies of Tom Uzzell's letter to go along with Bill's many letters of solicitation, and most especially, dealing with the time-consuming task of tracking, recording, and acknowledging the stock payments that were slowly trickling in. She was, as she noted in a mid-January apology to Bill Ruddell, late in responding to his most recent letter because she was literally "running around in circles."[44]

Both Bill and Hank were anxious to move the project forward as quickly as possible, so to assist Ruth with this daunting job, they turned to Bill Ruddell's wife, Kathleen, for help with the typing job. Years later, she confirmed she "typed some of that first book," noting that, "I helped them when they were needy. Bill and Hank, they would bring me papers up to Hackettstown and I would sit at the typewriter and I would type them out for them."[45]* Weeks later, the printer of the book at Cornwall Press would be given a heavily marked up copy of the text rather than a clean retyped version, so Kathleen's mention here of "that first book" can only mean she was asked to do some of the typing required for the pre-publication multilith printing.

This use of a typist other than Ruth Hock for this final version of the text for the Multilith copy is confirmed by the "Works Publishing, Inc. Report of June 30, 1940," which has one disbursement line item for "R. Hock, Secretary" ($2,563.50) and another for a "Typist" ($60.00).[46]

The Multilith Printing

Today it is hard to imagine a world where copies aren't readily available by simply pushing a button. But that kind of convenience wasn't available until the introduction of the Xerox 914 copy machine in mid-September 1959.[47] Twenty years earlier, things were much more time-consuming, laborious, complicated, and expensive.

Pre-publication copies of the book *Alcoholics Anonymous* are variously described in contemporary correspondence and later recollections as being "mimeograph copies,"[48] "photo-lith copies"[49] and "multilith copies."[50] But the most definitive description of how the book was printed comes from the last paragraph of the "Foreword" that explicitly states it is a "multilith volume," a description confirmed in the June 1940 financial report prepared for Works Publishing listing an expense line item for "Multilith (Pre-publication printing)."[51]

"Multilith" was the brand name of a popular offset printing press and in 1939, something of a generic name (along with "mimeo") for short-run printing. The offset process was economically efficient, but only if more than 100 copies were required.

---

* I am grateful to Jared L, the eminent Pennsylvania A.A. historian, for bringing this interview to my attention. It should be mentioned that Hackettstown is more than forty miles from Newark, so this was no casual trip to make, likely in Hank's car, although rail service was also available.

Printing began with the creation of a plate with the appropriate image that was secured to the cylinder of the press. It was possible to type onto a special plate to put directly onto the press,[52] but Ruth and Kathleen created typed pages for the printer so the process here required the use of "a photographic negative . . . a thin zinc plate made from a series of negatives, and the actual printing of this zinc plate on an offset press"[53] (hence the appearance of the term "photo-lith" in a few contemporary letters). Once installed on the press, the plate attracted ink to the appropriate areas of the image and then transferred "a reverse image in ink onto a rubber blanket wrapped around a cylinder. The wet impression was then offset from the blanket to a sheet of paper." The press was typically capable of turning out six thousand copies an hour if there were no interruptions to change the plate.[54]

After the pages were printed, they were collated into sets and unprinted covers of either "red or blue cardboard"[55] were added before each copy was punched for binding and then bound with a red plastic 'comb' whose teeth fit into the holes punched down the left-hand side of the book.* The resultant copies were clearly an interim production and looked nothing like a professionally bound book, a fact explicitly noted by Frank Amos in his February 21, 1939 letter to Willard Richardson. "They are quite legible," he said, "but of course are put up in cheap form and cannot be compared in attractiveness and readability to the final printed volume."[56]

This letter to Richardson allows us to pinpoint the date of the Multilith printing with some accuracy. On Thursday, February 16, Amos had sent a letter to Miss Dorothy Critchfield and mentioned that the book "is about ready for press,"[57] while his Tuesday, February 21 letter informs Richardson that "the photolith copies of the book are now completed." Frank included a copy of the book with his letter telling the clergyman "if you will let me or Bill know how many of these photo-lith copies you would like to have, he will see that you get them at once." Given that Richardson would have received one of the first copies of the book once it was available, the delivery of the pre-publication Multilith copies to Bill and Hank happened on either Monday, February 20 or the morning of Tuesday, February 21.

How Many Copies and Whether for Loan or Sale?

Amos's assertion that the books had been cheaply printed raises the question of just how much the printing might have cost. Bill later noted that many A.A.s objected to this printing because it "would consume still more time and money,"[58] but it is hard to imagine these objections—if they did occur—even slowing down Bill and Hank once they made up their mind to issue a pre-publication copy of the book. In fact, the cost of the Multilith printing was $165—almost exactly $1 a page.[59]

Much less easy to resolve is the question of how many copies one-dollar-a-page would have purchased in early 1939. Contemporary price lists for offset printing would

---

* This comb binding is typical of those still produced using a GBC (General Binding Corporation) punch and binding machine. The only noteworthy difference between this and the Multilith Copy is that the current standard calls for nineteen small rectangular holes to be punched along the left edge of the pages. The Multilith Copy—produced before this became the standard—had twenty-two holes along the edge. See the original 1934 patent for comb binding at https://www.google.com/patents/US1970285 (retrieved April 7, 2017).

be helpful in answering this question, but even an exhaustive search of the legendary holdings at the New York Public Library shed no useful light on the issue. The library does hold a New York City contract entitled "Price List for Department Printing" covering the period April 1938 to March 1939, but this document unhelpfully lists the price of 100 offset copies as $2.33 per page,[60] which was clearly not the case here.

Without reliable contemporary pricing information, we are left with Bill Wilson's later comments—the earliest known reference appears ten years after the fact[61]—in which he consistently claimed 400 copies of the book had been printed.[62] However, Jim Burwell in his 1947 talk said there were just 200 copies printed[63] and Frank Amos in a March 21, 1939 letter to the trustees of the Alcoholic Foundation states that 300 copies of the book were available for distribution: "Some 300 copies of this job have been placed in the hands of all kinds of people—alcoholics, Christian ministers, physicians, authors, book reviewers and prominent men and women—whose reactions are eagerly awaited."[64] The fact that Frank's letter was written just one month after the book was released lends a certain (but not definitive) credibility to his claim that 300 Multilith copies of the book were printed.

There are yet even further complications to this question. When Jim Burwell had his personal copy of the Multilith Copy rebound sometime in the 1950s or 1960s, he instructed the binder to print "ALCOHOLICS ANONYMOUS, Book No. 2 of the First Hundred Mimeographed Copies" in gilt lettering on the front cover.* Presuming some semblance of accuracy, Jim's title might mean that just one hundred copies of the book were bound by the printer for his first delivery; but it might also mean there were two or more press runs of the book necessitated by the growing number of copies going out the door to potential reviewers. While there is no other mention or hint of multiple press runs in the records, there is some physical evidence for this possibility since the title page of the Multilith copy exists in two states. Some copies read "Alcoholic's Anonymous" (note the apostrophe, which is frequently deleted in pencil when it does appear), while others have the grammatically correct title "Alcoholics Anonymous."

Usually when variations such as this occur, bibliographers presume that the incorrect printing has priority, the later state reflecting the fact that someone noticed the error and made a correction. But Burwell's copy—which has the handwritten statement on the title page claiming it is "Copy No. 2 of the First Hundred"—has no apostrophe. This calls into question either the usual understanding of priority in printings (which is admittedly more a rule-of-thumb than a hard and fast rule) or Burwell's claim that his copy was the #2 copy. While Jim's statements of fact are frequently fallacious, his contention that he possessed the second copy distributed is somewhat credible since the address he has written for himself on the inside front cover is Hank Parkhurst's house, where he was living at the time. Given his prominent role within the group and

---

* The Burwell copy is in the author's collection. It was this question of just how many Multilith copies were printed that provided the initial impetus for researching this book. As a rare book dealer, when I first acquired Burwell's copy of the Multilith printing I was more than a little curious to know exactly how rare it was. Was it one of 100, 200, 300, or 400 copies? My original trip to the A.A. Archive in New York City was in the hope that I might be able to locate the original $165 invoice that would tell me the length of the press run. Alas, no such invoice has been preserved, so the question of how many copies were printed remains one of inference, speculation, and controversy.

his daily proximity to Hank, Jim would have certainly been given one of the very first copies to come off the press.

Other archived copies of the book provide no further evidence regarding priority or the question of multiple press runs. The A.A. Archive in New York City holds three copies of the Multilith Printing, two with the apostrophe in the title and one without. The Stepping Stones Archive has two copies, one with an apostrophe and one without. The copy where all of the suggestions for changes were collected—so beautifully reproduced in Hazelden's *The Book That Started It All*—has an apostrophe, which had been definitively edited out in pencil.

While the two different title pages could imply two different press runs for the book (whatever the priority), page 54 in the front of the book (the next to last page in "To Wives") is printed much lighter than any other in the book and this is uniformly true of the three copies in the New York archive, the two held at Stepping Stones, the Burwell copy, and the copy reproduced in *The Book That Started It All*. Since it is all but impossible that two different press runs would make the same inking error, the only logical conclusion is that the bulk of the book was printed during a single press run, with some other explanation being required to explain the differences in the title pages.

When all is said and done, the question of the number of copies printed and the reason for the two states of the title page continue to be mysteries.

"Loan Copy" or Priced for Sale?

This leaves just one remaining controversy surrounding the Multilith printing. Bill Wilson's repeatedly claimed that in order "to avoid any cloud on our copyright, these multilith copies were marked 'Loan Copy.'"[65] This insistence seems to have been driven by the realization that the closing parenthetical statement in the "Foreword"—"(This multilith volume will be sent upon receipt of $3.50, and the printed book will be mailed, at no addition cost, as soon as published.)" —showed a clear intention to sell the book and therefore left them open to the valid charge of having published their book without benefit of any copyright protection.*

While this problem was most likely noticed sometime in the 1940s, by 1954 Bill Wilson was clearly anxious about the issue, asking Dorothy Snyder in a recorded interview: "By the way, can you remember if those copies were marked 'Loan' copies, was there a stamp on it, can you recall?" Dorothy could not, replying emphatically: "No, I don't remember a loan copy at all."[66] Bill simply dropped the topic.

There is no "Loan Copy" stamped on any of the covers of the copies preserved in the New York archive, in the Stepping Stones archive, or the Burwell copy. Currently the only known copy showing this stamp is the one reproduced in *The Book That*

---

* This caused significant problems for A.A. over the coming years and there is a wealth of information available online regarding these issues—which are far outside the scope of this book. One of the most concise presentations of these problems can be found in Mitchell K's statement in his article "The A.A. German Court Case" where he notes: "The fact is the AA book's copyright registration was allowed to lapse both on the First Edition and Second Edition. Upon investigation, it has been proven that indeed, there never was a valid copyright on the AA book. Several independent Intellectual Property (copyright) lawyers were consulted and they have found that since the original Multilith Manuscript was published, distributed and sold without any notice of copyright or notice that it was a review or loan copy, it was immediately placed in the public domain since early 1939. According to the Copyright Act of 1909, any publication that was published without these notices forfeited the right of copyright." (http://silkworth.net/mitchellk/articles/aagerman_courtcase.html - retrieved April 11, 2017).

Started It All and, just to be completely accurate, that copy is stamped "Loan<u>ed</u> Copy" rather than "Loan Copy."

But more important, that stamped cover is suspiciously un-punched—meaning it was never an integral part of a comb-bound book.

CHAPTER TWENTY-NINE

Promoting and Editing
the Multilith Copy

~March 1939~

Bill and Hank received the Multilith copies on Monday, February 20 (or early Tuesday morning at the latest) and began to distribute them immediately. Among the first recipients were the foundation members: Amos, Richardson, Chipman, and Strong. Frank Amos seems to have been in charge of this distribution, as can be seen from his previously quoted February 21 letter to Willard Richardson.[1] Just one month earlier, Richardson, Chipman, and Strong had each bought stock in Works Publishing Co. and made a commitment to promote the book as much as they possibly could. Now was the time to follow through on that promise.

Leonard Strong's Publicity Efforts

Within that group, Leonard Strong seems to have been the most ambitious in his efforts to get publicity for the book. The day he received a copy of the Multilith printing he wrote a letter to Meredith Wood, an old high school acquaintance who just happened to be Vice President of the Book of the Month Club. Strong told Wood this unexpected communication was intended to be "a letter of introduction for my brother-in-law, Mr. William G. Wilson" but he realized "it is just possible that I may have to reintroduce myself and recall to you our school days together at Prospect Heights School in Brooklyn." He then told Wood that "Mr. Wilson would like a brief interview with you" to relate some of "the rather remarkable recoveries" which have taken place for over one hundred medically incurable men and women during the past four years. After mentioning the group would soon be publishing a book, he told Wood "it occurs to me that to have your opinion would be desirable and it is just possible that the book may be of value to the Book of the Month Club."[2]

This was an amazing personal connection and it fit in perfectly with Hank's dream that the book would become a runaway bestseller. With the burning issue of Prohibition just six years in the past, it was not beyond the realm of possibility that *Alcoholics Anonymous* actually might be chosen as the Club's monthly offering. While there is no evidence either confirming or denying a meeting between Bill Wilson and Meredith Wood, if it did happen and if the book had been selected it would have automatically been made available to the 360,000 members enrolled in the Book of the Month Club in 1939.[3]

Whether or not Hank Parkhurst had a hand in this appeal to the Club, he definitely offered Leonard Strong some specific advice for the letter he sent two weeks later to Erdmann Brandt, an associate editor for the *Saturday Evening Post*.[4] The day before the letter was to be sent, Parkhurst wrote Dr. Strong giving him precise instructions on what to say, what not to say, and how to say it: "If I were writing to a friend at the Saturday Evening Post," Hank said, "I do not believe I would mention editorial matter in the letter. I would suggest a letter somewhat along the following lines."[5] This was followed by four short paragraphs that Strong adopted wholesale except for the addition of his own opening sentence: "You may remember me speaking of some work with alcoholics, some time since." The letter went on—exactly as Hank's suggested—to say that a copy of the "pre-publication multilith copy of ALCOHOLICS ANONYMOUS" would soon arrive under separate cover and that Strong unequivocally vouched for the authenticity of the recoveries described in the book. He then coyly asked "As a matter of information I wonder if it would be possible for you to let me know the number of replies the Saturday Evening Post received in response to an article published last February under the title 'The Unhappy Drinker.'"[6*]

This last was pure Hank Parkhurst. In his prospectus for the One Hundred Men Corporation written a few months earlier, he explicitly referred to this article, noting that "the Post commented that more inquiries came to them from this than from any other article they had ever printed."[7] Strong's closing question was nothing more than an unsubtle reminder of just how popular articles on the drink problem had proven to be for the *Post* in the recent past.

Even though Parkhurst was still confident *Readers Digest* would soon publish an article on the book, he saw no reason why he shouldn't try to parlay the popularity of this topic into another article in *The Saturday Evening Post*. Hank was certain the discovery of a cure for alcoholism was a subject that popular magazines would naturally jump at. Of course the *Post* famously did publish an article on A.A. which generated tremendous growth in the movement, but that did not appear until March 1, 1941. Leonard Strong's 1939 appeal apparently fell on deaf ears.

Strong was nothing if not persistent. On April 3 he also sent a pre-publication copy to Dr. E. E. Duffell, an official at the American Osteopathic Association (to which Leonard belonged), vouching for "the authenticity of the statements made there-in."

---

* 'The Unhappy Drinker' article actually appeared in the *Saturday Evening Post* on January 15, 1938.

His hope was that Duffell would "find it as gripping as I have" and also think it was appropriate for review in the Association's Journal.[8]

A. LeRoy Chipman also actively promoted the book, most particularly to Harry Emerson Fosdick, the famous pastor of Rockefeller's Riverside Church. In late September, Bill had told Dr. Bob that Chipman was planning to enlist Fosdick's support and his hope was that the minister would become so enthusiastic about their new method of recovery that he would try to convince John D. Rockefeller Jr. to donate more money to the cause.[9] On March 9 Fosdick reported to Chipman that he had read the Multilith copy "with keen interest. It certainly is a stirring document," he said and noted "I should think that its printing and wide distribution would do a great deal of good." He was enthusiastic enough about what he had read to ask if he should return this copy or if he was "at liberty to put it into the hands of a family where I think it would be of use?"[10] However, the Reverend Fosdick's enthusiasm did not result in the much hoped-for appeal to Rockefeller or, if he did make such an appeal, his efforts were unsuccessful.

Copies Sent to Professionals, Stockholders, and A.A. Members

Wilson later noted that Multilith copies were also sent to a wide variety of professionals,[11] a group that included doctors, psychiatrists, judges, and members of the clergy.[12] The main purpose, he said, was to ensure the book didn't contain any medical errors that would make them look foolish, and to discover if there was anything in the text "that might offend our friends in religion."[13] Of course his secondary purpose was the hope that once these people read the book, they would then generate some pre-publication 'buzz' about it within their own professional communities.

It's not clear exactly how the distribution to medical, legal, and religious leaders was carried out. It is likely that some (perhaps most?) copies were delivered in person with a verbal explanation of the purpose of this review copy. If other copies were mailed out to these professionals, whatever standard letter sent with the enclosed manuscript has not been preserved in any of the A.A. archives.

Copies were also sent to everyone who had bought stock in Works Publishing to reassure them that the book project was still firmly on track and that the publication date was fast approaching. In addition, copies went to several prospects in the hopes that this would encourage them to invest.[14]

Finally, "all of the A.A. members"[15] received Multilith copies, but here the purpose was primarily to solicit comments and critiques about the content of the book. In New York, many of these copies would have been hand-delivered, but some were mailed to the more remote members. For instance, Bill Ruddell, who lived in Hackettstown, New Jersey—more than fifty miles from New York City—received his copy by mail,[16] making it probable that other similarly distant members also received their Multiliths via the US Postal Service.

As Wilson had noted in his November 26 letter to Bob Smith, the "next step is to make, after one editing, photolithic copies of the whole works. There will be plenty of copies for everyone and then there will be no excuse for people not saying what they think. Or, as the wedding ceremony says, 'Forever hold thy peace.'"[17]* Feedback from Akron had been slim to none in the past and this was going to be their last chance to have any say about what went into the book explaining their program of recovery. If nothing else, Bill expected people to take an interest in the final edits made to their own stories, telling Frank Amos in late February that a trip to Akron was necessary so he could have "a final discussion with the men there on their personal stories which are to appear in the book."[18]

Bill Goes to Akron for Feedback on the Book

There is no record of whether copies were mailed to Ohio—individually or in bulk—or if they were personally delivered by Bill Wilson when he finally made his visit to Akron on March 1. Bill had originally planned to make this all-important final review visit to Ohio in mid-December,[19] but the writing of the Twelve Steps (and the two dependent chapters) along with the subsequent editing process had forced him to reschedule the trip repeatedly. With the Multilith copies now printed, Wilson headed out to Akron to gather whatever critiques and criticisms he could elicit from the Ohio members.

The day after he left, Lois wrote Bill a charming and loving letter. "I miss you such a lot already, much much more than I have for a long time," she said. "I can't tell you dear how much I appreciate your wonderful love and how sweet your parting was. It all makes me very happy dear and I am so proud to be your wife." The letter goes on to recount the antics of the drunks (sober and otherwise) who were constantly trekking through their home in Brooklyn—one wanting to borrow money, another trying to sell his story to a newspaper, while a third was hoping to get this enterprising fellow drunk enough to be admitted to Bellevue Hospital. She also tells Bill that she and Hank had been planning a dinner out alone that night, but they were now being joined by Morgan Ryan and perhaps Ray Campbell. Bill had only been gone one day, but it had been an eventful one.[20]

Dr. Bob's Payments Are Reduced

Getting feedback on the Multilith printing wasn't the only problem Bill had to face once he arrived in Akron. He also had the unpleasant task of telling Bob Smith that his regular $200 monthly payment from the Rockefeller funds was going to be reduced to just $50 a month for the next two months. In the week just before the Multilith copies became available, Wilson made two visits to Frank Amos's office where he pleaded that funds "be sent to [Fitz] Mayo to help in the work he and Mrs. Rankin [were] doing in Washington," while also explaining the desperation of his own financial situation. He had already received Charles Towns's last payment and he "badly" needed "an extra $100 to pay his insurance, due March 1, and to cover the expenses of a trip to Akron and back."[21]

---

*   Wilson had used almost identical language three weeks earlier in his November 3, 1938 letter to Smith (GSO, Box 59, Folder B(1), Document 1938-172).

In response to these pleas, Amos decided to reduce Smith's payment, while simultaneously sending Fitz Mayo and Bill Wilson checks for $100 each. Reporting this to Richardson, Amos said that when Bill had suggested this desperately needed redistribution, he proposed Dr. Bob's monthly check be reduced to $100. However, Amos told Richardson that he "was inclined to cut this in half, that is, $50 a month for two months," noting that in the end, both he and Wilson were "confident that Dr. Smith can carry on fairly well for probably three or four months without getting into a serious situation."[22]

Unfortunately Dr. Bob did not share their cool confidence in his ability to survive on just $50 a month. No sooner had Wilson left Akron than Smith wrote Frank Amos asking that some of the money be restored, implying it was vital to their ongoing work with alcoholics.

> I understand the exchequer of the Foundation is at a very low ebb and I also realize some of the boys there are in quite deplorable condition financially, which happens to be my condition also. I have no way of knowing who needs help the most.
>
> However, I would say that if it is at all possible for you to help me out a bit it would be much appreciated.
>
> We are still plugging along at about the usual clip. One chap left the hospital yesterday and there are still two left. We have a doctor from Cleveland who seems excellent timber. He'll certainly be in a wonderful position for good if he catches fire and I rather think he will.[23]

This request was either ignored or denied since there is no record of a larger payment going to Dr. Bob in either March or April 1939.

The Ohio Folks Are Happy with the Book but Not with Selling Stock

Regarding their plans for launching the book, Bill had obviously tried to do one of his traditionally flamboyant selling jobs, proudly assuring the Akron members they would soon receive some amazing national publicity. Dr. Bob made note of this in his letter to Amos, telling him, "Hope the boys will succeed in getting sufficient gratuitous advertising to speed up the sale of the book," This referred to the *Readers Digest* article Bill and Hank had been promised once the book was published, but that upcoming splash of publicity didn't seem to generate much positive excitement in Akron. Instead, it elicited some of the same concerns and complaints that had been raised in the past about the impossibility of responding to the flood of requests they would surely receive once the article appeared.

In relation to the book itself, Smith told Amos that "everyone seems to like the book very much and I think it will prove itself a very useful agent."[24] Once again, the Ohio response was negligible and confined to the fact that everyone was happy with what they had seen. This last minute comment by Smith—just weeks before the book was to appear—confirms Wilson's later note that when he asked Akron for "checking and criticism" on the manuscript, he got "nothing but the warmest support."[25]

But, while the Multilith copies and news of the coming national publicity produced little response, the fact that Hank and Bill had been selling stock in a company to publish *Alcoholics Anonymous* most certainly did. As Bob told Frank: "Some hard feeling among the boys over the way the book was financed but I guess that was the only solution possible. Looks OK to me."[26]

When the idea of selling stock had been proposed in October, Smith advised against sharing that information with anyone in Ohio,[27] so this was the first time they were being told about the sale of stock in Works Publishing Co. When Bill Wilson did finally reveal they were selling shares to finance the book, it created an immediate furor. Selling stock meant that money (and worse, profits!) were going to be an integral part of the enterprise and the Ohio members were unalterably opposed to mixing finance with spirituality, no matter how great the need might be. Bill's news confirmed their worst fears about him and about the terrible things being done in the name of their Fellowship back in New York City—things certain to destroy their simple program of recovery. These hard feelings over money continued to simmer and finally boiled over with the lurid accusations made by Clarence Snyder throughout the 1940s (and beyond), claiming that Bill Wilson was consistently taking large amounts of cash out of A.A.'s coffers to line his own pockets.[28*]

Dorothy Snyder Promotes the Book

But, however upset Clarence may have been by the financial contamination of their spiritual program, his wife, Dorothy, was very interested and deeply committed to circulating the Multilith copies once she had them in hand. In a 1954 interview she told Bill: "I don't know how many copies we had, but I know that I personally had about 10 copies to be passed around for people to read and criticize."[29] Dorothy was not only aggressive about getting these copies into the hands of local doctors and ministers, she even tried to solicit advance orders for the book.

> I was pounding the streets trying to show different book stores the Multilith copy. I went down to the public library and tried to get orders; of course, we wanted to get orders so that we'd have money too, and nobody would even listen to me and they looked at me like I was Salvation Nell and I began to think I really should have a tambourine.[30]

However unsuccessful Dorothy's sales efforts may have been, she did make one extremely important and consequential convert in Cleveland. "I took the Multilith copy to the Rev. Dilworth Lupton," she said "and he read it and he said he would definitely come to one of our meetings, he did and he was so impressed . . ." This was no small accomplishment. The Reverend Lupton was "one of the really big Protestant ministers in Cleveland"[31] and he had formerly been stridently antagonistic toward A.A., viewing

---

* While this controversy is beyond the scope of this book, it is worth noting that open examinations of A.A. financials by Clarence and others—made in the 1940s and clearly showing that all expenses were valid—has done nothing to allay the spread of this story, another A.A. myth being that Bill Wilson was making money off the Fellowship from the very beginning.

it as just another subset of the Oxford Group. But having read the book and attended a meeting or two, Lupton changed his mind and publicly demonstrated his reversal by preaching a sermon entitled "Mr. X and Alcoholics Anonymous."[32] This dramatic public support led directly to a series of five articles favorable to A.A. that ran on the editorial pages of the *Cleveland Plain Dealer* in October and November of 1939—articles that were directly responsible for an explosion of Alcoholics Anonymous membership in Cleveland in late 1939 and early 1940.

Another Failed Attempt to Get Ford's Endorsement

Wilson left Akron and headed for Detroit to make one final attempt to connect with Henry Ford and hopefully convince him to write a Preface for the book. Frank Amos had given Bill a letter of introduction addressed to two advertising executives he knew at Ford, asking them to grant Wilson an interview. The two men, Colin Campbell and Ben Donaldson, met Bill for lunch, where he told them his own story and detailed the growth of the A.A. Fellowship over the past four years. He ended his presentation by giving them a Multilith copy to read before they came to a decision about recommending the book to Ford.

Both men read the book, but once again Bill's hopes of securing a Preface by Ford were dashed. Colin Campbell found the book something of a chore to read, unenthusiastically informing Frank Amos that "by reading 'Alcoholics Anonymous' over the weekend, I kept my promise to Mr. Wilson." He was underwhelmed by a number of things in the book, especially the fact that during their lunch he had "felt the tremendous power of the message" Bill was delivering, but "in reducing this message to print I feel that most of this power is lost." He damned the writing with the faintest possible praise, calling it "sufficiently workman-like" and then noting that, in his opinion, beyond those whose lives were directly touched by alcoholism, this "book would have practically no interest."[33]

Given this scathing review, Campbell clearly had no intention of passing the manuscript along to the legendary head of the company with a recommendation that he become involved in the project. Bill Wilson's long-standing belief that if he could only get Ford's attention, he would surely raise his powerful voice in support of their solution for alcoholism was decisively crushed.

Good News From Lois

While in Michigan, there was at least one consolation for Bill when he received another loving letter from Lois ("I love you and miss you so much") recounting details of what had been happening in New York while he was away. Besides "a fine Tuesday night gang meeting," she had received Ray Furlong's story for the book (published as "Another Prodigal Son") which she judged to be "very good" and noted that "there seemed to be lots of good reports of the book. Dr's in all directions seem to be taking an interest." But perhaps most interesting, Lois reports she had delivered "a long dissertation on married love to Hank," adding that "whether the latter had anything to do with the great improvement in Hank I don't know, but he spent last night and is to spend tonight out in Montclair. He is cheerful with Kathleen and calls her dear and honey."[34]* The Parkhursts were back together again and Lois was, if nothing else, happy to have one less drunk in the house to care for, feed, and clean up after.

More Stories Arrive

Besides Ray Furlong's story, nine other new stories arrived throughout late February and March and all of these were eventually published in the first edition of the book. While the twenty stories that appeared in the back of the Multilith Copy were predominantly from Ohio (fourteen vs. six from New York), these ten new arrivals were more heavily weighted toward the East (six from New York, three from Ohio, and one supposedly written by a California member). Once Del Tryon's story was withdrawn, that left a total of twenty-nine stories (sixteen from Ohio, twelve from New York, and one from California) that appeared in the back section of the Big Book when it was first published.

All of these continued to appear throughout all sixteen printings of the first edition except for the California story entitled "Lone Endeavor," which was cut from the book when the second printing went to press in 1941—and for good reason. Jim Burwell provides the liveliest account of this story.

> One [of the Multilith copies] created quite an amusing incident for it got into the hands of a patient in a psychopathic hospital in California. This man immediately caught fire and religion all in one fell swoop. He wrote and told us about the wonderful release he had from alcohol through our new Alcoholics Anonymous multilith. Of course all of us in New York became highly excited and wires bounced back and forth between us and our new convert regarding this miracle that happened 3,000 miles away. This man wrote the last personal history in the book while he was still in California called the Lone Endeavor. Our New York Groups were so impressed by his recovery that we passed the hat and sent for him to come East as an example. This he did, but when the boys met him at the bus station the delusion faded, for he arrived stone drunk and as far as I know, never came out of it.[35]

For all its entertainment value, Jim's story makes at least one serious mistake. The man from California, Pat Cooper, did not write that story himself and send it off before his own inauspicious arrival; it was Ruth Hock's only unassisted contribution to the book. The Newark office had receive a letter from Cooper's mother claiming he had miraculously recovered from his drinking problem because of the book and Hock wrote back requesting more details. According to Ruth, Bill thought it would make an

---

* Someone later wrote "in Akron" on the archived original of this letter, but the date and the lack of the usual closing reminder to "give my love to Anne and Bob and all the rest of the gang" (see the March 2, 1939 letter to Bill previously quoted in this chapter and other letters sent to Akron over the years) confirms that this letter was sent to Bill in Detroit rather than while he was "in Akron."

"interesting" addition to the book, especially because it confirmed that someone could get sober remotely with nothing more than the book to rely on. Once she had all the relevant details, Ruth wrote the story herself without any further consultation with the Coopers. But given the disastrous outcome—as so colorfully related by Jim—she admitted that "the next time the Book was rewritten, that was left out. It was very well left out . . ."[36]

Hank and Bill Meet with Cornwall Press and *Readers Digest*

After his failed trip to Detroit, two important things demanded Bill's attention once he was back in New York City. First of all, Hank had made an appointment for them to meet with Edward Blackwell, the president of Cornwall Press, at his corporate offices on West 26th Street in Manhattan. They needed to finalize the arrangements for printing the book. Hank and Bill had met with Blackwell "months before"[37]— most likely on the recommendation of Richard J. Walsh, the owner of the John Day Publishing Company—when the printer had advised them how much it would cost for Cornwall to produce their book. Now, with a much more accurate idea of the length of the text, they sat down with Blackwell to iron out all the details for the printing. There are no contemporary records mentioning this meeting, but Bill supplied a number of colorful details in his *Alcoholics Anonymous Comes of Age* account.

> Henry and I went to New York and soon found ourselves face to face with Edward Blackwell, president of the Cornwall Press. In high spirits, we told him we were ready to go.
>
> Mr. Blackwell wanted to know how many copies we wished. With the promised Readers Digest article in mind, we were still thinking of carloads. Though doubtless impressed, Mr. Blackwell suggested 5,000 copies for the first printing. Then he asked what financial terms we were able to make. We cautiously let it be known that our cash was temporarily low. Pointing out what the Readers Digest article would do for us, Henry mentioned a figure of $500 for our first down payment on the 5,000 books. Mr. Blackwell was startled and looked it. "What about that Rockefeller connection?" he asked. We replied that we had better hold that in reserve; that we were trying to manage this thing on our own if we could. Mr. Blackwell, having already caught the A.A. spirit, said with a twinkle in his eye, "Well, I guess that will do. I'm glad to give you a hand." So the presses were set to roll . . .[38]

Typical of Bill, this is surely a sanitized version of what actually happened. In addition to how unlikely it would be to have such an easy and painless negotiation, contradictory facts arise elsewhere. For instance, in one of his earlier versions of this story, Bill says Hank was the one who made the suggestion for an initial press run of 5,000 copies, and he also notes that they had "leaned rather heavily on our connection with Mr. Rockefeller" in order to convince Edward Blackwell that the small $500 down payment should be perfectly acceptable given their close connection to the wealthiest man in the country.[39]

And, while $500 is a lovely round number, that too is a problem. For instance, Wilson elsewhere claimed they told Blackwell that "currently, the bank account is a little low, but we could put $200 down" for the printing.[40] But the most believable—though not exactly clear—evidence regarding the amount of the down payment comes from the Cornwall Press invoice issued on April 10 (the day the book was published). There it says that Blackwell received a check for $794.66 on March 27 as "payment on a/c [account]" and this is the only such payment recorded by the printer before the publication date. On the original archived copy of that invoice, this same number has been penciled in the margins opposite a $311.85 charge for "7 plate boxes @ 1.25 not on est.," as if to imply that the cost of these plates was somehow covered by a portion of that check.[41] But $311.85 and $500.00 do not equal $794.66, so the reason for this strange, uneven amount remains a mystery. Perhaps it was just every last penny Hank Parkhurst had at that moment in his Works Publishing checking account—and Blackwell accepted that amount as a good faith gesture.

A Disappointing Meeting with Readers Digest

Bill's second important meeting after his return from Detroit was with *Readers Digest*. Once again, there is no mention of this meeting in the contemporary documents, but Wilson provides his detailed description of what happened that day in Pleasantville, NY, in *Alcoholics Anonymous Comes of Age*:

> I will never know why, in all the time during which the book was in preparation, none of us had thought of getting in touch with the Readers Digest. Somehow the question of timing their article with the appearance of our book had not occurred to us. As Henry and I again rode up the parkway toward Pleasantville, we wondered about this. We estimated it might take them several months to produce the promised piece. But why worry; it was just a question of time, anyhow.
>
> We were greeted by Managing Editor Payne at the door of his office. He did not remember exactly who we were. Henry gaily remarked, "Well, Mr. Managing Editor, we are all ready to shoot." And Mr. Payne, nonplused, weakly replied, "Shoot what?" Hastily we brought him up to date, and the memory of our visit during the previous fall came back with a rush. "Of course, of course," he said. "I remember you now. You are the representatives of that fellowship of alcoholics. You wanted a Digest piece about your society and the book you are preparing. You will remember that I told you I had to check this up with our editorial staff. Well, I did. To my surprise, they did not like the idea at all. They did not think there would be much interest in a society of alcoholics. And they thought besides that the whole business would be controversial, medically and religiously speaking. And worst of all, I forgot to let you people know. I am so sorry."

This was shattering. Even the buoyant Henry was sunk. We protested, but it was no use. This was it. The book enterprise had collapsed.[42]

One can only imagine how much is left out of Wilson's simple declaration "We protested"—especially with the ever fiery and voluble Henry G. Parkhurst sitting in that meeting. Given Payne's contention that the editorial staff's reservations were based primarily on the possibility that the article would be "controversial, medically and religiously speaking" and the fact that the manuscript was even then being circulated to both of those professional communities for the express purpose of ensuring that no such controversies appeared in the final publication, Parkhurst must have been apoplectic and it seems unlikely he would have conceded this argument to Payne with any kind of gentlemanly grace.

The *Digest* article was the lynchpin in all Hank's arguments for buying the stock and he was counting on this national publicity to launch the book as a best seller. Given that dependence and having lost those arguments, it is not hard to imagine how shattering and shocking this news must have been to the two men and how they might so quickly conclude that the entire book enterprise had collapsed. The single most important pillar of their game plan for success had just vanished into thin air.

Bill says he and Hank left Pleasantville and rode back to New York in a daze, wondering how in the world they could possibly break this terrible news to the printer and to their stockholders. "What would we do? How could we face up to this catastrophe? . . . Soon 5,000 books would land in Cornwall's warehouse with no market whatever."[43] It was a disaster, but he reported that their homecoming

> proved less distressing than we expected. A few of our people grumbled and said, "We told you so," but nearly everybody else took a sporting attitude and asked what had become of our faith . . . Most cheering of all, Mr. Edward Blackwell said he had no intention of turning our book over to an outside publisher. He would see us through, he said. And so he did, for many an uncertain month and year to come.[44]*

It is hard to believe this brightly cheerful story, but there are no contemporary reports of stockholder's complaints, even though the often-stated expectation that they would soon be selling carloads of books had to be significantly revised along with any hope that the investors would soon be repaid the money they had sunk into the Works Publishing venture.

Suggested Edits Are Entered onto a Master Copy

As suggested changes for the book came in, they were handwritten into a single Multilith copy held in the Newark office. That copy, now referred to as "The Original Working Manuscript," was published in a 2010 facsimile edition by Hazelden Press as *The Book That Started It All: The Original Working Manuscript of* Alcoholics Anonymous.

---

* As noted on page 205 of *Pass It On:* "Bill never failed to express gratitude to Blackwell in later years. A.A. continued to have the Big Book printed at Cornwall Press for a long time after it became a steady seller, so the venture also became profitable for the company."

Because this copy contains both the suggestions which were accepted as well as those that were rejected, it presents "a rare and valuable snapshot taken from a few critical weeks in 1939 that dramatically captures the controversy and creativity that went into producing the book that would explain AA's program of recovery to the world."[45]*

However, those suggested edits were so numerous and, in some cases so important, that only an exhaustive scholarly investigation together with a genuinely critical evaluation could begin to do them justice. There is surely more than one doctoral dissertation waiting to be written about these pages, teasing out the lasting changes made to the emerging A.A. program, and tracing the impact they had on the direction and success of this uniquely American spiritual movement. Although the depth and breadth of these suggested edits preclude any kind of comprehensive survey, a few of the most important proposed changes deserve at least some mention here.

There is one entry in Bill Wilson's hand made with a green pencil and signed "WGW" (at the top of Del Tryon's deleted story)[46] along with a few minor corrections he made in the same green pencil to three pages of "Into Action."[47] Aside from these, the rest of the notations in the "Original Working Manuscript" have been made in black and red pencil—mostly in script, but some in print and a few in block lettering— and almost all can be easily identified as being written by Hank Parkhurst.** While there were almost no suggested changes for the stories in the back half of the book (Hank had already extensively edited them), hundreds of black pencil entries appear throughout the front half. The red pencil notations are, however, confined to just the first part of that front section—the last one showing up in the second paragraph of Chapter Six, "Into Action." Besides entering all of these suggested changes, Parkhurst further confirmed his position as the book's Managing Editor by signing his initials, "HGP," in the bottom corner of almost every page.***

Exactly how and when these suggestions were relayed to Hank is unknown, but the fact that he used both black and red pencils indicates that he made entries on at least two different occasions. In addition, there are several places where edits were originally made in red and then later overwritten in black[48]—indicating he revisited this task more than once with a black pencil in hand. In addition, Hank made frequent shifts between script and block lettering, suggesting he might have been entering these edits with some regularity during the last week of February and throughout the month of March.

---

* Anyone interested in the history of the writing of the Big Book cannot ignore this amazing facsimile copy. It provides a striking visual history of the arguments made and the decisions taken in the final days before *Alcoholics Anonymous* was published.

** One does not have to be a professional graphologist to identify Parkhurst's distinctive handwriting. A comparison of the suggestions entered in the "Original Working Manuscript" with the extensive sample of Hank's own handwriting (in script along with printed and block lettering) available in the several pages of his early-June, 1938 submission to Bill ("Hank's Ideas") provides easy matches for what appears here.

*** It is interesting to note that Bill Wilson's "WGW" initials appear on only one page of the expositional section of the "Original Working Manuscript." See *The Book That Started It All*, p. 74.

Hank Parkhurst's Edits

Parkhurst was especially ruthless in editing his own chapter, "To Employers." This he seemed to do willingly, noting at the top of the final blank page in the front of the "Original Working Manuscript" that his first task as editor was "1—Business chapter should be rewritten."⁴⁹ Hank rewrote "To Employers" with a vengeance, changing words and phrases with abandon while constantly making bold deletions of sentences, large parts of some paragraphs, and even the entire section containing the excellent ten point summary at the end of the chapter. This is an unexpected bit of humility from Hank, but perhaps he was trying to set an example for Bill Wilson who was much more reluctant to change anything he had already written.

But the single most important change made to the book during the review process was the addition of four completely new paragraphs that were added to "Bill's Story." These were written out across the first two blank pages of the "Original Working Manuscript" in Hank Parkhurst's distinctive hand, (with a number of abbreviations that are completed below with [bracketed] letters):

> Despite the living example of my fr[iend] there rem[ained] in me the vestiges of my old prejudice. The word God still aroused a cert[ain] antip[athy]. When the thought was expressed that there might be a God personal to me this feeling was intensified. I didn't like the idea. I could go for such concept[tions] as Cre[ative] Int[elligence], Universal M[ind] or Spirit of Nature but I resisted the thought of a Czar of the Heavens, however loving His sway might be. I have since talked with scores of men who f[e]lt the same way.
>
> My fr[iend] sug[gested] what then seemed a novel idea. He s[ai]d, "Why d[on']t you choose your own conc[eption] of God?"
>
> That stat[ement] hit me hard. It melted the icy intellectual mountain in whose shad[ow] I had lived and shivered many ye[a]rs. I stood in the sunlight at last.
>
> It was only a matter of being willing to bel[ieve] in a P[owe]r gr[eate]r than myself. Nothing more was req[uired] of me to make my beginning. I saw that growth could start from that point. Upon a found[ation] of comp[lete] willingness I mite [sic] build what I saw in my fr[iend]. Would I ha[ve] it? Of c[ou]rs[e] I w[o]u[l]d!⁵⁰

This entry raises a number of puzzling questions. Did Hank write it on his own? Or are all those abbreviations evidence that he was taking dictation from Bill? Were these words written out (or typed?) beforehand and then transcribed into the "Original Working Manuscript"? The only thing we know with certainty is that the insert was handwritten by Hank Parkhurst and approved by Bill Wilson for inclusion in his story.

While it is always possible this long insert had been previously written out by Bill, the idea of Wilson dictating this text to Hank is much less plausible. It just wasn't

Wilson's style to let a "first pass" go uncorrected (while Parkhurst was always much more confident about his own writing abilities). It is also possible Bill saw this as a necessary addition to correct an important omission from the earlier drafts of his story—perhaps something he had inadvertently left out. But, it should also be noted that this extremely open-ended and as-loose-as-possible approach to the Higher Power certainly sounds like something Hank would insist on adding to the book. However much the writing does not sound like a typical Hank Parkhurst effort, it is exactly the kind of position he had been so forcefully advocating for months.

Besides Parkhurst's strong desire to emphasize just how creative people could be when it came to their conception of a "Power greater than myself," this new text also filled a significant gap in "Bill's Story." As noted earlier, the two earliest versions of his story taken together contained close parallels to eleven of the Twelve Steps, leaving out only the Second Step. This handwritten insertion admirably corrects that omission and may have been added once it was noticed that the all-important Second Step was completely missing from his personal story.

Finally, there is the important question of whether or not this was something Ebby actually said to Bill when he visited him in Brooklyn in November 1934. The general consensus is that "Why don't you choose your own conception of God" is so far beyond the realm of anything preached by the Oxford Group that it is surely a later addition to the story.* To claim this critical part of the message of recovery had simply been forgotten and gone unmentioned up until this point—more than five years after the alleged conversation—strains Bill Wilson's credibility to the breaking point. The new text certainly fits well with the recently written Twelve Steps, but it hardly seems to be something that would have been said by Ebby Thacher in 1934.

But, however historically inaccurate this long addition may be, it is an accurate reflection of the group's more recent experiences working with newcomers. Offering the option of adopting virtually any reasonable concept of God as a starting point of sobriety was something that had worked so successfully that it was deemed worthy of being explicitly included in the book, and this was perhaps the most dramatically effective place to make that point.

The Catholic Church Weighs In

One critically important review of the Multilith copy was made by the Roman Catholic Archdiocese of New York. Most of the members of the Cleveland group that regularly drove to Akron on Wednesday nights were Catholics and they were being forbidden by their local priests to attend Oxford Group meetings; it was a clear violation of their membership in the Catholic Church. Nonetheless, they continued to attend the weekly Akron meetings—their sobriety depended on it—even if they did so with some reluctance and trepidation.[51] In those days, Catholics who openly participated in Protestant services could be refused absolution for their sins by their parish priest

---

*   See Bob K.'s *Key Players in AA History*, pp. 148–49 for an interesting discussion of this point and his note that Ebby "had no recollection" of ever saying such a thing at that meeting.

and denied the privilege of receiving communion at Sunday Mass. It was the local equivalent of excommunication.

Wilson later elaborated on the Catholic Church's rationale for this ban, explaining that when he

> first contacted the Oxford Groups, Catholics were permitted to attend their meetings because they were strictly non-denominational. But after a time, the Catholic Church forbade its members to attend and the reason for this seemed a good one. Through the Oxford Group teams, Catholic Church members were actually receiving very specific guidance for their lives; they were often infused with the idea that their own Church had become rather horse-and-buggy, and needed to be "changed." Guidance was frequently given that contributions should be made to the Oxford Groups. In a way, this amounted to putting Catholics under a separate ecclesiastical jurisdiction.[52]

Bill was tremendously worried about this, fearing that, just as they were prohibited from attending Oxford Group meetings, Catholics might also be forbidden to attend Alcoholics Anonymous meetings. Getting the Church's approval for the program outlined in the book or at least some solid assurance that there was nothing there that would prevent Catholics from attending A.A. meetings, was critically important to all of Wilson's plans for the Twelve Step program to become a universal method of recovery.*

How to discover if there was anything in the text "that might offend our friends in religion"[53] —in this case, specifically the Roman Catholic religion—was a challenging problem. First, they had to find a suitable way to approach the Church, and then they had to prepare themselves for the very real possibility of an unfavorable decision. In March 1939, Alcoholics Anonymous got lucky when a well-connected Catholic member joined the New York group. The liveliest version of this story (if somewhat marred by ethnic stereotypes) was delivered by Bill Wilson in 1951, recounting a tale that would be a bit hard to believe if it had not actually happened this way.

> And meanwhile, the Pope, he'd written off the Oxford Group and while we were now very much different, we had a big scare. And we said, "My God with all these carolers and Harps to come; if the Pope writes them off, we're going to be in an awful fix. This book has got to satisfy the Irish . . .
>
> [So] with great trepidation we laid hold of the only Irishman we had, who had just come out of Greystone Asylum, and we sent him over to the Catholic Committee on Publications in New York to see what the Committee thought about it. Well, of course we all had a bad case of the jitters. By some strange coincidence, we didn't just have any Catholic

members . . . we just got one in New York, this guy Morgan, who becomes quite the hero of this tale.

So our friend Morgan Ryan, he knows somebody on the Committee, you know how them Irishmen are; and he sneaks it over into the Committee and the Committee takes a look at it. And after a while Morgan comes in and says, "Boy," he said "It got by and how!" He said, "Of course the Bishop ain't gonna' put any imprimatur on it, but it's all in the clear."

So the Committee called in Mr. Ryan and they said, "Now this is an admirable work, the Church will have no objection to it. In fact, we have only one absolutely necessary change that has to be made in this book for Catholic reading."

So Mr. Ryan said, "Well, what is it?"

"Well," he said, "Right here in the first chapter, called 'Bill's Story,' you will find near the end a statement which reads like this." And they turned to the chapter which read: In a burst of extravagance of course, of rhetorical flourish, I had finished the chapter by saying, "We have found heaven, right here on this good old earth." So Morgan's priest friends on the Committee looked at him and said, "Now, Morgan, couldn't Mr. Wilson just shift that a little bit? Couldn't he change that word Heaven to Utopia? After all we clergymen are promising folks something much better later on. Moreover, we don't require it, and the chapter on meditation and prayer from the Catholic viewpoint, but maybe here a few little improvements that would interest you."

Well, the improvements were good and we slapped them right in.[54]

The original last paragraph in "Bill's Story" had actually said "Most of us feel we need look no further for Utopia, nor even for Heaven. We have it with us right here and now. Each day that simple talk in my kitchen multiplies itself in a widening circle of peace on earth and good will to men."[55] Although the change is not noted in "The Original Working Manuscript," the phrase "nor even for Heaven" was summarily dropped before the text of the Big Book was finalized.

Unfortunately it is impossible to identify those "few little improvements" on prayer and meditation suggested by the Catholic Committee, changes that Bill judged to be good and which he said were "slapped" right into the Eleventh Step section of the book. A quick glance at pages 71 and 72 of the Hazelden facsimile edition of the "Original Working Manuscript" shows why it is impossible to identify those Catholic changes. Both of these pages are "so loaded with cross-outs, inserts, and marginalia that it is even difficult for a reader familiar with the text to decipher it."[56] Whatever the Committee suggested is now lost in a morass of other comments and corrections.*

---

* In a conversation with the late Ernie Kurtz about this problem, he wondered aloud if perhaps an annotated copy of the Multilith printing might still be found in the archives of the Archdiocese of New York; an excellent suggestion that was never pursued.

In fact, this section on the Eleventh Step ("sought through prayer and meditation . . .") received more comments and suggestions than almost any other part of the book. Much of this was a negative response to Bill's attempt to accommodate the prayer and meditation practices that were still so common in Akron. There were many objections to this, some of them explicit comments labeling Wilson's writing as "Oxford Group" and "Group," along with a written complaint at the bottom of page 71 that "This is absolutely too Groupy" and noting there was more to be said about this "on the next page." Whatever changes the Catholic Committee on Publications suggested, it is hard to imagine that these challenging remarks were among the "little improvements" they requested. Instead, these pointedly anti Oxford Group annotations may have been made by Hank Parkhurst himself or included here in response to suggestions made by other members of the group (such as Jim Burwell), or perhaps they were in response to the extensive and comprehensive critique of the manuscript offered by the elusive Dr. Howard.

Significant Contributions from Dr. Howard

By far, the most comprehensive changes to the book were suggested by a man who is identified only as "Dr. Howard," a New Jersey psychiatrist who was given a Multilith Copy to review.[57] After reading it, the doctor was "greatly interested and enthusiastic,"[58] but he had a number of significant criticisms to offer. Most especially, he insisted that the tone of the book was far too dogmatic and directive. "His idea," Bill says, "was to remove all forms of coercion, to put our fellowship on a 'we ought' basis instead of a 'you must' basis."[59]

Doing so would mean the entire front half of the book would have to be reedited, page-by-page, taking out all of the directions, all the "yous," all of the "musts" and replacing them with much more suggestive language.

Bill Wilson would have none of it. He later claimed that he "argued weakly" against these changes, but "soon gave in."[60] However, Jim Burwell tells a different story, one that confirms Bill's ongoing reluctance to change anything he had already written and that—despite Burwell's frequent flights of historical fantasy—is likely to be much closer to the truth than Wilson's later claims. According to Jim, when they received Dr. Howard's extensive suggestions, Bill went "into a tizzy . . . He almost blew his top."[61] Here, so close to the publication date, "disaster nearly overtook us," he said, "for it threw Bill into a terrific mental uproar to have his baby pulled apart by an outside screwball psychiatrist, who in his opinion knew nothing about alcoholism."[62] But, Jim says, "after days of wrangling . . . Bill was finally convinced that all positive and must statements should be eliminated and in their place to use the word 'suggest' and the expression 'we found we had to.'"[63]

Wilson's dramatic capitulation on this vital issue was actually the result of an extraordinary power play made by Hank Parkhurst. On Friday March 24, 1939—just seventeen days before the book was actually published—Hank wrote a page-and-a-half memo recapping Dr. Howard's suggestions and effectively arguing for their inclusion in the book. He then told Bill that if he refused to make these changes himself, he would be forced to organize a committee to make those edits for him.[64]*

Typical of Hank, this is not the most well organized document, but its meaning and intent are perfectly clear nonetheless. He began with a one-line statement of Dr. Howard's objections:

> "Dogmatic; Marked by positive and authoritative assertion. As 'shown by God.'"

And then goes on to elaborate each of these points, insisting they be incorporated into the book.

According to Hank's summary (he had obviously spoken directly with Dr. Howard), the psychiatrist "claims that we stand on impregnable ground when we constantly talk about what some one of us did and let the man draw his own conclusions as to whether by doing the same thing he will or not receive the same thing." But, Dr. Howard notes that, instead of this open suggestive approach, the book repeatedly takes a directive tone, telling the reader "You do this or you do that." In his opinion, this means that the message instantly loses "a great deal of power." The psychiatrist said that, if the book is to have any hope of success with alcoholics, all of those authoritarian pronouncements must be deleted and replaced with statements such as "We did this or we did that and certain results followed."

In addition, the doctor felt the presentation of God was far too dogmatic and the constant mention of being "shown by God" was "entirely too much Oxfordism."[65] All of this had to be significantly toned down and made much more broadly spiritual. Dr. Howard had several suggestions for how to do this, one example of which was deleting the words "Heavenly Father" from the final sentence of Dr. Bob's story ("The Doctor's Nightmare") and replacing it with the word "faith." He thought the sentence would be much less off-putting to newcomers if it read "Your faith will never let you down" rather than Smith's original, "Your Heavenly Father will never let you down."**

In support of these religious objections, Hank argued that Bill needed to eliminate "any dogmatic statements or insinuations" which had crept into the text, but he needed to do so in such a way that none of those changes would "soften the religious implication" of the solution being offered. Religion wasn't the problem, but anything that was too much Oxford Group meant trouble.

Bookending this long recitation of the psychiatrist's objections, Hank had opened the paragraph by noting "Doctor Howard's position is that Mr. Wilson should not let himself be put in a position of being dogmatic anywhere in the book" and he then closed it by saying:

> The most impressive thing he said was "Mr. Wilson does not desire to be dogmatic and assume the position of God and every effort should be made to protect him from that pitfall." He said that in any writing, a

---

* The full text of this memo is reproduced in Appendix X on page 685.

** Neither this suggestion nor someone else's (Hank's?) proposal that three paragraphs be deleted from Dr. Bob's story were ever taken. (See *The Book That Started It All*, pp. 111, 112, and 116.)

position of that kind can creep in unconsciously, when a man thoroughly knows his subject even when a man is actually humble and is not that way.

Parkhurst was gently accusing Wilson of assuming "the position of God"—especially if he refused to make these changes to the text—while simultaneously offering Bill the olive branch of the doctor's presumption that he had surely never intended to be so autocratic in his writing. The author was, most likely, a humble man, but he had inadvertently and unconsciously gone off track and adopted a prose style that was far too omniscient and authoritarian.

Having so lucidly articulated Dr. Howard's criticisms, Hank began his second paragraph with the delivery of his ultimatum, saying that in his "personal opinion . . . Bill should take the book someplace where he can study it quietly with the attitude of changing any dogmatic statements or insinuations . . . Simply to change it where necessary from . . .You do this . . . to . . .We did this." His choice of the word "simply" here is a small, but emphatic rebuttal of Wilson's likely claim that it was just too great a task to take on at this late stage in the book's production. If that was Bill's position, Hank reminded him that "this suggestion of course covers only the first twelve chapters" since "a man can reveal himself in any way he chooses in the personal stories." But Hank wasn't concerned even if it *was* a monumental task. He was convinced these changes were absolutely essential because "we have in this book such a tremendous opportunity for good that no possibility should be overlooked, before it goes definitely to print."

If that wasn't enough to change Bill's mind, Hank openly threatened to take responsibility for the book's text—Wilson's "umpire" status—completely away from him. While Bill was doing his own review, he said, "certain men such as Frank Amos, Harry Brick, Jack Darrow, Doc. Smith, Horace Crystal, Paul Kellogg and any others who might be suggested could do the same thing. Then a meeting could be called for final discussion of these points and any changes made where this seemed right."[*]

Finally, in one of his typical closing paragraphs[66], Parkhurst tried to summarize the memo and bring "this proposal down to [a] concrete few words."

> A committee to study the book to change any "You do this or you must do that statements" or insinuations to, "We did this or we did that." Then at a meeting to decide by the vote of the majority the changes. ANY people who desire and will spend the necessary time to be able to serve on such a committee.[67]

Despite Wilson's repeated assertions that the book was such a tremendous group effort, the last thing he wanted was a committee to review those first twelve chapters and make substantive last-minute changes to them. Fortunately for Bill, there was really no time left for such a group to be organized, critically read over the text, and then gather for a vote on which of Dr. Howard's suggestions should or should not be

---

[*] Interestingly, the original typed document had read "any others who might be suggested <u>should</u> do the same thing. Then a meeting <u>should</u> be called"— but Hank had diplomatically hand corrected both of the words "should" to "could"—in an effort to tone down the level of his threat just a bit.

taken. In the face of Hank's audacious threat, Bill Wilson simply capitulated; he was, as he later said, "finally convinced"[68] and "soon gave in."[69]

At that point, the two men sat down and, with Hank's ever-argumentative presence, made all of those edits; changes which were, as Parkhurst had correctly realized, so absolutely essential to the book's future success.

Dr. Howard's True Identity

One tantalizing mystery that has plagued A.A. historians for decades is the identity of this Dr. Howard. The search has been complicated once again by Jim Burwell who claimed the doctor was the Chief Psychiatrist for the State of New Jersey.[70] However, there was no doctor named Howard serving on the staff of the Greystone Park Psychiatric Center in Morris Plains, NJ at this time (which had been earlier known as the State Asylum of the Insane and then later as the New Jersey State Hospital[71]).

This led some to speculate that the name was perhaps a pseudonym adopted by Dr. Marcus A. Curry, who was the Chief Psychiatrist at Greystone between 1936 and 1940. Or, reaching a bit farther afield, it has been suggested that Dr. Howard Haggard, the head of Yale's Laboratory of Applied Physiology at that time, might have been the pseudonymous "Dr. Howard."[72] However, in light of the evidence presented below, these are both rather unlikely candidates for the elusive psychiatrist.

Picking up on the chance that Howard may well have been the doctor's first (rather than his last) name, another possibility presents itself. Dr. Howard Hogan, an "A.A. doctor"[73] who was a member of the Fellowship in 1939, might be the person so frequently mentioned in the "Original Working Manuscript." We know that the group routinely called their Akron leader "Dr. Bob," so it is more than likely that Dr. Hogan was addressed by the New York members as "Dr. Howard." Confirming his status as a recovered alcoholic, Lois refers to him in her diary as "one of the gang"[74] —the word "gang" having been used in that same diary entry to explicitly refer to the A.A. group which met that day.

While this is an intriguing possibility, the fact that Dr. Hogan was a physician rather than a psychiatrist and that he lived in the Bronx rather than New Jersey[75], seriously challenges his candidacy for the role. In addition, while it is possible he was active with A.A. members in the first few months of 1939, he doesn't make his first appearance in Lois's diaries until August of that year (where he is mentioned four times[76]) and then again in a single entry made on March 29, 1941. Taken together, this would seem to eliminate him as the mysterious Dr. Howard.

In the Big Book chapter "A Vision For You" written in November of 1938, it mentions that "an A.A. member . . . was living in a large community . . . but a few weeks" before he "got in touch with a prominent psychiatrist" and persuaded him to adopt the program of recovery for his patients. This doctor was so impressed that he then convinced "the chief psychiatrist of a large public hospital" to do the same. As noted in an earlier footnote,** these events, which Bill says happened "only a few days ago at this

---

*   Dr. Howard's name explicitly appears at least twelve times on eleven different pages.

**   See p. 433.

writing,"[77] probably refers to Bill Ruddell and his recent move to Hackettstown, NJ. If that is true, Ruddell was the probable start of the chain of events that led to this "chief psychiatrist of a large public hospital" who is very likely the elusive Dr. Howard.

While Jim Burwell claimed Dr. Howard was the Chief Psychiatrist for the State of New Jersey, Bill Wilson said he was "a well-known psychiatrist of Montclair, New Jersey."[78] This would place the doctor much closer to New York City (Morris Plains is twenty miles farther west of Montclair) and makes it much more likely that Hank Parkhurst, who lived in Montclair at this time, could have given this local psychiatrist a copy of the Multilith printing to review and would have also been the person to whom the doctor directly submitted his opinions.

As far as being the "chief psychiatrist of a large public hospital" in Montclair, John B., a former A.A. Archivist for the State of New Jersey, recently did some excellent research, which unearthed the fact that in 1939, the thirty-eight-year-old Dr. James Wainwright Howard was working at Montclair's Mountainside Hospital (a substantial facility with 330 beds at that time[79]) as an Assistant Attending Psychiatrist, a position he held from 1934 to 1941.[80] More than any other candidate, this Dr. James Wainwright Howard meets almost all of the known criteria and appears to be most likely candidate for the Dr. Howard who so carefully read the manuscript and then made his insightful suggestions for change.

But whoever this "Dr. Howard" was, he did Alcoholics Anonymous an immeasurable service when he recommended removing all of the authoritarian language from the book and toning down the too obvious influence of the Oxford Group. In the end, the doctor's true identity is little more than an academic question since we really know nothing of substance about any of these candidates, and certainly nothing that might shine a helpful light on what led this insightful psychiatrist to advocate so strenuously for these important edits.

Works Publishing and the Foundation Get New Addresses

At the last minute, one small but telling change was made on the title page of the book. The address of Works Publishing Co. was changed from Hank's office at 17 William Street in Newark to a post office box in New York City. By this time, Parkhurst's business was bankrupt and it was clear that he would not be able to continue to maintain an office in Newark. Throughout early 1939, Hank was far behind on his rent and he "had a hard time keeping the sheriff out of [the] little cubicle of an office at 17 William Street."[81] In May, shortly after the book was published, the "landlord in Newark got really tough [and] the sheriff appeared with an eviction notice."[82] Hank and Ruth were forced to move to a "tiny room" down the hall, which they secured by making "a small down payment on the rent." But things were tenuous at best and Hank could only wonder "how many months it would be before the sheriff showed up once more."[83]*

A post office box was the easiest way to solve this problem, so in early April Hank secured two boxes (numbered 657 and 658) at the Church Street Annex Post Office. The first was for Works Publishing Co. and the other was the new address of the Alcoholic Foundation. Parkhurst paid the quarterly fee of $4 each and since one box was the responsibility of the Alcoholic Foundation, he asked Frank Amos to send him a $4 check to cover his out-of-pocket expense.[84]

A Sample of the Edited Text

Perhaps the best way to communicate the extent and importance of the edits made between the pre-publication printing and the final version of the book released on April 10 is to present a sample of text as it appeared in the Multilith copy with annotations showing all of the suggestions and changes. The beginning of Chapter Five, "How It Works," is one of the more heavily annotated parts of the book and it is also the section most frequently read at A.A. meetings. As such, this section should provide some accessible insight into the scale and scope of the whole editing process.

What follows here is the text as it appeared in the Multilith printing with the deletions noted by ~~strikeouts~~ and suggested edits appearing in ***bold italics*** along with suggested edits that were later crossed out in ~~***bold italic strikeouts***~~.

However there is one bit of writing on the first page of Chapter Five that requires some explanation before proceeding to the more familiar text. Across the top, Hank Parkhurst has written four lines in large script reading: "Should be / studied from / the mold / angle."[85] The mold angle? Fortunately, Hank supplied an explanation of what he meant by this phrase in another handwritten note that appears on the blank back side of the final story page in the book: "We have said constantly the trouble with org[anized] religion is that they try to dogmatically pour people into moulds. So why should we give specific instructions in the book such as saying do this and do that? You can obscure many alcoholics."[86]** There are also four other marginal notes about "mold" or "mould"—Hank was not consistent with his spelling; one appears opposite the Third Step prayer, two are next to the hour of review suggested after doing a Fifth Step, and one is written into the section on meditation.[87]

Parkhurst was still fighting for a more psychological program of recovery, here by attacking the very need for such an explicit Twelve Step program, one that insists people adopt some predetermined set of beliefs and actions before they can stop drinking. But at this point of the process, Hank was fighting a losing battle; it would mean completely rewriting (or perhaps even deleting) Chapters Five and Six, and that was something Bill Wilson would never have agreed to do.

---

* Bill Wilson regularly claimed that they moved to a smaller office down the street (see, for instance, *AACOA*, p. 176 and Bill Wilson speaking in Atlanta, Georgia, July 14, 1951 [recording acquired from Dicobe Media Inc., Bellevue NE, 68005]), but Merton M.'s exhaustive research into contemporary local business records confidently states that this "tiny room" was simply down the hall from the one from which they were being evicted (M., Merton, *Black Sheep*, p. 61).

** Obscure? Perhaps he meant 'confuse.'

Directly below this last-ditch effort to eliminate all formal structure from the program of recovery, the more familiar text of Chapter Five appears:

HOW IT WORKS

Rarely have we see person fail who has thoroughly followed our ~~directions~~ *path*. Those who do not recover are people who cannot or will not completely give themselves to this simple program, usually men and women who are constitutionally incapable of being honest with themselves. There are such unfortunates. They are not at fault; they seem to have been born that way. They are naturally incapable of grasping and developing a ~~way~~ *manner* of li~~f~~*ev*ing which demands rigorous honesty. Their chances are less than average. There are those, too, who suffer from grave emotional and mental disorders, but many of them do recover if they have the capacity to be honest.

Our stories disclose in a general way what we used to be like, what happened, and what we are like now. If you have decided you want what we have and are willing to go to any length to get it—then you are ready to ~~follow directions~~ *take certain steps*.

At some of these ~~you may~~ *we* balk~~ed~~. ~~You may think you can~~ *We thought we could* find an easier, softer way. ~~We doubt if you can,~~ *but we could not*. With all the earnestness at our command, we beg of you to be fearless and thorough from the very start. Some of us have tried to hold on to our old ideas and the result was nil until we let go absolutely.

Remember that ~~you are~~ *we* deal~~ing~~ with alcohol—cunning, baffling, powerful! Without help it is too much for ~~you~~ *us*. But there is One who has all power—That One is God. *May Y*~~y~~ou ~~must~~ find Him now!

Half measures ~~will~~ avail~~ed you~~ *us* nothing. ~~You stand~~ *We stood* at the turning point. ~~Throw yourself under~~ *We asked* His protection and care with complete abandon. *~~When we were receptive he responded.~~*

~~Now we think you can take it!~~ Here are the steps we took, which are suggested as ~~your~~ *a* Program of Recovery:

1. *We A*~~a~~dmitted we were powerless over alcohol—that our lives had become unmanageable.

2. Came to believe that a Power greater than ourselves could restore us to sanity.

3. Made a decision to turn our will and our lives over to the care ~~and direction~~ of God *as we understood Him.* [italics to be added noted in marginalia]

4. Made a searching and fearless moral inventory of ourselves.

5. Admitted to [*our understanding* suggested above, but crossed out] God, to ourselves, and to another human being the exact nature of our wrongs.

6. Were entirely ~~willing that~~ **ready to have** God remove all these defects of character. ["~~wouldn't anxious express greater humility~~" written above, but crossed out]

7. Humbly, ~~on our knees~~, asked Him to remove our ~~shortcomings holding nothing back~~. [The cross out for "shortcomings" has obviously been reconsidered since "shortcomings" is written back in just above it.]

8. Made a list of all persons we had harmed, and became willing to make ~~complete~~ amends to them all.

9. Made direct amends to such people wherever possible, except when to do so would injure them or others. [Directly beneath this—at the very bottom of this page—but with no obvious relationship to Step Nine, is written **His Divine Consideration** (perhaps a suggestion for the Third Step?)]

   [Here begins a new page. In the margins beside the next three Steps, the name **Buchman** has been written. In the top margin Hank has written **See inside back cover** and drawn a line connecting the two. The back cover of the book has unfortunately been lost so we have no idea exactly what connection it was that Hank wanted to point out between these three Steps and the founder of the Oxford Group.]

10. Continued to take personal inventory and when we were wrong promptly admitted it.

11. Sought through prayer and meditation to improve our **conscious** contact with God **as we understood**, praying only for knowledge of His will for us and the power to carry that out. [Above the word "God," ~~A Power above us~~ was written and crossed out.]

12. Having had a spiritual experience as the result of ~~this course of action~~, **these steps**, we tried to carry this message to ~~others, especially~~ alcoholics, and to practice these principles in all our affairs.

   [There is a vertical line beside the text of the Twelfth Step and an arrow pointing to the following two lines handwritten below and then crossed out: *~~Offered the simple kit of spiritual tools but no compulsion // could be said "we have tried to show others, especially alcoholics what etc.~~*

Many of us ~~You may~~ exclaim*ed*, "What an order! I can't go through with it." Do not be discouraged. No one among us has been able to maintain anything like perfect adherence to these principles. We are not saints. The point is, that we are willing to grow along spiritual lines. The principles we have set down are guides to progress. We claim spiritual progress rather than spiritual perfection.

Our description of the alcoholic, the chapter to the agnostic, and our personal adventures before and after, ~~have been designed to sell you~~ *was the way we determined* **made clear** three pertinent ideas:

(a) That ~~you are~~ *we were* alcoholic and ~~cannot~~ **could not** manage ~~your~~ *our* own lif~~e~~*ves*.

(b) That probably no human power ~~can~~ **could have** relieve*d* ~~your~~ alcoholism.

(c) That God ~~can and will~~ **could & did**.

[The word "God" had been circled in pencil and the word **Faith** written below it.]

If you are not convinced on these vital issues, you ought to re-read the book to this point or else throw it away!

[This entire sentence is circled in red pencil but not crossed out.][88]

All of these suggestions, all these changes, taken and not taken, make for fascinating reading on several levels.

The frequent substitutions of "we" for "you" that Hank had argued for so vehemently are strikingly evident, but none is more important than the insertion of the word "We" at the beginning of the First Step, an addition which has become a touchstone of recovery for many alcoholics ever since. There are also two significant deletions worth noting in Step Seven; gone is the requirement of getting "on our knees" along with the somewhat ominous "holding nothing back." The Eleventh Step shows the addition of the phrase "as we understood [Him]" carried over from the Third Step and, in the Twelfth Step, the direction to universally carry the message "to others" has been deleted.

The final section is also much changed. Gone is the rather crass reference to "selling" in the first of these paragraphs—although selling is such an ongoing theme in the book that only the most casual reader could have missed it at this point. Then, despite the edits made to (c), it has still not reached the final, slightly expanded form, "That God could and would if sought," which appeared in the book.* And the almost laughable final sentence—although only circled here—was, in fact, judiciously deleted.

---

* The further expansion of (c) to read "That God could and would if *He were* sought" did not appear until the first printing of the second edition in 1955.

Some of the suggestions not taken can be equally interesting. It seems that "When we were receptive he responded" was meant to be included just before the introduction of the Twelve Steps, but never made it into the final copy. Nor did the suggestion of adding the word "understanding" to Step Five and substituting "anxious" for "willing" in Step Six. The two other suggestions for softening the explicit references to God—"a Power above us" in Step Eleven and "Faith" in (c)—were also not taken.

All of this—and much more in this critically and historically important document—provides an exhaustive chronicle of the creative editing that was done in late February and throughout March 1939 to *Alcoholics Anonymous*, one of the most influential works on spirituality to be published in the twentieth century.

CHAPTER THIRTY

Publication Day

~Late March to April 1939~

Jim Burwell claimed there were "days of wrangling"[1] before Bill finally conceded to Hank's ultimatum and accepted Dr. Howard's changes to the manuscript. In another talk, he says he then needed "four or five days" to incorporate all of those edits into the book.[2] Actually, it took Bill just three or four days after Hank's threat to make those changes and then they had to sort out all the other suggestions offered into those they would adopt and those they would be rejecting. With those decisions made, nothing "remained except to prepare the printer's copy of the book." Bill said that at that point they "selected one of the mimeographs, and in Henry's clear handwriting all the corrections were transferred to it." But despite Parkhurst's alleged clear handwriting, Wilson claimed this copy was still "hardly legible and we wondered if the printer would take it, heavily marked up as it was."[3]

It should be noted that in 2004, when the "Original Working Manuscript" was first offered at a Sotheby's auction, it was bound in a later binding stating that it was, in fact, this printer's copy. However this claim is strongly contested in the first essay in the Hazelden facsimile edition, which concludes that it could not have been the printer's copy, noting that the typesetter "would have to have been a mind reader" to make any sense out of the mass of suggestions (including many not taken) that are written all over that particular copy.[4] Still, it is not hard to imagine that even after Hank had done his best to enter all of the accepted changes as neatly as possible, it would still appear to be a jumbled and hard-to-read mess (or as Bill described it, their "mangled but precious printer's copy"[5]).

The Annotated Manuscript Copy Goes to the Printer

With this fully annotated copy in hand, Bill, Hank, and Ruth set out in Hank's car on Wednesday, March 29 and drove sixty miles north to Cornwall, NY where the book was to be printed. They all went, Ruth said, because "we couldn't afford anyone to correct the pages as they came off, edit them, and so the three of us had gone up to work on that."[6] While the part about them not being able to afford a professional proofreader is certainly true, it is also clear that no one but these three would have been able to decide what was right and what was wrong in that growing stack of proof sheets. For anyone else to attempt to read and correct those pages was simply out of the question.

Bill claimed that Dorothy Snyder, who had been so enthusiastically promoting the Multilith copies in Cleveland just a few weeks earlier, joined them on this drive;[7] but Ruth Hock tells a different and, for all its detail, a much more plausible story about that day.

> We had gone up, the three of us, to Cornwall to do this [proofreading] and Dorothy Snyder . . . had a sister in [the] Bronx, New York and she had come to visit the sister and had met Bill, and she called Bill up and said she was in town and she would like to see him, and he said, up at Cornwall, "Come on up!" you know. And, I must say like most men of good taste, Bill liked pretty girls, too, and Dorothy was a lovely, warm, just humorous—full of humor, full of laughter person—and he liked Dorothy very much. So there we were, the four of us . . . "[8]

Whether Dorothy rode up with them or took a later train, Bill and Hank arrived in Cornwall and proudly presented their marked-up Multilith Copy to the print facility's manager and offered themselves and their two friends as proofreaders. The print manager was shocked with what they handed him, telling them he couldn't possibly set type from these impossible-to-read and disorderly pages. He insisted they return to New York, retype the entire manuscript, and then come back to Cornwall another day for the typesetting process. Parkhurst, ever impatient to start selling books, went into his high-pressure sales mode, defending his handiwork, and finally convinced the poor man "to begin setting the type in galley proofs, on the condition that the party would correct them on the spot, as they came off the press."[9] And so they did.

When Bill invited Dorothy to join them in Cornwall, he gallantly told her, "we could use your help and we'd love to see you."[10] This spur-of-the-moment invitation landed Dorothy Snyder right in the middle of the final editing session for *Alcoholics Anonymous* and it was an experience she claimed to remember vividly—even several years later. In a 1954 interview, she provides an animated eye-witness account of exactly how those last-minute changes were made. Speaking to Bill, she said:

> I can still see you. We were reading parts, different phrases to you and you would weigh those phrases, did this really say what you meant? would it really help somebody? would it offend this group, that group or the other

groups? And after one of those discussions, Hank was sort of pounding at you that a certain phrase was perhaps too strongly put. I can still hear you say, well, I don't want the thing to be so insipid that they don't get the idea of what they have to do to get sober![11]

What a wonderfully vivid and lively picture she paints: "I can still see you . . . I can still hear you . . . "! And, listening to this, Bill made no objection or correction to any of Dorothy's memories. He only acknowledged the fact that, yes, even during those final moments, Hank Parkhurst was still fighting for his own point of view, which he now characterized as Hank's desire to "water it down."[12]—something Wilson was just not going to allow at this final stage in the process.

Bill claims the first thing they did when they arrived in Cornwall was to "check in at the town's only hotel,"[13] but it is possible—based on their subsequent lack of cash to pay the hotel bill—that this might not have been the original plan. It is more likely their commitment to help the typesetter decipher the messy printer's copy and then check all the galley proofs required so much extra time that they had to stay overnight, at which point the four of them would have checked into the local hotel.

This overnight stay in Cornwall raises some interesting questions about the status of Parkhurst's and Hock's relationship at this time. It had only been a few weeks since Hank had reconciled with Kathleen, and it is hard to imagine her being comfortable with him spending a night away in the same hotel as Ruth. But whatever was or was not going on between these two at this point, Dorothy's presence seems to have precluded the possibility of any planned or even spontaneous adulterous behavior.

Bill, Ruth, and Dorothy Bond, and with Hank, Correct the Printer's Proof

The four spent the day working with the Cornwall Press compositors and then they all had dinner together[14] before turning in for the night—a night which produced a charming story about Bill Wilson and these two ladies. Although Ruth and Dorothy had just met, they "immediately developed a perfect rapport," so much so that Ruth claimed it was "as though we had known each other all our lives."[15] This was fortunate since the two women were to share not just a room, but a large bed for the night.

Ruth says once they got to their room, she and Dorothy "were talking, and talking, and talking"[16] and then "this must have been 1:30 or 2:00 o'clock in the morning—there was a knock on the door, and it was Bill."[17] Hank was fast asleep somewhere else in the hotel, but Bill was wide-awake and he just couldn't sleep. "He had a tray with a pot of coffee and cups in his hands," she said, "and we were in a room with one big double bed, so Bill just got right in the middle, and there we were! And we talked the rest of the night—the three of us—in that position." Their conversations, she said, "wandered over everything" and the three of them "just enjoyed that night thoroughly."[18]

However indecent that might sound—especially in light of Bill's later (though undocumented) reputation as a chronic womanizer—it was actually nothing of the sort. In a letter to Wilson almost twenty years later, Ruth Hock mentioned the "night the three of us spent in that bedroom in Cornwall!" and called it "one of the most satisfying and joyous memories of my life." "How wicked that sounds," she said, "but how innocent and wonderful it really was."[19] Wilson agreed with her, calling it "one of my precious moments."[20]

Charles Towns Finances the Trip

It took two days for the proofs to be printed and properly corrected. The number of changes was so extensive that Cornwall Press charged Works Publishing Company an additional $33 for "Author's corrections" on their April 10 printing bill, noting this represented 13.2 hours of time at "2.50 per est."[21] But with that job finally done, the group faced a serious problem: They didn't have enough money among them to check out of the hotel. Bill's later story about this dilemma offers a somewhat strange and unexpected insight into how Hank Parkhurst understood his Higher Power at this time.

> By now our money supply was gone. The hotel bill was going to be twice as much as the cash we had. To Ruth and Dorothy and me this seemed pretty awkward, but Henry stated confidently that God would provide. Henry had lately adopted the comforting theory that if God wanted something done we only had to keep running up bills which eventually He would pay. This was a heartening example of faith, but it did leave the practical question of who would be God's agent in the matter of the money.[22]

The question of agency was decided after Bill Wilson drove back to New York City on Friday, March 31 to see if he could borrow the money from Charles Towns. "Maybe good old Charles Towns would be the man," he wrote. "So it fell my lot to go to New York and put the touch on him. Mr. Towns was not too favorably impressed when he heard where we stood, but he came through with the hotel bill and about a hundred dollars to spare."[23] Towns wrote Bill a generous check for $200 to cover the hotel bill,[24] leaving enough over that Wilson, Parkhurst, and Hock could split the remainder among themselves as they drove back to New York "in high spirits."[25]

High spirits, indeed. Dorothy Snyder provides one more wonderful snapshot from that eventful week, a moment that perfectly captures Wilson's hopes and anxieties during those final few days before the book was published. In her interview, she asked him:

> Do you remember a few days after [Cornwall] that I was walking down the street with you, I can still see you, you must have had a premonition of what this A.A. was really going to be because you shuddered all of a sudden, pulled up the collar of your coat and said, "Good God, Dorothy, suppose this thing really does catch on? And if there are people that really want to stay sober!"[26]

An amazing image: Bill Wilson shudders and turns up his collar against the almost overwhelming thought of what might happen if they were successful. Even more charming and revealing, Dorothy says that after this brief moment of uncertainty, they looked each other and "we both laughed."[27]

More Money Raised, Delivery of the Books Arranged

Back in New York, Bill was still soliciting letters of introduction from Wall Street friends that he used to arrange interviews with potential donors or investors.[28] Hank was no less busy on the financial front, writing one of his typically tortuous business letters ("in order to clarify this point, suppose I use an example") to Wallace von Arx, setting out the terms of the financial agreement they had reached. Von Arx agreed to loan Works Publishing $1,200 and immediately wrote a check for $315 with the understanding that the company would call on part or all of an additional $885 if and when it became necessary. Parkhurst promised von Arx preferential stock options in consideration for this loan and assured him he would be appointed as Treasurer of Works Publishing once the business was officially incorporated.[29] (This arrangement with Wally seems to be the likely source of the miraculous $500 that appeared just two weeks later to finance Hank's most ambitious promotional campaign—the mailing of 20,000 postcards to every doctor east of the Mississippi.)[30]

On Friday, April 7 Ruth Hock wrote Edward Blackwell instructing him to deliver six copies of the book to Frank Amos and twelve to Willard Richardson. "It is Mr Parkhurst's understanding," she said, "that these will be delivered on Monday, April 10th without fail." Amos was planning to take all six copies with him when he left for Ohio the next day. Two of Richardson's copies were for his personal use, while the rest had been ordered by the Alcoholic Foundation. On that same day, Hank wrote to both Amos and Richardson telling them of the book's imminent arrival and requesting payment as soon as possible.

On Saturday, Amos wrote a long letter to Willard Richardson who was sick at home in Montclair, NJ, relating all of these details, but advising him to stay home until he was fully recovered. Amos reported that he had called Chipman the night before and made arrangements for him to take delivery of the books at Rockefeller Center on Monday morning and immediately send out five of those copies to "Dr. Fosdick; Rev. M. J. Lavelle, at St. Patrick's Cathedral; Mrs. Ballard; Mrs. Charles F. Burke, at 375 Riverside Drive; Mr. Scott." He instructed Chipman to inscribe each of these "on the front fly leaf something like: 'Compliments of the ALCOHOLICS ANONYMOUS.'" He then advised Richardson that "You—Chipman, Wilson, Parkhurst between you—will know the best use to make of the other five copies" (those purchased by the Alcoholic Foundation.) Frank added a hasty handwritten postscript to the bottom of this typed letter in his florid hand: "You may want to place a copy in Mr. Junior's hands."[31] This was an excellent afterthought: Certainly, one of the very first people who should see this remarkable new book promoting a proven solution to the drink problem was John D. Rockefeller Jr. It might just begin to melt his icy refusal to give A.A. any more money.

The Book Is Printed

Cornwall Press printed 4,650 copies of the book, charging Works Publishing a total of $1,783.15.* The invoice credited Hank's March 27 check for $794.66 along with two April 10 payments totaling $89.60 for delivered books. This left an outstanding balance of $898.89. Despite all their financial difficulties, Works had actually managed to pay half of the printing cost outright. But, because of the rather large outstanding balance, Cornwall decided to minimize their exposure by binding only 1,000 copies of the book. The remaining copies were stored as loose sheets until they were needed, at which time more money would have to be paid on account to cover that binding. (It would have cost Works Publishing an additional $593.25 to have all 4,650 copies bound at this time.)

Besides the extra $33 already noted for "Author's corrections," there are four surprising charges for overtime on the invoice totaling $410.60. Parkhurst had clearly authorized these extra expenses since the line items note they were levied "to make date, as agreed to."[32] Why Hank was willing to pay an exorbitant 30 percent premium for overtime—$410 was truly a significant amount of money in 1939—just so that he could hit an April 10 publication date is unknown. Perhaps he was so confident the books would soon be selling "by the carload" that he considered those extra expenses to be all but inconsequential.

Whatever the rush might have been, the books—bound by Cornwall's Manhattan-based binder[33]—were available on Monday, April 10. That morning, the printer delivered six copies to Frank Amos's office and twelve to Rockefeller Center for Willard Richardson. Wilson and Parkhurst drove down to the Cornwall office, picked up 112 copies of the new book, and then hurried back to the William Street office in Newark—almost certainly in a state of high excitement. For some unexplained reason, they returned the next day and picked up an additional three copies. This brought the total number of books released to 133 with the balance of 867 bound copies being held in stock.[34]

A Dust Jacket Is Chosen

It should be noted that these 133 copies were not delivered in the brightly colored dust jackets used for all sixteen printings of the first edition. Those covers weren't printed until the following week and Works Publishing was billed

---

* The "Works Publishing, Inc. Report of June 30, 1940," (GSO, Box 22, Reel 10 / 8.1 [Folder 2] The Alcoholic Foundation: 1939–1940) claims that the first printing of the book produced 4,730 copies, but the invoice issued on April 10, 1939 specifically notes 4,650 copies and all the following charges are based on that number. Where those extra eighty copies might have come from is a mystery.

an additional $147.47 for them on April 17.[35] Instead, the copies delivered during the week of April 10 were all shipped in glassine wrappers,[36] i.e., thin, almost transparent paper coverings used to protect a book without a dust jacket. Although there is no record of a glassine wrapped copy ever appearing in the collectible book market, should one someday surface, it could rightly claim to be one of the exceedingly rare "first edition, *first issue*" copies of *Alcoholics Anonymous*.

The dust jacket was designed by Ray Campbell, an early A.A. member whose story, "An Artist's Concept" appears in the first edition of the Big Book.[37] Although Ray's creation of the book's cover is noteworthy, his more lasting impact comes from the quote he inserted just below the title of his story.

> There is a principle which is a bar against all information, which is proof against all arguments and which can not fail to keep a man in everlasting ignorance—that principle is contempt prior to investigation.
>
> - Herbert Spencer

The English philosopher and biologist, Herbert Spencer, never actually said this, but that fact was not noticed for decades.* The spurious quote became a favorite among A.A. members and was frequently cited when talking to newcomers. When Ray Campbell's story was dropped from the second edition, so many protested the loss of the quote that it was added—in the 1959 third printing of the second edition—to the bottom of "Appendix II: Spiritual Experience" where it has continued to appear ever since—still incorrectly attributed to Herbert Spencer.

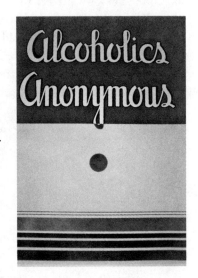

Ray's first design for the book's dust jacket was an art deco illustration of a man with clenched fists and a look of fierce determination on his face, striding purposefully away from a bottle of alcohol in which another smaller man is trapped. The title "Alcoholics Anonymous" was boldly scripted in red letters across this image with the additional words "Their Pathway to a CURE" in the lower right-hand corner.

There are no contemporary records indicating why this design was rejected (could it have been the prominent use of the word "cure" that sabotaged this effort or did someone just not like the graphic or perhaps even the idea of a graphic illustration?). It was replaced by a much simpler design dominated by two brightly colored red and yellow bands with the book's title printed in white script across the top half. Ray's use of these loud colors made the jacketed book distinctive and hard-to-miss when it was

---

* After years of fruitlessly searching throughout his works, A.A. historians finally conceded that the quote did not come from Spencer. Its true origin was decisively resolved in 2005 when Michael St. George published his scholarly (and humorously titled), seventy-page paper, "The Survival of a Fitting Quotation" (Spencer *did* invent the phrase "survival of the fittest") showing that something close to that was originally written in 1794 by the British theologian, William Paley and then modified to its modern form by the Rev. William H. Poole in 1879. (See http://silkworth.net/fitquotation.pdf - retrieved July 2, 2017; also Dodd, *The Authors*, p. 46.)

put on display and this encouraged A.A. members to begin calling it the "circus" dust jacket.[38]

Although a professional, Ray Campbell wasn't paid in cash for this work. Instead, he was issued four shares of Works Publishing Co. stock (face value of $100) to compensate him "for services rendered" on "art work on paper book jacket."[39]

The Book Is Delivered and Distributed

Every author distinctly remembers the first time they held a copy of their first book in their hands. It is beyond memorable; it's exciting, seductive, and gratifying in the extreme. *Me . . . a published author!* Bill Wilson had just such a moment on the morning of Monday, April 10, 1939, as he unpacked the books from Cornwall Press. *Alcoholics Anonymous, The Story of How More Than One Hundred Men Have Recovered from Alcoholism* was no longer just a dream, or a text in need of constant revision and correction, or a project that might be completed sometime in the distant future. Instead, finally, right here and now, there was this tangible, almost vibrant thing, a real book that he could pick up, hold in his hands, leaf through and shamelessly admire while savoring some of the words that *he* had written. It was, indeed, a big book, something with heft and substance, in a beautiful red cloth binding with the words "Alcoholics Anonymous" boldly embossed on the front cover in bright gold letters. At such a moment, how could he not have wondered once again: "Good God . . . suppose this thing really does catch on? And if there are people that really want to stay sober!"[40] It must have felt as if he was holding a miracle in his hands, a miracle that brought with it the promise of recovery for thousands upon thousands of suffering alcoholics all over the country.

Ever mindful of his debt to Lois and of the many sacrifices she had made to bring him to this point, Bill carefully set aside the first book out of the box and saved it until December when he presented it to her as a special Christmas gift with this heartfelt inscription on the front fly leaf:

> "To Lois / One whose loving / care and fortitude in / our dark days together / made these pages possible. / So to her, this first / book of the first edition / is lovingly and / thankfully given. / Bill. / In memory of / "The Fifth Christmas" / 12/25/39."*

On one level, the book was Wilson's gift to the world, and his hopes for what it might accomplish in the years to come could not have been far from his mind that morning. But the fact that Bill's first thought was of his wife, Lois, and of how much he owed her as he held that first copy in his hands, makes this one of the more poignant and tender moments in A.A.'s early history.

As more and more books were unpacked, Hank and Bill wrapped and labeled copies to be mailed out the next morning to those who had told their personal stories for the book and to the stockholders. Most of these first one hundred and twelve copies were

---

* This copy is currently preserved at the Stepping Stones Archive in Katonah, NY.

already owed *gratis* to the people who had so generously supported the book project and would, therefore, add no cash to Works Publishing's empty coffers. The first twenty-nine books were gifted to the alcoholics in New York and Ohio who had contributed their stories. Another forty copies were wrapped and sent out to the non-alcoholics who had purchased stock in Works Publishing Company.* Factoring in the copy Bill had set aside for Lois, this leaves just forty-two copies available for sale on the first day of publication, which at full list price would have been worth just a little under $150.

Money was still the critical problem. Desperately trying to remedy this, Ruth Hock spent Monday morning collecting and processing checks that had just arrived to pay for shares of stock already sold. That day's mail brought four final stock payments totaling $310, so Ruth typed up letters thanking each of these subscribers for their money and promising them that the "stock certificates will be issued as soon as all subscriptions are in and [the] corporation is formed."[41] With revealing candor about just how little cash they actually had in reserve, she told one of these new stockholders that "your check was used to cover the first withdrawal of one hundred books and we have them on hand today. Your copy will be forwarded by mail tomorrow."[42]

Copyright Is Assigned as Ownership Is Disputed

There was one other pressing problem demanding their immediate attention: No one had bothered to secure a copyright for the book. So the first package Ruth mailed out that day contained two copies of the book along with a check. Under separate cover, a letter went to Fitz Mayo in Washington, DC with the following instructions:

> We are forwarding to you today, two copies of "Alcoholics Anonymous" and a check for $2.00, and wonder if you would do something which would be <u>very</u> helpful at this end. It is important that "Alcoholics Anonymous" be registered at the Copywright [sic] Office in Washington, D. C. in the name of Works Publishing Company at the earliest possible moment, and this could be accomplished most speedily through you. The fee is $2.00 and both books must be submitted with whatever forms they may require.
>
> The two books for copywright [sic] purposes are coming forward to you marked special handling, special delivery, so will you rush them through for us?
>
> A book for you and also one for Florence** are also in the mail, but regular delivery.

---

* In a July 1947, *Grapevine* article, "Book Publication Proved Discouraging Venture," Bill Wilson claimed that copies were sent out to all forty-nine stockholders at this time. But, while there eventually were forty-nine stockholders, some, like Marty Mann, bought stock after the April 10 date, six had written stories for the book (and would not therefore have been doubly gifted), Willard Richardson and the Foundation had already received their copies, and there was a double entry in the stockholder's list for Wallace von Arx. The forty copies noted here is a best guess for how many books were actually sent off to stockholders on publication day.

** Florence Rankin was in Washington assisting Fitz Mayo in his attempts to start a local group there (see Dodd, *The Authors*, pp. 10–11).

Will you let us know the minute you have "Alcoholics Anonymous" registered?[43]

Fitz duly registered the book, but it took him a few days to get the job done. The books Ruth mailed on Monday were marked "special handling, special delivery," so Fitz almost certainly had them in hand by Wednesday. Still, it wasn't until April 19, a full week later, that his application and affidavit were noted as received and accepted by the Register of Copyrights office. It is interesting, given Ruth's instructions that the book should be registered in the name of Works Publishing Company, that the official document filed by Fitz listed the owner of the copyright as "Wm. G. Wilson, trading as Works Publishing Co." and specifically identified "Wm. G. Wilson" as the author of the book.*

While that was all still in process, Bill Wilson signed over his rights in the book to Hank Parkhurst, Wally von Arx, and Ruth Hock as the trustees of the soon to be incorporated Works Publishing Company. He did this in exchange for the promise of "one third of the stock to be issued:"

April 14, 1939

Henry G. Parkhurst,
Wallace von Arx,
R. E. Hock, as Trustees.

I hereby assert and warrant that I am the Author of the book "Alcoholics Anonymous" and own the copywright *[sic]* to said book.

As owner, I hereby sell, assign, and transfer all my right, title and interest in the copywright *[sic]* of said book "Alcoholics Anonymous" to you, as Trustees.

It is my understanding that, in consideration for the foregoing sale, assignment, and transfer, immediately upon the formation of a corporation, you will transfer this copywright *[sic]* ownership to the corporation (Works Publishing Co. Inc. to be formed) and that one third of the stock to be issued in the corporation to be formed will be issued to me in full payment of this copywright *[sic]* and all authorship claims.

Should my death occur before the corporation is formed, this same one third stock is to be issued in the name of Lois B. Wilson as an outright gift and to figure in no way in my estate.[44]

This was just one more step in the ongoing complications regarding the ownership of the book and the arguments that would swirl around the outstanding shares of stock in Works Publishing Company over the next several months. These disagreements would soon consume a tremendous amount of Bill's and Hank's attention and then grow so contentious that they would become key factors in the breakdown of their four-year

---

* Scans of both sides of the original stamped "Application for Registration for Book Now First Published in the United States" were supplied to the author by one of the great collectors of A.A. historical materials, Arthur S. of Arlington, TX.

friendship, eventually resulting in the complete dissolution of the vibrant partnership which had been so essential to the creation and publication of the Big Book.

Promoting the Book

But Hank wasn't particularly worried about the distribution of stock on April 10. Instead, he was completely focused on sales. With the book finally in hand, his main responsibility that day was to launch a marketing campaign announcing this new and proven solution for alcoholism and telling people it could be found in a just-published book called *Alcoholics Anonymous*. Parkhurst decided he needed to put "the Standard Oil promotion on it," so he went as full out as they could possibly afford, creating a small display ad which was submitted to the *New York Times*, where it ran—surrounded by a jagged-edged border—on the morning of Tuesday, April 11:[45]

> Have you an
> ## ALCOHOLIC PROBLEM?
>
> ALCOHOLICS ANONYMOUS—the story of
> *precisely how*
> **more than 100 men have recovered from alcoholism.**
>
> *For information write*
> **WORKS PUBLISHING COMPANY**
> **Church Street Annex P. O. Box 657, New York, N.Y.**

Note that Hank has slipped the extra word "precisely" into the title of the book and even emphasized it with italics. This is simply repeating a word used in the book's Foreword that says the "main purpose" of *Alcoholics Anonymous* is "To show other alcoholics PRECISELY HOW WE HAVE RECOVERED." Parkhurst seems to have thought this promise of clear-cut instructions should have been included in the book's title, so he simply added it into the title when he created this ad.

The advertisement cost Works Publishing $200[46] and the expense was justified not only by the large number of responses they expected to receive (there are at least forty post cards and letters generated by this ad preserved in the GSO archive),[47] but also in the hope that spending money with the advertising department of the *New York Times* would increase their chance that "the newspaper of record" would decide to review the book.[48] This ploy worked since the *Times* did review the book two and a half months later on June 25. It was even a fairly positive review, calling *Alcoholics Anonymous* an "extraordinary book" and describing the method of recovery as being based on "a deep psychological foundation" while giving only passing attention to the spiritual aspects of the program.[49]

Hank's $200 investment seems to have paid off handsomely.

The Program of Recovery Is Now Available to All

By now, it should be clear just how central and supremely important the date April 10, 1939, is to the history of Alcoholics Anonymous. It can hardly be overstated. Before that day, it would have been impossible to describe "precisely" what all these men were doing to stay sober. While there was some modicum of consistency in Akron (largely because they were so deeply embedded in the Oxford Group), the New Yorkers were far more free-wheeling, making generous allowances for Hank Parkhurst's broadly psychological approach and even tolerating an outspoken atheist within their midst. The difference between the two groups and the ways in which they formulated and practiced their respective programs of recovery at this time was enormous. Bill Wilson admitted all this when he claimed that the publication of the book ended their "flying blind period" and allowed them to enter "a new phase."[50] But this almost casual passing reference does not even begin to do justice to the reality of the situation—either before or after the book.

The book changed EVERYTHING.

Suddenly there was a definite program of recovery to follow, one with twelve clearly articulated steps to be taken if you wanted to move from drunkenness to sobriety, along with three central chapters explaining in detail exactly what had to be done to put those Twelve Steps into practice. *None* of that had been offered to the world or clearly explained prior to April 10, 1939.

While the day Ebby Thacher first visited Bill Wilson at his home in November 1934 or the day they met at Towns Hospital in mid-December 1934 are essential events in A.A. history, they do not qualify as "founding" moments. Then, they were just two men trying to work a still-undefined spiritual program in the hope that they would be able to stay sober themselves. In addition, Ebby and Bill never set out together to convert other drunks with their new method of maintaining sobriety and of course there is the uncomfortable fact that Ebby drank again in April 1937 (and many times after that).

June 10, 1935 is almost universally acknowledged as A.A.'s "Founders' Day" because it is the day on which Dr. Bob Smith is reputed to have finally stopped drinking. This was a significant milestone in the early evolution of A.A., especially because Wilson and Smith immediately began to approach other drunks, preaching a message of spiritual recovery—and doing so with some success. And the fact that both Bob and Bill stayed sober right up until the day their deaths was essential to the credibility and the respectability of their program.

Still, both of those men, along with the people they helped to get sober, were truly "flying blind" during this period, making things up as they went along, noticing what worked and what didn't, adjusting whatever seemed necessary and right, all in the desperate hope that they could somehow steer themselves and their friends down an increasingly better and safer road to recovery. "Flying blind" means just that: being unsure of exactly where you are, what you are doing, where you are going and how you are going to get there—but doing your best to figure it all out anyway.

But from the moment it was published, the Big Book ended all that confusion. It presented a definite, concrete, specific program that incorporated only the best of those disparate, sometimes confusing, and often experimental efforts. Suddenly, the Fellowship could declare with the utmost clarity and certainty:

> If you have decided you want what we have and are willing to go to any length to get it—then you are ready to take certain steps.
>
> At some of these we balked. We thought we could find an easier, softer way. But we could not. With all the earnestness at our command, we beg of you to be fearless and thorough from the very start. Some of us have tried to hold on to our old ideas and the result was nil until we let go absolutely.
>
> Remember that we deal with alcohol—cunning, baffling, powerful! Without help it is too much for us. But there is One who has all power— That One is God. May you find Him now!
>
> Half measures availed us nothing. We stood at the turning point. We asked His protection and care with complete abandon.
>
> Here are the steps we took, which are suggested as a program of recovery:[51]

That ringing declaration of hope was followed by the numbered Twelve Steps, along with forty-five pages of explicit instructions on how to make those steps a working part of your sobriety—and your life.

As such, Monday, April 10, 1939 must surely be recognized as The Founding Day—the day on which the movement known as Alcoholics Anonymous *truly* came into being.

Aftermath

~April 1939~

In one of his more florid moments, Bill Wilson described *Alcoholics Anonymous* as "our chip of a book" that would soon be launched "on the great world tide of alcoholism."[1] Just one month after it was published, this vision of the book's impact was validated when that tide actually began to take a noticeable turn. After years of there being just two A.A. meetings in the world, a third group was established in Cleveland on May 11, 1939, and the Big Book played a pivotal role in its creation.

Without the book, that third meeting would never have been started.

The Cleveland Group Breaks with Akron

By April 1939, the Cleveland contingent—which began when Clarence Snyder got sober on February 11, 1938[2*]—had grown to fourteen alcoholics.[3] This was the direct result of Snyder's relentless recruiting skills and he would go on to become one of A.A.'s most successful early promoters. These men (along with some of their wives) would get into their cars every Wednesday night and drive forty miles south to Akron for the meeting at T. Henry Williams's house. According to Clarence, the majority of the Cleveland men were Catholics and they had been told "they were about to be excommunicated from their Roman Catholic Church if they continued to attend Oxford Group meetings."[4] He had spoken with Dr. Bob about this critical problem and suggested that the only solution was for the "Alcoholic Squad" to sever all ties with the Protestant Group. Otherwise, he claimed, these men would have to stop coming

---

*   Clarence's story, "Home Brewmeister," appeared in the first, second, and third editions of *Alcoholics Anonymous*.

to their meetings and would therefore be likely drink again—something which was completely unacceptable to the evangelical Clarence.

Dr. Bob is Unsympathetic to Catholic Members' Dilemma

According to Snyder, Smith's stated position was that "we're not keeping the Catholics out—the church is keeping them out," claiming this was something "we can't do anything about."[5] Dr. Bob was not going to quit the Oxford Group. He did not want "to be disrespectful to the very Oxford Group people who had saved his life" and therefore "nothing at all could, or would be done" to resolve the impossible religious conflict in which the Cleveland Catholics found themselves.[6] As reported by Clarence's sponsee, friend, and biographer, Mitchell K.:

> Doc [Smith] felt that since there was nothing else to offer these alcoholics that differed in any way from what they now had in the Oxford Group, he could offer Clarence no solution. No solution other than to keep talking with the Church officials in an effort to change their minds and hearts. "Otherwise," Doc told Clarence, "if the Church did not change their minds, the men had but two choices. Remain with the Oxford Group and probably risk excommunication, or very simply, leave the Church."[7]

Dr. Bob could not have been more unsympathetic and indifferent to these men's plight and both of his proposed solutions were harsh indeed. He had no intention of severing his intimate ties with the Oxford Group, even if that refusal effectively excommunicated every Roman Catholic member from the Fellowship of Alcoholics Anonymous by raising an insurmountable barrier between their faith and his group's collective efforts to stay sober. Dr. Bob Smith did not seem to share Bill Wilson's compelling vision of a greater and greater inclusiveness.

Deeply troubled by Smith's lack of understanding and more than a little angry about his insensitivity, Snyder began to worry out loud about this dilemma. He finally decided that if Dr. Bob would not change his mind, the only solution was for them to make a complete break with the Akron group. But there was a practical problem that had to be overcome first: none of the recovering alcoholics in Cleveland had a house big enough to comfortably accommodate the new group. In the course of one of his outspoken rants about this difficulty—Clarence was never one to hide his light under a bushel—the wife of a man who had recently gotten sober generously offered their large Cleveland home as a meeting place.

Armed with this new possibility, at the next regular Wednesday meeting held on May 3, 1939, Clarence confronted Dr. Bob, making one last plea for him to change his mind:[8]

> I says, "Doc you know these fellows can't come." I says, "They can't belong to the Oxford Group." I says, "We don't need all this folderol of the Oxford Group. We can eliminate a lot of this stuff. We have a book now with these Twelve Steps, and we have the Four Absolutes, and anyone can live with that."

4444

He says, "Well you can't do that," he says, "you can't break this thing up."

I says, "We're not breaking anything up. All I'm interested in is something with more universality so that anybody can belong whether they have a religion or believe in anything or not. They can come."

He says, "Well you can't do that."

I says "We're gonna do something."

And he says, "Like what?"

And I says, "Well we'll see like what!"[9]

A Contentious Decision: The Big Book vs. the Oxford Group

On the way home that night, the Cleveland contingent made their regular pit stop for ice cream and a critical discussion of the night's meeting and what had transpired there.[10] Over coffee and ice cream, Clarence related the results of his most recent attempt to reason with Bob Smith and then declared that this left them with just one option—they had to start their own meeting in Cleveland. He told the group they would be using the new book, *Alcoholics Anonymous*, the Twelve Steps, and the Four Absolutes as the foundation of their sobriety. With those three pillars of support firmly in place, there was no need for them to rely on the Oxford Group, nor would they have to tolerate any preachy non-alcoholic Oxford Group members in the meeting. It was going to be an "alcoholics only" group. Most important, it would be a meeting that Catholic members could attend without fear of being excommunicated or of being asked to renounce their faith in order to stay sober.

This proposal generated some serious discussion that quickly turned into loud arguments. Bill Jones, Lloyd Tate, and Charles Johns all opposed the idea, claiming they would never attend such a meeting. The three men made it clear that if Clarence did break with the Akron Oxford Group, they would boycott his new group and continue to drive down to Akron every week to attend the 'real' meetings being held at T. Henry Williams's house. But despite all their strident objections, these three did not carry the day. The rest of the group was more than willing to go along with the proposal and in the end, a majority voted for Clarence's idea.[11] Snyder now had a clear mandate to proceed with his plan.

The following Wednesday, May 10, the Cleveland group once again drove down to Akron and at the end of the meeting Clarence rose and announced that this would be "the last time the Cleveland contingent would be down to the Oxford Group as a whole."[12] He told Dr. Bob that most of the group was going to meet the following night up in Cleveland.

> "We're gonna start our own group in Cleveland . . . . This is not gonna be an Oxford Group. It's gonna be known as Alcoholics Anonymous. We're taking the name from the book; and only alcoholics and their families

are welcome. Nobody else . . . We're gonna meet at 2345 Stillman Road, Cleveland Heights, at Al and Grace G[olrick].'s home."

Doc [Smith] stood up and said, "You can't do this."

Clarence replied, "There's nothing to talk about."[13]

At this point the meeting "almost turned into a riot."[14] "The roof came off the house," Snyder said, with someone shouting at him "Clarence, you can't do this," to which he replied that it was already too late. "It's done" he said. "We've got to talk about this!" they pleaded. "It's too late,"[15] he said, and at that, "the Cleveland Group got up as a whole and walked out."[16]

Clarence's plan was nothing less than heresy to the Oxford Group believers. The Akron men had been successfully staying sober on Oxford Group principles and practices for years now, practices and principles that were barely mentioned in this new book from New York. To the proud defenders of the Oxford Group, Clarence Snyder's announcement was the equivalent of the Protestant Reformation that split Christendom in two forever. They were convinced his new meeting was going to shatter the group's unity and take the Fellowship away from the things that had worked so well for them in the past. It just couldn't be allowed.

The Akron Group Invades Cleveland

However riotous the Wednesday night meeting may have been, it was "not as much of a riot as the one which occurred the next day in Cleveland"[17] when the Akronites—both alcoholics and non-alcoholics—"invaded the [Golrick] house and tried to break up [the] meeting."[18] Forever after, Clarence Snyder claimed that what happened in Cleveland on May 11, 1939 was the first official A.A. meeting ever held—a contention that is more than a little self-serving (Clarence always loudly insisted he was a "co-founder" of Alcoholics Anonymous based on his creation of that meeting) and one that has been disputed repeatedly over the years. But whatever its actual position in A.A. history might be, what Snyder called "The first A.A. meeting in the world"

> was not uneventful . . . the entire group from Akron showed up the next night and tried to "discourage" the Cleveland meeting from happening. Discourage was a very mild term, according to Clarence; and he used it sarcastically. He said: "The whole group descended upon us and tried to break up our meeting. One guy was gonna whip me. I want you to know that this was all done in pure Christian love. A.A. started in riots. It rose in riots."[19]

Dorothy Snyder later confirmed her husband's account, saying that "all the strict Oxford Group contingent came up from Akron and was very bitter and voluble. They felt we were being extremely disloyal to everyone in doing this."[20] Clarence provided a more contemporary account in a letter he wrote to Hank Parkhurst just three and a half weeks after the incident, delivering a first-hand report on what happened at that first Cleveland meeting and its immediate aftermath.

Bill Jones and I and Clarace Williams, and etc., etc. had a knockdown dragged out affair a couple of weeks ago and they have chosen to leave us alone and confine their activities elsewhere. We lost the activities of three or four rummies but I guess it had to be that way. Life is too short and there is too much to be done to spend any time or energy carrying on any comedy or petty business with any Oxford Group or any other group. As I analyze it, the main trouble was the Oxford Group wants the bows and along with perhaps some resentment or jealousy connected with the fact that I happened to be the gonoph that took the initiative to get our Cleveland gang started . . . I really had to play a little rough for a few weeks and really got some belting around but everything is hotsy totsy now. We have about fifteen or sixteen fellows now who are all 100% in my corner so we are now able to go ahead and really get things done.[21]

In that same letter, Snyder gave Parkhurst some interesting details about how different things were in the Cleveland meetings now that they had jettisoned all the Oxford Group "rigmarole that is offensive to other people"[22] and based their program exclusively on the Big Book and the Twelve Steps.

Our policy will be mainly this—not too much stress on spiritual business at meetings.* Have discussion after meetings of any business or questions arising. Plenty of fellowship all the time. Leaders of meetings have been chosen so far by seniority in the bunch. Cooperation in visiting at the hospital, so as not to gang up on a patient—but rather try to see him one or at the most two fellows at a time. We have an ideal hospital set up and have an alcoholic physician in attendance. Doc Smith came up and talked to the superintendent of the hospital and the resident physician last week and they are very sympathetic and enthusiastic. We have had one patient through the mill there already and expect two or three more this coming week . . . The man who lines up the new patient assumes the responsibility for him, for visitors, dollars, etc.** After he is defogged we feel him out, then give him the book, and lots of conversation. Our book certainly has been a tremendous help. We also contact the family when he is in the hospital and give them conversation and the book . . . By the way I am enclosing a check for four books—please send them on as soon as possible—we need them.[23]

Clearly Dr. Bob had overcome whatever resentment he may have had over the schism, or at least surrendered to the irreversibility of the new situation. And Snyder was obviously proud they had been able to make acceptable local hospital arrangements

---

* This is in stark contrast to Akron meetings where "not too much was said about alcoholism or drinking in the testimonials. 'That was conversation the alcoholics had among themselves. T. Henry was apt to have a number of Oxford Group guests who were visiting. Their witnessing would have nothing to do with alcohol.'" (*Dr. Bob and the Good Oldtimers*, pp. 140–41).

** This practice of the man who brings a new patient into the hospital being responsible for whatever payment might be needed is the reputed source of the phrase and practice of "sponsorship" in A.A. If you "sponsored" a man into the hospital, then you were responsible for him, his hospital bill should that be needed, and the guidance of his practice in Alcoholics Anonymous immediately afterward.

for the treatment of drunks who in the past, were always driven to Akron to be taken care of by Bob Smith directly.

Dr. Bob Breaks with the Oxford Group as the Cleveland Model Thrives

The fallout from this Cleveland 'heresy' was profound, far-reaching, and swift. In late November or (more likely) early December,* after Bob and T. Henry "had argued over it all for a month or so," a final joint meeting was held at the Williams's house and the group voted. "The ones who were going to stay with T. Henry—okay. And the ones we were going with Doc—okay. That's the way they said goodbye."[24] Bob Smith severed all their formal ties to the local Oxford Group and adopted a model similar to the one being used in Cleveland. While it is possible this was Dr. Bob surrendering to the inevitable, an early A.A. member contended that the final break actually was because Anne Smith argued the case with the two most important women in the Akron Oxford Group.

> Bob E. felt that the women had a lot to do with the final split. This belief was not farfetched. The wives all considered themselves members of A.A. and had a great deal to say. Furthermore, Anne was extremely protective of Dr. Bob, who evidently was taking quite a beating at the time . . .

> "Henrietta [Seiberling] didn't like the book," said Bob . . . "She and Anne had a little falling-out over that. Then Clarace Williams and Anne had a falling-out over something. What it was, no one ever found out.

> "There were some hot conversations on the telephone. It was a three-way thing between Clarace, Henrietta, and Anne. The women decided it, as was usually the case in things like that."[25]

Whatever the exact circumstances, it was a painful emotional experience for everyone involved. The "Alcoholic Squad" first moved into the Smith's small house on Ardmore Avenue, but it was far too small to be practical and after just two meetings there they moved their weekly meetings to King School.**

But, as is obvious from the vote, this move did not mean that every member of the "Alcoholic Squad" stopped attending Oxford Group meetings at T. Henry's house. One A.A. member from Cleveland, who came into the Akron Oxford Group as late as

---

* T. Henry and Clarace Williams visited New York City from September 29 to October 6, 1939 and spent several days with the Wilsons where they discussed how "things are muddled up in Akron." (Lois's diary, October 3, 1939). Clearly the issues revolved around Clarence Snyder and his accusations about money, because on October 4, they all went "to the book office and showed them the works [Works?] cause there is quite a misunderstanding in Akron about the whole thing." (Lois's diary, 1939). Five weeks later the Wilsons visited Akron from November 11 to November 20 and on Wednesday, November 15 they had a "grand meeting where T. Henry told about [the] Foundation and [the] Book and Bob about finances. I spoke too." (Lois's diary, 1939). Given that evidence, the earliest the "Alcoholic Squad" could have abandoned T. Henry's for Dr. Bob's house would have been on the Wednesday following a 'vote' meeting that might have been held on November 22. This would mean the earliest possible date for the first Akron alcoholics-only meeting would have been November 29, 1939. However, one participant remembered only two meetings at the Smith house before moving to King School and another mentions there being a Christmas tree in the house. (*Dr. Bob and the Good Oldtimers*, pp. 218–19). This would make the likeliest date for that first non-Oxford Group A.A. meeting in Akron to be either December 13 or 20, 1939.

** See *Dr. Bob and the Good Oldtimers*, pp. 218–19 for an interesting account of the break and the immediate aftermath with meetings at Dr. Bob's house and their move to Kings School.

August 1940, recounted what happened to him the day after he left the hospital and went to his first meeting at T. Henry's house in Akron:

> So, I went to the first meeting with Lloyd Tate and found that one meeting would be in charge of the Oxford Groupers and another in charge of the alcoholics—plenty of whom still supposed that they were Oxford Groupers. Anyhow a man and his wife had charge of this [Oxford Group] program and they almost out-did Billy Sunday. And the more they talked, the less I liked it. Anyhow, after they finished, a young man, younger than I, sitting next to me said, "Have you had a personal experience with Jesus Christ?" I said, "No." And he said, "That shows how far you've got to go."
>
> After the meeting, T. Henry said, "How did you like it?" I said, "I got quite a dose of religion from the leaders." I asked who that guy was sitting back there, and couldn't decide if he had helped me decide to come back or not to come back. I told him what he had said, and T. Henry said, "Well, he doesn't drink, but he has a lot of problems of his own, so forget it."
>
> Anyhow, I stayed there [in the Akron Oxford Group] for about a year and a half. And then about 6, 7 or 8 of us [alcoholics] decided to have our own [Oxford Group meeting] in Cleveland . . .[26]

He goes on to note that this Cleveland Oxford Group meeting for alcoholics continued "for several years" before "by common consent we disbanded the group" and joined the existing A.A. groups then meeting in the Cleveland area.

However heretical Clarence's new meeting may have been at first, it was firmly launched and continued to successfully guide its members in sobriety using nothing more than the Four Absolutes, the Twelve Steps, and the Big Book. It was a formula that worked spectacularly well. The Cleveland group began doubling in size with amazing rapidity, so much so that they quickly split into three groups (reputedly driven by Clarence's abrasive personality and his dictatorial attitude) and within a very short time, there were more A.A. members in Cleveland than the New York and Akron groups combined. As summarized by the eminent A.A. historian, Ernest Kurtz:

> Alcoholics Anonymous had come into a clear existence of its own. The book presenting its program had been published. Its final separation from Oxford Group sponsorship had been successfully completed. Most importantly, a new group flourished in a new city under the sole name "Alcoholics Anonymous," and without any direct impetus from either of A.A.'s co-founders.[27]

Akron Is Slow to Adopt the Big Book

Clarence had enthusiastically adopted the Twelve Steps found in the Big Book as the foundation for their Fellowship. But Akron was much less willing to embrace the book, a reluctance captured in an interview Bill Wilson did in June 1954 with Bill van Horn (who first got sober in July 1937[28] and whose story, "A Ward of the Probate Court" appeared in the first edition of the Big Book).

> BW. When the book came out, was it used at first very much around here? In some respect it marked a departure from the Oxford Group, strictly speaking, although the same principles were there, but a little different stress. Was the book used to any extent in the beginning?...

> BvH. Well, we'd be sponsoring a person, and I'd give him a book, and we'd try to get everybody to buy one, but a lot of them didn't . . . We tried to use the book and I would say, "Start and read Doc's story first through the personal stories, and then go into the theory." I always recommended that... The only thing that I remember about the book when I first read it was the stories. It took me three years, I think, before I got into the story behind it.

> BW. Then after the book was out for a while, do you remember that there was a lot of differences of opinion that began to grow up about it? As to what the Foundation was, and what the book was?

> BvH. I don't remember, Bill.[29]

When Wilson pressed Van Horn for more details on the early reception of the book in Akron, he simply refused to answer the question, replying diplomatically: "I don't remember, Bill."

While this is just one man's experience, it is almost shocking to hear that the only thing van Horn considered to be of any value in the book was the stories and most especially, Dr. Bob Smith's story. The front part of the book, which contained "the theory" and "the story behind" the stories, was considered to be decidedly secondary if not irrelevant. Certainly irrelevant enough that van Horn did not get around to reading about "the steps we took which are suggested as a Program of Recovery" until sometime in 1942.

Bill and Lois Become Vagabonds

But even before this serious schism in Ohio, radical changes had come to the New York group. When Lois's father died in September 1936, he left her the family home at 182 Clinton Street in Brooklyn. Unfortunately, the house came with a mortgage and the Wilsons were unable to keep up the payments. The bank eventually foreclosed, but having no ready buyer, they allowed Bill and Lois to stay on a month-to-month basis for a monthly rent of $20.[30] But Bill noted that even this small amount was hard to meet because throughout that time, "the need for money was simply terrific."[31]

Then, just as the book was being published, "the bank got very restless about Clinton Street and they decided to take their beating on the mortgage." They had found a willing buyer and the Clinton Street townhouse was "sold over our heads" as the Wilsons were literally set out into the street.[32] They had been given notice to vacate the premises by Monday, May 1,[33] but they were completely moved out a few days before that deadline. As Lois so tersely noted in her diary entry for Wednesday, April 26: "Left 182 for good. Went to Parkhursts." This was an extremely abrupt departure and their precarious financial situation meant, as Bill commented with painful honesty, "there wasn't enough money to even get our goods into storage. We had to go on the cuff with the drayman." Summing up this desperate and depressing experience, he concluded ruefully: "So climaxed four years of Alcoholics Anonymous."[34]

A.A. members were appalled by this sudden reversal and quickly rose to the occasion, pledging monthly contributions to the "Bill and Lois Improvement Fund," which on the first accounting amounted to over $140 a month.[35] How faithfully or how long these payments were made is unknown, but we do know that for the next two years, Bill and Lois Wilson "would have no permanent home of their own; they would live as vagabonds, first with one A.A. family, then with another."[36] By Lois's best estimate, they had something like fifty temporary homes over the next twenty-four months.[37]

Dispossessed of its regular Brooklyn home, the Tuesday night meeting was moved to Hank Parkhurst's house in Montclair, New Jersey on May 2, 1939.[38]

Hank Loses His Wife and His Sobriety

But an even more momentous disaster was looming on the horizon for the New York group. While Hank Parkhurst kept busy throughout May trying to drum up sales for the book and solicit financial support for the Wilsons, there was serious trouble brewing at home. Fortunately, now that Lois was relieved of all her duties with the resident drunks at Clinton Street, she began to make longer and more regular entries in her diary (which had been infrequent and brief throughout 1938 and early 1939). Several of these provide valuable details about the events that led up to Hank Parkhurst's return to drinking.*

On Sunday June 4, 1939, Lois simply noted that "Hank and Kathleen are on the outs again," but then on Tuesday, June 13, she reports she and Kathleen had attended a meeting at Bert Taylor's apartment on 72nd Street in New York City and that Kathleen had "stayed in town to go to a broadcast with some of the gang and ride back later with Morgan Ryan. But it rained so hard that she and Jean and Tyler Miller and Margaret spent the night in Bert's apartment." When the Wilsons arrived back in Montclair, they "found Hank in a murderous mood because Kathleen had just phoned him [to say] she was staying at Bert's apartment."

The next day, marital warfare in the Parkhurst household escalated significantly. According to Lois:

> We stayed all night with Hank trying to calm him down. But he was determined he was going to leave Kathleen and get a divorce. Got the children up early in the morning and he and Bill drove them to the

---

* Lois's 1939 diary provides a wealth of details on everyday events, people, and A.A. meetings throughout—most of which is irrelevant to the topic here, but which would provide important information to any historian attempting to chronicle the activities and growth of A.A. during the months immediately following the book's publication.

Ruddells in Hackettstown so they would be away from the fracas. It seemed to be the lesser evil cause at first he was asking to hide them out some place. Kathleen was of course awfully upset when she and Jean arrived to find the children gone.[39]

Things deteriorated further between the feuding couple—to the point where Kathleen felt she had no choice but to move out. A friend of hers had a house that would be empty from the last week in June through the end of August and she offered it to Kathleen, who readily accepted. Lois helped her pack and once that job was done on June 17, Hank brought the two boys back from Hackettstown. Kathleen moved out two days later, once again with Lois's help.[40]

Lois Wilson makes no explicit mention in her diary of the couple's troubles over the next two months, but she helped Kathleen pack up and move out of that temporary residence on August 31—presumably back into the Montclair house with Hank. Once they were back together, the ongoing battles intensified and this soon led to some terrible consequences for Hank. Lois provides some concrete details of that sad story in a half-dozen entries in her 1939 diary.

Tuesday September 5th: Harold, Emily and I drove to the meeting at the new meeting place Steinway Hall. Over 60 people there. Went home with the McDougall's. Soon after we arrived Kathleen phoned to say she thought Hank was drunk.

Wednesday September 6th: Bill and I planned to go out to Green Pond but because of the uncertain situation about Hank we decided to stay a day. Hank drunk phoned Bill in the afternoon. After a lot of phoning Bill found him and brought him back to McDougall's and put him to bed . . . In the afternoon we went around to Kathleen's . . .

Thursday September 7th: Hank still pretty drunk but after many delays we finally reached this camp, this grand camp of Frank Plummer's at Lake Swannanoa, 9 miles from Newfoundland [NJ]. Frank drove Bill and Hank and the bags in a station wagon while Laura and I drove up in Hank's car. In evening Hank's still slightly drunk told Bill and me the story of his life.

Friday September 8th: Hanks sober. Straightened things up at camp and swam and lay in sun and ate a picnic lunch. . . . late afternoon Hank left for East Orange. He needs to take the youngsters to outfit them for school tomorrow and then return . . .

Sunday September 10th: Hank arrived sober but jittery. Couldn't reach Kathleen and the children . . . Hank went back to East Orange and the McDougall's drove us over to the meeting at the Volentines. 55 there. Spent the night there. Kathleen and the children and Ed Eschman have been to Green Pond where Hank tried to get them. She is not coming to meetings for a while.

Monday September 11th: Marguerite and Bob Volentine drove us back to camp. Bill and I had supper in front of the fireplace then went to bed early. Grand day, first real fall weather. Hank didn't come back so Bill will have to walk to the bus, 5 miles, tomorrow in order to have lunch with Popsy Maher to go to the meeting.

After this, Hank disappears from her diary for more than a week. The next mention of either Parkhurst occurs on Friday, September 22 when Lois stopped at a lawyer's office "to sign an affidavit for Hank and Kathleen's divorce." Hank had proceeded with his plan to get a divorce, although for some unexplained reason, the "Petition for Divorce" was actually filed by Kathleen rather than Hank. The court accepted the petition on September 23, 1939.[41]

There were further accusations and counter-accusations filed regarding money during the proceedings. In an "Answering Affidavit to Petition for Divorce" dated October 2, Hank claimed he had been employed by Works Publishing Company up until the end of May 1939, but the job had paid him "little more than sufficient to cover my expenses." He said he had found work on July 1 as a salesman in the Newark office of the Tax Research Bureau Institute of America, but that position was just temporary and ended on September 9.[*] Hank then landed a commissions-only job selling oil burners for Jersey Oil Heating of Irvington, NJ, and he was still employed there on the date of the petition. He also noted that he was then living "in a furnished room in East Orange, New Jersey, [50 Beech Street] for which I pay the sum of Seven ($7.00) Dollars per week."[42]

Things were getting worse and worse for his friend and Bill was powerless to help him. Hank had started these divorce proceedings because he wanted to marry Ruth Hock, but now that he was drinking, Ruth "demurred and . . . there was quite an impasse." Hank presumed he would be opening a new Works Publishing office somewhere in New Jersey and that Ruth Hock would operate the book business from that new location. But Bill had decided to move the business "together with Ruth if she would come" to an office close to their post office box in New York City.[43] Hank objected violently. Such a move would not only separate him from the woman he loved, but also from Works Publishing which he believed would be the source of some substantial future income. When Ruth agreed to move to New York rather than into some new office with Hank, Wilson says that Parkhurst "began to blame me because Ruth wouldn't marry him."[44]

As bad as this confusing and painful personal situation must have been, the finances of Works Publishing Company were in even worse shape. A shareholder's meeting was held sometime in late 1939 (likely in October, shortly after the *Liberty Magazine* article appeared with a favorable article about A.A.) and Hank was asked to make an accounting.

> But he couldn't make an accounting because a great many of the records had mysteriously disappeared. He said he thought Standard Oil detectives

---

[*] Since this corresponds with the week when he was known to be drinking heavily, he may well have been fired from that job.

were after him and had broken into our office and taken them out, so to reconstruct what payments had been paid in and paid out was a very difficult job. The strain increased terrifically . . . [as] the boys put him badly on the spot. He began to be wildly excited. Silkworth [had] warned me against him, calling him a paranoid. I didn't know what that meant at the time. Silky warned that he might even be murderous.[45]

Parkhurst's murderous and paranoid behavior became even more apparent several months later when the divorce petition finally made its way onto the court's calendar. On May 9, 1940, the day before the trial, Lois met with Hank to "talk about his divorce for which I am to be a witness tomorrow,"[46] but it is unclear whether or not Hank knew Lois would be testifying on Kathleen's behalf before that meeting. Lois does not mention what the tone and temper of the meeting was, although Hank's behavior the next day suggests it was not a very friendly or pleasant conversation.

On Friday, May 10, Lois's diary recounts the dramatic events that transpired as the Parkhursts finally obtained their divorced.

Last night when we reached MacDougall's we found Frank [Plummer?] was raving drunk and threatening to break up the court proceeding tomorrow and of course wanting to see us. We are fed up with Hank drunk so we sent him a wire. Bill phoned Kathleen but Wally [von Arx]* answered and we advised her to delay her divorce until Hank is sober for he is wild enough to hurt her. Wally was furious and said he would have me subpoenaed and hung up. So under the circumstances Bill thought we ought to get out of the state as he did not want me to be mixed up in it. So we came back here to Volentines. This AM, I phoned Mort Eisener, Kathleen's lawyer, and he understood my not wanting to be a witness as did Kathleen when I phoned her. The divorce went through all right without me. Drove Bill to the bridge and then later phoned him up in time for supper. Bill phoned his mother not to come to Green Pond for a day or so until we know more about Hank for he's been anxious to go to Green Pond and might arrive there drunk anytime . . .

The next day, the Wilsons learned that "Hank had been put in the hospital by Henry Heller whom Hank had gone to see." Parkhurst had promised to stay four days so they now felt it would be "safe to bring mother W[ilson]" up to the camp.[47] But Hank didn't stay in the hospital as promised, which Bill and Lois discovered when they tried to visit him there the next day and "found [that] he had left. So [we] went to his apartment and wonder of wonders Carolyn Wright from Cleveland was there nursing him. Hank had wired her to come. She was tremendously flustered and seemed all atwitter about Hank. Will wonders never cease?"[48]

Carolyn Wright was Dorothy Snyder's sister and she soon became Hank's second wife.

---

* Wally von Arx was Kathleen's next husband.

Hank Breaks with Bill and A.A. before His Tragic Death

There is obviously far more to this story—including a number of historically important things that occurred during these same thirteen months after *Alcoholics Anonymous* was published—but those events are far beyond the scope of this book and, more important, were not part of the extensive primary document research done for this project. Certainly a history of the period from April 10, 1939 to July 28–30, 1950 (when Dr. Bob made his last public appearance at the First A.A. International Convention and where the Twelve Traditions were formally adopted) is a story that deserves to be told. But that history needs to be written by someone ambitious enough to wade through and then judiciously evaluate the small mountain of archived documents from that period before beginning such a book.

In the interest of closure, the only thing we have addressed here are the documented facts surrounding Hank Parkhurst's return to drinking less than five months after *Alcoholics Anonymous* was published. The downfall of this man who was so responsible for the creation of the Big Book and who forced such significant and far-reaching changes to some of Bill Wilson's more dogmatic positions was a tragedy of the first order and a living testimony to the power of active alcoholism. Hank's continued drinking was an event that colored so much of what came before—and after.

Once Hank Parkhurst returned to drinking, his relationship with Bill Wilson and the Fellowship of Alcoholics Anonymous became increasingly confrontational. Early on and still drinking, he left New Jersey and visited Clarence Snyder in Cleveland where the two men eventually became business partners. From there, they began a relentless campaign of spreading anti-Wilson stories and propaganda. Their collaboration and the fallout of that partnership are essential elements to any comprehensive history of A.A. during the 1940s.

Parkhurst found himself far from the fold and he languished there for years, seething with resentments. One story Clarence Snyder told about the mid-1940s provides gripping testimony to the depth of Hank's ongoing belligerence and his animosity toward both Bill Wilson and Alcoholics Anonymous.

> But he never would have anything to do with A.A. I remember quite some time later, a couple of years or so later, I was traveling up through that way and we were in New Haven [Connecticut] one time and we went to a meeting and he went with me to the meeting just for the fun of it, to see what was going on. He hadn't been in A.A. at all, all this time. So we went up in this club on Orange Street in New Haven and there's a picture of Bill up there, hanging on the wall, and Hank got over, looking at it, and he acted real stupid like a drunk just coming in. He didn't tell people who he was or anything, he just acted like he's some new guy coming in. And he says "Who is that guy up there?" and some guy, breathless, he says "That's Bill Wilson," [like he was] a god, you know. Holy Jeez! So [Hank] says to him "What about him, who is he?" So the guy starts explaining what a wonderful guy this Bill Wilson is and . . . Hank says "Well, how

does he come in here? Does he walk up those stairs or does he just float in the window?" . . .[49]

Hank Parkhurst had two other wives before he remarried Kathleen late in life. He died after a long illness at Glenwood Sanitarium in Trenton, New Jersey on January 18, 1954. He was fifty-seven years old.[50]

One of A.A.'s Co-founders
Hank Parkhurst is the most forgotten man in A.A. history. Had he stayed sober, he would surely be hailed today as one of the movement's co-founders. Instead, his name and place in the official story have been all but eliminated and he is best known—by those who remember him at all—as the "Co-founder Who Drank." Hank's slip was catastrophic and the price he paid—both personally and historically—was severe.*

Hopefully, this book provides ample testimony to the fact that Henry G. Parkhurst deserves a well-researched, full-length biography. He was not just important, influential, and interesting; he was a man whose direct contribution allowed A.A. to first survive and then emerge from its "flying blind" period with a clearly articulated program of recovery that was accessible, accommodating, and far more effective than the one Bill Wilson would have supplied had he been left on his own.

Hank Parkhurst was central, essential, and invaluable to the creation of Alcoholics Anonymous and as such, can rightfully claim substantial credit for saving the lives of millions of drunks worldwide. Without him, it is possible there would not have even been a worldwide movement for us to talk about.

Changes to the First Edition through Multiple Printings

Edits to the text of the Big Book did not end with its publication. There were a number of major changes made during the sixteen printings of the first edition (1939–1955) and some less striking ones made to early printings of the second edition (1955–1974). A few of these deserve mention here.

The second printing of the first edition appeared in March 1941, more than two years after the book was first released. Sales had been slow—they did not go out the door "by the carloads"—but the extremely favorable *The Saturday Evening Post* article by Jack Alexander published on March 1, 1941, produced a flood of requests for the book.

The changes made to the text for the second printing were among the most substantive ever made. Most important, the wording of the Twelfth Step was changed from "Having had a spiritual experience as the result of these steps . . ." to "Having had a spiritual awakening as the result of those steps . . ." And, at the end of this Step, an asterisk was added sending readers to the bottom of the page where they were directed to the newly added "Appendix II" in the back of the book, which at this point, lacked

---

* As of this writing, there is not even a Wikipedia page devoted to Hank Parkhurst and his life.

the formal title ("Spiritual Experience") that was added to the first printing of the second edition in 1955.

The softening of the result of working the Steps from spiritual "experience" to spiritual "awakening" was critical and necessary. As Wilson noted in the new Appendix, the edit was required because "our first printing gave many readers the impression that these changes, or religious experiences, must be in the nature of sudden and spectacular upheavals." Bill went on to explain that "Happily for everyone, this conclusion is erroneous" and noting that "among our rapidly growing membership of some 2000 alcoholics such transformations, though frequent, are by no means the rule. Most of our experiences are what the psychologist William James calls the 'educational variety' because they develop slowly over time.'"*

This small change would have the profound effect of making the Twelve Step program of recovery even more accessible to a vast number of future members—most especially to those who were "agnostically inclined" (as Wilson first wrote in the earliest version of the Appendix). Bill's original edits to this piece have been preserved and they provide some interesting insights into his March 1941 thinking on the issue. (As before, deletions are noted by ~~strikeouts~~ and additions by ***bold italics***):

> The terms "spiritual experience" and "spiritual awakening" are used many times in this book which ~~shows,~~ upon careful reading, ***shows*** that the personality change sufficient to bring about recovery from alcoholism has manifested itself among us in many different forms.

> ~~Nevertheless~~ ***Yet*** it is true that our first printing gave many readers the impression that these personality changes, or religious experiences, must be in the nature of sudden and spectacular upheavals. Happily for ~~those agnostically inclined~~ ***everyone***, this conclusion is erroneous.

> In the first few chapters a number of sudden revolutionary changes are described. Though it was not our intention to create such an impression, many alcoholics have nevertheless concluded that in order to recover they must acquire an immediate and overwhelming "God-consciousness" followed at once by a vast change in feeling and outlook.

> Among our ***rapidly growing*** *[note this insertion does not appear to be Bill Wilson's handwriting]* membership of ***some*** *[ditto]* 2,000 alcoholics such transformations, though frequent, are by no means the rule. Most of our experiences are what the psychologist William James calls the "educational variety" because they develop slowly over a period of time. Quite often friends of the newcomer are aware of the difference long before he is himself. He finally realizes that he has undergone a profound alteration in his reaction to life; ~~and~~ that such a change could hardly have been brought about by himself alone. What often takes place in a few months could seldom have been accomplished by years of self discipline.

---

* This quoted phrase, "educational variety," has yet to be found in any of William James writings.

With few exceptions our members find they have tapped an unsuspected inner resource which they presently identify with their own conception of a Power greater than themselves.

Most of us think this awareness of a Power greater than ourselves the essence of spiritual experience. Our *more* religiously ~~inclined~~ members call it "God-consciousness."

Most emphatically we wish to say that any alcoholic capable of honestly facing his problems in the light of our experience can recover provided he does not close his mind to all spiritual concepts. He can only be defeated by an attitude of intolerance or belligerent denial.

Page 2.

We find that no one need have difficulty with the spiritual side of the program. <u>Willingness, honesty and open mindedness are the essentials of recovery. But these are indispensable.</u> [Note: underlining is in pencil][1]

This new 1941 Appendix lacked not only its later full title, but also the quote attributed to Herbert Spencer, which wasn't added to "Spiritual Experience" until the third printing of the second edition in 1959.[*]

It should also be noted that the change of the word "these" to "those" became a touchstone for argument over the next several years. Saying the necessary "spiritual awakening" was "the result of <u>those</u> steps" rather than "<u>these</u> steps" effectively eliminated the practice of carrying the message to other alcoholics as a step that contributed to one's spiritual awakening. Since elsewhere in the book, Bill had placed primary importance on working with others as a way to grow spiritually and to ensure sobriety,[**] it could be argued that changing the demonstrative pronoun to "those" had completely removed this important Step from the basic, proven message that A.A. was trying to deliver regarding the road to recovery.

The word "those" continued to be used in the final fifteen printings of the first edition and also in the first printing of the second edition, but was changed back to the original "these" in the second printing of the second edition (1957) and has remained so ever since. That change in the pronoun successfully re-incorporated the necessity of working with others into the list of things an alcoholic must do to in order to have the desired result, i.e., a "spiritual awakening."

Another substantive change in the second printing of the first edition was the deletion of the last story in the book, "Lone Endeavor," the one Ruth wrote based on correspondence with a drunk named Pat Cooper and his mother in California. Besides the fact that Pat never wrote that story, he had showed up in New York City drunk and had struggled to stay sober ever since, so the story was summarily removed and never again appeared in the Big Book.

---

[*] See p. 579 for more details on this quote and its eventual addition to the book in 1959.

[**] "I soon found that when all other measure failed, work with another alcoholic would save the day" (*Alcoholics Anonymous*, 4th edition, "Bill's Story," p. 15) and "Practical experience shows that nothing will so much insure immunity from drinking as intensive work with other alcoholics. It works when other activities fail." (Ibid., "Working With Others," p. 89).

The other important changes made during the next fifteen printings of the first edition (other than the ongoing cosmetic updates to the numbers of people sober and a few other variables) came in the eleventh printing in June 1947. There were five places in the text where the hyphenated word "ex-alcoholic" had appeared and this was obviously a problem given the Fellowship's growing insistence that "once an alcoholic, always an alcoholic." In the eleventh printing, three of these phrases were changed to read "ex-problem drinker," one was changed to "understanding fellows" and the final one became a "non-drinking doctor."[52] The book would never again lend credibility to the idea that there was such a thing as an "ex-alcoholic."

Finally, it should be mentioned that what became the often-cited "first 164 pages" of the Big Book were originally the "first 179 pages." The reduced number did not appear until the second edition in which all of the text was reformatted. One reason for the revised page count was that in all of the first edition printings, "The Doctor's Opinion" had started on page 1 and "Bill's Story" appeared on page 10. In the second edition, for reasons still unknown, Wilson changed the numbering on Dr. Silkworth's contribution to roman numerals and started his own story on page 1. That change has been preserved in all subsequent printings.

In addition to the few other edits and additions already noted for the second edition, the title of Bob Smith's story was changed from "The Doctor's Nightmare" to "Doctor Bob's Nightmare"—reflecting his increased stature in the program since the book was first published. This was augmented by a new eleven-line introduction to the story noting that Dr. Bob was "A Co-founder of Alcoholics Anonymous" along with praise for his tireless efforts in reaching out to alcoholics throughout the fifteen years of sobriety he had enjoyed before his death in 1950.

No Substantive Changes after the Second Edition

Following the publication of the second edition, resistance to further changes to the text of the Big Book grew among the membership and became increasingly militant. This was documented in the "Preface" to the second edition.

> Because this book has become the basic text for our Society and has helped such large numbers of alcoholic men and women to recovery, there exists a sentiment against any radical changes being made in it. Therefore, the first portion of this volume, describing the A.A. recovery program, has been left largely untouched.[53]

This same statement has been repeated in the "Preface" of both the third and fourth editions.

In recent years, there have been a number of General Service Conference advisory actions insisting that the basic text "remain as is" without *any* further modifications, let alone "radical changes." When the first printing of the fourth edition appeared in October 2001, it was noticed that the punctuation had been changed in "Dr. Bob's Nightmare." The changes had been made by the Trustee's Literature Committee with the understanding they were authorized to do so, just so long as those changes corrected existing errors. The 2003 General Service Conference subsequently voted to allow those changes to stand, but the next year, the Conference passed an advisory action that restored the original punctuation.

Bill Wilson was well aware of this worshipful enshrinement of the text of the Big Book and he was not particularly happy about it. Bill felt strongly that the program had become "frozen" by the membership and it was the primary reason why he wrote another book, *Twelve Steps and Twelve Traditions*, published in 1953, fourteen years after the Big Book.

In 1952, in response to an A.A. member's question about the program and the Big Book, Bill noted:

> As to changing the Steps themselves, or even the text of the A.A. book, I am assured by many that I could certainly be excommunicated if a word were touched. It is a strange fact of human nature that when a spiritually centered movement starts and finally adopts certain principles, these finally freeze absolutely solid. But what can't be done respecting the Steps themselves—or any part of the A.A book—I can make a shift by writing these pieces which I hope folks will like. [54]

Those pieces were gathered together the next year and polished into *Twelve Steps and Twelve Traditions*. But nine years later, when his second book was just eight-years-old, Bill once again revisited this phenomenon of freezing.

> As time passes, our book literature has a tendency to get more and more frozen—a tendency for conversion into something like dogma. This is a trait of human nature which I'm afraid we can do little about. We may as well face the fact that A.A. will always have its fundamentalists, its absolutists, and its relativists. [55]

Indeed.

The Big Book—one of the central texts in the history of twentieth century spirituality—has now acquired the status of "Holy Writ" for millions of people worldwide and it is unlikely it will ever be updated. This despite the fact that it is littered with words and expressions incomprehensible to modern readers, sexist language and stereotypical gender roles offensive to twenty-first century women, and a limited range of beliefs in a providential God offered as the only acceptable way to understand a "Power greater than ourselves."

There is a Buddhist parable that may be relevant here:

> You may remember the story of how the devil and a friend of his were walking down the street, when they saw ahead of them a man stoop down and pick up something from the ground, look at it, and put it away in his pocket. The friend said to the devil, "What did that man pick up?" "He picked up a piece of Truth," said the devil. "That is very bad business for

you, then," said his friend. "Oh, not at all," the devil replied, "I am going to let him organize it."[56]

A Best-Selling Book That Saves Lives

In 2011, *Time* magazine included *Alcoholics Anonymous* on its list of "The 100 Best and Most Influential Books" written since the magazine was founded in 1923. The following year, the Library of Congress selected the Big Book for its list of the 88 "Books That Shaped America." Despite never being on the best seller list, *Alcoholics Anonymous* continues to be one of the best-selling books of all time. Over the years, it has literally been printed by the carloads and over thirty-seven million copies have been sold as of this writing.[57] The book, which has been translated into an impressive seventy languages, still sells well in hardcopy despite its ready availability online for free.

Most important, however, is the fact that since it was first published in early 1939, the Big Book has shown millions of people a precise and proven path to continuous sobriety through a spiritual awakening, allowing them to live sane, fulfilling, and fruitful lives without alcohol. We have no idea how many millions of recoveries have been effected by *Alcoholics Anonymous* since the book was published, but if an exact number were known it would be staggering. A.A. currently reports the Fellowship has well over 2,100,000 sober and active members.[58]

It was the writing and publication of the Big Book—more than anything else—that made all of that possible.

Finally (and once again) . . .

"I'd just like to spin some yarns and they will be a series of yarns which cluster around the preparation of the good old book, *Alcoholics Anonymous*. Some people reading the book now, they say, well, that this is the A.A. Bible, and when I hear that, it always makes me shudder because the guys who put it together weren't a damn bit biblical. I think sometimes some of the drunks have an idea that these old timers went around with almost visible halos and long gowns and they were full of sweetness and light. Oh boy, how inspired they were, oh yes. But wait till I tell you . . ."

Bill Wilson
Speaking in Fort Worth, TX
June 12, 1954

"Well, this is switching back, but one of the things I feel vitally important is to get the story of how the book was actually written. We get so many distorted stories on the [West] Coast. People talk about the one hundred men that wrote the book. Actually, there weren't a hundred, as Bill will bear me out, but he said one hundred to make it sound good as though it really was going to work. The people talk as though there were one hundred men, that all went saintly and were taken straight up to heaven and God just guided Bill's hand—that Bill just sat there and let the words come through. Actually, it wasn't anything like that at all."

Dorothy Snyder
Interviewed by Bill Wilson
August 30, 1954

No . . . it wasn't anything like that at all . . .

Frank Amos's Notes on Akron, Ohio Survey

(Unedited Version)

This is a copy of the typed document (GSO, Box 22, Reel 10/8.1 The Alcoholic Foundation: 1937–1938, Documents P-7 through P-10).

NOTE 1: This document differs from the final version of the Amos Report that can be found in the GSO files (Box 59, 1938, Folder B, First Two Chapters of the Proposed Book; Trust Indenture, Documents 1938-9 to 1938-12).

*NOTE 2: The text that was edited out of that final version (or that was modified in some way, for instance, by using all capital letters) has been indicated with **bold, underlined, italicized text.***

[*handwritten in upper right-hand corner*] February / 1938 / 1938

NOTES
On
AKRON, OHIO SURVEY
by
FRANK **B.** AMOS

The self-styled **ALCOHOLIC GROUP** of Akron, Ohio and vicinity, came into being through the visit of William G. Wilson of Brooklyn.

Wilson was an alcoholic of years experience who, through a definite religious experience—with which we are all acquainted—and which is testified to by Dr. William D. Silkworth, psychiatrist at the Charles B. Town [sic—**with handwritten 's' added here**] Hospital, 293 Central Park West, New York, had visited Akron on business. Following out one of the essential points in the technic [sic] of reforming incurable alcoholics, Wilson had sought out an "incurable" like himself to "**W**ork on." [sic] Through one of the Christian Ministers he located Dr. Robert H. Smith, a proctologist (rectal surgeon), who for years had been an alcoholic and whose practice as a result had been just about xxxxx ruined. Smith was ready for such an approach and within a short time followed completely in Wilson's footsteps.

> Robert H. Smith, M.D.—Dr. Smith is 59 years old; preliminary college education at Dartmouth, then at University of Michigan, then at University of Chicago. After practicing a period he took special training in proctology at Jefferson Medical College Hospital, Philadelphia. I checked up on Dr. Smith as follows:

> Dr. G. A. Ferguson—one of Ohio's foremost eye specialists, located at Akron. Dr. Ferguson—a man of probably 45—told me Dr. Smith was a brilliant and skillful surgeon. He stated, said there were [sic] no better in his line, within his knowledge. He stated, however, that for years, Smith's drinking had grown worse, that he, Ferguson, had at different times carted him home drunk as had other doctor friends. As a result his medical brothers and his patients had about lost confidence in him solely because of his drunkenness. Nearly three years ago, he said, Smith had stopped drinking and ever since had been regaining the confidence of all. He was still today, said Ferguson, just as skillful a surgeon and regarded as highly by the profession as he was in his earlier days. Ferguson had learned of the work Smith was xxx doing with alcoholics. Said he didn't fully understand it, but that it worked - **h**e was for it—and had unbounded admiration for Smith both professionally and in this work. He stated further that Smith was called upon to give so much of his time, free, to this work with alcoholics that it was very difficult for him to handle enough professional business to make a decent living. He thought it was vital for Smith to continue this work but needed help so he could better organize it personally and improve his practice.

> Dr. Howard Searl—General practitioner at xxx Cuyahoga Falls, Aged about 35. Searl had been an alcoholic and had been cured by Smith and his friends activity and the Christian technique prescribed. Searl said that Smith stood at the top of his profession. He said Smith was the keystone of the alcoholic reform movement there and that something must be done to help him so he could regain more of his remunerative practice and still give much of his time to this work. At present his work with alcoholics

was taking an average of 10 _xx_ hours a day. Searl thought Smith should head a small hospital for this purpose.

Judge Benner—Formerly Probate Judge and for 40 years Chairman of the Board of the Akron City Hospital. Benner is credited with having put this hospital in the position of being one of the finest in the mid-west. Benner said that only physicians of the highest standing were permitted on their staff, and that Smith stood at the top professionally.

Page 2

Benner said further that he knew all about Smith's alcoholic troubles; had seen him come out of them and was with him 100% in his fine work. His Board, he said, was proud to give Smith fullest privileges in handling alcoholics at City Hospital. He didn't claim to understand the method but whatever it was he said it worked and he was for it. Benner impressed me as an able judge and lawyer probably in his sixties.

Mrs. Henrietta Seiberling—_Dauter [ght added above in Frank Amos's hand]_ -in-law of F. A. Seiberling. _Mrs. S_ has been active in the Oxford Group. Had become well acquainted with Mrs. Smith while the Doctor was drinking heavily. She had seen Smith come out of it and ever since had _[sic]_ been a supporter of the alcoholic group, _in-so-far_ as she could help. She expressed unstinted admiration for Dr. Smith and the entire group who have followed him.

T. Henry Williams—Formerly Chief Engineer of the National Rubber Machinery Co., now one of the owners of a rival rubber machinery company. Mr. and Mrs. Williams are devout and practical Christians. They have become so impressed with the work of Smith and his associates that they turn over their home to them twice weekly for religious and social gatherings.

Alcoholic Group

There are now some fifty men, and, I believe, two women former alcoholics, all considered practically incurable by physicians, who have been _refromed [corrected above to "or" in Frank Amos's hand]_ and so far have remained teetotalers. A list of some of them is attached giving their business, the length in months they been "dry," the period in years they were drinking, and their present age. [_NOTE: no such list is attached here or could be found elsewhere in the AA Archive at GSO. That list has, however been preserved in the Rockefeller Archive collection._] I met and talked with about half of these men with their wives and, in one or two cases, their mothers. They told me varying stories, many of them almost miraculous, but all remarkably alike in the technique used and the system followed. Briefly this system is:

1. An alcoholic must realize that he is an alcoholic, incurable from a medical viewpoint and that he must never again drink anything with alcohol in it;

2. He must surrender himself absolutely to God realizing that in himself there is no hope;

3. Not only must he want to stop drinking permanently, but he must remove from his life other sins such as hatred, adultery and others which frequently accompany alcoholism. Unless he will do this, absolutely, Smith and his associates refuse to work with him.

4. He must have devotions every morning—a "quiet time" of prayer, and some reading from the Bible or other religious literature. Unless this is faithfully followed, there is grave danger of backsliding;

5. He must be willing to help other alcoholics get straightened out. This throws up a *prtective [an 'o' has been added from the left in Frank Amos's hand* barrier and strengthens his own will-power and convictions;

6. It is important, but not vital, that he meet frequently with other reformed alcoholics and form both a social and religious comradeship;

7. Important, but not vital, that he attend some religious service at least weekly.

All the above is being carried out faithfully by the Akron group and not a day passes when there is not one or more new "victim" to work on with Smith as their leader by common consent.

Page 3

Dr. Smith's position

Previous statements give a good idea, I hope, of Dr. Smith's present importance in this work at Akron. There are other able men in the group but they all look to him for leadership. There are a few from Cleveland but they have not yet found a leader there. Non-alcoholics, Christian ministers, Oxford groupers, Christian Scientists *practitioners* and others have tried and failed. Apparently with most of these cases it takes a former alcoholic to turn the trick with an alcoholic, and a fine *P*hysician of excellent standing, himself formerly an alcoholic and possessed of natural leadership qualities has proved ideal.

Only one other of the alcoholic group knew why I was there—that was Paul *xxxxx* Stanley who was at the meeting we had in Rockefeller Center. I was introduced as a friend of "Bill" Wilson's (whom they all know and who is the unofficial leader in New

York), and as a Christian Laymen *[sic]* deeply interested in their work. In private talks with many of them, without any prompting on my part, they emphasized how vital Smith was at this time—to their work. Several told me they knew he was sacrificing his professional and remunerative work for this and that something must be done to help him handle both with *['*out' *handwritten above with a caret below]* spoiling either. I didn't ask the rank and file for solutions. I did'nt *[sic]* regard it wise to even intimate that funds might be available for fear some short-sighted individual might feel that if one man was paid something, then others of them who give many hours to this work might also deserve remuneration. This of course would ruin one of the finest features of this movement   the voluntary Christian service for sick humanity which they themselves need to keep them permanently "On the wagon."

But Paul Stanley ~~put it this way~~ *[crossed out and "says" handwritten above]* "Most of us have our jobs and can make a good living. I am an insurance man and can go out aggressively for business. Smith as a reputable and ethical physician can't be an ambulance chaser or advertise himself. All he can do is to meet regularly with physicians, keep up his professional contacts, since from that source he, as a rectal surgeon, must get most of his surgical patients. At present his income is so low that he can't keep an office secretary and finds it difficult to meet his necessary home expenses. Either we must help him or he must give up most of this alcoholic work." Stanly feels it would be criminal, at this time, to lose Smith as their leader. Mr. Williams—with whom I discussed the same *xxxxxx* matter, *xxxxxxxx* stating that I was speaking for four Christian laymen who were interested, expressed practically the same ideas as Stanley.

Suggested Methods

At our meeting in Rockefeller Center, Wilson and Stanley had suggested that perhaps a small hospital of from 30 to 50 beds could be established at Akron and Smith put in charge. Their idea was that this could be used primarily for handling cases from outside of Akron, which when cured and trained could go home and continue the work in their communities. They thought that without any publicity, except by word-of-mouth, patients could be secured from big corporations and other sources where ample funds to pay for hospitalization, would be available. With this in mind I visited two sites which would cost probably from $75,000.00 to $100,000.00 to purchase and equip. Later some plan like this may be advisable but, in my opinion we are not ready to recommend this.

[NOTE: the above paragraph has a handwritten line down the left-hand edge and the word "Omit" written beside it in Frank Amos's distinctive hand.]

A second plan I considered was to continue just as at present with the hospitalization at the City Hospital, thus not involving any added expense for that (it costs xxxxx about $8.00 a day and requires from 5 to 8 days on an average). Then secure a smaller home with nice suroundings [sic] with accomadations [sic] for ten or twelve to use as a recuperating home for those who need it. A man (former alcoholic) and his wife could run this with a maid and a cook. Probably one or two unmarried former alcoholics, [sic] could reside there. Such a place *probably could be purchased, furnished, and equipped for not over $25,000 to $30,000 and if done, should be with the firm understanding that it must be self-supporting exfept [sic] perhaps for whatever would be supplied Dr. Smith as outlined in the next paragraph.*

[NOTE: the above paragraph has a handwritten line down the left-hand edge and the word "Omit" written beside it in Frank Amos's distinctive hand.]

Page 3 *[sic]*

~~A third plan—which could be worked with or without the second plan, would be to~~ *[crossed out and above it written in Frank Amos's distinctive hand:* I suggest that we try to*]* arrange on a confidential basis, with only a small carefully selected committee knowing anything about it, for a monthly remuneration for Dr. Smith for a period of at least two years until the whole proposition could get well going and perhaps be absolutely self-supporting in every way.

Dr, Smith has a wife—a lovely, cultured lady who supports him to the limit in this work—and a son and daughter around the ages of 18 and 20. His modest home is mortgaged and he has not been able to keep it in proper repair.

He needs a competent secretary not only to receive his calls when not in the office (his office hours are from 2 to 4 P.M.), but one who is thoroughly sympathetic with this work and who could handle a lot of assignments and details with other reformed alcoholics, in routing them to see patients, ***passing on his sinrtcutions [sic—for instructions] etc***, etc. which Smith himself has to do now. Mrs. Smith has her hands full with the home and with her work with wives of alcoholics, also with an occasional woman alcoholic who turns up. Smith says that men can rarely work satisfactorily with women alcoholics. The sex ***xxxx*** problem makes it difficult. He, as a physician, can and has helped, but his wife and other wives must handle most of this, for which there is a growing need. Such a secretary would cost about $1,200.***00*** a year. Smith needs to keep a good car—he now drives an Oldsmobile of ***xxxxxxxxxx*** somewhat ancient vintage— to afford swift, safe, prompt transportation. He needs better office facilities not only for his regular paying patients, but to better handle these ex-alcoholics who come to him daily for inspiration and instruction. ***[Note: this last sentence has been handwritten and inserted here from the lower margin of the sheet in Frank Amos's distinctive hand]*** Altogether I think a sum of around $5,000.***00*** a year for ~~at least~~ two years should be made available to help make up for his loss of practice, to pay a secretary, and to meet expense which he cannot possibly handle under present circumstances. I am sold on attempting this at once. ~~The other suggestions can be worked out later, after more analysis and consultation.~~

Local Support—For reason which I can explain verbally, not much local financial support can be secured at present. I believe within two years much, if not all, needed support can be secured.

~~Other Locations—The situation right here in New York, also down in Maryland deserve consideration. They can be taken up later but should not be overlooked.~~

Hank's May Letter to Bert Taylor on "The Publishing Firm"

~*May 1938*~

The letter below, Document #8, is to be found in GSO, Box 59, Folder D.2—a small collection of miscellaneous correspondence from 1937 to 1939 that was previously misfiled. The contents of that folder are noted as being: "Originally Located in Boxes marked 'Marty Mann Collection.' / Extent: 1 Folder; 26 pages / Filed with Alcoholic Foundation Corr. 8/2/07."

May 1938 *[handwritten in upper right corner]*

Copy to Bill Wilson

Mr. Herbert F. Taylor
129 E. 69ᵗʰ St
New York City

Dear Bert & Bill:

Just to see if we are thinking alike.

My understanding is that a non-profit foundation is to be formed for the purpose of disseminating funds for the furtherance of work among alcoholics. I understand that donations are to be solicited to this fund for the purpose of financing the writing and publishing of a book for alcoholics. The minimum amount to be secured for this publishing work to be $15,000.00. When the book is published any remainder of the donations to be returned pro-rata to the subscribers. The first profits from the sale of the book to be pro-rated among these subscribers. If the private marketing organization secures the promotion and sale of the book, they are to repay out of their profits the amount of money advanced for market investigations, promotions and writing of the book.

To make this concrete, we will suppose that $15,000.00 is loaned for production of the book. We will further suppose that $10,000.00 is expended—and that the book is ready for distribution. In this case one third of the donation money would immediately be returned to the subscribers and for the purpose of the illustration we will suppose that the marketing concern have assured the fund of 50¢ profit per book. In this case, this 50¢ accruing to the fund for the first 20,0000.00 [sic] books would be returned to the initial subscribers.

Now we have the situation of the initial subscribers having been entirely paid off and the $10,000.00 would be entirely between the fund and the publishing firm. In this case all net profits of the publishing firm would go to the fund to the amount of $10,000.00—this in addition to the 50¢ per book, assured profit to the fund. To simplify all of the above, if the book is profitable the fund will receive 50¢ for every book that has been issued. The expense of writing and marketing would have been entirely paid out of the profits secured by the marketing company.

I understand that you are going to approach a certain individual for the sum of $500.00—who would put this $500.00 in for immediate promotional work?

Sincerely,

Hank [his signature]

HGP:RH

May to June 1938 Versions of "There Is A Solution" and "Bill's Story"

Text taken from a copy of the typed transcript of the first two chapters of the book (GSO, Box 59, 1938, Folder B, First Two Chapters of the Proposed Book; Trust Indenture, Documents 1938-53 to 1938-75)

NOTE: *This copy is in an 8½" x 11" format while the original from which it was photocopied was typed on 8½" x 14" paper necessitating two copy pages for each page of the original.*

ALCOHOLICS, ANONYMOUS.
[written in pencil using block letters]

CHAPTER 1.
THERE IS A SOLUTION

"I have never seen one single case in which alcohol mindedness was established in the sense you have it, that ever recovered - - that ever recovered. *[sic]*" These fateful words were spoken to a man we know, some seven years ago. The speaker was a noted doctor and psychologist having world eminence in his specialty. The man to whom he spoke, like many of us before and since, had searched the whole world for the solution of his alcoholic problem. He was a man of ability, good sense, and high character. He had for many years before his encounter with this noted doctor, floundered desperately from one sanitarium to another. He had consulted several of the best known American psychologists and on their recommendation, he had gone to Europe and confined himself for a year in an institution there, at the same time, being under the care of this celebrated physician.

Though many bitter experiences had given him ground for skepticism, he left the place with unusual confidence. He felt that his physical and mental condition was unusually good and that above all he had acquired such a profound knowledge of the inner workings of his mind and its hidden springs, that a relapse was unthinkable. Nevertheless, he was drunk in a few weeks, and more baffling still, he could give no satisfactory explanation of why he became that way. So he went back to his doctor whom he had come to admire greatly, and asked him point blank why he could not recover. Why was it that a person such as he, who wished above all things to regain his self control, who seemed to be so rational and well balanced with respect to other problems of life, had proved to be non compis mentis with respect to alcohol. He begged the doctor to tell him the real truth, and he got it. In the doctor's judgment he was utterly hopeless, could never regain his position in society, and he would have to place himself permanently in an institution or hire a bodyguard if he expected to live long. That was the opinion of a great physician rendered after long observation and strenuous work with our friend.

But our friend lives and is a free man. He does not have to have a bodyguard, nor is he confined. There is no place on this earth where he cannot go with complete assurance that disaster shall not again overtake him, provided he remains willing to maintain a certain simple attitude.

We, of ALCOHOLICS ANONYMOUS, now know at least one hundred men who were every bit as hopeless as our friend and they are free men also. They have an answer for this terrific problem that really works.

We are 'run of the mine' [sic] Americans. All sections of this broad land of ours are represented, and many of its occupations. Among us is to be found nearly every conceivable

Page 2

political, economic, social and religious background and shade of belief. We are a crowd of people who would normally mix like oil and water, but there exists among us nevertheless a fellowship, a friendliness, and an understanding which is indescribably wonderful. We are something like the passengers of a great liner, the moment after shipwreck has been averted. Camraderie [sic], celebration, joyousness and democracy pervade the whole ship from the steerage to the Captain's table. Unlike people on shipboard in such a time, these feelings and sentiments do not abate as we commence to go our several ways.

There are potent reasons why these things are so. In the first place, we have been through many shipwrecks, and at long last there has been the final one at which it seemed we must certainly perish. We have been the victims of a common calamity and have collectively experienced almost every known variety of human misadventure and misery. We have inhabited sanitariums, insane asylums, and occasionally the jails. We have felt the pangs of remorse as shadows have deepened over our disintegrating lives and homes. We are sure that hell promises no more exquisite mental and physical tortures that *[sic]* we have survived. Ask anyone who has had delirium tremens or who has come anywhere near them. We have seen undertaking after undertaking and ambition after ambition destroyed or snuffed out, and that usually at the very point of success. We do not know many alcoholics who have been afraid to die, but we are acquainted with some who have tried it, and who were at the time, sorry they failed. Most of us, in earlier years, have thought well of our abilities, our qualities, and our futures. The hard thing to take has been the gradually dawning realization that these things were not much longer to be. Those successive smashing blows to our pride and self sufficiency have been among the hardest things to bear. Consequently, one important ingredient of the powerful cement which now binds us, is the feeling that we have been victims of a common disaster, even thought self inflicted.

However common to all of us these troubles have been, they would of themselves, never have bound us together as we are now joined. The tremendous fact for every one of us has been the discovery of a common solution—a way out with which we can absolutely agree, and upon which we can join in brotherly and harmonious action. This is the great news that we are confident this book will bear to those who suffer as we have.

An illness of this sort—and we have come to believe it is an illness, involves those about us in a way that no other human sickness is capable of doing. If a person, for instance, has cancer, all are sorry for him, and no one is angry or hurt. Presently he dies off honorably enough, and after the

Page 3

anguish of parting has worn away, people murmur, "Wasn't it too bad about Jim". But with the alcoholic illness, there goes a seemingly never ending annihilation of all the things worth while in life, which encompasses all who are near and dear to the sufferer. Misunderstanding, fierce resentment, financial insecurity, warped lives of blameless children, sad wives and parents, disgusted friends and employers—anyone could increase this list indefinitely.

Therefore we are certain that this volume should attempt to inform, instruct and comfort all of those who are or who may be affected, and that is pretty much everyone. As a group we have had four years of intensive and unique experience on which to draw. During this time we have most intimately touched some two hundred cases of acute alcoholism. The approach to these situations has been unusual in that it has always consisted of men having found the answer for themselves, carrying the message to others as a part of the maintenance of their own cure. Scarcely a day passes that some of us are not in contact with those who are trying to rid themselves of this appalling state of affairs. We have found for ourselves great satisfaction in the knowledge that we may be so happily and peculiarly useful to others. Where you have one alcoholic approaching another upon the basis which we are about to discuss, things are possible and results follow which hitherto have been virtually impossible. Many highly competent psychologists who have attempted to deal with us, rather fruitless *[sic]* we are afraid, complain that it is almost impossible to persuade one of us to honestly and without reserve, to *[sic]* discuss his or her situation. Strangely enough, so people think, wives, parents and intimate friends, find us even more unapproachable than does the psychiatrist and the doctor.

On the contrary, an ex-alcoholic who has found this solution, and who is properly armed with certain medical and psychiatric information can almost invariably win the complete confidence of another one in a few hours. Until that very high degree of mutual understanding is reached, little or nothing can be accomplished. The fact that the man who is making the approach has had the same difficulty, that he very obviously knows what he is talking about, that his whole deportment and attitude shouts at the new prospect that here is a man with a real answer, that there are no fees to pay, no axes to grind, nor people to please, nor sermons to be listened to, nor moralizings to be endured, nor any attitude of holier than thou, nor anything whatever except the sincere desire to be helpful, and to lay at the feet of another the same simple kit of tools which has enabled us to literally take up our beds and walk.

Page 4

None of us are making a vocation of this work, nor do we think it would increase its effectiveness if we did. We feel that the elimination of the liquor problem is but a beginning. A much more important demonstration of the principles upon which we became well lies before us in our respective homes, occupations and affairs. Every one of us spends much of his spare time in the sort of effort which we are going to describe to you. A few of us are fortunate enough to be so situated that we can give nearly all of our time. If we kept on in the way we are going, there is little doubt that much good will result, but the problem would hardly be scratched. Those of us who live in large cities are frequently overcome by the reflection that within gunshot of us there are hundreds dropping into oblivion this very minute who would recover if they were fortunate enough to have the opportunity we have enjoyed. How then shall we present the thing which has been so freely given us to those otherwise splendid people who want victory of John Barleycorn, but who are now discovering that apparently there is no such thing.

We realize that should a description of our work get into the ordinary channels of publicity in such a way as to involve our personal identities, more harm than good might be done. In all probability we would be besieged by great numbers of people who would only imagine they wish to give up drinking, or whose families think they ought to stop, or who are too badly impaired mentally, or whose alcoholism is complicated by other abnormal conditions of mind or body rendering their condition nearly impossible to deal with at all. And though we treated only with those cases who really want to recover and who are not too seriously handicapped in other ways than alcoholism, we could not begin to deal with them on a personal basis. There are not enough of us, nor have we accumulated the experience that would probably be necessary. Yet, the desire to get this message to thousands of people who could make use of it bears down with great weight upon us all.

We have come to the conclusion that our dilemma may be partially solved by the publication of an anonymous volume such as you are about to read, setting forth the problem as it looks to us, bringing then to bear upon it our combined experience and knowledge, which ought to suggest a definite program of action and attitude for everyone concerned in a drinking situation. In so doing we realized that we are amateurs and that we have a very great deal to learn period. Of necessity there will have to be a great deal of discussion in these pages of matters medical, psychiatric, social and religious. We are keenly aware that these subjects, from their very nature, are highly controversial. Nothing would please us so much as to write a book which would contain no basis for contention

Page 5

or argument, and we are going to do our utmost to achieve that ideal, knowing however, the impossibility of its complete attainment.

It is our sincere belief that the activities and attitudes which have proven vital to the successful solution of our drinking problem ought not to conflict at any point with the views of honest men of good will the world over whatever their race, creed or color. This is the spirit in which we shall try to proceed, remembering always that we may be mistaken here and there on factual matters concerning which there can be honest differences of opinion. We are most anxious not to appear in a role of those who would preach or reform, as we deem such attitudes ill befit the kind of people we have been and to some extent still are.

For example, it is rather surprising to most of us that we have not developed a downright hatred for John Barleycorn and all his works, that we have not become intolerant and impatient with those who like to drink, for many sincerely believe that they should not *[be]* deprived of an age old privilege and pleasure just because a lot of people are softened and made sick by it. We are sure that we have a way of life which, if adopted generally, would render excessive drinking a stupid and impossible practice. Most of us strongly feel that real tolerance of other people's shortcomings and viewpoints, and a decent respect for the opinions of mankind, are qualities which greatly enhance our usefulness to others, for in the last analysis our very lives as ex-alcoholics depend upon the constant thought of others, and how we may help meet their needs.

If you have read this far, you have commenced to ask yourself why it is that all of us became so desperately ill from drinking. Doubtless you are still more curious to discover how and why, in the face of expert medical opinion to the contrary, we have all recovered from an utterly hopeless condition of mind and body. If you are an alcoholic who wants to get over it, you are already beginning to ask yourself—"What do I have to do?"

The main purpose of this book is to exhaustively, definitely and specifically answer those questions and to let you know what you can do about it.

Before going on to a detailed discussion, it may be well to briefly summarize the answers as we see them.

How many times people have said to us—"I can take it or leave it alone"—"Why don't you drink like a gentleman or quit"—"That fellow can't handle his liquor"—"Why don't you try beer and wine?"—"Lay off the hard stuff" "His will power must be weak"—"Look what he's doing to his family"—"Why did he start drinking when he knew his wife would leave and the boss would fire him"—Or again—"I drink a quart of whiskey a day and never get drunk, but if that

Page 6

fellow Jones drinks two cocktails, he's sure to be drunk for a week, there must be something wrong with his will power"—"He could stop it if he wanted to"—"She's such a sweet girl, I should think he'd stop for her"—"The doctor told him that if he ever drank again it would kill him, but there he is, all lit up again"—

Now these are commonplace expressions with respect to drinkers, which you hear all the time. Back of them is a world of ignorance and of complete misunderstanding as to what the trouble really is. We see that these expressions pertain to people who each react very differently to alcohol. We observe in them the moderate drinker who has little trouble in abandoning liquor altogether, if any good reason appears why he should do so. Then we have the man who boasts control over his quart a day, and he may have only a bad habit which will gradually impair him somewhat physically and mentally. Perhaps it will cause him to die a few years before his time. If a sufficiently strong reason, such as ill health, falling in love, change of environment, the warning of a doctor, puts in an appearance, this fellow can also stop, although he may find it difficult and troublesome, and may discover it advantageous to get some medical or psychiatric aid.

But what about the true alcoholic who may have started off as a moderate drinker, who may or may not have become a continuous hard drinker, but who, at some stage in his drinking career begins to lose all control of his liquor consumption once he starts to drink. Here is the fellow who has been puzzling you especially in this matter of this lack of control, who does absurd incredible and tragic things while drinking. He is so often Dr Jekyll and Mr. Hyde. He is seldom pleasantly intoxicated; almost always, he is more or less insanely drunk. His disposition while drinking does not square at all with the man you know when sober. When normal he may be one of the finest fellows in the world, yet let him drink for a day and he frequently becomes disgustingly, and even dangerously anti-social. He has a positive genius for getting tight at exactly the wrong moment, particularly when some important decision or engagement has to be met. He is often perfectly sensible and well balanced concerning everything in the world save liquor. With respect to that he is incredibly dishonest and selfish. He frequently has ahead of him a promising career, and no matter what his station in life, or his educational and intellectual station, he almost invariably possesses special abilities, skills or aptitudes. How often have we seen him use these gifts to build up a very promising prospect for his family and himself, then pull the structure down on his own head by a senseless series of sprees. He is the fellow who goes to bed so in-

Page 7

toxicated that he ought to sleep the clock around, yet we find him feverishly searching the house early next morning for a bottle he misplaced the night before. If he can afford it, the chances are better than even that during his drinking spells, he has liquor concealed all over his house to be absolutely sure that no one gets his entire supply away from him to throw it down the waste pipe.

Every business mans convention presents much the same spectacle. Certain individuals are always found, going about from room to room in the early morning, sometimes shaking like the proverbial aspen leaf. They tell you they are dying for a drink and can't wait until the bar opens. This is very annoying to their brother business men who may have been twice as indiscreet the night before, but who still want to sleep, and who on awaking have no more inconvenience than a headache and the foolish feeling that they were much too skittish last evening.

As matters grow worse for our alcoholic friend, he begins to use a combination of high-powered sedative and liquor to quiet his nerves enough so that he can go to work. Then comes those days when he simply cannot make it and he gets drunk all over again. Finally he begins to appear at hospitals and sanitariums, or he gets in his doctor who gives him a dose of murphine [sic] and some high voltage sedative to taper off with. He leaves the poor fellow with a parting lecture on the evils of strong drink, and an admonition that he must use his will power, and if he cannot drink like a gentleman, he must leave it alone. This is by no means a comprehensive picture of the true alcoholic as our behavior patterns vary considerably. The description should suffice for the moment to roughly identify him in the mind of the reader.

But you are asking yourslef [sic]—"Why does he behave like this? If hundreds of experiences have shown him that one drink means another debacle with all its attendant suffering and humiliation, how is it that he takes that one drink? What has become of the common sense and will power that he frequently displays with respect to other matters? Perhaps there never will be a full answer to your questions. Psychiatrists and medical men vary considerably in their opinions as to why the alcoholic reacts differently than other people and why, once a certain point is reached, all of the kings horses and all of the kings men can seem to do nothing about it whatever. We have, out of our own experiences and observations of each other arrived at some pretty definite conclusions which we are confident are in the main, correct. While they may not entirely square with what the doctors say, they do meet our needs, and they do make sense to us, and we are positive that nine out of ten serious drinkers who honestly review their own experience will agree with us.

Page 8

To begin with, it is self evident that the reaction of our bodies and nervous systems to alcohol has become radically different, in fact very abnormal as compared with the ordinary person, or with even many hearty drinkers. It often takes ten or fifteen years of stiff drinking to bring about this condition in a body predisposed to alcoholism. Most of us now realize that our reaction to alcohol was somewhat abnormal from the very beginning; that we were actually 'hooked' and diseased by it long before grave symptoms, or incapacity to tend to business put in an appearance. The nature of these symptoms and the bodily conditions which seem to lie back of them we shall cover later on. It is enough to say here that we believe ourselves to have been bodily sick and not just foolish at the times we have been drinking.

We know that if the alcoholic keeps away from drink, he does not get sick. Equally positive are we that once he takes any alcohol whatever into his system, something happens both in the bodily and mental sense, which makes it virtually impossible for him to stop after he has had any alcohol whatever. We believe that the experience of any alcoholic will abundantly confirm what has just been said.

All of these observations would be quite academic and pointless if our friend never took the first drink, thereby setting in motion the terrible cycle that everyone has seen so many times. Therefore, the real problem of the alcoholic centers in his mind rather than in his body. If you ask him why he started on that last bender the chances are that he will offer you any one of a hundred alibis, many of which we shall list further on. Sometimes these excuses have a certain plausibility, but none of them really makes sense in the light of the havoc an alcoholic's drinking bout creates. They sound to you like the philosophy of the man who, having a headache, beat himself on the head with a hammer so that he couldn't feel the ache, together with the vague notion that it might feel better when he stopped. If you draw this fallacious reasoning to the attention of an alcoholic, he will laugh it off, or become irritated and refuse to talk. Perhaps, once in a great while, he may tell you the truth. And the truth, strange to say, is usually that he has no more idea why he took that first drink than you have. It is true, that numbers of drinkers have excuses with which they are some of the time satisfied. But in their hearts, they really do not know why they do it. As a class, once the disease has a real hold, they are a terribly baffled lot. Nearly all of them have the obsession that somehow, some day, they will beat the game, which deep down in them, they suspect has them down for the count.

But how surely they have already gone with the wind few of them realize. In a vague way their families and their friends sense that these people are abnormal and everybody hopefully waits the day when the sufferer will rouse himself from his lethargy and assert his power of will.

The tragic thing is, if the man be a real alcoholic, that happy day will never arrive. In the early part of this chapter, we cited the case of a friend who was frankly told of his utter hopelessness by a physician who is possibly the world's leading authority on the subject. At a certain point in the drinking of every alcoholic, he passes into a state where the most powerful desire to stop drinking is of absolutely no avail, and let us again emphasize that this unhappy situation has already arrived in virtually every case long before it is suspected. The fact is, that all of us for reasons which are yet obscure, have entirely lost the power of choice with respect to alcoholic drinks. Our so called will power with respect to that area of thinking and action becomes virtually non-existent. We are unable at certain times, no matter how well we understand ourselves, to bring into our consciousness with sufficne [sic] force, the memory of the suffering and humiliation of even a week or a month ago. The almost certain consequences that follow taking a glass of beer do not crowd into the mind and deter us. If these thoughts do occur, they are vague or hazy and become readily supplanted with the old threadbare idea that this time we shall handle ourselves like other people There is a complete failure of the kind of defense that would keep one from putting his hand on a hot stove. The alcoholic says to himself in the most casual way—"It won't burn me this time, so here's how!—Or perhaps he doesn't think at all. How many times have many of us begun to drink in this nonchalant way, and then after the third or fourth pounded on the bar and said to ourselves,—"For God's sake, how did I ever get started again,"—only to have that thought supplanted by—"Well I'll stop with the sixth drink"—or—"What's the use anyhow."

When this sort of thinking is fully established in an individual with alcoholic tendencies, he has become, in our opinion, just like our friend who consulted the great doctor. He has placed himself beyond all human aid, and unless locked up, is virtually certain to die, or to go permanently insane. It is a very grim business indeed. These are the stark and ugly facts which have been confirmed in hundreds of thousands of cases throughout history, and but for the grace of God, would have had one hundred more convincing demonstrations among us.

But there is a solution, and how glorious was the knowledge of it to us. Almost none of us liked the self searching, the levelling [sic] of our pride, the confession of our sins of omission and commission which the process requires for

its successful consummation, but we saw that it really worked in others, and we had come to believe in the hopelessness and futility of life as we had been living it. When, therefore, we were approached by others in whom the problem had been solved, there was nothing left for us to do but accept the proposals placed before us. We have found a heaven right here on this good old earth and have been literally rocketed into a fourth dimension of existence that none of us had dreamed could be a fact.

And the GREAT FACT is just this and no less; that all of us have had deep and effective religious experiences which have in every case revolutionized our whole attitude toward life, toward our fellows and toward God's great universe.

It is possible that this announcement has given you a severe jolt, followed by thoughts something like these—"Oh, so that's what it is, I'm so disappointed, I had begun to think these fellows knew what they were talking about." But let us assure you that you should be cheered up, for if you are a non-alcoholic, you don't have to have it if you don't want it, though we confess we should like to see you follow suit, for we think no one should miss THE GREAT REALITY which we have been lucky enough to find. The central fact of our lives today is the absolute certainty that the Creator of you and me has entered into our hearts and lives in a way which is to us new and beautiful and has there commenced to accomplish those things which by no stretch of the imagination were we humanly capable of.

If by chance you are, or have begun to suspect that you are, an alcoholic, we think there is no tenable middle of the road solution. You are in a position where life is becoming impossible, and if you have passed into the region from which there is no return through human aid, you have just two alternatives. One is to go on to the bitter end, blotting out the consciousness of your intolerable situation as best you can. Or, you can surely find what we have foudn [sic], if you honestly want to, and are willing to pay the price. After years of living on a basis which now seems to us wholly false, you are not going to get rightly related to your Creator in a minute. None of us has found God in six easy lessons, but He can be found by all who are willing to put the task ahead of all else.

On the bare chance that our alcoholic readers still think they can do without God, let us complete for you the conversation which our friend was having with the celebrated European man of medicine. As you will recall, the doctor said—"I never have seen one single case in which alcohol mindedness was established in the sense you have it that ever recovered." Naturally our friend felt at that moment as though the gates of hell had closed on him with a

Page 11

sickening clang. He then said to the doctor, "Is there no exception?" The doctor answered, "Yes, there is. The sole exceptions in cases such as yours have been occurring now and then since early times. Sporadically, here and there, once in a while, alcoholics have had what are called vital religious experiences. I am not a religious man, to me these occurrences are a phenomena [sic]. They appear to be in the nature of huge emotional displacements and rearrangements. Ideas, emotions and attitudes which were once the guiding forces of the lives of these men, are suddenly cast to one side and a completely new set of conceptions and motives commence to dominate them. In face [sic], I have been trying to produce some such emotional rearrangement within you. With many types of individuals the methods which I have been employing are successful, but they are never successful with an alcoholic of your state of mine [sic]."

Upon hearing this, our friend was somewhat relieved as he reflected that after all he was a very good church member, but his hope was promptly dashed by the doctor, who told him that his faith and his religious convictions were very good as far as they went, but that in his case they did not spell the vital religious experience so absolutely imperative to displace his insanity with respect to matters alcoholic.

You and I would say that the patient was on a very hot spot, that it [sic] probably what he did say and feel. So have we, when it began to look to us as though we must have a vital religious experience or perish. Our friend did finally have such an experience and we in our turn have sought the same happy end, with all of the ardor of drowning men clutching at straws. But what seemed at first to be a flimsy reed has proved to be a loving and powerful hand of God. A new life has been given us, or if you please, a design for living that really works.

That distinguished American psychologist, Mr. William James, once wrote a book called—"Varieties of Religious Experience", which indicates a multitude of ways in which men have found God. As a group, or as individuals, we have no desire to convince anyone that the true God can only be discovered in some particular way. Anyone who has talked with all of us would soon be disabused of the idea. If what we have learned, and felt, and seen, means anything at all, it indicates that all of us, whatever our race, creed or color, are the children of a living Creator with whom we may form a new relationship upon very simple and understandable terms, the moment any of us become willing enough and honest enough to do so. Therefore, we waste no time in the kind of religious disputation which has so frequently torn people apart.

Page 12

We have concluded that it is no concern of ours as a group what religious bodies we shall identify ourselves with as individuals. We feel that should be entirely ones own affair which he is bound to decide for the best in the light of his past association, his newly found religious experience, his convictions and preferences, and above all, his future usefulness. Not all of us have joined religious bodies, but we are nearly all agreed that by so doing, each would be taking a step toward new growth and availability for God's purpose.

The nect [sic] few chapters are the personal narratives of several of us. In these accounts each person will describe in his own language and from his own point of view the way in which he happened to find the living God. We propose to have told in these pages a good number of stories, that the reader may get a fair cross section and a clear cut idea of what has really happened, and why we think it happened. We hope that no one will be disturbed that these stories contain so much self revelation of the kind that some people might feel in bad taste or unnecessary. Non-alcoholic readers must bear in mind that we hope many men and women desperately in need will read these pages. It is only by disclosing ourselves and our problems to complete view that many of them will be persuaded to say—"Yes that's me. I must have this thing."

Text taken from the earliest version available in the Stepping Stones Archive (AA 501.1, Alcoholics Anonymous—Early Drafts of Chapter "There Is a Solution," Box 13, Folder 24).

NOTE: *Stepping Stones holds another version in that same folder which, based on a careful comparison of the edits that have been done to the text, is a later version The single version preserved at the GSO Archive in New York City is even later than this second Stepping Stones copy.*

Permission is required from the Stepping Stones Foundation for any further use, display, or duplication of the following material.

CHAPTER 2.

At the age of ten I went to live with my grandfather and grandmother—their ancestors settled the section of Vermont in which I was to grow up. Grandfather was a retired farmer and lumberman; he nurtured me on a vigorous pioneering tradition. I see, now, that my grandfather was the kind of man who helped make America.

Little did anyone guess I was to be of the war generation, which would squander the savings, the pioneering traditions and the incredible stamina of your grandfather and mine. Ambitious but undisciplined—that was I. There was a genius for postponing, evading and shirking; but a certain dogged obstinacy and persistence drove me to succeed at special undertakings upon which my heart was set.

Especially did I revel in attacking the difficult or the impossible. Grandfather said, for instance, that no one but an Australian could make and throw the boomerang. No school work done, no wood box filled and little sleep was there, until a boomerang had circled the church steeple, returning to almost decapitate [sic] him. Having accomplished this, my interest ceased.

So it was with my ambition to be a ball player; for I was finally elected captain of the team at the little Seminary I attended after leaving country school. Someone told me I could never sing, so I took up voice until I had appeared in a recital, then, as with the boomerang, my interest ended abruptly. I had commenced to fuss with the violin. This became such an obsession that athletics, school work, and all else went by the board much to everyone's consternation. I carried fiddling so far I failed to graduate. It was most embarrassing, for I was president of the Senior Class. So collapsed a certain legend of infallibility I had built around myself. Repairing this failure, I attempted to enter a leading technical school. Because of fierce enthusiasms I had displayed for matters chemical and electrical, It [sic] was assumed I was destined to become an engineer. At Boston, I failed the entrance examinations dismally. My people were heartbroken and my self sufficiency got another severe deflation.

Finally I commenced electrical engineering at an excellent military college, where it was fervently hoped I would get disciplined. No such thing happened. As usual I had good grades when interested but often failed when not. There was an illuminating instance concerning my calculus teacher. Not one formula would I learn, until all of the theory underlying the subject was made clear. At the library, I pored over the researches of Leibniz and Newton,

Page 13

whose genius had made calculul [sic] possible. Loving controversy, I argued much with my instructor, who quite properly gave me a zero, for I had solved only the first problem of the course. At this juncture, and quite conveniently for me, the United States decided to go to war.

We students bolted, almost to a man, for the First Officers Training Camp at Plattsburgh. I was commissioned second Lieutenant of artillery, electing that branch rather than aviation or infantry. For when I lay in my bunk at night, I had to confess I did not want to be killed. This suspicion of cowardice bothered me, for it couldn't be reconciled with the truly exalted patriotism which took possession when I hadn't time to think. Later, under fire abroad, I was relieved to learn I was like most men; scared enough, but willing to see it through. I was assigned to a post on the New England coast. The place is famous for its Yankee trading and whaling traditions.

Two far reaching events took place here. I married; had my first drink and liked it. My wife was city bred. She represented a way of life for which I secretly longed. To be her kind meant fine houses, servants, gay dinners, cultivated conversation and a much envied sophistication. I often felt a woeful lack of poise and polish. These inferiorities were later to drive me cityward in quest of success, as I suppose they have many a country boy.

War fever ran high, and I was flattered that the first citizens of the town took us to their homes and made me feel comfortable and heroic. So here was love, applause, adventure, war; moments sublime with intervals hilarious. I was part of life at last.

My gaucheries and ineptitudes magically disappeared, as I discovered the Siphon and the Bronx Cocktail. Strong warnings and the prejudices of my people concerning drink evaporated.

Then came parting with its bizarre mixture of sadness, high purpose and the strange elation which goes with adventure having fatal possibilities. many of us sailed for 'Over There'. Loneliness seized me, only to be whisked away by my charming companion, Prince Alcohol.

We were in England. I stood in Winchester Cathedral with head bowed, in the presence of something I had never felt before. Where now was the God of the preachers? Across the Channel thousands were perishing that day. Why did He not come? Suddenly in that moment of darkness - He was there! I felt an enveloping comforting Presence. Tears stood in my eyes. I had glimpsed the great reality.

Much moved, I wandered through the Cathedral yard. My attention was caught by a doggerel on an old tombstone.

> "Here lies a Hampshire Grenadier
> Who caught his death
> Drinking cold small beer
> A good soldier is ne'er forgot
> Whether he dieth by musket
>   or by pot."

My mood changed. A squadron of fighters roared overhead. I cried to myself, "Here's to Adventure". The feeling of being in the great presence disappeared.

Homecoming arrived at last. Twenty two and a veteran of foreign wars! I fancied myself a leader, for had not the men of my battery given me a special token of appreciation? Leadership, I imagined, would place me at the head of vast enterprises which I would manage with the assurance of a great pipe organist at his stops and keys.

Soon enough, I was brought to earth. A position at half the army pay, from which I was presently discharged as a poor and rebellious bookkeeper, was the first salutation of unsentimental industry. My resentment was so great I nearly turned Socialist; which in Vermont is downright treason. Humiliation and more came when my wife got a much better job and commenced to pay the bills. I fancied my new city friends were snickering at my predicament. Unwillingly, I had to admit, that I was not trained for anything. What then to do?

Somehow I would show these scoffers. The old driving determination to display my mettle rose. I determined to take anight [sic] law course. Then came employment as a criminal investigator for a surety company. The drive for what I though [sic] success was on. The world would see that I was important after all. My work took me about Wall Street. Little by little I got interested in what went on there. Most people lost but some became rich. Why not I, [sic] Economics and business became studies as well as the law.

Characteristically, I nearly failed my law course. At one of the finals I was too drunk to think or write. Though drinking was not continuous, it frequently disturbed my wife. We had long talks, when I would still her forebodings by saying men of genius conceived their vast projects when jingled; that the most majestic constructions of philosophic thought were so derived.

When the law course was done, I knew the profession was not for me. The inviting maelstrom of The Street had me in its grip. Business and financial

leaders were my heroes. Reminiscent of the boomerang episode, I became wholly absorbed and fascinated. Out of this tissue of drink and speculation I commenced to forge the weapon that one day would turn in its flight, and all but cut me to ribbons.

Both at work, and living modestly, my wife and I saved $1,000.00. It went into utility stocks then cheap and rather unpopular. I rightly imagined that they would some day have a great rise. Failing to persuade my broker friends to send me out looking over factories and managements, my wife and I decided to go anyhow. I had a theory people lost money in stocks by not knowing markets, managements and the ideas at work in a given situation. I was to discover lots more reasons later on.

We quit our positions and off we romped on a motorcycle and sidecar stuffed with a tent, blankets, change of clothes, and three huge volumes of a financial reference service. Our friends almost wanted a lunacy commission appointed. Perhaps they were right. There had been some success at speculation, so we had a little money though we once worked on a farm for a month to avoid drawing on our capital. It was the last honest manual labor for many a day. The whole Eastern United States was covered in a year. At the end of it, strangely enough, my reports sent back to Wall Street procured for me a position there, and the use of what seemed to me a large sum of money. The exercise of an option brought in more money and we had several thousand dollars profit.

For the next few years fortune threw money and applause my way. I had arrived. My judgment and ideas were followed by many to the tune of paper millions. The great boom of the late twenties was seething and swelling. Drink was taking an important and exhilirating [sic] part in my life. Loud talk in the jazz places uptown—we all spent in thousands, and chattered in millions. Scoffers could scoff and be damned. Of course they didn't, and I made a host of fair weather friends.

My drinking assumed more serious proportions, going on all day and nearly every night. Remonstrance of my cooler associates terminated in a row, and I became a lone wolf. There were many unhappy scenes in our apartment. This, by the way, was large, for I had rented two, and had the wall between knocked out. There had been no great infidelity. Loyalty to my wife, and sometimes extreme drunkenness, kept me out of those scrapes.

In 1929 I contracted the golf fever. That is a terrible illness. We went at once to the country, my wife to applaud while I overtook Walter Hagen. Liquor caught up with me much faster than I came up behind Walter. I began

Page 16

to be jittery in the morning. Golf permitted drinking both by day and night. It was fun to carom around the exclusive course which had inspired such awe in me as a lad. I acquired the impeccable coat of tan seen upon the well-to-do. With amused skepticism the local banker watched me whirl fat checks in and out of his till.

Abruptly in October, 1929, the whirling movement ceased. Hell had broken loose on the New York Stock Exchange. After one of those days of inferno I wobbled from a hotel bar to a brokerage office. It was eight o'clock - five hours after the market close. The ticker still clattered. I was staring at an inch of the tape. It bore the inscription PFK - 32. It had been 52 that morning. I was done and so were many friends. The papers said men were already jumping to death from those towers of Babel that were High Finance. That disgusted me. Going back to the bar I felt glad I would not jump. My friends had dropped several millions since ten o'clock - so what? Tomorrow was another day. As I drank, the old fierce determination to win came back.

Next morning I called a friend in Montreal. He had plenty of money left, so he thought I had better come up. By the following spring we were living in our accustomed style. It was like Napoleon returning from Elba. No St. Helenn [sic] for me. But I soon excelled as a serious and frivolous drinker, and my generous friend had to let me go. This time we stayed broke.

We went to live with my parents-in-law. I found a job; then lost it through a brawl with a taxi driver. Mercifully no one knew I was to have no real employment for five years nor hardly to draw a sober breath. My wife began to work in a department store, coming home exhausted to find me drunk. I became a hanger on at brokerage places, less and less desired because of my habits. Liquor ceased to be a luxury; it was a necessity. 'Bathtub' gin, two bottles a day, and often three, got to be routine. Sometimes a small deal would net a few hundred dollars, and I would pay the bars and delicatessen. Endlessly this went on, and I began to wake early, shaking violently. A tumbler full of gin followed by half a dozen bottles of beer would be required if I ate any breakfast. I still thought I could control the situation. There were periods of sobriety which would renew my wife's hope.

But things got worse. The house was taken over by the mortgage holder, my mother -in- law died, my wife became ill, as did my father-in-law.

Then I had a promising business opportunity. Stocks were at the low point of 1932, and I had somehow formed a group to buy. I was to share

Page 17

generously in the profits. I went on a prodigious bender, and that chance vanished.

I woke up. This had to be stopped. I saw I could not take even one drink. I was through forever. Before then, I had written lots of sweet promises, but my wife happily observed that this time I meant business. And so I did.

Shortly afterward I came home drunk. There had been no fight. Where had been my high resolve? I simply didn't know. It hadn't even come to mind. Someone pushed a drink my way, and I had taken it. Was I crazy? I began to wonder, for such an appalling lack of perspective came near being just that.

Sticking to my resolve I tried again. Some time passed. Confidence began to be replaced by cocksureness. I could laugh at the bars. Now I had what it takes! One day I walked into a place to telephone. In no time I was beating on the bar asking myself how it happened. As the whisky rose to my head I told myself I would manage better next time, but I might as well get good and drunk then. I did just that.

The remorse, horror and hopelessness of next morning is unforgettable. The courage to do battle was not there. My brain raced uncontrollably. There was a terrible sense of impending calamity. I hardly dared cross the street, lest I collapse and be run down by an early morning truck, for it was scarcely daylight. An all night place supplied me with a dozen glasses of ale. My writhing nerves were stilled at last. A morning paper told me the market had gone to hell again. Well, so had I . The market would recover but I wouldn't. That was a hard thought. Should I kill myself? No, not now. Then a mental fog settled down. Gin would fix that. So two bottles and - oblivion.

The mind and body is a marvelous mechanism, for mine endured this agony for two years more. Sometimes I stole from my wife's slender purse when the morning terror and madness were on me. Again I swayed dizzily before an open window, or the medicine cabinet where there was poison, cursing myself for a weakling. There were flights from city to country and back, as my wife and I sought escape. Then came the night when the physical and mental torture was so hellish I feared I would burst thru my window, sash and all. Somehow I managed to drag my mattress to a lower floor lest I suddenly leap. A doctor came with a heavy sedative. Next day found me drinking both gin and sedative without the usual penalty. This combination soon landed me on the rocks, and my wife saw something had to be done and quickly. People feared for my sanity, and so did I. When drinking, which was almost always, I could eat little or nothing. I was forty pounds under weight.

Page 18

My brother -in -law is a physician. Through his kindness I was placed in a nationally known hospital for the mental and physical rehabilitation of alcoholics. Under the so-called bella donna treatment my brain cleared. Hydro therapy and mild exercise helped much. Best of all, I met a kind doctor who explained, that though selfish and foolish, I had also been seriously ill, bodily and mentally. It relieved me somewhat to learn that in alcoholism, the will is amazingly weakened concerning drink, though frequently remaining strong in other respects. My incredible behavior in the face of a desperate desire to stop was explained. Understand ing myself, now, I fared forth in high hope. For three or four months the goose hung high. I went to town regularly and made a little money. Surely this was the answer. Self- Knowledge.

But it was not, for the frightful day came when I drank once more. The curve of my declining moral and bodily health fell like a ski jump. After a time I returned to the hospital. This was the finish, the curtain, so it seemed to me. My weary and despairing wife was informed that it would all end with heart failure during delirium tremens. Or I would develop a wet brain, perhaps within a year. She would soon give me over to the undertaker or the asylum. It was not necessary to tell me. I knew, and almost welcomed the idea. It was a devastating blow to my pride. I, who had thought so well of myself and my abilities, of my capacity to surmount obstacles, was cornered at last. Now I was to plunge out into the dark, joining that endless procession of sots who had gone on before. I thought of my poor wife. There had been much happiness after all. What would I not give to make amends? That career I'd set my heart upon, that pleasant vista, was shut out forever. No words can tell of the loneliness and despair I found in that bitter morass of self pity. Quicksand underlay me in all directions. I had met my match. I had been overwhelmed. King Alcohol was master.

Trembling, I stepped from the place a broken man. Fear sobered me for a bit. Then came the insidious insanity of that first drink, and on Armistice Day, 1934, I was off again. Everyone became resigned to the certainty that I would have to be shut up some where, or stumble along to a miserable end. How dark it is before morning comes! In reality, this was the beginning of my last debauch. I was soon to be catapulted into what I like to call the fourth dimension of existence. I was to know happiness, peace and usefulness, in a way of life that is incredibly more wonderful as time passes.

Near the end of that bleak November I sat drinking in my kitchen. With a certain satisfaction I reflected there was enough gin concealed about the house to carry me through that night and the next day. My wife was at work. I

Page 19

wondered whether I dared hide a full bottle near the head of our bed. I would need it before daylight.

My musing was interrupted by the telephone. The cheery voice of an old school friend asked if he might come over. <u>He was sober</u>. It was years since I could remember his coming to New York in that condition. I was amazed. He had been committed for alcoholic insanity. So rumor had it. I wondered how he had escaped. Of course he would have dinner. Then I could drink openly with him. Unmindful of his welfare, I thought only of recapturing the spirit of other days. There was that time we had chartered an airplane to complete a jag. Another glass stirred my fancy. His coming was an oasis in this drear [sic] desert of futility. The very thing - - - an oasis! Drinkers are like that.

The door opened. He stood there, fresh skinned and glowing. There was something about his eyes. He was inexplicably different. What had happened?

I pushed a drink across the table.

"Not now" he said.

Disappointed but curious, I wondered what had got into the fellow. He wasn't himself.

"Come, what's all this about", I queried.

He looked straight at me. Simply, but smilingly he said, "I've got religion".

I was aghast. So that was it—last summer an alcoholic crackpot; now I suspected a little cracked about religion—he had that starry- eyed look. The old boy was on fire alright. But bless his heart, let him rant! Besides, my gin would last longer.

He did no ranting. In quite a matter of fact way, he related how two men had appeared in court, persuading the judge to suspend his commitment. They had told of a simple religious idea and a practical program of action. That was months ago and the result was self evident. It worked.

He had come to pass his experience along to me - if I cared to have it.

I was shocked but interested. Certainly I was interested. I had to be, for I was hopeless.

He talked for hours. Childhood memories rose before me. The sound of the preacher's voice which one could hear on still Sundays, way over there on the hillside; the proffered temperance pledge I never signed; my grandfathers [sic] good natured contempt of some church fold and their doings; his insistence that the spheres really had their music; his denial of the preacher's right to tell him how he must listen; his fearlessness as he spoke of these things just before he died; such recollections welled up from the past. They made me swallow hard.

Page 20

That war- time day in old Winchester Cathedral came back again.

In a power greater than myself I had always believed. I had often pondered these things. I was not an atheist. Few people really are, for that means blind faith in an illogical proposition; that this universe originated in a cipher, and aimlessly rushes nowhere. My intellectual heroes, the chemists, the astronomers even the evolutionist, suggested vast laws and forces at work. Despite contra indications, I had little doubt that a mighty purpose and rhythm underlay all. How could there be so much of precise and immutable law, and no intelligence? I simply had to believe in a Spirit of the Universe, which knew neither time nor limitation. But that was as far as I had gone.

With preachers, and the world's religions, I parted right there. When they talked of a God personal to me, which was love, superhuman strength and direction, I became irritated, and my mind snapped shut against such theory.

Of Christ, I conceded the certainty of a great man, not too much followed by those who claimed Him. His moral teaching - most excellent. I had adopted those parts which seemed convenient and not too difficult. The rest were disregarded.

The wars which had been fought, the burnings and chicanery that religious dispute had facilitated, made me sick. I honestly doubted whether the religions of mankind had done any good on balance. Judging from what I had seen in Europe and since, the power of God in human affairs was negligible; the Brotherhood of Man a grim jest. If there was a Devil he seemed the Boss Universal, and he certainly had me.

But my friend sat before me, and he made the point blank declaration that God had done for him what he could not do for himself. His human will had failed. Doctors had pronounced him incurable. Society was about to lock him up. Like myself he had admitted complete defeat. In effect he been raised from the dead; suddenly taken from the scrap-heap to a level of life better than the best he had ever known.

Had this power originated in him? Obviously it had not. There had been no more power in him than there was in me at that minute; and this was none at all.

That floored me. It began to look as though religious people were right, after all. Here was something at work in a human heart which had done the impossible. My ideas about miracles were drastically revised right then. Never mind the musty past; here sat a miracle directly across the kitchen table. He shouted great tidings, straight out of the here and now!

Page 21

I saw that my friend was much more than inwardly reorganized. It went deeper than that. He was on a completely different footing. His roots grasped a new soil.

Thus was I convinced that God is concerned with us humans, when we want Him enough. At long last I saw; I felt, I believed. Scales of pride and prejudice fell from my eyes. A new world came into view.

The real significance of my experience in the Cathedral burst upon me. For a brief moment, I had needed and wanted God. There was a humble willing ness to have Him with me - and He came. But soon the sense of His presence had been blotted out by worldly clamors - mostly those within myself. And so it had been ever since. It was simple as that. How blind I had been.

At the hospital I was separated from King Alcohol for the last time. Treatment seemed wise then, for I showed signs of delirium when I stopped drinking.

There I humbly offered myself to God, as I then understood Him, to do with me as He would. I placed myself unreservedly under His care and direction. I admitted for the first time, that of myself I was nothing; that without Him I was lost. I ruthlessly faced my sins of omission and commission, and became willing to have my new -found Friend take them away, root and branch. My schoolmate visited me, and I fully acquainted him with my problems and deficiencies. We made a list of people I had hurt or toward whom I felt resentment. I expressed my entire willingness to approach these individuals, admitting my wrong. Never was I to be critical of them. I was to right all such matters to the utmost of my ability. I was to test my thinking by the new God consciousness within. Common sense would thus become uncommon sense. I was to sit quietly when in doubt, asking only for direction and strength to meet my problems as He would have me. Never was I to pray for myself, except as my requests bore on my usefulness to others. Then only might I expect to receive. But that would be in great measure.

My friend promised when those things were done I would enter upon a new relationship with my Creator; that I would have the elements of a way of life which answered all my problems. Belief in the power of God, plus enough willingness, honesty and humility to establish and maintain the new order of things, were the essential requirements. Simple but not easy; price [sic] had to be paid. It really meant the obliteration of self. I had to quit playing God. I must turn in all things to the Father of Light who presides over us all.

These were revolutionary and drastic proposals, but the moment I fully accepted them the effect was electric. There was a sense of victory, followed by such a peace and serenity as I had never known. There was utter confidence. I felt lifted up, as though the great clean wind of a mountain top blew through and through. God comes to most men gradually, but His impact on me was sudden and profound.

For a moment I was alarmed, and called my friend the Doctor to ask if I were still sane. He listened in wonderment as I talked.

He finally shook his head, saying: "Something has happened to you I don't understand. But you had better hang on to it. Anything is better than the way you were." The good doctor now sees many men have such experiences. He knows they are real.

While I lay in the hospital the thought came that there were thousands of hopeless alcoholics who might be glad to have what had been so freely given me. Perhaps I could help some of them. They in turn might work with others. My friend had emphasized the absolute necessity of my demonstrating these principles in all my affairs. Particularly was it imperative to work with others, as he had worked with me. Faith without works was dead, he said. And how appallingly true for the alcoholic! For if an alcoholic failed to perfect and enlarge his spiritual life through work and self sacrifice for others, he could not survive the certain trials and low spots ahead. If he did not work he would surely drink again, and if he drank he would surely die. Then faith would be dead indeed. With us it is just like that!

My wife and I abandoned ourselves with enthusiasm to the idea of helping other alcoholics to a solution of their problems. It was fortunate, for my old business associates remained skeptical for a year and a half, during which I found little work. I was not too well at the time, and was plagued by waves of self-pity and resentment. This sometimes nearly drove me back to drink. I soon found that when all other measures failed, work with another alcoholic would save the day. Many times I have gone to my old hospital feeling terribly. On talking to a man there, I would be amazingly lifted up and set on my feet. It is a design for living that works in the tough spots.

We commenced to make many fast friends and a fellowship has grown up among us of which it is a wonderful thing to feel a part. The joy of living we really have, even under pressure and difficulty. I have seen one hundred families set their feet in the path that really goes somewhere; have seen the most impossible domestic situations righted; feuds and bitterness of all sorts wiped out. I have seen men come out of asylums, and resume a vital place in

the lives of their families and communities. Business and professional people have regained their standing. There is scarce any form of human misadventure and misery which has not been overcome among us. In a Western city and its environs, there are sixty of us and our families. We often meet informally at our houses, so that newcomers may find what they seek. Gatherings of twenty to sixty are common. We are growing in numbers and power.

An alcoholic in his cups is an unlovely creature. Our struggles with them are variously strenuous, comic and tragic. One poor chap committed suicide in my home. He could not, or would not, see what we behold.

There is, however, a vast amount of fun about it all. I suppose some would be shocked at our seeming worldliness and levity. But just underneath one finds a deadly earnestness. God has to work twenty four hours a day in and through us, or we perish.

Most of us feel we need look no further for Utopia, nor even for Heaven. We have it with us on this good old Earth, right here and now. Each day that simple talk in my kitchen multiplies itself in a widening circle of peace on earth and good will to men.

Thomas Thacher's Introduction to "Victors Anonymous"

~No date, but likely June, 17 or 20, 1938~

Text from the original typed document (Stepping Stones: WGW/LBW 102.7, Box 25, Folder 30, Correspondence—General—"Letters to Us" 1938-1941 Friends/Associates)

Permission is required from the Stepping Stones Foundation for any further use, display, or duplication of the following material.

Dear Bill—This is a hurried suggestion along the lines we talked—The suggested title and signatures are merely thoughts that occurred and like the rest of the outline below may not fit the picture at all—Best to Lois.

Tom Thacher.

[this is hand-written in black ink along the top of the sheet]

ALCOHOLISM

"I have never seen one single case, in which alcohol-mindedness was established in the sense you have it, THAT EVER RECOVERED."

That statement addressed to one man, by an eminent physician, applies just as directly to several hundreds of thousands of our fellow citizens, and unfortunately will soon be applicable to a half million more that are fast succumbing to the ravages of alcohol.

INCURABLE

More than three years ago a hopeless alcoholic found a haven of self control. Starting from a man to man basis, using the approach and appeal of one alcoholic victim to another, a circle of self control and right living has multiplied.

To-day this circle numbers over 100 healthful, happy and capable citizens, that formerly in the clutches of alcohol, had been despaired of by their loved ones and friends.

ONE HUNDRED MEN have been returned to Society as useful members.

ONE HUNDRED FAMILIES of every FAITH and CREED are happily reunited.

ANONYMOUS

These men are bonded together in a common cause and for a common purpose—TO HELP THEIR FELLOW MAN.

By trial and error method, by combining their own experiences, reactions and appeals, by analyzing success and failure a definite procedure has been developed producing truly remarkable results.

These men have unselfishly given of their lives and resource, are daily making contribution and sacrifice, and with a simple Christian spirit are bringing back to worthwhile living those weaker human beings who have fallen by the wayside.

ONE HUNDRED MEN
by
VICTORS ANONYMOUS

[NOTE: here and in the three subsequent uses of the word "VICTORS," it has been written in by hand using block letters in black ink. This writing was done only after the word "ALCOHOLICS" had been erased in each of those cases.]

Each man is writing a brief outline of his life, experience, failure and the HOW and from WHENCE the spirit of righteous living was reborn in him.

The stories will be collated and edited, together with research as to the desease *[sic]* of alcoholism, the benefits of psychoanalysis and medical treatment, as the work of VICTORS ANONYMOUS.

An understanding of the desease *[sic]* of ALCOHOLISM is essential to every one touched in its path, a knowledge of this ILLNESS, its cause, treatment and cure is vital to wives, relatives, friends and employers.

PROGRAM

To perform the general work, to establish the right publicity contacts, to accomplish the necessary research, to combine and edit the story of these ONE HUNDRED CASES will require outside financial assistance.

There is a dire need for a volume of this kind, a composite story of the rehabilitation of one hundred men each written just as it occurred in his individual life.

Nothing like this has ever been done before—Writers and editors who have read parts of the work predict an earnest demand and sensational sale *[this last word written in by hand above this spot in the text]* for the book.

It is necessary to raise funds to finance the preparation and publication of this book and VICTORS ANONYMOUS seek the aid of men in sympathy with this aim, who will do a constructive part toward *[this last word written in by hand above this spot in the text]* the mental and physical deliverance of fellow human beings from their shame, inferiority and degradation.

The proceeds from the sale of this book will all be turned in to a FOUNDATION, administered by well known and responsible people, that will be dedicated to the perpetuation of SELF CONTROL and the RIGHT METHOD OF LIVING.

VICTORS ANONYMOUS.

Excuse the stereographic work please *[this is hand-written in black ink along the left edge of the sheet]*

[SIDE 2]:
[preprinted letterhead]:

THOMAS O. THACHER	7433
Investments	Telephone DIgby 4-7434
Thirty-Two Broadway	7435
New York	

Hank Parkhurst's Outline
for the Book

Text from the original typed document (Stepping Stones: AA 501.1, Box 13, Folder 16;
Publications—Alcoholics Anonymous [1939]—Outline of chapters)

Permission is required from the Stepping Stones Foundation for any further use,
display, or duplication of the following material.

CHAPTER ONE
Introduces Alcoholics Anonymous. There follows a description of ourselves, the
alcoholic problem and our solution. The chapter is general and casts a shadow of that
to follow.

Chapter Two.
Narrative One. An alcoholics life experience—How he found the answer.

Chapters Three to Ten, Inclusive.
The narrator of the first story introduces others, who will tell what they were like and
what they have found. Comments at end of each story emphasizing and analyzing
points.

Chapters Eleven to Fifteen, Inclusive.

These will contain groups of stories written by alcoholic men and women. Twenty cases or more will be covered with appropriate comment.

Chapter Sixteen.

Most of us were honest in being agnostic. This chapter is so directed.

Chapter Seventeen.

Testimony of a well known physician who has specialized a lifetime with alcoholics. At his hospital he has seen many of us recover whom he has pronounced incurable. It will also cover the problem in lay language from the medical and psychiatric point of view.

Chapter Eighteen.

Devoted to the vagaries of the alcoholic mind, bearing especially on mental and emotional states. Having observed each other under new conditions, we think our experiences will be of immense benefit to alcoholic readers. It will give the medical profession the intimate view of these mens minds they so much desire.

Chapter Nineteen.

Having secured the confidence of the alcoholic reader we tell him just what he can do about it. Detailed instructions for working out his situation with his priest, pastor, reader *[sic?]*, wife or best friend will be given. Our experience shows that a man can do this if he follows directions. Great numbers can be touched by the book in this fashion.

Chapter Twenty.

We observed that once an alcoholic has a spiritual experience he must throw himself into work for others. It is preferable that he work with other alcoholics for he can do things which no one else can do. This chapter will detail just how to help others and build up a new group of friends. This chapter will give a blind address, to which an alcoholic who has recovered, and is helping others, may write. When the correspondence indicates real results, we shall contact and draw them into fellowship.

Chapter Twenty One.

Dealing with wives, relative and friends, showing them how they may help.

Chapter Twenty Two.

Herein employers will be given the new view of alcoholism as it affects their interests. Many specific suggestions will be made, as to how in the best interest of all, the employer may handle the myriad situations which are so baffling to him at present.

Chapter Twenty Three.

We shall emphasize that we have no cure all. The sufferer must be willing to recover and cannot be too much handicapped by other great mental and nervous abnormalities. Our failures with many such types will be analyzed at length. We have learned more from our failures than our successes. This should be a valuable chapter for new men and women, that they may recognize their handicaps and may readily perceive the difficulties of those they seek to help.

Chapter Twenty Four.

This chapter will disclose our life as a group, our work as a group, our present situations, and our attitude toward the outside world of life and business. We shall show how our simple common denominator works in the every day world.

Chapter Twenty Five.

A chapter devoted to the potential alcoholic; that he and others may definitely recognize the symptoms before great consequences develop

Frank Amos's "History of the Alcoholics Movement . . ."

Text from the original typed document (GSO, Box 59, 1938, Folder B, First Two Chapters of the Proposed Book; Trust Indenture, Documents 1938-117 to 1938-124)

[handwritten in blue ink at top right of sheet]   8/19/38

History of the Alcoholics movement up to the formation of the Alcoholic Foundation on Aug. 11, 1938.

During December 1937, Mr. Wm. G. Wilson arranged an appointment, through a mutual friend Dr. L. V. Strong, with Mr. W. S. Richardson at 30 Rockefeller Plaza, New York City. To Mr. Richardson, Mr. Wilson told briefly the story of how, after many vain attempts to discontinue the use of alcohol, he had achieved what he believed was a permanent cure, through what he termed a religious or spiritual process.

Mr. Wilson's story was so sincere and was so convincing, that Mr. Richardson called in for a consultation, Mr. Albert L. Scott, Mr. A. Leroy Chipman, and Mr. Frank B. Amos. It was decided that a dinner conference would be held to which Mr. Wilson would bring a group of his ex-alcoholic friends who had had experiences similar to his, and after this dinner, these friends could tell more in detail of their experiences and the work they were endeavoring to do to help other alcoholics who, like themselves, were apparently incurable medically or through any other known methods of treating alcoholics.

This meeting was held in December 1937. Present at it, aside from Messrs. Scott, Richardson, Chipman, and Amos, were two other non-alcoholics, Dr. W. D. Silkworth and Dr. L. V. Strong, and the following ex-alcoholics, Wm. G. Wilson, Henry G. Parkhurst, Wm. J. Ruddell, Ned Pointer and Joe Taylor, all of New York and vicinity; Mr. J. H. F. Mayo of near Baltimore, Md; Dr. Robert H. Smith and J. Paul Stanley of Akron, Ohio.

The conference, held in the board room on the 56th floor at 30 Rockefeller Plaza, New York City, lasted five hours, and during it the experiences of some of the ex-alcoholics were told. Dr. Silkworth, Psychiatrist at Charles B. Towns Hospital, New York which is rated as a leading hospital in this country for the treatment of alcoholics, made the statement that he had treated a number of these ex-alcoholics present, some of them several times, and that not one of them, in his opinion, could have been permanently cured by any means known to medical

Page 2

science or to Psychiatry. He went on to state without reservation that while he could not tell what it was that these men had which had effected their "cure," yet he was convinced they were cured and that whatever it was, it had his complete endorsement. He stated that alcoholism is, medically, an incurable disease. These statements from an outstanding Psychiatrist and a leading authority on the treatment of alcoholism, made a profound impression upon the non-alcoholics present.

Immediately following this meeting, Mr. Amos brought to the attention of Mr. Wilson a friend of Mr. Amos's who had graduated from the same college, and who appeared to be a hopeless alcoholic in a desperate condition from every viewpoint. Mr. Wilson's reply was that almost every person, at all active in life, either had a relative or a friend in such a condition, and that he would be very glad to talk to Mr. Amos's friend and start work with him, providing this friend was willing. A meeting was arranged and within a two weeks [sic] period, this friend accepted without reservation the principles of the "cure" by a religious or spiritual approach. Over eight months have elapsed since that time, and there is every evidence that this party is permanently cured, although it is the policy of these ex-alcoholics through their own experience in working with other alcoholics, not to accept any alcoholic as permanently cured until a considerable period of time has elapsed. That period usually ranges from two to three years. The present leaders of the movement, all of them ex-alcoholics, have been teetotalers for periods ranging from two to four years.

The methods and the approach used are practical and spiritual but are not in accordance with any hard and fast dogma or rule of thumb procedure. It is not the purpose here to outline the varied methods employed, or the basic principles of this "cure." This will all appear in the stories of a large number of these ex-alcoholics which are now being written, and it is hoped will be published in book form for general distribution in the summer of 1939.

Following the meeting of the fourteen gentlemen in Rockefeller Plaza, Messrs. Scott, Richardson, Chipman and Amos, met in consultation to try to

Page 3

determine what steps, if any, could be taken to help this movement. It had been stressed by the leaders that commercialization of this movement must, at all hazards, be avoided. Furthermore, they believed that early publicity would be ruinous. It had been estimated that there are probably a million people in the United States who either are incurable alcoholics, or who are rapidly approaching that condition. It was obvious that too much publicity early in the development of the movement would result in the few present workers being swamped with requests from relatives and friends, and from alcoholics themselves, and as a consequence, the whole movement probably would bog down.

It was pointed out also that a great many elements entered into the successful carrying on of this work. Alcoholics who were reasonably normal mentally in other ways, and who genuinely wanted to be cured of their alcoholism, were the type with whom they had achieved their greatest success. On the other hand, alcoholics who were mentally defective, or who were definitely psycopathic [sic], had proven very difficult problems, and so far the percentage of 'cures' had been very low among these cases.

Therefore, any steps taken were to be weighed very carefully, and it was believed progress should be slow and just as sure as possible.

The members of this self styled Alcoholic Squad emphasized that they did not want this movement connected directly or indirectly with any religious organization or cult. They strongly stressed the fact that they had no connection whatever with any so-called orthodox religious denomination, or with the Oxford Movement [sic], or with Christian Science or any other organized movement. It is interesting to note that among the present group of some 110 ex-alcoholics, there are those who thought they were atheists, others had various religious backgrounds—Christian Science, Catholic, Episcopal, Lutheran, Methodist, Presbyterian, Baptist, etc.

It was also emphasized that these ex-alcoholics were in no way, shape or form attempting to practice medicine. They were, when possible, cooperating with physicians and psychiatrists. Any practicing physician, who had been an alcoholic,

Page 4

could of course use his medical knowledge to advantage.

At the meeting of the fourteen in December, Mr. Scott who by common consent was presiding, requested the ex-alcoholics present to state what, if any, ideas they had as to the assistance the non-alcoholics present could render.

The unusual situation at Akron, Ohio was then brought to light. Mr. Wm. G. Wilson, who initiated this movement, had, early in the period of his own emancipation, visited

Akron on business, where it was necessary for him to remain several weeks. Following out one of the principles of what might be termed the "technique of remaining cured," Mr. Wilson immediately endeavored to get acquainted with one or more individuals who, like himself in previous experiences, were suffering from what appeared to be incurable alcoholism. Through his inquiries, he was directed to Dr. Robert H. Smith, a prominent Proctologist, (Rectal Surgeon) of Akron. For many years Dr. Smith had been an alcoholic, and his situation was growing so bad, that his practice, despite his high professional standing and expert surgical ability, had just about been destroyed. Not only had Dr. Smith tried every medical aid available, but he had earnestly studied every religious angle known to him, to his family, and to his closest friends, but without success. His religious studies however had prepared him completely for Mr. Wilson's approach, and within a short time, not only did he accept this spiritual method of eliminating the alcoholic disease, but within a short time became a leader of an ex-alcoholic group which now numbers over seventy who, it is believed, are permanently cured. Nearly all of these seventy ex-alcoholics live in Akron or Cleveland, or within a short distance from those cities.

Dr. Smith had plunged into this work so earnestly, and the general business conditions in the Akron section were so bad, that it was obvious that he could not both continue his work leading the alcoholic group in the eastern Ohio section and at the same time build up his practice in Proctology to the point where he could make even a bare living.

Messrs. Scott, Richardson, Chipman and Amos, in discussing these reports

Page 5

decided to ask Mr. Amos to visit Akron and make a careful survey of the situation there. Mr. Amos's expenses were financed by the other three. This trip was made about the 1st of February, 1938. In Akron Mr. Amos consulted with the Chairman of the Board of Trustees of the Akron city Hospital, of which Dr. Smith was a staff member, with outstanding physicians, business men, lawyers,, and religious leaders. Without exception, Dr. Smith's professional and personal standing was affirmed as of the best. The marvelous work that he and his associates were doing was gradually becoming known and was meeting with approval. His leadership of the Akron work at this time and for some time to come was universally regarded as vital to the continued success of the movement.

The Akron alcoholics group was holding meetings weekly in the home of a friend. These meetings were attended by the alcoholics themselves, and members of their families. "Prospects" were invited whenever, in the opinion of the workers, they were of the type that could be helped.

In many respects these meetings have taken on the form of the meetings described in the Gospels of the early christians [sic] during the first century, but they have avoided some of the methods used by the Oxford Movement [sic] which, particularly with this class of people, had proved a handicap. Mr. Amos was invited to attend such a meeting, at which there were between fifty and sixty present.

The total result of this three day survey made by Mr. Amos at Akron caused him to report on his return that a work was being done there which was little short of miraculous, and which deserved financial support if it was to be continued, under Dr. Smith's leadership. This report was accepted by the other three, (Messrs. Scott, Richardson and Chipman), and as a result a contribution was received sufficient to bolster the work at Akron until May 1st, 1939. This appeared for the time being to take care of only the minimum needs of the Akron situation.

In the meantime, it daily became more clear that the situation in Metropolitan New York, in Maryland, in Washington D. C. and elsewhere on the eastern coast, likewise required financial support. Meetings being held weekly in

Page 6

various homes, several of which Mr. and Mrs. Amos attended. The time, effort and strength taken in visiting hospitals, meeting new "prospects," and thus endeavoring to save human lives from the oblivion of alcoholism, made it impossible for particularly three of the leaders to give any attention to speak of to a remunerative profession or business. The three men who had been most active in promoting the work backed strongly by a much larger group, were and are Wm. G. Wilson, Henry G. Parkhurst, and J. H. Fitzhugh Mayo. Mr. Wilson and Mr. Parkhurst had been very successful business men; Mr. Mayo a farmer and salesman. Through their alcoholism, they had lost practically all of their holdings, and had been thrown out of their professional and business circles. All of them staged a comeback, and it was quite evident that if they concentrated their attention exclusively on professional and business activity, they could soon be self supporting. But the need for their services in promoting this work among alcoholics, and the increasing successes which they were achieving, made it seem almost imperative for them, at this period at least, to give up remunerative work necessary to provide financially for their families even the minimum requirements. The only alternative appeared to provide financial support for them, at least the minimum amount.

In addition to this, while most of the alcoholics who had been rehabilitated through these methods and ministrations were men of exceptional ability, and had been good money makers, yet, because of their alcoholism the large majority of them had become destitute financially, it became quite evident that some of these men must have financial help while they were recovering and gradually getting back on their feet in a business way.

Most of the financial help as has been given so far, has come from the meager funds of other alcoholics, provided at great sacrifice. In some cases it was only natural that this might cause complication in the families of some of the alcoholics and develop one of the serious elements which might cause a breakdown in morale and spiritual power, and thus result in a return to the hopeless alcoholic state.

Through the efforts, particularly of Messrs. Wilson and Parkhurst, small sums of money have been secured by gifts and loans from outside sources, and plans were made in the Spring of 1938 to start a definite campaign among people who it was believed would be interested in this movement, and who would be able to contribute toward it.

It was decided also that steps should be taken toward the publishing of a book which would serve as a textbook for those seeking rehabilitation through this religious and spiritual approach. The net profits from the sale of this book would go into the alcoholic fund.

To accomplish both of these objectives, and with the long range view in mind of carrying on whatever was necessary and wise to promote this cause, it was decided to form an unincorporated, non-profit, non-sectarian, charitable organization under the laws of the State of New York, which would have general supervision of this work, and to which contributions could be made, which contributions would be accepted by the Federal and State governments as legal, income tax exemptions.

Mr. John E. F. Wood an Attorney on the staff of Root, Clark, Buckner & Ballantine, Attorneys of New York City, who had knowledge of this movement and sympathy for it, was approached and requested to give legal advice. Upon his advice, after thorough consultation with various of the ex-alcoholics and with interested parties mentioned above, it was decided to form what is known as a Trust. Mr. Wood drew up the Trust Indenture in legal form, and it became effective when signed by the following as Trustees: Williard [sic] S. Richardson, Frank B. Amos, John E. F. Wood, Wm. J. Ruddell and Robert E. [sic] Smith.

Appended to this historical statement is a document containing a tentative outline by chapters of the proposed book to be published by Alcoholics Anonymous. With it appears the statement of what has been done, how this work has been undertaken and how it may be promoted.

The first two chapters of the proposed book are also given. Chapter #1 headed, "There is a Solution," and Chapter #2, the very gripping story of Wm. G.

Wilson, which story is substantially the same as that which was told to Mr. Richardson in December 1937.

0

------------------- ----------------------

0

Prepared by
Frank B. Amos
[both lines in black ink and Frank Amos's characteristic florid hand]

Bill Wilson's "Sheep and Goats" Letter

*Text from the original typed document (GSO, Box 59, 1938, Folder B[1], Documents 1938-145 to 1938-151). [**NOTE**: These pages should have been numbered 1938-147 to 1938-153 but have been incorrectly numbered—duplicating the two numbers used to identify the previous document]*

[printed letterhead with penciled cross out of the top line and typed "xx" for the street address on the second line.]

~~Henry G. Parkhurst, Inc.~~
~~Eleven Hill Street~~—Newark, New Jersey
17 William Street

Sept. 26, 1938

Mr. Frank Amos,

570 Lexington Ave.,
New York City.

Dear Frank:

Pursuant to your suggestions, I am outlining the position with reference our alcoholic work, of Fitz Mayo, Hank Parkhurst, and myself.

So far as I can see, we three have "Sold all our sheep and goats."

Fitz Mayo has gradually liquidated his live stock, equipment and farm. His house only is left. His wife's income has dropped from a living competence to about $500.00 a year. He is also in debt to his sister. I don't know the amount. Two children are in boarding school. The third is diabetic and requires much medical care. This means that Fitz is in way over his head, for he has no income of his own at all. So he must now secure employment, or else be enabled to continue alcoholic work on a basis that would carry him along.

There are two possibilities that he can go on with his alcoholic work. One is that The Alcoholic Foundation supply him funds. The other concerns a group of Washington business men who are considering setting up a community house and farm for alcoholic rehabilitation. They seem seriously inclined, but at the moment their leader is ill. It is unlikely they can consider the matter before October 15th. There is better than a good chance this will solve Fitz's problem. Failing these sources of income he may be lost to us so far as much alcoholic work is concerned. When our book comes out we shall surely need man power of his kind. He can scrape by for a while on $200.00 a month, but will need more eventually.

Hank Parkhurst's situation is this. Two years ago I raised some money which set him up on business at Newark, N.J. "The best laid plans o' mice and men gang aft agley!" So did ours. The business resulting supports only its four salesmen, two of these being ex-alcoholics. It does not support Hank or me, nor does it carry our office and secretary since the slump of last year. Hence Hank has no income and is running into debt at an alarming rate. He is at least two thousand dollars in the hole now.

Business sense dictated we close the Newark office several months ago, or that Hank make a salary connection with an oil company in that area, this company to carry his office expense as part of the agency. I talked him out of that, feeling that his services and perhaps these very office facilities, were going to be badly needed in the alcoholic work, which would obviously expand so much on publication of our book.

Without someone like him I would be left to gather the material, to write the book, and to look after the publicity and distribution of the volume, pretty much alone. There is no one in our crowd who has been sober long enough, has the business capacity and energy, and would be available, save Hank.

[page 2 with headers:]

Mr. Amos   Page 2.

But that would be nothing, compared with the labor entailed by the huge volume of inquires and pleas for assistance which will surely descend upon us when the book is out. The situation would be chaotic. The work would assuredly suffer. It now costs about $600.00 per month to carry Hank, the office, and a secretary who is highly competent and already thoroughly understands our alcoholic work. If money is available I am in favor of continuing this arrangement, though three thousand dollars may be spent before the office is of maximum usefulness. This does not mean that the plant is idle, meanwhile. Hank is now doing a great deal for our effort to raise money, to prepare the publicity, and in the general work, where he is most effective with business men of his own type. In Montclair where he lives, three men of this description came to his attention only yesterday through his family physician. The office is now useful to me because I am dictating the book there and looking after an ever increasing correspondence.

We shall have to have an office in a few months anyhow, and if this one is liquidated, it will cost two thousand dollars to duplicate the equipment and furnishings we now possess. Therefore the net cost, viewed in this light, of carrying Hank and these facilities for five months, would be only one thousand dollars. Last, but not least, if we decide to publish and promote the sale of our own book, Hank's services will be invaluable, for we have no one else of his experience and energy. These are the reasons why I have been making every effort to keep Hank in our active picture.

To maintain the status quo we have both borrowed too much and have run up far too many bills. To go deeper into our creditors would be grossly unfair to them.

My own picture is as follows. Last fall, following the market collapse, my Wall Street income stopped. I have since been made Director of a promising company in the midwest, the Pierce Governor Company. Director's fees are nominal, though I may at a later time make some money out of this connection. As the company is a substantial one, I might be able to secure a position with them, but that would require so much travel that book writing would be out of the question. Despite the slump there, it is possible I could make a connection in Wall Street, for I once more enjoy the confidence of people in that business. But if steadily employed, it is evident I could do little for our alcoholic situation in the sense it now demands attention.

During the past year, so that I could keep on and have a free hand with this work, I have gone fifteen hundred dollars into debt. I have given my personal notes for twelve hundred dollars. This money was shared with Hank and Fitz. Contributions amounting to fifteen hundred dollars were secured from Mr. Charles B. Towns. This money was likewise divided among the three of us and has all been spent.

Nevertheless I feel duty bound to get the book out, for men everywhere are entitled to know what we know as soon as we can get the information to them. Considered in this light my personal inconvenience does not matter much. The sole question with us is: What is best for His work? In the past year we have tried hard to keep that thought before us. Which brings me to a discussion of our relations with Mr. Towns.

About a year ago, before we met you gentlemen, Mr. Towns asked me to join forces with him. It was a logical move, for hospitalization is vital to our work. We knew from personal experience that his treatment is of the best and worth the money he asks. We were satisfied he ran an ethical and honest

[page 3 with headers:]

Mr. Amos   Page 3.

establishment. At that time our work had been going on at his hospital for three years. In spite of some early skepticism, both he and Dr. Silkworth had been most kind and considerate. Therefore we could consistently recommend the place to any alcoholic.

It was plain as a pikestaff that if we permitted Mr. Towns to publicize what had happened even in a modest and perfectly ethical manner, his place would soon be overflowing. That meant that its monthly income would increase maybe five thousand dollars. And perhaps more by now for his has additional floor space easily available.

That might have solved our money problem. It would have launched us upon a venture which should have provided ample funds and increasing income. I think Mr. Towns would not have hesitated to take us into partnership. Almost any sanitarium proprietor would be glad to do so. It is obvious that the results we are getting would fill several places like Towns could it honestly be said that many of the patients really got well. It is certain that if we permitted even discreet publicity, we couldgreatly *[sic]* increase Mr. Towns income at any time. I strongly feel, when the time is right, that income arising from our interests in such places will make The Alcoholic Foundation self supporting. But hasty commitments of this sort, entered into before the public fully understands us, might prove harmful.

So the situation last fall was that Mr. Towns desired more patients and we badly needed money. It was clear even then, however, that Mr. Towns had a genuine personal interest in what we were doing and was prepared to help us in every possible way, whether he got any money return or not. He is a man who really likes to help people. What he has since done confirms that opinion of him.

We did not go along with Mr. Towns at that time because we felt there was a better way. We did not want any man's chance of finding his God and getting over his alcoholism prejudiced by accusations, however ill-founded, that we were too commercial. On this point we have been bending over backward ever since and I am very glad we have. But our financial backs have been broken with the bending!

Nevertheless, I am still of the view that the <u>very</u> best interests of our work demand that we carry it on independently as possible of money considerations. This is especially true at present for we are about to bring our situation to the attention of the general public. It would be disadvantageous to to [sic] [be] obliged to make this appearance with our hands extended for money. Racketeering has been so prevalent in the alcoholic field that some alcoholics and their families would be skeptical of a message which purports to be free as the air, yet seeks contributions, or recommends places of treatment. The fact that our approach is a religious one might give those having anti-religious sentiments an opportunity to air their disbelief in us were we too aggressive about money.

Were we as well known as the Red Cross these things would not be true. But to some extent it is self evident that we shall handicap our progress if we try to become self supporting or openly solicit the public at this time.

For the present an ideal arrangement would be for us to have access to adequate funds given by understanding people, quietly and without expectation of personal publicity or reward. Such contributions ought not to commit us to or identify us with any person or institution. To become publicly identified or committed in any quarter would be to arouse needless prejudice somewhere. This

[page 4 with headers:]

Mr. Amos   Page 4.

might prevent some alcoholics from adopting our solution. Some might die because we had launched this project in a short sighted fashion. I have been discussing an ideal set up but perhaps we cannot have that. It may be better to compromise or do with less in the best interests of the men we are trying to reach.

We could well use thirty thousand dollars during the coming year to place the knowledge of our solution in every home and to follow up this initial step. It will be unfortunate if we bring out a book which is sure to create a huge demand for help, at least by correspondence, and then be totally unprepared to take care of the situation. Though the book alone will undoubtedly do much good, it will fall short of this objective if publication finds us without men or money to carry it through. It is imperative we be ready. This is no time to bog down. The next six months are critical. The general work ought to be pushed and a foundation built that will withstand the pressure which is inevitably coming.

It is inconceivable to us, when we observe the amounts of money raised for other purposes, that we cannot quite readily secure adequate funds to carry forward a work of the probable importance of this one.

This ought to be especially true when it is considered that we aim at eventual self support. [Note: the underlining is by hand in dark blue ink.]

But it has not been as easy as it looked to Hank, Fitz, and myself. We have been trying to raise money for two months, and I am rather ashamed to say that outside of Mr. Towns generous contributions, we have not secured a red cent. Obviously, we have not yet discovered how to go about it. Though it is mainly our responsibility, we have not begun to discharge it. We simply have not reached the right people in the right way. Upon this point we badly need some new ideas.

As there are no funds yet in sight to carry the work upon the ideal basis we would like, we are plainly faced with the question as to whether we should go ahead on something less than an ideal basis. Or shall we stick to our vision of the ideal yet accomplish little or nothing for lack of money.

For example, we could let the status of the work revert to where it was a year ago. Those of us now active could go back to business. In that event we might continue to grow at such a rate that perhaps several hundred more men would be reached over the next few years. But what shall we say of the many thousand who might pass out of the picture just because we failed to let them know? May they not be obliged to suffer because we are now too timid, too conservative, or too fearful of what people may say?

And again, the great risk of the laissez faire course is that we might be at any time subjected to undesirable publicity. It might be of a sort which would irrevocably distort our situation in the public mind. In this fashion, a damaging and chaotic situation can arise at any minute. Does it not seem imperative we take the opportunity, while there is still time, to tell our story first? Would it not be infinitely better for us to publicly state our case and ask the public point blank for funds than to have the whole thing garbled because of our inactivity or timidity. *[sic—no question mark]* At least the truth would be told. In the long run that should hurt no one.

Even under these less than ideal conditions, many alcoholics would see

[page 5 with headers:]

Mr. Amos   Page 5.

that we were telling the truth. The truth would surely make some of them well. I should dislike starting off in this fashion, but does it not seem likely that more good would result than could possibly come out of a policy of drifting? Would we not more nearly approximate the main idea which is to effectively get our message to those who need it as rapidly as possible?

Assuming that the Trustees, by private contribution, think it unlikely we can take care of the situation, should we not consider other means?

The New York Herald Tribune, for example, seems willing to carry an article descriptive of our work, which would guardedly disclose our need for funds. I refer to their Sunday Magazine called "This Week." This section of the Tribune is widely syndicated. It has a weekly circulation of seven millions. Perhaps it would bring our work to the attention of several hundred thousand families where the alcoholic problem exists. The managing editor of "This Week" thinks that twenty thousand of them would get in touch with us. We could offer these families, say five of the vital chapter of our book in photo-lithographic form. We could frankly let them know about our finances and the necessity for money to publish the book and take care of this aftermath. We could ask them one dollar for these chapters, which is the price of a pint of cheap whiskey. Some of them would be skeptical and keep on buying the whiskey instead of the chapters, but perhaps thousands of homes would request this material. The chapters themselves should speak for our good intentions and allay any suspicion that we are primarily in the book business. I feel that numbers of men might get well on this basis alone. At least a spiritual beginning would be made in many homes. A demand for the entire book would be created among the very people who need it most. In a modest way our work and its needs would be brought to public attention. People disposed to make contributions might get in touch with us. Hope would be brought at an early date to homes where there is now none. Admittedly, this is not the best possible approach, but would it not be better than to drift? Frankly, I don't know. We would much like the advice of the Trustees on this point.

Though such a program would surely bring in some funds, there might not be enough profit to carry us until the book is out. In this connection it may be that we can get Mr. Towns to take care of whatever deficit there is. Among those making inquiry there might be many to whom we could properly recommend the Towns treatment, for it has distinct advantages over ordinary hospitalization. Moreover, such men coming into Towns could be brought into contact with the New York fellowship. This would be beneficial, for the men here are not getting enough personal work to do. We could easily handle ten new cases a week here in New York on the spare time of our group. It may be objected this would put us under too much obligation to Mr. Towns. So it might, though we are sure he would never take advantage of us. Yet, we would want to do all we honestly could for him. Certainly this is not a perfect program, but assuming we could carry it out, would it not be better than to drift and run the risks of so doing? Again, I am not sure. What do the Trustees think?

Still another course can be pursued. That would be for me to concentrate entirely on the book, letting Fitz, and Hank, and the office drop out of active participation. They have indicated their willingness to do the thing this way if it appears best. They think the book should be brought out whatever happens.

Should the Trustees decide the book is all that can be handled for the present, the question still remains as to how I shall live and pay the necessary incidental expenses. These expenses, allowing myself two hundred and fifty dollars a month to cover everything, will amount to fifteen hundred dollars for six months,

[page 6 with headers:]

Mr. Amos   Page 6.

though I am hopeful of doing the work in less time. I am reluctant to borrow any more money, as it would not be right to prejudice my present creditors to such an extent. It may be The Alcoholic Foundation will receive enough contributions to carry me. If this does not happen, there are other possibilities. I might raise money on a few personal belongings and ask members of our group to contribute small sums. If it comes down to that, we can get the book done by this means. The only certainty of funds in this connection is Mr. Towns. I think he is willing to finance the completion of the book, if no other way can be found. This situation is a bit urgent as I have no funds at the present time.

To sum up then; It seems doubtful whether the status quo of all three of us can be maintained during the month of October for less than one thousand dollars. That would be six hundred to Hank and the office, two hundred to Fitz and two hundred to me. Perhaps Fitz can get through October without any more money, though he could certainly use it. In any event he will be flat on November first, unless the Washington business men pick up the load.

With the forgoing in mind, does it not seem proper that the Trustees consider and perhaps come to some conclusion at their next meeting on the following questions:

1. Assuming that contributions can be obtained, should the Foundation attempt to maintain the three of us in active work for, let us say, six months?

2. Should the Trustees decide that status quo should be maintained, how are we going to do that for the month of October?

3. Do the Trustees think there is a real liklehood *[sic]* that we can maintain the status quo ($1,000.00 a month) for six months on the basis of private contributions only?

4. In the event the Trustees think it improbable we can maintain the status quo for six months by private contribution, what is their pleasure with respect to the proposal we augment our income through the Herald Tribune publicity, the sale of book chapters, and perhaps a closer working arrangement with Mr. Towns?

5. If the Trustees think it impossible or undesirable to maintain the status quo by any of the foregoing methods, what do they think of the proposal that I continue alone on the book?

6. If it is decided I continue on the book, what is their advice as to how I should be financed? Should I immediately commit myself to Mr. Towns or not?

I have been reluctant to discuss our personal situations at such length, but feel that the Trustees should have all of the facts before them. Though I have expressed some personal views, I would like to make it clear I shall not be at all disturbed if they are vetoed. Hank and Fitz and I are sensible that our thinking, at this time of financial embarrassment, may be warped. We would like the Trustees to help us guard against this possibility. We must, at all costs, avoid being

[page 7 with headers:]

Mr. Amos   Page 7.

driven into arrangements we might later regret.

Though we are grateful we have you gentlemen to go to, we do not want to cast too much responsibility on the shoulders of our ever-willing Trustees.

Let us say once more how much we appreciate the time and devotion which you Frank, Mr. Richardson, Mr. Chipman, Mr. Scott, and Mr. Wood have given this undertaking. Please do not take our problems too seriously.

After all, God has a way of working things out if we are willing to be used as He would like.

Sincerely yours,

William G. Wilson

WGW:RH

APPENDIX VIII

Hank Parkhurst's Proposed Q&A Chapter

Text from the re-typed document (GSO, Box 59, 1939, Folder C, Documents 1939-11 to 1939-25) with no date indicated.

NOTE: *The [bracketed italicized numbers] following each question do **not** appear in the original document. They are used here only as a convenience for any reference to their location within the Q&A chapter.*

A QUESTION AND ANSWER SECTION HAS BEEN PROPOSED
FOR THE BOOK

As follows ------- Any Suggestions?

What is your answer when asked to have a drink? *[1]*
On the first invitation I refuse. If there is insistence I explain I cannot handle it and a drink would eventually lead to a bender. If the party is interested, I explain I am one of the unfortunate people whom alcohol seems to poison much in the way certain pollens poison hay fever sufferers.

What are people's reaction when you explain you are an alcoholic? *[2]*
I have never seen it fail to arouse sympathetic interest and respect for meeting the question honestly.

How long since you had a drink? *[3]*
Three and a half years.

Don't you ever desire a drink? *[4]*
Of course, Seldom a day passes when I do not wish I could drink.

Do all alcoholics who have used this method with *[sic]* **they could drink?**
[5]
No. The desire to drink seems to be taken away instantaneously in some cases. Others lose it after a period of months.

What is there about liquor or the use of it you still desire? *[6]*
I miss the glow of well-being which comes from two or three drinks; the instant removal of tiredness or worries.

How then do you account for not drinking when you admit you miss those things? *[7]*
I believe some power outside of me has straightened my thinking in regard to the inevitable results of one drink.

Were the inevitable results of one drink pointed out to you before? *[8]*
Yes. A Psychiatrist in whom I had the greatest confidence labored far beyond his fees to prove to me the consequences of a single drink. This worked in some cases, but was useless when certain crises arose.

Have you met similar crises during the period of sobriety? *[9]*
Yes and worse. Two in particular have been worse than,

[Page 2]

[page header] 2.

or as bad as, any which caused me to drink before.

Did any of your friends, who are members of Alcoholics Anonymous, drink again? *[10]*
Yes. Many of them have had what we call slips.

What do you think causes slips? *[11]*
There are so many things, it is hard to define. Generally, I believe the man has been missing some of the more important points such as passing this on to another alcoholic, not putting first things first, dishonesty with self or others, not joining in the fellowship , getting angry at people or conditions, boredom, etc.

What do you mean by stating a man should pass this on to another alcoholic? *[12]*

This solution came to me for nothing. Every time I pass it on, I have done some good for another alcoholic and increased my own chances of not drinking.

Where would a man find people to pass this on to? *[13]*

Hospitals, Doctors, Priests, Ministers, Psychiatrists, etc. When people realize I am not interested in financial return, they generally cooperate.

How does dishonesty cause slips? *[14]*

Sometimes dishonesty sets up another cycle of shrinking from things which eventually leads to the desire to excape *[sic]* through drink.

What do you mean by putting "first things first"? *[NOTE: quotation marks added by hand.]* *[15]*

If a man is suffering from an incurable disease, I claim the first and most important for him is to do everything possible to recover from that disease. If a man is suffering from alcoholism, I believe the most important thing to him should be his recovery from his malady. In other words, first things first. Recovery should come before a job and everything else, for if the man does not recover, he will have no job or anything else anyway, An alcoholic is generally inclined to forget that he has spent many years getting into his present condition and is impatient for all difficulties to clear up immediately.

Why would not joining the fellowship cause slips? *[16]*

The best percentage of success has been obtained in localities where a meeting is held and a crowd of Alcoholics Anonymous gather for a good time and fellowship

[Page 3]

[page header]   3.

about one evening a week. Where men consistently pass up this fellowship on the basis of being tired or busy, I have noticed they are generally in danger of a slip.

Why would anger at people or conditions cause slips? *[17]*

When a man is griped at things, conditions, or people, he gets into a state of mind which separates him from the power that keeps him sober.

What are the results if an individual does slip? *[18]*

If a man sincerely wants to get well, I believe he will pick himself up and try to analyze the reason for the slip and carry on. The experience of the slip will undoubtedly help him to be stronger in the future. Generally, I believe a slip proves to a man irrevocably that he is an alcoholic and cannot handle liquor. In only one case have we seen such a case of discouragement result from a slip that the man simply continued drinking.

You speak at length of slips, it would appear that slips are common. Is that so? *[19]*

I would estimate that fifty percent who have accepted our method, have had no slips, and that everyone who has been sincere in their desire to recover has been so much better there is no comparison, even though they have slipped.

Why does boredom cause slips? *[20]*

To be brutally frank, I believe the man who gets plastered because he has become bored is generally a snob. He thinks he is a little better than the people whom he contacts and so he gets bored. While I do not claim that everyone in the fellowship must like every other person, I do believe that if a person sincerely searches for admirable qualities in other people, he will be able to find them. If a man really tries to help another person or persons, I believe life becomes so interesting he has no time to be bored.

How do you avoid criticizing people who may be wrong, and being wrong somehow hurting you? *[21]*

I ask myself—where am I wrong in this situation? If I examine the situation hard enough I find that I am at least somewhat to blame. It does not matter what percentage of blame is mine.; the fact that I am at least partially to blame tells me I must right this before I can afford to criticize another. This is an exceptionally hard attitude to reach and after three and half years, I have only partially learned it.

[Page 4]

[page header]   4.

Does not that attitude of placing yourself in the wrong tend to make you dishonestly submissive? *[22]*

Plain human nature will take care of seeing that I do not become a Casper Milquetoast. I look on this attitude as something like a brake which will not allow me to come to a full stop, but will keep me from lashing out and piling another wrong on top of the original wrong.

Does not this whole teaching tend to make you more introvertive? *[sic]* *[23]*

With the fellowship which has been built up of men who have suffered from the same malady as I, with the necessity of passing this along, I cannot become more introvertive *[sic]*, I believe this tends to make me more of an extrovert.

Are you not afraid that continuous repression of your alcoholism will result in one tremendous bust? *[24]*

Maybe it will, but so what? I have had three and a half years of sobriety which is a lifetime record for my adulthood. However, I have noticed that when one of our number has a big slip, he comes back stronger than ever.

If this works so well with alcoholics why would it not work with other who are in trouble? *[25]*

Undoubtedly it would. We see many of our families use the same approach to reach a happier way of existence.

If it could be successfully applied in other ways, whoy *[strikeout and y are hand written]* **do you limit your work to alcoholics and those close to alcoholics?** *[26]*

There are several reasons. Because of the things I have done, I am particularly able to interest alcoholics. Second, I am not a part, or trying to be a part of any religious movement. Third, one of the strongest things to me is the fellowship which has been built among men who have a common problem. Fourth, and most important to me, is the fact that working with alcoholics gives focus to my work and does not spread or diffuse it.

Did your drinking result in marital difficulties? *[27]*

Yes. My home was broken up.

Did this solution cure your marital difficulties? *[28]*

No, but it did give me a greater and more clearly defined picture of those difficulties. I have the feeling that whatever is right is bound to work out providing I can keep

[Page 5]

myself in the right frame of mind. I spent twenty years scrambling my marriage and making a mess of my life. I cannot expect immediate solution of all of my difficulties. However, my whole situation is less complicated today.

Have your financial problems been solved since your recovery? *[29]*
Most certainly not. I spent twenty years involving myself in all kind of difficulties with the help of alcohol. The only thing I can claim is that if I had gone on drinking, my financial difficulties would have been much worse today. You might call that a negative gain.

If your difficulties have not been solved, are you not inclined to think the way you are living is not worth while? *[30]*
Not at all. It is the first things first with me. I feel positive that if I go along doing the best I can and keeping myself in the right frame of mind, I will be rewarded exactly to the extent which I deserve. And when I do get those things I deserve, I will know they are not based on petty politics, pull or dishonest acts which are bound to come back later and smack me down.

Have you ever nearly slipped? *[31]*
Yes. Several times.

How did you escape? *[32]*
The first time I phoned one of the other alcoholics and told him I was afraid I was going to take a drink. He asked if I would wait until he got out to the house, and I agreed. When he arrived we talked over the desire and the things which were bothering me and strangely, the desire left me. Another time, I called one of the gang and he suggested reading the Bible and praying before I took the first drink. I never took that drink. The third time, I made careful plans and then simply told one of the bunch I was going to. Instead of getting all excited, he simply said, "So what. Go ahead and have a couple for me." I took a nap and when I woke up I could laugh at it, the desire was gone. Another time when in the biggest crisis of my life, which previously would undoubtedly have cause me to drink, I got to work helping others before the desire even had a chance to start to bother me.

[Page 6]

[page header] 6.

I understand that most alcoholics get into sexual messes. Is that true? *[33]*
Yes.

What is your attitude about possible future sexual troubles? *[34]*

If you are speaking of unfaithfulness, I feel the same way about that as I do about liquor. I am taking no stand on this question. I can only say I hope I will not get mixed up in any such difficulties. On the other hand, I have seen married men nearly thrown into an alcoholic slip by a sexual mix-up and the soundest advice I have heard given was, "you are terribly upset because you have been trying to live in the perfection of Jesus Christ and now that you find you are not as perfect as He was, are you going to add more troubles, such as drinking will bring? Or are you going to pick yourself up and be better in the future? Not better as the world sees it, but better as your vision of yourself sees it?"

How important is the fellowship? *[35]*

I think it is one of the most important elements. It allows newcomers to look us over, it allows the members of the fellowship to discuss their problems with others who have had similar problems. Many men get away from the weekly meetings, haven't time for one reason or another, and in most cases, I notice they have an eventual slip.

What are these weekly meetings? *[36]*

I am only familiar with them in three localities. At one of these, members who are interested decide who is to lead the meeting after the group gathers. He leads the group in the Lord's Prayer and then asks different ones to tell their stories. The meeting is closed with the Lord's Prayer. In the other two localities, the meeting is generally just a social get-together where the gang sits around and talks, sometimes in a large circle, sometimes in small groups. Occasionally this evolves into a meeting where some members tell their stories.

Why do you tell your story? *[37]*

I know my own story and when I am asked to tell it, it is generally because someone thinks it will be helpful to some of the newcomers. Actually all we have is the ability and

[Page 7]

[page header]   7.

willingness for each to tell their own story. The attitude is more or less, "Here is what I was . . . Here is what I did . . . Here is what happened . . . And here I am." By this telling of stories, newcomers may more or less identify themselves or things they have done with those things we did. As long as we stick to our own story, we are never in danger of preaching.

What is your opinion of psychoanalysis? *[38]*

I think anything which enables a person to better understand themselves and their thought processes, is well worth while. After the analysis I understood myself better and could identify more of my thoughts, though it still left me with nothing to tie to but myself. And I had always failed myself before.

What is your opinion of psychiatrical *[sic]* **treatment?** *[39]*

Same as psychoanalysis.

What do you regard as your greatest future dangers? *[40]*

I am still somewhat apprehensive about any success which might be thrown my way. I am afraid that success would build in me an inclination to deprecate the things I have learned to be so helpful in sustaining me in adversity. On the other hand, I am told that no real lasting success can come my way until I am ready for it.

What was the hardest lesson for you to learn? *[41]*

To keep first things first. I am apt to forget that as an alcoholic I was useless in a business way, to my family and friends. Only a*[s]* *[sic]* a nonalcoholic can I live a useful and happy life. Therefore, business, other people's actions, finances, in fact everything is based upon my remaining a nondrinker. So anything I do, anything which I might say was of prime importance is apt to throw me if I do not keep first things first *[sic for this entire sentence]*. Of course, that means for me to keep proper relation with the Power that enabled me to recover.

Do you realize that men who make a study of mental activities might say you are hypotizing *[sic]* **yourself?** *[42]*

The only answer I can make is the one a good friend of mine who is a psychiatrist made to me a year ago. He said, "I have believed you were hypnotizing yourself, but all I can say today is, if that is so, there has been such an improvement in you and these other fellows, that I hope you all keep right on hypnotizing yourselves." Which is his way of saying that no matter what it is, it works!

Isn't this nothing more or less than old fashioned revivalism? *[43]*

[Page 8]

[page header]   8.

I am forced to say..So What? It works! There is nothing that could place me in a more untenable position or make me do more ridiculous things than I did when in the grip of uncontrolled drinking.

Do you claim you are cured? *[44]*

No. I go around with somewhat the state of mind that I have been reprieved. If I take a drink I know I will call off that reprieve and yet I never have the feeling that I am fighting off liquor. I abused it, therefore the privilege of its use has been taken away from me.

What is your opinion of doctors and medical treatment for the alcoholic? *[45]*

I think they most definitely have their place in any program of recovery. They can bring the physical man back into such shape that he can think straight.

Because your present attitudes are so different from your former actions and thoughts, don't you ever fell *[sic]* **like a hypocrite?** *[46]*

Oh boy, and how. That is one of my most difficult problems. Knowing myself so well and knowing my own thoughts and struggles, I am terribly embarrassed when anyone attempts to pin any roses on me. All I know is that I am somewhat better than I was before, but the improvement is so small and all of my reactions are so human, I don't want to be forced into any pose of being good.

If this is so essentially religious, don't you ever feel any antipathy toward the ministers because they did not bring it to your attention? *[47]*

No. I tried ministers. They worked hard with me, but I simply refused to see. I think the main reason for this is that none of the ministers were alcoholics. Thank God.

Outside of the Bible what book has been the most helpful to you? *[48]*

Thomas Mason's...................

Do you go to church? *[49]*

Not regularly, but more than before. Probably I will become a regular church goer, but just at the moment (I may be fooling myself, but) I believe I am doing some church work every day. What I am trying to express is that every man should work that problem out for himself.

[Page 9]
[page header]   9.

You say that having gripes against people, things or conditions, are dangerous. Don't you ever have them? *[50]*

Sure, and plenty of them. But I identify them as gripes and know I should not have them. Before I was always so anxious to prove myself right that the gripe kept getting worse and worse. Now I know I'm griped about something, and that I'm probably wrong, so it does not have a chance to rise to the dangerous stage.

Do you ever lose your temper? *[51]*
And how. I blow sky high many times. But today I have the ability to apologize afterwards and admit my wrong. This is not an excurse for loss of temper, but these lapses do not harm me as much as formerly.

Are you ever tempted to preach? *[52]*
Plenty. Advice is so easy to give and another's dangers are so apparent that it is a human temptation.

When a man calls to tell you he is on the verge of a slip, what do you do for him? *[53]*
That is hard to define. So much depends on the man himself. One thing I always do is to say a silent prayer and ask him to get all his gripes off his chest. However, I usually tell him it may be right for him to go on a bender because I feel it may be necessary to prove certain things. I cannot get excited because anyone is going to get drunk. As I look at it, that will not presage the coming of the end of the world. I find that when a man is talking to someone who understands and actually does not care whether he is going to get drunk, he is apt to get his thinking on the right track and will not go on the bender.

When a man goes ahead anyway and then calls you up to tell you he has slipped, what do you tell him? *[54]*
I tell him not to bother me. I'm not in the business of pinning up anybody's diapers. When he gets through and sincerely wants to quit drinking, give me a ring and I'll see if I can be helpful.

When a man has had a slip should he attempt to hide it? *[55]*
We have found that to be one of our greatest dangers. The man is so ashamed of it, he generally has been so proud of his record that the temptation is great to pass it off. This, of course, is going right back to the old ways and

[Page 10]

[page header] 10.

is dangerous. If a man slips, my attitude is . . . So what? that isn't important, what is important is whether he is going to slip again. *[sic to that entire last sentence]* I clearly remember what a man once told me. He said, "An alcoholic who thinks no one knows about his drinking is like an ostrich with his behind in the air and his head in the sand."

Why do alcoholics give up such chances for improvement of position, for happiness, just for a drink? Why can't they go on the wagon and stay there like other human beings when they see the terrible consequences of their drinking? *[56]*

If you could answer that you would be on the trail of one of the best answers to—why an alcoholic. *[sic]*

Do you think you will ever be able to drink again? *[57]*

That is one of the greatest dangers. Many of our crowd have held on to the idea that some day, when certain financial conditions, when certain marital conditions, or something else is different, they would be able to drink again like a normal human being. Until that is knocked out of their heads and until they themselves know they can never drink again, their recovery is generally only temporary.

What do you see in the future for yourself? *[58]*

I am not interested in trying to see into the future for myself. If my recovery is maintained, I know that the future must hold better things in the way of real accomplishment and happiness than the past.

Have you any doubts as to the permanency of sudden conversion? *[59]*

Less now than formerly. I have seen too many of them stick. The extent, quality, and the permanence of any man's conversion is his own business. Again you might say . . . No matter what it is, it works.

Do you study the Bible? *[60]*

If you mean regularly, no. On the other hand, I have read the Bible a great deal more, and with more understanding the past three years, than all my life before. However, many of the fellowship are constant students of the Bible. A man's religious study, I believe, is entirely his own affair.

Is the Bible confusing to you? *[61]*

Yes, many times. Probably though because I am iconoclastic

[Page 11]

and do not study it enough.

How often do you pray? *[62]*

Many times a day.

What is your prayer? *[63]*

Thy Will Be Done . . . AND MEAN IT.

What is your vision of, or what do you understand, by God? *[64]*

That is unexplainable. When I begin to worry about that, I generally realize I am getting into a field where far greater minds than mine have argued and failed for years. I understand God as a great, indefinable, unexplainable Power which will help me if I keep in tune with it.

What do you think of a newcomer's chance of recovery through this method? *[65]*

I believe that to be unpredictable although I have yet to see a failure where a man sincerely wanted to get well and where he would follow strictly the experience of the rest of the men who have recovered.

Do you suggest this indiscrimately *[sic]* **to men you believe to be alcoholics?** *[66]*

No. Generally I talk to the man, and if he expresses interest, I tell him my story.

How do you present this to a man? *[67]*

First I tell him my story up to the time I discovered I was an alcoholic. By telling him my story, my drinking exploits, the tales of the shakes, how I hid bottles, etc. *[sic to this entire sentence]* Then I generally steer the talk to the subject of alcoholism. If the man decides that he is an alcoholic, (that is a thing I cannot decide for him) I tell him how I got well and the cases of others who got well. I then put him in touch with other members of our fellowship. If the man wants it, he can get it.

What do you believe identifies an alcoholic? *[68]*

I believe an alcoholic, broadly speaking, is a man who cannot control his drinking. He cannot stop drinking when he knows that more will harm him. Nor can he stop drinking when he actually wants to.

[Page 12]

[page header]   12.

Were you ever hospitalized? *[69]*

Yes. Many times.

Are you on the wagon? *[70]*

No. I say this because I do not desire to take any positive position with myself in regard to liquor. In other words, I am not fighting liquor.

In former times when you were on the wagon, did you ever feel sorry for yourself because you could not join in a group of drinking friends? *[71]*
Many times, because I had an unconscious feeling that they were pitying my weakness of will power in that I could not handle my liquor without going on the wagon.

Do you feel sorry for yourself now when you are with drinking companions? *[72]*
Occasionally, but I laugh at the emotion. I know now that will power nor *[sic]* habit have anything to do with my being an alcoholic.

Did your wife go on the wagon when you quit drinking? *[73]*
Yes.

Was it helpful to you? *[74]*
Yes. On the other hand, what she did or did not do was not the main thing. I was told that if I were placing responsibility on any human being, I was on the wrong track. However, I believe her action was very helpful.

Do you or your friends in Alcoholics Anonymous hate liquor? *[75]*
Personally I serve liquor in my home to people who can control the use. Some of the group however have a hatred for what liquor has done to them.

Don't you think and talk of alcoholism too much? *[76]*
Maybe you're right. Anyway you are talking like a lot of our wives.
On the other hand, I have recovered and the thing is should I talk about it a great deal, or should I not talk about it at all, and do a lot of drinking?

[Page 13]

[page header]   13.

Do you ever get into arguments? [77]
Many of them, but I am slowly learning the futility.

Have you caught yourself doing anything dishonest or selfish? *[78]*
Plenty of times. In those cases I try to undo the harm I may have done.

When other men in this fellowship start to expound their ideas as to the way a man should meet certain problems, etc.. what do you do? *[79]*
Most likely I interrupt with an idea of my own which I think is better but I am slowly learning to listen and keep to my own story exclusively.

Do you see any difficulties ahead for this work? *[80]*

Only from two angles. First, enough money may not be available to do the things which would result in the saving of many lives now. Eventually yes, but at least a limited amount of money is necessary now in order to consolidate what has been gained and learned. Second, I believe great difficulties would arise if too much organization were interjected into it.

What in your opinion is the greatest necessity on this alcoholic work? *[81]*

Public understanding. By that I mean it would make it much easier for the alcoholic to recover if the public had the same understanding of the alcoholic malady as they have of diabetes. One of the greatest sources of annoyance to the alcoholic is the practically universal belief on the part of the public that the alcoholic is weak-willed or suffering from a habit.

Do you say there should be no organization? *[82]*

No. Every work of any kind needs at least a simple organization for officiency *[sic]*. However, I believe the organization should be kept to the simplest possible form in order that no conflict be established with any organized religion. The strength of this, as I see it, is that it is extra religious work which can be co-ordinated with any organized religion and should be welcomed by them.

[Page 14]

[page header]   14.

What is The Alcoholic Foundation? *[83]*

Until this time, the work has been carried forward by private contributions from the people who have benefited. However, with the necessity for funds to spread the work further, it was thought wise to set up a foundation to handle any contributions which might come in.

How many men are there on The Alcoholic Foundation? *[84]*

It consists of seven men at present. Four nonalcoholic prominent business or professional men, and three alcoholics. It is stated in the article of trust that nonalcoholic members shall always be in the majority of at least one.

Do the members of The Alcoholic Foundation serve without pay? *[85]*
Yes.

Are the contributions to The Alcoholic Foundation deductible on income tax? *[86]*
Yes.

What will be done with the money donated to The Alcoholic Foundation?
[87]
If anyone is interested in making a donation, one of the members of the Foundation will be glad to answer any questions.

Is there anything to join? *[88]*
Of course not. There is no membership list, or anything to sign.

Do you ever tell a man he is an alcoholic? *[89]*
No. That is strictly a matter for him to decide. We tell him what we did and why we are sure we are alcoholics. He must decide for himself whether he is an alcoholic.

Do you identify different kinds of drinking? *[90]*
The casual drinker who takes an occasional drink. The social drinker who drinks when socially inclined. The heavy drinker who drinks a great deal. And the alcoholic.

Do you have any religious services? *[91]*
If you mean in the sense of organized religion, no. I believe our meetings are more or less the get-together

[Page 15]

[page header]   15.

of a fellowship.

Have you had any problems with divorced men? *[92]*
Yes. The main problem is to get them to put first things first. They have, through alcohol, broken up a home which they loved and have been divorced by a loved one. They so many times feel that now they are different, all of the things they have thrown away should be given back to them immediately. It is so hard for them to realize that proper recovery and holding it is more important than anything else.

What do you mean by the beer experiment? *[93]*
Many times a fellow gets the idea if he had always stayed on beer, he would not have had his trouble. Or he has the idea that beer will not harm him. They generally try to drink nothing but beer and end up on liquor. Or they get as bad on beer as on anything else. Having learned their lesson, they generally say they tried the beer experiment.

To what do you attribute your not drinking now? (Another member answers) *[94]*

When leaving institutions I had no one to talk to about my problems. I was afraid to phone people for fear they would recall something I had done. I feel, however, that I have made up for it by doing time in the laughing academy. Because of my fear, I would phone someone I had met in the institution. Loneliness, I guess you would call it, and the other bird from the cuckoo hatch would feel the same way. Since meeting this crowd, there has been no barrier of what I have done because they understood and generally can match my experience with something as bad or worse.

The Edited Text of "The Car Smasher"

An eighteen-page, handwritten document by Dick Stanley that has been edited by Hank Parkhurst (Stepping Stones, AA 501.1—Publications—Alcoholics Anonymous— Stories? (handwritten copies), Box 13, Folder 12).

Permission is required from the Stepping Stones Foundation for any further use, display, or duplication of the following material.

*The text below is annotated in three ways. The ~~double lined cross-outs~~ were made by Hank Parkhurst directly onto the original copy. The ~~single line deletions~~ were made to the text sometime after this, but before it was printed in the book, Alcoholics Anonymous, in April 1939. The words that appear in **bold italics** were added to the text as it first appeared in that book:*

During the first week of March, 1937, through the grace of God, I ended 20 years of a life made practically useless ~~by my not being able to do~~ **because I could not do** two things.

First, ~~being~~ **I was** unable to not take a drink.

Second, ~~being~~ **I was** unable to take a drink without getting drunk.

Perhaps a third as important as ~~these~~ **the other** two should be added; my being unwilling to admit either of the first two.

~~As a~~ *With the* result I kept trying to drink without getting drunk, and kept making a nightmare of my life, causing suffering and hardship to all those relatives and friends who tried so hard to help me and whom, when I was sober, I took the greatest pleasure in pleasing.

~~As a boy, I had taken a pledge in a religious church not to drink until I was 21. This pledge, I kept.~~

The first time I drank anything strong, *[page 2]* or in greater quantity than a glass of beer, I got disgustingly drunk ~~whereas the other fellows had a drink and went on into dinner. I stayed in the bar and as each group came in, I had a drink with them and when the groups failed to arrive fast enough, I went on myself with the result I~~ *and* missed the dinner *which had been* arranged ~~by a church~~ for me ~~because I was shortly to be married~~ *in honor of my coming marriage*.

I had to be taken home and remained in bed the following day; ~~far~~ more sick than I thought a human could be and live. ~~But~~ *Yet*, until two years ago *I* periodically ~~having been doing~~ *did* the same thing.

Making money was always pretty easy when I was sober and worked. ~~When I was nineteen, through the help of a friend, I acquired a piece of land, cut it into lots, sold it and within a year had made a profit larger than most successful men made~~ *[page 3]* ~~their first ten business years. I bring this up only to show one more reason why I should have no drink[?].~~

All right when sober—absolutely helpless with a drink aboard. But I seemed to have had the idea that making money or a living was something to take or let alone.

~~I started building some houses and buying and selling real estate~~ *I got into the real estate business*—~~began to~~ neglect business, sometimes with four houses under construction, wouldn't see any of them for a week or even longer—sometimes paid good money for an option, ~~then~~ *and* forgot to exercise it. ~~In spite of a generally rising market, anything you got could be turned at a profit (1914 to 1918), in five years I not only had lost and spent all I had made, but my huge original profit [too] and I was several hundred dollars in debt.~~ *I made and lost plenty of money in the market*.

Understand, I wasn't actually drunk all of this time but there seemed always to be an excuse to have a drink, and this first one, more and more often lead to my becoming drunk.

~~There was always some sort of excuse for the first drink and always a special reason why I got drunk. "Drank on an empty stomach"—"Drank in a warm place and it hit me when I went into the cold"—"Drank in a cold place and it hit me when I went into a warm room." Always explaining how and why that particular time was special and I believed these things.~~

As time went on, periods between drunks got shorter and I was full of fear; fear that I wouldn't be able to do anything I agreed to do; fear of meeting men; worrying about what they might know of my drinking and its results; all of which made me quite ~~as useless when I was sober as when drunk~~ *useless whether I was sober or drunk*.

Thus I drifted. Breaking promises to my wife, my mother, and a host of *[page 5]* other relatives and friends who stood [???] from me and tried harder than humans ~~could~~ *should* be expected to, to help me.

~~Through the efforts of a friend, I secured a position as broker of a commodity used extensively in my home city and did pull myself together for a short period due to a wartime personnel adjustments [sic]. I was advanced rapidly—and shortly became a Western manager—which necessitated my being away from home frequently—and things got no better fast. I did get business when I worked during this period in spite of sad neglect. I kept fooling people—most of all me for a couple of years—~~

I always seemed to pick the most inopportune time for a binge—an important business deal to be closed might find me in another city. Once ~~upon~~ *when* entrusted to purchase for ~~one of the largest and most important consumers of~~ *[page 6]* ~~the commity [sic] I dealt in~~ *a large customer*, I agreed to meet his representative in New York. ~~I went to New York, stayed a week, but~~ I ~~had~~ spent the time waiting for a train ~~in Pittsburgh~~ in a bar; *arrived in New York tight*; stayed tight the week; and came home by ~~way of Chicago~~ **a route** twice the distance from New York ~~to my home city~~.

~~Might work~~ *Worked* weeks, by long distance, wire, letters, and personal calls, to contact possible business connections under proper conditions and finally succeeded, only to show up tight or get tight and insult the man whose friendship, or respect meant so much.

Each time there was ~~always~~ the feeling of regret, inability to understand why, but a firm determination that it would never happen again—but it did—in fact the periods between became increasingly shorter, and the duration of each binge *[page 7]* longer. ~~and time required in recurring long [???] until there would be two to four days of hard drinking, two or three days of tapering off, a week after that when I [???] unable to face anyway which was just dandy for those with whom I was working.—~~

During the aforementioned period, I had spent thousands of dollars, my home was broken up—~~smashed up~~; a half dozen *cars smashed up; I had* times been picked up by police—*for* driving while intoxicated, plain drunk—had sponged and borrowed money; cashed rubber checks—*and* made such a general nuisance of myself that I ~~had~~ lost all ~~of~~ the friends I had. At least they felt unwilling to be a party to financing me while I made a more complete ass of myself. And I, on my side was ashamed to face any of them when I was sober. ~~So for a large part stayed out in the country, sponging a living from relatives, about as useless~~ *[page 8]* ~~as it is possible to be.~~

~~Even during this period, though I had several opportunities, worked one business selling lots and stayed sober long enough to make several hundred dollars. I had a stake and was going to use it for a fresh start. Had a nice car and enough to tide me through~~

~~a dull winter. Smashed the car up. Kept drinking the reserve until by Christmas I didn't have enough left to buy my children presents.~~

~~The year numanistic[?] gold craze hit the country, a long-time friend gave me a job selling them in six or eight weeks I had another stake amounting to several hundred dollars, another car and just about the same thing happened.~~

~~I cite all these details to bring out first that everyone gave me every chance ten-fold that I deserved. That when I worked,~~ *[page 9]* ~~I could make money but despite all that I had been taught, I still drank and when I drank I [????].~~

~~I had jobs secured for me through friends~~ *My friends secured jobs for me; I* made good on them for a ~~period~~ *time,* ~~one in a factory.~~ I ~~had~~ advanced *quickly* to night superintendent *in a factory but* it wasn't long until I ~~turned up~~ *was* missing, or worse, turning up drunk; was warned—warned again; finally fired. I was later rehired as a factory hand and mighty glad to have it—advanced again—~~got my old job back and~~ then *back to the bottom—always* ~~went through~~ the same process.

~~I cite all this detail to bring out first that everyone gave me every chance to [???] that I deserved. Second, that when I worked I could get results. Third that in spite of all I should have, in fact, had learned, time after time I had lost everything in days that it had taken me months to acquire.~~

*[page 10]*I ~~still~~ drank *continuously* and when I drank, sooner or later, and generally sooner, I got drunk and threw everything away.

During the early part of 1935 my brother secured my release from the city jail. On that day *by sincere but non-alcoholic friends* I was shown what might be done about my drinking with the help of God.

I asked for this help, gratefully accepted it, and in addition to losing my desire for drink, asked for and received the same help in other matters. I ~~was again working in a factory as a [???], the lowest form of animal life in the industry and thankful for it.~~ ~~Happy that I was earning~~ *I began to earn* my living and in my new found security, was unashamed to meet people I had avoided for years ~~and I might say in passing that without exception they were so glad that I had taken a turn for the better each one wanting~~ *[page 11]* ~~to encourage me.~~ *with happy results.*

Things continued well, I had two or three advancements to better jobs with greater earning power. My every need was being met—~~so long as I asked for acceptance, I found now [???] and acknowledged his divine help~~ *as long as I accepted and acknowledged the Divine Help* which was so generously given.

I find now, as I look back, that this period covered about six or eight months, then I began to think how smart I *[underlined in original]* was; to wonder if my superiors realized what they had in me; if they were not pretty small about the money they paid me; as these thoughts grew, my feeling of gratefulness grew less. I was neglecting to ask for help—when I received it as I ~~did always~~ *always did,* I neglected to acknowledge it. Instead I took great credit ~~unto me~~ *[page 12] for myself.* ~~During this period which covered four to six months, making about a year—that I hadn't had a drink—~~I began to take credit for the non-drinking ~~experiment~~ too—it came to me ~~more~~ strongly that I had conquered the drinking habit *myself*—I became convinced of my great will power.

Then ~~came a warm day—and as I left the factory~~—someone suggested a ~~cool~~ glass of beer—I had one—~~no more.~~ This was even better than I thought—I could take a drink and not get drunk. So another day, another beer until it was regular every day—~~and once or twice two beers—and no drunk.~~ Now I was indeed in the saddle ~~as concerned~~ **concerning** drink—could take it or ~~let~~ *leave* it alone.

~~On the chance of boring the reader to show you the extent one will go to fool himself, I relate the following~~ *[page 13]* ~~experience. I had been getting my beer regularly as I left the factory each day. In fact the beer would come to mind pretty often for the last two hours working period each day- one day—I wondered if this beer thing was getting to be an uncontrollable habit—I decided to find out so instead of my usual beer—~~

Just to prove it to myself, I decided to march right past the place I usually stopped ~~at~~ *for beer,* and I felt pretty good as I went to the parking lot ~~securing~~ *for* my car. The longer I drove the greater was my pride that I had finally licked liquor—I was sure ~~that~~ I had—so sure in fact that ~~in as much as I had licked it~~ I stopped ~~at the last place before reaching home~~ and had a beer *before I went home.* ~~And so I continued stopping for my beer almost every day and a few times had a shot of whiskey.~~ *In my smugness I continued to drink beer and began occasionally to drink liquor.*

~~And~~ So it went until ~~as~~ inevitably, *[page 14]* ~~"as the sun follows darkness"~~ *"as darkness follows the sun,"* I ~~drank on an empty stomach and~~ got drunk—*and* ~~I~~ was right where I had been fifteen years before, ~~drinking a little from time to time and~~ slipping into a binge every now and ~~again~~ *then*—never knowing when they would come—nor where I would wind up.

This ~~went on for some time, six or eight months~~ *lasted about eight months*—I didn't miss much time from work—did *spend* one ten day stretch in the hospital ~~from~~ *after* a beating I got while drunk—was warned a few times by my superiors ~~in the factory~~—but was "getting by."

In the meantime I had heard of ~~a man~~ *some men* who, like myself, were what I had always scoffed at being—alcoholics. I had been invited to ~~join~~ *see* them ~~at this time,~~ *but* after twenty years ~~of drinking,~~ I felt there was nothing wrong with me *[last four words underlined in the original, but not in printed text].* They *[italics added in printed text]* might need it; *they [italics added in printed text]* might be queer; but not me. *[page 15]* I wasn't going to get drunk again.

Of course I did, again and again, until ~~one binge lasted over a week and these guys~~ *these men* not only contacted me but took me under their wing.

~~I went into a hospital and after a couple of days~~ *After a few days* of "degoofing" *in a hospital*, these men ~~one by one~~ came in *to me one by one* ~~and~~ told me of their experiences ~~except for local duration and intensity they told me the same stories I would have told, part, in fact, I have told you.~~ They didn't ~~preach~~ *lecture*—didn't tell me I should quit ~~or why I should quit. Any of us had known more reasons why we should have quit in ten seconds than anyone else, [those who were not] not rummies like ourselves could have thought of in ten years.~~ But they did tell me how *[italics added in printed text]* to quit. THAT WAS IMPORTANT and simple too.

[page 16] ~~It was simply to acknowledge~~ *Their suggestion was that we simply acknowledge* we had made a pretty dismal failure of our lives, ~~to~~ *that* accept as truth and act upon what we had always been taught~~, always had~~ *and* known, that there was a kind and merciful God; that we were His children; and, that if we would let Him, He would help us.

I had certainly made a mess of my life. From the age of 20 I had thrown aside everything God had seen fit to endow me with. Why not avail myself of this all wise, ever-present help?

This I did. I ask for, accept, and acknowledge this help, and know that so long as I do, I shall never take a drink and what is more important, though impossible without the first, all other phases of my life have been helped.

There ~~is~~ *are*, it seems to me, four steps to be taken by one who is a victim of alcoholism.

First: Have a real desire to quit.

Second: Admit you can't. (This is ~~the~~ hardest.)

Third: Ask for His ever present help.

Fourth: Accept and acknowledge this help.

~~I might say in passing that alcoholics are not the only people this help is available for. I know personally many people that have never taken a drink who have experience as great or at least as any alcoholic. The process is the same "ask and you shall receive."~~

[page 17] ~~Surely I had made a mess out of my life from the age of 20, had thrown aside everything God had seen fit to endow me with. Why not avail myself of this all wise, ever-present help in God?~~

~~This I did. I ask for, accept, and acknowledge this help, and I know that as long as I do, I shall never take a drink and what is more important, though impossible without the first, all other phases of my life have been changed.~~

~~In my work at the factory and my relations with the people there and away from my work are so much more pleasant and profitable though this didn't always mean money. I am happy to be able in at least some of my applications [sic], am able to send my daughter to a~~ *[page 18]* ~~University. Three or more years ago, though I have wanted her~~

to go, I wouldn't have felt competent to guarantee one week's board for [????]. With this help, my work is better, I am some use and I am paying off my obligations fully. It's true, but when more speed is required, means will be provided. I am supremely happy, something I'd never known before except as a boy. I thank God for all this and I hope this poor effort may reach someone who is looking as I was, someone who is hooked as I was hooked and help them to find, as I have found, the only real cure for the drink habit I have ever heard of and that he may know the joy that I have known in his release from it.

Typed Memo to Bill Wilson

~March 24, 1939~

Text from the original document (Stepping Stones, AA 501.1: Publications—Alcoholics Anonymous (1939)—Correspondence and promotion material . . . , Box 13, Folder 15.)

Permission is required from the Stepping Stones Foundation for any further use, display, or duplication of the following material.

NOTE: *This has been transcribed with all the errors in spacing, spelling, punctuation and wording exactly as they appear in the original document.*

3/24/39

Dogmatic;   Marked by positive and authoritative assertions. As " shown by God."

Doctor Howards position is that Mr. Wilson should not let himself be put in a position of being dogmatic anywhere in the book. That instead of saying to any person . . . " You do this or You do that." . . . the whole attitude should be we did this or we did that and received certain blessings from God . . . That on account of the great possibilities for good in the book it should be studied from the standpoint of humility and " we did this and we did that" and God gave us certain things. He claims that we stand on impregnable ground when we constantly talk about what some one of us did and let the man draw his own conclusions as to whether by doing the same thing he will or not receive the same thing. He further says that if we say . . . "You do this or You do that" instead of . . . " We did this or we did that and certain results followed" . . . we have lost a great deal of power. The most impressive thing he said was . . . " Mr. Wilson does not desire to be dogmatic and assume the position of God and every effort should be made to protect him from that pitfall. He said that in any writing, a position of that kind can creep in unconsciously, when a man thoroughly knows his subject even when a man is actually humble and is not that way.

My personal opinion is as follows: EVERY personality should be laid aside because when personalities enter opinions become colored. Therefor Bill should take the book someplace where he can study it quietly with the attitude of ~~taking from it~~ changing *[handwritten above the strikeout]* any dogmatic statements or insinuations. In no sense of the word to soften the religious implications. Simply to change it where necessary from . . . You do this . . . to . . . we did this. At the same time certain men such as Frank Amos, Harry Brick, Jack Darrow, Doc. Smith, Horace Crystal, Paul Kellogg and any others who might be suggested ~~should~~ could *[handwritten above the strikeout]* do the same thing. Then a meeting ~~sh~~ould *[the "sh" had been overwritten with a "c"]* be called for final discussion of these points and any changes made where this seemed right. In my opinion

[page 2]

3/24/39

we have in this book such a tremendous opportunity for good that no possibility should be overlooked, before it goes definitely to print.

This suggestion of course covers only the first twelve chapters.

A man can reveal himself in anyway he chooses in the personal stories.

To bring this proposal down to concrete few words.

A committee to study the book to **xxxxxx** *[heavy typed strikeout obliterating original text]* change any " You do this or you must do that statements or insinuations to, " We did this or we did that."

Then at a meeting to decide by the vote of the majority the changes. ANY people who desire and will spend the necessary time to be able to serve on such a committee.

Bibliography

Primary Sources

AA Main Events: A transcription of a recording made by Bill Wilson on November 2, 1954. GSO, Box 29, Reel 13 / 17.2 Bill's Fact Sheets of AA Main Events (1934-1941) and StSt (Stepping Stones Foundation Archives—see StSt below), AA 401 – Alcoholics Anonymous – History – William G. Wilson – Main Events; AA Box 6, Folder 22.

Amos, Frank, "History of the Alcoholics [sic] movement up to the formation of the Alcoholic Foundation on Aug. 11, 1938," Original Typed Document with the handwritten date 8/19/38, GSO, Box 59, 1938, Folder B(1), 1938-117 to 1938-124.

GSO: The Archives at the General Service Offices of Alcoholics Anonymous, 475 Riverside Drive, 11th Floor, New York, NY, 10115.

Lois Wilson's Diaries: StSt (Stepping Stones Foundation Archives—see StSt below) LBW 201.10 Diaries 1935, LBW Box 11-B Folder 3 [includes 1936 materials]; Diaries 1937 same box but Folder 4; LBW Diaries 1937-1940 (Typescript edited by Lois, 1 of 2), 206.10, LBW, Box 11-A, Folder 7.

Oral History Transcriptions, Made by Bill Wilson in 1954 in preparation for *AA Comes of Age*, GSO, Transcribed Oral Interviews: Box 1 of 2, Draft "Cassidy" Through "Murphy," Box 1: 304680980 and Box 2 of 2, Draft "Ridgway" through "Wilson," Box 2: 304680981. NOTE: These boxes contain the original 8½" x 14" drafts. GSO also preserves retyped 8½" x 11" versions of these interviews (which impacts the page citations).

RAC: The Rockefeller Archive Center, 15 Dayton Avenue, Sleepy Hollow, NY, 10591.

Rockefeller Foundation Charter, available online at:

http://www.rockefellerfoundation.org/uploads/files/30ff1883-9e8f-44fd-9dd9-8bf2d6803578.pdf (retrieved September 23, 2010).

StSt: Stepping Stones Foundation Archives, Stepping Stones, the historic home of Bill and Lois Wilson, 62 Oak Road, Katonah, NY, 10536, steppingstones.org.

Secondary Sources

Alcoholics Anonymous, Works Publishing Company, New York City, 1939 (First Edition)

Alcoholics Anonymous, Alcoholics Anonymous World Services, Inc., New York City, 2001 (Fourth Edition)

Alcoholics Anonymous Comes of Age, A Brief History of A.A. (referred to in the notes as *AACOA*), Alcoholics Anonymous World Services, Inc., New York, 1957.

The Book That Started It All: The Original Working Manuscript of Alcoholics Anonymous, Hazelden, Center City, Minnesota, 2010.

A.A. Grapevine, (the monthly journal of Alcoholics Anonymous), published June, 1944, to the present.

[Anonymous] *What is the Oxford Group?*, Oxford University Press, London, 1933 (available online in pdf format - http://www.siestakeybeachmeeting.com/index_htm_files/What_Is_The_Oxford_Group.pdf)

B., Mel., *Ebby: The Man Who Sponsored Bill W.*, Hazelden, Center City, Minnesota, 1998.

Burwell, Jim, "Speech by Mr. James Burwell, Meeting of Alcoholics Anonymous, March 14, 1947, Hope Manor, 2200 West 7th, Los Angeles, California," Brown University Library Archival and Manuscript Collection, available online at: http://library.brown.edu/cds/catalog/catalog.php?verb=render&id=1264698468343875&view=pageturner&pageno=1

> "The Evolution of Alcoholics Anonymous, a history of A.A." by Burwell that grew out of a speech he delivered on March 14, 1947 at Hope Manor, 2200 West 7th Street, Los Angeles, California. This greatly edited version of that speech (the exact date of the revisions is unknown, but likely 1947 or 1948) was subsequently privately printed and widely distributed. (StSt, AA 401, Box 5, Folder 20. Also available at: http://www.barefootsworld.net/aa-jb-evolution.html.)

Chernow, Ron, *Titan: The Life of John D. Rockefeller, Sr.*, Random House, New York, 1998.

Chesnut, Glenn F., "Jim Burwell: early AA's first famous atheist" (http://hindsfoot.org/atheistburwell.html - retrieved July 4, 2012)

Dodd, Fiona, *The Authors*, iUniverse, Inc. Bloomington, IN, 2013.

Dr. Bob and the Good Oldtimers, Alcoholics Anonymous World Services, Inc., New York, 1980.

Finan, Christopher M., *Drunks: An American History* Beacon Press, Boston, 2017.

Fitzpatrick, Michael, *Dr. Bob & Bill W. Speak: AA's Cofounders Tell Their Stories,* Hazelden, Center City, MN, 2012.

Fosdick, Raymond B. and Scott, Albert L., *Toward Liquor Control,* Harper & Brothers, New York, 1933.

Fosdick, Raymond B., *John D. Rockefeller, Jr., A Portrait,* Harper & Brothers, New York, 1956.

Hartigan, Francis, *Bill W., A Biography of Alcoholics Anonymous Cofounder Bill Wilson,* Thomas Dunne Books, St. Martin's Griffin, New York, 2001.

Hock, Ruth, "A Discussion of the Big Book," a talk given at Glendale, CA on March 12, 1978; 28-page transcript copy in the Akron Archives. Also available on YouTube under the title "Ruth H. AA's First Secretary shares the history of Alcoholics Anonymous" - http://www.youtube.com/watch?v=mxVkTNgOhy0 – retrieved September 27, 2013.

Hunter, Charlotte, Jones, Billye & Zieger, Joan. *Women Pioneers in 12 Step Recovery,* Hazelden, Center City, MN, 1999.

James, William. *The Will to Believe*, Longmans Green and Co, New York, 1897.

K., Bob, *Key Players in AA History*, AA Agnostica, Canada, 2015.

K., Mitchell, *How It Worked, The Story of Clarence H. Snyder,* AA Big Book Study Group, Washingtonville, NY, 1999.

Kitchen, V. C., *I Was a Pagan,* Harper & Brothers, New York, 1934.

Kurtz, Ernest, *Not-God, A History of Alcoholics Anonymous,* Hazelden, Center City, MN, 1991 (Expanded Edition).

Levine, Harry G., "The Birth of American Alcohol Control: Prohibition, the Power Elite and the Problem of Lawlessness," *Contemporary Drug Problems*, Spring, 1985, pp. 63-115

(http://dragon.soc.qc.cuny.edu/Staff/levine/The-Birth-of-American-Alcohol-Control.pdf - retrieved October 18, 2010).

Lincoln, Samuel B., *Lockwood Greene, The History of an Engineering Business, 1832-1958,* Stephen Greene Press, Brattleboro, VT, 1960.

M., Merton, *Black Sheep, A History of Alcoholics Anonymous in New Jersey and Surrounding Vicinity 1935-1950,* [A valuable but unfinished and unpublished manuscript in the author's possession. Merton did some truly remarkable in-depth research on early A.A. in New Jersey, including courts records, real estate listings and a wealth of other sources that had been all but untouched for decades.]

Maxwell, Milton A., "The Washingtonian Movement," *Quarterly Journal of Studies on Alcohol*, Volume II, 1950, pp. 410-452.

Moore, Jay D., *Alcoholics Anonymous and the Rockefeller Connection,* Shut up and Get in the Car Publishing, Albuquerque, NM, 2015.

Neidhardt, Gary W., *King Charles of New York City,* Author House, Bloomington IN, 2015.

Newton, James D., *Uncommon Friends, Life with Thomas Edison, Henry Ford, Harvey Firestone, Alexis Carrel, & Charles Lindbergh,* Harcourt, Inc. San Diego / New York / London, 1987.

Okrent, Daniel, *Last Call, The Rise and Fall of Prohibition,* Scribner, New York, 2010.

Pass It On, The story of Bill Wilson and how the A.A. message reached the world, Alcoholics Anonymous World Services, Inc., New York, 1984.

Peabody, Richard R., *The Common Sense of Drinking,* Little, Brown, and Company, Boston, 1931.

Pittman, Bill, *AA The Way It Began,* Glen Abbey Books, Seattle, 1988 [Reissued with the same pagination in 1999 by Hazelden as *The Roots of Alcoholics Anonymous*].

Rockefeller, John D., Jr., Foreword to *Toward Liquor Control,* Harper & Brothers, New York, 1933.

Silkworth, William D., "Alcoholism as a Manifestation of Allergy," *Medical Record, A National Review of Medicine and Surgery,* The Medical Journal and Record Publishing Company, Inc., New York, Volume 145, January to June, 1937, pp. 249-251.

"Reclamation of the Alcoholic," *Medical Record, A National Review of Medicine and Surgery,* The Medical Journal and Record Publishing Company, Inc., New York, Volume 145, January to June, 1937, pp. 321-324.

"A New Approach to Psychotherapy in Chronic Alcoholism," *The Journal-Lancet,* Minneapolis, Volume 59, No. 7, July 27, 1939, pp. 312-314.

"Psychological Rehabilitation of Alcoholics," *Medical Record, A National Review of Medicine and Surgery,* The Medical Journal and Record Publishing Company, Inc., New York, Volume 145, July 19, 1939, pp. 321-324.

Smith, Bob & **Windows, Sue Smith,** *Children of the Healer,* Parkside Publishing Corporation, Park Ridge, Illinois, 1992.

Thomsen, Robert, *Bill W.,* Hazelden, City Center, Minnesota, 1999.

White, William L., *Slaying the Dragon: The History of Addiction Treatment and Recovery in America,* Second Edition, Chesnut Health Systems, Bloomington IL, 2014.

Wilson, Lois. "Bill's Wife Remembers When He and She and the First A.A.'s Were Very Young," A.A. *Grapevine,* Christmas Issue, 1944.

Diary of Two Motorcycle Hobos, Privately printed and distributed by Lois Wilson, Christmas, 1973. (StSt, LBW, Box 23, Writings 1925–1927—Diary of Two Motorcycle Hobos)

Lois Remembers, Al-Anon Family Group Headquarters, Inc., Virginia Beach, Virginia, 1979.

Wilson, William G., "The Fellowship of Alcoholics Anonymous," a speech given at the Yale School of Alcohol Studies, June 1944; published as the last lecture in *Alcohol, Science and Society Twenty-nine Lectures with Discussions as Given at the Yale Summer School of Alcohol Studies,* Quarterly Journal of Studies on Alcohol, New Haven, 1945.

"The Book Is Born," A.A. *Grapevine,* October 1945. Reprinted in *The Language of the Heart,* A.A. Grapevine, Inc., New York, 1988, pp. 9-12.

"Lack of Money Proved A.A. Boon," A.A. *Grapevine,* June 1947. Reprinted in *The Language of the Heart,* A.A. Grapevine, Inc., New York, 1988, pp. 57-61.

"Book Publication Proved Discouraging Venture," A.A. *Grapevine,* July 1947. Reprinted in *The Language of the Heart,* A.A. Grapevine, Inc., New York, 1988, pp. 105-108.

Twelve Steps and Twelve Traditions, Alcoholics Anonymous Publishing, Inc., [New York], [1953].

"A Fragment of History: Origin of the Twelve Steps," an article in the A.A. *Grapevine,* July 1953. Reprinted in *The Language of the Heart,* A.A. Grapevine, Inc., New York, 1988, pp. 195-202.

"How the Book Alcoholics Anonymous Came About," Bill W.'s Speech at the Texas State AA Convention, June 12, 1954, transcribed in *The Book That Started It All,* pp. 205-218.

"Bill W.'s Talk to the Manhattan Group, New York City, N.Y., 1955." Transcript available online at http://www.silkworth.net/aahistory/manhattan_group_1955.html (retrieved September 10, 2010.)

The Language of the Heart: Bill W.'s Grapevine Writings, A.A. Grapevine, Inc., New York, 1988.

Bill W. My First 40 Years, Hazelden, Center City, Minnesota, 2000.

The A.A. Service Manual combined with Twelve Concepts for World Service, Alcoholics Anonymous World Services, Inc., New York, 2009.

Endnotes

Chapter One. Challenging the Creation Myths

1 *Alcoholics Anonymous* (4th edition), "How It Works," p. 60.

2 Ibid., "There Is A Solution," p. 20, which is just one of many references to the importance of being "useful to others" in this book.

3 Ibid., "Foreword to the Second Edition," p. xvii.

4 *Pass It On*, pp. 237–38.

5 *Alcoholics Anonymous* (4th edition), "Bill's Story," pp. 8–10.

6 Ebby Thacher speaking in Memphis, Tennessee, 1958 [tape: 26:30 to 29:27] (http://www.xa-speakers.org – retrieved April 26, 2013). See also Fitzpatrick, *Dr. Bob & Bill W. Speak*, pp. 14–24, which presents an account based on "Ebby's own words, extracted from eight separate recordings and combined here."

7 Ebby Thacher speaking in Iowa, 1960 (GSO, Oral History Files, Thacher, Edwin Ebby / 1897-1962, p. 3).

8 Ebby Thacher speaking at the Jefferson Hotel, St. Louis, Missouri at the 1955 International Convention (GSO, Oral History Files, Thacher, Edwin Ebby / 1897-1962, p. 6). *NOTE*: There is a transcript of one other talk by Ebby given in Fort Worth, TX, June 1954 in this same GSO folder

9 Lois Wilson to Elise, Edith and Helen (StSt, LBW 210, Box 48, Folder 1).

10 *Alcoholics Anonymous*, (4th edition), "Foreword to the Second Edition," pp. xvi–xvii.

11 Ebby Thacher speaking in Iowa, 1960 (GSO, Oral History Files, Thacher, Edwin Ebby / 1897-1962, p. 3).

12 *Alcoholics Anonymous*, (4th edition), "Foreword to the Second Edition," p. xvi.

13 For the details found in the two preceding paragraphs, see *Alcoholics Anonymous*, (4th edition), "A Vision For You," pp. 153–55.

14 *Alcoholics Anonymous*, (4th edition), "Doctor Bob's Nightmare," pp. 179-180.

15 Perhaps the best source for more details on this information is the original Yahoo AAHistoryLovers Board. See for instance, http://health.groups.yahoo.com/group/AAHistoryLovers/message/4672 (retrieved October 10, 2010).

16 *Alcoholics Anonymous*, (4th edition), "Foreword to Second Edition," p. xvii. For more details on "A.A. number three," see also "A Vision for You," pp. 156–58 along with the personal story, "Alcoholics Anonymous Number Three," pp. 182–92.

17 For Dr. McKay, see Bill Wilson to Lois Wilson, May 1935 (StSt, WGW 102.4, Box 27, Folder 71); for Eddie Reilly see AA Main Events, 1935, Point 14 and *Dr. Bob and the Good Oldtimers*, pp. 77-81. Fitzpatrick, *Dr. Bob & Bill W. Speak* has a lovely account of this incident related by Dr. Bob's son (pp. 71–72).

18 Lois's Diary for 1935 notes that Bill left for Akron on Sunday, April 21 and returned on either Saturday, August 24 or Sunday, August 25 (StSt, LBW 201.10, Biographical – Diaries 1936 *[which includes the diary for 1935]*, Box 11-B, Folder 3).

19 AA Main Events: 1935, Points 3 ("no success at all"), 16, 18 & 19; 1936, Points 4 & 8 ("the failure rate was immense"); 1937, Point 5 ("the percentage of failures was immense") & Point 13.

20 Bill mentions at least one visit to Akron "in the fall of that year [1936]" (AA Main Events, 1936, Point 7).

21 *Alcoholics Anonymous*, (4th edition), "Foreword to the Second Edition," p. xvii.

22 AA Main Events, 1935, Points 17, 18 & 20; 1936, Points 3 & 8.

23 Ibid., 1934, Points 5 & 6; 1935, Points 15 & 17; 1936, Points 3 & 8.

24 Ibid., 1937, Point 2.

25 John 13:35: "By this shall all men know that ye are my disciples, if ye have love for one another." (King James translation)

26 Wikipedia, The Oxford Group, Named Article (retrieved May 18, 2013).

27 Ibid.

Chapter Two. The Akron Vote

1 AA Main Events, 1937, Points 6 & 7; Bill Wilson speaking in Fort Worth, Texas, June 12, 1954 ("How the Book Alcoholics Anonymous Came About," in *The Book That Started It All*, p. 205); *AACOA*, p. 76.

2 Bill Wilson speaking in Fort Worth, Texas, June 12, 1954 ("How the Book Alcoholics Anonymous Came About," in *The Book That Started It All*, p. 205); *AACOA*, p. 76.

3 AA Main Events, 1937, Point 8; Wilson, "The Book Is Born."

4 AA Main Events, 1937, Point 8. Bill Wilson speaking in Fort Worth, Texas, June 12, 1954 ("How the Book Alcoholics Anonymous Came About," in *The Book That Started It All*, p. 205); Wilson, "The Book Is Born."

5 Wilson, "The Book Is Born;" *AACOA*, p. 144.

6 *AACOA*, p. 76.

7 Ibid., Bill Wilson speaking in Fort Worth, Texas, June 12, 1954 ("How the Book Alcoholics Anonymous Came About," in *The Book That Started It All*, p. 205).

8 Wilson, "Lack of Money Proved AA Boon."

9 Wilson, "The Book Is Born."

10 Ibid. [Note: this is a direct quote].

11 Ibid.

12 Ibid.

13 *AACOA*, p. 144.

14 Bill Wilson speaking in Fort Worth, Texas, June 12, 1954 (How the Book Alcoholics Anonymous Came About," in *The Book That Started It All*, p. 206); *AACOA*, p. 76.

15 *AACOA*, pp. 86 & 144; Wilson, "The Book Is Born."

16 AA Main Events, 1937, Point 10; *AACOA*, p. 144.

17 Bill Wilson speaking in Fort Worth, Texas, June 12, 1954 ("How the Book Alcoholics Anonymous Came About," in *The Book That Started It All*, p. 206); Wilson, "Lack of Money Proved AA Boon."

18 Wilson, "Lack of Money Proved AA Boon."

19 Ibid., *AACOA*, p. 144.

20 Bill Wilson speaking in Fort Worth, Texas, June 12, 1954 ("How the Book Alcoholics Anonymous Came About," in *The Book That Started It All*, p. 206).

21 Wilson, "Lack of Money Proved AA Boon."

22 *AACOA*, p. 144.

23 Bill Wilson speaking in Fort Worth, Texas, June 12, 1954 ("How the Book Alcoholics Anonymous Came About," in *The Book That Started It All*, p. 206).

24 Wilson, "The Book Is Born."

25 Bill Wilson speaking in Fort Worth, Texas, June 12, 1954 ("How the Book Alcoholics Anonymous Came About," in *The Book That Started It All*, pp. 206-207); Wilson, "Lack of Money Proved AA Boon"; *AACOA*, pp. 144–45.

26 AA Main Events, 1937, Point 9 [Note: this is a direct quote].

27 Wilson, "Lack of Money Proved A.A. Boon."

28 *AACOA*, p. 144.

29 Wilson, "Lack of Money Proved AA Boon"; Wilson, "The Book Is Born."

30 *AACOA*, p. 146; Wilson, "The Book Is Born"; Wilson, "Lack of Money Proved AA Boon."

31 Bill Wilson speaking in Fort Worth, Texas, June 12, 1954 ("How the Book Alcoholics Anonymous Came About," in *The Book That Started It All*, p. 206).

32 AA Main Events, 1937, Point 11; *AACOA*, p. 145.

33 *AACOA*, p. 145; Bill Wilson speaking in Fort Worth, Texas, June 12, 1954 (How the Book Alcoholics Anonymous Came About," in *The Book That Started It All*, p. 207).

34 *AACOA*, p. 145.

35 Ibid., Bill Wilson speaking in Fort Worth, Texas, June 12, 1954 ("How the Book Alcoholics Anonymous Came About," in *The Book That Started It All*, p. 206).

36 AA Main Events, 1937, Point 11; Bill Wilson speaking in Fort Worth, Texas, June 12, 1954 ("How the Book Alcoholics Anonymous Came About," in *The Book That Started It All*, pp. 206–07); *AACOA*, p. 145.

37 Ibid.

38 *AACOA*, p. 145; Bill Wilson speaking in Fort Worth, Texas, June 12, 1954 ("How the Book Alcoholics Anonymous Came About," in *The Book That Started It All*, p. 207).

[39] *AACOA*, p. 146.

[40] AA Main Events, 1937, <u>Point 11</u>.

[41] Bill Wilson speaking in Fort Worth, Texas, June 12, 1954 ("How the Book Alcoholics Anonymous Came About," in *The Book That Started It All*, p. 207).

[42] *AACOA*, p. 145.

[43] Ibid.

[44] Ibid.

[45] Ibid., AA Main Events, 1937, <u>Point 11</u>, p. 145.

[46] Wilson, "The Book Is Born."

[47] Ibid., AA Main Events, 1937, <u>Point 11</u>.

[48] Wilson, "The Book Is Born"; *AACOA*, p. 144.

[49] *AACOA*, p. 145.

[50] Ibid.

[51] Ibid.

[52] Bill Wilson speaking in Fort Worth, Texas, June 12, 1954 ("How the Book Alcoholics Anonymous Came About," in *The Book That Started It All*, p. 207).

[53] Ibid.

[54] Ibid., Wilson, "The Book Is Born."

[55] AA Main Events, 1937, <u>Point 11</u>; Wilson, "The Book Is Born."

[56] *AACOA*, p. 145.

[57] *AACOA*, pp. 145-146; Bill Wilson speaking in Fort Worth, Texas, June 12, 1954 ("How the Book Alcoholics Anonymous Came About," in *The Book That Started It All*, p. 207).

[58] AA Main Events, 1937, <u>Point 11</u>; Wilson, "Lack of Money Proved AA Boon"; *AACOA*, p. 146.

[59] Bill Wilson speaking in Fort Worth, Texas, June 12, 1954 ("How the Book Alcoholics Anonymous Came About," in *The Book That Started It All*, p. 207); Wilson, "Lack of Money Proved AA Boon"; *AACOA*, p. 146.

[60] AA Main Events, 1937, <u>Point 6</u>.

[61] Lois's Diary, 1937.

[62] Lois's Diary, July 16, 1937.

[63] Dr. R. H. Smith to Bill [Wilson], September 27, 1937 (StSt WGW 102 – Correspondence General – Smith, Robert Holbrook – Letters to WGW 1937 [4], WBW Box 9, Folder 4).

[64] Paul and Hildreth [Stanley] to William G. Wilson, October 6, 1937 (StSt WGW 102.7 Correspondence – General – Friends/Associates [1937], WGW, Box 25, Folder 29).

[65] AA Main Events, 1936, <u>Point 7</u>.

[66] Lois's Diary, August 11 & 15, 1937.

[67] For Fitz Mayo inclusion in this group, see Lois's 1937 Diary entry for October 10.

[68] Lois's Diary, October 8, 1937.

[69] AA Main Events, 1937, <u>Point 6</u>.

70 Lois's 1937 Diary entry for July 16. For further details, see also Lois's 1937 Diary entries for July 9 & 21.

71 AA Main Events, 1937, Point 6; http://www.mutual-funds-advisor.com/mutual-fund-history/stock-market-crashes.html (retrieved October 1, 2010).

72 Lois's Diary, October 8, 1937.

73 Ibid., October 9, 1937.

74 Recorded interview with Kathleen Ruddell (GSO, CD 769; Tape 2: A.A. Niles Peebles Research – Mrs. Bill Ruddell [1978]).

75 Lois's Diary, October 10, 1937.

76 Ibid., October 16, 1937.

77 List of Akron Members and their length of sobriety (RAC, Family, Group 2 OMR, Series P, Box 42, Folder 458).

78 Minutes of the First Meeting of the Alcoholics Foundation (GSO, Box 59, 1938, Folder B, Documents 1938-18a and 1938-19).

79 Wilson, "The Book Is Born."

80 Wilson, "Lack of Money Proved A.A. Boon."

81 Bill Wilson speaking in Fort Worth, Texas, June 12, 1954 ("How the Book Alcoholics Anonymous Came About," in *The Book That Started It All*, p. 205).

82 AA Main Events, 1937, Point 8.

83 *AACOA*, pp. 76 & 144 respectively.

84 Lois's Diary, October 16 & 17, 1937.

Chapter Three. Meeting Mr. Richardson

1 Wilson, "Lack of Money Proved A.A. Boon."

2 Lois's Diary, October 17, 1937.

3 Lois Wilson's "AA and Al-Anon Historical Events (Taken from my Diaries and Other Sources)" notes December 1936 as the date when this occurred (StSt LBW 203, LBW, Box 32, Folder 5, p.1); Reprinted in *Lois Remembers*, p. 197; see also AA Main Events, 1937, Point 12 which confirms the 1936 date.

4 AA Main Events, 1937, Point 12.

5 Ibid., Point 14.

6 Ibid.

7 Ibid.

8 The Honor Dealers Business Plan, "History" section, (StSt, Personages – Henry G. [Hank] Parkhurst – Honor Dealers Business Plan and Correspondence, AA 329, Box 4a).

9 Wm. G. Wilson to Dr. Esther L. Richards, July 22, 1938 (GSO, Box 59, 1938, Folder B, Document 1938-76 to 1938-78).

10 Hank [Parkhurst] to Bill [Wilson], November 21, 1936, (StSt, Personages – Henry G. Parkhurst – Honor Dealers Correspondence, AA 329, Box 4a, Folder 1).

11 Bill Wilson to Hank Parkhurst, April 9, 1940, (GSO, Box 60, Folder B, Works Publishing Correspondence).

12 "A Discussion of the Big Book," a talk by Ruth Hock, Glendale, CA, March 12, 1978; transcript copy in the Akron Archives, pp. 6–7. Also available on YouTube under the title "Ruth H. AA's First Secretary shares the history of Alcoholics Anonymous" - http://www.youtube.com/watch?v=mxVkTNgOhy0 – retrieved September 27, 2013.

13 Henry G. Parkhurst to Wm. G. Wilson, March 24, 1937 (GSO, Box 200, Folder I, Bill: Business with Hank P. / 1937-1950).

14 Bill Wilson to Hank Parkhurst, April 1, 1937 (GSO, Box 200, Folder I, Bill: Business with Hank P. / 1937-1950).

15 WGW to Horace Andrews, Jr., May 17, 1937 (GSO, Box 200, Folder I, Bill: Business with Hank P. / 1937-1950).

16 "A Discussion of the Big Book," a talk by Ruth Hock, Glendale, CA, March 12, 1978; transcript copy in the Akron Archives, pp. 6–7. Also available on YouTube under the title "Ruth H. AA's First Secretary shares the history of Alcoholics Anonymous" - http://www.youtube.com/watch?v=mxVkTNgOhy0 – retrieved September 27, 2013.

17 Burwell, "Evolution," p. 3 and his Big Book Story, "The Vicious Cycle," (2nd through the 4th editions).

18 GSO, Box 200, Folder I, Bill: Business with Hank P. / 1937-1950.

19 See, for instance, *AACOA*, p. 159.

20 Hank [Parkhurst] to Bill [Wilson], November 21, 1936 (StSt, Personages – Henry G. Parkhurst – Honor Dealers Correspondence, AA 329, Box 4a, Folder 1).

21 Ibid.

22 The promotional Q&A document is partially preserved on the reverse side of several pages in the "The One Hundred Men" document prepared by Ruth Hock in January 1939, presumably in an effort to economize on paper expenses (GSO, Box 59, 1939, Folder C, 1939-26 to 1939-32). [Note that the current copy preserved in the GSO archive is a Xerox and the copier failed to make copies of the verso of the typed sheets. The originals are now preserved off site.]

23 Ruth [Hock] Crecelius to Bill Wilson, November 10, 1955 (StSt, AA 326, Box 4, Folder 17).

24 Lois Wilson, "History for Book," four typed sheets, p. 1 (StSt Al-Anon 800, Box 1, Folder 6).

25 Lois's Diary, April 26, 1939.

26 Bill Wilson speaking to the Manhattan Group, New York City, December, 1955 (retrieved from http://recoveryspeakers.com/bill-w-1955-manhattan-group-about-the-early-days/).

27 Ruth [Hock] Crecelius to Bill Wilson, November 10, 1955 (StSt, AA 326, Box 4, Folder 17).

28 AA Main Events, 1937, Point 14.

29 In Jim Burwell's personal copy of the Multilith copy of the Big Book, he has written his name and address on the inside front cover: "J. M. Burwell / 344 N. Fullerton Ave. / Montclair N. J." This was Hank Parkhurst's home address at the time (Jim's book is currently in the author's private collection).

30 Burwell, "Evolution," p. 2.

31 AA Main Events, 1937, Point 14.

32 Ibid., *AACOA*, pp. 146–47.

33 Finan, *Drunks*, p. 27.

34 AA Main Events, 1937, Point 16.

35 Lois's Diary, September 18, 1937.

36 *A.A. Service Manual*, p. S3.

37 See Kurtz, *Not-God*, p. 14 and n. 26 on p. 310 for an interesting discussion of Bill's three (or four?) visits to Towns Hospital.

38 Minutes of Trustee Meeting of the Alcoholic Foundation, January 18, 1939 (GSO, Box: Alcoholic Foundation, Minutes 1939).

39 *AACOA*, p. 147; Bill Wilson speaking in Fort Worth, Texas, June 12, 1954 ("How the Book Alcoholics Anonymous Came About," in *The Book That Started It All*, p. 207).

40 Bill Wilson's Talk in Memphis, September 19, 1947, 1:20:50 to 1:24:30 (http://beyondhumanaid.weebly.com/bill-w-memphis-1947.html - retrieved October 30, 2015); Leonard & Dorothy Strong's 1978 Interview with Niles Peebles (GSO, CD 619, Track 1, [22:10 – 24:20]).

41 These 'quotes' are a blend of separate comments that can be found in *AACOA*, p. 147, AA Main Events, 1937, Point 17, and Bill Wilson speaking in Fort Worth, Texas, June 12, 1954 ("How the Book Alcoholics Anonymous Came About," in *The Book That Started It All*, p. 208).

42 Chernow, *Titan*, p. 187.

43 Ibid., p. 191.

44 Okrent, *Last Call*, pp. 39, 133, 233, 300, 350–51. Okrent's book is a fascinating and compelling history of Prohibition and is highly recommended for anyone interested in the important historical context in which Alcoholics Anonymous's "new cure" for alcoholism was offered.

45 These 'quotes' are a blend of separate comments that can be found in *AACOA*, p. 147, AA Main Events, 1937, Point 17, and Bill Wilson speaking in Fort Worth, Texas, June 12, 1954 ("How the Book Alcoholics Anonymous Came About," in *The Book That Started It All*, p. 208).

46 GSO, Box 59, Folder A, Reel 28, 1937-1.

47 Bill Wilson speaking in Fort Worth, Texas, June 12, 1954 ("How the Book Alcoholics Anonymous Came About," in *The Book That Started It All*, p. 208).

48 Amos, "History," p. 1. Frank Amos's eight-page "History" is an invaluable record of the ten-month period preceding its August 1938, composition. Its value lies not only in the fact that it is a contemporary document, but also because Amos insisted it be checked for accuracy by both Hank Parkhurst and Bill Wilson before he had the final copy typed up (see Frank B. Amos to Henry G. Parkhurst, August 22, 1938, GSO, Box 59, 1938, B[1] 1938-116).

49 Ibid.

50 Bill Wilson speaking in Fort Worth, Texas, June 12, 1954 ("How the Book Alcoholics Anonymous Came About," in *The Book That Started It All*, p. 208).

51 AA Main Events, 1937, Point 19.

[52] Lois Wilson's "AA and Al-Anon Historical Events (Taken from my Diaries and Other Sources)" (StSt LBW 203, LBW, Box 32, Folder 5, p. 1); Reprinted in *Lois Remembers*, p. 197.

[53] "W. S. Richardson, Clergyman," Dead, Obituary, *The New York Times*, November 23, 1952.

[54] Fosdick, *John D. Rockefeller, Jr.*, p. 54.

[55] Ibid., pp. 61–62

[56] Ibid., pp. 61–62, 76–77, 81.

[57] "W. S. Richardson, Clergyman, Dead," Obituary, *The New York Times*, November 23, 1952; Personal salutations can be found throughout RAC, Family, Group 02, Series N, Box 095, Folder 0775; Hired in 1912: W. S. Richardson to [Charles O.] Heydt, August 28, 1912, (RAC, Family, Group 02, Series H, Box 100, Folder 0762); The Rockefeller Foundation Charter, p. 4; Executive Director (RAC, Details Page of online listing for: Rockefeller – Related Special Collections, 2B 04, Laura Spelman Rockefeller Memorial, 1918-1949).

[58] Starr J. Murphy to [Charles O.] Heydt, September 9, 1919 and Memorandum by John D. Rockefeller, Junior, May 23, 1923, (RAC, Family, Group 02, Series O, Box 001, Folder 0001).

[59] Advisory Committees [Report], March 14, 1931, (RAC, Family, Group 02, Series O, Box 001, Folder 0001).

[60] Arthur W. Packard to John D. Rockefeller, Jr., October 4, 1934, (RAC, Family, Group 02, Series O, Box 001, Folder 0002).

[61] November 1, 1937 (StSt, WGW 102, Correspondence General – Smith, Robert Holbrook – Letters to WGW 1937 [4], Box 9, Folder 4).

[62] GSO, Box 59, Folder A, Reel 28, 1937-2.

[63] [Dr. Leonard Strong] to W.S. Richardson, November 12, 1937; W.S. Richardson to Dr. Leonard V. Strong, November 13, 1937 (GSO, Box 59, Folder A, Reel 28, 1937-3 & 1937-4).

[64] AA Main Events, 1937, Point 25.

[65] Bill Wilson speaking in Fort Worth, Texas, June 12, 1954 ("How the Book Alcoholics Anonymous Came About," in *The Book That Started It All*, p. 208).

[66] StSt, WGW 102, Correspondence General – Smith, Robert Holbrook – Letters to WGW 1937 (4), Box 9, Folder 4.

[67] November 23, 1937 (GSO, Box 59, Folder D.2, Letter 20).

[68] November 24, 1937 (GSO, Box 59, Folder D.2, Letter 19).

[69] November 26, 1937 (GSO, Box 59, Folder D.2, Letter 21).

[70] November 30, 1937 (StSt, WGW 102, Correspondence General – Smith, Robert Holbrook – Letters to WGW 1937 [4], Box 9, Folder 4).

[71] December 6, 1937 (GSO, Box 59, Folder D.2, Letter 22).

[72] W. S. Richardson to William G. Wilson, December 7, 1937 (GSO, Box 59, Folder D.2, Letter 23).

Chapter Four. The Rockefeller Dinner

[1] Lois's Diary, December 12, 1937.

[2] Amos, "History," p. 1 provides the most complete and reliable list of the eight attendees at this first Rockefeller dinner. Note that Frank Amos spelled Ned's last name "Poynter" (see Amos, "History," p. 1), but Bill and Lois always wrote "Pointer."

[3] AA Main Events, 1937, Point 22.

[4] Lois Wilson to Bill Wilson, February 27, 1938 (StSt, LBW 202.4 in WGW 102.4, Box 27, Folder 111).

[5] July 2, 1936 (StSt, WGW 102.4, Box 27, Folder 99).

[6] Ebby Thacher to Bill Wilson, August 18, 1936 (StSt, AA 302, AA Box 1, Folder 14 Personages – Ebby Thacher – WGW Correspondence 1936-1937); Lois Wilson to Bill Wilson, September 12, 1936 (LBW 202.4 in WGW 102.4, Box 2, Folder 110).

[7] *AACOA*, p. vii; *Lois Remembers*, p. 87.

[8] Wilson, *Bill W., My First 40 Years*, p. 148.

[9] *AACOA*, p. 13.

[10] *Alcoholics Anonymous* (4th edition), Foreword to the Second Edition, p. xvi; *AACOA*, pp. 67–68.

[11] Lincoln, *Lockwood Greene*, pp. 647 & 780.

[12] John D. Rockefeller, Jr. to Albert L. Scott, February 3, 1934 (RAC, Family, Group 02, Series C, Box 069, Folder 0521).

[13] Albert L. Scott to John D. Rockefeller, Jr., December 26, 1934; John D. Rockefeller, Jr. to John R. Todd, December 28, 1934 (RAC, Family, Group 02, Series C, Box 069, Folder 0521).

[14] John D. Rockefeller, Jr. to G. H. Smith, February 15, 1933 (RAC, Family, Group 02 OMR, Series P, Box 41, Folder 448).

[15] *Toward Liquor Control*, Foreword, p. ix.

[16] "Albert L. Scott, 67, Engineer," Is Dead in the *New York Times*, March 3, 1946.

[17] Albert L. Scott to John D. Rockefeller, Jr., October 15, 1945 (RAC, Family, Group 02, Series N, Box 084, Folder 0679).

[18] *AACOA*, p. 15; Named Wikipedia entry for "Riverside Church" (retrieved October 10, 2010).

[19] AA Main Events, 1937, Point 20 and many supporting real estate correspondence and documents archived in the RAC.

[20] Rockefeller-Chipman Correspondence, 1906-1920 (RAC, Family, Group 2 OMR, Series P, Box 41, Folder 448).

[21] J[ohn] D. R[ockefeller] Jr., Memorandum, September 4, 1935 (RAC, Family, Group 2 OMR, Series N, Box 93, Folder 760).

[22] Bible Classes: Rockefeller-Chipman Correspondence, 1906-1920 (RAC, Family, Group 2 OMR, Series P, Box 41, Folder 448); "Riverside Church Elects Officers," in *The New York Times*, December 11, 1930.

[23] Edward Lathrop Ballard to John D. Rockefeller, Jr., July 30, 1931 (RAC, Family, Group 2 OMR, Series N, Box 93, Folder 760).

[24] John D. Rockefeller, Jr. to Virgil J. Johnson, July 7, 1950; Robert W. Gumbel to John P. Hodgkin, March 10, 1962 (RAC, Family, Group 2 OMR, Series N, Box 93, Folder 760).

[25] Chernow, *Titan*, pp. 238, 308.

[26] "Advertising News and Notes," August 18, 1938; "News and Notes of the Advertising Field," June 16, 1939 in *The New York Times*.

[27] Short speech before the April, 1951 General Services Conference (GSO, AA Conference 1951, Ref #0002, Tape 2 of 11, [B side], 1:03:37).

[28] AA Main Events, 1937, Point 20.

[29] *Toward Liquor Control*, pp. vii-ix.

[30] Bill Wilson speaking in Fort Worth, Texas, June 12, 1954 ("How the Book Alcoholics Anonymous Came About," in *The Book That Started It All*, p. 208).

[31] AA Main Events, 1937, Point 21.

[32] Amos, "History," p. 1.

[33] Ibid., p. 2.

[34] Ibid., pp. 1-2

[35] Ibid.

[36] Ibid., p. 2.

[37] *AACOA*, p. 148.

[38] This 'quote' rearranges the words used in *AACOA*, pp. 148–49.

[39] *AACOA*, p. 149.

[40] This 'quote' is a blend of separate comments that can be found in Bill Wilson speaking in Fort Worth, Texas, June 12, 1954 ("How the Book Alcoholics Anonymous Came About," in *The Book That Started It All*, p. 209); *AACOA*, p. 149; AA Main Events, 1937, Point 24 and Wilson, "Lack of Money."

[41] This 'quote' is a blend of separate comments that can be found in Bill Wilson speaking in Fort Worth, Texas, June 12, 1954 ("How the Book Alcoholics Anonymous Came About," in *The Book That Started It All*, p. 209); *AACOA*, p. 149; AA Main Events, 1937, Point 24 and Wilson, "Lack of Money."

[42] *AACOA*, p. 149.

[43] Ibid., Wilson, "Lack of Money."

[44] This 'quote' is a blend of separate comments that can be found in *AACOA*, p. 149; Wilson, "Lack of Money"; AA Main Events, 1937, Point 25. See also "Notes on Akron, Ohio Survey by Frank Amos," (GSO Box 22, Reel 10 / 8.1 The Alcoholic Foundation: 1937-1938, p. 3). *NOTE*: This document is the *second* copy of Amos's "Notes" preserved in the archives and is the unedited version which contains many extra details that did not make their way into the final version that went to John D. Rockefeller, Jr..

[45] AA Main Events, 1937, Point 25.

[46] Amos, "History," p. 4; *AACOA*, p. 149; Wilson, "Lack of Money"; AA Main Events, 1937, Point 25.

[47] "Notes on Akron, Ohio Survey by Frank Amos," [unedited version] (GSO Box 22, Reel 10 / 8.1 The Alcoholic Foundation: 1937-1938, p. 3).

[48] November 24, 1937 (GSO, Box 59, Folder D.2, Letter 19).

[49] Amos, "History," pp. 3-4.

[50] AA Main Events: 1935, Points 3 ("no success at all"), 16, 18 & 19; 1936, Points 4 & 8 ("the failure rate was immense"); 1937, Point 5 ("the percentage of failures was immense") & Point 13.

[51] Amos, "History," p. 2.

[52] Ibid.

[53] December 17, 1937 (GSO, Box 59, Folder D.2, Document 24).

[54] StSt, WGW/LBW 102.7, Box 25, Folder 29.

[55] Amos, "History," p. 2.

[56] Lois's Diary, December 14, 1937.

[57] Transcript of Remarks Henrietta B. Seiberling [June 1971] (StSt, AA 324a, Box 4, Folder 13: Personages – Henrietta Seiberling – Recollections to her son, John F. Seiberling, May 1972).

[58] See Kurtz, *Not-God*, p. 66 and especially p. 315, n. 64 for some interesting information and insight on Henrietta Seiberling.

[59] Lois's Diary, December 15, 1937.

[60] December 1937 (StSt, LBW 203, Box 35, Folder 4).

[61] Lois's Diary, December 1937 (GSO, Box 201, Folder A, Lois's Diaries – 1937).

Chapter Five. Dr. Bob's Hospital

[1] Willard S. Richardson to William G. Wilson (StSt, WGW/LBW 102.7, Box 25, Folder 29).

[2] W. S. Richardson to [William] Wilson, January 15, 1938 (GSO, Box 59, 1938, Folder B, Document 1938-6).

[3] Amos, "History," pp. 2–3.

[4] GSO, Box 59, Folder D.2, Document 3.

[5] GSO, Box 59, 1938, Folder B, Document 1938-6,

[6] Amos, "History," pp. 4–5.

[7] GSO, AA Conference 1951, Frank Amos's comments, Ref #0002, Tape 2 of 11, [B side], 1:03:37.

[8] Printed program for the "*Twelfth Anniversary of the forming of Alcoholics Anonymous*" held in Cleveland on June 14–15, 1947 (Brown University Library, Chester H. Kirk Collection, Clarence Snyder Box). *[Special thanks to Narcotics Anonymous historian, Chris B. of Raleigh, NC, for providing this reference.]*

[9] Reported by A.A. Historian Mel Barger on his personal experience when he first joined A.A. (DVD of a video interview with David Lester, June 9, 2013; The Roots of Recovery, Sound Solutions Recording).

[10] *AACOA*, p. 165; *Lois Remembers*, p. 114.

[11] Video interview, October 22, 2013.

[12] Bill Wilson, Founder's Day Speech, Akron, OH, June 1959.

13 "Epic Gathering Marks Tenth Anniversary," A.A. *Grapevine*, Volume II, No. 2, July, 1945, p. 1.

14 *AACOA*, p. 107.

15 "Epic Gathering Marks Tenth Anniversary," A.A. *Grapevine*, Volume II, No. 2, July, 1945, p. 6.

16 GSO File Folder marked: Recording of T. Henry Williams, December 12, 1954, p. 9.

17 See for instance, *AACOA*, pp. 64, 262, & 264 and *Alcoholics Anonymous*, (4th edition), "There Is A Solution" p. 28.

18 "How 14 California Groups Grew to 22," A.A. *Grapevine*, Volume I, No. 8, January, 1945, p. 6.

19 The Gospel of John, Verse 1:23, King James translation.

20 GSO, Box 59, Folder D.2, Documents 1 & 2.

21 [Dr.] Bob [Smith] to Bill [Wilson], February 17, 1938 (StSt, WGW Series 102, Box 9, Folder 5).

22 "Notes on Akron, Ohio Survey / by / Frank Amos," [unedited version], p. 3 (GSO, Box 22, Reel 10 / 8.1 The Alcoholic Foundation: 1937-1938, P-7 to P-10).

23 Ibid.

24 Ibid.

25 [Dr.] Bob [Smith] to Bill [Wilson], November 22, 1937 (StSt, WGW 102, Correspondence General – Smith, Robert Holbrook – Letters to WGW 1937 (4), Box 9, Folder 4).

26 "Notes on Akron, Ohio Survey / by / Frank Amos," [unedited version], p. 2 (GSO, Box 22, Reel 10 / 8.1 The Alcoholic Foundation: 1937-1938, P-7 to P-10).

27 Ibid.

28 Ibid.

29 RAC, Family, Group 2 OMR, Series P, Box 42, Folder 458.

30 [Dr.] Bob [Smith] to Bill [Wilson], February 17, 1938 (StSt, WGW Series 102, Box 9, Folder 5).

31 "Notes on Akron, Ohio Survey / by / Frank Amos," [unedited version], p. 3 (GSO, Box 22, Reel 10 / 8.1 The Alcoholic Foundation: 1937-1938, P-7 to P-10).

32 [Dr.] Bob [Smith] to Bill [Wilson], February 17, 1938 (StSt, WGW Series 102, Box 9, Folder 5).

33 Ibid.

34 "Notes on Akron, Ohio Survey / by / Frank Amos," [unedited version], p. 2 (GSO, Box 22, Reel 10 / 8.1 The Alcoholic Foundation: 1937-1938, P-7 to P-10).

35 [Dr.] Bob [Smith] to Bill [Wilson], February 17, 1938 (StSt, Series 102, Box 9, Folder 5).

36 Ibid.

37 *Dr. Bob and the Good Oldtimers*, p. 136.

38 Amos, "History," p. 5.

39 "Notes on Akron, Ohio Survey / by / Frank Amos," [unedited version], pp. 2 (GSO, Box 22, Reel 10 / 8.1 The Alcoholic Foundation: 1937-1938, P-7 to P-10).

40 "Epic Gathering Marks Tenth Anniversary," A.A. *Grapevine*, Volume II, No. 2, July, 1945, p. 6.

41 AA Main Events, 1938, Point 1.

42 "Notes on Akron, Ohio Survey / by / Frank Amos," [unedited version], pp. 1-2 (GSO, Box 22, Reel 10 / 8.1 The Alcoholic Foundation: 1937-1938, P-7 to P-10).

43 RAC, Family, Group 2 OMR, Series P, Box 42, Folder 458.

44 [Dr.] Bob [Smith] to Bill [Wilson], February 17, 1938 (StSt, WGW Series 102, Box 9, Folder 5); "Notes on Akron, Ohio Survey / by / Frank Amos," [unedited version], pp. 1-2 (GSO, Box 22, Reel 10 / 8.1 The Alcoholic Foundation: 1937-1938, P-7 to P-10).

45 [Dr.] Bob [Smith] to Bill [Wilson], February 17, 1938 (StSt, WGW Series 102, Box 9, Folder 5).

46 Ibid.

47 AA Main Events, 1938, Point 1.

48 "Notes on Akron, Ohio Survey / by / Frank Amos," [unedited version], p. 3 (GSO, Box 22, Reel 10 / 8.1 The Alcoholic Foundation: 1937-1938, P-7 to P-10).

49 Kurtz, *Not-God*, pp. 66 & 330, n. 23.

50 "Notes on Akron, Ohio Survey / by / Frank Amos," [unedited version], p. 3 (GSO, Box 22, Reel 10 / 8.1 The Alcoholic Foundation: 1937-1938, P-7 to P-10).

51 Ibid., p. 4.

52 Ibid.

53 Amos, "History," p. 5.

54 AA Main Events, 1938, Point 2.

55 "Notes on Akron, Ohio Survey / by / Frank Amos," [unedited version] (GSO, Box 22, Reel 10 / 8.1 The Alcoholic Foundation: 1937-1938, P-7 to P-10). For Richardson's condensation see AA Main Events, 1938, Point 3.

56 RAC, Family, RG2, OMR, P, Welfare-General, Box 42, Folder 458.

57 GSO, Box 59, 1938, Folder B, Document 1938-15.

58 AA Main Events, 1938, Point 5.

Chapter Six. The Alcoholic Fund

1 Lois Wilson to Bill Wilson, February 27, 1938 (StSt, LBW 202.4 in WGW 102.4, Box 27, Folder 111). The letter is to Bill in Maryland and, at the end, Lois thanks him "for the wire from Akron."

2 AA Main Events, 1938, Point 6.

3 Ibid.

4 AA Main Events, 1938, Point 7.

5 Lois's Diary, March 13, 1938; AA Main Events, 1938, Point 7.

6 AA Main Events, 1938, Point 9.

7 Lois's List of Historical Dates Oct 1937 to May 1945: February 4, 1938 (StSt, LBW 203, Box 35, Folder 4) has a parenthetical remark that Gussie was the one responsible for convincing Richardson to go along with the idea of a foundation.

[8] Lois's Diary, March 15, 1938.

[9] AA Main Events, 1938, Point 9.

[10] Ibid.

[11] "Bill's Wife Remembers When He and She and the First A.A.'s Were Very Young," A.A. *Grapevine*, Christmas Issue, 1944. p. 1.

[12] Ibid.

[13] Ibid.

[14] Lois's 1938 Diary.

[15] Lois's Diary, March 18, 1938.

[16] Lois Wilson to Bill Wilson, March 21, 1938 (StSt, LBW 202.4, Box 27, Folder 112).

[17] Lois's 1938 Diary.

[18] Henry G. Parkhurst to Frank Amos, March 16, 1938 (GSO, Alcoholic Foundation Correspondence, Box 59, Folder D-2, Documents 6 & 7).

[19] Ibid.

[20] Ibid for this and all the quotes in the preceding eight paragraphs.

[21] "A Discussion of the Big Book," a talk by Ruth Hock, Glendale, CA, March 12, 1978; transcript copy in the Akron Archives, p. 13. Also available on YouTube under the title "Ruth H. AA's First Secretary shares the history of Alcoholics Anonymous" - http://www.youtube.com/watch?v=mxVkTNgOhy0 – retrieved September 27, 2013.

[22] Ibid, p. 23.

[23] For the salary, see Ruth Hock's 1978 Interview with Niles Peebles, GSO, CD 873, Track 1, [13:10]. For the $3 increase see Ruth Hock to Bill Wilson, November 10, 1955 (StSt, AA 326, Box 4, Folder 17).

[24] "A Discussion of the Big Book," a talk by Ruth Hock, Glendale, CA, March 12, 1978; transcript copy in the Akron Archives, p. 8. Also available on YouTube under the title "Ruth H. AA's First Secretary shares the history of Alcoholics Anonymous" - http://www.youtube.com/watch?v=mxVkTNgOhy0 – retrieved September 27, 2013.

[25] Ibid, pp. 8–9

[26] Florence Rankin to Bill Wilson, September 24, 1937 (StSt, WGW 102.7, Box 25, Folder 29).

[27] "A Discussion of the Big Book," a talk by Ruth Hock at Glendale, CA, March 12, 1978; transcript copy in the Akron Archives, p. 23. Also available on YouTube under the title "Ruth H. AA's First Secretary shares the history of Alcoholics Anonymous" - http://www.youtube.com/watch?v=mxVkTNgOhy0 – retrieved September 27, 2013.

[28] Ibid.

[29] Ibid, p. 7.

[30] Ruth Hock to Bill Wilson, November 10, 1955 (StSt, AA 326, Box 4, Folder 17).

[31] "A Discussion of the Big Book," a talk by Ruth Hock, Glendale, CA, March 12, 1978; transcript copy in the Akron Archives, p. 7. Also available on YouTube under the title "Ruth H. AA's First Secretary shares the history of Alcoholics Anonymous" - http://www.youtube.com/watch?v=mxVkTNgOhy0 – retrieved September 27, 2013.

[32] GSO, Box 59, 1938, Folder B, Document 1938-16.

[33] GSO, Box 59, 1938, Folder B, Document 1938-18.

34 This was a joint checking account set up for Amos, Richardson and Chipman (Frank Amos to Willard Richardson, August 19, 1938, GSO, Box 59, 1938, Folder B[1], Document 1938-114. See also Record of Contributions and Payments to Alcoholic Fund by Frank Amos (GSO, Box 59, 1938, Folder B[1], Document 1938-196).

35 AA Main Events, 1938, Point 13.

36 Pittman, *AA The Way It Began*, p. 86.

37 *AACOA*, p. 100.

38 Pittman, *AA The Way It Began*, pp. 157-158.

39 *AACOA*, pp. 99–100.

40 *AACOA*, pp. 100–01 and *Twelve Steps and Twelve Traditions* (1ˢᵗ edition), pp. 140–42. The biblical quote is from the Gospel of Luke 10:7 (King James Translation).

41 *AACOA*, p. 101; *Twelve Steps and Twelve Traditions* (1ˢᵗ edition), pp. 140–42.

42 Ibid., *Lois Remembers*, p. 107.

43 William G. Wilson to Frank Amos, September 26, 1938 (GSO, Box 59, 1938, Folder B[1], Document 1938-145 to 151, page 3).

44 T. G. Lewis (Manager of Towns Hospital) to W. G. Wilson, April 3, 1957 (GSO, Box 27A, Reel 12 / 13.2[1] Miscellaneous – unmarked materials) which has information regarding the dates and the individual check stubs written by Charles Towns to Bill Wilson and A.A.. Confirmed receipt by Amos can be found in two of his handwritten tallies for the Alcoholic Fund (GSO, Box 59, 1938, Folder B[1], Documents 1938-195 & 1938-196).

45 Royalties paid to Bill and Dr. Bob, listing of (GSO, Box 200, Folder F). In addition, distribution of money by the Alcoholic Fund and later the Alcoholic Foundation to Wilson, Parkhurst and Mayo correspond almost exactly to this and future contributions made by Charlie Towns.

46 Bill to Darling Suzie, March 21, 1938 (GSO, Box 200, Folder J / Bill and Lois: Correspondence between, / 1935-1939).

47 Wilson, "The Book Is Born."

48 Lois's Diary, 1938.

49 Ibid.

50 Bill Wilson speaking in Fort Worth, Texas, June 12, 1954 ("How the Book Alcoholics Anonymous Came About," in *The Book That Started It All*, p. 216).

51 Oral History Transcriptions, Transcript Record of Wally [Gillam], Akron, Ohio, 12/12/54 (GSO, Box 1 of 2, Box 1: 304680980)

52 Lois Wilson to Bill Wilson, April, [21 or 22], 1938 (StSt, LBW 202.4 in WGW, Box 27, Folder 113).

53 Lois Wilson to Bill Wilson, April 25*[sic]*, 1938 (StSt, LBW 202.4 in WGW, Box 27, Folder 114).

54 During the first week of June 1938, Lois's diary records a "Picnic at Parkhursts" on Sunday, June 5 and a "Seminar" held, presumably in Brooklyn, on Tuesday, June 7. From that point on, "seminars" were always held on Tuesdays.

55 Lois Wilson to Bill Wilson, April 25*[sic]*, 1938 (StSt, LBW 202.4 in WGW, Box 27, Folder 114); Lois Wilson to Bill Wilson, April 28, 1938 (StSt, LBW 202.4 in WGW, Box 27, Folder 115).

Chapter Seven. Bill's Stories

1 Bill Wilson to Dr. Bob Smith, [June 22, 23 or 24], 1938 (GSO, Box 59, 1938, Folder B, Documents 1938-25 to 1938-30).

2 Ibid.

3 Ibid.

4 Hank [Parkhurst] to Herbert F. Taylor [and Bill Wilson], [May, 1938] (GSO, Box 59, Folder D.2, Document 8).

5 Ibid for this and the five preceding paragraphs.

6 Frank Amos to Willard Richardson, July 7, 1938 (GSO, Box 59, 1938, Folder B, Document 1938-37) and three handwritten documents detailing the income and expenses of the Alcoholic Foundation (GSO, Box 59, 1938, Folder B[1], Documents 1938-194, 195 & 196) up to 12/28/38, 2/27/39 and 7/2/38 respectively.

7 *AACOA*, p. 152.

8 AA Main Events, 1938, Point 12.

9 AA Main Events, 1938, Point 13.

10 T. G. Lewis (Manager of Towns Hospital) to W. G. Wilson, April 3, 1957 (GSO, Box 27A, Reel 12 / 13.2[1] Miscellaneous – unmarked materials) which contains detailed information regarding the dates and what was written on the individual check stubs.

11 William G. Wilson to Frank Amos, September 26, 1938 (GSO, Box 59, 1938, Folder B[1], Document 1938-145 to 151, page 3).

12 Bill Wilson to Dr. Bob Smith, [June 22, 23 or 24], 1938 (GSO, Box 59, 1938, Folder B, Documents 1938-25 to 1938-30).

13 Ibid.

14 Burwell, "Speech at Hope Manor," p. 11: "So, he sold Bill the idea of writing a couple of chapters."

15 Bill Wilson to Dr. Bob Smith, [June 22, 23 or 24], 1938 (GSO, Box 59, 1938, Folder B, Documents 1938-25 to 1938-30).

16 *Lois Remembers*, p. 197: "May 20 [1938]: Bill starts writing the Big Book."

17 Strangely, this manuscript is not to be found in either the GSO or Stepping Stones archives. See, however, Wilson, *Bill W. My First 40 Years*, Appendix B (pp. 186–99) for a facsimile of each page along with a transcription of the text. Online sites that have the full text of this story can be found by searching "it was a hot night in the midsummer of 1934" (using quotation marks as shown). NOTE that "legal" sheets of paper are 8½" x 14" (i.e., 3" longer than the standard American piece of paper).

18 Ibid., pp. 186–87.

19 Ibid., pp. 188–99.

20 Ibid., pp. 198–99.

21 Bill Wilson to Dr. Bob Smith, [June 22, 23 or 24], 1938 (GSO, Box 59, 1938, Folder B, Documents 1938-25 to 1938-30).

22 Ruth [Hock] Crecelius to Bill Wilson, November 10, 1955 (StSt, AA 326, Box 4, Folder 17).

23 Ibid.

24 http://www.barefootsworld.net/images/aa_strange_obsession.jpg (retrieved October 1, 2011). A black-and-white copy of all eight hand-written pages can be found in Wilson, *Bill W. My First 40 Years*, <u>Appendix B</u> (pp. 186-199).

25 Bill Wilson to Dr. Bob Smith, [June 22, 23 or 24], 1938 (GSO, Box 59, 1938, Folder B, Documents 1938-25 to 1938-30).

26 StSt, WGW 103, Box 31, Folder 3: Writings 1939 *[sic]* - Original story [incomplete; typescript; 36 pp., 1180 lines].

27 "Original Story," pp. 2–3 (StSt, WGW 103, Box 31, Folder 3)

28 [First Two Chapters of Proposed Book], p. 11 (GSO, Box 59, 1938, Folder B, Documents 1938-53 to 1938-75).

29 "Original Story," p. 30 (StSt, WGW 103, Box 31, Folder 3).

30 Ibid., p. 31.

31 *Alcoholics Anonymous* (4th edition), "Bill's Story," pp. 10 & 14 respectively.

32 Ibid., "Into Action," p. 84.

33 "Original Story," pp. 30[31], 31[32], 33-34. (StSt, WGW 103, Box 31, Folder 3).

34 Ibid. pp. 11–12.

35 Ibid., p. 30 [31].

36 *Alcoholics Anonymous* (4th edition), "Into Action," p. 85.

37 Transcript of Tape of Ebby Thacher in the Jefferson Hotel, St. Louis, Missouri at the 1955 St. Louis International Convention, p. 3 (GSO, Oral History Files, File folder: Thacher, Edwin Ebby / 1897-196).

38 Ebby Thacher speaking in Memphis in 1958 (XA-Speaker.org, *Five Years in Texas*, 25:00 minutes into the talk)

39 [First Two Chapters of Proposed Book], "There Is A Solution," p. 11 (GSO, Box 59, 1938, Folder B, Documents 1938-53 to 1938-75).

40 "A Discussion of the Big Book," a talk by Ruth Hock, Glendale, CA, March 12, 1978; transcript copy in the Akron Archives, p. 8-9. Also available on YouTube under the title "Ruth H. AA's First Secretary shares the history of Alcoholics Anonymous" - http://www.youtube.com/watch?v=mxVkTNgOhy0 – retrieved September 27, 2013.

41 Ibid, p. 14. For Bill's dislike for traditional dictation, see Ruth [Hock] Crecelius to Bill Wilson, November 10, 1955 (StSt, AA 326, Box 4, Folder 17).

42 "A Discussion of the Big Book," a talk by Ruth Hock, Glendale, CA, March 12, 1978; transcript copy in the Akron Archives, p. 8. Also available on YouTube under the title "Ruth H. AA's First Secretary shares the history of Alcoholics Anonymous" - http://www.youtube.com/watch?v=mxVkTNgOhy0 – retrieved September 27, 2013.

43 Ibid, p. 24.

44 "Original Story," p. 30 [31] (StSt, WGW 103, Box 31, Folder 3).

Chapter Eight. "There Is a Solution"

1 *Dr. Bob and the Good Oldtimers*, Alcoholics Anonymous World Services, Inc., New York, 1980, p. 155; *Lois Remembers*, p. 171 and, more specifically, Oral History Transcriptions, Transcript Record of Bob Evans, Akron, Ohio, 6/18/54 (GSO, Box 1 of 2, Box 1: 304680980) where Bill says: "…but still nominally up to the time the

book came out, you were still Oxford Groups and didn't have the nerve to tell T. Henry you weren't." to which Bob replies: "That's right. We were Oxford Groupers— the Alcoholic Squad of the Oxford Group until we physically moved out." (which, by the way, didn't happen until December of 1939). Also of interest is Bill's comment that "Out there they still talked and acted as though they were Oxford Groupers." (AA Main Events, 1937, Point 2.)

2   *Dr. Bob and the Good Oldtimers*, p. 158.

3   [Dr.] Bob [Smith] to Bill [Wilson], February 17, 1938 (StSt, WGW 102, Box 9, Folder 5).

4   *Dr. Bob and the Good Oldtimers*, p. 136.

5   "Notes on Akron, Ohio Survey / by / Frank Amos," [unedited version], p. 2 (GSO, Box 22, Reel 10 / 8.1 The Alcoholic Foundation: 1937-1938, P-7 to P-10).

6   Oral History Transcriptions, Transcript Record of Bob Evans, Akron, Ohio, 6/18/54 (GSO, Box 1 of 2, Box 1: 304680980)

7   Oral History Transcriptions, Transcript Record of Wally [Gillam], Akron, Ohio, 12/12/54 (GSO, Box 1 of 2, Box 1: 304680980)

8   *Dr. Bob and the Good Oldtimers*, p. 101.

9   GSO filing cabinet drawer marked "Oral Histories," Folder marked: Murphy, Dorothy Snyder / Akron OH / August 30, 1954, p. 14. Also quoted in *Dr. Bob and the Good Oldtimers*, p. 101.

10 Bob Evans to Nell Wing, March 14, 1975 (StSt, AA 401, History – Recollections of Early AA [Various], Box 6, Folder 9).

11 Oral History Transcriptions, Transcript Record of Bob Evans, Akron, Ohio, 6/18/54 (GSO, Box 1 of 2, Box 1: 304680980)

12 *Dr. Bob and the Good Oldtimers*, pp. 137–41.

13 GSO filing cabinet drawer marked "Oral Histories," Folder marked: Murphy, Dorothy Snyder / Akron OH / August 30, 1954, p. 14. Quoted (with editorial changes) in *Dr. Bob and the Good Oldtimers*, Alcoholics Anonymous World Services, Inc., New York, 1980, p. 101.

14 *Lois Remembers*, pp. 91 & 93.

15 Ibid., pp. 93–94.

16 AA Main Events, 1935, Points 17.

17 [Bill Wilson – Autobiographical Recording] – Writings 1954 – Recollections of his early life – recorded with Ed Bierstadt at Hotel Bedford Sept. 1954 (StSt, WGW 103, Box 31, Folder 15).

18 *Bill W. My First 40 Years*, pp. 159–60; Kurtz, *Not-God*, p. 314 n.57; *AACOA*, p. 74.

19 AA Main Events, 1935, Point 18.

20 Ibid., Point 20.

21 *Alcoholics Anonymous* (1st edition), "The Unbeliever," p. 205.

22 Ibid., "Our Southern Friend," p. 237.

23 William J. Ruddell to William G. Wilson, January 26, 1957 (GSO, Box 29, Reel 13, 17.3 History Book, A.A. Comes of Age: Correspondence with Members Mentioned in Book, pp. 42–43)

24 AA Main Events, 1935, Point 17-19 & 1936, Point 3; Kurtz, *Not-God*, p. 45; *Lois Remembers*, pp. 103–104.

25 AA Main Events, 1936, Point 8.

26 William J. Ruddell to William G. Wilson, January 26, 1957 (GSO, Box 29, Reel 13, 17.3 History Book, A.A. Comes of Age: Correspondence with Members Mentioned in Book, pp. 42–43).

27 Bill Wilson to McGhee Baxter, October 30, 1940 (GSO, Box 54, Reel 25, Folder G, Richmond, VA, pp. 23–24).

28 Ibid.

29 *AACOA*, p. 74.

30 Ibid., pp. 74–75.

31 Oral History Transcriptions, Transcript Record of Wally [Gillam], Akron, Ohio, 12/12/54 (GSO, Box 1 of 2, Box 1: 304680980); *AACOA*, pp. 74–75.

32 "Notes on Akron, Ohio Survey / by / Frank Amos," [unedited version], p. 3 (GSO, Box 22, Reel 10 / 8.1 The Alcoholic Foundation: 1937-1938, P-8).

33 Oral History Transcriptions, Transcript Record of Wally [Gillam], Akron, Ohio, 12/12/54 (GSO, Box 1 of 2, Box 1: 304680980); *AACOA*, pp. 74–75.

34 Bill Wilson to McGhee Baxter, October 30, 1940 (GSO, Box 54, Reel 25, Folder G, Richmond, VA, pp. 23-24).

35 *AACOA*, p. 13.

36 Ibid.

37 *Alcoholics Anonymous* (4th edition), "Foreword to the Second Edition," p. xvi.

38 AA Main Events, 1935, Point 18.

39 Ibid., Point 20.

40 *Alcoholics Anonymous* (4th edition), "More About Alcoholism," p. 33.

41 Silkworth, "Reclamation of the Alcoholic," p. 323.

42 Ibid.

43 This 'quote' combines separate comments that are found in *Pass It On*, p. 317-318 and a recorded talk by Barry L. at the Montreal International Convention, July 1985 speaking on the origins of the Third Tradition (retrieved from www.xa-speakers.org on December 30, 2011).

44 *AACOA*, p. 81.

45 Rosa Burwell's August 31, 1978 Interview with Niles Peebles (GSO, CD 1009, Track 2, [10:30]).

46 Unless otherwise noted, the details and quotes used here on Jim Burwell are from his story "The Vicious Cycle," which has appeared in the second, third and fourth editions of the Big Book (*Alcoholics Anonymous*, 4th edition, pp. 219–31).

47 This is an undated handwritten document entitled "Jimmy" that was most likely composed sometime between the publication of the Big Book in April 1939 and the early to mid-1940s (for the writing almost certainly predates Burwell's well publicized late 1940s history, "The Evolution of Alcoholics Anonymous.") It is a very roughly written piece—with additions, deletions and non-sequiturs—that has been lightly edited here for smoother reading (StSt, AA 501.1, Box 13, Folder 22, Publications – Alcoholics Anonymous – Stories? [handwritten, copies]).

[48] AA Main Events, 1938, Point 22.

[49] *Bill W., My First 40 Years,* pp. 119–20.

[50] "Notes on Akron, Ohio Survey / by / Frank Amos," [unedited version], p. 2 (GSO, Box 22, Reel 10 / 8.1 The Alcoholic Foundation: 1937-1938, P-7 to P-10).

[51] Ibid.

Chapter Nine. Hank's Ideas

[1] "There Is A Solution," first version, (StSt, AA 501.1, Alcoholics Anonymous – Early Draft of Chapter "There Is A Solution," Box 13, Folder 24, p. 2).

[2] *AACOA,* p. 163.

[3] A Question and Answer Section Has Been Proposed for the Book, p. 11 (GSO, Box 59, 1939, Folder C, Document 1939-11 to 1939-25).

[4] "Hank's ideas," StSt, AA 501.1 – Alcoholics Anonymous – Hank Parkhurst's ideas [handwritten pencil], AA, Box 13, Folder 19, p. 1.

[5] Ibid.

[6] "Hank's ideas," "Suggestion for Chapter 1", p. 5.

[7] "Hank's ideas," p. 10.

[8] Ibid., p. 11.

[9] Dodd, *The Authors,* pp. 81-82; *Alcoholics Anonymous,* (4th edition), "A Vision For You," p. 158.

[10] "Hank's ideas," p. 3.

[11] "Hank's ideas," pp. 8a, 8b & 9.

[12] [Anonymous], *What is the Oxford Group,* p. 9.

[13] "Original Story," p. 30 (StSt, WGW 103, Box 31, Folder 3).

[14] "Original Story," pp. 30–[34] (StSt, WGW 103, Box 31, Folder 3).

[15] *AACOA,* p. 163.

[16] A Question and Answer Section Has Been Proposed for the Book, p. 11 (GSO, Box 59, 1939, Folder C, Document 1939-11 to 1939-25).

[17] Quoted from page 3 (the "Questions + Answers" page) of Hank's notes.

[18] AA Main Events, 1938, Point 12.

[19] "Hank's ideas," p. 2.

[20] Ibid., p. 4a.

[21] AA Main Events, 1938, Point 17.

[22] "Hank's ideas," p. 4b.

[23] Ibid., p. 6.

[24] Bill Wilson to Mrs. Phil Crecelius [Ruth Hock], October 17, 1955 (GSO, Box 29, Reel 13, 17.4 The Twelve Steps: How Written, p. 18).

[25] Ibid. See also the first full paragraph on *AACOA,* p. 166 for some other speculations on this question, all of which are inaccurate to one degree or another.

[26] "There Is A Solution" p. 1 (GSO, Box 59, 1938, Folder B, Documents 1938-53 to 1938-75)

27 Bill Wilson to Dr. Bob Smith, [June 24, 25 or 26], 1938 (GSO, Box 59, 1938, Folder B, Documents 1938-25 to 1938-30).

28 "Hank's ideas," p. 7.

29 *Alcoholics Anonymous* (4th edition), "More About Alcoholism," p. 33.

30 Ibid., "The Vicious Cycle," p. 228.

31 Ibid.

32 Wilson, "The Fellowship of Alcoholics Anonymous," 1944 (page 10 of the online version; available at http://www.barefootsworld.net/aabw1944talk.html - retrieved July 4, 2012).

33 *Alcoholics Anonymous* (4th edition), "The Vicious Cycle," p. 228.

34 Ibid, Wilson, "The Fellowship of Alcoholics Anonymous," 1944 (page 10 of the online version; available at http://www.barefootsworld.net/aabw1944talk.html - retrieved July 4, 2012).

35 AA Main Events, 1937, Point 13.

36 *Twelve Steps and Twelve Traditions*, (1st edition), p. 148.

37 Wilson, "The Fellowship of Alcoholics Anonymous," 1944 (page 9 of the online version available at http://www.barefootsworld.net/aabw1944talk.html - retrieved July 4, 2012).

38 Ibid., pages 9–10.

39 *Twelve Steps and Twelve Traditions*, (1st edition), p. 148.

40 *Alcoholics Anonymous* (4th edition), "The Vicious Cycle," p. 228.

41 Ibid., pp. 228–29.

42 Ibid., p. 229.

Chapter Ten. The Outline

1 AA Main Events, 1938, Point 12.

2 "There Is A Solution," first version, (StSt, AA 501.1, Alcoholics Anonymous – Early Draft of Chapter "There Is a Solution," Box 13, Folder 24, p. 12).

3 For Maguire on the Advisory Committee at Chase see *Who's Who in America*, (Volume 20, 1938-1939, H-P, The A. N. Marquis Company, Chicago, 1938, p. 1610). For "the Rockefeller Bank," see Chernow, *Titan*, p. 664.

4 GSO, Box 59, 1938, Folder B, Document 1938-22.

5 [June 24], 1938 (GSO, Box 59, 1938, Folder B, Document 1938-30a.)

6 Wm. G. Wilson to Jeremiah D. Maguire, August 6, 1938 (GSO, Box 59, 1938, Folder B(1), Document 1938-105).

7 Mel B., *Ebby*, p. 65.

8 Ibid., p. 77. See Lois's Diary, June 23, 1937, for Ebby's trip to Towns Hospital.

9 Lois's Diary, 1938.

10 Mel B., *Ebby*, p. 80.

11 Lois's Diary, June 16, 1938.

12 Mel B., *Ebby*, pp. 19, 20 & 35

13 Lois's Diary, December 1937 (GSO, Box 201, Folder A, Lois's Diaries – 1937).

14 All quotes in this and the preceding seven paragraphs are from [June 17, 18 or 20], 1938, Thomas O. Thacher to Bill Wilson (StSt, WGW/LBW 102.7, Box 25, Folder 30, Correspondence – General – "Letters to Us" [1938-1941 Friends/Associates]).

15 All quotes in this and the preceding three paragraphs are from [June 17, 18, or 20], 1938, Thomas O. Thacher to Bill Wilson (StSt, WGW/LBW 102.7, Box 25, Folder 30, Correspondence – General – "Letters to Us" [1938-1941 Friends/Associates]). For Hank's use of "One Hundred Men" as the name of the proposed corporation see One Hundred Men, Inc. (GSO, Box 59, 1939, Folder C, Document 1939-26 to 1939-32)

16 StSt, AA 501.1, Box 13, Folder 16; Publications – Alcoholics Anonymous [1939 (sic)] – Outline of chapters. *NOTE*: this [1939] designation in the Stepping Stones archive is troublesome because there is no date whatsoever on this document. The designation might be read as indicating that the outline was done in 1939 or that it is an outline of the book published in 1939. If the intention was to date this document from some time in 1939, then it is clearly in error. The outline is self-evidently the one that was sent to both Jeremiah Maguire and Dr. Bob Smith and also to Frank Amos on or just before June 24, 1938.

17 *AACOA*, p. 159.

18 *Alcoholics Anonymous* (4th edition), "There Is A Solution," pp. 20–21 and "To Wives," 108–114 respectively.

19 Bill Wilson to Dr. Bob Smith, [June 22, 23, or 24], 1938 (GSO, Box 59, 1938, Folder B, Document 1938-25 to 1938-30).

20 Wm. G. Wilson to R. A. Furlong, July 15, 1938 (GSO, Box 59, 1938, Folder B, Document 1938-42).

21 Bill Wilson to Dr. Bob Smith, [June 22, 23, or 24], 1938 (GSO, Box 59, 1938, Folder B, Document 1938-25 to 1938-30).

22 *Alcoholics Anonymous* (4th edition), "How It Works," p. 58.

23 Bill Wilson to Dr. Bob Smith, [June 22, 23, or 24], 1938 (GSO, Box 59, 1938, Folder B, Document 1938-25 to 1938-30, p. 4). *NOTE*: The GSO Archive contains a very bad copy of the original five-page letter along with a later retyped six-page copy (hence the archive's numbering of 1938-25 to 30 for this document) with many of the typos corrected. All quotes here are from this retyped and corrected version that is presented here piecemeal, but in the proper order and complete.

24 "Hank's ideas," StSt, AA 501.1 – Alcoholics Anonymous – Hank Parkhurst's ideas [handwritten pencil], AA, Box 13, Folder 19, p. 11.

25 The fourth point noted in Frank Amos's February report to John D. Rockefeller outlining the seven basics of the Akron program: "[The alcoholic] must have devotions every morning—a 'quiet time' of prayer, and some reading from the Bible or other religious literature. Unless this is faithfully followed, there is grave danger of backsliding." ("Notes on Akron, Ohio Survey / by / Frank Amos," [unedited version], (GSO, Box 22, Reel 10 / 8.1 The Alcoholic Foundation: 1937-1938).

26 [Anonymous], *What is the Oxford Group*, p. 42.

27 This last p.s. quote is taken from the uncorrected copy of the original letter held by GSO (Box 59, 1938, Folder B, Document 1938-25 to 1938-30).

28 GSO, Box 59, 1938, Folder B, Document 1938-23 & 1938-24.

29 For the dates of Scott's absence see W. S. Richardson to John D. Rockefeller Jr., February 23, 1938 ((RAC, Family, RG2, OMR, P, Welfare-General, Box 42, Folder 458).

30 AA Main Events, 1938, <u>Points 12 & 13</u>. Albert L. Scott, To Whom It May Concern, July 1, 1938 (GSO, Box 59, 1938, Folder B, Document 1938-50).

31 Lois's Diary, June 25, 1938.

32 Lois's List of Historical Dates Oct 1937 to May 1945: June 27, 1938 (StSt, LBW 203, Box 35, Folder 4).

33 Lois's Diary, June 27, 1938.

Chapter Eleven. Chasing Testimonials

1 AA Main Events, 1938, <u>Point 12</u>.

2 Lois's Diary, July 1 & July 11, 1938.

3 *Lois Remembers*, p. 101.

4 Ibid.

5 *Alcoholics Anonymous* (1st edition), "Our Southern Friend," p. 238.

6 Lois Wilson to Bill Wilson, February 27, 1938 (StSt LBW 202.4 in WGW Box 27, Folder 111).

7 Lois Wilson to Bill Wilson, March 21, 1938 (StSt LBW 202.4 in WGW Box 27, Folder 112).

8 *Alcoholics Anonymous* (1st edition), "Our Southern Friend," pp. 238–39.

9 Lois's Diary, March 29, 1937.

10 *AACOA*, p. 18.

11 Minutes of the First Meeting of the Alcoholics Foundation (GSO, Box 59, 1938, Folder B, Document 1938-18a).

12 Bill Wilson to Robert H. Smith, July 15, 1938 (GSO, Box 59, 1938, Folder B, Document 1938-47); Lois's List of Historical Dates (LBW 203, Box 35, Folder 4): ". . . Charles Hedges sobered in 1937"; Charles C. Hedges to Bill Wilson, 1937, (StSt, WGW 102.7, Box 25, Folder 29).

13 Bill Wilson to Robert H. Smith, July 15, 1938 (GSO, Box 59, 1938, Folder B, Document 1938-47).

14 Ibid.

15 Named Wikipedia article (retrieved March, 25, 2013).

16 Bill Wilson to Robert H. Smith, July 15, 1938 (GSO, Box 59, 1938, Folder B, Document 1938-47).

17 Ibid.

18 Ibid.

19 Outline: Chapter Twenty Three (StSt, AA 501.1, Box 13, Folder 16; Publications – Alcoholics Anonymous [1939 – (sic)] – Outline of chapters).

20 Esther L. Richards, M.D. to William G. Wilson, August 9, 1938 (GSO, Box 59, 1938, Folder B[1], Document 1938-110).

21 See, for instance, "A Discussion of the Big Book," a talk by Ruth Hock, Glendale, CA, March 12, 1978; transcript copy in the Akron Archives, p. 10. Also available on YouTube under the title "Ruth H. AA's First Secretary shares the history of Alcoholics Anonymous" (http://www.youtube.com/watch?v=mxVkTNgOhy0 – retrieved September 27, 2013).

22 *Alcoholics Anonymous* (4th edition), "How It Works," p. 58.

23 For Ebby's presence at this follow-up meeting, see William G. Wilson to Dr. Esther L. Richards, September 28, 1938 (GSO, Box 59, 1938, Folder B[1], Document 1938-154).

24 Bill Wilson to Dr. Charles & Mrs. Margaret Hedges, July 15, 1938 (GSO, Box 59, 1938, Folder B, Document 1938-42).

25 Frank B. Amos to W. S. Richardson, July 7, 1938 (GSO, Box 59, 1938, Folder B, Document 1938-37). Towns had made contributions to Amos of $500 each on April 1 and May 18: See T. G. Lewis to W. G. Wilson, April 3, 1957 (GSO, Box 27A, Reel 12 / 13.2[1] Miscellaneous – unmarked materials).

26 *Patterson's American Educational Directory*, volume XXIX (American Education Company, Chicago, 1932), p. 750.

27 See, for instance: http://www.thepeoplehistory.com/1938.html (retrieved March 27, 2013).

28 Lois's Diary.

29 July 14, 1938 (GSO, Box 59, 1938, Folder B, Document 1938-39).

30 Ibid.

31 Wm. G. Wilson to Dr. Leslie B. Hohman, July 15, 1938 (GSO, Box 59, 1938, Folder B, Document 1938-40).

32 Bill Wilson to Dr. Charles & Mrs. Margaret Hedges, July 15, 1938 (GSO, Box 59, 1938, Folder B, Document 1938-42).

33 Named Wikipedia article (retrieved March 29, 2013).

34 Bill Wilson to Dr. Charles & Mrs. Margaret Hedges, July 15, 1938 (GSO, Box 59, 1938, Folder B, Document 1938-42)

35 Wm. G. Wilson to Albert L. Scott, July 15, 1938 (GSO, Box 59, 1938, Folder B, Document 1938-44)

36 GSO, Box 59, 1938, Folder B, Document 1938-50.

37 Wm. G. Wilson to W. S. Richardson, July 15, 1938 (GSO, Box 59, 1938, Folder B, Document 1938-46)

38 In his August 19, 1938 document, "History of Alcoholics movement . . .," Amos talks about "meetings being held weekly in various homes" and notes that "several of which Mr. and Mrs. Amos attended." (GSO, Box 9, 1938, Folder B[1], Document 117-124, pp. 5–6).

39 Bill Wilson to Frank Amos, July 15, 1938 (GSO, Box 59, 1938, Folder B, Document 1938-43)

40 *Alcoholics Anonymous* (1st edition), "Another Prodigal Son," pp. 360–63.

41 Ibid.

42 Wm. G. Wilson to R. A. Furlong, July 15, 1938 (GSO, Box 59, 1938, Folder B, Document 1938-42).

⁴³ C.E.B. Ward to Wm. G. Wilson, July 6, 1938 (GSO, Box 59, 1938, Folder B, Document 1938-35).

⁴⁴ Wm. G. Wilson to C.E.B. Ward, July 15, 1938 (GSO, Box 59, 1938, Folder B, Document 1938-45).

⁴⁵ Named Wikipedia articles for both men (retrieved April 4, 2013).

⁴⁶ Bill Wilson to Dr. Robert Smith, July 15, 1938 (GSO, Box 59, 1938, Folder B, Document 1938-47).

⁴⁷ Bill Wilson to Jeremiah T. Maguire, July [23 or 24], 1938 (GSO, Box 59, 1938, Folder B, Document 1938-34).

⁴⁸ M., Merton, *Black Sheep*, p. 93.

⁴⁹ *AACOA*, p. 175-176. In addition to this, Bill claimed in his June 12, 1954 Fort Worth talk that this eviction happened shortly after Gabriel Heatter's radio interview of April 25, 1939 (Bill Wilson speaking in Fort Worth, Texas, June 12, 1954 ("How the Book Alcoholics Anonymous Came About," in *The Book That Started It All*, p. 215).

⁵⁰ GSO, Box 59, 1938, Folder B, Document 1938-51.

⁵¹ Wm. G. Wilson to Dr. Esther L. Richards, July 22, 1938 (GSO, Box 59, 1938, Folder B, Document 1938-76 to 1938-78).

⁵² Dr. Esther Richards to William. G. Wilson, August 9, 1938 (GSO, Box 59, 1938, Folder B, Document 1938-110).

⁵³ Charles B. Towns to Bill Wilson, July 25, 1938 (GSO, Box 59, 1938, Folder B, Document 1938-80).

⁵⁴ One preserved copy of Dr. Esther Richards to William G. Wilson July 18, 1938 (GSO, Box 59. Folder B, Document 1938-79) has the handwritten notation at the bottom: "Note: this letter sent with prospectus for proposed book—two chapters—plus Mr. Towns and Dr. Silkworth's recommendations."

⁵⁵ Named Wikipedia article (retrieved April 15, 2013).

⁵⁶ GSO, Box 59. Folder B, Document 1938-82.

⁵⁷ GSO, Box 59. Folder B, Document 1938-52.

⁵⁸ [undated], GSO, Box 59. Folder B, Document 1938-49.

Chapter Twelve. The Alcoholic Foundation

¹ Okrent, *Last Call*, pp. 133 & 304.

² Wikipedia, Henry Ford, Named Article (retrieved June 30, 2013).

³ *The Decatur Evening Herald*, February 9, 1931, p. 6.

⁴ "Obituary Record of Graduates of Yale University Deceased During the Year 1947-1948," (*Bulletin of Yale University*, Series 45, 1 January, 1949, Number 1, pp. 100–01).

⁵ A host of details about Dr. Frank J. Sladen's career can be found online at http://www.henryford.com/body.cfm?id=47766 (retrieved July, 3, 2013).

⁶ All of the quotes so far in this chapter are from Wm. G. Wilson to Mr. Charles Parcelles [*sic*], July [*but really August*] 1, 1938 (GSO, Box 59, 1938, Folder B, Documents 1938-31 to 1938-34).

⁷ Charles B. Towns to Henry Ford, November 16, 1938 (GSO, Box 59, Folder D.2).

8   See the transcript of Archie's Christmas Day talk in 1948 (http://www.silkworth.net/
    aagrowth/mich_Detroit_ArchieT.html) which places this trip in March 1939, a date
    that corresponds with Lois's diary entry noting that "Bill left for Akron" on March
    1, 1939. The two men would have been in Detroit together on Monday and Tuesday,
    March 6 and 7.

9   Bill Wilson to Dr. Bob Smith, [June 22, 23 or 24], 1938 (GSO, Box 59, 1938, Folder B,
    Document 1938-25 to 1938-30).

10 Bill Wilson to Dr. Bob Smith, July 15, 1938 (GSO, Box 59, 1938, Folder B, Document
    1938-47).

11 GSO, Box 59, 1938, Folder B(1), Document 1938-106.

12 Amos, "History," p. 7.

13 *AACOA*, p. 152.

14 Bill Wilson speaking in Fort Worth, Texas, June 12, 1954 ("How the Book Alcoholics
    Anonymous Came About," in *The Book That Started It All*, p. 210).

15 *AACOA*, p. 152.

16 The Alcoholic Foundation, Trust Indenture (GSO, Box 59, 1938, Folder B, Documents
    1938-86 to 1938-104, p. 3).

17 Ibid., p. 2.

18 *AACOA*, p. 152.

19 The Alcoholic Foundation, Trust Indenture (GSO, Box 59, 1938, Folder B, Documents
    1938-86 to 1938-104).

20 Robert H. Smith to whom it may concern, August 11, 1938 (GSO, Box 59, 1938,
    Folder B[1], Document 1938-114).

21 Minutes of the First Meeting of the Alcoholics Foundation (GSO, Box 59, 1938,
    Folder B, Document 1938-18a).

22 Ibid.

23 Ibid, Supplemented with verbiage from the original handwritten notes from the First
    Meeting of the Alcoholic Foundation (GSO, Box 59, 1938, Folder B, Document
    1938-19).

24 *Alcoholics Anonymous* (1st edition), p. 25 with similar citations on pp. 168 & 176. In all
    other editions these references can be found on pp. 15, 153, and 162 respectively.

25 Henry G. Parkhurst to Frank Amos, March 16, 1938 (GSO, Box 59, 1938, Folder B,
    Document 1938-13/14).

26 Minutes of the First Meeting of the Alcoholics Foundation (GSO, Box 59, 1938,
    Folder B, Document 1938-18a).

27 Lois's Diary, August 13, 1938.

28 Minutes of the second meeting of The Alcoholic Foundation (GSO, Box 59, 1938,
    Folder B[1], Document 1938-115[a]).

29 Frank B. Amos to W. S. Richardson, August 19, 1938 (GSO, Box 59, 1938, Folder
    B[1], Document 1938-114). For the last accounting, see Frank B. Amos to W. S.
    Richardson, July 7, 1938 (GSO, Box 59, 1938, Folder B, Document 37).

30 [Dr.] Bob [Smith] to Bill [Wilson], February 17, 1938 (StSt, WGW Series 102, Box 9,
    Folder 5).

31 "Hank's ideas," (StSt, AA 501.1 – Alcoholics Anonymous – Hank Parkhurst's ideas [handwritten pencil], AA, Box 13, Folder 19. "Suggestion for Chapter 1," p. 5).

32 Victor G. Heiser to William G. Wilson, August 2, 1938 (GSO, Box 59, 1938, Folder B, Document 1938-83).

33 Wm. G. Wilson to Donald McClain *[sic]*, September 8, 1938 (GSO, Box 59, 1938, Folder B[1], Document 1938-135 & 136). The correct spelling of the recipient's name is "MacLean" (see his obituary in the January 29, 1958 issue of *The Times Record* of Troy, NY, page 13).

34 Wm. G. Wilson to J.H.F. Mayo, August 8, 1938 (GSO, Box 59, 1938, Folder B[1], Document 1938-109).

35 Wm. G. Wilson to Dr. Victor G. Heiger *[sic]*, August 8, 1938 (GSO, Box 59, 1938, Folder B, Document 1938-84).

36 Wm. G. Wilson to J.H.F. Mayo, August 8, 1938 (GSO, Box 59, 1938, Folder B[1], Document 1938-109).

37 Wm. G. Wilson to Donald McClain *[sic]*, September 8, 1938 (GSO, Box 59, 1938, Folder B[1], Document 1938-135 & 136).

38 *Life* magazine July 5, 1937, p. 20.

39 Wm. G. Wilson to Donald McClain *[sic]*, September 8, 1938 (GSO, Box 59, 1938, Folder B[1], Document 1938-135 & 136).

40 Wm. G. Wilson to Dr. Robert A.*[sic]* Smith, August 29*[sic?]*, 1938 (GSO, Box 59, 1938, Folder B[1], Document 1938-127 & 128).

41 Wm. G. Wilson to Donald McClain *[sic]*, September 8, 1938 (GSO, Box 59, 1938, Folder B[1], Document 1938-135 & 136).

42 Lois's Diary, 1938; August 13: "Bill went to Maryland"; August 23: "Bill and Fitz arrived [back in Brooklyn]."

43 Wm. G. Wilson to Donald McClain *[sic]*, September 8, 1938 (GSO, Box 59, 1938, Folder B[1], Document 1938-135 & 136).

44 Wm. G. Wilson to Dr. Robert A.*[sic]* Smith, August 29*[sic?]*, 1938 (GSO, Box 59, 1938, Folder B[1], Document 1938-127 & 128).

45 Wm. G. Wilson to Donald McClain *[sic]*, September 8, 1938 (GSO, Box 59, 1938, Folder B[1], Document 1938-135 & 136).

46 Ibid.

47 Lois's Diary, 1938.

48 H. Edmund Bullis to J. Fitzhugh Mayo, August 26, 1938 (GSO, Box 59, Folder B[1], Document 1938-125).

49 Wm. G. Wilson to Dr. Robert A.*[sic]* Smith, August 29 *[sic?]*, 1938 (GSO, Box 59, 1938, Folder B[1], Document 1938-127 & 128).

50 Lois's Diary, 1938, August 30: "Bob and Annie and little Bob arrive to spend 2 or 3 days. Seminar"; September 2: "Smiths left…"

51 Wm. G. Wilson to Dr. Robert A.*[sic]* Smith, August 7, 1938 (GSO, Box 59, Folder B[1], Document 1938-106).

52 Lois's Diary, 1938, August 30.

53 Henry G. Parkhurst to Mr. Dewitt Wallace, September 1, 1938 (GSO, Box 59, Folder B[1], Document 1938-129)..

54 Wm. G. Wilson to R. Smith, September 8, 1938 (GSO, Box 59, Folder B[1], Document 1938-134).

55 Bill Wilson to Dr. Robert Smith, July 15, 1938 (GSO, Box 59, 1938, Folder B, Document 1938-47).

56 Wm. G. Wilson to R. Smith, September 8, 1938 (GSO, Box 59, 1938, Folder B[1], Document 1938-134).

57 Wm. G. Wilson to Donald McClain [sic], September 8, 1938 (GSO, Box 59, 1938, Folder B[1], Document 1938-135 & 136).

58 Wm. G. Wilson to Dr. R. Smith, September 27, 1938 (GSO, Box 59, 1938, Folder B[1], Document 1938-153).

59 Bill [Wilson] to [Mrs. Fitz] Elizabeth [Mayo], October 13, 1938 (GSO, Box 59, 1938, Folder B[1], Documents 1938-168 & 169).

60 William G. Wilson to Frank Amos, September 26, 1938 (GSO, Box 59, 1938, Folder B[1], Documents 1938-145 to 151). [NOTE: These pages should have been numbered 147–153, but have been incorrectly numbered duplicating the two numbers used to identify the previous document in this folder.]

61 Bill Wilson to Agnes Mayo, November 3, 1938 (GSO, Box 59, 1938, Folder B[1], Document 1938-173).

62 Bill [Wilson] to [Mrs.] Elizabeth [Mayo], October 13, 1938 (GSO, Box 59, 1938, Folder B[1], Documents 1938-168 & 169).

63 Ibid.

64 Bill Wilson to Agnes Mayo, November 3, 1938 (GSO, Box 59, 1938, Folder B[1], Document 1938-173).

Chapter Thirteen. *This Week* Magazine

1 Wm. G. Wilson to Dr. Robert A.[sic] Smith, August 29 [sic?], 1938 (GSO, Box 59, 1938, Folder B[1], Document 1938-127 & 128).

2 Wm. G. Wilson to Donald McClain [sic], September 8, 1938 (GSO, Box 59, 1938, Folder B[1], Document 1938-135 & 136).

3 Frank B. Amos to Albert L. Scott, June 24, 1938 (GSO, Box 59, 1938, Folder B, Document 1938-23 & 1938-24).

4 Printed promotional stock prospectus entitled "Alcoholics Anonymous," a prospectus for The One Hundred Men Corporation (GSO, Box 59, 1939, Folder C, Document 1939-144 to 157, p. 12).

5 Wm. G. Wilson to Floyd W. Parsons (GSO, Box 59, Folder B, Document 1938-85).

6 Ruth [Hock] Crecelius to Bill Wilson, November 10, 1955 (StSt, AA 326, Box 4, Folder 17).

7 "A Discussion of the Big Book," a talk by Ruth Hock, Glendale, CA, March 12, 1978; transcript copy in the Akron Archives, p. 6. Also available on YouTube under the title "Ruth H. AA's First Secretary shares the history of Alcoholics Anonymous" - http://www.youtube.com/watch?v=mxVkTNgOhy0 - retrieved September 27, 2013.

8 StSt, AA 501.1, Alcoholics Anonymous – Early Draft of Chapter "There Is A Solution," AA Box 13, Folder 24.

9 Ibid.

10 GSO, Box 59, 1938, Folder B, Document 1938-53 pp. 9-10.

11 Wm. G. Wilson to Frederick W. Yeager, September 8, 1938 (GSO, Box 59, Folder B[1], Document 1938-133).

12 Fredrick W. Yaeger, Jr. to Wm. G. Wilson, September 9, 1938 (GSO, Box 59, Folder D.2, Document 12).

13 William G. Wilson to Frank Amos, September 26, 1938 (GSO, Box 59, Folder B[1], Document 1938-145 to 1938-151, p 4).

14 Bill Wilson to Fitz Mayo, September 8, 1938 (GSO, Box 59, Folder B[1], Document 1938-137).

15 For Watson, see, for instance, *The Sunday Spartanburg Herald-Journal*, November 13, 1938, p. 4; for Woodward, see the named Wikipedia article (retrieved September 4, 2013).

16 William G. Wilson to Frank Amos, September 26, 1938 (GSO, Box 59, Folder B[1], Document 1938-145 to 1938-151, p 4).

17 Ibid, p. 5.

18 Ibid, pp. 1–2.

19 Bill Wilson to Dr. Bob Smith, [June 24, 25 or 26], 1938 (GSO, Box 59, 1938, Folder B, Documents 1938-25 to 1938-30).

20 Gerald Mygatt to Silas Bent, September 19, 1938 (GSO, Box 59, Folder B[1], Document 1938-140).

21 William G. Wilson to Frank Amos, September 26, 1938 (GSO, Box 59, Folder B[1], Document 1938-145 to 1938-151, p. 5).

22 Gerald Mygatt to Silas Bent, September 19, 1938 (GSO, Box 59, Folder B[1], Document 1938-140).

23 Lois's Diary, September 19, 1938.

24 Gerald Mygatt to Silas Bent, September 20, 1938 (GSO, Box 59, Folder B[1], Document 1938-141).

25 Silas [Bent] to Billikins [Bill Wilson], September [21], 1938, (GSO Box 59, Folder B[1], Document 1938-139).

26 Minutes of the Alcoholics Foundation, September 23, 1938 (GSO, Box 59, Folder B[1], Documents 1938-145 & 146).

27 John D. Rockefeller to Willard Richardson, March 17, 1938 (GSO, Box 59, Folder B, Document 1938-15).

28 Minutes of the Alcoholics Foundation, September 23, 1938 (GSO, Box 59, Folder B[1], Documents 1938-145 & 146).

29 William G. Wilson to Frank Amos, September 26, 1938 (GSO, Box 59, Folder B[1], Documents 1938-145 to 1938-151).

30 All previous quotes from this letter come from: William G. Wilson to Frank Amos, September 26, 1938 (GSO, Box 59, Folder B[1], Documents 1938-145 to 1938-151).

31 Bill Wilson to Silas Bent, September 27, 1938 (GSO, Box 59, Folder B[1], Document 1938-143).

32 William G. Wilson to Dr. R. Smith, September 27, 1938 (GSO, Box 59, Folder B[1], Document 1938-153).

33 Ibid.

34 Frank B. Amos to Albert L. Scott, October 4, 1938 (GSO, Box 59, Folder B[1], Documents 1938-157 & 158).

35 This and previous quotes here are from: Frank B. Amos to Albert L. Scott, October 4, 1938 (GSO, Box 59, Folder B[1], Documents 1938-157 & 158).

36 Thomas O. Thacher to Bill Wilson (StSt, WGW/LBW 102.7, Box 25, Folder 30, Correspondence – General – "Letters to Us" [1938-1941 Friends/Associates]).

37 Mrs. William Brown Meloney to Willard S. Richardson, November 25, 1938 (GSO, Box 59, Folder B[1], Document 1938-184).

38 Wm. G. Wilson to Gerald Mygatt, November 10, 1938 (GSO, Box 59, Folder B[1], Document 1938-180).

39 Mrs. William Brown Meloney to Willard S. Richardson, November 25, 1938 (GSO, Box 59, Folder B[1], Document 1938-184).

40 Suggested letter to Mrs. Wm. Brown Meloney, [no date] (GSO Box 59, Folder B[1], Document 1938-182) and Mr. Richardson to Mrs. William Meloney, November 16, 1938 (GSO, Box 59, Folder B[1], Document 1938-183).

41 *Alcoholics Anonymous* (1st edition, 2nd printing, 1941), p. 391: "Now we are Two Thousand. March, 1941."

Chapter Fourteen. "More About Alcoholism" and "We Agnostics"

1 See for instance *AACOA*, p.16.

2 "A Discussion of the Big Book," a talk by Ruth Hock, Glendale, CA, March 12, 1978; transcript copy in the Akron Archives, p. 24. Also available on YouTube under the title "Ruth H. AA's First Secretary shares the history of Alcoholics Anonymous" - http://www.youtube.com/watch?v=mxVkTNgOhy0 – retrieved September 27, 2013.

3 AA Main Events, 1938, Point 21.

4 Outline: Chapter Six (StSt, AA 501.1, Box 13, Folder 16; Publications – Alcoholics Anonymous [1939 – (sic)] – Outline of chapters).

5 *The Book That Started It All*, p. 59.

6 I am grateful to Merton M. for bringing this suggestive quote to my attention on page 49 of his *Black Sheep* manuscript.

7 GSO Box 59, Folder B[1], Document 1938-153.

8 Bill Wilson to Dr. R. H. Smith (GSO, Box 59, Folder D, Document 1938-172).

9 "There Is A Solution" (GSO, Box 59, 1938, Folder B, First Two Chapters of the Proposed Book; Trust Indenture, Documents 1938-53 to 1938-75, p. 9).

10 All quotes in this section from "More About Alcoholism" can be found in *The Book That Started It All*, pp. 46-51.

11 William G. Wilson to Dr. R. Smith, September 27, 1938 (GSO Box 59, Folder B[1], Document 1938-153).

12 "There Is A Solution" (GSO, Box 59, 1938, Folder B, First Two Chapters of the Proposed Book; Trust Indenture, Documents 1938-53 to 1938-75, p. 10).

13 All quotes in this section from "We Agnostics" can be found in *The Book That Started It All*, pp. 52–59.

14 William James, *The Will to Believe*, Longmans Green and Co, New York, 1897, p. 1.

15 Speech at convention dinner of New York State League of Women Voters, Albany, N.Y., December 2, 1927.

16 Again, all quotes in this section from "We Agnostics" can be found in *The Book That Started It All*, pp. 52-59.

17 AA Main Events, 1938, <u>Point 26</u>; Ruth Hock's 1978 Interview with Niles Peebles (GSO, CD 876, Track 1, 18:15 to 18:45).

18 AA Main Events, 1938, <u>Point 26</u>.

19 William G. Wilson to Dr. R. Smith, September 27, 1938 (GSO Box 59, Folder B[1], Document 1938-153).

20 *Alcoholics Anonymous* (1st edition), pp. 195–96.

21 Bill Wilson to Silas Bent, September 27, 1938 (GSO, Box 59, Folder B[1], Document 1938-143).

22 AA Main Events, 1938, <u>Point 26</u>.

23 William G. Wilson to Dr. R. Smith, September 27, 1938 (GSO Box 59, Folder B[1], Document 1938-153).

24 AA Main Events, 1938, <u>Point 21</u>.

Chapter Fifteen. The One Hundred Men Corporation

1 Frank B. Amos to Albert L. Scott, October 4, 1938 (GSO, Box 59, Folder B[1], Documents 1938-157 & 158).

2 January 7, 1939: Memorandum on One Hundred Men Inc. (GSO, Box 59, 1939, Folder C, Documents 1939-26 to 1939-32, 3rd filed copy with this same identifying numbers, pp. 4-5). This is a strange and singular document, different from any other that we have seen in the GSO archive. The original is a cut-and-pasted affair with many sections affixed to the back sides of some old Honor Dealers promotional materials done in a Q&A format. Bill Wilson has made extensive handwritten edits to this first (but filed third) version of the document. Cut and pasted into the middle of all the other cut and pasted information about One Hundred Men Corporation is a typed transcript of Bill's side of a much earlier (internal evidence places it solidly in October 1938) phone conversation with Frank Amos. Perhaps Wilson dictated this to Ruth Hock at that time in an effort to get his 'talking points' properly organized before making this important call to Frank. The second version of this document (but the first one filed using these reference numbers in the GSO folder) has been typed incorporating Wilson's handwritten edits, but still preserving the transcript of Bill's side of the Amos phone conversation in the middle of all the other, unrelated memorandum materials. The final copy saved at GSO (filed second) incorporates a number of small edits and finally deletes the phone conversation from the One Hundred Men Corporation Memorandum. *NOTE*: It would be interesting to know if this practice of preparing a typescript for upcoming important conversations was a typical or frequent practice for Bill Wilson, but, if it was, this is the only such example to be preserved in the 1937, 1938, and first six months of 1939 documents archived at GSO.

3 Bill Wilson speaking in Atlanta, GA, July 14, 1951 (GSO, CD, BW115)

4 William G. Wilson to Frank Amos, September 26, 1938 (GSO, Box 59, Folder B[1], Document 1938-145 to 1938-151, p. 2).

[5] See Bill's four letters of October 11, 1938 to various people seeking contributions or appointments (GSO, Box 59, Folder B[1], Documents 1938-161-164).

[6] William G. Wilson to Frank Amos, September 26, 1938 (GSO, Box 59, Folder B[1], Document 1938-145 to 1938-151, p. 2) mentions this as Wilson's and Parkhurst's current plan tentatively noting: "if we decide to publish and promote the sale of our own book . . ."

[7] *AACOA*, p. 153.

[8] AA Main Events, 1938, <u>Point 15</u>. For Hank's presence at this meeting, see the printed prospectus for the One Hundred Men Corporation entitled "Alcoholics Anonymous" (GSO, 1939-144-157, p. 8) which notes that Eugene Exman "talked to two members of Alcoholics Anonymous."

[9] Bill Wilson speaking in Atlanta, GA, July 14, 1951 (GSO, CD, BW115).

[10] *AACOA*, p. 153.

[11] AA Main Events, 1938, <u>Point 15</u>.

[12] Bill Wilson speaking in Atlanta, GA, July 14, 1951 (GSO, CD, BW115).

[13] *AACOA*, p. 153.

[14] Bill Wilson speaking in Fort Worth, Texas, June 12, 1954 ("How the Book Alcoholics Anonymous Came About," in *The Book That Started It All*, p. 211).

[15] Ibid.

[16] *AACOA*, p. 153.

[17] Printed promotional stock prospectus entitled "Alcoholics Anonymous," p. 8 (GSO, Box 59, Folder C [1], Documents 1939 – 144 to 157).

[18] *AACOA*, p. 153.

[19] AA Main Events, 1938, <u>Point 15</u>.

[20] Bill Wilson speaking in Fort Worth, Texas, June 12, 1954 ("How the Book Alcoholics Anonymous Came About," in *The Book That Started It All*, p. 211).

[21] *AACOA*, p. 154.

[22] Ibid.

[23] Ibid.

[24] Bill Wilson to Jack Alexander, December 13, 1949 (GSO, Box 29, Folder 17.1, AA History: Miscellaneous Materials, p. 2).

[25] Bill Wilson speaking in Fort Worth, Texas, June 12, 1954 ("How the Book Alcoholics Anonymous Came About," in *The Book That Started It All*, p. 211).

[26] William G. Wilson to Frank Amos, September 26, 1938 (GSO, Box 59, Folder B[1], Document 1938-145 to 1938-151, pp. 1-4) claims that Fitz, Hank and Bill would require $1,000 a month ($200/$600/$200) to maintain themselves while the book was being prepared.

[27] *AACOA*, p. 154.

[28] Ibid.

[29] Ibid., p. 156.

[30] Ibid, p. 154.

[31] Bill Wilson speaking in Atlanta, GA, July 14, 1951 (GSO, CD, BW115).

[32] Ibid.

33 *AACOA*, p. 154.

34 Ibid., p. 155.

35 Ibid.

36 Bill Wilson to Jack Alexander, December 13, 1949 (GSO, Box 29, Folder 17.1, AA History: Miscellaneous Materials, p. 2).

37 William G. Wilson to Frank Amos, September 26, 1938 (GSO, Box 59, Folder B[1], Document 1938-145 to 1938-151, pp. 1–4)

38 *AACOA*. p. 155.

39 T. G. Lewis to Bill Wilson, April 3, 1957 (StSt, WGW 102.2, Box 22, Folder 6: Correspondence – Chronological Files – TOD-TYL). Also see GSO, Box 59, Folder B[1], Documents 1938-194 to 196 for three handwritten accounts by Richardson and Amos of the receipts and payments up to that time.

40 William G. Wilson to Frank Amos, September 26, 1938 (GSO, Box 59, Folder B[1], Document 1938-145 to 1938-151, pp. 2–6)

41 Charles B. Towns to William Wilson, October 4, 1945 (GSO, Box 65, Folder C [2 of 2] / 1945 – Alcoholic Foundation Inc. / Pages 116-262 / July – December, p. 162).

42 T. G. Lewis to Bill Wilson, April 3, 1957 (StSt, WGW 102.2, Box 22, Folder 6: Correspondence – Chronological Files – TOD-TYL).

43 Bill Wilson to Frank Amos, January 4, 1939 (GSO, Box 59, 1939, Folder C, Document 1939-7 to 1939-10).

44 Charles B. Towns to William Wilson, October 4, 1945 (GSO, Box 65, Folder C [2 of 2] / 1945 – Alcoholic Foundation Inc. / Pages 116-262 / July – December, p. 162).

45 Ibid.

46 Bill Wilson to Charles B. Towns, October 18, 1938 (GSO, Box 59, Folder B[1], Document 1938-170).

47 September 27, 1938 (GSO Box 59, Folder B[1], Document 1938-153).

48 GSO, Box 59, Folder B[1], Document 1938-171.

49 Charles B. Towns to William Wilson, October 4, 1945 (GSO, Box 65, Folder C [2 of 2] / 1945 – Alcoholic Foundation Inc. / Pages 116-262 / July – December, p. 162).

50 Bill Wilson to Jack Alexander, December 13, 1949 (GSO, Box 29, Folder 17.1, AA History: Miscellaneous Materials, p. 2).

51 *AACOA*, p. 155.

52 AA Main Event, 1938, Point 16.

53 *AACOA*, pp. 154–155.

54 Ibid.

55 Ibid.

56 January 7, 1939, Memorandum on One Hundred Men Inc. (GSO, Box 59, Folder C [1], Documents 1939-26 to 32, pp. 2 & 5). NOTE this information is taken from the first of three similar documents filed in the GSO folder with the same Document identification numbers.

57 *AACOA*, p. 155-156.

58 AA Main Events, 1938, Point 16.

59 January 7, 1939, Memorandum on One Hundred Men Inc. (GSO, Box 59, 1939, Folder C, Documents 1939-26 to 1939-32, p. 6). As noted in an earlier endnote [#2] for this chapter, this quote comes from the cut-and-pasted document containing a transcript of Bill Wilson's October, 1938 telephone conversation with Frank Amos.

60 *AACOA*, p, 156.

61 AA Main Events, 1938, Point 16.

62 *AACOA*, p, 156.

63 AA Main Events, 1938, Point 17.

64 *AACOA*, p, 157.

65 Ibid.

66 Bill Wilson speaking in Fort Worth, Texas, June 12, 1954 ("How the Book Alcoholics Anonymous Came About," in *The Book That Started It All*, p. 211).

67 Hank [Parkhurst] to Herbert F. Taylor [and Bill Wilson], [May, 1938] (GSO, Box 59, Folder D.2, Document 8).

68 T. G. Lewis to Bill Wilson, April 3, 1957 (StSt, WGW 102.2, Box 22, Folder 6: Correspondence – Chronological Files – TOD-TYL).

69 *AACOA*, pp. 155-156.

70 Typed prospectus for The One Hundred Men Corporation (GSO, Box 59, 1939, Folder C, Document 1939-26 to 1939-32, p. 2). *NOTE 1:* There are four different versions of this typed prospectus in the GSO files, three using the same reference numbers and the fourth unnumbered. The first, second, and third (which has Bill Wilson's hand corrections to it) all have this quote. However, the revelation of this gift of 400 shares to Wilson and Parkhurst has been deleted from the fourth, unnumbered version preserved in that file (which is, surprisingly, almost certainly the earliest version since it mentions only five chapters being completed). *NOTE 2:* This distribution of stock was also explicitly reported in the June 30, 1940 Report on Works Publishing, Inc: "dividends . . . on the total stock outstanding, of which it was planned that cash subscribers were to have one-third, Mr. Wm. G. Wilson, author, one-third, and Mr. Henry G. Parkhurst, business manager, one-third." (StSt, AA 500, Box 13, Folder 1, p. 3).

71 Wm. G. Wilson to Frank B. Amos, January 4, 1939 (GSO, Box 59, 1939, Folder C, Document 1939-7 to 1939-10, pp. 1–2).

72 Typed prospectus for The One Hundred Men Corporation (GSO, Box 58, 1939, Folder C, the fourth, unnumbered copy, p. 7); also, Printed promotional stock prospectus entitled "Alcoholics Anonymous" (GSO, Box 59, 1939, Folder C, Documents 1939-144 to 157, p. 11).

73 *Pass It On*, p. 195. *NOTE:* The extremely inadequate (and annoying) endnotes regarding sources in this book make no reference to this quote, but in two unpublished typescripts of earlier versions of the book seen by the author, the quote is credited to a phone interview conducted by Mel Barger with Hank's son, Henry Parkhurst, on September 7, 1981.

74 *AACOA*, pp. 156–57.

75 Bill Wilson speaking in Fort Worth, Texas, June 12, 1954 ("How the Book Alcoholics Anonymous Came About," in *The Book That Started It All*, p. 211).

76 *AACOA*, p. 155.

77 Ibid.

78 Printed promotional stock prospectus entitled "Alcoholics Anonymous" (GSO, Box 59, 1939, Folder C, Documents 1939-144 to 157, p. 8).

79 See the Wikipedia article entitled "The Good Earth" (retrieved May 7, 2014).

80 Printed promotional stock prospectus entitled "Alcoholics Anonymous" (GSO, Box 59, 1939, Folder C, Documents 1939-144 to 157, p. 8).

81 Ibid.

82 *AACOA*, p, 155.

83 Ibid., pp. 155, 157.

84 Bill Wilson speaking in Fort Worth, Texas, June 12, 1954 ("How the Book Alcoholics Anonymous Came About," in *The Book That Started It All*, p. 211); *AACOA*, pp. 157–58.

85 *AACOA*, p. 155.

86 AA Main Events, 1938, Point 18.

87 *AACOA*, p. 158.

88 Printed promotional stock prospectus entitled "Alcoholics Anonymous" (GSO, Box 59, 1939, Folder C, Documents 1939-144 to 157, p. 7); Bill Wilson to Frank Amos, January 4, 1939 (GSO, Box 59, 1939, Folder C, Document 1939-7 to 1939-10).

89 Named entry in *Gale Encyclopedia of Occultism and Parapsychology* (Gale Group, Farmington Hills, MI, 2001, 5th Edition, p. 523) – available online in pdf format (retrieved May 5, 2014).

90 Printed promotional stock prospectus entitled "Alcoholics Anonymous" (GSO, Box 59, 1939, Folder C, Documents 1939-144 to 157, p. 7).

91 Ibid.

92 Ibid.

93 Bill Wilson to Frank Amos, January 4, 1939 (GSO, Box 59, 1939, Folder C, Document 1939-7 to 1939-10).

94 Ibid.

95 Ibid.

96 Ibid.

97 Bill Wilson speaking in Fort Worth, Texas, June 12, 1954 ("How the Book Alcoholics Anonymous Came About," in *The Book That Started It All*, p. 212).

98 GSO, Box 59, Folder B[1], Document 1938-129.

99 *AACOA*, p. 158.

100 Bill Wilson speaking in Fort Worth, Texas, June 12, 1954 ("How the Book Alcoholics Anonymous Came About," in *The Book That Started It All*, p. 212).

101 AA Main Events, 1938, Point 18.

102 Bill Wilson speaking in Atlanta, GA, July 14, 1951 (GSO, CD, BW115).

103 *AACOA*, p. 158.

104 Bill Wilson speaking in Atlanta, GA, July 14, 1951 (GSO, CD, BW115).

105 Bill Wilson speaking in Fort Worth, Texas, June 12, 1954 ("How the Book Alcoholics Anonymous Came About," in *The Book That Started It All*, p. 212).

[106] Bill Wilson speaking in Atlanta, GA, July 14, 1951 (GSO, CD, BW115).

[107] Bill Wilson speaking in Fort Worth, Texas, June 12, 1954 ("How the Book Alcoholics Anonymous Came About," in *The Book That Started It All*, p. 213).

[108] Bill Wilson to Frank Amos, January 4, 1939 (GSO, Box 59, 1939, Folder C, Document 1939-7 to 1939-10).

[109] Bill Wilson speaking in Atlanta, GA, July 14, 1951 (GSO, CD, BW115).

[110] Bill Wilson to Frank Amos, January 4, 1939 (GSO, Box 59, 1939, Folder C, Document 1939-7 to 1939-10).

[111] Bill Wilson speaking in Fort Worth, Texas, June 12, 1954 ("How the Book Alcoholics Anonymous Came About," in *The Book That Started It All*, p. 212).

[112] AA Main Events, 1938, Point 18.

[113] Bill Wilson speaking in Atlanta, GA, July 14, 1951 (GSO, CD, BW115).

[114] Ibid.

[115] *AACOA*, p. 158.

[116] Bill Wilson to Frank Amos, January 4, 1939 (GSO, Box 59, 1939, Folder C, Document 1939-7 to 1939-10).

[117] *AACOA*, p. 158.

[118] Bill Wilson speaking in Fort Worth, Texas, June 12, 1954 ("How the Book Alcoholics Anonymous Came About," in *The Book That Started It All*, p. 212).

[119] *AACOA*, p. 158-159.

[120] AA Main Events, 1938, Point 18.

[121] *AACOA*, p. 156.

[122] Printed promotional piece entitled "Alcoholics Anonymous," a prospectus for The One Hundred Men Corporation (GSO, Box 59, 1939, Folder C, Document 1939-144 to 157). *NOTE*: The placement of this document among the 1939 materials held at the GSO archives is wrong. The prospectus claims that "ten chapters have now been written" which would clearly make this a late November 1938 document rather than a January 1939 production.

[123] Typed prospectus for The One Hundred Men Corporation (GSO, Box 59, 1939, Folder C, following Document 1939-26 to 1939-32). *NOTE 1*: This typed prospectus is actually an unnumbered document that appears after three similar (but textually different) documents that share the same identifying numbers in the GSO archive. These three are all dated January 7, 1939 and are different versions of a "Memo" explaining the current status of The One Hundred Men Corporation. This much earlier typed prospectus—almost certainly from mid- to late October—can be found following these three in the archive folder. The reason for claiming this is a "mid- to late October" document is the fact that this typed version states that "five chapters have now been written," clearly fixing it in that timeframe (and not in the January sequence within which it has been filed in the archive).

[124] "Hank's ideas," (StSt, AA 501.1 – Alcoholics Anonymous – Hank Parkhurst's ideas [handwritten pencil], AA, Box 13, Folder 19. "Suggestion for Chapter 1 –" p. 5).

[125] AA Main Events, 1938, Point 18.

[126] Silkworth, "Reclamation of the Alcoholic," April 21, 1937 in *Medical Record, A National Review of Medicine and Surgery*, The Medical Journal and Record Publishing Company, Inc., New York, Volume 145, pp. 321–24.

 the rest of the Akron group

127 "Hank's ideas," (StSt, AA 501.1 – Alcoholics Anonymous – Hank Parkhurst's ideas [handwritten pencil], AA, Box 13, Folder 19. "Sales Promotion Possibilities," p. 4a).

128 Ibid.

129 All quotes in this section without other attributions, come from the Typed Prospectus for The One Hundred Men Corporation (GSO, Box 59, 1939, Folder C, following Document 1939-26 to 1939-32).

130 Printed promotional piece entitled "Alcoholics Anonymous," a prospectus for The One Hundred Men Corporation (GSO, Box 59, 1939, Folder C, Document 1939-144 to 157).

131 AA Main Events, 1938, Point 20.

132 For the initial subscription payments on November 15, see a spate of letters written by Ruth Hock to a variety of subscribers in February, March, and April 1939 acknowledging and/or requesting time payments (GSO, Box 59, 1939, Folders C & C(1), Documents 1939-3, -39, -42, -50, -51, -52, -53, -160, -161, -167, -168, -169, -184,-185 & -265).

133 AA Main Events, 1938, Point 20.

134 List of $25.00 Par Value – Non-Assessable – Shares of Stock Subscribed for – Works Publishing Co., (GSO, Box 61, Folder D, 1940 - Works Publishing Company, Document 1940-76 to 79).

135 Ibid.

136 Ibid.

Chapter Sixteen. Meanwhile, Out in Akron . . .

1 *Lois Remembers*, p. 112: "Most of the New York members agreed with the group publication idea; so did Bob in Akron, but *the rest of the Akron group* thought it a dangerous undertaking." [Italics added]

2 List of $25.00 Par Value – Non-Assessable – Shares of Stock Subscribed for – Works Publishing Co., (GSO, Box 61, Folder D, 1940 - Works Publishing Company, Document 1940-76 to 79).

3 AA Main Events, 1938, Point 21.

4 Ibid.

5 *Lois Remembers*, p. 112.

6 *AACOA*, pp. 155–56.

7 Minutes of the Alcoholic Foundations, September 23, 1938 (GSO, Minutes: Alcoholic Foundation / 1938-1944 / Duplicates) quoting Dr. Robert Smith's September 3 letter making this request. NOTE The original letter is actually dated September 8 (GSO, Box 59, Folder B[1], Document 1938-132).

8 *AACOA*, pp. 155–56.

9 Ibid., p. 164.

10 Ibid.

11 GSO filing cabinet drawer marked "Oral Histories," Folder marked: Murphy, Dorothy Snyder / Akron OH / August 30, 1954, p. 25.

12 Smith & Windows, *Children of the Healer*, pp. 49 & 132.

13 Bill Wilson to Dr. R. H. Smith, November 3, 1938 (GSO, Box 59, Folder B[1], Document 1938-172) acknowledges receipt of some "personal stories from Akron."

14 Smith & Windows, *Children of the Healer*, p. 49.

15 GSO filing cabinet drawer marked "Oral Histories," Folder marked: Murphy, Dorothy Snyder / Akron OH / August 30, 1954, p. 26

16 Ibid., p. 25.

17 Ibid.

18 Oral History Transcriptions, Transcript Record of William Van Horn, Akron, Ohio, 6/19/54 (GSO, Box 1 of 2, Box 1: 304680980, pp. 16–17).

19 Oral History Transcriptions, Transcript Record of Bob Evans, Akron, Ohio, 6/18/54 (GSO, Box 1 of 2, Box 1: 304680980, pp. 11-12).

20 Ibid.

21 Oral History Transcriptions, Transcript Record of William Van Horn, Akron, Ohio, 6/19/54 (GSO, Box 1 of 2, Box 1: 304680980, p. 17): "Bill Wilson: Of course, Doc told me that he had talked to Jim and that Jim was doing this work."

22 GSO filing cabinet drawer marked "Oral Histories," Folder marked: Murphy, Dorothy Snyder / Akron OH / August 30, 1954, p. 25.

23 Oral History Transcriptions, Transcript Record of William Van Horn, Akron, Ohio, 6/19/54 (GSO, Box 1 of 2, Box 1: 304680980, p. 17) *NOTE*: Doppler's name is sometimes spelled Doeppler in other references to him.

24 Smith & Windows, *Children of the Healer*, p. 49.

25 *Dr. Bob and the Good Oldtimers*, p. 154.

26 *Lois Remembers*, p. 113.

27 GSO filing cabinet drawer marked "Oral Histories," Folder marked: Murphy, Dorothy Snyder / Akron OH / August 30, 1954, p. 25.

28 Ibid: "He wrote his story, then he withdrew it, then put it in again, then he went through it again . . ."

29 Signed and notarized statement by Sue Smith Windows (Dr. Bob's adopted daughter) dated January 7, 1999 (see http://www.orange-papers.org/orange-bigbook.html for a link to this document). Sue Windows is hardly a reliable source for information on the writing of the Big Book—she is a 'hostile witness' at best and her loathing for Bill Wilson is palpable, as any reading of her testimony here and elsewhere will demonstrate—but the details she presents here on Del Tryon's story sound not just plausible, but correct.

30 GSO filing cabinet drawer marked "Oral Histories," Folder marked: Murphy, Dorothy Snyder / Akron OH / August 30, 1954, p. 25.

31 Smith & Windows, *Children of the Healer*, p. 132.

32 Dodd, *The Authors*, p. 3.

33 Ibid.

34 See a facsimile of these pages in *The Book That Started It All*, pp. 172–75.

35 "Hank's ideas," StSt, AA 501.1 – Alcoholics Anonymous – Hank Parkhurst's ideas [handwritten pencil], AA, Box 13, Folder 19, p. 11.

36 Dodd, *The Authors*, p. 81. *Alcoholics Anonymous*, (4th edition), "A Vision For You," p 158.

37 Dodd, *The Authors*, p. 82.

38 Smith & Windows, *Children of the Healer*, p. 132.

39 Dodd, *The Authors*, p. 82. In at least this one case, Wilson was playing the part that Jim Scott had played in 1938–1939.

40 Interview with Kathleen Treat (Earl's wife), July 29, 1985 (Chicago Area Nineteen Archives transcript) – available on AAHistoryLovers Forum, Message 10162 @ https://groups.yahoo.com/neo/groups/AAHistoryLovers/conversations/topics/161 (retrieved July 26, 2014).

41 *Alcoholics Anonymous*, "He Sold Himself Short" (2nd & 3rd editions, p. 293; 4th edition, p. 264).

42 Ibid, p. 264 & 265 respectively.

43 GSO, Box 59, 1938, Folder B[1], Document 1938-172.

44 Oral History Transcriptions, Transcript Record of William Van Horn, Akron, Ohio, 6/19/54 (GSO, Box 1 of 2, Box 1: 304680980, p. 17).

45 *AACOA*, p. 164.

46 Oral History Transcriptions, Transcript Record of William Van Horn, Akron, Ohio, 6/19/54 (GSO, Box 1 of 2, Box 1: 304680980, p. 17): "I wrote mine and pitched it in."

47 Bill Wilson to Dr. Bob Smith, [June 22, 23 or 24], 1938 (GSO, Box 59, 1938, Folder B, Documents 1938-25 to 1938-30).

48 Sue Windows Smith, *Children of the Healer*, p. 42.

49 Wm. G. Wilson to Dr. R. Smith, September 27, 1938 (GSO, Box 59, 1938, Folder B[1], Document 1938-153).

50 Bill Wilson to Dr. Bob Smith, [June 24, 25 or 26], 1938 (GSO, Box 59, 1938, Folder B, Documents 1938-25 to 1938-30).

51 Bill Wilson to Dr. R. H. Smith, September 27, 1938 (GSO, Box 59, Folder D, Document 1938-172).

52 Bill Wilson to Bob Smith, November 3, 1938 (GSO, Box 59, 1938, Folder B[1], Document 1938-172).

53 William Wilson to W. R. Jones, November 3, 1938 (GSO, Box 59, 1938, B[1], Document 1938-174).

54 Oral History Transcriptions, Transcript Record of Bob Evans, Akron, Ohio, 6/18/54 (GSO, Box 1 of 2, Box 1: 304680980, p. 11).

55 AA Main Events, 1938, Point 21.

56 *AACOA*, p. 159.

57 Bill Wilson to Bob Smith, November 9, 1938 (GSO, Box 59, 1938, Folder B[1], Document 1938-178).

58 Bill Wilson to Bob Smith, November 9, 1938 (GSO, Box 59, 1938, Folder B[1], Document 1938-178).

59 GSO, Box 59, 1938, Folder B[1], Document 1938-201).

Chapter Seventeen. "Working with Others"

1 Wm. G. Wilson to Dr. R. Smith, September 27, 1938 (GSO, Box 59, 1938, Folder B[1], Document 1938-153).

2 *Lois Remembers*, p. 113.

[3] AA Main Events, 1938, <u>Point 20</u>.

[4] Ibid.

[5] "A Discussion of the Big Book," a talk by Ruth Hock, Glendale, CA, March 12, 1978; transcript copy in the Akron Archives, p. 6. Also available on YouTube under the title "Ruth H. AA's First Secretary shares the history of Alcoholics Anonymous" - http://www.youtube.com/watch?v=mxVkTNgOhy0 – retrieved September 27, 2013

[6] Ruth [Hock] Crecelius to Bill Wilson, November 10, 1955 (StSt, AA 326, Box 4, Folder 17).

[7] Pittman, *AA The Way It Began*, p. 179; quoting from phone interviews with Ruth Hock conducted in December 1981 and July 1982.

[8] Bill Wilson to Dr. Bob Smith, November 3, 1938 (GSO, Box 59, 1938, Folder B[1], Document 1938-172).

[9] "A Discussion of the Big Book," a talk by Ruth Hock, Glendale, CA, March 12, 1978; transcript copy in the Akron Archives, p. 6. Also available on YouTube under the title "Ruth H. AA's First Secretary shares the history of Alcoholics Anonymous" - http://www.youtube.com/watch?v=mxVkTNgOhy0 – retrieved September 27, 2013.

[10] Bill Wilson to Lois Wilson, May, 1935 (StSt, WGW 1024, Box 27, Folder 72).

[11] [Bill Wilson – Autobiographical Recording] – Writings 1954 – Recollections of his early life – recorded with Ed Bierstadt at Hotel Bedford Sept. 1954 (StSt, WGW 103, Box 31, Folder 15).

[12] Ibid.

[13] Bill Wilson speaking before the National Committee on Alcoholism, March 30, 1956 in New York City (see AAHistoryLovers message #1695; https://groups.yahoo.com/neo/groups/AAHistoryLovers/conversations/messages/1695 - retrieved November 3, 2014) and Bill Wilson speaking in Chicago, February, 1951 (http://www.silkworth.net/aahistory/billw2/need1951.html - retrieved November 3, 2014).

[14] *Pass It On*, p. 137

[15] *Alcoholics Anonymous* (4th edition), "A Vision For You," pp. 153–55.

[16] All quotes in this section from "Working With Others" can be found in *The Book That Started It All*, pp. 73–79.

[17] See the interviews of several early Ohio members done by Bill Wilson in 1954 which record many instances of this 'hospital approach' (GSO filing cabinet drawer marked "Oral Histories").

[18] Wm. G. Wilson to Mr. Charles Parcelles [sic], July [but really August] 1, 1938 (GSO, Box 59, 1938, Folder B, Documents 1938-31 to 1938-34).

[19] *The Book That Started It All*, p. 56.

[20] *Alcoholics Anonymous* (4th edition), p. 85.

Chapter Eighteen. "To Wives"

[1] *Dr. Bob and the Good Oldtimers*, p. 241.

[2] Ibid., p. 242.

[3] Ibid., p. 98

[4] Ibid., pp. 97–98.

5 Ibid., p. 244.

6 Ibid., p. 241.

7 Ibid., p. 244.

8 Ibid., p. 241.

9 Ibid., p. 247.

10 Ibid., pp.180–81. With thirty-five years of continuous sobriety. (http://www. barefootsworld.net/aasylviak.html - retrieved November 11, 2014).

11 Ibid., p. 180.

12 Ibid., p. 241.

13 Ibid., p. 242.

14 "Notes on Akron, Ohio Survey / by / Frank Amos," [unedited version], p. 4 (GSO, Box 22, Reel 10 / 8.1 The Alcoholic Foundation: 1937-1938, P-7 to P-10).

15 *Dr. Bob and the Good Oldtimers*, p. 241.

16 Ibid., p. 242.

17 [Bill Wilson – Autobiographical Recording] – Writings 1954 – Recollections of his early life – recorded with Ed Bierstadt at Hotel Bedford Sept. 1954 (StSt, WGW 103, Box 31, Folder 15); *The Authors*, p. 10; *Alcoholics Anonymous* (1st edition), "A Feminine Victory," pp. 221.

18 *Alcoholics Anonymous* (1st edition), "A Feminine Victory," pp. 221–22.

19 For instance in Dodd, *The Authors*, p. 45.

20 Bill Wilson to Dr. Bob Smith, [June 22, 23 or 24], 1938 (GSO, Box 59, 1938, Folder B, Document 1938-25 to 1938-30).

21 *Lois Remembers*, p. 114.

22 Hartigan, *Bill W.*, p. 114.

23 *Lois Remembers*, p. 114.

24 Hartigan, *Bill W.* pp. 114–15.

25 Ibid., p. 114

26 *Pass It On*, p. 200.

27 Hartigan, *Bill W.*, p. 114.

28 All quotes in this section on "To Wives" are from the Multilith edition and can be found in *The Book That Started It All*, pp. 80-87.

29 *Alcoholics Anonymous* (4th edition), "More About Alcoholism," p. 31.

30 Outline: Chapter Twenty One (StSt, AA 501.1, Box 13, Folder 16; Publications – Alcoholics Anonymous [1939 – (sic)] – Outline of chapters) *[Hank's Chapter #21]*.

31 *Alcoholics Anonymous* (4th edition), pp. 20–21.

32 Hartigan, *Bill W.* p. 115.

33 *Alcoholics Anonymous* (4th edition), pp. 20–22.

Chapter Nineteen. "The Family Afterward" and the Authorship Question

1 All quotes in this section on "The Family Afterward" are from the Multilith edition and can be found in *The Book That Started It All*, pp. 88–93.

2 As previously noted, all quotes in this section on "The Family Afterward" are from the Multilith edition and can be found in *The Book That Started It All*, pp. 88–93.

3 A phrase that Bill used in two letters to Dr. Bob at this time: November 3, 1938 (GSO, Box 59, 1938, Folder B[1], Document 1938-172) and November 9,1938 (GSO, Box 59, 1938, Folder B[1], Document 1938-178).

4 Bill Wilson to Bob Smith, November 9, 1938 (GSO, Box 59, 1938, Folder B[1], Document 1938-178).

5 AA Main Events, 1938, Point 21.

6 *AACOA*, p. 159.

7 Bill Wilson to Bob Smith, November 3, 1938 (GSO, Box 59, 1938, Folder B[1], Document 1938-172).

8 "Foreword to First Edition" of *Alcoholics Anonymous* (reprinted in every edition of the book).

9 AA Main Events, 1938, Point 21.

10 Bill Wilson speaking in Fort Worth, Texas, June 12, 1954 ("How the Book Alcoholics Anonymous Came About," in *The Book That Started It All*, p. 213).

11 *AACOA*, p. 160.

12 Burwell, "Speech at Hope Manor," p. 11.

13 Bill Wilson to Bob Smith, November 3, 1938 (GSO, Box 59, 1938, Folder B[1], Document 1938-172).

14 Bill Wilson speaking to the Manhattan Group, New York City, December, 1955 (retrieved from http://recoveryspeakers.com/bill-w-1955-manhattan-group-about-the-early-days/).

15 Jim Burwell speaking in Sacramento, CA on June 15, 1957 (retrieved from www.xa-speakers.org on May 23, 2015).

16 Burwell, "Speech at Hope Manor," p. 9

17 *AACOA*, p. 159.

18 Burwell, "Evolution," p. 3

19 Bill Wilson to Bob Smith, November 3, 1938 (GSO, Box 59, 1938, Folder B[1], Document 1938-172). Also referred to in Bill's letter to Bob on September 27, 1938 as "the original dictation."

20 Ruth [Hock] Crecelius to Bill Wilson, November 10, 1955 (StSt, AA 326, Box 4, Folder 17).

21 *AACOA*, pp. 11 & 16.

22 "A Discussion of the Big Book," a talk by Ruth Hock, Glendale, CA, March 12, 1978; transcript copy in the Akron Archives, p. 24. Also available on YouTube under the title "Ruth H. AA's First Secretary shares the history of Alcoholics Anonymous" - http://www.youtube.com/watch?v=mxVkTNgOhy0 - retrieved September 27, 2013.

23 AA Main Events, 1938, Point 26.

24 "Hank's ideas," StSt, AA 501.1 – Alcoholics Anonymous – Hank Parkhurst's ideas [handwritten pencil], AA, Box 13, Folder 19, p. 8a.

25 *AACOA*, p. 163.

26 "Hank's ideas," StSt, AA 501.1 – Alcoholics Anonymous – Hank Parkhurst's ideas [handwritten pencil], AA, Box 13, Folder 19, p. 8a.

27 Ibid.

28 *Alcoholics Anonymous* (4th edition), "Working With Others," p. 102.

29 Bill Wilson speaking in Fort Worth, Texas, June 12, 1954 ("How the Book Alcoholics Anonymous Came About," in *The Book That Started It All*, p. 213).

30 AA Main Events, 1938, Point 21.

31 *AACOA*, p. 160.

32 See, for instance, *Alcoholics Anonymous* (4th edition), pp. 3, 68–70, 74, 81–82, 106, 111, & 124–125 [this quote].

33 StSt, WGW 103, Box 31, Folder 3: Writings 1939 *[sic]* - Original story [incomplete; typescript; 36 pp., 1180 lines]. p. 15.

34 [First Two Chapters of Proposed Book], "Bill's Story," p. 15 (GSO, Box 59, 1938, Folder B, Documents 1938-53 to 1938-75).

35 *The Book That Started It All*, p. 2. *NOTE* that the same text appears in *Alcoholics Anonymous* (4th edition), "Bill's Story," p. 3.

36 AA Main Events, 1938, Point 26; Ruth Hock's 1978 Interview with Niles Peebles (GSO, CD 876, Track 1, 18:15 to 18:45).

37 "A Discussion of the Big Book," a talk by Ruth Hock, Glendale, CA, March 12, 1978; transcript copy in the Akron Archives, p. 12. Also available on YouTube under the title "Ruth H. AA's First Secretary shares the history of Alcoholics Anonymous" - http://www.youtube.com/watch?v=mxVkTNgOhy0.

38 M., Merton, *Black Sheep*, p. 58.

39 *Lois Remembers*, p. 129.

40 M., Merton, *Black Sheep*, p. 58.

41 Hunter et al., *Women Pioneers*, p. 84.

42 *Lois Remembers*, p. 129.

43 Hunter et al., *Women Pioneers*, p. 84.

44 Ruth Hock's 1978 Interview with Niles Peebles (GSO, CD 866, Track 1, 12:00 to 14:15).

45 Ibid.

46 Hunter et al., *Women Pioneers*, p. 84.

47 *Pass It On*, p. 229.

48 Ruth Hock's 1978 Interview with Niles Peebles (GSO, CD 866, Track 1, 12:00 to 14:15).

49 *Lois Remembers*, p. 129–30.

Chapter Twenty. Hank Parkhurst:
Managing Editor and "To Employers"

1 Frank B. Amos to Albert L. Scott, June 24, 1938 (GSO, Box 59, 1938, Folder B, Document 1938-23 & 1938-24).

2 Typed prospectus for The One Hundred Men Corporation (GSO, Box 59, 1939, Folder C, following Document 1939-26 to 1939-32, p. 8). *NOTE*: This typed prospectus is actually an unnumbered document that appears after three similar (but textually different) documents that share the same identifying numbers in the GSO archive.

3 Bill Wilson to Dr. Bob Smith, [June 22, 23 or 24], 1938 (GSO, Box 59, 1938, Folder B, Document 1938-25 to 1938-30).

4 Arthur E. Scott to Mr. [Bill] Wilson, October 12, 1938 (GSO, Box 59, 1938, Folder B[1], Document 1938-166 & 1938-167).

5 LVS [Leonard V. Strong] to Meredith Wood, Vice President, Book of the Month Club, February 21, 1939 (GSO, Box 59, 1939, Folder C, Document 1939-54).

6 Henry G. Parkhurst to Mrs. Janet M. Blair, November 7, 1938 (GSO, Box 59, Folder E.2, LETTERS – November 7, 1938 – July 24, 1939).

7 *Lois Remembers*, p. 115.

8 AA Main Events, 1938, <u>Point 26</u>; Ruth Hock's 1978 Interview with Niles Peebles (GSO, CD 876, Track 1, 18:15 to 18:45).

9 "A Discussion of the Big Book," a talk by Ruth Hock, Glendale, CA, March 12, 1978; transcript copy in the Akron Archives, p. 9. Also available on YouTube under the title "Ruth H. AA's First Secretary shares the history of Alcoholics Anonymous" - http://www.youtube.com/watch?v=mxVkTNgOhy0 – retrieved September 27, 2013.

10 H.G.P. [Henry G. Parkhurst] to Wm. G. Wilson, January 5, 1939 (GSO, Box 59, 1939, Folder C, Document 1939-6).

11 *The Liberator Magazine*, August, 1922, p. 32.

12 *A Writer's Digest*, September, 1933.

13 Ibid. See also "Uzzell, Thomas H.," *Fiction Mag Index, Chronological List* (http://www.philsp.com/homeville/FMI/d/d3810.htm - retrieved July 27, 2015) and UNZOrg (http://vkproduction.com/Author/UzzellThomasH - retrieved August 3, 2015) for these references.

14 Uzzell's advertisement for his services as "Literary Critic" in *A Writer's Digest*, September, 1933.

15 *The Minnesota Alumni Weekly*, June 12, 1926, "*If You* Want to *Write* Real Fiction *Stories* That Sell, *Thomas Uzzell ('09)* Will Help You *Do* So," p. 557.

16 *The Brooklyn Daily Eagle Educational Directory Section*, August 28, 1930, p. 16.

17 Henry G. Parkhurst to Mrs. Janet M. Blair, November 7, 1938 (GSO, Box 59, Folder E.2, LETTERS – November 7, 1938 – July 24, 1939).

18 *The Evening Star*, Peekskill, NY, Tuesday, July 10, 1965: "Mrs. Janet Blair Dies; Secretary to Authors."

19 See the many archived and scanned letters to and from Janet Blair in the Ida Tarbell archives preserved at Tarbell's alma mater, Allegheny College (http://sites.allegheny.edu/tarbell/) and also among the Ida M. Tarbell Papers to be found at Ohio University.

20 Wikipedia, Ida Tarbell, Named Article (retrieved July 28, 2015).

21 *The American Experience*, Biography: Ida Tarbell (http://www.pbs.org/wgbh/americanexperience/features/biography/rockefellers-tarbell/ - retrieved July 28, 2015).

22 *The Evening Star*, Peekskill, NY, Tuesday, July 10, 1965: "Mrs. Janet Blair Dies; Secretary to Authors."

23 Wikipedia, "Life Begins at 40," Named Article (retrieved July 30, 2015).

24 Wikipedia, Walter B. Pitkin, Named Article (retrieved July 30, 2015).

25 Uzzell's advertisement for his services, offering "Professional Training" in writing in *The Editor*, July 15, 1922, The Literary Marketplace section, p. IV.

26 Uzzell's advertisement for his services as "Literary Critic" in *A Writer's Digest*, September, 1933.

27 Uzzell's advertisement offering his services for "training beginners . . . in story writing by mail" in The Bookman, February 1922, The Bookman Advertiser section.

28 Lois's Diary, 1939, March 1.

29 List of $25.00 Par Value – Non-Assessable – Shares of Stock Subscribed for – Works Publishing Co., (GSO, Box 61, Folder D, 1940 - Works Publishing Company, Document 1940-76 to 79).

30 William G. Wilson to Frank Amos, September 26, 1938 (GSO, Box 59, Folder B[1], Documents 1938-145 to 1938-151).

31 List of $25.00 Par Value – Non-Assessable – Shares of Stock Subscribed for – Works Publishing Co., (GSO, Box 61, Folder D, 1940 - Works Publishing Company, Document 1940-76 to 79).

32 Ibid.

33 Wm. G. Wilson to Dr. Esther L. Richards, July 22, 1938 (GSO, Box 59, 1938, Folder B, Document 1938-76 to 1938-78). OR perhaps, as noted elsewhere, it was only the $20,000 reported by Silas Bent in his "There Is Hope" article in *The Hackettstown Courier-Post*, Thursday, January 19, 1939 (GSO, Album of Reprints; StSt, AA 501.1, Box 13, Folder 15).

34 The Honor Dealers Business Plan, "History" section, (StSt, Personages – Henry G. [Hank] Parkhurst – Honor Dealers Business Plan and Correspondence, AA 329, Box 4a).

35 William G. Wilson to Frank Amos, September 26, 1938 (GSO, Box 59, Folder B[1], Documents 1938-145 to 1938-151

36 Wm. G. Wilson to Mr. Charles Parcelles *[sic]*, July *[but really August]* 1, 1938 (GSO, Box 59, 1938, Folder B, Documents 1938-31 to 1938-34).

37 StSt, AA 501.1, Box 13, Folder 16; Publications – Alcoholics Anonymous [1939] – Outline of chapters.

38 *Lois Remembers*, p. 114.

39 Ruth Hock Crecilius to Bill Wilson, December 4, 1955 (StSt, WGW 102.2. Correspondence – Chronological Files – CRA-CUY, Box 14, Folder 2)

40 All quotes in this section from "To Employers" can be found in *The Book That Started It All*, pp. 94–101.

Chapter Twenty-One. "The Q&A Chapter"

1 A Question and Answer Section Has Been Proposed for the Book (GSO, Box 59, 1939, Folder C, Document 1939-11 to 1939-25).

[2] January 7, 1939: Memorandum on One Hundred Men Inc. (GSO, Box 59, 1939, Folder C, Documents 1939-26 to 1939-32, 3rd filed copy with this identifying number). This document, as noted in an earlier footnote, is a cut-and-paste affair with many sections affixed to the back side of some old Honor Dealers promotional materials done in this Q&A format. Unfortunately, we can only see these five and a half questions in this "found" material.

[3] "Hank's ideas," (StSt, AA 501.1 – Alcoholics Anonymous – Hank Parkhurst's ideas [handwritten pencil], AA, Box 13, Folder 19, p. 3).

[4] For these quotes and those that follow from this proposed chapter, see A Question and Answer Section Has Been Proposed for the Book (GSO, Box 59, 1939, Folder C, Document 1939-11 to 1939-25).

[5] *Alcoholics Anonymous* (4th edition), "There Is A Solution," p. 27 and "More About Alcoholism," p. 35 (in the story of Jim who put the whiskey in his milk).

[6] *AACOA*, p. 163.

[7] The Multilith printing version of "To Employers" found in *The Book That Started It All*, p. 97.

[8] www.dictionary.com definition (retrieved August 20, 2015).

[9] *Alcoholics Anonymous* (4th edition), p. 44.

[10] Quoted from the Multilith edition version of Chapter Five which can be found in *The Book That Started It All*, p. 58.

[11] Quoted from the Multilith edition version which can be found in *The Book That Started It All*, p. 79.

[12] "Hank's ideas," (StSt, AA 501.1 – Alcoholics Anonymous – Hank Parkhurst's ideas [handwritten pencil], AA, Box 13, Folder 19, p. 3).

[13] Dodd, *The Authors*, pp. 43–44.

[14] Horace Maher's Original Handwritten Notes on the Q&A Chapter, 3 pages (GSO, Box 59, 1939, Folder C, no number assigned, but the first document in this folder) for this quote and all that follow from this document quoted in this section.

[15] *Alcoholics Anonymous* (1st edition), "On His Way," p. 377.

[16] Ibid., p. vii.

Chapter Twenty-Two. "A Vision for You"

[1] Writings – *Lois Remembers* – Ebby's Calendar, p. 2 (StSt, LBW 203, Box 32, Folder 4).

[2] Ebby Thacher recording his memories (with Bill Wilson sitting in) at Fort Worth during the Texas State Convention, 1954 (GSO, Oral History Files, Thacher, Edwin Ebby / 1897-1962, p. 13). See also Mel B, *Ebby*, p. 80.

[3] Lois's Diary, 1938, November 1.

[4] Ebby in Fort Worth, 1954 (GSO, Oral History Files, Thacher, Edwin Ebby / 1897-1962, p. 14); Mell B. *Ebby*, p. 81.

[5] Lois's Diary, 1938, November 7.

[6] Ibid., November 8: "Bill sent Ebby and Brooke drunk away."

[7] Ebby in Fort Worth, 1954 (GSO, Oral History Files, Thacher, Edwin Ebby / 1897-1962, p. 14); Mel B. *Ebby*, p. 81.

8   Mel B., *Ebby*, p. 82.

9   Ebby in Fort Worth, 1954 (GSO, Oral History Files, Thacher, Edwin Ebby / 1897-1962, p. 14); Mel B. *Ebby*, pp. 81–82.

10 *Lois Remembers*, p. 130.

11 Mel B., *Ebby*, pp. 82–86.

12 Bill Wilson speaking before the New York City Medical Society on Alcoholism, April 28, 1958 (pamphlet: *Three Talks to Medical Societies by Bill W., Co-Founder of AA*, Alcoholics Anonymous Work Services, Inc., p.15 – available online at A.A.'s website).

13 *Alcoholics Anonymous* (4th edition), "Bill's Story," p. 15 and "Working With Others," p. 89.

14 *Lois Remembers*, p. 118.

15 Charles B. Towns to William Wilson, October 4, 1945 (GSO, Box 65, Folder C (2 of 2) / 1945 – Alcoholic Foundation, Inc. / Pages 116-262 / July – December, p. 162).

16 Wm. G. Wilson to Frank B. Amos, January 4, 1939 (GSO, Box 59, 1939, Folder C, Document 1939-7 to 1939-10, p. 3).

17 Ibid.

18 GSO, Box 59, 1938, Folder D.2, Page 11.

19 Wm. G. Wilson to Frank B. Amos, January 4, 1939 (GSO, Box 59, 1939, Folder C, Document 1939-7 to 1939-10, p. 3).

20 *AACOA*, pp. 159–60.

21 "Hank's Ideas," StSt, AA 501.1 – Alcoholics Anonymous – Hank Parkhurst's ideas [handwritten pencil], AA, Box 13, Folder 19, Suggestion for Chapter -," p. 5.

22 StSt, AA 501.1, Box 13, Folder 16; Publications – Alcoholics Anonymous [1939 (sic)] – Outline of chapters.

23 All quotes in this section of "A Vision For You" are from the Multilith edition and can be found in *The Book That Started It All*, pp. 102-108.

24 AA Main Events, 1938, <u>Point 21</u>: "The Akron people, still thinking they were Oxford Groupers, and dubious of the doings in New York subscribed no money whatever."

25 Again, all direct quotes in this section from "A Vision For You" are from the Multilith edition and can be found in *The Book That Started It All*, pp. 102–08.

26 *AACOA*, p. 176.

27 Wm. G. Wilson to Frank B. Amos, January 4, 1939 (GSO, Box 59, 1939, Folder C, Document 1939-7 to 1939-10, p. 3).

28 Ibid.

29 Ibid.

30 GSO File Folder marked: Ernie Galbraith / Akron OH Former / Husband Sue Windows, December 11, 1954 (Session II), p. 4.

31 Volume 113(16), October 14, 1939 (available online at http://silkworth.net/ bbreviews/01007.html (retrieved October 21, 2015).

32 Bill Wilson to Dr. Bob Smith, December 13, 1938 (GSO, Box 59, 1938, Folder B(1), Document 1938-191).

33 GSO, Box 59, 1938, Folder B(1), Documents 1938-190 and 1938-188 respectively.

34 Ibid plus Document 1938-189 (*NOTE*: these three GSO documents include all eleven telegrams).

Chapter Twenty-Three. Writing the Twelve Steps

1 Bill Wilson, "A Fragment of History: Origin of the Twelve Steps" (A.A. *Grapevine*, July 1953; *Language of the Heart*, p. 201).

2 AA Main Events, 1938, Point 22: "By December 1938 I had probably reached what is now Chapter 5 in the book. The chapter that carries AA's Twelve Steps." See also the calendar of events in *AACOA*, p. vii and *Lois Remembers*, p. 198.

3 Bill Wilson speaking in Fort Worth, Texas, June 12, 1954 ("How the Book Alcoholics Anonymous Came About," in *The Book That Started It All*, p. 213).

4 Ibid.

5 *AACOA*, pp. 159–60.

6 GSO, Box 29, Folder 17.1, AA History: Miscellaneous Materials, p. 2.

7 Bill Wilson speaking in Fort Worth, Texas, June 12, 1954 ("How the Book Alcoholics Anonymous Came About," in *The Book That Started It All*, p. 213).

8 Ibid.

9 Bill Wilson speaking in New York City, November 12, 1953 (GSO, CD BW 11).

10 *AACOA*, pp. 159–60.

11 Ibid, p. 161.

12 Bill Wilson, "A Fragment of History: Origin of the Twelve Steps" (A.A. *Grapevine*, July 1953; *Language of the Heart*, p. 201).

13 Bill Wilson speaking in Fort Worth, Texas, June 12, 1954 ("How the Book Alcoholics Anonymous Came About," in *The Book That Started It All*, p. 213); Bill Wilson to Jack Alexander, December 13, 1949 (GSO, Box 29, Folder 17.1, AA History: Miscellaneous Materials, p. 2).

14 Bill Wilson, "A Fragment of History: Origin of the Twelve Steps" (A.A. *Grapevine*, July 1953; *Language of the Heart*, p. 201); Bill Wilson to Jack Alexander, December 13, 1949 (GSO, Box 29, Folder 17.1, AA History: Miscellaneous Materials, p. 2).

15 Bill Wilson speaking in Fort Worth, Texas, June 12, 1954 ("How the Book Alcoholics Anonymous Came About," in *The Book That Started It All*, p. 213).

16 Bill Wilson speaking to the Manhattan Group, New York City, December, 1955 (http://recoveryspeakers.com/bill-w-1955-manhattan-group-about-the-early-days/ - retrieved December 2, 2015).

17 Ibid.

18 Bill Wilson, "A Fragment of History: Origin of the Twelve Steps" (A.A. *Grapevine*, July 1953; *Language of the Heart*, p. 200).

19 AA Main Events, 1938, Point 22.

20 Bill Wilson speaking in Atlanta, Georgia, July 14, 1951 (recording acquired from Dicobe Media Inc., Bellevue NE, 68005).

21 Bill Wilson speaking in Fort Worth, Texas, June 12, 1954 ("How the Book Alcoholics Anonymous Came About," in *The Book That Started It All*, p. 213) and Bill Wilson speaking to the Manhattan Group, New York City, December, 1955 (http://recoveryspeakers.com/bill-w-1955-manhattan-group-about-the-early-days/ - retrieved December 2, 2015).

22 Bill Wilson, "A Fragment of History: Origin of the Twelve Steps" (A.A. *Grapevine*, July 1953; *Language of the Heart*, p. 201).

23 AA Main Events, 1938, Point 22.

24 *AACOA*, p. 160.

25 Bill Wilson's talk at the National Clergy Conference on Alcoholism, 1960 (http://www.silkworth.net/religion_clergy/01052.html - retrieved November 6, 2015).

26 *AACOA*, p. 160.

27 Bill Wilson, "A Fragment of History: Origin of the Twelve Steps" (A.A. *Grapevine*, July 1953; *Language of the Heart*, p. 201).

28 *AACOA*, p. 160. A direct quote.

29 Ibid. Also a direct quote.

30 Ibid. p. 161.

31 Bill Wilson speaking in Fort Worth, Texas, June 12, 1954 ("How the Book Alcoholics Anonymous Came About," in *The Book That Started It All*, p. 213).

32 Bill Wilson speaking to the Manhattan Group, New York City, December, 1955 (http://recoveryspeakers.com/bill-w-1955-manhattan-group-about-the-early-days/ - retrieved December 2, 2015).

33 *AACOA*, p. 160.

34 Ibid, p. 161.

35 Bill Wilson, "A Fragment of History: Origin of the Twelve Steps" (A.A. *Grapevine*, July 1953; *Language of the Heart*, p. 201).

36 *AACOA*, p. 160.

37 Bill Wilson, "A Fragment of History: Origin of the Twelve Steps" (A.A. *Grapevine*, July 1953; *Language of the Heart*, p. 201).

38 *AACOA*, p. 161.

39 AA Main Events, 1938, Point 22.

40 Bill Wilson's talk at the National Clergy Conference on Alcoholism, 1960 (http://www.silkworth.net/religion_clergy/01052.html - retrieved November 6, 2015).

41 AA Main Events, 1938, Point 22.

42 Bill Wilson's talk at the National Clergy Conference on Alcoholism, 1960 (http://www.silkworth.net/religion_clergy/01052.html - retrieved November 6, 2015).

43 *AACOA*, p. 161.

44 Bill Wilson, "A Fragment of History: Origin of the Twelve Steps" (A.A. *Grapevine*, July 1953; *Language of the Heart*, p. 201).

45 Bill Wilson speaking in New York City, November 12, 1953 (GSO, CD BW 11).

46 Bill Wilson's talk at the National Clergy Conference on Alcoholism, 1960 (http://www.silkworth.net/religion_clergy/01052.html - retrieved November 6, 2015).

47 Bill Wilson speaking in Fort Worth, Texas, June 12, 1954 ("How the Book Alcoholics Anonymous Came About," in *The Book That Started It All*, p. 213).

48 Paul Kirby Hennessy to Bill [Wilson], October 19, 1948 (GSO, Box 29, Reel 13, 17.4 The Twelve Steps: How Written).

49 Ibid.

50 *AACOA*, p. 160.

51 Bill Wilson speaking in Fort Worth, Texas, June 12, 1954 ("How the Book Alcoholics Anonymous Came About," in *The Book That Started It All*, p. 213).

52 Bill Wilson speaking to the Manhattan Group, New York City, December, 1955 (http://recoveryspeakers.com/bill-w-1955-manhattan-group-about-the-early-days/ - retrieved December 2, 2015).

53 *AACOA*, pp. 165–66.

54 Ibid., p. 165.

55 Ibid., pp. 163–64.

56 Bill Wilson speaking in Long Beach, July 2, 1960 (GSO, CD IC 60/24).

57 AA Main Events, 1938, Point 22.

58 Bill Wilson's talk at the National Clergy Conference on Alcoholism, 1960 (http://www.silkworth.net/religion_clergy/01052.html - retrieved November 6, 2015).

59 *AACOA*, p. 161.

60 Wikipedia, Sam Shoemaker, Named Article – retrieved November 7, 2015.

61 Glenn Chesnut's comment can be found on the Yahoo AAHistoryLovers board, June 12, 2014, Message #10034 (https://groups.yahoo.com/neo/groups/AAHistoryLovers/conversations/messages/10034 - retrieved November 15, 2015).

62 *AACOA*, p. 160.

63 Ibid.

64 American Journal of Psychiatry, Vol. 106, 1949, "The Society of Alcoholics Anonymous," by William W., (read at the 105th Annual Meeting of the American Psychiatric Association, Montreal, Quebec, May 23-27, 1949). Available online at http://www.silkworth.net/aahistory/billw2/societyofaa.html - retrieved September 3, 2016.

65 *AACOA*, p. 160.

66 Ibid.

67 Kurtz, *Not-God*, p. 331, n. 32.

68 *AACOA*, p. 160.

69 There are two identical incomplete copies of "Me and John" in the Stepping Stones folder (only two pages each), both typed on 8½" x 11" paper. The third copy of the story is complete, six pages long and on 8½" x 14" sheets. This last copy is deeply indented (2") and has each line numbered, i.e., it has been typed in that same strange format that the earliest, long version of "Bill's Story" is preserved.

70 StSt, AA 501.1, Box 13, Folder 25: Alcoholics Anonymous – Early drafts of Our Southern Friend, Me and John (Barleycorn).

71 *Lois Remembers*, p. 113.

72 *The Book That Started It All*, p. 135.

73 "Notes on Akron, Ohio Survey / by / Frank Amos," [unedited version], p. 3 (GSO, Box 22, Reel 10 / 8.1 The Alcoholic Foundation: 1937-1938, p. 2).

74 Bill Wilson speaking in Fort Worth, Texas, June 12, 1954 ("How the Book Alcoholics Anonymous Came About," in *The Book That Started It All*, p. 213).

75 Bill Wilson, "A Fragment of History: Origin of the Twelve Steps" (A.A. *Grapevine*, July 1953; *Language of the Heart*, p. 201).

76 Bill Wilson speaking in Fort Worth, Texas, June 12, 1954 ("How the Book Alcoholics Anonymous Came About," in *The Book That Started It All*, p. 213).

Chapter Twenty-Four. Editing Bill's Steps

1 *AACOA*, pp. 161–62.

2 The Multilith edition of *Alcoholics Anonymous*, p. 26 (*The Book That Started It All*, p. 58).

3 *AACOA*, p. 17.

4 Bill Wilson to Dr. Bob Smith, November 3, 1938 (GSO, Box 59, 1938, Folder B[1], Document 1938-172).

5 Thomas Keane Birrell speaking in North Carolina in 1963[?] (GSO CD 51, quote from 18:30 to 19:20).

6 Bill Wilson speaking in Fort Worth, Texas, June 12, 1954 ("How the Book Alcoholics Anonymous Came About," in *The Book That Started It All*, p. 213.

7 Ruth [Hock] Crecelius to Bill Wilson, November 10, 1955 (StSt, AA 326, Box 4, Folder 17).

8 *AACOA*, p. 162. See also p. 17.

9 Ibid., p. 162.

10 Ibid., pp. 162–63.

11 See item #4 in "Notes on Akron, Ohio Survey / by / Frank Amos," [unedited version], p. 3 (GSO, Box 22, Reel 10 / 8.1 The Alcoholic Foundation: 1937-1938, p. 2) and several of the interviews Bill did with Ohio oldtimers in 1954 (GSO Archives). This was later confirmed by Bill Wilson in his talk, "The Fellowship of Alcoholics Anonymous by W.W. as given at the Yale School of Alcohol Studies, June 1944:" "It could not have been presented at first, but sooner or later in his second, third, or fourth year, the A.A. will be found reading his Bible quite as often – or more – as he will a standard psychological work" (http://www.barefootsworld.net/aabw1944talk.html - retrieved December 22, 2015).

12 *AACOA*, p. 17.

13 *Lois Remembers*, p, 101.

14 *AACOA*, p. 17. The "hot argument" between these two is also noted in a different speech by Bill Wilson quoted in Hunter et al., *Women Pioneers*, p. 81.

15 AA Main Events, 1938, Point 22.

16 Bill Wilson, "A Fragment of History: Origin of the Twelve Steps" (A.A. *Grapevine*, July 1953; *Language of the Heart*, p. 201).

17 *AACOA*, p. 163.

18 Bill Wilson speaking to the Manhattan Group, New York City, December, 1955 (http://recoveryspeakers.com/bill-w-1955-manhattan-group-about-the-early-days/ - retrieved December 2, 2015).

19 Bill Wilson speaking in Fort Worth, Texas, June 12, 1954 ("How the Book Alcoholics Anonymous Came About," in *The Book That Started It All*, p. 213).

20 Bill Wilson speaking in Atlanta, Georgia, July 14, 1951 (recording acquired from Dicobe Media Inc., Bellevue NE, 68005).

21 AA Main Events, 1938, Point 22 and Bill Wilson speaking to the Manhattan Group, New York City, December, 1955 (http://recoveryspeakers.com/bill-w-1955-manhattan-group-about-the-early-days/ - retrieved December 2, 2015).

22 "Bill's Story," pp. 20 – 21 (GSO, Box 59, 1938, Folder B, First Two Chapters of the Proposed Book; Trust Indenture, Documents 1938-53 to 1938-75).

23 Hunter et al., *Women Pioneers*, p. 81.

24 Bill Wilson to Dr. Bob Smith, [June 24, 25 or 26], 1938 (GSO, Box 59, 1938, Folder B, Documents 1938-25 to 1938-30).

25 Bill Wilson's talk at the National Clergy Conference on Alcoholism, 1960 (http://www.silkworth.net/religion_clergy/01052.html - retrieved November 6, 2015).

26 Bill Wilson speaking in Atlanta, Georgia, July 14, 1951 (recording acquired from Dicobe Media Inc., Bellevue NE, 68005).

27 Oral History Transcriptions, Transcript Record of Wally [Gillam], Akron, Ohio, 12/12/54 (GSO, Box 1 of 2, Box 1: 304680980).

28 Bill Wilson's talk at the National Clergy Conference on Alcoholism, 1960 (http://www.silkworth.net/religion_clergy/01052.html - retrieved November 6, 2015).

29 Bill Wilson speaking in Atlanta, Georgia, July 14, 1951 (recording acquired from Dicobe Media Inc., Bellevue NE, 68005). See also AA Main Events, 1938, Point 22 for the same kind of comment.

30 Bill Wilson, "A Fragment of History: Origin of the Twelve Steps" (A.A. *Grapevine*, July 1953; *Language of the Heart*, p. 201).

31 Bill Wilson speaking to the Manhattan Group, New York City, December, 1955 (http://recoveryspeakers.com/bill-w-1955-manhattan-group-about-the-early-days/ - retrieved December 2, 2015).

32 Bill Wilson, "The Dilemma of No Faith," A.A. *Grapevine*, April 1961 (http://www.barefootsworld.net/aadilemmanofaith.html - retrieved December 22, 2105).

33 Bill Wilson, "A Fragment of History: Origin of the Twelve Steps" (A.A. *Grapevine*, July 1953; *Language of the Heart*, p. 201).

34 Bill Wilson speaking to the Manhattan Group, New York City, December, 1955 (http://recoveryspeakers.com/bill-w-1955-manhattan-group-about-the-carly-days/ - retrieved December 2, 2015).

35 Bill Wilson's talk at the National Clergy Conference on Alcoholism, 1960 (http://www.silkworth.net/religion_clergy/01052.html - retrieved November 6, 2015).

36 Burwell, "Speech at Hope Manor," p. 16.

37 *Alcoholics Anonymous*, (2nd, 3rd & 4th editions), p. 248, 248, & 229 respectively.

38 "Original Story," p. 30 (StSt, WGW 103, Box 31, Folder 3).

39 [First Two Chapters of Proposed Book], p. 21 (GSO, Box 59, 1938, Folder B, Documents 1938-53 to 1938-75).

40 Bill Wilson to Mrs. Phil Crecelius [Ruth Hock], October 17, 1955 (GSO, Box 29, Reel 13, 17.4 The Twelve Steps: How Written, p. 18).

41 Ruth [Hock] Crecelius to Bill Wilson, October 31, 1955 (StSt, WGW 102.2, Box 14, Folder 1-9).

42 Bill Wilson to Ruth [Hock] Crecelius, November 7, 1955 (StSt, WGW 102.2, Box 14, Folder 1-9).

43 Bill Wilson's talk at the National Clergy Conference on Alcoholism, 1960 (http://www.silkworth.net/religion_clergy/01052.html - retrieved November 6, 2015).

44 In Jim Burwell's personal copy of the Multilith copy of the Big Book, he has written his name and address on the inside front cover: "J. M. Burwell / 344 N. Fullerton Ave. / Montclair N. J." This was Hank Parkhurst's home address at the time (Jim's book is currently in the author's private collection).

45 *AACOA*, pp. 166–67. See also Hunter et al., *Women Pioneers*, p. 81 where a quote from Bill makes the same point, but in slightly different language: "Fitz . . . wanted a powerfully religious document. Henry, a former atheist, fell into a hot argument with him. He was positive we would scare off alcoholics by the thousands when they read those Twelve Steps, and he quoted a newcomer named Jimmy B. who emphatically shared that view."

46 Bill Wilson speaking in Long Beach, July 2, 1960 (GSO, CD IC 60/24).

47 Bill Wilson speaking in Atlanta, Georgia, July 14, 1951 (recording acquired from Dicobe Media Inc., Bellevue NE, 68005).

48 GSO, Box 59, Folder B(1), Document 1938-191.

49 *AACOA*, p. 162.

50 *Dr. Bob and the Good Oldtimers*, p. 153.

51 *Dr. Bob and the Good Oldtimers*, pp. 154–55.

52 Wilson, "The Book is Born."

Chapter Twenty-Five. "How It Works" and "Into Action"

1 All quotes here from "How It Works" come from the Multilith printing of the book and can be found in *The Book That Started It All*, pp. 58–64.

2 Esther L. Richards, MD to William G. Wilson, August 9, 1938 (GSO, Box 59, 1938, Folder B[1], Document 1938-110).

3 All quotes here from "Into Action" come from the Multilith printing of the book and can be found in *The Book That Started It All*, pp. 65–72.

4 "Notes on Akron, Ohio Survey / by / Frank Amos," [unedited version], p. 3 (GSO, Box 22, Reel 10 / 8.1 The Alcoholic Foundation: 1937-1938, p. 2).

5 "Hank's ideas," StSt, AA 501.1 – Alcoholics Anonymous – Hank Parkhurst's ideas [handwritten pencil], AA, Box 13, Folder 19, p. 8a.

Chapter Twenty-Six. The Book Goes to the Editor and Is Approved by the Board

1 Recorded interview with Kathleen Ruddell (GSO, CD 769; Tape 2: A.A. Niles Peebles Research – Mrs. Bill Ruddell (1978). This tradition was also practiced in Akron (see *Dr. Bob and the Good Oldtimers*, p. 148).

2 StSt, WGW 102.7, Box 25, Folder 30.

3 Frank Amos [to the Trustees and Advisory Committee of the Alcoholic Foundation], January 6, 1939 (GSO, Box 59, 1939, Folder C, Document 1939-5).

4 Ibid.

5 Ibid.

6 Ibid.

7 For this and all other quotes from this letter see: Wm. G Wilson to Frank B. Amos, January 4, 1939 (GSO, Box 59, 1939, Folder C, Document 1939-7 to 10).

8 Quoting Marcus Tullius Cicero: "The sinews of war are infinite money" or "Endless money forms the sinews of war," *Fifth Philippic*, ii, 5 (Loeb Classic Library 189: *Cicero Philippics 1-6*, Cambridge, MA, Harvard University Press, 2010, p. 249).

9 Charles B. Towns to Bill Wilson, October 19, 1938 (GSO, Box 59, Folder B[1], Document 1938-171).

10 "The Annual Reports of the Postmaster General," 1922, pp. 23-24 and 1949, pp. 20-21. Interestingly, much of this inter-city traffic was carried by over twenty-seven miles of pneumatic tubes connecting the general post office in Brooklyn with twenty-two of the larger postal stations in Manhattan. (See "The Annual Report of the Postmaster General," 1939, p. 62 and a Wikipedia article entitled: Pneumatic Tube Mail in New York City).

11 H.G.P. [Henry G. Parkhurst] to Wm. G. Wilson, January 5, 1939 (GSO, Box 59, 1939, Folder C, Document 1939-6).

12 Ibid.

13 Secretary [Ruth Hock] to Wm. J. Ruddell, January 11, 1939 (GSO, Box 59, 1939, Folder C, Document 1939-33).

14 Secretary [Ruth Hock] to Clayton D. Quaw, January 11, 1939; Secretary to John S. Parker, January 11, 1939; Secretary to F.E. Miller, January 17, 1939 (GSO, Box 59, 1939, Folder C, Documents 1939-34 to 36).

15 GSO, Minutes: Alcoholic Foundation 1939-1944 Duplicates; Folder: Alcoholic Foundation Trustees' Meeting 1939 (January 18, 1939).

16 Ibid.

17 Dodd, *The Authors*, p. 13.

18 *Alcoholics Anonymous* (1st edition), pp. 252–53.

19 *Alcoholics Anonymous* (4th edition), pp. 39–43.

20 GSO, Minutes: Alcoholic Foundation 1939-1944 Duplicates; Folder: Alcoholic Foundation Trustees' Meeting 1939 (January 18, 1939).

21 Ibid.

22 Ibid.

23 Secretary [Ruth Hock] to A. LeRoy Chipman, January 24, 1939; Secretary to Willard Richardson, January 24, 1939; R. Hock to L. V. Strong, February 3, 1939 (GSO, Box 59, 1939, Folder C, Documents 1939-37, 1939-38 & 1939-43).

24 *The Hackettstown Courier-Post*, Thursday, January 19, 1939 (GSO, Album of Reprints; StSt, AA 501.1, Box 13, Folder 15).

25 Ibid.

Chapter Twenty-Seven. Editing the Manuscript

1 Henry G. Parkhurst to Mrs. Janet M. Blair, November 7, 1938 (GSO, Box 59, Folder E.2, LETTERS – November 7, 1938 – July 24, 1939).

2 H.G.P. [Henry G. Parkhurst] to Wm. G. Wilson, January 5, 1939 (GSO, Box 59, 1939, Folder C, Document 1939-6).

3 Burwell, "Evolution," p. 4.

4 Burwell, "Speech at Hope Manor," p. 14.

5 Ruth [Hock] Crecelius to Bill Wilson, November 10, 1955 (StSt, AA 326, Box 4, Folder 17 p. 4).

6 *Pass It On*, p. 204.

7 Pittman, *A.A., The Way It Began*, p. 181 and the supporting endnotes 216 & 227 on pp. 228 & 229 respectively.

8 AA Main Events, 1938, Point 26. Wilson confirms that Uzzell was responsible for his story being moved to the front of the book in his December 13, 1949 letter to Jack Alexander (GSO, Box 29, Folder 17.1, AA History: Miscellaneous Materials, p. 2).

9 *AACOA*, p. 165; *Lois Remembers*, p. 114.

10 [First Two Chapters of Proposed Book], pp. 12-13 (GSO, Box 59, 1938, Folder B, Documents 1938-53 to 1938-75).

11 The Multilith edition of *Alcoholics Anonymous*, p. 1 (*The Book That Started It All*, p. 33).

12 Ibid., pp. 5 – 6 (*The Book That Started It All*, pp. 37 – 38).

13 [First Two Chapters of Proposed Book], pp. 13-14 (GSO, Box 59, 1938, Folder B, Documents 1938-53 to 1938-75).

14 StSt, AA 501.1, Alcoholics Anonymous – Early Draft of Chapter "There Is A Solution," AA Box 13, Folder 24.

15 Ibid.

16 GSO, Box 59, 1938, Folder B, Document 1938-53.

17 *The Book That Started It All*, p. 44.

18 StSt, AA 501.1, Alcoholics Anonymous – Early Draft of Chapter "There Is A Solution," AA Box 13, Folder 24.

19 Ibid.

20 GSO, Box 59, 1938, Folder B, Document 1938-53 pp. 9–10.

21 *The Book That Started It All*, p. 44.

22 Ruth [Hock] Crecelius to Bill Wilson, November 10, 1955 (StSt, AA 326, Box 4, Folder 17 p. 4).

23 Ruth [Hock] Crecelius to Bill Wilson, November 10, 1955 (StSt, AA 326, Box 4, Folder 17 p. 4).

24 Burwell, "Evolution," p. 4.

25 Ruth [Hock] Crecelius to Bill Wilson, November 10, 1955 (StSt, AA 326, Box 4, Folder 17 p. 4).

26 AA Main Events, 1938, Point 26.

27 GSO, Box 59, 1939, Folder C, Document 1939-44.

28 GSO, Box 59, Folder E.2, LETTERS – November 7, 1938–July 24, 1939.

29 Memo from Janet Blair to Authors, no date (GSO, Box 59, 1939, Folder C, Document 1939-45).

30 Janet Blair to Wm. G. Wilson (GSO, Box 59, Folder E.2, LETTERS – November 7, 1938 – July 24, 1939).

31 Frank B. Amos to W. S. Richardson, February 21, 1939 (GSO, Box 59, 1939, Folder C, Document 1939-55).

32 "Works Publishing, Inc., Report of June 30, 1940," (GSO, Box 22, Reel 10 /8.1 [Folder 2] The Alcoholic Foundation: 1939-1940, p. 4).

33 Burwell, "Evolution," p. 4. He makes the same claim in his "Speech at Hope Manor," p. 14.

34 *A Writer's Digest*, September, 1933.

35 Wm. G. Wilson to Frank B. Amos, January 4, 1939 (GSO, Box 59, 1939, Document 1939-7 to 1939-10, p. 1).

36 Four documents relating to this December 5, 1938 loan can be found in GSO, Box 200, Folder I, Bill: Business with Hank P. /1937-1950.

37 November 7, 1938 (GSO, Box 59, Folder E.2, LETTERS – November 7, 1938 – July 24, 1939).

38 GSO, Box 59, Folder E.2, LETTERS – November 7, 1938 – July 24, 1939.

39 Ibid.

40 July 24, 1939 (GSO, Box 59, Folder E.2, LETTERS – November 7, 1938 – July 24, 1939).

41 *AACOA*, p. 164.

42 StSt, AA 501.1, Box 13, Folder 17: Publications – Alcoholics Anonymous (1939) – An Alcoholic's Wife [handwritten draft with edits by Bill*[sic]*; 4pp].

43 StSt, AA 501.1, Box 13, Folder 18: Publications – Alcoholics Anonymous (1939) – The Car Smasher [handwritten draft; 18pp].

44 StSt, AA 501.1, Box 13, Folder 21: Publications – Alcoholics Anonymous (1939) – The Rolling Stone Bill Tate [handwritten draft; 13pp].

45 StSt, AA 501.1, Box 13, Folder 20: Publications – Alcoholics Anonymous (1939) – Hindsight – Myron? [handwritten draft; 15pp].

46 Ibid.

47 StSt, AA 501.1, Box 13, Folder 25: Publications – Alcoholics Anonymous (1939) – Early drafts of Our Southern Friend; Me and John [Barleycorn].

48 Bill Wilson to Dr. Bob Smith, [June 22, 23 or 24], 1938 (GSO, Box 59, 1938, Folder B, Document 1938-25 to 1938-30).

Chapter Twenty-Eight. The Multilith Printing

1 November 3, 1938 (GSO, Box 59, 1938, Folder B[1], Document 1938-172).

2 *ACCOA*, pp. 164-165.

3 Burwell, "Evolution," p. 4.

4 *AACOA*, p. 165.

5 Minutes of the Alcoholic Foundation (GSO, Box 59, 1939, Folder C, Document 1939-44a).

[6] Ibid.

[7] Ibid.

[8] GSO, Box 59, 1939, Folder C(1), Document 1939-158.

[9] GSO, Box 59, 1939, Folder C(1), Document 1939-159.

[10] AA Main Events, 1938, Point 17. See also *AACOA*, p. 157.

[11] *Pass It On,* p. 195.

[12] Bill Wilson to Dr. Bob Smith, [June 22, 23 or 24], 1938 (GSO, Box 59, 1938, Folder B, Document 1938-25 to 1938-30).

[13] *Pass It On*, p. 202.

[14] Handwritten Notes by H. R. Maher on the Proposed Q&A Section of the Book (GSO, Box 59, 1939, Folder C, No assigned number or date, but the first document in this folder).

[15] AA Main Events, 1939, Point 26.

[16] "Hank's ideas," StSt, AA 501.1 – Alcoholics Anonymous – Hank Parkhurst's ideas [handwritten pencil], AA, Box 13, Folder 19, p. 7.

[17] Bill Wilson to Mrs. Phil Crecelius [Ruth Hock], October 17, 1955 (GSO, Box 29, Reel 13, 17.4 The Twelve Steps: How Written, p. 18).

[18] AA Main Events, 1939, Point 26.

[19] Mrs. Phil Crecelius [Ruth Hock] to Bill Wilson, November 10, 1955 (GSO, Box 29, Reel 13, 17.4 The Twelve Steps: How Written, p. 18).

[20] Bill Wilson to Mrs. Phil Crecelius [Ruth Hock], October 17, 1955 (GSO, Box 29, Reel 13, 17.4 The Twelve Steps: How Written, p. 18).

[21] AA Main Events, 1939, Point 28.

[22] AA Main Events, 1939, Point 29. See also *AACOA,* p. 166.

[23] *AACOA*, p. 166.

[24] Original Western Union Telegram from Fitz [Mayo] to Henry G. Parkhurst (GSO, Box 59, 1939, Folder C, Document 1939-46).

[25] *AACOA*, p. 166.

[26] Ibid, AA Main Events, 1939, Point 29.)

[27] M., Merton, *Black Sheep*, p. 58. Merton notes that Kathleen filed for divorce on September 20, 1939 and that Lois's affidavit was taken by Kathleen's lawyer, Mortimer Eisener, on September 22. See also Lois's diary entries for September 22, 1939 and May 10, 1940 for more details on this affidavit and for Lois's reluctant role in the Parkhurst divorce proceedings.

[28] Hunter et al., *Women Pioneers*, p. 84.

[29] Lois's Diary, 1939.

[30] In her March 11, 1939 letter, Lois tells Bill that Hank had left Brooklyn and returned to Montclair the night before. (StSt, LBW 202.4 in WGW Box 27, Folder 116).

[31] "Hank's ideas," StSt, AA 501.1 – Alcoholics Anonymous – Hank Parkhurst's ideas [handwritten pencil], AA, Box 13, Folder 19, p. 1.

[32] June 24, 1938 (GSO, Box 59, 1938, Folder B, Document 1938-23 & 1938-24).

[33] July 18, 1938 (GSO, Box 59, 1938, Folder B, Document 1938-51).

[34] GSO, Box 59, 1938, Document 1938-52.

[35] All quotes here from "The Doctor's Opinion" are from the Multilith edition version of that chapter that can be found in *The Book That Started It All,* pp. 29–32.

[36] "Psychological Rehabilitation of Alcoholics," *Medical Record, A National Review of Medicine and Surgery,* The Medical Journal and Record Publishing Company, Inc., New York, Volume 145, July 19, 1939, pp. 321-324.

[37] *AACOA,* p. 170.

[38] Printed promotional stock prospectus entitled "Alcoholics Anonymous" (GSO, Box 59, 1939, Folder C, Documents 1939-144 to 157, p. 10) and also Typed prospectus for The One Hundred Men Corporation (GSO, Box 59, 1939, Folder C, following Document 1939-26 to 1939-32). *NOTE*: This typed prospectus is actually an unnumbered document that appears after three similar (but textually different) documents that share the same identifying numbers in the GSO archive.

[39] AA Main Events, 1937, Point 23: "we would need some sort of textbook"; Frank Amos, "History of the Alcoholics movement up to the formation of the Alcoholic Foundation on Aug. 11, 1938," (GSO, Box 59, 1938, Folder B, First Two Chapters of the Proposed Book; Trust Indenture, Documents 1938-117 to 1938-124): "a book which would serve as a textbook"; AA Main Events, 1938, Point 26: "Others wanted it titled like a textbook."

[40] Bill Wilson speaking in Atlanta, GA, July 14, 1951 (GSO, CD, BW115).

[41] *AACOA,* p. 170.

[42] Ibid.

[43] See, for instance, his handwritten note to Ruth: "Miss H / No grammatical changes please" on Lloyd Tate's story (StSt, AA 501.1, Box 13, Folder 21: Publications – Alcoholics Anonymous (1939) – The Rolling Stone Bill Tate [handwritten draft; 13pp]).

[44] Secretary [Ruth Hock] to Wm. J. Ruddell, January 11, 1939 (GSO, Box 59, 1939, Folder C, Document 1939-33).

[45] GSO, CD 769; Tape 2: A.A. Niles Peebles Research – Mrs. Bill Ruddell (1978).

[46] GSO, Box 22, Reel 10 / 8.1 (Folder 2), The Alcoholic Foundation: 1939-1940, Document P-88 to P-92, p. 4.

[47] Xerox 914, Named Article, Wikipedia (retrieved November 10, 2016).

[48] *AACOA,* p. 165 and the title of the new binding prepared under Jim Burwell's direction for his personal copy, which reads "ALCOHOLICS ANOUNYMOUS, Book No. 2 of the First Hundred Mimeographed Copies" (author's collection). *NOTE*: Copies of the pre-publication book were definitely not mimeographed. They have the distinctive look of being offset-ink printed.

[49] William G. Wilson to Frank Amos, September 26, 1938 (GSO, Box 59, 1938, Folder B[1], Documents 1938-145 to 151; Bill Wilson to Bob Smith, December 13, 1938 (GSO, Box 59, Folder B(1), Document 1938-191); Frank Amos to Willard Richardson, February 21, 1939 (GSO, Box 59, 1939, Folder C, Document 1939-55).

[50] At least six references in contemporary records from Bill Ruddell's letter to Hank Parkhurst (February 27, 1939) to Leonard Strong's to Erdman Brandt (March 8, 1939) along with further mentions in Burwell's "Evolution" and Wilson's AA Main Events.

[51] "Works Publishing, Inc. Report of June 30, 1940," (GSO, Box 22, Reel 10 / 8.1 (Folder 2), The Alcoholic Foundation: 1939-1940, Document P-88 to P-92, p. 4).

[52] *Before Photocopying: The Art & History of Mechanical Copying, 1780-1938*, Oak Knoll Press, New Castle, Delaware, 1999. p. 151. See also *Office Duplicating*, Walter Dorwin Teague, Special Edition, 1939, pp. 41–42.

[53] *Before Photocopying: The Art & History of Mechanical Copying, 1780-1938*, Oak Knoll Press, New Castle, Delaware, 1999, p. 152.

[54] Ibid. See also *Office Duplicating*, Walter Dorwin Teague, Special Edition, 1939, p. 36.

[55] *Lois Remembers,* p. 115.

[56] GSO, Box 59, 1939, Folder C, Document 1939-55.

[57] GSO, Box 59, 1939, Folder C, Document 1939-48.

[58] *AACOA*, p. 165.

[59] "The "Works Publishing, Inc. Report of June 30, 1940," which explicitly stated "Multilith (Pre-publication printing) . . . 165" (GSO, Box 22, Reel 10 / 8.1 (Folder 2), The Alcoholic Foundation: 1939-1940, Document P-88 to P-92, p. 4).

[60] NYPL, *I p.v. 170, p. 16.

[61] Bill Wilson to Jack Alexander, December 13, 1949 (GSO, Box 29, Folder 17.1, AA History: Miscellaneous Materials).

[62] AA Main Events, 1939, Point 27; *AACOA*, p. 165.

[63] Burwell, "Speech at Hope Manor," p. 16.

[64] GSO, Box 59, 1939, Folder C, Document 1939-170 to 1939-172, p. 2.

[65] AA Main Events, 1939, Point 27. See also *AACOA*, p. 165.

[66] GSO filing cabinet drawer marked "Oral Histories," Folder marked: Murphy, Dorothy Snyder / Akron OH / August 30, 1954, p. 18.

Chapter Twenty-Nine. Promoting and Editing the Multilith Copy

[1] GSO, Box 59, 1939, Document 1939-55.

[2] February 21, 1939 (GSO, Box 59, 1939, Folder C, Document 1939-54).

[3] http://www.fundinguniverse.com/company-histories/book-of-the-month-club-inc-history/ (retrieved August 7, 2015).

[4] https://www.geni.com/people/Erdmann-Brandt/6000000003588375549 (retrieved April 18, 2017).

[5] Henry Parkhurst to Dr. L. V. Strong, March 7, 1939 (GSO, Box 59, 1939, Folder C, Document 1939-164).

[6] Leonard V. Strong, Jr. to Erdmann Brandt, March 8, 1939 (GSO, Box 59, 1939, Folder C, Document 1939-165).

[7] Printed promotional stock prospectus entitled "Alcoholics Anonymous" (GSO, Box 59, 1939, Folder C, Documents 1939-144 to 157, p. 7).

[8] April 3, 1939 (GSO, Box 59, 1939, Folder C, Document 1939-77).

[9] William G. Wilson to Dr. R. Smith, September 27, 1938 (GSO, Box 59, Folder B[1], Document 1938-153).

[10] Harry E. Fosdick to A. LeRoy Chipman, March 9, 1939 (GSO, Box 59, 1939, Folder C, Document 1939-166).

[11] *AACOA*, p. 165.

12 AA Main Events, 1939, <u>Point 27</u>.

13 *AACOA*, p. 165.

14 Burwell, "Evolution," p. 5.

15 *AACOA*, p. 165.

16 Bill [Ruddell] to Hank [Parkhurst], February 27, 1939 (GSO, Box 59, 1939, Folder C, Document 1939-158): "Am looking forward to getting the multilith copy of the book you're sending."

17 GSO, Box 59, Folder B(1), Document 1938-191.

18 Frank Amos to Willard Richardson, February 21, 1939 (GSO, Box 59, 1939, Folder C, Document 1939-55).

19 Hank Parkhurst to Janet Blair, November 7, 1938 (GSO, Box 59, Folder E.2, LETTERS – November 7, 1938 – July 24, 1939, p. 1).

20 March 2, 1939 (StSt, LBW 202.4 in WGW Box 27, Folder 116).

21 Frank Amos to Willard Richardson, February 21, 1939 (GSO, Box 59, 1939, Folder C, Document 1939-55).

22 Ibid.

23 Bob [Smith] to Frank [Amos], March 9, 1939 (GSO, Box 59, 1939, Folder C, no document number, but appearing in chronological order with the other materials in this folder). See also GSO, Box 33, Reel 15, /25.3 Dr. Bob and NY Headquarters, 1938-1940 for a copy of the original handwritten letter.

24 Ibid.

25 *AACOA*, p. 159.

26 Bob [Smith] to Frank [Amos], March 9, 1939 (GSO, Box 59, 1939, Folder C, no document number, but appearing in chronological order with the other materials in this folder). See also GSO, Box 33, Reel 15, /25.3 Dr. Bob and NY Headquarters, 1938-1940 for a copy of the original handwritten letter.

27 *AACOA*, pp. 155–56.

28 See *AACOA*, pp. 193-195 and, most especially, the recorded interviews with Clarence Snyder, (GSO, CDs 614. 615, 616 & 647 [throughout]; A.A. Niles Peebles Research – Clarence Snyder [1978]).

29 GSO filing cabinet drawer marked "Oral Histories," Folder marked: Murphy, Dorothy Snyder / Akron OH / August 30, 1954, p. 18.

30 Ibid. p. 19.

31 Ibid.

32 *Dr. Bob and the Good Oldtimers*, p. 205. See also *AACOA*, pp. 20–21.

33 Colin C. Campbell to F. B. Amos, March 21, 1939 (GSO, Box 59, Folder D.2, Document 16).

34 Lois to Bill darling, March 11, 1939 (StSt, LBW 202.4 in WGW Box 27, Folder 116).

35 Burwell, "Evolution," pp. 4-5.

36 "A Discussion of the Big Book," a talk by Ruth Hock, Glendale, CA, March 12, 1978; transcript copy in the Akron Archives, p. 23. Also available on YouTube under the title "Ruth H. AA's First Secretary shares the history of Alcoholics Anonymous" - http://www.youtube.com/watch?v=mxVkTNgOhy0 – retrieved September 27, 2013.

37 AA Main Events, 1939, <u>Point 30</u>.

38 *AACOA*, pp. 169–70.

39 AA Main Events, 1939, <u>Point 30</u>. See also Bill Wilson speaking in Fort Worth, Texas, June 12, 1954 ("How the Book Alcoholics Anonymous Came About," in *The Book That Started It All*, p. 214).

40 Bill Wilson speaking in Atlanta, Georgia, July 14, 1951 – recording acquired from Dicobe Media Inc., Bellevue NE, 68005.

41 Original Pre-printed Invoice from Cornwall Press to Works Publishing Co., #85-D dated April 10/39 with Typed and Handwritten Details (GSO, Box 59, 1939, Folder C, Document 1939-189).

42 *AACOA*, pp. 171–72.

43 Ibid.

44 Ibid, p. 172.

45 *The Book That Started It All*, p. 1.

46 Ibid., p. 172.

47 Ibid., pp. 66–68.

48 See for instance *The Book That Started It All*, pp. 54–55.

49 Ibid., p. 26.

50 Ibid, pp. 24–25 and also p. 38 for the notation "Inst > #1" in the appropriate spot in the text.

51 Kurtz, *Not-God*, p. 76; K., Mitchell, *How It Worked*, pp. 84-86.

52 Bill Wilson's talk at the National Clergy Conference on Alcoholism, 1960 (http://www.silkworth.net/religion_clergy/01052.html - retrieved November 6, 2015).

53 *AACOA*, p. 165.

54 Bill Wilson speaking in Atlanta, Georgia, July 14, 1951 (recording acquired from Dicobe Media Inc., Bellevue NE, 68005). See also *AACOA*, pp. 168-169 and *Pass It On*, pp. 201-202 for less expansive versions of this same story.

55 *The Book That Started It All*, p. 39.

56 Ibid, p. 8.

57 *AACOA*, pp.167-168; *Pass It On*, p. 204.

58 Burwell, "Evolution," p. 4.

59 *AACOA*, p. 167.

60 Ibid, p. 168.

61 Burwell, "Speech at Hope Manor," p. 15.

62 Burwell, "Evolution," p. 4.

63 Ibid.

64 StSt, AA 501.1, Box 13, Folder 15: Publications – Alcoholics Anonymous (1939) – Correspondence and promotion material.

65 Burwell, "Evolution," p. 4.

66 See his May 1938 letter to Bert and Bill (Appendix II) where he closes by saying "to simplify all of the above" and the end of the Multilith version of his "To Employers" chapter where he writes, "Being a business man, you might like to have a summary of this chapter" (*The Book That Started It All*, p. 100).

67 StSt, AA 501.1, Box 13, Folder 15: Publications – Alcoholics Anonymous (1939) – Correspondence and promotion material.

68 Burwell, "Evolution," p. 4.

69 *AACOA*, p. 168.

70 Burwell, "Evolution," p. 4; "Speech at Hope Manor," p. 15.

71 See the named Wikipedia article for "Greystone Park Psychiatric Hospital" (retrieved June 4, 2017).

72 Both of these suggestions—along with another for a Dr. Howard W. S. Potter of New Jersey—come from Jared L., an A.A. historian from Pennsylvania whose knowledge of early A.A. history is formidable and deep. (See AAHistoryLovers message 6028 [https://groups.yahoo.com/neo/groups/aahistorylovers/conversations/messages/6028 – retrieved June 9, 2017] and also AAHistoryLovers2 messages 303 & 304 [https://groups.yahoo.com/neo/groups/AAHistoryLovers2/conversations/messages/303] – retrieved June 9, 2017).

73 *Lois Remembers*, p. 198. See also Lois's Diary, August 18, 1939.

74 August 20, 1939.

75 Based on the 1940 census records. (See https://groups.yahoo.com/neo/groups/AAHistoryLovers2/conversations/messages/28 - retrieved June 9, 2017.)

76 Lois's Diaries, 1939: August 13, 15, 18 & 20.

77 *Alcoholics Anonymous*, (4th edition), p. 163.

78 *AACOA*, p. 167. See also AA Main Events, 1939, Point 2.

79 *American Medical Directory*, American Medical Association, Chicago, 1938, p. 1048.

80 *Biographical Directory of Fellows and Members of the American Psychiatric Association*, The American Psychiatric Association, New York, 1950, p. 368. (See http://hindsfoot.org/docu1.html for an online reproduction of this cited listing.)

81 *AACOA*, p. 11.

82 Ibid., p. 176.

83 Ibid.

84 Hank [Parkhurst] to Frank Amos, April 7, 1939 (GSO, Box 59, 1939, Folder C[1], Document 1939-179).

85 *The Book That Started It All*, p. 58.

86 Ibid., p. 190.

87 Ibid., pp. 60, 66, & 71 respectively.

88 Ibid., pp. 58–59.

Chapter Thirty. Publication Day

[1] Burwell, "Evolution," p. 4.

[2] Burwell, "Speech at Hope Manor," p. 16.

[3] *AACOA*, p. 169.

[4] *The Book That Started It All*, pp. 7–8.

[5] *AACOA*, p. 170.

[6] Recorded interview with Ruth Hock (GSO, CD 866; Track 4, 4:20-7:00: A.A. Niles Peebles Research – 1978)

[7] *AACOA*, p. 170.

[8] "A Discussion of the Big Book," a talk by Ruth Hock, Glendale, CA, March 12, 1978; transcript copy in the Akron Archives, pp. 10-11. Also available on YouTube under the title "Ruth H. AA's First Secretary shares the history of Alcoholics Anonymous" - http://www.youtube.com/watch?v=mxVkTNgOhy0 – retrieved September 27, 2013.

[9] Hunter et al., *Women Pioneers*, p. 82.

[10] Recorded interview with Ruth Hock (GSO, CD 866; Track 4, 4:20-7:00: A.A. Niles Peebles Research – 1978).

[11] GSO filing cabinet drawer marked "Oral Histories," Folder marked: Murphy, Dorothy Snyder / Akron OH / August 30, 1954, pp. 28–29.

[12] Ibid., p. 29.

[13] *AACOA*, p. 170.

[14] Recorded interview with Ruth Hock (GSO, CD 866; Track 4, 4:20-7:00: A.A. Niles Peebles Research – 1978).

[15] "A Discussion of the Big Book," a talk by Ruth Hock, Glendale, CA, March 12, 1978; transcript copy in the Akron Archives, p. 11. Also available on YouTube under the title "Ruth H. AA's First Secretary shares the history of Alcoholics Anonymous" - http://www.youtube.com/watch?v=mxVkTNgOhy0 – retrieved September 27, 2013.

[16] Recorded interview with Ruth Hock (GSO, CD 866; Track 4, 4:20-7:00: A.A. Niles Peebles Research – 1978).

[17] "A Discussion of the Big Book," a talk by Ruth Hock, Glendale, CA, March 12, 1978; transcript copy in the Akron Archives, p. 11. Also available on YouTube under the title "Ruth H. AA's First Secretary shares the history of Alcoholics Anonymous" - http://www.youtube.com/watch?v=mxVkTNgOhy0 – retrieved September 27, 2013.

[18] Recorded interview with Ruth Hock (GSO, CD 866; Track 4, 4:20-7:00: A.A. Niles Peebles Research – 1978).

[19] October 3, 1957 (StSt, WGW 102.2, Correspondence – Chronological files – CRA-CUY, Box 14, Folder 2).

[20] GSO filing cabinet drawer marked "Oral Histories," Folder marked: Murphy, Dorothy Snyder / Akron OH / August 30, 1954, pp. 28–29.

21 Original Pre-printed Invoice from Cornwall Press to Works Publishing Co., #85-D dated April 10/39 with Typed and Handwritten Details (GSO, Box 59, 1939, Folder C, Document 1939-189).

22 *AACOA,* pp. 170–171.

23 Ibid., p. 171.

24 T. G. Lewis to W. G. Wilson,April 3, 1957 (GSO, Box 27A, Reel 12 / 13.2[1] Miscellaneous – unmarked material) that notes a personal $200 check to Bill Wilson dated March 31, 1939.

25 *AACOA,* p. 171.

26 GSO filing cabinet drawer marked "Oral Histories," Folder marked: Murphy, Dorothy Snyder / Akron OH / August 30, 1954, p. 29.

27 Ibid.

28 Ashley E. Pidgeon to Harris Thurston, April 3, 1939 (GSO, 1939, Box 59, Folder C[1], Document 1939-176).

29 April 7, 1939 (GSO, 1939, Box 59, Folder C[1], Document 1939-178).

30 *AACOA,* pp.174-176; *Pass It On,* pp. 207–10.

31 April 8, 1939 (GSO, 1939, Box 59, Folder C[1], Document 1939-182 & 1939-183).

32 Original Pre-printed Invoice from Cornwall Press to Works Publishing Co., #85-D dated April 10/39 with Typed and Handwritten Details (GSO, Box 59, 1939, Folder C, Document 1939-189).

33 Cornwall Press to Works Publishing Company, April 28, 1939 (GSO, 1939, Box 59, Folder D, Reel 28, Document 1939-250).

34 Original Pre-printed Invoice from Cornwall Press to Works Publishing Co., #85-D dated April 10/39 with Typed and Handwritten Details (GSO, Box 59, 1939, Folder C, Document 1939-189).

35 Cornwall Press Monthly Statement dated April 29, 1939 citing Invoice #158-D dated April 17 for the dust jackets (GSO, 1939, Box 59, Folder D, Reel 28, Document 1939-271).

36 Cornwall Press Pre-printed Delivery Form with handwritten details dated April 10, 1939 (GSO, 1939, Box 59, Folder C[1], Document 1939-188).

37 *Alcoholics Anonymous,* 1ˢᵗ edition, p. 380–85.

38 Dodd, *The Authors,* p. 47.

39 See the list of shareholders in Works Publication dated May 15, 1940 (GSO, Box 61, Folder D, 1940 – Works Publishing Company, p. 79.)

40 GSO filing cabinet drawer marked "Oral Histories," Folder marked: Murphy, Dorothy Snyder / Akron OH / August 30, 1954, p. 29.

41 Secretary [Ruth Hock] to Fred D. Schnegge Co. Inc., April 10, 1939 (GSO, Box 59, Folder C [1], 1939-185).

42 Secretary [Ruth Hock] to Wm. Currie, April 10, 1939 (GSO, Box 59, Folder C [1], 1939-187).

43 Secretary [Ruth Hock] to John Henry Fitzhugh Mayo, Esq., April 10, 1939 (GSO, Box 59, Folder C [1], 1939-190).

44 GSO, Box 59, Folder C [1], 1939-191.

45 There is an unnumbered copy of the ad clipped from the newspaper along with the original proof sheet for the advertisement listed as Document 1939-192 found in GSO, 1939, N. Y. Times Ads and Order Forms, Box 59, Folder D.1.

46 AA Main Events, 1939, <u>Point 15</u>.

47 GSO, 1939, N. Y. Times Ads and Order Forms, Box 59, Folder D.1.

48 AA Main Events, 1939, <u>Point 15</u>.

49 See http://silkworth.net/bbreviews/01001.html (retrieved July 5, 2017) for the complete text of the review.

50 *Alcoholics Anonymous*, 4th edition, "Foreword to Second Edition," p. xvii.

51 Ibid. "How It Works," pp. 58-59.

Chapter Thirty-One. Aftermath

1 Original Typed Document: One Hundred Men, Inc. January 7, 1939 (GSO, Box 59, 1939, Folder, 1939-126 to 1939-132); *Alcoholics Anonymous*, 4th edition, "A Vision For You," p. 153.

2 Dodd, *The Authors*, p. 111.

3 K., Mitchell, *How It Worked*, p. 135.

4 Ibid.

5 *Dr. Bob and the Good Oldtimers*, p. 163.

6 K., Mitchell, *How It Worked*, p. 136.

7 Ibid., p. 85.

8 This date is based on the time sequence described on page 138-139 of *How It Worked* by Mitchell K.

9 Ibid., p. 139.

10 Ibid., p. 136.

11 Ibid., pp. 139–40; see also Recorded interview with Clarence Snyder (GSO, CD 615; Track 1 [9:30-10:50]: A.A. Niles Peebles Research – Clarence Snyder – April 24, 1978).

12 K., Mitchell, *How It Worked*, p. 140.

13 Ibid.

14 Ibid.

15 *Dr. Bob and the Good Oldtimers*, p. 164.

16 K. Mitchell, *How It Worked*, p. 140.

17 Ibid.

18 *Dr. Bob and the Good Oldtimers*, p. 164.

19 K., Mitchell, *How It Worked*, p. 142.

20 *Dr. Bob and the Good Oldtimers*, p. 165.

21 Clarence Snyder to Hank Parkhurst, June 4, 1939 [Scanned copy of letter supplied to the author by the eminent A.A. historian, Arthur S. of Arlington, TX]. Partially quoted in both *How It Worked*, p. 142 and *Dr. Bob and the Good Oldtimers*, p. 167.

22 *Dr. Bob and the Good Oldtimers*, p. 163.

23 Clarence Snyder to Hank Parkhurst, June 4, 1939 [Scanned copy of letter supplied to the author by the eminent A.A. historian, Arthur S. of Arlington, TX].

24 *Dr. Bob and the Good Oldtimers*, p. 218.

25 Ibid., pp. 216–17.

26 GSO filing cabinet drawer marked "Oral Histories," Folder marked: Kewley, Joseph / Cleveland OH / 1954 Interview, pp. 26–28.

27 Kurtz, *Not-God*, p. 82.

28 List of Akron Members and their length of sobriety (RAC, Family, Group 2 OMR, Series P, Box 42, Folder 458). According to Dodd (*The Authors*, p. 21) van Horn's date of continuous sobriety is in question: "Bill's sobriety date is uncertain. He joined the Fellowship in 1937, and slipped, but was known to be active in the program by September 1937."

29 Oral History Transcriptions, Transcript Record of William van Horn, Akron, Ohio, 6/19/54 (GSO, Box 2 of 2, Box 1: 304680980, pp. 17-18).

30 http://www.steppingstones.org/loisstory.html (retrieved July 17, 2017); AA Main Events, 1937, Point 15.

31 AA Main Events, 1937, Point 15.

32 AA Main Events, 1939, Point 32.

33 *AACOA*, p. 173; Thompson, *Bill W.*, p. 258.

34 AA Main Events, 1939, Point 32. See *AACOA*, p. 173 for a more detailed account by Bill.

35 Hank Parkhurst to Frank Amos, May 15, 1939 (GSO, Box 22, Reel 10 / 8.1 [Folder 2] The Alcoholic Foundation: 1939-1940).

36 *Pass It On*, p. 213.

37 Ibid., p. 214.

38 *AACOA*, p. 11.

39 Lois's Diary, June 14, 1939.

40 Ibid., June 15, 16, 17, 19, & 21, 1939.

41 M., Merton, *Black Sheep*, pp. 39–41.

42 Ibid., pp. 40–41.

43 AA Main Events, 1939, Points 17 & 18.

44 Ibid., Point 19.

45 Ibid.

46 Lois's Diary.

47 Ibid., May 11, 1940.

48 Ibid., May 12, 1940.

49 Recorded interview with Clarence Snyder, GSO, CD 614; Tape 2: A.A. Niles Peebles Research – Clarence Snyder (1978); [4:50-6:25].

50 Dodd, *The Authors*, p. 8.

51 StSt, AA 501.1, Box 13, Folder 26, two 8½" x 11" typed pages with hand corrections by Bill Wilson.

52 *Alcoholics Anonymous*, 1st edition, 11th printing, pp. 28, 30, 271, 272, & 330 respectively.

53 *Alcoholics Anonymous*, 2nd edition, p. xi.

54 Kurtz, *Not-God*, p. 356, n. 67.

55 Kurtz, *Not-God*, p. 356, n. 67 quoting Bill Wilson to Howard Edminster, February 6, 1961 (GSO, Box 31, 19.3 Faith and the Question of No Faith).

56 Stephen Batchelor, *Confessions of a Buddhist Atheist,*. Spiegel & Grau, New York, 2010, p. 236.

57 Wikipedia "List of Best Selling Books" has the Big Book in the #14 position on its list of "Best-Selling Regularly Updated Books." (https://en.wikipedia.org/wiki/List_of_best-selling_books#Between_30_million_and_50_million_copies - retrieved July 24, 2017).

58 http://www.aa.org/assets/en_US/smf-53_en.pdf (retrieved July 24, 2017).

Index

Note: "Bill" refers to Bill Wilson, "Dr. Bob" refers to Bob Smith, "Ebby" refers to Ebby Thacher, and "Hank" refers to Hank Parkhurst.

on religion vs. psychology, 144, 460–61 (*see also* "There Is A Solution")

tolerance by, 137, 140, 432

Tuesday night meetings/format, 175, 199n, 216, 247, 595

unstable people excluded, 206

New York City, 235, 497, 746n10

New York City Health Commissioner, 38

New York Times, 112, 193, 241, 256, 501, 540, 583

New York University, 286

New Yorker Magazine, 172, 531

"Notes on Akron" (Amos), 69, 73–83, 452, 607–12

O

Okrent, Daniel: *Last Call*, 699n44

One Hundred Men. See *Alcoholics Anonymous*

One Hundred Men Corporation (*later* Works Publishing), 142n, 289–314, 299n

formation, 109, 298–99

memorandum to Amos, 289–90, 723n2

name change (*see* Works Publishing)

ownership, 301–3

prospectus/stock sales, 111, 197n, 255n, 297–304, 308–14, 391–92, 498, 540, 548, 726n70, 728nn122–23, 729n134

"On His Way" (Maher), 419n, 456, 519–20, 524

osteopathic medicine, 37n

"Our Southern Friend" (Mayo), 23n, 134, 202, 450–51, 455, 524–25

outline (*Alcoholics Anonymous*), 177–99

abandoned, 394

as establishing the book's contents, 183–87

full text, 641–43

Hank as author, 179

Oxford Group

and A.A., 3–4

absence from the Big Book, 154n

in Akron (*see under* Akron A.A. group)

Bill's involvement with (*see under* Wilson, Bill)

Catholic Church on, 560–61, 563, 587–88

Christian foundation of, 11–12, 123, 129, 136, 694n25

Cleveland group opposed, 590

evangelicalism of, 469

focus on wealthy Christians, 78n, 129

founding, 12

Four Absolutes, 11–12, 127–29, 154n, 166–67, 414n, 451, 588–89, 593

goal of revolutionizing society, 15n

and guidance from God, 132, 135, 191–92, 487

influence on A.A., 12

I Was a Pagan, 12n, 123n

in New York (*see under* New York A.A. group)

on religion as cure for alcoholism, 138

and Ebby Thacher, 6–7

Oxford Movement, 63n

P

Paine, Kenneth, 306–8

Paley, William, 579n

Parcells, Charles, 229–32

Parker, John, 498

Parker, Sterling, 20, 22–23, 25, 26n, 27, 33

Parkhurst, Henry G. ("Hank")

and A.A., break with, 599

on the Advisory Board, 238–40

Alcoholic Fund proposed, 92–93

Bill prodded to resume writing by, 271–72

Bill's break with, 583, 599–600

as Bill's friend and right-hand man, 4, 21, 31, 34–35, 124, 158

Bill's writing criticized by, 286–87

on Burwell's final drunk, 174–75

business background, 31–32, 391 (*see also* Honor Dealers)

as a co-founder of A.A., 69–70, 600

contributions to the Big Book, 272 (see also under *Alcoholics Anonymous*; "Hank's Ideas"; outline)

Cornwall visit for final edits, 574–76

and the One Hundred Men
Corporation, 302–3
professionalization of A.A. opposed,
43–44
on Prohibition, 56
and Richardson, 38–39, 41–42, 83–85,
714n25
Riverside Church supported by, 54
at the Rockefeller dinner, 53, 56
and Albert Scott, 53–54
temperance supported, 39, 56–57
wealth, 39
Rockefeller, John D., Sr., 39, 41, 55, 388
Rockefeller Archives (Sleepy Hollow, NY),
1n
Rockefeller Center (NYC), 39–40, 53–54,
57, 60, 65–66, 68, 75, 239–41, 245, 257,
323, 577–78, 610–11
Rockefeller dinner (December 1937) and
meetings
A.A. attendees, 51, 53
A.A. proposal and Rockefeller men's
response, 51, 53, 57–60
alcoholic hospital proposed for Akron
("Akron Report"), 60–62, 69
awaiting the decision, 65–67
clarifications discussed, 62–63
confusion about, 85n
Dr. Bob's secrecy about, 60–61, 65–66,
71, 75–76, 82–83
follow-up Akron trip by Amos (*see
under* Amos, Frank)
follow-up correspondence between Bill
and Richardson, 64, 67–69
medical attendees, 53
planning, 42–43, 45–49, 51
Rockefeller attendees, 53–57
Rockefeller Jr.'s decision and
contribution, 85–86, 97–98, 254, 264
Sunday night set-up meeting, 51–52
test case proposed, 63–65
Rockefeller family, 39–40, 42, 229
Rockefeller Foundation, 38, 40–43, 170, 210
"The Rolling Stone" (Tate), 455, 519–20,
523
Roosevelt, Franklin D., 210, 235n, 254

Root, Clark, Buckner, and Ballantine
(NYC), 235
Root, Elihu, Jr., 235n
Root, Elihu, Sr., 235n
Royalties on the Big Book, 291–92, 294,
298, 303, 319, 425, 495–96, 707n45
Ruddell, Bill, 22–23, 25, 501–2
on the Advisory Board, 528
Akron visit, 22–23, 25, 27n
as Alcoholic Foundation chairman and
trustee, 237, 239–40, 257, 299n, 499n,
528
at American Saw Mill Machinery, 502n
"A Business Man's Recovery," 20, 23,
23n, 134, 456
in Hackettstown, 433n, 502n, 566–67
Multilith edition received, 549, 752n16
at the Rockefeller dinner, 51, 53
role in the New York A.A. group, 23
sobriety, 20, 499n
stock shares bought, 314n, 391
surrender to God, 134
on Works Publishing, 529–30
Ruddell, Kathleen, 22, 23, 25, 27n, 134,
595–96
Ryan, Morgan, 550, 561–62

S

Saturday Evening Post, 193, 197n, 270, 310,
548, 600
sauerkraut, tomatoes, and corn syrup
treatment for cravings, 435–36
School of Journalism (Columbia University),
286n, 388
scientific inquiry, open-mindedness of,
283–84
Scott, Albert, 501n
on A.A.'s need to be self-supporting,
265–68, 289
on the Advisory Board, 238–39
Alcoholic Foundation supported, 83–85
and Amos, 83, 196–98
Bill's thank-you letter, 210–11
letter of introduction for fundraising,
211